Grade 7

Annotated Teacher's Edition

Prentice Hall
Writing and Grammar
Communication in Action

Put Students' Words Into Action!

A new approach to language learning designed to produce competent, confident communicators.

- Active learning for today's middle school students.
- Systematic Learning Strategies.
- Easy-to-use handbook style saves time.
- Teacher's Edition provides all the support.

⌐3-Part Organization ──────────

Prentice Hall Writing and Grammar: Communication in Action is conveniently divided into the following three sections for ease of use:

- **Writing:** Guides students through each step of the writing process with an emphasis on revision.
- **Grammar:** Provides more grammar practice than any other program, including unique hands-on grammar activities.
- **Academic and Workplace Skills:** Focuses on practical, real-world skills for today's multimedia generation.

Prentice
Hall

Grade 6-Copper   ISBN: 0-13-043346-2
Grade 7-Bronze   ISBN: 0-13-043347-0
Grade 8-Silver   ISBN: 0-13-043348-9

3 4 5 6 7 8 9 10
05 04 03 02 01

Put Students' Words Into Action!

Only Prentice Hall Writing and Grammar: Communication in Action...

- Engages today's students with active, hands-on learning.

- Provides extensive practice opportunities and strategies for all stages of the writing process.

- Saves time with its easy-to-use handbook style.

Connections that make instruction relevant for today's students

10.1 Model from Literature

In his Newbery Award-winning book, Holes, Louis Sachar introduces readers to Stanley, a boy who is always in the wrong place at the wrong time. In this excerpt from the book, Stanley is in a boys' camp in the desert. He gets a lecture from the head counselor that sounds like an essay on how to survive in the camp.

▲ Critical Viewing
Why might a person need directions for how to survive in this environment?
[Analyze]

*How to Survive
Camp Greenlake*
from Holes

GRAMMAR IN LITERATURE

from "The Cat Who Thought She Was a Dog and the Dog Who Thought He Was a Cat"

Isaac Bashevis Singer

In this passage, notice that *peasant*, a common noun, is often used in place of the proper noun Jan Skiba. The proper noun is also capitalized. Look for other common and proper nouns in this paragraph.

Once there was a poor *peasant*, Jan Skiba by name. He lived with his wife and three daughters in a one-room hut with a straw roof, afar from the village. The house had a bed, a bench bed, and a stove, but no mirror. A mirror was a luxury for a poor *peasant*. And why would a *peasant* need a mirror? Peasants aren't curious about their appear-

Connect to the Language Arts

Connections to literature, writing, and grammar show students the relevance of what they learn.

Grammar in Your Writing
Using Commas to Separate Items in a Series

Use commas to separate items in a series, or list. Separating the items with commas makes your meaning absolutely clear to readers. Look at the following examples.

Examples:

Commas separate individual items in a series:
Add the sugar, baking soda, baking powder, and salt.

Commas separate groups of words in a series:
Begin by gathering your tools, reviewing the recipe, and preheating the oven.

  Note: Some writers use a comma before the *and* that connects the last two items in the series. (See the commas following *baking powder* and *recipe* in the examples above.) Others do not use a comma before the final *and*. Follow your teacher's directions about whether to use the comma before the *and*.

Find It in Your Writing Review your essay and circle any lists or series of items. Remember that the series can include either individual words or groups of words. Check that you have correctly used commas to separate the items in each series or list that you find.

Find It in Your Reading Read "How to Survive Camp Greenlake" on pages 12–13. Find an example of commas used to separate items in a s...

Engage Students

Address varied learning styles by actively involving students with Hands-on Grammar activities.

Hands-on Grammar

Subject-Verb Agreement Color Match
  Cut three strips of paper of equal length. Draw a blue line across the center of one. Draw a red line across the center of the other. Fold the strip into thirds, as shown in the illustration. Then, write a sentence with a singular subject, a singular verb form, and a phrase across the blue line. Write the subject in the first fold, the verb in the second, and the remaining words in the third fold. Write the same sentence on the strip with the red line, but use a plural subject and plural verb form. Next, cut each strip on the folds. Finally, try to line up the parts of the sentence. You will find that you can't create a color match between a singular subject and a plural verb form.

The Minister	attends	every session

The Ministers	attend	every session

The Ministers	attends	every session

Find It in Your Reading Do this activity with a sentence from the Grammar in Literature passage from "Glory and Hope," on page 578. If the sentence has too many phrases, just use the subject and verb.

Find It in Your Writing Review a recent piece of writing in your portfolio. Use this activity with several sentences from the piece.

Prentice Hall
WRITING and GRAMMAR
Communication in Action
Bronze Level

Grammar Exercise Workbook

Two practice pages for each grammar concept

Prentice Hall

What Is a Comparison-and-Contrast Essay?

A **comparison-and-contrast essay** analyzes the similarities and differences between two or more things. It can help you to decide which bicycle to buy. A good comparison-and-contrast essay can even change your perspective—as when a reviewer compares the latest hit song with an old album, letting you hear the startling similarities. A comparison-and-contrast essay includes

- a topic involving two or more things that are neither nearly identical nor extremely different.
- details illustrating both similarities and differences.
- clear organization that highlights the points of comparison.

To learn the criteria on which your essay may be evaluated, see the Rubric for Self-Assessment on page 166.

Types of Comparison-and-Contrast Essays

In addition to an ordinary comparison-and-contrast essay, some specialized essays also use comparison and contrast:

- **Product comparisons** compare two or more products, providing up-to-date information on each and discussing the advantages and disadvantages of purchasing each one.
- **Plan evaluations** compare two or more alternative plans or decisions, discussing the circumstances and comparing the advantages and disadvantages of each plan.

Writers in
ACTION

In his books and articles, Richard Lederer compares English to other languages and different English words to each other. He knows the value of saying more in fewer words:

". . . writing is hard work, and writing concisely is even more difficult."

PREVIEW
Student Work
IN PROGRESS

To develop your comparison-and-contrast writing skills, follow the work of Dylan Parker of Carr Lane VPA Middle School in St. Louis, Missouri. In this chapter, Dylan uses featured prewriting, drafting, and revising techniques to develop the comparison-and-contrast essay "Skateboards for Success." At the end of the lesson, you can read Dylan's completed essay.

Comparison-and-Contrast Essay • 151

Connect to Students' Lives

An authentic student model in every writing chapter tracks the development of one student's writing through a particular writing mode.

Persuasion in Everyday Life

Whenever you argue with a friend over which movie to see or debate the merits of one musical group over another, you're using persuasive skills. **Persuasion** is writing or speaking that attempts to convince others to accept a position or take a desired action. Effective persuasion can decide a defendant's fate in a trial, lead to a change in government leadership, or even end a war.

Engage Today's Multimedia Generation

Media and Technology Skills workshops teach students relevant, real-world skills and offer a full array of on-line and multimedia resources.

Prentice Hall
WRITING and GRAMMAR
Communication in Action

Media and Technology Skills

Using Computer Technology
Activity: Getting Help On-line

Computer programs typically come with built-in "how-to's"—on-line help the user can access while using the program. On-line help lets you learn as you work. It is as though the computer were a teacher and a tool rolled into one! By mastering Help, you can turn problems with computers into opportunities to learn.

Learn About It

Balloon Help Turn Balloon Help on or off through a program's menu bar. With Balloon Help on, a balloon appears whenever you roll your mouse pointer over a button, dialogue box, or other feature. Each balloon contains a brief description identifying the function of the feature on which the pointer is resting.

On-line Manuals To consult the on-line manual for a program, select "Help" from the menu bar. "Contents" lists topics by category. "Index" lists topics alphabetically and often provides a Search feature that allows you to search for a particular subject.

Other Kinds of Help Often, the best troubleshooting tips come from the program's "Read Me" file. You may open a "Read Me" file in a text-editor program. Software also comes with a printed manual, which offers detailed information on operating the program.

Apply It Choose an application, such as a word-processing program, to which you have access. Think of a difficulty you have had using the program or a question you might have about the program's use. Use two or more forms of help to solve the problem or answer the question. Take notes in a graphic organizer such as the one to the right. Then, write a mini-manual explaining how to use these different ways of getting help.

Computer Help
Built-in Help
• Balloon Help
• On-line manuals
Other Kinds of Help
• "Read Me" files
• Printed manuals

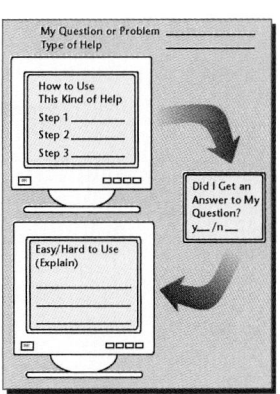

My Question or Problem _____
Type of Help _____

How to Use
This Kind of Help
Step 1 _____
Step 2 _____
Step 3 _____

Did I Get an
Answer to My
Question?
y ___ /n ___

Easy/Hard to Use
(Explain)
_____
_____
_____

Media and Technology Skills • 219

More Practice and Revision Support

Practice, Practice, and More Practice

More grammar exercises than any other program provide the practice your students need to improve their grammar skills and apply them in writing and speaking.

14.2 PRONOUNS

Section 14.2 Section Review

GRAMMAR EXERCISES 18–24

Exercise 18 Identifying Personal Pronouns Identify the personal pronoun in each sentence.

1. My brother and sister want to become pharmacists. They must attend a college of pharmacy.
2. After finishing a five-year program, he will graduate.
3. They must complete a one-year internship before becoming pharmacists.
4. She may choose from many schools.
5. All of them offer similar programs.

Exercise 19 Identifying Antecedents of Personal Pronouns Fill in the blank with the appropriate personal pronoun. Circle the antecedent of the pronoun you supply.

1. Radiologists must attend medical school. __?__ spend five years studying radiology.
2. If my brother studies radiology, __?__ will have to complete a residency program.
3. My aunt is a radiologist. __?__ has her own practice.
4. After completing __?__ residency, radiologists may decide to specialize.
5. __?__ may choose to teach instead.

Exercise 20 Recognizing Types of Pronouns Identify the pronouns in the sentence... demonstrative, interro...

1. My brother is in h... to study forensic...
2. That is the study...
3. It helps police off...
4. You may have se... about "crime doct...

5. Who wants to know more?
6. These are copies of fingerprints.
7. Each is unique.
8. Whose is this fingerprint?
9. What can we learn from fingerprints?
10. Few can identify a fingerprint.

Exercise 21 Revision Practice Replace each italicized noun in the sentences below with the type of pronoun indicated in brackets. Some sentences may have to be rewritten as questions. Revise punctuation as needed.

1. *Family practitioners* [personal] provide primary medical care.
2. Family doctors know *famil...* [personal] patients.
3. *Dedication* [demonstrative]... son they enter the field.
4. *Family practitioners* [interr... refer patients to a specialis...
5. *General practitioners* [inde... had many years of medical...

Exercise 22 Find It in... Reading Identify three pers... nouns in the excerpt from "The... Thought She Was a Dog . . ." o...

Exercise 23 Find It in... Writing In your own writin...

Section 14.1

Section Review

GRAMMAR EXERCISES 6–12

Exercise 6 Identifying Nouns Identify the nouns in each sentence.

1. Dogs require attention, including proper feeding and medical care.
2. Dogs need regular exercise.
3. Puppies need a combination of solid foods and milk as they grow.

Exercise 9 Revision Practice Copy the following paragraph. Replace the italicized words with proper nouns of your choice.

A dog came to *the town*. He walked up *a street* and down *another street*. *The man,* who lived at the end of *the street,* watched the dog approach.

Exercise 10 Find It in Your Reading Identify two proper nouns, two common nouns, one compound noun, and one collective noun in the following excerpt from "The Cat Who Thought She Was a Dog . . . ":

Burek had to be tied outside, and he howled all day and all night. In their anguish, both the dog and the cat stopped eating.

When Jan Skiba saw the disruption the mirror had created in his household, he decided a mirror wasn't what his family needed.

Exercise 11 Find It in Your Writing Look through your writing portfolio. Find five common nouns, two proper nouns, one collective noun, and one compound noun in your own writing.

Exercise 12 Writing Application Write about a dog you've known or read about. Use at least two compound nouns, one collective noun, and two proper nouns.

Chapter 14

Chapter Review

GRAMMAR EXERCISES 25–36

Exercise 25 Identifying Nouns in Sentences Identify the nouns in each sentence below.

1. The pack of wolves chased the rabbit.
2. The rabbit, filled with fear, ran away.
3. Because of their hunger, the wolves continued to hunt.
4. They found no more prey in the forest.
5. The howls of the hungry animals showed their frustration.

Exercise 26 Identifying Nouns in Paragraphs Identify the nouns in the paragraph below.

Wolves are wild animals that look similar to dogs. A wolf has fur that can be white, black, or gray. Wolves travel in packs, using their speed and strength to hunt as a group. They live in most climates, but rarely in deserts or tropical forests.

Exercise 27 Identifying Common and Proper Nouns Identify the nouns in each sentence below. Then, tell whether each noun is *common* or *proper.*

1. My sister Lucy, my mother, and I took our cat to the animal hospital.
2. The hospital is in Philadelphia.
3. We took the cat on the train.
4. The train passed through cities in New York and New Jersey.
5. Our cat Trudy needed special surgery.
6. Dr. Kim, the veterinarian, was very kind.
7. While we waited, my mother and I read a magazine.
8. We saw a dog that looked like a character from the movie *Benji.*
9. A poodle sat on a chair next to us.
10. Before we returned home, we stopped to see the Liberty Bell.

Exercise 28 Identifying Collective Nouns Identify the collective noun in each sentence below.

1. My class went on a trip to the animal hospital last week.
2. The team of veterinarians sees many types of patients.
3. Yesterday, they treated a group of monkeys from the zoo.
4. Sometimes, they go to farms to check a herd of cattle.
5. My family brought our cat to this animal hospital.

Exercise 29 Identifying Compound Nouns Identify the compound noun in each sentence below.

1. My sister-in-law brought a new cat home from the pound.
2. They told her that a police officer had found the cat.
3. It does not get along with the sheepdog in the house.
4. She brought it to the middle school where she teaches.
5. On the way home, they crossed the George Washington Bridge.

Exercise 30 Identifying Personal Pronouns Identify each personal pronoun below as *first person, second person,* or *third person.* Then, tell whether the pronoun is *singular* or *plural.*

1. you
2. she
3. their
4. our
5. them
6. I
7. his
8. yours
9. mine
10. we

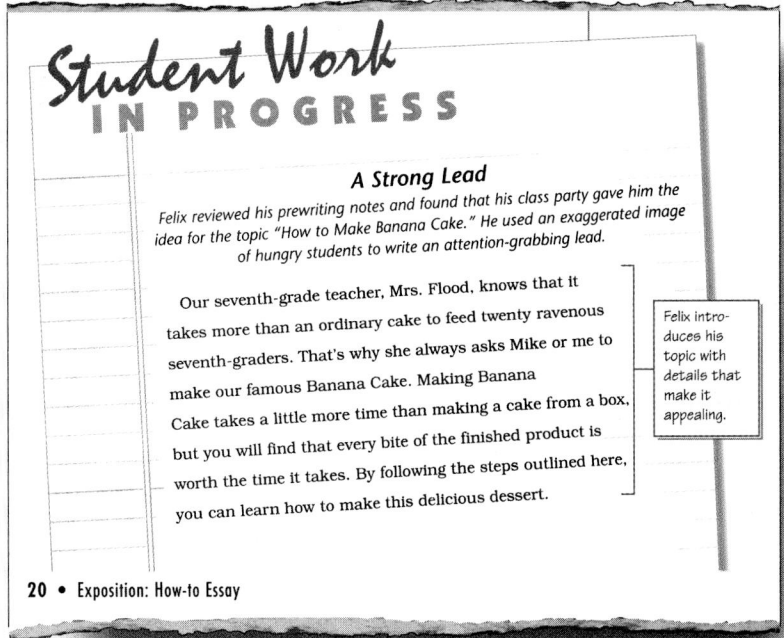

Student Work
IN PROGRESS

A Strong Lead

Felix reviewed his prewriting notes and found that his class party gave him the idea for the topic "How to Make Banana Cake." He used an exaggerated image of hungry students to write an attention-grabbing lead.

Our seventh-grade teacher, Mrs. Flood, knows that it takes more than an ordinary cake to feed twenty ravenous seventh-graders. That's why she always asks Mike or me to make our famous Banana Cake. Making Banana Cake takes a little more time than making a cake from a box, but you will find that every bite of the finished product is worth the time it takes. By following the steps outlined here, you can learn how to make this delicious dessert.

> Felix introduces his topic with details that make it appealing.

More Strategic Revision

More systematic, hands-on revision strategies help students examine what they write and how to improve it.

Revising

Looking at Overall Structure

Add an Introduction and Conclusion

After writing your first draft, reread your how-to essay, looking for ways to improve and polish it. You will probably recognize that you don't want to jump right in with step one and end abruptly at the last step. Instead, give a general overview of your topic in an introduction. Then, explain the different steps in the body of the essay and review, summarize, or briefly comment on the procedures in a conclusion.

Revision Strategy
◆ **Write a Strong Lead**

Begin with an image or idea that "leads" your reader into the essay. Look through your prewriting notes to find details that remind you why you enjoy the activity or why you decided to write about your topic. The detail that grabbed your interest may spark your audience's interest as well. Use one of these details to make that first sentence an attention grabber!

Analyzing Your Paragraphs
Identify Paragraph Purpose

Once you're comfortable with the general structure of your paper, carefully focus on each individual paragraph. The purpose of each paragraph will determine the words or phrases that may need to be added to make your meaning clearer.

Revision Strategy
◆ **Use Steps, Stacks, Chains, and Balances**

• **Steps** If the paragraph is explaining a step or several related steps for which time order is important, make sure you have indicated the sequence. Use words such as *first, next,* and *finally.*

• **Stacks** If the paragraph explains how one part of a process contributes to another, show the connection between ideas with words such as *and, furthermore,* and *for instance.*

• **Chains** If the paragraph explains the cause-and-effect relationship between steps, use words such as *so, because,* and *consequently.*

• **Balance** If the paragraph shows choice or contrast, use words such as *but, however, on the other hand,* and *rather.*

▶ Critical Viewing Do you think these boys successfully followed the directions for making a cake? **[Evaluate]**

Student Work
IN PROGRESS

A Strong Lead

Felix reviewed his prewriting notes and found that his class party gave him the idea for the topic "How to Make Banana Cake." He used an exaggerated image of hungry students to write an attention-grabbing lead.

Our seventh-grade teacher, Mrs. Flood, knows that it takes more than an ordinary cake to feed twenty ravenous seventh-graders. That's why she always asks Mike or me to make our famous Banana Cake. Making Banana Cake takes a little more time than making a cake from a box, but you will find that every bite of the finished product is worth the time it takes. By following the steps outlined here, you can learn how to make this delicious dessert.

> Felix introduces his topic with details that make it appealing.

20 • Exposition: How-to Essay

Unmatched Assessment Preparation

Assessment resources that you and your students need to succeed

Standardized Test Preparation Workshops

Standardized Test Preparation Workshops after each chapter provide unmatched preparation for PSAT, SAT, ACT, AP, state, and local standardized tests.

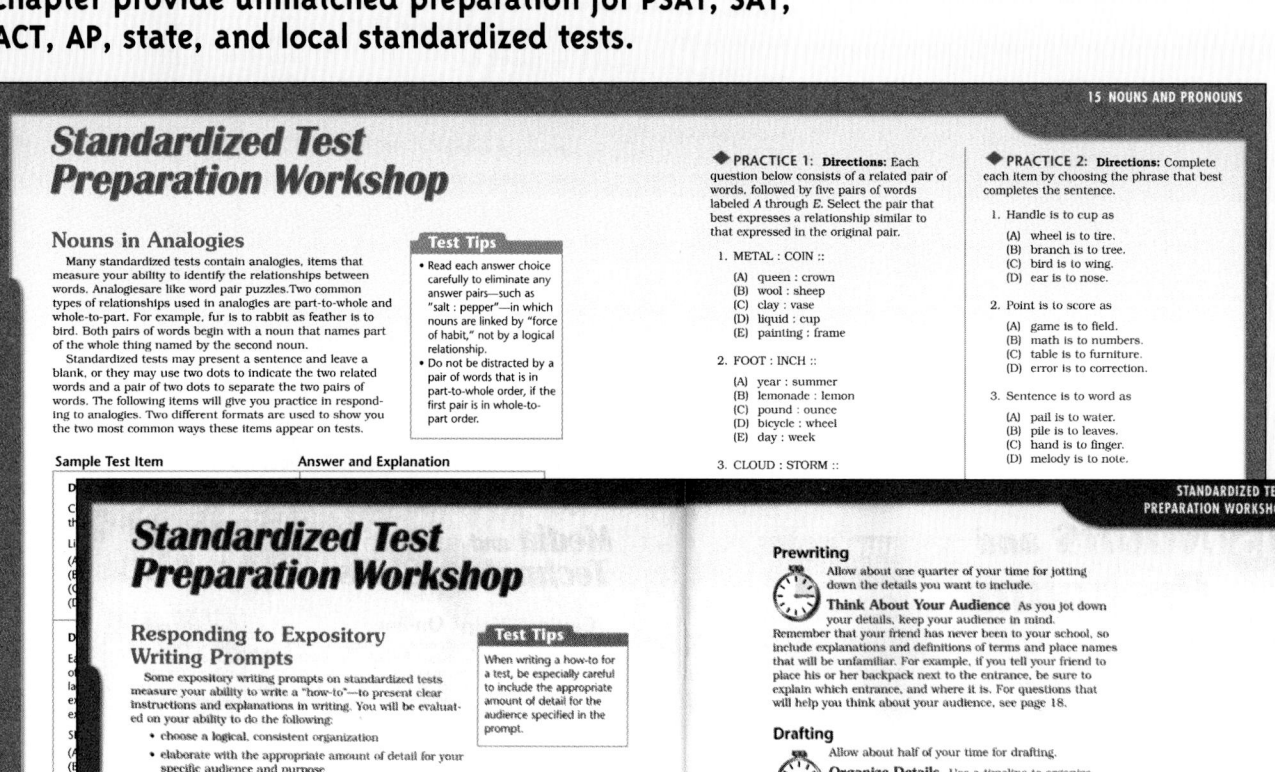

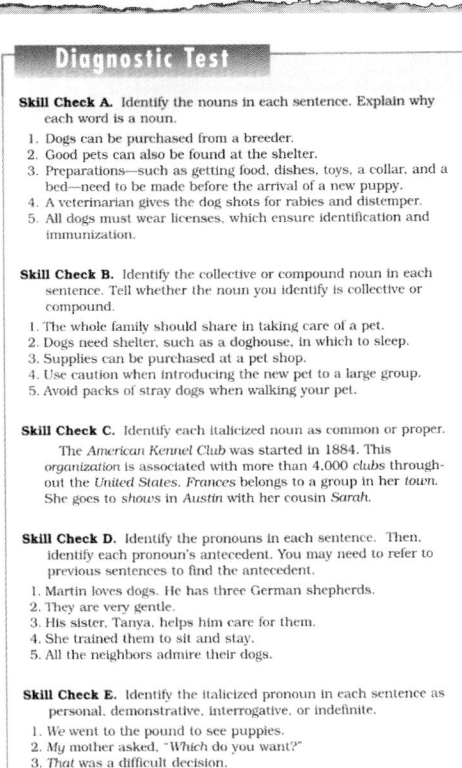

Diagnostic Test

Skill Check A. Identify the nouns in each sentence. Explain why each word is a noun.

1. Dogs can be purchased from a breeder.
2. Good pets can also be found at the shelter.
3. Preparations—such as getting food, dishes, toys, a collar, and a bed—need to be made before the arrival of a new puppy.
4. A veterinarian gives the dog shots for rabies and distemper.
5. All dogs must wear licenses, which ensure identification and immunization.

Skill Check B. Identify the collective or compound noun in each sentence. Tell whether the noun you identify is collective or compound.

1. The whole family should share in taking care of a pet.
2. Dogs need shelter, such as a doghouse, in which to sleep.
3. Supplies can be purchased at a pet shop.
4. Use caution when introducing the new pet to a large group.
5. Avoid packs of stray dogs when walking your pet.

Skill Check C. Identify each italicized noun as common or proper.

The *American Kennel Club* was started in 1884. This *organization* is associated with more than 4,000 *clubs* throughout the *United States*. *Frances* belongs to a group in her *town*. She goes to *shows* in *Austin* with her cousin *Sarah*.

Skill Check D. Identify the pronouns in each sentence. Then, identify each pronoun's antecedent. You may need to refer to previous sentences to find the antecedent.

1. Martin loves dogs. He has three German shepherds.
2. They are very gentle.
3. His sister, Tanya, helps him care for them.
4. She trained them to sit and stay.
5. All the neighbors admire their dogs.

Skill Check E. Identify the italicized pronoun in each sentence as personal, demonstrative, interrogative, or indefinite.

1. *We* went to the pound to see puppies.
2. *My* mother asked, "*Which* do you want?"
3. *That* was a difficult decision.
4. *Those* pups were so cute I wanted them all.
5. *Each* had *its* special qualities.

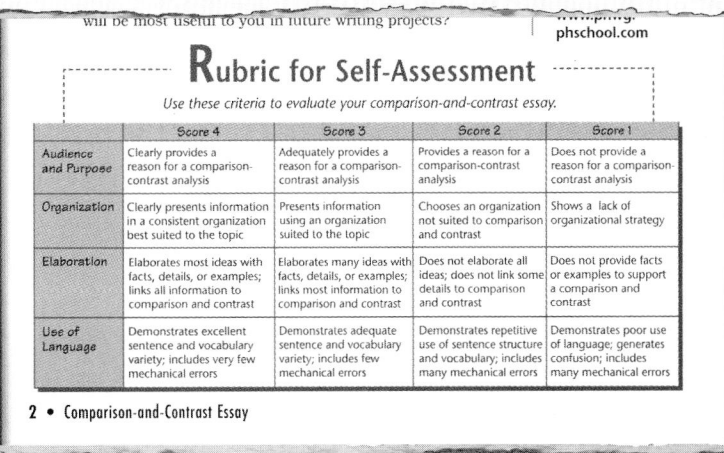

will be most useful to you in future writing projects?

www.phschschool.com

Rubric for Self-Assessment

Use these criteria to evaluate your comparison-and-contrast essay.

	Score 4	Score 3	Score 2	Score 1
Audience and Purpose	Clearly provides a reason for a comparison-contrast analysis	Adequately provides a reason for a comparison-contrast analysis	Provides a reason for a comparison-contrast analysis	Does not provide a reason for a comparison-contrast analysis
Organization	Clearly presents information in a consistent organization best suited to the topic	Presents information using an organization suited to the topic	Chooses an organization not suited to comparison and contrast	Shows a lack of organizational strategy
Elaboration	Elaborates most ideas with facts, details, or examples; links all information to comparison and contrast	Elaborates many ideas with facts, details, or examples; links most information to comparison and contrast	Does not elaborate all ideas; does not link some details to comparison and contrast	Does not provide facts or examples to support a comparison and contrast
Use of Language	Demonstrates excellent sentence and vocabulary variety; includes very few mechanical errors	Demonstrates adequate sentence and vocabulary variety; includes few mechanical errors	Demonstrates repetitive use of sentence structure and vocabulary; includes many mechanical errors	Demonstrates poor use of language; generates confusion; includes many mechanical errors

2 • Comparison-and-Contrast Essay

Success for all Students

Accommodate your students' diverse needs by customizing instruction with assignments that address different ability levels and learning styles.

Diagnostic Tests

Diagnostic Tests before each grammar chapter help you assess students' skill levels and identify areas for improvement.

Flexible Assessment Options

Develop confident and successful test-takers with a variety of test-taking opportunities.

Time-Saving Options!

Save time with an easy-to-use handbook style and a variety of integrated ancillary support options.

21.1 THE FOUR FUNCTIONS OF A SENTENCE

GRAMMAR IN LITERATURE

from **Tiger:**
A Biography of Tiger Woods
John Strege

In the following passage, the last sentence is an imperative sentence. The other sentences Earl [Tiger Woods's father] speaks are declarative. Since many imperative sentences

An imperative sentence gives an order or a direction and ends with either a period or an exclamation mark.

Most imperative sentences start with a verb. In this type of imperative sentence, the subject is understood to be *you.*

IMPERATIVE: Follow my instructions carefully.
Run as hard as you can!

Notice the punctuation at the end of these examples. In the first sentence, the period suggests that a mild command is being given in an ordinary tone of voice. The exclamation mark at the end of the last sentence suggests

Easy-to-use

handbook style gives you and your students immediate access to review sections when necessary.

Chapter 7 Time and Resource Manager

	LESSON FOCUS	PRINT AND MEDIA RESOURCES
DAY 1	**Introduction to Persuasive Essays** Students learn elements of persuasive essays and analyze the Model From Literature (pp. 128–133).	Writers at Work Videotape, Persuasion Writing Lab CD-ROM, Persuasion
DAY 2	**Prewriting** Students choose and narrow a topic, consider their audience and purpose and gather information (pp. 134–138).	Teaching Resources: Writing Support Transparencies, 7-A-E; Writing Support Activity Book, 7-1
DAY 3	**Drafting** Students organize their ideas and write their first drafts (pp. 139–140).	Teaching Re... Support Activ...
DAY 4	**Revising** Students revise their drafts in terms of overall structure, paragraphs, sentences and word choice (pp. 141–145).	Teaching Re...
DAY 5	**Editing and Proofreading; Publishing and Presenting** Students check their work for accuracy and correctness and present their final drafts (pp. 146–147).	Teaching Re... Writing Asses... Persuasion

	LESSON FOCUS	P...
DAY 1	**Drafting** Students review characteristics for persuasive writing, select topics and write drafts.	Writing Lab... Writers at W... Teaching Re... Writing Supp...
DAY 2	**Revising to Presenting** Students work individually or with peers to revise, edit and proofread their work for presentation.	Teaching Re... Scoring Rubri... Scoring Rubri...

HOMEWORK
Have students complete any stage of the lesson for homework.

TECHNOLOGY
Students can complete any stage of the lesson on computer. Have them print out their completed work.

FEATURES
Extend coverage the Humanities (... Standardized Tes...

7 PERSUASION

INTEGRATED SKILLS COVERAGE TEKS CORRELATIONS	BLOCK SCHEDULING
Integrating Grammar 3A–B Avoiding Adverb Clauses, SE p. 143 Revising Titles, SE p. 146	**Pacing Suggestions** **For 90-minute Blocks** • Have students complete the Prewriting and Drafting stages in a single period. • Focus one class period on Revising and Editing and Publishing and Presenting. Allow at least 30 minutes for peer revision.
Reading-Writing Connection 6F, 8A Reading Strategy, SE p. 130 Writing Application, SE p. 135	**Resources for Varying Instruction** • Writing Lab CD-ROM If your students have access to...

PREPARE and ENGAGE

Save time

with point of use support.

Chapter 2 A Walk Through the Writing Process

▶ **Lesson Objectives**

1. To understand that writing is a process.
2. To learn that there are two main types of writing, reflexive and extensive.
3. To review the stage in the writing process.
4. To become familiar with strategies for generating topic ideas.
5. To learn ways to narrow a list of topic ideas.
6. To create an audience profile.
7. To learn strategies for gathering details.
8. To practice organizing information.
9. To review strategies for creating a first draft, including the use of writing hook, and the SEE method.
10. To become familiar with strategies for revising first drafts.
11. To learn strategies for analyzing paragraphs and improving sentences.
12. To learn strategies for refining word choice.
13. To understand the peer revision process.
14. To apply strategies for collecting, refining, and assessing writing projects.

Critical Viewing
Relate Students' answers will vary, but they should identify both positive and negative writing habits they have.

The Process of Writing

There are five stages of the writing process.

• **Prewriting** Freely exploring topics, choosing a topic, and beginning to gather and organize details before you write.
• **Drafting** Getting your ideas down on paper roughly in the format you intend for the finished work.
• **Revising** Correcting any major errors and improving the form and content of the writing.
• **Editing and Proofreading** Polishing the writing and fixing errors in grammar, spelling, and mechanics.
• **Publishing and Presenting** Sharing your writing with others.

These stages may seem sequential, but writers often move among the various stages as they work. For example, as a question detail once writers, they often discover that their initial vision is their presenting work, to gather more information.

A Guided Tour

Use this chapter as a guided tour to the writing process. Take a close look at the steps presented here. Learn new strategies, look at the way another writer has used them, and try them yourself. When you apply these strategies to your own writing process, the improved quality of your final work will treat surprise you.

Types of Writing

One way to study types of writing is to analyze them by **mode**—the form or shape that writing takes. The list below allows the results of writing you'll encounter in this book.

Another way to learn more about writing is to consider the source or the inspiration and the intended audience. For example, when you write **reflexively**, you choose what to write, when, how to use, and whether to share your writing. Reflexive writing such as a diary, or a journal entry, is done yourself and for your self. In **extensive** writing, you write for others. It is usually responding to a school assignment that will be read by a general audience. Extensive writing begins with others and is the others. It can take many forms, including poems, essays, and much reviews.

▲ **Critical Viewing**
How does one craft writing process help to complete your success as a writer? [Relate]

MODES OF WRITING

Narration
Description
Persuasion
Exposition
Research
Response to Literature
Poetry and Plays
Writing for Assessment

PREPARE and ENGAGE

Play "Pass a Word." Write 30 different words on small pieces of paper. Put the papers into a container and choose one student as Player 1. Explain that you will take a word from this container and read it aloud. As soon as Player 1 hears the word, he or she should "Blurt out" whatever word or phrase comes to mind. Proceed with Player 2. Next, have Player 1 choose and read a word for Player 2. Player 2 blurts a word or phrase. Repeat this process until all students have had a chance to both choose and blurt a word.

Explain that students will use a writing strategy that is similar to "Blurt a Word." In this strategy, called freewriting, students quickly write down whatever thoughts come to mind. Freewriting boosts students' creativity and confidence while also providing them with ideas for topics to write about.

Activate Prior Knowledge

Write the words Reflexive and Extensive on the chalkboard in column heads. Explain that reflexive writing is writing that students choose to do. Under the Reflexive head, write writing a note to a friend. Extensive writing is writing that students are asked to do. Under the Extensive head, write writing a thank you note to a guest speaker. Invite students to share on their own life experiences with writing to add examples under both heads.

TIME AND RESOURCE MANAGER

In-Depth Coverage	Accelerated Pace
• Cover pp. 14–33 in class. • Review the illustrations on p. 14 and the diagram on p. 15. • Point out that this chapter will walk students through the writing process.	• Have students read pp. 14–33 on their own.

Choose from

in-depth, accelerated, or block-scheduling lesson plans to best meet your needs and the needs of your students.

Make planning easier
with a wealth of integrated ancillary support.

Multimedia Instruction for the Future!

Connect to today's multimedia generation with a variety of fully-integrated technology practice and support options.

Prentice Hall's Internet Homepage

brings the world of writing to your students through support and extension activities and related links.

Resource Pro

helps you manage your lesson planning and resources with a simple click of a mouse.

Formal Assessment CD-Rom

allows you to gauge your students' ability levels and establish your own skills objectives.

TEACHING RESOURCES

Writing

Writing Support Activity Book
Topic Bank for Heterogeneous Classes
Multigenre Research Project

Grammar, Usage, and Mechanics

Grammar Exercise Workbook, Teacher's Edition
Daily Language Practice
Hands-on Grammar Activity Book
Extra Grammar and Writing Exercises

Academic and Workplace Skills

Academic and Workplace Skills Activity Book, Teacher's Edition
Vocabulary and Spelling Practice Book, Teacher's Edition
Reading Support Practice Book, Teacher's Edition

Assessment

Standardized Test Preparation Workbook, Teacher's Edition
Writing Assessment and Portfolio Management
Formal Assessment/Assessment Resources Software CD-ROM

Professional Resources

How to Manage Instruction in the Block
How to Assess Student Work
Putting Patterns to Work
Kick Off for Success: Organizing for School
Hearing All Sides: Resolving Conflict

ADDITIONAL ANCILLARIES

Workbooks

Hands-on Grammar Activity Book
Writing Support Activity Book
Grammar Exercise Workbook
Reading Support Practice Book
Vocabulary and Spelling Workbook
Academic and Workplace Skills Workbook
Standardized Test Preparation Workbook

Transparencies

Writing Support Transparencies
Daily Language Practice Transparencies
Grammar Exercises Answers on Transparencies
Scoring Rubrics on Transparencies

Technology

Writing and Grammar Interactive CD-ROM
    Writing Lab CD-ROM
    Language Lab CD-ROM
Interactive Writing and Grammar Web site
Resource Pro CD-ROM (including Test Bank)
Writers at Work Videotape

Spanish Support
Extra Grammar and Writing Exercises
Multigenre Research Writing

Correlation to the Six Traits Analytical Model

Chapter	Ideas	Organization	Voice	Word Choice	Sentence Fluency	Conventions
1 The Writer in You			p. 3			
2 A Walk Through the Writing Process						
2.1	pp. 16–20	p. 20				
2.2	p. 22	p. 21	p. 21			
2.3	pp. 23–24			p. 23, p. 25	p. 24	
2.4						
Spot/Hum.	p. 28					p. 26
3 Paragraphs and Compositions						
3.1	pp. 33–35	p. 36				
3.2	p. 37	pp. 38–39				
3.3			p. 42	p. 42	p. 42	p. 43
Spot/Hum.	p. 44					
4 Narration: Autobiography						
4.1	pp. 50–51	pp. 50–51				
4.2	pp. 52–55		p. 55			
4.3	pp. 56–57	p. 56				
4.4	p. 58	pp. 59–60		p. 61	p. 60	
4.5						p. 63
4.6	p. 64	p. 64		p. 64		p. 64
4.7	p. 65	p. 65				
Spot/Hum.	p. 68					
5 Narration: Short Story						
5.1	pp. 74–77	pp. 74–77				
5.2	p. 78, pp. 80–81	p. 80	p. 80			
5.3	p. 83	p. 82				
5.4	p. 85	p. 84		pp. 87	p. 86	
5.5						p. 88
5.6	p. 89	p. 89	p. 89	p. 89		p. 89
5.7	pp. 90–91	pp. 90–92		p. 91		
Spot/Hum.	p. 94					
6 Description						
6.1	pp. 100–101	p. 101		p. 101		
6.2	pp. 102–105		p. 104	pp. 103–104		
6.3	pp. 103–104	p. 103		p. 107		
6.4	pp. 109–110	p. 108		p. 109, pp. 112–113		p. 111
6.5						p. 114
6.7	p. 117	p. 117		pp. 116–117		
Spot/Hum.	p. 120					
7 Persuasion						
7.1	pp. 126–127	pp. 126–127	pp. 126–127	pp. 126–127		
7.2	pp. 128–131		p. 130			
7.3	p. 133	p. 132				
7.4	pp. 134–136	pp. 134–136		p. 138	p. 137	p. 137
7.5						p. 139
7.6	p. 140	p. 140	p. 140	p. 140		
7.7	pp. 142–143	pp. 141–143		pp. 142–143		
Spot/Hum.	p. 146					
Media/Tech.	p. 147			p. 147		
8 Exposition: Comparison and Contrast						
8.1	pp. 152–153	pp. 152–153				
8.2	pp. 154–156	p. 157	p. 157			
8.3	p. 159	p. 158				
8.4	p. 160, p. 162	pp. 160–162		p. 164	p. 163	p. 163
8.5						p. 165
8.6	p. 166	p. 166		p. 166	p. 166	p. 166
8.7	pp. 167–168	pp. 167–168				
Spot/Hum.	p. 170					

Chapter	Ideas	Organization	Voice	Word Choice	Sentence Fluency	Conventions
9 Exposition: Cause and Effect						
9.1	pp. 176–177					
9.2	pp. 178–9, pp. 180–1		p. 181			
9.3	pp. 182–183	p. 182				
9.4	p. 185	pp. 184–185		p. 186, p. 188		pp. 186–187
9.5						p. 189
9.6	p. 190	p. 190		p. 190		
9.7	p. 192	p. 191				
Spot/Hum.	p. 194					
10 Exposition: How-to Essay						
10.1	pp. 200–201	pp. 200–201				
10.2	pp. 202–205		p. 204			
10.3	p. 207	p. 206		p. 207		
10.4		pp. 208–209		p. 212	p. 210	p. 211
10.5						p. 214
10.6	p. 215	p. 215		p. 215	p. 215	
10.7		p. 216				
Spot/Hum.	p. 218					
11 Research Report						
11.1	pp. 224–226	pp. 224–226			p. 225	
11.2	pp. 228–9, pp. 230–1					
11.3	pp. 232–233	p. 232				
11.4	p. 238	pp. 234–235		pp. 237–238	pp. 236–237	p. 237
11.5						p. 239
11.6	p. 240	p. 240			p. 240	p. 240
11.7	pp. 241–242	pp. 241–242				
Spot/Hum.	p. 244					
12 Response to Literature						
12.1	pp. 250–251	p. 250				
12.2	pp. 252–257		p. 255			
12.3	pp. 258–259					
12.4	pp. 260–261	p. 260			pp. 262–263	
12.5				p. 263		p. 263, p. 264
12.6	p. 265	p. 265		p. 265	p. 265	p. 265
12.7	pp. 266–268	p. 266, p. 268				
Spot/Hum.	p. 270					
13 Writing for Assessment						
13.1	pp. 276–278					
13.2	pp. 279–280	p. 279				
13.3	pp. 281–282	pp. 281–282				
13.4				p. 282		p. 283
13.5	p. 284	p. 284	p.284	p. 284	p. 284	p. 284
13.6	pp. 285–286	pp. 285–286				
Spot/Hum.						
14 Nouns and Pronouns						
14.1				pp. 296–299		pp. 296–299
14.2				pp. 301–302		pp. 305–307
15 Verbs						
15.1				p. 316, p. 318		
15.2				p. 324		p. 320, pp. 322–323
15.3						pp. 326–328
16 Adjectives and Adverbs						
16.1				p. 336		p. 338, pp. 340–346
16.2				p. 351		pp. 348–350
17 Prepositions						
17.1						p. 362
17.2						pp. 366–367

Correlation to the Six Traits Analytical Model

Chapter	Ideas	Organization	Voice	Word Choice	Sentence Fluency	Conventions
18 Conjunctions and Interjections 18.1 18.2				pp. 381–382		pp. 376–377
19 Basic Sentence Parts 19.1 19.2 19.3 19.4 19.5					p. 405	pp. 392–393 p. 396 p. 400, 402 pp. 406–408 pp. 410–414, pp. 416–418
20 Phrases and Clauses 20.1 20.2						pp. 426–8, pp. 430–2 pp. 438–9, pp. 441–3
21 Effective Sentences 21.1 21.2 21.3 21.4					p. 460, p. 462 pp. 465–466	pp. 456–457 pp. 469–471, pp. 473–476, pp. 478–479
22 Using Verbs 22.1 22.2						pp. 492–3, pp. 495–6 p. 500, p. 502, p. 504, pp. 508–511
23 Using Pronouns						pp. 520–521, p. 523, p. 525
24 Making Words Agree 24.1 24.2						pp. 534–536, pp. 538–539, pp. 542–543 pp. 548–9, p. 551
25 Using Modifiers 25.1 25.2						pp. 560–565 pp. 567–568
26 Punctuation 26.1 26.2 26.3 26.4 26.5						pp. 580–582 p. 585, pp. 587–588, p. 590, pp. 592–596 p. 600, pp. 602–604 pp. 606–609, p. 611, pp. 614–616 pp. 618–626
27 Capitalization						pp. 636–645, p. 647
Sentence Diagraming Workshop						pp. 656–665
28 Speaking Listening, Viewing and Representing 28.1	p. 787, pp. 790–791	pp. 789–790	pp. 788–790	pp. 788–790	pp. 788–790	
29 Vocabulary and Spelling 29.1 29.2 29.3 29.4				pp. 692–694 pp. 695–697 pp. 698–701		pp. 702–710
30 Reading Skills 30.1 30.2 30.3	pp. 719–720 pp. 721–723 p. 727, pp. 730–731	p. 726		p. 721, p. 725		
31 Study, Reference, and Test-Taking Skills						

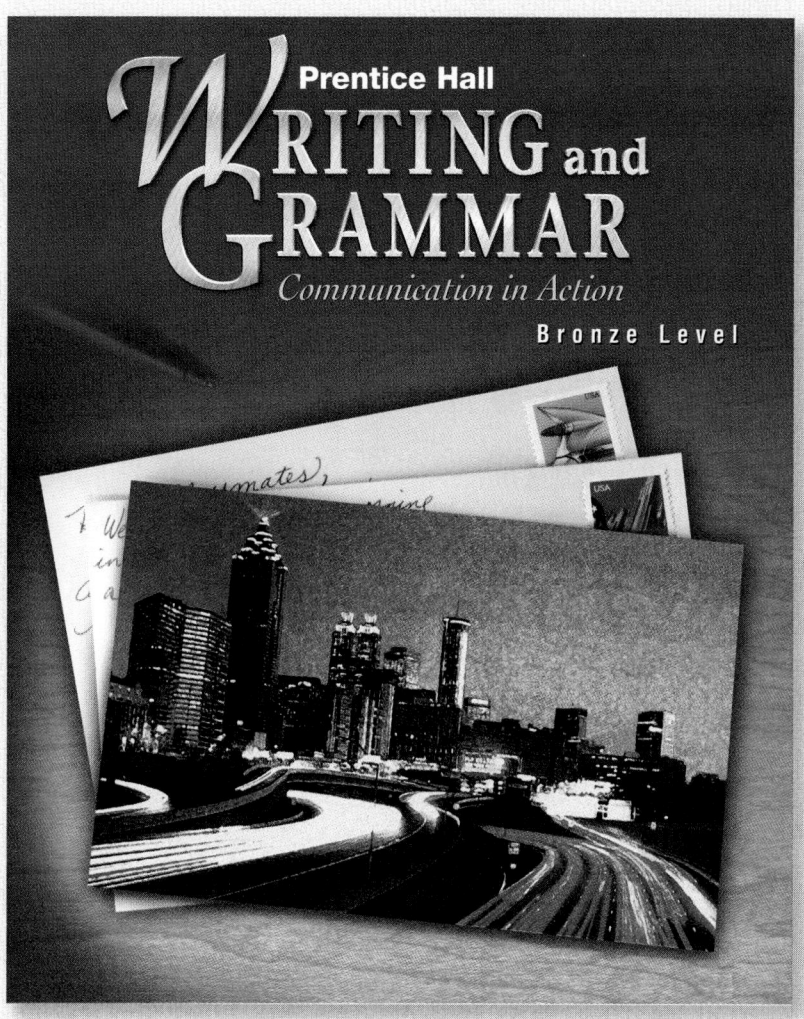

Prentice Hall

WRITING and GRAMMAR

Communication in Action

Bronze Level

Bronze Level

Prentice Hall

Upper Saddle River, New Jersey
Needham, Massachusetts
Glenview, Illinois

ISBN 0-13-436963-7

5 6 7 8 9 10   05 04 03 02 01

Prentice
Hall

WRITING and GRAMMAR
Communication in Action

Copper
Bronze
Silver
Gold
Platinum
Ruby
Diamond

Program Authors

The program authors guided the direction and philosophy of *Prentice Hall Writing and Grammar: Communication in Action.* Working with the development team, they contributed to the pedagogical integrity of the program and to its relevance to today's teachers and students.

Joyce Armstrong Carroll

In her forty-year career, Joyce Armstrong Carroll, Ed.D., has taught on every grade level from primary to graduate school. In the past twenty years, she has trained teachers in the teaching of writing. A nationally known consultant, she has served as president of TCTE and on NCTE's Commission on Composition. More than fifty of her articles have appeared in journals such as *Curriculum Review, English Journal, Media & Methods, Southwest Philosophical Studies, Ohio English Journal, English in Texas,* and the *Florida English Journal.* With Edward E. Wilson, Dr. Carroll co-authored *Acts of Teaching: How to Teach Writing* and co-edited *Poetry After Lunch: Poems to Read Aloud.* Beyond her direct involvement with the writing pedagogy presented in this series, Dr. Carroll guided the development of the Hands-on Grammar feature. She co-directs the New Jersey Writing Project in Texas.

Edward E. Wilson

A former editor of *English in Texas,* Edward E. Wilson has served as a high-school English teacher and a writing consultant in school districts nationwide. Wilson has served on the Texas Teacher Professional Practices Commission and on NCTE's Commission on Composition. With Dr. Carroll, he co-wrote *Acts of Teaching: How to Teach Writing* and co-edited the award-winning *Poetry After Lunch: Poems to Read Aloud.* In addition to his direct involvement with the writing pedagogy presented in this series, Wilson provided inspiration for the Spotlight on Humanities feature. Wilson's poetry appears in Paul Janeczko's anthology *The Music of What Happens.* Wilson co-directs the New Jersey Writing Project in Texas.

Gary Forlini

Gary Forlini, a nationally known education consultant, developed the grammar, usage, and mechanics instruction and exercises in this series. After teaching in the Pelham, New York, schools for many years, he established Research in Media, an educational research agency that provides information for product developers, school staff developers, media companies, and arts organizations, as well as private-sector corporations and foundations. Mr. Forlini was co-author of the *S.A.T. Home Study* program and has written numerous industry reports on elementary, secondary, and post-secondary education markets.

National Advisory Panel

The teachers and administrators serving on the National Advisory Panel provided ongoing input into the development of *Prentice Hall Writing and Grammar: Communication in Action.* Their valuable insights ensure that the perspectives of teachers and students throughout the country are represented within the instruction in this series.

Dr. Pauline Bigby-Jenkins
Coordinator for Secondary English
    Language Arts
Ann Arbor Public Schools
Ann Arbor, Michigan

Lee Bromberger
English Department Chairperson
Mukwonago High School
Mukwonago, Wisconsin

Mary Chapman
Teacher of English
Free State High School
Lawrence, Kansas

Jim Deatherage
Language Arts Department
    Chairperson
Richland High School
Richland, Washington

Luis Dovalina
Teacher of English
La Joya High School
La Joya, Texas

JoAnn Giardino
Teacher of English
Centennial High School
Columbus, Ohio

Susan Goldberg
Teacher of English
Westlake Middle School
Thornwood, New York

Jean Hicks
Director, Louisville Writing Project
University of Louisville
Louisville, Kentucky

Karen Hurley
Teacher of Language Arts
Perry Meridian Middle School
Indianapolis, Indiana

Karen Lopez
Teacher of English
Hart High School
Newhall, California

Marianne Minshall
Teacher of Reading and Language Arts
Westmore Middle School
Columbus, Ohio

Nancy Monroe
English Department Chairperson
Bolton High School
Alexandria, Louisiana

Ken Spurlock
Assistant Principal
Boone County High School
Florence, Kentucky

Cynthia Katz Tyroff
Staff Development Specialist
    and Teacher of English
Northside Independent School District
San Antonio, Texas

Holly Ward
Teacher of Language Arts
Campbell Middle School
Daytona Beach, Florida

Grammar Review Team

The following teachers reviewed the grammar instruction in this series to ensure accuracy, clarity, and pedagogy.

Kathy Hamilton
Paul Hertzog
Daren Hoisington
Beverly Ladd

Karen Lopez
Dianna Louise Lund
Sean O'Brien

CONTENTS IN BRIEF

Chapters 14–27

Part 2: Grammar, Usage, and Mechanics . . 292

Chapters 28–31

Part 3: Academic and Workplace Skills . . 666

Resources:

Contents in Brief • vii

CONTENTS
PART 1: WRITING

INTEGRATED SKILLS

INTEGRATED SKILLS

INTEGRATED SKILLS

Chapter 4 Narration

Autobiographical Writing 48

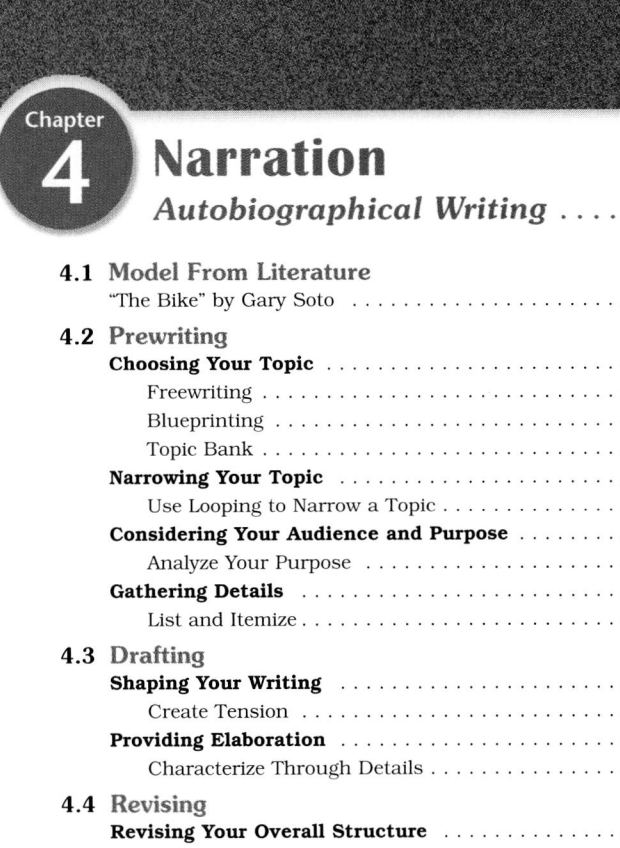

Student Work IN PROGRESS

Featured Work:
"To the Dogs"
by Emily Taylor Speer
Hildebrandt Intermediate
School
Spring, Texas

INTEGRATED SKILLS

Contents • ix

Chapter 5 Narration

Short Story 72

INTEGRATED SKILLS

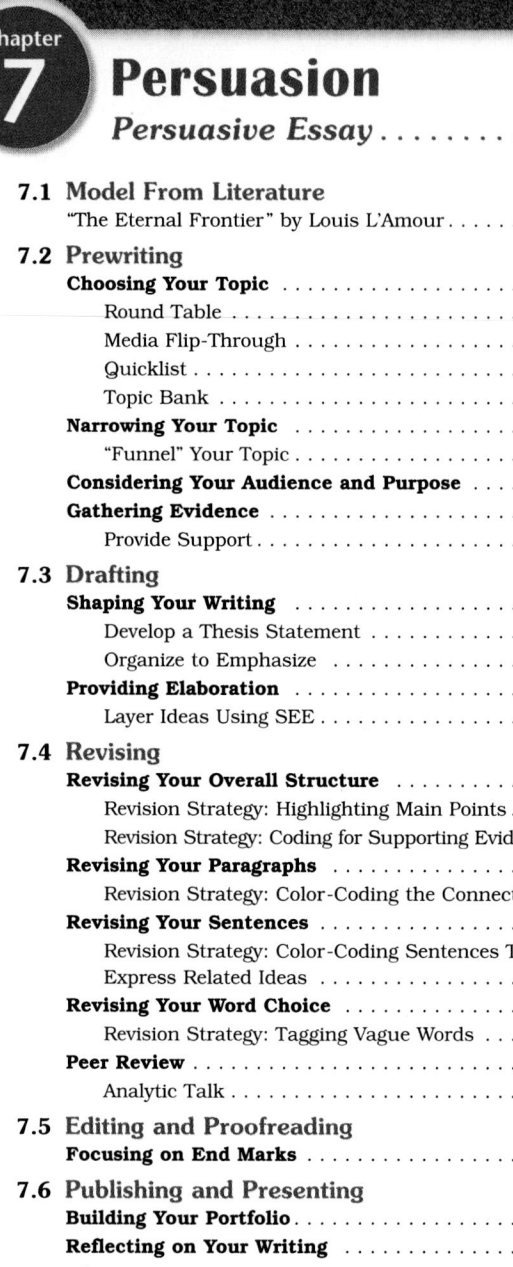

INTEGRATED SKILLS

Contents • xiii

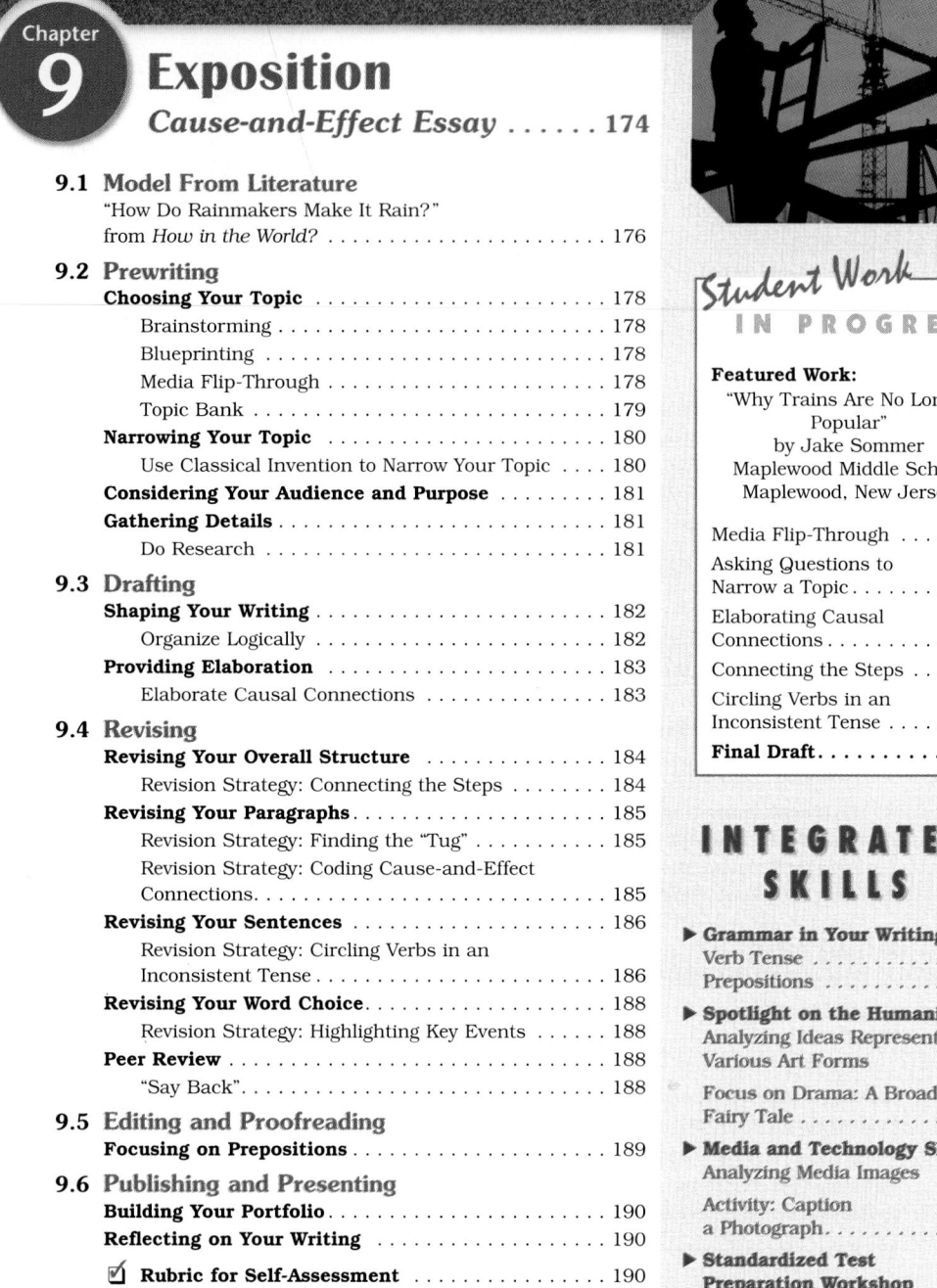

Chapter 10 Exposition

How-to Essay 198

INTEGRATED SKILLS

Contents • **xv**

Chapter 11 Research Report ...222

Student Work
IN PROGRESS

Featured Work:
"Built to Survive: Whales"
by Jamie Barraclough
Los Alamos Middle School
Los Alamos, New Mexico

INTEGRATED SKILLS

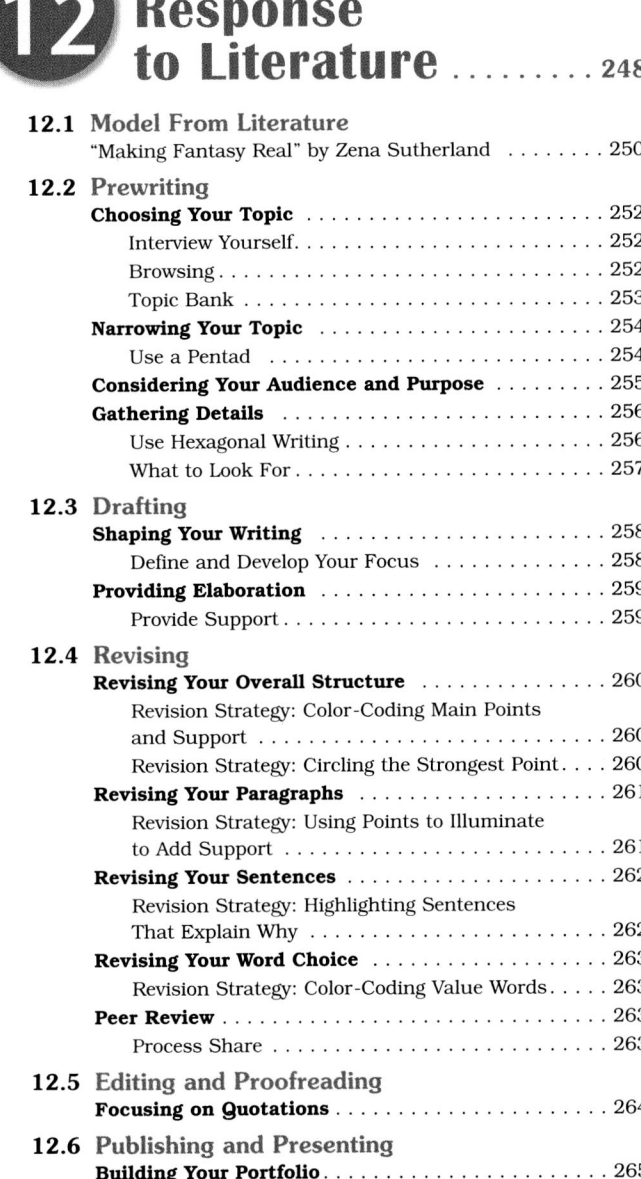

Student Work
IN PROGRESS

Featured Work:
"Frogs vs. Flowers"
by Jade Yamamoto
Calvary Lutheran School
Indianapolis, Indiana

INTEGRATED SKILLS

Contents • xvii

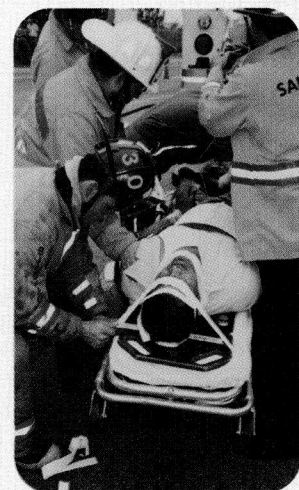

Contents • xxiii

▶ *Lesson Objectives*

1. To understand writing as a recursive process and to develop ownership of their own writing processes

2. To write in a variety of forms, including narrative, descriptive, persuasive, expository, and literary texts, and to develop skills in writing for assessment

3. To analyze works of literature and student drafts as models and examples of specific writing strategies

4. To develop voice and adjust their writing to various audiences and purposes

5. To develop research skills and to use writing as a tool for learning

6. To apply specific prewriting strategies for generating and narrowing writing topics

7. To use graphic organizers and other methods for organizing and supporting ideas in drafting

8. To approach revision in a systematic way in terms of overall structure, paragraphs, sentences, and word choice

9. To edit and proofread drafts to ensure appropriate usage and accuracy in spelling and the conventions and mechanics of written English

10. To understand rubrics and to use them to evaluate their own writing and the writing of others

The Students, Eduard Von Gebhardt

PART 1

Writing

Responding to Fine Art

The Students **by Eduard Von Gebhardt**

Use this painting to start a discussion about the process of writing.

1. Have students examine the painting on pages xxvi–1. You might use the following questions to prompt discussion:

   What are some of the objects that you see in the painting? What are each of these two men doing? How can you tell?

2. Have students describe each of the two figures, using details from the painting to support their responses. Ask students why they think the figure on the right is looking off so intently into the distance.

3. Encourage students to discuss how this painting pertains to the writing process. Students may say that the two men are students, possibly engaged in research for a writing project. Other students may say that the men are simply reading, which pertains to the last stage of the writing process, publishing and presenting.

In-Depth Lesson Plan

	LESSON FOCUS	PRINT AND MEDIA RESOURCES
DAY 1	**Introduction to The Writer in You** Students learn about writing in everyday life and about the qualities of good writing (pp. 2–3).	**Writers at Work Videotape,** Selected Segments
DAY 2	**Developing Your Writing Life** Students discuss ways to keep track of ideas and reading and writing sources, learn different approaches to writing and different ways to plan for writing (pp. 4–6).	**Teaching Resources:** *Writing Support Transparencies,* 1-A; *Writing Support Activity Book,* 1-1
DAY 3	**Collaboration and Publishing** Students discuss the value of collaboration with peers and research publishing opportunities (pp. 7–9).	**Teaching Resources:** *Formal Assessment,* Ch. 1

Accelerated Lesson Plan

	LESSON FOCUS	PRINT AND MEDIA RESOURCES
DAY 1	**Introduction to The Writer in You** Students review how writing is used in everyday life and what some qualities of good writing are (pp. 2–3).	**Writers at Work Videotape,** Selected Segments
DAY 2	**Developing Your Writing Life Through Collaboration and Publishing** Students learn how to keep track of ideas, learn about different writing approaches, discuss collaboration, and research publishing opportunities (pp. 4–9).	**Teaching Resources:** *Writing Support Transparencies,* 1-A; *Writing Support Activity Book,* 1-1; *Formal Assessment,* Ch. 1

Options for Adapting Lesson Plans

HOMEWORK

Have students complete any stage of the lesson for homework.

FEATURES

Extend coverage with Spotlight on the Humanities (p. 10), Media and Technology Skills (p. 11), and the Standardized Test Preparation Workshop (p. 12).

TECHNOLOGY

Students can complete any stage of the lesson on computer. Have them print out their completed work.

INTEGRATED SKILLS COVERAGE

Viewing and Representing
Critical Viewing, SE pp. 2, 5, 6, 7, ATE p. 10
Analyzing How Meaning is Communicated through the Arts, SE p. 10

Speaking and Listening
ATE p. 8

Technology
SE p. 11

Real-World Connection
ATE p. 5

Workplace Skills
Integrating Workplace Skills, ATE p. 13

ASSESSMENT SUPPORT

Standardized Test Preparation, SE p. 12

Standardized Test Preparation Workbook, pp. 1–2

Formal Assessment, Ch. 1

Writing Assessment and Portfolio Management

MEETING INDIVIDUAL NEEDS

Less Advanced Students, ATE p. 4. See also Ongoing Assessment, ATE p. 6.

ESL Students, ATE p. 5

Logical/Mathematical Learners, ATE p. 6

Interpersonal Learners, ATE p. 7

Verbal/Linguistic Learners, ATE p. 9

BLOCK SCHEDULING

Pacing Suggestions
For 90-minute Blocks
- Have students complete the Introduction and Prewriting stages in a single period.
- Focus one class period on Drafting, Collaborating, and Publishing. Allow at least 30 minutes for peer revision.

Professional Development Support
- *How to Manage Instruction in the Block* This Teaching Resource provides management and activity suggestions.

MEDIA AND TECHNOLOGY

For the Teacher
- *Writers at Work* **Videotape**
- *Resource Pro* **CD-ROM**

WRITING AND GRAMMAR WEB SITE

The Interactive Writing and Grammar Web site provides a wide array of support for students, teachers, and parents. Writing support includes:

- Interactive revision checkers
- Scoring rubrics with complete models

www.phschool.com

LITERATURE CONNECTIONS

Related selections from *Prentice Hall Literature: Timeless Voices, Timeless Themes*, Bronze Level:
"Two Kinds" from *The Joy Luck Club*, Amy Tan, ATE p. 3
"Winter" Nikki Giovanni, ATE, p. 9

1. To understand the purposes and value of writing to explain, describe, report, and narrate.
2. To understand and use writing strategies such as brainstorming, notetaking, and logs.
3. To understand and use resources as needed for writing, revising, and editing final drafts.

Critical Viewing

Speculate Students' responses will vary, but make sure they support their responses with details from the photograph.

Chapter

1 The Writer in You

▲ Critical Viewing
Do you think this student is writing to himself or to someone else? Why? [Speculate]

Which words describe you? You are a student, a friend, and a reader. You might also be a dancer, a singer, a dog walker, or a skater. There's one more word that describes you, whether you realize it or not: You are a *writer*.

Writing in Everyday Life

You probably write every day. Think about all of the ways you write. At school, you take notes and answer quiz questions. You write essays, poems, and stories. At home, you jot down phone messages and shopping lists. You may send your friends e-mail. You may even keep a journal. These are just a few of the ways you write. You also write for special reasons. Have you ever written a letter to complain about a product? Maybe you have written an essay or a poem for a contest.

2 • The Writer in You

⏱ TIME AND RESOURCE MANAGER	
In-Depth Coverage	**Accelerated Pace**
• Go over pp. 2–9 in class. • Use the reflecting questions on p. 9 for class discussion, asking students to share their responses.	• Have students read pp. 2–9 on their own. • Ask students to select a reflecting question (p. 9) and write a one-paragraph response.

Why Write?

You write for the same reason you talk—to communicate. Through writing, you can communicate what you think, what you know, and how you feel. Furthermore, writing allows you to communicate—to yourself or to others—across time and space. You can write a postcard about a vacation adventure and send it to a friend three states away. A story you write could entertain many classmates over the course of the school year. The notes you write in class today will help you remember tonight what was discussed.

What Are the Qualities of Good Writing?

Ideas   Good writing begins with interesting ideas. Explore topics that you find interesting and that you think will interest others. Focus on presenting information that will be new and fresh to readers. You will lose readers if you are simply telling them something they already know.

Organization   Organization refers to the way in which the ideas and details are arranged in a piece of writing. To enable readers to follow your ideas, choose an organization that makes sense for your topic, and stick with that organization throughout the piece of writing.

Voice   Just as you have a distinctive way of expressing yourself when you speak, you can develop a distinctive voice as a writer. Your voice consists of the topics you choose, the attitude you express toward those topics, the words you use, and the rhythm of your sentences. By developing your own voice, you let your personality come through in your writing.

Word Choice   Words are the building blocks of a piece of writing. By choosing precise and vivid words, you will add strength to your writing and enable readers to follow your ideas and picture in their minds the things that you describe.

Sentence Fluency   In a piece of writing, it is not only important that the words blend together smoothly—it is also important that the sentences flow well from one to another. By using a variety of sentences—different lengths and different structures—and using transitions to connect them, you will create a smooth rhythm in your writing.

Conventions   Conventions refer to the grammatical correctness of a piece of writing. Don't let errors in grammar, usage, mechanics, and spelling interfere with your message.

Writers in
ACTION

"*Always write honestly and be true to what you need to write. . . . Don't ever try to copy anybody. Find out what is unique about the way you see the world and [realize] that only you can say it.*"

—*Amy Tan*

Learn More

You'll take a closer look at the step-by-step process for achieving these qualities in Chapter 2, "A Walk Through the Writing Process," page 14.

The Writer in You • 3

PREPARE and ENGAGE

Interest GRABBER   Tell students that the word *write* is derived from far older words that originally meant "to cut or scratch." Ask students to speculate how cutting or scratching might have related to writing. (Students might suggest that early forms of writing were cuts and scratches in wood, clay, and stone.)

Activate Prior Knowledge

Point out that just the thought of writing scares some people. That's usually because they are afraid they can't think of a good idea to write about. Remind students that brainstorming is a good way to come up with ideas because:

- *it gets the creative juices flowing.*
- *it's fun.*
- *it's risk-free (in brainstorming, all ideas are good ideas).*
- *it lets other people do some of the work for you, by contributing ideas you might not think of on your own.*

Invite students to brainstorm theme titles that could fit the following categories:

- *Bad Hair Days*
- *The World of the Yo-Yo*
- *Oops!*

More About the Writer

It is not always easy to discover what it is "you need to write" and how to write in a way "that only you can say it." Amy Tan struggled with these issues herself. She tried many different schools and worked at a variety of jobs before she found her true "voice" as a writer. That voice was powerful when it finally emerged. Amy Tan's first novel, *The Joy Luck Club,* was a bestseller and even inspired a movie by the same name. Students can find "Two Kinds" from *The Joy Luck Club* by Amy Tan in *Prentice Hall Literature: Timeless Voices, Timeless Themes.*

Developing Your Writing Life

After you review the strategies for developing writing, ask students the following questions:

- *How do you get your best ideas for writing?* (while taking a shower, "sleeping" on it, talking with a friend)

- *If you're upset about a situation, how might writing about your thoughts and feelings help?* (gives you a chance to let off steam; brings up points you hadn't thought of; demands that you think with your head as well as your emotions)

Customize for
Less Advanced Students

Have students create a simple journal page. Ask them to estimate how many times they'll need to write something during the next 24 hours, then note that number at the top of the page. Have students keep the folded page in their pockets or backpacks, making a notation every time they write something during the next 24 hours. They should record all kinds of writing, including notes to friends, phone numbers, and homework assignments. Ask students to share their journal results in class. How do the actual results compare with the estimates?

Developing Your Writing Life

Writing is already part of your life. By consciously choosing to develop your writing life, you will become a better writer and a better communicator.

Keep Track of Your Ideas

You probably come up with writing ideas all the time without even realizing it. Here are some strategies for keeping track of thoughts, feelings, and inspirations that you have, so that you can use them when you write:

Notebook or Journal Carry a small notebook wherever you go. Make a habit of writing down interesting facts and other tidbits. You might jot down an account of the day's events, make a quick sketch of a scene, or paste clippings from newspapers and magazines in your notebook.

Learning Log Writing about something can help you understand it. A learning log is a special tool that writers can use to think about information they collect. Open your learning log anytime you learn something new—from a fascinating historical fact to a new soccer play. Record the information you've acquired and capture your thoughts about it and how it relates to your life. When you look back at your learning log, you will find a lot of ideas that made your mind click. One of the topics could help you launch a brand-new writing project.

Keep Track of Your Writing and Reading

Writing Portfolio Maintaining a portfolio is one important way in which you can become a more effective writer. Reviewing past work and strategies can help you make writing decisions that will work for you. Your portfolio can include finished writing as well as notes and drafts.

Reader's Journal Author Amy Tan advises writers to "read a lot and know what you like to read." You can use a reader's journal to keep track of your reading. Write down memorable quotations, reactions to characters, and responses to the message of a piece.

Clipping File Start a file of newspaper and magazine articles you've read to keep track of issues and events that matter to you. If you have permission, clip articles from the source. Otherwise, make a photocopy. Jot down notes about your reactions and thoughts on the copy. When you are looking for a writing topic, review the articles in your clipping file to spark ideas.

Try Different Approaches

Every writer is different. Develop your own personal approach to writing, one that reflects your tastes and preferences. Here are some ideas:

Getting Started How will you begin? You might decide to sit in a quiet place and just think. Perhaps music helps you get your ideas flowing. Another alternative is called *freewriting*. To freewrite, simply write whatever comes to mind. Don't stop to think or edit—just write.

Finding Ideas Ideas are all around you if you know where to look. You may get a great idea watching television or reading a magazine. If you keep a learning log or journal, you may turn to its pages to find inspiration for your writing.

Writing a Draft Some writers like to take their notes and write a complete first draft. They write in order from beginning to end. Other writers prefer to work out one idea at a time. They might begin in the middle or even at the end. Try both strategies to see which one you prefer.

Improving Your Work You may want to finish your draft and then go back and make changes, or you may make changes while you draft. You can draft on your own, or you can ask a classmate to help you find unclear passages or ideas that need support.

Sharing Your Work As you develop as a writer, you'll explore different ways of sharing your work. You may consider certain types of writing more personal and choose to keep them to yourself. On the other hand, you may write other pieces that you want to share, not only with family and friends but with an even wider audience. There are many ways for you to share your work—student publications, Internet Web sites, and group readings, among others.

◀ Critical Viewing
For what types of writing would the setting in which this girl is writing be appropriate? Explain. **[Analyze]**

Real-World Connection

Ask a student to name one career he or she might be interested in. Ask the other students to think of types of writing that might be required in that career. (reports, memos, proposals, minutes) Repeat this process with several more students. Point out how writing is an important skill in almost any occupation. Challenge students to think of an occupation that does *not* include any writing.

Critical Viewing

Analyze Students may say that the setting is appropriate for informal types of writing, such as letters or a journal, or for getting started and finding ideas for an essay.

Customize for
ESL Students

Students from other cultures have some advantages when it comes to thinking of topics to write about:

• Being a member of an ethnic culture can provide unique perspectives on everyday subjects such as holidays, school, and family life.

• Many students can write about their travels and experiences visiting or living in foreign countries.

• Students often have special experience or expertise writing in a particular style unique to their culture, such as storytelling or certain forms of poetry.

Plan to Write

Teaching Resources: Writing Support Transparency 1-A; Writing Support Activity Book, 1-1

1. Ask each student to write down one thing he or she is really skilled at, such as blading, drawing, playing a musical instrument, or reading.

2. Invite volunteers to share what they wrote. Discuss these questions:

   - *Did practice have anything to do with your success? How?*
   - *What preparations do you make when you are going to perform this skill?*
   - *How do you make sure you have time to do this skill?*

3. Go over the information on the page, pointing out how practice, preparation, and scheduling are important to developing good writing skills.

Critical Viewing

Compare Students should say that you need to wear the proper protective gear when skating and you need to skate in a safe area.

Customize for
Logical/Mathematical Learners

Provide students with blank one-month calendars. Have the students record a typical daily schedule on each calendar day. Then ask students to work ten hours of writing activities into their schedule for the month. Students should specify the day, length of time, and type of writing for each of the ten entries. For example, a student might write this entry on one of the Mondays:

6:30 P.M.–7:15 P.M. Write e-mail notes to friends.

Plan to Write

If you wanted to become a better inline skater, you would set aside time to skate every day. Make writing a part of your routine. Set aside some time every day to write in your notebook or journal. Choose a place where you are comfortable writing. When you have long-term writing assignments, create a plan and organize yourself so that you can focus on the writing, rather than on the deadline.

Choose the Right Spot Your surroundings can really affect the way you write. Pick a spot where you won't be interrupted. You might write in a quiet library or study area. You might prefer to work in your own room with music playing in the background.

Come Prepared It can be very frustrating to have to stop writing once your ideas are flowing, so gather your equipment before you begin. Make sure you have enough paper and a pen that works. In fact, bring along an extra pen, just in case. If you're using a computer, bring along a disk to back up your work.

Budget Your Time A deadline doesn't have to create stress. Writers can use deadlines to plan and budget their writing time. If you have a long-term goal, it's a good idea to divide it into several short deadlines. Use a calendar to help you plan your writing process. For example, suppose an essay is due on November 18. You can set deadlines for starting your research, writing a first draft, revising, and proofreading. Leave a little extra room in your schedule so that you can adjust the deadlines. Some tasks may take more or less time than you originally predicted.

▲ Critical Viewing
How do the headings "Choose the Right Spot" and "Come Prepared" apply to inline skating as well as to writing? [Compare]

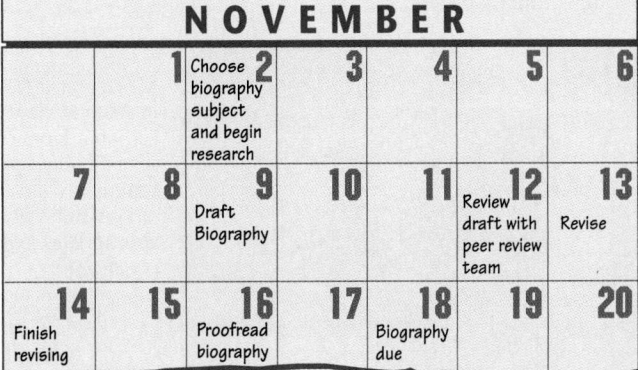

NOVEMBER						
	1	**2** Choose biography subject and begin research	**3**	**4**	**5**	**6**
7	**8**	**9** Draft Biography	**10**	**11**	**12** Review draft with peer review team	**13** Revise
14 Finish revising	**15**	**16** Proofread biography	**17**	**18** Biography due	**19**	**20**

6 • The Writer in You

☑ **ONGOING ASSESSMENT: Monitor and Reinforce**

If students have difficulty understanding how they can plan to write, try one of the following options.

Option 1 Ask students to review any journals, logs, or portfolios from previous years. Have them list the ways they could have made the writing process easier for themselves.	**Option 2** Ask students to write a brief description of their own writing process: how they get started, organize ideas, draft and so on.

Work With Others

You don't have to write by yourself. Including other people in the writing process can help you grow as a writer.

Group Brainstorming Sometimes, the best way to get started is to bounce ideas around among a group of people. When you sit in a group and let ideas flow freely, building on them without stopping, you are brainstorming. A group might begin by brainstorming on a broad topic, such as pets or sports. Hearing other people's thoughts can help you come up with new, interesting ideas.

Collaborative and Cooperative Writing

There are many ways that writers can work together on a project. A team of writers working on a poem might take turns suggesting lines. A team writing a research report might work differently, with each member writing a different section of the finished work. By working together, a group can benefit from the individual strengths of each writer.

Peer Reviewers It can be very helpful to ask another writer to help you review your work. A fresh pair of eyes can often catch mistakes that you might miss. A peer reviewer can help you see both strong and weak points in your writing.

Writers in **ACTION**

"Every time we work on our writing, it has more meaning. And it becomes something more beautiful."

—*Denise Chávez*

▼ Critical Viewing
Do you think these students are brainstorming, drafting, or reviewing a draft? Why? **[Analyze]**

Work With Others

1. Explain to students that writing can be a collaborative process.
2. Ask students why they think it might be helpful to have input from others. (Other people can give you a different perspective on a topic.)

Critical Viewing

Analyze Students may say that the group is reviewing a draft because there is written work in front of them and they are looking at it carefully.

More About the Writer

Denise Chávez was born and raised in New Mexico, where she was steeped in the tradition of oral storytelling of nearby Mexico. She has written numerous plays and novels, including *Face of an Angel.*

Customizing for
Interpersonal Learners

Divide the class into small groups. Assign one of the following "professionals" to each group:

- *football player*
- *mystery writer*
- *truck driver*
- *software engineer*
- *travel agent*
- *drummer for a rock band*

Explain that each group's mission is to convince its professional that he or she must collaborate with others in order to be successful. Have each group write down five convincing reasons, then share them with the class.

Publish Your Work

1. If students want to have a piece of writing published, they should first identify likely publishers. The student's work should match what the company publishes. Students should check that potential publishers publish writings from students their age and publish the genre (poetry, fiction) of the work the student has created.

2. Students may also request writer's guidelines from publishers, so the work is submitted in the correct format.

3. Ask students to research the writing opportunities listed, then identify one of the listings they would be most likely to contact if they wanted their work to be published. Students may share their answers in class.

Integrating Speaking and Listening Skills

Have partners locate one example of student-published writing. Ask them to take turns reading the selection aloud to each other, then answer these questions:

What did you like about the selection?

What didn't you like about the selection?

Why do you think the publishers chose this particular work?

Publish Your Work

There is nothing like finding an audience for your writing. You can find many publishing opportunities. Browse the Web for sites that accept student writing. Look for writing contests. Submit a letter, an editorial, or an article to your local newspaper. Here are some ways in which you might consider publishing your work:

Periodicals

- "In Your Own Write": READ, c/o Weekly Reader Corporation, 245 Long Hill Road, Middletown, CT 06457
- Creative Kids, P.O. Box 8813, Waco, TX 76714-8813
- Skipping Stones, P.O. Box 3939, Eugene, OR 97403

On-line Publications

- Stone Soup: http://www.stonesoup.com/
- MidLink Magazine: http://longwood.cs.ucf.edu:80/~MidLink/

Contests

- Annual Poetry Contest, National Federation of State Poetry Societies, 3520 State Route 56, Mechanicsburg, OH 43044
- *Seventeen* Magazine Fiction Contest, *Seventeen* Magazine, 850 Third Avenue, New York, NY 10022
- National Written & Illustrated By . . . Awards Contest for Students: Landmark Editions, Inc., 1402 Kansas Avenue, Kansas City, MO 64127

Your Name
Your Street
Your City, State, and ZIP Code

Place Stamp Here

Creative Kids
P.O. Box 8813
Waco, TX 76714-8813

Writers in Action

Careers in Writing, Writing in Careers

Many people earn their living as writers. When we think of writers, we most often consider novelists and other literary writers. However, there are many other types of professional writers. These include screenwriters, speechwriters, and people who write advertisements. In addition, writing is an important part of many other occupations—from accounting to zoology.

In the chapters of this book, you'll meet professionals who use different types of writing on the job. These "Writers in Action" include the following:

Will Hobbs, a young-adult novelist, fills his works with vivid descriptions that help readers accompany his characters on their adventures.

Denise Chávez, a poet and playwright, uses writing to take her readers on fascinating, believable journeys.

Richard Lederer, a weekly newspaper columnist and essayist, writes entertaining and amusing articles about the English language.

Dimitri Ehrlich, a music critic, writes reviews that help music fans decide which CDs to purchase.

Joseph Bruchac, a noted poet and a supporter of Native American causes, uses writing for a wide range of purposes—from entertaining audiences to swaying opinions.

Ellie Fries, a director of education at an aquarium, writes the information aquarium visitors need in order to understand an exhibit.

Nikki Giovanni, a well-known poet, shares her ideas and experiences in verse.

Jane Choi, a brochure writer for an arts society, uses writing to raise money for her organization.

Reading how these professionals use writing may help you imagine new directions for your own future in writing.

Reflect on Your Writing

You can learn a lot about your own writing by asking yourself a few questions. Try these for starters:

- What kinds of writing do you like to do?
- Where is your favorite place to write?
- What kind of writing would you like to learn to do?
- What would you say in a fan letter to your favorite author?

Writers at Work Videotape

Use the Writers at Work video to learn more about these writers and the writing techniques that they use.

Will Hobbs

Dimitri Ehrlich

Nikki Giovanni

The Writer in You • **9**

Lesson Objectives

1. To interpret and evaluate the array of media that people use to express themselves.
2. To write about art forms.

Step-by-Step Teaching Guide

Analyzing How Meaning Is Communicated Through the Arts

1. You may want to have students work in groups to explore each art form in greater depth. Students can research what makes their art form unique from other art forms, and the ways in which artists have used the particular art form to express themselves.

2. Each group can then present their findings to the class. Encourage groups to bring in examples, if possible.

Viewing and Representing

Activity Encourage volunteers to present their journal entries to the class.

Critical Viewing

Interpret Students may say that the fact that Virgil is leading Dante illustrates the connection between different time periods and art forms.

Spotlight on the Humanities

Analyzing How Meaning Is Communicated Through the Arts

Introducing the Spotlight on the Humanities

Writing is just one form of self-expression—there are many others. In the Spotlight on the Humanities features, you will learn about connections between different forms of creative expression in the arts. Photography, dance, music, fine art—these are just a few of the vast array of media that allow us to express ourselves. Each medium has its own unique characteristics.

- **Fine art** creates meaning through color, line, texture, and subject. Paintings, sketches, sculpture, and collage are just a few examples of the many types of fine art.
- **Photography** uses still images to create meaning. Although a photograph captures only still images on film, photographers express ideas through subject, composition, and lighting.
- **Theater** creates meaning through the performances of actors on a stage. Using props, scenery, sound effects, and lighting, drama brings a story to life. In some cases, music and dance are incorporated into the story line.
- **Film** captures ideas and stories through sound and motion. Like dramatic theater, most film tells stories and uses setting, costumes, and characterization to develop a story. A filmmaker can create a unique point of view using camera angles along with lighting and sound techniques.
- **Music** uses sound to create meaning. Whether presented as an oboe solo, an operatic aria, or a symphony, music can create moods or present variations on a theme.
- **Dance** creates meaning through organized movement. It can be performed by a single person, a pair, or larger groups.

Writing Activity In a journal entry, consider which of these art forms is most familiar to you and which you would like to explore.

▲ Critical Viewing
This engraving is one artist's interpretation of a famous work of literature in which Dante, a medieval writer, is guided by Virgil, a writer from ancient Roman times. How does this artwork illustrate the connections between different time periods and art forms? [Interpret]

Media and Technology Skills

Making Technology Work for You

Activity: Identify Appropriate Technology

In the "old days," you probably would have handwritten all of your papers. If you wanted to share them with others, you would probably have had to read them aloud. Today, you have many more options for drafting, publishing, and presenting your work.

Learn About It Today's vast array of technology makes writing and other forms of communication faster and easier than ever before. Below are just some of the tools available.

- **Writing tools** Word-processing programs allow you to store and retrieve text as well as to create, draft, and edit a piece of writing. Desktop-publishing programs let you add pictures to your writing and customize the layout (appearance and arrangement) of your work.

- **Audiovisual tools** Several tools allow you to record images and sound. A video camera captures moving images as well as sound. A still camera records still images, which can be displayed on their own or projected in a series with a slide projector. A tape recorder can be used to take notes or to play background music or sound effects for a multimedia presentation.

- **Virtual resources** The Internet is an extensive computer network that allows you to access and to post information, pictures, and so on. E-mail is a way to send and receive messages nearly instantaneously over the Internet.

Evaluate It Find out what technology tools are available in your school or local library. Talk to the librarian and other students who have used these tools. Ask for a demonstration and browse instruction manuals. Then, use a chart like the one above to plan how you might use these tools to produce or enhance a presentation or report. Compare your chart with the chart of a classmate who has also done this activity.

Available Technologies

Writing Tools
- Word Processing
- Desktop-publishing programs

Virtual Resources
- The Internet
- E-mail
- Electronic databases

Audiovisual Tools
- Video cameras
- Still cameras
- Slide projectors
- Overhead projectors
- Tape recorders

Report Title: <u>How to Grow Tomatoes</u>

Type of Technology	Advantages for My Report	Disadvantages for My Report
the Internet	• I can search gardening Web sites for information. • I can post my report on a Web page and invite people to give feedback. • I can e-mail an expert if I have a technical question.	• There might be too much information to review. • It may not always be clear how reliable the sources are.

▶ *Lesson Objectives*

1. To learn about the different technologies available that make the writing process easier.
2. To organize information about these technologies in a graphic organizer.

Step-by-Step Teaching Guide

Making Technology Work for You

Teaching Resources: Writing Support Transparency 1-B; Writing Support Activity Book, 1-2

1. If possible, bring in some examples of available technologies to the classroom.

2. You may want to have students work in groups to explore the advantages and disadvantages of several technologies for the same topic.

3. Have students create a chart or other organizer that lists the technologies best suited for different kinds of writing. Students can refer to these charts in the future.

Lesson Objectives

1. To respond to a writing prompt on a standardized test.
2. To communicate effectively by using correct grammar and standard usage.

Step-by-Step Teaching Guide

Writing for Standardized Tests

Teaching Resources: Standardized Test Preparation Workbook, pp. 1–2

1. Guide students through the different writing stages and the time they should plan on spending for each stage.
2. Read aloud the sample writing situation. Have students identify the purpose for writing. (to explain Amy Tan's quotation)
3. Have students respond to the writing prompt within the class time.

Standardized Test Preparation Workshop

Writing for Standardized Tests

As you have learned in this chapter, writing is an important part of your daily life. Your ability to communicate through writing is often measured when you respond to a writing prompt on a standardized test. When scorers evaluate your writing, they will look for evidence that you can

- respond directly to the prompt.
- make your writing thoughtful and interesting.
- organize your ideas so that they are clear and easy to follow.
- develop your ideas thoroughly by using appropriate details and precise language.
- stay focused on your purpose for writing by making sure that each sentence you write contributes to your composition as a whole.
- communicate effectively by using correct spelling, capitalization, punctuation, grammar, usage, and sentence structure.

The process of writing for a test, or any kind of writing, can be divided into stages. Plan to use a specific amount of time for prewriting, drafting, revising, and proofreading.

Following is an example of one type of writing prompt you might find on a standardized test. Use the suggestions on the next page to help you respond. The clocks next to each stage show a suggested plan for organizing your time.

Sample Writing Situation

Read the following quotation:

"Find out what is unique about the way you see the world and [realize] that only you can say it."
　　　　　　　　　—Amy Tan

What do you think Tan's advice means to student writers? Write an essay in which you explain the quotation. Support your interpretation with examples from your own experiences and from literature.

Prewriting

 Allow approximately one fourth of your time for prewriting.

Identify Your Topic Explore the quotation by breaking it into parts. Write the quotation on a piece of paper. Circle the word in the quotation that is most meaningful to you. Freewrite on that word for two or three minutes. Reread the quotation and, using some words from your freewriting, restate the quotation in your own words. Write this sentence at the top of your paper.

Gather Details Begin listing experiences from your own writing life that show the truth of the quotation as you have restated it. Then, jot down the titles of stories and novels, as well as the names of authors, that can be used as examples.

Organize Details Group details into a few broad categories. Write a sentence about each category that explains what the details in the category have in common. For example, concerning one group of details, you might write that knowing about a topic makes it easier for you to write about it. For another group of details, you might write that the more interested you are in a subject, the more time you will be willing to spend writing about it. Use these sentences to plan the framework of your essay.

Drafting

 Allow almost half of your time for drafting.

Write an Introduction Grab your reader's attention by beginning your introduction with a strong lead— an attention-getting first sentence. You might use a startling statement or an unusual observation that is related to the quotation. Then, give the quotation and explain how it is connected to your lead. Finally, give your interpretation in a sentence or two.

Support Your Interpretation Each supporting paragraph should begin with a topic sentence that supports your interpretation. Develop each topic sentence with details and examples.

Revising, Editing, and Proofreading

 Allow just over a fourth of your time for revising. Use the last few minutes to proofread your work.

Review Details and Language Review your response for details that do not directly support your interpretation, and remove them. Make sure that you use language that is appropriate for a formal test response.

 **Make Corrections** Check for errors in spelling, grammar, and punctuation. When making changes, place a line through text that you want to eliminate. Use a caret (^) to indicate places where you would like to add words.

Integrating Workplace Skills

Tell students that understanding and following the various stages of the writing process isn't only important in test situations. As they may know, most jobs involve some form of writing. Any form of writing can benefit from the kind of knowledge measured by a standardized test.

Chapter 2

Time and Resource Manager

In-Depth Lesson Plan

	LESSON FOCUS	PRINT AND MEDIA RESOURCES
DAY 1	**Introduction to the Writing Process** Students discuss types of writing and review the steps in the writing process (pp. 14–15).	
DAY 2	**Prewriting** Students discuss strategies for choosing and narrowing a topic, linking audience and purpose, and gathering and organizing details (pp. 16–20).	*Language Lab* **CD-ROM,** Composing **Teaching Resources:** *Writing Support Transparencies,* 2-A–F; *Writing Support Activity Book,* 2-1–4
DAY 3	**Drafting** Students learn ways to get the reader's attention and to use elaboration (pp. 21–22).	
DAY 4	**Revising** Students review strategies for revising and for conducting peer reviews (pp. 23–25).	**Teaching Resources:** *Writing Support Transparencies,* 2-G–H
DAY 5	**Editing and Proofreading; Publishing and Presenting** Students review what to look for when proofreading and learn ways to build and organize a portfolio (pp. 26–27).	**Teaching Resources:** *Formal Assessment,* Ch. 2

Accelerated Lesson Plan

	LESSON FOCUS	PRINT AND MEDIA RESOURCES
DAY 1	**Introduction, Prewriting, and Drafting** Students review the steps in the writing process and learn strategies for finding and narrowing a topic, for writing for an audience, and for providing elaboration (pp. 14–22).	*Language Lab* **CD-ROM,** Composing **Teaching Resources:** *Writing Support Transparencies,* 2-A–F; *Writing Support Activity Book,* 2-1–4
DAY 2	**Revising to Presenting** Students discuss strategies for revising, conducting peer reviews, proofreading, and organizing a portfolio (pp. 23–27).	**Teaching Resources:** *Formal Assessment,* Ch.2; *Writing Support Transparencies,* 2-G–H

Options for Adapting Lesson Plans

HOMEWORK

Have students complete any stage of their lesson for homework.

FEATURES

Extend coverage with Spotlight on the Humanities (p. 28), Media and Technology Skills (p. 29), and the Standardized Test Preparation Workshop (p. 30).

TECHNOLOGY

Students can complete any stage of the lesson on computer. Have them print out their completed work.

INTEGRATED SKILLS COVERAGE

Viewing and Representing
Critical Viewing, SE pp. 14, 28
Recognizing Common Subjects in Art, SE p.28
ATE p. 28

Speaking and Listening
ATE p. 18

Vocabulary Skills
ATE pp. 19, 27

Technology
SE p. 29

Real-World Connection
ATE p. 21

Workplace Skills
ATE p. 17

ASSESSMENT SUPPORT

Standardized Test Preparation, SE p. 30
Standardized Test Preparation Workbook, pp. 3–4
Formal Assessment, Ch. 2
Writing Assessment and Portfolio Management

MEETING INDIVIDUAL NEEDS

ESL Students, ATE pp. 16, 25
Bodily/Kinesthetic Learners, ATE p. 17
Less Advanced Students, ATE pp. 20, 31. See also Ongoing
Assessments, ATE pp. 17, 22, 24

BLOCK SCHEDULING

Pacing Suggestiong
For 90-minute Blocks
• Have students complete the Prewriting and Drafting stages in a single period.
• Focus one class period on Revising and Editing and Publishing and Presenting. Allow at least 30 minutes for peer revision.

Professional Development Support
• *How to Manage Instruction in the Block* This Teaching Resource provides management and activity suggestions.

MEDIA AND TECHNOLOGY

For the Student
• *Language Lab* CD-ROM, Composing

For the Teacher
• *Resource Pro* CD-ROM

WRITING AND GRAMMAR WEB SITE

The Interactive Writing and Grammar Web site provides a wide array of support for students, teachers, and parents. Writing support includes:

• Interactive revision checkers
• Scoring rubrics with complete models

www.phschool.com

LITERATURE CONNECTIONS

Related selection from *Prentice Hall Literature: Timeless Voices, Timeless Themes,* Bronze Level:
"The Hummingbird That Lived Through Winter," William Saroyan, SE p. 21

A Walk Through the Writing Process

Lesson Objectives

1. To understand that writing is a process.
2. To learn that there are two main types of writing: reflexive and extensive.
3. To review the steps in the writing process.
4. To become familiar with strategies for generating topic ideas.
5. To learn ways to narrow a list of topic ideas.
6. To create an audience profile.
7. To learn strategies for gathering details.
8. To practice organizing information.
9. To practice strategies for creating a first draft, including the use of enticing leads and the SEE method.
10. To become familiar with strategies for revising first drafts.
11. To learn strategies for analyzing paragraphs and improving sentences.
12. To learn strategies for refining word choice.
13. To understand the peer revision process.
14. To apply strategies for collecting, refining, and assessing writing projects.

Critical Viewing

Relate Students' answers will vary, but they should identify both positive and negative writing habits they have.

Whatever your final product, the writing process—a systematic approach to writing —can help you get there. From prewriting to publishing and presenting, knowing and using the stages of the writing process will help you do your best on any writing project.

▲ **Critical Viewing** How does your own writing process help or complicate your success as a writer? **[Relate]**

Types of Writing

One way to study types of writing is to analyze them by **mode**—the form or shape that writing takes. The list below shows the modes of writing you'll encounter in this book.

Another way to learn more about writing is to consider the source of the inspiration and the intended audience. For example, when you write **reflexively,** you choose what to write, what format to use, and whether to share your writing. Reflexive writing, such as a diary or a journal entry, is from yourself and for yourself. In contrast, when you write **extensively**, you are usually responding to a school assignment that will be read by a general audience. Extensive writing begins with others and is for others. It can take many forms, including poems, essays, and movie reviews.

MODES OF WRITING

Narration
Description
Persuasion
Exposition

Research
Response to Literature
Poems and Plays
Writing for Assessment

14 • A Walk Through the Writing Process

⏱ TIME AND RESOURCE MANAGER

In-Depth Coverage	Accelerated Pace
• Go over pp. 14–15 in class. • Review the illustrations on p. 14 and the diagram on p. 15. • Point out that this chapter will walk students through the writing process.	• Have students read pp. 14–15 on their own.

The Process of Writing

These are the stages of the writing process:

- **Prewriting** Freely exploring topics, choosing a topic, and beginning to gather and organize details before you write
- **Drafting** Getting your ideas down on paper roughly in the format you intend for the finished work
- **Revising** Correcting any major errors and improving the form and content of the writing
- **Editing and Proofreading** Polishing the writing and fixing errors in grammar, spelling, and mechanics
- **Publishing and Presenting** Sharing your writing with others

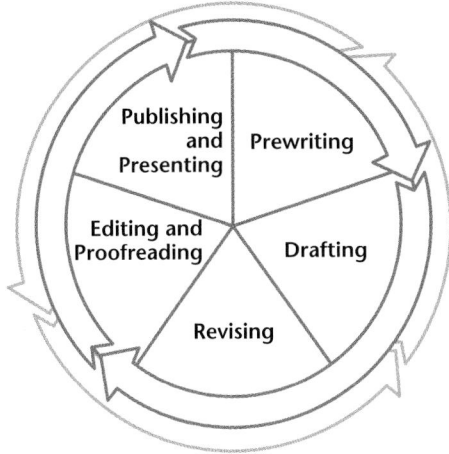

These steps may seem sequential, but writers often move among the various stages as they work. For example, as reporters draft news stories, they often discover that they must return to their prewriting work to gather more information.

A Guided Tour

Use this chapter as a guided tour to the writing process. Take a close look at the steps presented here. Learn new strategies, look at the way another writer has used them, and try them yourself. When you apply these strategies to your own writing process, the improved quality of your final draft may surprise you.

PREPARE and ENGAGE

Interest GRABBER Play "Blurt a Word." Write 30 different words on small pieces of paper. Put the papers into a container and choose one student as Player 1. Explain that you will take a word from the container and read it aloud. As soon as Player 1 hears the word, he or she should "blurt out" whatever word or phrase comes to mind. Proceed with Player 2. Next, have Player 1 choose and read a word for Player 2. Player 2 blurts a word or phrase. Repeat this process until all students have had a chance to both chose and blurt a word.

Explain that students will use a writing strategy that is similar to "Blurt a Word." In the strategy, called freewriting, students quickly write down whatever thoughts come to mind. Freewriting boosts students' creativity and confidence while also providing them with ideas for topics to write about.

Activate Prior Knowledge

Write the words *Reflexive* and *Extensive* on the chalkboard as column heads. Explain that reflexive writing is writing that students choose to do. Under the Reflexive head, write *writing a note to a friend.* Extensive writing is writing that students are asked to do. Under the Extensive head, write *writing a thank-you note to a guest speaker.* Invite students to draw on their own life experiences with writing to add examples under both heads.

What Is Prewriting?

Teaching Resources: Writing Support Transparency 2-A

1. Have a student draw a blueprint or floor plan of your classroom on the chalkboard. Invite other students to mark particular points on the blueprint that have special meaning to them. Have these students explain why they marked the points. For example, a student might mark the computer station and explain that it's a place where time seems to fly. Another student might mark the doorway and say that it stands for freedom, since this is the last class of the day.

2. Discuss how marking a blueprint can lead to interesting writing topics. (It pushes students to view everyday places and activities in new ways.)

3. Point out that sometimes writers come up with topics that are too big to write about. As an example, write *teenagers* on the chalkboard. Explain that this is a topic too large to cover in a theme or research paper. Ask students to list some additional examples of topics that are too broad.

4. Topics that are too broad can still be put to good use. Ask students to choose one of the topics on the chalkboard, then brainstorm a list of narrower topics contained within or related to the broad one.

> *Examples: teenage sports, teenagers who get good grades, problems of teenagers.*

Customize for
ESL Students

As the class brainstorms for topics in step 2 above, have students take note of words or phrases they don't understand and words they would like to add to their vocabulary. Assign students to work in pairs to find meanings for the unfamiliar words and phrases. For homework, ask them to practice spelling their new vocabulary words and use them in sentences.

2.1 What Is Prewriting?

A blank piece of paper can challenge even the most seasoned writer. Writers may struggle over what to write, or they may wonder how much they can say about a topic. Prewriting helps to make the task less overwhelming. Just as athletes and musicians prepare for a performance by practicing and planning, you can warm up to write with your own set of strategies and routines.

Choosing Your Topic

Before you can begin writing, you need a topic. Generally, the best topics are those that you find interesting. That is why it is important to take time to explore ideas, issues, and experiences that are important to you. To generate a topic, you can use a wide variety of strategies. Try this sample strategy:

SAMPLE STRATEGY

Blueprinting Draw the floor plan of a place that is important to you. You might map out your home, your school, or a local park. Then, jot down memorable events that these places suggest. You can then review your list to choose a topic for your writing. In this sample, the writer listed ideas that the blueprint sparked. From that list, she highlighted a topic to develop.

BLUEPRINTING TO FIND A TOPIC

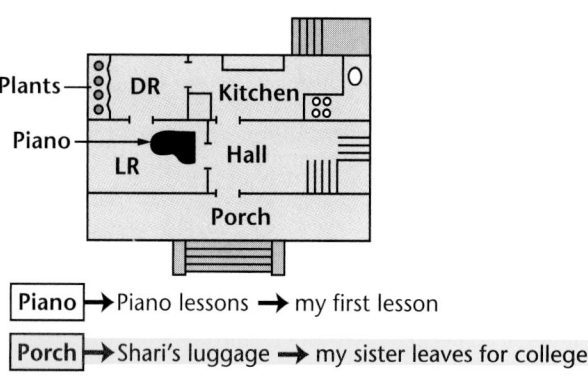

Piano → Piano lessons → my first lesson

Porch → Shari's luggage → my sister leaves for college

Learn More

For additional prewriting strategies suited to specific writing tasks, see Chapters 4-13.

⏱ TIME AND RESOURCE MANAGER	
In-Depth Coverage	**Accelerated Pace**
• Go over pp. 16–17 in class. • Review the diagram on p. 16 and the topic list on p. 17. • Have students respond in writing to items 1 and 2 on p. 20.	• Have students read pp. 16–17 on their own. • Have students work independently to narrow the topic "high school" by using the strategy of listing.

Narrowing Your Topic

While you may initially be inspired to write on a broad topic like "museums" or "vacations," you'll quickly find that such an undertaking can be too much of a challenge. A topic that is too broad can force you to write a draft that is either too general or too long. Narrow your general topic into something more manageable. Look at these examples of broad and narrow topics. Then, try the listing strategy for narrowing a topic.

BROAD TOPIC: Museums
NARROW TOPIC: Boston's Museum of Fine Arts
NARROWER TOPIC: The Impressionist exhibit at Boston's Museum of Fine Arts

BROAD TOPIC: Vacations
NARROW TOPIC: Vacations to take with your family
NARROWER TOPIC: Enjoying a family vacation at the beach

SAMPLE STRATEGY

Listing To take a closer look at your subject and all the specific ideas it may include, jot down your broad topic at the top of a page. Then, list people, places, and things that may be associated with this broad topic. Finally, look for connections between items on your list. Choose a topic based on the connections you find.

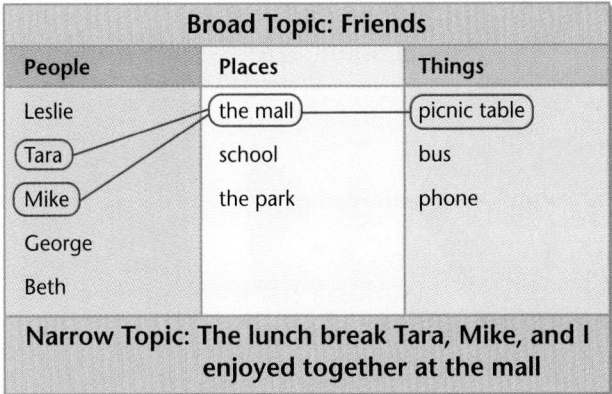

Broad Topic: Friends		
People	**Places**	**Things**
Leslie	the mall	picnic table
Tara	school	bus
Mike	the park	phone
George		
Beth		

Narrow Topic: The lunch break Tara, Mike, and I enjoyed together at the mall

---

Narrowing Your Topic

1. Have students look at the topics listed in their textbooks.
2. Ask students which topic they would rather use for an essay.
3. Guide students to see that a topic that is too broad will make writing a very difficult task.

Listing

Teaching Resources: Writing Support Transparency 2-B; Writing Support Activity Book, 2-1

Tell students not to be concerned with the order of items when they use this strategy. The important point is to get one's ideas down on paper and then look for connections.

Integrating Workplace Skills

People who write articles for magazines must constantly come up with fresh ideas. For instance, one writer has been asked to write an article about a new restaurant that features local jazz bands. What prewriting strategies could this writer use to get some ideas? (drawing a blueprint to help identify special points of interest in the restaurant; making a list of all the topics that relate to the restaurant, such as food, music, and decor)

Customize for
Bodily/Kinesthetic Learners

In step 1 of the Step-by-Step Teaching Guide on page 16, ask students to walk to two or three locations instead of marking them on the floor plan. At each location, have these students briefly explain why this spot is significant to them.

☑ ONGOING ASSESSMENT: Monitor and Reinforce

If students have difficulty with listing, try the following option.

Have students work in pairs to use the listing strategy to narrow a topic of your choice, such as after-school sports or vacations.

Considering Your Audience and Purpose

Teaching Resources: Writing Support Transparency 2-C

1. Make sure that students understand that the people and the reasons for which they are writing have a significant impact on the style and content of their writing.

2. You may want to have students create audience profiles for the following hypothetical audiences:
   - *a fourth-grade class*
   - *parents*
   - *local officials*

3. In order to help students understand how their purpose for writing affects what they write, ask students to consider the following question:

   If you were going to write an entertaining and informative essay about a trip to Europe, what kind of tone would you take in your essay? Why?

Integrating Speaking Skills

Write the following sentence on the chalkboard:

A googol is a number that is equal to one and contains 100 zeros.

Challenge students to role-play explaining the concept of a googol to these various audiences:

- *a third-grader*
- *a college math professor*
- *their best friend*
- *their math teacher*

Point out and discuss ways students took into account the audiences' knowledge and language level.

Prewriting Tip

Ask students to describe briefly their audience and purpose at the top of their first draft.

For example:

Audience: School principal

Purpose: To propose opening the weight room to students after school

As students gather details and begin to write, this visual reminder will help them keep their focus.

2.1

Considering Your Audience and Purpose

Once you've pinpointed your topic, give yourself a little more direction. When you identify your **audience**—the people who will read your work—you can plan how you'll communicate with them. When you identify your **purpose**—the reason you are writing—you can plan what you'll communicate.

Consider Your Audience Tailor your draft to meet the needs of your audience. Avoid words that are too sophisticated, but don't "talk down" to your readers. Strike a balance by identifying your readers, their language level, and their knowledge. Keep this information in mind as you draft.

Consider Your Purpose Focus on why you are writing. You may want to entertain, persuade, or reflect on your experiences. This purpose will guide the kind of information you include.

Link Topic With Audience and Purpose You can use most topics to suit a variety of audiences and purposes. This chart shows how one soccer game could inspire several different forms of writing.

MATCHING TOPIC, AUDIENCE, AND PURPOSE

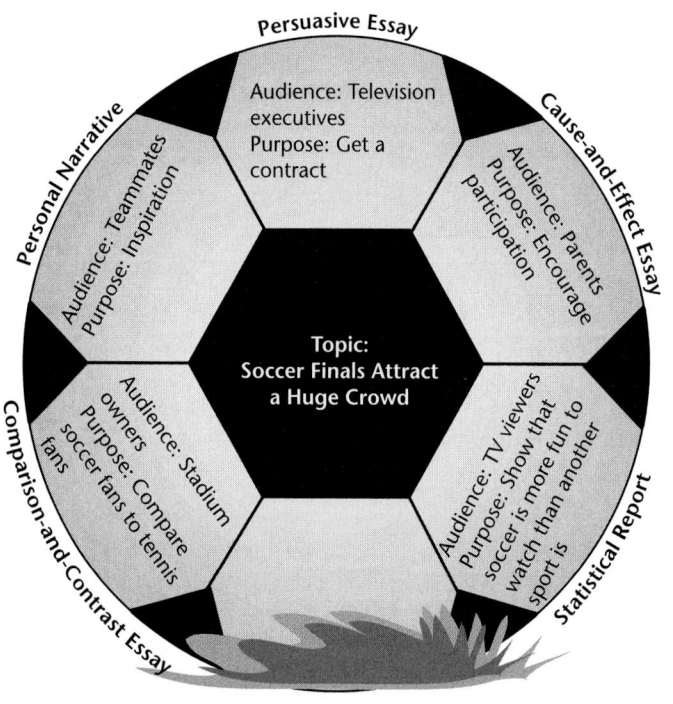

Persuasive Essay — Audience: Television executives Purpose: Get a contract

Personal Narrative — Audience: Teammates Purpose: Inspiration

Cause-and-Effect Essay — Audience: Parents Purpose: Encourage participation

Comparison-and-Contrast Essay — Audience: Stadium owners Purpose: Compare soccer fans to tennis fans

Statistical Report — Audience: TV viewers Purpose: Show that soccer is more fun to watch than another sport is

Topic: Soccer Finals Attract a Huge Crowd

18 • A Walk Through the Writing Process

⏱ TIME AND RESOURCE MANAGER	
In-Depth Coverage	**Accelerated Pace**
• Go over pp. 18–20 in class. • Review the samples provided on pp. 18–20. • Have students respond in writing to items 3–7 on p. 20.	• Have students read pp. 18–20 on their own. • Have students choose a short story or poem, then use a hexagonal to analyze it.

Gathering Details

Just as you assemble the ingredients you need before you bake, gather the materials you need before you write. Whether you want to tell a compelling story, describe an event clearly, or argue a position, collect as many relevant ideas and facts as you can to improve your writing. You may have to conduct research or talk to other people. The work you do in this phase will make the job of writing easier. Try these sample strategies:

SAMPLE STRATEGY

The Reporter's Formula To clarify the basics of your topic, use the first five questions most reporters ask. The Reporter's Formula is based on the five W's—the *who, what, where, when,* and *why* an event happened. After you have the simple answers, gather more details to round out your ideas.

SAMPLE STRATEGY

Hexagonal Writing When writing about literature, use a prewriting technique called hexagonal writing to focus your attention. Complete the six sides of the hexagon by following the directions in the diagram at right. The details and responses you create with this tool will help you give a thoughtful, thorough analysis. After you respond to each side of the hexagon, you may want to focus on a particular aspect of the novel, play, short story, or other literature you address.

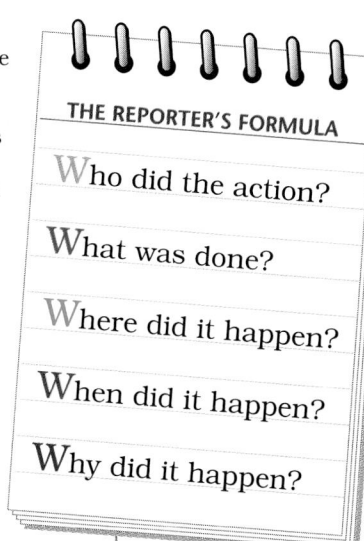

THE REPORTER'S FORMULA

Who did the action?

What was done?

Where did it happen?

When did it happen?

Why did it happen?

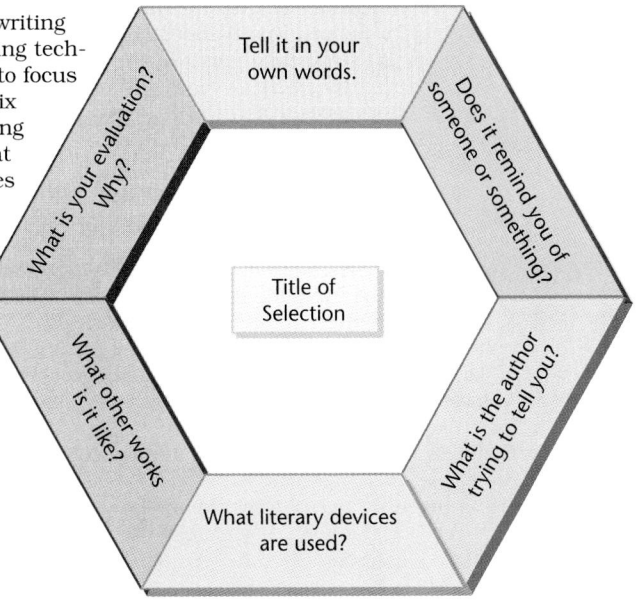

Tell it in your own words.

Does it remind you of someone or something?

What is your evaluation? Why?

Title of Selection

What is the author trying to tell you?

What other works is it like?

What literary devices are used?

The Reporter's Formula; Hexagonal Writing

Teaching Resources: Writing Support Transparencies 2-D–E; Writing Support Activity Book, 2-2–3

1. Write the following on the chalkboard: 5 W's. Explain that the *W's* stand for the Reporter's Formula of *who, what, where, when,* and *why.* Give one student a short newspaper article to read aloud. Have the other students raise their hands each time they hear one of the 5 W's covered in the article.

2. Draw an unlabeled hexagon on the chalkboard. Explain that hexagonal writing is a technique to help students write about literature. Call on students to come to the chalkboard and add the labels for the hexagon, as shown in the diagram on the page. Point out that this technique helps students analyze poems, stories, and other types of writing.

Integrating Vocabulary Skills

Hex- The prefixes *hex-* and *hexa-* mean "six." That's why a six-sided figure is called a hexagon. Explain to students that any unfamiliar word that contains *hex-* or *hexa-* carries a clue about its meaning. Here are some examples:

- *hexachloride—a type of chloride that has six atoms of chlorine*
- *hexapod—a six-legged insect*
- *hexarchy—a group of six kingdoms*

Make a Timeline

Teaching Resources: Writing Support Transparency 2-F; Writing Support Activity Book, 2-4

1. Write an unlabeled timeline on the chalkboard. Ask students to copy the blank timeline onto papers at their desks.

2. Have students write their date of birth at the beginning of the timeline (left side) and today's date at the end (right side). Ask students to mark and label on the timeline three important events in their lives.

3. Invite a volunteer to share his or her timeline with the class. After the student explains the timeline, ask these questions:

   • *If you had to choose one of the events to write a story about, which would it be?*

   • *Would you include any events that took place before or after the one you marked on the timeline?*

   • *Imagine "zooming in" on that main event, then creating another timeline. How would this second timeline be marked? In hours? Days? Weeks? Months?*

4. Point out how creating timelines can help students organize the events in a story.

Customize for
Less Advanced Students

Have students work in pairs to complete items 2, 3, and 6 of Applying the Prewriting Strategies on page 20.

2.1

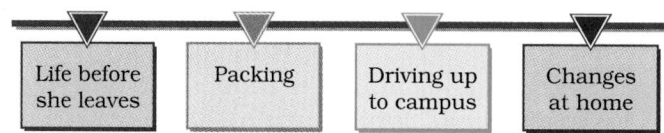

SAMPLE STRATEGY

Timeline When you share information with readers, it is best to present details in a way that makes your ideas easy to follow. To identify the details and their sequence in your writing, consider creating a timeline. This can be an especially useful tool as you gather details for a narrative. The model below shows how one writer planned to narrate the events surrounding a sister's departure for college.

A TIMELINE OF EVENTS
When a Sister Leaves for College

| Life before she leaves | Packing | Driving up to campus | Changes at home |

▶ **APPLYING THE PREWRITING STRATEGIES**

1. Make a blueprint of a place that is important to you. Then, label your blueprint with the people, events, objects, and memories you associate with the place you blueprinted. Identify the topic you would choose based on this exercise.

2. Use the listing strategy to narrow your topic. Jot down people, places, things, and events you associate with the word you choose. Make connections between items on the list. Then, identify a topic narrow enough to address in an essay.

3. Identify two different audiences for a report you might write on a hobby. Then, create two different audience profiles.

4. For each audience and purpose listed below, identify three details you might include in an essay about traffic safety:
   a. To warn children about crossing the street
   b. To persuade town officials to install a traffic light
   c. To tell friends about a frightening personal experience.

5. Answer the Reporter's Formula questions to gather details for an account of a sporting event.

6. Complete a hexagon for a short story you have recently read.

7. Using the story line of a television show or a film you have seen recently, sketch out a timeline of the main events.

2.2 *What Is Drafting?*

Shaping Your Writing

Focus on the Form As you draft, remember the mode of writing you have chosen. Each form of writing has a specific set of rules: persuasion has to convince, mystery has to surprise, and narration has to tell a story. Whatever your final product, keep this focus in mind as you draft.

Pull Readers in With an Enticing Lead Pay special attention to the first paragraph of your writing. Start with an interesting opener that will provoke your audience to keep reading. To create a strong introduction, consider beginning with a quotation, a shocking fact, or a dazzling description.

WRITING MODELS

Faced with a smooth and featureless span of wall, some climbers would see just one available course of action: Panic, scream "Falling!" and let go, making their belay partner lower them down. Not you.

> —Paul Scott, "So You Want to Be a Superstar"

The writer leads with the excitement of a risky situation.

There was a hummingbird once which in the wintertime did not leave our neighborhood in Fresno, California.

I'll tell you about it.

> —William Saroyan, "The Hummingbird That Lived Through Winter"

Saroyan addresses his audience directly, inviting readers to enjoy the story that will follow.

He found me crying one day as I sat on the swing in our backyard. My brother, sister, and I had long ago worn out the other swing and the see-saw. Only the rusty slide and one wooden swing remained on the old frame, testimony to the childhood we had recently left behind.

> —Rachel Martinez Hulsey, "Cenicienta"

This lead uses description and a compelling last line to ease the reader into the events to be addressed.

Shaping Your Writing

1. On the chalkboard, write the names of several forms of writing, including exposition, such as a how-to essay; persuasion, such as a political speech; narration, such as a short story; and description, such as a travel brochure.

2. Call on a student to read aloud the first sample lead. Ask students what catches their attention in this lead. (the use of *you*; description of a high-risk situation) Finally, ask students which writing form they think the lead is introducing. (Possible answers: exposition, short story, travel)

3. Repeat step 2 with the second and third sample leads.

Real-World Connection

Have students scan newspaper and magazine stories for examples of both good and bad leads. Encourage them to share their findings with the class and explain why each example is either good or bad.

Connections With Literature

Students can find the complete text of William Saroyan's "The Hummingbird That Lived Through Winter" in *Prentice Hall Literature: Timeless Voices, Timeless Themes, Bronze.*

⏱ TIME AND RESOURCE MANAGER

In-Depth Coverage	Accelerated Pace
• Go over pp. 21–22 in class. • Have students respond in writing to Applying the Drafting Strategies on p. 22.	• Have students read pp. 21–22 on their own.

Using the SEE Method

1. Review the SEE method. Write the following heads on the chalkboard:

   Statement, Extension, Elaboration.

2. Under the Statement head, write the following sentence:

   The wind screamed around us.

3. Ask students to think of and jot down one or more extensions.

   Example: The storm was getting stronger.

   Invite students to share their extensions and write them under the appropriate head on the chalkboard.

4. Ask students to think of ideas for elaboration and jot them down.

   Example: Lightning seared the sky, thunder roared, and hail drove our feeble shelter down to the ground.

   Have students share their elaborations by writing them on the chalkboard.

Drafting Tip

Remind students that they can use strategies such as drawing a blueprint or using the reporter format in the drafting stage of the writing process. These strategies will especially help them with elaboration.

2.2

Providing Elaboration

To make your writing as strong as it can be, include details and explanation to allow readers to understand your subject. Add information to help readers imagine the action you describe, see the connections you make, or evaluate your opinion. The SEE method is one of many strategies that can help you strengthen your writing.

SAMPLE STRATEGY

Using the SEE Method

When you use the SEE method (Statement, Extension, Elaboration), you strengthen your writing by providing a greater depth of information. Begin with a statement that conveys a main idea. Write an extension by restating or explaining the first sentence. Elaborate further by providing even more details about the main idea. Think of the SEE method as a way to shed more light on your subject. Look at this example:

STATEMENT: The space launch was a success.

EXTENSION: It was a picture-perfect start for the mission to Mars.

ELABORATION: The weather worked in the astronauts' favor, all systems worked well, and the engineers in Mission Control reported no problems as the shuttle escaped the Earth's atmosphere.

Statement   Extension   Elaboration

▶ APPLYING THE DRAFTING STRATEGIES

1. Write an exciting or interest-grabbing lead for a description of a sunrise.
2. Complete the sentences below. Then, using the SEE method, elaborate on each one.
   (a) The ___?___ is my favorite musical instrument.
   (b) If I had an extra hour every day, I would ___?___ .

Learn More

Each writing chapter provides elaboration strategies suited to specific writing modes.

☑ ONGOING ASSESSMENT: Monitor and Reinforce

If students have difficulty applying the SEE method, try one of the following options.

Option 1 Have students select and read an essay from *Prentice Hall Literature: Timeless Voices, Timeless Themes,* Bronze. Ask students to identify the author's statement, extension, and elaboration in a paragraph of their choice.	**Option 2** Have students make a blank flow chart with three squares. Label the first "statement," the second "extension," and the third "elaboration" to help students see how the statement is "built upon" elaborated ideas.

2.3 *What Is Revising?*

Color-Coding Clues for Revision

To use the stages of the writing process most effectively, devote full attention to the revision process. Focus your review by asking specific questions about your draft. The word **ratiocination** (rash´ ē äs´ ə nā´shen) means "thinking logically." Apply ratiocination to your writing by marking your draft with color-coded clues that will help you isolate specific problems and then make informed decisions about revising. These are sample revision strategies suited to color-coding:

- Circling vague words
- Bracketing transitions
- Highlighting topic sentences

Revision sections in chapters 4–13 include strategies for revising structure, paragraphs, sentences, and word choice.

Revising Your Overall Structure

When you review the organization of your writing, make sure that ideas flow logically from start to finish. Consider reordering paragraphs to make the argument more logical or adding information to fill holes in organization.

SAMPLE STRATEGY

▶ **REVISION STRATEGY**
Highlighting Topic Sentences

To see the structure of your writing, use a highlighter to mark sentences that state the main idea of each body paragraph in your draft. Evaluate the order of the sentences you've highlighted, and rearrange the paragraphs as needed. In the example shown at right, the writer decided to switch the order of body paragraphs to make ideas flow more smoothly. Transitions help to make the structure more obvious to readers.

Writers in ACTION

William Zinsser, a writer on writing, says this about the act of revision: "The writer must . . . constantly ask himself: What am I trying to say? Surprisingly often, he doesn't know. Then he must look at what he has written and ask: Have I said it?"

Topic: The Internet is a great place to access timely information.

Most importantly,
∧ Most newspapers and networks have Web sites to post updates to news stories. . . .

Ease of use is one feature.
∧ You can use the Internet from the comfort of your home. . . .

Accessing daily information is another value of the Internet.
∧ You can find almost anything you want on-line. Biographies, weather reports, and transcripts of Congressional hearings are available at the click of a mouse. . . .

What Is Revising? • 23

Step-by-Step Teaching Guide

Color-Coding Clues for Revision; Highlighting Topic Sentences

Teaching Resources: Writing Support Transparency 2-6

1. Ask students why they sometimes use highlighters to mark text as they read. (to call attention to important points, words they want to remember, facts they want to include in a research paper) Tell students that they will also learn to use color to highlight, or call attention to, certain aspects of their writing.

2. Highlighting topic sentences is one way to use color when revising a piece of writing. As a quick review, ask students to find the topic sentence in the paragraph called A Guided Tour on page 15. (The first sentence is the topic sentence.)

More About the Writer

William Zinsser is a professional journalist (as well as a former writer and editor for the *New York Herald Tribune*) who has written extensively on the writing process.

⏱ TIME AND RESOURCE MANAGER

In-Depth Coverage	Accelerated Pace
• Go over pp. 23–25 in class. • Have students complete the Applying the Revision Strategies activity on p. 25.	• Have students read pp. 23–25 on their own.

Making Paragraphs Apply; Vary Sentence Beginnings

1. Lead students in developing a list of questions they could ask themselves to help analyze paragraphs. For instance, students might ask if any paragraphs:

   - *seem incomplete*
   - *seem too long*
   - *are not really relevant to the topic*

   Invite students to add more questions.

2. Help students focus on sentences by asking them to develop questions they could ask themselves. For instance, students might ask if a sentence:

   - *fits better in another paragraph*
   - *elaborates on the topic sentence*
   - *starts the same way as too many other sentences in the paragraph*
   - *is the same length as all the other sentences in the paragraph*

2.3

Revising Your Paragraphs

Take a closer look at each paragraph in your writing. To make each element of your writing contribute successfully to the draft, you may have to change some of your paragraphs.

▶ REVISION STRATEGY
Making Paragraphs Apply

Once you've completed your first draft, analyze whether each paragraph is doing what you want it to do. Write the purpose or function of each paragraph on a piece of paper. Then, fill out the paragraph's qualifications. (You may want to copy the "application form" shown here.) If you find that a paragraph is missing an important point, look to see whether you can pull in a sentence from another paragraph near the one you are analyzing.

Paragraph Application

Job: _to show that walking is good exercise_

Qualifications:

1. _Example of someone who has benefited from walking_

2. _Fact that demonstrates walking is good_

Revising Your Sentences

When you focus on your writing at the sentence level, try to enliven it by breaking repetitive patterns. One way to find these patterns is to analyze sentence beginnings.

SAMPLE STRATEGY

▶ REVISION STRATEGY
Color-Coding to Vary Sentence Beginnings

To evaluate the variety of your sentence beginnings, use red to circle the first word of each sentence in your draft. Review the words to identify any pattern your draft includes. For example, you may have begun many sentences with the word *I* or *The.* To improve your draft, insert phrases or clauses that break the pattern. Look at this example:

START WITH *I*:	*I* like watching movies.
START WITH A PHRASE:	*On snow days,* I like watching movies.
START WITH A SUBORDINATING CONJUNCTION:	*Even though they sometimes scare me,* I like watching movies.

24 • A Walk Through the Writing Process

∨ ONGOING ASSESSMENT: Monitor and Reinforce

If students have difficulty varying sentence beginnings, try the following option.

For sentences that require a varied form, have students write three or four possible alternatives. Then have students select the best variation.

Revising Your Word Choice

Take a closer look at the language you have used to be sure that you express your ideas effectively. Look for places in your draft where an added detail can bring an idea to life or where an accurate or precise verb can replace a vague one.

▶ **REVISION STRATEGY**
Circling "To Be" Verbs

"To be" verbs, such as *am, is, are, was, were, be, being,* and *been,* are often the words you choose first, but they don't provide the power that action verbs do. Circle the *to be* verbs in your draft, and then challenge yourself to change some of them to more vivid action verbs. You may need to rewrite the sentences when you change the verb. Look at these examples:

"TO BE" VERB: The stadium traffic *was* horrendous.
ACTION VERB: The traffic *inched* around the stadium.

Peer Review

During the revising stage, get someone else's opinion. A partner's fresh approach may reveal issues in your draft that you were too close to see.

Provide a Specific Task Ask your peer reviewer to discuss one part of your writing. Consider these focused options:

Focusing Peer Review	
Purpose	**Ask**
Evaluate introduction	What did the introduction suggest about the topic of the paper?
Check if more details are needed	What do you want to know more about?
Check which parts need to be clearer	Which parts were confusing? Why?

Make the Final Decision Consider your reviewer's responses to your writing, but do not feel obligated to make every suggested change. Make those revisions that you think will improve your draft.

▶ **APPLYING THE REVISION STRATEGIES**

Using the first draft of an essay or story you have recently written, try the revision strategies introduced in this chapter. When you have finished, identify the one that worked best for you.

🌐 Learn More

For extensive instruction on verbs see Chapter 15.

Circling "To Be" Verbs

1. In writing, not all words are created equal. Precise, colorful action words are usually the best choice.

2. Have students brainstorm for a list of qualities they can look for when refining the words in their writing. The list might include words that:
   - *help paint word pictures*
   - *show action*
   - *are vivid—full of life and color*
   - *are precise*
   - *describe details*
   - *trigger our senses—hearing, seeing, smelling, touching, and tasting*

Peer Review

Teaching Resources: Writing Support Transparency 2-H

1. Write this short story title on the chalkboard: "Whose School Is It, Anyway?"

2. Ask students, *What do you think about my title for a short story?* Don't elaborate with additional information; just ask for feedback. Students will probably have trouble commenting because they are not being asked a specific question.) Point out why "what do you think?" is not the best question to use in peer review because it invites subjective, nonspecific answers.

3. Invite students to help you create a list of better peer review questions that you should have asked about your title, such as:
   - *From the title, who do you think is the story's intended audience?*
   - *Does the title sound interesting enough that you'd want to read the first few sentences of the story?*
   - *What do you think of how the title sounds when it's read aloud?*

Customize for
ESL Students

Lead students in review of the forms of *be* by asking them to complete the following sentences.

I _____ feeling fine now. (am)

I _____ sick last week. (was)

You _____ looking a little pale. (are)

You _____ fine yesterday. (were)

He _____ complaining of a headache today. (is)

Focusing on Proofreading

1. Review with students the categories for proofreading.

2. Explain to students that it is difficult to notice mistakes in one's work after having looked at it so much.

3. Encourage students to set their work aside for a day before proofreading it. This way they can approach their writing with "fresh" eyes.

2.4 *What Are Editing and Proofreading?*

After you are satisfied with the content of your draft, edit and proofread your writing to make it presentable to readers. Whether you're correcting a letter to a friend, an application essay, or a brochure in support of a candidate, strive to make your writing error-free.

Focusing on Proofreading

Get in the habit of looking closely at your work. Each writing chapter offers a focus, providing closer instruction about a specific topic you can check in your draft. Use the suggestions you find there, but do not limit your proofreading to these topics. Instead, correct all errors you see. Following are the broad categories for proofreading:

Check Spelling To catch spelling errors, focus on each word separately. For this task, avoid getting distracted by content. Consider reading your paper last word to first.

Review Capitalization and Punctuation Check that you have properly capitalized proper nouns and words that begin sentences. Then, evaluate and correct your use of parentheses, quotation marks, commas, semicolons, colons, and other punctuation marks.

Confirm Grammar and Usage Use a usage handbook to correct troublesome language and grammatical structures. To start, confirm that you have written in complete sentences. Then, analyze agreement between subjects and verbs, and check pronoun references.

Check the Facts To be sure that the information you present is accurate, use an accuracy checklist like the one shown here. When necessary, consult encyclopedias and library sources to confirm the details you include.

Make It Legible If your work is handwritten, be sure that every word is readable. When you correct an error in your final draft, cross out the error and insert new information neatly.

> **Accuracy Checklist**
> ✓Names
> ✓Dates and titles
> ✓Statistics
> ✓Exact wording of quotations
> ✓Ideas that are not your own

▶ **APPLYING THE EDITING AND PROOFREADING STRATEGIES**

Using a draft you have recently written, use the proofreading tips on this page. Circle your corrections in red, and note how many improvements careful proofreading generated.

ⓛ Learn More

For extensive instruction on grammar, usage, and mechanics conventions, see Chapters 14–27.

⏱ TIME AND RESOURCE MANAGER	
In-Depth Coverage	**Accelerated Pace**
• Go over pp. 26–27 in class. • Have students complete the Applying the Strategies activities on pp. 26 and 27.	• Have students read pp. 26–27 on their own.

2.5 *What Are Publishing and Presenting?*

Moving Forward

This walk through the writing process gives you just a taste of the strategies and techniques you can use as part of your writing process. Each of the chapters in Part 1 will teach you specific strategies suited to specific forms of writing.

Building Your Portfolio Keep your finished writing products in a folder, a box, or another safe, organized container. With all your work in one place, you can easily see your growth as a writer. You can also use your portfolio as a treasure chest of ideas. Set aside a section of your portfolio for prewriting activities, partly finished pieces of writing, and photographs that inspire ideas.

Reflecting on Your Writing Every time you write, you can learn from your experience. In addition to discovering information about your topic, take the time to consider what you gained from using the writing process. Questions at the end of each chapter will help you to reflect on your experiences.

Assessing Your Writing At the end of each chapter, you will find a *rubric*, or set of criteria, on which your work can be evaluated. Refer to the rubric throughout the writing process to make sure that you are addressing the main points of the particular mode you are using.

▶ APPLYING THE PUBLISHING AND PRESENTING STRATEGIES

1. Review the prewriting activities you used in this introductory walk-through. Put it in your portfolio as an inspiration for a later piece of writing. Talk with a partner about the activities you selected.
2. To begin reflecting on your own writing process, jot down a response to one of these questions. Save your writing in your portfolio:
   - What is your greatest strength as a writer?
   - Which writing experience in your life did you enjoy most? Why?

PORTFOLIO

Publishing and Presenting

1. Tell students to look back on their writing every so often to see how their writing has changed and developed.
2. Encourage them to record their thoughts about changes in their writing.

Integrating Vocabulary Skills

Students keep photos, clippings, and other writing ideas in one section of their portfolios. Encourage them to keep a vocabulary list in this section too. When students come across interesting words they want to remember, they can add them to the list. When they write, they can get out their list to see if any of the words enhance a particular piece they are writing.

Ask students if they learned any words in this chapter that they'd like to keep in their portfolios. Possibilities include *googol, extensively, reflexively, hexagon.*

Lesson Objectives

1. To evaluate and interpret subject matter across different media, including photography, literature, and film.

2. To write a journal entry about a photograph.

Step-by-Step Teaching Guide

Recognizing Common Subjects in Art

1. Choose one of the Spotlight elements for class discussion, or have students work individually or in groups on the element of their choice. Give students the initiative to find the necessary books, photographs, and videos.

2. Interested students may want to research for more information about Erwitt and his work. Encourage students to look for more examples of his work.

3. Aside from London, ask students if they can think of other novels and stories in which dogs play a central role.

4. Students may want to compare the film version of *Old Yeller* with the original novel. Have students research other films with dogs as their subject matter.

Viewing and Representing

Activity Encourage volunteers to bring in their photographs and read their journal entries to the class.

Critical Viewing

Respond, Analyze Students' responses will vary. Make sure they support their responses with details from the photograph.

Spotlight on the Humanities

Recognizing Common Subjects in Art

Focus on Photography: Elliott Erwitt

When you approach the writing process, you choose a topic, develop your idea, and decide how you want to present your work to your audience. Artists use similar processes to plan, create, and show their work. American photographer Elliott Erwitt was a photojournalist for such magazines as *Time* and *Life*, and he found inspiration in the objects and events around him. Erwitt has photographed people and places all over the world. In contrast to his work in the news media, Erwitt's dogs have provided a personal inspiration. Whenever he can, Erwitt adds a humorous touch to his pictures. He has had exhibitions all over the world, including the Museum of Modern Art in New York and the Art Institute of Chicago.

▲ Critical Viewing
What is your first reaction to this photograph by Elliott Erwitt? What detail created this response?
[Respond, Analyze]

Literature Connection Dogs provide a common subject in the arts. Jack London (1876–1916) wrote *The Call of the Wild* (1903), narrating the adventures of a sled dog named Buck. After he is stolen from his home, Buck is forced to work in the Klondike. Eventually, the dog courageously journeys to freedom in the wild. London's story was originally serialized in *The Saturday Evening Post* from June 20 to July 18, 1903.

Film Connection Beyond photography and novels, dogs have also found their way onto the silver screen. *Old Yeller*, a classic motion picture created by media genius Walt Disney, was released in 1957. The film tells the story of a boy named Travis and the dog, Old Yeller, that he adopts. Set in Texas in the nineteenth century, the film starred Fess Parker, Dorothy Maguire, and Chuck Connors. Disney found his inspiration in the original story by Fred Gipson.

Writing Process Activity: Choosing a Topic Through Photograph Review

If the saying "every picture tells a story" is true, you probably have countless stories in photo albums and boxes. Choose a picture you like, and jot down several writing ideas that it brings to mind. Write a journal entry to explore your ideas, or keep the list in your portfolio for development later.

Media and Technology Skills

Using Technology for Writing

Activity: Build an Electronic Portfolio

With today's word-processing software, you can effortlessly jot down, edit, save, and retrieve ideas. To make the most of writing on a word processor, build an electronic portfolio to store your work.

Learn About It Create a single folder for all your writing work. For each new project, create a subfolder. It can hold all your files for the project, including your prewriting notes, drafts, and revisions. Here are suggestions for arranging these files:

- **Prewriting** Create a subfolder for inspirations. Store freewriting notes, topic ideas, and miscellaneous notes here. Access these files when you want to begin a new writing project.

- **Drafting** The draft of a short essay may require only one file. In contrast, a research report may be better suited to several files—one for your introduction, one for the body of your work, and one for the conclusion. When you are ready to print a single draft, copy and paste the text into one main file. Store all the files in a folder that indicates the name or subject of the work.

- **Revising** Whenever you revise, save a new version of the file so that you can track the changes. An easy way to do this is to add a number to the end of the file name. Every time you create a new version, increase the number by one. Move your old drafts to a folder called Old Drafts.

Useful Functions

Editing
- Cut—deletes a selected section of text and stores it temporarily so that you can paste it elsewhere
- Copy—duplicates a selected section of text
- Paste—inserts previously cut or copied text

Saving
- Save—stores a file and any changes to it
- Save As—lets you save a new version of a file

Retrieving
- File Find—enables you to search for a file even if you remember only part of its name
- Text Find—helps you find specific text

📁 my writing	
Name	**Date Modified**
▽ 📁 Project 1 – Descriptive Essay	Oct 17
📄 Ideas	Oct 5
▽ 📁 Old Drafts	Oct 14
📄 Rocky Mountain Park	Oct 9
📄 Rocky Mountain Park.1	Oct 14
📄 Rocky Mountain Park.2	Oct 17
▷ 📁 Project 2 – Haiku Poem	Nov 11

Apply It Use this organizational plan for your next writing assignment. Then, get together with classmates to discuss the positive and negative features of storing your work electronically.

Media and Technology Skills • 29

Using Technology for Writing

Teaching Resources: Writing Support Transparency 2-1

1. Most students will be familiar with the various functions of word-processing programs.

2. If some students are not as familiar as others, consider pairing more knowledgeable students with less knowledgeable ones as you work through the activity.

3. Remind students that they will need to rename their files each time in order not to overwrite their drafts. Tell them they may want to use the current date in each of their file names to keep track of their drafts.

► *Lesson Objectives*

1. To use the writing process to respond to writing prompts.

Using the Writing Process to Respond to Writing Prompts

Teaching Resources: Standardized Test Preparation Workbook, pp.3–4

1. Have a volunteer read aloud the writing prompt.

2. Tell students to either underline or circle the important information in the prompt that they will use to guide their responses.

3. Ask students what form of writing their responses will take. (a letter) Ask them what the purpose of their letters will be. (to explain features of the community center to the town council and to persuade them to adopt these features)

4. Remind students that their letters will require convincing reasons to support their main points.

Standardized Test Preparation Workshop

Using the Writing Process to Respond to Writing Prompts

Many standardized tests include writing prompts that offer specific topics for you to address. Use the writing process to generate thoughtful, well-elaborated responses. You will be evaluated on your ability to do the following:

• Address the situation, problem, or question presented.

• Choose a logical, consistent organization for your ideas.

• Elaborate with the appropriate amount of detail for your specific audience and purpose.

• Use complete sentences and follow the rules of grammar.

• Use correct spelling and punctuation.

The process of writing for a test, or any kind of writing, can be divided into stages. Plan to use a specific amount of time for prewriting, drafting, revising, and proofreading.

Following is an example of one type of writing prompt that you might find on a standardized test. Use the suggestions on page 31 to help you respond. The clocks next to each stage show a suggested plan for organizing your time.

Sample Writing Situation

Your town has just received a grant to build a community center that would include a teen wing. Write a letter to the town council in which you explain what features you believe would most benefit teenagers in your community. Support your ideas with convincing reasons.

Test Tip

Although you won't have extensive time to devote to each stage of the writing process, take the time to prewrite and revise. Each of these steps will help you create a better final draft.

✐ **TEST-TAKING TIP**

Carefully review with students the information on page 31. Explain to them that prewriting and drafting are the most important stages because it is in these stages that students will explore and develop their writing topics. Revising, editing, and proofreading are like the icing on the cake. They are important stages in the process, but without solid organization and elaboration, a test essay will be found lacking.

Prewriting

Allow about one fourth of your time for prewriting.

Focus Your Topic There are probably many things that you would like to see in a town teen center. List all the possibilities. Then, review them, eliminating those that are unrealistic, extremely costly, or too difficult to create. From this list, choose a few programs that you would like to see in the center.

Consider Audience and Purpose As you begin to gather details for your response, keep in mind the audience indicated in the prompt. Many of the members of the town council may not know what interests teens, and you may have to include details that will educate them. Be sure to include information that will persuade them to implement your ideas.

Choose an Organization To make your letter effective, organize ideas to make them easy to follow. For this assignment, identify the suggestions you will make, and plan to present them in order of increasing importance.

Drafting

Allow almost half your time for drafting.

Build Your Authority As a person who might visit the teen center, you are the perfect spokesperson for your interests. Start off with an introduction that shows your audience why they should consider your ideas. Then, devote a paragraph to each idea you suggest. End with a conclusion that politely encourages action.

Elaborate With Details An important part of your letter will be the details that you use to prove your points. Include examples or information that will help the council members understand your points. Use the SEE method to elaborate ideas in your writing. Review page 22 to see an example of this drafting technique.

Revising, Editing, and Proofreading

Allow about one fourth of your time for revising. Use whatever time remains to proofread your work.

Check Diction Your letter is addressed to a governing committee. Make sure that the words you have chosen reflect respect for your readers. Delete any slang and define any terms your audience may not know.

Make Corrections Review your paper for spelling and punctuation errors. Make all corrections neatly. Cross out text with a single line, and use a caret (^) to indicate insertions neatly.

Customizing for
Less Advanced Students

Explain to students that graphic organizers are a helpful way to explore, narrow, and organize a topic for writing. Encourage students to think about the kinds of organizers they might use during the prewriting stage of the process.

In-Depth Lesson Plan

	LESSON FOCUS	PRINT AND MEDIA RESOURCES
DAY 1	**Introduction and Topic/Support Sentences** Students learn the characteristics of a paragraph. They also learn the function of topic sentences and support sentences in a paragraph (pp. 32–36).	*Language Lab* CD-ROM, Building Paragraphs Teaching Resources *Writing Support Tranparencies,* 3-A–B
DAY 2	**Paragraph Unity and Types** Students learn how to construct an effective paragraph through principles of unity and coherence. They also learn about the types of paragraphs (pp. 37–41).	*Language Lab* CD-ROM, Building Paragraphs Teaching Resources *Writing Support Tranparencies,* 3-C
DAY 3	**Style** Students learn about sentence variety, diction, and tone, and about the characteristics of formal and informal English (pp. 42–43).	*Language Lab* CD-ROM, Building Paragraphs Teaching Resources *Formal Assessment,* Ch. 3

Accelerated Lesson Plan

	LESSON FOCUS	PRINT AND MEDIA RESOURCES
DAY 1	**Introduction Through Topic/Support Sentences** Students learn the characteristics of paragraph writing and construct topic and supporting sentences (pp. 32–36).	*Language Lab* CD-ROM, Building Paragraphs
DAY 2	**Paragraph Unity and Types Through Style** Students learn that effective paragraph writing depends upon unity and coherence in presenting content. They also learn about sentence variety, diction, tone, and formal and informal English (pp. 37–43).	*Language Lab* CD-ROM, Building Paragraphs Teaching Resources *Formal Assessment,* Ch. 3

Options for Adapting Lesson Plans

HOMEWORK

Have students complete any stage of the lesson for homework.

FEATURES

Extend coverage with Spotlight on the Humanities (p. 44), Media and Technology Skills (p. 45), and the Standardized Test Preparation Workshop (p. 46).

TECHNOLOGY

Students can complete any stage of the lesson on computer. Have them print out their completed work.

INTEGRATED SKILLS COVERAGE

Viewing and Representing
Critical Viewing, SE pp. 32, 44
Analyzing Artistic Composition, SE p.44, ATE p. 44

Vocabulary
ATE p. 41

Technology
SE p. 45

Workplace Skills
ATE p. 35

Real-World Connection
ATE p. 42

ASSESSMENT SUPPORT

Standardized Test Preparation, SE p. 46
Standardized Test Preparation Workbook, pp. 5–6
Formal Assessment, Ch. 3

MEETING INDIVIDUAL NEEDS

Less Advanced Students ATE p. 34. See also Ongoing
Assessments, ATE pp. 36, 38, 43.
Verbal/Linguistic Learners ATE p. 34
More Advanced Students ATE p. 40

BLOCK SCHEDULING

Pacing Suggestions
For 90-minute Blocks
• Have students complete the Introduction and Topic/Support
 Sentences stages in a single period.
• Focus one class period on paragraph unity, the types of
 paragraphs, and style.

Professional Development Support
• *How to Manage Instruction in the Block* This Teaching
 Resource provides management and activity suggestions.

MEDIA AND TECHNOLOGY

For the Student
• *Language Lab CD-ROM,* Building Paragraphs

For the Teacher
• *Resource Pro* CD-ROM

WRITING AND GRAMMAR WEB SITE

The Interactive Writing and Grammar Web site provides a wide
array of support for students, teachers, and parents. Writing
support includes:

• Interactive revision checkers
• Scoring rubrics with complete models

www.phschool.com

LITERATURE CONNECTIONS

Related selections from *Prentice Hall Literature: Timeless Voices, Timeless Themes,* Bronze:
from "Melting Pot," Anna Quindlen, SE p. 33
from "All Summer in a Day," Ray Bradbury, SE p. 33
from *Winslow Homer: America's Greatest Painter,* H. N. Levitt, SE p. 40

▶ **Lesson Objectives**

1. To recognize unity and coherence as features of effective paragraphs.
2. To identify the three types of paragraphs.
3. To identify the topic sentence or main idea in a paragraph.
4. To write a topic sentence that serves as the basis for writing an effective topical paragraph.
5. To recognize patterns of paragraph organization.
6. To practice writing a topical paragraph.
7. To identify functional paragraphs and explain how they relate to the overall piece of writing.
8. To divide a long paragraph into paragraph blocks.
9. To analyze paragraph style in terms of sentence variety, diction, and tone.

Critical Viewing

Connect Students may say that, like a building, a paragraph needs a solid foundation (topic sentence or main idea), a plan for how it will turn out, building materials (words, details, sentence structures) that suit the purpose, and a dedicated "boss" to see the project through from beginning to end.

Chapter 3 Paragraphs and Compositions
Structure and Style

▲ **Critical Viewing**
Explain the ways in which constructing a building is like constructing an effective paragraph or composition. **[Connect]**

A **paragraph** is a unit of expression—a group of related sentences that focus on a main idea or thought. By using paragraphs when you write, you break information into logical, meaningful sections. The content and organization of what you write determine where you will break your writing into paragraphs.

Just as a group of related sentences work together to form a paragraph, groups of related paragraphs work together to form a composition. There are many kinds of compositions. They include various types of essays, research reports, and responses to literature. Although fictional works are not usually called compositions, these works also depend on the logical use of paragraphs to present ideas in an organized way. The specific types of compositions will be covered in the chapters that follow.

32 • Paragraphs and Compositions

⏱ TIME AND RESOURCE MANAGER	
In-Depth Coverage	**Accelerated Pace**
• Go over pp. 32–36 in class. • Have students complete the exercises on pp. 34–36. Discuss the results in class.	• Have students read pp. 32–36 on their own. • Have students complete the exercises on pp. 34–36 independently.

3.1 Writing Effective Paragraphs

Stating the Main Idea in a Topic Sentence

Most paragraphs have a main idea. Often, this main idea is directly stated in a single sentence called the **topic sentence.** The rest of the sentences in the paragraph support or explain the topic sentence, providing support through facts and details.

Sometimes, the main idea of a paragraph is implied. An **implied main idea** is not directly stated. Instead, the sentences communicate the main idea by working together to present the details and facts that allow the reader to infer the main idea.

WRITING MODELS

from Melting Pot
Anna Quindlen

Change comes hard in America, but it comes constantly. The butcher whose old shop is now an antiques store sits day after day outside the pizzeria here like a lost child. The old people across the street cluster together and discuss what kind of money they might be offered if the person who bought their building wants to turn it into condominiums. The greengrocer stocks yellow peppers and fresh rosemary for the gourmands, plum tomatoes and broadleaf parsley for the older Italians, mangoes for the Indians. He doesn't carry plantains, he says, because you can buy them in the bodega.

> In this passage, the stated topic sentence is shown in blue italics.

from All Summer in a Day
Ray Bradbury

Margot stood alone. She was a very frail girl who looked as if she had been lost in the rain for years and the rain had washed out the blue from her eyes and the red from her mouth and the yellow from her hair. She was an old photograph dusted from an album, whitened away, and if she spoke at all her voice would be a ghost. Now she stood, separate, staring at the rain and the loud wet world beyond the huge glass.

> In this passage, all the sentences work together to illustrate the implied main idea of the paragraph: Margot is a delicate, unhappy loner who is different from the others.

Writing Effective Paragraphs • 33

Writing a Topic Sentence

1. The topic sentence does not have to be the first sentence in a paragraph. It sometimes works as the last sentence. But it should not be hidden in the middle.

2. For nonfiction that explains, it is helpful for readers to find the topic sentence at the beginning.

3. Review the chart with students.

Customize for
Less Advanced Students

Have partners work on Exercise 3 together. Have students draft their own sentences and then collaborate on the final versions.

Customize for
Verbal/Linguistic Learners

After students finish writing their sentences in Exercise 3, invite them to read their paragraphs aloud to the class.

Answer Key

▶ Exercise 1

The first sentence is the topic sentence.

▶ Exercise 2

Possible response: English is the most widely-spoken language in the world.

▶ Exercise 3

Answers will vary.

3.1

▶ Exercise 1 Identifying a Stated Topic Sentence Identify the stated topic sentence of the following paragraph.

The first house I remember was kind of boxy and looked pretty much like its neighbors. However, because it was the house I grew up in, it seemed unique to me. I can still see the blue door with our house number on it, the lilac bushes my sister and I raided for bouquets each spring, and the driveway where we played hopscotch.

▶ Exercise 2 Identifying an Implied Main Idea Identify the implied main idea of the following paragraph.

English is the first or official language of over sixty countries. In fact, one out of every seven people in the world understands or speaks English. Schoolchildren who live in countries where English is not the official language are often required to study it. More than half of the world's newspapers, books, magazines, radio programs, and mail are communicated in English.

Writing a Topic Sentence

When you outline a topic or plan an essay, you identify the main points you want to address. Each of these points can be written as a **topic sentence**—a statement of the main idea of a topical paragraph. You can organize your paragraph around the topic sentence.

A good topic sentence tells readers what the paragraph is about and the point the writer wants to make about the subject matter. The chart below offers some tips for writing a strong topic sentence.

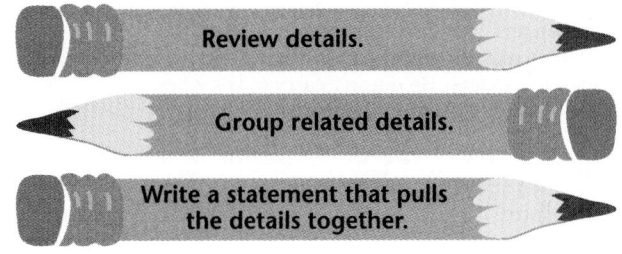

Review details.

Group related details.

Write a statement that pulls the details together.

▶ Exercise 3 Writing Topic Sentences Write a topic sentence for a paragraph on each of the following topics.
1. The condition of your locker.
2. The typical weather in your area.
3. How you are similar to or different from your best friend.
4. Why the last movie you saw was or was not a good one.
5. What makes your school unique?

Writing Supporting Sentences

Whether your topic sentence is stated or implied, it guides the rest of the paragraph. The rest of the sentences in the paragraph will either develop, explain, or support that topic sentence.

You can support or develop the idea by using one or more of the following strategies:

Use Facts Facts are statements that can be proven. They support your key idea by providing proof.

TOPIC SENTENCE: Our football team is tough to beat.
SUPPORTING FACT: It wins almost all of its games.

Use Statistics A statistic is a fact, usually stated using numbers.

TOPIC SENTENCE: Our football team is tough to beat.
SUPPORTING STATISTIC: The football team's record is 10–1.

Use Examples, Illustrations, or Instances An example, illustration, or instance is a specific thing, person, or event that demonstrates a point.

TOPIC SENTENCE: Our football team is tough to beat.
ILLUSTRATION: Last week, the team beat the previously undefeated Tigers in an exciting upset game.

Use Details Details are the specifics—the parts of the whole. They make your point or main idea clear by showing how all the pieces fit together.

TOPIC SENTENCE: Our football team is tough to beat.
DETAIL: There were only seconds left in last week's game when the quarterback threw the winning pass.

Exercise 4 **Writing Supporting Sentences** Write two supporting sentences for each of the following topic sentences. Use a variety of types of support.
1. Good habits promote good health.
2. Everyone has a different style.
3. You get out of an experience what you put into it.
4. Doing well in school requires effort and a good attitude.
5. My favorite sport is fun to watch.

Writing Supporting Sentences

1. Write the following topic sentence on the chalkboard:
   Seventh graders are super.
2. Write the following column heads on the chalkboard:
   Facts-Statistics-Examples, Illustrations, Instances-Details.
3. Have students brainstorm for items they can write in each column that would support the topic sentence. For example:
   Facts: The result of a classroom vote on the subject was unanimous.
   Statistics: 20 students are on the honor roll, in the band, play sports.

Integrating Workplace Skills

Having effective strategies, or plans, is important for preparing for careers. For example, many students use strategies such as these:
• *getting special training in a career area*
• *getting a college degree*
• *learning how to work with people on teams*

What are additional strategies students can use as they plan for adulthood?

Answer Key

Exercise 4

Answers will vary.

1. Ask students these questions about topic sentence placement:

   • *Where might you find a topic sentence in a paragraph? (beginning, middle, end)*

   • *What is the function of a topic sentence placed at the beginning of a paragraph? (introduction)*

   • *Why might a writer place a topic sentence in the middle of a paragraph? (when it is necessary to lead up to the idea)*

   • *What is the function of a topic sentence placed at the end of a paragraph? (emphasis)*

2. Write TRI vertically on the board. Ask volunteers to complete the acronym and explain the steps in their own words.

3. Discuss the IIT pattern next. Ask students when this pattern might be most effective (to build a case for an idea, to surprise people with a conclusion, etc.).

4. Tell students that whenever they write a paragraph, they should reread it and ask themselves these questions:

   • *Does each sentence support or expand the topic sentence or unstated main idea?*

   • *Does each sentence closely connect with the sentences before and after it?*

Answer Key

Answers will vary. The TRI order is 1. Team sports . . ., 2. Working as part . . ., 3. The player who . . . Students should add transitions and two additional supporting details to the paragraphs. Then, they should reorganize their paragraphs using a variation of the TRI pattern.

3.1

Placing Your Topic Sentence

Frequently, the topic sentence appears at the beginning of a paragraph. Topic sentences can, however, be placed at the beginning or at the end of the paragraph. Place your topic sentence at the beginning of a paragraph to focus readers' attention. Place your topic sentence in the middle of a paragraph when you must lead into your main idea. Place your topic sentence at the end of a paragraph to emphasize your main idea.

Paragraph Patterns Sentences in a paragraph can be arranged in several different patterns, depending on where you place your topic sentence. One common pattern is the TRI pattern (Topic, Restatement, Illustration).

• **T**opic sentence (State your main idea.)
• **R**estatement (Interpret your main idea; put it in other words.)
• **I**llustration (Support your main idea with facts and examples.)

T	Participating in after-school clubs is one of the ways you can meet new people. Getting involved in extracurricular
R	activities brings you in contact with a wide range of individuals. The drama club, for example, brings together
I	students from several different grades.

Variations on the TRI pattern include sentence arrangements such as TIR, TII, or ITR.

I	This month alone the service club at our high school delivered meals to thirty shut-ins.
I	In addition, members beautified the neighborhood with new plantings.
T	If any school-sponsored club deserves increased support, the service club does.

▶ **Exercise 5** Placing Topic Sentences Arrange the sentences below in a TRI pattern. Add transitions as needed. Include two additional details to support the topic sentence. Then, reorganize the sentences in a variation of TRI.

• Team sports teach cooperation.
• The player who passes the ball contributes as much to the team's success as the player who scores the goal.
• Working as part of a team, a player learns to work for a common goal, rather than a personal one.

☑ **ONGOING ASSESSMENT: Monitor and Reinforce**

If students are having trouble differentiating topic and supporting sentences, try the following strategy.

Have students work in pairs to find examples of effective paragraphs in a magazine article. Have them identify topic and supporting sentences in these paragraphs. Ask students to note whether topic sentences are stated or implied. You may also want to ask students where in the paragraph the topic sentence is found.

3.2 Paragraphs in Essays and Other Compositions

Unity and Coherence

Achieve Unity

In a paragraph that has **unity,** all the sentences relate to the main idea. They either develop, support, or explain the main idea. To achieve unity in your paragraphs, refer to your topic sentence as you draft. Be sure that each point is related to your topic. When you revise a paragraph, strengthen unity by deleting any sentences or details that do not develop, support, or explain the main idea. In the following paragraph, one sentence is marked for deletion because it interferes with the unity of the paragraph.

WRITING MODEL

When choosing a pet, consider the space and time you have available. If you live in a small apartment and don't have a lot of extra time, you should not choose a pet that requires a lot of exercise and affection. A dog, for instance, is probably not the best choice if you don't have time to take it outside to walk and play. It's also expensive to take a dog to the veterinarian. A goldfish, on the other hand, is happy if you feed it once a day and keep its bowl clean.

▶ **Exercise 6** Revising for Unity On a separate sheet of paper, copy the following paragraph. Mark for deletion any sentences that interfere with the unity of the paragraph.

Orchestras consist of four main groups, or sections, of instruments. These sections are string, woodwind, brass, and percussion. The string section is made up of violins, violas, cellos, and basses. My sister plays the violin, and I play the cello. The woodwinds are flutes, oboes, clarinets, and bassoons. The oboe has a unique sound. The brass section contains trumpets, French horns, trombones, and tubas. Percussion instruments include drums, bells, cymbals, gongs, triangles, tambourines, and xylophones. Many schools offer programs in which students can learn one of these instruments.

Paragraphs in Essays and Other Compositions • 37

TIME AND RESOURCE MANAGER

In-Depth Coverage	Accelerated Pace
• Go over pp. 37–41 in class. • Have students complete the exercises on pp. 37–41.	• Have students read pp. 37–41 on their own. • Have students complete the exercises on pp. 37–41 independently.

PREPARE and ENGAGE

Interest GRABBER Write the following sentences on the board:

I like to eat ice cream. I went on vacation in the mountains. I like watching documentaries.

Ask students to explain why these sentences do not make sense together. Then, ask them for changes that might make the sentences fit together better.

Activate Prior Knowledge

Have students bring in short newspaper and magazine articles. Ask them to identify the main idea of the first paragraph. Then, ask them to identify the introduction, body, and conclusion of the article.

TEACH

Step-by-Step Teaching Guide

Unity and Coherence

1. Ask students why they think unity and coherence are so important to effective paragraphs.

2. To reinforce this importance, copy the paragraph in the middle of page 37 on the chalkboard, but rearrange the order of the sentences.

3. Have a volunteer read the paragraph.

Teaching From the Model

Have a student read aloud the model, first with the deleted sentence and then without. Do students agree that the sentence interrupts the flow of the paragraph?

Answer Key

▶ **Exercise 6**

Students should mark the fourth, sixth, and last sentences for deletion.

Creating Coherence

1. Review the different types of paragraph organization.

2. Ask students to name different kinds of writing and the type of organization best suited for each.

Answer Key

Answers will vary.

3.2

Create Coherence

A paragraph has coherence when the ideas are arranged in a logical order and the sentences are connected so that it is clear to a reader how ideas are related. The type of organization you choose depends on your topic and purpose. When you draft, order the sentences in a paragraph so that one leads logically to the next. Use transitional words and phrases to indicate the connections between ideas.

TYPES OF ORGANIZATION

- **Chronological Order:** Details are arranged in order of time—what happens first, next, and last. This type of organization is useful for writing about events and explaining processes.

  Common transitions for indicating chronological relationships include *first, second, then, next, finally, before, after, at the same time, later, immediately, soon,* and *recently.*

- **Spatial Order:** Details are presented in order of how they relate to one another physically. This type of organization is frequently used in descriptions of places and things, and may also be used in giving directions.

  Common transitions for indicating spatial relationships include *through, next to, above, below, in front of, behind, outside, inside, in the middle, near, past,* and *beyond.*

- **Order of Importance:** Details are presented in increasing or decreasing order of importance. This type of organization is especially effective in persuasive writing.

  Common transitions for indicating relative importance include *first, primarily, most important, in addition, also,* and *significantly.*

- **Cause-and-Effect Order:** Details are presented to show how one event or circumstance leads to or is the result of another. This type of organization is used to explain a process or the analysis of an event.

  Common transitions for indicating relative importance include *therefore, because, if, then, due to, so,* and *thus.*

► **Exercise 7** Revising for Coherence On a separate sheet of paper, revise the following paragraph to create coherence. If necessary, reorder sentences. Add transitions to show connections.

If you have never been hiking, you should start with an easy trail. Some beginners have started off on a trail that is too difficult. They quickly become discouraged. Keep at it. You will build stamina and endurance. You will be able to tackle more difficult trails. Don't fall into the beginner's trap of thinking that hiking is easy. You need to become familiar with the woods. You need to know your own limitations.

38 • Structure and Style

☑ ONGOING ASSESSMENT: Monitor and Reinforce

If students have difficulty creating coherence, try the following option.

Have students carefully read a sample paragraph, looking for relationships between the sentences. Have them note any relationship they find. Then they can use appropriate transitional words and phrases to indicate these relationships.

Understanding the Parts of a Composition

To *compose* means to put the parts together—to create. Most often, *composing* refers to the creation of a musical or literary work—a composition. You may not think of the reports, essays, and test answers you write as literary works, but they are compositions. To write an effective composition, you must understand the parts.

The Introduction

The **introduction** does what its name suggests: It introduces the topic of your composition. An effective introduction begins with a strong **lead,** a first sentence that captures readers' interest. The lead is followed by the **thesis statement,** the key point of your composition. Usually, the thesis statement is followed by a few sentences that outline how you will make your key point.

The Body

The **body** of a composition consists of several paragraphs that develop, explain, and support the key idea expressed in the thesis statement. The body of an essay should be **unified** and **coherent.** In the same way that the sentences of a paragraph work together to support the topic sentence, the paragraphs in a composition work together to support the thesis statement. The topic of each paragraph should relate directly to the thesis statement and be arranged in a logical organization.

The Conclusion

The **conclusion** is the final paragraph of the essay. The conclusion restates the thesis and sums up the support. Often, the conclusion includes the writer's reflection or observation on the topic. An effective conclusion ends on a memorable note, with a quotation, a call to action, or a forceful statement.

▶ **Exercise 8** Planning a Composition On a separate sheet of paper, outline the parts of a composition on a topic that interests you. Write a thesis statement and a possible lead for the introduction. Write a topic sentence for each of several paragraphs that support your thesis statement. Then, choose a quotation or write a forceful statement that you might use in the conclusion.

Step-by-Step Teaching Guide

The Parts of a Composition

1. Explain to students that writing gains effectiveness through coherence and organization.
2. Review with students the parts of a composition. Ask them why they think each part belongs where it does.

Answer Key

▶ **Exercise 8**

Answers will vary.

Recognizing Types of Paragraphs

Teaching Resources: Writing Support Transparency 3-C

1. Reinforce the difference between topical and functional paragraphs by explaining to students that a *topical* paragraph centers on a *topic,* while a *functional* paragraph performs a specific *function.*

2. Encourage students to copy the information from their textbooks into their notebooks, possibly in chart form.

Customize for
More Advanced Students

Ask students to locate examples of each type of functional paragraph in a selection from *Prentice Hall Literature: Timeless Voices, Timeless Themes,* Bronze. Have pairs of students share their choices with each other.

Teaching From the Model

Have a student read aloud the selection "Winslow Homer: America's Greatest Painter." Lead students in analyzing the purpose of the italicized paragraph. Ask students to back up their opinions with facts and details. A student may point out, for example, that the paragraph makes a transition between describing Winslow (a young boy who wasn't interested in school and who wanted only to fish and draw) and giving insight into the Winslow family (they were poor, and the father's attempt to get rich quick set the family back even farther).

3.2

Recognizing Types of Paragraphs

There are several types of paragraphs you can use in your compositions and creative writing.

Topical Paragraphs

A topical paragraph is a group of sentences that contains one key sentence or idea and several sentences that support or develop that key idea or topic sentence.

Functional Paragraphs

Functional paragraphs serve a specific purpose. They may not have a topic sentence, but they are unified and coherent because the sentences (if there is more than one) are clearly connected and follow a logical order. Functional paragraphs can be used for the following purposes:

- **To create emphasis** A very short paragraph of one or two sentences lends weight to what is being said because it breaks the reader's rhythm.

- **To indicate dialogue** One of the conventions of written dialogue is that a new paragraph begins each time the speaker changes.

- **To make a transition** A short paragraph can help readers move between the main ideas in two topical paragraphs.

WRITING MODEL

from Winslow Homer: America's Greatest Painter
H. N. Levitt

When he was six, the family moved to Cambridge, directly across the street from Harvard College. Sometimes Winslow's dad would suggest that the boy consider attending Harvard someday. But it was no use. All young Winslow wanted to do was fish and draw.

After a while, the family realized there was something special about Winslow, because that's all he would do—fish and draw, day in and day out, all year long.

But even if Homer had wanted to go to college, there would have been no money for it. When Homer was 13, his dad sold all and left to make his fortune in the California gold rush. He came back a few years later empty-handed.

> The functional paragraph, highlighted in blue italics, provides a transition between Winslow's boyhood and teen years.

Exercise 9 Identifying Functional Paragraphs Skim a magazine or newspaper article to find one example of a functional paragraph that creates emphasis and one example of a functional paragraph that makes a transition. Explain to a partner how the paragraph works in the context of the longer piece of writing.

Paragraph Blocks

Sometimes, you may have so much information to support or develop a main idea that it "outgrows" a single paragraph. When a topic sentence or main idea requires extensive explanation or support, you can develop the idea in a paragraph block—several paragraphs that work together and function as a unit. Each paragraph in the block supports the key idea or topic sentence. By breaking the development of the idea into separate paragraphs, you make your ideas clearer.

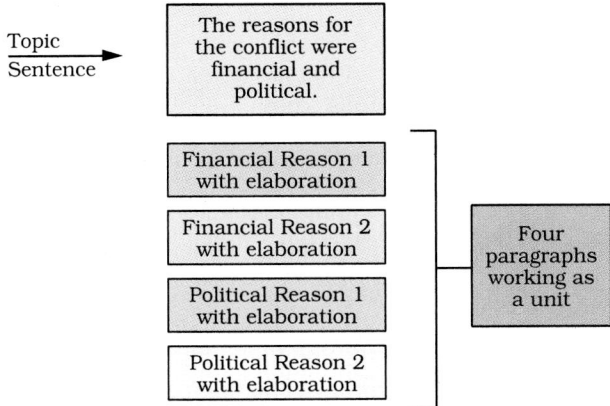

Exercise 10 Identifying Paragraph Blocks Look through magazine articles, factual reports, and short stories to find examples of paragraph blocks. Photocopy the works in which you find your example, and mark each block with a brace { }. Underline the topic sentence for the block. Next to each paragraph in the block, write a phrase describing its relationship to the main idea of the block.

> **Exercise 9**

You may want to circulate around the classroom as pairs share their paragraphs to check on students' work.

> **Exercise 10**

You may want to have students work with partners to check each other's work.

Step-by-Step Teaching Guide

Paragraph Blocks

1. Explain to students that when paragraphs get to be too long, they are more difficult to read.

2. Bring in a newspaper or magazine article and distribute copies to students. Work with the class to identify paragraph blocks that develop a topic sentence or main idea.

Integrating Vocabulary Skills

Block The word *block* originally meant "tree trunk." Later it came to mean "a solid mass of wood or stone." Would that mean that a paragraph block is a "solid mass of paragraphs"? Yes, if the paragraphs are constructed solidly, with each sentence and paragraph tightly linked to the one before and the one after.

Write the word *style* on the chalkboard. Lead a rapid-fire brainstorm in which students call out words or short phrases that mean "style" to them.

Activate Prior Knowledge

Ask students what they think the word *tone* means in the context of a piece of writing. Encourage students to provide examples from their experiences.

TEACH

Step-by-Step Teaching Guide

Writing Style

1. Explain that a writer's style is composed of the three elements listed: sentence variety, diction, and tone.

2. Remind students that a writer's style can change from piece to piece, and is dependent on the purpose for writing. For example, if a student wanted to persuade the school board to adopt a new after-school program, he or she would not use a sarcastic tone in his or her writing.

3. Divide the class into three groups. Assign one of the style qualities (sentence variety, diction, and tone) to each group. Ask the groups to come up with a description of their assigned quality in their own words. Have them share their descriptions with the class.

Real-World Connection

Professional writers or people who do a lot of writing in their jobs usually develop a recognizable style. Many writers can switch styles to fit their audiences or the particular piece they are working on. Encourage students to think about style when they read articles, stories, and books. Is the style friendly? Sassy? Tongue-in-cheek? Bold?

Answer Key

▶ Exercise 11

Responses will vary.

3.3 *Writing Style*

Developing Style

Your style is the way you express yourself—in the clothes you wear, the music you listen to, and the way you fix your hair. Style also refers to the way you express yourself in writing. Several qualities contribute to the style of your writing.

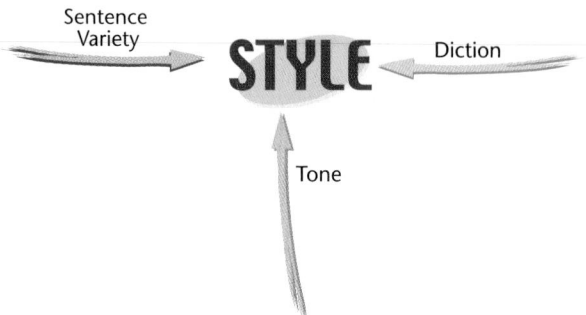

Sentence Variety The different CDs in your music collection reflect your musical taste and style. You have a "collection" that contributes to your writing style as well. When you write, use a variety of sentence types, lengths, and structures. A paragraph or an essay composed of all short sentences will be choppy; too many long sentences will make a composition boring and difficult to follow. Vary sentences to create a rhythm and emphasize your most important points.

Diction *Diction* refers to the words you choose to use when you write. You can use words with positive connotations or associations for an upbeat style, or you can use words with negative connotations if you are trying to make a point about a problem or situation. The sounds of words can also contribute to the style of a paragraph.

Tone Tone is your attitude toward your subject. You may view your subject with fondness, disapproval, or humor. If you are writing an explanation of a process, your paragraphs will have a serious, formal tone. If you are writing a letter to a friend, your paragraphs will have a casual, friendly tone.

▶ Exercise 11 **Writing a Paragraph** Read the two Writing Models on page 33. Study the sentence lengths and structures, the word choice, and the tone of each. Discuss with a partner how the styles of the two paragraphs are similar and different. Then, write a paragraph of your own, modeled on the style of one of the paragraphs you read.

42 • Structure and Style

⏱ TIME AND RESOURCE MANAGER

In-Depth Coverage	Accelerated Pace
• Go over pp. 42–43 in class. • Have students complete the exercises on pp. 42 and 43. Discuss their responses in class.	• Have students read pp. 42–43 on their own. • Have students complete the exercises on pp. 42 and 43 independently.

Using Formal and Informal English

Standard English may be formal or informal. Use formal English when you want to discuss a subject in a serious way. Use informal English for casual writing, or when you want your writing to resemble conversation.

The Conventions of Formal English

Use formal English for reports, persuasive essays, business letters, and most of your school assignments. When writing in formal English, observe the following conventions:

- Do not use contractions.
- Do not use slang.
- Use standard English usage and grammar.

Informal English

Informal English is the casual language you hear in everyday conversation. In writing, you may use informal English for friendly letters, casual notes, humorous writing, some narratives, and in dialogue. When writing in informal English, you can

- use contractions.
- use popular expressions and slang.

FORMAL ENGLISH: Please consider me for the position of lifeguard. I am well qualified and dependable.

INFORMAL ENGLISH: I'd love to land the lifeguard job. I'd be a super lifeguard. I'm dependable—my pals say they know they can count on me.

Exercise 12 Using Formal and Informal English On a separate sheet of paper, rewrite the following sentences. Use formal English for those written in informal English. Use informal English for those written in formal English.

1. Check out the show at seven.
2. This rule is such a drag.
3. I am writing to complain that you did not return my call.
4. My friends who participated were disappointed in the experience.
5. I can't believe that everyone isn't knocked out by how cool the movie is.

Writing Style • 43

Using Formal and Informal English

1. Ask students what the words *informal* and *formal* mean.

2. Have students skim through *Prentice Hall Literature: Timeless Voices, Timeless Themes,* Bronze to find examples of both kinds of language. Tell students to share their examples with the class.

3. Lead students in a discussion of why certain situations require the use of formal English. Encourage students to come up with situations in which formal English is required, and situations in which informal English is acceptable.

Answer Key

Exercise 12

Answers will vary. Sample responses are given.

1. You should watch the show at seven o'clock.
2. This rule is difficult for me to remember.
3. Why didn't you call me back?
4. My friends who went hated it.
5. I do not understand why other people did not enjoy the movie.

☑ ONGOING ASSESSMENT: Monitor and Reinforce

If students are having difficulty understanding diction, as well as when it is appropriate to use formal English, try one of the following strategies.

Option 1 Identify three potential audiences for students: a close friend, a parent, a teacher. Have them write three short paragraphs stating why they want to go to an amusement park, changing the language for the three different audiences.

Option 2 Since it is likely that formal English will be more difficult than informal, ask students to write a paragraph in formal English. Then have students exchange papers and assess the level of formality in the writing, noting any contractions or slang. Review in class how slang terms can be "translated" into formal language.

Lesson Objectives

1. To analyze artistic compositions in different media.
2. To write about a dance performance.

Analyzing Artistic Composition

1. Choose one of the Spotlight elements for class discussion, or have students work individually or in small groups on the element of their choice. Give students the initiative to find the necessary books, recordings, and videotapes.

2. Interested students can research the life and work of Anna Pavlova.

3. Encourage students to find out more information about the life and work of Saint-Saëns. Interested students can locate recordings of his considerable musical output.

4. Have students locate photography books that contain the work of Doris Ulmann. Interested students may want to compare her portraits with her other work.

Viewing and Representing

Activity Make sure students do not choose a performance that is too difficult about which to write. Have students research for background information regarding the composition they are analyzing to help guide their responses.

Critical Viewing

Analyze Students may say that both types of compositions have a form and style.

Spotlight on the Humanities

Analyzing Artistic Composition

Focus on Dance: Anna Pavlova

In a written composition, sentences and paragraphs work together to create a clear, unified piece of writing focused on a central idea. In dance, each movement contributes to the overall "composition." Each new step adds strength and beauty to the dance as a whole.

The ballet world produced a magnificent Russian dancer in Anna Pavlova (1881–1931). In 1907, she danced what was to become a signature piece for her called "The Dying Swan," with music by Camille Saint-Saëns. Pavlova toured the world and became an international ballet phenomenon. She continued to dance until illness prevented her from performing. She died of pneumonia, and reports were that on her death bed, she asked to have her swan costume brought to her. She felt unable to give up her love of dance.

Music Connection At the age of two, Frenchman Camille Saint-Saëns (1835–1921) began learning the piano, and by the time he was ten, he had memorized all of Beethoven's piano sonatas. Not only did he write the music for Anna Pavlova's signature dance, but he also wrote his Second Piano Concerto in seventeen days in 1868.

Photography Connection Known for her photographs of Anna Pavlova and other artists of her day, Doris Ullman (1882–1934) established herself as an important portrait photographer in the 1920's. Although her portraits of the famous were well published, Ullman spent most of her career photographing farm workers and street scenes.

Writing Activity: Analyze Composition

View a video of a group dance performance. Look for ways that the dancers work together to create a unified effect. For example, one dancer's outstretched arm may point toward another dancer in the group. Several dancers may perform the same step at different times. Identify specific examples of how the "parts" of the dance you view work together. Write notes on what you observe, and use your notes to give a presentation to your class or a small group. Show the video as part of your presentation.

Pavlova as Bacchante, Sir John Lavery, Glasgow Art Gallery and Museum, Scotland

▲ **Critical Viewing**
Explain by referring to the painting the elements that a visual composition shares with a written composition. **[Analyze]**

Media and Technology Skills

▶ **Lesson Objectives**

1. To evaluate the ways in which different media present information.

2. To analyze the way in which different media inform.

Evaluating Information Media

Activity: Comparing and Contrasting Newscasts

Media is a general term used to label a broad range of communication delivery forms that provide the public with information, opinions, and ideas. One service provided by most kinds of media is to report and analyze world, national, and local events.

Think About It The types of information media differ in depth of coverage and in tone and method of presentation.

- **Print media** come in several formats, including newspapers and magazines. Newspapers may be distributed daily or weekly. Often, they provide ongoing coverage that is updated with each new publication. The tone is objective, except in sections that are specifically devoted to editorials and opinions. Magazines are usually published weekly or monthly. They may provide more depth of coverage than do broadcast media, but they cannot update information as frequently. Both newspapers and magazines use typefaces to stress headlines or key points. Photographs usually accompany articles.

- **Broadcast media** reach you by electronic means such as television or radio. Broadcast media combine elements of sound, images, and live narration to report the news. Television newscasts are broadcast several times daily and may show live coverage of an event while an anchor gives details and analysis. Although radio coverage provides verbal information only, it often provides the most frequent updates. The technology of the Internet allows users to access full coverage of any story at any time of day.

Types of Media

Print
- Books
- Magazines
- Newspapers
- Photography
- Print Advertisements

Broadcast
- Film
- Radio
- Television
- Internet Broadcasts

News story: _____

The New News

Print-Media Source: _____

Images: _____

Facts Included: _____

Most Memorable Detail: _____

Broadcast-Media Source: _____

Images: _____

Facts Included: _____

Most Memorable Detail: _____

Analyze It Using charts like these, compare the coverage of the same news story in a print-media source and in a broadcast-media source. Consider how the different approaches affect the way you view the information being presented.

Step-by-Step Teaching Guide

Evaluating Information Media

Teaching Resources: Writing Support Transparency, 3-D; Writing Support Activity Book 3-1

1. You may want to introduce the topic to the class by bringing in a newspaper article and a videotape of a television news report on the same event or subject.

2. Encourage students to analyze the similarities and difference among types of formats within the same medium.

Media and Technology Skills • 45

Analyzing Strategy, Organization, and Style

1. Reinforce that students will be confronted with test questions that address strategy, organization, and style.

2. Explain to students that choosing the logical sentence sequence for the sample item is much like filling in a timeline.

3. Students should use context clues to determine the most coherent and unified order. Some students may benefit from rewriting the paragraph in a few different ways to see which version reads the best.

Standardized Test Preparation Workshop

Analyzing Strategy, Organization, and Style

Standardized tests often measure your knowledge of writing an effective paragraph. These types of test items consist of a paragraph in which each sentence is numbered and specific questions based on the paragragh. These test questions often ask about the writer's strategy, organization, sequence of sentences, and choice of words, and about the overall style of the paragraph. The following are three types of questions that you will need to answer:

- **Strategy questions** ask whether a given revision is appropriate in the context of the essay.

- **Organization questions** ask you to choose the most logical sequence of ideas or to decide whether a sentence should be added, deleted, or moved.

- **Style questions** focus on your analysis of the writer's point of view and the use of appropriate and effective language for the intended audience.

The sample test item will give you practice in answering questions on writing strategy, organization, and style.

Sample Test Item	Answer and Explanation
Read the paragraph, and then answer the question that follows. (1) New members were welcomed at the meeting. (2) The year's first meeting of the school literary magazine was productive. (3) By the close of the meeting, each committee had several new and enthusiastic members. (4) Over thirty new students attended, expressing their interest in producing the magazine. Choose the most logical sentence sequence. **A** 2, 4, 1, 3 **B** 3, 1, 2, 4 **C** 2, 4, 3, 1 **D** Correct as is.	The correct answer is *A.* In order to arrange the information in the paragraph in a logical sequence, 2 should begin the paragraph as a topic sentence. 4, 1, and 3 must appear in this sequence to support the topic sentence and follow a logical order.

✎ TEST-TAKING TIP

Encourage students to jot down notes and mark the text as they read each test item. For example, they may want to highlight the topic sentence, which will help them identify supporting sentences as well as the appropriate organization for the paragraph. In addition, students should make note of the writer's choice of sentence style and overall tone, which will help students evaluate the writer's style.

Practice 1 **Directions:** Read the passage, and then answer the questions that follow. Choose the letter of the best answer.

(1) Robert Frost explores humanity's shared experiences of life against a natural background in his poems. (2) Most frequently, Frost sets his work in the stark natural landscape of rural northern New England. (3) It is very cold in the winter here and the region often sees a great deal of snow. (4) There, isolated from America's bustling cities, Frost's speakers confront difficult and life-changing choices—which road to take, what commitments to honor, how connected each person should be to others. (5) This region is known for its natural beauty, harsh winters, and picture-postcard villages. (6) Frost likes to use these settings and themes for his poems.

1 Which of the following is the most logical sentence sequence for this paragraph?
A 4, 5, 6, 1, 2, 3
B 2, 3, 1, 5, 6, 4
C 1, 2, 3, 5, 4, 6
D 1, 4, 5, 6, 2, 3

2 Which of the following parts is irrelevant and could be deleted from the paragraph?
F Part 5
G Part 2
H Part 3
J Part 4

3 If the writer wanted to add more information about specific poems by Frost, which of the following would be most appropriate?
A Frost has written several poems that can be found in his collections.
B One such poem, "Stopping by Woods on a Snowy Evening," is an example of a man gaining insight into his life during a personal moment with nature.
C Some poems describe working on the land.
D One of Frost's most famous poems is "The Road Not Taken."

4 Which of the following sentences would best conclude the paragraph?
F Sentence 6
G By using these rural settings as a backdrop, Frost emphasizes the natural life processes that cause the narrator of the poem to make certain choices and confront challenges.
H These settings are fitting for a writer from New England.
J The stark beauty of New England is the theme of most of his works.

5 Which phrase BEST identifies the author's purpose?
A To entertain
B To inform
C To criticize
D To persuade

6 The tone of this passage can be described as—
F persuasive
G emotional
H whimsical
J admiring

Answer Key

▶ **Practice 1**
1. C
2. H
3. B
4. H
5. B
6. J

In-Depth Lesson Plan

	LESSON FOCUS	PRINT AND MEDIA RESOURCES
DAY 1	**Introduction to Autobiographical Writing** Students learn key elements of autobiographical writing and analyze the Model from Literature (pp. 48–51).	*Writers at Work* **Videotape,** Narration *Writing Lab* **CD-ROM,** Narration
DAY 2	**Prewriting** Students choose a topic based on a place, idea, or person, consider their audience and purpose, and gather details (pp. 52–55).	**Teaching Resources** *Writing Support Transparencies, 4-A–D; Writing Support Activity Book, 4-1* *Writing Lab* **CD-ROM,** Narration
DAY 3	**Drafting** Students identify characters and conflicts within their chosen topic, and write their first drafts (pp. 56–57).	**Teaching Resources** *Writing Support Transparencies, 4-E–F; Writing Support Activity Book, 4-2* *Writing Lab* **CD-ROM,** Narration
DAY 4	**Revising** Students revise their drafts in terms of overall structure, paragraphs, sentences, and word choice, and eliminate irrelevant details (pp. 58–62).	**Teaching Resources** *Writing Support Transparencies, 4-G–I;* *Writing Lab* **CD-ROM,** Narration *Language Lab* **CD-ROM,** Capitalization
DAY 5	**Editing and Proofreading; Publishing and Presenting** Students check their work for accuracy and correctness and present their final drafts (pp. 63–64).	**Teaching Resources** Scoring Rubrics on Transparency, Ch. 4; *Formal Assessment,* Ch. 4

Accelerated Lesson Plan

	LESSON FOCUS	PRINT AND MEDIA RESOURCES
DAY 1	**Introduction Through Drafting** Students review characteristics of autobiographical writing, select topics, and write drafts (pp. 48–57).	*Writers at Work* **Videotape,** Narration *Writing Lab* **CD-ROM,** Narration **Teaching Resources** *Writing Support Transparencies, 4-A–F; Writing Support Activity Book, 4-1–2*
DAY 2	**Revising Through Presenting** Students work individually or with peers to revise, edit, and proofread their work for presentation (pp. 58–64).	**Teaching Resources** *Writing Support Transparencies, 4-G–I; Scoring Rubrics on Transparency,* Ch. 4; *Formal Assessment,* Ch. 4

Options for Adapting Lesson Plans

HOMEWORK

Have students complete any stage of the lesson for homework.

FEATURES

Extend coverage with Connected Assignment (p. 67), Spotlight on the Humanities (p. 68), Media and Technology Skills (p. 69), and the Standardized Test Preparation Workshop (p. 70).

TECHNOLOGY

Students can complete any stage of the lesson on computer. Have them print out their completed work.

INTEGRATED SKILLS COVERAGE

Integrating Grammar
Nouns, SE p. 61; Capitalization of Proper Nouns, SE p. 63
Grammar and Style, SE p. 58

Reading/Writing Connection
Reading Strategy, SE p. 50
Writing Application, SE p. 51

Viewing and Representing
Critical Viewing, SE pp. 48, 50, 57, 62, 66, 68
Use Visuals to Extend Meaning, SE p. 68
Produce Visuals to Make Meaning, SE p. 69

Speaking and Listening ATE, p. 63

Technology SE pp. 56, 64, 69

Language Highlight ATE p. 51

Real-World Connection ATE, pp. 54, 60

BLOCK SCHEDULING

Pacing Suggestions
For 90-minute Blocks
• Have students complete the Prewriting and Drafting stages in a single period.
• Focus one class period on Revising and Editing and Publishing and Presenting. Allow at least 30 minutes for peer revision.

Resources for Varying Instruction
• *Writing Lab* CD-ROM If your students have access to hardware, a 90-minute block provides an ideal opportunity for them to work on computer.
• *Writers at Work* Videotape Show the Narration segment in class.

Professional Development Support
• *How to Manage Instruction in the Block* This Teaching Resource provides management and activity suggestions.

ASSESSMENT SUPPORT

Standardized Test Preparation SE p. 70; ATE pp. 55, 62
Standardized Test Preparation Workbook, pp. 7–8
Scoring Rubrics on Transparency, Ch. 4
Formal Assessment, Ch. 4
Writing Assessment and Portfolio Management

MEDIA AND TECHNOLOGY

For the Student
• *Writing Lab* CD-ROM, Narration

For the Teacher
• *Writers at Work* Videotape, Narration

MEETING INDIVIDUAL NEEDS

Less Advanced Students ATE p. 71. See also Ongoing Assessments ATE pp. 53, 57, 59, 64.
Gifted/Talented Students ATE p. 55
Visual/Spatial Learners ATE p. 69
ESL Students ATE, pp. 56, 57
Bodily/Kinesthetic Learners ATE, p. 57
Verbal/Linguistic Learners ATE p. 51

WRITING AND GRAMMAR WEB SITE

The Interactive Writing and Grammar Web site provides a wide array of support for students, teachers, and parents. Writing support includes:

• Interactive revision checkers
• Scoring rubrics with complete models

www.phschool.com

LITERATURE CONNECTIONS

Related selections from *Prentice Hall Literature: Timeless Voices, Timeless Themes*, Bronze:
"Oranges" and "Seventh Grade," by Gary Soto, SE p. 51
"A Day's Wait," by Ernest Hemingway, SE p. 53

Lesson Objectives

1. To understand the characteristics of autobiographical writing.

2. To write to express, discover, record, develop, reflect on ideas, and to problem solve.

3. To select and use voice and style appropriate to audience and purpose.

4. To produce cohesive and coherent written texts by organizing ideas, using effective transitions, and choosing precise wording.

5. To capitalize correctly to clarify meaning.

6. To generate ideas and plans for writing using prewriting strategies such as brainstorming and graphic organizers.

7. To revise selected drafts by adding, deleting, and rearranging text.

8. To use available technology to create, revise, edit, and publish texts.

9. To proofread his/her own writing and that of others.

10. To apply criteria to evaluate writing.

11. To analyze published examples as models for writing.

12. To describe how media help to represent or extend the text's meanings.

Chapter 4 Narration
Autobiographical Writing

Untitled, Pascal Milelli, Courtesy of the artist

Autobiographical Writing in Everyday Life

"Wait till you hear this!" Every day, you tell friends and family about events in your life. You might tell your parents about why it took so long to walk the dog. You might write a letter or send e-mail to friends, telling them about a trip you took last weekend.

Writing about the events in your life is a good way to share your life with others. It is also a way to discover more about yourself. When you start writing about events in your life, you may find yourself recalling details that you might otherwise have forgotten. Writers of all types use autobiographical writing as a way to understand themselves and their past.

▲ **Critical Viewing**
Name three events suggested by this painting. Which one do you think would make an interesting topic for an autobiographical narrative? Explain. **[Draw Conclusions]**

Critical Viewing

Draw Conclusions Students may mention owning a pet, going to an amusement park, or playing sports.

⏱ TIME AND RESOURCE MANAGER	
Resources **Technology:** Writers at Work videotape	
In-Depth Coverage	**Accelerated Pace**
• Cover pp. 48–51 in class. • Show Autobiography section of the Writers at Work videotape. • Read Model From Literature (pp. 50–51) in class and use it to discuss elements of autobiographical writing. • Discuss examples of autobiographical writing, such as letters, journals, and memoirs.	• Have students read pp. 48–51 on their own. • Discuss definitions and types of autobiographical writing in class. • Assign Model From Literature for independent reading.

What Is Autobiographical Writing?

Autobiographical writing tells the story of an event or person in the writer's life. Writing autobiography is like showing a special object or photo to friends—it is a way of sharing your life. Writing autobiography is also like looking in the mirror—it is a way of asking and answering the question, "Who am I?" Autobiographical writing includes

- a clear sequence of events involving the writer.
- a problem or conflict, or a clear contrast between past and present viewpoints.
- vivid details portraying people and places.

To see the criteria on which your narrative may be judged, see the Rubric for Self-Assessment on page 64.

Types of Autobiographical Writing

These are a few types of autobiographical writing:

- **Autobiographical incidents,** which are also called **personal narratives,** tell the story of a specific event in your life.
- **Autobiographical narratives** or **sketches** describe a time or a group of events in your life, offering insight into them.
- **Reflective essays** recount an experience and give your thoughts on its meaning.
- **Memoirs** are the true story of your relationship with a person, place, or animal, including your thoughts and feelings about the relationship.

PREVIEW
Student Work
IN PROGRESS

To create a piece of autobiographical writing, follow the models of the strategies in this lesson. You will trace the progress of Emily Taylor Speer, a student at Hildebrandt Intermediate School in Spring, Texas. As you'll see, Emily used featured prewriting, drafting, and revising techniques to develop her autobiographical essay, "To the Dogs." You can read her final piece at the end of the chapter.

Writers in ACTION

Gary Soto, author of short stories and poems, often writes about his past. He knows that good autobiographical writing cannot be a simple list of events but must engage the reader's interest. He arranges events in his autobiographical writing almost as if he were writing a short story:

"What I do as a memoirist or an essayist is that I try to slice up my life in a way that would be interesting to others...."

Interest GRABBER List the titles of several famous autobiographies on the chalkboard. You might include *Desert Exile: The Uprooting of a Japanese-American Family* (Yoshiko Uchida), *I Always Wanted to Be Somebody* (Althea Gibson), *Autobiography* (Benjamin Franklin), *I Never Had It Made* (Jackie Robinson), *The Story of My Life* (Helen Keller), and *Little House in the Big Woods* (Laura Ingalls Wilder). Have students compare their impressions of these titles. What do the titles suggest about the books? About the writers? Help them see that people write about their own lives for a great variety of reasons.

Activate Prior Knowledge

Ask students to share what they recall about the autobiographies they have read. Ask them to think about what makes an autobiography interesting to read. This class discussion should get students thinking about what they might want to write about themselves.

More About the Writer

Gary Soto finds plenty of material for stories and poems in his past. He writes about young people like those he grew up with in southern California. Early in his career, Soto wrote harshly of the difficulties of being poor and Mexican American. Over the years, his writing has become softer and more humorous.

☑ ONGOING ASSESSMENT: Diagnose

Use one of the following options to diagnose students' current level of proficiency in autobiographical writing.

Option 1 Ask students to select the strongest example of his or her autobiographical writing from last year. Read these samples to determine which students might need extra support in developing an autobiographical piece.

Option 2 After students read "The Bike," have them write down the main conflict and three details that support it. Students might need extra support in elaborating and in choosing details that are relevant to the main conflict.

Reading\Writing Connection

Reading: Make Predictions

Tell students that predictions are educated guesses about what will happen next in a story. Readers make predictions based on hints and clues provided by the writer. Have students read the first paragraph of "The Bike." Ask them to share their predictions and give reasons for them. (Possible response: This story will not be a happy one, because the narrator says that his bike got him nowhere.)

Critical Viewing

Speculate Students may say dogs running loose, traffic, or pedestrians.

Step-by-Step Teaching Guide

Engage Students Through Literature

1. Work through the text and marginal notes. Ask questions based on the notes. For instance, you might discuss the conflict mentioned in the first note on page 50. Have students trace this conflict through the story and see how it keeps them interested in the story.

2. Have students think about topics this story suggests for their own writing. Possible topics include a bike accident, confronting something they are afraid of, the consequences of ignoring a parental warning, or a first meeting with a newcomer to your block.

 **4.1** # Model From Literature

In this autobiographical account, short-story writer and poet Gary Soto (1952–) re-creates a memorable experience.

Reading Writing Connection

Reading Strategy: Predict As you read "The Bike," **make predictions**. Come up with answers to the question, "What will probably happen next?" As you read further, compare your answers to what actually happens.

▲ **Critical Viewing** What problems might a kid on a bike such as this one encounter? [Speculate]

The Bike

Gary Soto

My first bike got me nowhere, though the shadow I cast as I pedaled raced along my side. . . .

Going up and down the block was one thing, but taking the first curve, out of sight of Mom and the house, was another. I was scared of riding on Sarah Street. Mom said hungry dogs lived on that street, and red anger lived in their eyes. Their throats were hard with extra bones from biting kids on bikes, she said.

But I took the corner anyway. I didn't believe Mom. Once she had said that pointing at rainbows caused freckles, and after a rain had moved in and drenched the streets, after the sparrows flitted onto the lawn, a rainbow washed over the junkyard and reached the dark barrels of Coleman pickles. I stood at the window, looking out, amazed and devious, with the devilish horns of my butch haircut standing up. From behind the window, I let my finger slowly uncurl like a bean plant rising from earth. I uncurled it, then curled it back and made a fist. I should remember this day, I told myself.

I pedaled my squeaky bike around the curve onto Sarah Street, but returned immediately. I braked and looked back at where I had gone. My face was hot, my hair sweaty, but nothing scary seemed to happen. The street had looked like our street: parked cars, tall trees,

Soto's effective opener leaves readers curious to find out why the bike didn't get Soto anywhere. He also creates a conflict: He is afraid of riding around the corner, but he also wants to go there.

Details about Soto's mother, such as the stories she tells, help to characterize her—she is an imaginative woman.

Soto links each detail in this paragraph to the central conflict—his fear of biking around the corner.

50 • Autobiographical Writing

a sprinkler hissing on a lawn, and an old woman bending over her garden. I started again, and again I rode the curve, my eyes open as wide as they could go. After a few circle eights I returned to our street. There ain't no dogs, I told myself. I began to think that maybe this was like one of those false rainbow warnings.

. . . I again tore my bike around the curve onto Sarah Street. I was free. The wind flicked my hair and cooled my ears. I did figure eights, rode up the curbs and onto lawns, bumped into trees, and rode over a garden hose a hundred times because I liked the way the water sprang up from the sprinkler after the pressure of my tires. I stopped when I saw a kid my age come down a porch. His machinery for getting around was a tricycle. Big baby, I thought, and said, "You can run over my leg with your trike if you want." I laid down on the sidewalk, and the kid, with fingers in his mouth, said, "OK."

He backed up and slowly, like a tank, advanced. I folded my arms behind my head and watched a jay swoop by with what looked like a cracker in its beak, when the tire climbed over my ankle and sparks of pain cut through my skin. I sat up quickly, my eyes flinging tears like a sprinkler.

The boy asked, "Did it hurt?"

"No," I said, almost crying.

The kid could see that it did. He could see my face strain to hold back a sob, two tears dropping like dimes into the dust. . . .

. . . I got on my bicycle and pedaled mostly with the good leg. The few tears still on my eyelashes evaporated as I rode. I realized I would live. I did nothing fancy on the way home, no figure eights, no wiggling of the handlebars, no hands in my pockets, no closed eye moments.

Then the sudden bark of a dog scared me, and my pants leg fed into the chain, the bike coming to an immediate stop. I tugged at the cuff, gnashed and oil-black, until ripping sounds made me quit trying. I fell to the ground, bike and all, and let the tears lather my face again. I then dragged the bike home with the pants leg in the chain. There was nothing to do except lie in the dirt because Mom saw me round the corner from Sarah Street. I laid down when she came out, . . . and I didn't blame the dog or the stupid rainbow.

Writing Strategy: Help Readers Make Predictions To help readers make predictions as they read your autobiographical narrative, include clues. For instance, Gary Soto leaves a clue about how his story ends when he writes "My first bike got me nowhere."

To read more of Gary Soto's reflections on his life, see the poem "Oranges" and the story "Seventh Grade." You can find these selections in *Prentice Hall Literature: Timeless Voices, Timeless Themes,* Bronze.

At the end of his autobiographical narrative, the conflict is resolved: Fear "wins," since Soto's overconfidence has gotten him into trouble.

Model From Literature • 51

Teaching From the Model

Point out that "The Bike" describes an everyday occurrence in the life of an ordinary person. Students who are sure that their lives are not exciting enough to interest readers should find this encouraging. Remind them that an autobiographical story need not detail an event of major importance.

Customize for
Verbal Learners

As students read "The Bike," point out slang expressions and colloquialisms such as *ain't no dogs, trike,* and *I laid down.* Have students substitute standard English words and expressions for Soto's. Discuss which version they prefer, and why. Ask them why Soto chose to use slang expressions. Then ask them to consider whether they will want to use dialect, slang, or colloquial speech in their essays, and why it might be appropriate.

Responding to Literature

Ask students to think about how Soto builds suspense and increases readers' interest in the story of "Oranges" or "Seventh Grade." Why do we care about the characters? What moment makes us most eager to find out how the story ends? Encourage students to look for such a climax in other narratives and apply the idea to their own work.

Language Highlight

Similes Remind students that a simile is a comparison that uses the words *like* or *as.* Have them find two similes in Soto's work and explain what they mean. Encourage them to use a simile to make a memorable comparison in their own writing. (Possible answers: I let my finger slowly uncurl like a bean plant rising from earth; He backed up and slowly, like a tank, advanced.)

Reading\Writing Connection

Writing Strategy: Help Readers Make Predictions

Remind students to provide clues to readers as they draft and revise their essays.

Prewriting

Prewriting: Freewriting

1. Remind students that exploration does not have to be the physical act of going to a new place. People can explore ideas in a conversation, or they can explore the past by reading and studying about it.

2. Tell students to think about all different kinds of exploring as they write.

Prewriting: Blueprinting

Teaching Resources: Writing Support Transparency 4-A

1. Display the transparency to show how Emily used blueprinting to come up with a topic.

2. Suggest that students who are inspired by favorite places go back and visit these places (if they are nearby), rather than drawing their blueprints or maps from memory. Students might draw everything they remember first, then revisit the place. They may find discrepancies between memory and reality.

3. Challenge them to think about why their memories don't match what they see is actually there. This exercise will help them focus on their topics and decide how to present them.

Choosing Your Topic

To choose a topic for autobiographical writing, think of times when you learned something, solved a problem, or gained an insight. Use these strategies to select a topic:

Strategies for Generating a Topic

1. **Freewriting** Write whatever comes to mind in response to the word *explore*. Then, reread what you have written, and circle the most interesting idea. Use the events connected to this idea as the inspiration for your topic.

2. **Blueprinting** Think of places that are important to you, such as your house or a place you go to with friends. Draw a map of this place, marking different areas. For each location, list connected memories. Choose a memory from this list as your topic.

**Writing Lab
CD-ROM**

For more help finding a topic, use the activities and tips in the Choosing Your Topic section of the Narration lesson.

Name: Emily Taylor Speer
Hildebrandt Intermediate School
Spring, TX

Blueprinting
Here is how Emily used blueprinting to come up with a topic:

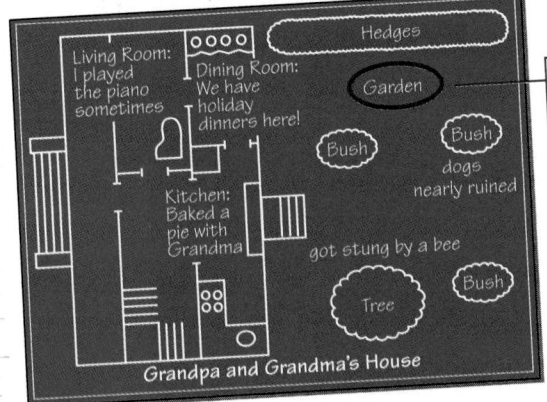

Living Room: I played the piano sometimes

Dining Room: We have holiday dinners here!

Hedges

Garden

Bush

Bush
dogs nearly ruined

Kitchen: Baked a pie with Grandma

got stung by a bee

Tree

Bush

Grandpa and Grandma's House

Emily decided to write about some of the events that had taken place in her Grandpa's garden.

52 • Autobiographical Writing

🖋 **Writing Support Transparencies**
Use the transparencies for Chapter 4 to facilitate the teaching of strategies.

Resources
Print: Writing Support Transparencies 4-A–D; Writing Support Activity Book 4-1
Technology: Writing Lab CD-ROM, Narration

In-Depth Coverage	Accelerated Pace
• Cover pp. 52–55 in class. • Have students use the looping technique to narrow their topics.	• In class, discuss how to identify a good autobiographical writing topic. • Have students list possible topics. • Ask students to submit topic proposals for your review.

TOPIC BANK

If you're having trouble finding a topic, consider the following possibilities:

1. **A Present That You Received** Think of a present you received that made you happy or proud or that disappointed you. Write about the occasion, the person who gave you the present, and your reaction to it.

2. **An Important Event** What happened and how did you feel the first time you went to the dentist? What was your experience the first time you went to a store by yourself? Write about one of these events, or choose a similar one.

Responding to Fine Art

3. Describe the weather in this painting and its overall mood. What might the girl be doing? Describe the details that lead you to answer as you do. Then, think of a day in your own life that had similar weather or a similar mood, or on which you felt as this girl might. Write about this day.

Responding to Literature

4. Read "A Day's Wait" by Ernest Hemingway. In this story, the main character's reaction to the situation is very different from the narrator's. After reading the story, write about a time when your reactions to an event or situation were very different from the reactions of other people. You can find "A Day's Wait" in *Prentice Hall Literature: Timeless Voices, Timeless Themes*, Bronze.

March Wind, ©Robert Vickrey/Licensed by VAGA, New York, NY

✔ Cooperative Writing Opportunity

5. **Autobiography of a School Year** With a group, write about important or interesting events in the last school year. Each group member can write about a different aspect of school life: assemblies, school trips, sports, class projects, and so on. Artistic group members can draw pictures to illustrate the work. Assemble your work in a folder or binder and share it with others.

Responding to Fine Art

March Wind by Robert Vickrey

Teaching Resources: Writing Support Transparency 4-B

1. You can use this artwork as a starting point to help students find a relevant topic for autobiographical writing.

2. Students may want to look through art books or visit a local museum to study the paintings. They need not look for exact parallels with their own experiences. They may find that even abstract works of art can trigger associations and memories.

Responding to Literature

Have students keep a list of some of Hemingway's specific, concrete nouns as they read "A Day's Wait." Discuss how these nouns help them form mental images of the scenes he describes. Students will concentrate on precise nouns later in this lesson as they revise their drafts.

Spotlight on the Humanities

For additional topic suggestions, refer students to the Spotlight on the Humanities on page 68.

✔ ONGOING ASSESSMENT: Monitor and Reinforce

If you observe that some students are having difficulty coming up with a topic, use one of the following options.

Option 1 If many students are having trouble, brainstorm with the class for more topic ideas. Then, suggest that students choose a topic from this new list.

Option 2 Tell students that, like taking a photograph, writing an autobiographical piece is a good way to preserve a memory. Encourage them to write about an occasion they want to be sure to remember for a long time to come.

Prewriting: Use Looping to Narrow a Topic

Teaching Resources: Writing Support Transparency 4-C

1. Display the transparency or draw students' attention to the model at the bottom of the page. Help them see how Emily narrowed her topic by focusing on and expanding the most interesting detail each time. General memories of her grandparents might have been too broad a topic, so she decided to focus on a specific story about her grandfather.

2. Students might try looping as a paired activity. Have them exchange papers with partners after freewriting for five minutes. Each student can read his or her partner's paper and choose the most interesting detail. Students can then take back their own papers and expand on the chosen detail for another five minutes. Partners can repeat this step one more time. Students may find that a reader's curiosity sparks memories they might not have thought of writing about.

Real-World Connection

Bring in two or three news articles about the same event. Make sure they came from sources whose intended audiences differ, such as *The New York Times* and a news magazine for teens. Read them with students and discuss the ways each article appeals to its targeted audience.

⏱ TIME SAVERS!

Writing Support Transparencies
Use the transparencies for Chapter 4 to teach these strategies.

4.2

Narrowing Your Topic

Once you've chosen a topic, uncover the story that is hidden within it. For instance, the event of going to a concert includes many parts. The real story, however, might focus on the moment when you thought your friend had forgotten the tickets! Peel away details from your topic to include only points that create or enrich a story. Use the strategy of "looping."

Use Looping to Narrow a Topic

Here are the steps for looping:

1. Write freely on your topic for about five minutes.
2. Circle the most interesting or important word or phrase.
3. Write for five minutes on this main focus.
4. Circle your new main focus.

If the new focus is narrow enough, use it as your topic. Otherwise, continue looping until you find a narrow topic.

Student Work IN PROGRESS

Name: *Emily Taylor Speer*
Hildebrandt Intermediate School
Spring, TX

Looping

Here is how Emily used looping to narrow a broad topic.

Grandpa and Grandma have a really big garden. It's got big bushes and trees as well as flowers. I used to hide in the bushes from my brother. Last time I was there, we found a big mess in the garden. Grandpa figured that the dogs must have gotten in, and used the garden as a pit stop.

Lots of dogs lived in the neighborhood. They come by Grandpa's house all the time. The man next door had Spanky, but Spanky is always on a leash. The woman across the street had Lucky and Buddy.

Focused Topic: There was the time Grandpa tried to stop the neighborhood dogs from messing up his lawn. I helped.

54 • Autobiographical Writing

Considering Your Audience and Purpose

Your **audience**—the readers for whom you are writing—will determine how casual or formal your writing should be. Your **purpose** for writing should also affect your writing. Autobiographical writing can entertain, share an insight, or celebrate a person in your life. Before you draft, decide on your purpose.

Analyze Your Purpose

Use the following chart to see how your purpose should shape your writing.

If your purpose is to . . .	then organize your writing to . . .	Include details that . . .
tell an exciting, amusing, or moving story about yourself	build to a climax without giving away your ending.	create suspense, sympathy, or humor.
share an insight you have had	build up to the lesson you learned.	emphasize the contrast between your previous and your present points of view.
celebrate a person in your life	dramatically show the person's character, building up to the most revealing details.	reveal the character of this person.

Gathering Details

Next, find details to enrich your writing. For instance, if you were telling the story of the time your friend misplaced the tickets for a concert, you might describe the look of impatience on the usher's face as your friend looked through her pockets. Listing and itemizing will help you gather such details.

List and Itemize

Here are the steps for listing and itemizing:

1. Spend five minutes listing ideas connected to your topic.
2. Look over your list. Circle the most important items.
3. Look for connections among the phrases you've circled.
4. Highlight details that will add to the story you want to tell.

STANDARDIZED TEST PREPARATION WORKSHOP

Responding to a Narrative Writing Prompt
Standardized tests often require students to respond to a writing prompt that takes the form of narrative writing. Share the following prompt with students:

Many of our experiences in life teach us valuable lessons. Often, we do not learn the value of the lesson until later.

Choose an experience from your own life in which you learned a valuable lesson. Tell about the experience and what you learned from it.

Step-by-Step Teaching Guide

Prewriting: Considering Your Audience and Purpose; Gathering Details

Teaching Resources: Writing Support Transparency 4-D; Writing Support Activity Book, 4-1

1. Display the transparency. On the chalkboard, write the following question: "What do I want to share with my readers?"

2. Go back to the list of famous autobiographies in the Interest Grabber activity on page 49 of this chapter. Jackie Robinson, for example, focused on his experiences as a man who paved the way for the Civil Rights movement. Yoshiko Uchida wrote about the heartbreak of being Japanese in America after Pearl Harbor, along with the joys of having a close family. Ask students to name the probable audience and purpose of these works.

3. Direct students' attention to the board. Ask them to discuss with partners why their topic is important to them and what aspect of it will be of the greatest interest to readers.

4. To help them gather details, students may find it helpful to make word webs about different aspects of their topics. For instance, they can make a web for each character in the story they will recount. Students can write the character's name in the center of the web, then add details on lines radiating outward. They can elaborate on these details in the empty space around the web. Students can then cross out any details that they feel are not relevant to the character's in the story.

Customize for
Gifted/Talented Students

Ask students why many writers alter or build on their own experiences. Have students examine their topics with this concept in mind. Challenge them to write alternative versions of some parts of their work, using their imagination to build on real events and make them as interesting as possible.

Drafting: Shaping Your Writing

Teaching Resources: Writing Support Transparency 4-E; Writing Support Activity Book 4-2

1. Help students see that conflict is what moves a plot along and motivates characters. Much of the reader's interest in a piece of writing stems from his or her response to the conflicts it presents. Conflicts need not be full-scale wars; they can be any struggle between two forces. Conflict can occur inside a character's mind, or it can occur between two characters. If a student has ever faced a difficult decision, the choice and consequences might be an excellent topic for an autobiographical essay.

2. Have students share examples of internal and external conflicts in selections they've read so far this year.

3. Display the transparency and distribute the blank graphic organizer to students. When building an essay around a central conflict, students may find that chronological order is a good way to organize it. By recounting events in the order in which they happened, students show how the conflict began, how it developed, and how it was resolved. Students may have other ideas about how to tell their stories. Present this as one model they may want to follow.

Customize for
ESL Students

Students learning English are understandably focused on remembering one English equivalent for a word; for example, *gato* (or *chat* or *katze*) = cat. In other words, they look for the denotation. Help them with the secondary definitions of words. In this case, *conflict* also means opposing ideas or desires.

4.3 Drafting

Shaping Your Writing

Create Tension

Most stories, even incidents taken from life, create tension to keep readers interested. The most important form of tension is *conflict*.

Conflict A conflict is a struggle between opposing forces. If an obstacle prevents a character from getting what he or she wants, there is a conflict.

Contrasting Viewpoints Not every autobiographical piece has an obvious conflict. For example, your recollection of childhood games might not include a struggle. To keep your reader interested, though, you might write about the day when you realized that you were too old for some games. Here, the tension lies between your old and new ways of looking at the world.

Use a Conflict Map You can help focus your thoughts about conflict or other forms of tension by drawing a conflict map like the one below.

CONFLICT MAP

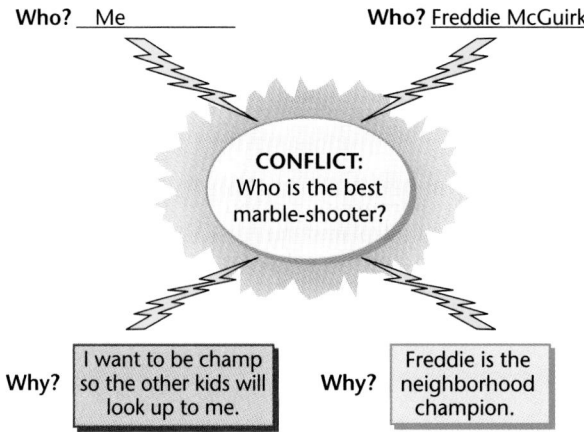

Who? __Me_____   Who? Freddie McGuirk

CONFLICT:
Who is the best marble-shooter?

Why? I want to be champ so the other kids will look up to me.

Why? Freddie is the neighborhood champion.

Create a Sequence of Events Arrange in sequence the events related to your conflict or change of viewpoint. These events should lead up to the point at which you solved the problem—the resolution of the conflict—or to the point at which your viewpoint changed—a moment of insight.

56 • Autobiographical Writing

Technology Tip

You can use the "Table" feature of a word-processing program to track a conflict. Make a column for each character involved. In separate rows, list the reasons they are involved in the conflict. Then, make a new column for each new action that deepens or resolves the conflict. Enter each action in the same row as the reasons it involves.

⏱ TIME AND RESOURCE MANAGER

Resources
Print: Writing Support Transparencies 4-E–F; Writing Support Activity Book 4-2
Technology: Writing Lab CD-ROM, Narration

In-Depth Coverage	Accelerated Pace
• Cover pp. 56–57 in class. • Discuss how students can use details to make characters come alive.	• Encourage students to use conflict maps to increase tension in their drafts.

Providing Elaboration

As you draft, you will realize you cannot say everything about your subject. One well-chosen detail, though, can conjure up an entire person or place.

Characterize Through Details

Characterizing details—Uncle Bob's laugh like a horse's whinny or Aunt Betty's careful way of walking—can create a strong, vivid image. For each important person in your autobiographical work, find a characterizing detail. Ask yourself these questions:

- What two details would I use to describe this person to a friend?
- What does this person look like?
- What is unique about this person's behavior?
- What kind of personality does this person have?
- How does this person sound?
- What expressions or words does this person frequently use?

As you draft, pause occasionally and review what you have written about other characters. Add any characterizing details that will help create a vivid picture for readers.

▲ **Critical Viewing** Describe two details in this photograph that could be used to characterize this man. **[Analyze]**

Student Work IN PROGRESS

Name: *Emily Taylor Speer*
Hildebrandt Intermediate School
Spring, TX

Adding Characterizing Details

Look at the details Emily added to her draft to characterize her grandfather, painting a picture of a careful, meticulous person.

Grandfather was a good worker. We ~~tied the stuff,~~ which looked like small, round balls, all over his bushes and trees. We followed the instructions and spaced them apart as the box directed.

> spent hours

> carefully tying the stuff

> conscientiously exactly

Drafting: Characterize Through Details

Teaching Resources: Writing Support Transparency 4-F

1. Discuss with students the importance of making characters come alive on the page.
2. Display the transparency and ask students how the details Emily added help create a vivid picture of her grandfather.

Critical Viewing

Analyze Students may say that his smile hints he has a good sense of humor and his skin reveals that he is old.

Customize for
Bodily/Kinesthetic Learners

Have partners act out some of the scenes in their essays. Students should try to convey as much as they can of the characters' personalities. After acting out the scenes, students can reread their drafts and determine how to make the characters on the page as three-dimensional and alive as those acting in the scene.

Customize for
ESL Students

Remind students that a person's speech is an important characterizing detail. When writing dialogue, students might want to share it with a more fluent English speaker to make sure the words convey the intended tone.

☑ **ONGOING ASSESSMENT: Monitor and Reinforce**

If students are having difficulty developing a clear central conflict for their work, try the following strategy.

Have students write a brief "statement of conflict." Tell them that the statement should include a goal, a problem, and a choice. In other words, the main character should have a goal,	face a problem that prevents him or her from reaching that goal, and then make a choice about how to overcome that problem.

⊘ **TIME SAVERS!**

▧ **Writing Support Transparencies**
Use the transparencies for Chapter 4 to teach these strategies.

📖 **Writing Support Activity Book**
Use the graphic organizers for Chapter 4 to facilitate these strategies.

Revising: Identifying Connections to Conflict

Teaching Resources: Writing Support Transparency 4-G

1. Remind students that even though they may have a lot to say, some details may not be relevant to the central conflicts around which their essays are built.

2. Ask students whether they have ever listened to a story that went on for much too long and bored them. Help them see that one thing that bores readers is tangents—side issues that are not relevant to the main plot. A concise piece of writing should include only the relevant details.

3. Display the transparency to show students how Emily strengthened her paragraph.

4. Have students apply the revision strategy described on this page to the model on pages 50–51 of this chapter. Discuss with them how each paragraph sticks to the main point—the narrator's challenge to his mother's warning and the consequences of his behavior. Challenge students to make sure that every paragraph in their own essays meets the same standard.

4.4 Revising

Revising Your Overall Structure
Link Details to the Central Conflict

Keep your reader eager to read—right up to your final resolution or insight! Make sure the details in your autobiographical story are connected to the central conflict or tension.

▶ **REVISION STRATEGY**
Identifying Connections to Conflict

On an index card, write a sentence summing up your conflict or change of viewpoint. Run the card down your draft. Read each paragraph and label it to show its connection with the conflict or change. A connected paragraph may

- provide information necessary to understand the conflict.
- show events that make the conflict worse.
- show how the conflict is resolved or explain the insight.

If a paragraph is not clearly related to the central conflict, rewrite it or consider deleting it.

Grammar and Style Tip

As you add and delete material to make your revisions, make sure you shape the material into complete sentences.

Student Work
IN PROGRESS

Name: Emily Taylor Speer
Hildebrandt Intermediate School
Spring, TX

Identifying Connections to Conflict
Emily decided to strengthen the connection of this paragraph to the conflict.

Conflict:
My grandfather who wants a neat lawn vs the dogs, who mess it up. ➡

who always prized his lawn and shrubbery.
My grandfather was a ~~very tall man.~~ ∧
~~Everybody who met him liked him. He had a~~
garden. Nearly all of the neighborhood agreed,
well maintained
there was no lawn more ~~beautiful~~ than Bob ∧
Speer's. It had the reputation of being the   NEEDED INFORMATION
best in the neighborhood. ~~My grandmother~~
~~worked in it, too, but it was mostly my grandfather's.~~

58 • Autobiographical Writing

⏱ TIME AND RESOURCE MANAGER

Resources
Print: Writing Support Transparencies 4-G–I
Technology: Writing Lab CD-ROM, Narration

In-Depth Coverage	Accelerated Pace
• Cover pp. 58–62 in class. • Discuss the revision process with students. Review conflicts and transitions and how they can improve a piece of writing. • Review the idea that precise nouns strengthen writing. • Help students identify vague, general nouns they should revise.	• Have students brainstorm possible criticism of their writing. • Have students work independently to revise their writing.

Revising Your Paragraphs

Strengthen Coherence

A paragraph should not be a clump of sentences that just happened to spring up in the same place. Like plants in an orderly garden, each sentence should clearly belong with the others in the paragraph. Check the connection of each sentence to the main idea of the paragraph by "weeding" paragraphs.

▶ **REVISION STRATEGY**
Coding for Coherence: "Weeding" Paragraphs

For each paragraph, jot a brief phrase on a sticky note summing up its main idea. Stick the note by the paragraph. (For a functional paragraph, identify the main function of the paragraph. See Chapter 3 for more on functional paragraphs.)

Go back over each paragraph. For each sentence in the paragraph, first read the phrase on the sticky note, then read the sentence. Place a check mark over any sentence that seems odd or out of place when read after your main idea.

When you are finished, review each checked sentence. Eliminate it if it does not belong in the paragraph, or rewrite it to make clear its connection to other sentences.

**Language Lab
CD-ROM**

For additional help with coherent paragraphs, complete the Coherence in Paragraphs lesson in the Building Paragraphs unit.

Revising: Coding for Coherence

Teaching Resources: Writing Support Transparency 4-H

1. Ask students why people pull out weeds in their gardens. (Weeds can hurt the good plants and flowers, and they don't look as nice as the plants and flowers.)

2. Display the transparency to show students how to "weed" paragraphs of out-of-place sentences.

WEEDING PARAGRAPHS

Main Topic: The City Botanical Garden is a fun place to visit.

If someone invited you on a trip to the City Botanical Garden, you might think, "Boring."

I have to admit that I wasn't exactly looking forward to my first visit.

Once you see the amazing insect-eating pitcher plant, though, you'll realize the Garden is not just about pretty flowers.

One bad thing about the Garden is the price of the refreshments.

From weirdly shaped cacti to delicate orchids, the Garden can show you sights you never imagined—at least not on Earth!

Revising • 59

✓ **ONGOING ASSESSMENT: Monitor and Reinforce**

If students are having trouble revising their sentences to show the order of events in the story in the order in which they occur, try the following strategy.

Have students list each event in their narrative on a separate note card. Direct them to lay out the cards in the order in which events occurred. Once they have the cards in order, students should number them sequentially. Then, have them compare the sequence of note cards to their drafts. Do the events occur in the same order in the cards and on the draft? If not, have them locate the problem and then correct it.

🕐 **TIME SAVERS!**

🔖 **Writing Support Transparencies**
Use the transparencies for Chapter 4 to teach these strategies.

Revising: Coding Events for Transitions

Teaching Resources: Writing Support Transparency 4-I

1. Explain that transitions get a reader from one place to another. A transition can be as simple as the sentence "I went outdoors." This sentence can transport a reader from a conversation in the kitchen to a fight at the bus stop. It tells the reader that the setting has shifted because a character has moved from one place to another.

2. Display the transparency and lead students through the model.

Real-World Connection

Journalists are often forced to limit their stories and articles to a certain number of lines of copy because of the great number of articles that have to be printed in each issue of a newspaper. Therefore, they must write concisely; each word must carry its full weight in a sentence. A precise noun or verb takes up much less room than a vague word that has to be modified by two or three other words. "The man sprinted down the street" is more vivid—and shorter—than "The man ran as fast as he possibly could down the street."

4.4

Revising Your Sentences

To help readers follow your story, make sure your sentences show the order of events and the connections between them. Add transitional words or phrases to clarify these connections.

Kinds of Transitions

Show Sequence	Identify Cause and Effect	Show Comparison and Contrast	Identify Conclusions
first, next, then, finally, before, after, soon	since, because, if	like, also, similarly, although, however, despite, but, on the other hand	therefore, thus, so, consequently, as a result

▶ **REVISION STRATEGY**
Coding Events for Transitions

Select a paragraph in your draft. Circle each sentence that tells of an event. Number the circled sentences in the order of the events they narrate. Then, reread the paragraph. If the connection between circled sentences is clear, draw a link in a new color between the circles. If the connection is not clear, add a transition. You can use the transitions listed above.

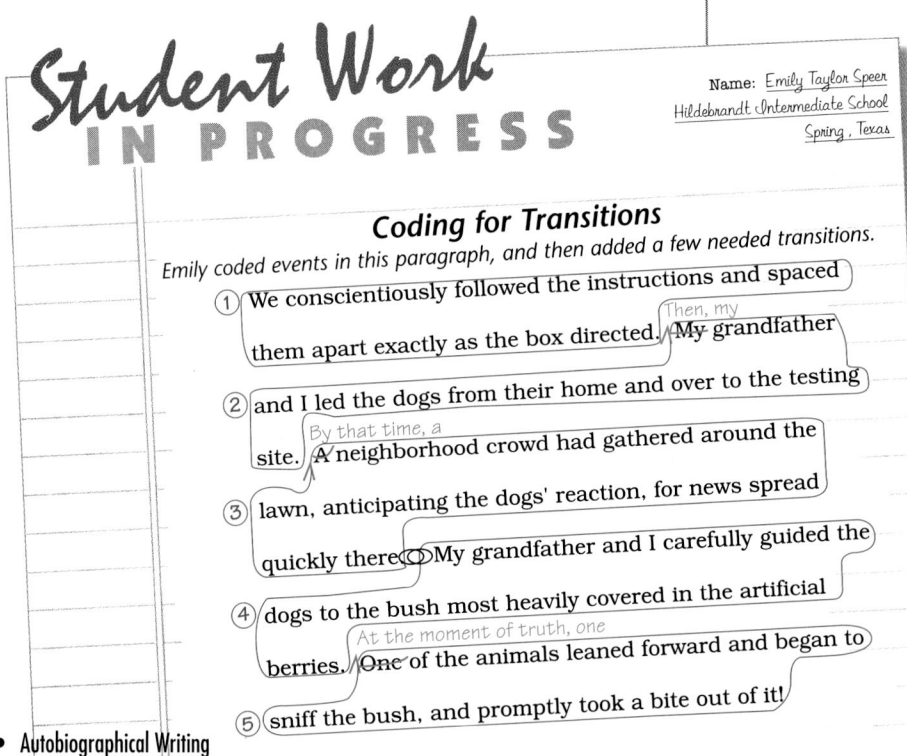

Student Work IN PROGRESS

Name: *Emily Taylor Speer*
Hildebrandt Intermediate School
Spring, Texas

Coding for Transitions

Emily coded events in this paragraph, and then added a few needed transitions.

① We conscientiously followed the instructions and spaced them apart exactly as the box directed. *Then, my* My grandfather

② and I led the dogs from their home and over to the testing site. *By that time, a* A neighborhood crowd had gathered around the

③ lawn, anticipating the dogs' reaction, for news spread quickly there. My grandfather and I carefully guided the

④ dogs to the bush most heavily covered in the artificial berries. *At the moment of truth, one* One of the animals leaned forward and began to

⑤ sniff the bush, and promptly took a bite out of it!

⏱ TIME SAVERS!

🎞 **Writing Support Transparencies**
Use the transparencies for Chapter 4 to teach these strategies.

Revising Your Word Choice

Use Precise Nouns

Precise language helps a reader understand your ideas and picture the scenes you have described. A **precise noun** is a noun that stops readers from asking *what kind?* For instance, the word *dog* would leave a reader wondering, "What kind of dog? What does it look like?" A precise noun like *collie* or *poodle* gives the reader enough information.

VAGUE:	There was a lot of **stuff** strewn about the garage.
PRECISE:	Old **tires,** greasy **rags,** and crumpled **candy wrappers** were strewn about the garage.
GENERAL:	At 9:00, I finished the **book** I was reading.
PRECISE:	At 9:00, I finished the **mystery** I was reading.

▶**REVISION STRATEGY**

Color-Coding Nouns for Precise Word Choice

Using a red pencil, draw boxes around the first ten nouns in your draft. Evaluate whether these nouns are vague. If so, improve your word choice by replacing them with more precise nouns.

Research Tip

Look up a vague word in a thesaurus to find precise words with which you can replace it. (Always check the meaning of a synonym in a dictionary before using it.)

Grammar in Your Writing
Nouns

A **noun** is a part of speech that names a person, place, or thing (including a quality, an idea, or an action). Here are some examples of nouns:

People	Places	Things	Ideas/Qualities	Actions
teacher	Florida	bicycle	beauty	running
Dr. Cassidy	riverbank	childhood	kindness	hunting
sister	downtown	T-shirt	clarity	writing
Steven	Lake Erie	joy	freedom	relaxing

Notice that nouns can name concrete things (those that can be experienced with the five senses) or abstract things (periods of life like "childhood" or feelings like "joy").

Find It in Your Reading Review "The Bike" by Gary Soto on page 50. Find three examples of precise nouns.

Find It in Your Writing Identify the first ten nouns in your draft. For each, explain which of the five categories (above) it belongs to.

To learn more about nouns, see Chapter 14.

Revising • 61

Step-by-Step Teaching Guide

Revising: Color-Coding Nouns

1. Give students examples of imprecise nouns, such as *boy, song, house,* and *room.* Challenge students to come up with at least two specific nouns for each of these. (Possible responses: *toddler, bully; jingle, aria; cottage, mansion; kitchen, attic*)

2. As students look at the nouns they color-coded in their drafts, have them think about how they would describe each one. For instance, if a student used the word *fence,* have him or her think about what kind of fence it is. A student may choose to describe it with adjectives *(picket fence)* or by substituting a more specific noun *(barricade).*

Step-by-Step Teaching Guide

Grammar in Your Writing: Nouns

1. Tell students that the word *noun* comes from a word that means *name.* Nouns are naming words; they identify the people, places, and things we think about and talk about.

2. Point out to students that even the categories of nouns—people, places, and things (including ideas and qualities)—are themselves nouns.

3. Ask students to suggest other nouns for each of the categories. You may also want to suggest nouns and have students identify the categories.

Find It in Your Reading

Possible responses: *Mom, freckles, junkyard, sprinkler, tricycle, tank, ankle*

Find It in Your Writing

Go over students' drafts individually with them. Discuss their evaluations of the nouns they used. Help them understand that precise nouns can help make writing more clear and concise.

Peer Review

1. If time permits, have students choose partners for this activity rather than working in small groups. Students can read each other's essays silently. This way, they can take as much time as they need, pay closer attention to details, and be sure they don't miss anything.

2. Encourage partners to discuss both essays after they have read each other's work. Students may have questions and concerns besides nouns. Partners should feel free to point out unclear transitions, vague descriptions, gaps in chronology, or other issues that they find puzzling.

Critical Viewing

Hypothesize Students may say the girls appear to be having fun. Helping a friend makes you happy.

4.4

Peer Review

Highlight

After you've finished revising on your own, you can still use the help of other readers. Often, a classmate can see a possible improvement that you have overlooked.

Read your entire narrative to a small group. Group members should simply listen the first time. Then, read your narrative a second time. This time, listeners should write down the nouns you use that could be made more precise—nouns that leave them wondering *what kind?* or *which one?*

When you have finished reading, have listeners repeat back to you the nouns they wrote down. Highlight them on your paper. Consider changing the highlighted words to more precise nouns.

✍ Collaborative Writing Tip

In a peer review session, express your criticisms as suggestions for improvement —not as negative comments.

▼ **Critical Viewing** Describe the mood of the girls in this picture. Explain what might be enjoyable about helping someone improve his or her draft. **[Hypothesize]**

62 • Autobiographical Writing

✎ STANDARDIZED TEST PREPARATION WORKSHOP

Mechanics Standardized tests often ask students to find mistakes in sentences and passages. Use this model to demonstrate how to find a mistake in capitalization.

Read the following passage and determine which sentence contains a mistake in capitalization.

A My train went over the Brooklyn bridge.

B I gazed out the window as the train rumbled along.

C I saw the full moon reflected in the East River.

D The two people behind me were speaking Russian in low voices.

Students should choose item **A**. Since the Brooklyn Bridge is a specific bridge, both words should be capitalized.

4.5 **Editing and Proofreading**

Before you create your final draft, carefully check for errors in spelling, grammar, punctuation, and usage.

Focusing on Capitalization

As you check your work, ask yourself:

• Have I capitalized the first word of each sentence?
• Have I capitalized the names of people and places?

Clocking Form a circle with three classmates. Each student should pass his or her draft to the right. Then, each student should check the draft for correct capitalization, highlighting possible errors. Pass the papers again, and check for run-on sentences. Pass them again, and check for sentence fragments. Each writer should look over the highlights on his or her draft and correct any errors.

Grammar in Your Writing
Capitalization of Proper Nouns

Capitalize words when they serve as the name (or part of the name) by which someone or something is called.

I took a walk with Grandpa.
We went to the Rocky Mountains on vacation.

Do not capitalize words that do not serve as a name, unless they appear at the beginning of a sentence.

I took a walk with my grandfather.
We went to the mountains on vacation.

Find It in Your Reading Review "The Bike" by Gary Soto on page 50. Choose five capitalized words, ignoring words that start sentences and the title. For each word, explain whether it is the name of a specific person, place, or thing. If it is not, explain why the word has been capitalized.

Find It in Your Writing Choose five words in your draft that you have capitalized. Write down the reason you have capitalized each. Then, choose five words you have not capitalized, and write down why. Correct any mistakes you may discover in your draft.

To learn more about capitalization, see Chapter 27.

Editing and Proofreading • **63**

TIME AND RESOURCE MANAGER

Resources
Technology: Writing Lab CD-ROM, Narration

In-Depth Coverage	Accelerated Pace
• Cover pp. 63–66 in class. • Distribute and review Proofreading Checklist and Correction Marks. • Have students edit and proofread their essays in class.	• Have students review pp. 63–66. • Have students edit and proofread their essays on their own. • Respond to individual editing needs.

Grammar in Your Writing: Capitalization of Proper Nouns

1. Explain to students that nouns are either common or proper. A proper noun names a specific person, place or thing.

2. Write the following examples on the board:
   Common: garden, general, collie, country, bridge
   Proper: Chicago Botanic Garden, General Robert E. Lee, Lassie, Ecuador, Golden Gate Bridge

3. Point out that, not only are the proper nouns capitalized, but all parts are capitalized: *General Robert E. Lee, Golden Gate Bridge,* etc.

Find It in Your Reading

Mom—name by which mother is called

Sarah Street—name of specific street

Coleman—brand name of pickle

Find It in Your Writing

Students should think carefully about their reasons for using proper nouns. Is it necessary to mention the type of car a character drives? The brand of peanut butter he or she uses? What, if anything, do these details reveal about the character?

Integrating Speaking Skills

Encourage students interested in giving dramatic readings of their essays to rehearse before reading in class. Students can find an audience of friends or family members for this purpose. After the rehearsal, students should ask the audience questions such as these:

• Did I speak clearly and audibly?

• Did I capture the characters' personalities as I read their dialogue?

• Did I stumble over words or phrases?

Students should try one more rehearsal after receiving comments from the audience. Then they should be ready to read aloud in class.

Publishing and Presenting

1. Work individually with students interested in giving dramatic readings of their essays. Discuss the difference between listening to a work and reading it. Since reading aloud always takes longer than reading silently, students may need to shorten their essays for this purpose.

2. Work with students to tighten up their essays, making sure that only the most dramatic and interesting sections remain. Students may need more distinct transitions for the script versions of their essays.

3. Students may want to work with partners to illustrate a book of their autobiographical works. The partner should read the full text carefully, noting any ideas he or she has for illustrations.

ASSESS

Assessment

Teaching Resources: Scoring Rubrics on Transparency, 4; Formal Assessment, Chapter 4

1. Display the Scoring Rubric transparency and review the criteria in class.

2. Before students proceed with self-assessment, you may wish to review the Final Draft of the Student Work in Progress on pages 65–66. Have students score the Final Draft in one or more of the rubric categories. For example, how would students score the piece in terms of audience and purpose?

3. In addition to student self-assessment, you may wish to use the following assessment options:

   • Score student essays yourself, using the rubric and scoring models from Writing Assessment.

   • Review the Standardized Test Preparation Workshop on pages 70–71 and have students respond to a writing prompt within a time limit.

   • Administer the Chapter 4 Test from Formal Assessment in Teaching Resources to assess students' grasp of concepts presented.

64

Publishing and Presenting

Building Your Portfolio

Here are some ideas for presenting your autobiographical writing:

1. **Perform a Dramatic Reading** Read your writing aloud to the class or to a group. Read expressively, matching your tone to the quality of the events that you are narrating—happy, sad, or funny.

2. **Send Your Story to a Magazine** Type your work neatly, and mail it to a magazine that publishes student writing. Include a brief letter that tells who you are and why you think your story should be published.

Reflecting on Your Writing

Reflect on your writing experience by answering the following questions in your writing journal or notebook:

• As you thought about and wrote about your topic, what new insights occurred to you?

• How did focusing on conflict help you structure your story?

📭 Internet Tip

To see an autobiographical narrative scored according to this rubric, visit www.phschool.com

Rubric for Self-Assessment

Use the following criteria to evaluate your autobiographical piece.

	Score 4	Score 3	Score 2	Score 1
Audience and Purpose	Contains an engaging introduction; successfully entertains or presents a theme	Contains a somewhat engaging introduction; entertains or presents a theme	Contains an introduction; attempts to entertain or to present a theme	Begins abruptly or confusingly; leaves purpose unclear
Organization	Creates an interesting, clear narrative; told from a consistent point of view	Presents a clear sequence of events; told from a specific point of view	Presents a mostly clear sequence of events; contains inconsistent points of view	Presents events without logical order; lacks a consistent point of view
Elaboration	Provides insight into character; develops plot; contains dialogue	Contains details and dialogue that develop character and plot	Contains details that develop plot; contains some dialogue	Contains few or no details to develop characters or plot
Use of Language	Uses word choice and tone to reveal story's theme; contains no errors in grammar, punctuation, or spelling	Uses interesting and fresh word choices; contains few errors in grammar, punctuation, and spelling	Uses some clichés and trite expressions; contains some errors in grammar, punctuation, and spelling	Uses uninspired word choices; has many errors in grammar, punctuation, and spelling

64 • Autobiographical Writing

☑ ONGOING ASSESSMENT: Assess Mastery

Use one of the following options to assess final drafts of students' autobiographical writing.

Self Assessment Ask students to score their works using the rubric on this page. Then have students write a paragraph reflecting on the most valuable thing they learned in completing this piece.	**Teacher Assessment** You may wish to use the rubric and the scoring models provided in Writing Assessment, Bronze Level, to score the autobiographical writing.

Student Work
IN PROGRESS

4.7

FINAL DRAFT

To the Dogs

Emily Taylor Speer
Hildebrandt Intermediate School
Spring, Texas

My grandfather was a man who had always prized his lawn and shrubbery. Nearly all of the neighborhood agreed, there was no lawn more well maintained than Bob Speer's. It had the reputation of being the best in the neighborhood. One summer, several of the neighbors' dogs seemed to form a similar opinion. They flocked to his yard every day, using it as a pit stop. Being the creative man that he was, Grandpa asked for my help, and we began testing a series of methods to make his yard lose its appeal. We tried sprays, statues, plants, and even asked the owner of the most frequent pests, two huge, intimidating Dobermans, to reroute their morning walk. One attempt after the other failed.

Notice how Emily introduces the conflict between her grandfather and the dogs in the very first paragraph.

Teaching from the Final Draft

1. Help students recognize the elements of good autobiographical writing demonstrated by this model.
   - The title catches a reader's interest.
   - The subject is one that many of the writer's peers will enjoy reading about.
   - The conflict is clearly presented.
   - The writing is well organized and it describes the events in the order in which they occurred.

2. Go through the marginal notes with students. Have students try to similarly annotate their own work or that of a partner. These margin notes will give them a good idea of what to look for.

Integrate Social Studies Skills

Have students find and read an autobiography written by a historical figure they admire or find interesting. They need not read an entire book; they can read just a chapter or two. Have them write brief essays evaluating these autobiographies for presentation of conflict, use of specific nouns, organization, effective leads, and overall level of interest.

Critical Viewing

Evaluate Answers will vary, but make sure students support their opinions.

4.7

Ready to surrender, we were desperate when the answer appeared, a small ad for a "miracle repellent" at the bottom of the classifieds.

Grandpa was a perfectionist. We spent hours carefully tying the repellent, which looked like blueberries, around the vicinity of the house and yard, and all over the bushes and the trees. We conscientiously followed the instructions and spaced them apart exactly as the box directed. Then, my grandfather and I led the dogs from their home and over to the testing site. By that time, a neighborhood crowd had gathered around the lawn, anticipating the dogs' reaction, for news spread quickly there. My grandfather and I carefully guided the dogs to the bush most heavily covered in the artificial berries. At the moment of truth, one of the animals leaned forward and began to sniff the bush, and promptly took a bite out of it! The crowd was silent. Then the dog hiked its leg and clearly marked its territory!

I was devastated that the foolproof plan had failed, but Grandpa just shrugged and said, "Well, we've learned our lesson."

"What lesson?' I asked.

"Never succumb to the pull of an advertisement, however strong," he said." And, more important—let the dogs have their fun."

In the second paragraph, Emily heightens the tension by elaborating on the steps that she and her grandfather took. The reader asks: Will the plan work?

The conflict is resolved. The dogs "win." Note the final functional paragraph, in which Grandpa humorously accepts the resolution.

▼ **Critical Viewing**
Does this picture of a Doberman increase your appreciation of Emily and her grandfather's experiment? Explain. **[Evaluate]**

Connected Assignment *Firsthand Biography*

A **firsthand biography** is your account of someone you know. It shares your unique perceptions of the person. To write a firsthand biography, focus on a series of events during your acquaintance with your subject. A firsthand biography includes

- use of the first-person point of view ("I").
- a well-organized retelling of events in the life of the subject.
- insights from the writer's perspective.

Prewriting List people who are important in your life—relatives, friends, teachers, coaches, and so on. Select one as your topic. Jot down impressions of your subject and your interactions with him or her.

Know	Want to Know	Learned
Ms. Grundy is a great English teacher. She makes the stories seem really important and alive.	• Did she read a lot as a kid? • Did she have a great English teacher like herself? • How did she become an English teacher?	

Then, arrange to talk with your subject. Ask questions about his or her life and the experiences you have shared. Use a K-W-L chart to help prepare these questions.

Drafting Organize the information you have gathered in logical sequence. Determine the focus of your biography—your subject's most memorable personality trait or accomplishment—and organize your writing to develop that focus. Conclude with your strongest story about, or insight into, your focus. As you draft, elaborate on each main point with your own observations.

Revising and Editing When you have finished your first draft, review it. Make the following revisions:

- Rearrange paragraphs as necessary to make sure you narrate events in sequence. (If you tell an event out of sequence, make sure that you have good reason and that you handle the transition clearly to avoid confusion.)
- Check for places where you can clarify the order of events by adding transition words, such as *first, then, next,* and *after.*
- Then, look for places where you can elaborate on your main points. *Show* your subject's characteristics by adding descriptions, dialogue, and illustrative stories.

Publishing and Presenting After revising, proofread your biography. Consider presenting a copy of it to an organization to which your subject belongs, such as a school or civic group.

▶ Lesson Objectives

1. To write a firsthand biography appropriate to audience and purpose.
2. To generate ideas using graphic organizers and interviews.
3. To revise and organize paragraphs in logical sequence using effective transitions.
4. To publish a biography for an audience.

Step-by-Step Teaching Guide

Firsthand Biography

Teaching Resources: Writing Support Transparency 4-J; Writing Support Activity Book 4-3

1. Display the transparency and give students copies of the blank organizer. Have a volunteer familiar with the KWL chart lead the class through the way to use the chart to organize information.
2. Suggest that students review strategies from Chapter 4 to help them with the activity.
3. Students may want to exchange their papers with partners for a peer review.
4. When students have finished, you may want to create a class display of firsthand biographies. Invite children to illustrate their work or to bring in photographs of the subjects of their biographies.

1. To interpret the ways photographers represent meaning.
2. To evaluate how different media inform.
3. To select photographs that communicate meaning.

Critical Viewing

Interpret Students may refer to the fact that Chanel is looking off camera to the right.

Step-by-Step Teaching Guide

Use Visuals to Extend Meaning

1. Choose one of the Spotlight elements for class discussion, or have students work individually or in groups on the element of their choice. Give students the initiative to find the necessary books or reference materials.

2. You may want to bring in a book of Abbott's work to show students.

3. Have students research to find other portraits of famous people taken by Abbott. What do these portraits "say" about the subjects?

4. Interested students can find out more information about Le Gallienne and the American Repertory Theatre.

Viewing and Representing

Activity Students can put their photographs and essays into book form. Suggest that students refrain from gluing or taping their photos in their books, in case their families want them back.

Spotlight on the Humanities

Use Visuals to Extend Meaning

Focus on Photography: Berenice Abbott

Just like an autobiographical narrative, a picture "tells a story." Photographer Berenice Abbott (1898–1991) used pictures to tell the story of a few artistic and literary figures who lived in Paris in the 1920's. James Joyce, the writer; Jean Cocteau, the filmmaker; and Eva Le Gallienne, the actress, are just a few of the luminaries she captured on film.

After living in Paris for many years, Abbott returned home to New York City in 1929 and began photographing the New York City land-scape in all its variety. In the 1950's, Abbott merged photography with scientific principles and began photographing scientific subjects. She filled three high-school books on physics with these photographs.

Art Connection In 1927, Abbott photographed the famous fashion designer Coco Chanel (1883–1971). Born in France, Chanel was the leading fashion designer of her day, promoting necklaces and belts and short hairstyles for women. One early suc-cess was a loose-fitting sweater with a belted skirt. Chanel's revo-lutionary designs carried a feeling of simplicity, opposing the flam-boyant styles popular in the early part of the twentieth century. Her influence on clothing design can still be seen in fashion today.

Theater Connection Abbott also photographed actress, direc-tor, and producer Eva Le Gallienne (1899–1991). Cofounder of the American Repertory Theatre in 1946, Le Gallienne estab-lished herself as one of the leading American actresses of the twentieth century. Born in London, England, she lived in America throughout most of her professional career. She believed strongly in repertory theater and translated many of the works of classic playwright Henrik Ibsen.

Autobiographical Writing Activity: Photo Essay

Compile a collection of photographs that illustrate memorable moments in your life. Then, write a short paragraph to accompa-ny each photograph so that you create an autobiographical photo essay of your life. Share your photo essay with your classmates.

▲ **Critical Viewing** How does Abbott use Coco Chanel's pose in this photo-graph to suggest that Chanel is a cre-ative woman with a vision? **[Interpret]**

Media and Technology Skills

Produce Visuals to Make Meaning

Activity: Create a Photo Essay

Like Berenice Abbott (previous page), you can use a camera to reveal something unique about a person. Learn more about taking photographs, and create your own photo essay.

Learn About It Read through the owner's manual of your camera to familiarize yourself with its features. If you are using a 35-mm camera, learn about the effects of film speed, f-stop, and aperture. Get the help of an experienced user of the camera if necessary.

Experiment To get to know your camera well, take lots of photos under different conditions—for example, pictures of an object at various distances in various lighting. Keep a log of the conditions under which you took each shot and the results they produced.

Creating Meanings Different uses of the camera create different meanings. For example, a picture taken on a sunny day creates a different effect from one taken on a cloudy day. See the sidebar for other ways in which pictures create meaning.

Apply It Take a series of photographs that reveal something about a family member or friend. Choose objects, places, and events that tell something about the person, and photograph the person in connection with them. Use a chart like the one below to plan your pictures. Display your results to the class.

Types of Images

Action Shot
A shot of a person performing a specific action. The photograph must include enough background to make the circumstances clear.

Portrait
A close-up of a person or his or her face. The person's pose can suggest a great deal about him or her. A person looking directly at the camera may appear frank and friendly; a person staring off to the side or out a window may appear thoughtful or moody.

Still Life
A shot of a group of objects. A still life is generally an exercise in composition (the arrangement of objects for effect). It can also be used to show something about the owner of the objects.

Aspect of Person	Type of Photograph	Special Considerations
Dad coaches baseball.	Action Shot	• Take the picture on a sunny day. • Show players to make clear what the event is. • To make Dad's role clear, I should take a picture of him correcting somebody's batting stance.

1. To evaluate how media inform and create meaning.
2. To produce visuals to extend meaning.
3. To assess how a presentation contributes to a message.

Step-by-Step Teaching Guide

Produce Visuals to Make Meaning

Teaching Resources: Writing Support Transparency 4-K; Writing Support Activity Book 4-4

1. Display the transparency and give students copies of the blank organizer. Tell students that by planning the photograph ahead of time, they can ensure a better result.

2. You may want to bring in a camera to demonstrate proper use to students. If possible, bring in an automatic and a manual camera.

3. Before students take their photographs, you may want to bring in books that contain examples of different photographic styles and subject matter. Students can look through magazines and newspapers to find examples to bring into class.

4. Encourage students to take a look at some "how-to" photography manuals to give them more background information about taking photographs.

Customizing for
Visual/Spatial Learners

Some students may benefit from sketching the subject of their photographs before taking the photo. Encourage them to be as detailed as possible about the angles, framing, and lighting. This will provide them with a "blueprint" for the final product.

1. To write in a style appropriate to audience and purpose.
2. To use prewriting strategies to gather details.
3. To organize details to produce cohesive and coherent text.
4. To revise the draft for progression and logical support of purpose.

Using Narration to Respond to Writing Prompts

Teaching Resources: Standardized Test Preparation Workbook, pp. 7–8

1. Have students copy down the bulleted list of information on this page. This should help them remember the important features of narrative writing.

2. Have a volunteer read aloud the writing prompt to the class. Ask students to identify the form their writing will take, the audience for their writing, and their purpose for writing. Remind them to keep these factors in mind when responding to the prompt. Students should see that their writing will take the form of a letter, and will involve both narrative and persuasive forms of writing.

3. Review the suggested percentages of time students should set aside for each stage of the writing process.

4. Have students respond to the prompt, completing it within the class period.

Standardized Test Preparation Workshop

Using Narration to Respond to Writing Prompts

The writing prompts on standardized tests often measure your ability to write a narrative or to use elements of narrative writing for a specific purpose. The following are the criteria upon which such writing will be evaluated:

- Organizes details in a meaningful and coherent sequence.
- Tailors word choice and style to the purpose and audience named in the response. For example, a letter to the school board should be more formal than one to a friend.
- Uses appropriate transitions to create a unified, coherent narrative.
- Elaborates on events with the effective use of description, characterization, and other details.
- Uses correct grammar, spelling, and punctuation.

Following is an example of a writing prompt that requires you to use elements of narrative writing. Use the suggestions on the following page to help you respond. The clocks show the suggested percentage of your test-taking time to devote to each stage.

Test Tip

Before drafting, jot down a list of supporting details. Then, choose the strongest details to include in your narrative.

Sample Writing Situation

Extracurricular activities are an important part of middle school. Often, they require so much time and dedication that, if you are not careful, your grades can suffer. Think about your experiences balancing school work and outside commitments, and then respond to the following prompt.

Your school has just added your favorite extracurricular activity to the after-school program. You are already involved in two other activities but don't want to miss this opportunity. Your parents are concerned that you are involved in too many activities outside school. Write a letter to your parents in which you persuade them that you are responsible enough to participate in these activities and maintain good grades. To support your position, include accounts of past situations in which you successfully took on responsibility.

70 • Autobiographical Writing

✍ TEST-TAKING TIP

Remind students that good organization is key to writing effectively. Students can create brief outlines to help them organize their thoughts. Aside from the overall chronological order, students should remember to support each of their main points, since they want to persuade their parents in the letter. Suggest that students use some of the writing strategies they have learned in this chapter to help them with all of the stages in the writing process.

Prewriting

Allow close to one fourth of your time for prewriting.

Gather Details Begin to gather information about your experiences with responsibility. Using the strategy of listing and itemizing, focus on examples in which you successfully handled a few responsibilities at the same time. (To see the steps for listing and itemizing, refer to page 55.)

Consider Your Audience and Purpose As you begin to gather details for your narrative, keep in mind the audience and purpose indicated in the prompt—persuading your parents. A respectful tone is appropriate, but you may be less formal than if you were writing to a stranger.

Drafting

Allow almost half of your time for drafting.

Organization After you have gathered details, make an outline to organize them. Each story you tell to support your main idea should be organized in chronological order. Alternatively, you may introduce each story by summarizing the most important aspect, presenting less important details later. If you present more than one story, save the story that makes the strongest case for last.

Introduction, Body, and Conclusion After organizing details, begin drafting. Start off with an introductory paragraph that uses an example, an exaggeration, or another attention-grabbing device to establish your purpose in writing. In the body paragraphs, tell the stories that establish your capacity for responsibility. Connect each to your main purpose. Finally, sum up your letter by restating your evidence and what it supports.

Revising, Editing, and Proofreading

Allow almost one fourth of your time to revise and edit. Use the last few minutes to proofread your work.

Strengthen Your Case Review your draft. Neatly add in details to strengthen your persuasive case. Cross out any details that do not support your purpose. Change language that is inappropriately infomal for your audience. Add transitions where necessary to keep ideas flowing smoothly.

Make Corrections Check for errors in spelling, grammar, and punctuation. When making changes, place one line through text that you want to eliminate and enclose it in brackets. Use a caret (^) to indicate the places at which you want to add words.

Time and Resource Manager

In-Depth Lesson Plan

	LESSON FOCUS	PRINT AND MEDIA RESOURCES
DAY 1	**Introduction to Narration: Short Story** Students learn key elements of short story writing and analyze the Model From Literature (pp. 72–77).	*Writers at Work* **Videotape,** Narration
DAY 2	**Prewriting** Students use freewriting to help select a short story topic (pp. 78–81).	**Teaching Resources** *Writing Support Transparencies,* 5-A–D; *Writing Support Activity Book,* 5-1 *Writing Lab* **CD-ROM,** Narration
DAY 3	**Drafting** Students identify the characters, setting, conflict, and other plot elements, and write their first drafts (pp. 82–83).	**Teaching Resources** *Writing Support Transparencies,* 5-E–F; *Writing Support Activity Book,* 5-2 *Writing Lab* **CD-ROM,** Narration
DAY 4	**Revising** Students revise their stories to strengthen characterizations and make plot action move vivid (pp. 84–87).	**Teaching Resources** *Writing Support Transparencies,* 5-G–H; *Writing Support Activity Book,* 5-3 *Writing Lab* **CD-ROM,** Narration
DAY 5	**Editing and Proofreading; Publishing and Presenting** Students edit their stories, focusing on the punctuation of dialogue, and present their final drafts (pp. 88–89).	**Teaching Resources** *Scoring Rubrics on Transparency,* Ch. 5; *Formal Assessment,* Ch. 5

Accelerated Lesson Plan

	LESSON FOCUS	PRINT AND MEDIA RESOURCES
DAY 1	**Introduction Through Drafting** Students review characteristics of short story narration, select story characters and conflict, and write drafts (pp. 72–83).	**Teaching Resources** *Writing Support Transparencies,* 5-A–F; *Writing Support Activity Book,* 5-1–2 *Writers at Work* **Videotape,** Narration *Writing Lab* **CD-ROM,** Narration
DAY 2	**Revising Through Presenting** Students work individually or with peers to revise, edit, and proofread their work for presentation (pp. 84–89).	**Teaching Resources** *Writing Support Transparencies,* 5-G–H; *Writing Support Activity Book,* 5-3; *Scoring Rubrics on Transparency,* Ch. 5; *Formal Assessment,* Ch. 5 *Writing Lab* **CD-ROM,** Narration

Options for Adapting Lesson Plans

HOMEWORK

Have students complete any stage of the lesson for homework.

FEATURES

Extend coverage with Connected Assignment (p. 93), Spotlight on the Humanities (p. 94), Media and Technology Skills (p. 95), and the Standardized Test Preparation Workshop (p. 96).

TECHNOLOGY

Students can complete any stage of the lesson on computer. Have them print out their completed work.

INTEGRATED SKILLS COVERAGE

Integrating Grammar
Identifying Action Verbs, SE p. 87
Punctuating Dialogue, SE p. 88
ATE p. 92

Reading/Writing Connection
Reading Strategy, SE p. 74
Writing Application, SE p. 77

Viewing and Representing
Critical Viewing, SE pp. 72, 74, 76, 77, 81, 83, 86, 90, 92, 93, 94
Analyze Visual Meaning, SE p. 95; ATE p. 94

Speaking and Listening
ATE, p. 91

Technology   SE p. 85, 89; ATE, p. 76

Language Highlight   ATE, p. 79

Real-World Connection   ATE, p. 83

BLOCK SCHEDULING

Pacing Suggestions
For 90-minute Blocks
• Have students complete the Prewriting and Drafting stages in a single period.
• Focus one class period on Revising and Editing and Publishing and Presenting. Allow at least 30 minutes for peer revision.

Resources for Varying Instruction
• *Writing Lab* **CD-ROM** If your students have access to hardware, a 90-minute block provides an ideal opportunity for them to work on computer.
• *Writers at Work* **Videotape** Show the Narration segment in class.

Professional Development Support
• *How to Manage Instruction in the Block* This Teaching Resource provides management and activity suggestions.

ASSESSMENT SUPPORT

Standardized Test Preparation SE p. 96; ATE p. 75
Standardized Test Preparation Workbook, pp. 9–10
Scoring Rubrics on Transparency, Ch. 5
Formal Assessment, Ch. 5
Writing Assessment and Portfolio Management

MEDIA AND TECHNOLOGY

For the Student
• *Writing Lab* **CD-ROM**, Narration

For the Teacher
• *Writers at Work* **Videotape**, Narration

MEETING INDIVIDUAL NEEDS

Less Advanced Students ATE p. 76. See also Ongoing Assessments ATE pp. 73, 76, 79, 80, 83, 86, 89.
ESL Students ATE pp. 77, 78
Bodily/Kinesthetic Learners ATE p. 80
Gifted/Talented Students ATE p. 81
Visual/Spatial Learners ATE p. 82
Interpersonal Learners ATE p. 85
More Advanced Students ATE p. 97

WRITING AND GRAMMAR WEB SITE

The Interactive Writing and Grammar Web site provides a wide array of support for students, teachers, and parents. Writing support includes:

• Interactive revision checkers
• Scoring rubrics with complete models

www.phschool.com

LITERATURE CONNECTIONS

Related selections from *Prentice Hall Literature: Timeless Voices, Timeless Themes*, Bronze:
"The Third Level," by Jack Finney, SE p. 75
"Mother to Son," by Langston Hughes, SE p. 79

▶ **Lesson Objectives**

1. To write a narrative short story.

2. To read to appreciate the writer's craft and interpret the meaning of what they have read.

3. To use prewriting strategies to generate ideas for topics.

4. To identify conflict within a story.

5. To select and use voice and style appropriate to audience and purpose.

6. To generate plans for writing using listing and itemizing.

7. To develop drafts by categorizing and providing elaboration.

8. To revise drafts by building to a climax, improving characterization, combining sentences, and using vivid verbs.

9. To edit and proofread to correct punctuation of dialogue.

10. To use available technology for publishing and presenting.

Critical Viewing

Speculate Students' responses will vary but should involve the two figures in the painting.

Early Carolina Morning, 1978, Romare Bearden, ©Romare Bearden Foundation/Licensed by VAGA, New York, NY

Chapter 5 Narration
Short Story

Short Stories in Everyday Life

Even if you've never *written* a story, you've probably *told* many stories. Perhaps you've made up a bedtime story to tell a younger brother. Maybe you've amused friends with the tale of the night you found a bat flying around your bedroom.

Storytelling comes naturally to us. The first stories were probably told around campfires, but these days stories are told around kitchen or cafeteria tables—or even passed around by e-mail. Every year, thousands of stories are published in books and magazines.

In this chapter, you'll learn strategies for writing a short story that captures your readers' interest—and may even take them somewhere they've never been before.

▲ **Critical Viewing**
What story do you imagine this painting is "telling"? **[Speculate]**

72 • Narration

⏱ TIME AND RESOURCE MANAGER

Resources
Technology: Writers at Work videotape

In-Depth Coverage	Accelerated Pace
• Cover pp. 72–73 in class. • Show Narration section of the Writers at Work videotape. • Read literature excerpt (pp. 74–77) in class, and use it to brainstorm short story ideas with students. • Discuss examples of short stories students know about or have brought to class.	• Have students read pp. 72–77 on their own. • Discuss definitions and types of short stories in class. • Assign Model From Literature for independent reading.

What Is a Short Story?

A **short story** is a brief, creative narrative—a retelling of events arranged to hold a reader's attention. From the Arctic tundra to a steamy rain forest, a short story can send you places you've never been. By letting you enter the lives of its characters, a short story reminds you that you can always be more than who you are today.

Most short stories include

- one or more characters (the people, animals, or other creatures involved in the story).
- a conflict or problem that keeps the reader asking, "What will happen next?"
- a beginning that introduces the characters and setting and establishes the conflict.
- a middle in which the story reaches a high point—usually, some type of conflict.
- an ending in which the conflict is resolved and loose ends are tied up.

To learn the criteria on which your short story may be evaluated, see the Rubric for Self-Assessment on page 89.

Types of Short Stories

The following are some of the different kinds of short stories:

- **Realistic stories** take place in familiar neighborhoods with people just like the ones you know.
- **Fantasy and science-fiction stories** take you to worlds that exist only in the mind—a far-off galaxy or a future Earth.
- **Adventure stories** immerse you in exciting action played out by larger-than-life heroes.

Writers in ACTION

Ray Bradbury has been writing science fiction since he was a high-school student in the 1930's and has published more than 500 short stories. Here is what he has said about how he gets the ideas for his stories:

"My stories run up and bite me in the leg—I respond by writing down everything that goes on during the bite. When I finish, the idea lets go and runs off."

PREVIEW *Student Work* IN PROGRESS

In this chapter, you'll see how Elisabeth Laskey, a student at Gray-New Gloucester Middle School in Gray, Maine, developed her short story "Showing Amanda the Ropes." You'll follow her work in progress, including the strategies she used to come up with a topic and revise her first draft. At the end of the chapter, you'll read her finished short story.

Short Story • **73**

Reading\Writing Connection

Reading: Interpret

Explain to students that, in order to understand how a story is "built," they need to interpret, or figure out, what an author accomplishes with each detail or event. Suggest that students be aware of how they get to "know" the people and places of the story.

Teaching from the Model

Use this Model From Literature as a means of reinforcing the ways short stories use carefully chosen details to give a sense of characters' lives. In a novel, readers would probably learn all about Larry's life at school, his father's job as a detective, and his mother's concerns about his safety. Instead, in this short story, Asimov uses one incident to provide a window onto all of these issues.

Critical Viewing

Infer Students may note that the building has many windows through which criminals could enter. There are also places to hide, such as beneath the arch.

Step-by-Step Teaching Guide

Engage Students Through Literature

1. Read this short story aloud, or have students read it aloud.

2. Pause while reading to use the margin notes to help students interpret the story.

3. By the end of page 74, ask what students have already learned about Larry, the boy in the story. (He is a good student and waits for what he wants.)

4. At the middle of page 76, ask what new things students know about Larry. (He has a good imagination and knows how to reason and interpret.)

5. After reading the story, ask if anyone figured out the location of the diamond before Larry did.

continued

5.1 Model From Literature

Isaac Asimov (1920–1992) was celebrated for his science-fiction and detective stories, as well as for his popular accounts of science.

Reading\Writing Connection

Reading Strategy: Interpret

As you read, **interpret,** or restate the meaning of what you have read. Ask yourself: Why did this event happen? Why did the writer add that detail? For example, in "Sarah Tops," you might restate the significance of the narrator's decision not to linger at the museum as follows: The narrator is smart and responsible. You can also interpret the writer's decision to add this detail: He wants the reader to sympathize with the narrator.

▲ **Critical Viewing** Citing details from this photograph, explain whether a museum seems a likely place for a crime. **[Infer]**

Sarah Tops

Isaac Asimov

I came out of the Museum of Natural History and was crossing the street on my way to the subway, when I saw the crowd about halfway down the block; and the police cars, too. I could hear the whine of an approaching ambulance.

For a minute I hesitated, but then I walked on. The crowds of the curious just get in the way of officials trying to save lives. My Dad, who's a detective on the force, complains about that all the time, and I wasn't going to add to the difficulty myself.

I just kept my mind on the term paper I was going to have to write on air-pollution for my seventh-grade class and mentally arranged the notes I had taken on the Museum program on the subject.

Of course, I knew I would read about it in the afternoon papers. Besides, I would ask Dad about it after dinner. Sometimes he

The opening paragraph draws the reader in by presenting signs of excitement without any explanation.

By revealing the narrator's thoughts, the writer shows the narrator's character —he is responsible and intelligent.

talked about cases without giving too much of the real security details. And Mom and I never talk about what we hear, anyway.

After I asked, Mom looked kind of funny and said, "He was in the museum at the very time."

I said, "I was working on my term paper. I was there first thing in the morning."

Mom looked worried. "There might have been shooting in the museum."

"Well, there wasn't," said Dad soothingly. "This man tried to lose himself in the museum and he didn't succeed."

"I would have," I said. "I know the museum, every inch."

Dad doesn't like me boasting, so he frowned at me. "The thugs who were after him didn't let him get away entirely. They caught up with him outside, knifed him, and got away. We'll catch them, though. We know who they are."

He nodded his head. "They're what's left of the gang that broke into that jewelry store two weeks ago. We managed to get the jewels back, but we didn't grab all the men. And not all the jewels either. One diamond was left. A big one—worth thirty thousand dollars."

"Maybe that's what the killers were after," I said.

"Very likely. The dead man was probably trying to cross the other two and get off with that one stone for himself. They turned out his pockets, practically ripped off his clothes, after they knifed him."

"Did they get the diamond?" I asked.

"How can we tell? The woman who reported the killing came on him when he was just barely able to breathe. She said he said three words to her, very slowly. 'Try. . . Sarah . . . Tops.' Then he died."

"Who is Sarah Tops?" asked Mom.

Dad shrugged. "I don't know. I don't even know if that's really what he said. The woman was pretty hysterical. If she's right and that's what he said, then maybe the killers didn't get the diamond. Maybe the dead man left it with Sarah Tops, whoever she is. Maybe he knew he was dying and wanted to give it back and have it off his conscience."

"Is there a Sarah Tops in the phone book, Dad?" I asked.

Dad said, "Did you think we didn't look? No Sarah Tops, either one *P* or two *P*'s. Nothing in the city directory. Nothing in our files. Nothing in the FBI files."

Mom said, "Maybe it's not a person. Maybe it's a firm. Sarah Tops Cakes or something."

"Could be," said Dad. "There's no Sarah Tops firm, but there are other kinds of Tops and they'll be checked out for anyone working there named Sarah. It'll take days of dull routine."

These paragraphs are part of the exposition: They introduce us to the characters.

The author uses dialogue to give information and move the story along.

These paragraphs establish the conflict: The police need to locate the missing diamond, but the only clue they have is mysterious and confusing.

To read another short story involving a mystery, see "The Third Level" by Jack Finney. You can find this short story in *Prentice Hall Literature: Timeless Voices, Timeless Themes, Bronze.*

Model From Literature • 75

---

6. Discuss how Asimov used a small incident and a brief period of time as his plot and setting. He did not include extra information that would have cluttered the story.

7. Remind students that short stories require writers to give a lot of essential information in a small amount of text. Explain that as they write their own short stories, they will have to be aware of which details to include about characters and setting.

More About the Writer

Isaac Asimov (1920–1992) was born in Russia and moved to the United States when he was three. He began his first short story when he was only 11 years old. During his life, he wrote more than 400 books. His specialty was science fiction. His love of science and his imagination prompted him to write about the wonders of robots, computers, and space travel before they became everyday realities. He wrote his first science fiction story when he was 17 years old, which he submitted in person to a magazine called *Astounding Science Fiction.* The story was not accepted, but the editor of the magazine encouraged Asimov in his writing, and he went on to win a host of literary awards, including the National Science Fiction Writers Award.

Responding to Literature

"The Third Level" is a mystery story that involves traveling back in time. Students may want to compare the ways in which both short stories rely on a mystery to advance the plot.

STANDARDIZED TEST PREPARATION WORKSHOP

Grammar and Usage Standardized tests require students to identify correctly punctuated sentences. Ask students to choose the best way to punctuate the following sentence.

The girls prepared their science experiments carefully. Because they were hoping for a good grade.

A The girls prepared their science experiments carefully, because they were hoping for a good grade.

B The girls prepared their science experiments carefully; because they were hoping for a good grade.

C The girls prepared their science experiments carefully because, they were hoping for a good grade.

D Correct as is

The correct answer is item **A** because it connects two independent clauses with a comma and a conjunction.

Teaching From the Model

Use this section of the story to preview the concept of building suspense toward a climax, which is one of the skills students will be learning in this chapter. Ask how they feel about the mystery of "Sarah Tops." What do they think that name could mean? Point out that the writer has provided a mystery to keep the reader engaged. Explain that writers use many different techniques for building suspense. Have students think of some other ways a writer might build suspense in a short story.

Integrating Technology Skills

Even if students live in New York City, they may not be familiar with the setting of the story, the American Museum of Natural History. Suggest that they visit the museum's Web site (www.amnh.org) to learn about this exciting place. Discovering that it contains one of the world's best and biggest dinosaur exhibits may be the clue they need to figure out Asimov's surprise ending.

Customize for
Less Advanced Students

Review plot structure: problem, rising action, climax, falling action, solution. Use the margin notes to help students identify parts of this short story for each part of the plot. (Problem: a stolen diamond has disappeared, the only clue is confusing; rising action: Larry thinks about the problem and has some ideas; climax: Larry has an idea, which he keeps to himself; solution: Larry finds the diamond.)

Critical Viewing

Analyze Students should note that *top* is used as a surname and as a spinning toy.

I got an idea suddenly and bubbled over. "Listen, Dad, maybe it isn't a firm either. Maybe it's a *thing*. Maybe the woman didn't hear 'Sarah Tops' but 'Sarah's top'; you know, a *top* that you spin. If the dead guy has a daughter named Sarah, maybe he gouged a bit out of her top and stashed the diamond inside and . . ."

Dad pointed his finger at me and grinned. "Very good, Larry," he said. "A nice idea. But he doesn't have a daughter named Sarah. Or any relative by that name as far as we know. We've searched where he lived and there's nothing reported there that can be called a top."

"Well," I said, sort of let down and disappointed, "I suppose that's not such a good idea anyway, because why should he say we ought to try it? He either hid it in Sarah's top or he didn't. He would know which. Why should he say we should *try* it?"

And then it hit me. What if . . .

Dad was just getting up, as if he were going to turn on television, and I said, "Dad, can you get into the museum this time of evening?"

"On police business? Sure."

"Dad," I said, kind of breathless, "I think we better go look. *Now.* Before the people start coming in again."

"Why?"

"I've got a silly idea. I . . . I . . . "

Dad didn't push me. He likes me to have my own ideas. He thinks maybe I'll be a detective, too, some day. He said, "All right. Let's follow up your lead whatever it is."

He called the museum, then we took a taxi and got there just when the last purple bit of twilight was turning to black. We were let in by a guard.

I'd never been in the museum when it was dark. It looked like a huge, underground cave, with the guard's flashlight seeming to make things even darker and more mysterious.

We took the elevator up to the fourth floor where the big shapes loomed in the bit of light that shone this way and that as the guard moved his flash.

▶ **Critical Viewing** Name each meaning of the word *top* discussed in the story. Explain how the discussion of different possible meanings catches readers' interest and builds suspense. **[Analyze]**

76 • Short Story

As the narrator asks his father questions, the conflict is deepened. A few explanations of the clue have been checked, but no answer has turned up.

The narrator's clever explanation helps increase the tension. The reader wants him to solve the crime but is disappointed at this first attempt.

At the turning point, or climax, of the story, the reader's suspense is at its greatest. The narrator's unfinished sentence "What if . . ." begins the falling action.

Details such as the guard's use of a flashlight and the description of the fossils give the reader a vivid sense of the setting.

✓ ONGOING ASSESSMENT: Monitor and Reinforce

After previewing the Model From Literature, you may anticipate some students may have difficulty with some proper names and other words. Use one of the following options.

Option 1 If students read the model independently, have them list any unfamiliar words they encounter. Then go over pronunciations and definitions in class.	**Option 2** If you or a prepared student read the model aloud in class, take time to define unfamiliar words as they are encountered. Words such as *thugs, conscience, vertebrae,* and *triceratops* may need definition.

◀ **Critical Viewing**
How does Asimov
"spell out" the name
of one of the
dinosaurs in this pic-
ture without giving
away the ending?
[Summarize]

"Do you want me to put on the light in the room?" he asked.

"Yes, please," I said.

There they all were. Some in glass cases; but the big ones in the middle of the large room. Bones and teeth and spines of giants that ruled the earth hundreds of millions of years ago.

"I want to look close at that one," I said. "Is it all right if I climb over the railing?"

"Go ahead," said the guard. He helped me.

I leaned against the platform, looking at the grayish plaster material the skeleton was standing on.

"What's this?" I said. It didn't look much different in color from the plaster on which it was lying.

"Chewing gum," said the guard, frowning. "Those darn kids . . . "

"The guy was trying to get away and he saw his chance to throw this . . . keep it away from *them* . . . ." Before I could finish my sentence Dad took the gum from me. He squeezed it, then pulled it apart. Something inside caught the light and flashed. Dad put it in an envelope. "How did you know?" he asked me.

"Well, look at it," I said.

It was a magnificent skeleton. It had a large skull with bone stretching back over the neck vertebrae. It had two horns over the eyes, and a third one, just a bump, on the snout. The nameplate said *Triceratops*.

At the resolution of the story, the narrator finds the diamond.

The resolution is completed with the explanation of the dying man's last words.

Writing Application: Help Your Readers Interpret As you write your short story, emphasize details that will help readers interpret your characters' personalities and actions. You can emphasize a detail by discussing it at length, or by leaving out key information about it so that a reader's curiosity will be aroused.

Prewriting: Freewriting

1. Students are accustomed to writing things that will be evaluated and graded. Explain that freewriting is not good or bad, or right or wrong. It is a prewriting activity intended to let their words and ideas flow naturally onto the page. Emphasize that the point of freewriting is to come up with many ideas.

2. Before they begin and after they finish, tell students that they may not find a topic in their freewriting. Sometimes story ideas come from freewriting and sometimes they don't.

Prewriting: Magazine Flip-Through

1. Bring in as many different kinds of magazines as possible. Students should have a wide range of materials to scan for topic ideas.

2. Explain that short story topics can come out of anything that makes them think or have an emotional reaction, so they should mark any images, phrases, sentences, or pages that trigger a response of any kind.

Prewriting: Writing Round

Teaching Resources: Writing Support Transparency 5-A

1. Divide students into groups.

2. Students can say their sentences, with one group member acting as the recorder, or each student can write a sentence and pass the paper to the next person.

3. Display the transparency to show how a writing-round session helped Elizabeth.

Customize for
ESL Students

Being self-conscious and stopping to think or fret defeats the purpose of freewriting. Students can freewrite in a mixture of languages, then think about how to translate the useful ideas into English later.

78

5.2 Prewriting

Choosing Your Topic

Writers like Ray Bradbury may wait for a story idea to "bite them on the leg" (see page 73), but most of us need specific strategies for finding a topic, such as the following:

Strategies for Generating a Topic

1. **Freewriting** Set a timer for five minutes, and write down anything that comes to mind. Afterward, choose the most interesting idea for a story.

2. **Magazine Flip-Through** Grab a pile of magazines, and flip through them, looking for photographs, articles, or ads that spark your interest—or your scorn. Use sticky notes to mark your finds. Later, review the flagged pages, and take notes on the most promising ideas for your story.

3. **Writing Round** Form a circle with three or four classmates. One student begins by saying the first sentence of a story, and then each student adds another sentence, with one student writing it all down. Afterward, one student should read the story aloud. Use one of the details in the group story as a springboard for your own story.

Writing Lab CD-ROM

For more help finding a topic, use the activities and tips in the Choosing a Topic section of the Creative Writing lesson.

Name: Elisabeth Laskey
Gray-New Gloucester Middle School
Gray, ME

Writing Round

These are the notes from a writing-round session that helped Elisabeth come up with the topic for her story.

Sam: It was the first week of August.

Eleanor: My family was going on vacation.

Ahmed: I was looking forward to it, but I knew I was going to miss my friends.

Elisabeth: So I asked my parents if I could invite my best friend to come with us.

Talking about summer vacation made Elisabeth remember a weekend trip to her aunt's cottage with her friend Amanda, and she decided to write a story about something that had happened while they were there.

78 • Short Story

⏱ TIME AND RESOURCE MANAGER

Resources
Print: Writing Support Transparencies 5-A–D; Writing Support Activity Book, 5-1
Technology: Writing Lab CD-ROM, Narration

In-Depth Coverage	Accelerated Pace
• Cover pp. 78–81 in class.	• In class, discuss how to create and choose a good short story topic.
• Guide students through the Strategies for Generating a Topic.	• Have students list possible topics.
• Help students make some initial decisions about narrative elements by creating conflict diagrams.	• Ask students to submit topic proposals for your review.
• Have students use listing and itemizing to generate details before they begin drafting.	
Option Students having difficulties may adopt topics from the Topic Bank.	

TOPIC BANK

If you're having trouble finding a topic, consider the following possibilities:

1. **Your Own Life** A short story can be based on your own experiences. Choose an object in your room that brings back memories of an event or a person in your life. Write a story about this object and the experience it evokes. You might even tell the story from the object's point of view.

2. **Your Own Community** Write a fantasy story set in your community or school in the future. As you plan your story, think about what will be different in the future and what will stay the same.

Responding to Fine Art

3. Write a story based on this painting. Your story might be the tale you imagine the storyteller is telling. Alternatively, your story might use the setting and characters depicted in the painting.

Responding to Literature

4. Read the poem "Mother to Son" by Langston Hughes. Write a short story telling what happened either before or after this mother spoke these words to her son. You can find "Mother to Son," as well as background information on the poet, in *Prentice Hall Literature: Timeless Voices, Timeless Themes,* Bronze.

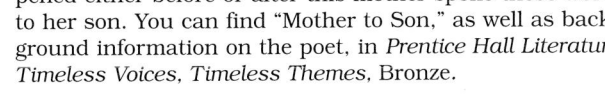

Storyteller, Velino Shije Herrera, National Museum of American Art, Washington, DC

☑ Cooperative Writing Opportunity

5. **Collaborative Story** After participating in a writing-round session (see page 78), have each member complete the story the group has begun. Have a group discussion about the differences among the stories. Determine which were the most successful elements in each story. Afterward, illustrate the stories, and bind them in a collection. Present the collection to the school library for display.

Prewriting • 79

Prewriting: Developing Narrative Elements

Teaching Resources: Writing Support Transparency 5-C; Writing Support Activity Book 5-1

1. Write the word *conflict* on the board and ask students what it means. As you discuss the definition, elicit that conflict exists when people have different and opposing goals, or when they are prevented from achieving their goals by particular obstacles. Emphasize that in literature, conflict is not (necessarily) a fight. The struggle can be with things (nature, a handicap) or ideas (should I or shouldn't I?), as well as people.

2. Display the transparency. Use "Sarah Tops" as a means of showing how conflict helps a story move forward. Point out that Larry's father the detective brought home an unsolved problem: He had not recovered an expensive diamond from one of his robbery cases. Reading about how the characters try to resolve this conflict is what makes the story interesting.

3. Distribute copies of the blank organizer. Have them fill in the main character's name, what that character wants, and then, in the middle of the chart, the obstacles that separate the character from what he or she wants.

4. Next, ask them to consider who they want their audience to be. If they are writing for other teens, they might include details that would be different than if they were writing for their parents.

Customize for
Bodily/Kinesthetic Learners

Have students work in pairs or groups of three to act out the conflicts they are imagining for their short stories as represented in their conflict diagrams. The groups can present their silent reenactments, and classmates can make guesses about the nature of the central conflict.

Developing Narrative Elements

The best stories just fly along. As you read a well-written story, you might forget you are turning pages—they may seem to turn themselves! The secret of all this movement is a kind of "story motor"—the conflict. By finding the conflict inside your story idea, you can get your story moving.

Identify Conflict

A **conflict** is a struggle between two opposing forces. A character's conflict may be *external*, as when a sheriff has a conflict with an outlaw, or *internal*, as when an outlaw struggles with his conscience.

Using a Conflict Diagram To identify the conflict in a story, ask yourself these questions:

1. What does the main character want?
2. Who or what is preventing that character from getting what he or she wants?

Use a conflict diagram to find answers to these questions. Here's one based on "Sarah Tops" by Isaac Asimov (see page 74):

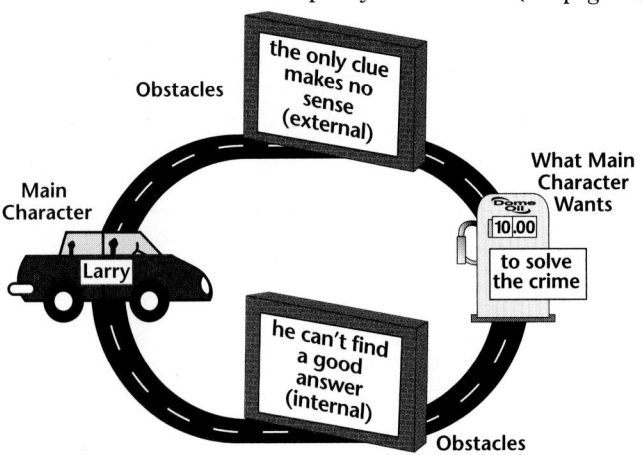

Considering Your Audience and Purpose

Your **audience**—who your readers are—should affect the details you include in your story. If your readers are other teenagers, they will probably understand a reference to a particular band. If you're writing for a wider audience, though, you will have to explain more about the band and its music.

Your **purpose** also affects the details you include. Consider whether you simply want to entertain or whether you also want to convey a theme—an insight or question about life.

Writing Lab CD-ROM

For more on developing narrative elements, as well as on considering your purpose, see the Developing Narrative Elements and the Considering Audience and Purpose sections in the Narration lesson.

☑ ONGOING ASSESSMENT: Monitor and Reinforce

Students often misinterpret the literary connotation of the word *conflict* to mean simply an argument or fight. To help them understand the word in the context of storytelling and plot, try one of the following strategies.

Option 1 Have students write a journal entry on the topic of something that they want but do not have yet in their lives. Tell them to include a description of the obstacles they face in achieving their goal. Point out that their desire for something and the obstacles in the way are an example of conflict.

Option 2 Make a class list of books that most students have read, fairy tales with which they are familiar, or even movies they have recently seen. Identify the central conflict of some of these stories. Help students see that in the context of storytelling and plots, conflicts include much more than just arguments and fights.

Gathering Details

Your next step is to begin gathering details to include in your story. Here is a strategy that will help you get started:

Use Listing and Itemizing

To use the strategy of listing and itemizing, follow these steps:

1. Quickly jot down a list of everything that comes to mind about a general idea.
2. Circle the most interesting item on the list.
3. "Itemize" that item—create another list of everything that comes to mind about it.
4. After you've generated several lists in this way, look for connections among all the circled items on your lists. These connections will help you decide which details to include in your story.

LISTING AND ITEMIZING

a man is caught in a flood
a man is caught in a fire
a man is stranded on an island
a man is locked out of his house
a man is caught in an avalanche

the man nearly drowns
the man's dog nearly drowns
the man's house is nearly ruined

he's an inventor
he has invented something valuable
he has to finish building it before someone else creates it
the flood has destroyed most of his work

▲ **Critical Viewing**
If this man was a character in a story, what kind of conflict—external or internal—do you imagine he would be experiencing? **[Analyze]**

Critical Viewing

Analyze Students may explain that the man in the photograph is experiencing the external conflict of protecting himself and his home from the flood. Some may note an internal conflict created by losing his home or possessions.

Step-by-Step Teaching Guide

Prewriting: Use Listing and Itemizing

Teaching Resources: Writing Support Transparency 5-D

1. Tell students that once they have a story idea, they can start thinking about what details they want to include in their story. Display the transparency to show students the process of listing and itemizing.

2. Refer to "Sarah Tops" to help students understand what you mean by details. Have them skim the story and list details on the chalkboard.

3. Circle one item on this list and use itemizing to provide more details about it. Point out that listing and itemizing allow a writer to look at the details that spring from different parts of a single existing detail.

4. Explain to students that they will now be trying to expand their own list of details for their own stories. Ask them to list all the different ideas they have connected to their own story, then circle one of the items on that list.

5. Ask them to make a list of all the details and ideas that come to mind in relation to the item they just circled.

6. Explain that exploring all the connections among possible details for their story may also give them ideas about what to write.

Customize for
Gifted/Talented Students

Write each of the following words on slips of paper: *iguana, cello, grapefruit, pogo stick, vulture, asparagus*. Fold the papers and have students take one. Challenge them to write as many details as they can think of about their word.

Drafting: Create a Plot

Teaching Resources: Writing Support Transparency 5-E; Writing Support Activity Book 5-2

1. Remind students that they have already begun to think about the main conflict of their story. They now need to explore how their plot, which develops the conflict, is going to move from the beginning of the story right through to the end.

2. Display the transparency and give students copies of the blank organizer.

3. Tell students to review what they chose as the main conflict of their own stories and then fill their plot diagram.

4. Tell students to start drafting their story using the plot diagram as a way of organizing the story's narrative. Remind them to use their lists of details as material for the descriptions they include in their writing.

Customize for
Visual/Spatial Learners

Provide art materials, including drawing paper, rulers, and markers or crayons. Let students illustrate their plot diagrams with pictures of the action, or images that represent the different elements of the plot. These can be hung around the room, museum style, so classmates can see the color and movement of other students' stories as they imagine them.

Drafting

Shaping Your Writing

Once you have come up with the main conflict in your story, you are ready to organize and draft.

Create a Plot

Begin by mapping out your plot. A **plot** is the arrangement of actions in the story, but it is more than a simple sequence. In most stories, the plot follows this pattern:

- The **exposition** introduces the main characters and their basic situation, including the central conflict.
- This **conflict** develops and intensifies during the rising action, which leads to
- the **climax** (the high point of suspense), followed by
- the story's **falling action,** which leads to
- the **resolution,** in which the conflict is resolved in some way (the good guy wins, a compromise is reached, and so on).

Using a Plot Diagram Map out the events in your story using a diagram like the one below. Refer to it as you draft.

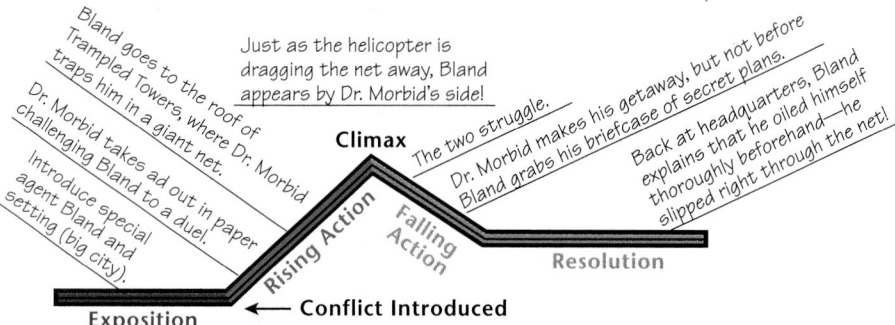

Focusing on Conflict and Resolution As you write, make sure that the events you include help develop the story's conflict and create suspense about how that conflict will be resolved.

To help you work toward a resolution, expand the Conflict Diagram you created in the Prewriting section. Add a resolution box at the top. Brainstorm for an ending in which the main character overcomes or is defeated by the obstacle he or she faces.

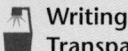 **Writing Support Transparencies**
Use the transparencies for Chapter 5 to teach these strategies.

 Writing Support Activity Book
Use the graphic organizers for Chapter 5 to facilitate these strategies.

Resources
Print: Writing Support Transparencies 5-E–F; Writing Support Activity Book 5-2
Technology: Writing Lab CD-ROM, Narration

In-Depth Coverage	Accelerated Pace
• Work through the plot diagram strategy (p. 82) with the entire class, using the transparency. • Have students write their own short story draft in class. • Help students use details of character and setting after reviewing the characterization model with them (p. 83). **Option** Have students work in groups or independently with the Writing Lab CD-ROM.	• Have students review pages 82–83 independently, then write their own first short story draft. • Respond to individual drafting issues as needed.

Providing Elaboration

Use Details to Define Character and Setting

As you draft your story, try to make your characters and setting come to life by including vivid details.

Telling and Showing You can present setting or character traits and reactions directly by **telling** what a place or a character is like— "The ocean was pretty" or "Amanda was afraid."

It is often better to reveal characters and setting indirectly by **showing** what they are like. Instead of *telling* us that your character is happy, you can *show* that happiness through her light, skipping footsteps or her chirpy voice.

As you draft, pause occasionally, and review what you have written. Add details that reveal the mood of a place, what your characters look like, how they talk and act, what they think and feel, and how others react to them.

▼ Critical Viewing
Judging from this illustration, how is the conflict in this tall tale resolved? **[Interpret]**

from *Swamp Angel* by Anne Isaacs, illustrated by Paul O. Zelinsky, illustrations copyright ©1994 by Paul O. Zelinsky

Student Work IN PROGRESS

Name: *Elisabeth Laskey*
Gray-New Gloucester Middle School
Gray, ME

Adding Characterizing Details
Elisabeth added characterizing details as she drafted.

"Of course! It'll be fun!" Amanda held the worn rope in her hands.

"Okay, I'll just watch," I said, peering down at the churning water far below.

Amanda's hands tightened on the rope as she prepared to swing off. ~~Suddenly she was afraid.~~ Now that we were on top, the bank seemed higher and steeper, and a quick gust of wind caused huge waves to crash toward us.

Looking below, she gulped and hesitated.

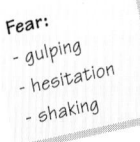

Fear:
- gulping
- hesitation
- shaking

Drafting • 83

Drafting: Use Details to Define Character and Setting

Teaching Resources: Writing Support Transparency 5-F

1. Remind students that they have begun to think about the details of their stories (they made lists of possible details and itemized them). Now they can focus their writing by collecting details related directly to character and setting from the first draft of their stories. Tell students that the process of adding more details to a draft of writing is called elaboration.

2. Display the transparency. Ask students how Elisabeth's additional details improve her characterization of Amanda.

3. Have students draw a circle with their main character's name in the center. Remind them that, as they think of details they might want to tell readers about their characters, they can add more circles and connect the ones that seem to go together.

4. Have students repeat this process, using the story's setting in the center circle and adding details as they did with the character's name.

5. Point out that writers can engage readers by including details and using action verbs. These make characters come alive.

Critical Viewing

Interpret Students may suggest that the conflict is resolved through fierce determination and confidence.

Real-World Connection

Bring in some catalogs and pass them around. Have students notice that the descriptions of items include details to make them sound more interesting and attractive. "Blue pajamas with dogs" is less tempting than "Cozy flannel pajamas with puppies frolicking on a blue background. Dog biscuit–shaped buttons complete the look. Woof!" Details are important in menus too. "Burger with topping" sounds less tasty than "Quarter pound prime ground beef with melted cheese, grilled onions."

✓ **ONGOING ASSESSMENT: Monitor and Reinforce**

If students have difficulty using details to define character and setting, try the following option.

Write these two sentences on the board:

Amanda tried to show that she wasn't afraid.

Amanda smiled as her hands tightened on the rope.

Ask which sentence gives a more vivid idea of Amanda's character. Elicit that in the first sentence, the writer gives it away by simply telling how Amanda feels. In the second sentence, however, we guess that she's afraid because the writer says how she looks and acts.

Revising: Build to a Climax

Teaching Resources: Writing Support Transparency 5-G; Writing Support Activity Book 5-3

1. Tell students that good writers make their readers want to keep reading. Keeping a reader's interest can be achieved by having a good conflict, which may involve a problem to be solved, characters who want different things, or an obstacle to be overcome. Remind students that the climax is the moment when the central conflict of a story takes its most dramatic turn and determines the outcome of the plot.

2. Display the transparency and give students copies of the blank organizer. Explain that building the conflict of a story toward a climax is an important part of keeping readers interested.

3. Provide students with two different colored highlighters. Have students review their own drafts while studying the plot diagrams they made for themselves. Tell them to find where they first start writing about the resolution of their story and have them mark it with an "R."

4. Students may need help understanding setup and payoff as applied to their own short stories. Remind them of the line "Try Sarah Tops" in the literature model and how it leads to the word *triceratops,* which can be considered the payoff to the setup of the story (the setup being, What does "Try Sarah Tops" mean?).

5. Tell them to highlight the setup and payoff in their own drafts. As they count the paragraphs between their setup and payoff, remind them that the purpose of building toward a climax is to keep their readers interested. Encourage them to give themselves some room to develop their plot as it moves from setup to payoff.

Revising Your Overall Structure

Build to a Climax

A good story builds to a single most exciting moment, called the **climax**. The secret of building to a climax is **pacing**—introducing important information or new twists at the right spots. To evaluate the pacing of your story, first consider this example:

SETTING THE RIGHT PACE

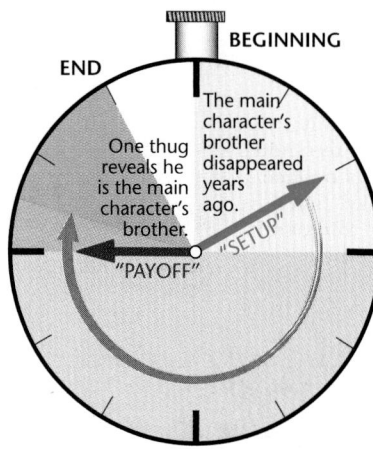

4. RESOLUTION: The two brothers defeat the thugs and return with the money and the thugs' treasure to their family.

3. CLIMAX: The family cannot pay the ransom. The young man worries that the thugs will soon find all the money. One of the thugs, though, is the hero's brother. He offers to help him.

END / **BEGINNING**

The main character's brother disappeared years ago.

One thug reveals he is the main character's brother.

"PAYOFF" / "SETUP"

1. EXPOSITION: The hero must take all of his family's money out of the bank so the family can escape from a dangerous city. We learn that the hero's brother disappeared years ago.

2. RISING ACTION: On his way back from the bank, the hero is captured by thugs. The thugs hold him for ransom. He tries various ways to escape.

The reader learns at the beginning that the brother is missing. The early placement of this fact makes the ending believable. Notice, too, that the thug reveals his identity right at the climax. This placement adds surprise to the climax.

Evaluate the pacing of your own story, using this strategy:

▶ **REVISION STRATEGY**
Using Clues to Evaluate Pacing

To "time" the pacing of your story, take the following steps:
1. Mark the resolution of your story with the letter *R*.
2. Highlight the "setup" for the resolution (facts that make the resolution possible or believable—see diagram above).
3. In a second color, highlight the "payoff" (the point connecting the setup and the resolution—see diagram above).
4. Count paragraphs between the setup and the resolution. If there are too few, the setup may not seem believable.
5. Measure the distance between the payoff and the resolution. If it is too great, the story may drag.
6. Move your setup and payoff to the most effective spots.

84 • Short Story

⏱ TIME AND RESOURCE MANAGER

Resources
Print: Writing Support Transparencies 5-G–H; Writing Support Activity Book 5-3
Technology: Writing Lab CD-ROM, Narration

In-Depth Coverage	Accelerated Pace
• Work through revision strategy with the entire class. • Use the relevant transparencies to demonstrate strategies for analyzing overall structure, time pacing (p. 84), improving characterization (p. 85), and word choice (p. 87).	• Assign students to review pp. 84–87 independently. • Have students revise their short stories independently.

Revising Your Paragraphs

Improve Characterization

Add details to bring characters to life. Use "Points to Illuminate" to find the best places to add information.

▶ **REVISION STRATEGY**
Using Points to Illuminate

Cut out a five-pointed star from construction paper. Label the points *appearance, actions, words, thoughts,* and *perceptions of others.*

Slide the star down your draft as you look for a place where your characters might "show themselves" more. Attach the star at such a place with a glue stick, and circle the point representing the kind of detail you will add. Repeat the process until you've read through your entire story. Then, go back and add the missing information.

Technology Tip

Your word-processing program may include a "track changes" function that highlights the inserts and cuts you've made. Use this function while revising, and you can decide later whether you want to "accept" or "reject" your first revisions.

Student Work IN PROGRESS

Name: *Elisabeth Laskey*
Gray-New Gloucester Middle School
Gray, ME

Using Points to Illuminate

Elisabeth used points to illuminate to improve her characterization of Amanda.

Suddenly two elderly couples appeared,

one man holding a camera.

"Do you girls mind if we take a picture of

you jumping from a rope?" asked the

gentleman with the camera.

∧Amanda gave me a quick glance. *she quavered.*
∧"Sure, why not?" ~~Amanda said.~~∧The pressure

was on.

She clutched the rope, and tension seemed

to swell over her body. Every eye focused on

She stood boldly, but *A sidelong glance told*
her.∧I saw the fear in her eyes.∧ *me that she would*
welcome a way out.

appearance
others ✩ actions
thoughts words

appearance
others ✩ actions
thoughts words

Revising • 85

Revising: Using Points to Illuminate

Teaching Resources: Writing Support Transparency 5-H

1. Display the transparency. Ask students to cut out a number of stars—five to begin with—just big enough to fit in the margins of their rough drafts. Have students label each point of the star using the five words they see in the example: *appearance, actions, words, thoughts, others.* (Since stars are small, you may want to suggest that students use the abbreviations *ap., ac., wo, th, o,* writing the full word with its abbreviation on the board.)

2. Explain that in the revision process, writers often add details or elaborate on existing ones to make their characterizations even stronger.

3. Because students already have a draft of their story and have included some details about their characters, they can reread what they've written and become more precise in their descriptions.

4. Ask them to reread their stories, looking for places where they could reveal more about their characters by adding details.

5. Provide them with glue sticks so that they can glue the stars next to the places in the text where they might want to add characterization details. When they've found a place where they might add detail, tell them to circle the point of the star that describes what kind of detail they are considering adding.

6. Now students can write new sentences or add words and phrases to add to the depth of characterization in their drafts.

Customize for
Interpersonal Learners

Students can trade papers with partners to discuss which of their characters seem like real people and which need more details to illuminate their personalities.

Revising: Combine Sentences for Variety

1. Read aloud each of the sample sentences. Ask students what they think is meant by "choppy." *(Their responses may include too short, repetitive, ends too quickly, and so on.)*

2. Have students use their "spy cameras" to find choppy sentences in their own drafts. Any sentences that fit into the window might be too short. Tell them to underline these short sentences as they move through the draft.

3. After they are finished, review the different ways they can combine sentences. Then have them read the sentences they underlined to see whether they need to be combined.

4. Stress that not all short sentences should be combined. Good writers use a mixture of different kinds and lengths of sentences to prevent their writing from becoming boring.

Critical Viewing

Analyze Students might combine sentences this way:

There is a man in a wheelchair. The man is holding a camera.

There is a man in a wheelchair who is holding a camera.

Accept all correct responses.

5.4

Revising Your Sentences
Combine Sentences for Variety

Writing too many short sentences in a row will produce a "choppy" effect. To avoid choppiness and create a smoother, more varied writing style, combine related sentences. Here are some simple techniques:

Add a coordinating conjunction (*and, but, for, nor, or,* or *yet*).

CHOPPY: I knew Cassie was my friend. I had no idea just how loyal she was.

COMBINED: I knew Cassie was my friend, **but** I had no idea just how loyal she was.

Use a subordinating conjunction, such as *when* or *because.*

CHOPPY: I heard the disappointment in Sam's voice. I knew he couldn't go to the movies.

COMBINED: **When** I heard the disappointment in Sam's voice, I knew he couldn't go to the movies.

Cross out repeated words and phrases.

CHOPPY: My mom said we could go to the park. ~~She said we could go to the park~~ in an hour.

COMBINED: My mom said we could go to the park in an hour.

Use a clause that begins with *who, which,* or *that.*

CHOPPY: We went to a beautiful beach. The beach has huge white dunes.

COMBINED: We went to a beautiful beach **that** has huge white dunes.

▶ **REVISION STRATEGY**
Using a "Spy Camera"

Cut a 1-inch by 2-inch window in an index card to create a "spy camera." Then, slide the camera around your draft, framing each paragraph in turn. Underline the sentences in each in alternating colors. Use the lengths of the lines to evaluate sentence length and revise as needed. Finally, think of a way to combine at least two of the sentences in each cluster.

🔵 **Learn More**

To learn more about subordinating conjunctions, see Chapter 20.

▼ **Critical Viewing**
In two short sentences, describe what's going on in this picture. Then, combine your sentences, using one of the techniques explained on this page. **[Analyze]**

☑ **ONGOING ASSESSMENT: Prerequisite Skills**

Students' writing may contain choppy sentences because they are not comfortable with compound sentences, clauses, and conjunctions. You may find it helpful to review the following to assure coverage of prerequisite knowledge.

In the Textbook	Print Resources	Technology
Effective Sentences, pp. 465–468	Grammar Exercise Workbook, pp. 93–94	Language Lab CD-ROM, Problems with Sentences; On-Line Exercise Bank, Section 21.3

Revising Your Word Choice

Use Vivid Verbs

You can keep your story exciting by using vivid verbs. Replace colorless verbs like *said*, *was*, and *went* with strong, colorful verbs like *quavered*, *radiated*, and *rocketed*.

▶ **REVISION STRATEGY**
Circling Verbs

Circle the first ten verbs in your story. Evaluate whether each verb vividly expresses your meaning. Replace any overused verbs with vivid ones.

Peer Review

Highlight Passages

Read your draft aloud twice to a group of classmates, pausing after the first reading. Before the second reading, ask the group to write down any passages that they like or that they want to know more about. Afterward, take their comments. Underline passages they like, and highlight those they want to know more about. Consider their feedback as you revise.

Language Lab CD-ROM

For more on using vivid verbs, see the Using Verbs lesson and the Vivid and Precise Verbs lesson.

Grammar in Your Writing
Identifying Action Verbs

A **verb** is a word that expresses an action or a state of being. Every sentence includes at least one verb that tells us something about the subject of the sentence. An **action verb** tells what action the subject is doing.

Physical/Visible Actions		Mental Actions	
run	walk	remember	believe
jump	slide	wish	wonder
breathe	float	think	hope
hide	bang	want	worry
tremble	hug	study	dream

Find It in Your Reading Find three action verbs in "Sarah Tops" by Isaac Asimov on page 74. For each action verb, name the subject that is performing the action.

Find It in Your Writing Underline five action verbs in your story. If you can't find five different action verbs, consider whether you've overused certain verbs, and find replacements if necessary.

To learn more about verbs, see Chapter 15.

Revising • 87

Revising: Use Vivid Verbs

1. Remind students that verbs describe actions or states of being. Tell them that if their verbs don't move, their stories don't move either. If they use the same verbs over and over, or if they use uninteresting verbs, it will make readers less excited about their stories.

2. Write the following sentences on the board:

   I said that I was late and ran toward my car.

   I shouted that I was late and sprinted toward my car.

3. Read the sentences aloud and ask the class which verbs are different in the second sentence. Ask them which sentence seems more exciting. Elicit that the verbs *shouted* and *sprinted* are more active and exciting then the verbs *said* and *ran*. Point out that by changing only a few verbs, they can add excitement to their stories.

Grammar in Your Writing: Identifying Action Verbs

1. Remind students that an action verb tells what action the subject of the sentence is doing.

2. Encourage students to add other verbs to the two categories.

Find It in Your Reading

Some possible choices are: *came, was crossing, saw, hear, hestitated, save, ask, talk,* etc. You may want to ask students how the action verbs they found move the story forward.

Find It in Your Writing

Have students work in small groups. Assign each group a less vivid verb, such as *walk, sit, say.* Ask each group to think of at least 10 action verbs to replace their assigned word. For example, *race, scramble; perch, slouch; squawk, announce.* Groups can write their lists with markers on large paper and post them around the room for the class to use as inspiration.

Grammar in Your Writing: Punctuating Dialogue

1. Tell students that no matter how good their stories are, if they are full of punctuation mistakes, readers will struggle to understand them. Punctuating dialogue correctly is especially important because it lets readers know who is saying what.

2. Review the rules of punctuating dialogue in the student book, and then write the following sentences on the board:

   I said good morning! I raced over here as quickly as I could. I was getting worried, he replied solemnly. I'm glad you're here."

3. Ask students what it was like reading those sentences. How did it affect their ability to understand what was written? Point out the significant difference between *"I said, 'good morning'!"* and *I said, "Good morning!"* Work with them to fix the sentences and rewrite them on the board.

   I said, "Good morning! I raced over here as quickly as I could."

   "I was getting worried," he replied solemnly. "I'm glad you're here."

4. Have students look carefully at the punctuation in their drafts, paying close attention to the guidelines provided.

5. Remind students to begin a new paragraph whenever the speaker changes.

Find It in Your Reading

Answers will vary. Make sure students can explain why the dialogue is punctuated the way it is.

Find It in Your Writing

You may want to have students complete this activity with a partner.

5.5 # Editing and Proofreading

Errors in spelling, punctuation, grammar, and usage are just as important to eliminate in a short story as they are in other forms of writing.

Focusing on Dialogue

As you proofread your story, pay close attention to the correct punctuation of **dialogue**—a character's speech.

Grammar in Your Writing
Punctuating Dialogue

When you write **dialogue,** you present words exactly as the character would say them. Here are some guidelines for punctuating dialogue:

Enclose dialogue in quotation marks.

"I'm taking an acting class on Thursdays," Yuki told me.

Don't use quotation marks when you report only the general meaning of a character's speech, not the exact words.

Yuki told me she was taking an acting class on Thursdays.

If dialogue comes *after* the words announcing speech, use a comma before the quote.

Max whispered, "I have no idea where the ruby ring could be."

If dialogue comes *before* the words announcing speech, use a comma, question mark, or exclamation point at the end of the quote—never a period.

"I have no idea where the ruby ring could be," whispered Max.

"I have no idea where the ruby ring could be!" screamed Max.

"Do you think Mr. Collins stole it?" asked Max.

Find It in Your Reading Find three examples of dialogue in "Sarah Tops" by Isaac Asimov on page 74. Explain why each is punctuated as it is.

Find It in Your Writing Highlight each instance of dialogue in your story, and circle the words announcing speech. Correct the punctuation if necessary.

To learn more about punctuating dialogue, see Chapter 26.

⏱ TIME AND RESOURCE MANAGER

Resources
Print: Scoring Rubrics on Transparency 5; Formal Assessment, Chapter 5
Technology: Writing Lab CD-ROM, Narration

In-Depth Coverage	Accelerated Pace
• Cover pp. 88–92 in class, including Grammar in Your Writing. • Distribute and review Proofreading Checklist. • Give step-by-step coverage to Publishing and Presenting (p. 89). • Analyze in class the final draft on p. 90. • Have students edit and proofread their short stories in class.	• Assign pages 88–92 for independent review. • Have students independently edit and proofread their short stories. • Respond to individual editing issues as needed.

5.6 *Publishing* and *Presenting*

Building Your Portfolio

Here are some ideas for presenting your short story:

1. **Submit Your Story** Submit your story to a school literary magazine, a national publication, an on-line journal, or a contest. (See page 8 for suggestions, or ask your teacher or librarian.)
2. **Give a Reading** Read your story aloud to your class or to a group of friends. Prepare posters announcing your reading, and distribute signed copies of your story at the event.

Reflecting on Your Writing

Jot down your thoughts on the experience of writing a short story. Begin by answering these questions:

- Based on your own writing experience, what advice would you give another student who is about to write a story?
- Has writing your own short story changed your experience reading short stories written by others? Explain.

🖳 Internet Tip

To read a short story scored according to this rubric, visit **www.phschool.com**

Rubric for Self-Assessment

Use the following criteria to evaluate your short story.

	Score 4	Score 3	Score 2	Score 1
Audience and Purpose	Contains an engaging introduction; successfully entertains or presents a theme	Contains a somewhat engaging introduction; entertains or presents a theme	Contains an introduction; attempts to entertain or to present a theme	Begins abruptly or confusingly; leaves purpose unclear
Organization	Creates an interesting, clear narrative; told from a consistent point of view	Presents a clear sequence of events; told from a specific point of view	Presents a mostly clear sequence of events; contains inconsistent points of view	Presents events without logical order; lacks a consistent point of view
Elaboration	Provides insight into character; develops plot; contains dialogue	Contains details and dialogue that develop character and plot	Contains details that develop plot; contains some dialogue	Contains few or no details to develop characters or plot
Use of Language	Uses word choice and tone to reveal story's theme; contains no errors in grammar, punctuation, or spelling	Uses interesting and fresh word choices; contains few errors in grammar, punctuation, and spelling	Uses some clichés and trite expressions; contains some errors in grammar, punctuation, and spelling	Uses uninspired word choices; has many errors in grammar, punctuation, and spelling

Publishing and Presenting • 89

✓ ONGOING ASSESSMENT: Assess Mastery

Use one of the following options to assess final drafts of students' short stories.

Self Assessment Ask students to score their story using the rubric provided. Then have students write a single paragraph reflecting on the most valuable thing they learned in completing this story.

Teacher Assessment You may wish to use the rubric and the scoring models provided in Writing Assessment, Narration, to score students' work.

Publishing and Presenting

1. If students want to submit their stories to an outside publication, have them find out the rules, such as maximum length, if they have to send a letter first (called a *query* by publishers), and so on. This information should be included in each issue of the magazine.
2. If students want to give a reading, ask them whom they decided their audience would be.
3. Students can illustrate their stories, design a cover, and create their own minibooks.
4. If several students wrote on the same general topic or genre—animals, sports, mystery—they could combine them as a book.

ASSESS

Assessment

Teaching Resources: Scoring Rubrics on Transparency 5; Formal Assessment, Chapter 5

1. Display the Scoring Rubric transparency and review the criteria in class.
2. Before students proceed with self-assessment, you may wish to review the Final Draft of the Student Work in Progress on pages 90–92. Have students score the Final Draft in one or more of the rubric categories. For example, how would students score the story in terms of audience and purpose?
3. In addition to student self-assessment, you may wish to use the following assessment options:
   - Score student stories yourself, using the rubric and scoring models from Writing Assessment.
   - Review the Standardized Test Preparation Workshop on pages 96–97 and have students respond to a writing prompt within a time limit.
   - Administer the Chapter 5 Test from Formal Assessment in Teaching Resources to assess students' grasp of concepts presented.

Teaching From the Final Draft

1. Help students see that "Showing Amanda the Ropes" incorporates key elements of narration and the short story:

   • Conflict in the form of a personal obstacle has been given to one of the main characters. Amanda wants to have fun and show off for the tourists, but she is frightened of using the rope to jump into the water.

   • The pace of the story moves quickly from the setup— Amanda spots the rope—to the introduction of the conflict, to the climax in which she overcomes her fears and jumps in, and then finally to the resolution in which the narrator acknowledges her friend's courage.

   • The story is filled with details of both character and setting. Readers know that Amanda is quiet and shy, as well as that she's never been on a Maine ocean island. Readers also know that the sun is beating down with "fiery fists," and that there are trees and steep banks by the ocean.

2. Ask students if the story was too short or too long or just about the right length. Have them explain their answers by referring back to the idea of pacing in a short story.

3. Ask students if there are details they would like to know more about or details that they feel the writer could have left out. What other changes would they like to see in this short story? Ask them how they might apply these changes to their own writing.

Critical Viewing

Relate Students' responses will vary. Make sure student support their answers.

FINAL DRAFT

◄ **Critical Viewing**
Does this look like a setting where you'd like to spend time? Why or why not? **[Relate]**

View of Bear Island Harbor, c. 1950, Fairfield Porter, Courtesy Martha Parrish & James Reinish, Inc., New York

Showing Amanda the Ropes

Elisabeth Laskey
Gray-New Gloucester Middle School
Gray, Maine

Hopping off the boat, I skipped up the wharf ahead of my best friend, Amanda, eager to give her the experience of a lifetime. We were here on Bustin's Island to spend the weekend at my aunt's cottage. This was Amanda's first time on a Maine ocean island, but it wasn't mine. I had been here many times before, and I was prepared to show her the ropes.

Elisabeth's first paragraph grabs the reader's interest. It is also part of her exposition. She tells us who the two main characters are and establishes the story's setting.

90 • Short Story

Amanda had always been the quiet, shy type, but on that weekend I saw a different side of her. Who would have ever thought that Amanda would be teaching me the ropes?

It was late afternoon on our second day there, and the sun was beating down with fiery fists. Amanda and I were sitting on the dock, just listening to the calm lapping of waves against the shore. Suddenly, peals of laughter and loud splashing broke the serenity.

On the next beach, three teenage boys were taking turns swinging from a steep bank by a rope tied to an overhanging tree. At the farthest point from the shore, they would drop to the ocean at least ten feet below.

"Hey, that looks like fun!" Amanda exclaimed. She watched excitely as a tall, lanky boy swayed in the breeze and hurtled toward the water with his arms and legs flailing wildly. I had to admit that it did look like a lot of fun. I knew it was safe, because my aunt had told my cousin he could jump there.

"Maybe they'll let us take a turn," Amanda said hopefully. She seemed fascinated by the whole idea. I didn't believe those boys would actually let us use their rope, but we could ask, anyway.

With swimsuits on, we made our way over to the next beach, but by the time we got there, the guys had left.

"Good! Now we have it all to ourselves," she said cheerfully. With that, she began climbing, and I followed her to the top of the bank.

"Are you sure you really want to do this?" I asked.

"Of course! It'll be fun!" Amanda held the worn rope in her hands.

"Okay, I'll just watch," I said, peering down at the churning water far below.

Amanda's hands tightened on the rope as she prepared to swing off. Looking below, she gulped and hesitated. Now that we were on top, the bank seemed higher and steeper, and a quick gust of wind caused huge waves to crash toward us.

Suddenly two elderly couples appeared, one man holding a camera.

"Do you girls mind if we take a picture of you jumping from the rope?" asked the gentleman with the camera.

Amanda gave me a quick glance. "Sure, why not?" she quavered. The pressure was on.

She clutched the rope, and tension seemed to swell over her body. Every eye focused on her. She stood boldly, but I saw the fear in her eyes. A sidelong glance told me that she would welcome a way out.

Here, the narrator's question helps "set up" the story's climax.

The vivid verb beating—and the image of the sun as an angry person—help the reader picture the scene.

These details of setting help create the story's conflict.

Elisabeth uses dialogue to show character and move the action along.

Here's the story's conflict: Amanda wants to jump but must first overcome her fear. Her conflict is internal. We also learn about her character: She appears easygoing but takes on more than she can handle.

The writer presents several details— including Amanda's appearance, speech, and the narrator's perceptions—that reveal her fear and her desire to seem bold.

Student Work in Progress • 91

Integrating Speaking, Listening, and Viewing Skills

Because "Showing Amanda the Ropes" includes an abundance of dialogue and action, it lends itself to an active reader's theater performance. Students can take these parts: narrator, Amanda, three teenage boys, man with camera, group of tourists. Encourage students to have fun acting out swinging from a rope, landing in the water, gliding off the rock, and so on.

She froze. The awkward moments of silence made everyone uneasy. Finally the tourists grew impatient and began to walk away.

"Wait!" Amanda called to them.

In a sudden spring of action, she gripped the rope and glided off the rock. Sailing through the air, she held her head high. At just the right moment she let go of the rope and fell into the water with a mighty splash. When her head reappeared, I saw a smile of triumph spread across her face.

She did it! I couldn't help but smile. My timid friend had conquered her fear and taken the risk. Amanda had more courage than I had ever imagined, and I admired her.

Amanda's "frozen moment" heightens tension, building toward a climax.

Here, at the climax of the story, the reader's curiosity about what will happen next is highest. The resolution follows in the very next paragraph—Amanda jumps!

Connected Assignment *Dramatic Scene*

Like a short story, a drama presents a narrative. A dramatic script is a guide for actors to act out a story. Elements of drama include

• dialogue—or speech—for one or more characters.

• directions, when needed, for how the characters speak, where they are on stage, and what actions they perform.

Prewriting Imagine two characters who are in conflict. Write down important details about each character, and write a brief description of their conflict.

MODEL

from **The Monsters Are Due on Maple Street**
Rod Serling

In this passage, notice how stage directions and the iden-
tity of each speaker are set off from the spoken dialogue:

[*The people stare at* STEVE. *He stands for a moment by the car, then walks toward the group.*]

STEVE. I don't understand it. It was working fine before . . .

DON. Out of gas?

STEVE. [*Shakes his head*] I just had it filled up.

Drafting Note where your characters are and what activity they are engaged in. As you draft, "overhear" their conversation in your mind and write out what each says. Then, go back and add directions specifying how lines should be spoken; what the scenery is like; what actions characters perform, and so on.

Revising and Editing Read the draft of your scene aloud. Revise lines that do not sound as though your characters would say them, or that do not express the characters' situations and attitudes forcefully enough.

Publishing and Presenting With a classmate, act out your dialogue for the class.

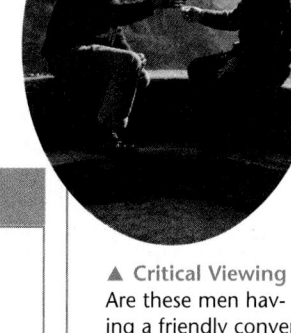

▲ **Critical Viewing**
Are these men having a friendly conversation, or are they in conflict? Point out details justifying your answer. [**Evaluate**]

▶ *Lesson Objectives*

1. To write a dramatic scene, using dialogue and stage directions, appropriate to audience and purpose.

2. To use prewriting strategies to generate ideas and plans for writing.

3. To develop drafts by adding, elaborating, deleting, combining, and rearranging text.

4. To revise and edit drafts for coherence and to ensure standard usage.

Step-by-Step Teaching Guide

Dramatic Scene

1. In order to help students familiarize themselves with dramatic scenes, bring in a few examples for students to read aloud, or encourage students to bring in their own examples.

2. Remind students that as they work on developing their drafts they should try to add as many stage directions as possible.

3. When students have revised their drafts, have them work with other students to stage their dramatic scene. Listening to other people read the dialogue may help the students further refine the scene.

4. Encourage interested students to work on further developing their dramatic scenes. As they continue working on them, they can present them to the class.

Critical Viewing

Evaluate Answers will vary. Be sure students give reasons, based on the picture, for their answers.

Lesson Objectives

1. To write a short tale based on *The Thousand and One Nights*.
2. To evaluate the purposes and effects of various media.
3. To use media to compare ideas.

Critical Viewing

Interpret Students might say that the painting creates an exotic, graceful, or mysterious mood.

Step-by-Step Teaching Guide

Analyzing Themes Across Cultures

1. Choose one of the Spotlight elements for class discussion, or have students work individually or in groups on the element of their choice. Give students the initiative to find the necessary book, tapes, or recordings.

2. Interested students may want to read some of the tales from *The Thousand and One Nights*.

3. Students may be able to find video recordings of the ballet. Encourage them to research the history of the ballet as well.

4. In addition to listening to Rimsky-Korsakov's suite, have students research the background to this piece of music. Encourage students to compare the pieces of the suite to the corresponding stories in *The Thousand and One Nights*.

Viewing and Representing

Activity Have students focus on the mood and atmosphere created by the music. Encourage them to imagine possible actions that could take place to the music. Students can then use this information in their own tales. Invite volunteers to read their tales to the class.

Spotlight on the Humanities

Analyzing Themes Across Cultures

Focus on Oral Tradition: Scheherazade

You may have enjoyed writing one short story, but imagine having to tell a new one every night for a thousand and one nights! According to legend, Scheherazade does exactly that.

The sultan Shahriyar plans to execute Scheherazade. Scheherazade, though, tells the sultan a cliff-hanging story every night. Eager to hear the ending of the story, he puts off the execution by a day in exchange for Scheherazade's promise to continue the tale on the following night. In this way, Scheherazade saves her life (and shows the power of a good story). The tales she tells, as well as the story of her telling them, are known as *The Thousand and One Nights* or *The Arabian Nights' Entertainment.*

Scheherazade's colorful stories existed in the Middle East as early as the ninth century. Originally, they were passed from one teller to another. Eventually, they were copied down. Their origins vary: Indian, Persian, Egyptian, Arabian, and Turkish influences weave through the work. These tales have given the world such familiar characters as Sinbad the Sailor, Ali Baba and the forty thieves, and Aladdin and his magic lamp.

Ballet Russian choreographer Michel Fokine created the ballet *Scheherazade* in 1910 for the famous producer of dance, Sergey Diaghilev.

Music Composer Nikolay Rimsky-Korsakov of Russia created his symphonic suite *Scheherazade* in 1888. It is considered one of the most popular orchestral works ever written. Rimsky-Korsakov uses **leitmotif**—the repetition of melodic elements—to create his musical pictures.

Narrative Writing Activity: Tale for a Character

Listen to an excerpt from Rimsky-Korsakov's *Scheherazade*, taking notes on images it conjures up in your mind. Using these notes, write a tale involving a character from the tales.

▲ **Critical Viewing**
What mood does this painting of the ballet *Scheherazade* create? [Interpret]

▼ **Critical Viewing**
What themes in *The Arabian Nights' Entertainment* might have interested composer Rimsky-Korsakov? [Speculate]

Critical Viewing

Speculate Students might say that the themes of adventure and intrigue may have interested Rimsky-Korsakov.

Media and Technology Skills

▶ **Lesson Objectives**

1. To write an analysis of a cartoon.
2. To interpret and evaluate the various ways cartoons represent meanings.
3. To evaluate the effects of various media.

Analyzing Visual Meanings

Activity: Follow Events in Animated Cartoons

A cartoon may be goofy, but it includes the same elements as a short story—character, setting, theme, and plot. To appreciate cartoons, learn about the storytelling techniques they use.

Think About It Cartoonists use many special storytelling devices to "jump" between events, including the following:

- **Cutting Between Viewpoints** A cartoon can create interest by making a sudden shift from one point of view to another. For example, a superhero rushes to save a child. Suddenly, the screen flashes to a villain leaving a bank with a large bag in his hand. The viewer realizes that while the hero was saving the child, she did not see the villain rob the bank.

- **Cliffhanger** Just at the moment when it appears that the hero is about to meet his doom, the screen flashes to show the search party looking for him. The viewer doesn't find out until later what happened to the hero. This device creates suspense.

- **Flashback** While a character in the present tells a story or reminisces about the past, the cartoon may "flashback" to the past, showing you past events as if they were occurring in the present.

- **Farcical Rhythm** Some cartoons jump from one scene to another in which a character tries to outwit a goofy hero and is instead outwitted. A cartoonist will generally "one-up" each scene with the next. That is, if the first scene involves a small explosion, the next will involve a larger explosion. The second scene might move at a faster pace than the first. In the zaniest cartoons, the final scenes take place at lightning speed, with characters trading places or moving from victory to defeat in dizzying alternation.

Your Turn As you watch a cartoon, complete a chart like the one shown. Then, using the chart, write an analysis explaining the storytelling devices the cartoon used. Evaluate the effectiveness of each.

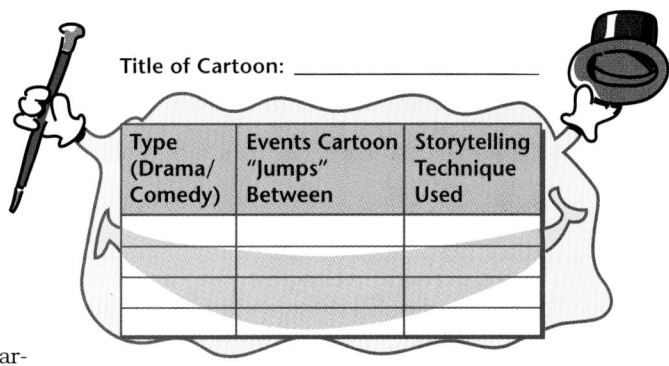

Title of Cartoon: _____

Type (Drama/ Comedy)	Events Cartoon "Jumps" Between	Storytelling Technique Used

---

Tips for Analyzing Events in a Cartoon

- Identify the relationship between characters. Which one is the hero and which is the villain? Which one is the frustrated hunter and which is the fool he or she never catches?

- In zany repetitive cartoons, pay attention to the differences between scenes. Does the frustration of one character build? Does the "cleverness" of his or her attacks increase? Does the pacing grow more frenzied?

Step-by-Step Teaching Guide

Analyzing Visual Meanings

Teaching Resources: Writing Support Transparency 5-I; Writing Support Activity Book 5-4

1. Review with students the types of techniques that cartoons use to tell stories.

2. If possible, bring in examples that students can analyze and evaluate as a class, or have students bring in examples of their favorite cartoons.

3. Display the transparency and give students copies of the blank organizer. You may want to complete a chart as a class using one of the examples you or your students provided.

4. Encourage students to research the subject of the animated cartoon at the library to learn more.

Media and Technology Skills • 95

Lesson Objectives

1. To respond to texts by making observations, interpreting, connecting, and comparing ideas and themes.

2. To write to express, using voice and style appropriate to audience and purpose.

Responding to Prompts About Short Stories

Teaching Resources: Standardized Test Preparation Workbook, pp. 9–10

1. Have volunteers read the sample prompts.

2. Explain to students that they will be writing a short response to the short story "Sarah Tops." There is no right or wrong response. However, students need to make sure that they support their responses with details from the story.

3. Guide students through the information on page 97, pointing out the amount of time they should spend on each stage of the writing process.

4. Assign a writing prompt for completion during class time.

Standardized Test Preparation Workshop

Responding to Prompts About Short Stories

Learning how the elements of a short story work together will help you write about short stories. Some standardized tests require you to write a short response to a story you have read. Before responding to a test prompt on a short story, think about the following elements of the story:

- **Plot** is the sequence of events in the story, arranged to catch your interest and maintain suspense.

- **Characters** are the people, animals, or other beings that take part in the story's action.

- **Setting** is the time and place in which the events occur.

- **Theme** is the message about life that the story conveys.

As you read the story, think about how each element helps create an effective short story. As you write, concentrate on creating a unified response in which you use details from the story to respond to the prompt.

Choose one of the following sample prompts for the short story "Sarah Tops" on page 74, and write a short response. Use the suggestions on the following page to help you respond. (The clocks show the suggested percentage of your test-taking time to devote to each stage.)

Test Tip

Look over the test questions before you read a passage. That way, you will know to which details you should pay special attention as you read.

Sample Writing Situation

> In "Sarah Tops," the main interest of the plot is whether the narrator succeeds in solving the case. His first few guesses are wrong or have already been thought of by others. When he has his final insight, he does not tell anyone what it is right away. Explain how, by presenting the narrator's insight in this way, the author creates suspense.

> The reader sides with the narrator of "Sarah Tops," hoping that he will solve the case. Explain what facts about the narrator make him an appealing character. Pay special attention to his relationship with his father. Explain how, if his attitude toward his father or his father's treatment of him were different, the reader might think he was just a "know-it-all."

96 • Short Story

✍ TEST-TAKING TIP

In addition to reading the prompt carefully, tell students they should also jot down notes that list the important details they are being asked to address. Encourage students to mark up the question, underlining, circling, or highlighting any important information that will help them respond to the story appropriately.

For example, in the first prompt, the important detail that students must address is how the author creates suspense through the narrator's insight. Students' responses should not stray from that topic.

Customizing for
More Advanced Students

Have students write a brief essay in which they evaluate how writing a short story helps them better analyze and evaluate short stories that they read.

Prewriting

Allow nearly one fourth of your time for prewriting.

Map Out Story Details Identify the element of the story on which the prompt focuses. Then, use a graphic organizer to gather details about this element. For instance, if the prompt asks about plot, use a plot diagram. (To see an example of a plot diagram, refer to page 82.) If the prompt asks about a character, you might use a cluster diagram.

Select Important Details Review your notes and reread the prompt. Then, circle details in your notes that will help you to respond. For instance, if you chose the prompt about the narrator's character, you might circle your note about his concern to stay out of the way of the police: It shows that he has self-control.

Drafting

Allow almost half of your time for drafting.

Outline Your Response Review your notes, and jot down a brief outline organizing your main points in logical order. If you are discussing plot, chronological order (the order in which events occur) might be the best choice. If you are discussing character, order of importance (from least to most important characteristics) might be an effective choice.

Elaborate After organizing details, begin drafting. Make sure that you state each of your main points clearly. For each main point, offer as many supporting illustrations or examples from the story as you can. At the same time, make sure you clearly show the connection of each detail to the prompt.

Revising, Editing, and Proofreading

Allow almost one fourth of your time to revise and edit. Use the last few minutes to proofread your work.

Strengthen Your Introduction and Conclusion Reread your introduction and conclusion. Make sure each includes a clear statement of the topic of your paper. This statement should reflect the prompt to which you are responding.

Strengthen Support Review each paragraph in your draft. Add any support you need to provide for each main point. Consider deleting paragraphs for which you cannot find supporting details.

Make Corrections Check for errors in spelling, grammar, and punctuation. When making changes, place one line through text you are deleting. Use a caret (^) to indicate where you are adding words.

Standardized Test Preparation Workshop • 97

In-Depth Lesson Plan

	LESSON FOCUS	PRINT AND MEDIA RESOURCES
DAY 1	**Introduction to Description** Students learn key elements of a description essay and analyze the Model From Literature (pp. 98–101).	*Writers at Work* **Videotape**, Description *Writing Lab* **CD-ROM**, Description
DAY 2	**Prewriting** Students use freewriting to choose a topic, consider their audience and purpose, and gather details (pp. 102–105).	**Teaching Resources** *Writing Support Transparencies 6-A-C; Writing Support Activity Book, 6-1–2* *Writing Lab* **CD-ROM**, Description
DAY 3	**Drafting** Students choose a method of organization and write their first drafts (pp. 106–107).	**Teaching Resources** *Writing Support Transparencies, 6-D;* *Writing Lab* **CD-ROM**, Description
DAY 4	**Revising** Students revise their essay by rearranging and grouping details, sentences, or entire paragraphs (pp. 108–113).	**Teaching Resources** *Writing Support Transparencies, 6-E–H;* *Writing Lab* **CD-ROM**, Description
DAY 5	**Editing and Proofreading; Publishing and Presenting** Students proofread their work with a focus on commas, and present their final drafts (pp. 114–115).	**Teaching Resources** *Scoring Rubrics on Transparency,* Ch. 6; *Formal Assessment,* Ch. 6 *Writing Lab* **CD-ROM**, Description

Accelerated Lesson Plan

	LESSON FOCUS	PRINT AND MEDIA RESOURCES
DAY 1	**Introduction Through Drafting** Students review characteristics of descriptive writing, select topics, and write drafts (pp. 98–107).	**Teaching Resources** *Writing Support Transparencies, 6-A–D; Writing Support Activity Book, 6-1–2* *Writers at Work* **Videotape**, Description *Writing Lab* **CD-ROM**, Description
DAY 2	**Revising Through Presenting** Students work individually or with peers to revise, edit, and proofread their work for presentation (pp. 108–115).	**Teaching Resources** *Writing Support Transparencies, 6-E–H; Scoring Rubrics on Transparency,* Ch. 6; *Formal Assessment,* Ch. 6 *Writing Lab* **CD-ROM**, Description

Options for Adapting Lesson Plans

HOMEWORK

Have students complete any stage of the lesson for homework.

FEATURES

Extend coverage with Connected Assignment (p. 118), Spotlight on the Humanities (p. 120), Media and Technology Skills (p. 121), and the Standardized Test Preparation Workshop (p. 122).

TECHNOLOGY

Students can complete any stage of the lesson on computer. Have them print out their completed work.

INTEGRATED SKILLS COVERAGE

Integrating Grammar
Adjectives, SE pp. 113, 114
Using Commas With Two or More Adjectives, SE p. 114

Reading/Writing Connection
Reading Strategy, SE p. 100
Writing Application, SE p. 101

Viewing and Representing
Critical Viewing, SE pp. 98, 100, 101, 104, 106, 112, 116, 117, 118, 120
Comparing Interpretations of Nature, SE p. 120, ATE p. 120

Speaking and Listening
ATE p. 114

Real-World Connection ATE p. 110

Vocabulary Skills ATE p. 112

Technology SE pp. 108, 112, 115

ASSESSMENT SUPPORT

Standardized Test Preparation, SE p. 122, ATE pp. 105, 112
Standardized Test Preparation Workbook, pp. 11–12
Scoring Rubrics on Transparency, Ch. 6
Formal Assessment, Ch. 6
Writing Assessment and Portfolio Management

MEETING INDIVIDUAL NEEDS

Less Advanced Students ATE pp. 103, 108   See also Ongoing Assessments ATE pp. 103, 104, 107, 109, 111, 113
Visual/Spatial Learners ATE, p. 101
ESL Students ATE p. 101
More Advanced Students ATE p. 117

BLOCK SCHEDULING

Pacing Suggestions
For 90-minute Blocks
• Have students complete the Prewriting and Drafting stages in a single period.
• Focus one class period on Revising and Editing and Publishing and Presenting. Allow at least 30 minutes for peer revision.

Resources for Varying Instruction
• *Writing Lab* CD-Rom If your students have access to hardware, a 90-minute block provides an ideal opportunity for them to work on computer.
• *Writers at Work* Videotape Show the Description Section in class.

Professional Development Support
• *How to Manage Instruction in the Block* This Teaching Resource provides management and activity suggestions.

MEDIA AND TECHNOLOGY

For the Student
• *Writing Lab* CD-ROM, Description

For the Teacher
• *Writers at Work* Videotape, Description
• *Resource Pro* CD-Rom

WRITING AND GRAMMAR WEB SITE

The Interactive Writing and Grammar Web site provides a wide array of support for students, teachers, and parents. Writing support includes:

• Interactive revision checkers
• Scoring rubrics with complete models

www.phschool.com

LITERATURE CONNECTIONS

Related selections from *Prentice Hall Literature: Timeless Voices, Timeless Themes,* Bronze:

"Fog," Carl Sandburg, SE p. 100
"Four Skinny Trees," Sandra Cisneros, SE p. 100
"All Summer in a Day," Ray Bradbury, SE p. 103

▶ *Lesson Objectives*

1. To write a descriptive essay appropriate to audience and purpose
2. To read to appreciate the writer's craft and to analyze models for writing
3. To use prewriting strategies to generate ideas and plan
4. To develop drafts by categorizing ideas and organizing them into paragraphs
5. To use adjectives appropriately to make writing vivid or precise
6. To revise drafts by elaborating, deleting, and rearranging text
7. To edit and proofread to ensure standard English usage and grammar
8. To evaluate how well one's writing achieves its purposes
9. To refine selected work for publication

Critical Viewing

Connect Students may say that the scene is majestic, awe-inspiring, or beautiful.

Chapter 6 Description

▲ **Critical Viewing**
What words would you use to describe the scene that the artist is painting? **[Connect]**

Description in Everyday Life

When you talk with your friends and family, you naturally describe things—a spectacular play on the soccer field, the sound of a musical group, the taste of a food you like or dislike, or the way the weather makes you feel.

As you talk, your words, gestures, and tone of voice blend together to create an impression of what you have seen, heard, tasted, touched, or smelled. When you write a description, however, you must rely on words alone. Just as an artist uses paint to create a picture, a writer uses words to create a description. By choosing your words well, you can help a reader to experience in his or her imagination what you have experienced in your own life.

⏱ TIME AND RESOURCE MANAGER

Resources
Technology: Writers at Work videotape, Description

In-Depth Coverage	Accelerated Pace
• Cover pp. 98–101 in class.	• Discuss definitions and types of descriptive writing in class.
• Show Description section of the Writers at Work videotape.	• Assign Model From Literature for independent reading.
• Read literature excerpt in class and use it to brainstorm with students for descriptive topics.	• Have students read pp. 98–101 on their own.
• Discuss examples of descriptive writing you or students bring to class.	

What Is Descriptive Writing?

Descriptive writing creates a picture of a person, place, thing, or event. Like a painting, descriptive writing opens a door for a reader's imagination. Through that door might come the steam of savory dishes, the rattle of pot lids, or the "skritchy" rasp of a scouring pad. It might also let through a writer's wonder at a sunrise or gloom when it rains. Most descriptive writing includes

- vivid sensory details—details appealing to one or more of the five senses.
- a clear, consistent organization.
- links between sensory details and the feelings or thoughts they inspire.
- a main impression to which each detail adds.

To learn the criteria on which your description will be assessed, see the Rubric for Self-Assessment on page 115.

Types of Descriptive Writing

Your descriptive writing may be one of several types:

- **Descriptions of people or places** portray the physical appearance of a person or place and show readers why the subject is important or special.
- **Remembrances** capture a memorable experience in the writer's life; they may describe a specific moment or a longer period of time.
- **Observations** describe an event that the writer has personally witnessed.
- **Vignettes** capture a single moment in the writer's life, painting a picture with words.

Writers in ACTION

Will Hobbs's novels, such as **Bearstone,** *are rich with descriptions of the outdoors. As he writes, Hobbs draws on his personal experiences hiking in the wild country of Alaska and in the mountains of Colorado and California. He realizes the power of using sensory details:*

"Descriptive writing is really using the five senses. When you write with the five senses, your description becomes real."

PREVIEW Student Work IN PROGRESS

Kaitlin Crockett, a student at Baypoint Middle School in St. Petersburg, Florida, wrote a description of her grandparents' house. In this chapter, you will see her work in progress, including the strategies she used to choose her topic, to organize details, and to revise her work. You'll find her finished description at the end of this chapter.

Reading: Infer

Let students know that to infer is to draw conclusions based on information not directly stated. Making inferences from texts can add greatly to a reader's understanding. For example, the excerpt reports several things Uncle Henry says and does without stating directly what kind of person he is. As students read the passage, have them note the details that help them infer Henry's qualities as a leader, a businessman, and an uncle.

Step-by-Step Teaching Guide

Engage Students Through Literature

1. Read through the text and marginal notes with the whole class.

2. Ask students to identify details in the opening paragraph that make them want to go on reading.

3. As students read, have them list the details about Uncle Henry that Callaghan gives. Ask students how these details contribute to the reader's picture of Uncle Henry.

4. Have students think about possible subjects this story suggests for their own writing.

Critical Viewing

Analyze Students should include the sounds of the water and the water wheel, the smell and feel of the water and the wood, and the texture of the stone and wood.

Responding to Literature

Ask students to identify the key images in "Fog" by Carl Sandburg and "Four Skinny Trees" by Sandra Cisneros. Then, have them explain which words the poets use to make the images vivid and lively.

6.1 Model From Literature

In his short story "Luke Baldwin's Vow," Morley Callaghan uses descriptive writing to create memorable characters. In this excerpt, Callaghan creates a picture of Uncle Henry using sensory details as well as descriptions of Henry's behavior and interactions with others.

Reading Writing Connection

Reading Strategy: Infer A writer does not spell out all the information you need to know about a character. To understand a character fully, **make inferences,** or draw conclusions, based on the details the writer provides. For instance, knowing that Luke is mindful of his promise to his father, you might make the inference that he is a serious boy.

▲ **Critical Viewing**
What details appealing to the senses would you include in a description of the place in this picture? **[Analyze]**

Luke Baldwin's Vow

Morley Callaghan

That summer when twelve-year-old Luke Baldwin came to live with his Uncle Henry in the house on the stream by the sawmill, he did not forget that he had promised his dying father he would try to learn things from his uncle: so he used to watch him very carefully.

Uncle Henry, who was the manager of the sawmill, was a big, burly man weighing more than two hundred and thirty pounds, and he had a rough-skinned, brick-colored face. He looked like a powerful man, but his health was not good. He had aches and pains in his back and shoulders which puzzled the doctor. The first thing Luke learned about Uncle Henry was that everybody

LITERATURE

For other examples of descriptive writing, see the poem "Fog" by Carl Sandburg and the poem "Four Skinny Trees" by Sandra Cisneros in *Prentice Hall Literature: Timeless Voices, Timeless Themes, Bronze.*

100 • Description

had great respect for him. The four men he employed in the sawmill were always polite and attentive when he spoke to them. His wife, Luke's Aunt Helen, a kindly, plump, straightforward woman, never argued with him. "You should try and be like your Uncle Henry," she would say to Luke. "He's so wonderfully practical. He takes care of everything in a sensible, easy way."

Luke used to trail around the sawmill after Uncle Henry not only because he liked the fresh clean smell of the newly cut wood and the big piles of sawdust, but because he was impressed by his uncle's precise, firm tone when he spoke to the men.

Sometimes Uncle Henry would stop and explain to Luke something about a piece of timber. "Always try and learn the essential facts, son," he would say. "If you've got the facts, you know what's useful and what isn't useful, and no one can fool you."

He showed Luke that nothing of value was ever wasted around the mill. Luke used to listen, and wonder if there was another man in the world who knew so well what was needed and what ought to be thrown away. Uncle Henry had known at once that Luke needed a bicycle to ride to his school, which was two miles away in town, and he bought him a good one. He knew that Luke needed good, serviceable clothes. He also knew exactly how much Aunt Helen needed to run the house, the price of everything, and how much a woman should be paid for doing the family washing. In the evenings Luke used to sit in the living room watching his uncle making notations in a black notebook which he always carried in his vest pocket, and he knew that he was assessing the value of the smallest transaction that had taken place during the day.

This description is organized in order of importance. It moves from physical details about Uncle Henry to deeper insights into his character.

The writer links sensory details to the feelings they inspire in Luke.

These details contribute to the reader's main impression—Uncle Henry is a strong, solid character, a little larger than life.

Reading / Writing Connection

Writing Application: Help Your Readers Make Inferences As you draft your description, include details that will help readers make inferences about the feelings you connect with the person, place, or object you describe.

▶ **Critical Viewing** Find two details in this photograph that match the description of Uncle Henry. [Connect]

Model From Literature • 101

Teaching From the Model

Help students to understand how Callaghan's descriptions increase a reader's interest in the events coming up in the story. Ask students to predict what will happen next. Which details in the passage helped them come to that particular conclusion?

Customize for
Visual/Spatial Learners

Have students discuss what the illustration on page 100 adds to their impressions of Callaghan's writing. Ask them how Callaghan uses words to create pictures for the reader. Can students think of ways to do this in their own writing?

More About the Writer

Morley Callaghan was born to Irish immigrant parents in Toronto, Ontario, Canada. Callaghan began his career as a reporter for the *Toronto Daily Star.* He went on to write realistic short stories and novels about problems in contemporary life.

Customize for
ESL Students

You may want to pair ESL students with students who are more fluent in English. Have partners read the model to each other, paying particular attention to nouns and adjectives in the narrative's descriptive detail. Each student should make sure that his or her partner can summarize the passage.

Critical Viewing

Connect Students may say that the man in the photo is large and rough-skinned.

Reading\Writing Connection

Writing Application: Help Your Readers Make Inferences

Review the inferences students made about Uncle Henry. Remind them of the value of including details in their writing that will help their readers draw similar conclusions.

1. You may wish to assign or suggest a freewriting topic drawn from recent events in your community or at your school.

2. Make sure students recognize they are only expected to generate possible topics at this stage, not begin writing their descriptions.

1. You may wish to provide students with paper for this activity.

2. Stress to students the importance of not worrying about the quality of their drawing. This activity is like freewriting with pictures.

Teaching Resources: Writing Support Transparency 6-A; Writing Support Activity Book 6-1

1. Display the transparency. Point out that Kaitlin decided to narrow her focus to one kind of event: family journeys. This narrower focus keeps her timeline manageable. Other sample topics for timelines include: baseball games I've played in or seen, family moving days, or baby-sitting adventures.

2. Gives students a copy of the blank Timeline (6-1). Have students fill in the organizer with events from their own lives.

Choosing Your Topic

You will find it easiest to describe an event, person, or place that has special meaning for you. To uncover your special topic, use these strategies:

Strategies for Generating a Topic

1. **Freewriting** Set a clock for five minutes. Then, write whatever comes to mind. You might want to start with a general idea, such as *friends*, *places*, or *holidays*. During freewriting, focus more on the flow of ideas than on spelling or punctuation. After five minutes, review your writing and choose as your topic an object, place, person, or event you mention.

2. **Drawing** Think about a general idea, such as *good times*, *adventures*, or *solving problems*. Draw the people, scenes, and places that come to mind. Don't worry about drawing well—just doodle! At the end of five minutes, review your drawings. Select the person, place, or event of which a drawing reminds you as your topic.

3. **Timeline** Make a timeline of events in your life. Then, choose a person or place associated with one event as the topic of your description.

Writing Lab CD-ROM

For more help finding a topic, explore the activities and suggestions in the Choosing a Topic section of the Description lesson.

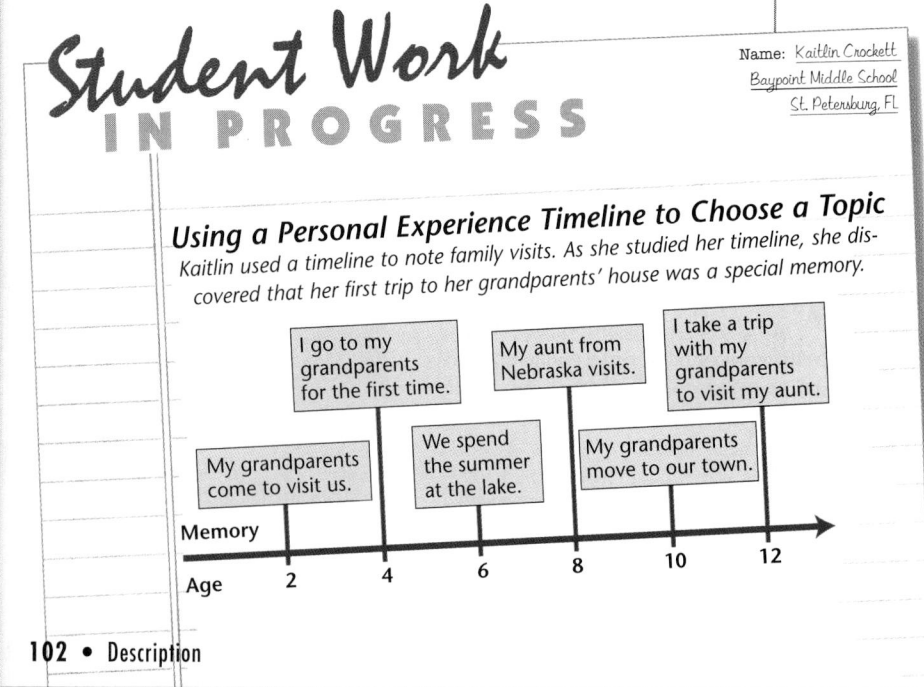

Student Work IN PROGRESS

Name: Kaitlin Crockett
Baypoint Middle School
St. Petersburg, FL

Using a Personal Experience Timeline to Choose a Topic
Kaitlin used a timeline to note family visits. As she studied her timeline, she discovered that her first trip to her grandparents' house was a special memory.

102 • Description

⏱ TIME SAVERS!

 **Writing Support Transparencies**
Use the transparencies for Chapter 6 to teach these strategies.

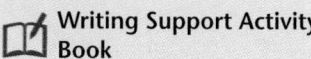 **Writing Support Activity Book**
Use the graphic organizers for Chapter 6 to facilitate these strategies.

⏱ TIME AND RESOURCE MANAGER

Resources
Print: Writing Support Transparencies 6-A–C; Writing Support Activity Book, 6-1
Technology: Writing Lab CD-ROM, Description

In-Depth Coverage	Accelerated Pace
• Cover pp. 102–105 in class. • Guide students through the Strategies for Generating a Topic. • Have students use the "zoom in" technique to narrow their topics. • Work through the cubing process in class to gather details.	• In class, discuss how to identify a good descriptive writing topic. • Ask students to submit topic proposals for your review. • Have students work independently to narrow their topics and gather details.

TOPIC BANK

If you're having trouble finding a topic, consider these possibilities:

1. **Description of a Remarkable Place** Think of the most fascinating, most comfortable, or weirdest place you have ever visited. List qualities and features that give the place its special character. Then, write a description that will allow a reader to share your impressions of the place.

2. **Remembrance or Vignette** Describe a special moment or person in your life. (You might browse through family photo albums or videotapes for ideas.) Include details that show why the person or event is special to you.

Responding to Fine Art

3. Respond to this painting of Fort George Hill. Take notes on the scene it shows, describe the colors the artist uses, and note the mood these colors create. Also note the patterns or movement the objects in the painting create. Does space in the painting seem empty or full? Pull these details together in a written description.

Fort George Hill, 1915, Preston Dickinson, Munson-Williams-Proctor, Courtesy Martha Parrish & James Reinish, Inc., New York

Responding to Literature

4. Read Ray Bradbury's story "All Summer in a Day." Pay special attention to his descriptions of rain. Then, write a description of another kind of weather, such as a windy day. Following Bradbury's example, use musical language to make your description ring. You can find Bradbury's story in *Prentice Hall Literature: Timeless Voices, Timeless Themes*, Bronze.

☑ Cooperative Writing Opportunity

5. **Travel Brochure** With a group, create a travel brochure for your community. Brainstorm a list of places of interest, such as historic sites, libraries, museums, stores, and so on. Each group member should write a description of a different place on the list. Assemble the group's descriptions into a brochure illustrated with photographs and maps.

Prewriting • 103

Responding to Fine Art

Fort George Hill, 1915, by Preston Dickinson
Teaching Resources: Writing Support Transparency 6-B

1. Display the transparency, and ask students what details seem most important. How does the artist use color and shape to emphasize those details?

2. Encourage students interested in describing a work of art to visit a local museum. This will enable them to see the true colors of a painting, to observe the texture of the paint, to walk around a piece of sculpture and view it from all sides, and to compare multiple works by a single artist. Remind students to take careful notes.

Responding to Literature

Ray Bradbury's story will help students understand how a piece of writing benefits from vivid descriptions and details. In the story Bradbury imagines conditions of life on the planet Venus. Although the Venus he describes is completely unlike the real planet, his version is so specifically described that it seems real.

Spotlight on the Humanities

For additional topic suggestions, see the Spotlight on Humanities on page 120.

Customize for
Less Advanced Students

Students who have trouble finding a topic may want to imagine a place and then describe it.

☑ ONGOING ASSESSMENT: Monitor and Reinforce

If you observe that students are having difficulty coming up with a topic, use one of the following options.

Option 1 Work with the whole class on one idea from the Topic Bank or from ideas suggested by students.	**Option 2** If Topic Bank ideas seem too difficult, suggest that students try an assignment from the Topic Bank in the Teaching Resources.

1. As students look through the hole in the card, they will discover that it cuts off most of their view of a subject, forcing them to focus on one detail at a time.

2. After completing discussion of the Critical Viewing question, have students use the camera technique on particular subjects they wish to describe.

Prewriting: Considering Your Audience and Purpose

1. Have students ask themselves, "What is important to me about this person/place/event?" Then jot down their ideas. This will help them determine the main impression they want to produce.

2. Let students know that an entertaining description of an event should be full of exciting, action-packed, or funny details for readers to enjoy. An informative description of a person should include details about important events in his or her life.

Critical Viewing

Analyze Students should notice the two parts consist of students in the lunch line and cafeteria workers on the other side. Details will vary.

6.2

Narrowing Your Topic

Once you've chosen a topic, you may find that it is too broad to describe well. For instance, to describe your entire school building in detail, you would have to write many pages. "My school building" is too general a topic.

Narrow a broad topic by dividing it into parts and focusing on one of them. For instance, the topic "my school building" might be divided into such subtopics as "my homeroom," "the cafeteria," and so on. By focusing on one narrow topic, you can write a more effective description. Use an index-card "camera" to zoom in on just the right part of your topic.

Zoom in to Narrow a Topic

Cut a small hole in an index card to make a "camera." Look through the "camera lens" (the hole) at the subject or at a picture of the subject you wish to describe. (If you are describing a past event or a place or person you cannot revisit, draw pictures of your subject. Use your camera to zoom in on your drawings.) Focus first on one part of your subject and then another. Which details are specific to one part? Which are common to all parts? After observing various aspects of your subject, choose the most interesting one as your topic.

Considering Your Audience and Purpose

Your **audience**—those who will read your description—should affect the details you include. Before you begin drafting, think about how familiar your audience is with your topic. If your audience is unfamiliar with your topic, give basic details about it. If they are very familiar with your topic, focus on the details that show a unique or unexpected side of it.

Your **purpose** in writing a description is to let readers experience in their imaginations what you have experienced with your senses. You can best achieve your purpose by including vivid sensory details—details appealing to the senses—and by using colorful words and comparisons.

▲ Critical Viewing Create an index-card camera as described on this page. Use it with this photograph. List two parts of this scene, and three details you notice for each part. [Analyze]

104 • Description

ONGOING ASSESSMENT: Monitor and Reinforce

If you notice that some students are having difficulty narrowing their topics, then use one of the following options.

Option 1 Have students create a word web with their general topics listed in the center oval. Suggest that they fill in the remaining ovals with details related to this topic. They then can choose one of the details to help them narrow their topics.	Option 2 Have students work with a partner. Each partner can ask questions about the topic, point out details that seem especially interesting, and give the other student ideas for narrowing his or her topic.

Gathering Details

Descriptive writing creates a vivid picture using sensory details. A sentence telling how something looks, smells, feels, sounds, or tastes gives a sensory detail, as in this example:

NO SENSORY DETAILS:	The car turned the corner sharply.
ADDED SENSORY DETAILS:	The flaming red car screeched around the corner, leaving only the stench of burning rubber.

Sensory details paint a scene. Other details, such as emotions, deepen a reader's experience of the scene. Use cubing to pull together different kinds of details to use in your description.

Use Cubing to Gather Details

Follow these steps to "cube" your subject:
1. **Describe it.** Explain how it looks, sounds, feels, tastes, or smells.
2. **Associate it.** List feelings or stories it calls to mind.
3. **Apply it.** Show how it can be used or what it does.
4. **Analyze it.** Divide it into parts.
5. **Compare and contrast it.** Compare it with a related subject.
6. **Argue for or against it.** Show its good and bad points.

☑ Collaborative Writing Tip

Practice cubing a topic with a group of classmates. Choose an object or place familiar to all, and name details for each side of the cube. Take special note of details your classmates contribute that you did not consider.

Prewriting: Use Cubing to Gather Details

Teaching Resources: Writing Support Transparency 6-C; Writing Support Activity Book, 6-2

1. Display the transparency, which demonstrates the making of a cube.

2. Rephrase the six steps of the cubing strategy as questions: What does your subject look like? What things or feelings do you associate with it? What kinds of things could you do with or to your subject? How could you break your subject up into parts? What might you compare or contrast it with? How could you persuade a reader to like or dislike your subject?

3. Point out that Kaitlin has written notes on each of these six questions. Be aware that, depending on their topics, students may not have notes for all six steps.

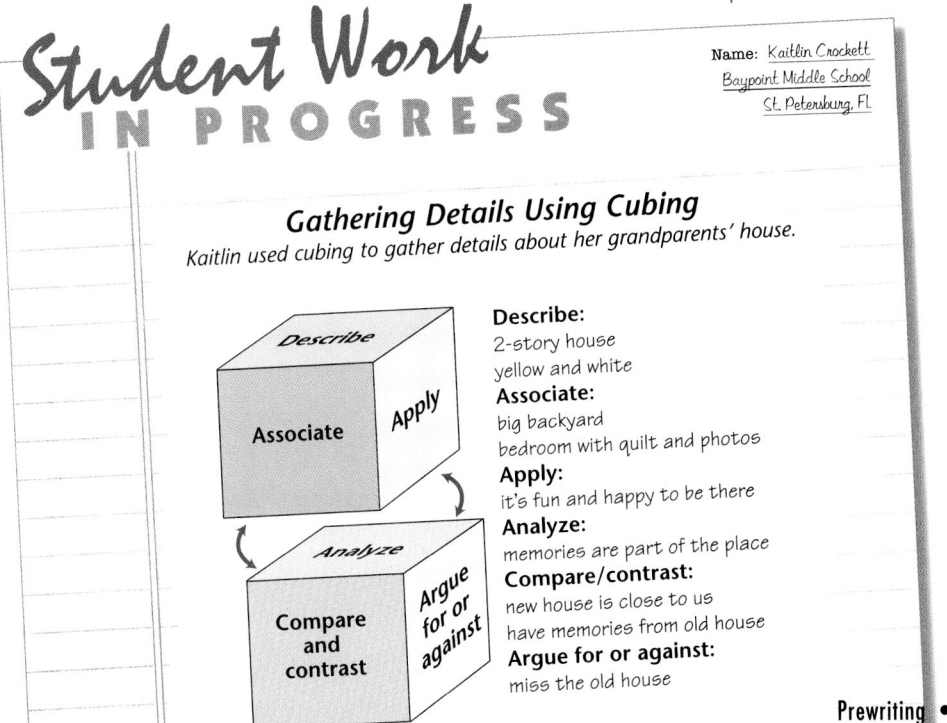

Student Work **IN PROGRESS**

Name: Kaitlin Crockett
Baypoint Middle School
St. Petersburg, FL

Gathering Details Using Cubing

Kaitlin used cubing to gather details about her grandparents' house.

Describe:
2-story house
yellow and white
Associate:
big backyard
bedroom with quilt and photos
Apply:
it's fun and happy to be there
Analyze:
memories are part of the place
Compare/contrast:
new house is close to us
have memories from old house
Argue for or against:
miss the old house

Prewriting • 105

◇ STANDARDIZED TEST PREPARATION WORKSHOP

Organization Some standardized tests require students to use their organizational abilities. Share the following sample test question with students:

(1) My mother grew up on a chicken farm.
(2) On the weekends, she would help my grandfather gather eggs from the chicken coops.
(3) She moved to the farm with her family when she was just a little girl. (4) The farm was in Toms River, New Jersey.

Choose the most logical sentence sequence.

A 1, 4, 3, 2   **C** 1, 2, 4, 3

B 2, 3, 4, 1   **D** Correct as is

The correct answer is **A**. Sentence (2) interrupts the logical time frame and belongs at the end of the paragraph.

Drafting: Shaping Your Writing

1. Discuss the three methods of organization listed on the page. Have students turn back to the Model From Literature (pages 100–101) and identify its method of organization. (Order of importance; details build in importance until the reader has a clear picture of Uncle Henry.) Help students see that any of these three methods can work well for a variety of topics.

2. As they start listing details about their topics, students may find word webs helpful. They can write their main topic, such as "World Series, Game 4," in a central oval and note details associated with it on spokes. They can then list these details in order of importance, choosing which ones are the most important. They will use these details to create their main impression.

Critical Viewing

Apply Students may say the main impression is that the dog is lovable. He has very sweet eyes and a friendly face.

6.3 # Drafting

Shaping Your Writing

Once you have gathered the details you will use in your descriptive writing, you can begin drafting. Your descriptive writing will take your readers on a journey to see new places or people. To make sure they don't get lost, organize your details clearly.

Organize to Make Your Ideas Clear

The order in which you present details depends largely on the topic that you are describing. Using the following information, choose an organization plan that fits your topic.

Spatial Order
- Present details from left to right, front to back, or bottom to top.
- Use for descriptions of places or objects.

Chronological Order
- Present events in the order in which they occur.
- Use for a remembrance or other story.

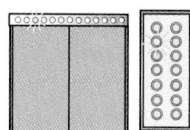

Order of Importance
- Present least important details at the beginning and strongest observations at the end.
- Use to lead readers to your main impression.

Create a Main Impression

Choose details for your description that will help create a main impression of your subject.

For instance, if you were describing a dog, you might want to leave readers with an impression of the dog as a small bundle of energy. To do so, you might describe its shaggy hair flying, its high-pitched yips, and its short legs blurring as it zips around. You might then tie these details together by calling the dog a "flying furball."

106 • Description

▼ Critical Viewing Explain what main impression is created by this photograph. Describe two details that help create this impression. **[Apply]**

Resources
Print: Writing Support Transparency 6-D
Technology: Writing Lab CD-ROM, Description

In-Depth Coverage	Accelerated Pace
• Cover pp. 106–107 in class. • Discuss ways of organizing details with students. • Help students link sensory details to facts and images in their drafts.	• Assign pp. 106–107 for independent student review. • Have students write their first drafts.

Providing Elaboration

Build Upon Details

By using sensory details, you create a clear picture of your subject. By elaborating on details as you draft, you bring your picture to life.

"Depth-charging" is one strategy you can use to build sensory impressions into a vivid picture.

Using Depth-Charging To depth-charge as you draft, pause at the end of a paragraph. Circle the detail in the paragraph that you find most compelling. It might be a word that suggests a strong feeling or a vivid sensory detail.

Next, draw an arrow from the circled word to a blank line. Write a new sentence telling more about the quality, action, or thing named by the circled word. Next, circle the most compelling word in your new sentence. Draw an arrow to a new line, and write a sentence giving more information about this second circled word. Review your paragraph, and decide whether it should include your new sentences.

Drafting: Using Depth-Charging

Teaching Resources: Writing Support Transparency 6-D

1. Display the transparency to show how depth-charging focuses attention on sensory details and helps develop these details in greater "depth." Point out how Kaitlin worked from the general impression of the village to a specific image of the children who gave her that impression.

2. Guide students through another example. For instance, if a student wrote about the thrill of catching a fly ball in the stands at the World Series game, sensory details might include the *thwack* of the ball in the glove, the applause of the nearby fans, or the feel of the ball's leather cover.

Student Work
IN PROGRESS

Name: Kaitlin Crockett
Baypoint Middle School
St. Petersburg, FL

Depth-Charging to Build Upon Sensory Details

This is how Kaitlin used depth-charging to elaborate on her impressions of a toy village in her grandparents' home. Later, she incorporated these new details in her final draft.

The (village) children, dressed in their warm coats and bundled with scarves and mittens, enjoyed ice skating on the glimmering icy pond or building a snowman in the soft, white snow.

The village seemed so (cozy.)

When I was little, I used to wish I lived in one of those houses, happy and safe in their perfect little world.

Drafting • 107

☑ **ONGOING ASSESSMENT: Monitor and Reinforce**

If you observe that students are having difficulty building upon sensory details, try the following strategy.

Have students work in pairs and trade drafts. Each student circles two details that he or she finds most compelling. Then pairs return their papers so that students can elaborate upon the particular details.

🕐 **TIME SAVERS!**

📖 **Writing Support Activity Book**

Use the graphic organizers for Chapter 6 to facilitate these strategies.

📑 **Writing Support Transparencies**

Use the transparencies for Chapter 6 to teach these strategies.

1. Encourage students to read their drafts once, put them away, and wait a few hours or overnight before rereading them. This wait will give them a fresh perspective and make it easier for them to re-enter their writing.

2. As students reread their drafts, have them highlight related details, and decide whether these belong together. Then they can go back to cut and paste these details together.

3. If students are working on word processors, remind them that they can use the cut and paste commands to rearrange details, sentences, or whole paragraphs.

Customize for
Less Advanced Students

Encourage students to keep in mind the feelings that prompted them to choose their topics. Their revisions should help their readers better understand those feelings and impressions.

6.4 Revising

After your first draft is done, it's time to review your description. As you reread your work, pretend that you are a reader who has never seen or experienced what you are describing. Consider first what changes to your organization would help such a reader experience what you describe.

Revising Your Overall Structure
Analyze Your Organization Plan

Review your entire description to be sure you used your chosen method of organization consistently. Group related details, rather than scattering them throughout your draft. Use cutting and pasting to move and regroup details as needed.

▶ **REVISION STRATEGY**
Cutting and Pasting for Order

Make an extra printout or a photocopy of your draft. Reread your work, noting details that concern the same person, place, thing, or idea. If you find related details far apart in your draft, they may be in the wrong place. Consider putting them together. Cut each misplaced detail out of your photocopied draft and tape it to your original draft next to the related details with which it belongs.

CUTTING AND PASTING

Covered in hard scales from its head to its tail, a crocodile is like an armored tank. Its mouth bristles with sharp teeth. No other reptile seems quite as fierce.
    A crocodile's mouth is its main weapon—for grabbing and tearing. A crocodile can also use its long, blunt head to knock an animal as big as a zebra off its feet. It has long, sharp claws.

It has long, sharp claws.

Technology Tip

If you created your draft with a word processor, underline or highlight related details that are in different parts of your draft. Save a copy of your file under a different name, and cut and paste to rearrange details. If you want to restore a paragraph, you can always copy it from your original file.

108 • Description

⏱ TIME AND RESOURCE MANAGER

Resources
Print: Writing Support Transparencies 6-E–H
Technology: Writing Lab CD-ROM, Description

In-Depth Coverage	Accelerated Pace
• Cover pp. 108–113 in class. • Review Grammar in Writing, p. 113.	• Assign pp. 108–113 for independent student review. • Have students work in small groups for peer review. • Ask students to revise their drafts.

Evaluate Your Main Impression

Consider whether each detail you have included supports a main impression. You may need to add or replace details to create or focus a main impression. Code details to make sure your main impression is strong.

▶ REVISION STRATEGY
Circling Details to Strengthen a Main Impression

On a note card, write down your main topic. Underneath, write down the main impression that you want your draft to provide. For instance, your topic might be "basketball" and the main impression might be "nonstop excitement."

Next, run your note card down your draft, stopping at each line in turn. At each line, ask yourself, "Does this detail support my main impression?" Circle in colored pencil those details that do not. Then, review your circled details.

If a circled detail does not add to your main impression and does not give information your reader needs, then either

- consider eliminating it, or
- consider rewording the detail using more vivid language. You might consider using the depth-charging strategy to elaborate on these details further (see page 107).

Step-by-Step Teaching Guide

Revising: Circling Details to Strengthen a Main Impression

Teaching Resources: Writing Support Transparency 6-E

1. Display the transparency. Help students understand that even though details may be accurate, well expressed, and interesting, they may not be relevant to the main impression. Descriptive writing should always focus on the main impression. Details that do not help to build to this impression may distract the reader.

2. Have students look at the changes Kaitlin made to her description of her grandparents' house. Have students evaluate these changes. Is the writing stronger? Is Kaitlin making a more clearly focused impression on her readers? If students answer no, ask them what they would have done differently.

Student Work
IN PROGRESS

Name: *Kaitlin Crockett*
Baypoint Middle School
St. Petersburg, FL

Circling Details to Strengthen a Main Impression

Kaitlin identified a few details that did not clearly contribute to her main impression of her grandparents' house. She rewrote sentences, elaborated, and eliminated unnecessary details to strengthen her impression of a cheerful, well-kept house.

I remember how their two-story house looked. ~~They lived there~~
It was freshly painted with light yellow and white paint.
~~a long time.~~ ~~It was yellow and white.~~ My grandfather liked to
The newly mowed lawn was neatly trimmed, and bright flowers bloomed
work in the yard. ~~He still gardens where they live now.~~
on the porch. Squash and other vegetables filled the garden.

Main Impression:
bright, cheery, well-kept home

☑ ONGOING ASSESSMENT: Monitor and Reinforce

If students have difficulty determining if a detail is relevant, try one of the following options:

Option 1 Have students ask themselves questions like the ones that follow to help them evaluate the details in their writing: How does this detail contribute to the main impression? Is there another way I could state the detail that would contribute more to the main impression?	**Option 2** Have students consider their audience in assessing details. This may determine the level of detail in their writing. For instance, if they were writing for a audience of young children, would their writing be more or less detailed?

⏱ TIME SAVERS!

Writing Support Transparencies
Use the transparencies for Chapter 6 to teach these strategies.

Revising: Use Functional Paragraphs

Teaching Resources: Writing Support Transparency 6-F

1. Display the transparency to show students how paragraphs can have different purposes. A transitional paragraph, for instance, helps get readers from one section of the text to another.

2. Have students reread their paragraphs and note in the margin each paragraph's purpose. Have them think about whether any of these paragraphs fits the functions described on this page. If not, do students feel they need to add functional paragraphs? Are there gaps in their writing that they need to fill?

Real-World Connection

Television news anchors often have to help viewers make connections between different parts of stories being presented. For example, an anchor can give a brief verbal introduction. This may be followed by a background report and then an interview. The anchor will appear between the two to explain the connection between the background and the interview. All of the anchor's speeches can be considered functional paragraphs. They connect the various parts of the whole story.

6.4

Revising Your Paragraphs
Use Functional Paragraphs

A **topical paragraph** develops or supports one main idea. A **functional paragraph** adds emphasis or makes a transition. A functional paragraph may be one sentence or a series of sentences. It may be a character's words (dialogue), or it may be in the writer's voice. Although most of the paragraphs in your description are probably topical paragraphs, you can add functional paragraphs to "spice up" your writing. Here are some examples:

FUNCTIONAL PARAGRAPHS

Arouse or sustain interest:
That old house on the edge of town looks pretty enough—until you get close.

Present a special effect:
There was a huge ker-PLOP!! as wet snow spattered all over the sidewalk.

Emphasize a point:
I have never eaten clams again.

Present dialogue:
"Look out!" he yelled. "She's about to blow!"

Functional Paragraphs

Provide a transition:
Bob was not the only one out in the storm that night. Others had their own reasons for braving the wind and snow.

Show a shift from one speaker to another:
It was up to Betty to calm them down. Her voice cracked through their chatter like a whip.

▶ **REVISION STRATEGY**
Adding Functional Paragraphs

As you reread your draft, look for surprising or especially interesting details. You can emphasize a surprising detail by writing a functional paragraph to introduce it. Look also for places where you need to make a transition. You can add a functional paragraph to guide a reader smoothly from one part of your description to another.

Learn More

To learn more about topical and functional paragraphs, see Chapter 3.

Revising Your Sentences

Eliminate Run-on Sentences

When writing a description, you'll probably want to pack sentences full of vivid details. It's easy to let these sentences become run-ons. A run-on sentence is two or more complete sentences written as though they were a single sentence.

RUN-ON: I went to my grandma's, we ate then it was time to go.

POSSIBLE CORRECTION: I went to my grandma's. We ate until we couldn't eat another bite. Soon it was time to go.

▶ REVISION STRATEGY
Color-Coding Clues to Eliminate Run-ons

Read your draft aloud slowly. As you read, mark the places where you pause the longest with red dot stickers. Use yellow dots to mark shorter pauses. Review your draft. See whether you have written a period for each red sticker. Consider adding a period if the words before the dot express a complete thought. Capitalize the word following the period. For each yellow sticker, consider whether you need to add a comma.

Language Lab CD-ROM

For additional practice eliminating run-on sentences, complete the Language Lab lesson on Run-on Sentences in the Problems With Sentences unit.

Student Work
IN PROGRESS

Name: *Kaitlin Crockett*
Baypoint Middle School
St. Petersburg, FL

Color-Coding Pauses to Eliminate Run-ons
Here are some of the pauses Kaitlin marked in her writing. Notice where she added periods and commas.

There was a store with a red awning , and the train station was busy with travelers● the figures of people , placed along shelves, looked like they were busily working in the big city.

Revising: Eliminate Run-on Sentences

1. Make sure students can recognize run-on sentences. Students' writing may be full of long sentences and compound sentences that are not necessarily run-ons.

2. Have students go through their drafts, using the color-coding strategy to mark possible run-on sentences. Have them read these sentences aloud. This test should help them decide whether a sentence can stand as it is.

Revising: Color-Coding Clues to Eliminate Run-ons

Teaching Resources: Writing Support Transparency 6-G

1. Display the transparency to show students how periods and commas can be added to eliminate run-ons.

2. Have a volunteer read aloud the run-on, so that students understand a pause is needed between the two separate ideas.

☑ ONGOING ASSESSMENT: Prerequisite Skills

If students have difficulty identifying run-on sentences in their own writing, you may find it helpful to review the following to assure coverage of prerequisite knowledge.

In the Textbook	Print Resources	Technology
Effective Sentences, pp. 469–483	Grammar Exercise Workbook, 99–102	Language Lab CD-ROM, Problems With Sentences; On-Line Exercise Bank, Section 21.4

⏱ TIME SAVERS!

 **Writing Support Transparencies**
Use the transparencies for Chapter 6 to teach these strategies.

Revising: Checkmarking Empty Words

Teaching Resources: Writing Support Transparency 6-H

1. Write a few phrases or sentences such as *very tired, really big,* and *I liked it a lot* on the chalkboard. Challenge students to give synonyms. (Possible suggestions: exhausted, weary; huge, enormous, vast; I thought it was marvelous, I was impressed.) Have students discuss the difference between the original phrases and their suggested replacements. What makes the replacement words better?

2. Display the transparency to illustrate how Kaitlin checkmarked and replaced empty words in her draft.

3. Emphasize that the word with the most syllables is not necessarily the most precise or the best one to use in a particular sentence. Students should try to find the word that best expresses their meaning, regardless of length.

Integrating Vocabulary Skills

Using a Thesaurus After students have checkmarked the empty words in their drafts, encourage them to look in a thesaurus for suggested synonyms. This activity will help students build vocabulary. Encourage students to check any new words they think they would like to use in a dictionary to be sure these words express exactly what they want to say.

Critical Viewing

Relate Most students will say they would also prefer having the group make suggestions.

6.4

Revising Your Word Choice

Use Precise Words

You wouldn't want to buy a container of juice only to find that it was full of water. Don't give your readers a description full of watered-down words. For instance, *nice* is a watered-down adjective. Replace it with a precise adjective, such as *generous* or *helpful*—adjectives that describe a specific quality.

Sometimes, writers try to "juice up" their writing by using empty words and phrases such as *very* and *a lot.* None of these empty words, however, is as powerful as a precise one. If you use these empty words in your description, you need to eliminate them and use more precise words to express your meaning.

▶ **REVISION STRATEGY**
Checkmarking Empty Words

Reread your draft, and place a check mark over any use of the words *very, really,* or *a lot.* Next, reread each sentence containing a checked word. Think of the strong image or important information that you want the sentence to express. Choose a precise word or phrase to help convey that image or information, and use it in the sentence. Then, delete the empty word.

▲ **Critical Viewing** Imagine reading your work to these reviewers. Explain whether you would prefer them just to point out problems in your work or to suggest solutions as well. **[Relate]**

Student Work
IN PROGRESS

Name: *Kaitlin Crockett*
Baypoint Middle School
St. Petersburg, FL

Checkmarking Empty Words

Kaitlin checkmarked her empty words and deleted them. Then, she found precise words to "juice up" her sentences. Notice the other replacements she considered.

curtained
~~large~~
A ~~really big~~ window almost filled the wall in the kitchen.

glistened
~~shone~~
Rays of sunshine ~~came~~ through the windowpanes ~~very~~

~~brightly.~~ Through the window you could see the great

expanse of the backyard where my grandfather and I used

every visit
to pick raspberries and play catch ~~a lot~~.

112 • Description

🖊 STANDARDIZED TEST PREPARATION WORKSHOP

Grammar Standardized tests often ask students to identify a particular grammatical element in a sentence. Ask students to find the adjective in the following sentence.

I had so many distracting thoughts, that I gazed out the window instead of working.

A distracting   **B** thoughts
C window   **D** instead

The correct answer is item **A**. *Distracting* modifies *thoughts.* Items **B** and **C** are nouns. Item **D** is an adverb.

Grammar in Your Writing: Adjectives

1. Use the chart to review adjectives.

2. Remind students of the distinction between adjectives and adverbs. Adjectives modify only nouns and pronouns. If a descriptive word modifies any other part of speech, it is an adverb.

Find It in Your Reading

Possible answers:

> *What kind?: big, burly, rough-skinned, brick-colored*
>
> *Which one?: that, his, first, your*
>
> *How many?: two hundred and thirty, four*
>
> *How much?: a piece*

Find It in Your Writing

Go over students' drafts individually. Discuss their evaluations of the nouns in their drafts. Assure students that adjectives may just add unnecessary or irrelevant details, and a more precise noun may be used, *roadster* for the less precise *car,* for example.

Grammar in Your Writing
Adjectives

If you use precise adjectives in your description, they will make your meaning clear. Adjectives are *modifiers*. **Adjectives** modify (slightly change) the meaning of a noun or pronoun by answering one of these four questions:

What Kind?	
oak table	*glimmering* pond
Which One?	
their house	*each* cottage
How Many?	
two shelves	*several* children
How Much?	
more time	*smaller* amount

Find It in Your Reading Review "Luke Baldwin's Vow" by Morley Callaghan on page 100. For each of the four questions—*What kind? Which one? How many? How much?*—identify one adjective used in the story to answer that question.

Find It in Your Writing Review your draft to identify seven nouns (words naming a person, place, or thing). Did you use adjectives to tell more about the thing each noun names? If not, evaluate whether the noun is precise enough or whether an adjective is needed.

For more on adjectives, see Chapter 16.

Peer Review

Analytic Talk

In a small group, read your revised draft twice. Ask the group members just to listen the first time you read. The second time, ask them to take notes on effective parts and on parts where they want to know more. Afterward, the group can discuss the description, responding to these questions:

1. What did I like in the beginning of the description? In the middle? In the end?

2. What did I want to hear more about? Did a lack of information make me feel as if I had been left hanging at the end?

Consider your peers' responses as you revise your draft further. Look for ways to improve parts they found unclear or ineffective.

Revising: Peer Review

1. You may want to have students choose partners for this activity, rather than working in small groups, so that everyone's writing will get more time and attention.

2. Encourage students to supply reasons for their analysis of others' work. Articulating their reasons for suggesting changes to a piece of writing will improve students' active reading skills.

☑ ONGOING ASSESSMENT: Prerequisite Skills

If students are having difficulty with adjectives, you may find it helpful to review the following to assure coverage of prerequisite knowledge.

In the Textbook	Print Resources	Technology
Adjectives and Adverbs, pp. 336–347	Grammar Exercise Workbook, pp. 21–30	Language Lab CD-ROM, Adjectives; On-Line Exercise Bank, Section 16.1

Editing and Proofreading: Commas

1. Remind students that a comma indicates a pause. Have a volunteer read aloud the text below the head "Color-Coding Clues for Commas." Point out the pauses at the commas.

2. Have the student read the sentences again without pausing. Have students discuss why these commas are there.

Grammar in Your Writing

1. If students are not sure if two adjectives are of equal rank, have them reverse the order of the words. If the meaning does not change, they should use a comma to separate the adjectives.

2. Write a noun on the board and have students suggest two or three adjectives to modify it. Then, work through the ordering of the adjectives.

3. Remind students that *a* and *the* are adjectives that always come first and never require a comma, even if commas are needed between the other adjectives in the phrase.

Find It in Your Reading

The adjectives *kindly, plump,* and *straightforward* are of equal rank. Therefore, Callaghan separates them with commas.

Find It in Your Writing

After students have reviewed their drafts, they can exchange papers with partners and check each other's results.

Integrating Speaking Skills

Have students choose partners and alternate reading and listening to paragraphs of their work. The reader should pause at each comma in the text as it is written. The listener should note any pauses that seem unnecessary, as well as any places he or she thinks the reader should have paused. Have students work together to add or delete commas to revise

114

6.5 Editing and Proofreading

Proofread your description carefully to eliminate any errors in grammar, spelling, or punctuation. Errors can be distracting. For instance, missing commas may confuse readers.

Focusing on Commas

Commas signal readers to pause slightly. They are also used to prevent confusion. Color-code your draft to find places where you may need to add commas.

Color-Coding Clues for Commas

Using a colored pencil, circle adjectives wherever you use two or more of them in a row. Read the information below, and then review what you have circled. Add any commas you need.

Grammar in Your Writing
Using Commas With Two or More Adjectives

Adjectives are words that tell *what kind, which one, how many,* or *how much.* When two or more adjectives appear in front of the noun they modify, you may need to add a comma between them.

Use a comma to separate adjectives of equal rank. Adjectives of equal rank are those you can write before a noun in any order without changing the meaning of the phrase. For instance, "a colorful, handmade quilt" and "a handmade, colorful quilt" have the same meaning. *Colorful* and *handmade* are adjectives of equal rank. Separate them with a comma.

Do not use commas to separate adjectives that must stay in specific order. For instance, you should not use a comma between the adjectives *this* and *heavy* in the phrase "this heavy mug."

Find It in Your Reading Review "Luke Baldwin's Vow" by Morley Callaghan on page 100. Copy the sentence that describes Aunt Helen. Explain why the adjectives are separated by commas.

Find It in Your Writing Review your draft to find places where you use two or more adjectives before a noun. Determine whether the adjectives are of equal rank or whether they need to appear in a specific order. Be sure you have used commas to separate adjectives of equal rank.

For more information on commas, see Chapter 26.

114 • Description

⏱ TIME AND RESOURCE MANAGER

Resources
Print: Scoring Rubrics on Transparency, Chapter 6 Writing Assessment: Scoring Rubric and Scoring Models for Descriptive Essay
Technology: Writing Lab CD-ROM, Description

In-Depth Coverage	Accelerated Pace
• Cover pp. 114–115 in class. • Have students edit and proofread their essays in class. • Review Rubric for Self-Assessment in class. • Have students present final drafts.	• Have students review pages 114–115 independently. • Have students edit and proofread their essays on their own. • Have students present final drafts.

6.6 Publishing and Presenting

Building Your Portfolio

1. **Publish in a Newspaper** If you've written a description of a person, place, or event in your school, submit your piece to the school newspaper or magazine.

2. **Create an Illustrated Booklet** You can make your description more interesting for readers by adding photos and drawings to illustrate specific details or your main impression. Find images in magazines or create your own. Assemble your words and pictures in a booklet.

Reflecting on Your Writing

Jot down your thoughts about what you learned from writing a description. Include a copy of this reflection in your portfolio. Begin by answering these questions:

- Did describing your subject lead you to new insights about it? Explain.

- Which strategy for revising might you recommend to a friend? Why?

 Internet Tip

To see examples of descriptive writing scored according to this rubric, visit **www.phschool.com**

Rubric for Self-Assessment

Use the following criteria to evaluate your description.

	Score 4	Score 3	Score 2	Score 1
Audience and Purpose	Creates a memorable main impression through effective use of details	Creates a main impression through use of details	Contains extraneous details that detract from main impression	Contains details that are unfocused and create no main impression
Organization	Is organized consistently, logically, and effectively	Is organized consistently	Is organized, but not consistently	Is disorganized and confusing
Elaboration	Contains rich sensory language that appeals to the five senses	Contains some rich sensory language	Contains some rich sensory language, but it appeals to only one or two of the senses	Contains only flat language
Use of Language	Uses vivid and precise adjectives; contains no errors in grammar, punctuation, or spelling	Uses some vivid and precise adjectives; contains few errors in grammar, punctuation, and spelling	Uses few vivid and precise adjectives; contains some errors in grammar, punctuation, and spelling	Uses no vivid adjectives; contains many errors in grammar, punctuation, and spelling

---

Publishing and Presenting

1. If students are interested in having their work published more widely than in a school publication, have them discuss it with you. Suggest journals, Internet sites, or community newspapers that might publish outstanding student work.

2. Students may want to illustrate their descriptions. Students should read the full text carefully, noting any ideas he or she has for illustrations. Students should note places in the text where an illustration could enhance the text for a reader. Do students feel that photographs, drawings, or some other medium would best illustrate the description?

ASSESS

Assessment

Teaching Resources: Scoring Rubrics on Transparency, 6; Formal Assessment, 6

1. Display the Scoring Rubric transparency and review the criteria with students.

2. Before students proceed, you may wish to review the Final Draft of the Student Work in Progress on the following pages. Have students score the Final Draft in one or more of the rubric categories.

☑ ONGOING ASSESSMENT: Assess Mastery

Use one of the following options to assess final drafts of students' descriptive essays.

Self Assessment Have students score their essays using the rubric provided. Then have students write a brief paragraph reflecting on the most valuable thing they learned in completing this essay.	**Teacher Assessment** You may wish to use the rubric and scoring models provided in Writing Assessment to score the descriptive essays.

Teaching From the Final Draft

Help students recognize the elements of good descriptive writing demonstrated by this final draft.

- The subject is one that many of the writer's peers can identify with.
- The opening paragraph makes the main impression of the topic clear.
- Sensory details throughout the writing support the main impression.
- The writing is clearly organized in spatial order, describing the house one area at a time.
- The adjectives are specific and concrete.

Critical Viewing

Analyze Students may say that the house connotes wealth because it is very large and well-kept.

6.7 *Student Work*
IN PROGRESS

FINAL DRAFT

House of Memories

Kaitlin Crockett
Baypoint Middle School
St. Petersburg, Florida

When I think of my grandparents' old house, I remember a cheery atmosphere with lots of laughs and smiles filling the air. It was always a fun and happy place. When I found out my grandparents were selling their house, I was happy that they were going to be moving here. I was sad, though, that I would never see them in their old place again.

I remember how their two-story house looked. It was freshly painted with light yellow and white paint. My grandfather liked to work in the yard. The newly mowed lawn was neatly trimmed, and bright flowers bloomed on the porch. Squash and other vegetables filled the garden.

116 • Description

▲ Critical Viewing
What is your main impression of this house? Cite two details contributing to this impression. [Analyze]

In her introduction, Kaitlin starts to create a main impression of her grandparents' house—it had a "cheery atmosphere."

Kaitlin supports her main impression with phrases such as freshly painted, light yellow, *and* neatly trimmed.

A curtained window almost filled the wall of the kitchen. Rays of sunshine glistened through the windowpanes. Through the window you could see the broad expanse of the backyard where my grandfather and I used to pick raspberries and play catch every visit.

In the dining room, the big oak table was draped with a white lace tablecloth ruffling over the edge. The table was neatly set with flowered china and polished silver. Soon, the table would be filled with delicious homemade breads, piping hot dishes, and freshly baked apple pie. We were always ready to indulge. Next to the table, on two white wooden shelves, sat my grandmother's toy village. Each cottage was beautifully painted. There was a store with a red awning, and the train station was busy with travelers. The figures of people, placed along the shelves, looked as if they were busily working in the big city. The little children, dressed in their warm coats and bundled with scarves and mittens, smiled as they ice skated on the glimmering icy pond or built a snowman in the soft white snow. The village seemed so cozy. When I was little, I used to wish I lived in one of those houses, happy and safe in their perfect little world.

Downstairs in the basement a stone fireplace blazed with reds and oranges. A comfortable, overstuffed couch sat in a corner. Along the opposite wall, my grandfather's tools hung in shiny rows above his old wooden workbench. The smell of saw-dust and oil meant he kept busy fixing and building things.

Upstairs, on the second floor, a small bedroom nestled in the corner. The bed was covered with a colorful, handmade quilt, and old photographs filled the oak nightstand. This was the bedroom I stayed in during overnight visits. It was so exciting having a room of my own, like at home, but different.

My grandparents now live just around the corner from us. I enjoy spending time with them and get to see them more often. I still miss that house, but I will always remember the good times I had there with my grandparents.

Kaitlin uses spatial order, organizing her description of the house room by room.

Sensory details such as bundled with scarves and mittens *and rich adjectives like* glimmering *make the description of the village vivid.*

Kaitlin builds up her sensory description with her feelings and imaginings about the toy village.

Kaitlin concludes by exploring how her memories of her grandparents' old house make her feel.

▶ Critical Viewing
In what ways is this room similar to or different from the one described by Kaitlin? [**Compare**]

Student Work in Progress • 117

Critical Viewing

Compare Students may say that it is similar in that many of the objects described by Kaitlin are there, such as the table. The room is different in that it seems more modern than the one Kaitlin describes.

Customize for
More Advanced Students

Have students locate a short piece of descriptive writing that they think is especially well done. It may be a short story, an article, or some other fairly brief work. Students may write brief essays analyzing how effectively it describes its main topic. Remind students to provide support for their opinions.

Lesson Objectives

1. To write a poem appropriate to audience and purpose
2. To recognize the distinguishing features of poetry
3. To revise selected drafts by adding, elaborating, deleting, combining, and rearranging text

Step-by-Step Teaching Guide

Poem

Teaching Resources: Writing Support Transparency, 6-I; Writing Support Activity Book, 6-3

1. You may want to bring in a sample of short poems to help students choose topics of their own.

2. Display the transparency and give students copies of the blank organizer. As students work on choosing and narrowing their topics, make sure they focus on a topic that can be explored adequately in a short poem. Encourage students to review their webs to see if they can break down further one of the details in the outer ovals. If they can, they may want to choose this detail as their topic.

Critical Viewing

Apply Students may say that the columns cascade down like snow or that the tall trees loom larger than life over the house.

Connected Assignment
Poem

The best descriptions are often found in poems. While "poetry" may sound fancy, it is part of the beat of your life. Skip-rope chants, birthday greetings, television jingles, the latest rap single—wherever words mingle, chiming and rhyming, poetry is taking place.

A **poem** is a creation made of words chosen for their sound and associations—even their looks—as well as their meaning. It uses words to suggest strong images and feelings. Most poems include one or more of these features:

- words arranged for a rhythmical, visual, or musical effect
- figures of speech such as
  - similes (comparisons of unlike things using *like* or *as)*
  - metaphors (comparisons of unlike things that do not use *like* or *as)*
  - personifications (descriptions of a nonhuman thing as if it were a person)
- a repeated pattern of lines and stanzas (groups of lines)

Write your own poem, using the strategies suggested below:

Prewriting Choose a topic to write a poem about. You might

- describe a place, object, animal, or person.
- tell a story, either one you have heard or one from your life.

Focus on one aspect of your topic—an event or a particular feature. Then, find a striking contrast between this aspect of your subject and another one. For instance, your poem might contrast a flower's timeless beauty with the short time it blooms. This contrast is your focused topic.

Next, use a web like this one to gather details. Write your topic in the middle. Use connecting circles to explore related details.

Drafting Once you have gathered details, choose a form in which you will present them. There are several forms from which you can choose, including those listed on page 119.

Early Houses, 1913, Lawren S. Harris, Robert and Signe McMichael, McMichael Canadian Art Collection

▲ Critical Viewing
Find two musical-sounding phrases for this scene, drawing on the features the artist emphasizes. **[Apply]**

DARK

LIGHT

moves silently, quickly, like smoke

sunlight: like a pool of golden syrup

dark like smoke

likes lying in the sunlight

CONTRAST
my cat: loves light, but he is dark and full of secrets

looks at me sometimes like he knows something I don't

sleepy

- **Rhyming poems** follow a regular pattern. Each line has a designated number of accented syllables (beats). Designated lines end with rhyming words. For instance, in "Pete at the Zoo" (below), Gwendolyn Brooks rhymes every other line. Her odd-numbered lines have four beats each. Her even-numbered lines have three.

- **Free-verse poems** do not rhyme and do not follow a regular pattern of beats. The poet must still pay close attention to the sounds and rhythms of the lines.

- **Haiku** are three-line poems in a traditional Japanese form. The first line contains five syllables, the second contains seven syllables, and the third has five syllables.

Look over poems you like, and choose one in order to copy its pattern of rhyming, rhythm, or repetition.

As you draft, incorporate details from your web and create the contrast you chose as your focus. Create strong images using figurative language such as metaphors and similes. Create musical effects by using words beginning with the same sound.

MODEL

Pete at the Zoo
Gwendolyn Brooks

I wonder if the elephant
Is lonely in his stall
When all the boys and girls are gone
And there's no shout at all,
5 And there's no one to stamp before,
No one to note his might.
Does he hunch up, as I do,
Against the dark of night?

Revising and Editing Once your first draft is on paper, go through your poem line by line. Focus on these revisions:

- **Replace vague words with precise ones.** Replace any worn-out expressions you have used with fresh ways of expressing your ideas.

- **Make sure that you have followed your chosen form.** Read your poem out loud, tapping as you go. Mark lines where there are too many or too few beats, or where the right rhythm is lacking. For a rhyming poem, check the last word of each line to make sure the right lines rhyme.

Publishing and Presenting Post a copy of your poem on a class bulletin board, or send it to a publication.

Connected Assignment: Poem • 119

Poem

1. Encourage students to select a poetic form that works well with their topics. For instance, a haiku works well with a single, fleeting image.

2. You may wish to review figurative language with students. Explain that a simile compares two unlike things, using the word *like* or *as*:

   The sunrise was like an orange flare.

3. A metaphor directly sets up a comparison between two unlike things:

   Her voice was sweet music.

4. As students review their drafts, have students circle or underline vague words or clichés. Then have them go back and replace these words. Remind them to use a thesaurus to help choose more vivid and precise words.

5. When students are done, encourage volunteers to read aloud their poems to the class.

Critical Viewing

Synthesize Students' responses will vary.

Step-by-Step Teaching Guide

Comparing Interpretations of Nature

1. Choose one of the Spotlight elements for class discussion, or have students work individually or in groups on the element of their choice. Give students the initiative to find the necessary books, videotapes, or pictures.

2. Students may want to research more information about O'Keeffe and her paintings.

3. Encourage students to check the school or local library for books containing Stieglitz's photographs. Do students notice any consistent themes in his work? Is there a discernable style?

4. Encourage students to check the school or local library for a recording of Grofé's suite. Interested students may also want to look for other musical compositions with similar subject matter.

Viewing and Representing

Activity Remind students that they will be "translating" musical and visual experiences into words. Encourage volunteers to share their comparisons with the class.

Critical Viewing

Interpret Students may say that she is relaxed because her hands are open and not clenched shut.

Spotlight on the Humanities

Comparing Interpretations of Nature

Focus on Fine Art: Georgia O'Keeffe

As you may have realized while writing a description, what your *mind* sees—the patterns you notice in things—is as important as what your *eye* sees. American artist Georgia O'Keeffe (1887–1986) excelled at seeing with her mind, finding new forms in nature.

O'Keeffe worked in oil paint and watercolors. Many of her paintings are nearly abstract—while they suggest particular scenes and objects, they also explore colors and shapes for their own sake. The paintings seem to discover something new about nature, expressing patterns lying behind the objects we ordinarily see.

O'Keeffe was one of a few women artists who achieved international recognition during her career. She is best known for her paintings of flowers and of natural forms found in the American Southwest.

Photography Connection Alfred Stieglitz (1864–1946), one of the masters of photography in the twentieth century, first brought O'Keeffe's work to the public when he showed it in his small Gallery 291 in New York. He later married O'Keeffe. One of his portraits of her is shown on this page (right).

Music Connection In 1931, Ferde Grofé composed his popular *Grand Canyon Suite.* His piece shares its title with a series of watercolors of Southwestern landscapes attributed to O'Keeffe. Like O'Keeffe, he was inspired by the elements of nature in the Southwest.

Descriptive Writing Activity: Comparison of Images in Music and Art

Listen to Grofé's *Grand Canyon Suite.* Then, view reproductions of O'Keeffe's paintings of the Southwest. Write an essay comparing the visions of this region that O'Keeffe and Grofé create.

Spring, ©1922, Georgia O'Keeffe, Frances Lehman Loeb Art Center, Vassar College, Poughkeepsie, New York

▲ **Critical Viewing** What natural objects can you discover in this painting? Describe how each is related to other forms in the painting. **[Synthesize]**

▶ **Critical Viewing** What do Georgia O'Keeffe's hands in this portrait suggest about her mood? **[Interpret]**

120 • Description

Media and Technology Skills

▶ **Lesson Objectives**

1. To assess how language, medium, and presentation contribute to the message
2. To evaluate the purposes and effects of various media

Analyzing Visual Meanings

Activity: Analyze Camera Techniques in a Movie

In a description, the details the writer chooses to include shape your idea of what is being described. Using a camera, a movie-maker can also shape your idea of a person, place, or event. Learn to identify the camera techniques used in movies and to recognize the effects they create.

Think About It Here are some important camera techniques:

Close-up Shots In a close-up shot, the person or thing filmed takes up most of the screen. The close-up shot tells you that what you are looking at is important. In a mystery movie, a director might use a close-up shot of someone's ring to let you know it is a clue. The shot also lets you see the ring in detail.

Zoom In When the camera zooms in on a person or thing, the image moves closer and closer. Like a close-up, a zoom shot tells you that you are looking at something important. It also increases the intensity or suspense of the moment. When the bad guys make a getaway, the camera might zoom in on their speeding car.

Zoom Out In zooming out, the camera begins with a tight focus on a single subject. Then, the image moves farther away and takes in more of the surrounding area. This shot shows how a person or thing fits into—or doesn't fit into—its environment. For example, an elderly person listening to a lecture may not seem unusual, but if the camera pulls away and shows him sitting among high school students, it might be funny, or touching.

Watch It Watch a movie, either on video or at the theater. Take notes on the camera techniques used. (Concentrate on the beginnings and endings of scenes and on moments of high drama.) Choose one example each of a close-up, a zoom in, and a zoom out. Describe the scene, and explain how the camera technique influenced your response to it.

Other Camera Techniques

Pan The camera moves from left to right over a person, place, or thing. A pan may be used to show the scope or full setting of something.

Aerial View The camera looks down from a point high above the subject. The shot gives a broad view of the setting and may emphasize the power of the camera—and the viewer—to see more than the characters can see.

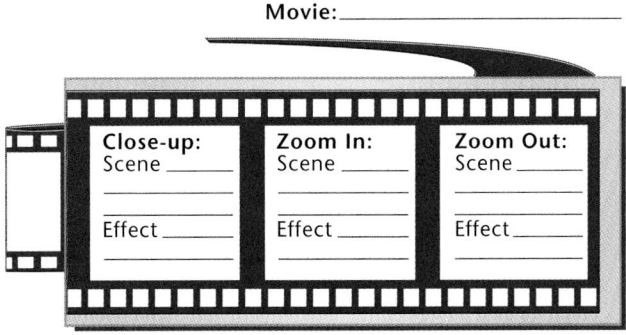

Movie:_____

Close-up:
Scene _____
_____
Effect _____
_____

Zoom In:
Scene _____
_____
Effect _____
_____

Zoom Out:
Scene _____
_____
Effect _____
_____

Step-by-Step Teaching Guide

Analyzing Visual Meanings

Teaching Resources: Writing Support Transparency, 6-J; Writing Support Activity Book, 6-4

1. Display the transparency to the class. Explain to students that the techniques described in the textbook are just a few of the many that filmmakers can use to help communicate ideas and feelings.

2. Students may have difficulty understanding the different techniques. If you have access to a video camera, you may want to bring it into class to demonstrate some of these techniques for students.

3. Encourage students to take detailed notes when watching their chosen movies. Suggest that they watch the movie on video. This way they can pause and rewind the movie while taking notes on the techniques used in the scene. Students can use the blank organizer to take notes.

Lesson Objectives

1. To revise selected drafts by adding, elaborating, deleting, combining, and rearranging text
2. To revise drafts for coherence, progression, and logical support of ideas

Step-by-Step Teaching Guide

Strategy, Organization, and Style Skills

Teaching Resources: Standardized Test Preparation Workbook, pp. 11–12

1. Call students' attention to the test tip on the page. Remind them that they should read the directions and the entire passage before attempting to answer the questions.

2. Draw students' attention to question 2. The two sentences have been combined into one in a few different ways. Explain to students that B expresses a similar meaning to A, but that A expresses it more precisely and with fewer words. C is not correct because *while* implies that both actions were done simultaneously.

Standardized Test Preparation Workshop

Strategy, Organization, and Style Skills

To write a good description, you need to organize details effectively. Some standardized test items measure organizational abilities along with other writing skills. Such items consist of a passage followed by questions, which include:

- *strategy* questions, asking if a given revision is appropriate
- *organization* questions, focusing on logical sequence
- *style* questions, focusing on point of view and word choice.

Test Tip

Read the entire passage before answering questions. You need to understand the author's purpose in the entire passage before deciding how to revise it.

Sample Test Items	Answers and Explanations
Read the passage, and then answer the questions that follow. (1) John cultivated the ground in preparation for planting. (2) He carefully placed a tulip bulb with the pointed side facing up in each hole. (3) He dug holes six inches deep and six inches apart. (4) He then buried each bulb. **1** Choose the most logical sentence sequence. **A** 2, 4, 1, 3 **B** 1, 3, 2, 4 **C** 2, 1, 3, 4 **D** Correct as is	The correct answer is *B*. Part (2) must follow part (3) because John could not have placed the bulbs until he had dug the holes. Part (1) describes the first step in planting, and part (4) describes the last event that occurred.
2 Which of the following is the best way to write parts (2) and (3)? **A** He dug holes six inches deep and six inches apart and placed a tulip bulb, pointed side up, in each. **B** He dug holes six inches deep and six inches apart, and he carefully placed a tulip bulb with the pointed side facing up in each hole. **C** He dug holes six inches deep and six inches apart, while carefully placing a tulip bulb with the pointed side facing up in each hole. **D** Correct as is	The correct answer is *A*. Although the other answers express similar meanings, this choice is the best way to combine the two sentences. It best conveys the order of steps without repeating words unnecessarily.

122 • Description

TEST-TAKING TIP

Tell students that when a test question involves chronological organization (such as Sample Test Item 1 above), it's a good idea to use a graphic organizer. A flow-chart or other diagram can help students visualize the correct order of events. Draw a flow-chart on the chalkboard and have volunteers come up to list in order each of the four sentences in the first sample test item.

Practice 1 **Directions:** Read the passage, and then answer the questions that follow. Choose the letter of the best answer.

(1) After researching avocados, I found out that they are the fruit of a tropical American tree. (2) It is <u>oval</u> shaped. (3) It can have black or green skin. (4) It has a bland green pulp and a large seed. (5) I decided to use the seed to grow an avocado plant.

(6) My original assignment was simply to find out from where a food <u>item</u> in my refrigerator came. (7) I had chosen to find out more about an avocado because it is one of my favorite foods. (8) Was it grown on a vine, a tree, or a shrub? (9) Was it a fruit or a vegetable?

(10) First, I removed the seed from the avocado and placed it, wide end down, in a wide-mouthed jar. (11) It took a while before I saw roots, and a few weeks later the stem pushed its way through the <u>top</u> of the seed. (12) I added an inch of water. (13) I was then able to plant it in soil and watch it grow.

1 Which of the following is the best order for the paragraphs?
  A 1, 2, 3
  B 3, 2, 1
  C 1, 3, 2
  D 2, 1, 3

2 Which of the following would be the best way to write parts 2, 3, and 4 ?
  F It is oval shaped, can have black or green skin, has a bland green pulp, and contains a large seed.
  G It is oval shaped, and it can have black or green skin. It has a bland green pulp and a large seed.
  H It is oval shaped, and can have black or green skin. It also has a bland green pulp and a large seed.
  J An avocado has an oval shape, black or green skin, a bland green pulp, and a large seed.

3 Which of the following sentences should be inserted between parts 7 and 8?
  A I didn't know anything about avocados.
  B My choice was not a good one.
  C To complete my assignment, I needed to answer a few questions.
  D I had a lot of questions.

4 In part 7, which of the following should be deleted to eliminate irrelevant information?
  F because it is one of my favorite foods
  G about an avocado
  H I had chosen
  J to find out more about an avocado

5 If the author wanted to include scientific information about the growth of the avocado seed in paragraph 3, which of the following would be appropriate?
  A The roots looked like spaghetti hanging from the bottom of the seed.
  B I used toothpicks to hold the end of the avocado seed in the water.
  C It seemed to take forever before the roots began to grow.
  D The epicotyl, the upper part of the seed embryo, pushed the plumule, or leaf-bud, through the seed coat.

6 Choose the most logical sentence sequence for paragraph 3.
  F 10, 11, 12, 13
  G 10, 12, 11, 13
  H 13, 10, 11, 12
  J 12, 11, 13, 10

7 In which part should the underlined word be replaced by a more precise word?
  A Part 2
  B Part 6
  C Part 11
  D Correct as is

Standardized Test Preparation Workshop • **123**

Answer Key

Practice 1
1. D
2. J
3. D
4. F
5. D
6. G
7. B

In-Depth Lesson Plan

	LESSON FOCUS	PRINT AND MEDIA RESOURCES
DAY 1	**Introduction to Persuasion: Persuasive Essay** Students learn key elements of persuasive writing and analyze the Model From Literature (pp. 124–127).	*Writers at Work* **Videotape**, Persuasion *Writing Lab* **CD-ROM**, Persuasion
DAY 2	**Prewriting** Students brainstorm to select and narrow topics for a persuasive essay (pp. 128–131).	**Teaching Resources** *Writing Support Transparencies, 7-A–D; Writing Support Activity Book, 7-1–2* *Writing Lab* **CD-ROM**, Persuasion
DAY 3	**Drafting** Students organize their persuasive evidence to support a thesis and write a first draft (pp. 132–133).	**Teaching Resources** *Writing Support Transparencies, 7-E–F;* *Writing Lab* **CD-ROM**, Persuasion
DAY 4	**Revising** Students revise their essay, focusing on effective organization (pp. 134–138).	**Teaching Resources** *Writing Support Transparencies, 7-G–I;* *Writing Lab* **CD-ROM**, Persuasion
DAY 5	**Editing and Proofreading; Publishing and Presenting** Students edit their essays and present their final drafts for submission to local publications (pp. 139–140).	**Teaching Resources** *Scoring Rubrics on Transparency, Ch. 7; Formal Assessment, Ch. 7* *Writing Lab* **CD-ROM**, Persuasion

Accelerated Lesson Plan

	LESSON FOCUS	PRINT AND MEDIA RESOURCES
DAY 1	**Introduction Through Drafting** Students review persuasive writing, select a thesis and supporting evidence, and write drafts (pp. 124–133).	**Teaching Resources** *Writing Suppport Transparencies, 7-A–F; Writing Support Activity Book, 7-1–2* *Writers at Work* **Videotape**, Persuasion *Writing Lab* **CD-ROM**, Persuasion
DAY 2	**Revising Through Presenting** Students work individually or with peers to revise, edit, and proofread their work for presentation and submission to local publications (pp. 134–140).	**Teaching Resources** *Writing Support Transparencies, 7-G–I; Scoring Rubrics on Transparency, Ch. 7; Formal Assessment, Ch. 7* *Writing Lab* **CD-ROM**, Persuasion

Options for Adapting Lesson Plans

HOMEWORK
Have students complete any stage of the lesson for homework.

FEATURES
Extend coverage with Connected Assignment (p. 144), Spotlight on the Humanities (p. 146), Media and Technology Skills (p. 147), and the Standardized Test Preparation Workshop (p. 148).

TECHNOLOGY
Students can complete any stage of the lesson on computer. Have them print out their completed work.

INTEGRATED SKILLS COVERAGE

Integrating Grammar
Compound Sentences, SE p. 137
End Marks, SE p. 139

Reading/Writing Connection
Reading Strategy, SE p. 126
Writing Application, SE p. 127

Viewing and Representing
Critical Viewing, SE pp. 124, 126, 132, 141, 142, 143, 146

Speaking and Listening
ATE pp. 134, 136, 146

Vocabulary
ATE pp. 127, 149

Real World Connection
ATE pp. 132

ASSESSMENT SUPPORT

Standardized Test Preparation SE p. 148, ATE p. 138
Standardized Test Preparation Workbook, pp. 13–14
Scoring Rubrics on Transparency, Ch. 7
Formal Assessment, Ch. 7
Writing Assessment and Portfolio Management

MEETING INDIVIDUAL NEEDS

Less Advanced Students, See Ongoing Assessments ATE pp. 127, 129, 133, 135, 137, 140
Visual/Spatial Learners, ATE pp. 127, 145
ESL Students, ATE p. 138, 149
Bodily/Kinesthetic Learners, ATE p. 139
More Advanced Students, ATE p. 142

BLOCK SCHEDULING

For 90-minute Blocks
- Have students complete the Prewriting and Drafting stages in a single period.
- Focus one class period on Revising and Editing and Publishing and Presenting. Allow at least 30 minutes for peer revision.

Resources for Varying Instruction
- *Writing Lab* **CD-ROM** If your students have access to hardware, a 90-minute block provides an ideal opportunity for them to work on computers.
- *Writers at Work* **Videotape** Show the Persuasion segment in class.

Professional Development Support
- *How to Manage Instruction in the Block* This Teaching Resource provides management and activity suggestions.

MEDIA AND TECHNOLOGY

For the Student
- *Writing Lab* **CD-ROM**, Persuasion

For the Teacher
- *Writers at Work* **Videotape**, Persuasion
- *Resource Pro* **CD-ROM**

WRITING AND GRAMMAR WEB SITE

The Interactive Writing and Grammar Web site provides a wide array of support for students, teachers, and parents. Writing support includes:
- Interactive revision checkers
- Scoring rubrics with compelte models

www.phschool.com

LITERATURE CONNECTIONS

Related selections from *Prentice Hall Literature: Timeless Voices, Timeless Themes,* Bronze:
"I Am a Native of North America," Chief Dan George, SE p. 127
"Icarus and Daedelus," Greek myth, SE p. 129

▶ **Lesson Objectives**

1. To write to influence, such as to persuade, argue, and request.

2. To select and use voice and style appropriate to audience and purpose.

3. To generate ideas and plans for writing by using prewriting strategies such as brainstorming, graphic organizers, notes, and logs.

4. To produce cohesive and coherent written texts by organizing ideas, using effective transitions, and choosing precise wording.

5. To revise selected drafts by adding, elaborating, deleting, combining, and rearranging text.

6. To use available technology to support aspects of creating, revising, editing, and publishing texts.

7. To proofread his/her own writing and that of others.

8. To respond in constructive ways to others' writing.

9. To analyze published examples as models for writing.

10. To select, organize, or produce visuals to complement and extend meanings.

Critical Viewing

Speculate Students may say that persuasive words are powerful and can have a strong impact on people's actions.

Chapter 7 *Persuasion*
Persuasive Essay

▲ **Critical Viewing** John F. Kennedy was famous for his use of persuasive words. Why might persuasive words like his be remembered for years after they were uttered? **[Speculate]**

Persuasion in Everyday Life

A word is more than just a sound. "Words may be deeds," said Aesop, the ancient Greek fable writer. Said at the right time, they make things happen. Your words might persuade a friend to let you borrow her bike. They might encourage family members to watch a particular television show. When you use words to influence the actions and opinions of others, you are using **persuasion**.

You can find persuasion in writing all around you—in a magazine advertisement or a newspaper editorial, in a movie review or an advice column—even on a box of cereal. By encouraging action or changing people's views, persuasive writing turns words into deeds.

124 • Persuasion

⏱ **TIME AND RESOURCE MANAGER**

Resources
Technology: Writers at Work videotape, Persuasion

In-Depth Coverage	Accelerated Pace
• Cover pp. 124–127 in class. • Show Persuasion section of the Writers at Work videotape. • Read literature excerpt (pp. 126–127) in class, and use it to brainstorm with students for persuasion ideas. • Discuss examples of persuasive writing or speeches you or students bring to class.	• Have students read pp. 124–127 on their own. • Discuss definition and types of persuasive essays in class. • Assign Model From Literature for independent reading.

What Is a Persuasive Essay?

A **persuasive essay** is a brief work in which a writer presents the case for or against a particular position. An effective persuasive essay includes

- a clear statement of the writer's position on an issue with more than one side.
- facts, examples, and other details supporting the writer's position.
- a clear organization.

To see the criteria on which your persuasive essay may be assessed, see the Rubric for Self-Assessment on page 140.

Types of Persuasive Writing

Here are a few other common types of persuasive writing:

- **Persuasive letters** are written to persuade a decision-maker to support a particular cause or measure.
- **Editorials** give and support an opinion on a current issue. They may appear in newspapers, magazines, or on television or the radio.
- **Political speeches** are delivered by a politician to win support for a policy or a position.
- **Public-service announcements** are radio or television commercials designed to persuade and educate the public.

Writers in
ACTION

American history brims with powerful persuasive speakers. William Jennings Bryan (1860–1925), a politician and fiery speechmaker, knew that persuasion combines argument and emotion:

"An orator is a man who says what he thinks and feels what he says."

PREVIEW
Student Work
IN PROGRESS

Use the sample strategies and tips in this lesson to improve your skills at writing persuasively. You'll follow the featured prewriting, drafting, and revising techniques used by Josh McWhirter, a student at College Station Junior High in College Station, Texas, to develop his persuasive essay. His final draft appears at the end of the chapter.

PREPARE and ENGAGE

Interest GRABBER Ask students to imagine that they have witnessed President Kennedy give a speech about the United States' desire to land on the moon, and that they are talking with friends afterwards. What would they say to persuade their friends of the wisdom or the folly of attempting a moon landing? Have students jot down notes for preparing their arguments.

Activate Prior Knowledge

Remind students that they most likely use persuasive tactics every day while interacting with family and friends. Invite them to share an incident in which they tried to persuade someone to do something. What arguments did they use? Were they successful or unsuccessful? How might they have been more successful?

More About the Writer

William Jennings Bryan was born in 1860 in Salem, Illinois. After receiving a degree in law, he entered a long and distinguished career in politics. He was also active as an orator, author, lecturer, publisher, and philosopher.

☑ ONGOING ASSESSMENT: Diagnose

Use one of the following options to diagnose students' current level of proficiency in persuasive writing.

Option 1 Ask each student to select the strongest example of his or her persuasive writing from last year. Review these samples to determine which students will need extra support in developing a persuasive essay.	**Option 2** Ask students to write a sentence persuading a friend to join the debating team. Then have them list three reasons or items of evidence that support that sentence. Students who have difficulty completing this exercise might need extra support in the elaboration phase of the writing process.

Reading\Writing Connection

Reading: Writer's Purpose

A writer's purpose is his or her reason for writing. This purpose often has an impact on a writer's style as well as on the content. What clues can students find to help them determine L'Amour's purposes for writing?

Teaching From the Model

After they read just three lines of the essay, have students stop and predict what the rest of it will be about. They will probably say that the author will elaborate on why space is the next frontier. Point out that the author states his position very quickly and clearly. How does this make the essay easier to read?

Step-by-Step Teaching Guide

Engage Students Through Literature

1. Read the essay aloud, or ask students to take turns reading portions of it.

2. Lead students in discussion by asking questions such as:
   - Do you agree with L'Amour's opinion about where the future lies? Why, or why not?
   - Do you think L'Amour adequately answers the question about attending to problems on Earth? Why, or why not?

3. Encourage students to brainstorm for other topics for persuasive essays. Here are some possibilities:
   - Use and conservation of natural resources
   - Advertising in schools
   - Equal access to computer technology

4. Students may add these ideas to their own banks of persuasive topics. Remind them that they are most likely to write a successful persuasive essay if they choose a topic on which they have strong opinions.

Novelist Louis L'Amour (1908–1988) set his action-packed bestsellers in the frontier days of the Old West. His fascination with the idea of the frontier also led him to write persuasively on the "New Frontier"—outer space.

Reading Writing Connection

Reading Strategy: Understand a Writer's Purpose A writer's **purpose**—to inform, to entertain, to argue for a position—affects the facts, arguments, and images he or she uses. When you read, formulate an idea of the writer's purpose. Test whether it is effectively achieved as you read. For instance, L'Amour's purpose is to encourage support for the space program. With this in mind, you can evaluate his comparison between those who oppose exploring space and babies clinging to their mothers.

The Eternal Frontier

Louis L'Amour

The question I am most often asked is, "Where is the frontier now?"

The answer should be obvious. Our frontier lies in outer space. The moon, the asteroids, the planets, these are mere stepping stones, where we will test ourselves, learn needful lessons, and grow in knowledge before we attempt those frontiers beyond our solar system. Outer space is a frontier without end, the eternal frontier, an everlasting challenge to explorers not [only] of other planets and other solar systems but also of the mind of man.

All that has gone before was preliminary. We have been preparing ourselves mentally for what lies ahead. Many problems remain, but if we can avoid a devastating war we shall move with a rapidity scarcely to be believed. In the past seventy years we have developed the automobile, radio, television, transcontinental and transoceanic flight, and the electrification of the country, among a multitude of other such developments. In 1900 there were 144 miles of surfaced road in the United States. Now there are over 3,000,000. Paved roads and the development of the automobile have gone hand in hand, the automobile being civilized man's antidote to overpopulation.

126 • Persuasive Essay

▲ **Critical Viewing**
Find a passage in the essay that captures the spirit of the photograph. **[Connect]**

The author begins with an attention-grabbing question—and a provocative answer. This answer is his thesis statement—the statement of his position.

L'Amour presents evidence in the form of facts and statistics to support his argument that we are ready for a new challenge.

Critical Viewing

Answers include: "we have a driving need to see what lies beyond" and "Mankind is not bound by [our world's] atmospheric envelope or its gravitational field, nor is the mind of man bound by any limits at all."

What is needed now is leaders with perspective; we need leadership on a thousand fronts, but they must be men and women who can take the long view and help to shape the outlines of our future. There will always be the nay-sayers, those who cling to our lovely green planet as a baby clings to its mother, but there will be others like those who have taken us this far along the path to a limitless future.

We are a people born to the frontier. It has been a part of our thinking, waking, and sleeping since men first landed on this continent. The frontier is the line that separates the known from the unknown wherever it may be, and we have a driving need to see what lies beyond. . . .

A few years ago we moved into outer space. We landed men on the moon; we sent a vehicle beyond the limits of the solar system, a vehicle still moving farther and farther into that limitless distance. If our world were to die tomorrow, that tiny vehicle would go on and on forever, carrying its mighty message to the stars. Out there, someone, sometime, would know that once we existed, that we had the vision and we made the effort. Mankind is not bound by its atmospheric envelope or by its gravitational field, nor is the mind of man bound by any limits at all.

One might ask—why outer space, when so much remains to be done here? If that had been the spirit of man we would still be hunters and food gatherers, growling over the bones of carrion in a cave somewhere. It is our destiny to move out, to accept the challenge, to dare the unknown. It is our destiny to achieve.

Yet we must not forget that along the way to outer space whole industries are springing into being that did not exist before. The computer age has arisen in part from the space effort, which gave great impetus to the development of computing devices. Transistors, chips, integrated circuits, Teflon, new medicines, new ways of treating diseases, new ways of performing operations, all these and a multitude of other developments that enable man to live and to live better are linked to the space effort. Most of these developments have been so incorporated into our day-to-day life that they are taken for granted, their origin not considered.

If we are content to live in the past, we have no future. And today is the past.

Writing Application: Help Readers Understand Your Purpose To help readers understand the purpose of your essay, begin with a statement of your issue and your position on it.

LITERATURE

To read another example of persuasive writing on a social theme, see the essay "I Am a Native of North America" by Chief Dan George in *Prentice Hall Literature: Timeless Voices, Timeless Themes,* Bronze.

With language such as "Out there, someone, sometime" and a dramatic contrast between the "tiny vehicle" and the "mighty message," L'Amour invites the reader to feel the heroic spirit of exploration.

L'Amour organizes his essay logically according to the different kinds of argument he uses. First, he makes an inspiring argument about the human spirit. Here, he adds a strong, practical argument.

He concludes with a stirring phrase summing up his main argument.

Model From Literature • 127

More About the Writer

Louis L'Amour's many jobs—longshoreman, lumberjack, elephant handler, miner, boxer—provided him with a rich well of experience on which to draw as he wrote about the Old West. The tough-but-romantic heroes of his novels had straightforward views on right and wrong as well as a respect for the natural environment. From 1953 until his death in 1988, L'Amour consistently turned out three novels a year. Each sold millions of copies.

Responding to Literature

Ask students to identify the position for which Chief Dan George argues in "I Am a Native of North America." Then, have them identify two images and one argument he uses to support his points.

Integrating Vocabulary Skills

Greek and Latin Roots Students may be interested in using a dictionary to find the derivation of these words associated with space exploration: *asteroid* (star-like), *planet* (wanderer), and *gravity* (heavy).

Customize for
Visual/Spatial Learners

Have students organize L'Amour's argument in a T-chart. On the left side, have them list his main points. On the right, have them list the evidence he uses to support each point.

Reading\Writing Connection

Writing Application: Help Readers Understand Your Purpose

Have students locate a sentence or two from L'Amour's essay that help them understand his purpose. Ask students how they might begin a persuasive essay about the importance of wearing a bicycle helmet.

Step-by-Step Teaching Guide

Prewriting: Round Table

1. You may wish to have students engage in round-table discussion in small groups. Suggest that each group choose a member to write down topics as they are suggested.

2. If many students choose the same topic, encourage them to pursue different aspects of that topic. For example:
   - Newspapers provide more accurate news than the Internet does.
   - The role of newspapers has declined in the last few years.

Step-by-Step Teaching Guide

Prewriting: Media Flip-Through

1. If students are using the media flip–through strategy, suggest that they look through several different newspapers or magazines in the library or the Internet.

2. Remind them that newspapers may cover similar stories in different ways. Reading multiple accounts of a story or issue may broaden their understanding of it.

Step-by-Step Teaching Guide

Prewriting: Quicklist

Teaching Resources: Writing Support Transparency 7-A

1. Display the transparency to show students how Josh used the quicklist to organize his ideas.

2. Ask students to share some of the topics on their quicklists. Provide time for students who choose the same topics to engage in a discussion or debate that might help them further develop their ideas.

Choosing Your Topic

To create a powerful persuasive essay, write on an issue about which you care. Use the following strategies to choose a good topic. (Remember, your issue must have more than one side.)

Strategies for Generating a Topic

1. **Round Table** With a group of classmates, hold a round-table discussion of problems in your school and community. Raise as many different issues as possible. Jot down topics on which you have strong feelings. Choose among these subjects for your essay topic.

2. **Media Flip-Through** Your city government announces a budget crisis. A slumping basketball team trades its key forward. Every day, controversies blare from newspapers and television sets. Over the course of a few days, flip through newspapers, watch TV, and listen to the radio for possible topics. Choose one that interests you.

3. **Quicklist** Fold a piece of paper lengthwise in three. In the first column, write a list of issues and ideas that interest you. In the second, write a descriptive word for each. In the third, give an example supporting that description. Review your list, and decide which topic interests you most.

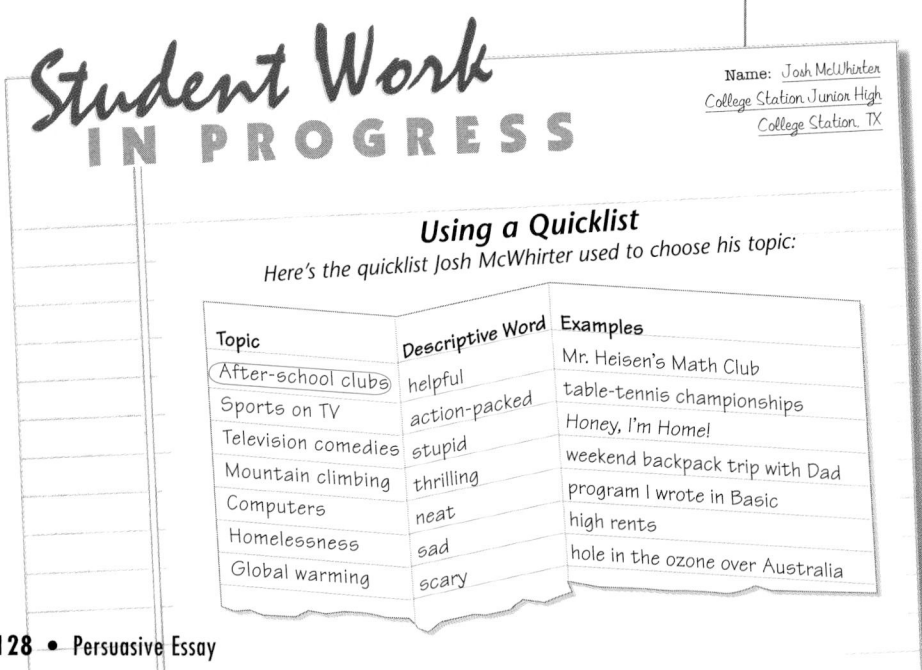

Student Work IN PROGRESS

Name: Josh McWhirter
College Station Junior High
College Station, TX

Using a Quicklist

Here's the quicklist Josh McWhirter used to choose his topic:

Topic	Descriptive Word	Examples
After-school clubs	helpful	Mr. Heisen's Math Club
Sports on TV	action-packed	table-tennis championships
Television comedies	stupid	Honey, I'm Home!
Mountain climbing	thrilling	weekend backpack trip with Dad
Computers	neat	program I wrote in Basic
Homelessness	sad	high rents
Global warming	scary	hole in the ozone over Australia

128 • Persuasive Essay

⏱ TIME AND RESOURCE MANAGER

Resources
Print: Writing Support Transparencies 7-A–D; Writing Support Activity Book 7-1–2
Technology: Writing Lab CD-ROM, Persuasion

In-Depth Coverage	Accelerated Pace
• Cover pp. 128–131 in class. • Guide students through the strategies for generating topics. • Have students use the "funneling" method for narrowing their topics. • Have students complete their "funnels" and begin to gather evidence. **Option** Students having difficulties may adopt topics from the Topic Bank.	• In class, discuss how to choose a good topic for a persuasive essay. • Invite students to list possible topics. • Ask students to submit proposed topics for your review.

TOPIC BANK

If you're having trouble finding a topic, consider these possibilities:

1. **Editorial on School Issues** Choose an issue in your school, such as lunch quality or prices, class schedules, or transportation. Argue for the current policy or for a better one.

2. **Persuasive Essay on Kindness to Animals** Some argue that the laws protecting animals from unkind treatment should be expanded. Do research on the issue, and write an essay for or against new laws to protect animals.

Responding to Fine Art

3. Take notes on this painting to determine its mood—whether it captures the festive bustle of business or the confusing clamor of sales hype. Review your notes, and reflect on the advertisements that surround us. Should such advertising be reduced? Write a persuasive essay defending your views.

Responding to Literature

4. Read the Greek myth "Icarus and Daedalus." In the role of lawyer, write a statement either condemning or defending Daedalus for his role in Icarus' fall. You can find "Icarus and Daedalus" in *Prentice Hall Literature: Timeless Voices, Timeless Themes*, Bronze.

August Bargain Days, John Ward Lockwood, Collection of The McNay Art Museum

☑ Cooperative Writing Opportunity

5. **Radio Documentary on Required Courses** In a group, investigate which classes are required in your school and which are not. Divide the following tasks: analyzing the benefits and drawbacks of not requiring music, art, or drama courses; analyzing the benefits and drawbacks of requiring math, science, and foreign languages; and so on. Group members should each draft a section of the documentary. Tape the documentary, and play it for the class.

Prewriting • 129

Responding to Fine Art

August Bargain Days by John Ward Lockwood
Teaching Resources: Writing Support Transparency 7-B

1. Display the transparency and engage students in a discussion about it. The following questions may be used to prompt discussion:
   - What persuasive word is emphasized in the painting? How are the people in the painting responding to this persuasion? What other words might the store owners have posted to persuade customers to enter the store?

2. Encourage students to brainstorm topics that the art brings to their minds. Here are some possibilities:
   - Advertising strategies
   - Shopping as a pastime
   - Overconsumption of goods

3. Students may include these topics in their data banks and add ideas of their own.

Responding to Literature

Icarus, son of Daedalus, perished when he flew too near the sun while wearing the feather-and-wax wings constructed by his father. Students might read the myth and then write a persuasive essay on whether or not Daedalus should have trusted the boy to follow his instructions.

Spotlight on Humanities

For additional topic suggestions, refer students to the Spotlight on Humanities on page 146.

☑ ONGOING ASSESSMENT: Monitor and Reinforce

Students may need to review the elements of a good topic for a persuasive essay. Use the following strategy to help them remember three important characteristics of a good topic.

Encourage students to imagine that they are asking for something they want or need, such as a computer game or a musical instrument. Students will realize that such a request contains many of the elements of a good topic for a persuasive essay:

1. The subject is likely to be of high interest to both the speaker and the listener.

2. There are two distinct sides to the request. The speaker must anticipate possible objections and address them.

3. Facts must be gathered and presented logically for the best result.

 **Writing Support Transparencies**
Use the transparencies for Chapter 7 to teach these strategies.

Step-by-Step Teaching Guide

Prewriting: "Funnel" Your Topic

Teaching Resources: Writing Support Transparency 7-C; Writing Support Activity Book 7-1

1. Draw students' attention to the graphic organizer. Ask a volunteer to explain the function of a funnel. (to catch and direct a downward flow; for example, funneling water into a car's radiator)

2. Work through the steps of "funneling" with students, emphasizing how the topic progresses from broad to narrow.

3. Ask volunteers to share their topics. You and the class can help each volunteer determine whether his or her proposed topic is narrow enough. If proposed topics are too broad, use the "funneling" process to narrow them.

4. Remind students that keeping audience and purpose in mind will help to narrow the topic.

Step-by-Step Teaching Guide

Prewriting: Considering Your Audience and Purpose

Encourage students to think about their intended audience. This will help them as they determine what kind of information to include in their essays and how they will convince these intended readers.

Narrowing Your Topic

Once you've chosen an issue, narrow your focus. For example, the topic "violence in the media" includes violence on news reports, in movies, on TV, and so on. To write an effective essay, you might focus on violence in television shows.

One strategy for narrowing your topic is the "funnel."

"Funnel" Your Topic

Here's how to "funnel" your topic. First, draw a funnel shape, as shown below. Then,
1. Write your general topic above the funnel mouth.
2. Off to the side, divide your topic into parts.
3. Select one part to focus on. Write it on the first line.
4. Note causes and effects connected with this subtopic.
5. Describe one cause or effect on the second line.
6. Formulate a narrowed topic based on the previous entries.

TOPIC FUNNEL

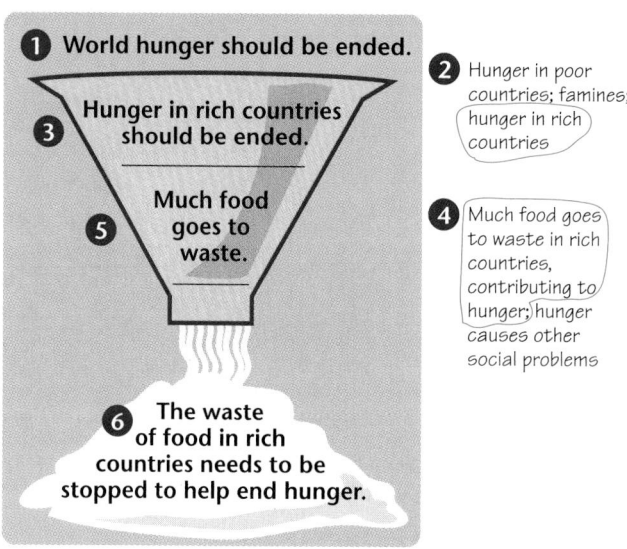

Considering Your Audience and Purpose

Your purpose in writing a persuasive essay is to convince readers. Knowing your audience will help achieve this purpose. As you gather details and draft, keep the following questions in mind: What will your readers think is important? To what kind of reasoning and language will your readers respond?

⏱ TIME SAVERS!

 Writing Support Transparencies
Use the transparencies for Chapter 7 to teach these strategies.

 Writing Support Activity Book
Use the graphic organizers for Chapter 7 to facilitate these strategies.

Gathering Evidence

Provide Support

To persuade readers, you must provide support for your position. Types of support include the following:

- **Logical arguments:** *The town needs money. A skating rink will bring in money. Therefore, we should build a rink.*
- **Statistics:** *Eighty percent of the voters support a rink.*
- **Expert opinions:** *Professor Irving Hud argues that public recreational facilities will improve business in our town.*
- **Personal observations:** *Every day, I see kids hanging out with nothing to do. A skating rink will give them an outlet.*
- **Charged language and striking images:** *Our "sleepy little town" is starting to wake up. We can turn over and go back to sleep—or we can get up and do what needs doing.*

Do research on your topic, and complete a T-chart to gather support for your position.

Completing a T-Chart Write your topic at the top of a sheet of paper. Fold the paper in half to create two columns. At the top of the first column, write "Pro," and jot down support for your position. At the top of the second column, write "Con," and jot down any evidence that might be used to argue against your idea.

Writing Lab CD-ROM

For more on gathering evidence, use the activities and suggestions in the Gathering Evidence section of the Persuasion lesson.

Research Tip

To gather more evidence, ask your librarian for help using indexes to magazines and newspapers. Use these sources to find facts or statistics that will convince your reader.

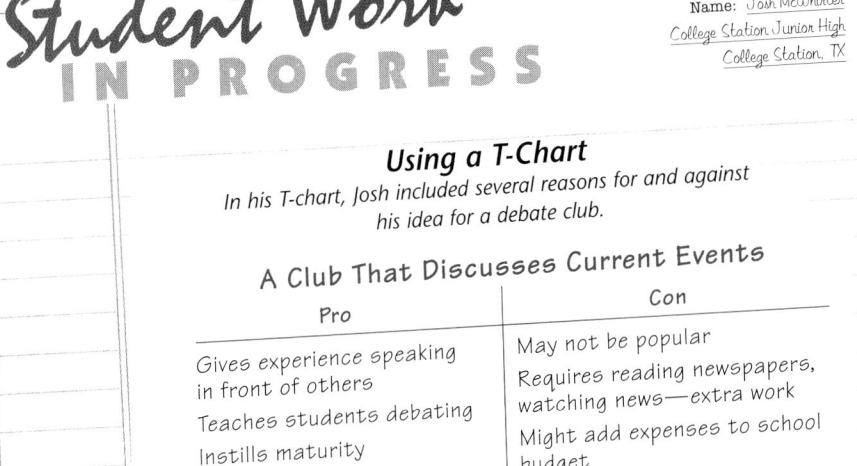

Student Work
IN PROGRESS

Name: Josh McWhirter
College Station Junior High
College Station, TX

Using a T-Chart

In his T-chart, Josh included several reasons for and against his idea for a debate club.

A Club That Discusses Current Events

Pro	Con
Gives experience speaking in front of others	May not be popular
Teaches students debating	Requires reading newspapers, watching news—extra work
Instills maturity	Might add expenses to school budget
Helps teach current events	

Prewriting • 131

Step-by-Step Teaching Guide

Prewriting: Using a T-Chart to Gather Evidence

Teaching Resources: Writing Support Transparency 7-D; Writing Support Activity Book 7-2

1. Encourage students to give other examples for each of the types of support. You might also ask them to identify the type of support illustrated in each of these sentences from a persuasive essay on the topic of teaching children to read in kindergarten:

   - I've seen my five-year-old sister trying to read (personal observation)
   - Almost 75% of five-year-olds . . . (statistics)
   - A study at Iowa State University shows that . . . (expert opinion)
   - Kindergartners are eager to read, and eager students learn more quickly. (logical)
   - Children who cannot read will soon lose their way on the road to education. (charged language and striking images)

2. Tell students that using a T-chart is another way to gather evidence. A T-chart that lists the arguments for and against the subject of a persuasive essay can help the writer present a more thorough case.

3. Display the transparency. Have students fill out the T-chart for their persuasive essay topics.

4. Point out to students that the title at the top of a T-chart can be the start of a position statement, or thesis statement.

Integrating Workplace Skills

Tell students that many professions require the ability to speak and write persuasively. Discuss with them when people in each of these fields might need persuasive skills: law, medicine, teaching, sales, and architecture. Students may suggest other professions as well.

131

Drafting: Organize to Emphasize

Teaching Resources: Writing Support Transparency 7-E

1. Help students develop the title of their T-chart into a thesis statement.

2. Suggest that students organize the points of evidence from their T-charts into statements for and against their thesis statement.

3. Display the transparency. Help students determine the strength of their arguments and organize them appropriately on the chart. Have them work with a partner to determine which points help support their arguments and which make their arguments less persuasive.

Critical Viewing

Analyze Students may answer that a lawyer tries to keep the interest and attention of a jury by using the techniques of a storyteller. Like a story, or even like a song, a lawyer's words may start off slowly and accelerate, sweeping the jury along, and building interest and suspense until the conclusion.

Real-World Connection

Explain to students that many writers and speakers follow this pattern in a presentation: First, tell the audience what you will present (the introduction). Then, present the information (the body of the article or speech). Finally, tell the audience what you have presented (the conclusion). Ask students why this pattern is often an effective one.

7.3 Drafting

Shaping Your Writing

Develop a Thesis Statement

The evidence you have gathered will support your position. To keep your position clearly before your readers, review your notes and develop a thesis statement—one clear sentence that sums up your argument. Include this statement in your introduction.

Organize to Emphasize

The ideas in a persuasive essay are like notes in a piece of music. Properly organized, they will build to a stirring climax.

To create a rhythm in your paper, identify the strongest point on your T-chart. Also, note the strongest arguments against your position. Then, consider using the following organization:

CREATING A RHYTHM FOR YOUR ARGUMENTS

I. Introduction
- Open with a striking image or other attention grabber.
- Present your thesis statement.

II. First Set of Arguments
- Begin to win your reader over by presenting most of your arguments.

III. Acknowledging the Opposition
- Present the strong arguments against your position.
- Refute these arguments. Show that they are illogical or misstate facts, or that your ideas outweigh them.

IV. Strongest Argument
- Introduce the strongest argument for your position. You might note that even if your other arguments were bad, this argument alone would prove your case.
- Present your strongest argument.

V. Conclusion
- Summarize your arguments.
- Restate your thesis.
- Close with a memorable image, brief story, or phrase.

132 • Persuasive Essay

▲ **Critical Viewing**
Why is it important for a lawyer, such as the one in the photograph, to create a rhythm in his or her arguments before a jury? **[Analyze]**

⏱ TIME SAVERS!

📄 **Writing Support Transparencies**
Use the transparencies for Chapter 7 to teach these strategies.

⏱ TIME AND RESOURCE MANAGER

Resources
Print: Writing Support Transparencies 7-E–F
Technology: Writing Lab CD-ROM, Persuasion

In-Depth Coverage	Accelerated Pace
• Cover pp. 132–133 in class. • Discuss the purpose and development of thesis statements with students. • Help students layer their ideas in paragraphs.	• Ask students to submit their layered paragraphs for peer editing or for your review.

Providing Elaboration

Like a piece of music, a persuasive essay has a rhythm. If you make a point without providing support, though, it is as though you missed a beat. Supporting details include logical arguments, statistics, stories from personal experience, colorful images, and charged words and phrases.

As you draft, use the SEE technique to keep the beat and supply supporting details.

Layer Ideas Using SEE

To layer a paragraph, begin with the main idea. Then, create layer after layer to elaborate that idea. Follow these steps:

State the main idea for the paragraph.

Extend the idea. You might give your opinion on the idea, restate it with a new emphasis, or apply it to an example.

Elaborate on the idea in one or more sentences. Provide support for the idea or your view of it, referring to your T-chart.

Drafting: Layer Ideas Using SEE

Teaching Resources: Writing Support Transparency 7-F

1. Display the transparency. With students, work through the steps Josh took in layering his paragraph.

2. Discuss how to extend an idea. Present this idea to students: Most schools have several extracurricular activities. Ask them to give examples and opinions to extend the idea.

3. Discuss how to elaborate on an idea. Present this idea to students: It's important for students to feel connected to their school. Ask them to suggest ideas that support that statement and help answer the question *Why?*

4. You may choose to write students' answers on the Layering Chart Transparency.

Student Work IN PROGRESS

Name: Josh McWhirter
College Station Junior High
College Station, TX

Layering Ideas

Josh wrote his essay on a debate club he called the "DCE." He elaborated on the main idea of the paragraph below by providing supporting details.

Statement: Finally, the DCE program will help students get over the fear of expressing their ideas aloud. **Extension:** Students need to find ways to conquer this fear. **Elaboration:** In classes, when I'm being graded, I often find myself shaking with fear. I also find that I can't think clearly about whatever subject I'm presenting. The best part about the DCE program is that it gives the student a chance to think about a subject and then discuss it in a nonpressured environment.

> Josh states the main idea of his paragraph in the first sentence.

> Josh's extension of his main idea emphasizes one aspect of it—students need help getting over their fear.

> The support Josh provides includes: a reference to his personal experience ("I often find myself shaking with fear"); a logical argument (speaking in a setting without pressure will help students gain poise speaking before others); and instances of vivid or charged language ("shaking with fear").

Drafting • 133

☑ ONGOING ASSESSMENT: Monitor and Reinforce

If you observe that students are having difficulty elaborating on their ideas, try the following strategy:

Have students list their main ideas. Then, have each read in turn a main idea along with a supporting detail. Invite suggestions from the rest of the class for other supporting details. Have the class also ask questions about the idea to elicit further support.

Revising: Analyze the Organization

1. Tell students that a persuasive argument needs to be well organized in order for it to be effective. Otherwise, readers will have trouble following the argument and are less likely to be convinced by it.

2. Have a volunteer read aloud the information in the chart.

3. Have students review their own work and apply the highlighting strategy. Tell them to look out for similar points that can be grouped together, rather than handled separately. Then have them go over their points one more time to make sure that there is a logical flow from one point to the next.

Integrating Speaking and Listening Skills

Suggest that students read aloud to a friend the drafts of their persuasive essays. Encourage them to solicit the friend's suggestions about organization.

7.4 Revising

Once you've written your first draft, look for ways to make it better. Start by reviewing the overall structure of your essay and paragraphs.

Revising Your Overall Structure

Analyze the Organization

As you reread your draft, look at the arrangement of your main points. Is it logical? Is it effective? Do your main points build toward a climax, with your strongest point last? Each point in your essay is like a rung in a ladder leading readers to your viewpoint—each must be in the proper position. To check your organization, highlight your main points.

▶ **REVISION STRATEGY**
Highlighting Main Points

Highlight the main points you have used to convince your readers. Then, number each in order. Next, look at the connections between your main points. For instance, will readers understand main point 3 if you haven't explained main point 4? If not, you should probably move point 4 before point 3. Write down any changes you need to make to the order of your points in the margin of your draft. Refer to this chart for more ideas about how points might connect.

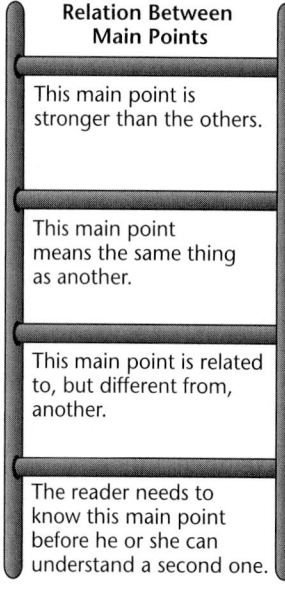
Relation Between Main Points

This main point is stronger than the others.

This main point means the same thing as another.

This main point is related to, but different from, another.

The reader needs to know this main point before he or she can understand a second one.

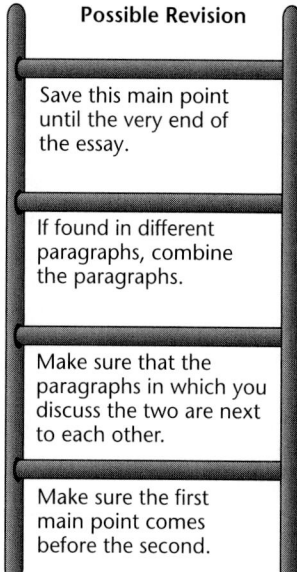
Possible Revision

Save this main point until the very end of the essay.

If found in different paragraphs, combine the paragraphs.

Make sure that the paragraphs in which you discuss the two are next to each other.

Make sure the first main point comes before the second.

134 • Persuasive Essay

⏱ TIME AND RESOURCE MANAGER

Resources
Print: Writing Support Transparencies 7-G–I
Technology: Writing Lab CD-ROM, Persuasion

In-Depth Coverage	Accelerated Pace
• Cover pages 134–138 in class. • Discuss the revision process with students and review the idea that a persuasive essay's main points need support. • Encourage students to anticipate reader response to their arguments, and to order their rebuttals accordingly. • Help students identify the points in their essays that need strengthening.	• Have students brainstorm for possible reader criticism of their essays. • Encourage students to work independently to revise their essays.

Check Support

Now that you've located your main points, make sure that they are well supported with evidence.

▶ REVISION STRATEGY
Coding for Supporting Evidence

Review each highlighted main point. Mark places where you might add supporting evidence using the following symbols:

▲ Specific example   ■ Expert opinion   ✳ Striking image

● Logical argument   ▼ Personal observation

▬ Measurable fact   ★ Charged language

Review your prewriting notes to find the supporting facts and other details you need to add.

Revising: Coding for Supporting Evidence

Teaching Resources: Writing Support Transparency 7-G

1. Display the transparency. Ask them to identify the changes Josh made. Do these changes make Josh's argument more persuasive?

2. As students review their work, they should code the evidence for each of their main points. Then they can go back and focus their attention on the weak or absent evidence.

3. Remind students that it is not a bad idea to eliminate any points in their arguments that are not well supported. It is better to omit the idea than to have a weak link in one's argument.

Student Work
IN PROGRESS

Name: Josh McWhirter
College Station Junior High
College Station, TX

Coding for Supporting Evidence
Though Josh noted that he had strong support for the main idea of this paragraph, he found two places where he could add more. He added a specific example and a logical argument.

First of all, the program will teach students the art of debating. Adults and students should know how debating works. Important groups of people use debating to make decisions that affect you and me and everybody else.∧

▲ Let's say that someone has written a law to decrease the minimum driving age. Most likely, this law will never make it past the Senate, but it is still important to know that someone has written and proposed this law. And it's important for students to know how to debate and discuss this proposed law.

> To keep his reader's attention, Josh added an example of "decisions that affect you and me."

The DCE will teach students how to engage in a good argument, rather than a fight. They'll learn that they cannot debate current events by saying, "I think that's bad," or by engaging in unpleasant argument.∧

●
★ By teaching students to listen to each other and to respond to disagreements with reasoned arguments, debating will teach maturity.

> Josh added a logical argument supporting the idea that learning to debate is good. He also used the charged, positive word *maturity.*

Revising • 135

Step-by-Step Teaching Guide

Revising: Color-Coding the Connections

Teaching Resources: Writing Support Transparency 7-H

1. Remind students that in order to persuade readers, their paragraphs must logically follow one another. If a paragraph interrupts flow of their writing, the persuasiveness of their arguments may suffer.
2. Display the transparency. Ask students how Josh's revision strengthens the persuasiveness of his argument.
3. Suggest that students locate phrases in their paragraphs that signal a shift from one part of the topic to another. Examples might include *on the other hand, however, secondly.*
4. Encourage them to add transition words to the beginning of their paragraphs, if needed. This will help create smoother transitions between ideas.

Integrating Speaking and Listening Skills

By listening to politicians and other public speakers, students can note how these professionals connect ideas to create unity in their speeches. Encourage them to jot down transition words and phrases they hear.

TIME SAVERS!

Writing Support Transparencies
Use the transparencies for Chapter 7 to teach these strategies.

7.4

Revising Your Paragraphs

Check Unity

Check the flow of your writing. The space between paragraphs is like a curve in a road. Readers need a sign showing which way the argument is turning. If the turn is not marked, the readers may go off the road! Code the connections between paragraphs. Then, mark turns by adding transitions.

REVISION STRATEGY
Color-Coding the Connections

Highlight the sentence that expresses the main idea of each paragraph. In the margin, code the connection between each idea and the one before it, referring to the chart below. Then, add transitional words or sentences to signal the turns.

Code	Connection	Transition Words
A	**Adds** to, or elaborates on, the previous main idea	*for example, in one case, furthermore*
C	Offers a **contrast**, objection, exception	*in contrast, however*
N	Introduces a **new** idea	*in addition, finally, first (second, third), in the first place*
S	**Sums** up previous ideas	*in conclusion*

Student Work IN PROGRESS

Name: Josh McWhirter
College Station Junior High
College Station, TX

Coding Connections Between Paragraphs

Josh discovered that this paragraph offered an objection to the position he defended in the previous paragraph. He added a needed transition.

C ~~Afterschool~~ It's true that after-school programs can be difficult to set up and keep going. Even if a club is popular at the beginning, students can lose interest. . . .

Revising Your Sentences

Combine Sentences to Show Connections

A persuasive argument is composed of connected ideas. By combining sentences, you can show these connections clearly.

▶ **REVISION STRATEGY**
Color-Coding Sentences That Express Related Ideas

Reread each paragraph, looking for sentences that express ideas that add to each other. For instance, two sentences that support the same idea add to each other. Underline these sentences in blue. Underline in red any pairs of sentences that express opposing ideas. For instance, one sentence might give an objection to the other. Then, consider combining sentences underlined in the same color.

IDEAS THAT ADD TOGETHER:	The town already permits skating on the lake. We don't have the money to open a rink.
COMBINED:	The town already permits skating on the lake, **and** we don't have the money to open a rink.
OPPOSING IDEAS:	The town won't permit skating on the lake. We don't have the money to open a rink.
COMBINED:	The town won't permit skating on the lake, **but** we don't have the money to open a rink.

Grammar in Your Writing
Compound Sentences

To join two thoughts, you can create a **compound sentence**—a sentence containing two or more independent clauses.

An **independent clause** is a clause that can stand on its own as a complete sentence. Two independent clauses may be joined in a single sentence with a semicolon or with a comma followed by a coordinating conjunction: *and, but, or, for, so,* or *yet.*

┌──── independent clause ────┐ ┌──── independent clause ────┐
A skating rink is a good idea; we should open one now.

┌──── independent clause ────┐ ┌──── independent clause ────┐
A skating rink is a good idea, **yet** no one will vote to pay for one.

Find It in Your Reading Find a compound sentence in "The Eternal Frontier" by Louis L'Amour on page 126. Identify each independent clause.

Find It in Your Writing Circle three compound sentences in your draft. If you cannot find any, consider combining sentences.

For more on compound sentences, see Chapter 20.

Combine Sentences to Show Connections

1. Have a volunteer read aloud the example sentences.
2. Ask students how the ideas in the first sentence are connected and how the ideas in the second are opposed.

Step-by-Step Teaching Guide

Grammar in Your Writing

1. You may wish to remind students that a sentence must contain a subject and a verb.
2. Point out that a persuasive essay or any other kind of writing may be clearer when related ideas are combined into compound sentences. As an example, write these sentences on the board:

   The architect designed a new cafeteria. It didn't look big enough on the plans.

   The architect designed a new cafeteria, but it didn't look big enough on the plans.

3. Tell students that combining the sentences into a compound sentence with a coordinating conjunction makes clearer the relationship between the two sentences.

Find It in Your Reading

[independent clause:] We landed men on the moon; [independent clause:] we sent a vehicle beyond the limits of the solar system, a vehicle still moving farther and farther into that limitless distance.

Find It in Your Writing

You may want to have students exchange drafts to check each other's work.

☑ ONGOING ASSESSMENT: Prerequisite Skills

If students have difficulty with compound sentences, refer them to the following to assure coverage of prerequisite skills.

In the Textbook	Print	Technology
Effective Sentences, pp. 465–468	Grammar Exercise Workbook, pp. 93–94	Language Lab CD-ROM, Problems With Sentences; On-Line Exercise Bank, Section 21.3

Revising: Tagging Vague Words; Peer Review

Teaching Resources: Writing Support Transparency 7-I

1. Read the following movie review to students and ask them whether they would see it or avoid it:

   The movie was fine, had good actors, and had an interesting plot. The scenery was nice, too.

2. Point out that words such as *fine, good, interesting,* and *nice* are vague words that convey little information.

3. Display the transparency. Ask students what other precise words Josh might have chosen.

4. Have students reread the drafts of their persuasive essays and look for vague words that do not help persuade the reader. In addition to tagging, they can circle these words and then replace them with more vivid, persuasive language.

5. Remind students who are reviewing a classmate's work to offer concrete suggestions for revision. For instance, a comment such as "A more specific word than *pretty* would clarify your meaning. What do you mean by *pretty*?" might be helpful.

Customize for
ESL Students

ESL students may benefit from additional suggestions for precise words. Explain how to use a thesaurus to find words to substitute for vague words such as *good, bad, right,* and *wrong.*

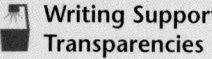

7.4

Revising Your Word Choice

Use Persuasive Language

When you write to persuade, use precise words and phrases to point the readers in a clear direction. For instance, when you describe a "good" candidate, you may actually mean a *trustworthy, intelligent,* or *issue-oriented* one. A "bad" plan may be *poorly thought out, unfair,* or *unworkable.*

▶ REVISION STRATEGY
Tagging Vague Words

Use sticky notes to mark places in which you use general evaluative words like *good, bad, right,* and *wrong.* Ask, "Good or bad in what way?" to find more precise words.

Technology Tip

Use the thesaurus feature in your word-processing program to find specific alternatives to general words. (Always check the meaning of a new word in a dictionary before using it.)

Student Work
IN PROGRESS

Name: Josh McWhirter
College Station Junior High
College Station, TX

Tagging Vague Words

In an analytic talk session, Josh's peer reviewers noted a few places in which Josh used vague words. Josh made improvements based on their comments.

The DCE will teach students how to engage
in a ~~good~~ argument rather than a fight.
        civilized

good
In what way?
– peaceful
– civilized

They'll learn that they cannot debate current

events by saying, "I think that idea is bad," or
                      aggressive and rude
by engaging in ~~unpleasant~~ argument.

unpleasant
In what way?
– rude
– aggressive
– dangerous

Peer Review

Analytic Talk

Read your revised draft twice to a small group of peers. Before the second reading, ask listeners to jot down words or phrases to help them comment on some part of your draft. Listeners should use these questions as a guide:

1. Was the opening clear and interesting?
2. Did I get lost during the reading? If so, where?
3. What did I find most convincing? Least convincing?

138 • Persuasive Essay

Combining Sentences to Show Connections
Many standardized tests require students to revise sentences for clarity and sense. Use the following sample test item to give students practice in this skill.

Read the two sentences below. Then decide which compound sentence correctly connects those sentences.

Students need to develop debating skills.

A debating club will help them.

A Students need to develop debating skills, and a debating club will help them.

B Students need to develop debating skills, but a debating club will help them.

C Students need to develop debating skills, or a debating club will help them.

D None of the above

Item **A** is the correct choice. Because the two ideas build on one another, they are correctly joined with *and.*

7.5 Editing and Proofreading

You want your essay to persuade readers that your position is correct—not that your spelling needs improvement. Review your draft closely for errors in spelling, punctuation, grammar, and usage.

Focusing on End Marks

Persuasive writers use sentences to make statements, to ask questions, and to exclaim in the heat of an argument. Make sure that you use the correct end mark for each kind of sentence.

Language Lab CD-ROM

For more practice with punctuation, complete the unit on Punctuation.

Grammar in Your Writing
End Marks

Sentences must be concluded with one of three **end marks:** the period (.), the question mark (?), or the exclamation mark (!).

- Use a **period** to indicate the end of a statement or a directive.

  Statement of fact Newspapers contain facts about current events.
  Directive Next, watch as many news programs as you can.

- Use a **question mark** to indicate the end of a direct question.

  Direct question Why shouldn't students learn in a relaxed setting?

- Use an **exclamation mark** to indicate strong feeling or urgency.

  Sentence with strong feeling There are only three days left!

  Urgent directive Give us a chance!

Find It in Your Reading Find two question marks in "The Eternal Frontier" by Louis L 'Amour on page 126, and explain why the author uses them. Find a sentence for which an exclamation mark might be appropriate. Explain your choice.

Find It in Your Writing Read your draft aloud with expression. If your voice rises at the end of a sentence, check whether you need a question mark. If you emphasize a phrase, think about using an exclamation mark.

For more on end marks, see Chapter 26.

Editing and Proofreading • 139

Step-by-Step Teaching Guide

Editing and Proofreading: End Marks

1. You may wish to provide in-class access to such reference books as *The Chicago Manual of Style.*

2. Explain to students that it is often difficult to note typographical errors in their own writing, because they will tend to see what they meant to write. Encourage them to trade essays with a partner for proofreading.

3. Students also can put their work aside for a while and then return to it later. They will find it easier to notice mistakes and errors with a fresh pair of eyes.

Step-by-Step Teaching Guide

Grammar in Your Writing

1. Tell students that reading their essays aloud to themselves with expression will help them determine whether they have used the correct punctuation at the end of sentences.

2. Remind students to use exclamation marks sparingly. An essay riddled with exclamation marks can defeat the purpose of emphasizing the most-important points.

Find It in Your Reading

Louis L'Amour uses question marks in the first and seventh paragraph to spark questions in readers' minds and to introduce his own answers to those questions. One place L'Amour might have used an exclamation mark to indicate his strong feelings is after the next-to-last sentence .

Find It in Your Writing

Have students meet with partners and read each other's draft aloud, listening closely to the reader's tone. If it does not change to reflect the more dramatic sentences, these sentences may need to be punctuated differently or even rewritten.

Customize for
Bodily/Kinesthetic Learners

Suggest that students create movements to represent end punctuation marks.

⏱ TIME AND RESOURCE MANAGER

Resources
Print: Scoring Rubrics on Transparency, Chapter 7; Formal Assessment, Ch. 7
Technology: Writing Lab CD-ROM, Persuasion

In-Depth Coverage	Accelerated Pace
• Cover page 139–143 in class. • Review the Rubric for Self Assessment on page 140. • Have students edit and proofread their essays in class. **Option** Students can work on their own with the editing and evaluation sections of the Writing Lab CD-ROM.	• Assign pages 139–143 for students to review independently. • Have students independently edit and proofread their essays. • Respond to students' individual editing issues.

Publishing and Presenting

1. Ask students to remember the audience they wish to reach. Encourage them to explore ways to reach their intended readers. For example, a local newspaper, community newsletter, or school publication may be good vehicles.

2. Remind students that most community action involves persuasive writing. Fund-raising for charities, campaigning for votes, and petitioning authorities for changes all rely on persuasive writing. Students can find examples in direct-mail appeals, flyers, letters to the editors of publications, and opinion columns.

ASSESS

Assessment

Teaching Resources: Scoring Rubrics on Transparency 7; Formal Assessment, Chapter 7

1. Display the Scoring Rubric transparency and review the criteria in class.

2. Before students proceed with self-assessment, you may wish to review the Final Draft of the Student Work in Progress on pages 141–143. Have students score the Final Draft in one or more of the rubric categories. For example, how would students score the essay in terms of audience and purpose?

3. In addition to student self-assessment, you may wish to use the following assessment options:

   • Score student essays yourself, using the rubric and scoring models from Writing Assessment and Portfolio Management.

   • Review the Standardized Test Preparation Workshop on pages 148–149 and have students respond to a persuasive writing prompt within a time limit.

   • Administer the Chapter 7 Test from Formal Assessment in Teaching Resources to assess students' grasp of concepts presented.

7.6 Publishing and Presenting

Building Your Portfolio

Give your persuasive essay a chance to change someone's mind—publish or present it! Consider these suggestions:

1. **Send a Letter** If you have written about a local problem, such as a dangerous traffic intersection, find a person or agency with authority over the situation. Then, send that authority your persuasive essay with a cover letter. Share your essay and any response with the class.

2. **Create a List-Serve** Encourage the exchange of ideas by making a list-serve, or discussion space, on the Internet or school server. Ask a teacher or administrator to help sponsor the list-serve. Post your essay, inviting responses.

Reflecting on Your Writing

Write out some of your thoughts about your experience writing a persuasive essay. Start off by answering these questions:

• What did you learn about your subject as you wrote?

• What part of the writing process seemed hardest for you?

Consider including this reflection in your portfolio.

Internet Tip

To review persuasive essays scored according to this rubric, visit www.phschool.com

Rubric for Self-Assessment

Evaluate your persuasive essay using the following criteria:

	Score 4	Score 3	Score 2	Score 1
Audience and Purpose	Provides arguments, illustrations, and words that forcefully appeal to the audience and effectively serve persuasive purpose	Provides arguments, illustrations, and words that appeal to the audience and serve the persuasive purpose	Provides some support that appeals to the audience and serves the persuasive purpose	Shows little attention to the audience or persuasive purpose
Organization	Uses clear, consistent organizational strategy	Uses clear organizational strategy with occasional inconsistencies	Uses inconsistent organizational strategy	Shows lack of organizational strategy; writing is confusing
Elaboration	Provides specific, well-elaborated support for the writer's position	Provides some elaborated support for the writer's position	Provides some support, but with little elaboration	Lacks support
Use of Language	Uses transitions to connect ideas smoothly; shows few mechanical errors	Uses some transitions; shows few mechanical errors	Uses few transitions; shows some mechanical errors	Shows little connection between ideas; shows many mechanical errors

140 • Persuasive Essay

✓ ONGOING ASSESSMENT: Assess Mastery

Use one of the following options to assess students' final drafts.

Self-Assessment Ask students to score their essay using the rubric provided.	**Teacher Assessment** Use the rubric and scoring models provided in Writing Assessment, Persuasive Essay to score students' work.

7.7 *Student Work* IN PROGRESS

FINAL DRAFT

◀ Critical Viewing
How might Josh caption this photograph to use it as supporting evidence for his position? [Apply]

Learning to Speak Up: the DCE

Josh McWhirter
College Station Junior High
College Station, Texas

To start people talking, all it takes is the right question: Is it right for the United States to intervene in foreign conflicts? What is the role of government in education? Questions like these can set off endless controversy. They can also lead to real-life decisions that affect all of us. Discussing and debating are two very important activities in the United States and in the world. The Senate discusses and debates. The United Nations discusses and

This opening hooks readers with questions. It introduces the main topic and leads into the thesis statement.

Step-by-Step Teaching Guide

Teaching From the Final Draft

1. Explain to students how Josh has layered ideas in his persuasive essay by stating main ideas, extending the ideas, and then elaborating on the ideas. Ask them to cite examples of this in his essay.

2. Have students make a list of Josh's main points. Discuss why he presented them in the order he did.

3. Make sure students notice that Josh's persuasive essay closes on a positive note by mentioning some traits that schools want to promote in students: social skills, patience, maturity, and intelligence. Have them check their own essays to ensure they too have provided a strong closing.

Critical Viewing

Apply Students may suggest something like this: "Members of the DCE Club enjoy a lively discussion and debate of current events."

141

◄ **Critical Viewing**
Which of Josh's argu-
ments does this pho-
tograph illustrate?
[Analyze]

debates. Even families discuss and debate current events at the
dinner table.

Realizing the importance of discussion and debate, I have come
up with a great idea for an after-school program. I call it "DCE,"
or "Discussion of Current Events." Students will come after school
to a room with a circular table, so everybody can see one another.
As soon as students are ready and seated, the teacher running
the program will select a student to bring up a current event.
Each student will have a chance to express his or her views on
the subject. I think this program would be great for the school
and the students alike for several important reasons.

First of all, the program will teach students the art of debating.
Adults and students should know how debating works. Important
groups of people use debating to make decisions that affect you
and me and everybody else. Let's say that someone has written a
law to decrease the minimum driving age. Most likely, this law
will never make it past the Senate, but it is still important to
know that someone has written and proposed this law. And it's
important for students to know how to debate and discuss this
proposed law. The DCE will teach students how to engage in a
civilized argument, rather than a fight. They'll learn that they cannot debate current events by saying, "I think that's bad," or by
engaging in aggressive and rude argument. By teaching students
to listen to each other and to respond to disagreements with reasoned arguments, debating will teach maturity.

Second, the DCE will make students more aware of current
events. The program is based on discussing anything and everything in the news. Because students will have to know about current events, they will start reading newspapers and watching tele-

*The second para-
graph begins with
Josh's thesis
statement.*

*To support his argu-
ment, Josh presents
the first of three
main points.*

*Using the charged
words* civilized, *on
the one hand, and*
aggressive *and* rude,
*on the other, Josh
sets up a persuasive
contrast.*

*Josh uses a transi-
tion word,* second, *to
signal his turn to a
new argument.*

Critical Viewing

Apply Students may say that law-making bodies often argue a great deal over important issues. Good debating skills can help a law-maker persuade others to share his or her point of view.

vision news or listening to the radio to find out what's going on. Newspapers and television or radio news are great sources for current events in this country and around the world. In the DCE program, students will also learn about current events from other students. Remember, the biggest influence on the government is the people, and people must be informed.

Finally, the DCE program will help students get over the fear of expressing their ideas aloud. Students need to find ways to conquer this fear. In classes, when I'm being graded, I often find myself shaking with fear. I also find that I can't think clearly about whatever subject I'm presenting. The best part about the DCE program is that it gives the student a chance to think about a subject and then discuss it in a nonpressured environment. The student can express an opinion to a group of people that really care and really listen. This can be very good for a student's morale, especially for a shy student who has trouble speaking in front of other people. Trust me, many students (and adults, too) have this problem. It's a problem that can be overcome when the listeners are actually listening, not snickering.

By refuting opposing views, Josh strengthens his own position.

It's true that after-school programs can be difficult to set up and keep going. Even if a club is popular at the beginning, students can lose interest and drop out. Also, these programs are sometimes expensive and can add too much to our school budget. These are good reasons to question starting up another after-school club. The DCE program deserves special consideration, though, because it might be very popular. After all, students like to discuss and even argue. They just need a place to go and a little direction to help guide the discussion. And my program would not be very expensive, since we wouldn't travel and the program doesn't need any extra equipment.

Josh's concluding statement is forceful and shows his confidence in his idea.

This school needs some extracurricular activities that involve social skills, patience, maturity, and intelligence, and we can start with DCE.

▶ Critical Viewing
Explain the power of debating skills in law-making bodies such as the United Nations, shown here. **[Apply]**

Student Work in Progress • 143

1. To understand the major ideas and supporting evidence in spoken messages.
2. To write to influence such as to persuade, argue, and request.
3. To generate ideas and plans for writing by using prewriting strategies.
4. To compare and contrast print, visual, and electronic media.

Step-by-Step Teaching Guide

Persuasive Advertisement

Teaching Resources: Writing Support Transparency, 7-J; Writing Support Activity Book, 7-3

1. Bring in a variety of advertisements from a range of media, or have students bring in examples they find in newspapers, in magazines, on TV, and on the Internet. Discuss the various persuasive techniques used. If you have access to ads in languages other than those spoken by students, present them and then have students figure out their meaning relying on visual images alone.

2. Remind students that their ads need not be for a product or service, but can also be a public service announcement.

3. If students will be completing the activity in groups, you may want to have them hold round tables to help choose topics.

4. Create a classroom display of the various ads when students have completed the activity. Ask students which ads they find the most persuasive and why.

Connected Assignment
Persuasive Advertisement

You may not read a persuasive essay every day, but there's one kind of persuasive writing you can hardly avoid—advertisements. Day after day, advertisements flood into our lives, from full-page ads in magazines to 30-second television commercials to posters in bus shelters.

An **advertisement** is a persuasive message in print or broadcast form, sponsored by an individual, a business, or another group to achieve a particular end, such as selling a product or spreading a specific view. Advertisements may include

- the use of visual, musical, or dramatic elements, such as pictures, jingles, and skits.
- a **"concept,"** or central theme. (A commercial for an automobile, for instance, might focus on *luxury* by showing a ride along a beautiful, sunlit country road, or it might focus on *power* by showing a fast ride on a rough mountain track.)
- a **"hook,"** such as a catchy jingle, a memorable slogan, or an attention-grabbing image.
- appeals to people's concern with their image (for example, how beautiful, responsible, or wealthy they appear).
- **charged language**—words that imply a certain view of a product or issue.
- repetition of key elements, such as words or music, to ensure that the advertisement is memorable.

Create your own advertisement, following the strategies outlined here:

Prewriting First, make up a product, service, or a position to advertise.

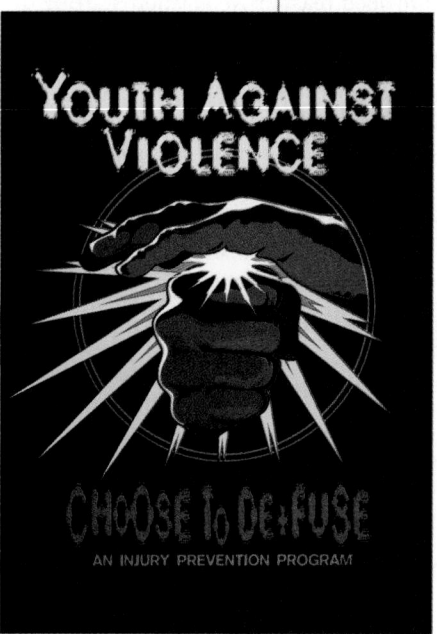

MODEL

The concept of this anti-violence poster is that being against violence is an exciting, powerful stand. The hook is the slogan "Choose to Defuse," combined with the comic book style drawing.

Once you have chosen something to advertise, select your medium: magazine advertisement or television or radio commercial. Next, invent a "concept" for your campaign. For instance, you might decide that the room-cleaning service you are advertising should appeal to students' laziness.

After creating a concept, sum it up in a hook—such as a slogan, jingle, or photograph. Then, list art, music, images, or special effects you wish to include. To help you gather ideas, use a chart like the one below.

Drafting As you draft, focus on presenting your "concept" clearly by using easily interpreted images (for instance, a cowboy), situations (for example, a fancy party), and phrases.

For a **television commercial,** create a storyboard—drawings laid out comic-strip style to show the sequence of visuals. Follow your storyboard in drafting your script—the dialogue to be spoken by actors. Indicate music and special effects in your script.

For a **print ad,** use heads (words set in larger type) to grab readers. Feature your hook in one or more of these heads. Then, lay out your ad to achieve an eye-catching look, arranging pictures and text and selecting typestyles for the best effect.

Revising and Editing Review your draft to ensure that events or ideas are organized logically. Make sure your "concept" is clearly presented. Cut material that distracts from your message.

Publishing and Presenting Consider recording your broadcast commercial or creating a poster of your print ad and presenting it to the class.

Customizing for
Visual/Spatial Learners

For students who wish to write a TV commercial. you may want to bring in examples of storyboards. Many storyboards can be found in media books or animation books. Explain to students that storyboards lay out the basic sequence of events from shot to shot, similar to a blueprint.

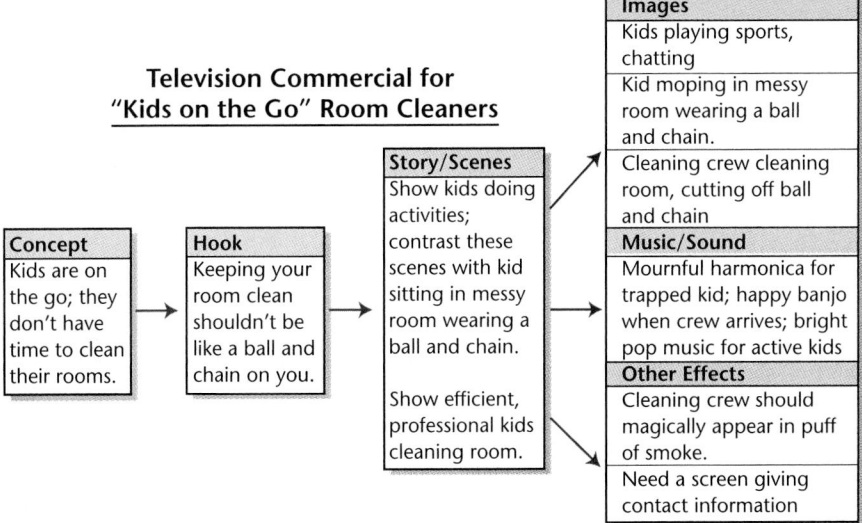

Television Commercial for "Kids on the Go" Room Cleaners

Concept
Kids are on the go; they don't have time to clean their rooms.

Hook
Keeping your room clean shouldn't be like a ball and chain on you.

Story/Scenes
Show kids doing activities; contrast these scenes with kid sitting in messy room wearing a ball and chain.

Show efficient, professional kids cleaning room.

Images
Kids playing sports, chatting

Kid moping in messy room wearing a ball and chain.

Cleaning crew cleaning room, cutting off ball and chain

Music/Sound
Mournful harmonica for trapped kid; happy banjo when crew arrives; bright pop music for active kids

Other Effects
Cleaning crew should magically appear in puff of smoke.

Need a screen giving contact information

Connected Assignment: Persuasive Advertisement • 145

Lesson Objectives

1. To evaluate media presentations.
2. To analyze ideas as presented in various media.

Critical Viewing

Interpret Students may say that the portrait conveys Puccini's intensity and seriousness.

Evaluating Peformances

1. Choose one of the Spotlight elements for class discussion, or have students work individually or in groups on the element of their choice. Give students the initiative to find the necessary books, videotapes, or recordings.

2. Interested students can visit the library to find out more about Maria Callas. In addition to filmed performances, there are a few documentary films about her. Encourage students to think about what a singer brings to the music that he or she sings.

3. If students watch the film *A Room With a View,* encourage them to think about the effects of Puccini's music. Why do they think the filmmakers chose his music for their film?

Listening and Representing

Activity Explain to students that they should familiarize themselves with the libretto before they begin listening to the opera of their choice. This way, they will be able to follow the action while listening to the music. Encourage students to play clips from Puccini's work as part of their presentations.

Critical Viewing

Interpret Students may say the cover creates a sad or serious mood.

Spotlight on the Humanities

Evaluating Performances

Focus on Music: Giacomo Puccini and Opera

The words in an essay may hold great persuasive power, but perhaps nothing moves an audience as directly as music. In an opera, the persuasive force of music is combined with a story (often tragic) acted out by singers. Though the stories may be hard to believe, many spectators find the emotions portrayed in opera overwhelmingly convincing.

The first operas were written in the 1590's and 1600's in Italy. A chorus would sing parts telling the story, while soloists would sing of their character's feelings. A small orchestra or a harpsichord accompanied the singers.

Italian opera blossomed in the nineteenth century. Composer Giacomo Puccini (1858–1924) brought a new sense of realism (*verisimo*) and theater to opera. His works include *Madama Butterfly* (1904), *Tosca* (1900), and *La Bohème* (1896)—all ending with the tragic death of the heroine!

Literature Connection One of Puccini's most successful interpreters, and one of the most important contributors to the art of opera, was singer Maria Callas (1923–1977). A talented actress as well as a gifted singer, she played tragic parts like Turandot in Puccini's opera of that title. Fortunately, videos and recordings exist of her performances, preserving her art for the future.

Film Connection Music from Puccini's *Gianni Schicchi* (1918) and *La Rondine* (1917) is woven beautifully throughout the film *A Room With a View* (1986). Directed by James Ivory and produced by Ismail Merchant, the film gives evidence of the lasting emotional power of Puccini's music.

Persuasive Writing Activity: Presentation on Opera

Listen to a section of an opera by Puccini. Then, in a brief presentation, persuade classmates of the value of listening to his work.

▲ **Critical Viewing** What qualities does this portrait of Puccini convey? **[Interpret]**

G. PUCCINI TURANDOT

EDIZIONI RICORDI

▶ **Critical Viewing** What mood does this cover for *Turandot* create? **[Interpret]**

146 • Persuasive Essay

Media and Technology Skills

► **Lesson Objectives**

1. To evaluate how different media forms influence and inform.

2. To assess how language, medium, and presentation contribute to the message.

Analyzing Bias in the Media
Activity: Evaluating Objectivity of News Reports

If someone gets up at a meeting and starts making a speech, you can recognize his or her persuasive purpose right away. Persuasion takes subtler forms as well. When a news report that claims to be objective actually takes a side, that report is said to be **biased**—it has a concealed persuasive purpose. Learn to detect bias in the news.

Think About It Bias in the news may take a few forms:

- **Loaded language** is the use of emotionally charged words to suggest a view of a subject without supporting the view with argument or evidence. For example, a news report on youth curfew laws might use the phrase "rowdy youths" without documenting any rowdy behavior.

- **Hasty generalizations** appear when a general statement is made based on only a few cases. For example, the news report on curfews might state that "Unsupervised teenagers are likely to turn to crime."

- **Inflammatory images** show actions or events that will elicit strong emotions from an audience, such as teenagers causing mischief. If an inflammatory image does not illustrate a specific fact in a news report, if the circumstances in which it was taken are not made clear, or if there are few contrasting images, then its use may reflect bias.

- **One-sided presentations** appear when all or most of the facts and images accompanying a report support a certain response to the story. Objective news reporting generally involves presenting more than one side of any controversial issue.

Evaluate It Fill out a chart like this one for a magazine article, a newspaper article, and a television news segment.

Review your chart and write a brief evaluation of how biased or objective each report was.

Other Forms of Bias

- **Opinions stated as facts** Example: "The best solution is to . . ."
- **Story "angle"** Example: The writer might report on efforts to save an endangered animal, stressing its uniqueness but not mentioning the potential harm it might cause humans.
- **Relative weight given an aspect of a story** Example: A newspaper editor features on the front page the damage done by protesters while "burying" in the back pages reports about new developments in the issue they are protesting.

Step-by-Step Teaching Guide

Analyzing Bias in the Media

Teaching Resources: Writing Support Transparency 7-K; Writing Support Activity Book 7-4

1. Present newspaper articles or videotaped segments of news programs that display bias. Choose features on subjects of potential interest to students.

2. Have students discuss the views promoted by each piece.

3. Display the transparency. As a class, evaluate the objectivity of one of the examples you have displayed.

BIAS DETECTOR

Source: _____ Report on:_____

Loaded Language	Hasty Generalizations	Inflammatory Images	One-sided Presentation: Y/N

Media and Technology Skills • 147

Lesson Objectives

1. To write to influence such as to persuade, argue, and request.

2. To write in a style appropriate to audience and purpose.

3. To produce a coherent written text by organizing ideas, using effective transitions, and choosing precise wording.

Step-by-Step Teaching Guide

Responding to Persuasive Writing Prompts

Teaching Resources: Test Preparation Workbook, pp. 13–14

1. Explain to students that it is important to address the question in the time allotted. Therefore, students should plan each stage of the writing process so that they do not run the risk of not finishing in time.

2. Remind students that length is not important. The longer of two essays may not necessarily be the more persuasive one. The key is writing for one's audience, choosing precise words that strengthen one's argument, and supporting one's main points.

3. Assign one of the prompts in the textbook and have students write a brief essay.

Standardized Test Preparation Workshop

Responding to Persuasive Writing Prompts

The writing prompts on standardized tests often measure your ability to write persuasively. Your writing will be evaluated according to your demonstrated ability to:

- use language and arguments appropriate to the purpose and audience named in the prompt.
- use a consistent method of organization suited to the topic, such as pro-and-con organization.
- present effective support of arguments using descriptions, facts, and other details.
- use correct grammar, spelling, and punctuation.

Practice for such tests by responding to the following sample persuasive writing prompt. Use the suggestions on the following page to help you respond. The clocks suggest the portion of your allotted time that you should devote to each stage.

Test Tip

When responding to a persuasive essay prompt, be especially careful to take into account any arguments suggested in the prompt against your position.

Sample Prompts

For thousands of years, people have wondered about distant stars and planets. Many people believe that the information gained about the universe through space exploration is important enough to justify support of the space program. Others regard space exploration as frivolous, saying that it diverts money from practical needs, such as education and care of the elderly.

Choose between the following writing prompts:

- State your position on public funding for the space program in a letter to a school astronomy club.
- State your position on public funding for the space program in a letter to your legislator.

148 • Persuasive Essay

✎ TEST-TAKING TIP

When writing a persuasive essay, students should not underestimate the importance of arguments that oppose their own. Many times, it is a good idea to acknowledge these counter arguments and offer reasons as to why they are not valid. This will make students' arguments more powerful and persuasive because they are directly confronting the opposition.

Ask students to identify some of the counter arguments they may have to deal with in responding to either of the prompts in their textbooks.

Prewriting

 Allow close to one fourth of your time for prewriting.

Consider Your Audience and Purpose Your purpose is to convince your readers that your position on the space program is the correct one. If you choose to write for members of an astronomy club, you can assume that they support space exploration. If you choose to write to a legislator, you can assume that he or she is interested in balancing various interests against one another. These facts about your audience should shape the kind of support you offer and the tone of your letter. For instance, if you were persuading the astronomy club not to support space exploration, you would probably want to suggest alternative ways to gather astronomical information.

Gather Support Use a T-chart to gather logical arguments, facts, examples, and strong images or phrases on both sides of the issue. Look for ways to refute the strongest arguments against your position. (See p. 131 for more information on using a T-chart.)

Drafting

Allow almost half of your time for drafting.

 **Introduce and Develop Your Position** Begin by writing an interest-grabbing introduction in which you present your position with a strong image or story. Then, develop support for your position in the body of your response. Refer to your T-chart for details as you write. Before the end, introduce opposing arguments and refute them. You might save your strongest argument for the end of your response. In your conclusion, sum up your main points and restate your position.

Elaborate to Add Precise Language and Detail As you draft, make sure you include descriptive details and use precise words to make your writing vivid. Choose illustrations and descriptive words that will appeal to your chosen audience. Astronomy club members might like the sound of *far-sighted*. Legislators might prefer the sound of *responsible*.

Revising, Editing, and Proofreading

 Allow almost one fourth of your time to revise. Use the last few minutes to proofread your work.

Evaluate Details and Word Choice Eliminate any details that are distracting or irrelevant. Change language that is inappropriate for your audience. Also, note places in your paper where you have used vague words, such as *good, bad, right,* and *wrong*. Replace them with precise words by answering the question, "Good (or bad) in what way?"

 **Work Neatly** Check your work for errors in grammar, spelling, or punctuation. When making changes, place one line through the text to eliminate and use a caret (^) to indicate insertions.

Integrating Vocabulary Skills

Persuasive Language Read the following two sentences to students and ask them which one they find more persuasive:

I guess you could say that after-school reading would help students read better.

Without a doubt, after-school reading programs would have a direct impact on improving students' reading abilities.

Explain to students that vague language can only serve to undermine the strength of an argument in a persuasive essay.

Customizing for
ESL Students

Students learning English may feel threatened by standardized essay questions. When practicing the test questions in class, allow students to use a thesaurus to help them replace vague words.

Time and Resource Manager

In-Depth Lesson Plan

	LESSON FOCUS	PRINT AND MEDIA RESOURCES
DAY 1	**Introduction to Comparison-and-Contrast Essay** Students learn key elements of comparison-and-contrast exposition and analyze the Model From Literature (pp. 150–153).	*Writers at Work* **Videotape**, Exposition: Making Connections *Writing Lab* **CD-ROM**, Exposition: Making Connections
DAY 2	**Prewriting** Students choose an expository topic, consider their audience and purpose, and gather details (pp. 154–157).	**Teaching Resources** *Writing Support Transparencies*, 8-A–D; *Writing Support Activity Book*, 8-1–3; *Writing Lab* **CD-ROM**, Exposition: Making Connections
DAY 3	**Drafting** Students choose a method of comparison-and-contrast organization and write their first drafts (pp. 158–159).	**Teaching Resources** *Writing Support Transparencies*, 8-E *Writing Lab* **CD-ROM**, Exposition: Making Connections
DAY 4	**Revising** Students revise their drafts for organization and clarity, and to strengthen their introductions and conclusions (pp. 160–164).	**Teaching Resources** *Writing Support Transparencies*, 8-F–G *Writing Lab* **CD-ROM**, Exposition: Making Connections
DAY 5	**Editing and Proofreading; Publishing and Presenting** Students proofread their work and present their final drafts in public readings (pp. 165–166).	**Teaching Resources** *Scoring Rubrics on Transparency*, Ch. 8; *Formal Assessment*, Ch. 8 *Writing Lab* **CD-ROM**, Exposition: Making Connections

Accelerated Lesson Plan

	LESSON FOCUS	PRINT AND MEDIA RESOURCES
DAY 1	**Introduction Through Drafting** Students review characteristics of comparison-and-contrast exposition, select topics, and write drafts (pp. 150–159).	*Writers at Work* **Videotape**, Exposition: Making Connections *Writing Lab* **CD-ROM**, Exposition: Making Connections **Teaching Resources** *Writing Support Transparencies*, 8-A–E; *Writing Support Activity Book*, 8-1–3
DAY 2	**Revising Through Presenting** Students work individually or with peers to revise, edit, and proofread their work for presentation (pp. 160–166).	**Teaching Resources** *Writing Support Transparencies*, 8-F–G; *Scoring Rubrics on Transparency*, Ch. 8; *Formal Assessment*, Ch. 8 *Writing Lab* **CD-ROM**, Exposition: Making Connections

Options for Adapting Lesson Plans

HOMEWORK
Have students complete any stage of the lesson for homework.

FEATURES
Extend coverage with Connected Assignment (p. 169), Spotlight on the Humanities (p. 170), Media and Technology Skills (p. 171), and the Standardized Test Preparation Workshop (p. 172).

TECHNOLOGY
Student can complete any stage of the lesson on computer. Have them print out their completed work.

INTEGRATED SKILLS COVERAGE

Integrating Grammar
Subject-Verb Agreement, SE. p. 163
Pronoun-Antecedent Agreement, SE. p. 165
Grammar and Style, SE p. 164; ATE p. 168

Reading/ Writing Connection
Reading Strategy, SE, p.152
Writing Application, SE, p. 153

Viewing and Representing
Critical Viewing, SE pp. 150, 152, 153, 158, 160, 164, 167, 168, 169, 170
Evaluating Performances, SE p. 170

Speaking and Listening ATE, p. 156

Technology SE pp. 157, 166, 171; ATE p.165

Workplace Skills
Integrating Workplace Skills, ATE p. 168

ASSESSMENT SUPPORT

Standardized Test Preparation SE, p. 172, ATE pp. 156, 163
Standardized Test Preparation Workbook, pp. 15–16
Scoring Rubrics on Transparency, Ch. 8
Formal Assessment, Ch. 8
Writing Assessment and Portfolio Management

MEETING INDIVIDUAL NEEDS

ESL Students ATE pp. 155, 158, 173
Verbal/Linguistic Learners ATE p. 157
Visual/Spatial Learners ATE p. 158
Less Advanced Students ATE p. 162. See also Ongoing Assessments, ATE pp. 157, 159, 162, 166, 169
More Advanced Students ATE p. 171

BLOCK SCHEDULING

Pacing Suggestions
For 90-minute Blocks
• Have students complete the Prewriting and Drafting stages in a single period.
• Focus one class period on Revising and Editing and Publishing and Presenting. Allow at least 30 minutes for peer revision.

Resources for Varying Instruction
• *Writing Lab* CD-ROM If your students have access to hardware, a 90-minute block provides an ideal opportunity for them to work on computer.
• *Writers at Work* **Videotape** Show the Exposition: Making Connections segment in class.

Professional Development Support
• **How to Manage Instruction in the Block** This Teaching Resource provides management and activity suggestions.

MEDIA AND TECHNOLOGY

For the Student
• *Writing Lab* **CD-ROM**, Exposition: Making Connections

For the Teacher
• *Writers at Work* **Videotape**, Exposition: Making Connections
• *Resource Pro* **CD-ROM**

WRITING AND GRAMMAR WEB SITE

The Interactive Writing and Grammar Web site provides a wide array of support for students, teachers, and parents. Writing support includes:

• Interactive revision checkers
• Scoring rubrics with complete models

www.phschool.com

LITERATURE CONNECTIONS

Related selections from *Prentice Hall Literature: Timeless Voices, Timeless Themes,* Bronze:
"Fable," by Ralph Waldo Emerson, SE p. 153
Greek myths of Phaëton and Persephone, SE p. 155

Lesson Objectives

1. To recognize and produce the elements of an effective comparison-and-contrast essay.

2. To write to inform such as to explain, describe, report, and narrate.

3. To select and use voice and style appropriate to audience and purpose.

4. To produce cohesive and coherent written texts by organizing ideas, using effective transitions, and choosing precise wording.

5. To employ standard English usage in writing for audiences, including subject-verb agreement, pronoun referents, and parts of speech.

6. To generate ideas and plans for writing by using prewriting strategies such as brainstorming, graphic organizers, notes, and logs.

7. To revise drafts for coherence, progression, and logical support of ideas.

8. To apply criteria to evaluate writing.

9. To analyze published examples as models for writing.

Critical Viewing

Compare and Contrast Students may say the overall composition, the triptych-like structure, and the subject matter are the same. The colors, the mood, and the contrast between light and dark are different.

Chapter 8 *Exposition*
Comparison-and-Contrast Essay

The King of Prospect Park Triptych, 1994 (light), Anders Knutsson, Courtesy of the artist.

The King of Prospect Park Triptych, 1994 (dark), Anders Knutsson, Courtesy of the artist.

▲ **Critical Viewing**
This painting may be viewed under ordinary light (top) or in the dark (below). List three similarities and three differences between the two views. **[Compare and Contrast]**

Comparison-and-Contrast Writing in Everyday Life

If you move to a new home, you can't help but compare your new neighborhood to your old one. Maybe you miss the corner store, but welcome a new friend across the street. You don't have to move, though, to start comparing. Making decisions means making comparisons. "I'll wear sneakers today," you might decide—comparing them to the sandals you wore the day before.

A comparison-and-contrast essay builds on such everyday comparisons. By creating new comparisons, writers can help us make decisions or see old things in fresh ways.

150 • Exposition

⏱ TIME AND RESOURCE MANAGER

Resources
Technology: Writers at Work videotape, Exposition: Making Connections

In-Depth Coverage	Accelerated Pace
• Cover pp. 150–153 in class. • Show Exposition: Making Connections section of the Writers at Work videotape. • Read Model From Literature (pp. 152–153) in class. • Discuss examples of comparisons and contrasts you or students bring to class. **Option** Have students work individually or in groups on the Exposition: Making Connections section of the Writing Lab CD-ROM.	• Have students read pp. 150–153 on their own. • Discuss definitions and types of comparison-and-contrast essays in class. • Assign Model From Literature for independent reading.

What Is a Comparison-and-Contrast Essay?

A **comparison-and-contrast essay** analyzes the similarities and differences between two or more things. It can help you to decide which bicycle to buy. A good comparison-and-contrast essay can even change your perspective—as when a reviewer compares the latest hit song with an old album, letting you hear the startling similarities. A comparison-and-contrast essay includes

- a topic involving two or more things that are neither nearly identical nor extremely different.

- details illustrating both similarities and differences.

- clear organization that highlights the points of comparison.

To learn the criteria on which your essay may be evaluated, see the Rubric for Self-Assessment on page 166.

Types of Comparison-and-Contrast Essays

In addition to an ordinary comparison-and-contrast essay, some specialized essays also use comparison and contrast:

- **Product comparisons** compare two or more products, providing up-to-date information on each and discussing the advantages and disadvantages of purchasing each one.

- **Plan evaluations** compare two or more alternative plans or decisions, discussing the circumstances and comparing the advantages and disadvantages of each plan.

Writers in **ACTION**

In his books and articles, Richard Lederer compares English to other languages and different English words to each other. He knows the value of saying more in fewer words: ". . . writing is hard work, and writing concisely is even more difficult."

PREVIEW

Student Work **IN PROGRESS**

To develop your comparison-and-contrast writing skills, follow the work of Dylan Parker of Carr Lane VPA Middle School in St. Louis, Missouri. In this chapter, Dylan uses featured prewriting, drafting, and revising techniques to develop the comparison-and-contrast essay "Skateboards for Success." At the end of the lesson, you can read Dylan's completed essay.

Comparison-and-Contrast Essay • 151

Reading: Identify Main Points

A good reader will try to identify the author's main points. The main point of a piece of writing often is found in the first paragraph. The conclusion usually will restate this main point. Ask students why they think the main points usually appear in these locations. As students read the Model From Literature, have them write down the main point and at least two details that support it.

TEACH

Step-by-Step Teaching Guide

Engage Students Through Literature

1. Read the essay aloud or have prepared volunteers do so.

2. Review the logical points the author makes by asking students the following questions:

   - Why does the ball come off an aluminum bat harder? (The bat compresses more, giving more kinetic energy to the ball.)

   - What is a "sweet spot"? (It is a place with fewer energy-sucking vibrations.)

   - What is the main advantage and disadvantage of an aluminum bat? (An aluminum bat enables batters to hit the ball harder, but it is more dangerous to fielders.)

3. Review the author's method of organization. (Each paragraph addresses a different point about bats.)

Critical Viewing

Apply Students may say they would prefer to use the aluminum bat since they can hit the ball harder with it.

8.1 Model From Literature

Laura Allen (1972–) is a former editor of the magazine Superscience. *In this article, she uses research results from a new "field" of science—sports physics. Physics is the study of the natural laws governing the motion of physical bodies. For a physicist, the world can be described in terms of simple mathematical formulas. For a sports fan, the world is a more colorful—and rougher—place. The physicist watches a fly ball and sees a sphere traveling along a mathematical curve. The sports fan sees a game-clinching homer.*

Sports physics combines these two views into one. It is the study of the laws of physics as they apply to the actions of objects and materials in sports. The sports physicist studies how balls travel through the air, how pucks slide across the ice, and how the material of a gym floor affects the bounce of a ball. Sports officials may use the findings of physicists to make decisions about equipment and regulations.

Reading Writing Connection

Reading Strategy: Identify Main Points
By **identifying an author's main points**—the points he or she wants you to remember—you can better understand the information presented. For instance, in "Bat Attacks?" you might identify one main point as follows: The amount of energy a bat gives a ball determines how fast the ball travels.

▲ **Critical Viewing**
After reading this essay, which bat would you rather use—the one pictured here, or the one on the next page? Explain. [Apply]

Bat Attacks?

Laura Allen

If you play baseball, you may swing an aluminum bat. Metal bats make balls fly faster than wooden bats, and that has some baseball officials worried. They say metal bats just might seriously injure players.

Slugging a ball gives it *kinetic energy*—the energy of motion. The more kinetic energy a ball has, the harder it strikes a player who misses a catch!

The author uses the point-by-point method of organizing a comparison. She compares each feature of the two bats in turn.

152 • Comparison-and-Contrast Essay

If you use a wooden bat, the baseball compresses briefly. (The bat does too, but only slightly.) The compression causes friction in the ball, transforming some kinetic energy into heat. That means less kinetic energy for a fast hit.

But an aluminum bat compresses much more than the baseball does. "That's because metal bats are more *elastic* (springy) than wooden bats," says Yale University baseball physicist Robert Adair. Unlike a solid wooden bat, aluminum bats are hollow inside. The compressed bat bounces back like a trampoline, giving the ball an added thrust forward. That's why pro players don't use aluminum—there'd be too many home runs!

[Both a metal bat and a wooden bat have "sweet spots."] A metal bat[, though,] sports larger sweet spots than wooden bats. That's another reason metal bats slug balls so fast. Sweet spots are areas on a bat that drive the farthest hits.

Any bat vibrates along its length when struck, says Adair. But at the sweet spots, there are no energy-sucking vibrations. That leaves more energy to send the ball sailing.

But a metal bat is stiffer (lengthwise) than a wooden bat. Stiff bats vibrate less *overall*. So aluminum bats may guarantee you a home run, but there's a tradeoff—if the ball hits a player, you've struck him or her out.

Most coaches haven't noticed an increase in injuries. But batter beware!

LITERATURE

For a different kind of comparison-and-contrast writing, see the poem "Fable" by Ralph Waldo Emerson in *Prentice Hall Literature: Timeless Voices, Timeless Themes*, Bronze.

The writer elaborates on the main idea here by explaining what a "sweet spot" is and why larger sweet spots make a metal bat so powerful.

The writer concludes with a point of high interest—the very power that makes a metal bat a home-run hitter may also make it dangerous to other players.

Writing Application: Help Readers Identify Main Points As you write your own comparison-and-contrast essay, make sure to help readers identify main points. You can do this by using transition words such as *first, second,* and *third,* or phrases such as "in addition," "by contrast," or "at the same time."

▶ **Critical Viewing** Judging from the essay, is this batter's chance of hitting a home run greater or less than if he were swinging a wooden bat? [Deduce]

153

Teaching From the Model

Point out to students the conciseness with which the author writes. She announces her purpose, makes her point, and draws conclusions in a tightly written essay full of details which support her points.

Responding to Literature

Explain to students that the comparison-and-contrast approach can be found in many different types of literature. Emerson's poem "Fable" relies on this approach in order to make a poignant point about the importance of all things on Earth, both great and small.

Real-World Connection

Ask students who play baseball to describe their experiences with aluminum and wooden bats. How do they compare? How are they different? Which do they prefer, and why?

Reading\Writing Connection

Writing Application: Help Readers Identify Main Points

Have students review Allen's essay to see how she helps readers identify her main points.

Critical Viewing

Deduce Students should say the batter's chance is greater.

Prewriting

Prewriting: Quicklist

1. Use the sample below to begin a chart for students on the board.

2. Ask students to suggest more choices, and then have them work individually to list additional descriptions and examples.

Choices	Descriptions	Examples
movie	very scary	girl standing with back to open window

Prewriting: BUT Chart

Teaching Resources: Writing Support Transparency, 8-A; Writing Support Activity Book, 8-1

1. Display the transparency. Have a volunteer read the things Dylan listed that are similar. Have another volunteer read the differences.

2. Point out to students how contrast is the primary element here, highlighting how related things are different. Ask students to suggest some topics from this list and then have them make a BUT Chart of their own.

Choosing Your Topic

Use these strategies to find an interesting comparison-and-contrast topic:

Strategies for Generating a Topic

1. **Quicklist** Fold a piece of paper in thirds lengthwise. In the first column, write a list of recent choices you have made—for instance, products you have bought. In the second column, next to each choice, write a descriptive phrase. In the third column, give an alternative to your choice. Review your list, and choose the most interesting topic.

2. **BUT Chart** Fold a piece of paper in half. Write the word *BUT* down the middle. In the left column, list items with something in common. Write down differences among them in the right column. Choose your topic from this list.

Writing Lab CD-ROM

For more help finding a topic, explore the activities and suggestions in the Choosing a Topic section of the Exposition: Making Connections lesson.

Student Work IN PROGRESS

Name: *Dylan Parker*
Carr Lane VPA Middle School
St. Louis, MO

Using a BUT Chart

Here is how Dylan used a BUT chart to come up with a topic:

Things That Are Similar	**BUT**	Differences Between Them
My skateboard and Jimmy's skateboard: board plus 4 wheels		Jimmy's has a slick deck. My board is just wood. My board has high-quality wheels. Jimmy's board has cheap wheels.
Monday morning and Saturday morning: we wake up, eat breakfast, and leave the house		Mondays, we all grab our own breakfast. Saturdays, we make breakfast for Mom. Mondays, I have to get up at 6:00 (groan!). Saturdays, I sleep until 9:00 AT LEAST.

 **Writing Support Transparencies**
Use the transparencies for Chapter 8 to teach these strategies.

📖 **Writing Support Activity Book**
Use the graphic organizers for Chapter 8 to facilitate these strategies.

⏱ TIME AND RESOURCE MANAGER

Resources
Print: Writing Support Transparencies, 8-A–D; Writing Support Activity Book, 8-1–3
Technology: Writing Lab CD-ROM, Exposition: Making Connections

In-Depth Coverage	Accelerated Pace
• Cover pp. 154–158 in class. • Work through the Quicklist or BUT Chart strategy with the class (p. 154). • Use the Responding to Fine Arts Transparency to generate additional topics. • Do the Venn Diagram activity in class.	• Discuss strategies for generating topics. • Have students work independently to choose and narrow their topics. • Have students work with partners to focus on audience, purpose, and gathering details.

TOPIC BANK

If you're having trouble finding a topic, consider one of the following suggestions:

1. **The Book or the Movie?** It's fascinating to see how writers make a movie from a book—or a book from a movie. What is stressed? What is left out? What is added? Compare and contrast a book and the movie that was made from it. Explain which you enjoyed more, and why.

2. **Saturday Morning and Monday Morning** You wake up in the same body on the same planet—but a lot of other things may be different between Saturday morning and Monday morning. Write an essay comparing the two mornings.

Responding to Fine Art

3. Jot down similarities and differences between the two objects in this painting and among different parts of the canvas. Explore the reasons the artist might have included apparently dissimilar objects. How is the shape of the flowers similar to that of the skull? How are their meanings different? Write an essay comparing and contrasting the parts of this painting or comparing this painting with another by Georgia O'Keeffe.

Responding to Literature

4. Read the Greek myths of Phaëton and Persephone. Compare the characters, the mistakes they make, and their fates. You can find these myths in *Prentice Hall Literature: Timeless Voices, Timeless Themes*, Bronze.

Summer Days, 1936, Georgia O'Keeffe, Collection of Whitney Museum of American Art, New York

☑ Cooperative Writing Opportunity

5. **Travel Brochure** The mountains and the seashore are both attractive places to visit. With a group, compare and contrast these two vacation destinations. Divide your group into two smaller groups. One subgroup can write about the similarities, the other about the differences. Present your work to the class as an illustrated folder or pamphlet.

Prewriting • 155

Responding to Fine Art

Summer Days, 1936 by Georgia O'Keeffe

Teaching Resources: Writing Support Transparency, 8-B

1. Display the transparency, and ask students what they think is depicted in the painting.

2. Ask students what topics for a comparison-and-contrast essay are suggested by the painting.

Customize for *ESL Students*

Suggest that students compare and contrast a characteristic of their original language or culture with a notable part of the English language or American culture.

Responding to Literature

Read the myths with students and use questions such as the following to guide them in a discussion about the characters and events.

• What mistake does Phaëton make, and what happens to him?

• What causes Phaëton to act as he does?

• What explains Persephone's fate?

• Who is responsible for what happens to Persephone?

• Remind students who want to write about these myths to take notes during this discussion.

Spotlight on the Humanities

For additional topic suggestions, refer students to the Spotlight on Humanities on page 170.

155

Prewriting: Cubing to Narrow a Topic

Teaching Resources: Writing Support Transparency, 8-C; Writing Support Activity Book, 8-2

1. Discuss the necessity of narrowing topics. Ask which is a more appropriate topic for an essay, and why: "How to Bake" or "How to Make Chocolate Chip Cookies"? "Dogs" or "Housebreaking Your New Puppy"?

2. Cubing is a prewriting strategy designed to help students examine a subject from six different angles in order to develop a thorough understanding of it.

3. Point out how each step of cubing fleshes out unique details of the topic: *describe* yields a basic description; *associate* and *apply* bring in other related elements; *analyze* and *compare/contrast* explore similarities and differences; *argue* yields a point of view.

4. Display the transparency. Review Dylan's use of cubing to narrow his too-broad topic of "Skateboards."

Integrating Speaking and Listening Skills

Ask students to think of a time a friend told them a story that seemed to go on for so long that it was hard to figure out the point of the story. Ask them to identify the qualities that made it hard to follow. Explain that even in the casual stories and anecdotes we tell to friends, it helps to be organized, provide lively detail, and get to the point. Listeners appreciate it as much as readers.

8.2

Narrowing Your Topic

Once you've chosen a topic, consider whether it is too broad to cover in a brief essay. Use cubing to narrow your topic.

Use Cubing to Narrow a Topic

To "cube" a topic, follow these steps:

1. **Describe it** to someone who is not familiar with it.
2. **Associate it** with someone, something, or some event in your life.
3. **Apply it,** explaining what you can do with it, on it, or to it.
4. **Analyze it** by breaking it into parts.
5. **Compare and contrast it** with things that are similar and different.
6. **Argue for or against it**, explaining good and bad points.

Circle details from your cube to create a focused topic.

Writing Lab CD-ROM

For more suggestions on how to narrow a topic for comparison and contrast, play the clip and use an activity under Narrowing a Topic in the Exposition: Making Connections lesson.

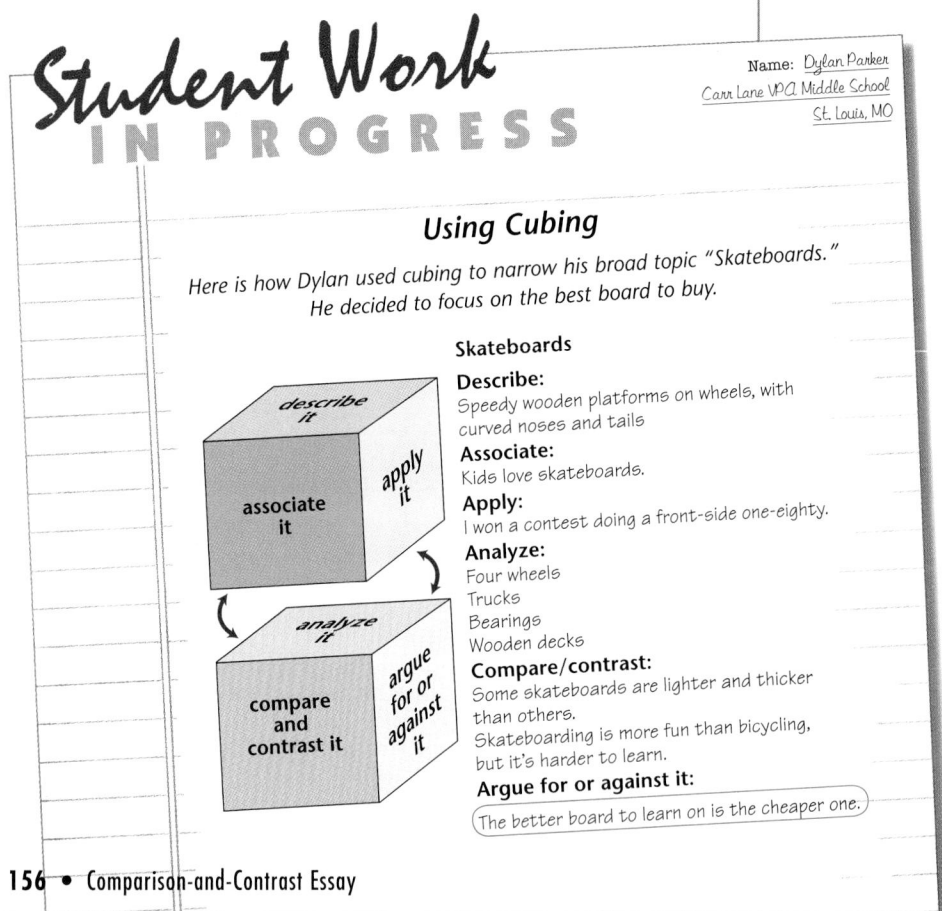

Student Work
IN PROGRESS

Name: *Dylan Parker*
Carr Lane VPA Middle School
St. Louis, MO

Using Cubing

Here is how Dylan used cubing to narrow his broad topic "Skateboards."
He decided to focus on the best board to buy.

Skateboards

Describe:
Speedy wooden platforms on wheels, with curved noses and tails

Associate:
Kids love skateboards.

Apply:
I won a contest doing a front-side one-eighty.

Analyze:
Four wheels
Trucks
Bearings
Wooden decks

Compare/contrast:
Some skateboards are lighter and thicker than others.
Skateboarding is more fun than bicycling, but it's harder to learn.

Argue for or against it:
The better board to learn on is the cheaper one.

156 • Comparison-and-Contrast Essay

✎ **STANDARDIZED TEST PREPARATION WORKSHOP**

Expository Writing Prompts Writing prompts on standardized tests often ask students to write expository pieces. Share the following sample prompt with students:

Poets rely on language to express themselves in unique ways.

Choose two short poems you have read in class that share similar themes. Compare and contrast the form and style of each poem and how these elements contribute to the theme.

Considering Your Audience and Purpose

Your **audience**—who your readers are—and **purpose**—your reason for writing—should determine your choice of details and writing style. Before you begin writing, consider what details and vocabulary will best suit your audience's level of knowledge. Also, examine your purpose.

Analyze Your Purpose

Answer the following questions before you gather details and draft:

- Am I trying to **persuade** my audience to do or believe something? *If so, emphasize details that prove your case.*

- Will my writing **instruct** my readers, providing them with information? *If so, think of questions that your readers would probably ask, and answer them in your essay.*

- Will I **entertain** my readers—make them laugh or share a personal experience or insight? *If so, use vivid language to convey the humor, beauty, or other qualities of your subject.*

Gathering Details

For a comparison-and-contrast essay, focus on gathering details that show similarities and differences between your subjects.

Use a Venn Diagram

Draw two large circles that overlap in the middle, like the ones below. Fill in details about your two subjects, using the middle for features they have in common.

VENN DIAGRAM

Everyday Meals

any day
my family sits in kitchen together
use everyday plates
wear everyday clothes
eat good food
talk about our days

cook and eat food clean up

Holiday Meals

holiday
grandparents, aunts, uncles, cousins sit in dining room
use good china and tablecloths
dress extra nicely
eat great holiday food
talk about family news and history

Technology Tip

If the subject of your topic is not always accessible to you, film it with a video camera to record its details. For example, if you are comparing and contrasting dawn and dusk at a nearby lake, record the sights and sounds there at each time of day. Review the tape to recall concrete details when you begin to write.

Prewriting: Considering Audience and Purpose

1. Explain to students that knowing one's audience often can help narrow the topic because it helps determine which details need to be included.

2. Have students write a "statement of purpose" for their essays. They might start with these words: "The purpose of my essay is to . . ." Make sure their statements make some mention of both the topic and the audience. For example: "The purpose of my essay is to pursuade my classmates to vote for me, rather than for my opponent."

3. After they write their drafts, have students reread their statements. Do their essays achieve the intended purpose?

Prewriting: Gathering Details

Teaching Resources: Writing Support Transparency, 8-D; Writing Support Activity Book, 8-3

1. Display the transparency and discuss how to properly use a Venn diagram.

2. Give students copies of the blank organizer. Have students complete a Venn diagram for their own topics.

Customize for
Verbal/Linguistic Learners

Have students identify a person for whom they want to write. Encourage them to script a dialogue with the person about their topic. What kinds of questions does he or she ask? What tone seems most appropriate to use? The answer to these questions will help guide the content and tone of their essays.

☑ ONGOING ASSESSMENT: Monitor and Reinforce

When writing in class, students sometimes abandon their own voices and write in forced "grown up" voices they think will please their teacher. To help break this pattern try one of the following options.

| **Option 1** Tell students to direct their writing toward a particular friend or family member. As they write, encourage them to think about what would interest this person in terms of topic, details, tone, and language. | **Option 2** To emphasize that we often speak differently to different audiences, have students work in pairs and describe their day to one another. The first time, have them imagine they are talking to a close friend; the second, a parent. In what ways did the descriptions differ? |

Drafting: Shaping Your Writing

1. Explain to students that the point-by-point method works best when there are only one or two features, or when the closeness of the comparison or the distance of the contrast is a main point of the essay.

2. Discuss that for complex topics, it can get confusing to switch back and forth comparing and contrasting individual details. Similarly, in relatively simple topics, the thrust of the comparison/contrast can get lost if the block method is used instead of the point-by-point method.

3. Have students work with partners to determine which type of organization would best suit their topics.

Critical Viewing

Speculate Students may say they are deciding which destination is easier to get to, which will be cheaper, and which will be more fun.

Customize for
ESL Students

Review signal words with students. These words can help students keep track of the ideas in their writing, and they can be helpful for readers too. Encourage students to keep a list in their notebooks as a reference guide. *First, second, next, then,* and *last* show order. *And, also, same, like,* and *similarly* show comparison. *But, however, different,* and *on the other hand* show contrast.

Customize for
Visual/Spatial Learners

Have students complete a thorough outline once they have decided which organizing method to use. It should include more details and examples than the sample outlines on this page. Seeing the information in this concrete form will help them locate gaps or weak areas in their essays.

8.3 Drafting

Shaping Your Writing

You cannot simply write down all the details you have gathered and call the result an essay. First, you must organize these details logically, so that a reader can assemble them into a clear picture of your subject.

Select an Effective Organization

There are two main ways to organize a comparison: the block method and the point-by-point method.

Block Method

- Present all details about one subject first.
- Next, present all the details about the second subject (then, about the third, fourth, and so on).

▲ **Critical Viewing**
If the people in the photograph are choosing among destinations, what three aspects of their choices are they probably discussing? **[Speculate]**

EXAMPLE: **Steam Engine vs. Gas Engine**
  A. Steam engine
   1. fuel
   2. operation
   3. efficiency

  B. Gas engine
   1. fuel
   2. operation
   3. efficiency

The block method works well if you are writing about more than two things or if your topic is complex.

Point-by-Point Method

- First, discuss one aspect of both subjects.
- Next, discuss another aspect of both subjects, and so on, for each important aspect of the topic.

EXAMPLE: **Snow-Skiing vs. Water-Skiing**
  A. Different equipment
   1. snow-skiing
   2. water-skiing

  B. Length of time to learn
   1. snow-skiing
   2. water-skiing

Choose a method of organization suited to your topic. Then, make an outline arranging details according to this method.

158 • Comparison-and-Contrast Essay

⏱ TIME AND RESOURCE MANAGER

Resources
Print: Writing Support Transparencies, 8-E
Technology: Writing Lab CD-ROM, Exposition: Making Connections

In-Depth Coverage	Accelerated Pace
• Cover pp. 158–159 in class. • Discuss the block and point-by-point methods with students. Have individual conferences with students as needed to determine which method they should use. • Have students write their drafts in class. • Demonstrate the technique of layering details using the transparency.	• Have students review pp. 158–159 independently, then write their first comparison-contrast draft. • Respond to individual drafting issues as needed.

Providing Elaboration

As you draft your essay, incorporate the details you have gathered, following the organization you have chosen. Think of yourself as an artist, adding vivid images, interesting examples, and clear reasons like touches of color on a canvas. Layering is a technique for writing in this careful and colorful way.

Layer Ideas Using SEE

To layer a paragraph, begin by writing out the main idea. Then, elaborate on—give more details about—that idea.

State the main idea of the paragraph in a sentence.

Extend your main idea. You might restate it with a new emphasis, show how it applies in a particular case, or distinguish it from another point.

Elaborate on your main idea in one or more sentences. Give examples, explanations, or other supporting details.

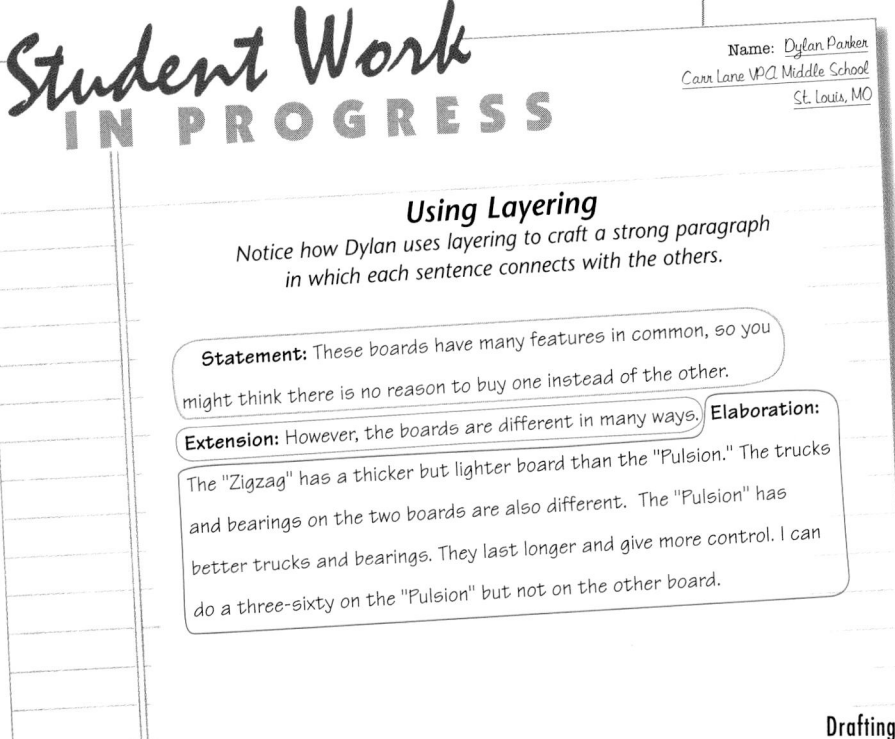

Student Work
IN PROGRESS

Name: *Dylan Parker*
Carr Lane VPA Middle School
St. Louis, MO

Using Layering

Notice how Dylan uses layering to craft a strong paragraph in which each sentence connects with the others.

Statement: These boards have many features in common, so you might think there is no reason to buy one instead of the other.

Extension: However, the boards are different in many ways. **Elaboration:** The "Zigzag" has a thicker but lighter board than the "Pulsion." The trucks and bearings on the two boards are also different. The "Pulsion" has better trucks and bearings. They last longer and give more control. I can do a three-sixty on the "Pulsion" but not on the other board.

Drafting • 159

Drafting: Providing Elaboration

Teaching Resources: Writing Support Transparency, 8-E

1. The **SEE** acronym is a useful structure because it helps students both identify and expand upon the main idea in each paragraph.

2. Display the transparency. Point out how Dylan identifies the main idea and then extends it by pointing out that there are differences. In the remaining sentences, he elaborates with details showing the differences between the two skateboards.

3. If students have trouble stating the main idea of a paragraph, they should consider revising it for clarity before extending or elaborating in any way.

Elaboration Tip

Students can use the familiar strategy of freewriting to come up with details to enhance their topic. Give them three minutes to write down anything and everything they can think of about their topic. Then they can review what they have listed and choose items to include in their writing.

Language Highlight

Acronyms Explain to students that *SEE* is an example of an *acronym,* or a word formed from the first letters of a series of words. *Radar* and *sonar* are both acronyms. Have students find out which words they come from. Can they think of more examples of acronyms?

☑ **ONGOING ASSESSMENT: Monitor and Reinforce**

If you find that students have difficulty elaborating on their ideas, try one of the following strategies.

Option 1 Interpersonal learners might benefit from conversing with another student about their topics. Give them a few minutes to have a conversation, and encourage their partners to ask probing questions about the topic at hand.	**Option 2** Students might need to learn more about their topics before they can write about them. If possible, give students time to conduct research in the school library or on the Internet. Remind them to take notes.

Revising: Revising Your Overall Structure

1. Tell students that the purpose of revision is to make a piece of writing better, by cleaning up errors, organizing details, and sharpening word choice.

2. Point out that a message makes better sense when related details are grouped together. It also conveys that a writer has a clear understanding of his or her topic. This strategy will be particularly helpful for visual learners.

3. Suggest that students try to put themselves in their readers' shoes and imagine that they know nothing about their topics. As they read their essays, they should ask themselves which parts, if any, might not be clear to a novice.

Critical Viewing

Apply Students may say that this skateboarder is more likely to use a "Pulsion."

8.4 Revising

Once you have completed your draft, begin revising your work. Michelangelo, the great Italian artist of the Renaissance, once said that his sculpture was inside the piece of marble before he began to work. He simply chipped away until it revealed itself. There is a good essay hidden in what you have written. Chip away at problems in your draft to reveal it.

Revising Your Overall Structure
Check the Effectiveness of Your Organization

A consistent organization that builds to a point helps readers understand and enjoy a comparison-and-contrast essay. Make sure that you have followed the block or the point-by-point method consistently. Also, make sure that your essay is balanced—that it includes an equal amount of information on both of the subjects you are comparing. Color-code details to make sure your essay is well-organized and balanced.

▶ **REVISION STRATEGY**
Color-Coding Details for Effective Organization and Balance

Highlight in one color the details pertaining to one of the items you are comparing. Use another color to highlight points about the other item.

- If most details in one color are grouped together, review stray details in that color: Do they make sense where they are placed, or should they be joined with the others?

- If one color alternates with another regularly, review longer clumps of a single color: Should these clumps be broken up, with some details moved elsewhere?

If you notice that you have more highlights in one color than in another, add details about the item for which there are fewer highlights.

▶ Critical Viewing Read the "Student Work in Progress" on the next page. Which skateboard model is this skateboarder more likely to use, and why? [**Apply**]

160 • Comparison-and-Contrast Essay

⏱ TIME AND RESOURCE MANAGER

Resources
Print: Writing Support Transparencies, 8-F–G
Technology: Writing Lab CD-ROM, Exposition: Making Connections

In-Depth Coverage	Accelerated Pace
• Cover pp. 160–164 in class. • Work through Revising strategies with students. • Use the relevant transparencies to demonstrate strategies for revising organization and achieving balance, tagging high points, and revising paragraph structure and sentences.	• Assign students to review pp. 160–164 independently. • Have students revise their comparison/contrast essays independently.

Revise Your Introduction and Conclusion

Review your **lead**—your introductory paragraph. If it seems boring to you, consider adding interest with a statement that invites your reader in, such as "You may think all mountain bikes are alike." You could also start off with a strong image or a surprising comparison.

Next, review your conclusion. It should leave your readers with a vivid image or with something to think about. If it does not, consider "tagging high points" to help create such a conclusion.

▶ **REVISION STRATEGY**
Tagging High Points

As you reread your draft, use a sticky note to flag any points of comparison or contrast that stand out as vivid, especially important, or surprising. Consider moving such a point to the end and building up to it.

Writers in
ACTION

Richard Lederer knows the importance of revising for any writer. Like others, he notes that writing only becomes effective after the revision stage:
"Good writing is rewriting. A writer is someone who will work for great lengths of time so that it looks easy."

Student Work
IN PROGRESS

Name: Dylan Parker
Carr Lane VPA Middle School
St. Louis, MO

Tagging High Points
Dylan tagged high points in his draft and moved one for an effective conclusion.

. . . To slide, the skateboarder rides the board in the air while part of it slides along a curb or even the railing on some stairs. I can do more tricks on a "Pulsion," because it has better trucks and wheels. I'm glad I started on a "Zigzag," though, because you can pick up tricks faster on a light, thick board.

I should save this point for the end, because it is an important point. Saving it till the end will be effective in another way, as well. First, readers will learn that the "Pulsion" is a better board, and then they will be surprised that I recommend the "Zigzag" for amateurs.

Conclusion
It sounds like the "Pulsion" is a much better board. Actually, it is not the best board for a beginner. If you are just starting out, you should get the "Zigzag" board. It is made thicker and lighter, and it is more affordable than the "Pulsion." If you learn with a thick but light board, you will be able to do tricks much more easily. This brand was my first board, and now I'm a great skater!

Revising • 161

Step-by-Step Teaching Guide

Revising: Revise Your Introduction and Conclusion

1. Explain that introductions and conclusions are the first and last impressions the reader receives. A strong introduction pulls the reader in and makes him or her want to keep reading. A strong conclusion leaves a final favorable impression.

2. Have partners take turns reading their introductions and making suggestions for improvement. Then have them repeat the process with the conclusions.

Step-by-Step Teaching Guide

Revising: Tagging High Points
Teaching Resources: Writing Support Transparency, 8-F

1. Discuss with students the importance of saving the strongest point for last. Point out how Dylan moved one of the high points from the body of the essay to the conclusion to provide a more effective and powerful ending.

2. Remind students that after they tag their strong points of comparison or contrast, they shouldn't be concerned with moving all of them to the end of their essays. While it is important to build up to a strong conclusion, the body of their essays should offer strong points that can be summarized and revisited in their conclusions.

 TIME SAVERS!

Writing Support Transparencies
Use the transparencies for Chapter 8 to teach these strategies.

Revising: Check Your Paragraph Structure; Marking Paragraph Patterns

Teaching Resources: Writing Support Transparency, 8-G

1. Remind students that each new idea in their essays requires a new paragraph. Display the transparency. Have students compare the paragraphs in "Bat Attacks?" with those in Dylan's essay. Laura Allen includes a lot of short, compact paragraphs. Dylan's paragraphs are longer and more detailed, and there are fewer of them. In both selections, each paragraph addresses a new idea.

2. Review the **TRI** structure with students. Make sure students understand that a topic sentence states the main idea of the paragraph.

3. **R** stands for restatement of the main idea in the topic sentence. The goal is to reinforce the main idea in the reader's mind. Point out how Dylan's restatement reinforces the idea that "Pulsion" and "Zigzag" skateboards have many features in common.

4. The **I** is for details that illustrate the main idea. Tell students it is crucial to include details that support the main idea of the paragraph. Have students point out the details Dylan uses to illustrate his main idea.

5. Have students apply the **TRI** strategy to their essays.

Customize for
Less Advanced Students

Make sure students are familiar with main ideas and topic sentences. Use Dylan's essay as an example. Show students how the first sentence expresses his main idea, that the skateboards have many things in common. To reinforce, have students reread some of the instructional paragraphs in the chapter of the textbook. Ask them to identify the main idea of each.

8.4

Revising Your Paragraphs
Check Your Paragraph Structure

Most paragraphs in your essay probably contain

- **T:** a **topic** sentence, stating the main idea.
- **R:** a **restatement** of the main idea in the topic sentence.
- **I:** **illustrations** of the main idea (including facts, examples, descriptions, and so on).

EXAMPLE: **T**—Not all brands of cat food are alike.

R—Some brands are tastier than others.

I—My cat will eat a quart of Brand X, even if he has eaten an hour earlier. He won't touch Brand Y, though, even if he is starving.

Read the *I* sentences above. On their own, they do not make a good paragraph. In paragraphs that explain main ideas, use at least one sentence of each kind, even if their order varies. Mark paragraph patterns to help strengthen paragraphs.

▶ **REVISION STRATEGY**
Marking Paragraph Patterns

Mark each of your sentences as a *T*, an *R*, or an *I*. Review your draft. If you find a group of *I*'s, make sure there is a *T* they support. If you find a *T* by itself, add an *I* sentence.

Student Work
IN PROGRESS

Name: Dylan Parker
Carr Lane VPA Middle School
St. Louis, MO

Marking Paragraph Patterns

Dylan marked a paragraph in his draft, adding a needed topic sentence.

The "Pulsion" skateboard and the "Zigzag" skateboard have many things in common. Both have the basic features that every skateboard has. **T R**

Each ~~skateboard~~ has four rubber wheels. The wheels are held onto the board by metal trucks, or axles. They both have bushings and pads for the trucks. These parts are like cushions that help the trucks work smoothly and last longer. Both skateboards have ball bearings to keep the wheels rolling fast. **I I I I**

> Dylan noticed that this paragraph contained only "illustrations," so he added two sentences: a statement of the main idea of the paragraph, along with a restatement of that main idea.

162 • Comparison-and-Contrast Essay

☑ **ONGOING ASSESSMENT: Monitor and Reinforce**

If students are having difficulty identifying the main idea of a paragraph, use one of the following options.

Option 1 Have students read one paragraph from the Model From Literature. Ask them what the paragraph is about. Then have them identify the sentence that says this.	**Option 2** Have students work in pairs to review their paragraphs. A fresh pair of eyes can help a student identify the main idea of a paragraph.

Collaborative Writing Tip

Form a group and read one another's work. Each member should mark topic sentences and underline sentences illustrating a point. Then, trade papers, and have others make recommendations based on the markings.

Revising Your Sentences
Combining Sentences
Using Compound Subjects

When you mention a similarity between two things, you can often cover it in one sentence by using a compound subject.

TWO SENTENCES: Water-skiing is fun. Snow-skiing is fun, too.

COMBINED WITH COMPOUND SUBJECT: Both **water-skiing and snow-skiing** are fun.

By combining sentences in this way, you can eliminate unnecessary wordiness. Use the following strategy to help.

▶ **REVISION STRATEGY**
Circling Repetitive Sentences

Review your draft, looking for places where you say the same thing about two items, each in its own sentence (see the example above). Circle these sentences. Review them, and see whether you can combine such sentences using a compound subject.

Language Lab CD-ROM

For additional help in subject-verb agreement, complete a lesson in the Language Lab unit on Subject-Verb Agreement.

Grammar in Your Writing
Subject-Verb Agreement: Compound Subjects

A **compound subject** consists of two subjects joined by a conjunction such as *and, or,* or *nor.* When the subjects joined are singular, two simple rules will help you make sure that a compound subject agrees with its verb:

Two or more singular subjects joined by *and* take a plural verb.

EXAMPLE: Swimming *and* tennis are both fun sports.

Two or more singular subjects joined by *or* or *nor* take a singular verb.

EXAMPLES: A swimming lesson *or* a tennis lesson is good exercise.
Neither a swimming lesson *nor* a tennis lesson is a waste of time.

Find It in Your Reading Read "Bat Attacks?" by Laura Allen on page 152. Identify one compound subject and the verb it takes. Explain what form the verb has—plural or singular—and why.

Find It in Your Writing Identify any singular subjects joined by *and, or,* or *nor* in your draft. Identify the verb for each. Is the verb plural or singular? Does it agree with the subject? Correct any errors you find.

For more on subject-verb agreement, see Chapter 24.

Revising • 163

Grammar in Your Writing: Subject-Verb Agreement: Compound Subjects

1. Students sometimes have difficulty understanding why mistakes in grammar detract from an essay. It is important that they understand the concept of credibility. Many readers associate grammatical mistakes with general incompetence. If the writer is careless about or ignorant of grammar, then the reader often will not trust what the writer has to say about the topic.

2. Use the following examples for extra practice with subject-verb agreement. Have students look for errors, especially with irregular verbs, in their own drafts.

   That book goes here. (singular)
   Those books go here. (plural)

3. Write the following examples on the board for practice on agreement with compound subjects. Have students look for errors of this nature in their drafts.

   Dawn and Carolyn are good friends.
   Dawn or Carolyn is making dinner.

4. The rules here apply to singular subjects combined in compound subjects. You may wish to point out to students that plural subjects take plural verbs when combined. The most confusing situation—when a singular and a plural subject are combined with *or*—is covered on p. 538, along with additional examples of agreement with compound subjects.

Find It in Your Reading

Compound subject and verb: Both a metal bat and a wooden bat have "sweet spots!" The verb *have* is plural because the subjects are joined by *and.*

Find It in Your Writing

Have students exchange papers with partners to check that they have both correctly identified compound subjects and chosen the correct verb to agree with these subjects.

STANDARDIZED TEST PREPARATION WORKSHOP

Grammar and Usage Many standardized tests require students to identify errors in sentences. Problems with subject-verb agreement are among the items included in these sentences. Following is a sample test item. Ask students to identify the sentence containing an error in subject-verb agreement.

A The book about dogs and cats is on the top shelf in my bedroom.

B Tom or Hannah are responsible for baking the cakes.

C Micki or Roger has the helmet you need.

D Roses and lilies are my favorite flowers.

Item **B** is incorrect because compound subjects connected by the conjunction *or* take a singular verb. Show students that the subject in item A is *book,* not *cats and dogs.*

163

Revising: Revising Your Word Choice; Peer Review

1. Write the following sentences on the board and read them aloud:

   John went to the store. Then John went to his friend Rita's house. John and his friend went to the swimming pool.

2. Ask students to identify the problems with the example. (short sentences; the word John is used three times) Ask for suggestions for rewriting to avoid repetition.

   John went first to the store then to his friend Rita's house. John and Rita went to the swimming pool.

3. Point out that using pronouns and different verbs can help add variety and avoid repetition.

4. Have students work in small groups to complete the peer review exercise. Suggest that students take notes on a sheet of paper with two columns headed *Alike* and *Different* to help them keep track of comparisons and contrasts in each essay.

5. This peer review exercise is dependent on students paying close attention to one another's work. Some students may want to work with a partner rather than in a group.

Critical Viewing

Relate Some students may say that they would feel comfortable because the people in the group look friendly and they're all working together.

Revising Your Word Choice
Avoid Unnecessary Repetition

It is important to include everything you want to say in your essay, but you don't have to say it twice! Check your writing for unnecessary repetition. A good way to spot redundancy is to read your work aloud.

▶ **REVISION STRATEGY**
Reading Aloud for Repeated Words

Read your work aloud, underlining any nouns, verbs, or adjectives you use more than once. (You can ignore commonly repeated words such as *the*, *a*, and *of*.) After you have marked your repeated words, evaluate each to determine whether you should replace the word with a synonym.

Peer Review
Summarize

In a small group, read your comparison-and-contrast essay twice, asking group members to listen the first time and to respond the second time. After the second reading, ask your classmates to summarize:

• the main similarities you discuss

• the main differences you discuss.

If your group cannot easily summarize your essay, review your writing again to make sure you have used well-organized paragraphs to develop your topic.

Grammar and Style Tip

One way to avoid repeating the same noun is to use a pronoun in its place. Another is to use a referring term, such as "the former," "the latter," or "the first one." (For more about pronouns, see Chapter 14.)

◀ **Critical Viewing** Would you feel comfortable having this group summarize your essay? Give two details from the photograph to explain your response. **[Relate]**

8.5 Editing and Proofreading

Carefully review your draft for errors in spelling, grammar, punctuation, and usage.

Focusing on Pronouns

Check your draft to make sure that you have used the correct pronoun for each antecedent.

Grammar in Your Writing
Pronoun-Antecedent Agreement

Pronouns are words that take the place of a noun or nouns.

SINGULAR		PLURAL	
Personal	**Possessive**	**Personal**	**Possessive**
I, me	my, mine	we, us	our, ours
you	your, yours	you	your, yours
he, she, it him, her	his, hers, its	they them	their, theirs

A pronoun must agree with its antecedent in both **person** and **number**. A **first-person** pronoun refers to the person speaking; a **second-person** pronoun refers to the person spoken to; and a **third-person** pronoun refers to the person, place, or thing spoken about.

INCORRECT: A *skateboarder* should wear a helmet. You would be a fool not to. (third person/second person)

CORRECT: A *skateboarder* should wear a helmet. He or she would be a fool not to. (third person/third person)

Number indicates whether a pronoun is **singular** (referring to one) or **plural** (referring to more than one).

INCORRECT: A *person* should practice their tricks. (singular/plural)

CORRECT: A *person* should practice his or her tricks. (singular/singular)

Find It in Your Reading Review "Bat Attacks?" by Laura Allen on page 152. Find two examples of pronouns. Identify their antecedents.

Find It in Your Writing Find three pronouns and their antecedents in your draft. For each, determine whether they agree in person and number.

For more on pronouns and their antecedents, see Chapter 24.

Editing and Proofreading • 165

⏱ TIME AND RESOURCE MANAGER

Resources
Print: Scoring Rubrics on Transparency, Chapter 8; Formal Assessment, Ch. 8
Technology: Writing Lab CD-ROM, Exposition: Making Connections

In-Depth Coverage	Accelerated Pace
• Review pp. 165–168 in class. • Distribute and review Proofreading Checklist. • Read and discuss Publishing and Presenting (p. 166). • Analyze in class the Final Draft on p. 167. • Have students edit and proofread their essays.	• Assign pp. 165–168 for independent review. • Have students independently edit and proofread their essays. • Respond to individual editing issues as needed.

Grammar in Your Writing: Pronoun-Antecedent Agreement

1. Make sure students understand that the antecedent is the word for which a pronoun stands. It usually comes before the pronoun in a sentence.

2. Share the following examples with students to help reinforce the concept of pronoun-antecedent agreement:

   I take care of <u>my</u> dog. (first person, singular)

   <u>Susan</u> takes care of <u>her</u> cat. (third person, singular)

   <u>June and I</u> take care of <u>our</u> pets. (first person, plural)

3. In addition to agreement, students should examine their pronouns for clarity. Does each one have a clear antecedent? If not, encourage students to rephrase the sentence.

Find It in Your Reading

There are numerous examples of pronoun usage in "Bat Attacks?" The author writes in the second person, making frequent use of *you*. The subject of the essay, metal and wood bats, is frequently referred to in the third person as *it*. In the first paragraph, baseball officials are *they*. Have students share some examples they find in "Bat Attacks?"

Find It in Your Writing

Students can work in pairs to help each other check for pronoun-antecedent agreement in their essays.

Integrating Technology Skills

Remind students that using the spell check function on the computer is not "cheating." In fact, students should get in the habit of spell checking everything they compose on the computer. However, the spell check is not a substitute for proofreading. On some computers, this function will not pick up errors in grammar, punctuation, or usuage.

165

Publishing and Presenting

1. Publishing is the reward of the writing process. Brainstorm with students for different ways they can share their essays. Possible ideas include giving public readings, posting essays on a relevant Web site, or e-mailing them to a friend.

2. If students choose to present their work to the class, discuss with them any visual aides they could add to their essays, such as photos or drawings, or graphs to enhance their presentations.

ASSESS

Assessment

Teaching Resources: Scoring Rubrics on Transparency, 7; Formal Assessment, Chapter 7

1. Display the Scoring Rubric transparency and review the criteria in class.

2. You may wish to review the Final Draft of the Student Work in Progress. Encourage students to score the Final Draft in at least two categories. Ask them to explain their reasoning.

3. In addition to student self-assessment, you may wish to use the following assessment options:

   • Score student essays yourself, using the rubric and scoring models from Writing Assessment.

   • Review the Standardized Test Preparation Workshop on pages 172–173 and have students respond to an expository writing prompt within a time limit.

   • Administer the Chapter 8 Test from Formal Assessment in Teaching Resources to assess students' grasp of concepts presented.

8.6 Publishing and Presenting

Building Your Portfolio

Consider these ideas for publishing and presenting your work:

1. **Be a Consumer Watchdog** If your essay contains information useful to consumers, form a Consumer Information Panel with classmates. Read your essays to the class, using visual aids to help convey the facts you've gathered.

2. **Present to Your Family or Friends** If you wrote about something in your own life, arrange to read your essay aloud to family or friends. Ask audience members to share their reactions.

Reflecting on Your Writing

Write down a few notes on your experience with comparing and contrasting, answering the questions below.

• Did the process of comparing and contrasting lead you to new ideas about your topic? Explain.

• What was the most important improvement you made to your essay when revising? Explain.

🖳 Internet Tip

To review a comparison-and-contrast essay scored according to this rubric, visit **www.phschool.com**

Rubric for Self-Assessment

Use the following criteria to evaluate your comparison-and-contrast essay:

	Score 4	Score 3	Score 2	Score 1
Audience and Purpose	Clearly attracts audience interest in the comparison-contrast analysis	Adequately attracts audience interest in the comparison-contrast analysis	Provides a reason for the comparison-contrast analysis	Does not provide a reason for a comparison-contrast analysis
Organization	Clearly presents information in a consistent organization best suited to the topic	Presents information using an organization suited to the topic	Chooses an organization not suited to comparison and contrast	Shows a lack of organizational strategy
Elaboration	Elaborates ideas with facts, details, or examples; uses all information for comparison and contrast	Elaborates most ideas with facts, details, or examples; uses most information for comparison and contrast	Does not elaborate all ideas; does not use enough details for comparison and contrast	Does not provide facts or examples to support a comparison and contrast
Use of Language	Demonstrates excellent sentence and vocabulary variety; includes very few mechanical errors	Demonstrates adequate sentence and vocabulary variety; includes few mechanical errors	Demonstrates repetitive use of sentence structure and vocabulary; includes many mechanical errors	Demonstrates poor use of language; generates confusion; includes many mechanical errors

166 • Comparison-and-Contrast Essay

☑ ONGOING ASSESSMENT: Assess Mastery

Use one of the following options to assess final drafts of students' comparison-and-contrast essays.

Self-Assessment You may wish to use the rubric and the scoring models provided in Writing Assessment, Bronze Level, to score the essays.	**Teacher Assessment** Use the rubric and the scoring models provided in Writing Assessment, Comparison-and-Contrast Essay to score students' work.

8.7 Student Work
IN PROGRESS

FINAL DRAFT

Skateboards for Success

Dylan Parker
Carr Lane VPA Middle School
St. Louis, Missouri

Lots of kids are interested in learning to skateboard because they see how much fun skateboarding is. They may not know which is the best skateboard to buy, though. Anyone who is interested in skateboarding needs to compare the different brands of skateboards that are out there. Different features are good for different levels of skaters. I have owned two good models, one called the "Pulsion" and the other called the "Zigzag."

The "Pulsion" skateboard and the "Zigzag" skateboard have many things in common. Both have the basic features that every skateboard has. Each has four rubber wheels. The wheels are held onto the board by metal trucks, or axles. They both have bushings and pads for the trucks. These parts are like cushions that help the trucks work smoothly and last longer. Both skateboards have ball bearings to keep the wheels rolling fast.

The deck is the part of the skateboard that you stand on. Both the "Pulsion" and the "Zigzag" have wooden decks instead of "slick" ones. (A slick deck is also made of wood, but it has plastic along the bottom.) The deck of each has a nose, which is the front curve, and a tail, which is the curve in back. Both models come with grip tape on the boards. A skateboarder needs grip tape to help him or her stay on when doing tricks on the skateboard.

Some skateboard brands do not put a design on the bottom of the deck, but these two do. Both skateboards are represented by a cartoon of an alien on their decks.

▲ **Critical Viewing**
Judging by Dylan's essay, why might this skateboarder prefer the "Pulsion"? **[Apply]**

In his introduction, Dylan draws his audience in by noting a problem his readers may face. He also introduces the two items he is going to compare.

Following a point-by-point organization, Dylan first discusses the features the two boards share with all others. In this next paragraph, he compares other basic features of the two.

Critical Viewing

Apply Students may say that the "Pulsion" is a better board for the experienced skater.

Step-by-Step Teaching Guide

Teaching From the Final Draft

1. As students read the final draft, have them refer to the margin notes to guide their reading. See that students identify the point-by-point organizational structure that Dylan chose.

2. Discuss the strong points of the essay. Point out the casual but interesting introduction; the tight, point-by point comparison Dylan employs; and the separate grouping of contrasting points in the next to last paragraph. Finally, help students appreciate how Dylan keeps readers interested and provides a surprise ending by saving the high point for last.

3. Encourage students to similarly annotate their own essays, pointing out features such as the following: strong introduction, method of organization, similarities, differences, and strong conclusion.

Student Work in Progress • 167

Integrating Grammar Skills

Ask students to find the compound subjects in Dylan's final essay. ("The 'Pulsion' skateboard and the 'Zigzag' skateboard"—paragraph 2, first sentence; "Both the 'Pulsion' and the 'Zigzag'"—paragraph 3, second sentence; "The 'Zigzag' and the 'Pulsion'"—paragraph 6, first sentence; "The trucks and bearings"—paragraph 7, fourth sentence) If students mention "a 'shove it' or a flip" (paragraph 5, seventh sentence), point out that this isn't the subject of the sentence; the subject is *you*.

Integrating Workplace Skills

Explain to students that most jobs require intelligent decision making. Decision making relies on the ability to compare and contrast information. Doctors decide whether to prescribe medicine A or B; lawyers decide which witness to question; quarterbacks decide to whom they should pass the football. Ask other students to think of similar examples in other fields.

Critical Viewing

Compare and Contrast Suggested response: The use in the picture is flashier and more dangerous than the ordinary use. It involves riding on two wheels, while the ordinary use involves riding on all four wheels.

Both skateboards go very fast. Both are easy to control. Using either a "Pulsion" or a "Zigzag," I can do many tricks. For instance, I can do an ollie, a "shove it," a kick flip, a heel flip, a front-side one-eighty, and a nose slide. An ollie is the basic skateboarding trick. To ollie, the skateboarder jumps up. As he or she jumps, he or she snaps the tail of the skateboard so that it comes up with the skateboarder. When a skateboarder does a "shove it" or a flip, he or she turns the board around or over while it is in the air. When a skateboarder does a one-eighty, he or she spins his or her body around while in the air. To slide, the skateboarder rides the board in the air while part of it slides along a curb or even the railing on some stairs.

The "Zigzag" and the "Pulsion" are easy to find. They are sold at almost every skateboarding store. The companies have professional representatives and are known by skaters all across the United States of America.

These boards have many features in common, so you might think there is no reason to buy one instead of the other. However, the boards are different in many ways. The "Zigzag" has a thicker but lighter board than the "Pulsion." The trucks and bearings on the two boards are also different. The "Pulsion" has better trucks and bearings. They last longer and give more control. I can do a three-sixty on the "Pulsion" but not on the other board. The grip tape on the two boards is also different. The "Pulsion" has grip tape like sandpaper, and the "Zigzag" grip tape is just like regular paper stuck onto the board.

It sounds like the "Pulsion" is a much better board. Actually, it is not the best board for a beginner. If you are just starting out, you should get the "Zigzag" board. It is made thicker and lighter, and it is more affordable than the "Pulsion." If you learn with a thick but light board, you will be able to do tricks much more easily. This brand was my first board, and now I'm a great skater! When you are a beginner, you should go with an inexpensive board first, and then, once you've gotten more advanced in your skills, you can get a more expensive skateboard. If you choose the right board, you will learn faster and save money!

▲ **Critical Viewing** Compare this use of a skateboard with a more ordinary use. **[Compare and Contrast]**

Here, Dylan turns to the important differences between the two boards. He keeps the point toward which he is building —which board is better to buy?—in the reader's mind.

Dylan presents the high point of his comparison—the better, more expensive board is actually not better for a beginner!

Connected Assignment *Consumer Report*

Need advice on purchasing a product? It's helpful to turn to a **consumer report**—a comparison of the strengths and weaknesses of different products and the advantages of using one over another. Useful consumer reports feature

- a detailed comparison of two or more similar products.
- a rating of the products, backed by facts.

Prewriting To choose a topic, consider these suggestions:

- **A Recent Purchase** Choose an important purchase you or your family has recently made. Write a report evaluating the product and an alternative.
- **Report on Music Magazines** Choose two magazines that cover music. Compare the type of stories they publish, their advertising, and their features. Recommend one to readers.

Once you have chosen a topic, focus on only a few items— for example, if your topic is CD-players, focus on two in the same price range. Then, jot down a description of who will use your report on an index card: What are their needs? How much money do they have to spend? To meet your audience's needs, consult this card as you gather details.

To gather the details you need, read brochures, user guides, and magazine articles. Record details in a Venn diagram like the one shown.

Drafting After you've gathered and organized all of the information you need, begin drafting. Write the body of your consumer report first. Then, create an introduction that leads into it and a conclusion in which you make your recommendation.

Revising and Editing After completing a draft, check it against your audience description. Is there information you have not included that your readers need to make a good decision? If so, add these details. Have you included details your readers don't need? If so, consider deleting them.

Publishing and Presenting After revising your consumer report, proofread it for errors in spelling, grammar, or punctuation. Consider publishing it on a class consumer Web site.

▲ **Critical Viewing**
Describe a time when you felt as the person in this picture appears to. **[Relate]**

VENN DIAGRAM

CD-Player A
- three-disc changer
- separate bass and treble speakers
- a tone control with five bands
- no bass enhancement

- two built-in tape decks
- built-in radio
- portable

CD-Player B
- five-disc changer
- one speaker for both bass and treble
- "Busta Bass" bass
- no tone controls

Lesson Objectives

1. To compare and contrast musicals as portrayed in different media.
2. To assess how language, medium, and presentation contribute to the message.
3. To write a comparison and contrast essay.

Critical Viewing

Speculate Students may say they might be making fun of a stodgy or pompous person.

Evaluating Performances

1. Choose one of the Spotlight elements for class discussion, or have students work individually or in small groups on the element of their choice. Give students the initiative to find the necessary books, videotapes, or pictures.

2. Interested students can research more information about various forms of orientalism, including any visual examples they find. Have students consider why they think European culture at that time became so fascinated with things Asian.

3. There have been a number of other film adaptations of Gilbert and Sullivan musicals, including *The Mikado.*

4. Students also may be interested in seeing *Topsy Turvy,* a film based on the lives and works of Gilbert and Sullivan.

Viewing and Representing

Activities Encourage interested students to give a class presentation of their comparisons, playing sequences from their chosen films to illustrate their points.

Critical Viewing

Analyze Elements of japonisme include the fan, the cherry blossoms, and the vase on the mantelpiece.

Spotlight on the Humanities

Evaluating Performances

Focus on Music: Gilbert and Sullivan

Sometimes, one movie may remind you of another. When you compare and contrast the two, you may realize that one movie is making fun of the other!

Two masters of the sneaky art of making fun by making comparisons were British composers William Gilbert (1836–1911) and Arthur Sullivan (1842–1900). In their musical comedies, they spoofed everything from the plays about pirates popular at the time (*The Pirates of Penzance*) to the Victorian craze for Japanese culture (*The Mikado*).

Gilbert and Sullivan's comedies are in a form called operetta—a mix of songs and spoken dialogue. (Musically and in subject matter, operetta is lighter than its cousin, opera.) Their fourteen operettas are still performed today.

Art Connection In *The Mikado*, Gilbert and Sullivan made fun of a fashionable fascination with all things Asian, a trend that was underway in England by 1875. The preoccupation with Japanese art, especially ceramics and pottery, was called **japonisme**. Using Japanese and other elements, mid- to late Victorian decorators favored a lush, cluttered look in interior furnishings.

Film Connection In 1983, a film version of Gilbert and Sullivan's *The Pirates of Penzance* was released starring Kevin Kline and Angela Lansbury. Spawned by the successful New York stage production of the operetta at The New York Shakespeare Festival, the film captures the whimsical Gilbert and Sullivan style.

Comparison-and-Contrast Writing Activity: Compare Two Versions of a Musical

Choose a musical that you've seen both on film and in the theater, or in two different movie versions. Write a comparison and contrast of the two versions, explaining which you prefer.

◄ **Critical Viewing** What type of person might Gilbert and Sullivan be making fun of with this character? **[Speculate]**

The Little White Girl, James Abbott McNeill Whistler, Tate Gallery, London

▲ **Critical Viewing** What elements of japonisme can you find in this painting? **[Analyze]**

Media and Technology Skills

Comparing Media

Activity: Comparing Book and Movie Versions

Books don't always stay on the page. Sometimes, a movie maker takes a favorite story and puts it on screen. There are a few ways in which movie makers change stories when they film them.

Learn About It

- **Form** Books unfold in the mind. Anything that can engage the mind—an exciting scene, a poetic description, a scientific explanation—can find a place in one book. A movie, though, holds viewers' attention through images of action. Movie makers do not often include parts of a book that cannot be shown in actions.

- **Time** Movie makers often leave out events that appear in a book. They will also eliminate characters or combine them. The reason is simple: While a reader can read a book over the course of days, putting it down, then picking it up again, most movies are viewed continuously. A movie rarely exceeds two hours in length. To hold to this time, movies include only essential parts of a story.

- **Image and Sound** While a writer shapes your appreciation of a person or event with well-chosen words, movie makers make use of actors' abilities, various camera techniques (close-ups on faces, panoramic views of backgrounds), and the pacing of shots to create drama, mood, and character. A movie maker can also add a piece of lush orchestral music to create romantic longing or a deafening explosion to create excitement.

- **Audience** To help pay for their cost, movies must make a great deal of money during their short "run." For this reason, movie makers try to appeal to current tastes. They may change the period in which a story is set. They may cast the latest star in a role, disregarding the physical appearance of the character in the book.

Evaluate It Watch a movie production of a book you have read. Take notes using a chart like the following. Then, write a brief evaluation of the two versions, explaining which you preferred and why.

Book
Characters: _____
Plot: _____
Setting: _____

Movie
Characters: _____
Plot: _____
Setting: _____

Similarities/ Differences
_____
_____
_____

▶ **Lesson Objectives**

1. To compare and contrast a film with the written version of the story.
2. To evaluate the similarities and differences of the ways in which films and novels tell stories.

Step-by-Step Teaching Guide

Comparing Media

Teaching Resources: Writing Support Transparency, 8-1; Writing Support Activity Book, 8-5

1. Review with students the ways in which film adaptations can differ from their original novel versions.

2. Encourage students to think about the ways in which information can be conveyed in film and the novel. How do these differences affect the story being told in each medium?

3. Display the transparency and distribute the blank graphic organizers. Have students use the organizers to jot down some of their initial thoughts on the films and novels of their choice.

Customize for *More Advanced Students*

Some students may know that not all situations involve a novel being adapted for the screen. Sometimes, a popular film is adapted into a novel in a process known as *novelization*. Encourage students to evaluate films that have been novelized. Does the relationship between the two media differ when it is the film that is adapted into a novel?

Lesson Objectives

1. To select and use a style appropriate to audience and purpose.

2. To produce cohesive and coherent written texts by organizing ideas, using effective transitions, and choosing precise wording.

3. To revise drafts for coherence, progression, and logical support of ideas.

Step-by-Step Teaching Guide

Expository Writing Prompts

Teaching Resources: Standardized Test Preparation Workshop, pp. 15–16

1. Tell students that the more information they can gather in the prewriting stage, the easier writing the essay will be. Remind them not to gather information in too much depth at this point; they will elaborate on this information in the drafting stage.

2. Stress the importance of sketching an outline. A good outline, which maps out the overall organization, will make writing the essay an easier task.

3. Ask students if they can think of any other transition words that they might use to show comparison-and-contrast relationships.

4. Have students answer the writing prompt within a class period.

Standardized Test Preparation Workshop

Responding to Expository Writing Prompts

The writing prompts on standardized tests often measure your ability to write an expository piece, such as a comparison-and-contrast essay. Your writing will be evaluated according to your ability to

- respond directly to the prompt, selecting only details directly connected to the topic.

- organize ideas so they are easy to follow.

- elaborate ideas through the use of appropriate details.

- unify your work through the use of transitions.

- write with few errors in spelling, grammar, usage, or mechanics.

Following is an example of an expository writing prompt. Use the suggestions on the following page to help you respond. The clocks show the suggested percentage of your test-taking time to devote to each stage.

Sample Writing Situation

Writers often use contrasting characters in their stories. By placing unlike characters together in a situation, they are able to emphasize the personality traits of each.

In "Rip Van Winkle" by Washington Irving, Dame Van Winkle and her husband Rip have very different personalities. Write an essay in which you compare and contrast the two characters. Use specific incidents from the story to support your analysis of each.

172 • Comparison-and-Contrast Essay

 TEST-TAKING TIP

Stress to students the importance of an overall plan of attack, like that discussed on page 173. Tell students to make sure they stick to their plans, which will help streamline the writing process. For instance, students should not spend time at the drafting stage worrying about the spelling of a certain word. The time for that will come later during the editing and proofreading stages.

Prewriting

Allow close to one fourth of your time for prewriting.

Use a Venn Diagram Gather information about the two characters using a Venn diagram. (To review an example of a Venn diagram, see page 157.)

Keep a Consistent Purpose As you begin to gather details for your essay, keep in mind your purpose in writing, set by the prompt. The sample prompt does not ask you to retell the story. Instead, it asks you to provide examples from the story that reveal the personalities of the two characters.

Drafting

Allow almost half of your time for drafting.

Organize Details Choose a method of organization. To use the block method, discuss all qualities of one subject first, then all qualities of the next subject. To use the point-by-point method, discuss each aspect of the two subjects in turn. After you choose a method, sketch an outline that fits your chosen method.

Elaborate After organizing details, write an introductory paragraph making a general statement about what the contrast between Irving's characters shows the reader. Then, follow your organization in presenting details that reveal the personality of each character. In your conclusion, sum up your essay by restating the lesson the comparison teaches.

Use Transitions As you draft, use transitional words to indicate the connections between ideas. The following words show comparison-and-contrast relationships: *however, nevertheless, yet, likewise, in the same way, on the contrary, similarly, instead,* and *nonetheless.*

Revising, Editing, and Proofreading

Allow almost one fourth of your time to revise and edit. Use the last few minutes to proofread your work.

Use Precise Language Review your paper for areas where your descriptions are vague. Decide on the best way to phrase each description, and then neatly add the new phrasing to your paper.

Make Corrections Check for errors in spelling, grammar, and punctuation. When making changes, place one line through text that you are eliminating. Use a caret (^) to indicate the places where you are adding words.

Customize for
ESL Students

Explain to students that most of their time should be spent drafting their essays, including choosing methods of organization and elaborating on their ideas. They should not spend valuable time agonizing over particular words or phrases.

Customize for
Less Advanced Students

Review with students how to create and complete a Venn diagram. Have students brainstorm for transition words supporting comparisons and contrast. Develop one list of transitions useful for items in the shared area of the circles and another list of transitions useful for contrasting items in the outer areas.

In-Depth Lesson Plan

	LESSON FOCUS	PRINT AND MEDIA RESOURCES
DAY 1	**Introduction to Cause-and-Effect Essays** Students learn key elements of cause-and-effect essays and analyze the Model From Literature (pp. 174–177).	*Writers at Work Videotape,* Exposition: Making Connections **Writing Lab CD-ROM,** Exposition: Making Connections
DAY 2	**Prewriting** Students choose and narrow a topic, consider their audience and purpose, and gather information (pp. 178–181).	**Teaching Resources** *Writing Support Transparencies 9-A–D; Writing Support Activity Book 9–1*
DAY 3	**Drafting** Students organize their ideas and write their first drafts (pp. 182–183).	**Teaching Resources** *Writing Support Transparencies 9-E*
DAY 4	**Revising** Students revise their drafts in terms of overall structure, paragraphs, sentences, and word choice (pp.184–188).	**Teaching Resources** *Writing Support Transparencies 9-F–H; Writing Support Activity Book 9–2*
DAY 5	**Editing and Proofreading; Publishing and Presenting** Students check their work for accuracy and correctness and present their final drafts (pp. 189–190).	**Teaching Resources** *Scoring Rubrics on Transparency,* Ch. 9; *Formal Assessment,* Ch. 9

Accelerated Lesson Plan

	LESSON FOCUS	PRINT AND MEDIA RESOURCES
DAY 1	**Introduction Through Drafting** Students review characteristics of cause-and-effect writing, select topics, and write drafts (174–183).	*Writers at Work Videotape,* Exposition: Making Connections **Writing Lab CD-ROM,** Exposition: Making Connections **Teaching Resources** *Writing Support Transparencies 9-A–E; Writing Support Activity Book 9–1*
DAY 2	**Revising Through Presenting** Students work individually or with peers to revise, edit, and proofread their work for presentation (pp. 184–190).	**Teaching Resources** *Writing Support Transparencies 9-F–H; Writing Support Activity Book 9–2; Scoring Rubrics on Transparency,* Ch. 9; *Formal Assessment,* Ch. 9

Options for Adapting Lesson Plans

HOMEWORK

Have students complete any stage of the lesson for homework.

TECHNOLOGY

Students can complete any stage of the lesson on computer. Have them print out their completed work.

FEATURES

Extend coverage with Connected Assignment (p. 193), Spotlight on the Humanities (p. 194), Media and Technology Skills (p. 195), and the Standardized Test Preparation Workshop (p. 196).

INTEGRATED SKILLS COVERAGE

Integrating Grammar
Verb Tense SE p. 187
Prepositions SE p. 189
ATE p. 183

Reading/Writing Connection
Reading Strategy SE p. 176
Writing Application SE p. 177

Speaking and Listening
ATE p. 175

Vocabulary
ATE p. 185

Workplace Skills
ATE p. 179

Technology
SE p. 190, ATE p. 184

Viewing and Representing
Critical Viewing SE pp. 174, 176, 182, 187, 188, 191, 192, 193, 194, 195
Analyzing Ideas Represented in Various Art Forms, SE p. 194
Analyzing Media Images, SE p. 195

ASSESSMENT SUPPORT

Standardized Test Preparation SE p. 196; ATE p. 186
Standardized Test Preparation Workshop pp. 17–18
Scoring Rubrics on Transparency, Ch. 9
Formal Assessment, Ch. 9
Writing Assessment and Portfolio Management

MEETING INDIVIDUAL NEEDS

Less Advanced Students ATE p. 186, 197. See also Ongoing Assessments, ATE pp. 177, 179, 181, 187, 190.
More Advanced Students ATE p. 197
ESL Students ATE p. 188

BLOCK SCHEDULING

Pacing Suggestions
For 90-minute Blocks
• Have students complete the Prewriting and Drafting stages in a single period.
• Focus one class period on Revising and Editing and Publishing and Presenting. Allow at least 30 minutes for peer revision.

Resources for Varying Instruction
• *Writing Lab* **CD-ROM** If your students have access to hardware, a 90-minute block provides an ideal opportunity for students to work on computer.
• *Writers at Work* **Videotape** Show the Exposition: Making Connections segment in class

Professional Development Support
• *How to Manage Instruction in the Block* This Teaching Resource provides management and activity suggestions.

MEDIA AND TECHNOLOGY

For the Student
• *Writing Lab* **CD-ROM,** Exposition: Making Connections
• *On-Line Exercise Bank,* Section 22.2

For the Teacher
• *Resource Pro* **CD-ROM**

WRITING AND GRAMMAR WEB SITE

The Interactive Writing and Grammar Web site provides a wide array of support for students, teachers, and parents. Writing support includes:

• Interactive revision checkers
• Scoring rubrics with complete models

www.phschool.com

LITERATURE CONNECTIONS

Related selections from *Prentice Hall Literature: Timeless Voices, Timeless Themes,* Bronze:
From "The Night the Bed Fell," James Thurber, SE p. 177
"Stopping by Woods on a Snowy Evening," Robert Frost, SE p. 179

▶ **Lesson Objectives**

1. To write to inform and explain in a style appropriate to audience and purpose.
2. To write to express, develop, and reflect on ideas.
3. To produce coherent text by organizing ideas using effective transitions and choosing precise wording.
4. To generate ideas for writing by using brainstorming, graphic organizers, and notes.
5. To develop drafts by organizing them into paragraphs.
6. To revise drafts by adding, elaborating, deleting, and rearranging text.
7. To demonstrate control of the English language and use verb tenses appropriately and consistently.
8. To proofread his/her writing.
9. To select and use reference materials and resources for writing, revising, and editing final drafts.
10. To respond in constructive ways to others' writings, and evaluate how well his/her own writing achieves its purposes.
11. To present information using available technology.
12. To analyze and evaluate how different media, such as print and photography, influence and inform.

Chapter 9 Exposition
Cause-and-Effect Essay

Cause-and-Effect Explanations in Everyday Life

A friend explains that her bike had a flat tire and that's why she didn't show up at the mall. Your brother arrives late for dinner and complains that his soccer game started an hour later than scheduled. These excuses are also **cause-and-effect explanations**—explanations of why something happened.

Without cause-and-effect explanations, there would be no excuses—but neither would there be sciences, plans, or games. Why hit a ball if you don't believe the bat will cause it to fly into the outfield? Why change the batteries if you don't think that electricity causes the flashlight to work? Cause-and-effect explanations help us make sense of our world and discover new possibilities.

▲ **Critical Viewing** Explain briefly what cause-and-effect relationships connect the subjects of these two photographs. **[Interpret; Connect]**

174 • Exposition

Critical Viewing

Interpret; Connect Students may say that the construction workers work on steel beams and, eventually, their labor will result in these high-rise buildings.

⏱ TIME AND RESOURCE MANAGER

Resources
Technology: Writers at Work videotape, Exposition: Making Connections

In-Depth Coverage	Accelerated Pace
• Cover pp. 174–177 in class. • Read literature excerpt (pp. 176–177) in class, and use it to brainstorm essay ideas with students. • Discuss examples of cause-and-effect essays students know about or have brought to class.	• Have students read pp. 174–177 on their own. • Discuss definitions and types of cause-and-effect essays in class. • Assign Model From Literature for independent reading.

What Is a Cause-and-Effect Essay?

Exposition is writing that informs or explains. A **cause-and-effect essay** is expository writing that explains the reasons why something happened or the results an event or situation will produce. A cause-and-effect essay might focus on causes, as in an explanation of why the days get shorter in the fall, or it might focus on effects, as in an essay on why chemicals are used in farming. In either case, a cause-and-effect essay explains one group of events or facts with another group.

Cause-and-effect essays include

- a well-defined topic that can be covered in a few pages.
- detailed, factual explanations of events or situations and the relationships among them.
- a clear organization with transitions that indicate the relationships among details.

Types of Cause-and-Effect Essays

The following are a few of the types of cause-and-effect essays you might write:

- **Science reports** describe a series of events (including experiments) and explain them according to natural laws.
- **Historical accounts** describe the causes or effects of an event, such as a war or an election.
- **Cause-and-effect investigations** describe the causes or effects of something you have noticed in your own life, such as a new road or a change in weather patterns.

Writers in ACTION

Music critic and expository writer Dimitri Ehrlich has written for a number of publications. His music reviews often analyze the causes of musical success or failure. Experience has taught him that writing is a process of reworking:

"I sit down and I create the raw material. Then I sit back and look at it, maybe I print it. . . . Then I will organize and I'll write a theme sentence at the beginning."

PREVIEW Student Work IN PROGRESS

Jake Sommer is a student at Maplewood Middle School in Maplewood, New Jersey. In his essay "Why Trains Are No Longer Popular," Jake looks at why train travel has become less popular than travel by car and plane. In this chapter, you will see how Jake used featured prewriting, drafting, and revising strategies to develop his final draft. At the end of the chapter, you can read Jake's completed essay.

Interest GRABBER Ask students to think about the most recent sporting event they have seen. Have students write the reasons why they think the winning team or athlete was successful over the opponent(s). Ask several students to share their responses with the class.

Activate Prior Knowledge

Ask partners to talk about the last time they did well on an exam. Instruct students to explain the events that led up to their success on the test and how their actions affected their performance. Discuss student responses as a class, emphasizing the relationship between students' behavior prior to the exam and their grade. Draw students' attention to the similarity between the way they described the reasons for their success on the exam and the necessary components of a cause-and-effect essay. Ask students to identify other events in everyday life they might analyze to determine cause, for example, a sporting event, a misunderstanding, an argument with a friend, a traffic jam, or being late. Point out to students that this kind of analysis of events and why they happened makes up the basis for a cause-and-effect essay.

More About the Writer

Dimitri Ehrlich is a music journalist who has also spent twenty years as a musician. His work has appeared in almost every major music and style magazine.

Integrating Speaking and Listening Skills

Point out to students that the entire experience of school can be seen as a series of cause-and-effect conversations with teachers and classmates. Discuss the ways school reinforces the speaking and listening skills needed to make cause-and-effect explanations.

☑ ONGOING ASSESSMENT: Diagnose

Use one of the following options to diagnose students' current level of proficiency in cause-and-effect writing.

Option 1 Ask each student to select the strongest example of his or her science or history report from last year. Hold conferences in which you review each student's sample. Use the conferences to determine which students will need extra support in developing skill at cause-and-effect writing.

Option 2 Ask students to write for 5 minutes on how much they have grown in the last year and what has changed in their life because of it. If students have difficulty completing this exercise, you will need to devote more time on the process of organizing and evaluating information.

TEACH

Reading\Writing Connection

Reading: Infer

Making inferences can also be called reading between the lines. Inferring the meaning of something described in a piece of writing involves drawing a conclusion by thinking about what the author does not say directly. Making inferences is central to the creation of a cause-and-effect essay because the writer may have to see the connection between causes and effects that are not obvious and then convey them to readers.

Teaching From the Model

Use this Model From Literature as a means of reinforcing the ways cause-and-effect essays use carefully chosen details to give a sense of what happens and why. This is obvious in nonfiction selections. It is just as important in fiction, but less obvious. Writers usually imply rather than state directly why characters act this way or feel that emotion.

Critical Viewing

Analyze Students may say that the rain caused this person to put on rain gear and carry an umbrella.

Step-by-Step Teaching Guide

Engaging Students Through Literature

1. Ask students what scientists say causes rain. Use their responses to point out the features of this particular cause-and-effect essay.

2. Ask students what they learned from this cause-and-effect essay. Make a two-column chart on the chalkboard labeled *Cause* and *Effect* and list students' responses.

3. Suggest that students use clue words that signal causes or effects. The essay contains *proved, only when, one way, since, the reason for, proved,* and *as long as*—all hints that a cause and/or an effect follows.

continued

Model From Literature

How in the World? is a collection of brief articles explaining various facts and phenomena—from why you don't fall out of a roller coaster when it turns upside down to how physicists count tiny nuclear particles.

This form of literature—brief scientific explanations for ordinary readers—has become quite popular. Its popularity shows the importance of science in our lives. It also shows people's need to understand the causes and effects that shape their world.

▲ **Critical Viewing** What are some cause-and-effect explanations that this photograph brings to mind? **[Analyze]**

◀ **Reading | Writing Connection**

Reading Strategy: Infer Even in a cause-and-effect essay, a writer cannot explain every detail. As a result, when you read you must **make inferences**—use explanations and details that are provided to draw conclusions about details that are left out. You can also use your knowledge and experiences to help you make inferences. As you read this essay, use your knowledge to make inferences about why scientists would attempt to cause rain.

How Do Rainmakers Make It Rain?

from **How in the World?**

. . . In 1946 Vincent Schaefer and Irving Longmuir started their work at the General Electric Research Laboratories in Schenectady, New York, which proved that rain clouds could be artificially encouraged to produce showers.

176 • Cause-and-Effect Essay

Clouds are made up of billions of particles of water too small to fall as rain. Only when the droplets grow to a quarter of a millimeter or more will they fall as a fine drizzle. Smaller droplets evaporate before reaching the ground.

One way the droplets grow is by freezing to form particles of ice. In a cloud containing some ice particles and some water droplets, the ice particles grow rapidly as the droplets evaporate and the vapor is transferred to the ice. Since the temperature of clouds is often below freezing it might be expected that the droplets would freeze easily. But the water can be 10 or 20 degrees below freezing (supercooled) without actually freezing.

The reason for this is that the water in clouds is absolutely pure, without any dust or other contaminants which can form the center of an ice crystal. If tiny particles are provided, the droplets freeze, grow quickly until they are large enough to fall, and then melt as the temperature rises, reaching the ground as rain.

Schaefer and Longmuir proved that small particles, usually of silver iodide, added to supercooled clouds could create rapidly growing ice crystals. These particles have been dropped from aircraft, carried by rockets or even released at ground level for air currents to carry them aloft.

In the [former] Soviet Union, 70mm artillery guns have been used to fire silver iodide particles into clouds, exploding at the right height to disperse the chemical.

As long as the clouds are supercooled the technique may work—increasing rainfall by up to a fifth. But since it is impossible to know how much rain would have fallen anyway there are still question marks over the method's economic effectiveness.

Reading Writing Connection

Writing Application: Help Readers Infer As you write your own cause-and-effect essay, help readers draw inferences by providing thorough evidence for your cause-and-effect explanation.

The authors present a sequence of causes and effects. First, they describe what needs to happen before rain will fall—water particles must grow in size. Next, they give one cause of this growth.

Here, the authors explain an additional condition needed to cause rain to fall.

By explaining what causes rain to fall naturally, the authors make it possible for readers to understand how scientists have tried to cause it to rain.

LITERATURE

To read a humorous example of cause-and-effect writing, see James Thurber's story "The Night the Bed Fell." This story can be found in *Prentice Hall Literature: Timeless Voices, Timeless Themes,* Bronze.

Model From Literature • 177

Step-by-Step Teaching Guide continued

4. Explain to students that as they write their own cause-and-effect essays, they will need to be aware of what details to include to make causes and effects clear to readers.

5. Refer to the list of types of cause-and-effect essays on page 175. Ask students which kind of essay they think "How Do Rainmakers Make It Rain?" is (part science, part investigation). Ask them which kind of cause-and-effect essay they think they might want to write.

Responding to Literature

James Thurber's "The Night the Bed Fell" is not cause-and-effect writing in the way students might expect. It is not scientific, factual, or even plausible! Yet the characters seem to spend their life devising reasons why weird things happen and trying to avoid their recurrence. It all makes a kind of lunatic sense—readers do see how the characters arrived at their conclusions, even if those conclusions are zany.

Reading\Writing Connection

Writing Application: Help Readers Inter

Tell students that readers have an easier time understanding a cause-and-effect explanation when the writer first gives a general principle or rule and then shows how it applies in a particular case. Readers can make inferences from the general principle to determine what effects a particular cause should have. Point out that, in the essay, the writers explain the principles behind rain before explaining how scientists make it rain.

☑ ONGOING ASSESSMENT: Monitor and Reinforce

After previewing the Model from Literature, you may anticipate some students may have difficulty with some proper names and other words. Use one of the following options.

Option 1 If students read the model independently, have them list any unfamiliar words they encounter. Then go over pronunciations and definitions in class.	**Option 2** If you or a prepared student read the model aloud in class, take time to define unfamiliar words as they are encountered. Words such as *contaminants* and *disperse* may need definitions.

Prewriting: Brainstorming

1. Explain to students that they should choose a topic for their cause-and-effect essay about which they are genuinely interested.

2. To help students generate ideas about possible topics, have them work in groups and choose a recorder who writes down all of the ideas generated by the group.

3. Instruct students to think of as many answers as they can to the following questions: "What causes X?" and "What are the effects of Y?"

4. Remind students that at this stage in their process, they should be thinking of many ideas without judging them.

5. Give groups 10 minutes to generate and record their responses. Then ask students to review their lists and circle all of the topics they think could be developed into cause-and-effect essays. Write these possible topics on the chalkboard.

6. Evaluate the viability of the possible topics as a class and cross out any that are too large, too small, or, now that they consider it, too boring.

7. Explain to students that they can choose their topic from one listed on the chalkboard or try other techniques to generate topics.

Prewriting: Blueprinting

Explain to students that they can use any place or structure: a sports stadium, a bridge, an amusement park, a museum, and so on.

Prewriting: Media Flip-Through

Teaching Resources: Writing Support Transparency 9-A

Display the transparency. Have students study Jake's notes from his Media Flip-Through. Suggest that they watch the news on TV tonight and flip through some magazines at home for inspiration.

9.2 Prewriting

Choosing Your Topic

Perhaps you have always wondered why leaves change color or why hair turns gray as people age. Choose a question that interests you as the topic of your essay. Use the following strategies to help stimulate ideas:

Strategies for Generating a Topic

1. **Brainstorming** In a group, brainstorm for topics by filling in the blanks in two questions: "What Causes X?" and "What Are the Effects of Y?" One member should list ideas on the chalkboard. Select your topic from those listed.

2. **Blueprinting** Draw the plan of a house, apartment, or other place you know, labeling each room or area. For each part of the plan, list connected people, things, words, or activities. Then, reread what you have written. Circle items about which you can ask, "What caused this?" or "What effects does this have?" Choose your topic from these items.

3. **Media Flip-Through** Sometimes you browse through the refrigerator looking for just the right snack. You can browse for writing ideas as well. Scan the newspaper, look through magazine racks, or go to the library. Skim for ideas until you find an interesting topic involving causes and effects.

Student Work
IN PROGRESS

Name: Jake Sommer
Maplewood Middle School
Maplewood, NJ

Media Flip-Through

Jake watched the news, looked at magazines, and poked around his house gathering topic ideas. From his notes, he selected the one that interested him most.

Ideas for Cause-and-Effect Essay

TV news story: Increases in airfares

Landfill article in <u>Newsweek</u> magazine

Radio: Diary from Kosovo

Conversation between Uncle Robert and Dad—
our team's offensive line

Radio documentary: people who watch and track trains

178 • Cause-and-Effect Essay

⏱ TIME AND RESOURCE MANAGER

Resources
Print: Writing Support Transparencies 9-A–D, Writing Support Activity Book 9-1

In-Depth Coverage	Accelerated Pace
• Cover pp. 178–181 in class. • Guide students through the Strategies for Generating a Topic. • Help students make some initial decisions about narrowing their topics by using Classical Invention on p. 180.	• In class, discuss how to create and choose a cause-and-effect essay topic. • Have students list possible topics. • Ask students to submit topic proposals for your review.

TOPIC BANK

If you're having trouble finding a topic, consider the following possibilities:

1. **Explanation of a Cycle** Choose a cycle, such as the life cycle of plants, the creation of new toys every year, or television show "repeats." Write an essay explaining what keeps the cycle going.

2. **Causes of Victory or Defeat** Write an explanation of the performance of a favorite team or athlete over a season or in a playoff. Explain how ability and other factors, such as the weather and level of confidence, shaped the outcome.

Responding to Fine Art

3. This painting hints at forces in the sky. Choose an event in the sky, such as the seasonal "movement" of the stars, a thunderstorm, or the Northern Lights, and explain what causes it.

Responding to Literature

4. Read Robert Frost's "Stopping by Woods on a Snowy Evening." Then, write about a time when you stopped in the middle of an activity. Explain what caused you to stop, what the effects of the pause were, and whether you felt as Frost did. You can find Frost's poem in *Prentice Hall Literature: Timeless Voices, Timeless Themes*, Bronze.

Aloha #6, Paul Brach, Courtesy Bernice Steinbaum Gallery, Miami, FL

☑ Cooperative Writing Opportunity

5. **Cause-and-Effect Pamphlet** With a group of classmates, choose a major event in history with many causes and effects, or select a broad topic with many subtopics—weather events, for example. Brainstorm a list of causes and effects. Then, each group member should choose a specific topic or set of causes and effects. Work individually to write cause-and-effect essays on your chosen topics. Then, regroup to revise the essays and assemble them into a pamphlet with a cover and contents page.

Responding to Fine Art

Aloha #6 by Paul Brach
Teaching Resources: Writing Support Transparency 9-B

Weather phenomena can make good topics for cause-and-effect essays. You can use this artwork to help students think about weather events and find a main focus for a cause-and-effect essay.

1. Display the transparency and ask students what kind of weather this sky suggests.

2. Ask what they think the arrow over the sky means.

3. Have students brainstorm a list of other events that occur in the sky, and write their ideas on the chalkboard.

4. Choose several topics and ask students to explain what causes these events to occur.

5. Explain that any one of these topics could serve as a main focus for a cause-and-effect essay.

Responding to Literature

Read Robert Frost's poem with the students and use questions such as the following to guide them in discussion:
• What does the speaker stop to do?
• What does the last speaker suggest the speaker is tempted to do?

Spotlight on the Humanities

For additional topics, refer students to the Spotlight on the Humanities on page 194.

☑ ONGOING ASSESSMENT: Monitor and Reinforce

If you observe that students lapse into the habit of always writing for their teacher, try one of the following options.

Option 1 Suggest that students write to a very specific audience of one—a relative, a friend, or a much younger person.	**Option 2** Have students write down a brief profile of their intended audience, including their level of education, skills, and background knowledge of the topic.

⏱ TIME SAVERS!

🔳 **Writing Support Transparencies**
Use the transparencies for Chapter 9 to teach these strategies.

Prewriting: Asking Questions to Narrow a Topic

Teaching Resources: Writing Support Transparency 9-C

1. Remind students that they will need to provide in-depth analysis of the causes and effects of the events they describe in their essay, and that they will need to focus their topic in order to do this.

2. Display the transparency. Review Jake's process of narrowing his too-big topic of trains.

3. Have students freewrite on the questions listed in the textbook. Afterward, they can circle the most interesting items in their answers and put them together to see if they all lead to a good topic.

4. Ask volunteers to tell the class their narrowed topic and explain the cause(s) and effect(s). Let the class offer constructive criticism on the pros and cons of the topic, along with ways to make it better or more workable.

Integrating Workplace Skills

All workers consider causes and effects. Doctors wonder what caused a disease and what effect a treatment will have. Car manufacturers add safety devices and see if the effect is fewer injuries. Clothing designers try to determine why a certain style is no longer popular. Restaurants raise (or lower) prices and watch if this affects customer satisfaction.

9.2

Narrowing Your Topic

Consider whether your topic is narrow enough to discuss thoroughly in a brief essay. A topic with many causes and effects, such as the causes of storms, is far too broad. However, the effects of a tornado would be appropriate. The following strategy will help you narrow your topic.

Use Classical Invention to Narrow Your Topic

In ancient Greece, thinkers developed the strategy of Classical Invention to analyze a topic. Here are the steps:

1. Replace the topic in the example below with your own topic, and answer the questions shown.

2. Review your responses, and circle a series of related events that catch your interest.

3. Write a statement summing them up. Use this as your narrowed topic.

Student Work
IN PROGRESS

Name: *Jake Sommer*
Maplewood Middle School
Maplewood, NJ

Asking Questions to Narrow a Topic
Here's how Jake focused his topic:

General Topic: Trains

- In what category does your topic belong?
  Hobbies (train counting, collecting models); transportation

- How is your topic similar to or different from others in the category?
  Hobbies: train counting is for outdoors; Transportation: trains carry groups of people—not like cars; Transportation: trains are not as popular as cars.

  Narrowed Topic
  Why are trains no longer popular?

- What causes and effects are involved with this topic?
  Causes: invention of steam engine; goods needed to be moved across the country quickly; invention of cars, trucks, and airplanes caused trains to become less popular. Effects: The U.S. was able to grow westward.

Considering Your Audience and Purpose

Identify your intended **audience**—your readers—and your **purpose** for writing. Answer these questions to help you choose words and details that fit your audience and purpose:

- How much do my readers know about my topic?
- With what type of language will they be most comfortable? Formal? Informal? A combination?
- In addition to informing my audience, what else do I hope to accomplish? Do I want my audience to accept a point of view or take action?

Gathering Details

Do Research

You may not know all the causes and effects you need to cover. Do research to fill in any gaps in your knowledge. Use library resources, on-line references, and primary sources—for example, interviews with experts or your own observations. Use a T-chart and note cards to help you gather details.

Use a T-Chart Focus your research by asking good questions. Draw a large T on a piece of paper. Write your topic above it. Label each side as shown below. List key causes and effects involved in your topic on either side. Fill in the answers as you do research.

Topic: **How the Sun Heats and Lights the Earth**

What causes _____?	What are the effects of _____?
1. the sun to rise and set: The Earth spins around on its axis.	**1. the sun rising and setting:** Day and night, warmth and light, cold and darkness result.
2. the sun to give heat and light: Atomic reactions, like a long-lasting explosion, go off inside the sun.	**2. the sun giving heat and light:** Animals and plants can live on Earth. Plants use sunlight to grow, and animals eat the plants.

 Research Tip

Encyclopedias on CD-ROM make browsing especially easy. Many allow you to begin by identifying an area of interest, such as Performing Arts, Science, Hobbies, Sports, or Pets. Then, you can scan the alphabetical list until something sparks your interest.

Prewriting: Do Research; Use a T-Chart

Teaching Resources: Writing Support Transparency 9-D; Writing Support Activity Book 9-1

1. Display the transparency and distribute copies of the blank organizer.

2. Ask students to list all the things that they already know about the causes and effects of the event that will be the main focus of their essay.

3. Now ask if the information they have written is sufficient to write their essay. (Most students should say no.)

4. Explain that students will probably have to do some research on their topic in order to write a cause-and-effect essay that contains enough detailed, factual explanation of the events they choose to write about and the relationships between them.

5. Remind students that these questions will guide their research on their topic, and that they need to consider their audience and purpose as they answer them.

☑ **ONGOING ASSESSMENT: Monitor and Reinforce**

Students often forget their sources when they work on topics that require research. To help them keep a record of where they collected their information, try the following strategies.

Option 1 Remind students that the details they gather on their T-charts will carry more weight if their sources are credited. Ask students what kinds of sources might have been used to find the information for the topic example in the T-chart, "How the Sun Heats and Lights the Earth."

Option 2 In class, have students prepare index cards with the numbers from their T-charts. They should label one set of cards *Causes* and the other *Effects*. By recording bibliographic information on these cards and matching them with the lists on their charts, they will be able to find their sources when they use them.

⏱ **TIME SAVERS!**

 **Writing Support Transparencies**
Use the transparencies for Chapter 9 to teach these strategies.

 Writing Support Activity Book
Use the graphic organizers for Chapter 9 to facilitate these strategies.

Drafting: Shaping Your Writing

1. Now that students have narrowed their topics, they will need to find a focus and organize their information logically. Because students may be covering a number of events in their essay, they may need to use a strategy to help them to organize their information.

2. Tell students that a focused cause-and-effect essay answers a single question that is interesting to them and that they think will be interesting to their audience.

3. Instruct students to review the information they have gathered on their topic and to formulate a single question that their essay will answer.

4. Have several students write their sentences on the chalkboard so that the class can evaluate them together for focus.

5. Explain that there can be multiple cause-and-effect relationships involved in their topic and that these relationships can be complicated. This means that students must keep their information organized as they write their essay.

6. Draw students' attention to the flowcharts in their textbooks, which show several causes leading to one effect and several effects resulting from one cause.

7. Have students draw their own flowcharts for the causes and effects they will explain, using the models in the textbook as examples.

Critical Viewing

Analyze Students may mention any of the various stages of the contraption shown.

Drafting

Shaping Your Writing
Organize Logically

Using the information you've gathered, begin writing your first draft. Start your essay with an introduction that includes a sentence or two summing up the main point you'd like to make about your topic. Then, organize your body paragraphs using these suggestions:

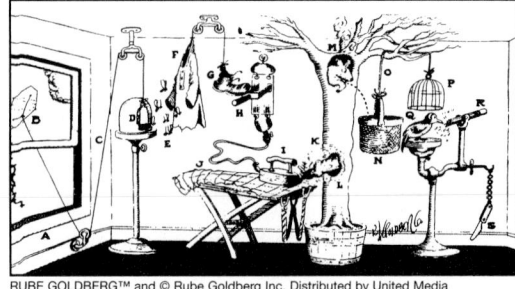

RUBE GOLDBERG™ and © Rube Goldberg Inc. Distributed by United Media

▲ **Critical Viewing** Describe two of the processes linking cause and effect in this cartoon. **[Analyze]**

Many Causes/Single Effect If you're writing about a single event with many causes—as illustrated in this diagram—devote one paragraph to each cause and follow these paragraphs with one paragraph about the effect.

CAUSE Sid sprains his ankle.

CAUSE Mary has the flu.

CAUSE Sam isn't allowed to play.

EFFECT The team loses an important game.

Single Cause/Many Effects If your topic involves a single event or situation that has produced many effects, devote one paragraph to each effect.

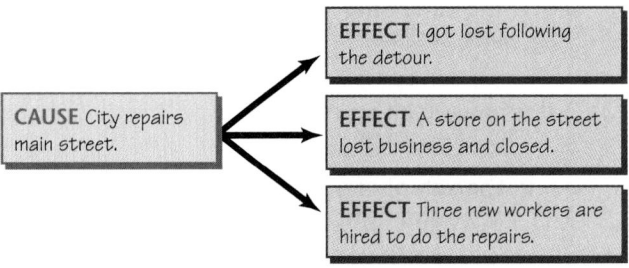

CAUSE City repairs main street.

EFFECT I got lost following the detour.

EFFECT A store on the street lost business and closed.

EFFECT Three new workers are hired to do the repairs.

Series of Causes and Effects If your topic consists of a series of causes and effects, organize your body paragraphs in chronological, or time, order.

182 • Cause-and-Effect Essay

⏱ TIME AND RESOURCE MANAGER

Resources
Print: Writing Support Transparency 9-E

In-Depth Coverage	Accelerated Pace
• Cover pp. 182–183 in class. • Work through the diagram for organizing events with entire class. • Have students write their own cause-and-effect essay draft in class. • Help students elaborate on the causal connections in their essays as they write.	• Have students review pp. 182–183 independently, then write their own cause-and-effect essay draft. • Respond to individual drafting issues as needed.

Providing Elaboration

Provide detailed explanations of each cause or effect. Make sure that your explanations include enough evidence to enable readers to follow the logic of the connections you're making.

Elaborate Causal Connections

Following are three different types of connections:

- **Natural laws** link some causes to their effects.

CAUSE AND EFFECT: The shape of a steel ship causes it to float.

EXPLAIN THE LOGIC: An object will float if the amount of fluid it pushes aside weighs more than it does. *(Law of Buoyancy)*

- **Physical processes** link some causes to their effects.

CAUSE AND EFFECT: Sunlight causes plants to grow.

EXPLAIN THE LOGIC: Chlorophyll in the plant uses energy from sunlight in a chemical reaction that nourishes the plant. *(Process: Photosynthesis)*

- **Motives and habits** usually explain the way people act.

CAUSE AND EFFECT: Unfair laws caused the colonists to revolt.

EXPLAIN THE LOGIC: The colonists wanted control over the laws by which they were ruled. *(The Desire for Freedom)*

As you draft, explain the logic of each causal connection you describe.

Student Work
IN PROGRESS

Name: Jake Sommer
Maplewood Middle School
Maplewood, NJ

Elaborating Causal Connections
As Jake drafted, he explained the logic of some causal connections:

Traveling by train then became the main source of transportation between small towns and from big cities to other cities. One important cause of the growth of the railroad was the convenience of train travel and shipping. By having trains everywhere, the people could travel thousands of miles in only days instead of weeks.

> To explain one reason for the growth of trains, Jake wrote a sentence about people's motives: People used trains because they liked the convenience of the railroad.

Drafting • 183

Step-by-Step Teaching Guide

Drafting: Elaborate Causal Connections

Teaching Resources: Writing Support Transparency 9-E

1. To illustrate the importance of showing causal connections between events and to heighten students' awareness of their audience, tell students about a cause-and-effect relationship without mentioning the logical connection between the two occurrences. For example, it snowed yesterday, and you didn't walk your dog. Explain that the snow was the cause, and not walking your dog was the effect.

2. Ask students to tell you how the cause led to the effect. (Students might guess but probably won't know the answer.)

3. Explain the logical connection. Your dog is terrified.

4. Tell students that this is an example of a tie between events that is explained by motives and habits.

5. Direct students to read about the three ties that can exist between events in their textbooks. Explain to students that they will need to provide this kind of explanation so that their readers can see the relationship between the events they describe in their essays.

6. Display the transparency of Jake's work in progress for an example of how to elaborate on causal connections.

7. Ask students to choose two causal connections in their own essay and elaborate on them by using the same technique.

Integrating Grammar Skills

Cause-and-effect essays provide an opportunity to help students strengthen their ability to use subordinating conjunctions. Write the following sentences on the chalkboard and then review the use of *because* as a subordinating conjunction:

The shape of a steel ship causes it to float.

A steel ship floats because of its shape.

Sunlight causes plants to grow.
Plants grow because of sunlight.

Revising: Connecting the Steps

Teaching Resources: Writing Support Transparency 9-F

1. Students need to make sure that the organization of their essay helps the reader to understand both the importance of the events and the order in which they occur.

2. Explain to students that the order in which they include events in their essay can either help or confuse readers.

3. Display the transparency. Go through Jake's process of connecting the steps in his essay.

4. Using Jake's work as a guide, tell students to highlight each sentence in their own text in which they sum up an event or condition.

5. Next, students can number these events or conditions in order of importance or occurrence and draw arrows to connect each step in numbered order.

6. Have students analyze their arrows and order by checking all arrows that point backward.

7. Ask students to think about why they ordered these events or conditions the way they did, and to change them if they cannot justify their decisions.

8. After students have established their final order, ask them to share their sequence with a partner, justifying their organizational decisions.

Technology Tip

If students are using a word-processing application on the computer, be sure they know how to highlight text and drag it to another location. This makes it easy to test various ways of ordering information.

⏲ TIME SAVERS!

🗒 **Writing Support Transparencies**
Use the transparencies for Chapter 9 to teach these strategies.

📖 **Writing Support Activity Book**
Use the graphic organizers for Chapter 9 to facilitate these strategies.

9.4 Revising

Revising Your Overall Structure

Check Logical Structure

Start revising by using this strategy to check that you have presented causes and effects in a logical sequence.

▶ **REVISION STRATEGY**
Connecting the Steps

Following is the procedure for "Connecting the Steps":

1. Highlight each sentence that sums up an event or condition.
2. Number each in the order of occurrence or importance.
3. Draw arrows connecting each step in numbered order.
4. If any arrows point backward, reorganize some of your details so that all of the arrows point forward.

Student Work
IN PROGRESS

Name: Jake Sommer
Maplewood Middle School
Maplewood, NJ

Connecting the Steps

When Jake saw arrows crisscrossing his draft, he realized he needed to rearrange sentences.

By the early 1900s, there were 252,000 miles of track. ³ The biggest advance in railroads came in 1869 when the transcontinental railroad was completed. It took seven years to build the tracks between the east coast and the west coast. Then came the Golden Age of Railroads. Before the Civil War there were approximately 31,000 miles of track. Traveling by train then became the main source of transportation between small towns and from big cities to other cities.

184 • Cause-and-Effect Essay

⏲ TIME AND RESOURCE MANAGER

Resources
Print: Writing Support Transparencies 9-F–H; Writing Support Activity Book 9-2

In-Depth Coverage	Accelerated Pace
• Cover pp. 184–188 in class. • Work through revision strategy with the entire class.	• Assign students to review pp. 184–188 independently. • Have students revise their cause-and-effect essays independently.

Revising Your Paragraphs

State Main Ideas Clearly

Simply by starting a new paragraph, you signal readers that a new idea is coming up. Effective writers state the main idea in each paragraph clearly. Use the following strategy to make sure that each of your paragraphs has a clearly stated main idea:

▶ **REVISION STRATEGY**
Finding the "Tug"

Reread each paragraph to find the main idea that draws your attention—the "tug" of the paragraph. Summarize this "tug" in one or two words in your margin. Then, check whether your paragraph includes a sentence that expresses this idea clearly. If not, craft a "tug" sentence, weaving it into the beginning, middle, or end of the paragraph.

The Earth is attracted to the sun by the force of gravity. This force keeps it from flying off into space. Gravity alone, though, would just pull the Earth straight into the sun. Inertia, the force that keeps the Earth speeding along through space, keeps it from falling into the sun.

Tug: There are two forces that cause the Earth to revolve around the sun.

Show Connections

Once you're confident that each paragraph has a topic sentence, use the following strategy to strengthen the connections among your other sentences:

▶ **REVISION STRATEGY**
Coding Cause-and-Effect Connections

Reread each paragraph. Each time you find a sentence describing a cause next to a sentence describing one of its effects, circle the space between those sentences. Go back and add transitions—such as *because of* and *as a result*—to help readers see cause-and-effect connections.

Revising: Find the "Tug"

Teaching Resources: Writing Support Transparency 9-G; Writing Support Activity Book 9-2

1. Remind students that a new paragraph signals a new idea. Every paragraph should contain a main idea and details to support it.

2. Display the transparency and give students copies of the blank organizer. Instruct students to reread each paragraph in their essay and ask themselves, "What is this paragraph about?" Their answer to this question is the "tug" for that paragraph, and they should annotate each paragraph by summarizing this "tug" in a few words in the margin of their paper.

Revising: Coding Cause-and-Effect Connections

1. Logical connectors are like street signs that help a reader know what to expect and see the logical connections between where they are and where they are going.

2. Instruct students to reread each paragraph in their essays to find sentences that describe causes and effects and that occur next to one another.

3. Tell students to circle the space between sentences that describe a cause and sentences that describe the effect of that cause when they appear next to one another. Then they can add appropriate transition words that show the cause-and-effect connections between these ideas.

Integrating Vocabulary Skills

Transition Words and Phrases
Transitions help the writer and the reader. As a class, make a list on chart paper to keep on display for students' reference. The chart might include these transitions: *first, next, then, finally, after, so, therefore, because of, thus, as a result, on account of, consequently, for example, that is, in other words.*

Revising: Circling Verbs in an Inconsistent Tense

Teaching Resources: Writing Support Transparency 9-H

1. Ask students to look back briefly at the Model From Literature. It used mostly forms of the past tense, because the authors were talking about things that already happened. When they compared the past to the present, they (correctly) used the present tense.

2. Display the transparency to show students how Jake evaluated the verb tenses in his draft.

3. A writer may need to shift from the dominant tense in order to show when events happened in relationship to one another. However, shifting tenses without warning or reason can seriously interfere with the meaning they are trying to convey.

4. To find verbs that shift tense without reason, it may be helpful for students to underline all the verbs in their text to determine the dominant tense they are using. Then they can circle all verbs that are not in this tense and determine whether each tense shift is necessary to show the order of events in their text.

5. Ask students to change the tenses that they shifted unnecessarily.

Customize for
Less Advanced Students

Students may have difficulty with correct subject-verb agreement. Review agreement rules and ask students to add a step in their revision process to check agreement. Encourage students to underline all verbs and check tense first, as tense will affect agreement. They can then circle all subjects. Finally, students can check that subjects and verbs agree. Review compound or difficult subjects: *A and B are, A or B is, neither A nor B is,* and so on.

9.4

Revising Your Sentences
Use the Appropriate Verb Tense

Generally, you should use one verb tense (your "dominant tense") consistently throughout your paper. However, to show the order of events, you sometimes need to shift tenses.

EVENTS AT DIFFERENT TIMES:	Because my puppy **chewed** (past) my catcher's mitt, I **need to** (present) buy a new one.
EVENTS THAT RECUR:	Yesterday, I **bought** (past) a new mitt. Because my puppy **chews** (present) my mitt every day, I **buy** (present) a new one every week.

▶ **REVISION STRATEGY**
Circling Verbs in an Inconsistent Tense

Review your essay to determine the tense of the majority of your verbs. Then, circle any verbs in a different tense. If these verbs do not show events at different times or show a recurring event, consider changing them to your dominant tense.

Student Work
IN PROGRESS

Name: Jake Sommer
Maplewood Middle School
Maplewood, NJ

Circling Verbs in an Inconsistent Tense

Jake's dominant tense was the past. He circled verbs in the present and future. He determined that these shifts in tense were necessary.

So what happened to the trains? By the 1970's, most of the private railroad companies went bankrupt and were sold to the U.S. government. The government created Amtrak to take over passenger operations for long-distance trips. Amtrak's 23,000 miles (go) to just 500 stations. Not many people (make) cross-country trips by train anymore. However, in the future, high-speed trains like they (have) in Europe and Japan (may come) to the U.S. and (spark) a revival of train travel.

✏ STANDARDIZED TEST PREPARATION WORKSHOP

Verb Tenses Standardized test questions may require students to identify whether a verb tense is correct. Provide students with opportunities to practice identifying past, present, and future tense verbs

Which verb below best completes this sentence?

Yesterday I ___ my first race.

A run   **C** ran

B had run   **D** have run

Students should recognize that **C** is the correct answer. It is the past tense of the verb *run*. The past tense is necessary because the action took place yesterday, which is in the past. Answers A, B, and D are the present, past perfect, and present perfect tenses respectively. The perfect tenses are used to express an event that took place before another, specific event.

Grammar in Your Writing
Verb Tense

Every verb has a few different forms, called tenses. The **tense** of a verb indicates the time when the action it expresses takes place—past, present, or future. (If the verb does not express an action, its tense tells when a fact or condition is the case.)

Forms of Regular Verb Tenses	
Tense	Forms of *Speak*
Present	I speak we speak you speak you speak he, she, it speaks they speak
Past	I spoke we spoke you spoke you spoke he, she, it spoke they spoke
Future	I will speak we will speak you will speak you will speak he, she, it will speak they will speak

Find It in Your Reading Read "How Do Rainmakers Make It Rain?" on page 176. Find one example each of the use of past, present, and future tenses. In each case, explain why the use of that tense is appropriate.

Find It in Your Writing Circle past events mentioned in your draft in one color, current events in another color, future events in a third, and recurring events in a fourth. Make sure you use a past tense for all past events, present tense for current or recurring events, and future tense for events that have not yet occurred.

To find out more about verb tense, see Chapter 22.

▶ Critical Viewing Write a sentence describing events suggested by this photograph. Use verbs in both the present and future tenses. **[Analyze]**

Revising • 187

Step-by-Step Teaching Guide

Grammar in Your Writing: Verb Tense

1. Go over the example on the page of tenses for the irregular verb *speak.*

2. Ask students to skim their essays for other irregular verbs. Write them on the chalkboard and have the class work together to list the past, present, and future forms, along with singular and plural forms.

Find It in Your Reading

There are many examples in the model. For example, the first sentence uses the past tense *(started).* The second paragraph contains the future tense *(will . . . fall).* The third paragraph uses the present tense *(is).*

Find It in Your Writing

Recurring or continuing events are more difficult to identify. To add to the possible confusion, an event can have continued in the past, be continuing now, or occur and continue in the future. Let students work in small groups and help one another check and correct their verbs.

Critical Viewing

Analyze Students may say that these curious cats find the fish so fascinating that they will probably want to catch it to get a closer look.

✓ ONGOING ASSESSMENT: Prerequisite Skills

Some students may have difficulty identifying the various forms for tenses. You may find it helpful to review the following to assure coverage of prerequisite knowledge.

In the Textbook	Print Resources	Technology
Using Verbs, pp. 490–517	Grammar Exercise Workbook, pp. 111–120	Language Lab CD-ROM, Using Verbs; On-Line Exercise Bank, Section 22

Revising: Use Precise Verbs

1. Challenge students to think of more verbs to use in the precise examples. For instance, *Sara slumped, lounged, sat at attention; Martha gulped, spilled; Anthony dog-paddled, torpedoed himself.*

2. Ask students to reread their essay and underline five sentences that describe key events. Instruct students to circle the verbs in these sentences.

3. In small groups, have students share their sentences. Instruct group members to brainstorm a list of more precise or vivid verbs that the writer might use to communicate his or her idea more effectively.

Customize for
ESL Students

The most important part of learning any language is acquiring vocabulary. Students may know many vivid verbs, but not in English. Encourage them to use a thesaurus, then check the definitions of words they don't know in a dictionary. It is not cheating to use a bilingual dictionary too—that is precisely why it was written.

Revising: "Say Back"

Remind students of the benefits of sharing their work both as readers and writers. Writers can get feedback about the clarity of their writing, the strengths and weaknesses in their writing, and suggestions for improvement. Readers can get ideas from reading the work of others and can practice the skill of evaluating writing, which they can later apply to their own writing.

Critical Viewing

Interpret Students may say that the three students listening appear to be bored. If they are not interested in the topic they will probably not listen carefully to the reader and provide useful feedback.

Revising Your Word Choice
Use Precise Verbs

In addition to using verbs in the correct tense, it is important to make your verbs as precise as possible. Notice how the verbs in these examples make the action much more vivid.

GENERAL: Sara **sat** in her chair.
PRECISE: Sara **slouched** in her chair.
GENERAL: Martha **ate** her soup.
PRECISE: Martha **slurped** her soup.
GENERAL: Anthony **swam** across the pool.
PRECISE: Anthony **splashed** across the pool.

Use the following strategy to help you revise key verbs to make them more precise:

▶ **REVISION STRATEGY**
Highlighting Key Events

Highlight five sentences in your draft that focus on key events, and examine the verbs you use in them. Replace general or vague verbs with vivid, precise ones.

Peer Review

After you've finished revising on your own, enlist some of your classmates to help you identify potential problems you may have missed. Follow this strategy:

"Say Back"

Read your essay aloud to a group of classmates. Ask them to write down things that stood out in your essay. Pause for one minute while they write. (Look at the clock; a minute is longer than it feels!) Then, read your essay a second time. Ask reviewers to tell you

- what causes you discuss.
- what effects these causes produce.
- anything about which they would like to know more.

What your reviewers tell you should match what you believe your essay says. If they do not mention an important cause or effect, consider adding more information about it or even reorganizing your draft to make connections between events clear.

▲ **Critical Viewing**
What is the mood of the peer review session in the photograph? Explain how this mood would affect the productivity of the session. **[Interpret]**

9.5 Editing and Proofreading

Just by changing one word, you can turn "the man in the moon" into "the man on the moon." The first is an imaginary figure. The second might be a real astronaut. A tiny preposition like *in* can make a big difference to readers. Carefully proofread your work. Focus on making certain that the prepositions you use express the relationship you intend.

Focusing on Prepositions

Review a list of common prepositions. Then, check your draft to make sure that, in each case, you have used the preposition that expresses your meaning. Also, make sure you have not used two prepositions where one will do.

Grammar in Your Writing
Prepositions

A **preposition** relates the noun or pronoun following it to another word in the sentence. Prepositions show relationships between things. Review the following examples:

on the table   above the table

under the table   around the table

Do not use two prepositions where one will do.

Avoidable: He fell **off of** the diving board.

Preferred: He fell off the diving board.

Avoidable: Margaret put the desserts **up on** the counter.

Preferred: Margaret put the desserts on the counter.

Find It in Your Reading Find three prepositions in "How Do Rainmakers Make It Rain?" on page 176. For each preposition, cite the two words in the sentence that it most clearly links.

Find It in Your Writing Highlight each preposition in your draft. In each case where you have highlighted two in a row, see whether you can use only one.

For more about prepositions, see Chapter 17.

Editing and Proofreading • 189

Editing and Proofreading

1. Instruct students to follow the same process to edit their own paper for appropriate and accurate use of prepositions.

2. If students notice that they have used the same few prepositions over and over, suggest that they find substitutes.

Grammar in Your Writing: Prepositions

1. Explain that prepositions show relationships between words in sentences. They usually answer the question *Where? When?* or *How?*

2. Students can recognize prepositions because they begin prepositional phrases. In *The book is on the desk, on* is the preposition, which answers the question *Where is the book? On the desk* is the prepositional phrase.

3. Warn students not to confuse prepositions with adverbs. In *The child fell down, down* is an adverb that describes or modifies the verb *fell.* If the sentence were *The child fell down the stairs,* then *down* would be a preposition, and *down the stairs* would be the prepositional phrase.

Find It in Your Reading

To is a preposition in, for example, *I rode my bike to the park.* But in the first sentence of "How Do Rainmakers Make It Rain?", *to produce* is an infinitive verb, so *to* is not a preposition. Possible responses include *to the ice, in clouds, at ground level.*

Find It in Your Writing

"In a row" means next to each other. There is nothing grammatically wrong with *Daisy spread the jelly on top of the peanut butter.* The prepositions are separated by *top,* which makes the sentence correct.

⏱ TIME AND RESOURCE MANAGER

Resources
Print: Scoring Rubrics on Transparency, Chapter 9; Writing Assessment: Scoring Rubrics and Scoring Models for Cause-and-Effect Essay

In-Depth Coverage	Accelerated Pace
• Cover pp. 189–192 in class. • Students edit and proofread their cause-and-effect essays in class. • Review Rubric for Self-Assessment in class. • Students present their final drafts.	• Assign pages 189–192 for independent review. • Students independently edit and proofread their cause-and-effect essays. • Respond to individual editing issues as needed.

Publishing and Presenting

1. Encourage students to take their essays and diagrams home with them to share with family members.

2. Students may want to create a full-fledged skit with costumes and scenery for an audience of other classes. They can also present their essays as a reader's theater for classmates.

3. It might be more appropriate to create several mini-magazines for cause-and-effect essays on similar topics, such as sports, science, and so on.

4. Suggest that students post their work on a Web site that focuses on their topic area.

ASSESS

Assessment

Teaching Resources: Scoring Rubrics on Transparency, 9; Formal Assessment, Chapter 9

1. Display the Scoring Rubric transparency and review the criteria in class.

2. Before students proceed with self-assessment, you may wish to review the Final Draft of the Student Work in Progress on pages 191–192. Have students score the Final Draft in one or more of the rubric categories. For example, how would students score the piece in terms of audience and purpose?

3. In addition to student self-assessment, you may wish to use the following assessment options:

   • Score student essays yourself, using the rubric and scoring models from Writing Assessment.

   • Review the Standardized Test Preparation Workshop on pages 196–197 and have students respond to a writing prompt within a time limit.

   • Administer the Chapter 9 Test from Formal Assessment in Teaching Resources to assess students' grasp of concepts presented.

190

9.6 Publishing and Presenting

Building Your Portfolio

Here are some ideas for presenting your cause-and-effect essay:

1. **Present a Diagram** On posterboard or an overhead slide, create a diagram of the causal chain in your essay. Read your essay aloud, pointing out appropriate parts of the diagram as you go.

2. **Produce a Skit** Prepare a brief skit in which you and several classmates act out the sequence of causes and effects in your essay. While a narrator reads your essay aloud, the actors might enact the events the narrator is describing.

Reflecting on Your Writing

Jot down a few notes on the experience of writing your essay. To get started, answer these questions:

• What did you enjoy about analyzing the cause(s) and effect(s) of your topic? What did you not enjoy?

• What was the most interesting thing you learned?

 **Internet Tip**

To see a cause-and-effect essay scored according to this rubric, visit **www.phschool.com**

Rubric for Self-Assessment

Use the following criteria to evaluate your cause-and-effect essay:

	Score 4	Score 3	Score 2	Score 1
Audience and Purpose	Consistently targets an audience through word choice and details; clearly identifies purpose in introduction	Targets an audience through most word choices and details; identifies purpose in introduction	Misses a target audience by including a wide range of word choice and details; presents no clear purpose	Addresses no specific audience or purpose
Organization	Presents a clear, consistent organizational strategy to show cause and effect	Presents a clear organizational strategy with occasional inconsistencies to show cause and effect	Presents an inconsistent organizational strategy; creates illogical presentation of causes and effects	Demonstrates a lack of organizational strategy; creates a confusing presentation
Elaboration	Successfully links causes with effects; fully elaborates connections among ideas	Links causes with effects; elaborates connections among most ideas	Links some causes with some effects; elaborates connections among some ideas	Develops and elaborates no links between causes and effects
Use of Language	Chooses clear transitions to convey ideas; presents very few mechanical errors	Chooses transitions to convey ideas; presents few mechanical errors	Misses some opportunities for transitions to convey ideas; presents many mechanical errors	Demonstrates poor use of language; presents many mechanical errors

190 • Cause-and-Effect Essay

✓ ONGOING ASSESSMENT: Assess Mastery

Use one of the following options to assess final drafts of students' essays.

Self Assessment Ask students to score their essay using the rubric provided. Then have students write a single paragraph reflecting on the most valuable thing they learned in completing this essay.	**Teacher Assessment** You may wish to use the rubric and the scoring models provided in Writing Assessment, Bronze Level, to score the essays.

9.7 Student Work IN PROGRESS

FINAL DRAFT

◄ **Critical Viewing**
Using details from this picture, explain the quantity of resources—time, money, and labor—that the country invested in creating a railway system. **[Hypothesize]**

Why Trains Are No Longer Popular

Jake Sommer
Maplewood Middle School
Maplewood, New Jersey

Passenger trains, commuter trains, freight trains, high-speed trains—I've always liked trains, but I've often wondered whatever happened to them. Why don't more people travel by train? Do they enjoy being cramped up in a car or an airplane for their long trips? Maybe they haven't enjoyed the comfort of a passenger train or the unique hospitality of the crew or the unforgettable sights out the window as the train slowly eases through a mountain pass. So I was thinking about these questions one day and decided to do some research on the rise and fall of trains.

Trains didn't arrive in the United States until almost 1830. At first, some people were afraid of this new form of transportation. They were used to horses and buggies, and they didn't like the

In his first paragraph, Jake introduces the main question that his essay will answer.

He organizes his explanation into a series of causes and effects. First, he looks at the causes of the rise of trains.

Step-by-Step Teaching Guide

Teaching From the Final Draft

1. Help students see that "Why Trains Are No Longer Popular" incorporates key elements of the cause-and-effect essay.

   • The topic is clear and implies that several causes and effects will be presented.

   • The introduction engages the reader by presenting a list of types of trains and then posing a question about their role today.

   • The body of the essay clearly explains causal connections for the decline of the train's popularity.

   • Finally, a short conclusion is given that restates the main topic and summarizes the causes and effects that contributed to the train's decline in popularity.

   continued

Critical Viewing

Hypothesize Students may say that the bridges, tracks, and trains were all made by thousands of people who took many years to develop the railway system.

191

2. Ask students if they think that the care with which Jake constructed his essay contributes to their understanding of why trains are no longer popular.

3. Explain that this is one of the reasons that it is important to write carefully—to help readers understand clearly the relationships between causes and effects. Not only must there be enough information, the writing also must be presented in such a way that causal relationships are clear.

4. Ask students if there are any changes they would recommend for this essay, to make it flow better or fine-tune the connections between the causes and effects presented. How might they apply these suggestions to their own writing?

Critical Viewing

Speculate Students may say that they would enjoy watching the scenery as the train passed through the countryside.

steam and sparks coming out of the trains. However, after about ten years, the railroads began to spread quickly across the country. By the time of the Civil War, trains were used to transport troops and supplies.

The biggest advance in railroads came in 1869 when the transcontinental railroad was completed. It took seven years to build the tracks between the east coast and the west coast. Then came the Golden Age of Railroads. Before the Civil War, there were approximately 31,000 miles of track, and by the early 1900's, there were 252,000 miles of track. Traveling by train then became the main source of transportation between small towns and from big cities to other cities.

One important cause of the growth of the railroad was the convenience of train travel and shipping. By having trains everywhere, people could travel thousands of miles in only days instead of weeks. Also, freight could be shipped from the East and Midwest to shopkeepers in the West.

Henry Ford changed everything by mass-producing the automobile. Because it cost him less to make cars, more people could buy them. By the early 1920's, cars and buses started to make trains less popular. Manufacturers used trucks to ship freight because it was cheaper and more reliable. Railroads might pick up freight only once a week, but trucks could come for pickups and deliveries every day. Railroads began their decline.

The last great era of trains was during World War II when trains were used to transport soldiers, arms, and supplies. By the end of the war, heavy use had damaged the rail system, but government money was being spent on building interstate highways and airports instead of on repairing the railroads.

The effect of having the interstate highways was staggering. Millions of dollars were taken from what would have been spent on railroad tickets and was used to buy cars. Americans chose driving over relaxing, leisurely train trips.

So what happened to the trains? By the 1970's, most of the private railroad companies went bankrupt and were sold to the U.S. government. The government created Amtrak to take over passenger operations for long-distance trips. Amtrak's 23,000 miles go to just 500 stations. Not many people make cross-country trips by train anymore. However, in the future, high-speed trains like they have in Europe and Japan may come to the U.S. and spark a revival of train travel. Then, people will know what it's like to see our beautiful country through the window of a train.

192 • Cause-and-Effect Essay

Jake elaborates on the effects of the success of railroads, using his research to give specific details about the length of track.

▲ Critical Viewing
What would you enjoy the most if you were able to travel across the United States by train? **[Speculate]**

Jake identifies a main cause—the rise of the automobile—and explains its logical connections with the decline of the railroad.

Connected Assignment

Documentary Video Script

You can often find examples of cause-and-effect writing just by flipping through the channels on your television set. Newsmagazine shows often contain video segments that explain the cause-and-effect relationships behind a news story.

A **documentary video script** outlines the words to be used, either those recorded in interviews or those written for a narrator. It also includes directions to the camera operators, the technicians who are providing sound and lighting, and the editor who will put the video together.

Challenge yourself to write a documentary video script. Use the suggestions that follow to guide you.

▲ **Critical Viewing**
Will the final documentary include every word this interviewee says? Explain your answer. **[Hypothesize]**

Prewriting Watch a television newsmagazine show. Note the alternation between narration and interview footage and the use of camera angles and sound. Then, choose a situation that interests you—for example, a current event or a technological advance—as your topic.

Next, conduct an investigation into your topic. Use a variety of sources—if possible, include interviews with experts or eyewitnesses. Take careful notes as you gather information. If possible, use an audio or video recorder to capture interviews.

Drafting Format your script to include the words spoken (interviews or commentary) and instruction for the creation and arrangement of visuals (video clips), including lighting and sound directions.

Organize your script to present facts in the most effective way. A chronological organization will allow you to trace how each cause triggered each effect. You might instead pinpoint a major event (an effect) and then examine the various causes that contributed to it.

Revising and Editing After drafting, read your script aloud and listen to how it sounds. Revise to make the segment flow better and to improve the connections among key ideas.

Publishing and Presenting If you have access to video equipment, produce your segment and show it to the class.

Connected Assignment: Documentary Video Script • **193**

▶ **Lesson Objectives**

1. To write a documentary video script appropriate to audience and purpose.
2. To use multiple sources to locate information relevant to research questions.
3. To use writing processes to develop and revise drafts.
4. To select, organize, and produce visuals to complement and extend meaning.

Step-by-Step Teaching Guide

Documentary Video Script

1. Identify documentaries students may watch on their own or bring videotapes to the class for group viewing.
2. To help students find a topic, suggest that they review strategies from Chapter 9.
3. Pair students to brainstorm information sources and develop interview formats.
4. If possible, show students the script of a documentary. Discuss how script writers indicate camera angles, sound effects, and lighting directions.
5. Encourage students to produce their segments. If possible, provide video equipment through the school or by rental from a local video shop. Explain or review basic functions of a video camera.

Critical Viewing

Hypothesize Students should say that the documentary will not use all of the interviewee's words. Some of what was said will be edited out.

Lesson Objectives

1. To evaluate the purposes and effects of various media forms.
2. To use media to compare ideas and points of view.
3. To compare and contrast media with written story.
4. To write to inform and explain.
5. To write a cause-and-effect essay.

Analyzing Ideas Represented in Various Art Forms

1. Choose one of the Spotlight elements for class discussion, or have students work individually or in groups on the element of their choice. Give students the initiative to find the necessary books, videotapes, and illustrations.

2. Invite interested students to view the musical *Once Upon a Mattress,* on video or if possible, in a live production. Do they think the production succeeds with contemporary audiences? Why or why not?

3. Have volunteers read aloud from a text version of Hans Christian Andersen's stories or play one of the many audiotaped recordings of these works. Ask students to compare and contrast several of the stories for style and theme.

4. Challenge students to locate examples of Edmund Dulac's illustrations. Then have them briefly research modern printing technology. How might Dulac's illustrations differ were he creating them today?

Viewing and Representing

Activity Have interested students create their own illustrations for a Hans Christian Andersen story.

Critical Viewing

Compare and Contrast Students' responses will vary. They should support their answers with details from the illustration and from the photograph.

194

Spotlight on the Humanities

Analyzing Ideas Represented in Various Art Forms

Focus on Drama: A Broadway Fairy Tale

Causes and effects occur in the literary world, as well as in history and science. For example, the creators of *Once Upon a Mattress* were deeply affected by the Hans Christian Andersen fairy tale "The Princess and the Pea"—so much so that they created a successful Broadway play based on it. Opening off-Broadway in 1959, the musical *Once Upon a Mattress* moved to Broadway and was nominated for two Tony Awards. With music by Mary Rodgers and lyrics by Marshall Barer, this musical made a star of the young Carol Burnett and continues to entertain audiences in productions all over the world.

Literature Connection Considered one of Denmark's greatest storytellers, Hans Christian Andersen (1805–1875) is primarily known for his fairy tales. Along with "The Princess and the Pea," Andersen wrote the fairy tales "The Snow Queen," "The Ugly Duckling," and "The Red Shoes," among others. In addition to his fairy tales, Andersen wrote poems and plays.

Art Connection Frenchman Edmund Dulac (1882–1953) illustrated Hans Christian Andersen's "The Princess and the Pea." He was one of the foremost illustrators and artists of the late nineteenth and early twentieth centuries. Dulac began his career as an illustrator just as a new technology for printing color illustrations began. With this process, colors were printed separately, allowing for clearer definition of the shapes on a page.

Cause-and-Effect Writing Activity: Diagraming Cause-and-Effect in Fairy Tales

Select a fairy tale. Create an illustrated diagram of causes and effects in the story. Read the story to the class, pointing out events on your diagram. Conclude with an observation about the importance of cause-and-effect relationships in fairy tales.

Illustration to "The Princess and the Pea" by Hans Christian Andersen, c. 1911, Edmund Dulac, Victoria & Albert Museum, London, UK

▲ **Critical Viewing** Compare the main impression created by the drawing of the princess with that created by the photograph from the play. [**Compare and Contrast**]

Media and Technology Skills

Analyzing Media Images
Activity: Captioning a Photograph

Television, newspapers, and magazines all use photographs to record events. Each image also makes a statement about the person, event, or situation it depicts. Learn more about how an image can cause a certain effect in those who view it.

Learn About It An effective photograph uses

- **a central point of interest**—the actions, objects, or people that the photograph focuses on. In this photograph by Dorothea Lange, the woman's face is the focus.

- **composition**—the placement of objects and the use of space and of light. For instance, in the photograph shown, the woman is centered between her children. She looks outward, while the children huddle inward. The space is full—the people take up most of the image. There is a contrast between the light on the woman's face and the shadows around it. All of these features emphasize how much depends on the mother's strength.

- **emotional impact.** A photograph can inspire fear, anger, pity, and other emotions. The photograph shown might inspire compassion.

- **choice of subject.** Photographs of widely differing scenes can be used to illustrate the same topic. This photo was used to show the plight of displaced farmers in the 1930's. Notice that a grim-faced woman was chosen as the subject. A photograph of men lounging about would make a different statement.

Apply It A caption is a statement describing a photograph and providing additional information. Select two photographs from the media and cover up their captions. Using a chart like the one below, take notes on them. Then, write your own caption for each. Compare yours with the published ones.

	What Is the Central Point of Interest?	Describe Its Composition	What Is Its Emotional Impact?	What Effect Does the Choice of Subject Have?
Photograph 1				
Photograph 2				

Types of Photographs

- **Candid**—shows natural, unposed behavior
- **Documentary**—records an event
- **Portrait**—portrays people
- **Abstract**—evokes mood
- **Landscape**—shows a place

▲ **Critical Viewing**
List three details in this photo that capture your interest. **[Analyze]**

▶ *Lesson Objectives*

1. To interpret important ideas gathered from media.
2. To evaluate the various ways visual image makers represent meanings.
3. To evaluate how different media forms influence and inform.
4. To generate ideas for writing with prewriting strategies.

Step-by-Step Teaching Guide

Analyzing Media Images

Teaching Resources: Writing Support Transparency 9-I; Writing Support Activity Book 9-3

1. Review the types of photographs people take and discuss likely purposes or applications for each.

2. Display a sampling of other photographs and ask students to identify their type and discuss their features.

3. Using the transparency, demonstrate the activity using one of the sample photographs. Provide copies of the blank organizer for students' use.

4. Review and, if possible, supply some appropriate sources for photographs. As students work, discuss their emotional reactions to the various photographs. How were the techniques discussed on this page used for emotional appeal? What, if any, other techniques were used?

5. After students complete their charts, have them read captions aloud to a partner and invite questions. Determine whether the published captions answered students' questions.

Critical Viewing

Analyze Students may mention the woman's hand at her mouth, the body language of the children, and the composition.

Lesson Objectives

1. To select and use voice and style appropriate to audience and purpose.

2. To generate plans for writing by using graphic organizers.

3. To produce cohesive and coherent written texts by organizing ideas, using effective transitions, and choosing precise wording.

4. To edit drafts for specific purposes such as to ensure appropriate word choice.

5. To employ standard English usage in writing for audiences.

Step-by-Step Teaching Guide

Expository Writing Prompts

Teaching Resources: Standardized Test Preparation Workbook, pp. 17–18

1. Emphasize with students that they should work methodically when writing for tests. Despite the limited time, rush often leads to errors. It is especially important to read the prompt carefully.

2. Remind students to use their scrap paper when creating a cluster diagram. Ideas can be listed with quick words or phrases only.

3. Review the different types of organization with students. Urge them to choose an organization they feel comfortable with—this will save time and help them stay focused.

4. Stress the importance of word choice when drafting an essay. Students have limited time for revision so careful word choice while drafting is helpful.

5. Provide ample timed-writing practice, using an appropriate time interval such as one class period.

Standardized Test Preparation Workshop

Responding to Expository Writing Prompts

Some writing prompts on standardized tests require you to show the relationships between causes and their effects. Your writing will be evaluated on your ability to

- respond directly to the prompt.

- make your writing thoughtful and interesting.

- organize ideas so they are clear and easy to follow.

- develop your ideas thoroughly by using appropriate details and precise language.

- stay focused on your purpose by making sure that each sentence contributes to your composition as a whole.

- use correct spelling, capitalization, punctuation, grammar, usage, and sentence structure.

Following is an example of an expository writing prompt. Use the suggestions on the following page to help you respond. When writing for a timed test, you should plan to devote a specified amount of time to prewriting, drafting, revising, and proofreading. The clocks next to each stage show a suggested percentage of time to devote to each stage.

Test Tips

- Make sure that you get enough rest the night before the test.
- Come prepared with pencils, pens, and scrap paper.

Sample Writing Situation

Writer Rudyard Kipling explores the conflict between natural enemies— a mongoose and a cobra— in his famous short story, "Rikki-tikki-tavi."

What causes the conflict between the mongoose Rikki-tikki-tavi and the cobra Nag in the short story? Use details and information from the story to explain why the two are natural enemies, what specifically causes the conflict in this story, and what causes the story to end as it does.

196 • Cause-and-Effect Essay

✎ TEST-TAKING TIP

Answering the question that has been asked may be the strategy most important to test-taking success. Tell students to look for key verbs that identify the required task. Urge them also to study the prompt for cues to format and necessary support. This will dictate details and word choice. Discuss the sample prompt and invite students to practice the strategy.

Sample Prompt: The key verb is *explain*. Essays must discuss the causes of situations and events in the story. The format is an essay and the required support is details from the story.

Prewriting

Allow close to one fourth of your time for prewriting.

Use a Cluster Diagram When gathering details for your cause-and-effect response, use a cluster diagram. Write each cause the prompt asks you to explain on a piece of paper and circle it. Then, write the effects of each cause in new circles. Draw lines linking effects to their causes.

Keep a Consistent Purpose As you gather details, include only those relevant to the prompt. The purpose assigned by the example prompt is to explain the cause-and-effect relationships in the story—not to retell every event that occurs in it.

Drafting

Allow almost half of your time for drafting.

Organizing Details When writing a cause-and-effect response, organize details in chronological order, the sequence in which they occurred. Organizing using this method will enable you to clearly show the relationship between causes and effects.

Use the Story as Support As you write the body of your response, elaborate your ideas using specific details and examples from the story to explain cause-and-effect relationships. Each time you mention an event, look for ways to explain its connection to the events before and after it.

Using Precise Language As you write, elaborate using precise, strong words. For example, if you are describing Nag's personality, use a strong word, such as *nasty*, instead of a weak and vague word, such as *bad*.

Revising, Editing, and Proofreading

Allow almost one fourth of your time to revise and edit. Use the last few minutes to proofread your work.

Make Clear Connections Review your draft. Add transitional words, such as *as a result, because of, before,* and *after,* where needed to indicate the cause-and-effect relations between events. Neatly cross out any details that do not support your purpose. Replace vague or general modifiers, such as *good,* with precise words, such as *brave.*

Make Corrections Review your response for errors in spelling, grammar, and punctuation. When making changes, draw a line through text that you want eliminated. Use a caret (^) to indicate the place where you would like to add words.

Review with students how to create and complete a cluster diagram. Discuss the way various transition words can support cause-and-effect explanations.

Challenge students to explain their writing process. Have them orally present their prewriting, drafting, and revising choices. Invite them to comment on how they might improve their process.

Time and Resource Manager

In-Depth Lesson Plan

	LESSON FOCUS	PRINT AND MEDIA RESOURCES
DAY 1	**Introduction to How-to Essays** Students learn key elements of how-to essays and analyze the Model From Literature (pp. 198–201).	*Writers at Work* **Videotape**, Exposition: Making Connections *Writing Lab* **CD-ROM**, Exposition: Making Connections
DAY 2	**Prewriting** Students choose and narrow a topic, consider their audience and purpose, and gather information (pp. 202–205).	**Teaching Resources** *Writing Support Transparencies* 10-A–C; *Writing Support Activity Book* 10-1 *Writing Lab* **CD-ROM**, Exposition: Making Connections
DAY 3	**Drafting** Students organize their ideas and write their first drafts (pp.206–207).	**Teaching Resources** *Writing Support Transparencies* 10 D–E; *Writing Support Activity Book,* 10-2 *Writing Lab* **CD-ROM**, Exposition: Making Connections
DAY 4	**Revising** Students revise their drafts in terms of overall structure, paragraphs, sentences, and word choice (pp. 208–213).	**Teaching Resources** *Writing Support Transparencies* 10-F–H *Writing Lab* **CD-ROM**, Exposition: Making Connections
DAY 5	**Editing and Proofreading; Publishing and Presenting** Students check their work for accuracy and correctness and present their final drafts (pp. 214–215).	**Teaching Resources** *Scoring Rubrics on Transparency,* Chapter 10; *Formal Assessment,* Ch. 10 *Writing Lab* **CD-ROM**, Exposition: Making Connections

Accelerated Lesson Plan

	LESSON FOCUS	PRINT AND MEDIA RESOURCES
DAY 1	**Introduction Through Drafting** Students review characteristics for how–to writing, select topics, and write drafts.	*Writers at Work* **Videotape**, Exposition: Making Connections *Writing Lab* **CD-ROM**, Exposition: Making Connections **Teaching Resources** *Writing Support Transparencies* 10-A–E; *Writing Support Activity Book* 10-1–2
DAY 2	**Revising Through Presenting** Students work individually or with peers to revise, edit, and proofread their work for presentation.	**Teaching Resources** *Writing Support Transparencies* 10-F–H; *Scoring Rubrics on Transparency,* Ch. 10; *Formal Assessment,* Ch. 10

Options for Adapting Lesson Plans

HOMEWORK

Have students complete any stage of the lesson for homework.

TECHNOLOGY

Students can complete any stage of the lesson on computer. Have them print out their completed work.

FEATURES

Extend coverage with Connected Assignment (p. 217), Spotlight on the Humanities (p. 218), Media and Technology Skills (p. 219), and the Standardized Test Preparation Workshop (p. 220).

INTEGRATED SKILLS COVERAGE

Integrating Grammar
Adverb Clauses and Phrases SE p. 211
Using Commas in a Series SE p. 214
Grammar and Style SE p. 217

Reading/Writing Connection
Reading Strategy SE p. 200
Writing Application SE p. 201

Speaking and Listening
ATE pp. 204, 206

Vocabulary Skills
ATE, p. 210

Workplace Skills ATE p. 219

Technology SE pp. 215, 219

Viewing and Representing
Critical Viewing SE pp. 198, 200, 201, 204, 209, 213, 218
Comparing Media SE p. 218

ASSESSMENT SUPPORT

Standardized Test Preparation Workshop SE p. 220; ATE p. 212
Standardized Test Preparation Workbook, pp. 19–20
Scoring Rubrics on Transparency, Ch.10
Formal Assessment, Ch. 10
Writing Assessment and Portfolio Management

MEETING INDIVIDUAL NEEDS

Less Advanced Students ATE pp. 208, 221. See also Ongoing Assessments, ATE pp. 203, 204, 209, 211, 215, 217.
More Advanced Students ATE pp. 207, 221
ESL Students ATE p. 212
Bodily/Kinesthetic Learners ATE p. 205
Spatial Learners ATE p. 206

BLOCK SCHEDULING

Pacing Suggestions
For 90-minute Blocks
• Have students complete the Prewriting and Drafting stages in a single period.
• Focus one class period on Revising and Editing and Publishing and Presenting. Allow at least 30 minutes for peer revision.

Resources for Varying Instruction
• *Writing Lab* **CD-ROM** If your students have access to hardware, a 90-minute block provides an ideal opportunity for students to work on computer.
• *Writers at Work* **Videotape** Show the Exposition: Making Connections segment in class

Professional Development Support
• *How to Manage Instruction in the Block* This Teaching Resource provides management and activity suggestions.

MEDIA AND TECHNOLOGY

For the Student
• *Writing Lab* **CD-ROM**, Exposition: Making Connections
• *On-Line Exercise Bank*, Sections 20.1, 20.2

For the Teacher
• *Writers at Work* **Videotape**, Exposition: Making Connections
• *Resource Pro* **CD-ROM**

WRITING AND GRAMMAR WEB SITE

The Interactive Writing and Grammar Web site provides a wide array of support for students, teachers, and parents. Writing support includes:

• Interactive revision checkers
• Scoring rubrics with complete models

www.phschool.com

LITERATURE CONNECTIONS

Related selections from *Prentice Hall Literature: Timeless Voices, Timeless Themes,* Bronze:
From "How to Enjoy Poetry," James Dickey, SE p. 201
"If—," Rudyard Kipling, SE p. 203

Chapter
10 **Exposition**
How-to Essay

▶ *Lesson Objectives*

1. To write a how-to essay appropriate to audience and purpose
2. To read to appreciate the writer's craft and to discover models for writing
3. To use prewriting strategies to generate ideas and plan
4. To organize prior knowledge of a topic with graphic organizers
5. To develop and revise drafts in terms of structure, paragraphs, sentences, and word choice
6. To edit and proofread to ensure standard English usage and grammar
7. To refine a how-to essay for publication
8. To apply criteria to evaluate writing

Critical Viewing

Connect Student responses might address basic bicycle maintenance topics such as "How to Replace a Bicycle Chain" or "How to Change a Tire on a Bicycle."

▲ Critical Viewing
What title would you give a how-to essay that might accompany this photo? **[Connect]**

How-to Essays in Everyday Life

You read "how-to's" all the time. The instruction booklet for a computer game, the directions on microwave popcorn, safety warnings, repair instructions, guidelines for caring for your bike or washing your clothes—these are all forms of writing that explain how to do something.

In your own life, you probably do a lot of explaining as well. You might explain to your teacher how you created invitations with your new word-processing program, or you might tell a friend the rules for street hockey before a pickup game. In this chapter, you will learn the process for writing a clear, effective how-to essay.

198 • Exposition

⏱ TIME AND RESOURCE MANAGER

Resources
Technology: Writers at Work Videotape, Exposition: Making Connections

In-Depth Coverage	Accelerated Pace
• Cover pp. 198–201 in class.	• Have students read pp. 198–201 on their own.
• Show the Exposition section of the Writers at Work Videotape.	• Discuss definitions and types of how-to essays in class.
• Read the Model From Literature in class and use it to brainstorm for how-to topics with students.	• Assign the Model From Literature for independent reading.

What Is a How-to Essay?

Writing that explains or informs is called expository writing. One of the most common types of expository writing is the how-to essay.

In a **how-to essay,** you explain how to do or make something. You break the process down into a series of logical steps and explain the steps in the order in which the reader should do them.

The following features are characteristics of a useful, effective how-to essay:

- a narrow, focused topic that can be fully explained in the length of an essay
- a list of materials needed
- a series of logical steps explained in chronological order
- details that tell *when, how much, how often,* or *to what extent*
- an essay format with an introduction, a body, and a conclusion.

To learn the criteria on which your how-to essay may be assessed, see the Rubric for Self-Assessment on page 215.

Types of How-to Essays

Following are some of the types of how-to essays you might write:

- How to do something ("How to Hit a Baseball")
- How to make something ("How to Make Trail Mix")
- How to improve a skill ("How to Improve Your Test Scores")
- How to achieve a desired effect ("How to Organize Your Locker")

PREVIEW
Student Work IN PROGRESS

Felix Espinoza, a student at Palo Alto Middle School in Killeen, Texas, wrote an essay explaining how to make his favorite cake. In this chapter, you will see his work in progress, including strategies he used to choose a topic, to gather details, to elaborate, and to revise his overall structure and his word choice. At the end of the chapter, you can read the completed essay Felix wrote.

Writers in **ACTION**

Richard Lederer writes how-to's that make learning fun! His humorous books and articles on the English language have helped many readers learn how to write and speak more effectively. He shares the following thoughts on expository writing:

"Expository writing is taking an idea or cluster of ideas and transferring it from the writer, as clearly as possible, to the reader, so that the reader participates in those ideas."

Interest GRABBER Ask students to imagine they are telling a new student the fastest way to get from English class to the school office. After they jot down the information, ask for volunteers to share and compare their "how-to" instructions. Help them to see that good directions are clear, accurate, and in the right sequence. Tell them that they will be writing a how-to essay that must have these same characteristics.

Activate Prior Knowledge

Ask students to recall the last time they showed a friend how to do something—to use some equipment, to play a game, to make something. What steps and what techniques were important in helping the friend learn? After discussing these issues, refer students to the characteristics of the how-to essay listed in the text.

More About the Writer

Richard Lederer has shared his fascination with the English language in more than ten books, including *The Miracle of Language* and *Anguished English.* He writes a weekly syndicated column "Looking at Language" and is well known as a speaker and presenter. Richard Lederer is featured in the Exposition section of the *Writers at Work* Videotape.

☑ ONGOING ASSESSMENT: Diagnose

Use one of the following options to diagnose students' current level of proficiency in expository writing.

Option 1 Ask students to provide you with a sample of expository writing from their previous year's writing portfolio. Individual conferences with students can help you to identify which of them may need extra help.	**Option 2** Have students write brief directions to help a new student get from English class to the school office (or a similar task). Use students' responses to diagnose their current proficiency in how-to writing.

Reading\Writing Connection

Reading: Identify Cause-and-Effect Relationships

Tell students that a cause is an event, condition, or situation that makes something happen. An effect is the result of a particular event, condition, or situation. For example, road repair work on a highway might be the cause of a big traffic backup. The work on the highway is the cause; the traffic backup is the effect.

Writers often show the cause-and-effect relationship between events. Understanding these relationships is an important reading comprehension skill.

As students read "Moving Mountains" have them indicate the cause of these effects:

The Himalayas are gradually losing mass.

The position of the block changes in the water.

Because of their loss of mass, the Himalayas' position on Earth is changing.

Step-by-Step Teaching Guide

Engage Students Through Literature

1. Read this excerpt aloud, or have a prepared student read it.

2. Use questions like these to prompt discussion:

   How easy do you think it would be to carry out this demonstration?

   What has the writer done to make it easier?

   Which parts of the essay are hard to follow?

   Which parts are easy to understand?

   What has the writer done to make the essay easy to follow?

3. Ask students to brainstorm for what the experiment might show about changes in the position of the Himalayas. Here are some possibilities:

   • The Himalayas will rise, just as the block in the experiment will rise as the sand is scraped off.

   • The Himalayas are growing even taller than they already are.

200

10.1 Model From Literature

In this how-to essay, science writer Janice VanCleave (1942–   ) lets readers see how erosion moves mountains.

Reading **Writing** **Connection**

Reading Strategy: Identify Cause-and-Effect Relationships
In this how-to essay, look for **cause-and-effect relationships**—explanations of *why* something happens or is done.

▲ **Critical Viewing**
What kind of force might it take to change the position of a mountain in the Himalayas, such as this one? **[Speculate]**

Moving Mountains

Janice VanCleave

The Himalayas, the highest mountain system in the world, lie just south of the Tibetan Plateau, where the Yangtze River originates. According to Professor Douglas Burbank of the University of Southern California, the normal process of erosion is affecting the Himalayas in two major ways. First, the enormous glaciers on the mountains are grinding down rock into huge amounts of gravel and silt, which are then washed away by streams and rivers. The Himalayas are gradually losing mass.

Second, the loss of mass is affecting the Himalayas' position on Earth's surface. Mountains are part of Earth's *crust*, or rigid outer layer. The crust floats on the *mantle*, a layer of molten rock, in the same way that a boat floats on an ocean.

How does the Himalayas' loss of mass affect its position on Earth's mantle? Try this demonstration to find out.

What You Need

- a lightweight wooden block measuring 5 centimeters by 10 centimeters by 5 centimeters (roughly 2 inches by 4 inches by 2 inches)
- a black marking pen
- a red marking pen
- masking tape
- sand
- a clear container twice as large as the wooden block
- a pencil and paper
- a tablespoon
- a ruler

200 • How-to Essay

VanCleave introduces the topic of her how-to essay by giving general background information.

She provides a cause-and-effect explanation to help explain erosion.

Here the writer lists all the materials the reader will need.

Critical Viewing

Speculate Students may suggest that only a massive, violent force could move a mountain. Others may realize that many small changes over time may also be sufficient.

What to Do

1. Fill the container about half full with water, and place a piece of masking tape down the outside of the container.
2. Starting at the top of the tape, mark it off in centimeters with the black pen. Mark the level that the water comes to with the red pen.
3. Place a piece of masking tape down one side of the wooden block and mark it off in centimeters with the black pen.
4. Float the wooden block in the container of water, and pour several spoonfuls of sand on top of the block. Using the red pen, record the level that the water comes to on the block and the level that the water now comes to in the container.
5. Use the spoon to scrape some sand from the top of the block into the water. Record the water level on the block and in the container again.
6. Scrape off some more sand and again record the water levels.

MODEL DEMONSTRATION: EROSION'S EFFECTS

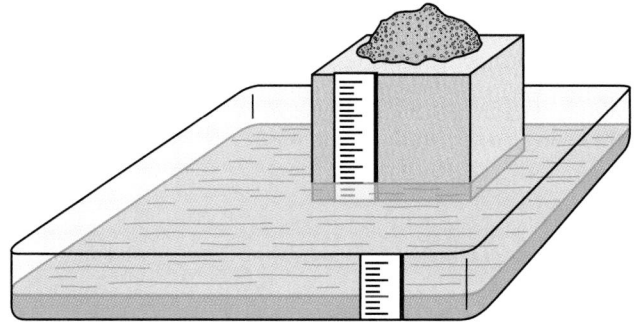

What Happens?

After you have completed the experiment, you have the information you need to understand the effect of erosion on the Himalayas. Interpret the experiment by answering these questions:

- What happens to the block as it loses sand to the water?
- How do the objects in this experiment compare to the Himalayas and Earth's mantle?
- What conclusions can you draw about the effect of erosion on the Himalayas?

Reading Writing Connection

Writing Application: **Help Readers See Cause-and-Effect Relationships** As you write your how-to essay, give reasons why following the exact order of steps is important.

The writer presents steps in logical order. She does not put too much information into a step, but instead focuses each step on one action or a group of closely related actions.

For an example of non-fiction that explains how to do something, read "How to Enjoy Poetry" in *Prentice Hall Literature: Timeless Voices, Timeless Themes*, Bronze.

The writer concludes by guiding the reader in drawing conclusions from the demonstration. This type of conclusion is appropriate for a how-to essay explaining how to conduct an experiment.

Teaching From the Model

This model from literature exemplifies some of the features of how-to writing:

- It begins by presenting a situation in which more information is needed. In this case, the writer will explan how to perform an experiment that will make it easier for the reader to understand the consequences of erosion.
- It clearly outlines the materials the reader will need.
- It presents the steps of the experiment in a logical sequence.

Responding to Literature

Let students know that topics for their how-to essays need not be limited to descriptions of physical activities. Students may enjoy James Dickey's approach to the how-to essay in "How to Enjoy Poetry" in *Prentice Hall Literature: Timeless Voices, Timeless Themes*, Bronze. Suggest that students jot down Dickey's essay headings to help them begin thinking about how to organize their essays.

More About the Writer:

Janice VanCleave has taught science in the public schools. The author of over 30 science books, she believes experiments are the best way to teach science. Her friends joke that they are never sure *what* she is growing in her refrigerator!

Reading\Writing Connection

Writing Application: Cause and Effect

Point out to students that often there is a cause-and-effect relationship between one step in a how-to procedure and the next. If you do X, Y will happen. Students will need to make this relationship clear as they write their how-to essays.

Prewriting: Invisible Ink

1. If you wish to have students do this activity in class, you might supply the carbon paper. Students working on a computer can write at the keyboard with the monitor turned off or darkened.

2. The point of this activity is to have students generate ideas without stopping to look at them. After they have finished, they can review their work and circle or highlight potential topic ideas.

Prewriting: List

Teaching Resources: Writing Support Transparencies 10-A; Writing Support Activity Book 10-1

1. Have students make four columns on a piece of paper. They might do this by folding a sheet of paper vertically and then folding it vertically again, creating four equal vertical columns when the paper is unfolded. Columns may be labeled people, places, things, and events. Alternatively, you may give them a copy of the organizer (10-1) in the *Writing Support Activity Book.*

2. As students list items in their columns, encourage them to allow their ideas to flow freely, without worrying about whether any one item will offer the perfect topic.

3. When students have finished their lists, ask them to look for connections among the listed items. Students should circle related items and draw lines connecting them.

4. Draw attention to the student work to show the student writer's connections. You can display Transparency 10-A to prompt students to make their own connections.

10.2 # Prewriting

Choosing Your Topic

The first step in writing a good how-to essay is to choose an appropriate topic. Choose a topic you know well enough to explain clearly. Also, make sure the topic you choose is simple enough that a reader can easily learn the steps involved by following your explanation. The following strategies will help you find a suitable topic:

Strategies for Generating a Topic

1. **Invisible Ink** Place a piece of carbon paper between two blank sheets of paper. Using a pen that has run out of ink, "write" on the blank top sheet. Begin by writing about any part of your day that you enjoy. After five minutes, look at what has been recorded on the carbon copy. Circle any words or sentences that suggest a topic for your essay. (You can also do this activity by writing on the computer with your monitor turned off. When you are finished, turn your monitor on to see what you have written.)

2. **List** Begin by making a list of people, places, things, and events that you associate with your home or school. Circle words and draw lines to show connections between items on the list. These links may suggest a topic. The model below shows an example of how listing led one student to a topic.

Writing Lab CD-ROM

For additional help choosing a topic, see the tips and strategies in the Choosing a Topic section of the Exposition: Giving Information lesson.

Student Work IN PROGRESS

Name: Felix Espinoza
Palo Alto Middle School
Killeen, TX

Listing to Discover a Topic

Felix listed the people, places, things, and events that he associates with school. He discovered connections by remembering that his classmate Mike helped him make a cake for the class party. This led him to choose "Making a Cake" as his topic.

People	Places	Things	Events
Mike	school	bus	soccer game
Mrs. Flood	classroom	locker	class party
Gary	soccer field	desk	
Maria		cake	
		movie	

202 • How-to Essay

⏱ TIME AND RESOURCE MANAGER

Resources
Print: Writing Support Transparencies 10-A–C; Writing Support Activity Book 10-1
Technology: Writing Lab CD-ROM, Exposition: Making Connections

In-Depth Coverage	Accelerated Pace
• Work through the Invisible Ink or the Listing strategy (p. 202) with the class. • Use the Responding to Fine Art transparency (p. 203) to generate additional topics. • Do the Itemizing activity (p. 205) in class.	• Discuss strategies for generating topics. • Have students work independently to choose and narrow their topics. • Have students work with partners to focus on audience, purpose, and gathering details.

TOPIC BANK

If you're having trouble coming up with a topic, think about the following possibilities:

1. **How to Make a Gift** Explain how readers can make a homemade gift, such as a collage, trinket box, picture, or beaded bracelet.

2. **How to Improve a Sports Skill** Explain how readers can improve a specific skill, such as making free throws in basketball, hitting a baseball or softball, or serving in tennis.

Responding to Fine Art

3. Look at the painting on this page. What steps might be involved in the activity portrayed? Write a how-to essay about what you think is happening in this painting or about some other process or activity involving a pet.

Responding to Literature

4. Read "If—" by Rudyard Kipling. Write a how-to essay explaining how readers can achieve one of the goals expressed in the poem. For example, you might write an essay explaining how to respond calmly in a crisis or how to avoid giving in to negative peer pressure. You can find "If—," as well as background on the poem and the poet, in *Prentice Hall Literature: Timeless Voices, Timeless Themes*, Bronze.

Man Playing With Dog, Serge Hollerbach, Courtesy of Sanders and Newman Gallery, PA

Cooperative Writing Opportunity

5. **How to Organize a Game for Young Children** With a group, explain how to organize a game for young children. Some group members can explain the equipment or playing area, others can draw diagrams or illustrations, and others can list and explain rules.

Responding to Fine Art

Man Playing With Dog by Serge Hollerbach

Teaching Resources: Writing Support Transparencies, 10-B

1. Display Transparency 10-B and engage students in discussion about it. You might use questions like these to prompt discussion:

   Is this the first time the man has played with this dog? How can you tell?

   What does the man's body language tell you about him and how he feels about the dog?

2. Ask students to brainstorm for "how-to" ideas suggested by this piece of art. Here are some possibilities:

   How to teach a dog to play catch.

   How to play safely with a dog.

   Students may include these topic ideas along with their own suggestions in their topic banks.

Responding to Literature

Students might use Rudyard Kipling's "If—" as a starting point for a how-to essay. Ask students whether they feel the poet left out any other elements of maturity that they consider crucial, and list these on the board. Do any of these ideas suggest to students a possible topic for their essays?

☑ ONGOING ASSESSMENT: Monitor and Reinforce

If students are having difficulty coming up with a topic, try the following strategy.

Work as a class to select and develop a single topic, choosing from the Topic Bank or from ideas suggested by students. (You will find additional topics in *Topic Bank for Heterogeneous Classes* in	Teaching Resources.) Working with a common topic will enable you to focus efficiently on specific issues, apply strategies more easily, and allow for effective collaboration during Prewriting.

⏱ TIME SAVERS!

Writing Support Transparencies
Use the transparencies for Chapter 10 to teach strategies.

Writing Support Activity Book
Use the graphic organizers for Chapter 10 to facilitate students' planning.

Prewriting: Narrowing Your Topic; Audience and Purpose

1. To help students narrow their topics, you might give examples such as the following:

Too broad:	*How to bake*
Narrow enough:	*How to bake apple pie*
Too broad:	*Taking care of fish*
Narrow enough:	*How to clean an aquarium*

2. Ask volunteers to share topics. You and the class members can help each volunteer determine whether his or her proposed topic is narrow enough.

3. If topics are too broad, list smaller elements of the topic on the board, and invite students to suggest which of these offer a more focused topic.

4. Analyzing the intended audience can also help students narrow a topic. As writers consider what they hope to communicate to the audience, they may see ways to focus and narrow their topics.

5. Give students this additional question to help them analyze their audience:

   What does my audience need or want to know?

Integrating Speaking and Listening Skills

It is not only in writing that it is important to keep topics sufficiently narrow. Tell students that if you are talking to a friend and have hours to share, you need not narrow your topic, but if you are speaking in front of a group, it is necessary to narrow your topic. Doing so enables you to say something meaningful on the topic you have selected while still making it possible to end the speech before your audience is asleep.

Critical Viewing

Analyze Students should be able to tell from the appearance of the kitchen and quality of tools and ingredients that this is probably an experienced cook. It is unlikely that he would need a lot of background on cooking.

204

10.2

Narrowing Your Topic

Once you have chosen a topic, evaluate whether it can be covered fully in an essay. Some topics are so broad that entire books could be written about them. For example, the topic "How to Get Organized" is too broad for an essay. The topic could be narrowed to focus on how to organize study time or how to organize a locker. If your topic is too broad, focus on a single, manageable aspect of the topic.

Considering Your Audience and Purpose

The topic you choose for your how-to essay reflects your purpose in writing. Your **purpose** is most likely to explain your topic. Considering your **audience**—the people who will be reading your essay—is not as simple, but it is one of the most important parts of writing a good how-to essay. Ask yourself the following questions when you think about your audience:

- **How much does my audience know about this topic?** Do they need a lot of background or just a little? Will they need definitions of any special terms I use?

- **What is the age of my audience?** Should I use simple vocabulary for young children, or can I use vocabulary appropriate for people my age or older?

- **What skills might my audience have?** Do they have the basic skills needed to learn what I am teaching?

Thinking about your audience may even lead you to change or further narrow your topic. For example, readers who are very familiar with cooking will not need to have special cooking terms or the names of utensils defined. If your audience is familiar with your topic, you might narrow the focus of your essay to a subtopic that requires special knowledge or expertise.

▼ **Critical Viewing** Based on what you see in this picture, do you think the man needs much background on cooking? **[Analyze]**

204 • How-to Essay

☑ **ONGOING ASSESSMENT: Monitor and Reinforce**

Students often lapse into the habit of always writing for the same audience: their teacher. To help break this pattern, try one of the following strategies.

Option 1 Tell students to write to a very specific audience—a relative or friend—or to a much younger person. Students may find that this will affect not only the level of detail and vocabulary, but also the level of formality or informality.

Option 2 Have students write down pertinent information about their intended readers and their own purposes in writing. You might create a short form (based on the questions on page 204) that students would fill out and attach to their final draft.

Gathering Details

Once you have identified your audience, you can focus on gathering details. Since your topic is an activity or skill that you know well, most of your details can be gathered from your own knowledge and experience. If you need help getting started, try the itemizing strategy.

Itemize to Gather Details

One way to start gathering details is to itemize. Begin with a simple list, such as materials or steps. Then, itemize each part of the list, generating specific details for each area. If you find your itemized lists are becoming too long or unmanageable, evaluate whether your topic is still too broad or whether you are including more details than your audience needs.

Writing Lab CD-ROM

To gather details appropriate for your audience, use the Audience Profile activity in the Writer's Toolkit.

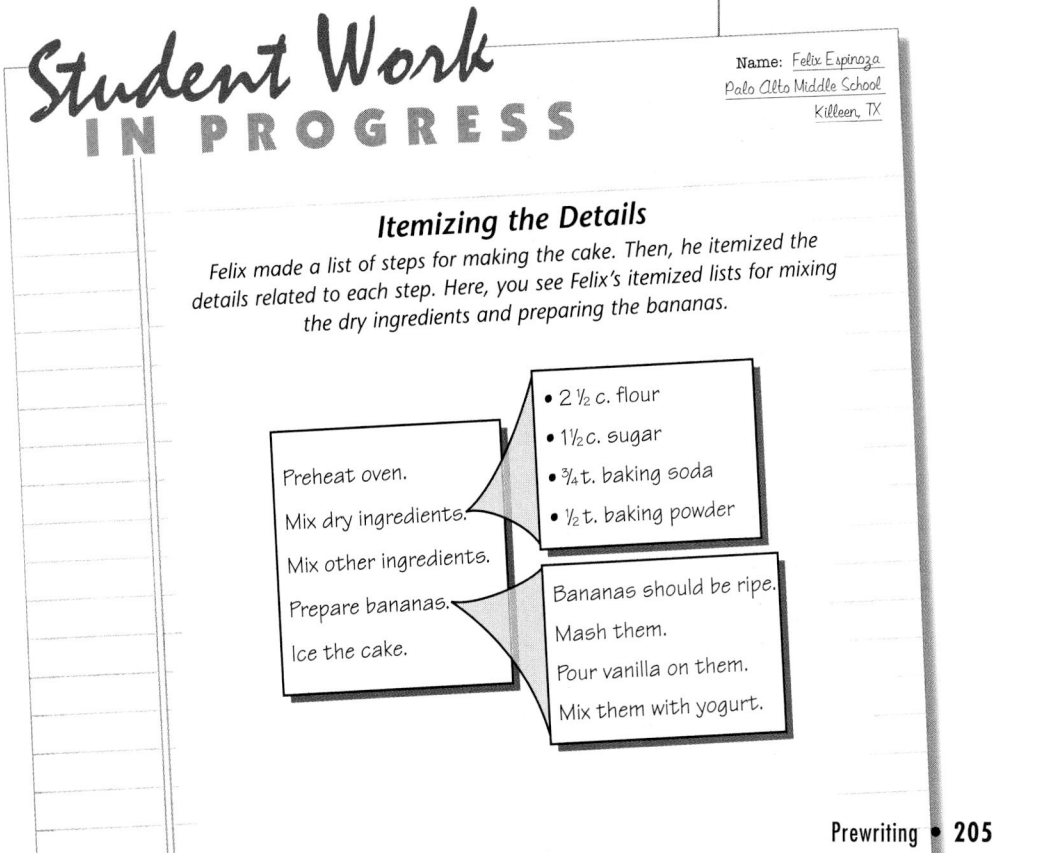

Student Work
IN PROGRESS

Name: *Felix Espinoza*
Palo Alto Middle School
Killeen, TX

Itemizing the Details

Felix made a list of steps for making the cake. Then, he itemized the details related to each step. Here, you see Felix's itemized lists for mixing the dry ingredients and preparing the bananas.

Preheat oven.

Mix dry ingredients.

Mix other ingredients.

Prepare bananas.

Ice the cake.

- 2 ½ c. flour
- 1½ c. sugar
- ¾ t. baking soda
- ½ t. baking powder

Bananas should be ripe.

Mash them.

Pour vanilla on them.

Mix them with yogurt.

Prewriting • 205

Step-by-Step Teaching Guide

Prewriting: Itemize to Gather Details

Teaching Resources: Writing Support Transparencies 10-C

1. Start this activity by having students make lists related to their topics. They can list the steps involved, the materials needed, or anything else that can be listed. Suggest that they write their lists with some space between each item.

2. As they examine each item on the list, they can add the details of each. In this way, they are gathering specific details for their essays.

3. Draw students' attention to the Student Work in Progress on this page, or display Transparency 10-C for an example of itemizing.

Customize for
Bodily/Kinesthetic Learners

Suggest to students that, if they are having difficulty remembering or relating all the steps in a process, they should go through the process—whether in reality or just acting it out—and record each step as they do or act it. Often, getting started with the actions will help them remember steps and give them clues to how to relate the process.

TIME SAVERS!

Writing Support Transparencies
Use the transparencies for Chapter 10 to teach strategies.

- Point out to students that a good way to be sure their details are in chronological order is to put them in a timeline.

- Give students activity page 10-2 from the *Writing Support Activity Book,* or have them write each step in their "how-to" on individual note cards and lay the cards out on their desks in chronological order. They can easily rearrange the cards as necessary, or add or combine steps.

- Display Transparency 10-D, the example on this page. Point out that the student writer needed to add a step and was easily able to do so.

Integrating Speaking and Listening Skills

Some students may find they can more readily talk about their topic than they write about it. Suggest that students first tell another student what they plan to write about. They might also use a tape recorder to "draft" their papers orally. Replaying their ideas may facilitate the actual writing process.

Customize for
Spatial Learners

Suggest that students sketch quick "storyboards" of the process they are trying to teach in their how-to essays. Then have them make notes under each scene, and compare these notes with their drafts to identify any missing steps in the process.

10.3 Drafting

Shaping Your Writing

Once you have gathered your details, you need to put them into some kind of order. Think of the details as a recipe for the ingredients in a cake. Throwing all the ingredients together without a plan just makes a mess. On the other hand, if you put the ingredients together in a logical way, following the recipe, and pour the batter into a pan for baking, you will make a cake that holds together. Drafting is the mixing and baking time in your writing process. It is the time for bringing the details together and making some sense of them.

Organize Details in Chronological Order

The logical organization for most how-to essays is chronological order. Because one step usually affects the following steps, explaining steps in time order will help readers follow the logical sequence. Organize the steps you wish to explain by creating a sticky-note timeline. If you don't have sticky notes, you can use note cards or slips of paper.

Use a Timeline to Organize Details By putting details on individual sticky notes or note cards, you can arrange the steps in order and add steps as needed. Notice how "Get a second bowl" can easily be added because each step is written on a separate note.

STICKY-NOTE TIMELINE

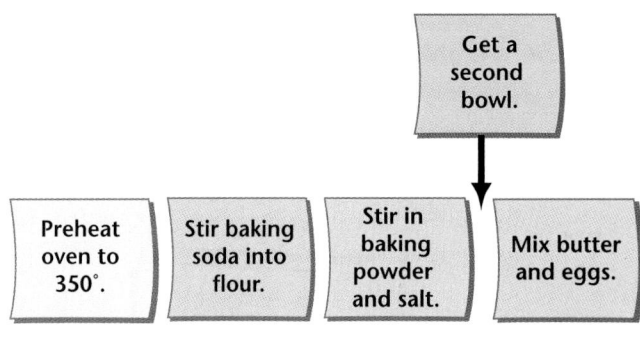

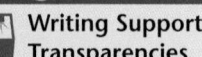
⏱ TIME AND RESOURCE MANAGER

Resources
Print: Writing Support Transparencies, 10-D–E; Writing Support Activity Book, 10-2
Technology: Writing Lab CD-ROM, Exposition: Making Connections

In-Depth Coverage	Accelerated Pace
• Work through the Timeline strategy with the entire class, using the transparency. • Have students write their how-to draft in class. • Demonstrate the techniques of "exploding the moment" using the transparency.	• Have students review pp. 206–207 independently and then write their first how-to draft. • Respond to individual drafting issues as needed.

Providing Elaboration

As your writing takes shape, you may find that parts of your explanation need more details. Through elaboration—the adding of details—you can help your readers understand exactly what is required at each step. Look for places where adding details—how much, how long, to what degree—will make your how-to essay more precise.

Add Details by "Exploding the Moment"

Cut out several "bursts" or "explosions" from colored paper. As you write your draft, pause occasionally to look for places where you can "explode a moment" in the directions by adding details that give more specific information. Use words that indicate actions, times, or amounts as clues showing where you may need to add information. Write additional details on the colored paper explosions, and lightly paste them to your draft. The example below shows how Felix added details to his draft by exploding the moment.

Student Work
IN PROGRESS

Name: *Felix Espinoza*
Palo Alto Middle School
Killeen, TX

Exploding the Moment

Felix pasted explosions on his draft to add details about parts of the process.

First, gather your ingredients. Then, preheat **to 350°** the oven. Mix together the flour, baking soda, and salt. Put ½ cup butter in a second bowl. Add eggs, and mix them. Set bowl aside. **beat for five minutes after adding each**
In a third bowl, mash the bananas. Add the vanilla and the yogurt. Combine the butter and eggs with the flour mixture. Put the bananas into the bowl. Stir it for a while. Then, add the rest. **until the mixture is smooth**

Drafting: "Exploding the Moment"

Teaching Resources: Writing Support Transparencies 10-E

1. Use Transparency 10-E to show students how "Exploding the Moment" might look in practice. Point out why the writer may have decided to add the "explosions" illustrated (vague point, detail needed to clarify, important element omitted).

2. Explain that using "explosions" can help add the kind of detail that makes writing successful. In a how-to piece, the success must not belong only to the writer, but also to the person following the instructions.

3. Suggest that students look first at verbs (*Is the way the action should be carried out clear?*) then nouns (*Can readers determine precisely what is being described?*) to determine if additional details are needed. However, do let them know that not every item will need explosion.

4. Students can create construction paper "explosions" to attach to their papers, or they can sketch them with colored markers.

Customize for
More Advanced Students

Suggest that students use business software to organize and draft their how-to essay. Spreadsheet software is ideal for helping students to visualize, organize, and record a sequence of actions.

Revising: Writing a Strong Lead

Teaching Resources: Writing Support Transparencies 10-F

1. Explain to students that they need to give readers a reason to keep reading. For a how-to piece, this "reason" can be a result the reader will see or a skill they will obtain by following the instructions.

2. Have students review their prewriting notes and add a sentence to the introduction that tells the reader why they enjoyed the activity described or why it is a good thing to know.

3. Ask students to review their introductions. Does the introduction engage the reader? Does it "hook" the reader into reading further? Suggest that they revise as necessary.

4. Use Transparency 10-F to point out that Felix used appealing details to create his strong lead.

Customize for
Less Advanced Students

To help students become more familiar with good beginnings, give them newspapers or magazines and ask them to highlight examples of strong leads in news reports and feature articles.

10.4 Revising

Revising Your Overall Structure
Add an Introduction and Conclusion

After writing your first draft, reread your how-to essay, looking for ways to improve and polish it. You will probably recognize that you don't want to jump right in with step one and end abruptly at the last step. Instead, give a general overview of your topic in an introduction. Then, explain the different steps in the body of the essay. Review, summarize, or briefly comment on the procedures in a conclusion.

▶ **REVISION STRATEGY**
Writing a Strong Lead

Begin with an image or idea that "leads" your reader into the essay. Look through your prewriting notes to find details that remind you why you enjoy the activity or why you decided to write about your topic. The detail that grabbed your interest may spark your audience's interest as well. Use one of these details to make that first sentence an attention grabber!

Student Work
IN PROGRESS

Name: Felix Espinoza
Palo Alto Middle School
Killeen, TX

Writing a Strong Lead

Felix reviewed his prewriting notes and found that his class party gave him the idea for the topic "How to Make Banana Cake." He used an exaggerated image of hungry students to write an attention-grabbing lead.

Our teacher, Ms. Tallman, knows that it takes more than an ordinary cake to feed twenty ravenous seventh-graders. That's why she always asks Mike or me to make our famous Banana Cake. Making Banana Cake takes a little more time than making a cake from a box, but you will find that every bite of the finished product is worth the time it takes. By following the steps outlined here, you can learn how to make this delicious dessert.

Felix introduces his topic with details that make it appealing.

208 • How-to Essay

⏱ TIME SAVERS!

🗒 **Writing Support Transparencies**
Use the transparencies for Chapter 10 to teach strategies.

⏱ TIME AND RESOURCE MANAGER

Resources
Print: Writing Support Transparencies, 10-F–H
Technology: Writing Lab CD-ROM, Exposition: Making Connections

In-Depth Coverage	Accelerated Pace
• Work through Revising (pp. 208–213) with the entire class. • Use the relevant transparencies to demonstrate strategies for analyzing overall structure (p. 208), sentence beginnings (p.210), and word choice (p. 212).	• Assign students review pp. 208–213 independently. • Have students revise their how-to essays after getting feedback from peer reviewers.

Revising Your Paragraphs

Identify Paragraph Purpose

Once you're comfortable with the general structure of your paper, carefully focus on each individual paragraph. The purpose of each paragraph will determine the words or phrases you may need to add to make your meaning clearer.

▶ **REVISION STRATEGY**
Using Steps, Stacks, Chains, and Balances

- **Steps** If the paragraph explains a step or several related steps for which time order is important, make sure you have indicated the sequence. Use words such as *first*, *next*, and *finally*.

- **Stacks** If the paragraph explains how one part of a process contributes to another, show the connection between ideas with words such as *and*, *furthermore*, and *for instance*.

- **Chains** If the paragraph explains the cause-and-effect relationship between steps, use words such as *so*, *because*, and *consequently*.

- **Balances** If the paragraph shows choice or contrast, use words such as *but*, *however*, *on the other hand*, and *rather*.

▶ Critical Viewing Do you think these boys successfully followed the directions for making a cake? **[Evaluate]**

Revising • **209**

Step-by-Step Teaching Guide

Revising: Steps, Stacks, Chains, and Balances

1. Students may try to explain too many steps in a process in a single paragraph, making the text confusing and hard to follow. Ask students to jot down how many steps are described in each paragraph in the body of their drafts.

2. Suggest that students limit the number of steps covered in each paragraph to no more than two or three.

3. Suggest that students note in the margin next to each paragraph what kind of information it contains—time order, connected elements of the process, cause-and-effect relationships, choice or contrast—to help them decide what clarifying or connecting words to use.

4. Marking paragraphs with a bracket ({) in the margins can help students to identify places where a single lengthy paragraph may be broken into two shorter and clearer paragraphs.

5. Ask students to examine their topic sentences carefully. Does each clearly state the paragraph's main idea?

Critical Viewing

Evaluate Students will probably note that the cake looks fine, indicating that the boys followed the directions correctly, but students may also note that the boys seem to have gotten carried away—and a little messy—with decorating it.

☑ **ONGOING ASSESSMENT: Monitor and Reinforce**

If you observe that students are having difficulty writing strong leads or identifying paragraph purpose, trying one of the following strategies.

Option 1 To help students identify details that would grab reader interest, have them exchange drafts with a partner. Each student identifies an attention grabber in the other's draft. Students then use this feedback in writing their leads.

Option 2 Distribute copies of how-to articles from newspapers or magazines and have students highlight the key words that keep readers focused (*first, for instance, because,* etc.).

Revising: Using Clues to Sentence Beginnings

Teaching Resources: Writing Support Transparencies 10-G

1. Before beginning the activity, ask students to quickly scan their drafts, looking only at the beginnings of sentences. Do they notice any patterns?

2. Display Transparency 10-G and review examples given on the transparency. Discuss with students how sentences have been improved. Ask what other changes might have been chosen instead.

3. Have students fold a piece of loose-leaf paper as indicated, and list the first word in each sentence. Invite several students to read their lists, and write these lists on the board. Circle words that are frequently repeated, such as *it, and, then,* or *next.*

4. Read an excerpt from your own or someone else's writing to show how, by varying sentence beginnings, writers can establish strong rhythms and reader interest, as well as giving how-to essays clearer sequence.

5. Adverb clauses and phrases can also be used to vary the beginnings of sentences. Review Grammar in Your Writing on page 211 to show students how they can enrich their writing.

Integrating Vocabulary Skills

In some cases, greater precision in a how-to essay can be achieved by using words that are more specific. Advise students in ways they might find additional words to help them describe a process. For example, they might turn to the work of other writers on a similar subject. In a recipe, one might need to *blend, fold, incorporate, cream,* or *whip.* Suggest that students record useful words they discover.

10.4

Revising Your Sentences

Vary Your Sentence Beginnings

Within each paragraph, look even more closely at the individual sentences. You may find that by varying the ways your sentences begin, you can make your meaning clearer and make your essay more interesting to read.

▶ **REVISION STRATEGY**
Using Clues to Sentence Beginnings

Fold a piece of lined loose-leaf paper in half lengthwise, then in half again, to make a long strip. Place the strip on the side of your draft. Write the first word of each sentence on its own line to create a list of first words. Review the list, and circle words that are repeated frequently. Rewrite or combine sentences to eliminate some of the words that appear more than once. Look at the following example to see how Felix revised his sentence beginnings:

Student Work
IN PROGRESS

Name: Felix Espinoza
Palo Alto Middle School
Killeen, TX

Varying Sentence Beginnings

Felix listed the first words of all the sentences in his draft. His list showed that he began more than one sentence with the verbs "put" and "add." He varied his sentence beginnings by using transitional words and prepositional phrases.

Put
Use
Add
Set
Put
Add

Put ½ cup butter in a second bowl. Then, Use an eggbeater to cream it. Add 2 eggs and beat for five minutes after adding each egg. Finally, Set this bowl aside, and get out a third bowl. Put the bananas into the third bowl. Add the vanilla and the yogurt.

Felix revised this sentence to begin with the prepositional phrase.

Felix added transitional words to these sentences to vary sentence beginnings and to make the order of the steps clearer.

Because Felix created variety by revising earlier sentences, he decided these could be left as they were.

210 • How-to Essay

Grammar in Your Writing
Adverb Clauses and Adverb Phrases

For many of the steps in your how-to essay, you may add words or groups of words that give more information about a step. **Adverb phrases** and **clauses** can be used to add details that tell *how, where, when, why,* and *under what circumstances* the step is being done. For example, in Felix's revision on the previous page, he uses the phrase "in a second bowl." This phrase acts as an adverb, telling where the reader should put the ingredients.

How: Beat the eggs with an eggbeater.

Where: In a third bowl, prepare the bananas.

When: Before you gather the ingredients, set the oven to preheat.

Why: Preheat the oven so the cake will bake evenly.

Under what circumstances: If the knife is clean, the cakes are finished.

When an adverb phrase or clause comes before the main clause in the sentence, set it off with a comma. When the phrase or clause follows the main clause, do not set it off with a comma.

Phrase follows the main clause:
Beat the eggs with an eggbeater.

Phrase comes before the main clause:
With an eggbeater, beat the eggs.

Adverb clause comes before the main clause:
Before you gather the ingredients, set the oven to preheat.

Adverb clause follows the main clause:
Set the oven to preheat before you gather the ingredients.

Find It in Your Reading Find one adverb phrase and one adverb clause in "Moving Mountains" by Janice VanCleave on page 200. Explain what information is added with each example you find.

Find It in Your Writing Identify three adverb clauses and three adverb phrases that you have used in your how-to essay. Find at least one of each that precedes the main clause. If you can't find three examples, consider whether you have given readers enough information about *how, when, where, why,* and *under what circumstances* they perform the required steps. Identify at least one sentence to which you can add an adverb phrase or clause to give more detail.

To learn more about adverb phrases and clauses, see Chapter 20.

Grammar in Your Writing: Adverb Clauses and Adverb Phrases

1. Have students note that the kind of information provided by the adverb phrases and clauses—how, where, when, why, and under what circumstances—is the kind of information journalists must provide in a news article.

2. Give students a copy of an article from your local newspaper. Have them underline adverb clauses and phrases in the article and then share their answers with the class.

3. Then have them cross out these clauses and phrases and reread the article. Discuss how the omission of adverb clauses and phrases affects its meaning. (The article is not very informative and it may be hard to understand.)

4. This activity will emphasize to students the importance of adverb clauses and phrases to help an essay better inform a reader.

Find It in Your Reading

In the first paragraph of the Model students will find three adverb phrases ("in the world" telling *where*; "in two major ways," telling *how*; and "by streams and rivers," telling *how*). They will find an adverb clause under "What Happens?" ("After you have completed the experiment," telling *when*).

Find It in Your Writing

After students have reviewed their essays for adverb phrases and clauses, have volunteers share with the class the revisions they have made.

☑ ONGOING ASSESSMENT: Prerequisite Skills

If students have difficulty with adverb phrases and clauses, you may find it helpful to review the following to assure coverage of prerequisite knowledge.

In the Textbook	Print Resources	Technology
Phrases and Clauses, pp.428–429, 441–442	Grammar Exercise Workbook, pp. 71–72, 81–82	On-Line Exercise Bank, 20.1, 20.2

Revising: Eliminating Repeated Words

Teaching Resources: Writing Support Transparencies 10-H

1. Using examples on Transparency 10-H, point out how repeated words hurt writing (by making it harder to read and less interesting for the reader) and how variety can make it better.

2. Have students go over their own writing, highlighting words that are repeated frequently.

3. After students have highlighted words they have repeated, have them evaluate which need to be replaced with synonyms, and which must be left alone for clarity. Then ask them to make appropriate replacements.

4. Invite some students to read both the old and the revised paragraphs. Invite students to comment on the improvement, and use these as models when making further changes.

5. Remind students that in a how-to essay, some words or terms must appear repeatedly, such as "eggs" or "teaspoon" in the student essay. Changes might be helpful, however, in how you phrase actions. For instance, by using "add" one place and "combine" in another, you make the reading more interesting, and may help readers to find their place in the list of instructions.

Customize for
ESL Students

Students learning English as a second language may use words repetitively because these are words of whose meaning they are sure. Students with a more limited English vocabulary may wish to use their lists to help them brainstorm for synonyms in their first languages, which they can then translate into English with the help of a dictionary.

10.4

Revising Your Word Choice
Eliminate Repeated Words

Varying your word choice is as important as varying your sentence beginnings. Variety is a quality of sophisticated, mature writing. Go back through your essay and look for overused words. One way to evaluate whether you have overused any words is to highlight repeated words.

▶ **REVISION STRATEGY**
Highlighting Repeated Words

Go through your essay, and use a highlighter to mark any nouns, verbs, or adjectives that you have used more than once. After marking repeated words, evaluate each use to determine whether you should replace the word with a synonym.

Writers in
ACTION

Good advice on revising your how-to essay comes from Sophocles, a writer of ancient Greece whose works are still read today. He said:

"One learns by doing a thing; for though you think you know it, you have no certainty until you try."

Take Sophocles' advice and try out your how-to essay with some classmates. Use this technique to be certain that you have included all the necessary steps and information.

Student Work
IN PROGRESS

Name: Felix Espinoza
Palo Alto Middle School
Killeen, TX

Highlighting Repeated Words

Felix went through his essay and highlighted verbs and nouns that he had used more than once. When he looked at the words he had highlighted, he realized that he was overusing the words make, mix, and bowl.

Combine
Make a mix of the dry ingredients in the first bowl
with the butter and egg mixture, and mix in the
create
second bowl well to make a smooth batter.

Felix eliminated a few uses of mix, make, and bowl. He realized he didn't need to repeat these words to make his meaning clear.

✏️ STANDARDIZED TEST PREPARATION WORKSHOP

Vocabulary Standardized test questions may require students to recognize multiple meanings of words. Provide students with opportunities to evaluate the appropriateness of words when their meanings shift. Write these sentence and word choices on the board. Ask students to find the word that fits in both of the sentences.

Mike poured the ___ into the cake pan.

The pitcher struck out the last ___ to end the game.

A mixture

B batter

C ingredients

D hitter

Students should recognize that item **B** is the only word that fits both sentences. A and C fit the first sentence but not the second, and D fits the second sentence but not the first. In the first sentence, *batter* means "a mixture of flour, milk, and eggs for baking." In the second sentence, it means "a player whose turn it is to bat in baseball."

Peer Review

Getting feedback from your classmates is especially helpful in revising a how-to essay. Because the purpose of a how-to essay is to explain, peer reviewers can give you objective opinions about how clear the explanation is and whether any additional information is needed.

Ask a Group to Try It Out

First, read your essay aloud to a small group of classmates as they listen. Then, read it aloud again, as if you were guiding the group through the activity or procedure you are explaining. Have the group go through the motions of each step, taking notes on where they are confused or unsure. After you have finished reading the essay a second time, ask reviewers to respond to the following questions:

- Which step or steps could have been explained more clearly?

- What was confusing about those steps?

- In which sections did you feel you needed more or less information? What information would you have added or eliminated?

- What other questions or comments do you have about the activity or process I explained?

Use the comments and questions to guide you in making a final revision of your essay.

**Writing Lab
CD-ROM**

Use the Language Variety Checker in the Writer's Toolkit to find words that you may have overused. Evaluate which ones you should replace with synonyms.

▼ **Critical Viewing** What procedures or processes do you find it helpful to try with a group of peer reviewers? **[Relate]**

Revising: Peer Review

1. Begin the peer review process by inviting students to identify a draft's strengths before zeroing in on its drawbacks.

2. Remind students that some errors will be corrected at the proofreading stage, and that the focus here should be on content.

3. Suggest that students who will be reading their drafts aloud prepare a short list of questions beforehand for their peer reviewers. See the four questions on page 213.

4. Point out that many comments made during peer review will be helpful to all students. Suggest that students note down important ideas raised in discussion, and consult them later.

Critical Viewing

Relate Answers will vary. Some students may find they learn more when group members take turns responding to specific questions about each essay. Others might prefer a less structured, more conversational meeting.

Editing and Proofreading: Commas

1. Editing and proofreading may be viewed as an extension of the paragraphing process. You might suggest that students check punctuation paragraph by paragraph.

2. Check that students look carefully at introductory or adverbial phrases. Does a paragraph explaining a sequence of actions in time have the necessary commas after the words *first, next,* or *finally*? Does a paragraph with stacks or chains of information have commas after *for example* or *consequently*?

Grammar in Your Writing: Using Commas to Separate Items in a Series

1. Remind students that a series consists of three or more items of the same kind. These items may be words, phrases, or clauses.

2. Write the following sentence on the board:

   We looked for that recipe in old cookbooks on the Internet and in magazines.

   Point out that as it is punctuated, the sentence contains only two distinct items: *old cookbooks on the Internet* and *magazines.*

3. Then challenge students to add commas so that this sentence contains three distinct items (commas should appear after *cookbooks* and after *Internet*). What are the three items? (*old cookbooks, the Internet, magazines*)

Find It in Your Reading

Students will find the first example of a series under "What You Need." They might rewrite part of the series as follows: "a lightweight wooden block, a black marking pen, and a red marking pen."

Find It in Your Writing

You may wish to have students exchange drafts with a partner to check for correct use of commas to separate items in a series.

10.5 # Editing and Proofreading

Errors in spelling, punctuation, grammar, or usage can create confusion. Proofread your essay to discover and eliminate these errors in your essay. Be especially careful that you have used commas correctly.

Focusing on Commas

As you proofread your how-to-essay, check to make sure that you have used commas where they are needed. As is explained on page 211, you might use commas to set off introductory adverb clauses. You will also need commas to separate items in lists.

Grammar in Your Writing
Using Commas to Separate Items in a Series

Use commas to separate items in a series, or list. Separating the items with commas makes your meaning clear to readers. Look at the following examples:

Commas separate individual items in a series:
Add the sugar, baking soda, baking powder, and salt.

Commas separate groups of words in a series:
Begin by gathering your tools, reviewing the recipe, and preheating the oven.

Note: Most writers use a comma before the *and* that connects the last two items in the series because it prevents misreading. (See the commas following *baking powder* and *recipe* in the examples above.) Some do not use a comma before the final *and* if the meaning is clear without one. Follow your teacher's directions about whether to use the comma before the *and*.

Find It in Your Reading Read "Moving Mountains" by Janice VanCleave on page 200. Find an example of items in a series, and rewrite part of the list using commas.

Find It in Your Writing Review your essay, and circle any lists or series of items. Remember that the series can include either individual words or groups of words. Check that you have correctly used commas to separate the items in each series or list that you find.

To learn more about the correct use of commas, see Chapter 26.

⏱ TIME AND RESOURCE MANAGER

Resources
Print: Scoring Rubrics on Transparency, Ch. 10; Formal Assessment, Ch. 10
Technology: Writing Lab CD-ROM, Exposition: Making Connections

In-Depth Coverage	Accelerated Pace
• Review pp. 214–215 in class, including Grammar In Your Writing. • Analyze the Final Draft (p. 216) in class • Have students revise and proofread their essays in class.	• Assign pp. 214–216 for independent review. • Have students independently edit and proofread their essays. • Respond to individual editing issues as needed.

10.6 Publishing and Presenting

Building Your Portfolio

Consider the following possibilities for publishing or presenting your how-to essay:

1. **Give a Demonstration**   Distribute copies of your how-to essay as a handout to accompany a demonstration of the activity you will explain. Your audience can follow along as you demonstrate the steps. Then, they can take your explanation with them to follow on their own.

2. **Make a Poster**   Make a poster of your topic, with pictures of each step of the activity. Copy your essay, and cut the paragraphs apart so they can be attached in appropriate places on the poster.

Reflecting on Your Writing

Write down a few thoughts about writing a how-to essay. You might start off by answering these questions:

- Did explaining an activity increase or decrease your enjoyment of the activity? Explain.

- After writing your essay, do you think the activity you explained would be difficult or easy to learn? Why?

 Internet Tip

To see model essays scored with this rubric, visit **www.phschool.com**

Rubric for Self-Assessment

Use the following criteria to evaluate your how-to essay:

	Score 4	Score 3	Score 2	Score 1
Audience and Purpose	Clearly focuses on procedures leading to a well-defined end	Focuses on procedures leading to a well-defined end	Includes procedures related to an end, but presents some vaguely	Includes only vague descriptions of procedures and results
Organization	Gives instructions in logical order; subdivides complex actions into steps	Gives instructions in logical order; subdivides some complex actions into steps	For the most part, gives instructions in logical order	Gives instructions in a scattered, disorganized manner
Elaboration	Provides appropriate amount of detail; gives needed explanations	Provides appropriate amount of detail; gives some explanations	Provides some detail; gives few explanations	Provides few details; gives few or no explanations
Use of Language	Shows overall clarity and fluency; uses transitions effectively; contains few mechanical errors	Shows some sentence variety; uses some transitions; includes few mechanical errors	Uses awkward or overly simple sentence structures; contains many mechanical errors	Contains incomplete thoughts and confusing mechanical errors

Publishing and Presenting • **215**

Publishing and Presenting

1. Review the presentation options on p. 215 and encourage students to consider finding more places to share their work.

2. In preparing their essays for publication, students may wish to add illustrations, graphs, or photographs to their essays.

ASSESS

Assessment

Teaching Resources: Scoring Rubrics on Transparency, Ch. 10; Writing Assessment and Portfolio Management; Formal Assessment, Ch. 10

1. Display the Scoring Rubric transparency and review the criteria in class.

2. Before students proceed with self-assessment, you may wish to review Felix's final draft on page 216. Have students score the final draft in one or more of the rubric categories.

3. In addition to student self-assessment, you may wish to:

   - score student essays yourself using the rubric and scoring models from *Writing Assessment and Portfolio Management.*

   - review the Standardized Test Preparation Workshop on pages 220–221 and have students respond to an expository writing prompt within a set time limit.

   - administer the Chapter 10 assessment from *Formal Assessment* in the Teaching Resources to assess students' grasp of concepts presented.

☑ ONGOING ASSESSMENT: Assess Mastery

Use one of the following options to assess final drafts of students' how-to essays.

Self-Assessment Ask students to score their essays using the rubric provided. Then have students write a paragraph discussing the most useful strategy they learned in writing a how-to essay.	**Teacher Assessment** Use the rubric and the scoring models provided in *Writing Assessment and Portfolio Management* to score students' work.

Teaching From the Final Draft

1. Help students see that "Banana Cake" incorporates key elements of the how-to essay:

   • The topic has been well chosen; the activity described is both appealing and manageable.

   • Audience and purpose have been carefully considered: the essay is clearly addressed to young people who enjoy eating and offers something good to eat.

   • The introduction engages the reader, and gives the reader a good idea of what is to come.

   • The body of the essay clearly explains the steps required to bake Banana Cake successfully. The steps of the process are presented in logical sequence, and all materials needed are clearly specified.

   • Finally, a short conclusion is given. It repeats the goal— having a tasty cake—and the benefit to the reader—eating it.

2. Ask students if they think that the care with which the essay has been constructed contributes to making them feel confident about being able to follow the instructions and get the result promised.

3. Explain that this is one of the reasons that it is important to write carefully—to instill confidence in the reader that you know your subject. Not only must there be enough information, it must be presented in such a way that it is obvious that thought has gone into the guidelines.

4. Ask students if there are any other changes they would recommend for this essay, to make it flow better or fine-tune the directions. How might they apply these suggestions to their own writing?

10.7 *Student Work*
IN PROGRESS

FINAL DRAFT

Banana Cake

Felix Espinoza
Palo Alto Middle School
Killeen, Texas

Our teacher, Ms. Tallman, knows that it takes more than an ordinary cake to feed twenty ravenous seventh-graders. That's why she always asks Mike or me to make our famous Banana Cake. Making Banana Cake takes a little more time than making a cake from a box, but you will find that every bite of the finished product is worth the time it takes. By following the steps outlined here, you can learn how to make this delicious dessert.

2 1/4 cups cake flour	1/2 cup butter, softened
1 1/2 cups sugar	2 eggs
3/4 teaspoon baking soda	1 cup mashed ripe bananas
1/2 teaspoon baking powder	1 teaspoon vanilla
1/2 teaspoon salt	1/4 cup yogurt

Before mixing the ingredients, set the oven to preheat to 350 degrees. (Preheating is important, because the cake will come out lopsided if it is not evenly baked.) Grease and flour two 9-inch round cake pans.

Start by mixing the dry ingredients. First, sift the cake flour into a large bowl. Next, add the sugar, baking soda, baking powder, and salt.

In a second bowl, put 1/2 cup butter. Use an eggbeater to cream it. Then, add 2 eggs and beat for five minutes after adding each egg. Finally, set this bowl aside, and get out a third bowl. Put the bananas into the third bowl. Add the vanilla and the yogurt.

Combine the dry ingredients with the butter and egg mixture, and mix well to create a smooth batter. Then, gradually pour the batter over the mashed banana. Mix the batter as you pour. When the batter is smooth and has no lumps, pour half of the cake mixture into each pan. Bake for one-half hour. Let the cake cool for one-half hour before icing.

After following these directions, you should end up with a treat. Ice the cake if you like. The final step is to cut a slice and enjoy it!

216 • How-to Essay

In the introduction, Felix tells readers why they should make the cake.

Felix puts the ingredients in list form.

Felix explains steps in chronological order. He uses words like first to make the order clear.

Because Felix's audience of classmates may not know which utensil to use, he tells them—an eggbeater.

Felix rounds off his essay with an inspiring conclusion.

Connected Assignment
Problem-and-Solution Essay

The purpose of a **problem-and-solution essay** is to describe a problem and offer one or more solutions to it. Like a how-to essay, a problem-and-solution essay describes an organized set of steps to achieve a result. Unlike a how-to essay, it must also explain why these steps will work. An effective problem-and-solution essay will:

Why It's a Problem	Problem	Possible Solution
Recycling is necessary—we're running out of places to put garbage.		Have inspectors spot-check people's trash and fine them if the recyclables are not sorted out.
Recycling is necessary—we may run out of some resources if we don't conserve them.	Many citizens don't take the time to sort out recyclables.	Hold a contest with a prize for the kid who turns in the greatest amount of recyclables to the center.

- clearly explain the problem.
- explain and defend the proposed solution.

Prewriting Choose a topic for your essay by browsing news sources. Choose a problem that grabs your interest.

Use a cluster diagram like the one above to gather details about your problem. Then, do research to find solutions. Gather facts, expert opinions, and other evidence for support.

Drafting After gathering facts, clearly state the problem and the solutions your essay will present. Include this statement in your introduction. At the beginning of your draft, provide any necessary background information. Then, lay out your solutions step-by-step, in a clear, well-organized manner. Support your solutions with evidence.

Revising and Editing Review your first draft. When you find a possible objection to a solution you offer, mention the objection in your draft. Answer it, or show that it is outweighed by other considerations. Finally, proofread your essay to eliminate errors in spelling, grammar, or punctuation.

Publishing and Presenting Consider submitting your completed essay to a school or local newspaper.

⚙ Grammar and Style Tip

By combining simple sentences into compound or complex sentences, you can emphasize the connections between problems and solutions. For more on sentence structure, see Chapter 20.

▶ Lesson Objectives

1. To write a problem-and-solution essay.
2. To generate and organize ideas with graphic organizers.
3. To use writing processes to develop and revise drafts.

Step-by-Step Teaching Guide

Problem-and-Solution Essay

Teaching Resources: Writing Support Transparencies 10-I; Writing Support Activity Book 10-3

1. Bring samples of problem-and-solution essays to class. Other sources for ideas are how-to or advice columns (on gardening, computers, auto repair) that appear in newspapers and magazines.
2. Suggest that students use the listing strategy on page 202 to generate their topics.
3. Display Transparency 10-I to demonstrate how a cluster diagram can aid in organizing details about a problem.
4. Give students copies of the blank organizer for their use as they gather information.
5. Allow class time for students to present their problem-and-solution essays.

1. To compare print and visual media.
2. To evaluate how different media influence and inform.
3. To write a how-to essay.

Comparing Media

1. Choose one of the Spotlight elements for class discussion, or have students work individually or in groups on the element of their choice. Give students the initiative to find the necessary books, videotapes, recordings, or pictures.

2. If students read Verne's novel *From the Earth to the Moon* and view Méliès's twenty-one minute film, have them compare the different moods of the written and visual versions.

3. Play the opening strains of *Also Sprach Zarathustra* for students and ask students what mood or emotion the music evokes. Then show the portions of Kubrick's film, *2001: A Space Odyssey,* where Strauss's music first occurs on the soundtrack. Ask students if they think the music fits the images on the screen.

Viewing and Representing

Activity Give interested students opportunity to make class presentations of their film/story research. Encourage them to show portions of the film in their presentations.

Critical Viewing

Compare Students may note that the film's satirical "moon rocket" bears a closer resemblance to a bullet than to the actual spacecraft shown in the photograph.

Spotlight on the Humanities

Comparing Media
Focus: Science Fiction in Film

It's easy enough to write a how-to essay on baking a cake—others can tell you how it's done. In 1865, though, no one had ever gone to the moon. It took a genius like Jules Verne (1828–1905), the early science fiction writer, to write a how-to on the subject: a novel called *From the Earth to the Moon.*

Much science fiction is like a how-to for what has never been done before. Using today's science, science fiction writers project future technologies and their effect on people's lives.

In 1902, one of the early masters of silent film, Frenchman Georges Méliès (1861–1938), followed Verne's "recipe" and made the short movie *A Trip to the Moon.* The recipe worked a little differently on screen—Verne's serious science fiction turned into hilarious satire. Méliès proved, though, that however far science fiction stretched the mind, the movies could teach the eye to keep up.

A number of Verne's works, including *A Journey to the Center of the Earth* (1864), were also made into movies. While these movies dealt in adventure, other science fiction movies explored people's fears. In the 1950's, movies such as *The Thing* (1951) explored the terrors science had unleashed—including nuclear war. Later, in 1968, Stanley Kubrick's highly acclaimed *2001: A Space Odyssey* showed a computer run amok, making decisions for the people it was meant to serve.

Music Connection In 1896, German composer Richard Strauss wrote *Also Sprach Zarathustra,* his famous tone poem (short musical piece). Matching the majesty of Kubrick's depictions of outer space, the work appeared as the theme of *2001: A Space Odyssey.*

Literature Connection Twentieth-century writers such as Isaac Asimov (1920–1992) and Ray Bradbury (1920–   ) brought science fiction beyond simple adventure stories, dealing with social issues and creating vivid characters.

Expository Writing Activity: Explanation of Special Effects Research special effects in films of the silent era. Write a how-to essay explaining the steps by which moviemakers created one of these special effects.

▼▲ **Critical Viewing** Compare Méliès's film version of a moon rocket with this photograph of a real space launch. [**Compare**]

Media and Technology Skills

Using Computer Technology

Activity: Getting Help On-line

Computer programs typically come with built-in "how-to's"— on-line help the user can access while using the program. On-line help lets you learn as you work. It is as though the computer were a teacher and a tool rolled into one! By mastering Help, you can turn problems with computers into opportunities to learn.

Learn About It

Balloon Help Turn Balloon Help on or off through a program's menu bar. With Balloon Help on, a balloon appears whenever you roll your mouse pointer over a button, dialogue box, or other feature. Each balloon contains a brief description identifying the function of the feature on which the pointer is resting.

On-line Manuals To consult the on-line manual for a program, select "Help" from the menu bar. "Contents" lists topics by category. "Index" lists topics alphabetically and often provides a Search feature that allows you to search for a particular subject.

Other Kinds of Help Often, the best troubleshooting tips come from the program's "Read Me" file. You may open a "Read Me" file in a text-editor program. Software also comes with a printed manual, which offers detailed information on operating the program.

Apply It Choose an application, such as a word-processing program, to which you have access. Think of a difficulty you have had using the program or a question you might have about the program's use. Use two or more forms of help to solve the problem or answer the question. Take notes in a graphic organizer such as the one to the right. Then, write a mini-manual explaining how to use these different ways of getting help.

Computer Help

Built-in Help
- Balloon Help
- On-line manuals

Other Kinds of Help
- "Read Me" files
- Printed manuals

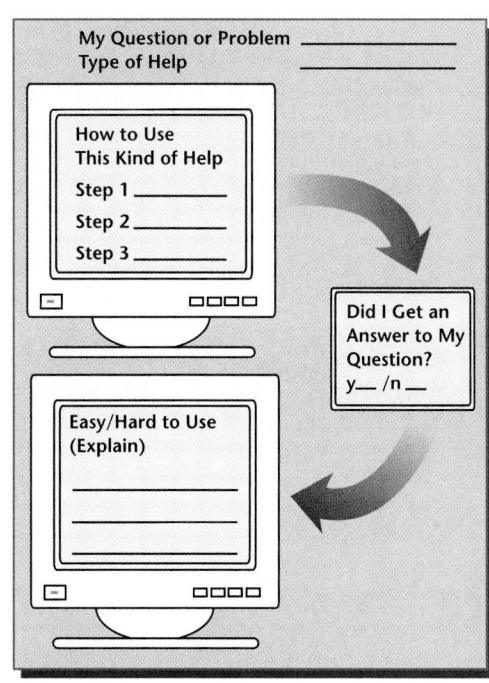

My Question or Problem _____
Type of Help _____

How to Use This Kind of Help

Step 1 _____
Step 2 _____
Step 3 _____

Did I Get an Answer to My Question?
y__ /n __

Easy/Hard to Use (Explain)
_____
_____
_____

Media and Technology Skills • 219

▶ Lesson Objectives

1. To understand and use on-line computer help resources.
2. To use technology for aspects of creating, revising, editing, and publishing.
3. To organize information with a graphic organizer.
4. To write a manual.

Step-by-Step Teaching Guide

Getting Help On-line

Teaching Resources: Writing Support Transparency 10-J; Writing Support Activity Book 10-4

1. Let students know that the "Help" function of a computer program is usually readily accessible from the document screen. Advise students to scan the menu or toolbar for the word "Help" or for a button with a symbol such as a question mark.

2. When students have accessed the Help function, they need not scroll at length through the list of topics. Most programs have a prompt screen in which students may enter the topic about which they need information.

3. When the topic is entered in the prompt screen, the program will provide detailed instructions on how to perform the required function. You may wish to give students copies of the graphic organizer (10-4) to help them record helpful information.

Integrating Workplace Skills

Tell students that most workplaces have internal, or in-house, publishing facilities for producing guidelines or instructional materials for employees. Point out that effective writing of this kind is often written in the style of a how-to essay. You may wish to obtain materials of this kind to share with students.

Lesson Objectives

1. To write a response to an expository prompt
2. To use prewriting strategies to generate ideas
3. To organize ideas to ensure logical progression and support for ideas
4. To demonstrate control of grammatical elements

Step-by-Step Teaching Guide

Responding to Expository Writing Prompts

1. During a class period, have students respond to the expository writing prompt on this page. Set a time limit so that students can become familiar with writing short pieces in a set time.

2. If you plan to give students an entire class period to respond to the prompt, prepare them by reviewing the requirements the day before.

3. Remind students that the key to writing for standardized tests is in preparation. Discourage the impulse to begin writing immediately—urge them to use these first impulses for note-taking and outlining. You might provide students with scrap paper for this purpose.

4. Remind students that different tests may require different things from them. Some tests require a clean, rewritten draft; others do not. Encourage them to read instructions carefully before they begin to write, and to budget their time accordingly.

Standardized Test Preparation Workshop

Responding to Expository Writing Prompts

Some expository writing prompts on standardized tests measure your ability to write a "how-to"—to present clear instructions and explanations in writing. You will be evaluated on your ability to do the following:

- choose a logical, consistent organization
- elaborate with the appropriate amount of detail for your specific audience and purpose
- use complete sentences and follow the rules of grammar
- use correct spelling and punctuation.

The process of writing for a test, or for any other kind of writing, can be divided into stages. Plan to use a specific amount of time for prewriting, drafting, revising, and proofreading.

Following is an example of one type of expository writing prompt you might find on a standardized test. Use the suggestions on the following page to help you respond. The clock icons suggest the portion of the test-taking time that you should spend on each stage.

Test Tip

When writing a how-to for a test, be especially careful to include the appropriate amount of detail for the audience specified in the prompt.

Sample Writing Situation

A friend of yours is about to start going to your school. Unfortunately, you won't be there to show him or her around on the first day. Write a letter to your friend explaining the morning procedures for your class or school.

220 • How-to Essay

✎ TEST-TAKING TIP

A clear understanding of the writing prompt is the first step to success on a written test. Tell students to make sure to identify the exact words in the prompt that specify audience, purpose, topic, and form. They might find it useful to mark these words on the prompt before they begin to plan their response.

Ask students to pick out the 3–5 key words in the sample test item on this page.

friend	the audience
letter	the required form
explaining	the purpose
morning procedures	the topic

Prewriting

 Allow about one fourth of your time for jotting down the details you want to include.

Think About Your Audience As you jot down your details, keep your audience in mind. Remember that your friend has never been to your school, so include explanations and definitions of terms and place names that will be unfamiliar. For example, if you tell your friend to place his or her backpack next to the entrance, be sure to explain which entrance and where it is. For questions that will help you think about your audience, see page 204.

Drafting

 Allow about half of your time for drafting.

Organize Details Use a timeline to organize your explanation in chronological order. Review the example timeline on page 206.

Elaborate Look over the steps you've outlined on your timeline. Add any "in-between" steps or any definitions that will make your explanation clearer. Look for places where you can add details about times and places.

Make Connections Readers find it easier to follow directions when you make connections between steps. Words like *next, then, instead,* or *after* help make these connections. As you draft, use transitional words such as these to help your friend follow your directions.

Revising, Editing, and Proofreading

 Allow almost one fourth of your time for revising.

Show Transitions Read over your work, looking for places where you should add a transitional word or more information about a step. You probably won't have time to copy your work over, so make sure you indicate the insertion neatly.

 Allow several minutes to give your work one final check for errors in spelling or punctuation.

Be Neat Put a single line through any misspelled word and neatly write the correct spelling above it. Make sure you have begun each sentence with a capital letter and that you have used the correct end punctuation for each sentence.

Customize for
Less Advanced Students

Help students budget their time as they respond to the prompt by announcing elapsed time at regular intervals and suggesting when students should be moving from one step of the process to another.

Customize for
More Advanced Students

To give students practice in "writing against the clock" set time limits for other writing tasks you assign for completion during class time. You might suggest that students set time limits themselves when writing independently.

11 Time and Resource Manager

In-Depth Lesson Plan

	LESSON FOCUS	PRINT AND MEDIA RESOURCES
DAY 1	**Introduction to Research Report** Students learn key elements of writing a research report and analyze the Model From Literature (pp. 222–227).	*Writers at Work* **Videotape**, Reports *Writing Lab* **CD-ROM**, Reports
DAY 2	**Prewriting** Students use listing, newswatch, and self-interview to choose a research topic (pp. 228–229).	**Teaching Resources** *Writing Support Transparencies*, 11-A–C; *Writing Support Activity Book*, 11-1–2 *Writing Lab* **CD-ROM**, Reports
DAY 3	**Drafting** Students narrow their topic, construct an outline, conduct research, and write their first drafts (pp. 230–233).	**Teaching Resources** *Writing Support Transparencies*, 11-D *Writing Lab* **CD-ROM**, Reports
DAY 4	**Revising** Students revise their drafts, using their outlines as guides (pp. 234–238).	**Teaching Resources** *Writing Support Transparencies*, 11-E–F *Writing Lab* **CD-ROM**, Reports
DAY 5	**Editing and Proofreading; Publishing and Presenting** Students edit their research reports, check their source citations, and present their final drafts (pp. 239–240).	**Teaching Resources** *Scoring Rubrics on Transparency*, Ch. 11; *Formal Assessment*, Ch. 11 *Writing Lab* **CD-ROM**, Reports

Accelerated Lesson Plan

	LESSON FOCUS	PRINT AND MEDIA RESOURCES
DAY 1	**Drafting** Students review characteristics of a research report, select and outline a topic, conduct research, and write a first draft (pp. 222–233).	**Teaching Resources** *Writing Support Transparencies*, 11-A–D; *Writing Support Activity Book*, 11-1–2 *Writing Lab* **CD-ROM**, Reports *Writers at Work* **Videotape**, Reports
DAY 2	**Revising to Presenting** Students work individually or with peers to review, edit, and proofread their work for presentation (pp. 234–240).	**Teaching Resources** *Writing Support Transparencies*, 11-E–F; *Scoring Rubrics on Transparency*, Ch. 11; *Formal Assessment*, Ch. 11 *Writing Lab* **CD-ROM**, Reports

Options for Adapting Lesson Plans

HOMEWORK

Have students complete any stage of the lesson for homework.

FEATURES

Extend coverage with Connected Assignment (p. 243), Spotlight on the Humanities (p. 244), Media and Technology Skills (p. 245), and the Standardized Test Preparation Workshop (p. 246).

TECHNOLOGY

Students can complete any stage of the lesson on computer. Have them print out their completed work.

INTEGRATED SKILLS COVERAGE

Integrating Grammar
Participial Phrases, SE p. 237
Punctuation of Titles, SE p. 239
Grammar and Style SE p. 235

Reading/Writing Connection
Reading Strategy, SE p. 224
Writing Application, SE p. 227

Viewing and Representing
Critical Viewing, SE pp. 222, 224, 227, 233, 234, 238, 241, 243, 244
ATE pp. 227, 244

Technology
SE pp. 239, 240, 245; ATE p. 226

Speaking and Listening
ATE p. 229

ASSESSMENT SUPPORT

Standardized Test Preparation SE p. 246; ATE pp. 226, 237

Standardized Test Preparation Workbook, pp. 21–22

Scoring Rubrics on Transparency, Ch. 11

Formal Assessment, Ch. 11

Writing Assessment and Portfolio Management

MEETING INDIVIDUAL NEEDS

More Advanced Students ATE p. 225
Verbal/Linguistic Learners ATE p. 230
Visual/Spatial Learners ATE p. 235
ESL Students ATE p. 242
Less Advanced Students See Ongoing Assessments, ATE pp. 231, 233, 235, 236, 240

BLOCK SCHEDULING

Pacing Suggestions
For 90-minute Blocks
• Have students complete the Prewriting and Drafting stages in a single period.
• Focus one class period on Revising and Editing and Publishing and Presenting. Allow at least 30 minutes for peer review.

Resources for Varying Instruction
• *Writing Lab* CD-ROM If your students have access to hardware, a 90-minute block provides an ideal opportunity for them to work on computer.
• *Writers at Work* Videotape

Professional Development Support
• *How to Manage Instruction in the Block* This Teaching Resource provides management and activity suggestions.

MEDIA AND TECHNOLOGY

For the Student
• *Writing Lab* CD-ROM, Reports
• *On-Line Exercise Bank*, Section 18.1

For the Teacher
• *Writers at Work* Videotape, Reports

WRITING AND GRAMMAR WEB SITE

The Interactive Writing and Grammar Web site provides a wide array of support for students, teachers, and parents. Writing support includes:

• Interactive revision checkers
• Scoring rubrics with complete models

www.phschool.com

LITERATURE CONNECTIONS

Related selections from *Prentice Hall Literature: Timeless Voices, Timeless Themes,* Bronze:

from *Tiger: A Biography of Tiger Woods,* SE p. 227
"Rikki-tikki-tavi," by Rudyard Kipling, SE p. 229

Lesson Objectives

1. To write to inform such as to explain, describe, report, and narrate.

2. To generate ideas and plans for writing by using prewriting strategies.

3. To select and use reference materials and resources as needed for writing, revising, and editing final drafts.

4. To apply criteria to evaluate writing.

5. To frame questions to direct research.

6. To evaluate his/her own research and frame new questions for further investigation.

7. To follow accepted formats for writing research, including documenting sources.

Critical Viewing

Analyze Students may mention having to use a typewriter in order to publish it. Students will probably mention that computers make this work much easier.

Chapter 11 *Research Report*

Le Roman, Rosa Ibarra

Research Reports in Everyday Life

How much does your world hold? You have your home, your school, your town—places you see every day. There are also the places you've never seen but about which you have learned something. They, too, are part of your picture of the world.

Research starts when you ask questions about that picture: "Where is Sri Lanka?" "Who is the leader of Germany?" As soon as you look for answers—in a library book, in an interview with an expert, or on the Internet—you are doing research. Each fact you learn adds to your picture of the world. Learn how to write an effective research report and expand your horizons.

▲ **Critical Viewing**
What does this painting suggest about the process of writing a research report? Name one resource you can use to help with this process. **[Analyze]**

222 • Research Report

⏱ TIME AND RESOURCE MANAGER

Resources
Technology: Writers at Work videotape, Reports

In-Depth Coverage	Accelerated Pace
• Cover pp. 222–223 in class. • Show the Research Report section of the Writers at Work videotape. • Read the Model From Literature (pp. 224–227) in class and use it to brainstorm research report ideas. • Discuss examples of research reports students may have done or read in the past.	• Have students read pp. 222–227 on their own. • Discuss definitions and types of research reports in class. • Assign Model From Literature for independent reading.

What Is a Research Report?

A **research report** presents information gathered from reference books, observations, interviews, or other sources. A good research report does not simply repeat information. It guides readers through a topic, showing them why each fact matters and creating an overall picture of the subject. An effective research report includes

- an overall focus or main idea.
- information gathered from a variety of sources.
- a clear organization and smooth transitions.
- facts and details to support each main point.
- accurate, complete citations identifying sources.

To learn the criteria on which your report may be evaluated, see the Rubric for Self-Assessment on page 240.

Types of Research Reports

Some types of reports you might write include the following:

- **Biographical sketches** report high points in the life of a notable person.
- **Reports of scientific experiments** present the setup and results of experiments.
- **Documented essays** use research to support a point or examine a trend.

Writers in ACTION

Ellie Fries writes "reports"— signs about the animals posted at the Aquarium for Wildlife Conservation in Brooklyn, New York. She focuses on the interests of her audience:

"The elements of the exhibit include, first and foremost, the animal. Well, what is a shark all about? What does it eat? Will it eat me? . . . So we think about what questions the visitors will have. Then we will have to research the answers. . . ."

PREVIEW Student Work IN PROGRESS

Jamie Barraclough, of Los Alamos Middle School in Los Alamos, New Mexico, wrote a research report about whales. In this chapter, you will see Jamie's work in progress, including strategies he used to choose a topic, focus his topic, elaborate, and revise. At the end of the chapter, you can read the final draft of the report Jamie wrote.

Research Report • 223

PREPARE and ENGAGE

 **Interest GRABBER** If possible, bring in a copy of a medical journal and an encyclopedia volume. Ask students if they are familiar with the type of information these books provide. Explain that these are examples of types of research reports.

Activate Prior Knowledge

Ask students to remember the last time they learned a fact about a topic or newsworthy person that surprised them or contradicted what they presumed to be true. How did they originally form their beliefs about this topic? How did they find the information that challenged those beliefs?

More About the Writer

Ellie Fries, Director of Education at the Aquarium for Wildlife Conservation, guided the development of interdisciplinary marine science programs that were linked to real-life experiences for school children, families, the public, and the teaching community.

☑ ONGOING ASSESSMENT: Diagnose

Use one of the following options to diagnose students' current level of proficiency in writing research reports.

Option 1 Ask each student to select the strongest example of his or her research writing from last year. Hold conferences in which you review each student's work. Use the conferences to determine which students will need extra support.

Option 2 Tell students to imagine that they will be writing a research report on a mammal native to their home state. Ask them to quickly list three or four questions they would answer in their reports. If students have difficulty, you may need to devote more time to the prewriting phase of the process.

Reading\Writing Connection

Reading Strategy: Question

As they read Standring's essay, have students divide a sheet of paper into two columns and list in one column any questions that come up as they read, such as "What do pandas eat?" Then have them place a check mark in the column opposite when and if the essay answers that question. This will help students recognize the importance of anticipating and answering questions in the research essay.

Step-by-Step Teaching Guide

Engage Students Through Literature

Use this Model From Literature as one way to help students generate a topic for their research essays.

1. Read aloud the first two pages, or have students take turns reading portions of the text.

2. Lead students in discussion using questions such as these:

   • *What are the ways that the author catches the reader's interest?*

   • *Did Standring provide enough information about pandas to give a thorough understanding of why they are endangered?*

   • *Do you think the research essay is an effective tool to help the future of the panda species?*

3. Ask students to brainstorm for other research topics. Here are some possibilities:

   • *What are the ways organizations like the WWF help in the fight for wildlife preservation and what are their goals for this century?*

   • *What previously endangered species was saved from extinction and how can this accomplishment serve as a model for the future?*

continued

 # Model From Literature

This report by nature writer Gillian Standring (1935–   ) offers a wealth of information about the giant panda.

 **Reading Strategy: Question** To get the most out of reading research reports, **ask questions.** After reading Standring's first paragraph, for example, you might ask, "Why have pandas become so rare?"

Pandas

Gillian Standring

Introducing Pandas The giant panda is one of the best-known animals in the world. It is also one of the rarest. In 1990 there were only about one thousand giant pandas living wild in China, and only fifteen in zoos outside China (Catton 93, 110–111). So if you have seen pandas in a zoo, you are very lucky.

. . . The first living pandas outside China were brought to the United States in 1936 and to Britain in 1938 (Angel 16–24). Ever since, the giant panda has been of great interest to scientists, zookeepers, and all animal lovers. Because it is so popular and so unusual, it was chosen as the symbol of the World Wildlife Fund (WWF), the world's best-known conservation organization.

Life in the Wild Pandas, unlike people, prefer to be cool and damp. Hot, dry weather is bad for them (Dudley 29). High up in the mountains of Sichuan in southwest China, there are thick, misty forests where it is always cool and damp. Pandas spend most of the year in these forests. In winter they come down to the lower slopes to get away from the deep snow and freezing cold (Dudley 30). There are few people living in this part of China.

Pandas are famous for eating bamboo. Their food grows all around them in the bamboo forests, so they never have to hunt

224 • Research Report

▲ **Critical Viewing**
Give two questions for research suggested by this photo. **[Question]**

Standring's introduction sets out her main idea—that the giant panda is a rare, special species.

Standring's report is ordered logically. First, she presents information on the habitat and life of pandas. After providing this necessary background, she discusses the specific reasons pandas are endangered.

Critical Viewing

Question Students' answers will vary. Suggested questions should refer to details of the photo; they might include "What do pandas eat?" and "What kind of place do pandas live in?"

for it. However, they like to eat only a few kinds of bamboo, and their digestion is not very good, so they spend almost all the day just eating (Angel 37–38). Pandas also eat grasses, roots, bulbs, and tree bark. Sometimes they catch little cane rats and fish. They often take long drinks from mountain streams and rivers (Dudley 36).

Why Are Pandas So Rare? Giant pandas have probably never been common anywhere. There are several reasons for this. They do not produce many babies (Laidler 133–134). As we have seen, they can live only in cool bamboo forests. Each panda needs a big area of forest to itself, and even large areas of suitable mountain forest have room for only a few pandas (Laidler 109–113).

Pandas also need plenty of their favorite bamboo. This plant has a very unusual way of growing. For perhaps a hundred years, bamboo plants spread by underground branches. Then suddenly, all the bamboo plants over a wide area flower, make seeds, and die. This leaves no food for the pandas until new plants grow from the seeds. Many pandas die of starvation when this happens, as it did in 1975–6 (Schaller 137).

For thousands of years, the giant panda's homeland in southwest China was very hard for people to reach, so it was left undisturbed for pandas and other wildlife. Now the millions of Chinese people need more land for their farms and villages. Modern roads help them to reach even the farthest mountains of Sichuan. As the people cut down the mountain forests, the pandas have fewer unspoiled bamboo groves to live in (Schaller 148–149).

Another reason why pandas are rare is that people have captured them from the wild. . . . The People's Republic of China banned the hunting of pandas in 1962. Now zoos can obtain pandas only as a gift from the Chinese people or from other zoos (Catton 110–111).

However, panda-hunting still goes on in spite of the ban. The pandas are not captured to be taken to zoos but are killed for their skins. Panda fur is too coarse to use for fur coats, but some people like to have a panda skin to decorate their home. In Japan people will pay a great deal (over $200,000) to have a black-and-white panda skin rug on the floor (Catton 110–115).

Of course, this hunting is against the law, and if the hunters are caught they are imprisoned for life or even sentenced to death. However, the hunters still manage to smuggle a few panda skins out of China (Catton 115).

Each paragraph discusses one main idea. Here, it is the panda's diet.

This section explains why pandas are endangered. This paragraph mentions several reasons. Each of the next two paragraphs explores an important reason in more detail.

Notice how Standring varies the structure of her sentences to keep the reader's interest as she presents explanations.

Using the word however, Standring "glues" this paragraph to the previous one.

4. Point out to students that Standring's research essay closely resembles an exhibit one might encounter at a zoo or natural history museum. She provides biological, historical, and ecological information on her subject to educate someone who has little prior knowledge of pandas.

5. To focus the discussion, ask questions such as these:

   - *How does Standring direct the reader to her essay's main focus, which is the preservation of the panda species?*

   - *Why does she provide information about the habits of the panda in the wild?*

   - *Why does she provide information about the steps being taken today to prevent extinction?*

   - *What effect does this information have on the reader?*

Customize for
More Advanced Students

Have students look up the Web site of the World Wildlife Fund. Have them pick five species that are currently on the most endangered list. Using a globe or map, have students locate and mark the countries where these endangered species are found and share their findings with the class.

Model From Literature • **225**

They take the risk because they are well paid by the people who want the panda skins.

Saving the Panda Although pandas are in danger from hunting, the main threat to them is the loss of their bamboo forests (Dudley 31–33). There is some good news for pandas, however. The Chinese people and international conservation organizations are working hard to protect them.

Now there are [thirteen] special panda reserves in China, where some [800] pandas are living in safety. The reserves were created to protect the pandas and the bamboo forests they need. The cutting down of bamboo and felling of trees by people is strictly controlled. Armed guards patrol the reserves to protect the pandas from hunters and to ensure that local people do not destroy the trees (Schaller 231–233).

Besides protecting the pandas, it is important to tell the local people why these animals are so special. So the people from 5,000 villages in Sichuan are taught about the need to protect pandas and how to care for starving pandas. They are told why they should not cut down trees and bamboo. If a panda causes damage to the local people's farm crops, the people are paid to cover the damage (Laidler 188–189).

The largest reserve, at Wolong, was created in 1975. In 1980, the Chinese government and WWF built a special panda-breeding and research center there (Laidler 177).

The Future for Pandas . . . [T]he giant panda's urgent need for help has brought together conservation workers, vets, scientists, zookeepers, and animal lovers from all over the world. The Chinese people and conservation organizations have managed to protect large areas of bamboo forest and guard the pandas that live in them. We have already found some ways of helping pandas to survive by studying them in the wild and in captivity.

If we can give enough support to the efforts to save pandas, perhaps in the next century there will be more pandas in the world than now. Then the panda on the WWF badge will be the symbol of a success story in wildlife conservation.

The writer uses facts and figures to support her statement that people are working hard to protect pandas.

Standring cites her sources for all specific facts that are not common knowledge. She uses the standard format for internal citations.

Works Cited

Angel, Heather. *Pandas*. Stillwater, MN: Voyageur Press, 1998.

Catton, Chris. *Pandas*. New York: Facts on File, 1990.

Dudley, Karen. *Giant Pandas*. Austin, TX: Raintree Steck-Vaughn, 1997.

Laidler, Keith and Liz. *Pandas: Giants of the Bamboo Forest*. London: BBC Books, 1992.

Schaller, George B. *The Last Panda*. Chicago: University of Chicago Press, 1993.

226 • Research Report

STANDARDIZED TEST PREPARATION WORKSHOP

Revising and Editing Some test questions measure a student's ability to revise and edit a passage. Share the following sample question with students:

(1) The giant panda is a bearlike animal, and can be recognized by its black and white coloring. (2) In 1972, the Chinese government gave two giant pandas to the United States. (3) The giant panda can grow to between 3 and 5 feet long, and can weigh from 200 to 300 pounds.

Which of the following is the **BEST** revision to the passage?

A Delete Sentence 1   **C** Delete Sentence 3

B Delete Sentence 2   **D** No change

Students should recognize that the correct choice is item **B**. The other sentences give factual information about the giant panda's physical characteristics.

Writing Application: **Help Readers Answer Questions** As you draft your report, think about questions your readers may have. Provide any necessary background and details. Consider providing some information in the forms of charts or graphs to which readers can refer as needed. For example, when Standring writes in her report that pandas have fewer bamboo groves to live in, readers may have questions about how much the habitat has diminished. A map like the one here allows interested readers to find out.

LITERATURE

To read another example of research writing, read *Tiger: A Biography of Tiger Woods*. You can find an excerpt from the book in *Prentice Hall Literature: Timeless Voices, Timeless Themes*, Bronze.

CHINA

■ Existing Panda Habitat
□ Approximate Prehistoric Distribution

CHINA · Beijing

0   500 Miles

Beijing

Wolong Reserve

Xi'an
● Qinling Mts.

Qionglai Mts.
Xiangling Mts.
Liangshan Mts.

Minshan Mts.
● Chengdu

● Chongqing

● Kunming

Huang Ho (Yellow River)

Yangtze River

Mekong River

Xun River

0   250   500 Miles
0   250   500 Kilometers

▲ **Critical Viewing** Using the map, estimate the percentage by which panda habitat has shrunk since prehistoric times. **[Analyze]**

Integrating Viewing and Representing Skills

Work with students to identify the features of the map: the "key," distance scale, inset, shadings, cities, rivers, mountains. Discuss how this visual aid adds to their understanding of the research report.

Responding to Literature

Suggest that students compare and contrast this report about pandas with the biography of the golfer Tiger Woods. Ask them to point out the similarities and differences in the two types of research writing. Similarities may include the need to collect details, access resources, and provide readers with factual information. Students may note that the Tiger Woods biography tells the story of a single person's life, while the research report about pandas educates readers about a species with which they may not be familiar. Reinforce the idea that students can choose which kind of research writing interests them more.

Critical Viewing

Analyze Students may estimate the percentage to be between 90 and 95.

Reading\Writing Connection

Writing Application: Help Readers Answer Questions

Tell students that their readers must go through the same process the students have gone through in assembling a report: taking in information, looking for connections, and reevaluating interpretations. Students can help show readers the way by thinking about the questions they had while doing research, and answering those questions for readers.

227

Prewriting

Choosing Your Topic

Use the following strategies to choose a research topic that interests you and on which enough information is available:

Strategies for Generating a Topic

1. **Listing** List ideas in response to one of the following: *animals, famous people,* or *science.* After writing for several minutes, review your list. Circle three ideas, and list words you associate with each. Then, draw lines between related items. Choose a topic from among these items.

2. **Newswatch** Skim recent magazines or newspapers, and listen to the news on radio and television. List people, places, events, or current issues of interest. Review your list, and choose your topic from among current news items.

3. **Self-Interview** Create a chart like the one below, and answer the questions shown. Circle words and draw lines to show connections between items on your list. Choose a topic from among these linked items.

Writing Lab CD-ROM

For more help finding a topic, explore the activities and tips in the Choosing a Topic section of the Reports lesson.

Student Work
IN PROGRESS

Name: Jamie Barraclough
Los Alamos Middle School
Los Alamos, NM

Conducting a Self-Interview

Jamie chose his topic, whales, from his self-interview answers after connecting his science teacher, Mrs. Mondello, with the film she had shown on ocean life.

People	Places	Things	Events
What interesting people do I know or know about?	What interesting places have I been to or heard about?	What interesting things do I know about or have I seen?	What interesting events have I experienced or heard about?
Mrs. Mondello	Grand Canyon	football	class trip to aquarium
Gloria	kitchen	flag	World Series
Davy Crocket	library	movie	craft fair
Gilles	ocean	clouds	
		whales	

228 • Research Report

Step-by-Step Teaching Guide

Prewriting: Listing

1. Tell students not to spend too much time thinking about "appropriate" responses. The point is to get as many ideas as one can down on paper.

2. Encourage students to look for interesting links and connections between their listed ideas to form into a topic.

Step-by-Step Teaching Guide

Prewriting: Newswatch

1. Encourage students to look through news media of both national *and* local focus. They should consult at least one of each of the different types of media: newspaper, newsmagazine, broadcast news, radio news, and on-line news sites.

2. Have students make a list of topics that interest them as they do their newswatch.

3. Remind them that a good topic for a news-related research essay raises and answers compelling questions or involves issues that affect many groups of people.

Step-by-Step Teaching Guide

Prewriting: Self-Interview

Teaching Resources: Writing Support Transparency 11-A; Writing Support Activity Book, 11-1

1. Display the transparency and distribute copies of the graphic organizer from the Writing Support Activity Book. Ask students to "interview" themselves by writing down what interests them, using as categories the headings shown on the chart. This self-interview is a technique to help them develop a research topic, so they should allow themselves to free-associate without editing.

2. After they have completed their self-interview, have students make connections among the various categories by circling and drawing lines where they see related topics.

3. Have students choose the most interesting of these subjects— the one that has the most connections in their list.

228

⏱ TIME AND RESOURCE MANAGER

Resources
Print: Writing Support Transparencies, 11-A–C; Writing Support Activity Book, 11-1
Technology: Writing Lab CD-ROM, Reports

In-Depth Coverage	Accelerated Pace
• Cover pp. 228–229 in class.	• In class, discuss how to create and choose a research report topic.
• Guide students through the Strategies for Generating Topics.	• Have students list possible topics.
• Help students make some initial decisions about narrowing their topics by using Classical Invention on p. 230.	• Ask students to submit topic proposals for your review.
• Encourage students to use a variety of sources and to use index cards for notes.	

TOPIC BANK

If you're having trouble finding a topic, consider the following possibilities:

1. **Biographical Sketch** Think of a famous person you admire. The person may be someone who is alive today or someone who lived long ago. Research this person's life, and then write a biographical sketch.

2. **Report on a Natural Phenomenon** What are volcanoes? Why do they erupt? Using library and Internet resources, write a report on volcanoes or another natural phenomenon.

Responding to Fine Art

3. Jot down notes describing the painting on this page. From your notes, choose a research topic about Native American life or traditions.

Responding to Literature

4. Read "Rikki-tikki-tavi" by Rudyard Kipling, and then write a report on one of the following topics: mongooses, poisonous snakes of India, or an aspect of everyday life in India today. You can find "Rikki-tikki-tavi" in *Prentice Hall Literature: Timeless Voices, Timeless Themes*, Bronze.

Our Home and Native Land, Danielle Hayes

☑ Cooperative Writing Opportunity

5. **Aquarium Display** As a group, develop the shark exhibit for an aquarium. Each group member should research one type of shark and find a photograph of it. Then, each group member should write an informative caption of two or three paragraphs to accompany the photograph. Work as a group to assemble the photographs and captions into an exhibit in which the "sharks" swim in an "aquarium."

Responding to Fine Art

Our Home and Native Land, by Danielle Hayes
Teaching Resources: Writing Support Transparency 11-B

1. Display the transparency and have students discuss what the painting means to them.

2. Ask students to brainstorm possible research topics suggested by this work of art.

Responding to Literature

Ask students how much of the information in Kipling's fictional short story they think is true. Kipling grew up in India, so he certainly had some firsthand experience with snakes and mongooses. Do they feel that the facts and information about the animals added to their enjoyment of the story?

Integrating Speaking and Listening Skills

Have interested students select a local nonprofit organization that supports a particular community interest (such as parks service, animal shelter, art museum, conservation group). Have them briefly interview a contact person there about an issue that is important to the mission of the organization. Based on this interview, students can generate a research essay topic. Urge them to share their completed essay with the organization.

Spotlight on the Humanities

For additional topic suggestions, refer students to the Spotlight on the Humanities on p. 244.

⏱ TIME SAVERS!

🗒 Writing Support Transparencies
Use the transparencies for Chapter 11 to teach these strategies.

📖 Writing Support Activity Book
Use the graphic organizers for Chapter 11 to facilitate these strategies.

Prewriting: Use Classical Invention

Teaching Resources: Writing Support Transparency 11-C; Writing Support Activity Book, 11-2

1. Display the transparency. Help students see that Jamie used these questions to narrow his topic by circling the details that struck him as especially interesting. After these items were circled, Jamie was able to identify links, or connections, among them. By summarizing the connections, he was able to narrow his topic.

2. Suggest that students use highlighters to color code the different details. They can use one color to highlight all linked details, and another color to highlight others. This will help them see which of their narrowed topics offers a greater amount of details to explore in their writing.

Customize for
Verbal/Linguistic Learners

Some students may benefit from being interviewed by a partner using the classical invention method. One student can ask the questions and record the interviewee's responses. Then students can switch roles.

Narrowing Your Topic

After choosing your topic, make sure it is narrow enough to cover in a short report. Use the strategy of "Classical Invention."

Use Classical Invention

Classical Invention is a strategy used by the ancient Greeks to explore a topic. To help you narrow your topic, answer questions about your topic like the ones shown in the Student Model below. Simply replace *whales* with your own topic.

Review your answers to these questions. Circle a series of related ideas that interest you. Sum these ideas up in a sentence. Use this sentence as the focus of your research paper.

Student Work
IN PROGRESS

Name: Jamie Barraclough
Los Alamos Middle School
Los Alamos, NM

Using Classical Invention

Jamie answered the Classical Invention questions for his general topic, whales. Then, for each detail on the list, he itemized more details.

General Topic: Whales

- In what general category does your topic belong?

  Whales are animals. They are mammals, just like dogs and cats. Most eat sea animals.

  Some whales eat big squid and fish. Others eat tiny plants and animals called plankton. They have a kind of strainer in their mouths.

- How is your topic like, or different from, other topics in this category?

  Unlike most other mammals, whales spend their entire lives in the sea. They do not have legs.

  Narrowed Topic
  What are the different kinds of whales and their different characteristics?

- Into what other topics can your topic be divided?

  There are different kinds of whales, like the bowhead, which has a funny head, and the sperm whale with its sharp teeth. Some whales have baleen instead of teeth.

  Baleen is what some whales use to get food, but these whales only eat plankton. Sperm whales don't have baleen, though. They have teeth.

- What cause-and-effect relationships are involved in your topic?

  Hunting and pollution are causing whales to become endangered.

230 • Research Report

TIME SAVERS!

Writing Support Transparencies
Use the transparencies for Chapter 11 to teach these strategies.

Considering Your Audience and Purpose

Your audience's background on your topic will determine which details you include. If your audience for a report on Indian tigers is a group of young children, you will probably want to explain where India is. For an older audience, you might omit this information but give more details about tigers.

Your purpose will also affect the details you use. For example, if your purpose in a report on recycling is to show its necessity, you might include facts on shrinking landfill areas.

Gathering Details

Use a Variety of Research Sources

Use a variety of sources to ensure that the information you present is accurate and balanced. Cross-check information from the Internet or an interview whenever possible by consulting printed sources. If you find differing versions of the facts, you might simply note the discrepancy in your report.

Take Notes

When you find information related to your topic, use index cards to take detailed notes. Follow these guidelines:

- Write one note on each card.
- Double-check the spelling of names and technical terms.
- Use quotation marks whenever you include exact words from your source in a report.
- On each card, record the title of the book or article and the page number, or write the name of the Web site or your interviewee.
- Create a source card for each book, article, or interviewee. For a source in print, list the author, title, publisher, and place and date of publication. For a Web site, list the title of the main page and the URL address (the address begins with "http://"). For an interviewee, list the person's name, address, and phone number, as well as the date of the interview.

As an alternative to note cards, you can photocopy pages from resources and highlight the information you plan to use. Include information about the source on the photocopy.

🖥 Research Tip

To search the Internet efficiently, use a search engine. Start by using search terms that are as specific as your topic permits. Scan the list of "hits," reading the descriptions of sites and eliminating any not clearly related to your topic. If you have not found any relevant sites by the third page of your search results, try a new search term.

Prewriting: Considering Your Audience and Purpose

1. Audience and purpose are the two key factors in determining the types of details that should be included in a research report.

2. *Audience* answers the question *Who will be reading my essay?* and should direct the writer toward selecting details appropriate for the age and background knowledge of his or her readers. *Purpose* answers the question *What do I want to accomplish with this report?* and should direct the writer toward selecting and including details that support his or her intention.

Prewriting: Use a Variety of Research Sources

1. You might want to schedule library time for students to collect data for their research essays.

2. Explain that students never can assume that any one research source is necessarily accurate. Responsible research techniques involve using multiple sources. When conducting their research, students should always cross-check a fact before using it in their essay.

3. To the same end, if students encounter differences in fact or opinion expressed in their research materials, they must make note of this in their essays.

Prewriting: Take Notes

1. Students must take notes on every fact or opinion they learn when they learn it. They should note the author, title, page number, and any other data that will enable someone to find the information.

2. This helps not only the reader but also the writer. Later, when students edit their reports, they may want to elaborate on something. They cannot do this if they do not know where to look.

☑ ONGOING ASSESSMENT: Monitor and Reinforce

Students often forget their sources when they work on topics that require research. To help them keep a record of where they collected their information, try one of the following strategies.

Option 1 Remind students that the details they gather on their index cards will carry more weight if their sources are credited. Ask students what kinds of sources might have been used to find the information in "Pandas" by Gillian Standring. Have them begin thinking about what sources they want to use for their own reports.

Option 2 Ask students what would happen if they published a biographical sketch about a famous person's life and then that person accused them of getting all the facts wrong. How would they defend themselves? Point out that a researcher with clear, organized notes should be able to provide specific sources for each and every fact. Ask them to think of other kinds of research writing that require well-documented sources.

Drafting: Develop a Main Idea or Thesis

1. Now that the research-gathering phase is complete, tell students it is now time to make crucial decisions concerning how the information is going to be organized and presented.

2. Tell students that by having already established their audience and purpose, developing a main idea is a matter of their putting their research findings into a usable structure with a strong and clear focus.

Drafting: Make an Outline

1. The note cards students used in their research gathering can now help them organize their information into a sensible structure for their essay. The first step is to order their cards into groupings by basic categories of information or ideas.

2. Then, students must decide how best to order these groups to suit their essay's topic, purpose, and audience. In other words, they must decide which things they are going to write about first, second, and so on.

3. After students have determined the essay's order, it is time to compose an outline. An outline is like a map or diagram that the writer uses throughout the writing process to ensure that all critical information is incorporated and that the essay truly sticks to a logical order and structure. Trying to write a research essay without an outline is like trying to go someplace you've never been without a map!

4. Have students study the example of an outline in the book. Point out the usefulness of Roman numerals, capital letters, and subheadings to organize information according to the most logical method.

11.3 Drafting

Shaping Your Writing

After you have gathered your information for a research report, you must decide how to organize and present it.

Develop a Main Idea or Thesis

Determine the overall focus of your report. For example, in a report about tigers, you could focus on their habitat requirements, or you could emphasize that illegal poaching contributes to their being endangered. Write a single sentence expressing your main idea. This sentence is called a **thesis statement.**

Make an Outline

Choosing a Method of Organization Group your notes by category. For instance, place all cards on tiger habitats in one group and all notes on their hunting strategies in another. Then, choose a method of organization that suits your topic.

- **Chronological Order** You might arrange details according to their sequence in time, as in writing a biographical sketch.

- **Ordering by Type** If your groups of notes are about ideas of equal importance, you might write about each one in turn. For a report on poisonous snakes in India, for example, you might separate your notes for cobras, for kraits, and for vipers into different folders.

Developing an Outline Referring to your chosen method of organization, develop an outline for your report. Use each category of notes as a main point on your outline. Use Roman numerals (I, II, III) to number your most important points. Under each Roman numeral, use capital letters (A, B, C) for the supporting details.

> Title of Your Report
>
> I. First main point
>   A. First supporting detail
>   B. Second supporting detail
> II. Second main point...

For help providing elaboration, read portions of your draft that you think might need clarification to a group of peers. Ask them if they found anything confusing or surprising in what you read. Use their comments to guide you as you add clarifications to your draft.

⏱ TIME AND RESOURCE MANAGER

Resources
Print: Writing Support Transparency 11-D
Technology: Writing Lab CD-ROM, Reports

In-Depth Coverage	Accelerated Pace
• Cover pp. 232–233 in class. • Have students write their own research report draft in class. • Help students listen for the "Huh?" in their own papers as they write. **Option** Have students work in groups or independently with the Writing Lab CD-ROM.	• Have students review pp. 232–233 independently, then write their own research report draft. • Respond to individual drafting issues as needed.

◄ Critical Viewing
Name two details about tigers that most people already know. Name one type of detail about which readers might need more information. **[Hypothesize]**

Providing Elaboration
Find Points for Clarification

After you write a paragraph, review it, looking for words you did not know before you started your report and for facts that might seem incredible. Consider the following sentence:

Less than a teaspoon of krait venom can kill a person.

Many readers will not know the word *krait*. Some will find it incredible that so little venom can be fatal. Add details to elaborate or clarify such points in your writing.

Student Work
IN PROGRESS

Name: Jamie Barraclough
Los Alamos Middle School
Los Alamos, NM

Finding Points to Clarify

As Jamie drafted, he found a few words, including baleen and krill, that he first learned while doing research on whales. He elaborated on them to help readers.

Instead of teeth,
Baleen whales have a unique physical feature. in their mouths

It is
They are called baleen, which grows down from their jaw in

with tiny spaces between them
long, narrow plates. Whales use their baleen to feed by

opening their mouths to let in lots of water. Then, they spit

out the water through the baleen, leaving plankton

, or tiny shrimp,
and krill in their mouths.

Drafting • 233

Revising: Matching Your Draft to Your Outline

1. The best way to revise an essay is to return to the original organizing principles on which the essay was structured. The outline was the "map" the writer used to create the essay, and it is now the tool to use in revising. Did the writer achieve his or her purpose? Did he or she fulfill the essay's outline?

2. Have students refer to their outlines as they read through their essay drafts. When they get to the end of each paragraph, they should check their outline to see if they covered all their important information and ideas. They should use the same notations they used in the outline (Roman numerals, capital letters, etc.) to mark the paragraphs so they can follow exactly how the essay corresponds to the outline. They should do this through the entire essay.

3. Students can refer to the questions listed in the textbook to evaluate whether their essay drafts have successfully conformed to their outlines. Are all the paragraphs tagged with the same numerals next to each other? What about the paragraphs with the same Roman numeral-capital letter combination? Does the sequence of numerals and letters match the outline?

4. It is now important to decide if the essay's deviations from the outline are changes for the better or worse. Students must make decisions about whether their essays are well organized and whether they need to add or omit information.

Critical Viewing

Infer Students' responses will vary. Make sure they respond with a feature that can be the topic of an entire paragraph.

11.4 Revising

Revising Your Overall Structure

Analyze Organization

During the drafting process, you used your notes to make an outline for your research report. Now that you have completed a first draft, you can analyze your organization to see whether you have achieved the best possible results.

▶ **REVISION STRATEGY**
Matching Your Draft to Your Outline

As you read through your report, stop at the end of each paragraph and refer to your outline. Mark each paragraph with the Roman numeral and capital letter from your outline that designate the subject of the paragraph.

For example, the following might be part of your outline:

I. Cobras
   A. front-fanged
   B. hunting method

In this case, you should mark a paragraph about the fangs of cobras "I.A." If your second paragraph discusses their hunting method, mark it "I.B.," and so forth.

When you have finished labeling each paragraph, review your labels. Ask yourself the following questions:

- Are all the paragraphs that are tagged with the same Roman numeral next to each other? Should they be?

- What about the paragraphs with the same Roman numeral-capital letter combination?

- Does the sequence of Roman numerals and capital letters in the report match the sequence on your outline? If not, is the change an improvement? Why or why not?

Reorganize the paragraphs in your draft to achieve the most effective organization.

▼ Critical Viewing Referring to this picture, name a feature of this snake that might appear as a main head on an outline. **[Infer]**

⏱ TIME AND RESOURCE MANAGER

Resources
Print: Writing Support Transparencies, 11-E–F
Technology: Writing Lab CD-ROM, Reports

In-Depth Coverage	Accelerated Pace
• Cover pp. 234–238 in class. • Use the relevant transparencies to demonstrate strategies for analyzing organization (p. 234), matching drafts to outlines (p. 234), and using transitions (p. 235). **Option** Divide the class into groups for peer review activities (p. 238).	• Assign students to review pp. 234–238 independently. • Have students revise their research reports independently.

Revising Your Paragraphs

Use Transitions

The space between paragraphs is like a joint in a piece of furniture. The glue you need to hold two paragraphs together—a transition—is a clear indication of their relationship.

Transitions are words, phrases, or whole sentences that clarify the relationships between ideas. For example, transitions like *at first, then, next,* and *finally* show a sequence of events. Transitions like *the reason that, consequently,* and *as a result* show cause and effect.

▶ **REVISION STRATEGY**
Finding the Glue Between Paragraphs

Read the final sentence of each paragraph. Then, read the opening sentence of the next paragraph. If one or both sentences clearly show the relationship between paragraphs, underline them in blue pencil. If you don't find a transition, draw a squiggly red line in the space between the paragraphs and add a word, phrase, or sentence to "glue" them together.

⚙ **Grammar and Style Tip**

Transitions make the connections between ideas "visible." If you have difficulty finding a transition to join two paragraphs, your ideas may not be well-connected. Consider rearranging such paragraphs so that you can connect them to others with transitions.

Student Work IN PROGRESS

Name: Jamie Barraclough
Los Alamos Middle School
Los Alamos, NM

Finding the Glue Between Paragraphs

Jamie found a few places where he needed transitions. He added words and phrases there to glue his paragraphs together.

Several of the toothed whales shoot a jet of water at the ocean floor. They use this jet to stir up prey hiding in the sand. These whales include the beluga and the narwhal. These whales also have very flexible necks that help them scan the ocean floor for food.

Other characteristics can help a whale live in a harsh environment.

The bowhead, for instance, has several interesting physical features that allow it to live in the Arctic all the time.

Revising • 235

Step-by-Step Teaching Guide

Revising: Finding the Glue Between Paragraphs

Teaching Resources: Writing Support Transparency 11-E

1. Transitions are necessary between paragraphs. Without transitions, the reader cannot follow the writer's train of thought. As in speech, thoughts must be shown to be connected and must flow from one to the next in a logical way.

2. The best way for students to make sure that an essay has transitions is to read the last sentence of one paragraph and the first sentence of the next. Is it obvious why one sentence/paragraph follows the other? Is the transition clear for the reader, or does it seem as if there is something missing connecting the two ideas?

3. Display the transparency. Ask students why they think Jamie made the changes he did.

4. Have students highlight their successful transitions in one color and their unsuccessful transitions in another color. This method will show them where to add information to make the transition.

Customize for
Visual/Spatial Learners

Encourage students to skim their drafts, highlighting or circling sentences that contain similar information. They can rearrange these sentences and use transitional words to connect them.

☑ **ONGOING ASSESSMENT: Prerequisite Skills**

Some students may have difficulty punctuating sentences with transitional words. You may find it helpful to review the following to assure coverage of prerequisite knowledge.

In the Textbook	Print Resources	Technology
Conjunctions and Interjections, pp. 376–380	Grammar Exercise Workbook, pp. 41–42	On-Line Exercise Bank, Section 18.1

⏱ **TIME SAVERS!**

📄 **Writing Support Transparencies**
Use the transparencies for Chapter 11 to teach these strategies.

Revising: Finding the Main Action in a Cluster

Teaching Resources: Writing Support Transparency 11-F

1. One way students can make their writing more interesting is to use varied sentence structures.

2. Display the transparency to show students how Jamie used color-coding to identify short sentences.

3. Encourage students to provide other ways Jamie could have combined these sentences.

4. Have students apply this strategy to their own drafts.

11.4

Revising Your Sentences
Vary Sentence Length

You can make your writing smoother and more interesting by varying your sentence structure and length.

▶ REVISION STRATEGY
Finding the Main Action in a Cluster

Select five paragraphs in your draft. In each, underline sentences in alternating colors (for example, underline the first sentence in green, the second in orange, the third in green, and so on). Then, review your coding. Circle any place where you find clusters of short lines. Reread the sentences in the cluster, and draw a rectangle around the sentence that expresses the main action or point. Then, try combining sentences by substituting a phrase for one sentence and adding it to the sentence expressing the main action.

Language Lab CD-ROM

For more practice varying sentences, complete the Varying Sentence Structure lesson in the Sentence Style unit.

Student Work IN PROGRESS

Name: Jamie Barraclough
Los Alamos Middle School
Los Alamos, NM

Combining Short Sentences

Jamie used color-coding to find this cluster of short sentences. He drew boxes around two main points in the paragraph. Then, he broke up the cluster by combining short sentences with the sentences expressing main points.

Having teeth allows these whales to eat chewy foods. These foods include squid and octopus. *such as* These creatures are abundant in the waters they *, which* inhabit. Several of the toothed whales shoot a jet *, such as the beluga and the narwhal,* of water at the ocean floor. They use this jet to stir up prey hiding in the sand. These whales include the beluga and the narwhal.

236 • Research Report

☑ **ONGOING ASSESSMENT: Monitor and Reinforce**

If students have difficulty identifying ways to combine short sentences, try the following option.

Have students work in pairs to review each other's color-coded work. Students can work together to find ways of combining the short sentences.

Grammar in Your Writing
Participial Phrases

A present participle is the *-ing* form of a verb. A past participle is the past form of the verb, often ending in *-ed* or *-d*. A **participial phrase** combines a present or past participle with other words and phrases. Participles and participial phrases act as adjectives: They answer the questions *What kind? Which one? How many?* or *How much?* about something in the sentence.

By using participial phrases, you can combine sentences, as in these examples:

SHORT SENTENCES:	The attorney spoke quietly. She summarized the case.
COMBINED:	The attorney, speaking quietly, summarized the case.
SHORT SENTENCES:	He found the ring. It was hidden in a trunk.
COMBINED:	He found the ring hidden in a trunk.

Notice that, as in the first example, a participial phrase can be created by replacing a verb (*spoke*) with its participial form (*speaking*).

Find It in Your Reading Find one participial phrase in the Student Work on page 241. Explain what information the phrase adds to the main action or point of the sentence.

Find It in Your Writing Identify three participial phrases that you have used in your research report. If you can't find three examples, consider whether you could use participial phrases to combine pairs or groups of short, choppy sentences.

To learn more about participial phrases, see Chapter 20.

Revising Your Word Choice

Look Up New Words

In doing research, you may have come across new words, including specialized terms or unfamiliar expressions. If you use these new words in your own report, consider whether they will be familiar to your audience. Code these terms, and consider adding a definition for each.

▶ **REVISION STRATEGY**
Color-Coding Technical Terms

Highlight any technical terms—terms specific to your topic—that you use in your report. Add a definition in parentheses after each highlighted word the first time it appears.

🖉 STANDARDIZED TEST PREPARATION WORKSHOP

Grammar and Usage Standardized tests often require students to identify correctly written sentences. Ask students to choose the best way to rewrite the following sentence:

The students walked quickly to the library, and they hoped they would find what they needed.

A The students walked quickly to the library, hoping that they would find what they needed.

B The students walked to the library. They hoped they would quickly find what they needed.

C The students walked quickly to the library to hope they would find what they needed.

D Correct as is

The correct answer is item **A**, which properly punctuates a sentence with a participial phrase. Items B and C are both punctuated correctly, but B changes the meaning of the sentences, and C does not make sense.

Step-by-Step Teaching Guide

Grammar in Your Writing: Participial Phrases

1. Explain that a participial is the past or present form of a verb, with the past participial ending usually in *-ed* or *-d*, and the present participial ending in *-ing*. Participial phrases answer the question *What kind? Which one? How many?* or *How much?* about the idea of the sentence.

2. Write the following sentences on the chalkboard:

   The clock was on the mantelpiece. It read six o'clock.

   The clock on the mantelpiece read six o'clock.

3. Explain that using participial phrases is a good way to make sure that sentences in an essay are varied and interesting.

Find It in Your Reading

Have volunteers read aloud the participial phrases they have found.

Find It in Your Writing

Students should be sure to punctuate the phrases correctly. If a phrase is nonessential—if it can be removed without changing the meaning of the sentence—it is set off by commas. If the phrase is essential, commas are not necessary.

Step-by-Step Teaching Guide

Revising: Look Up New Words

1. Remind students that their readers do not have as much knowledge as they do about the essay topic. As with checking transitions and sentence structure, word choice can be a source of confusion to the reader.

2. Have students read through their essay drafts and highlight any words that are not in common usage and that they think might not be known to their readers. Technical terms related to the subject matter often require explanation.

3. Have students add a definition in parentheses after each highlighted word the first time it appears.

Revising: Peer Review

1. After their careful revision process, students are now ready to take the last step in making sure that they have maintained their reader's interest and understanding and fulfilled the purpose of their essay. The best way to do this is to have someone listen to their essay read aloud.

2. Have students work in groups of four. Students take turns reading their report to the group. Listeners should write down summaries of the report's main ideas. Each main idea should be recorded as a single sentence.

3. Have group members share their summaries with the essay writer. These summaries will reveal exactly where their essay may need to be revised. If important ideas were missed or misunderstood by the group, more information or clarification in the essay may be necessary.

Critical Viewing

Analyze Students may say that players are running out of the dugout and some are hugging each other in victory.

11.4

Peer Review

Summarize

Join with a group of four other classmates. Read your entire report to the group, then pause, and read it a second time. After the second reading, each listener in the group should follow these steps:

1. Determine the main idea of your report.

2. Write the main idea as a single sentence.

3. Choose one word to express the main idea.

4. Think of a synonym for this word.

5. Share the sentences and words with the group and discuss differences among them.

If most listeners have stated a main idea different from the one you had in mind as you drafted, review your draft. Consider these possibilities:

- Your draft fully covers your original main idea. *If so, clarify the statement of your main idea in your introduction and conclusion.*

- Your classmates have discovered a main idea more closely reflected in your draft than the one you had in mind. *If so, revise your introduction and conclusion to include a statement of this main idea.*

Writers in
ACTION

Ellie Fries comments as follows on the importance of peer review:

"Having someone read your work is very important in reassuring you that you are doing the right thing, that your concepts are being developed in the way you want them to be."

▼ **Critical Viewing** In what way does this picture summarize the game that has just ended? **[Analyze]**

238 • Research Report

11.5 Editing and Proofreading

Focusing on Citations

In a research report, you must cite the sources for quotations, facts that are not common knowledge, and ideas that are not your own.

Internal Citations A basic form of citation is an internal citation in parentheses. An internal citation directly follows the information that came from the source cited. It includes the author's last name and the page number on which the information appears.

> "I tell my students that the American Indian has a unique investment in the American landscape" (Momaday 33).

Works Cited List Provide full information about the sources in an alphabetical "Works Cited" list at the end of your report. The following is an example of the correct form:

> Momaday, N. Scott. *The Man Made of Words.* New York: St. Martin's Press, 1997.

 **Technology Tip**

To format titles quickly in a word-processing program, check the Help feature to find the keyboard shortcut for italics. Use this shortcut when formatting the titles of long works.

Grammar in Your Writing

Quotation Marks and Underlining With Titles of Works

Underline (or style in italics) the titles of long written works and the titles of periodicals. Also, underline or italicize the titles of movies, television series, and works of music and art.

EXAMPLES: *The Sun Also Rises* (title of a book)
Mona Lisa (title of a painting)

Use quotation marks with the titles of short written works and Internet sites.

EXAMPLES: "Rikki-tikki-tavi" (title of a short story)
"My Home Page" (title of a Web site)

Find It in Your Reading Read the Works Cited list on page 242. Notice how italics and quotation marks are used for the titles of works.

Find It in Your Writing Review your essay to see whether you have used underlining and quotation marks correctly for the titles of works.

To learn more about the form for titles, see Chapters 26 and 27.

Editing and Proofreading: Focusing on Citations

1. The writer of a research report has a very important responsibility to inform the reader of his or her research sources wherever and whenever an idea, fact, or quote is given that is not the writer's own.

2. There are two reasons for citations. The first is to show that the writer did not "make it all up." Even experts use the previous findings of other experts to draw conclusions and make their points more forceful and credible. Second, readers who are interested in something in a report may want to know more. A source tells them exactly where to go.

Grammar in Your Writing: Quotation Marks and Underlining with Titles of Works

1. Explain to students that underlining is a way of indicating italics when they are writing or typing. Point out that, if they are using a word processor or computer that has the capability of making type italic, they should always choose italics, rather than underlining.

2. Tell students that while a magazine's name is italicized, the title of an article in the magazine would appear in quotation marks.

3. Write the following titles on the chalkboard and ask students to underline them or add quotation marks:

> <u>US News & World Report</u> (magazine)
>
> <u>60 Minutes</u> (television series)
>
> "To Build a Fire" (short story)
>
> <u>Hamlet</u> (play)
>
> "The Star-Spangled Banner" (song title)

Find It in Your Writing

If students are unsure of the correct formatting, have them work with a partner.

⏲ TIME AND RESOURCE MANAGER

Resources
Print: Scoring Rubrics on Transparency, Chapter 11; *Formal Assessment,* Ch. 11
Technology: *Writing Lab* CD-ROM, Reports

In-Depth Coverage	Accelerated Pace
• Review pp. 239–242 in class, including Grammar in Your Writing. • Distribute and review Proofreading Checklist. • Give step-by-step coverage to Publishing and Presenting (p. 240). • Analyze in class the final draft on p. 241. • Students edit and proofread their research reports in class.	• Assign pp. 239–242 for independent review. • Students independently edit and proofread their research reports. • Respond to individual editing issues as needed.

Publishing and Presenting

1. Students whose reports are on a similar topic (such as animals) can compile them into a book.

2. Students who wrote biographical reports about people who are alive can post them to a personal Web site.

ASSESS

Assessment

Teaching Resources: Scoring Rubrics on Transparency 11; Formal Assessment, Chapter 11

1. Display the Scoring Rubric transparency and review the criteria in class.

2. Before students proceed with self-assessment, you may wish to review the Final Draft of the Student Work in Progress on pp. 241–242. Have students score the Final Draft in one or more of the rubric categories. For example, how would students score the essay in terms of audience and purpose?

3. In addition to student self-assessment, you may wish to use the following assessment options:

   • Score student essays yourself, using the rubric and scoring models from Writing Assessment.

   • Administer the Chapter 11 Test from Formal Assessment in Teaching Resources to assess students' grasp of concepts presented.

11.6 Publishing and Presenting

Building Your Portfolio

Consider these suggestions for publishing and presenting:

1. **Create a "Wall of Fame"** In a group, create a bulletin-board display of biographical sketches. Mount each report along with a picture of the subject. Then, label each image with a descriptive title, such as "Famous Inventor."

2. **Design a Web Site** Join with classmates to plan a Web site for your reports. Create illustrations representing each page on the site and a chart showing how each links to the others. The group should find Web links to related Web sites for each report and design icons for each page.

Reflecting on Your Writing

In a brief reflective note, discuss what happened when you wrote your research report. Include this reflection in your portfolio. To get started, use the following questions:

• In the process of writing, what did you learn about the topic you chose?

• Which writing strategies would you recommend to others? Why?

▣ Internet Tip

To see a research report scored according to this rubric, visit **www.phschool.com**

Rubric for Self-Assessment

Use the following criteria to evaluate your research report:

	Score 4	Score 3	Score 2	Score 1
Audience and Purpose	Focuses on a clearly stated thesis, starting from a well-framed question; gives complete citations	Focuses on a clearly stated thesis; gives citations	Focuses mainly on the chosen topic; gives some citations	Presents information without a clear focus; few or no citations
Organization	Presents information in logical order, emphasizing details of central importance	Presents information in logical order	Presents information logically, but organization is poor in places	Presents information in a scattered, disorganized manner
Elaboration	Draws clear conclusions from information gathered from multiple sources	Draws conclusions from information gathered from multiple sources	Explains and interprets some information	Presents information with little or no interpretation or synthesis
Use of Language	Shows overall clarity and fluency; contains few mechanical errors	Shows good sentence variety; contains some errors in spelling, punctuation, or usage	Uses awkward or overly simple sentence structures; contains many mechanical errors	Contains incomplete thoughts and mechanical errors that make the writing confusing

---

☑ ONGOING ASSESSMENT: Assess Mastery

Use one of the following options to assess final drafts of students' research reports.

Self-Assessment Ask students to score their essay using the rubric provided. Then have students write a paragraph reflecting on the most valuable strategy they learned in completing this essay.	**Teacher Assessment** Use the rubric and the scoring models provided in Writing Assessment, Research Report to score students' work.

11.7 *Student Work*
IN PROGRESS

FINAL DRAFT

Built to Survive: Whales

Jamie Barraclough
Los Alamos Middle School
Los Alamos, New Mexico

Whales live in all the oceans of the Earth, both in the shallow
and deep waters as well as in Arctic and tropical waters. A
whale's physical features help it to survive and meet the challenges of its environment. All whales are aquatic mammals of the
Cetacean order. They are separated into two groups: the baleen
and the toothed. Whales range in body size from the largest mammal in the world (the blue whale) at over 100 feet long to whales
the size of a human—about six feet (Carwardine 14–19).

Instead of teeth, baleen whales have a unique physical feature
called *baleen*, which grows down from their jaw in long, narrow
plates with tiny spaces between them. Whales use their baleen to

*Jamie uses the first
paragraph to introduce
his research topic. The
second sentence states
the main idea or thesis
of the report—its over-
all focus.*

*Jamie's report is
organized by type—
he discusses each of
the main groups of
whales in turn.*

feed by opening their mouths to let in lots of water. Then, they spit out the water through the baleen, leaving plankton and krill, or tiny shrimp, in their mouths. Using the baleen for feeding allows this kind of whale to eat up to four tons of krill a day. Therefore, it makes sense that baleen whales such as the blue whale, the fin whale, the bowhead whale, the humpback whale, and the sei whale (to name just a few) grow to immense sizes (Carwardine 19–21). The blue whale has grooves running from under its chin to partway along the length of its underbelly. As in some other whales, these grooves expand and allow even more food and water to be taken in (Ellis 18–21).

On the other hand, the toothed whales such as the beluga, the narwhal, the Baird's beaked whale, and the orca are smaller in size. The sperm whale is an exception, growing up to 59 feet long (Whales in Danger). Having teeth allows these whales to eat chewy foods such as squid and octopus, which are abundant in the waters they inhabit (Carwardine 68–69). Several of the toothed whales, such as the beluga and the narwhal, shoot a jet of water at the ocean floor to stir up prey hiding in the sand. These whales also have very flexible necks that help them scan the ocean floor for food (Carwardine 190–191).

Other characteristics can help a whale live in a harsh environment. The bowhead, for instance, has several interesting physical features that allow it to live in the Arctic all the time. The first characteristic is the one from which this species gets its name. The bowhead uses its gigantic head, which is about 40 percent of its total body length, to punch through sheets of ice up to 12 inches thick. Bowheads need to do this to create an airhole in the ice. In addition, their layer of blubber, which is over 2 feet thick, allows them to live in extremely cold water (Whales in Danger).

Sperm whales also have a distinctive physical feature: a cavity in the head called the spermaceti organ, which is a large area full of tubes filled with a kind of yellow wax. This organ is thought to keep sperm whales afloat and to focus their sonar clicks (Whales in Danger).

Whales have many special features that make them well adapted to all of the oceans of the world. They are beautiful, gentle creatures in spite of their enormous size. They are also a critical part of the ocean ecology, living peacefully in their watery world.

Works Cited

Carwardine, Mark, Erich Hoyt, R. Ewan Fordyce, and Peter Gill. *The Nature Company Guides: Whales, Dolphins, & Porpoises.* New York: Time-Life Books, 1998.
Ellis, Richard. *Men and Whales.* New York: Knopf, 1991.
Whales in Danger. "Discovering Whales." http://whales.magna.com.au/DISCOVER

Jamie shows how the physical features of baleen whales help them fit into their environment— a main focus of his report.

The phrases "On the other hand" and "smaller in size" supply transitions, connecting this paragraph to the previous one.

This paragraph discusses a single main point: the unusual features of the bowhead whale.

Throughout his report, Jamie cites his sources for specific facts, using a standard format.

In his final paragraph, Jamie restates the main idea of his report, emphasizing the interest of his topic.

Jamie includes a "Works Cited" list at the end of his report, giving full publication information for each source he cites.

Connected Assignment *I-Search Report*

Even the driest research begins life as a lively question—"I wonder . . .?" An I-Search report tells the story of that curiosity. It begins with a topic of immediate concern to you and provides well-researched information on that topic. Unlike a research report, an I-Search report tells the story of your exploration of the topic, using the pronoun *I*. It gives

- your purpose in learning about the topic.
- the story of how you researched it.
- an account of what you learned.

Prewriting To choose a topic for your report, focus on subjects in which you have an immediate interest: the best CD player to buy, how to organize a neighborhood cleanup, what career to choose. Narrow your topic to a manageable size. Then, use a K-W-L chart to help you gather details about your topic. Record the steps you took to learn more about your topic and the practical lessons you learned.

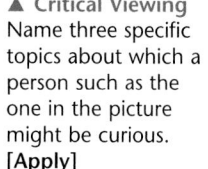

▲ **Critical Viewing**
Name three specific topics about which a person such as the one in the picture might be curious. **[Apply]**

Know	**W**ant to Know	**L**earned
Graphics programs let you create amazing pictures on the computer.	What are some of the basic programs?	
	What is the difference between bitmapped and vector art?	

Drafting Use an outline to organize your details clearly. In your outline, consider presenting the story of your interest in and research on your topic first, followed by a report of the information you found.

Revising and Editing Review your draft. Circle sentences that describe your research experience or the practical application of what you have learned. If you find long stretches without circles, consider adding more details about your research experience and the importance of information to you. Add transitions to connect parts of your report that present information with parts that tell the story of your research.

Publishing and Presenting After revising your I-Search report, consider posting it on a personal or school Web site to share your research and experiences with others.

▶ *Lesson Objectives*

1. To write an I-Search report.
2. To generate ideas and plans for writing by using prewriting strategies.
3. To develop and revise drafts.
4. To evaluate how well the writing achieves its purpose.

Step-by-Step Teaching Guide

I-Search Report

Teaching Resources: Writing Support Transparency 11-G; Writing Support Activity Book, 11-3

1. I-Search reports occur in journalism, where the journalist gives lively details of his or her own experiences in doing the research for the article. I-Searches are a popular form of biography writing, "undercover" reporting, and diary-format journalism in which the report is structured by the chronology of the reporter's investigation.

2. Another way to think about an I-Search report is that the writer's curiosity and experiences in doing the research are as important to the essay as the information given on the topic in question.

3. Have students use some of the topic development techniques described earlier in the chapter to develop their own I-Search subjects.

4. Display the transparency to demonstrate the elements of a KWL chart.

5. Give students copies of the blank organizer for them to use in developing their I-Search reports.

Critical Viewing

Apply Students may mention graphics software, public art, and painting techniques.

Lesson Objectives

1. To evaluate the purposes and effects of various media.

2. To use media to compare ideas.

3. To write a research report.

4. To frame questions to direct research.

5. To interpret and evaluate the ways visual image makers represent meanings.

Framing Questions to Direct Research

1. Choose one of the Spotlight elements for class discussion, or have students work individually or in groups on the element of their choice. Give students the initiative to find the necessary books, videotapes, or pictures.

2. Interested students can research more information about the original Broadway production.

3. Some students may want to compare the original story with the filmed version. You may want to have students read an excerpt from the novel and then show them the corresponding scene from the film version of *Oliver!*

4. You may want to bring in some examples of caricatures or have students find examples.

Viewing and Representing

Activities You may want students to familiarize themselves with the subject a bit more before they choose a question to research. When they are done, encourage volunteers to present their reports to the class.

Critical Viewing

Compare Students may say that the orphans in the film still are more exaggerated, especially in terms of their clothing, than the ones in the illustration.

Spotlight on the Humanities

Framing Questions to Direct Research

Focus on Theater: *Oliver!*

To tell even a sentimental story properly, you may need to do research into hard facts. The musical *Oliver!* tells the story of an orphan in nineteenth-century England who runs away from a cruel orphanage to rough-and-tumble London. The plot comes from Charles Dickens's novel *Oliver Twist,* but the costume and scenery designers had to find out about the clothes, buildings, and other details from Dickens's times. The research paid off. *Oliver!* hit the Broadway stage in 1963 and ran for 774 performances. With music and lyrics by Lionel Bart, it won a Tony Award for Best Composer and Lyricist, as well as Best Scenic Design.

Literature Connection British author Charles Dickens (1812–1870) wrote a number of novels that, like *Oliver Twist,* chronicle the sufferings of the poor. Here, Dickens drew on his own experiences. When he was a young child, his family hit financial hard times, and his father went to debtor's prison. Dickens himself, however, was a huge success as a writer. Among his most famous works are *A Christmas Carol, David Copperfield,* and *Great Expectations.*

Art Connection Dickens's popularity left its mark on the art of the day. Over four hundred portraits and caricatures of him were created during his lifetime! The illustrations of his works also include caricatures. For example, the drawing from *Oliver Twist* on this page caricatures orphanage officials. Dickens's original illustrators, George Cruikshank (1792–1878), who illustrated *Oliver Twist,* and Hablot K. Browne (1815–1882), who signed his work "Phiz," matched Dickens's distinctive style with their own.

Caricatures have a long history. Some caricatures protest or ridicule their subjects, commenting on character by distorting faces or figures. Others gently exaggerate a colorful personality.

Research Writing Activity: History of Caricatures

Come up with a question about the history of caricatures—for example, "When have caricatures been most popular?" Do research to find an answer, and write up your results in a report.

Etching from Charles Dickens's *Oliver Twist*

▲ **Critical Viewing** Compare the orphans in the still from the film version of *Oliver!* with the orphans in Cruikshank's illustration. **[Compare]**

Media and Technology Skills

Using On-line Sources in Research

Activity: Finding and Evaluating On-line Sources

The Internet can be a valuable research tool. Learn how to use it efficiently and critically.

Learn About It

Searching the Web To search for information on the Web, use a search engine. When you arrive at a search engine's home page, type your topic into the appropriate field, hit Enter, and a list of sites related to your topic will come up. If you are not familiar with different search engines, use the Search button on your browser.

Evaluating Sources Before using information from the Internet, evaluate the source from which it comes. Someone's personal home page may not be well researched. A site sponsored by a group with a product to sell or a cause to promote may not always give complete information. Reliable sites include those sponsored by

* the government (address ends in ".gov").
* nonprofit organizations (address ends in ".org").
* educational institutions (address ends in ".edu").
* publishers of educational or reference books, producers of educational television programs, news organizations, and so on.

Evaluate It Choose a topic, and gather information on it using the Internet. Record your search in a chart such as the one below. When you have explored four or more sites, write a brief essay in which you evaluate the credibility of each.

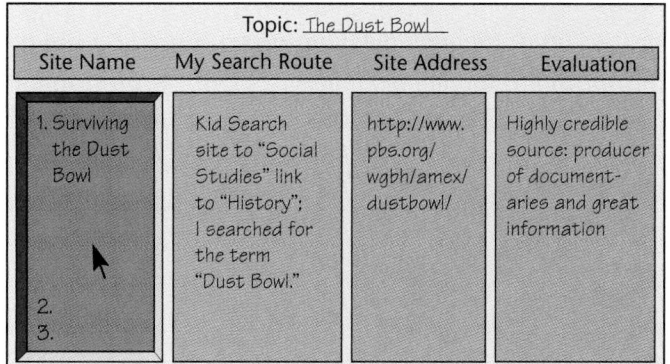

Topic: The Dust Bowl

Site Name	My Search Route	Site Address	Evaluation
1. Surviving the Dust Bowl	Kid Search site to "Social Studies" link to "History"; I searched for the term "Dust Bowl."	http://www. pbs.org/ wgbh/amex/ dustbowl/	Highly credible source: producer of documentaries and great information
2.			
3.			

Tips for On-line Research

* Web pages on a particular subject often have links to related sites. Use these links to quickly scout for more information. Use the Back button to return to the page listing the links.
* Use the Bookmark feature of your browser to record the address of any site that seems particularly useful. A bookmark makes returning to the site easy.
* Do not use sites that require personal information or a purchase. There are many free, reliable sources available.

▶ **Lesson Objectives**

1. To conduct research on the Internet.

2. To summarize and organize ideas gained from multiple sources in useful ways.

Step-by-Step Teaching Guide

Using On-Line Sources in Research

Teaching Resources: Writing Support Transparency 11-H; Writing Support Activity Book, 11-4

1. Chances are, some students are very familiar with doing searches on the Internet. You may want to have volunteers share their experiences of performing on-line searches.

2. Remind students that the more specific information they can provide, the more specific the results of their searches will be.

3. Explain to students that to evaluate sources means to judge the value and reliability of a particular source.

4. Display the transparency and distribute copies of the blank organizer. Guide students through the process of recording information on the chart.

Lesson Objectives

1. To respond in constructive ways to other's writing.
2. To revise and edit drafts for coherence, support of ideas, and to ensure standard usage.
3. To employ standard English usage in writing.

Step-by-Step Teaching Guide

Revising and Editing

1. Stress to students the importance of choosing the BEST choice among the four. More than one choice may work within the context of the passage, but only one will be the best.

2. Tell students that test items such as this one may also require them to check for standard usage. Draw their attention to the first test item of the Practice on the next page.

Standardized Test Preparation Workshop

Revising and Editing

One of the most important steps in research is revising the organization of your draft to present information in the clearest way possible. When taking a standardized test, you may be challenged by questions that test your ability to revise and edit a passage. The following sample test item shows one format for such questions.

Test Tip

When answering revising-and-editing questions, place each choice in the context of the passage before choosing an answer.

Sample Test Item

The following is from a report written by Will. As part of a peer conference, you must make suggestions about the report. Read the passage, and answer the question that follows.

1 Benjamin Franklin became clerk
2 of the Pennsylvania Legislature
3 in 1736 and Philadelphia
4 postmaster in 1737. He served in
5 both these positions for over
6 fifteen years. In 1753, he became
7 Deputy Postmaster General in
8 charge of all mail for the northern
9 colonies. Franklin's public
10 duties also led him to travel. In
11 1757, he sailed to England to
12 negotiate between the family of
13 William Penn and the state
14 government in a legal dispute.

1 Which of these sentences would make the **BEST** topic sentence for this paragraph? **A** Benjamin Franklin served in the Pennsylvania state government. **B** Benjamin Franklin had a genius for negotiating compromises. **C** Benjamin Franklin pursued an extensive career in public service. **D** Benjamin Franklin made many contributions to the postal system.	**Answer and Explanation** The correct answer is *C.* *A* concerns Franklin's service in the Pennsylvania government, which is covered in the paragraph, but the paragraph also describes other facets of his career in government. *B* does not make a good topic sentence for the paragraph because the paragraph says nothing to support the idea that Franklin was a successful negotiator. *D* does not make a good topic sentence because nothing is said about Franklin's contributions to the postal system, and the paragraph covers other parts of his career as well. *C* is the best choice because each sentence in the paragraph gives one or more details about Franklin's career in public service.

 TEST-TAKING TIP

Encourage students to mark up the passages they read in order to help focus their attention on important information. For example, in the passage on Benjamin Franklin, students might circle or underline *Pennsylvania Legislature, Philadelphia postmaster, Deputy Postmaster*

General, and *public duties.* This last piece of information should help students realize that the paragraph focuses on Franklin's public service, which would eliminate all choices except item **C.**

Answer Key

> **Practice**

1. B
2. G
3. A
4. H
5. C
6. F

> **Practice**   **Directions:** Read the following passage. Then, answer the questions below, choosing the letter of the best answer.

1 James Madison served as a
2 member of Congress, Secretary of
3 State, and as the fourth president
4 of the United States. He is a great
5 statesman. Madison entered
6 politics in 1774. Later, as an
7 assemblyman, he represented
8 Virginia at the drafting of the
9 Constitution. In Congress,
10 Madison proposed six of the
11 first ten amendments to the
12 Constitution, which are called the
13 Bill of Rights. For his contribution
14 to this important document, he
15 became known as "the father of
16 the Constitution" Columbia
17 Encyclopedia 1193. He was also
18 greatly involved in the war of
19 1812. Enduring defeat by the
20 British and the burning of
21 Washington, D.C., Madison
22 recruited soldiers from earlier
23 battles and trained new soldiers to
24 fight. The war finally ended with
25 victory for Americans with the
26 signing of the Treaty of Ghent in
27 1814.

1 What is the **BEST** change, if any, to make to the sentence in lines 4–5 ("*He . . . statesman*")?
  A Change *is* to **are**
  B Change *is* to **was**
  C Change *he* to **Madison**
  D Make no change.

2 Which of the following sentences would **BEST** fit after the sentence in lines 5–6 ("*Madison . . . 1774*")?
  F He was very successful in politics.
  G His first position was as an elected official to the Committee of Safety in Orange County, Virginia.
  H These committees provided local government.
  J Madison was born on March 16, 1751.

3 What is the **BEST** change, if any, to make at the beginning of the sentence in line 9 ("*In Congress, . . .*")?
  A Change *In Congress,* to **As a member of Congress,**
  B Change *In Congress,* to **During Congress,**
  C Delete *In Congress,*
  D Make no change.

4 Which of these sentences would **BEST** fit the ideas in lines 9–17 ("*In Congress . . . 1193*")?
  F The Bill of Rights describes the fundamental rights of the people and forbids government to violate these rights.
  G Madison lost an election because of his strong support for the Constitution.
  H Madison was a great political thinker.
  J Many of the ideas for the constitution were developed in ancient Greece and Rome.

5 Which is the **BEST** change, if any, that should be made to the sentence ("*For his . . . 1193*") in lines 13–17?
  A Delete *For his contribution to this important document,*
  B Change *Columbia Encyclopedia 1193* to **(Columbia Encyclopedia 1193)**.
  C Change *Columbia Encyclopedia 1193* to **(Columbia Encyclopedia, 1193)**.
  D Make no change.

6 Which of the following sentences would **BEST** conclude the passage?
  F After making great contributions to the development of America, Madison retired in 1817.
  G Madison did many great things.
  H Now we know why Madison is known as the father of the constitution.
  J Madison retired in 1817.

In-Depth Lesson Plan

	LESSON FOCUS	PRINT AND MEDIA RESOURCES
DAY 1	**Introduction to Response to Literature** Students learn key elements of responding to writing and analyze the Model From Literature (pp. 248–251).	*Writers at Work* **Videotape,** Response to Literature *Writing Lab* **CD-ROM,** Response to Literature
DAY 2	**Prewriting** Students choose and narrow a topic, consider their audience and purpose, and gather information (pp. 252–257).	**Teaching Resources** *Writing Support Transparencies,* 12-A–D; *Writing Support Activity Book,* 12-1–2; *Topic Bank for Heterogeneous Classes,* Ch. 12 *Writing Lab* **CD-ROM,** Response to Literature
DAY 3	**Drafting** Students organize their ideas and write their first drafts (pp. 258–259).	**Teaching Resources** *Writing Support Transparency,* 12-E–F; *Writing Support Activity Book,* 12-3 *Writing Lab* **CD-ROM,** Response to Literature
DAY 4	**Revising** Students revise their drafts in terms of overall structure, paragraphs, sentences, and word choice (pp. 260–263).	**Teaching Resources** *Writing Support Transparencies,* 12-G–H *Writing Lab* **CD-ROM,** Response to Literature
DAY 5	**Editing and Proofreading; Publishing and Presenting** Students check their work for accuracy and correctness and present their final drafts (pp. 264–265).	**Teaching Resources** *Scoring Rubrics on Transparency,* Ch. 12; *Formal Assessment,* Ch. 12 *Writing Lab* **CD-ROM,** Response to Literature

Accelerated Lesson Plan

	LESSON FOCUS	PRINT AND MEDIA RESOURCES
DAY 1	**Drafting** Students review characteristics of responding to literature, select topics, and write drafts (pp. 248–259).	**Teaching Resources** *Writing Support Transparencies,* 12-A–F; *Writing Support Activity Book* 12-1–3 *Writing Lab* **CD-ROM,** Response to Literature
DAY 2	**Revising to Presenting** Students work individually or with peers to revise, edit, and proofread their work for presentation (pp. 260–265).	**Teaching Resources** *Writing Support Transparencies,* 12-G–H; *Scoring Rubrics on Transparency,* Ch. 12; *Formal Assessment,* Ch. 12 *Writing Lab* **CD-ROM,** Response to Literature

Options for Adapting Lesson Plans

HOMEWORK

Have students complete any stage of the lesson for homework.

FEATURES

Extend coverage with Connected Assignment (p. 269), Spotlight on the Humanities (p. 270), Media and Technology (p. 271), and the Standardized Test Preparation Workshop (p. 272).

TECHNOLOGY

Students can complete any stage of the lesson on computer. Have them print out their completed work.

INTEGRATED SKILLS COVERAGE

Integrating Grammar
Combining Ideas in Complex Sentences, SE p. 263
Rules for Punctuating Quotations, SE p. 264

Reading/Writing Connection
Reading Strategy, SE p. 250
Writing Application, SE p. 251

Viewing and Representing
Critical Viewing, SE pp. 248, 250, 251, 255, 257, 259, 260, 266, 267, 268, 269, 270
Comparing Art With a Written Story, SE p. 270
Interpreting Literature in a Variety of Media, SE p. 271; ATE p. 270

Speaking and Listening
ATE p. 267

Real-World Connection
ATE p. 259

ASSESSMENT SUPPORT

Standardized Test Preparation SE p. 272; ATE p. 255
Standardized Test Preparation Workbook, pp. 23–24
Scoring Rubrics on Transparency, Ch. 12
Formal Assessment, Ch. 12
Writing Assessment and Portfolio Management

MEETING INDIVIDUAL NEEDS

Less Advanced Students ATE p. 255. See also Ongoing Assessments ATE pp. 253, 254, 259, 261, 262, 263, 265, 269
Gifted/Talented Students ATE p. 268
ESL Students ATE pp. 254, 273
Bodily/Kinesthetic Learners ATE p. 271
More Advanced Students ATE p. 273

BLOCK SCHEDULING

Pacing Suggestions
For 90-minute Blocks
• Have students complete the Prewriting and Drafting stages in a single period.
• Focus one class period on Revising and Editing and Publishing and Presenting. Allow at least 30 minutes for peer revision.

Resources for Varying Instruction
• *Writing Lab* CD-ROM If your students have access to hardware, a 90-minute block provides an ideal opportunity for students to work on computer.
• *Writers at Work* videotape Show the Response to Literature segment in class.

Professional Development Support
• *How to Manage Instruction in the Block* This Teaching Resource provides management and activity suggestions.

MEDIA AND TECHNOLOGY

For the Student
• *Writing Lab* CD-ROM, Response to Literature
• *On-Line Exercise Bank*, Sections 20.2 and 21.1

For the Teacher
• *Writers at Work* Videotape, Response to Literature
• *Resource Pro* CD-ROM

WRITING AND GRAMMAR WEB SITE

The Interactive Writing and Grammar Web site provides a wide array of support for students, teachers, and parents. Writing support includes:
• Interactive revision checkers
• Scoring rubrics with complete models

www.phschool.com

LITERATURE CONNECTIONS

Related selection from *Prentice Hall Literature: Timeless Voices, Timeless Themes*, Bronze:
"The Princess and the Tin Box," James Thurber, SE p. 251

► *Lesson Objectives*

1. To understand the characteristics of a written response to literature.
2. To choose and narrow a topic for a written response to literature.
3. To consider audience and purpose in developing a writing topic.
4. To apply strategies for gathering and organizing details.
5. To draft a response to literature through defining and developing your focus and categorizing ideas.
6. To evaluate and revise the overall structure of a draft response to literature.
7. To add support to paragraphs.
8. To combine sentences to show connections.
9. To use precise, concrete words that show opinion.
10. To benefit from the peer review process in the revision of a written response to literature.
11. To edit, proofread, and publish a written response to literature.

Critical Viewing

Interpret Students may explain that even though the boys in the picture are not talking, they may be sharing the same experience just by reading the same information.

Chapter 12 Response to Literature

▲ **Critical Viewing**
Explain how these two students might be sharing the same experience, even though they are both absorbed in reading. **[Interpret]**

Responses to Literature in Everyday Life

Reading is usually considered a solitary activity. Picture yourself reading a book in an empty room. Anyone who peeked in would have no way to tell what new adventures were beginning for you. Yet another person, miles away, might share the same images flashing before your mind—just by reading the same book.

When you respond to literature, you can test just how much of your experience of a book you share with others. In a response to literature, you tell readers "what the book was like." You might respond in a quick conversation with a friend or in a review you write for a magazine. Discussing your response brings you closer to other readers and helps show that when we read, we are rarely alone.

248 • Response to Literature

⏱ TIME AND RESOURCE MANAGER

Resources
Technology: Writers at Work videotape

In-Depth Coverage	Accelerated Pace
• Cover pp. 248–251 in class. • Show Response to Literature section of the Writers at Work videotape. • Read literature excerpt (pp. 250–251) in class and use it to brainstorm topics for response to literature with students. • Discuss examples of written responses to literature, such as book reviews and personal essays.	• Have students read pp. 248–251 on their own. • Discuss definitions and types of written responses to literature in class.

What Is a Response to Literature?

A **response to literature** is an essay or other type of writing that discusses what is of value in a book, short story, essay, article, or poem. A response might retell the plot of an exciting story, explain why a poem is beautiful, or show disappointment with a writer's latest play. A response to literature includes

- a strong, interesting focus on an aspect of the work.
- a clear organization that groups related details.
- supporting details for each main idea.
- a summary of important features of the work.
- a judgment about the value of the work.

To preview the criteria on which your response may be assessed, see the Rubric for Self-Assessment on page 265.

Types of Responses to Literature

In addition to a standard literary essay, there are other types of responses to literature:

- **Book reviews** give readers an impression of a book, encouraging them either to read it or to avoid reading it.
- **Letters to an author** let a writer know what a reader found enjoyable or disappointing in a work.
- **Comparisons of works** highlight specific features of two or more works by comparing them.

PREVIEW

Student Work
IN PROGRESS

Jade Yamamoto, a student at Calvary Lutheran School in Indianapolis, Indiana, wrote a response to two poems by Emily Dickinson. In this chapter, you will follow her work in progress and the strategies she used to choose a topic, to draft, and to revise her work. Her final draft appears at the end of the chapter.

Writers in ACTION

Naomi Long Madgett is a poet and publisher who reads and responds to hundreds of poems each week, deciding which poems to publish. This is how she sums up her response to poetry:

"If my mind's eye can get pictures or if I can hear sounds in the poem—or if the words used and the way the language is put together permit me to get a sense of feel, a sense of touch—the poem is much more vivid than one simply using ordinary language."

Response to Literature • 249

Interest GRABBER Ask students to think about going to the movies. Ask whether they talk over their reactions to the movies afterwards, or whether they read published reviews before or after seeing a film. Explain that these conversations and published reviews are responses to performances. They are conversations and writings about whether a person liked a movie, and why he or she did or did not. Students can now apply their movie-reviewing skills to literature.

Activate Prior Knowledge

Ask students what kinds of things they like to read. (Answers may include comic books, magazines, or books of various sorts.) Ask whether students ever discuss their reactions to various books with their friends. These conversations are verbal responses to literature. Students already know how to do this. Now they will apply that knowledge to writing a response to a work of literature.

More About the Writer

Naomi Long Madgett has published a number of collections of her poetry, including *Exits and Entrances* and *Octavia and Other Poems*. She has also published the *Student's Guide to Creative Writing*.

☑ ONGOING ASSESSMENT: Diagnose

Use one of the following options to diagnose students' current level of proficiency in responding to literature.

Option 1 Have each student select the strongest example of his or her response to literature from last year. Hold conferences to review each student's sample and to determine which students will need extra support.	**Option 2** Ask students to brainstorm for a list of reactions to a piece of literature they have read in class recently. What did they like about it? What didn't they like? If students have difficulty completing this exercise, you will need to devote more time to the prewriting phase of the process.

Reading Strategy: Identify Evidence

Explain that a written response to literature is filled with personal opinions. Emphasize that students cannot give just their opinions of books or poems; they must explain the reasons for these opinions. These reasons will convince a reader and strengthen a writer's argument. These reasons are called evidence.

Teaching From the Model

Zena Sutherland writes about the characters found in the work of Hans Christian Andersen. Analyzing Andersen's "genius for characterization," she details the ways in which he affects our perception of the world around us.

Critical Viewing

Analyze Students should mention the expression on Andersen's face as well as the fact that he is looking off to his side, as if lost in a daydream.

Step-by-Step Teaching Guide

Engage Students Through Literature

1. Point out that Sutherland writes about children's literature, but her intended audience is older.

2. Ask students to identify the literary device that Sutherland is analyzing in Andersen's work. (characterization)

continued

12.1 *Model From Literature*

Zena Sutherland (1915–) has written many works on children's literature. This excerpt is taken from one of them, Children and Books.

Reading Strategy: Identify Evidence
The writer of a response to literature or another piece of nonfiction should provide evidence to support each main point. As you read nonfiction, **identify the evidence** provided for better understanding. For instance, Sutherland claims that Hans Christian Andersen's "heroes and heroines are not stereotypes." You can better understand her claim by identifying her evidence—her descriptions of a few characters.

▲ **Critical Viewing**
Explain how the style of this portrait helps suggest Andersen's dreamy side. **[Analyze]**

Making Fantasy Real
Zena Sutherland

Hans Christian Andersen (1805–1875) was born in Odense, Denmark, of a peasant family. His . . . first book, a travel diary of a walking trip, appeared in 1829, published by himself, and his first volumes of *Fairy Tales, Told for Children* appeared in 1835. . . . Andersen poured himself into his writing; it became the vehicle for expressing his emotions, flashes of humor, commentaries on life, and the follies of humankind. Some of his stories are retellings of folktales: "Little Claus and Big Claus," "The Princess and the Pea," and "The Emperor's New Clothes." In these, Andersen took the traditional story and added to it his own interpretation of character, providing motivation for the action in the tale. The heroes and heroines are not stereotypes; they live and breathe and become individuals, named or not. The princess who can feel a pea under twenty mattresses can never be confused in our thinking with any other princess, sensitive though she may be. Andersen imparted such life to these characters that we feel empathy for the emperor and his courtiers, none of whom naturally wish to admit they are stupid or unfit for office.

But it is in Andersen's own creations, his literary fairy tales, that his genius for characterization is shown. As we read "The

Sutherland introduces her topic—Hans Christian Andersen's characters—in her first paragraph. She also makes clear her opinion of his work.

Sutherland organizes her response logically, moving from the least important to the most important aspects of Andersen's art of characterization. She emphasizes the way Andersen shapes our perceptions, linking each paragraph to her concluding point.

250 • Response to Literature

Little Mermaid," we shudder at the pain the mermaid must feel as she puts foot to ground[. A]nd yet, so persuasive is Andersen's art that, in spite of the physical agony, we still agree with her that the prince is worth dying for.

"The Ugly Duckling" is, rightly or wrongly, seen as symbolic of Andersen's own life. The animosity of the neighbors to the "different" one seems so natural that we wonder if we ourselves would have seen the promise implicit in the awkward creature. The conversations in the poultry-yard ring true both to human nature and to the human ear. What mother would not say, "He is my own child and, when you look closely at him, he's quite handsome . . ."? Because of Andersen, every "ugly duckling" promises a swan.

Andersen's ability to draw character does not rest on extensive description. In a few carefully chosen words he establishes important qualities, leaving our imaginations so stimulated that we supply the rest of the picture. Of the hero of "The Steadfast Tin Soldier" Andersen says, "he stood as firm and steadfast on his one leg as the others did on their two." The outward description is not important; what Andersen is emphasizing is the constancy of his character.

Andersen's fantasies do not lack supernatural beings or things, and many of them have otherworldly settings, talking animals, and personifications of inanimate objects. But his main contribution was to make us look more sharply at daily life through the window of his imagination.

Sutherland makes connections to real-life experiences. She also shows again how Andersen's characterization affects our perceptions.

Sutherland builds to her strongest point, showing that Andersen's insight into character helps change the way we see the world.

**Writing Application:
Provide Evidence** As you draft your own response to literature, provide your readers with evidence for each of your main points.

▶ Critical Viewing
What insight of Andersen's does this image represent?
[Interpret]

ⓁITERATURE

For a response to Andersen-style stories, see James Thurber's "The Princess and the Tin Box." You can find this response in *Prentice Hall Literature: Timeless Voices, Timeless Themes,* Bronze.

Model From Literature • 251

3. Work through the text and marginal notes with the whole class. Ask questions based on the margin notes.

More About the Writer

Aside from her *Children and Books,* Sutherland has also compiled four volumes *The Best in Children's Books: The University of Chicago Guide to Children's Literature* from 1966 to 1990.

Reading\Writing Connection
Writing Application: Provide Evidence

Tell students that responding to literature involves supporting your main points with evidence from the text(s) being analyzed. To an extent, this kind of writing has a persuasive dimension, and your readers will only be persuaded if you can support your ideas.

Critical Viewing

Interpret Students may say that this image represents the idea that we often see ourselves very differently than how others see us.

Responding to Literature

Explain to students that a response to literature need not take the form of an essay. Writers may write a new literary work as a way of commenting on or responding to other works. For example, James Thurber writes a fairy tale that has many of the same elements as one of Andersen's tales— a princess, a few princes, and a competition to see which prince will marry the princess. Thurber gives his story a surprising twist, though, that may make readers question the message in Andersen's tales.

Prewriting

Prewriting: Interview Yourself

As a variation on this strategy, students can interview partners, asking the questions listed. Talking to another person may bring out more ideas, or fuller answers. The interview might take an unexpected direction—students might have a strong agreement or disagreement over a particular book. This can be a fruitful source for writing, because a conversation may help them articulate their ideas better than a self-interview would.

Prewriting: Browsing

Teaching Resources: Writing Support Transparency 12-A

1. Discourage students from writing a response to literature based on an excerpt. Students who try this strategy should concentrate on short works such as poems, essays, or short stories. A response to only one chapter of a novel is not valid, because each part of a novel is affected by all the other parts. If students are working with a literature anthology in class, suggest that they browse through it to find a topic.

2. Display the transparency to show students how Jade used this strategy to explore the poetry of Emily Dickinson.

Choosing Your Topic

A good response to literature begins with a work to which you react strongly. Use these strategies to choose such a work:

Strategies for Generating a Topic

1. **Interview Yourself** Answer these questions: What is my favorite type of reading? (Give examples.) Which character from my reading would I like to be? Review your answers, and choose as your topic a work you mention.

2. **Browsing** Browse the literature section of a library or bookstore. Choose works you have already read or new short works by familiar authors (avoid works that will take too long to read). Flip through these works, taking notes. Write on the work that most interests you.

Writing Lab CD-ROM

For more help finding a topic, use the activities and tips in the Choosing a Topic section of the Response to Literature lesson.

Student Work
IN PROGRESS

Name: Jade Yamamoto
Calvary Lutheran School
Indianapolis, IN

Browsing

Looking through the poetry at the library, Jade found two poems by Emily Dickinson that seemed to have a common topic.

POEMS BY EMILY DICKINSON	NOTES
"I'm Nobody"	The frog is funny—he tries to get people's attention by croaking all the time.
"Success is counted sweetest"	People really want to succeed.
"He ate and drank the precious words"	Reading takes you places— in your mind.
"How many Flowers fail in Wood"	It's sad that flowers don't know how beautiful they are.

The first and last poems both seem to be about wanting or not wanting people to pay attention to you.

⏱ TIME AND RESOURCE MANAGER

Resources
Print: Writing Support Transparency 12-A–D; Writing Support Activity Book 12-1–2
Technology: Writing Lab CD-ROM, Responding to Literature

In-Depth Coverage	Accelerated Pace
• Cover pp. 252–257 in class. • Guide students through the Strategies for Generating Topics. • Have students use the pentad technique to narrow their topics. **Option** Students having difficulty may want to adapt topics suggested in the Topic Bank.	• In class, discuss how to identify a good topic for a response to literature. • Have students list possible topics. • Ask students to submit topic proposals for your review.

TOPIC BANK

If you're having trouble finding a topic, consider the following possibilities:

1. **Review a Favorite** Choose a favorite—or a disliked—book, short story, essay, or poem. Write a review of it for your classmates. What will they like about the piece? What will they dislike about it? Include details to support your point of view.

2. **Literary Log and Letters** Keep a daily log in which you take notes on the literature you are reading. At the end of a week, review your log. Write one letter to your teacher and one to a friend, in which you discuss what you've read.

Responding to Fine Art

3. Take notes on this painting, focusing on its mood or feeling. Then, decide what literary work you would associate with it. In an essay, compare the mood of the painting with that of the literary work. Use details from the painting and from the literary work to support your points.

Responding to Literature

4. Read O. Henry's story "After Twenty Years." Write an essay describing your response to the ending. Discuss how the ending changes the way you see the beginning. Then, explain how the order in which O. Henry presents information creates these effects. You can find the story in *Prentice Hall Literature: Timeless Voices, Timeless Themes*, Bronze.

Dormer, 1984–1987, Edward Rice, Morris Museum of Art, Augusta, Georgia

☑ **Cooperative Writing Opportunity**

5. **Panel Talk** Form a group with other students who are writing a response to the same work. Have each member write a paragraph about his or her reaction to the work. List discussion questions based on these statements. Then, hold a talk before the class to respond to these questions and to any others from the audience. Afterward, each member should write a complete response to the work.

Prewriting • 253

Step-by-Step Teaching Guide

Responding to Fine Art

Dormer, 1984–1987, by Edward Rice
Teaching Resources: Writing Support Transparency 12-B

You can use this artwork as a starting point to help students respond to a visual image.

Display the transparency and engage students in a discussion about it. Explain that a dormer is an upstairs window, usually in a bedroom.

• What do you think this bedroom looks like?

• Who do you think sleeps in this room?

• Does that person enjoy spending time in this room?

• What does he or she see out the window?

Responding to Literature

Suggest to students that they stop reading for a moment at the point where the policeman leaves and make a prediction about how "After Twenty Years" will end. Have them identify events that seem to confirm their prediction as the story continues. Then, have them identify the point at which the story "twists," creating surprise. After they have read the story, discuss how the conversation with the policeman at the beginning both prepares for the reading and keeps the reader from guessing how it will turn out.

Spotlight on the Humanities

For additional topic suggestions, refer students to the Spotlight on the Humanities on p. 270.

☑ ONGOING ASSESSMENT: Monitor and Reinforce

If you observe that some students are having difficulty coming up with a topic, use one of the following options.

Option 1 Suggest that students choose an idea from the Topic Bank. If many students have difficulty, work with the whole class on one idea selected from the Topic Bank or from ideas suggested by students.	**Option 2** If Topic Bank ideas seem too difficult, suggest that students try one of the assignments from the Topic Bank for Heterogeneous Classes in the Teaching Resources.

⏱ TIME SAVERS!

Writing Support Transparencies
Use the transparencies for Chapter 12 to teach these strategies.

Prewriting: Use a Pentad

Teaching Resources: Writing Support Transparency 12-C; Writing Support Activity Book 12-1

1. Display the transparency. Go over Jade's model of a pentad. Even though Jade is working on a poem that hints and suggests rather than tells, she can still apply a strategy that deals largely with "plot."

2. Give students copies of the blank organizer and have students narrow their topics as Jade did.

Customize for
ESL Students

If students are having difficulty choosing a piece of literature, suggest that they consider writers who share their backgrounds, for example, Gary Soto, Sandra Cisneros, Alice Walker, Toni Cade Bambara, Yoshiko Uchida.

12.2

Narrowing Your Topic

After you have chosen a work to which to respond, read or review it carefully. Once you have the work "under your skin," use a pentad to select an aspect on which to focus.

Use a Pentad

Draw a large five-pointed star as a graphic organizer. Label each point as follows:

- **Actors** Who did the action?
- **Acts** What was done?
- **Scenes** When or where was it done?
- **Agencies** How was it done?
- **Purposes** Why was it done?

Fill in each point of the star with details matching its label. Then, highlight details that connect in interesting ways. To create a focused topic, sum up your highlighted details in a sentence.

Collaborative Writing Tip

To help fill out your pentad, brainstorm with another student who has read the same work. Try out as many ideas as you can for difficult categories such as "Agencies."

Student Work IN PROGRESS

Name: Jade Yamamoto
Calvary Lutheran School
Indianapolis, IN

Using a Pentad

Jade narrowed her topic by creating a pentad and highlighting interesting details for each of the two poems she had selected. She made the pentad below for "I'm Nobody."

The speaker, the person she is talking to, other people, and the frog.

The speaker finds out the other person is "nobody," too. The other people will banish the two if they find out. The frog croaks all summer long to the bog.

Actors

Purposes

Acts

The "nobodies" want to stay private. The other people want to banish them. The frog wants to be admired for his croaking.

Agencies

Scenes

There isn't one really, except the bog.

Recognition—the speaker just knows the other person is a "nobody." Secrecy—the speaker and the other person don't tell anyone else they are "nobodies." Boasting—the frog croaks all summer long.

☑ ONGOING ASSESSMENT: Monitor and Reinforce

If you observe that students lapse into the habit of always writing for the teacher, try one of the following options.

Option 1 Suggest that students write to a very specific audience of one—a relative, a friend, or a much younger person.	**Option 2** Have students write down a brief profile of their intended audience, including their level of education, skills, and background knowledge of the topic.

Considering Your Audience and Purpose

After focusing your topic, think about your audience and your purpose for writing. Use your answers to the following questions to guide you as you gather details and draft:

- **Are my readers already familiar with this kind of work?** If so, give details showing what is unique about this work or about how it differs from others of its kind.

- **Are my readers unfamiliar with this kind of work?** If so, explain the basic purpose of the work—to tell a suspenseful story, to make music with words, and so on.

- **Are my readers practiced, older readers?** If so, you need not explain every detail. For instance, you might explain a character to these readers as follows: "Jake is a typical adventure-story hero—rugged and able to keep cool under pressure." You might then move on to discuss the plot.

- **Am I writing for less sophisticated readers?** To help these readers picture Jake, you might need to describe him more fully, giving specific examples that reveal his character.

- **Am I trying to persuade readers of something?** If your purpose is to persuade readers that the work is "worth reading" or "not worth reading," concentrate on examples supporting your opinion.

- **Am I trying to enhance readers' appreciation of the work?** If your purpose is to enhance appreciation, point out qualities and patterns in the work that a reader might not see.

◄ **Critical Viewing**
What type of literary work might these students enjoy reading? **[Speculate]**

Step-by-Step Teaching Guide

Prewriting: Considering Your Audience and Purpose

Ask students who their primary audience is. (Teacher and classmates) Have them answer the questions on the page with this audience in mind. Students should have a good idea of their classmates' level of familiarity with their topics. Remind them that teachers have not read everything ever written!

Critical Viewing

Speculate Students' responses will vary.

Customize for
Less Advanced Students

Students who do not do a great deal of reading for pleasure may have difficulty approaching this assignment. There is a book for everyone's taste. Reassure students that they do not have to impress you by pretending to like a difficult poet such as Dickinson. They can choose a scary story by Edgar Allan Poe, a mystery by Arthur Conan Doyle, a funny story by James Thurber, science fiction by Ray Bradbury, or even a silly poem by Shel Silverstein. Probe their interests. A student who just got a new kitten may respond to James Herriot. A student who wonders how things work may be captivated by a book by David Macaulay. These students may need a story or book for slightly younger readers—avoid telling them it's a "kids' book."

STANDARDIZED TEST PREPARATION WORKSHOP

Audience and Purpose Standardized tests frequently require students to respond to an essay prompt that specifies an audience and purpose.

Share the following sample prompt with students:

Your school's literary magazine wants to devote an entire issue to an American poet. Write a letter to the editors of the magazine in support of the poet of your choice.

Have students write a paragraph that identifies the audience and purpose for this prompt, and how these elements would influence their writing.

⏱ TIME SAVERS!

 Writing Support Transparencies
Use the transparencies for Chapter 12 to teach these strategies.

 Writing Support Activity Book
Use the graphic organizers for Chapter 12 to facilitate these strategies.

Prewriting: Use Hexagonal Writing

Teaching Resources: Writing Support Transparency 12-D; Writing Support Activity Book 12-2

1. Display the transparency and give students copies of the blank organizer.

2. Go over Jade's model to be sure that students understand how to use hexagonal writing. Point out that the hexagon poses specific questions about the work, and finding the answers to these questions (such as "What did I like about this work?") will force students to articulate their responses. This strategy will help them get over the difficulty of how to get started on their written responses to literature.

12.2

Gathering Details

To give readers a feeling for a work, and to support your judgments about it, you need to present examples. Review the work, taking notes to gather the details you will include in your response.

Use Hexagonal Writing

To gather details about various sides of your topic, use hexagonal writing. Take two different-colored sheets of construction paper. Cut out three triangles of equal size from each sheet. Using alternating colors, arrange the triangles to form a hexagon. Label each triangle as shown in the example below. Then look through the work to find details for each triangle.

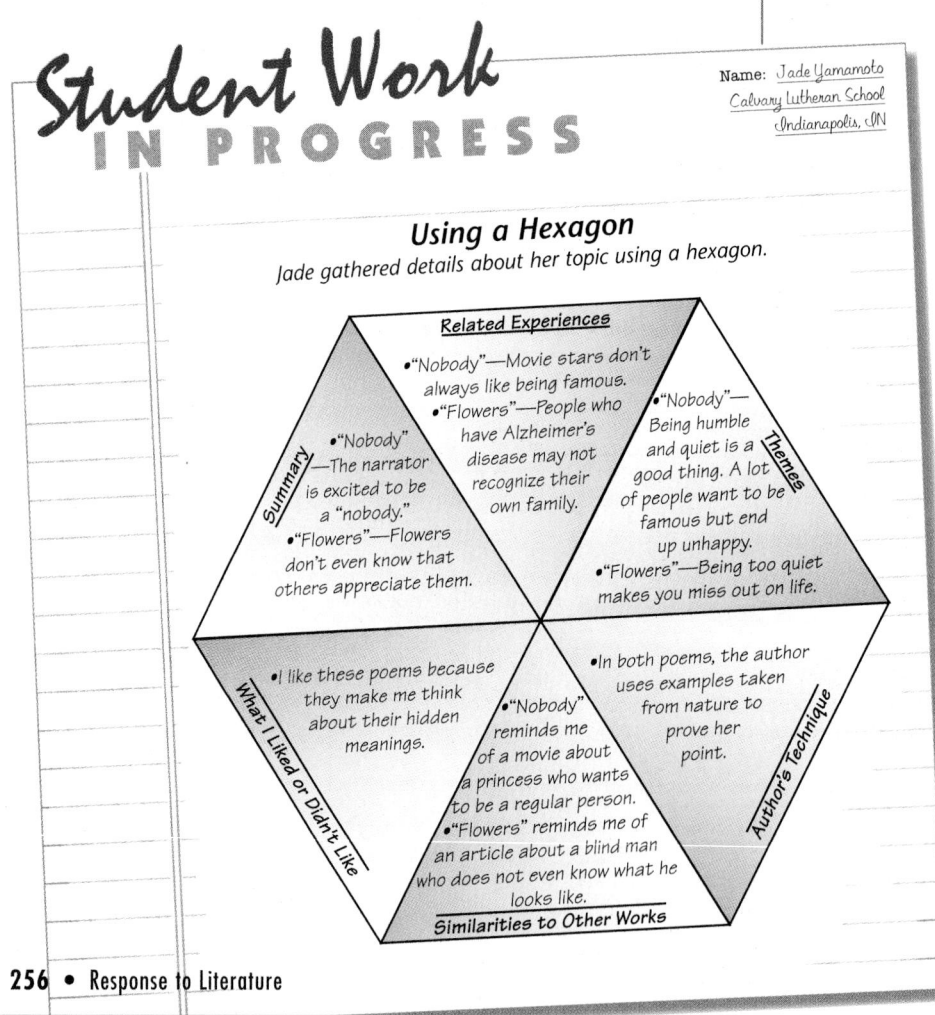

Student Work IN PROGRESS

Name: *Jade Yamamoto*
Calvary Lutheran School
Indianapolis, IN

Using a Hexagon
Jade gathered details about her topic using a hexagon.

Related Experiences
• "Nobody"—Movie stars don't always like being famous.
• "Flowers"—People who have Alzheimer's disease may not recognize their own family.

Summary
• "Nobody"—The narrator is excited to be a "nobody."
• "Flowers"—Flowers don't even know that others appreciate them.

Themes
• "Nobody"—Being humble and quiet is a good thing. A lot of people want to be famous but end up unhappy.
• "Flowers"—Being too quiet makes you miss out on life.

What I Liked or Didn't Like
• I like these poems because they make me think about their hidden meanings.

Similarities to Other Works
• "Nobody" reminds me of a movie about a princess who wants to be a regular person.
• "Flowers" reminds me of an article about a blind man who does not even know what he looks like.

Author's Technique
• In both poems, the author uses examples taken from nature to prove her point.

What to Look For

As you explore the work you've chosen, look for the following types of details. Jot down notes in the appropriate section of your hexagon.

Summary If you call a book exciting or boring, you need to tell readers about what happens in it. Begin gathering details by exploring the work on a literal level, and then summarize the work:

- Outline the main events, ideas, or images.
- Indicate how these events, ideas, or images are related.
- Briefly describe the characters in the work—the people involved in the story.

Related Experiences Often, a character's experience or a line from a poem reminds you of something in real life. Part of the impact of a work depends on what it shows us about the world. Jot down any experiences or associations from life that you connect with the work.

Themes Many works of literature suggest a question or lesson about life—a **theme.** To discover the theme of a work, look for patterns of events or contrasts between characters. For instance, if one character is greedy while another is generous, you can conclude that generosity is one theme of the work. If the greedy character comes to a bad end, the work may teach a lesson about greed. Write a single sentence that expresses the message or lesson of the work.

Author's Technique Writers create any number of special effects using words. Gather examples of some of these techniques, such as the following:

- A short story writer can create a tragic effect by timing an event just right.
- A poet creates effects using **figurative language**—musical phrases, colorful images, and surprising comparisons.

Similarities to Other Works When different writers address the same subject, the differences in what they write can show you what is special about each writer. Gather specific details about characters, events, or the writer's attitude that show how your chosen work compares with another.

Evaluation and Reaction Responding to a work of literature means telling readers what you thought of it. Find precise words to describe your reactions. Note examples showing exactly what you enjoyed or disliked in the work.

▲ **Critical Viewing**
If the man in this picture were a character in a story you had read, what details about him might you include in a response to the story? **[Analyze]**

What to Look For

1. Caution students not to retell the plot of a book or story and then stop. In a literary response such as a book review, writers need to give readers enough plot information to whet their appetites and to understand comments made about characterization or theme. A book report answers the question *What is this book about?* A response to literature answers the questions *How did this book make me feel? Why?* Its purpose is not to summarize, but to discuss, analyze, and evaluate.

2. Ask students to bring in movie reviews from newspapers or magazines. Use these reviews to demonstrate that retelling plot is only a small part of the purpose of a review and response. Writers tell readers only the bare outlines of a story, plus any particular details they want to focus on for comment. Explain that reviews of books make the same use of plot summary.

Critical Viewing

Analyze Students might describe the old man by comparing him to other characters in the story. Because of his age and rugged face, they may describe him as wise, rough, tired, or simply an old man with vivid and wild stories of the old days.

⏱ TIME SAVERS!

 Writing Support Transparencies
Use the transparencies for Chapter 12 to teach these strategies.

Writing Support Activity Book
Use the graphic organizers for Chapter 12 to facilitate these strategies.

Teaching Resources: Writing Support Transparency 12-E; Writing Support Activity Book 12-3

1. Ask what the word *focus* means to students. Bring a camera or binoculars to class. Have students look through the lens(es) and adjust the focus until they can see clearly. Draw the analogy between focusing with a camera and focusing with words. Just as the focus of a camera defines an image as sharply as possible, certain words can turn a vague verbal image into a clear, specific one.

2. Have students try to summarize their responses to literature in one sentence. This sentence should be the focus of their papers. It is their main idea—the point they want to build up to. This is the idea they will want to support with various details.

12.3 Drafting

Shaping Your Writing

After gathering details from the work, review your notes to find a focus for your response. Look for connections between details. Find the direction in which many details seem to point or the main idea that most seem to illustrate. Then, organize your writing around this main point, or focus.

Define and Develop Your Focus

A focus statement sums up your reaction to one aspect of the work. For instance, your topic might be a comparison of two characters:

UNFOCUSED RESPONSE: Cherry has dark hair. Sherri is blonde. Cherry likes adventure. Sherri likes to stay at home.

FOCUSED RESPONSE: Cherry is easier to like than Sherri. Cherry likes adventure. She always has something sassy to say when people bug her.

To define a focus, review your notes. Then, answer the questions shown here, writing your focus as a single sentence. Include this sentence in your introduction, and elaborate on it in the body of your essay.

QUESTIONS FOR DEFINING A FOCUS

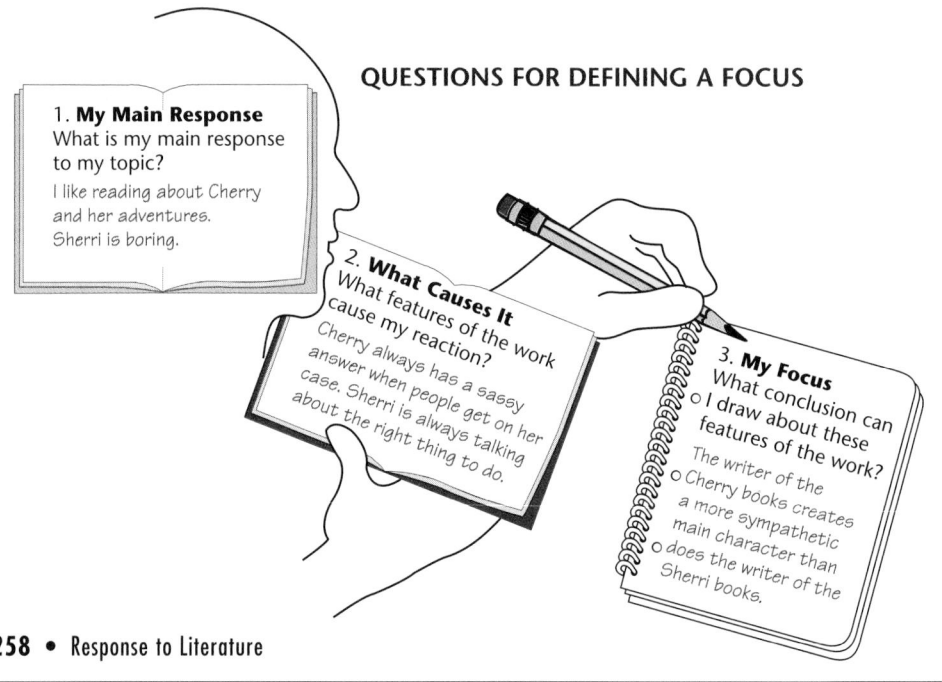

1. **My Main Response**
What is my main response to my topic?
I like reading about Cherry and her adventures. Sherri is boring.

2. **What Causes It**
What features of the work cause my reaction?
Cherry always has a sassy answer when people get on her case. Sherri is always talking about the right thing to do.

3. **My Focus**
What conclusion can I draw about these features of the work?
The writer of the Cherry books creates a more sympathetic main character than does the writer of the Sherri books.

258 • Response to Literature

⏱ TIME AND RESOURCE MANAGER

Resources
Print: Writing Support Transparency 12-E
Technology: Writing Lab CD-ROM, Response to Literature

In-Depth Coverage	Accelerated Pace
• Cover pp. 258–259 in class. • Discuss how students can use details to focus on particular elements of a literary work.	• Assign pp. 258–259 for independent student review. • Encourage students to use graphic organizers to help them focus their writing.

Providing Elaboration

You've gathered details related to your topic. As you draft, include these details in your response to help readers understand each main point. If necessary, return to the work to gather more support.

Provide Support

As you write, refer to your notes to find support for each main point. Include details such as:

- **Quotations** In a quotation, you take the exact words used in the work and include them in your draft. Use quotation marks to set off these words.

- **Summaries** A summary is a brief retelling of events or ideas.

- **Descriptions** Your own descriptions can help readers picture the setting of a work, its characters, and so on.

- **Comparisons** Writers often create contrasting characters, places, and ideas. By making comparisons between such features, you can better interpret the meaning of a work.

Pause occasionally while drafting, and review what you have written. Add any supporting details you need.

▲ **Critical Viewing** To which details in this photograph would you refer to show readers that these people are angry? **[Apply]**

Student Work
IN PROGRESS

Name: Jade Yamamoto
Calvary Lutheran School
Indianapolis, IN

Providing Support

After writing one paragraph, Jade reviewed it and added supporting details.

She shows her excitement in the line "Then there's a pair of us!" It's as if the speaker and the reader will make a secret club.

First, Dickinson makes being "nobody" seem fun. The speaker proudly says "'I'm Nobody'" in the very first line. She sounds excited when she discovers the reader also might be "Nobody." Later, she uses the phrases "How dreary" and "How public" to describe being famous. Being famous is not as fun as being "Nobody."

Drafting • 259

Step-by-Step Teaching Guide

Drafting: Providing Elaboration

Teaching Resources: Writing Support Transparency 12-F

1. Go over the four types of details with the class. Give examples of situations in which students might want to use each type of detail. If a student wanted to suggest that the language in Ernest Lawrence Thayer's poem "Casey at the Bat" was too melodramatic, for example, he or she might quote phrases such as "that stricken multitude" and "the maddened thousands" to support this point.

2. Display the transparency and review with students how Jade added supporting details.

3. Almost any response to a literary work includes a short summary. Provide students with a recent issue of the book section from the Sunday paper and let them examine the reviews. Warn students not to spend too much time retelling the story. Their summaries should include only enough information for the reader to understand their analyses.

Real-World Connection

Critics earn their livings responding to books, concerts, plays, movies, and so on. A critic's job is to give readers an idea of whether they want to see a particular performance or read a certain book. Critics must understand how to respond to literature and drama in ways that engage their readers without replacing the experience of reading the book or seeing the performance.

Critical Viewing

Apply Students will likely describe the angry faces, the individual yelling, the pointing, and angry gestures. Some may even describe anger in their eyes.

☑ **ONGOING ASSESSMENT: Monitor and Reinforce**

Students sometimes have problems recognizing the strengths and weaknesses of their evidence. If you find this is the case with your students, try the following strategy.

Have students work in pairs. Each student writes down his or her supporting points on note cards or self-sticking notes and asks the other student to place them in order of strongest to weakest.	Students can then discuss the effectiveness of their arrangements of supporting points before continuing to draft.

1. Even though students may have many things to say, some details may not be relevant to the central focus of their response to literature. Ask if any student has ever cried in exasperation, "But that's not the point!" during an argument. Help students see that sticking to the point is essential when making an argument or expressing an opinion about a literary work.

2. Using a photocopy of the text, have students color-code the literary model on pp. 250–251 for stray details. Ask if anyone found details he or she thought should have been eliminated. Students can then try the strategy on their own essays. Challenge them to make sure that every paragraph in their own essays can meet the same standard.

Critical Viewing

Compare and Contrast Students may say that, like the frog, this man is boasting by flexing his muscles.

12.4 Revising

Revising Your Overall Structure

A draft is just the first step in creating a response to literature. You have most of your ideas on paper. Now, you need to make sure that they will be clear to your readers. Start by reviewing your organization.

Analyze Your Organization

Your ideas may be good, but if the support for a particular point is scattered throughout your draft, it will be hard for your reader to piece the details together. Use the strategy of color-coding to improve organization.

▶ **REVISION STRATEGY**
Color-Coding Main Points and Support

As you read over what you have written, circle each main point in a different color. Underline sentences supporting a main point in the same color as that of the main point.

When you have finished color-coding, review your draft:

- If a paragraph is marked in a few different colors, consider reorganizing details so that all of the support for a main point is in the same paragraph.

- Consider eliminating any sentence that is neither circled nor underlined. If such a sentence states a new main idea, consider developing it in a paragraph of its own.

Build to a Point

Readers have a more enjoyable time reading a work when each paragraph carries them closer to a main point. Identify your strongest point, and consider reorganizing your draft to build to this point.

▶ **REVISION STRATEGY**
Circling the Strongest Point

Review your paper. Circle your strongest point—the one that is most interesting or that summarizes your other main ideas.

Move this point to the end of your piece. Add a transition sentence clearly explaining the relationship of this point to the rest of your ideas. Then, go back and add sentences to other paragraphs in your draft, linking them to this point. (Review "Making Fantasy Real" on page 250. Read the sidenotes that explain how Zena Sutherland links each paragraph to her concluding point.)

▼ Critical Viewing Compare this man's pose with the croaking of the frog described in the Student Work in Progress feature on page 261.
[Compare and Contrast]

⏱ TIME AND RESOURCE MANAGER

Resources
Print: Writing Support Transparency 12-G–H
Technology: Writing Lab CD-ROM, Response to Literature

In-Depth Coverage	Accelerated Pace
• Cover pp. 260–263 in class. • Discuss the revision process with students. Review supporting details and how they can improve writing. • Review how varying sentence length strengthens writing. • Help students identify short, overly simple sentences they could combine into longer ones.	• Assign pp. 260–263 for independent student review. • Have students brainstorm possible criticism of their writing. • Have students work independently to revise their writing.

Revising Your Paragraphs

Strengthen Support

Use the following strategy to ensure that you are providing enough support.

▶ **REVISION STRATEGY**

Using Points to Illuminate to Add Support

Review your draft, following these steps to illuminate it:

1. Cut out a five-pointed construction paper star for each of your main points. Write your main point in the center and label the points of each star as follows: *quotation, character, event, figure of speech,* and *theme.*
2. Find support in your draft for each main idea. Add a check to each star-point for which you find an example.
3. Use the unchecked points on your stars to assess your support. For example, if none of your stars have "Quotation" checked, consider adding a quotation to your response.

🛈 Research Tip

Use library resources to find essays on, or reviews of, the work to which you are responding. You can use quotations from an essay or review, properly cited, as additional support in your own response.

Step-by-Step Teaching Guide

Revising: Revising Your Paragraphs

Teaching Resources: Writing Support Transparency 12-G

1. Ask students how they feel when they are exchanging ideas or opinions with someone who refuses to give reasons for his or her opinions. Students should agree that this both frustrates them and makes them less willing to believe the other person's statements. Use this analogy to demonstrate why supporting details are essential. They make arguments more believable and provide more interest for a reader then do unsupported assertions.

2. Display the transparency. Go over the steps of the strategy of illuminating to add support, and take students through Jade's example. Point out that this strategy will force them to give reasons for all the statements they made in their essays.

Student Work
IN PROGRESS

Name: Jade Yamamoto
Calvary Lutheran School
Indianapolis, IN

Adding Support With Points to Illuminate

Jade used the strategy of illuminating and discovered that she had no support for the main idea in this paragraph. She decided to add a quotation.

The frog in "I'm Nobody" represents those who brag. Emily Dickinson shows us that those who boast just make , like a frog's croaking. They are like the frog that tells its name "the livelong June/ To an admiring Bog." a lot of noise. Boastful people try to win the compliments of others by making known their every little "amazing" feat.

☑ ONGOING ASSESSMENT: Monitor and Reinforce

If you observe that students are supporting their opinions only with more opinions, use the following strategy.

Select a newspaper column, editorial, or letter to the editor on some controversial local issue and work with the class to label each sentence with a "F" for fact or "O" for opinion. Then have students label their own draft in the same way. Any paragraph filled only with opinions will need better support.

⏱ TIME SAVERS!

 Writing Support Transparencies
Use the transparencies for Chapter 12 to facilitate teaching of adding support with points to illuminate and other strategies.

Revising: Revising Your Sentences

Teaching Resources: Writing Support Activity 12-H

1. Go over the list of words that explain *why* with the whole class. Students may be surprised to discover that there are so many ways to say *because*.

2. Have volunteers give before and after examples of sentences they combined. If they want to combine some but cannot figure out how, let the class help.

3. Display the transparency. Ask students how Jade's change strengthens her point.

12.4

Revising Your Sentences
Combine Sentences to Show Connections

For your writing to flow smoothly, you need to make the connections between ideas as clear as possible. One way to show connections is to combine short sentences into longer ones using connecting words—words that explain the relationships between ideas. (See the Grammar in Your Writing feature on the next page for an example showing how to combine sentences into complex sentences.)

▶ **REVISION STRATEGY**
Highlighting Sentences That Explain Why

Use a colored pencil to highlight points in your writing where you explain *why* something happened or *why* you reached a particular conclusion. At each of these *why* passages, see whether you can combine shorter sentences using one of these connecting words or phrases:

as a result of	for the purpose of
because	for the sake of/in order to
despite	since
due to	so that
even though	

Language Lab CD-ROM

For more practice combining sentences, complete the Combining Sentences lesson in the Sentence Style unit.

Student Work IN PROGRESS

Name: Jade Yamamoto
Calvary Lutheran School
Indianapolis, IN

Highlighting Sentences That Explain Why
In this passage, Jade used a connecting phrase to combine a short sentence with another one. The second sentence provides an explanation of the first.

We sometimes assume that being on top is what life is all about. ↳ because we ~~We~~ see famous people, in magazines and on TV, smiling and looking fabulous. "I'm Nobody" makes us think about whether fame is really so important.

☑ ONGOING ASSESSMENT: Monitor and Reinforce

If you find that students have difficulty identifying passages in their drafts that need more emphatic wording, use the following strategy.

As a variation of the "read aloud" strategy, students should listen to their draft being read by someone else. If particular statements do not sound as emphatic or persuasive as the writer intended, they should be marked. As students revise these key statements to make them more forceful, tell them to concentrate first on verbs, then on adjectives.

Grammar in Your Writing
Combining Ideas in Complex Sentences

To join two ideas, you can create a complex sentence. A **complex sentence** consists of one independent clause and one or more subordinate clauses. An **independent clause** can stand on its own as a sentence. A **subordinate clause** has a subject and a verb, but it cannot stand on its own. One way to form a complex sentence is to use a subordinating conjunction, such as *after, as, because, before, if, since, until, unless, when,* or *while.*

Separate: Emily Dickinson published only a handful of her own poems. It is amazing that she became so widely known.

Combined: Since Emily Dickinson published only a handful of her own poems, it is amazing that she became so widely known.

Find It in Your Reading Find one complex sentence in "Making Fantasy Real" by Zena Sutherland on page 250. Identify the clauses.

Find It in Your Writing Circle two complex sentences in your draft. If you cannot find any, consider combining sentences.

To learn more about complex sentences, see Chapter 20.

Revising Your Word Choice
Choose Precise Words for Evaluation

Use precise words to make your opinion about the work clear. Sharpen your word choice by color-coding value words.

▶ **REVISION STRATEGY**
Color-Coding Value Words

With a colored pencil, draw a box around words that express your opinion, such as *good* or *bad.* Replace general value words with precise ones. Here are some examples:

GENERAL: boring, wonderful
PRECISE: repetitious, plodding, gripping, colorful

Peer Review
Process Share

Read your draft to a small group. The group should ask the following questions and discuss your answers to them:

• What problems did writing pose? How did you solve them?

• What are you planning to do next?

Use the group's suggestions as you prepare your final draft.

Revising • 263

✓ **ONGOING ASSESSMENT: Prerequisite Skills**

If students have difficulty combining sentences, refer them to the following to assure coverage of prerequisite skills.

In the Textbook	Print Resources	Technology
Clauses, pp. 445–446 Effective Sentences, pp. 460–463	Grammar Exercise Workbook, pp. 89–90	On-Line Exercise Bank, Sections 20.2 and 21.2

Editing and Proofreading

1. Remind students that quotations are exact words. If they quote from literary works, students should be sure to quote accurately.

2. Students can also paraphrase—rewrite something in their own words. They should be careful about this, too. Changing a word or two and then pretending it is your own work is stealing. Here are valid and invalid paraphrases of Zena Sutherland's third sentence:

   Valid   *Andersen's writing expresses the full range of his feelings, insights, and complaints about life.*

   Invalid   *Andersen poured himself into his tales; they became the vehicle for expressing his feelings, flashes of humor, commentaries on life, and the follies of humankind.*

Grammar in Your Writing: Rules for Punctuating Quotations

1. If students are quoting dialogue between two characters, it will be clearer if they set these lines apart (even if there are only two of them) rather than run them into the text.

2. Show students how to quote several lines of poetry: as separate lines indented, or run into the text with a slash to show line breaks.

Find It in Your Reading

What mother would not say, "He is my own child and, when you look closely at him, he is quite handsome . . ."?

Andersen says, "he stood as firm and steadfast on his one leg as the others did on their two."

Find It in Your Writing

Students should correct any errors in punctuation.

12.5 Editing and Proofreading

After revising your response, proofread carefully to catch any errors in spelling, punctuation, or grammar. A response to a literary work will probably include a number of quotations from the work. Pay careful attention to the punctuation, indentation, and capitalization of quotations. The following suggestions can help:

Focusing on Quotations

Long quotations (four or more lines) from a literary work should be indented in your writing. Treat shorter quotations just like the dialogue of a story. Be sure that when you quote, you copy the words exactly as they appear in the work.

Grammar in Your Writing
Rules for Punctuating Quotations

The following are two ways to present quotations from a literary work:

Long quotations Introduce the quotation with a colon; indent the entire quotation on both sides.

> Max goes through a long debate with himself about the crime he wants to commit:
>
> He walked the streets, asking himself, "Do I really want to do it? If I steal the plans, I can make a lot of money. Jeanine can have the operation she needs." As he stared out over the city, Max felt desperate. "If I'm caught," he asked himself, "could my family bear the shame?"

Brief quotations Use quotation marks and commas to separate the quotation from the rest of a sentence. Use single quotation marks for a quotation within another quotation:

> The writer portrays Max's feelings clearly when she writes, "Max felt desperate. 'If I'm caught,' he asked himself, 'could my family bear the shame?'"

Find It in Your Reading In "Making Fantasy Real" by Zena Sutherland on page 250, find an example of a quotation and note how it is punctuated.

Find It in Your Writing Read over your response to literature, and check each quotation to be sure it is set off and punctuated correctly.

To learn more about punctuating quotations, see Chapter 26.

⏱ TIME AND RESOURCE MANAGER

Resources
Print: Scoring Rubrics on Transparency, Chapter 12; Formal Assessment, Ch. 12

In-Depth Coverage	Accelerated Pace
• Cover pp. 264–268 in class. • Distribute and review Proofreading Checklist and Correction Marks. • Have students edit and proofread their essays in class. **Option** Students can work on their own with the Editing and Evaluation sections of the Writing CD-ROM.	• Have students read pp. 264–268 on their own. • Have students edit and proofread their essays on their own. • Respond to individual editing needs.

12.6 Publishing and Presenting

Building Your Portfolio

Here are a few suggestions for publishing and presenting your response to literature:

1. **Post It at the Library** Arrange to post the responses of the class on a special bulletin board at your local or school library. Attach an eye-catching picture to each response. Students looking for recommendations for reading can browse the board.

2. **Publish It in a Newspaper** Contact the editor of a local paper, and arrange to publish the responses of the class in a weekly "Teen Book Reviews" column.

Reflecting on Your Writing

Jot down a few notes on your experience writing a response to literature. Start off by answering these questions:

• How did writing about the work help me understand it?

• Would I like to write my next response about the same kind of work or about a different kind? Why?

Add your reflection to your portfolio.

 Internet Tip

To see an essay scored according to this rubric, visit **www.phschool.com**

Rubric for Self-Assessment

Evaluate your response to literature using the following criteria.

	Score 4	Score 3	Score 2	Score 1
Audience and Purpose	Presents sufficient background on the work(s); presents the writer's reactions forcefully	Presents background on the work(s); presents the writer's reactions clearly	Presents some background on the work(s); presents the writer's reactions at points	Presents little or no background on the work(s); presents few of the writer's reactions
Organization	Presents points in logical order, smoothly connecting them to the overall focus	Presents points in logical order and connects many to the overall focus	Organizes points poorly in places; connects some points to an overall focus	Presents information in a scattered, disorganized manner
Elaboration	Supports reactions and evaluations with elaborated reasons and well-chosen examples	Supports reactions and evaluations with specific reasons and examples	Supports some reactions and evaluations with reasons and examples	Offers little support for reactions and evaluations
Use of Language	Shows overall clarity and fluency; uses precise, evaluative words; makes few mechanical errors	Shows good sentence variety; uses some precise evaluative terms; makes some mechanical errors	Uses awkward or overly simple sentence structures and vague evaluative terms; makes many mechanical errors	Presents incomplete thoughts; makes mechanical errors that create confusion

Publishing and Presenting • 265

☑ **ONGOING ASSESSMENT: Assess Mastery**

Use one of the following options to assess final drafts of students' response to literature.

Self-Assessment Ask students to score their essay using the rubric provided. Then have students write a single paragraph reflecting on the most valuable thing they learned in completing this essay.

Teacher Assessment You may wish to use the rubric and the scoring models provided in Writing Assessment, Response to Literature, to score students' work.

Publishing and Presenting

Teaching Resources: Scoring Rubrics on Transparency 12; Formal Assessment, Chapter 12

1. Students may want to start a book review section in the school paper or begin a literary magazine. Work with other teachers to support and encourage their efforts.

2. If students wrote about a work by a living author, they may want to send their response to him or her. They can write in care of the book's publisher.

3. Several classes can get together and organize and combine their responses in a loose-leaf binder they donate to the school librarian. When other students are searching for something to read, it may help them to know what works schoolmates liked and disliked.

ASSESS

Assessment

Teaching Resources: Scoring Rubrics on Transparency 12; Formal Assessment, Chapter 12

1. Display the Scoring Rubric transparency and review the criteria in class.

2. Before students proceed with self-assessment, you may wish to review the Final Draft of the Student Work in Progress on pp. 266–268. Have students score the Final Draft in one or more of the rubric categories.

3. In addition to student self-assessment, you may wish to use the following assessment options.

• Score student essays yourself, using the rubric and scoring models from Writing Assessment.

• Review the Standardized Test Preparation Workshop on pp. 272–273 and have students respond to a writing prompt within a time limit.

• Administer the Chapter 12 Test from Formal Assessment in Teaching Resources to assess students' grasp of concepts presented.

Teaching From the Final Draft

1. Help students recognize the elements of a thorough and thoughtful response to literature demonstrated by Jade's model.

   • The title catches a reader's interest.

   • Many of the writer's peers will find the subject interesting.

   • The writer's opinions are clearly presented and supported.

2. Go through the margin notes. Have students try to apply similar standards to their own work. These margin notes will give them a good idea of what to look for.

Critical Viewing

Speculate Students might explain that Dickinson is following her own advice of avoiding the extremes in attitude and self-portrayal. Her attitude is not too proud or boastful, nor is it too humble or quiet.

12.7 *Student Work*
IN PROGRESS

FINAL DRAFT

◄ **Critical Viewing**
Read Jade's essay. Then, using details from this photograph, explain whether you think Emily Dickinson followed her own advice about how best to live. **[Speculate]**

Frogs vs. Flowers

Jade Yamamoto
Calvary Lutheran School
Indianapolis, Indiana

In the two poems "I'm Nobody" and "How many Flowers fail in Wood," Emily Dickinson describes two paths that people can take to find an identity. She also shows where each leads. I like these poems because they teach important lessons about life.

"I'm Nobody" makes us think about society and our ideals today. This poem helps us to see that we all want to be "some-body." It makes us open our eyes to a major human interest: fame. We sometimes assume that being on top is what life is all about because we see famous people, in magazines and on TV,

Jade introduces the focus of her paper in her first paragraph. She will concentrate on the lessons that two Emily Dickinson poems teach about identity.

266 • Response to Literature

Integrating Speaking and Listening Skills

Some readers instantly respond in a positive way to Emily Dickinson's poetry. Others are alienated by it. One problem may be the eccentric punctuation. Have a volunteer rehearse and then read "I'm Nobody" aloud to the class. The reader should decide when to pause to make the poem's meaning clearer. Pauses may not (and should not) occur at every dash.

Critical Viewing

Interpret Students may explain that the frog is proud and boastful as he holds his head high and makes loud croaking noises so that others will notice how important he is.

I'm Nobody

Emily Dickinson

I'm Nobody! Who are you?
Are you—Nobody—Too?
Then there's a pair of us!

Don't tell! they'd banish us—you know!
5   How dreary—to be—Somebody!
How public—like a Frog—
To tell one's name—the livelong June—
To an admiring Bog!

smiling and looking fabulous. "I'm Nobody" makes us think about whether fame is really so important.

First, Dickinson makes being "nobody" seem fun. The speaker proudly says "I'm Nobody" in the very first line. She sounds excited when she discovers that the reader also might be "Nobody." She shows her excitement in the line "Then there's a pair of us!" It's as if the speaker and the reader will make a secret club. Later, she uses the phrases "How dreary" and "How public" to describe being famous. Being famous is not as much fun as being "Nobody."

This poem is not only about fame. It is also about the boastful. The frog in "I'm Nobody" represents those who brag. Emily Dickinson shows us that those who boast just make a lot of noise, like a frog's croaking. They are like the frog that tells its name "the livelong June/To an admiring Bog." Boastful people try to win the compliments of others by making known their every little "amazing" feat. After a while, they may fall into despair. I like the comparison of boasters to frogs because it is clever. It makes boasters look as ridiculous as a tiny frog who makes a big noise.

"I'm Nobody" praises those who are humble and quiet. I like the poem because it helps us see clearly what we already know: If you are truly friends with someone, it doesn't matter how important you are. The two of you will have a good time just being "nobodies."

Jade tells us what she likes about the poem, using the word clever *and, later, the phrase* helps us see clearly *as precise, evaluative terms.*

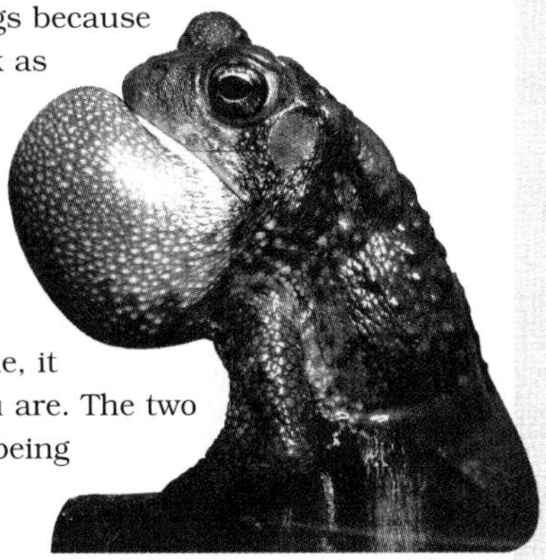

◄ **Critical Viewing** Using details from this photograph, explain why a frog is a good image to use for a boastful, self-important person. **[Interpret]**

12.7

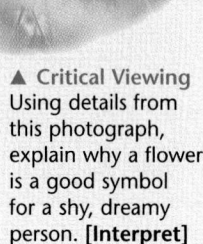

How many Flowers fail in Wood
Emily Dickinson

How many Flowers fail in Wood—
Or perish from the Hill—
Without the privilege to know
That they are Beautiful—

5   How many cast a nameless Pod
Upon the nearest Breeze—
Unconscious of the Scarlet Freight—
It bear to Other Eyes—

▲ **Critical Viewing** Using details from this photograph, explain why a flower is a good symbol for a shy, dreamy person. **[Interpret]**

Jade's response is clearly organized: First, she discusses one poem, and then she turns to the second poem.

In "How many Flowers fail in Wood," Dickinson describes "nobodies"; but here, it is the bad part of being a "nobody." Dickinson uses a flower to make her point. She wonders how many flowers die "Without the privilege to know/That they are Beautiful." She means that they never realize that others appreciate their beauty. She also says that many flowers may "cast a nameless Pod/Upon the nearest Breeze." This means that they spread their seeds without even thinking. Others may see the beauty of the seeds, but the flowers don't know it. They are "Unconscious." The flowers don't even realize that others see them.

Jade explains why the poem makes her sad by weaving together supporting details with her main points.

I thought the picture of these flowers was sad. Imagine never hearing anyone praise you. You might not be unhappy, but you would miss out on something enjoyable. Part of the beauty of life lies in interacting with the people around you. If you are too quiet, you end up missing out.

Jade concludes with a strong point, summing up the themes of the two poems to draw a lesson about life.

In these two poems, Emily Dickinson compares people's personalities to natural things. These things are a frog and a flower. The frog is a boaster, but the flower is all alone. Although boasting is not a good way to be with others, the opposite extreme, being meek and not calling attention to yourself, is almost just as bad. Instead, you should aim to strike a balance in your life between these two extremes. You should try to be good friends with someone instead of trying to impress people or ignoring them.

Connected Assignment *Movie Review*

Like a response to literature, a movie review starts with a basic response—did you enjoy the work?—and then explains the reasons for the response. A movie review features

- reactions to and an evaluation of the movie.
- details from the movie used to support your opinions.
- descriptions of and facts about the movie.

Prewriting Choose a movie that has left a lasting impression on you, and view it again. Record your general opinion of the movie in a Topic Web like the one on this page. Then, use the web to begin collecting details to explain your reaction. Include notes about the acting, lighting, pacing, music, use of camera techniques, and special effects, as well as notes on action and dialogue.

Drafting Before drafting, read a few movie reviews in a magazine or newspaper. (Avoid reviews of the movie you are reviewing.) Notice which aspects of a film they focus on, their language, and the support they give to their opinions.

Then, write the introduction to your own piece. Craft it to engage a viewer. Your introduction should include a statement of your general opinion of the film.

In the body of your review, develop your opinion of the movie. Provide examples that explain your reactions and opinions. As you develop your opinions, provide a summary of the movie and identify the actors. Conclude with a recommendation.

Revising and Editing Review your draft. If necessary, add information about the plot and the characters to help readers follow your points. Replace vague words, such as *entertaining* or *bad*, with forceful ones, such as *captivating* or *tedious*.

Publishing and Presenting After revising your movie review, submit it to a school or local newspaper. Compare your review to professionally written reviews of the same movie.

▲ **Critical Viewing**
Describe the reaction of one of these moviegoers. Then, write the introductory sentence of the review that this person might write of the movie.
[Speculate]

Movie: *Revenge of the Slime Mold*

Main Opinion: *Great special effects, but completely unbelievable plot, acting, and dialogue*

| **Special Effect:** The slime mold is frightening. It heaves, glistens, ripples, and bubbles as it moves. | **Plot:** The slime mold is defeated because it is allergic to the hero's brand of chewing gum. Come on! | **Acting:** Brent Wills thinks that frowning a little shows deep emotion. | **Dialogue:** "Dr. Quvark, for you that creature is just another science project run amok. For me, it's personal." |

▶ **Lesson Objectives**

1. To write a movie review appropriate to audience and purpose.
2. To produce cohesive and coherent written texts by organizing ideas, using effective transitions, and choosing precise wording.
3. To revise drafts for coherence, progression, and logical support of ideas.
4. To publish a movie review to an audience.

Step-by-Step Teaching Guide

Movie Review

Teaching Resources: Writing Support Transparency 12-I; Writing Support Activity Book 12-4

1. Supply students with several sample movie reviews. Choose films appropriate for students' age and maturity. Invite students to share knowledge of films if this is helpful. Discuss the sample reviews, highlighting elements.
2. Suggest that students review strategies from Chapter 12.
3. Display the transparency and model its use as students supply information from one of the films discussed in Step 1 or another they know well.
4. Give students copies of the blank organizer. Encourage them to use a pencil as they complete it, in order to make additions or corrections. They can also add cells if they need more space.
5. Help students identify the appropriate submissions editor at a local or school newspaper. Guide their efforts to organize a submission package.

Critical Viewing

Speculate Students' responses will vary.

Lesson Objectives

1. To compare and contrast visual media with written story.

2. To use media to compare ideas and points of view.

3. To interpret the various ways visual image makers represent meanings.

4. To write song lyrics.

Comparing Art With a Written Story

1. Choose one of the Spotlight elements for class discussion, or have students work individually, or in groups on the element of their choice. Give students the initiative to find the necessary art and literature books.

2. Interested students may want to view additional paintings by Matisse or others in the Fauves school. Suggest on-line museums and Web sites offering both information and images. Ask students to rate the sites they visit.

3. Select and then invite volunteers to read aloud a brief portion of *Metamorphoses.* Work together to paraphrase Ovid's views about the Icarus myth.

4. Discuss the story of Daedalus and Icarus. Ask students what lesson they feel the story teaches. Urge them to state that lesson in one or two sentences before attempting to complete the Writing Activity.

Critical Viewing

Interpret Students' responses will vary. Make sure they support their answers with details from the work.

Spotlight on the Humanities

Comparing Art With a Written Story

Focus on Art: Henri Matisse

Some people respond to a good story by telling their friends about it. Others respond by creating a new work of art. French painter Henri Matisse (1869–1954) responded to the myth of Icarus by creating the work in paper shown on this page, *Icarus.* Matisse's response to this classic myth is a work famous in its own right.

Considered one of the preeminent painters of the twentieth century, Matisse unleashed bright, untamed colors on his canvasses. His wild use of color earned him the name "King of the Fauves." (*Fauve* means "wild beast," and the Fauves were painters who used violent combinations of color.) After 1941, when he could no longer paint, Matisse continued to create by carving colored paper into various shapes and pasting them together in works like *Icarus.*

In the Greek myth to which Matisse responded, Icarus and his father, the inventor Daedalus, are held prisoner by King Minos of Crete. To escape, Daedalus builds two pairs of wings from wax and feathers. Despite Daedalus' warnings, Icarus flies too close to the sun. The sun melts the wax in his wings, and he falls into the sea. For Matisse and others, this flight and Icarus' end are rich symbols for human ambition and its limits.

Literature Connection The Roman poet Ovid (43 B.C.– A.D. 17) tells the story of Icarus in his greatest work, the *Metamorphoses,* a long poem retelling various Greek myths. Ovid was the first important writer to grow up in the Roman Empire. During the Middle Ages, people studied Ovid's writing for historical information. Many myths came to us through his work.

Response to Literature Writing Activity: Song Lyrics Based on the Myth of Icarus

The portrayal of Icarus in story may be different from Matisse's depiction. Read a version of the myth. Then, compare Matisse's Icarus with the Icarus in the story. (Pay special attention to the pose of Matisse's Icarus.) Write lyrics in which you contrast these two views of Icarus and present your own view.

Icarus, plate 8 of the 'Jazz' series, 1943, Henri Matisse, Arts Council Collection, Hayward Gallery, London, UK

▲ **Critical Viewing** Explain what Icarus' pose in Matisse's work tells you about his flight: Is he a helpless victim or a daring flyer? **[Interpret]**

Media and Technology Skills

Interpreting Literature in a Variety of Media

Activity: Creating a Multimedia Interpretation

Writing an essay or letter is only one way in which to respond to literature. You can also respond to a literary work by presenting it to others—and you can enhance your presentation by using a variety of media. When you create a multimedia presentation, you are actually creating an interpretation of the work—emphasizing the elements you find significant in it.

Learn About It

Learn How to Use Equipment As you plan your presentation, familiarize yourself with the equipment you will use—tape recorders, slide projectors, computer presentation software, and so on. Read the manuals, and ask questions of experienced users.

Use Audio Elements The center of your presentation is your reading of the work. Practice reading your chosen piece slowly and with expression. Incorporate other audio effects into your presentation as well. Choose a piece of music appropriate to the mood of the work. Working with a partner, or using a tape recorder that allows overdubbing, arrange for the right music to come in at the right spots in your reading. Consider adding other sound effects, too. (You may tape your reading along with your "soundtrack," or you may practice synchronizing it with your live reading.)

Use Visual Elements You can add to the words of the work by including visuals in your presentation. You might run a slide show as you read the work. You might videotape others acting out scenes and show the tape as you read. Make sure that the slide show or video is synchronized with your reading.

Apply It Choose a work of literature, and then plan a multimedia presentation of it using a storyboard organizer like this one. Follow your storyboard as you create your presentation.

Effects
Audio
Visual
Text

Scene 1   Scene 2   Scene 3

Tips for Creating a Multimedia Interpretation

- Choose a piece of literature you enjoy and know well. It is easier to read such a work effectively.
- If you use background music, make sure that it is not so loud that it drowns out your reading.
- If you use background visuals, make sure the images do not distract listeners from your reading. If you use complex or provocative images, introduce a few slight pauses in your reading to give listeners time to absorb what they are seeing and hearing.

▶ Lesson Objectives

1. To select, organize, and produce visuals to complement meaning.
2. To produce communications using technology and appropriate media.
3. To assess how language, medium, and presentation contribute to the message.
4. To present dramatic interpretations of literary works.

Step-by-Step Teaching Guide

Interpreting Literature in a Variety of Media

Teaching Resources: Writing Support Transparency 12-J; Writing Support Activity Book 12-5

1. Discuss the tips for creating a multimedia presentation.
2. Invite volunteers to discuss their experiences creating multimedia presentations, especially if they used the techniques discussed on this page. What worked? What didn't work?
3. If possible, bring in some of the equipment students will use and allow students to become familiar with it. Pair or group students of mixed techno-literacy to facilitate peer instruction.
4. Display the transparency and discuss its use with students. Urge students to plan their presentation on the organizer, noting how long each segment will take and what media it will contain.
5. Provide copies of the blank organizer and have students complete it as they develop their presentations. Invite pairs to review each other's storyboards for revisions prior to creating the actual presentations.

Customize for
Kinesthetic Learners

Encourage students to incorporate physical gesture and movement into their reading. Invite them to walk through the storyboard plan as they develop it, practicing their gestures and physically moving around in the performance area to activate equipment, point out visual elements, or engage audience participation.

1. To select and use voice and style appropriate to audience and purpose.

2. To use prewriting strategies to generate writing ideas and plans.

3. To use writing process strategies to revise and edit drafts.

4. To employ standard English usage in writing for audiences.

Step-by-Step Teaching Guide

Responding to Literature-Based Writing Prompts

Teaching Resources: Standardized Test Preparation Workbook, pp. 23–24

1. Remind students to focus on the specific audience and purpose outlined in the test prompt. In Literature-Based Prompts, especially, the audience may not be familiar with the text.

2. Urge students to follow the suggested time divisions until they have practiced enough to modify these for their own best pacing. It may seem risky to spend one quarter of the time planning, but a well-made plan is critical in timed writing situations.

3. Stress the importance of following the indicated format. When asked to write a letter, for example, students should follow letter writing conventions. Test examiners will respond not only to the content but to the student's knowledge and execution of standard English usages.

4. Review the hexagon from p. 256 with students and discuss its use. Point out to students that they may prewrite in whatever fashion is most effective for them. Their prewriting efforts will not be rated.

5. Provide timed writing practice at regular intervals. Begin by asking students to write about familiar and comfortable topics in order to focus on the process more than the content. Over time, move toward more challenging topics.

Standardized Test Preparation Workshop

Responding to Literature-Based Writing Prompts

Some standardized test questions evaluate your ability to respond to literature. Your response to this type of prompt will be evaluated on how well it shows your ability to

- respond directly to a prompt.

- organize ideas in a clear fashion.

- successfully apply concepts such as plot, setting, character, speaker, theme, mood, point of view, and figurative language.

- develop and support ideas thoroughly, using appropriate details and precise language.

- use correct spelling, capitalization, punctuation, and grammar.

The following is one type of literature-based writing prompt found on standardized tests. Although you will need to find in a literature anthology the poems suggested for this prompt, most tests will provide the literature to which you will respond. Respond to the prompt, using the suggestions on the following page. The clocks show the suggested percentage of your test-taking time to devote to each stage of the writing process.

Sample Writing Situation

Read the poems "Primer Lesson" and "Fog," both by Carl Sandburg. Then, respond to the following prompt:

In a letter to the poet, compare his use of figurative language in the two poems. In what way is the use of figurative language in the poems similar? In what way is it different? Then, explain which poem uses figurative language more effectively. Use details from the poems to support your response.

✐ TEST-TAKING TIP

Tell students that preparedness will help them overcome test-taking jitters. Encourage them to develop test-taking packets, including supplies such as a watch, pencils, erasers, and scrap paper. They might also include tissues and cough lozenges if these are permitted. Suggest that all prewriting work be completed on scrap paper and that organizers or lists be completed in pencil to allow for additions and changes.

Customize for
ESL Students

Review the difference between summarizing and responding to literature, providing or having students provide examples of each form. Tell students that they can improve their test-taking results with careful attention to required audience, purpose, and format. Review each of these elements for the sample prompt.

Customize for
More Advanced Students

Challenge students to develop their own test-taking time clock. They might practice with several different writing assignments. How much time do they need for each stage? Does this time requirement vary with the type of prompt? Have students prepare time guides to add to their test-taking packets.

Prewriting

Allow close to one fourth of your time for prewriting.

Use a Hexagon Read the two Sandburg poems twice. Then, gather details for your response. For each poem, you might sketch a hexagon like the one shown on page 256 and record details in it. Next, review the prompt. Circle items in your notes concerning the literary concept referred to: the author's use of figurative language. (If you cannot find such details, review the poems and take further notes on figurative language.)

Consider Your Audience Your audience, the poet, is named in the response. Because he presumably knows the poems and himself, do not include background information about the poem or its author in your response. Since you are writing to a respected person to whom you have not been introduced, use formal language and avoid slang or clichés.

Drafting

Allow almost half of your time for drafting.

Focus Your Response Review your prewriting notes. Then, write a sentence explaining which poem uses figurative language more effectively. Include this thesis statement in your introduction. To evaluate the poems, consider the following criteria for effective figurative language: It sums up an aspect of life as it creates an easily visualized image or while it catches the ear with the musical use of words.

Organize Details Make an outline listing main points followed by supporting details. Consider using the block method of organization, grouping details about each poem separately.

Elaborate As you draft your response, keep your audience (the poet) clearly in mind. For each point you make, refer to the poem directly, including direct quotations where suitable.

Revising, Editing, and Proofreading

Allow almost one fourth of your time for revising and editing. Use the last few minutes to proofread your work.

Strengthen Support After drafting, review your response. Eliminate details that do not support your focus. Identify points needing more support, and, referring to the poems, add supporting details. Leave a few minutes to proofread your work.

Make Corrections Check for errors in spelling, grammar, and punctuation. When making changes, draw a line through text that you want eliminated. Use a caret (^) to indicate places where you would like to add words.

Time and Resource Manager

In-Depth Lesson Plan

	LESSON FOCUS	PRINT AND MEDIA RESOURCES
DAY 1	**Introduction to Writing for Assessment** Students learn key elements of writing for assessment (pp. 274–275).	*Language Lab* **CD-ROM,** Building Paragraphs
DAY 2	**Prewriting** Students choose and narrow a topic, consider their audience and purpose, and gather information (pp. 276–278).	**Teaching Resources** *Writing Support Transparencies* 13-A–B; *Writing Support Activity Book* 13-1–2 *Language Lab* **CD-ROM,** Building Paragraphs
DAY 3	**Drafting** Students organize their ideas and write their first drafts (pp. 279–280).	**Teaching Resources** *Writing Support Transparency* 13–C *Language Lab* **CD-ROM,** Building Paragraphs
DAY 4	**Revising** Students revise their drafts in terms of overall structure, paragraphs, sentences, and word choice (pp. 281–282).	*Language Lab* **CD-ROM,** Building Paragraphs *Writing Lab* **CD-ROM,** Writer's Toolkit
DAY 5	**Editing and Proofreading; Publishing and Presenting** Students check their work for accuracy and correctness and present their final drafts (pp. 283–284).	**Teaching Resources** *Scoring Rubrics on Transparency,* Chapter 13; Formal Assessment, Ch. 13 *Writing Lab* **CD-ROM,** Writer's Toolkit

Accelerated Lesson Plan

	LESSON FOCUS	PRINT AND MEDIA RESOURCES
DAY 1	**Introduction Through Drafting** Students review characteristics for writing for assessment, select topics, and write drafts (pp. 274–280).	**Teaching Resources** *Writing Support Transparencies* 13-A–C *Language Lab* **CD-ROM,** Building Paragraphs
DAY 2	**Revising to Presenting** Students work individually or with peers to revise, edit, and proofread their work for presentation (pp. 281–284).	**Teaching Resources** *Scoring Rubrics on Transparency,* Chapter 13; Formal Assessment, Ch. 13 *Writing Lab* **CD-ROM,** Writer's Toolkit

Options for Adapting Lesson Plans

HOMEWORK

Have students complete any stage of the lesson for homework.

TECHNOLOGY

Students can complete any stage of the lesson on computer. Have them print out their completed work.

FEATURES

Extend coverage with Connected Assignment (p. 287), Spotlight on the Humanities (p. 288), Media and Technology Skills (p. 289), and the Standardized Test Preparation Workshop (p. 290).

INTEGRATED SKILLS COVERAGE

Integrating Grammar
Using Complete, Correct Sentences, SE p. 283

Technology
Using Technology to Support Learning, SE p. 289

Viewing and Representing
Critical Viewing, SE pp. 274, 275, 277, 279, 281, 285, 286, 287, 288

Comparing and Contrasting Print and Visual Media, SE p. 288

Real-World Connection
ATE p. 278

BLOCK SCHEDULING

Pacing Suggestions
For 90-minute Blocks
- Have students complete the Prewriting and Drafting stages in a single period.
- Focus one class period on Revising and Editing and Publishing and Presenting. Allow at least 30 minutes for peer revision.

Resources for Varying Instruction
- *Writing Lab* **CD-ROM** If your students have access to hardware, a 90-minute block provides an ideal opportunity for students to work on computer.

Professional Development Support
- *How to Manage Instruction in the Block* This Teaching Resource provides management and activity suggestions.

ASSESSMENT SUPPORT

Standardized Test Preparation SE p. 290; ATE p. 282

Standardized Test Preparation Workshop pp. 25–26

Scoring Rubrics on Transparency, Ch. 13

Formal Assessment, Ch. 13

Writing Assessment and Portfolio Management

MEDIA AND TECHNOLOGY

For the Student
- *Writing Lab* **CD-ROM,** Writer's Toolkit

For the Teacher
- *Resource Pro* **CD-ROM**

MEETING INDIVIDUAL NEEDS

Less Advanced Students ATE pp. 276, 291. See also Ongoing Assessments, ATE pp. 277, 280.

More Advanced Students ATE p. 283, 291

ESL Students ATE p. 277

Logical/Mathematical Learners ATE p. 289

Ongoing Assessments ATE pp. 275, 277, 280, 284

WRITING AND GRAMMAR WEB SITE

The Interactive Writing and Grammar Web site provides a wide array of support for students, teachers, and parents. Writing support includes:

- Interactive revision checkers
- Scoring rubrics with complete models

www.phschool.com

LITERATURE CONNECTIONS

Related selection from *Prentice Hall Literature: Timeless Voices, Timeless Themes,* Bronze:
From *The Taming of the Shrew,* William Shakespeare, SE p. 288.

▶ **Lesson Objectives**

1. To define writing for assessment.
2. To understand that persuasive, expository, comparison-and-contrast, and cause-and-effect writing are all part of writing for assessment.
3. To understand the following prewriting techniques: choosing and narrowing a topic, identifying purpose in writing, and gathering details.
4. To understand the following drafting techniques: finding a focus, planning organization, and providing elaboration.
5. To demonstrate the following revising techniques: checking introduction and conclusion; identifying main ideas and details; circling topic sentences; adding transitions; choosing precise and vivid words; and show, don't tell.
6. To demonstrate good editing and proofreading skills focusing on complete sentences.

Critical Viewing

Apply Students may mention that they should remember to stay focused, keep track of time, and so on.

Chapter 13 Writing for Assessment

Assessment in School

Writing is not just something you do in English class. Throughout your years in school, you will take essay tests in many subjects, including social studies, science, health, and even math. You may also take standardized writing tests that compare your writing skills with those of students across the state or nation.

The writing you do on these tests is called writing for assessment, and it requires special skills you can learn and practice ahead of time. This chapter will show you how to do your best work when you are writing for assessment.

▲ **Critical Viewing**
What advice might you give this student to help her prepare for writing tests? **[Apply]**

274 • Writing for Assessment

⏱ **TIME AND RESOURCE MANAGER**	
Resources **Technology:** Language Lab CD-ROM, Building Paragraphs	
In-Depth Coverage	**Accelerated Pace**
• Cover pp. 274–275 in class. • Discuss different types of writing for assessment.	• Have students read pp. 274–275 on their own. • Discuss definitions and types of writing for assessment.

What Is Writing for Assessment?

The word *assessment* means "measurement" or "evaluation." **Writing for assessment** is used to measure how much you have learned about a subject or to evaluate the development of your writing skills. Assessment may involve

- specific instructions about what to write, called the *writing prompt.*
- limited time in which to write.
- limited space in which to write.
- no use of textbooks, dictionaries, or other references.

To learn the criteria on which your writing for assessment may be judged, see the Rubric for Self-Assessment on page 284.

Types of Writing for Assessment

Writing prompts may call for the following kinds of writing:

- **Persuasive writing** requires you to support an opinion or position using persuasive language.
- **Expository writing** requires you to give information in a clear and well-organized fashion. It includes

    Comparison-and-contrast writing, which requires you to compare aspects of two or more subjects in an organized way.

    Cause-and-effect writing, which requires you to explain a process or series of events.

▲ Critical Viewing
This painting suggests that a clock helps us control the power of time, just as a steam engine uses the power of fire. How might keeping track of time during a test help you succeed on it? **[Interpret]**

PREVIEW
Student Work
IN PROGRESS

In this chapter, you'll follow the work of Brittany Wilson, a student at Stuart Middle School in Louisville, Kentucky, as she answers an essay question on a science test. You'll see the featured activities and strategies she uses to gather and organize details and draft her response. You can read her completed essay at the end of the chapter.

Writing for Assessment • 275

 **Interest GRABBER** Ask students to give a few reasons why someone might *like* taking tests. Elicit that tests do more than just make you worry about making mistakes or doing badly. They are also an opportunity to show what students have learned and to express themselves. Discuss what they can do to approach it more positively.

Activate Prior Knowledge

Ask students to remember an essay test or particular question they did well on. Discuss what they did to answer the question well. Elicit that it took more than knowing the material. They needed to be able to organize their ideas and express them clearly.

Critical Viewing

Interpret Students may say that keeping track of time assures you that you will have plenty of time to complete each step of the writing process.

☑ ONGOING ASSESSMENT: Diagnose

Use one of the following options to diagnose students' current level of proficiency in persuasive writing.

Option 1 Ask students to select the strongest example of his or her persuasive writing from last year. Hold conferences in which you review each students' sample. Use the conferences to determine which students will need extra support in developing a persuasive essay.

Option 2 Ask students to write a sentence persuading a friend to begin a program of physical fitness. Then have them list three reasons or items of evidence that support that sentence. If students have difficulty completing this exercise, you will need to devote more time to gathering evidence and elaboration of the process.

Prewriting: Choosing Your Topic

1. Time management is one of the most important strategies students should learn for test-taking situations. Talk with students about test panic. Discuss how the very nature of panic deprives them of the tools they need to make good decisions. You might want to amend the text to say the first rule is DON'T PANIC! The second rule is to keep track of the time.

2. The basis of most writing for assessment is information. In most cases, students should let their knowledge and comfort with the topics guide their choices.

3. Discuss a common error in writing for assessment—misreading, or misinterpreting the writing prompt. Remind them that skimming the writing prompts is a sure recipe for disaster. Most students should be able to remember a time when they didn't read a problem closely enough and found the perimeter of a circle when they were asked for the area. On the other hand, they should not take so long reading and puzzling over the prompts that they are rushed when they write.

Customize for
Less Advanced Students

Some students may have difficulty choosing an appropriate topic. Work with them to evaluate the topics in the Topic Bank. Then have students brainstorm for a list of possible topics. Have them go back through their lists and number the possibilities in the order in which they feel most comfortable with the topic.

Spotlight on the Humanities

For additional topic suggestions, refer students to the Spotlight on the Humanities on p. 288.

13.1 Prewriting

It is important to use your time wisely when you are writing for assessment, because your time is often limited. Before you begin, find out how much time you have to complete the test. Plan to spend about one fourth of that time on prewriting. If you have an hour for the test, for example, you can spend 15 minutes reviewing the questions and taking notes.

Choosing Your Topic

When you are taking a standardized test, you don't have to rack your brain to think of a topic: You'll be given a topic in the writing prompt. At most, you may have to choose among a few specific options.

Choosing a Writing Prompt If you do have a choice, carefully consider the topics and the types of writing required for each choice. Eliminate any question about which you do not know enough. Choose the topic that interests you most or about which you know the most.

If the writing prompt tells you who your readers will be, consider whether you feel more comfortable writing for adults or for peers, for people who are already familiar with a topic or for beginners who will need to have everything explained.

To practice writing for assessment, you might ask your teacher for a topic, or you can select from the following writing prompts:

Learn More

To learn more about studying for a test, see Chapter 31.

TOPIC BANK

1. **Explain a Process** Explain a process that you have learned about in science class, such as the circulation of blood in the human body or photosynthesis in plants.

2. **Compare and Contrast Leaders** Choose two important historical leaders. Compare and contrast their abilities and the importance of their respective contributions to history.

3. **Persuade a Historical Figure** Choose an important historical figure. Imagine that you meet this person just before he or she decides to perform one of his or her most memorable actions. Drawing on your knowledge of the person and of history, persuade the person to do or to refrain from doing the action.

276 • Writing for Assessment

⏱ TIME AND RESOURCE MANAGER

Resources
Print: Writing Support Transparencies 13-A–B; Writing Support Activity Book 13-1–2
Technology: Language Lab CD-ROM, Building Paragraphs

In-Depth Coverage	Accelerated Pace
• Cover pp. 276–278 in class. • Work through the strategies for choosing and narrowing a topic and gathering details. • Review the student example in the textbook, pointing out the application of prewriting techniques.	• Discuss strategies for generating topics. • Have students work independently to choose and narrow their topics. • Have students work with partners to focus on audience, purpose, and gathering details.

Narrowing Your Topic

When you are writing for a test, your possible topics are set for you. You still need to "narrow" the topic you choose by focusing on exactly what the prompt asks you to do.

Identify the Topic and Purpose

Before you start writing, read the prompt you have chosen carefully and identify each of the following:

- **The topic** is the subject about which you must write. Make sure that you consider all information given about the topic. For instance, an essay explaining why pioneers traveled west is different from an essay explaining what kinds of people became pioneers who traveled west. You may also need to choose among several subtopics. List them, and then choose the one about which you know the most.

- **Your purpose in writing** is identified by key words in the prompt. These words determine what information you should include and how you should organize it.

Key Words	What You Will Do
explain	give a clear, complete account of how something works or why something happened
compare and contrast	provide details about how two or more things are alike and how they are different
argue, convince, persuade	take a position on an issue and present strong reasons to support your side of the issue
summarize	tell the main events, points, or ideas of a topic and briefly describe the relationship between them
classify	organize information into categories based on important similarities and differences

Circle Key Words Study the chart above. Write out the prompt to which you are responding. Circle the key words. Then, find the interpretation of each key word in the chart. Next to the prompt, jot down the kind of information you will need to include in your answer.

You may discover that you were mistaken about the topic or the purpose for writing that was assigned by the prompt. If so, you may wish to choose another prompt.

▲ **Critical Viewing**
If the purpose of your writing is to inform this swimmer about a special swimming stroke, explain what information you would supply. **[Apply]**

Prewriting • 277

Step-by-Step Teaching Guide

Prewriting: Narrowing Your Topic

Teaching Resources: Writing Support Transparency 13-A

1. Remind students again of the importance of reading the writing prompts carefully. They need to read both for *content* and *direction.*

2. The direction is given by the key words shown on the chart. Review each of the key words. Tell students that understanding and following the directions of the key words is paramount. A brilliant description of a topic loses points if an explanation is called for.

3. Discuss the importance of considering both the topic and the key word in choosing a prompt. For instance: You may be very knowledgeable about western pioneers, but the prompt may prove difficult when you are asked to compare western pioneers with European immigrants, a topic about which you are less knowledgeable.

Customize for
ESL Students

Key words are worth spending some time on so that students have a complete understanding of them and how they differ. Tell students that these words will show up in almost every test-taking situation. Work with them individually or in small groups to assure their understanding of them.

Critical Viewing

Apply Students' responses might include arm and leg positions, breathing techniques, and so on.

☑ **ONGOING ASSESSMENT: Monitor and Reinforce**

If students have difficulty understanding how their writing can have more than one purpose, try the following option.

Give students possible situations in which they might write with more than one purpose, such as explaining why something happened in order to persuade someone. Work with them to think of other situations and to identify the purposes for writing.

Prewriting: Gathering Details

Teaching Resources: Writing Support Transparency 13-B; Writing Support Activity Book 13-1

1. Remind students that they need details, or facts, to answer a question. Broad generalizations will not answer the question if the key word is *explain* or *argue*.

2. Display the transparency. Review Brittany's topic web with students, pointing out how the details are already revealing the skeleton of an essay. Obviously Brittany knows enough about air pollution to write her essay, so she can stop her web here. She could also go on to web water and land pollution, to see if they spark more ideas. Again, she should not spend all day writing everything she knows about all three kinds of pollution. As soon as students find a topic that works, they should begin writing.

3. Give students copies of the blank organizer and have them gather details for their responses to their prompts.

Real-World Connection

Emphasize that students use the key words every day in their lives. They *explain* why they didn't clean their room. They *compare and contrast* last week's basketball game with this week's. They *describe* to a friend a new movie. They *argue* with parents, try to *convince* them to get a dog, or *persuade* them to let them stay out later.

13.1

Gathering Details

Now that you understand your topic and purpose, you can begin gathering details. The way in which you gather details will depend on your purpose in writing.

If a prompt asks you to create a piece of persuasive writing:

• Start by taking a position to defend.

• Then, list reasons that support your view.

If the prompt asks you to create a piece of informative writing:

• Begin by listing the main ideas.

• Then, list supporting details you would like to include.

When gathering details for a piece of informative writing, you might use a Topic Web such as the one below.

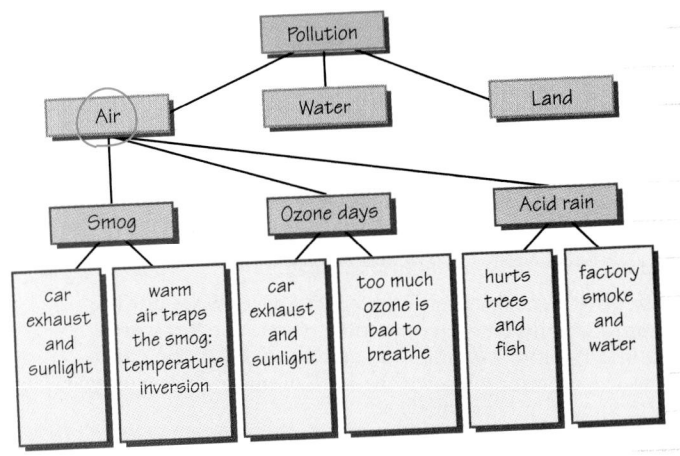

Student Work
IN PROGRESS

Name: *Brittany Wilson*
Stuart Middle School
Louisville, KY

Using a Topic Web to Gather Details

Brittany chose the following prompt: "Choose one form of pollution. Describe three of its effects and some possible solutions." She listed different forms of pollution in a Topic Web, chose one, and then gathered details about her topic.

13.2 Drafting

Allow about half of your testing time for drafting. If you have an hour for the test, for example, spend about half an hour writing your draft.

Shaping Your Writing

On a test, it's very important for your writing to have a clear direction and to be logically organized. Once you have gathered details, you're ready to organize your ideas.

Find a Focus

Any effective piece of writing, however short or simple, must have a guiding focus. Review the prompt you have chosen and the details you have gathered. Then, formulate the main idea of your response in a sentence. For instance, the prompt might ask you to support an idea for a school club. Your focus statement might read, "A book club will encourage reading."

Begin your draft with an introduction that includes your focus statement. Use an interesting image or fact to draw your reader in.

Plan Your Organization

Because your time is limited, choose a clear, simple method of organization. Here are some ideas for organizing an essay for assessment, depending on the prompt to which you respond:

- **Persuasive Writing Prompt** If the prompt asks you to persuade people about an issue, use an outline to organize your reasons, or simply number your ideas from least to most important.

- **Cause-and-Effect or How-to Writing Prompt** If the prompt asks you to explain a sequence of steps or events, you should organize your ideas in chronological order. Making a timeline is a quick way to do this.

- **Comparison-and-Contrast Writing Prompt** If the prompt asks you to compare two items, organize your ideas using either the block or the point-by-point method. To use the block method, make an outline grouping all details about one item, followed by all details about the other. To use the point-by-point method, make an outline that groups details about one aspect of both items, followed by details about another aspect, and so on.

▼ Critical Viewing
Draw a simple time-line charting the series of events suggested by this photo. [Infer]

Drafting • 279

Drafting: Shaping Your Writing

1. Drafting is the core activity in writing for assessment. It is also a place where students can lose time by trying to write the whole essay at once. At each different task they need to stay focused and keep from panicking.

2. Finding a guiding focus or thesis statement will guide the entire drafting process. Students should recognize the focus as their main idea—what the essay is mostly about—and state it in a single sentence.

3. Review each of the organization methods. Remind students that they have recently studied each of these types of writing and the techniques presented. Discuss why the outline method is best suited to the writing prompt.

4. Remind students of the importance of managing their time during the drafting process. Tell them that finding a focus statement quickly is important for time management. They can't write until they know what they are writing about.

Critical Viewing

Infer Students' charts may include the designer's drafting blueprints, material being purchased then delivered, construction work, and even a completed house at the end of the charts.

⏱ TIME AND RESOURCE MANAGER

Resources
Print: Writing Support Transparency 13-B
Technology: Writing Lab CD–ROM, Writer's Toolkit

In-Depth Coverage	Accelerated Pace
• Cover pp. 279–280 in class. • Work through finding a focus, planning, organization, and providing elaboration with students. • Have students write their draft in class. • Demonstrate the technique of providing elaboration using the transparency.	• Have students review pp. 279–280 independently, then write their first writing for assessment draft. • Respond to individual drafting issues as needed.

Drafting: Providing Elaboration

Teaching Resources: Writing Support Transparency 13-C

1. Main ideas need supporting details. Display the transparency. Go over Brittany's outline with students. Ask students which items are main ideas and which are supporting details. (One main idea is that a major cause of air pollution is the use of fossil fuels. Items 1 and 2 are details, examples of using the fossil fuels gas and coal, and so on.)

2. Use Brittany's outline to investigate facts, descriptions, and examples. A fact is that gas and coal are fossil fuels, fuels made from the decomposed remains of once-living things. A description could be how Los Angeles looks on a typical smoggy day. An example might be how an asthma sufferer feels on one of those days.

3. A good essay must include all these elements for balance and interest. An essay that contains only facts is boring. An essay that contains only examples is unconvincing.

13.2

Providing Elaboration

After organizing your ideas, study your timeline or outline. Find places where you can add details to strengthen your writing. Supporting details include the following:

- **Facts** If you are explaining a sequence of events or steps, provide facts showing why or how one event links to another. If you are writing to persuade, prove your points with evidence.

- **Descriptions** If you are comparing things, you need to describe them thoroughly. If you want to persuade, describe situations and ideas in positive or negative ways, in order to help your reader see your point of view.

- **Examples** To help readers grasp your meaning, give examples illustrating any general points you make.

Note supporting details on your outline or timeline in capital letters. As you draft, follow your organizer, and include supporting details.

Student Work IN PROGRESS

Name: *Brittany Wilson*
Stuart Middle School
Louisville, KY

Adding Supporting Details to an Outline

Brittany added supporting details about air pollution to her sentence outline, part of which is shown below.

Topic: Air Pollution

What are the major causes?
  – Use of fossil fuels
      1. Cars burning gas
      2. Factories burning coal

"FOSSIL FUEL" IS MADE OF THE BODIES OF ANCIENT ANIMALS.

BURNING FOSSIL FUELS MAKES CARBON MONOXIDE.

What are three effects?
  – Smog
      1. Cause: sunlight and car exhaust
      2. Warm air traps the smog (temperature inversion)
  – Ozone action days
      1. Cause: sunlight and car exhaust
      2. Too much ozone makes it hard to breathe
  – Acid rain . . .

OZONE IS A SPECIAL FORM OF OXYGEN.

WE NEED OZONE HIGH IN THE ATMOSPHERE.

280 • Writing for Assessment

☑ ONGOING ASSESSMENT: Monitor and Reinforce

Students sometimes have problems recognizing the strengths and weaknesses of their evidence. If you find this is the case with your students, try the following strategy.

Have students work in pairs. Each student writes down his or her supporting points on note cards or self-sticking notes and asks the other student to place them in order of strongest to weakest.

Students can then discuss the effectiveness of their arrangements of supporting points before continuing to draft.

13.3 Revising

Plan to spend approximately one fourth of your testing time on revising your work. Decide whether you will have time to copy a clean final draft or whether you need to make changes neatly on your first draft. On a school test, you may not have the time or the space to make a clean final draft. Some standardized tests, however, give you blank pages on which to draft and lined pages on which to copy your final work.

Revising Your Overall Structure

The teachers who evaluate your writing on a standardized test will look for a logically organized piece of writing that clearly follows the directions in the writing prompt.

▶ **REVISION STRATEGY**
Checking Your Introduction and Conclusion

Before you begin revising, read the writing prompt again. Then, read the first paragraph of your piece. Your introduction should

- clearly state what your draft explains or argues.
- accurately reflect the instructions in the writing prompt.
- capture interest with a fact, a question, or an example.

Now, look at your final paragraph. Your conclusion should

- restate what you have explained or argued in your draft.
- present a final thought about the subject or a call to action.

Revising Your Paragraphs

Identify Main Ideas and Supporting Details

When evaluating writing, teachers look closely at each paragraph. They expect to find a clear, well-expressed main idea supported by relevant details.

▶ **REVISION STRATEGY**
Checking Support

For each paragraph, identify the main idea, often stated in the topic sentence. If a paragraph does not have a topic sentence, it is best on a test to add one for clarity.

Then, check the details in each paragraph. Neatly cross out sentences that do not support the main idea. Consider replacing them with sentences offering more effective support.

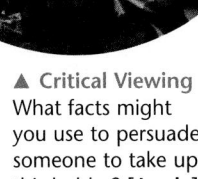

▲ Critical Viewing
What facts might you use to persuade someone to take up this hobby? **[Apply]**

Language Lab CD-ROM

For practice in identifying topic sentences, complete the Main Idea and Topic Sentence lesson in the Building Paragraphs unit.

Revising: Revising Your Overall Structure and Your Paragraphs

1. Explain to students that in test-taking situations, there may not be time to make a clean copy. It is a good idea to double-space the draft, so there is room to make legible changes.

2. Remind students of the importance of a strong introduction. All the items on the checklist are essential. If anything is missing, a revision is in order. The conclusion also needs to restate the thesis statement and end strongly.

3. Tell students to find the topic sentence in each paragraph and the details, examples, or facts that support the topic sentence. The topic sentence does not always need to appear in the first sentence of the paragraph, but it needs to be somewhere.

4. After circling their topic sentences, tell students to skim their essay, reading only the topic sentences. Though the style will not be smooth, a reader should be able to get the gist of the essay from just those sentences.

Critical Viewing

Apply Students may say that playing music can be very relaxing and fulfilling.

⏲ **TIME AND RESOURCE MANAGER**

Resources
Technology: Writing Lab CD-ROM, Writer's Toolkit; Language Lab CD-ROM, Building Paragraphs

In-Depth Coverage	Accelerated Pace
• Cover pp. 281–282 in class. • Work through revising strategy with the entire class.	• Assign students to review pp. 281–282 independently. • Have students revise their writing for assessment essays independently.

Revising: Revising Your Sentences

1. Have students decide how they organized their essay. For example, a compare-and-contrast essay will use words such as *alike, different, also, but, however.* Students may also have used a secondary structure, such as chronological order. If so, they can use time order transitional words too.

2. Precise and vivid descriptions add energy and information to essays. Compare *He was a big brown-and-white dog* with *He was a huge, 160-pound St. Bernard with brown and white markings.* The latter example gives detail and information and is more interesting to read.

3. Respecting the readers' intelligence means showing, not telling. Readers can draw obvious conclusions from well-described or well-argued situations. When a writer does more telling than showing, it reveals not just poor writing but also an uncertainty on the writer's part of the validity of the point being presented.

13.3

Revising Your Sentences

On a standardized writing test, teachers evaluate how well your writing hangs together—how easy it is to follow the flow of your ideas. They want to see clear relationships between one sentence and the next.

▶ REVISION STRATEGY
Adding Transitions

Reread each paragraph of your draft. Is there a clear, logical relationship between the sentences? If a sentence simply states a new idea without referring to words in the previous sentence, the relationship between the two sentences may not be clear. Consider adding a transitional word or phrase to indicate the relationship. For example, if you want to signal a cause or an effect, add transitions such as *for this reason, therefore,* or *as a result.* If you want to signal chronological order, add transitions such as *then, next, before, after,* or *finally.*

Revising Your Word Choice

Choose Precise and Vivid Words

Teachers will evaluate your writing for assessment to see whether you have a strong command of the English language. Use words that say precisely and vividly what you mean. When writing persuasively, make sure you have chosen words that will influence readers to accept your point of view.

▶ REVISION STRATEGY
"Show, Don't Tell"

Reread your draft, looking for sentences with general descriptive words, such as *good, bad, big,* and *small.* Think of the reasons you have used each word. Then, rewrite each of these sentences so that it shows why or how the general word applies.

For instance, you might write "This plan is very bad" because you know the plan will waste a lot of time. To show why the word *bad* applies, rewrite the sentence as follows: "This plan is inefficient." Consider the improvement in the following examples:

TELLING: Our current computer lab is too small. It is very old. The facilities are out of date.

SHOWING: In the computer lab, thirty students are crammed into a tiny classroom, with no space left for lab equipment. Plaster is crumbling off the walls in the hallway. The ancient wiring cannot handle the demands of a high-tech computer lab.

282 • Writing for Assessment

Writing Lab
CD-ROM

For more practice using transitions, see the Transition Word Bin in the Writer's Toolkit.

STANDARDIZED TEST PREPARATION WORKSHOP

Topic Sentences Standardized test questions may ask students to identify the topic sentence in a paragraph. Ask students to identify the topic sentence in the following paragraph.

(1) New York City has many famous sights. (2) But what makes the city such an exciting place is the people. (3) New Yorkers come from all over the country and all over the world. (4) They walk fast, talk loudly, and have opinions about everything.

A (1)   **C** (3)

B (2)   **D** (4)

The correct answer is item **B**. The first sentence has nothing to do with the information in the paragraph. The third and last sentences are details that support the idea of interesting people in New York City.

13.4 Editing and Proofreading

You may have the best ideas in the world, but evaluators can't take them seriously if you don't express yourself in complete, correctly punctuated sentences. Save a few minutes at the end of the test to proofread your work for errors in spelling, mechanics, grammar, and usage. Make sure that you have expressed yourself in complete sentences.

Focusing on Complete Sentences

Look over each sentence in your draft. Read it by itself, starting at the beginning and ending at the period. Ask:

- Does this sentence express a complete thought?
- Does it begin with a capital letter and end with a period?
- Is more than one idea squeezed into the sentence without proper punctuation—for instance, have you used a comma to join two sentences?

Correct any incomplete or run-on sentences you find, crossing out words and punctuation marks neatly with a single line, and marking insertions with a caret (^).

Grammar in Your Writing
Using Complete, Correct Sentences

Every **sentence** must express a complete thought. A fragment is a group of words, punctuated as a sentence, that does not express a complete thought. If you find any sentence fragments in your writing, correct them by adding a subject or a verb. You can also fix a sentence fragment by correctly connecting it to another sentence.

Sentence + Fragment:	We need a computer lab with enough space. And modern, up-to-date equipment, too.
Add Subject and Verb:	We need a computer lab with enough space. We also need modern, up-to-date equipment.
Combine Sentences:	We need a computer lab with enough space and with modern, up-to-date equipment.

Check to make sure that each sentence begins with a capital letter and ends with a period, question mark, or exclamation mark.

To learn more about using complete, correct sentences, see Chapter 19.

Editing and Proofreading • 283

Step-by-Step Teaching Guide

Editing and Proofreading

1. Students have already done the hard work of organizing, drafting, and revising. However, explain to them that errors will distract their readers and may even prevent them from understanding the essay.

2. Have students reread their drafts or encourage them to trade their drafts with partners. They should proofread the drafts, paying careful attention to complete sentences.

Step-by-Step Teaching Guide

Grammar in Your Writing: Using Complete, Correct Sentences

1. Write the following sentence fragments on the chalkboard and ask student to create two sentences and a combined sentence for each:

   The soccer field has holes and ruts. And little grass.

   (The soccer field has holes and ruts. It also has little grass.

   The soccer field has holes, ruts, and little grass.)

   The pizza was covered with pepperoni and mushrooms. But no anchovies.

   (The pizza was covered with pepperoni and mushrooms. It had no anchovies.

   The pizza was covered with pepperoni and mushrooms, but it had no anchovies.)

2. Point out that "expresses a complete thought" is also a key aspect of sentences. A phrase may have a verb and subject and still not express a complete thought (e.g., *unless you come, he wants*). So a sentence needs *both* to have a subject and verb *and* to express a complete thought.

Customize for
More Advanced Students

Challenge students to write a synopsis of their essay in five "sentences," but each one must be a run-on. Then they can trade papers with a partner, who rewrites the paragraph grammatically correct.

⏰ TIME AND RESOURCE MANAGER

Resources
Print: Scoring Rubrics on Transparency, Chapter 13; Writing Assessment: Scoring Rubric and Scoring Models for Writing for Assessment

In-Depth Coverage	Accelerated Pace
• Cover pp. 283–286 in class. • Review p. 283 in class, including Grammar in Your Writing. • Distribute and review Proofreading Checklist. • Review Rubric for Self-Assessment in class. • Students present their final draft.	• Assign pp. 283–286 for independent review. • Students independently edit and proofread their essays. • Respond to individual editing issues as needed.

Publishing and Presenting

1. Explain to students that reviewing previous essays can be very insightful because they will be viewing their work with fresh eyes.

2. Encourage students to reassess their strengths and weaknesses every so often to evaluate their progress.

ASSESS

Assessment

Teaching Resources: Scoring Rubrics on Transparency, 13; Formal Assessment, Chapter 13

1. Display the Scoring Rubric transparency and review the criteria in class.

2. Before students proceed with self-assessment, you may wish to review the Final Draft of the Student Work in Progress on pp. 285–286. Have students score the Final Draft in one or more of the rubric categories. For example, how would students score the essay in terms of audience and purpose?

3. In addition to student self-assessment, you may wish to use the following assessment options:

   • Score student essays yourself, using the rubric and scoring models from Writing Assessment.

   • Review the Standardized Test Preparation Workshop on pp. 290–291 and have students respond to a writing for assessment prompt within a time limit.

   • Administer the Chapter 13 Test from Formal Assessment in Teaching Resources to assess students' grasp of concepts presented.

13.5 Publishing and Presenting

Building Your Portfolio

Consider the following suggestions for publishing and presenting your work:

1. **Prepare for Future Exams** As you get ready to take other writing tests, review your essay. Recall what strategies worked for you when writing under time constraints. If you wrote on a topic covered in a particular class, study your test to refresh your memory about that topic.

2. **Organize a Class Discussion** In a group discussion, compare your responses with those of classmates. Discuss the reasons for the differences in the grades given for each. (Refer to the rubric below for ideas on what teachers look for in an essay written for assessment.)

Reflecting on Your Writing

Jot down your thoughts on writing an essay for assessment. Get started by answering these questions:

• What are your strengths and weaknesses as a test taker?

• Which strategy presented in this chapter might help you complete your next essay test?

Internet Tip

To view an essay written for assessment that has been scored according to this rubric, visit **www.phschool.com**

Rubric for Self-Assessment

Use the following criteria to evaluate the essay you have written for assessment.

	Score 4	Score 3	Score 2	Score 1
Audience and Purpose	Uses word choices and supporting details appropriate to the specified audience; clearly addresses writing prompt	Mostly uses word choices and supporting details appropriate to the specified audience; adequately addresses prompt	Uses some inappropriate word choices and details; addresses writing prompt	Uses inappropriate word choices and details; does not address writing prompt
Organization	Presents a clear, consistent organizational strategy	Presents a clear organizational strategy with few inconsistencies	Presents an inconsistent organizational strategy	Shows a lack of organizational strategy
Elaboration	Adequately supports the thesis; elaborates each idea; links all details to the thesis	Supports the thesis; elaborates most ideas; links most information to thesis	Partially supports the thesis; does not elaborate some ideas	Provides no thesis; does not elaborate ideas
Use of Language	Uses excellent sentence variety and vocabulary; includes very few mechanical errors	Uses adequate sentence variety and vocabulary; includes few mechanical errors	Uses repetitive sentence structure and vocabulary; includes some mechanical errors	Demonstrates poor use of language; includes many mechanical errors

284 • Writing for Assessment

☑ ONGOING ASSESSMENT: Assess Mastery

Use one of the following options to assess final drafts of students' essays.

Self-Assessment Ask students to score their essay using the rubric provided. Then have students write a single paragraph reflecting on the most valuable thing they learned in completing this essay.	**Teacher Assessment** You may wish to use the rubric and the scoring models provided in Writing Assessment, Ruby Level, to score the essays.

Critical Viewing

Interpret Students will probably say that the photo illustrates air pollution, and that the first sentence in the fourth paragraph justifies the answer.

13.6 Student Work IN PROGRESS

FINAL DRAFT

Air Pollution

**Brittany Wilson
Stuart Middle School
Louisville, Kentucky**

Writing Prompt Choose one form of pollution. Describe three of its effects and some possible solutions.

▲ **Critical Viewing** Cite details from Brittany's essay to identify the problem this photograph illustrates. **[Interpret]**

Air pollution is one of the major forms of pollution. By releasing chemicals into the air, we create problems such as smog, ozone action days, and acid rain. As widespread and dangerous as air pollution is, we can take some simple steps to help solve the problem, such as carpooling and controlling the amount of smoke coming from factories.

Much air pollution is caused by the burning of fossil fuels. Fossil fuels include gasoline, coal, and oil. They are called fossil fuels because they come from buried plants and animals that died millions of years ago.

When cars burn gas or when factories burn coal, they release carbon monoxide, hydrocarbons, and other harmful chemicals. These chemicals cause problems such as smog, ozone action days, and acid rain.

Smog is thick brown air that hangs over a city. It is made when the chemicals in car exhaust mix in the sunlight. Smog hurts people's eyes and makes it hard for them to breathe.

Smog would just blow away, except that sometimes there is a temperature inversion. In a temperature inversion, the air in the city is trapped by warmer air above the city. As a result, the air in the city cannot rise up and carry the smog away.

Brittany's introduction clearly identifies her focus: air pollution and three of its effects. This focus addresses the prompt.

Brittany organizes her response logically. First, she discusses a cause of air pollution; then, she discusses three of its effects.

The phrase "as a result" is a transition showing the connection between this sentence and the one before.

Step-by-Step Teaching Guide

Teaching From the Final Draft

1. Have students read Brittany's final draft. You can either read it aloud in class or have students read it together in small groups.

2. As students read the final draft, have them use the margin notes to guide their reading.

3. Point out the crisp introduction that states the main idea and tells the reader what she is going to read about.

4. Emphasize how directly Brittany follows the writing prompt, providing three effects of air pollution and possible solutions.

Teaching From the Final Draft

1. Have students identify the topic sentences in Brittany's paragraphs. Then ask them to find the supporting details for each paragraph.

2. Discuss Brittany's conclusion. Review how well Brittany restates her case and ends with a strong statement.

Critical Viewing

Draw Conclusions Students may suggest that because members of a carpool do not have to focus on the actual driving to and from work, carpooling allows for personal time both before and after their work day.

13.6

◄ **Critical Viewing** In addition to helping with the problem of air pollution, what other advantages might carpooling have, judging from this picture? **[Draw Conclusions]**

Another danger of air pollution is too much ozone. Ozone is a special form of oxygen. It is also caused by car exhaust and sunlight. We need ozone in the top part of the atmosphere. When there is too much of it lower down, it is just as bad to breathe as smog. In addition, you cannot see or smell ozone. Some cities have ozone action days. Scientists tell people when there will be too much ozone in the air.

A third danger caused by air pollution is acid rain. Chemicals in car fumes and factory smoke mix with water in the air. Together, they make burning acid. When the rain falls, it brings the acid down to the trees and ground. It hurts the trees. It can also kill fish in lakes. The acid rain washes into the water and changes the fishes' environment. One problem with acid rain is that it can fall far away from the factory that caused it. The wind can blow clouds with acid rain miles away from the factory before the acid rain falls.

To solve the problem of air pollution, people can carpool. This will limit the number of cars on the road polluting the air. People can also walk to places. That way, they can get some exercise. For each person walking, there would be one less car on the road. Another way to solve the problem would be to limit the amount of smoke that comes out of stacks at power plants. It is important to find a solution, because air pollution is a real danger to people's health and to nature.

Brittany supports her claim that acid rain is dangerous by explaining how it kills fish.

Brittany concludes with a restatement of the importance of her subject.

286 • Writing for Assessment

Connected Assignment *Open-Book Test*

When taking an open-book test, you can refer to a textbook or to class notes. You still need to complete the writing process in a limited time. Your answer should

- include facts, such as specific names, dates, events, or formulas, from your reference materials.

- present your own ideas based on the facts you present.

- sum up your main idea in a thesis statement.

- show a clear and logical organization.

Use these strategies to do your best on open-book tests:

Prewriting Organize your time well. Use a little more than one fourth of your time for prewriting.

Begin by outlining your answer to the question, as in the example on this page. Then, consult your reference materials for each specific point of your outline. If you are referring to a textbook, use the index to locate information quickly. As you gather details about each point, add them to your outline.

Drafting Next, allow half your time for drafting. Include these elements:

- **Thesis statement** Begin with an introduction that includes a thesis statement—a one-sentence statement that sums up your answer and that includes words from the question.

- **Elaboration** In the body of your paper, develop each main point of your outline. Include the specific details you have gathered from your reference materials.

- **Conclusion** In your final paragraph, sum up your answer to the question and your supporting reasons.

Revising and Editing
Allow one fourth of your time for revising.

Reread your essay. Check-mark points that lack sufficient support. Then, review marked paragraphs, and add details from your reference materials.

Publishing and Presenting Add your graded test to your portfolio.

▲ Critical Viewing
What advice for taking an open-book test might you give this student?
[Apply]

TOPIC: Circulation of Blood
I. The Heart
   A. The heart pumps blood throughout the body.
      1. made of ?   p. 48 – made of smooth muscle
      2. four chambers: atria and ventricles
   B. Sends some blood to lungs, some to body
II. Blood to the lungs
   A. The left atrium sends blood to the lungs.
      1. blood goes through the ? artery p. 50 – blood goes
      2. blood needs to go to the lungs, to lungs through
      because it is coming back from   pulmonary artery
      the body and all its oxygen is gone

Connected Assignment: Open-Book Test • 287

Lesson Objectives

1. To compare and contrast visual and electronic media with written story.
2. To analyze oral interpretations of literature.
3. To evaluate the purposes and effects of various media.
4. To write a letter.

Critical Viewing

Deduce Students should say that the woman in the center foreground is Kate. She is frowning and looks ill-tempered.

Step-by-Step Teaching Guide

Comparing and Contrasting Print and Visual Media

1. Choose one of the Spotlight elements for class discussion, or have students work individually or in groups on the element of their choice. Give students the initiative to find the necessary videotapes and books.

2. Interested students may wish to listen to the soundtrack of *Kiss Me Kate* or view a video of the play. Ask why they think this play was such a success.

3. Provide copies of an appropriate version of Shakespeare's play. Compare Shakespeare's language to that of the Broadway musical.

4. Invite volunteers to research either Shakespeare's play or *Kiss Me Kate.* What historical material influenced Shakespeare? How did the Broadway production develop?

5. If students view *10 Things I Hate About You,* invite them to present oral film reviews. Discuss whether students feel that the film depicts family relationships realistically.

Spotlight on the Humanities

Comparing and Contrasting Print and Visual Media

Focus on Theater: *Kiss Me Kate*

When one character "assesses" another, putting him or her to a test, it can make for great comedy. In the Broadway musical *Kiss Me Kate,* a sharp-tongued woman puts her husband to the test—and he passes with top grades.

The music for *Kiss Me Kate* was written by the great American composer Cole Porter, who wrote his first song when he was ten years old. This show is considered his best. Bella and Samuel Spewack wrote the book (the words spoken and sung by the characters).

The show opened in New York on December 30, 1948. By the time it closed, *Kiss Me Kate* had passed a popularity test of its own, running on Broadway for 1,077 performances.

Literature Connection In 1594, William Shakespeare wrote his comedy *The Taming of the Shrew,* on which *Kiss Me Kate* is based. The comedic play tells the story of the hot-tempered Katharina and her husband, Petruchio. Elements of *The Taming of the Shrew* are rooted in ancient folk tales.

Film Connection Director Gil Junger and cinematographer Mark Irwin loosely based their 1999 film *10 Things I Hate About You* on *The Taming of the Shrew.* The movie features an ill-tempered older sister and a favored younger one, just as in the play.

Assessment Activity: Proposal

Select a classic story you have read, and write a letter to a producer explaining why a Broadway-show version of the story will be a great success. Compare the show as you envision it to the original story.

▲ **Critical Viewing** Which one of these characters is Kate? Explain how you know. [Deduce]

▶ **Critical Viewing** Why might the idea of a woman who nastily rejects all suitors be of interest to playwrights? To what scenes might it lead? [Hypothesize]

288 • Writing for Assessment

Assessment Activity Interested students might prepare an oral presentation or storyboard sketches to accompany their letters.

Critical Viewing

Hypothesize Students may say that playwrights might enjoy the challenge of creating situations to change this character's reactions. The idea might lead to courtship and rejection scenes.

Media and Technology Skills

Using Technology to Support Learning

Activity: Explore Electronic Tests

These days, you can take all sorts of tests on a computer—academic standardized tests, school entrance exams, even tests for a driver's license. Most of the test-taking skills that apply to print tests also apply to tests taken on a computer. It is important, though, that you be familiar and comfortable with the computer test format before taking a test on-line.

Learn About It

Practice on the Computer If possible, practice beforehand using the computer on which you will be tested. For instance, if the test will be given in the school computer room, visit the room before the test. Start up the computer, use the mouse, and open and close applications. This will reduce stress you might feel during the test because of confusion about using the computer.

Read Instructions Carefully Some computer-based tests will not allow you to change an answer once you have selected it. Make sure that you read all instructions and tips carefully before taking the test. After you read the instructions, decide on the best strategy for answering questions on the test.

Take On-line Practice Tests Practice tests of various kinds are available on CD-ROM and on-line. You may practice with these tests to become comfortable with computer test taking, as well as to familiarize yourself with each particular kind of test. Practice programs also provide you with feedback on your answers to help you learn about the test and the subject matter covered.

Evaluate It With the help of a teacher or school librarian, find print and computer versions of practice tests. Take both tests, and complete the Venn diagram shown here, listing similarities between the two in the area where the two circles cross. Finally, write a summary in which you evaluate which type of test taking you prefer, and why.

PRINT TEST
- like the fact that you can turn back a page

- dislike the fact that both have complicated instructions

COMPUTER TEST
- like the fact that you don't have to worry about filling in the wrong blank

---

Step-by-Step Teaching Guide

Using Technology to Support Learning

Teaching Resources: Writing Support Transparency 13-D; Writing Support Activity Book 13-2

1. Review the tips on computer test taking.

2. Invite any students who have previously taken on-line tests to share their experiences with the efficacy of the tips outlined here. Ask them to suggest any additional tips and have a volunteer list these on the chalkboard.

3. Using a classroom, school, or public access computer, help students practice their basic computer skills. Also review the likely instructions in a test, e.g. how to indicate correct answers.

4. Display the transparency. Point out that students will use it *after* completing the activity. Reinforce the use of a Venn diagram by walking students through the included example.

5. Give students copies of the blank organizer for use in responding to the test-taking practice activity. Have students exchange completed Venn diagrams with a peer and discuss the responses.

Customize for
Logical/Mathematical Learners

Students who are advanced computer users may wish to search out additional on-line tests. Encourage these students to compare and contrast the located tests and rate these as useful practice vehicles.

Lesson Objectives

1. To answer different types and levels of questions
2. To read to take action and identify a response
3. To recognize and apply the conventions of written language including capitalization and punctuation

Step-by-Step Teaching Guide

Proofreading

1. Emphasize to students that care and accuracy should be their highest priorities when completing multiple-choice test questions. Students should check over completed items to make sure they have indicated the intended response. They should also verify that they have used the requested method (circling, underlining, etc.) to indicate that response.

2. Remind students to read the directions carefully before beginning. What exactly are they meant to look for among the answer alternatives?

3. Reassure students that when completing tests in pencil, as is usually required, they will have the opportunity to change responses. Stress the importance, however, of making changes neatly and completely.

4. Provide practice with this or other sample tests. Use a time interval suited to local and state testing procedures.

Standardized Test Preparation Workshop

Proofreading

Standardized test questions often measure your knowledge of basic spelling, punctuation, and capitalization rules. Use the following guidelines when answering these questions:

- When looking for punctuation errors, determine whether a mark is misplaced, missing, or unnecessary.

- To identify capitalization errors, look for errors in titles and proper nouns.

- When identifying spelling errors, look closely at each word.

The following sample test items will help you become familiar with the format of these questions.

Test Tip

Read each sentence from beginning to end before trying to determine what type of error exists in the underlined portion. Just reading the underlined phrase may not provide enough information for you to answer accurately.

Sample Test Items	Answers and Explanations

Directions Read the passage, and decide which type of error, if any, appears in each underlined section. Then, choose the letter that identifies the error type.
 	
Almost like a <u>combination of his too most</u>
(1)
famous <u>characters Sherlock Holmes</u> and Dr.
(2)
Watson, Sir Arthur Conan Doyle was both a
 	
mystery solver and a medical doctor.
 	
1   A   Spelling error
     B   Capitalization error
     C   Punctuation error
     D   No error
	The correct answer for section 1 is *A*. The word *too* should be spelled *two*.

2   F   Spelling error
     G   Capitalization error
     H   Punctuation error
     J   No error
	The correct answer for section 2 is *H*. A comma is needed after *characters* to introduce the appositive phrase *Sherlock Holmes and Dr. Watson.*

290 • Writing for Assessment

✎ TEST-TAKING TIP

Tell students that a common test-taking error is to indicate the response to one item on the answer chart for another item. Encourage students to use a piece of paper, ruler, or other flat object as a guide. Model how to place the paper over all items except the one being addressed (and those already completed). Demonstrate how to move the paper down the page as items are completed. Then invite students to practice this strategy on the test question provided.

Practice **Directions:** Read the passage, and decide which type of error, if any, appears in each underlined section. Then, choose the letter that identifies the error type.

Unlike Sherlock holmes, who catches
(1)
Culverton Smith in *the Dying Detective*
(2)
with a clever trick today's detectives often
(3)
use scientific evidence. They anaylze this
(4)
evidence with the help of forensic experts,

who study the chemical makeup of tiny
(5)
pieces of material—hair, fabric, or soil, for
(6)
example, from a crime scene to link it with

an accused criminal. They may also use:
(7)
fingerprints and shoe impressions to study
(8)
how a crime was commited.

1 A Spelling error
 B Capitalization error
 C Punctuation error
 D No error

2 F Spelling error
 G Capitalization error
 H Punctuation error
 J No error

3 A Spelling error
 B Capitalization error
 C Punctuation error
 D No error

4 F Spelling error
 G Capitalization error
 H Punctuation error
 J No error

5 A Spelling error
 B Capitalization error
 C Punctuation error
 D No error

6 F Spelling error
 G Capitalization error
 H Punctuation error
 J No error

7 A Spelling error
 B Capitalization error
 C Punctuation error
 D No error

8 F Spelling error
 G Capitalization error
 H Punctuation error
 J No error

1. B
2. G
3. C
4. F
5. D
6. H
7. C
8. F

Customize for
Less Advanced Students

Ask students which type of errors they find easiest to spot: spelling, capitalization, or punctuation. Encourage them to begin by searching for the error type they find easiest to locate. This will allow them to progress quickly through items they can answer, leaving more time for those presenting difficulty.

Customize for
More Advanced Students

Encourage students to feel comfortable choosing *No error* as the answer. Some test items will be correct and students who are proficient in spelling and mechanics should be able to recognize these correct items.

Lesson Objectives

1. To understand parts of speech and to apply relevant concepts

2. To use prepositional phrases to elaborate written ideas

3. To use conjunctions to connect ideas meaningfully

4. To write in complete sentences, varying the types such as compound and complex sentences

5. To understand verb tenses and use them appropriately and consistently

6. To write with increasing accuracy when using pronouns

7. To employ subject-verb and pronoun-antecedent agreement

8. To use adjectives (including comparatives and superlatives) and adverbs appropriately to make writing vivid and precise

9. To analyze works of literature as models of appropriate and effective English usage

10. To recognize appropriate English usage in their own writing

11. To use "hands-on" strategies to reinforce understanding of grammar and usage concepts

12. To master the conventions of capitalization, punctuation, and spelling

PART

2

Grammar, Usage, and Mechanics

Gardeners, 1995, Judy Byford, The Grand Design, Leeds, England

Grammar, Usage, and Mechanics • **293**

Responding to Fine Art

Gardeners **by Judy Byford**

Use this work of art to start a discussion about the functions of grammar, usage, and mechanics.

1. Have students examine the painting on pages 292–293. You might use the following questions to prompt discussion:

   What do you see happening in this painting? What details help you describe what is happening?

   How would you describe the style of this painting? Is it realistic? Is it realistic in the same way that a photograph is? What mood or atmosphere does the artist create in her work? How does the artist's use of color and line contribute to this mood or atmosphere?

2. In this garden (called a *topiary*), the gardeners have created distinct shapes and designs by pruning the bushes and trees. Ask students to relate this process to learning the functions of grammar, usage, and mechanics. Lead students to see that learning about these elements helps us to put together words to construct distinct sentences. Without these rules, we would have difficulty communicating and with and understanding one another.

Chapter 14 Time and Resource Manager

In-Depth Lesson Plan

	LESSON FOCUS	PRINT AND MEDIA RESOURCES
DAY 1	**Nouns** Students learn to identify and use common, proper, and compound nouns (pp. 296–300).	**Teaching Resources** *Grammar Exercise Workbook*, pp. 1–6; *Grammar Exercises Answers on Transparencies*, Ch. 14 ***Language Lab* CD-ROM,** Using Nouns; ***On-Line Exercise Bank***, Section 14.1
DAY 2	**Pronouns** Students learn to identify and use pronouns and their antecedents and do the Hands-On Grammar activity (pp. 301–309).	**Teaching Resources** *Grammar Exercise Workbook*, pp. 7–12; *Grammar Exercises Answers on Transparencies*, Ch. 14; *Hands-on Grammar Activity Book*, Ch. 14 ***Language Lab* CD-ROM,** Using Pronouns; ***On-Line Exercise Bank***, Section 14.2
DAY 3	**Review and Assess** Students review chapter and demonstrate mastery of use of nouns and pronouns (pp. 310–313).	**Teaching Resources** *Formal Assessment*, Ch. 14 ***On-Line Exercise Bank***, Sections 14.1–2

Accelerated Lesson Plan

	LESSON FOCUS	PRINT AND MEDIA RESOURCES
DAY 1	**Nouns and Pronouns** Students cover concepts and usage of nouns and pronouns as determined by Diagnostic Test (pp. 296–309).	**Teaching Resources** *Grammar Exercise Workbook*, pp. 1–12; *Grammar Exercises Answers on Transparencies*, Ch. 14; *Hands-on Grammar Activity Book*, Ch. 14 ***Language Lab* CD-ROM,** Using Nouns; Using Pronouns; ***On-Line Exercise Bank***, Section 14.1, 14.2
DAY 2	**Review and Assess** Students review chapter and demonstrate mastery of use of nouns and pronouns (pp. 310–313).	**Teaching Resources** *Formal Assessment*, Ch. 14 ***On-Line Exercise Bank***, Sections 14.1–2

Options for Adapting Lesson Plans

HOMEWORK
Have students complete any section of the chapter for homework.

FEATURES
Extend coverage with the Grammar in Literature feature (p. 299), and the Standardized Test Preparation Workshop (p. 312).

TECHNOLOGY
Students can use the On-Line Exercise Bank to complete the exercises on computer. The Auto Check feature will grade their work.

294a

INTEGRATED SKILLS COVERAGE

Grammar in Literature
SE p. 299

Reading
Find It In Your Reading, SE pp. 300, 308, 309

Writing
Find It In Your Writing, SE pp. 300, 308, 309, 311
Writing Application SE pp. 300, 309, 311
Integrating Writing Skills SE p. 303

Language
Language Highlight, ATE p. 304

Real-World Connection
ATE p. 302

Speaking and Listening
Integrating Speaking Skills ATE p. 302

Viewing and Representing Critical Viewing,
SE pp. 294, 298, 301, 307

ASSESSMENT SUPPORT

Standardized Test Preparation SE p. 312; ATE pp. 297, 304
Standardized Test Preparation Workbook, pp. 27–28
Formal Assessment, Ch. 14

MEETING INDIVIDUAL NEEDS

ESL Students ATE p. 298, 304
Less Advanced Students ATE p. 307. See also Ongoing Assessments, ATE pp. 298, 303, 305, 307, 308.
Linguistic Learners ATE p. 299
Spatial Learners ATE p. 305
Gifted and Talented Students ATE p. 297

BLOCK SCHEDULING

Pacing Suggestions
For 90-minute Blocks
• Administer the Diagnostic Test to students to determine instructional coverage
• Have students complete the necessary exercises in class. Use the Hands-on Grammar activity to provide a change of pace.

Resources for Varying Instruction
• *Language Lab* CD-ROM If your students have access to hardware, a 90-minute block provides an ideal opportunity for students to work on computer.

Professional Development Support
• *How to manage Instruction in the Block* This Teaching Resource provides management and activity suggestions.

MEDIA AND TECHNOLOGY

For the Student
• *Language Lab* CD-ROM Using Nouns, Using Pronouns
• *On-Line Exercise Bank,* Ch. 14

For the Teacher
• *Resource Pro* CD-ROM

WRITING AND GRAMMAR WEB SITE

The Interactive Writing and Grammar Web site provides a wide array of support for students, teachers, and parents. Grammar support includes:

• On-Line Exercise Bank with Auto Check scoring
• Diagnostic and assessment support

www.phschool.com

LITERATURE CONNECTIONS

Grammar in Literature selections from *Prentice Hall Literature: Timeless Voices, Timeless Themes,* Bronze:
From *"The Cat Who Thought She Was a Dog and the Dog Who Thought He Was a Cat,"* Isaac Bashevis Singer, SE p. 299

1. To understand what nouns and pronouns are, and how they are used in sentences
2. To recognize collective and compound nouns
3. To understand the difference between common and proper nouns and how the difference affects capitalization
4. To write with increasing accuracy when using pronoun case
5. To employ standard English usage in writing for audiences, including pronoun referents and parts of speech
6. To write to express, discover, record, develop, reflect on ideas, and to problem solve
7. To analyze a model from literature to reinforce concepts and improve one's own writing

Critical Viewing

Relate Students may include in their responses such nouns as *dog, puppy, fur, collar, tags, toy,* and *grass.*

Chapter 14 Nouns and Pronouns

▲ Critical Viewing
What nouns can you use to name the things in this picture? **[Relate]**

Nouns are words that name people, places, things, and ideas. Some nouns name things, such as dogs. There are many different kinds of dogs: collies, poodles, terriers, and more. The words that name all the different kinds of dogs and the places where they can be found are nouns. In this chapter, you will learn about different types of nouns, such as common and proper nouns, collective nouns, and compound nouns. You will also learn about **pronouns,** the words that are sometimes used to replace nouns.

294 • Nouns and Pronouns

☑ ONGOING ASSESSMENT: Diagnose

If students miss more than one item in each category, direct them to the relevant pages of the text and assign exercises for practice and review.

Nouns and Pronouns	Diagnostic Test Items	Teach	Practice	Section Review	Chapter Review
Skill Check A					
Nouns	A 1–5	p. 296	Ex. 1	Ex. 6	Ex. 25–26, 34
Skill Check B					
Collective Nouns	B 6, 8–10	p. 297	Ex. 2	Ex. 7, 10–11	Ex. 28
Compound Nouns	B 7	pp. 297–298	Ex. 3, 4	Ex. 7, 10–11	Ex. 29
Skill Check C					
Common and Proper Nouns	C 11–15	pp. 298–299	Ex. 5	Ex. 5–11	Ex. 27, 34

Diagnostic Test

Directions: Write all answers on a separate sheet of paper.

Skill Check A. Identify the nouns in each sentence. Explain why each word is a noun by telling whether it is a person, place, or thing.

1. Dogs can be purchased from a breeder.
2. Good pets can also be found at a shelter.
3. Preparations—such as getting food, dishes, toys, a collar, and a bed—need to be made before the arrival of a new puppy.
4. A veterinarian gives the dog shots for rabies and distemper.
5. All dogs must wear licenses, which ensure identification and immunization.

Skill Check B. Identify and label the collective or compound noun in each sentence.

6. The whole family should share in taking care of a pet.
7. Dogs need shelter, such as a doghouse, in which to sleep.
8. Supplies can be purchased at a pet shop.
9. Use caution when introducing the new pet to a large group.
10. Avoid packs of stray dogs when walking your pet.

Skill Check C. Identify each italicized noun as *common* or *proper*.

The (11) *American Kennel Club* was started in 1884. This (12) *organization* is associated with more than 4,000 clubs throughout the (13) *United States*. Frances belongs to a group in her (14) *town*. She goes to shows in (15) *Austin* with her cousin Sarah.

Skill Check D. Identify the pronouns in each sentence. Then, identify each pronoun's antecedent. You may need to refer to previous sentences to find the antecedent.

16. Martin loves dogs, and he has three German shepherds.
17. They are very gentle.
18. His sister, Tanya, helps him care for them.
19. She trained them to sit and stay.
20. The neighbor admires their dogs.

Skill Check E. Identify the italicized pronoun in each sentence as *personal, demonstrative, interrogative,* or *indefinite*.

21. *We* went to the pound to see puppies.
22. My mother asked, "*Which* do you want?"
23. *That* was a difficult decision.
24. Those pups were so cute *I* wanted them all.
25. *Each* had its own special qualities.

Nouns and Pronouns • 295

Answer Key

Diagnostic Test

Each item in the diagnostic test corresponds to a specific section in the nouns and pronouns chapter. This will enable you to tailor instruction to the particular needs of your students. See "Ongoing Assessment: Diagnose" below for further details.

Skill Check A

1. dogs—thing, breeder—person
2. pets—thing, shelter—place
3. preparations, food, dishes, toys, collar, bed, arrival, puppy—things
4. veterinarian—person; dog, shots, rabies, distemper—things
5. dogs, licenses, identification, immunization—things

Skill Check B

6. family—collective
7. doghouse—compound
8. pet shop—compound
9. group—collective
10. packs—collective

Skill Check C

11. American Kennel Club—proper
12. organization—common
13. United States—proper
14. town—common
15. Austin—proper

Skill Check D

16. he—Martin
17. they—German shepherds
18. his, him—Martin; them—German shepherds
19. she—Tanya; them—German shepherds
20. their—Martin and Tanya

Skill Check E

21. We, personal
22. Which, interrogative
23. that, demonstrative
24. I, personal
25. Each, indefinite

☑ ONGOING ASSESSMENT: Diagnose *continued*

Nouns and Pronouns	Diagnostic Test Items	Teach	Practice	Section Review	Chapter Review
Skill Check D					
Pronouns	D 16–20	p. 301		Ex. 21	Ex. 31, 32, 34, 36
Antecedents	D 16–20	pp. 302–303	Ex. 13	Ex. 19	Ex. 31
Skill Check E					
Personal Pronouns	E-21, 24–25	pp. 303–304	Ex. 14	Ex. 18–20, 22, 23	Ex. 30, 33
Demonstrative Pronouns	E-23	p. 305	Ex. 15		
Interrogative Pronouns	E-22	p. 306	Ex. 16	Ex. 20,23	
Indefinite Pronouns	E-25	pp. 306–307	Ex. 17		
Cumulative Reviews and Applications				Ex. 10–12 Ex. 21–24	Ex. 35–36

⏱ TIME SAVERS!

Answers on Transparency Use the Grammar Exercise Answers on Transparencies to facilitate correction by students.

On-Line Exercise Bank Have students complete the Diagnostic Test on computer. The Auto Check feature will grade their work for you!

PREPARE and ENGAGE

Interest GRABBER Have students look around the room for two minutes and then, without looking up, write a list of everything they remember seeing. (Acceptable items include anything present, such as people and objects, or anything represented, such as on a poster or by a map.) Have students share from their lists, or ask how many noticed specific things in the room. Point out to them that the things on their lists are nouns.

Activate Prior Knowledge

Ask students if they have ever taken part in coming up with a name, such as naming a new pet, discussing the name of a new baby with parents, or naming a favorite toy. Have them share some of their experiences: what was named and how was the name chosen?

TEACH

Step-by-Step Teaching Guide

Nouns

1. Explain that a noun is a word that we use to identify a person, place, thing, or idea.

2. Write the following sentences on the board, underlining the nouns and asking students why each functions as a noun:

   The <u>man</u> thought <u>obedience</u> was an important <u>quality</u> in a <u>dog</u>.

   <u>Jilly</u> took her <u>pet</u> to <u>school</u>.

Answer Key

Exercise 1

1. puppy—thing
2. leash—thing
3. trainer—person
4. tail—thing
5. family—thing or group of people
6. loyalty—quality or idea
7. yard—place
8. doghouse—thing or place
9. judge—person
10. show—thing

Section 14.1 Nouns

Nouns are naming words. Words such as *friend*, *sky*, *dog*, *love*, *courage*, and *Seattle* are nouns. They help people name what they are thinking or talking about.

▶ **KEY CONCEPT** A **noun** names a person, place, thing, or idea. ■

In English, most nouns fall into four main groups:

People, Places, Things, and Ideas

The nouns in the chart are grouped under four headings. You may know most of the nouns under the first three headings. You may not have realized that all of the words in the fourth group are nouns.

PEOPLE	
veterinarian	Americans
Dr. Robinson	leader
PLACES	
Lake Mead	kennel
classroom	Bunker Hill
THINGS	
bumblebee	motorcycle
collar	notebook
IDEAS	
strength	willingness
honesty	obedience

▶ **Exercise 1** Classifying Nouns Explain why each of the words below can function as a noun.

EXAMPLE: friendship
ANSWER: *Friendship* is a noun because it names a quality, an idea.

1. puppy
2. leash
3. trainer
4. tail
5. family
6. loyalty
7. yard
8. doghouse
9. judge
10. show

Theme: Dogs

In this section, you will learn about nouns. The examples, sentences, paragraphs, and exercises in this section are about dogs.

Cross-Curricular Connection: Science

▶ **More Practice**

Language Lab CD-ROM
• Using Nouns Lesson
On-line Exercise Bank
• Section 14.1
Grammar Exercise Workbook
• pp. 1–4

296 • Nouns and Pronouns

TIME AND RESOURCE MANAGER

Resources
Print: Grammar Exercise Workbook, pp. 1–6
Technology: Language Lab CD-ROM, Using Nouns; On-line Exercise Bank, Section 14.1

In-Depth Coverage	Accelerated Pace
• Work through all key concepts, pp. 296–299.	• Assign pp. 296–299, for independent student review.
• Assign and review Exercises 1–5.	• Assign Section Review Exercises 6–9, p. 300.
• Read and discuss Grammar in Literature, p. 299.	

Collective Nouns

A few nouns name groups of people or things. A *pack*, for example, is "a group of dogs that travel together." These nouns are called *collective nouns*.

▶ **KEY CONCEPT** A **collective noun** is a noun that names a group of people or things. ■

COLLECTIVE NOUNS		
club	herd	army
troop	orchestra	committee
class	team	group

▶ **Exercise 2** Recognizing Collective Nouns Each of the numbered groups of words below contains one collective noun. Write each collective noun on your paper.

EXAMPLE: bone   pack   collar

ANSWER: pack

1. collar   club   fur
2. team   dish   claw
3. ball   litter   toys
4. snout   group   paw
5. ribbon   brush   class

Compound Nouns

Sometimes two words are used together to form a new word with a different meaning. You know, for example, the two separate words *dog* and *house*. When they are used together, however, as in the sentence "The puppy sleeps in a doghouse," the combined words mean "a house for a dog." Together, the words take on a special meaning. A noun such as *doghouse* is said to be a *compound noun*.

▶ **KEY CONCEPT** A **compound noun** is a noun made up of two or more words. ■

COMPOUND NOUNS		
Separate Words	Hyphenated Words	Combined Words
post office	bull's-eye	flagship
middle school	daughter-in-law	railroad
Golden Gate Bridge	left-hander	doorknob

⚙ Grammar and Style Tip

Use collective nouns to replace the vague word *group* with a more specific one. For example, a *group* of dogs can be called a *pack*.

Nouns • 297

✎ STANDARDIZED TEST PREPARATION WORKSHOP

Grammar and Usage Many standardized tests require students to recognize parts of speech within the context of a passage. Use the following example to demonstrate.

There were hundreds of animals in the herd that ran across the plain at Yellowstone Park.

Which word in the above passage is a collective noun?

A Yellowstone Park   **C** animals

B herd   **D** hundreds

The correct answer is item **B**—the others are a compound proper noun (*Yellowstone Park*), and plurals (*animals, hundreds*).

> **Exercise 3**

1. purebreds, German shepherds
2. dewclaws
3. sheepdogs
4. sister-in-law, sheepdog
5. high school

> **Exercise 4**

1. greyhound
2. fox terrier
3. watchdog
4. bloodhound
5. dog-eared

Critical Viewing

Relate; Speculate The most common response will probably be *fire engine* (or *fire truck*), but any response that uses a compound noun for a vehicle (*bandwagon, hay cart*) is acceptable, since not all students will be familiar with this association for Dalmatians.

> ### Step-by-Step Teaching Guide

Common and Proper Nouns

1. Point out to students that they use common and proper nouns all the time.

2. Emphasize that a proper noun is a name that has been given to a specific person, place, or thing. A field of grass may be lovely, but only when someone gives it a name, like "Reed's Meadow," do you have a proper noun.

3. Write the sentence below on the board and point out which noun is proper (P) and which is common (C), then have students suggest other sentences that use both a common and a proper noun.

   The <u>town</u> (C) where I grew up is <u>El Paso</u> (P).

Customize for
ESL Students

Different languages handle proper nouns differently. For example, in English, we capitalize languages, but in French, Spanish, and Italian, languages are not capitalized. Because of these differences, students may need extra assistance in identifying nouns that must be capitalized.

> **Exercise 3** Identifying Compound Nouns Each of the following sentences has one or more compound nouns. Copy the sentences onto your paper, and underline each compound noun.

EXAMPLE: The dog dragged his blanket into the doghouse.
ANSWER: The dog dragged his blanket into the <u>doghouse</u>.

1. Some purebreds, such as German shepherds, are born with an extra claw on each paw.
2. These extra claws, called dewclaws, are usually removed by a veterinarian.
3. Other dogs, like sheepdogs, have different problems.
4. My sister-in-law has a sheepdog.
5. She found it behind the high school.

> **Exercise 4** Finding the Correct Form of Compound Nouns Use a dictionary to find the correct spelling of each of the compound nouns below. Write the correct form on your paper.

EXAMPLE: dog-catcher   dogcatcher   dog catcher
ANSWER: dogcatcher

1. greyhound   grey hound   grey-hound
2. foxterrier   fox-terrier   fox terrier
3. watch-dog   watch dog   watchdog
4. blood hound   bloodhound   blood-hound
5. dog-eared   dog eared   dogeared

Common and Proper Nouns

All nouns—even if they are collective or compound—can be classified as either *common nouns* or *proper nouns*.

> **KEY CONCEPT** A **common noun** names any one of a class of people, places, or things. A **proper noun** names a specific person, place, or thing. ∎

Common nouns are not capitalized unless they begin a sentence or a title. Proper nouns are always capitalized.

Common Nouns	Proper Nouns
writer	Mary Swenson
park	Yellowstone National Park
document	Declaration of Independence

▲ **Critical Viewing**
What compound noun names a vehicle in which you might see a Dalmatian?
[Relate; Speculate]

✓ **ONGOING ASSESSMENT: Monitor and Reinforce**

If students miss more than two items in Exercises 1–5, refer them to the following for additional practice.

In the Textbook	Print Resources	Technology
Section Review, Ex. 6–9, p. 300	Grammar Exercise Workbook, pp. 1–6	On-Line Exercise Bank, Section 14.1

GRAMMAR IN
LITERATURE

from **The Cat Who Thought She Was a Dog and the Dog Who Thought He Was a Cat**

Isaac Bashevis Singer

In this passage, notice that peasant, *a common noun, is often used in place of the proper noun* Jan Skiba. *The proper noun is capitalized, but the common noun is not. Look for other common and proper nouns in this paragraph.*

Once there was a poor *peasant, Jan Skiba* by name. He lived with his wife and three daughters in a one-room hut with a straw roof, far from the village. The house had a bed, a bench bed, and a stove, but no mirror. A mirror was a luxury for a poor *peasant*. And why would a *peasant* need a mirror? Peasants aren't curious about their appearance.

But this *peasant* did have a dog and a cat in his hut. The dog was named Burek and the cat Kot.

⯮ **Exercise 5** **Identifying Common and Proper Nouns** Copy each of the following nouns onto your paper. Place a *C* after each common noun and a *P* after each proper noun. Then, for each common noun, write a corresponding proper noun. For each proper noun, write a corresponding common noun.

EXAMPLE:	club
ANSWER:	club, C American Kennel Club

EXAMPLE:	United States
ANSWER:	United States, P country

1. statue
2. Latin
3. St. Bernard
4. state
5. street
6. Central Park
7. China
8. friend
9. lake
10. town

Ⓛ**ITERATURE**

You can read the complete selection "The Cat Who Thought . . ." in *Prentice Hall Literature: Timeless Voices, Timeless Themes,* Bronze.

⯮ **More Practice**

Language Lab CD-ROM
• Using Nouns Lesson
On-line Exercise Bank
• Section 14.1
Grammar Exercise Workbook
• pp. 5–6

Nouns • 299

Section Review

Each of these exercises correlates to the concepts in the section on nouns, pages 296–299. The exercises may be used for more practice, for reteaching, or for review of the Key Concepts presented. Answers for all chapter exercises are available in *Grammar Exercise Answers on Transparencies* in your Teaching Resources.

Answer Key

Exercise 6

1. Dogs, attention, feeding, care
2. Dogs, exercise
3. Puppies, combination, foods, milk
4. Dogs, rawhide strips
5. doghouse, heat, cold

Exercise 7

Collective nouns:
herd, flock

Compound nouns:
German shepherd, police officer, firefighters, fire engines, self-discipline

Exercise 8

Common nouns:
pieces, literature, dog, story, companion, story, dogs, suburbs, cities, loyalty, writers, qualities, dogs, dog, author, book

Proper nouns:
White Fang, Jack London, Yukon, James Herriot, William Armstrong, Millie, White House.

Exercise 9

Answers will probably reflect names and places familiar to students. Examples: A dog, Rover; the town, Smithville; a street, Main Street; another street, Central Street; The man, Mr. Valdez; the street, Main Street

Exercise 10

Find It in Your Reading
Proper nouns—Burek, Jan Skiba
Common nouns—day, night, anguish, dog, cat, disruption, mirror
Compound noun—household
Collective noun—family, household

GRAMMAR EXERCISES 6–12

Exercise 6 **Identifying Nouns**
Identify the nouns in each sentence.

1. Dogs require attention, including proper feeding and medical care.
2. Dogs need regular exercise.
3. Puppies need a combination of solid foods and milk as they grow.
4. Dogs enjoy rawhide strips.
5. A doghouse needs to be comfortable and insulated from heat and cold.

Exercise 7 **Identifying Collective and Compound Nouns** Copy the paragraph. Underline the collective nouns, and circle the compound nouns.

Several types of dogs are associated with occupations. The courage of the German shepherd is valuable to a police officer. Dalmatians are associated with firefighters and fire engines. Shelties can quickly organize a herd of sheep. A spaniel can point out a flock of birds without even seeing them. Working dogs, as well as their trainers, must have a great deal of self-discipline.

Exercise 8 **Distinguishing Between Common and Proper Nouns** Make a list of the common nouns and a separate list of the proper nouns in this paragraph:

Many pieces of literature celebrate the dog. *White Fang,* written by Jack London, is the story of a brave and loyal companion. The story is set in the Yukon, but dogs in suburbs and cities often display similar loyalty. Other writers who have written about the fine qualities of dogs are James Herriot and William Armstrong. Millie, a dog who lived in the White House, is listed as the author of her own book.

Exercise 9 **Revision Practice** Copy the following paragraph. Replace the italicized words with proper nouns of your choice.

A dog came to *the town*. He walked up *a street* and down *another street*. *The man*, who lived at the end of *the street*, watched the dog approach.

Exercise 10 **Find It in Your Reading** Identify two proper nouns, two common nouns, one compound noun, and one collective noun in the following excerpt from "The Cat Who Thought She Was a Dog . . . ":

Burek had to be tied outside, and he howled all day and all night. In their anguish, both the dog and the cat stopped eating.
When Jan Skiba saw the disruption the mirror had created in his household, he decided a mirror wasn't what his family needed.

Exercise 11 **Find It in Your Writing** Look through your writing portfolio. Find five common nouns, two proper nouns, one collective noun, and one compound noun in your own writing.

Exercise 12 **Writing Application** Write about a dog you've known or read about. Use at least two compound nouns, one collective noun, and two proper nouns.

Exercise 11

Find It in Your Writing
Answers will vary. Ask volunteers to share some of the collective and compound nouns they've used in their writing. If students are unable to find examples, encourage them to write two or three sentences that include collective and/or compound nouns.

Exercise 12

Writing Application
Suggest that students write first, then go back to locate the nouns. They can then substitute as needed to make sure they have the specified numbers and types of nouns.

Section 14.2 *Pronouns*

Pronouns are a very useful part of language. They save us from having to say many things twice. Notice the following sentence, for example: *The doctor said that the doctor needed assistance during the surgery.* By replacing the second "the doctor" with the word "he," the sentence becomes much clearer: *The doctor said that he needed assistance during the surgery.* In this section, you will learn how to identify and use different types of pronouns.

> **KEY CONCEPT** A **pronoun** is a word that takes the place of a noun or a group of words acting as a noun. ■

Pronouns make it possible to avoid using the same noun over and over. Read the following examples.

WITHOUT PRONOUNS:	The *firefighters* described how the *firefighters* did the *firefighters'* jobs.
WITH PRONOUNS:	The *firefighters* described how *they* did *their* jobs.

The pronouns *they* and *their* stand for the noun *firefighters* at the beginning of the sentence.

A pronoun can also take the place of a noun in an earlier sentence.

EXAMPLE: Finally, the *rescue worker* reappeared. *She* smiled to show the crowd that *she* was unharmed.

The pronoun *she*, used twice in the second sentence, takes the place of the noun *rescue worker* in the first sentence.

Once in a while, a single pronoun takes the place of a whole group of words.

EXAMPLE: *How they rescued Kim* is amazing. *It* is a story that will be told again and again.

In this example, the pronoun *it* in the second sentence takes the place of four words: *How they rescued Kim.*

Theme: Careers in Medicine

In this section, you will learn about pronouns. The examples, sentences, paragraphs, and exercises in this section are about careers in rescue, health, or medicine.

Cross-Curricular Connection: Science and Health

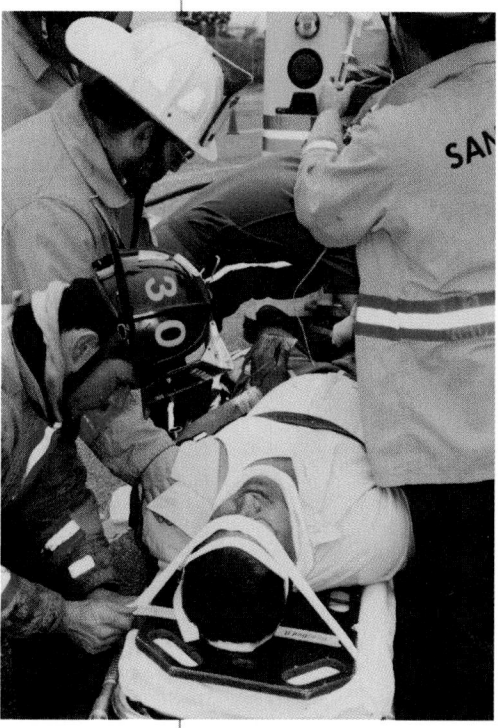

▲ Critical Viewing
What pronouns would you use to refer to the people in this picture? **[Analyze]**

Pronouns • **301**

PREPARE and ENGAGE

Interest GRABBER Ask students to write a paragraph about a friend or family member without ever using his or her name. Then ask students to share the words they used to indicate the individual about whom they wrote. Write on the board "pronouns" and "nouns," listing beneath each the words students suggest, as appropriate. Though most students will use pronouns, it is likely that nicknames, for example, will be used, as well. Simply list them under "nouns," then circle the list of pronouns at the end of the discussion.

Activate Prior Knowledge

Brainstorm for famous titles or lines in movies or books that use pronouns. ("*It,*" "*Them,*" "*They're here.*") Discuss what impact using the pronoun has in some of these cases. Ask students what we don't know from these titles or lines. (*We don't know who "it" or "they" are.*)

TEACH

Step-by-Step Teaching Guide

Pronouns

1. Point out to students that they already regularly use pronouns.
2. Emphasize that pronouns are similar to nouns in the way they are used in a sentence.
3. Explain that pronouns are related to nouns, in that they are used in place of nouns. Pronouns make speaking and writing easier.

Critical Viewing

Analyze Students will likely suggest *he, they, him, their.*

⏱ TIME AND RESOURCE MANAGER

Resources
Print: Grammar Exercise Workbook, pp. 7–12; Hands-on Grammar Activity Book, Ch. 14
Technology: Language Lab CD-ROM, Using Pronouns; On-Line Exercise Bank, Section 14.2

In-Depth Coverage	Accelerated Pace
• Work through all key concepts, pp. 301–307. • Assign and review Exercise 13–17. • Do the Hands-on Grammar Activity, p. 308.	• Assign pp. 301–307 for independent student review. • Assign Section Review Exercises 18–21, p. 309.

Antecedents of Pronouns

1. Remind students that pronouns are used to replace a noun or group of words acting as a noun. The name given to this replaced word (or group of words) is *antecedent*.

2. Explain that some pronouns are so common (such as *You* or *I*) that students may not realize that they're replacing a noun. In these cases the antecedents are understood—for example, if Bill Smith says "I," *Bill Smith* is the antecedent, and if he says to Rosa Chae, "You," *Rosa Chae* is the antecedent.

3. Point out that not every pronoun has a specific antecedent. With a pronoun like "everyone," for example, the antecedent is understood to be all the people in the group identified, whether the class or the world.

Critical Viewing

Speculate Students may relate the details of a house fire they've seen, an arson incident in the news, or other emergency that requires the presence of the fire department.

Real-World Connection

After responding to an emergency, firefighters file reports describing what happened and what they did. Discuss with students how confusion might occur if a pronoun's antecedents were unclear. (*The reader might not know who did what.*)

Integrating Speaking Skills

Tell students that, when speaking, varying the words used is as important as it is in writing. It is also important that people be able to tell what the antecedent for each pronoun is. However, when making a presentation, one can often make an antecedent obvious by pointing, using an overhead transparency, or finding some other way to direct an audience's attention to what is being spoken about.

14.2

Antecedents of Pronouns

The word or group of words that a pronoun replaces is called an *antecedent*.

▶ **KEY CONCEPT** An **antecedent** is the noun (or group of words acting as a noun) for which a pronoun stands. ■

 ANT.   PRON.   PRON.
The |firefighters| described how they did their jobs.

 ANT.   PRON.
Finally, the |rescue worker| reappeared. She appeared to be unharmed.

 ANT.   PRON.
|How Kim was rescued| is amazing. It is a story that will be told often.

Some kinds of pronouns will not have any antecedent.

EXAMPLE: *Everyone* knows what the truth is.

The indefinite pronoun *everyone* does not have a specific antecedent because its meaning is clear without one.

▼ Critical Viewing
Describe what you think has happened to cause this scene. What pronouns do you use in your description? **[Speculate]**

302 • Nouns and Pronouns

> **Exercise 13** Recognizing Antecedents Find the antecedent for each italicized pronoun in the following sentences, and write it on your paper. Some antecedents may appear in other sentences.

EXAMPLE: Martha explained how *she* won the contest.
ANSWER: Martha

1. Pastor Theodor Fliedner began *his* school of nursing in 1836.
2. Florence Nightingale received *her* formal training in nursing at Fliedner's school.
3. This famous reformer of nursing used *her* experience on battlefields during the Crimean War.
4. When *she* returned home, Nightingale established her training program at Saint Thomas's Hospital in London.
5. Any school for nursing can trace *its* pattern for training to Saint Thomas's Hospital in London.
6. In the 1800's, nurses received most of *their* training through apprenticeship programs.
7. An apprentice's training was only as good as the nurse overseeing *it*.
8. A nursing program is responsible for preparing *its* students for the demands of nursing.
9. Nurses have many responsibilities assigned to *them*.
10. *They* need technical knowledge as well as compassion.

> **More Practice**
> Language Lab
> CD-ROM
> • Using Pronouns lesson
> On-line
> Exercise Bank
> • Section 14.2
> Grammar Exercise
> Workbook
> • pp. 7–8

> **Exercise 13**
> 1. his—Theodor Fliedner
> 2. her—Florence Nightingale
> 3. her—Florence Nightingale
> 4. she—Florence Nightingale
> 5. its—school
> 6. their—nurses
> 7. it—training
> 8. its—program
> 9. them—nurses
> 10. They—nurses

Personal Pronouns

Personal pronouns are either singular or plural. Depending on to whom or what they refer, they are called *first-person*, *second-person*, or *third-person pronouns*.

KEY CONCEPT **Personal pronouns** refer to the person speaking (first person), the person spoken to (second person), or the person, place, or thing spoken about (third person). ■

Study the forms in the following chart:

PERSONAL PRONOUNS		
	Singular	Plural
First Person	I, me, my, mine	we, us, our, ours
Second Person	you, your, yours	you, your, yours
Third Person	he, him, his, she, her, hers, it, its	they, them, their, theirs

Pronouns • 303

Step-by-Step Teaching Guide

Personal Pronouns

1. Explain that a personal pronoun refers to the person or people speaking, the person or people spoken to, or the person or people, place or places, or thing or things spoken about.

2. Draw on the board a numeral *1*. Next draw an arrow leading away from the *1* and add a *2* at the point of the arrow. Then put a *3* a short distance away from the 1 and 2, but unconnected to them. Explain to students that this is one way they can remember personal pronouns: 1 (first person) is the speaker, 2 (second person) is the person to whom 1 is speaking, and 3 (third person) is outside the conversation, being spoken about.

3. Underscore that, while first- and second-person pronouns always refer to people, third-person pronouns can refer to places or things (*it*), as well as people (*he, she, him, her*).

Integrating Writing Skills

Explain that, whenever students use pronouns, they need to make sure that it is clear what the antecedent is. This is done either by having the pronoun close to the antecedent, or by making certain that nothing confusing is inserted between the antecedent and the pronoun. For example, in "Jana walked her dog," it is clear that *her* refers to Jana, because they are close together. If something gets inserted, it can be less clear: "Jana saw Melany while she was walking her dog." Do *she* and *her* refer to Jana or Melany?

ONGOING ASSESSMENT: Monitor and Reinforce

If students miss more than two items in Exercise 13, refer them to the following for additional practice.

In the Textbook	Print Resources	Technology
Section Review, Ex. 18, p. 309	Grammar Exercise Workbook, pp. 7–8	On-Line Exercise Bank, Section 14.2

Critical Viewing

Analyze Students may identify a friend or family member who helped or emergency personnel such as paramedics or ambulance driver. Pronouns would likely include *he, she, they, him, his.*

Customize for
ESL Students

In many languages there are two forms of "you"—singular and plural or formal. Make certain that non-English-speakers understand that in English we use "you" for both singular and plural. There are not different words for familiar and formal usage. This is as much a cultural issue as it is one of grammar. Make certain they understand that no disrespect is involved in using "you" for everyone. You might write on the board the forms of "you" in any languages represented in your class, then note that they all equal "you."

Answer Key

> **Exercise 14**

1. its—third person
2. their—third person
3. You—second person
4. Your—second person
5. My—first person
6. It—third person
7. them—third person
8. me—first person
9. Our—first person
10. She—third person

Language Highlight

While many of the world's languages have more than one way of saying "you," English currently has one. But English did have a singular and a plural *you* at one time. While it sounds very formal today, *thou* was the singular, familiar form, and *you* was the plural or formal form. *Thee* was an objective form (like *whom*), as in "I gave it to thee." *Thee* and *thou* would have been used with friends and family, and *you* would have been used when addressing a group, a stranger, or someone who deserved respect, such as a teacher.

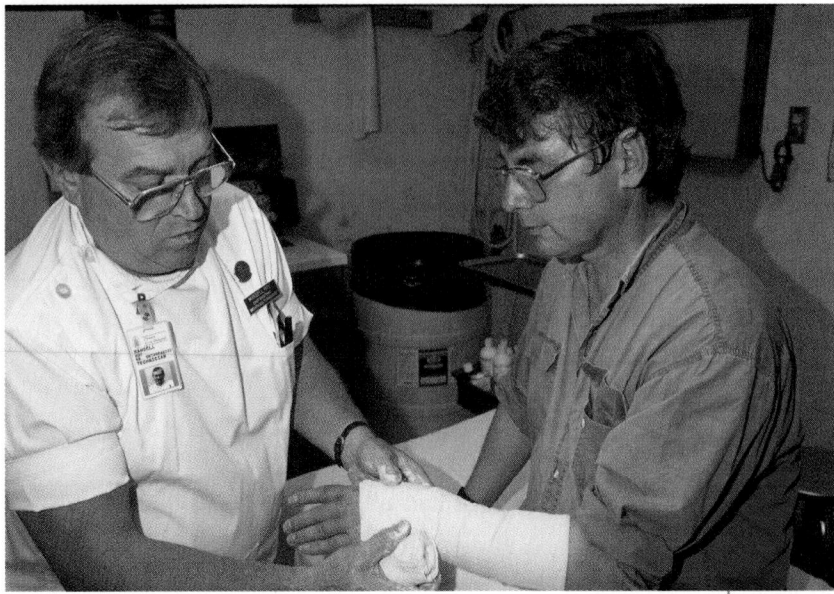

▲ **Critical Viewing** What other people besides a doctor and a physical therapist may have helped this man? What pronouns did you use in your answer? **[Analyze]**

> **Exercise 14** **Identifying Personal Pronouns** Copy the italicized pronoun in each of the following sentences onto your paper. Identify the pronoun as *first person, second person,* or *third person.*

EXAMPLE: The teacher asked *him* a difficult question.
ANSWER: him (third person)

1. Physical therapy received *its* start in the latter part of the nineteenth century.
2. Physical therapists teach *their* patients different forms of exercise.
3. *You* may be required to take courses in human anatomy.
4. *Your* training will include clinical instruction.
5. *My* physical therapist can offer treatment for different injuries.
6. *It* is used to improve strength, coordination, and endurance.
7. Many people say exercise has helped *them*.
8. A career in physical therapy interests *me*.
9. *Our* aunt will receive a degree in physical therapy after six years of college.
10. *She* looks forward to helping people recover from injuries.

304 • Nouns and Pronouns

✎ STANDARDIZED TEST PREPARATION WORKSHOP

Grammar and Usage Many standardized tests require students to identify the correct form of a pronoun for completing a sentence. Write the following on the board and ask students to identify the correct pronoun.

My brother and his friend want to be doctors someday. First, ___ have to get better grades in science.

A he   C they
B we   D I

Students should recognize that the correct choice is item **C.** The brother and the friend combined require a plural pronoun. "We" or "I" might need to get better grades, but there is no antecedent to connect with these pronouns.

Demonstrative Pronouns

> **KEY CONCEPT** A **demonstrative pronoun** points out a specific person, place, or thing. ∎

There are two singular and two plural demonstrative pronouns:

DEMONSTRATIVE PRONOUNS			
Singular		**Plural**	
this	that	these	those

A demonstrative pronoun generally appears at the beginning of a sentence, with its antecedent appearing later in the same sentence. However, sometimes the demonstrative pronoun will be placed after its antecedent.

BEFORE: *That* has always been my favorite *subject.*

AFTER: We met an EMT and a doctor. *These* were the most interesting guests.

> **Exercise 15** Recognizing Demonstrative Pronouns
> Identify five demonstrative pronouns in the following paragraphs:

Science and math are two of my favorite subjects. These are important studies for anyone planning a career in medicine. I hope to become a doctor, specializing in sports medicine. All medical students, no matter what specialty they plan to enter, must do well in all the sciences, as well as math. That is the reason I work hard to get good grades and understand the material. To do well in school, to get into a good pre-med program, and to eventually become "Dr. Sanabria"—those are my goals.

You may think this is too early to plan for college. Some students don't start thinking about their goals until high school. I know there are many careers open to me. I can always change my mind. For now, however, sports medicine is what I hope will be my career. That would be a dream come true.

ⓠ Learn More

The words *this, that, these,* and *those* can also function as adjectives. See Chapter 16 to learn more about pronouns used as adjectives.

▶ More Practice

Language Lab
CD-ROM
• Using Pronouns lesson
On-line
Exercise Bank
• Section 14.2
Grammar Exercise
Workbook
• pp. 9–10

Demonstrative Pronouns

1. Suggest that students imagine someone demonstrating a new product. Wouldn't the demonstrator point out that "this is a new feature," or "these are new functions"? Explain that some pronouns are called *demonstrative* because they demonstrate, or point out, someone or something.

2. Emphasize that, while most demonstrative pronouns appear at the beginning of a sentence, they often appear at the end of a question. (What is that? Whose are those?) In the case of questions, the antecedent appears in the answer.

3. Write the following sentences on the board, then have students identify the antecedents for each demonstrative pronoun.

   What are <u>those</u>? They are my new <u>books</u>.

   <u>This</u> is a beautiful <u>day</u>.

   Go to the <u>zoo</u>. <u>That</u> is a great place to learn about animals.

Customize for
Spatial Learners

Hand several students objects, such as a ruler, two or three books, a marker. You may want to have them stand at the front of the class. Then have other students form questions using appropriate demonstrative pronouns (What is that? What are those?) while pointing at the object(s) to be identified. Then have the students holding the objects respond using the appropriate demonstrative pronoun for what they are holding (This is a marker. These are books.).

Answer Key

> **Exercise 15**

These, That, those, this, That

☑ ONGOING ASSESSMENT: Monitor and Reinforce

If students miss more than two items in Exercises 14 or 15, refer them to the following for additional practice.

In the Textbook	Print Resources	Technology
Section Review, Ex. 18–20, p. 309	Grammar Exercise Workbook, pp. 7–10	On-Line Exercise Bank, Section 14.2

Interrogative Pronouns

1. Discuss with students how questions are formed (inverting the verb and subject—"*Claudia is . . .*" becomes "*Is Claudia?*"—or using a word that signals a question—*who, what, when, where, why*).

2. Explain that often a word that signals a question—an interrogative word—refers to or replaces a noun, which means that it is a pronoun.

3. Emphasize that not all interrogative words are pronouns.

4. Point out that one way to identify an interrogative pronoun is to try to reword a question as a response, with a noun in place of the pronoun: *Who is, Bill is; What are, Dogs are.* Since one o'clock is not a person, place or thing, it shows that "when" is not an interrogative pronoun.

5. Explain that, as a general rule, *who* is used as a subject —for example, "Who played the piano?" "Who walked the dog?"—while *whom* is an object, and will be used with a preposition—for example, *to whom, with whom, for whom.*

Answer Key

> **Exercise 16**

1. What
2. Which
3. Who
4. Whose
5. whom

Indefinite Pronouns

1. Ask students if they have ever said, "Everybody is doing it." Discuss why they use words like "everybody." (They are generalizing; there is no specific person they have in mind.)

2. Explain that not having a specific person, place, or thing in mind is one reason we use indefinite pronouns.

306

14.2

Interrogative Pronouns

To *interrogate* means "to ask questions."

> **KEY CONCEPT** An **interrogative pronoun** is used to begin a question. ■

All five interrogative pronouns begin with *w*:

INTERROGATIVE PRONOUNS				
what	which	who	whom	whose

Most interrogative pronouns do not have antecedents.

EXAMPLE: *What* did the doctor say?
    Which is the best treatment?
    Who wants to be a doctor?

> **Exercise 16**   Recognizing Interrogative Pronouns Identify the interrogative pronoun in each sentence below.

EXAMPLE: What happened to the cookies I baked?
ANSWER: What

1. What does a podiatrist do?
2. Which of these doctors treats foot diseases?
3. Who will be treated by a podiatrist?
4. Whose is the most difficult training?
5. From whom will you receive your podiatry training?

Indefinite Pronouns

> **KEY CONCEPT** An **indefinite pronoun** refers to a person, place, or thing that is not specifically named. ■

EXAMPLES: *Everything* is ready for the field trip.
    Everyone wants to see the medical center.

An indefinite pronoun can function either as an adjective or as the subject of a sentence.

ADJECTIVE: *Both* students want to be nurses.
SUBJECT: *Both* want to be nurses.

> **More Practice**
>
> **Language Lab CD-ROM**
> • Using Pronouns lesson
> **On-line Exercise Bank**
> • Section 14.2
> **Grammar Exercise Workbook**
> • pp. 9–12

---

3. Review the list of indefinite pronouns on page 307 and ask students if they regularly use these words. Ask them to suggest situations where they would want to use an indefinite pronoun in a sentence.

INDEFINITE PRONOUNS

Singular		Plural	Singular or Plural
another	much	both	all
anybody	neither	few	any
anyone	nobody	many	more
anything	no one	others	most
each	nothing	several	none
either	one		some
everybody	other		
everyone	somebody		
everything	someone		
little	something		

▶ **Exercise 17** **Recognizing Indefinite Pronouns** On your paper, write the indefinite pronoun you find in each sentence.

EXAMPLE: Each wanted to help Susan.

ANSWER: Each

1. One of the doctors is an optometrist.
2. Another is an ophthalmologist.
3. Both treat eye diseases.
4. Each must have a medical degree.
5. Everyone should have regular checkups.

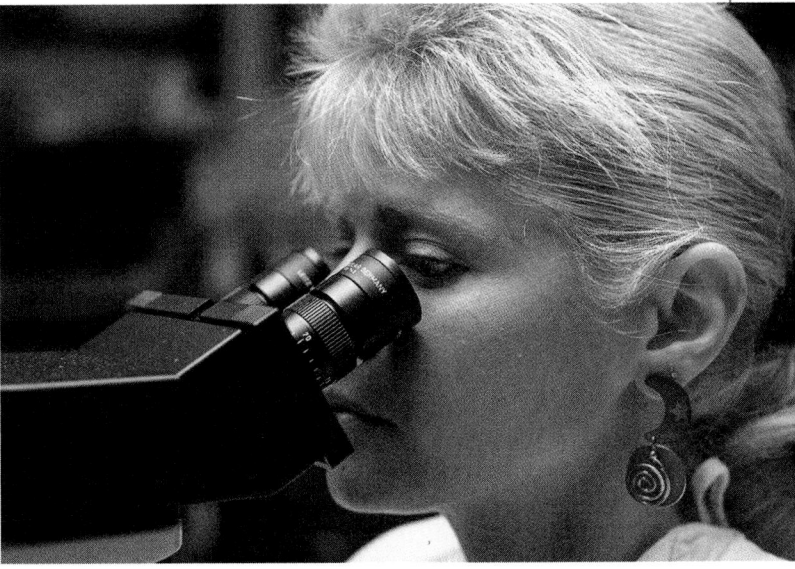

◀ **Critical Viewing**
What questions might this person be asking herself about what she sees? What interrogative pronouns might she use? **[Speculate]**

Pronouns • 307

Integrating Workplace Skills

Pronouns are important in news reporting. Journalists rely on interrogative pronouns to help develop stories. They generally avoid indefinite pronouns, because indefinite pronouns are not accurate enough for reporting the news. In addition, journalists need to be careful that readers can always tell what the antecedent is for a pronoun. If they report that "The mayor's dog chased a ball. He then went to work," we can guess that *he* probably refers to the mayor. However, the way the sentences are constructed, the antecedent for *he* is the dog. Imagine how embarrassing this type of mistake could be for a journalist.

Answer Key

▶ **Exercise 17**

1. One
2. Another
3. Both
4. Each
5. Everyone

Critical Viewing

Speculate Students may suggest questions about the things that she is seeing (What is it?) or the quality of how she is seeing it (Is it blurry or clear?).

Customize for
Less Advanced Students

For students who need additional practice with interrogative or indefinite pronouns, write the following sentences on the chalkboard, and have students pick the correct word. Feel free to add additional examples.

She threw the ball to (who/whom)? (whom)

(Is/Are) anyone going to the game? (Is)

(Who/Whom) is at the door? (Who)

Few (share/shares) my interests in botany. (share)

Everything (is/are) where (it/they) (belong/belongs). (is, it, belongs)

You called (who/whom) about the party? (whom)

☑ **ONGOING ASSESSMENT: Monitor and Reinforce**

If students miss more than two items in Exercises 16 or 17, refer them to the following for additional practice.

In the Textbook	Print Resources	Technology
Section Review, Ex. 20–21, p. 309	Grammar Exercise Workbook, pp. 9–12	On-Line Exercise Bank, Section 14.2

Nouns and Pronouns Circle Book

Teaching Resources: Hands-on Grammar Activity Book, Ch.14

1. Be sure that students have their Hands-on Grammar activity books or that you have prepared copies of the relevant pages for them. You will need pencils and scissors for this activity. It would also be a good idea to have prepared a circle book in advance, to show students the finished product.

2. After students have cut out the circles, make sure they fold the circles into fourths before labeling the sections.

3. After they have made the cut between sections 3 and 4, have students refold their circles into quarters before taping. If they put the folded circles next to each other, it should be obvious how taping section 3 (collective nouns) of one circle to section 4 (demonstrative nouns) of the next circle will create a "book."

Find It in Your Writing

If students are having difficulty identifying types of nouns and pronouns, encourage them to go back through this chapter looking at the examples and Key Concepts.

Find It in Your Reading

You may wish to suggest an additional selection, to help students find examples of all the various nouns and pronouns. Alternatively, you could simply encourage students to fill in the book as they read during the week, checking for correct entries at a later time.

14.2

Hands-on Grammar

Nouns and Pronouns Circle Book

1. Cut out two circles of equal size, at least 6 ½ inches in diameter. Fold each circle into fourths.

2. Label each fourth of the paper as shown.

3. Cut to the center of each circle along the line between sections 3 and 4, and then place the circles back to back, lining up the sections that are shown here in matching colors.

4. Tape the open edge of "Collective Nouns" to the open edge of "Demonstrative Pronouns." This creates a completed circle book.

5. On each section, write the definition of the type of noun or pronoun.

6. Fold your completed circle book, and keep it in your notebook. Add examples of each type of noun or pronoun as you find them.

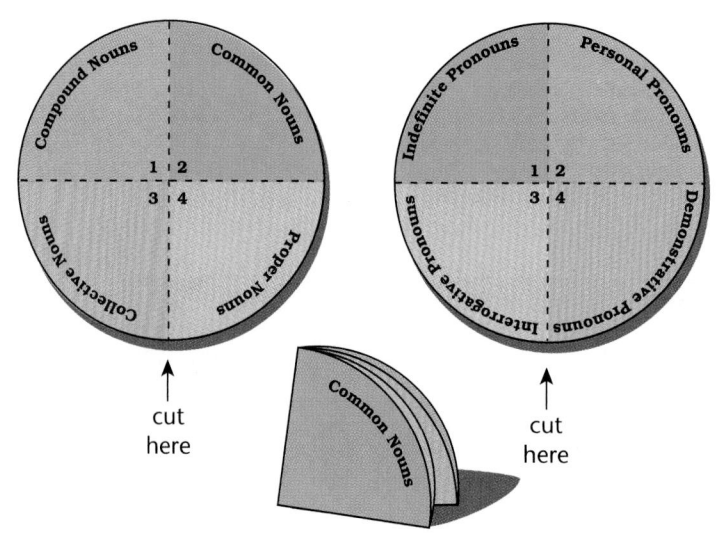

cut here   cut here

Find It in Your Writing Look through your portfolio to find examples of each kind of noun and each kind of pronoun. Write them down in the appropriate section of your circle book.

Find It in Your Reading Record examples of each type of noun and pronoun as you discover them in your reading. Start by recording examples from the Grammar in Literature example on page 299.

308 • Nouns and Pronouns

✓ **ONGOING ASSESSMENT: Monitor and Reinforce**

Use the following resources to assess student mastery of nouns and pronouns.

In the Textbook	Print Resources	Technology
Chapter Review, Ex. 30–34, pp. 310–311	Formal Assessment, Chapter 14	On-Line Exercise Bank, Sections 14.2

Section Review

GRAMMAR EXERCISES 18–24

Exercise 18 Identifying Personal Pronouns Identify the personal pronoun in each sentence.

1. My brother and sister want to become pharmacists. They must attend a college of pharmacy.
2. After finishing a five-year program, he will graduate.
3. They must complete a one-year internship before becoming pharmacists.
4. She may choose from many schools.
5. All of them offer similar programs.

Exercise 19 Identifying Antecedents of Personal Pronouns Fill in the blank with the appropriate personal pronoun. Circle the antecedent of the pronoun you supply.

1. Radiologists must attend medical school. ___?___ spend five years studying radiology.
2. If my brother studies radiology, ___?___ will have to complete a residency program.
3. My aunt is a radiologist. ___?___ has her own practice.
4. After completing ___?___ residency, radiologists may decide to specialize.
5. ___?___ may choose to teach instead.

Exercise 20 Recognizing Types of Pronouns Identify each of the pronouns in the sentences below as *personal, demonstrative, interrogative,* or *indefinite.*

1. My brother is in high school. He wants to study forensic medicine.
2. That is the study of medical evidence.
3. It helps police officers solve crimes.
4. You may have seen popular shows about "crime doctors."

5. Who wants to know more?
6. These are copies of fingerprints.
7. Each is unique.
8. Whose is this fingerprint?
9. What can we learn from fingerprints?
10. Few can identify a fingerprint.

Exercise 21 Revision Practice Replace each italicized noun in the sentences below with the type of pronoun indicated in brackets. Some sentences may have to be rewritten as questions. Revise punctuation as needed.

1. *Family practitioners* [personal] provide primary medical care.
2. Family doctors know *family doctors'* [personal] patients.
3. *Dedication* [demonstrative] is one reason they enter the field.
4. *Family practitioners* [interrogative] can refer patients to a specialist.
5. *General practitioners* [indefinite] have had many years of medical training.

Exercise 22 Find It in Your Reading Identify three personal pronouns in the excerpt from "The Cat Who Thought She Was a Dog . . ." on page 299.

Exercise 23 Find It in Your Writing In your own writing, find at least one example of each kind of pronoun.

Exercise 24 Writing Application Write a brief description about a person in a job that interests you. Identify the kinds of pronouns you use.

ASSESS and CLOSE

Section Review

Each of these exercises correlates to a concept in the chapter on pronouns, pages 301–308. The exercises may be used for more practice, for reteaching, or for review of the Key Concepts presented. Answers for all chapter exercises are available in *Grammar Exercises Answers on Transparencies* in your Teaching Resources.

Answer Key

Exercise 18

1. My; They
2. he
3. They
4. She
5. them

Exercise 19

1. They—radiologists
2. he—brother
3. She—aunt
4. their—radiologists
5. They—radiologists

Exercise 20

1. My, He—personal
2. That—demonstrative
3. It—personal
4. You—personal
5. Who—interrogative
6. These—demonstrative
7. Each—indefinite
8. Whose—interrogative, this—demonstrative
9. What—interrogative, we—personal
10. Few—indefinite

Exercise 21

1. They
2. their
3. That (or This)
4. Who
5. All

Exercise 22

Find It in Your Reading
He, their, his. (If students included the title in their search, they may also have "she.")

Exercise 23

Find It in Your Writing
Students' answers should include samples of each kind of pronoun, all correctly identified by type.

continued

Answer Key continued

Exercise 24

Writing Application
Emphasize to students the importance of making certain that each pronoun has an antecedent, and that the antecedents are close enough to the pronouns to make it easy to determine the connection. If there is time, you may wish to have volunteers share their descriptions with the class.

These exercises correlate to the concepts taught on nouns and pronouns, pages 296–309. The exercises may be used for more practice, for reteaching, or for review of the Key Concepts presented.

Answer Key

Exercise 25

1. pack, wolves, rabbit
2. rabbit, fear
3. hunger, wolves
4. prey, forest
5. howls, animals, frustration

Exercise 26

Wolves are wild animals that look similar to dogs. A wolf has fur that can be white, black, or gray. Wolves travel in packs, using their speed and strength to hunt as a group. They live in most climates, but rarely in deserts or tropical forests.

Exercise 27

(C = common, P = proper)

1. sister-C, Lucy-P, mother-C, cat-C, hospital-C (or possibly animal hospital identified as one compound noun, but still C)
2. hospital-C, Philadelphia-P
3. cat-C, train-C
4. train-C, cities-C, New York-P, New Jersey-P
5. cat-C, Trudy-P, surgery-C
6. Dr. Kim-P, veterinarian-C
7. mother-C, magazine-C
8. dog-C, character-C, movie-C, *Benji*-P
9. poodle-C, chair-C
10. home-C, Liberty Bell-P

GRAMMAR EXERCISES 25–36

Exercise 25 Identifying Nouns in Sentences Identify the nouns in each sentence below.

1. The pack of wolves chased the rabbit.
2. The rabbit, filled with fear, ran away.
3. Because of their hunger, the wolves continued to hunt.
4. They found no more prey in the forest.
5. The howls of the hungry animals showed their frustration.

Exercise 26 Identifying Nouns in Paragraphs Identify the nouns in the paragraph below.

Wolves are wild animals that look similar to dogs. A wolf has fur that can be white, black, or gray. Wolves travel in packs, using their speed and strength to hunt as a group. They live in most climates, but rarely in deserts or tropical forests.

Exercise 27 Identifying Common and Proper Nouns Identify the nouns in each sentence below. Then, tell whether each noun is *common* or *proper*.

1. My sister Lucy, my mother, and I took our cat to the animal hospital.
2. The hospital is in Philadelphia.
3. We took the cat on the train.
4. The train passed through cities in New York and New Jersey.
5. Our cat Trudy needed special surgery.
6. Dr. Kim, the veterinarian, was very kind.
7. While we waited, my mother and I read a magazine.
8. We saw a dog that looked like a character from the movie *Benji*.
9. A poodle sat on a chair next to us.
10. Before we returned home, we stopped to see the Liberty Bell.

Exercise 28 Identifying Collective Nouns Identify the collective noun in each sentence below.

1. My class went on a trip to the animal hospital last week.
2. The team of veterinarians sees many types of patients.
3. Yesterday, they treated a group of monkeys from the zoo.
4. Sometimes, they go to farms to check a herd of cattle.
5. My family brought our cat to this animal hospital.

Exercise 29 Identifying Compound Nouns Identify the compound noun in each sentence below.

1. My sister-in-law brought a new cat home from the pound.
2. They told her that a police officer had found the cat.
3. It does not get along with the sheepdog in the house.
4. She brought it to the middle school where she teaches.
5. On the way home, they crossed the George Washington Bridge.

Exercise 30 Identifying Personal Pronouns Identify each personal pronoun below as *first person*, *second person*, or *third person*. Then, tell whether the pronoun is *singular* or *plural*.

1. you   6. I
2. she   7. his
3. their   8. yours
4. our   9. mine
5. them   10. we

Exercise 28

1. class
2. team
3. group
4. herd
5. family

Exercise 29

1. sister-in-law
2. police officer
3. sheepdog
4. middle school
5. George Washington Bridge

Exercise 30

1. you—second person, singular and plural
2. she—third person, singular
3. their—third person, plural
4. our—first person, plural
5. them—third person, plural
6. I—first person, singular
7. his—third person, singular
8. yours—second person, singular and plural
9. mine—first person, singular
10. we—first person, plural

> **Exercise 31** Identifying Pronouns and Antecedents Identify the pronoun in each sentence below. Then, identify its antecedent. Remember that the antecedent may be in a previous sentence.

1. The doctor explained that she would order tests.
2. The tests would help her determine what was wrong.
3. She said they are very accurate tests.
4. These are the tests she ordered.
5. This is the medication she prescribed for the cat.

> **Exercise 32** Supplying Pronouns Read the paragraph. Identify the antecedent to which the missing pronoun refers. Then, supply the correct pronoun to fill in the blank.

My friend's father is a veterinarian. ___?___ works at the zoo. Our class took a trip to the zoo. ___?___ learned a lot about animals. We saw a family of monkeys. ___?___ were very funny. Some animals need to be vaccinated. The shots prevent ___?___ from getting sick. At five o'clock, we left the zoo. ___?___ closes to the public at that time.

> **Exercise 33** Classifying Pronouns Identify each underlined pronoun below as *personal, demonstrative, interrogative,* or *indefinite.*

1. <u>What</u> is a veterinarian?
2. <u>This</u> is the doctor who takes care of the animals.
3. <u>Everyone</u> in the office helps care for the animals.
4. <u>All</u> seem concerned and helpful.
5. <u>Whom</u> should <u>we</u> talk to about our cat?
6. <u>These</u> are <u>her</u> medical records.
7. Should <u>we</u> be concerned about <u>her</u> cough?
8. <u>That</u> is one of <u>my</u> biggest concerns.
9. The office staff was reassuring. <u>They</u> told us it's a common ailment.
10. <u>Which</u> is <u>your</u> cat?

> **Exercise 34** Using Nouns and Pronouns Revise the following paragraph. When it will improve the paragraph, replace nouns with pronouns and common nouns with proper nouns.

Last week, my family went to the animal shelter. The director of the shelter, Mr. Miller, said my family could choose a puppy. First, though, my family had to fill out a form. Then, the man took us to the puppy room. In the puppy room, Mr. Miller let my family play with the puppies. My brother liked the little brown mutt. My brother thought the little brown mutt was the cutest. My sister liked the little white poodle. My sister thought the little white poodle was the cutest. The man said my family could come back another day, but my family decided on the spot. My family took both of the puppies!

> **Exercise 35** Find It in Your Writing Look through your portfolio. Identify examples in your own writing of each type of noun and each type of pronoun. Challenge yourself to improve a piece of writing by replacing a vague common noun with a more specific proper noun or compound noun.

> **Exercise 36** Writing Application Write a short paper about an animal that interests you. Use at least one proper noun, one collective noun, and one compound noun. Identify where you have used each type of noun. Remember to use pronouns when they help you avoid awkward repetitions of nouns.

Chapter Review • 311

Answer Key continued

> **Exercise 35**

Find It in Your Writing
Students' responses will vary. Look for examples of each type of noun and pronoun in their work. Encourage them to also look for pronoun and antecedent pairs as they work to make their writing more precise.

> **Exercise 36**

Writing Application
Explain to students that the objectives of careful use of nouns and pronouns are increasing clarity while reducing awkwardness. There is always a chance that the message will get lost if writing is not clear, or that the reader will give up if the writing is too hard to get through.

> **Exercise 31**

1. she, doctor
2. her, doctor
3. She, doctor; they, tests
4. these, tests
5. this, medication; she, doctor

> **Exercise 32**

friend's father—He works at the zoo.
class—We learned a lot about animals.
monkeys—They were very funny.
animals—The shots prevent them from getting sick.
zoo—It closes to the public at that time.

> **Exercise 33**

1. What—interrogative
2. This—demonstrative
3. Everyone—indefinite
4. All—indefinite
5. Whom—interrogative; we—personal
6. These—demonstrative, her—personal
7. we—personal, her—personal
8. That—demonstrative, my—personal
9. They—personal
10. Which—interrogative; your—personal

> **Exercise 34**

Students' rewrites will vary; accept those with a sufficient number of changes to show understanding and correct usage. Note: "I" is never mentioned, so "they" or "them" could replace "we" or "us," because inclusion of the speaker is not obvious. One possible rewrite:

Last week, my family went to the animal shelter. The director of the shelter, Mr. Miller, said we could choose a puppy. First, though, we had to fill out a form. Then, Mr. Miller took us to the puppy room. There, he let us play with the puppies. My brother liked the little brown mutt. He thought it was the cutest. My sister liked the little white poodle. She thought it was the cutest. Mr. Miller said we could come back another day, but we decided on the spot. We took both of the puppies!

Step-by-Step Teaching Guide:

Nouns in Analogies

Teaching Resources: Standardized Test Preparation Workbook, pp. 27–28

1. Explain that an analogy item on a test expresses comparison between two pairs of words. In order to complete an analogy, students must determine the type of relationship in the first pair of words and then identify a second pair that has the same relationship. For example, the relationship of *cow* to *herd* is that of *part* to *whole*. Students should recognize that the same relationship exists between *bird* and *flock*.

2. Point out that students have studied in this chapter one type of noun that commonly appears in analogies—the collective noun.

3. Explain to students that there are many other types of analogies, but whole-to-part or part-to-whole are very common.

4. Encourage students to read test instructions carefully. Not all standardized tests are graded in the same way. Some tests do not penalize students for incorrect answers, so that they may increase their scores with a judicious guess.

5. Suggest that, if students get stuck on any questions, they go to the next question, then return to the difficult question(s) later.

6. You may wish to provide students with standardized test answer sheets so they can practice their test-taking skills.

Standardized Test Preparation Workshop

Nouns in Analogies

Many standardized tests contain analogies, items that measure your ability to identify the relationships between words. Analogies are like word-pair puzzles. Two common types of relationships used in analogies are part-to-whole and whole-to-part. For example, fur is to rabbit as feather is to bird. Both pairs of words begin with a noun that names part of the whole thing named by the second noun.

Standardized tests may present a sentence and leave a blank, or they may use two dots to indicate the two related words and a pair of two dots to separate the two pairs of words. The following items will give you practice in responding to analogies. Two different formats are used to show you the two most common ways these items appear on tests.

Test Tips

- Read each answer choice carefully to eliminate any answer pairs—such as "salt : pepper"—in which nouns are linked by "force of habit," not by a logical relationship.
- Do not be distracted by a pair of words that is in part-to-whole order if the first pair is in whole-to-part order.

Sample Test Items	Answers and Explanations
Directions: Complete each item by choosing the word that best completes the sentence. Library is to book as (A) artist is to painting. (B) art is to history. (C) page is to book. (D) museum is to painting.	The correct answer is *D*. The library is the whole that contains the part—book—and the museum is the whole that contains the part—painting.
Directions: Each question below consists of a related pair of words followed by five pairs of words labeled *A* through *E.* Select the pair that best expresses a relationship similar to that expressed in the original pair. SLEEVE : SHIRT :: (A) flag : country (B) tree : branch (C) window : house (D) temperature : fever (E) whale : fish	The correct answer is *C*. A sleeve is part of the whole shirt, so the answer should reflect a part-to-whole relationship. In *A*, the flag is a symbol for the country, not a physical part of it. In *B*, a tree is the whole of which the branch is a part. The relationship is the reverse of part-to-whole. *D* and *E* are incorrect because the word pairs do not express any kind of part-whole relationships.

312 • Nouns and Pronouns

✏ TEST-TAKING TIP

Tell students that in cases where the analogy uses part-to-whole or whole-to-part relationships, it is important to make sure that the parts are comparable.

For example, a foot is comparable to a paw or hoof, but not to a tail or wing. So an anaolgy of "foot is to human as" could be answered by "paw is to cat" but not by "tail is to cat," even

though this second example is a part to whole comparison

Point out that parts and wholes are not always obvious—sometimes "a part" means that which makes up the whole—cloth is "part" of a dress, because the dress is made of cloth. Therefore, "Cloth: dress" could be compared with "metal: spoon" or "leather: shoe."

Answer Key

▶ **Practice 1**
1. C
2. C
3. A
4. B
5. C

▶ **Practice 2**
1. B
2. C
3. D
4. A
5. C

▶ **Practice 1** Each question below consists of a related pair of words, followed by five pairs of words labeled *A* through *E*. Select the pair that best expresses a relationship similar to that expressed in the original pair.

1. METAL : COIN ::

   (A) queen : crown
   (B) wool : sheep
   (C) clay : vase
   (D) liquid : cup
   (E) painting : frame

2. FOOT : INCH ::

   (A) year : summer
   (B) lemonade : lemon
   (C) pound : ounce
   (D) bicycle : wheel
   (E) day : week

3. SAND : DUNE ::

   (A) water : ocean
   (B) thunder : lightning
   (C) stove : kitchen
   (D) flake : snow
   (E) rain : flower

4. WAR : BATTLE ::

   (A) fruit : pit
   (B) concert : song
   (C) soldier : courage
   (D) king : dignity
   (E) ship : sail

5. BOOK : LIBRARY ::

   (A) magazine : page
   (B) desk : school
   (C) money : bank
   (D) head : hat
   (E) disk : computer

▶ **Practice 2** Choose the phrase that best completes each sentence below.

1. Handle is to cup as

   (A) wheel is to tire.
   (B) branch is to tree.
   (C) bird is to wing.
   (D) ear is to nose.

2. Point is to score as

   (A) game is to field.
   (B) math is to numbers.
   (C) table is to furniture.
   (D) error is to correction.

3. Sentence is to word as

   (A) pail is to water.
   (B) pile is to leaves.
   (C) hand is to finger.
   (D) melody is to note.

4. Traffic is to car as

   (A) crowd is to person.
   (B) ocean is to boat.
   (C) motor is to gasoline.
   (D) dinner is to food.

5. Bird is to flock as

   (A) fan is to audience.
   (B) runner is to race.
   (C) student is to class.
   (D) letter is to number.

In-Depth Lesson Plan

	LESSON FOCUS	PRINT AND MEDIA RESOURCES
DAY 1	**Action Verbs** Students learn and apply the concept of action verbs and do the Hands-on Grammar activity (pp. 316–318).	**Teaching Resources** *Grammar Exercise Workbook*, pp. 13–14; *Grammar Exercises Answers on Transparencies*, Ch 15; *Hands-On Grammar Activity Book*, Ch. 15 *Language Lab* **CD-ROM,** Using Verbs; **On-Line Exercise Bank,** Section 15.1
DAY 2	**Linking Verbs** Students learn and apply concepts involving linking verbs and do Grammar in Literature (pp. 320–324).	**Teaching Resources** *Grammar Exercise Workbook*, pp.15–18; *Language Lab* **CD-ROM,** Using Verbs; **On-Line Exercise Bank,** Section 15.2
DAY 3	**Helping Verbs** Students learn and apply concepts using helping verbs (pp. 326–328).	**Teaching Resources** *Grammar Exercise Workbook*, pp.19–20; *Language Lab* **CD-ROM,** Using Verbs; **On-Line Exercise Bank,** Section 15.3
DAY 4	**Review and Assess** Students review chapter and demonstrate mastery of use of action, linking and helping verbs (pp. 330–333).	**Teaching Resources** *Formal Assessment*, Ch. 15

Accelerated Lesson Plan

	LESSON FOCUS	PRINT AND MEDIA RESOURCES
DAY 1	**Action Verbs and Linking Verbs** Students cover concepts and usage of action and linking verbs as determined by Diagnostic Test (pp. 316–324).	**Teaching Resources** *Grammar Exercise Workbook*, pp. 13–18; *Grammar Exercises Answers on Transparencies*, Ch 15; *Hands-On Grammar Activity Book*, Chapter 15 *Language Lab* **CD-ROM,** Using Verbs; **On-Line Exercise Bank,** Section 15.1–2
DAY 2	**Helping Verbs and Review and Assess** Students cover concepts and usage of helping verbs as determined by Diagnostic Test and review chapter and demonstrate mastery of concepts (pp. 326–333).	**Teaching Resources** *Grammar Exercise Workbook*, pp.19–20; *Grammar Exercise Answers on Transparency*, Ch. 15; *Language Lab* **CD-ROM,** Using Verbs; **On-Line Exercise Bank,** Section 15.3 *Formal Assessment*, Ch. 15

Options for Adapting Lesson Plans

HOMEWORK

Have students complete any section of the chapter for homework.

FEATURES

Extend coverage with the Grammar in Literature feature (p. 324), and the Standardized Test Preparation Workshop (p. 332).

TECHNOLOGY

Students can use the On-Line Exercise Bank to complete the exercises on computer. The Auto Check feature will grade their work.

INTEGRATED SKILLS COVERAGE

Grammar in Literature
SE p. 324

Writing
Find It In Your Writing, SE pp. 318, 319, 325, 329
Writing Application, SE pp. 319, 325, 329

Reading
Find It In Your Reading, SE pp. 318, 319, 325, 329

Language Highlight
ATE p. 321

Workplace Skills
Integrating Workplace Skills, ATE p. 327

Spelling
ATE p. 328

Viewing and Representing
Critical Viewing, SE pp. 314, 317, 321, 322, 324, 327, 328

Real World Connection
ATE p. 317

ASSESSMENT SUPPORT

Standardized Test Preparation SE p. 332; ATE pp. 323, 327
Standardized Test Preparation Workbook, pp. 29–30
Formal Assessment, Ch. 15

MEETING INDIVIDUAL NEEDS

Less Advanced Students, ATE p. 322. Also see Ongoing Assessment, pp. 317, 322, 324, 328
ESL Students ATE p. 318
Gifted and Talented Students ATE p. 324

BLOCK SCHEDULING

Pacing Suggestions
For 90-minute Blocks
- Administer the Diagnostic Test to students to determine instructional coverage
- Have students complete the necessary exercises in class. Use the Hands-on Grammar activity to provide a change of pace.

Resources for Varying Instruction
- *Language Lab* CD-ROM If your students have access to hardware, a 90-minute block provides an ideal opportunity for students to work on computer.

Professional Development Support
- *How to Manage Instruction in the Block* This Teaching Resource provides management and activity suggestions.

MEDIA AND TECHNOLOGY

For the Student
- *Language Lab* CD-ROM Action verbs, linking verbs, helping verbs
- *On-Line Exercise Bank,* Ch. 15

For the Teacher
- *Resource Pro* CD-ROM

WRITING AND GRAMMAR WEB SITE

The Interactive Writing and Grammar Web site provides a wide array of support for students, teachers, and parents. Grammar support includes:

- *On-Line Exercise Bank* with Auto Check scoring
- Diagnostic and assessment support

www.phschool.com

LITERATURE CONNECTIONS

Grammar in Literature selection from *Prentice Hall Literature: Timeless Voices, Timeless Themes,* Bronze:
"Melting Pot," by Anna Quindlen, SE p. 324

► *Lesson Objectives*

1. To recognize verbs and understand their function in sentences
2. To distinguish between action and linking verbs
3. To recognize helping verbs and understand their function in verb phrases
4. To employ standard English usage in writing for audiences, including parts of speech

Critical Viewing

Analyze Students may suggest verbs such as *cry, yell, cheer, celebrate,* and *rejoice.*

Chapter 15 Verbs

▲ Critical Viewing
Identify three verbs that could name actions by immigrants when they first saw the Statue of Liberty.
[Analyze]

Verbs are words that name an action or describe a state of being. They describe what is happening in the sentence. Every complete sentence needs to include at least one verb.

Some verbs describe specific actions. If you were writing about the migration of people to the United States from foreign countries, you might use verbs for the actions of immigrants. For instance, you might tell what these people did as they left their homelands and traveled to the United States.

In this chapter, you will learn about *action verbs* and *linking verbs* and the ways that these verbs can be used with *helping verbs* in verb phrases.

314 • Verbs

☑ **ONGOING ASSESSMENT: Diagnose**

If students miss more than one item in each category, direct them to the relevant pages of the text and assign exercises for practice and review.

Verbs	Diagnostic Test Items	Teach	Practice	Section Reviews	Chapter Review
Skill Check A					
Transitive and Intransitive Verbs	A 1–5	p. 316–317	Ex. 2	Ex. 5	Ex. 28
Skill Check B					
Action Verbs	B 6–7, 9, 12–14, 16, 19	p. 316	Ex. 1, 2	Ex. 3–4, 15	Ex. 27, 30–32
Linking Verbs	B 8, 11, 15, 17–18, 20	pp. 320–324	Ex. 10–13	Ex. 13–15	Ex. 29–32

Diagnostic Test

Directions: Write all answers on a separate sheet of paper.

Skill Check A. Write the action verb in each sentence below and label it *transitive* or *intransitive*.

1. Thousands of people entered the United States in the nineteenth century.
2. These immigrants traveled from many different countries all around the world.
3. Many brought customs and traditions from their native lands.
4. They envisioned new opportunities in the United States.
5. Whole families moved from their homeland for numerous reasons.

Skill Check B. Identify the underlined word or words in each of the following sentences as an *action verb* or a *linking verb*.

6. Some <u>left</u> their homeland to look for better jobs.
7. Many people <u>had</u> hopes of owning their own land.
8. The United States <u>was</u> a land of opportunity for countless numbers of people.
9. Many people <u>looked</u> for wealth in a new land.
10. Some <u>hoped</u> for adventure.
11. The immigrants <u>were</u> joyful and hopeful.
12. Some <u>fled</u> their country because of war.
13. Many people <u>moved</u> to the United States for religious freedom.
14. The people <u>walked</u> away from everything familiar to them.
15. Some immigrants quickly <u>felt</u> comfortable in their new land.
16. Some <u>describe</u> the United States as a tapestry of cultures.
17. Ellis Island <u>was</u> the first stopping place for many immigrants.
18. This location <u>became</u> known worldwide as the entry to America.
19. People from all walks of life <u>entered</u> America through Ellis Island.
20. Life in the United States <u>seemed</u> exciting to the new arrivals.

Skill Check C. Identify the helping verbs and the main verbs in the following sentences.

21. The immigrants must have been waiting to see the Statue of Liberty.
22. They had often heard stories about the great wealth in America.
23. They should have been warned about the immigration laws.
24. Everyone was being thoroughly checked for physical ailments.
25. The number of immigrants each year was being limited.

Verbs • 315

Answer Key

Skill Check A

1. entered—transitive
2. traveled—intransitive
3. brought—transitive
4. envisioned—transitive
5. moved—intransitive

Skill Check B

6. action
7. action
8. linking
9. action
10. action
11. linking
12. action
13. action
14. action
15. linking
16. action
17. linking
18. linking
19. action
20. linking

Skill Check C

21. must have been—helping; waiting—main
22. had—helping; heard—main
23. should have been—helping; warned—main
24. was being—helping; checked—main
25. was being—helping; limited—main

✓ ONGOING ASSESSMENT: Diagnose *continued*

Verbs	Diagnostic Test Items	Teach	Practice	Section Reviews	Chapter Review
Skill Check C					
Helping Verbs and Main Verbs	C 21–25	pp. 326–328	Ex. 20–22	Ex. 22–23	Ex. 33–34
Cumulative Reviews and Applications				Ex. 7–9, 17–19, 25–27	Ex. 36

⏱ TIME SAVERS!

Answers on Transparency Use the Grammar Exercises Answers on Transparencies for Chapter 15 to facilitate correction by students.

On-Line Exercise Bank Have students complete the Diagnostic Test on computer. The Auto Check feature will grade their work for you!

Ask volunteers to write on the chalkboard three things they did yesterday (walked to school, rode a bike, and so on). Have other students underline the words that show the action in the items listed. Remind students that these words are called *verbs*.

Activate Prior Knowledge

Ask students to name the two essential parts of every sentence. (Possible answers: a subject and a verb, a subject and a predicate.)

TEACH

Step-by-Step Teaching Guide

Action Verbs

1. Explain to students that action verbs are used to tell what someone or something does, did, or will do.

2. Write the following sentences on the chalkboard and have students identify the action verbs:

   I walked to the store.

   I thought about a friend.

3. Point out to students that, while the action in the first sentence (*walked*) can be seen, the action in the second sentence (*thought*) cannot. Ask students to think of verbs for other actions that can't be seen (e.g. *dream, wish, wonder, understand*).

4. Explain to students that verbs can be described as transitive or intransitive depending on whether they *transfer* action to another word (a noun or pronoun other than the subject) in a sentence. A way for students to remember this is that <u>trans</u>itive verbs <u>trans</u>fer action. Intransitive verbs do not.

Answer Key

Exercise 1

1. walked	6. cried
2. wondered	7. docked
3. lashed	8. adapted
4. completed	9. found
5. studied	10. helped

Section 15.1

Action Verbs

Verbs such as *walk, sailed, played, migrate, raced, crossed, learn,* and *arrive* all show some kind of action.

KEY CONCEPT An **action verb** tells what action someone or something is performing. ■

EXAMPLES: Father *packed* our suitcases.
  The ship *chugged* into the harbor.

The verb *packed* explains what Father did to the suitcases. The verb *chugged* tells what the ship did.
  Some actions, such as *sailed* or *mingled*, can be seen. Some actions, such as *believe* or *recall*, cannot be seen.

Exercise 1 Recognizing Action Verbs Copy the following sentences onto your paper. Underline the action verb in each sentence.

EXAMPLE: The ship from Barcelona <u>arrived</u> three hours late.

1. Lines of people walked to the ship for their voyage across the ocean.
2. On board, many passengers wondered about their new homeland.
3. The waves lashed at the ship during storms.
4. Eventually, the immigrants completed the journey.
5. From the decks, children and their parents studied the coastline of their new homeland.
6. Some cried at the sight of the Statue of Liberty.
7. The ships full of passengers docked in New York Harbor.
8. Families adapted to the new culture.
9. Most of the people found jobs in America.
10. Their previous skills helped some of them find jobs.

KEY CONCEPT A **transitive verb** is an action verb that directs action from the performer of the action toward the receiver of the action. The "receiver" of the action is a person, place, or thing—that is, a noun or pronoun. An **intransitive verb** expresses action or tells something about the subject of the sentence but does not direct action toward another noun or pronoun. ■

TRANSITIVE:	The captain *rang* the bell.
INTRANSITIVE:	The bell *rang* for dinner.
TRANSITIVE:	The captain *sailed* the ship.
INTRANSITIVE:	The ship *sailed* out to sea.

316 • Verbs

Theme: Immigration
In this section, you will learn about action verbs. The examples and exercises in this section are about immigration.

Cross-Curricular Connection: Social Studies

More Practice

Language Lab CD-ROM
• Using Verbs lesson
On-line Exercise Bank
• Section 15.1
Grammar Exercise Workbook
• pp. 13–14

⏱ TIME AND RESOURCE MANAGER

Resources
Print: Grammar Exercise Workbook, pp.13–14; Hands-on Grammar Activity Book, Chapter 15
Technology: Language Lab CD-ROM, Using Verbs; On-Line Exercise Bank, Section 15.1

In-Depth Coverage	Accelerated Pace
• Work through all key concepts, pp. 316–317.	• Assign pp. 316–317, for independent student review.
• Assign and review Exercises 1–2.	
• Do the Hands-on Grammar Activity, p. 318.	• Assign Section Review Exercises 3–6.

> **Exercise 2** Identifying Transitive and Intransitive Verbs
> Write the underlined action verb in each of the sentences below. After each verb, write *transitive* or *intransitive*. If you label a verb *transitive*, identify the noun toward which the action is directed.

EXAMPLE: Marcia <u>picked</u> a bushel of apples from the tree.

ANSWER: picked—transitive; action is directed at bushel

1. Early settlers <u>hoped</u> for new lives in the United States.
2. They <u>explored</u> the new territory.
3. Some colonists <u>sailed</u> back to their homelands.
4. The other immigrants <u>stayed</u> in the U.S. permanently.
5. These people <u>shared</u> a dream of a better life.
6. They <u>dared</u> to cross the ocean.
7. They <u>settled</u> in the new land.
8. All <u>built</u> new lives.
9. Some <u>regretted</u> their decision.
10. Most <u>believed</u> in the promise of America.

⚙ Grammar and Style Tip

Use vivid action verbs such as *dash, scurry*, and *rush* to convey the way an action happens.

◄ Critical Viewing
Name at least four action verbs that describe what people on this crowded ship are doing. **[Relate]**

Action Verbs • 317

Answer Key

► **Exercise 2**

1. hoped—intransitive
2. explored—transitive; action is directed at territory
3. sailed—intransitive
4. stayed—intransitive
5. shared—transitive; action is directed at dream
6. dared—intransitive
7. settled—intransitive
8. built—transitive; action is directed at lives
9. regretted—transitive; action is directed at decision
10. believed—intransitive

Critical Viewing

Relate Student responses may include verbs such as *staring, smiling, waiting, standing,* and *wondering*.

Real-World Connection

Remind students that using specific action verbs is important in many kinds of real-world writing. In expository writing, such as recipes and instructions, specific verbs such as *mix, pour,* or *refrigerate,* help to clarify the particular action that needs to be performed.

☑ **ONGOING ASSESSMENT: Monitor and Reinforce**

If students miss more than two items in Exercises 1 or 2, refer them to the following for additional practice.

In the Textbook	Print Resources	Technology
Section Review, Ex. 3–5, p. 319	Grammar Exercise Workbook, pp. 13–14	Language Lab CD-ROM, Using Verbs On-Line Exercise Bank, Section 15.1

⏱ **TIME SAVERS!**

🖼 **Answers on Transparency** Use the Grammar Exercises Answers on Transparencies for Chapter 15 to facilitate correction by students.

💻 **On-Line Exercise Bank** Have students complete the exercises on computer. The Auto Check feature will grade their work for you!

Action Verb Showdown

Teaching Resources: Hands-on Grammar Activity Book, Chapter 15

1. You can choose to have students complete this activity in small groups. Give each student a copy of the Hands-on Grammar activity sheet, Chapter 15.

2. Not all students will agree on the intensity of each verb. Suggest that students consult a dictionary for definitions to help them in cases of disagreement.

3. As students continue the activity, circulate around the classroom to make sure students are explaining their ratings adequately.

Find It in Your Reading

Have students work in groups to give a rating to the verb. Students can either agree upon a rating or choose the average of the group's ratings.

Find It in Your Writing

Have students circle or highlight the action verbs they find. For each verb they wish to replace, suggest that they make a short list of four to five alternatives. Then they can select the best choice.

Customize for ESL Students

Students who are not fluent in English may not be able to "rate" the intensity of verbs. For these students, simply brainstorm for a list of verbs, then hold a discussion about the intensity of those listed. You may want to have some students act out some verbs, to make differences clear (for example, *jump, hop, leap*).

⏱ **TIME SAVER!**

✋ **Hands-on Grammar**
Use the Hands-on Grammar activity sheet for Chapter 15 to facilitate this activity.

15.1

Hands-on Grammar

Action Verb Showdown

To increase your understanding of action verbs, create and play an Action Verb Showdown game.

Work with a partner to brainstorm for a list of action verbs. Give each verb a "rating" from 1 to 5, based on the intensity of the action. With your partner, discuss whether some mental actions, such as *ponder*, are more intense than some visible actions, such as *sit*. Come to an agreement with your partner about the rating for each verb.

VISIBLE ACTION		MENTAL ACTION	
sail	swim	remember	decide
rip	migrates	understand	hope
bring	smile	expect	think
traveled	cried	consider	forgot

When you have listed approximately fifty verbs, write each verb and its rating on a separate piece of paper. Fold each piece of paper so that the verbs and ratings cannot be seen. Then, put all the verbs into a container such as a shoebox or coffee can. To play, each partner takes one of the pieces of paper from the container. The partner with the action verb that has the highest action rating gets to keep both verbs if he or she can explain why one verb is rated higher than the other. Otherwise, return both verbs to the box.

Then, each player takes another verb from the container. Continue playing until all verbs are taken from the container.

To score, add up the activity ratings of the verbs that each player has. The player with the highest total wins.

Find It in Your Reading Read the excerpt from "Melting Pot" on page 324. Give a rating to the action verb that is repeated in the passage. Think of a similar or related verb to which you would give a higher rating.

Find It in Your Writing Review a piece of writing from your portfolio. Identify the action verbs you have used. Challenge yourself to replace any verbs that do not express the precise intensity of the action to which you are referring.

318 • Verbs

☑ **ONGOING ASSESSMENT: Assess Mastery**

Use the following resources to assess student mastery of action verbs.

In the Textbook	Technology
Chapter Review, Ex. 28–29, p. 330	On-Line Exercise Bank, Section 15.1

Section 15.1 *Section Review*

GRAMMAR EXERCISES 3–9

Exercise 3 Finding Action Verbs
Identify the action verbs in the sentences that follow. One sentence contains more than one verb.

(1) Teachers in neighborhood schools helped immigrants with their English. (2) Sometimes, they taught groups in the evenings and very early in the mornings. (3) Soon, many immigrants spoke and wrote in English. (4) Some older people stumbled over the strange new language. (5) Many immigrants helped each other with their new language.

Exercise 4 Identifying Action Verbs
Copy the headings below. Under *performer*, list who or what is performing the action. Under *action*, list the verb.

EXAMPLE: The captain shouted at the crew.
ANSWER: PERFORMER   ACTION
         captain   shouted

1. The first immigrants arrived from England.
2. The ship approached the harbor.
3. The mayor announced the arrival of the immigrants.
4. The people celebrated their arrival in America.
5. A committee greeted the immigrants.

Exercise 5 Recognizing Transitive and Intransitive Verbs
Label each underlined verb *transitive* or *intransitive*.

1. The Statue of Liberty <u>impressed</u> most immigrants.
2. They <u>asked</u> about its meaning.
3. The statue <u>stands</u> as a symbol of liberty.
4. France <u>gave</u> the statue to the United States as a gift.
5. Americans <u>appreciated</u> the gift and <u>built</u> the pedestal for the statue.

Exercise 6 Revision Practice: Verbs
Revise each sentence by replacing the underlined words with a single, precise verb.

1. The ship <u>moved gracefully</u> away from the dock.
2. The family <u>quickly and eagerly accepted</u> the chance to immigrate.
3. We <u>moved quickly</u> toward the refreshment stand.
4. We <u>noisily sipped</u> our sodas.
5. We <u>walked as if we were very tired</u> back to the boat.

Exercise 7 Find It in Your Reading
Identify two action verbs in this passage from "Melting Pot" by Anna Quindlen. Do not include the verb phrases *doesn't carry* and *can buy.*

The greengrocer stocks yellow pepper and fresh rosemary for the gourmands, plum tomatoes and broadleaf parsley for the older Italians, mangoes for the Indians. He doesn't carry plantains, he says, because you can buy them in the bodega.

Exercise 8 Find It in Your Writing
Look through your writing portfolio. Find three examples of transitive verbs and three examples of intransitive verbs.

Exercise 9 Writing Application
Write a paragraph about the people in your neighborhood, including at least two transitive verbs and two intransitive verbs.

ASSESS

Section Review
Each of these exercises correlates with a concept in the section on action verbs, pages 316–318. The exercises may be used for more practice, for reteaching, or for review of the Key Concepts presented.

Answer Key

Exercise 3
1. helped
2. taught
3. spoke, wrote
4. stumbled
5. helped

Exercise 4

Performer	Action
1. immigrants	arrived
2. ship	approached
3. mayor	announced
4. people	celebrated
5. committee	greeted

Exercise 5
1. transitive
2. intransitive
3. intransitive
4. transitive
5. transitive, transitive

Exercise 6
Answers will vary; samples are given.
1. The ship glided away from the dock.
2. The family grabbed the chance to immigrate.
3. We ran toward the refreshment stand
4. We slurped our sodas.
5. We trudged back to the boat.

continued

Answer Key continued

Exercise 7

Find It in Your Reading
stocks, says

Exercise 8

Find It in Your Writing
Have students place these verbs in a two-column chart, with one column labeled *Transitive* and the other *Intransitive.*

Exercise 9

Writing Application
When they finish, have students exchange paragraphs with a partner and underline the verbs in each other's work.

⏱ TIME SAVERS!

Answers on Transparency
Use the Grammar Exercises Answers on Transparencies for Chapter 15 to facilitate correction by students.

On-Line Exercise Bank
Have students complete the exercises on computer. The Auto Check feature will grade their work for you!

Interest GRABBER Ask two students to stand and link arms. Then, hold up a piece of chain or picture of a chain. Ask students how the word "link" applies to the interlocked segments of the chain (connect things). Ask them what they would expect a word to do if it were described as a "link" (connect things in a sentence).

Activate Prior Knowledge

Refer students to the chapter introduction. The first sentence says that verbs "name an action or describe a state of being." Ask students, if action verbs name actions, which verbs must describe a state of being (linking verbs). Ask students what they think "a state of being" might be (what a thing *is*). Answers will likely include forms of *be*. Point out that *be* is the most common linking verb.

TEACH

Step-by-Step Teaching Guide

Linking Verbs

1. Remind students that not all sentences contain an action. In some sentences, the subject is described or identified. To demonstrate this, ask a student how he or she feels today. Point out that in the response (I feel happy, I am tired), the subject is describing himself or herself, not performing an action.

2. To emphasize how a linking verb shows a relationship, write forms of the verb *be* on the chalkboard:

    were

    is

    are

3. Have students take turns providing words for both the right and left sides of each verb to create complete sentences.

4. Then have students replace each verb with an equal sign, noting that the sentences still make sense. Point out that this would not be possible with action verbs.

Section 15.2 # Linking Verbs

Some verbs do not show action. Instead, they link two parts of a sentence. These *linking verbs* thus show a relationship between words in a sentence.

KEY CONCEPT A **linking verb** connects a noun or pronoun with a word that identifies or describes it. ■

EXAMPLES: New York *is* a city.

The best swimmers *were* Margie and Pia.

Lucy *seems* unhappy.

Linking verbs act almost as equal signs. *City* identifies *New York*; *Margie* and *Pia* identify the *swimmers*; *unhappy* describes *Lucy*.

The Most Common Linking Verb

In English, the most common linking verb is *be*. This verb has many forms.

FORMS OF *BE*		
am	can be	have been
are	could be	has been
is	may be	had been
was	might be	could have been
were	must be	may have been
am being	shall be	might have been
are being	should be	must have been
is being	will be	shall have been
was being	would be	should have been
were being		will have been
		would have been

Exercise 10 Writing Sentences With Linking Verbs Write a sentence using each form of *be* listed below.

1. might have been
2. should have been
3. could be
4. were being
5. will be
6. has been
7. shall be
8. is being
9. would be
10. had been

Theme: Immigration

In this section, you will learn about linking verbs. The examples and exercises in this section are about immigration.

Cross-Curricular Connection: Social Studies

⏱ TIME AND RESOURCE MANAGER

Resources
Print: Grammar Exercise Workbook, pp. 15–18
Technology: Language Lab CD-ROM, Using Verbs; On-Line Exercise Bank, Section 15.2

In-Depth Coverage	Accelerated Pace
• Work through all key concepts, pp. 320–324. • Assign and review Exercises 10–13. • Read and discuss Grammar in Literature, p. 324.	• Assign pp. 320–324, for independent student review. • Assign Section Review Exercises 14–16.

Exercise 11 Recognizing Forms of the Linking Verb *Be*

Copy the following sentences onto your paper. Underline the form of *be* in each one. Then, draw an arrow connecting the words that are linked by the verb.

EXAMPLE: The immigrants <u>were</u> happy.

1. Ellis Island was the busiest immigrant processing center in the United States.
2. The Immigration Service determines whether immigrants will be citizens.
3. Citizenship may have been open to people of all origins.
4. However, not all immigrants would be able to receive it.
5. The children may be cranky from waiting in the long lines.
6. An elderly man is sick from the long trip.
7. It had been a difficult voyage.
8. Soon, he will be a citizen of the United States.
9. Most of the people with him are his cousins.
10. The new Americans must have been nervous.

More Practice

Language Lab CD-ROM
• Using Verbs lesson
On-line Exercise Bank
• Section 16.2
Grammar Exercise Workbook
• pp. 15–16

▼ **Critical Viewing**
In what ways did Ellis Island serve a linking role for American immigrants? **[Analyze]**

Linking Verbs • **321**

321

Other Linking Verbs

1. Explain to students that linking verbs other than *be* are often used to connect a subject with an adjective that modifies the subject. Write the following partial sentences on the chalkboard.

   1. The pudding ___ delicious.

   2. The roses ___ wonderful.

   Ask students to provide linking verbs to complete each sentence. (Sample responses: 1. tasted, looked; 2. smelled, looked)

2. Ask students to write their own sentences using three of the linking verbs shown on the page.

Critical Viewing

Analyze Make sure students use complete sentences to describe the actions and feelings of the immigrants. (Sample responses: The immigrants *were* restless as they waited in the crowded room. The immigrants *appeared* anxious as they waited to leave the reception area.)

Customize for
Less Advanced Students

After reviewing the material on linking versus action verbs, on page 323 of the text, have students take turns writing a pair of sentences with a partner using a form of one of the verbs listed below. One sentence should use the verb as an action verb; the other sentence should use it as a linking verb. The partners should then read the sentences and discuss how the verb is used in each one.

smell, turn, sound, taste, look, feel

15.2

Other Linking Verbs

Be is the most commonly used linking verb, but there are some other important linking verbs you should know.

OTHER LINKING VERBS		
appear	look	sound
become	remain	stay
feel	seem	taste
grow	smell	turn

Like *be*, these verbs are often used to link two parts of a sentence.

EXAMPLES: She later became a citizen.

The cream tastes sour.

The food stayed fresh and crisp.

▶ Critical Viewing Use linking verbs—such as *are, was, seem,* or *feel*—in sentences that describe the immigrants in a waiting room at Ellis Island. [**Analyze**]

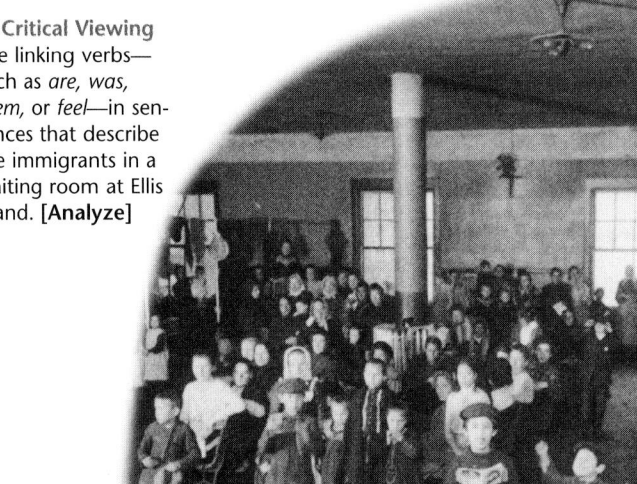

322 • Verbs

Internet Tip

To learn more about immigration, use search words such as *Ellis Island, immigration, emigration,* and *Immigration and Naturalization Service.*

✓ **ONGOING ASSESSMENT: Monitor and Reinforce**

If students miss more than two items in Exercises 9 and 10, refer them to the following for additional practice.

In the Textbook	Print Resources	Technology
Section Review, Ex. 14, p. 325	Grammar Exercise Workbook, pp. 15–16	Language Lab CD-ROM, Using Verbs On-Line Exercise Bank, Section 15.2

▶ **Exercise 12** Identifying Other Linking Verbs Copy each of the following sentences onto your paper. Underline the linking verb in each one. Then, draw arrows connecting the words that are linked by the verb.

EXAMPLE: During the storm, the road quickly <u>turned</u> muddy.

1. The atmosphere on the ship seemed exciting.
2. Everyone stayed quiet at the very beginning of the voyage.
3. The waves sounded rough and frightening to the passengers.
4. The captain appeared gruff.
5. The voyage became an adventure for the young children.
6. During the long trip, each child grew hungry and tired.
7. At that point, anything tasted delicious to them.
8. Regardless of their condition, the immigrants felt happy to be in the United States.
9. They remained hopeful.
10. Some immigrants looked discouraged because of the long delays.

Action Verb or Linking Verb?

Many of the twelve verbs in the preceding chart can be used as either linking verbs or action verbs.

LINKING: The bread *smelled* stale. (*Smelled* links *bread* and *stale*.)

ACTION: Charles *smelled* the sea air. (Charles is performing an action.)

LINKING: The Dutch bulbs *grow* tall. (*Grow* links *bulbs* and *tall*.)

ACTION: Annemarie *grows* tulips. (Annemarie is performing an action.)

To test whether a verb is a linking verb or an action verb, substitute *am, are,* or *is* for the verb. If the sentence with the new verb still makes sense, then the original verb is a linking verb.

LINKING	ACTION
Tina *felt* weak. (Tina *is* weak?) Yes, it's a linking verb.	Tina *felt* the cloth. (Tina *is* the cloth?) No, it's an action verb.

▶ **More Practice**

Language Lab CD-ROM
• Using Verbs lesson
On-line
Exercise Bank
• Section 16.2
Grammar Exercise Workbook
• pp. 17–18

Linking Verbs • 323

Answer Key

▶ **Exercise 12**

1. seemed; arrow connecting *atmosphere* and *exciting*
2. stayed; arrow connecting *Everyone* and *quiet*
3. sounded; arrows connecting *waves* and *rough, waves* and *frightening*
4. appeared; arrow connecting *captain* and *gruff*
5. became; arrow connecting *voyage* and *adventure*
6. grew; arrows connecting *child* and *hungry, child* and *tired*
7. tasted; arrow connecting *anything* and *delicious*
8. felt; arrow connecting *immigrants* and *happy*
9. remained; arrow connecting *They* and *hopeful*
10. looked; arrow connecting *immigrants* and *discouraged*

Step-by-Step Teaching Guide

Action Verb or Linking Verb?

1. Emphasize to students that it is what the verb *does* in the sentence that determines whether it is an action verb or linking verb.

2. Explain that the thing a linking verb *does* is *describe* or *rename* the subject, For example: "The flower smells nice" *describes* the subject; "It looks like a rose" *renames* the subject.

3. Point out that the easiest test is the one shown in the text—if you replace the verb in the sentence with *am, are,* or *is* and it still makes sense, the verb is being used as a linking verb. (Underscore that the new sentence doesn't have to be true, it just has to make sense. For example, "He looks like my brother" is not the same as "He is my brother," but both make sense.)

⬙ **STANDARDIZED TEST PREPARATION WORKSHOP**

Grammar and Usage Some questions on standardized tests measure a student's ability to recognize Standard English usage within the context of a passage.

Share the following example with students:

Nestor and I ___ late to the party if his father had not been able to drive us there.

Which of the following items best completes the sentence?

A will be   **C** would be

B were   **D** would have been

The correct choice is item **D**. Only item D is consistent with the time frame of the sentence—past perfect. The verb phrase *had not been able* indicates this time frame.

Grammar in Literature

1. Read or have a prepared student read the passage aloud.

2. Ask students to apply the *is/am/are* substitution test to verbs in the passage to confirm whether these verbs are linking verbs or action verbs.

More About the Writer

Anna Quindlen, winner of the Pulitzer Prize for Commentary in 1992, is a newspaper and magazine writer and the author of the novels *One True Thing* and *Black and Blue*. Quindlen's writing frequently explores the ways in which everyday life affects people differently.

Critical Viewing

Relate Students' verbs may include *shopping, walking, buying, selling, standing,* and *watching.*

Answer Key

Exercise 13

1. looked—AV
2. felt—LV
3. looked—LV
4. smelled—LV
5. appeared–LV
6. became—LV
7. appeared—AV
8. stayed—AV
9. grew—LV
10. grew—AV

Customize for
Gifted and Talented Students

Ask students to choose a writing sample from their portfolios and circle all the linking verbs the piece contains. Have them revise the work by rewriting several of the sentences that use linking verbs so that the sentences now contain action verbs. Explain that this may involve considerable revision. As an example, tell students that "It is a beautiful, sunny day" might be revised a "A cloudless sky stretches overhead, and the sun warms my face." Ask students to compare the revised work with the original and decide which is more interesting to read. Does relying less on *to be* verbs create more interest?

324

15.2

GRAMMAR IN LITERATURE

from **Melting Pot**
Anna Quindlen

Notice the linking verbs printed in blue in the passage and the action verbs printed in red. What words does each linking verb connect?

My children *are* upstairs in the house next door, having dinner with the Ecuadorian family that *lives* on the top floor. The father *speaks* some English, the mother less than that. The two daughters *are* fluent in both their native and their adopted languages, but the youngest child, a son, a close friend of my two boys, *speaks* almost no Spanish.

> **Exercise 13** Distinguishing Between Action Verbs and Linking Verbs On your paper, write the verb(s) from each of the sentences below. After each action verb, write *AV*, and after each linking verb, write *LV*.

EXAMPLE: Suddenly the sun broke through the clouds.
ANSWER: broke—AV

1. The father looked at his family.
2. He felt sad about leaving them.
3. His family looked so tiny from the ship.
4. The rain smelled fresh, like his new start.
5. The crowds on the ship appeared happy.
6. The immigrants became weary after the long journey.
7. Suddenly, the Statue of Liberty appeared through the fog.
8. Many immigrants stayed in New York.
9. They grew comfortable with their new surroundings.
10. Farmers grew vegetables to sell in the city.

324 • Verbs

Grammar and Style Tip

Avoid using too many linking verbs in your sentences. A balance of action verbs and linking verbs will help your writing sound varied and interesting.

▼ Critical Viewing
Identify four verbs that describe what the people in this picture from 1900 are doing. **[Relate]**

☑ **ONGOING ASSESSMENT: Monitor and Reinforce**

If students miss more than two items in Exercise 11, refer them to the following for additional practice.

In the Textbook	Print Resources	Technology
Section Review, Ex. 15–16, p. 325	Grammar Exercise Workbook, pp. 17–18	Language Lab CD-ROM, Using Verbs On-Line Exercise Bank, Section 15.2

Section 15.2 Section Review

GRAMMAR EXERCISES 14–19

Exercise 14 Identifying Linking Verbs Identify the linking verbs in the following sentences, and write them on your paper.

1. Immigrants are people who transfer residence from one country to another.
2. The first immigrants to the United States were western Europeans.
3. Up until 1860, most immigrants had been British, Irish, or German.
4. Many immigrants stayed loyal to their old customs.
5. Between 1890 and 1910, most new immigrants were from southern and eastern Europe.

Exercise 15 Recognizing Linking Verbs in a Paragraph Copy the following sentences onto your paper, and underline the linking verb in each one. Then, draw arrows connecting the words that are linked by the verb.

(1) Ellis Island is one of New York's most popular tourist attractions. (2) It seems very small when viewed from the island of Manhattan. (3) Liberty Island and Roosevelt Island are other islands near Manhattan. (4) Liberty Island has become a popular tourist site. (5) This and many more islands remain part of greater New York Harbor.

Exercise 16 Distinguishing Between Action Verbs and Linking Verbs Each underlined verb in the following sentences is either a linking verb or an action verb. On your paper, write each underlined verb and label it either *LV* for *linking verb* or *AV* for *action verb*.

1. Some new immigrants <u>felt</u> nervous.
2. Towns <u>grew</u> as more and more people <u>arrived</u> from Europe.
3. Adjusting to the new country <u>felt</u> strange.
4. Some did not <u>stay</u> long.
5. Nonetheless, America <u>remains</u> a nation of immigrants.

Exercise 17 Find It in Your Reading Identify the linking verb in each sentence of this passage from "Melting Pot" by Anna Quindlen.

My first apartment in New York was in a gritty warehouse district, the kind of place that makes your parents wince. A lot of old Italians lived around me, which suited me just fine because I was the granddaughter of old Italians.

Exercise 18 Find It in Your Writing Select a writing sample from your portfolio that contains sentences with linking verbs. Underline the linking verbs. Then, draw arrows connecting the words that are linked by those verbs.

Exercise 19 Writing Application Write a short description about the first place you remember living. Use at least three of the linking verbs from this list.

appeared	seemed
became	smelled
felt	sounded
grew	stayed
looked	tasted
remained	turned

ONGOING ASSESSMENT: Assess Mastery

Use the following resources to assess student mastery of linking verbs.

In the Textbook	Technology
Chapter Review, Ex. 33–34, p. 331	On-Line Exercise Bank, Section 15.2

ASSESS

Section Review

Each of these exercises correlates with a concept in the section on linking verbs, pages 320–324. The exercises may be used for more practice, for reteaching, or for review of the Key Concepts presented. Answers for all chapter exercises are available in *Grammar Exercises Answers on Transparencies* in your teaching resources.

Answer Key

Exercise 14

1. are
2. were
3. had been
4. stayed
5. were

Exercise 15

1. is; arrow connecting *Ellis Island* and *one*
2. seems; arrow connecting *It* and *small*
3. are; arrows connecting *Liberty Island* and *islands, Roosevelt Island* and *islands*
4. has become; arrow connecting *Liberty Island* and *site*
5. remain; arrows connecting *This* and *part, islands* and *part*

Exercise 16

1. felt = LV
2. grew = AV; arrived = AV
3. felt = LV
4. stay = AV
5. remains = LV

Exercise 17

Find It in Your Reading
The linking verb *was* is used twice in the passage.

Exercise 18

Find It in Your Writing
Students' writing samples should contain linking verbs. Ask volunteers what they notice about their use of linking verbs (e.g., which are most common, which work best, etc.).

Exercise 19

Writing Application
When they finish writing, have students exchange papers with a partner. Then, have them underline the linking verbs and draw arrows connecting the words that are linked by the verb.

Interest GRABBER Assign partners the following incomplete sentences. Have them brainstorm for five different ways to complete each sentence.

I ___ laughing at the comedian.

The trees ___ cut down last fall.

His pet iguana ___ called George.

Have students share their answers, and explain that the words they used are called *helping verbs.*

Activate Prior Knowledge

Ask students whether a verb can be made up of several words. Then have students write a sentence telling how they usually get to school. Have them underline the verb in the sentence. (Sample responses: I <u>ride</u> the bus.) Ask students to revise their sentences to explain how they will get to school tomorrow. (Sample response: I <u>will ride</u> the bus.) Discuss the words that now make up the verb.

TEACH

Step-by-Step Teaching Guide

Helping Verbs

1. Write a list of four verbs on the chalkboard, for example: *think, walk, forget,* and *tell.*

2. Have students brainstorm for ways to create verb phrases using these verbs, plus forms of *be* or other helping verbs found on the page.

3. Write some of these verb phrases on the chalkboard, clearly marking the helping verb(s) and main verb.

   Example: <u>have been</u> <u>walking</u>
           HV   MV

Section 15.3 # Helping Verbs

Sometimes, a verb in a sentence is just one word. Often, however, a verb will be made up of several words. This type of verb is called a *verb phrase.* A verb phrase can have one, two, or three helping verbs before the main part of the verb.

▶ **KEY CONCEPT** **Helping verbs** are added before another verb to make a **verb phrase.** ∎

The helping verbs in the following examples are italicized. Notice how they help to change the meaning of *put,* the key part of the verb.

EXAMPLES: put
               had put
               will have put
               might have put
               should have been put

Recognizing Helping Verbs

The various forms of *be* shown in the chart on page 320 are often used as helping verbs in front of other verbs. In the chart below, a number of different forms of *be* are used as helping verbs. All are italicized.

SOME FORMS OF *BE* USED AS HELPING VERBS	
Helping Verbs	**Main Verbs**
am	growing
has been	warned
was being	told
could have been	reminded
will have been	waiting

Some other common verbs are also used as helping verbs.

OTHER HELPING VERBS				
do	have	would	will	can
does	has	shall	might	could
did	had	should	must	may

326 • Verbs

Theme: Governments

In this section, you will learn about helping verbs. The examples and exercises in this section tell more about immigration.

•••••••••••••••••••••••

Cross-Curricular Connection: Social Studies

⏱ **TIME AND RESOURCE MANAGER**

Resources
Print: Grammar Exercise Workbook, pp.19–20
Technology: Language Lab CD-ROM, Using Verbs; On-Line Exercise Bank, Section 15.3

In-Depth Coverage	Accelerated Pace
• Work through all key concepts, pp. 326–328. • Assign and review Exercises 20–22.	• Assign pp. 326–328 for independent student review. • Assign Section Review Exercises 23–24, p. 329.

Exercise 20

1. <u>were</u> called
2. <u>had</u> entered
3. <u>would have been</u> known
4. <u>may have</u> arrived
5. <u>were</u> escaping

Exercise 21

1. <u>was</u> considered
2. <u>were being</u> passed
3. <u>were</u> tested, <u>could</u> read
4. <u>were</u> given
5. <u>should have been</u> warned

VERB PHRASES

Helping Verbs	Main Verbs
do	remember
has	written
would	hope
can	believe
may	attempt
must have	thought
should have	grown

Exercise 20 Identifying Helping Verbs On your paper, write the verb phrase in each sentence below. Underline the helping verbs.

EXAMPLE: Immigrants have been arriving in the United States for nearly two centuries.

ANSWER: <u>have been</u> arriving

1. Early arrivals in the United States from northern and western Europe were called old immigrants.
2. Many old immigrants had entered the country in the 1850's.
3. People from southern and eastern Europe would have been known as new immigrants.
4. The Carlucci family may have arrived before 1900.
5. The family members were escaping a terrible famine in their area of Italy.

Exercise 21 Finding Helping Verbs and Main Verbs Copy the sentences below onto your paper. Draw one line under each helping verb and two lines under each main verb.

(1) The large number of immigrants was considered a threat by some people already living in the United States. (2) New immigration laws were being passed by Congress. (3) Some immigrants were tested to see whether they could read English. (4) Health examinations were given to many others. (5) The immigrants should have been warned about the new requirements.

▼ Critical Viewing
Looking at the picture, list four verb phrases that answer the question, "What are they doing?" **[Analyze]**

More Practice

Language Lab CD-ROM
• Using Verbs lesson
On-line Exercise Bank
• Section 16.3
Grammar Exercise Workbook
• pp. 19–20

Critical Viewing

Analyze Students may answer the question with sentences such as the following: They *are checking* their vision. They *are being examined.*

Integrating Workplace Skills

Newscasters, sports broadcasters, and public address system announcers are some of the people who frequently have to describe events that are happening in real time. To do so, they form sentences using helping verbs and main verbs in the *-ing* form. Share these examples with students:

Foster *is running* downfield with the ball.

Tonight, representatives of the company <u>are speaking</u> with the public.

The train <u>will be leaving</u> from Track 10.

STANDARDIZED TEST PREPARATION WORKSHOP

Grammar and Usage Many standardized tests require students to recognize parts of speech in the context of a passage. Use the following example to demonstrate this type of question:

Only a few of the mountain climbers had experienced a Himalayan blizzard.

Which is the verb phrase in the passage above?

A Only a few
B experienced
C had experienced
D experienced a Himalayan blizzard

The correct answer is item **C.** The verb phrase is made up of the helping verb *had* and the main part of the verb, *experienced.* Remind students that verb phrases do not include the objects of verbs.

TIME SAVERS!

Answers on Transparency Use the Grammar Exercises Answers on Transparencies for Chapter 15 to facilitate correction by students.

On-Line Exercise Bank Have students complete the exercises on computer. The Auto Check feature will grade their work for you!

Helping Verbs Can Be Separated

1. Write the following sentences on the chalkboard. Then ask students to identify the words that make up the verb phrases.

   Marcus had asked us a question. (had asked)

   They can afford a new car. (can afford)

2. Modify the sentences as shown and again have students identify the verb phrase.

   Marcus had not asked us a question. (had asked)

   Can they afford a new car? (can afford)

3. Emphasize that the words that constitute the verb phrase remain the same. Words that separate the helping verb and the main part of the verb are not part of the verb phrase.

Answer Key

▶ **Exercise 22**

1. was increasing
2. were hoping
3. had passed
4. were being prohibited
5. were affected
6. had been established
7. would establish
8. could move
9. did agree
10. might have been concerned

Critical Viewing

Compare and Contrast Students may use phrases such as the following: These immigrants *are walking, had arrived;* on the previous page, immigrants *were waiting, were hoping.*

Integrating Spelling Skills

When the word *not* comes between a helping verb and the main part of the verb, it is often combined with the helping verb to form a contraction. For example: *I have not found the essay* becomes *I haven't found the essay.* Point out that when these contractions are formed, the spelling of the helping verb does not change: *are not = aren't, is not = isn't.* The only exception to this rule is *will not,* which becomes *won't.*

328

15.3

Helping Verbs Can Be Separated

Words in a verb phrase can sometimes be separated by other words. Very often, words such as *not, certainly,* and *seldom* come between a helping verb and the key part of the verb. In questions, verbs of two or more words are frequently separated. In the following examples, the parts of each verb phrase are italicized.

WORDS TOGETHER: They *must have been taken* by taxi to the airport.

WORDS SEPARATED: Marie *has* certainly not *contacted* us.
He *had* carefully *kept* all the records.
Can they really *build* their own home?

▶ **Exercise 22** **Finding Complete Verb Phrases** On your paper, write the complete verb phrase in each of the following sentences. Include all the helping verbs, but do not include any of the words that may separate the parts of the verb phrase.

EXAMPLE: Have you walked the dogs yet?
ANSWER: Have walked

1. After the Civil War, immigration from China was rapidly increasing.
2. The immigrants were, at first, hoping to work as laborers for the railroad.
3. Congress had, however, passed the Chinese Exclusion Act.
4. Some Chinese laborers were now being prohibited from coming to the United States.
5. Other groups of immigrants were also affected by new laws.
6. A ceiling had actually been established to limit immigration.
7. Government officials would soon establish quotas.
8. Only a limited number of immigrants could now move to the United States from other countries.
9. Some people did not agree with the limits.
10. Others might possibly have been concerned about job competition.

Spelling Tip

The word *immigrate* means to move into a new country. The word *emigrate* means to move out of a country.

▼ **Critical Viewing** List several verb phrases to describe the action in this picture. Then, compare them to the verb phrases you used to describe the action in the picture on the previous page. How do your lists compare? **[Compare and Contrast]**

✓ **ONGOING ASSESSMENT: Monitor and Reinforce**

If students miss more than two items in Exercises 19, 20, or 21, refer them to the following for additional practice.

In the Textbook	Print Resources	Technology
Section Review, Ex. 23–24, p. 329	Grammar Exercise Workbook, pp. 19–20	Language Lab CD-ROM, Using Verbs On-Line Exercise Bank, Section 15.3

Section 15.3 *Section Review*

GRAMMAR EXERCISES 23–27

Exercise 23 Recognizing Helping Verbs Write the helping verb(s) in each sentence below.

1. As the immigrants arrived in America, they would be taken to Ellis Island.
2. They had been gathered into large groups.
3. Impatient guards were shouting instructions to the nervous crowds.
4. Most of the people could not understand the guards who were directing them.
5. The immigrants had been carrying their bags for hours.
6. They were being led into a large room.
7. There, they were given a choice about their baggage.
8. They could check their bags, or they could carry them into the next room.
9. Numbered tags should have been placed on each bag.
10. Many of the tags were accidentally torn off.

Exercise 24 Finding Complete Verb Phrases Write the verb phrase in each of the following sentences, and underline the helping verbs. Do not include any of the words that may separate parts of the verb phrase.

1. The medical inspectors had stood on the balcony in the Great Hall.
2. The immigrants were being closely observed by the inspectors.
3. They would eventually be checked by each inspector.
4. Every person would be marked in chalk with a large letter.
5. The letter would designate the person's level of health.
6. The inspectors had been trained to spot illness or disease.

7. Some people with physical disabilities were marked with an "L" for "lame."
8. If they were found coughing, they would have been marked with "TB" for tuberculosis even if they did not have the disease.
9. Immigrants who were breathing heavily might have been unfairly marked with an "H" for heart disease.
10. People could not pass through customs if inspectors suspected they had a dangerous, contagious disease.

Exercise 25 Find It in Your Reading Identify two verb phrases in this passage from "Melting Pot" by Anna Quindlen. (One of the helping verbs is part of a contraction.)

Drawn in broad strokes, we live in a pressure cooker: oil and water, us and them. But if you come around at exactly the right time, you'll find members of all these groups gathered around complaining about the condition of the streets, on which everyone can agree.

Exercise 26 Find It in Your Writing Select a writing sample from your portfolio that includes at least three verb phrases composed of a helping verb and a main verb. Circle the verb phrases, and underline the helping verbs.

Exercise 27 Writing Application Imagine that you have just arrived at Ellis Island. Write a brief description of your feelings and impressions. Underline any verb phrases that you use.

Section Review • 329

ASSESS and CLOSE

Section Review

Each of these exercises correlates with a concept in the section on helping verbs, pp. 326–328. The exercises may be used for more practice, for reteaching, or for review of the Key Concepts presented. Answers for all chapter exercises are available in *Grammar Exercises Answers on Transparencies* in your teaching resources.

Answer Key

Exercise 23

1. would be
2. had been
3. were
4. could; were
5. had been
6. were being
7. were
8. could; could
9. should have been
10. were

Exercise 24

1. <u>had</u> stood
2. <u>were being</u> observed
3. <u>would be</u> checked
4. <u>would be</u> marked
5. <u>would</u> designate
6. <u>had been</u> trained
7. <u>were</u> marked
8. <u>were</u> found, <u>would have been</u> marked, <u>did</u> have
9. <u>were</u> breathing, <u>might have been</u> marked
10. <u>could</u> pass

Exercise 25

Find It in Your Reading
'll find (will find), can agree

Exercise 26

Find It in Your Writing
Explain to students that in formal writing, helping verbs usually should not be combined with other words to form contractions. Have them make sure they followed this rule in their portfolios.

Exercise 27

Writing Application
Ask volunteers to share their descriptions with the class. Discuss with students what helping verbs help them do (change time of action, add emphasis, and so on).

Each of these exercises correlates to a concept in the chapter on verbs, pages 316–329. The exercises may be used for more practice, for reteaching, or for review of the Key Concepts presented.

Answer Key

	Performer	Action
1.	Officials	detained
2.	The immigrants	went
3.	members	sat
4.	Men; boys	stayed
5.	Women; girls	stood
6.	families	reunited
7.	man	cried
8.	examiners	looked
9.	he	passed
10.	immigrant	smiled

Exercise 29

1. transitive   4. transitive
2. intransitive   5. intransitive
3. transitive

Exercise 30

1. were; arrow connecting *choices* and *limited*
2. seemed; arrow connecting *vendors* and *unkind*
3. tasted; arrow connecting *food* and *bad*
4. became; arrow connecting *Some* and *sick*
5. grew; arrow connecting *immigrants* and *angry*

Exercise 31

Answers may vary. Sample answers:
1. seemed—LV
2. stayed—AV
3. would be—LV
4. knew—AV
5. remained—LV
6. could be—LV
7. felt—LV
8. sounded—AV
9. were—LV
10. had become—LV

Chapter 15 Chapter Review

GRAMMAR EXERCISES 28–37

▶ **Exercise 28** Identifying Action Verbs On your paper, write the verb and the performer of the action in each sentence.

EXAMPLE: The women completed the voyage.

ANSWER: PERFORMER   ACTION
           women   completed

1. Officials detained more than twenty percent of the immigrants on Ellis Island.
2. The immigrants first went to a waiting room.
3. Family members often sat in separate places.
4. Men and boys stayed on one side of the room.
5. Women and girls stood on the other side of the room.
6. Usually, families reunited later in the day.
7. A young man cried quietly before his examination.
8. The medical examiners looked at him carefully.
9. At last, he passed the test.
10. The young immigrant smiled.

▶ **Exercise 29** Distinguishing Transitive and Intransitive Verbs In each sentence below, the verb is underlined. Label each verb *transitive* or *intransitive*.

1. Immigrants <u>took</u> a test to enter the United States.
2. Most people <u>worried</u> about the test.
3. Interpreters <u>helped</u> the nervous immigrants as much as possible.
4. Sometimes, the guards <u>asked</u> only a few questions of the immigrants.
5. The immigrants <u>answered</u> as well as they could.

330 • Verbs

▶ **Exercise 30** Identifying Linking Verbs Copy the sentences below onto your paper. Underline each linking verb, and draw an arrow connecting the words that are linked by the verb.

1. The food choices on Ellis Island were limited.
2. Some food vendors seemed unkind.
3. In addition, the food often tasted bad.
4. Some ate the food and became sick.
5. Many immigrants grew very angry at the poor treatment and long waits.

▶ **Exercise 31** Supplying Linking Verbs and Action Verbs On your paper, write the sentences, filling in the blanks with verbs from the following list. Use each verb only once. Then, indicate whether each verb is an action verb or a linking verb, based on its use in the sentence.

had become   stayed   would be   felt
seemed   appeared   remained   sounded
knew   could be   were

1. The twelve-year-old boy __?__ older than he was.
2. He __?__ with the other children in his family for the physical exam.
3. If he failed the exam, he __?__ heartbroken.
4. Sadly, the examiner __?__ he had to order the boy back to his homeland.
5. His grandfather __?__ ready to return with the boy.
6. It __?__ tragic to split up the family.
7. The rest of the family __?__ terrible about the situation.
8. The steamship officials __?__ as if they would pay for the return trip.
9. The boy and his grandfather __?__ hopeful about returning to America.
10. For them, Ellis Island __?__ a sad place.

Exercise 32
Identifying Action Verbs and Linking Verbs Write the verbs you find in the following sentences. Label each verb *LV* for *linking verb* or *AV* for *action verb*.

1. The young immigrant tasted new foods during his first days in America.
2. After he drank a glass of sour lemonade, the boy's face turned green.
3. A peddler's wagon appeared on the street where the boy lived.
4. The roasted meat on the wagon smelled wonderful.
5. Because of the smell, the boy grew hungry.

Exercise 33
Writing Action Verbs and Linking Verbs Write a verb to complete each sentence. Label each verb *LV* for *linking verb* or *AV* for *action verb*.

1. Suddenly, his stomach ___?___ very empty.
2. He ___?___ in his pocket to locate a coin.
3. He ___?___ his one coin over inside his pocket.
4. The boy ___?___ sadly at the peddler.
5. The boy ___?___ hungry.

Exercise 34
Recognizing Verb Phrases Write the verb phrase in each of the following sentences. Underline the helping verbs.

1. Europeans had sometimes waited for years to emigrate to the United States.
2. Some families may have been saving most of their working lives to make such a trip.
3. In some cases, they traveled many miles just to reach the ship that would carry them across the ocean.
4. Many surely must have thought that they should have stayed home.
5. However, most must have overcome their fears, because they eventually did board their ships.

Exercise 35
Identifying the Helping Verb and the Main Verb Write each verb phrase. Circle the helping verb(s), and underline the main verb.

1. The ship was rocking back and forth on the waves in the harbor.
2. The passengers had been told that they could leave the ship soon.
3. The immigrants should have disembarked hours ago.
4. They were hoping that relatives would greet them on the shore.
5. The relatives were huddled behind barricades.

Exercise 36
Writing Application Write a brief paragraph about one of your older relatives. Include sentences that contain action verbs, linking verbs, and verb phrases. Circle each verb you use.

Exercise 37
CUMULATIVE REVIEW
Nouns, Pronouns, and Verbs List the nouns, pronouns, and verbs that you find in the sentences below. Label each noun *CN* for *common noun* or *PN* for *proper noun*. For each pronoun, indicate its antecedent. For each verb, indicate whether it is an action verb or a linking verb. Identify the helping verb and the main verb in each verb phrase.

(1) Italians were one group of people who emigrated from Europe. (2) They had suffered from war in their homeland. (3) Sometimes, one person came to the United States ahead of his relatives. (4) My great-grandfather arrived at Ellis Island in 1908. (5) After he had worked for two years, he brought his wife to New York.

> **Exercise 32**
1. tasted—AV
2. drank—AV, turned—LV
3. appeared—AV
4. smelled—LV
5. grew—LV

> **Exercise 33**
Answers will vary, samples are given.
1. felt—LV
2. felt—AV
3. turned—AV
4. looked—AV
5. remained—LV

> **Exercise 34**
1. had waited
2. may have been saving
3. traveled, would carry
4. must have thought, should have stayed
5. must have overcome, did board

> **Exercise 35**
1. (was) rocking
2. (had been) told, (could) leave
3. (should have) disembarked
4. (were) hoping, (would) greet
5. (were) huddled

> **Exercise 36**
Writing Application
To extend the activity, have students apply the instructions for Exercise 34 to their paragraphs.

> **Exercise 37**
Cumulative Review
1. Nouns: Italians—PN, group—CN, people—CN, Europe—PN
   Pronouns: who—group
   Verbs: were—linking, emigrated—action
2. Nouns: war—CN, homeland—CN
   Pronouns: They—Italians, their—Italians
   Verbs: had suffered—action; had—helping, suffered—main
3. Nouns: person—CN, United States—PN, relatives—CN
   Pronouns: his—person
   Verbs: came—action
4. Nouns: great-grandfather—CN, Ellis Island—PN, 1908—PN
   Pronouns: My—(the writer)
   Verbs: arrived—action

continued

Answer Key continued
5. Nouns: years—CN, wife—CN, New York—PN
   Pronouns: he—great-grandfather, he—great-grandfather, his—great-grandfather
   Verbs: had worked—action; had—helping, worked—main; brought—action

Lesson Objectives

1. To use standard English usage, including subject-verb agreement
2. To use verb tenses appropriately and consistently
3. To answer different typed and levels of questions, such as multiple choice

1. As students examine the sample test item on this page, remind them to use context clues to help them determine the answer. Encourage them to read the whole sentence through before they pick an answer.

2. Encourage students to read carefully. If a sentence is part of a passage, look for clues in other sentences. For example, in the sample test item, all four answers could work in the sentence if there were no other clues. The clue to the tense of the passage occurs in the second sentence.

3. Point out that while the present tense verb is the clue in the sample item, there are other clues that might establish tense. Ask students what other clues might exist (time can be indicated by statements such as *yesterday, someday, tomorrow, next week, right now*).

4. Remind students that tense is not the only consideration when choosing the correct verb. Tell them to also be aware that agreement in number must be correct, as well. That is, if the subject is plural, the verb must be, too (e.g., "they are" not "they is").

Standardized Test Preparation Workshop

Standard Usage for Parts of Speech: Verbs

Some questions on standardized tests are designed to measure your ability to recognize standard English usage within the context of a written passage. Often, these questions are designed as fill-in-the-blanks. When using verbs—words that express actions or states of being—to complete sentences, read through the entire passage to get an idea of the writer's purpose. Then, eliminate those answers that would change the meaning of the sentence. Also, determine the time frame—past, present, future—of the sentence and eliminate verbs that do not indicate the appropriate tense.

The following test item will give you practice with the format used for items testing verb usage.

Test Tip

- When choosing verbs, make sure to read the whole passage that gives the context. There may be two verbs that could fit in the numbered space, but only one will make sense in the context of the passage.

Sample Test Item	Answer and Explanation
Directions: Read the passage, and choose the letter of the word or group of words that belongs in each space. An erupting volcano ____(1)____ great clouds of ash and gas into the atmosphere. Sometimes rivers of red-hot lava ooze from its opening. **A** shoots **B** will be shooting **C** shot **D** has been shooting	The correct answer is *A.* The verb *shoots* is consistent with the time of the passage, which is in the present. (Notice the present-tense verb *ooze* in the second sentence.) *Will be shooting* indicates a future action, and *shot* and *has been shooting* are past-tense forms.

✎ TEST-TAKING TIP

Remind students to carefully reread the sentence with their choice in place of the blank. This is a good way to double-check that their choice is correct.

Write the following example on the chalkboard:

We ___ lunch at noon next Sunday.

A have eaten	**C** will eat
B eat	**D** ate

The correct choice is item **C**. Students who may not have read carefully might choose item B, forgetting that *next Sunday* indicates the future.

Answer Key

1. C
2. F
3. A
4. F

1. C
2. F
3. A
4. J

> **Practice 1** **Directions:** Read each passage, and choose the letter of the word or group of words that belongs in each space.

Volcanoes ___(1)___ thousands of people, and they have caused great damage to property. Perhaps someday, we ___(2)___ to predict volcanic eruptions.

1 A will hurt
  B have been hurting
  C have hurt
  D hurt

2 F will learn
  G learn
  H learned
  J are learning

At this time, scientists ___(1)___ special technology to measure activity under the Earth's crust. They ___(2)___ not always entirely accurate.

3 A use
  B used
  C will use
  D were using

4 F are
  G is
  H were
  J will be

> **Practice 2** **Directions:** Read each passage, and choose the letter of the word or group of words that belongs in each space.

More and more people ___(1)___ the outdoors. The choices for enjoyable, healthful activities are endless. Some people ___(2)___ winter sports, such as cross-country skiing or snowboarding. Other people ___(3)___ warm-weather activities, such as baseball, swimming, or tennis. No matter what your seasonal preference is, you ___(4)___ sure there is an activity for you.

1 A enjoyed
  B is enjoying
  C are enjoying
  D would enjoy

2 F choose
  G chosen
  H would have chosen
  J might have chosen

3 A may prefer
  B preferred
  C have preferred
  D preferring

4 F will be
  G are
  H might be
  J can be

In-Depth Lesson Plan

	LESSON FOCUS	PRINT AND MEDIA RESOURCES
DAY 1	**Adjectives** Students learn to recognize adjectives and the nouns they modify and to distinguish between definite and indefinite articles, (pp. 334–339).	**Teaching Resources** *Grammar Exercise Workbook*, pp.21–30; *Grammar Exercises Answers on Transparencies*, Ch. 16 *Language Lab* **CD-ROM**, Using Modifiers; *On-Line Exercise Bank*, Section 16.1
DAY 2	**Adjectives** Students learn and apply concepts identifying nouns used as adjectives, and different types of adjectives (pp. 340–347).	**Teaching Resources** *Grammar Exercise Workbook*, pp.21–30 *Language Lab* **CD-ROM**, Using Modifiers; *On-Line Exercise Bank*, Section 16.1
DAY 3	**Adverbs** Students learn and apply concepts identifying and using adverbs, distinguishing between adjectives and adverbs and do the Hands-On Grammar activity (pp. 348–354).	**Teaching Resources** *Grammar Exercise Workbook*, pp. 31–36; *Hands-on Grammar Book*, Ch. 16 *Language Lab* **CD-ROM**, Using Modifiers; *On-Line Exercise Bank*, Section 16.2
DAY 4	**Review and Assess** Students review chapter and demonstrate mastery of use of adjectives and adverbs (pp.356–358).	**Teaching Resources** *Formal Assessment*, Ch. 16; *On-Line Exercise Bank*, Sections 16.1–2

Accelerated Lesson Plan

	LESSON FOCUS	PRINT AND MEDIA RESOURCES
DAY 1	**Adjectives** Students cover concepts and usage of adjectives as determined by Diagnostic Test (pp. 336–347).	**Teaching Resources** *Grammar Exercise Workbook*, pp.21–30; *Grammar Exercises Answers on Transparencies*, Ch. 16 *Language Lab* **CD-ROM**, Using Modifiers; *On-Line Exercise Bank*, Section 16.1
DAY 2	**Adverbs** Students cover concepts and usage of adverbs as determined by Diagnostic Test (pp.348–354).	**Teaching Resources** *Grammar Exercise Workbook*, pp. 31–36; *Hands-on Grammar Book*, Ch. 16 *Language Lab* **CD-ROM**, Using Modifiers; *On-Line Exercise Bank*, Section 16.2
DAY 3	**Review and Assess** Students review chapter and demonstrate mastery of use of adjectives and adverbs (pp.356–358).	**Teaching Resources;** *Formal Assessment*, Ch. 16; *On-Line Exercise Bank*, Sections 16.1–2

Options for Adapting Lesson Plans

HOMEWORK

Have students complete any section of the chapter for homework.

FEATURES

Extend coverage with the Grammar in Literature feature (p. 339), and the Standardized Test Preparation Workshop (p. 358).

TECHNOLOGY

Students can use the On-Line Exercise Bank to complete the exercises on computer. The Auto Check feature will grade their work.

INTEGRATED SKILLS COVERAGE

Grammar in Literature
SE p. 339

Reading
Responding to Literature SE pp. 339, 352
Find It In Your Reading, SE pp. 347, 352, 354

Writing
Responding to Literature SE pp. 339, 352
Find It In Your Writing, SE pp. 347, 354, 355
Writing Application SE pp. 347, 357

Language Highlight
ATE p. 338

Spelling
SE pp. 338, 351; ATE p. 344

Vocabulary
Integrating Vocabulary Skills ATE p. 346

Viewing and Representing
Critical Viewing, SE pp. 334, 337, 340, 343, 344, 349, 350

ASSESSMENT SUPPORT

Standardized Test Preparation SE p. 358; ATE pp. 341, 350
Standardized Test Preparation Workbook, pp. 31–32
Formal Assessment, Ch. 16

MEETING INDIVIDUAL NEEDS

Less Advanced Students, ATE pp. 337, 353. Also see Ongoing Assessment, pp. 339, 343, 351.
ESL Students, ATE pp. 338, 344
More Advanced Students, ATE p. 341
Bodily/Kinesthetic Learners, ATE p. 346
Gifted/Talented Students, ATE p. 337

BLOCK SCHEDULING

Pacing Suggestions
For 90-minute Blocks
• Administer the Diagnostic Test to students to determine instructional coverage.
• Have students complete the necessary exercises in class. Use the Hands-on Grammar activity to provide a change of pace.

Resources for Varying Instruction
• *Language Lab* **CD-ROM** If your students have access to hardware, a 90-minute block provides an ideal opportunity for students to work on computer.

Professional Development Support
• *How to Manage Instruction in the Block* This Teaching Resource provides management and activity suggestions.

MEDIA AND TECHNOLOGY

For the Student
• *Language Lab* **CD-ROM,** Using Modifiers
• *On-Line Exercise Bank,* Ch. 16

For the Teacher
• *Resource Pro* **CD-ROM**

WRITING AND GRAMMAR WEB SITE

The Interactive Writing and Grammar Web site provides a wide array of support for students, teachers, and parents. Grammar support includes:

• *On-Line Exercise Bank* with Auto Check scoring
• Diagnostic and assessment support

www.phschool.com

LITERATURE CONNECTIONS

Grammar in Literature selections from *Prentice Hall Literature: Timeless Voices, Timeless Themes,* Bronze:
"The Third Wish," by Joan Aiken, SE p. 339
"The Californian's Tale," by Mark Twain, SE p. 352

▶ *Lesson Objectives*

1. To recognize adjectives and the nouns they modify
2. To distinguish between definite and indefinite articles
3. To identify nouns and pronouns used as adjectives
4. To identify proper, compound, possessive, demonstrative, and interrogative adjectives
5. To recognize adverbs and the words they modify
6. To locate adverbs in sentences
7. To distinguish between adjectives and adverbs
8. To use adjectives and adverbs appropriately

Critical Viewing

Analyze Possible responses: pink, long-necked, strange, feathered

Chapter 16 Adjectives and Adverbs

▲ Critical Viewing
How many adjectives can you think of to describe the flamingo's appearance?
[Analyze]

Adjectives are words that describe. When used properly, they sharpen and polish the meaning of nouns and pronouns.

Adjectives help a writer paint a picture with words. For example, we get a clear picture of Hans Christian Andersen's ugly duckling because of the adjective *ugly*. If the waterfowl in the story had been a mallard duck instead of a swan, the best adjective to describe the duckling might have been *colorful*.

Adverbs, too, play an important part in sentences. Adverbs include words such as *carefully, often, seldom, finally, never, very,* and *soon*. Like adjectives, adverbs are modifiers. Adjectives can modify *two* different parts of speech—nouns and pronouns. Adverbs, on the other hand, can modify *three* different parts of speech—verbs, adjectives, and other adverbs. Using adverbs to modify words can create a more vivid picture in a reader's mind. For example, instead of writing, "Redwood trees grow in California," it would be more descriptive to write, "The giant redwood trees of Northern California tower majestically above the landscape."

In this chapter, you will learn how to use adjectives and adverbs.

334 • Adjectives and Adverbs

☑ ONGOING ASSESSMENT: Diagnose

If students miss more than one item in any category, direct them to the relevant pages of the text and assign exercises for practice and review.

Adjectives and Adverbs	Diagnostic Test Items	Teach	Practice	Section Review	Chapter Review
Skill Check A					
Adjectives	A 1–5	pp. 336–339	Ex. 1–2	Ex. 9–10	Ex. 29, 30
Skill Check B					
Nouns/Pronouns Used as Adjectives	B 6–10	pp. 340, 343–346	Ex. 3 Ex. 6–8	Ex. 11	Ex. 31
Skill Check C					
Compound and Proper Adjectives	C 11–15	pp. 341–342	Ex. 4–5	Ex. 12	Ex. 32

Diagnostic Test

Directions: Write all answers on a separate sheet of paper.

Skill Check A. Write the adjective(s) in the following sentences. Next to each one, write the noun it modifies.

1. Birds live in all parts of the world.
2. There are about 8,700 kinds of birds.
3. Many birds have gorgeous colors or sing sweet songs.
4. The fastest birds can reach speeds of more than 100 miles per hour.
5. Although every bird has wings, not all birds can fly.

Skill Check B. Write the nouns or pronouns used as adjectives in the following sentences. Next to each, write the noun it modifies.

6. Ducks, gulls, and herons are kinds of water birds.
7. Penguins can also be put into this category.
8. Bird-watchers have a special fascination for penguins.
9. Penguins use their wings as flippers when they swim.
10. A penguin's temperature doesn't change, despite its very cold surroundings.

Skill Check C. Copy the sentences below. Underline any compound adjectives, and circle any proper adjectives.

11. Like mammals, birds are warmblooded animals.
12. Some American water birds nest in seacoast habitats.
13. Birds belonging to the waterfowl family live in freshwater areas.
14. Many sandpipers and other arctic birds visit American and Canadian shores while traveling to winter homes in the tropics.
15. Some North American birds migrate to faraway Chile.

Skill Check D. Write the adverb(s) in each sentence below. Next to each, indicate whether it modifies a verb, an adjective, or another adverb.

16. Native Americans were among the very first people in California.
17. They hunted and fished skillfully for much-needed food.
18. Trappers traded with Native American groups for absolutely essential food.
19. Trappers were almost immediately followed to California by settlers from the East.
20. Many settlers traveled quite slowly by wagon to California.

Skill Check E. Label each underlined word *adverb* or *adjective*.

21. The journey was not an <u>easy</u> one.
22. Settlers worked <u>hard</u>.
23. After they had cleared the land, there was more <u>hard</u> work.
24. Settlers who arrived <u>late</u> in the year faced more difficulties.
25. <u>Gradually</u>, towns grew.

Adjectives and Adverbs • 335

Diagnostic Test

Each item in the diagnostic test corresponds to a specific concept in the adjectives and adverbs chapter. This will enable you to tailor instruction to the particular needs of your students. See "Ongoing Assessment: Diagnose" below for further details.

Skill Check A

1. all, parts; the, world
2. 8,700 kinds
3. Many, birds; gorgeous, colors; sweet, songs
4. fastest, birds; 100, miles
5. every, bird; all, birds

Skill Check B

6. water, birds
7. this, category
8. bird, watchers
9. their, wings
10. penguin's, temperature; its, surroundings

Skill Check C

11. <u>warmblooded</u>
12. (American), <u>seacoast</u>
13. <u>waterfowl</u>, <u>freshwater</u>
14. (American), (Canadian)
15. (North American), <u>faraway</u>

Skill Check D

16. very—adjective
17. skillfully—verb, much—adjective
18. absolutely—adjective
19. almost—adverb, immediately—verb
20. quite—adverb, slowly—verb

Skill Check E

21. adjective	24. adverb
22. adverb	25. adverb
23. adjective	

⏱ TIME SAVERS!

Answers on Transparency
Use the Grammar Exercises Answers on Transparencies for Chapter 16 to have students correct their own or one another's exercises.

On-Line Exercise Bank
Have students complete the Diagnostic Test on computer. The Auto Check feature will grade their work for you!

☑ ONGOING ASSESSMENT: Diagnose *continued*

Adjectives and Adverbs	Diagnostic Test Items	Teach	Practice	Section Review	Chapter Review
Skill Check D and E					
Adverbs	D 16–20 E 21–25	pp. 348–354	Ex. 16–22	Ex. 23–25	Ex. 33–35
Cumulative Reviews and Applications				Ex. 13–15, 26–28	Ex. 36

Write a series of nouns on the chalkboard, such as *tree, fish, potato,* and *dog.* Ask students to imagine what the items named look like, then to answer the following questions: *What kind of dog is it? Which tree is it? How many fish are there?* Explain that answers to these questions are adjectives. Adjectives modify nouns by describing them.

Activate Prior Knowledge

Write the following sentence on the chalkboard:

Go to the intersection, make a turn, and it will be the building.

Ask students how the absence of adjectives affects the sentence (there's not enough information to make this useful). Ask students to suggest adjectives that would make this sentence useful (sample: Go to the second intersection, make a left turn, and it will be the third building from the corner, the brick building with the white trim.

TEACH

Step-by-Step Teaching Guide

Adjectives

1. Review the word *modify* on the textbook page. Explain that adjectives make the words they modify more specific. Adjectives add details: color, shape, size, and condition. Write these examples on the chalkboard:

   less *sunlight*   blue *ribbon*

   that *potato*   three *frogs*

2. Emphasize that adjectives modify nouns and pronouns only. Adjectives usually answer one of the following questions about the noun or pronoun: *What kind? Which one? How many? How much?* Have students look at the examples on the chalkboard and decide which questions are answered.

Adjectives

Adjectives are used with nouns and pronouns.

> **KEY CONCEPT** An **adjective** is used to describe a noun or a pronoun. ■

Using Adjectives as Modifiers

To *modify* means to "change slightly." Adjectives modify nouns and pronouns by slightly changing their meanings. For example, when you hear the noun *house,* a certain picture of a house may come to mind. However, when you say "a small house," "a large wooden house," or "an old white colonial house," the adjectives change the picture slightly.

Adjectives usually answer one of these four questions about the nouns and pronouns they modify: *What kind? Which one? How many? How much?*

What Kind?	
new car	*striped* tie
Which One?	
this swan	*every* page
How Many?	
one hamburger	*many* geese
How Much?	
no food	*little* rain

When adjectives modify nouns, they usually come directly before the nouns. Occasionally, they may come after.

BEFORE: She saw a bright, smiling face.

AFTER: The room, narrow and dark, frightened us.

Adjectives may also modify pronouns. When they do, they usually come after a linking verb. Occasionally, they may come before.

AFTER: They are happy and talkative.

BEFORE: Quiet and sullen, he sat in a corner.

In this section, you will learn how adjectives are used to modify nouns and pronouns. The examples and exercises in this section are about birds that live on or near water.

Cross-Curricular Connection: Science

Grammar and Style Tip

The English language is full of descriptive clichés like *busy as a bee.* If you want to be fresh and original in your writing, try to avoid them and find vivid, precise adjectives instead.

⏱ TIME AND RESOURCE MANAGER

Resources
Print: Grammar Exercise Workbook, pp. 21–30
Technology: Language Lab CD-ROM, Using Modifiers; On-Line Exercise Bank, Section 16.1

In-Depth Coverage	Accelerated Pace
• Work through all key concepts, pp. 336–346.	• Assign pp. 336–346 for independent student review.
• Assign and review Exercises 1–8.	
• Read and discuss Grammar in Literature, p. 339.	• Assign Review Exercises 9–12, p. 347.

▶ **Exercise 1** Recognizing Adjectives and the Words They Modify Copy each of the following sentences onto your paper. Draw an arrow pointing from each underlined adjective to the noun or pronoun it modifies.

EXAMPLE: He has not been <u>well</u> for <u>several</u> months.

1. Ducks, geese, and swans are <u>aquatic</u> birds.
2. <u>All</u> waterfowl swim and float.
3. <u>These</u> birds have <u>webbed</u> feet.
4. Ducks are <u>smaller</u> than <u>other</u> waterfowl.
5. A <u>female</u> duck has <u>dull</u> feathers that blend in with <u>her</u> surroundings.
6. <u>Male</u> ducks, also called drakes, are slightly <u>larger</u> than the females and have more <u>colorful</u> feathers.
7. A mallard drake has <u>many</u> <u>green</u> feathers on its head.
8. <u>These</u> <u>colorful</u> birds are often called greenheads.
9. A mallard duck plucks feathers from <u>her</u> <u>own</u> body to build a <u>soft</u>, <u>warm</u> nest.
10. A <u>baby</u> mallard can already swim and feed itself when it is <u>one</u> day old.

▶ **More Practice**

Language Lab CD-ROM
• Using Modifiers lesson
On-line Exercise Bank
• Section 16.1
Grammar Exercise Workbook
• pp. 21–22

▼ Critical Viewing
Think of several adjectives to describe the color, shape, and size of the mallard drakes in the photo.
[Analyze]

Adjectives • 337

Customize for
Gifted/Talented Students

Read aloud the Grammar and Style Tip on p. 336. Give students a list of clichés such as *mad as a wet hen* and *mind like a steel trap*. Challenge them to come up with vivid adjectives to replace each cliché. (Possible responses for the two examples: *furious, outraged; incisive, keen*)

Answer Key

▶ **Exercise 1**

1. arrow from *aquatic* to *birds*
2. arrow from *All* to *waterfowl*
3. arrow from *These* to *birds*; arrow from *webbed* to *feet*
4. arrow from *smaller* to *Ducks*; arrow from *other* to *waterfowl*
5. arrow from *female* to *duck*; arrow from *dull* to *feathers*; arrow from *her* to *surroundings*
6. arrow from *Male* to *ducks*; arrow from *larger* to *ducks*; arrow from *colorful* to *feathers*
7. arrow from *many* to *feathers*; arrow from *green* to *feathers*
8. arrow from *These* to *birds*; arrow from *colorful* to *birds*
9. arrow from *her* to *body*; arrow from *own* to *body*; arrow from *soft* to *nest*; arrow from *warm* to *nest*
10. arrow from *baby* to *mallard*; arrow from *one* to *day*

Critical Viewing

Analyze Possible responses: colorful, gaudy, green, plump, big

Customize for

Less Advanced Students

Write the word *adjective* on the chalkboard. Pronounce the word and underline the first two letters. Remind them that to *add* means to increase or to join things together so that one has more. *Ad*jectives *add* detail to nouns so that one has a more precise idea of what the nouns mean. Remembering the idea of adding will help students remember what adjectives do.

Step-by-Step Teaching Guide

Using Articles

1. Ask volunteers to offer definitions of the word *definite*. ("sure"; "clear"; "exact") Point out that *indefinite* means just the opposite.

2. Explain that *the* is a definite article because it is exact. Point out that when *the* is used, additional information may be needed. For example, a speaker may have a specific sweater in mind, but information such as that it's blue, wool, or lying on the bed is needed to identify it to the hearer. Sometimes, the details are understood. For example, in *I'll get the car*, it is understood that the speaker means the car he or she drives; in *get out of the water*, the speaker means the specific water that you are in.

3. Indefinite articles, while still somewhat specific (that is, if one says *a dog* one doesn't mean anything other than *dogs*), are not as precise or specific as *the*.

4. Have a volunteer read the chart for using *a* and *an*. Emphasize that it is the sound that determines use.

Language Highlight

Students may see the article *an* used with the words *historic* or *historical* in books, or they may hear this usage on television newscasts and documentaries. Explain that this is an exception to the general rule about when to use *a* and *an*. Americans are more likely to use *a* with *historical*, but students may still see and hear the older usage, especially in scholarly or formal contexts.

Customize for
ESL Students

Many languages require that adjectives, including articles, agree in number and gender with the nouns they modify. In English, however, there is no such requirement. Demonstrate by writing on the board *the girl, the girls, the boy, the boys, the house, the houses*. Likewise, with indefinite articles: *a boy, a girl, a house*.

Using Articles

Three common adjectives—*the, a,* and *an*—are known as *articles*. Unlike other adjectives, which may sometimes come after the nouns they modify, articles always come before nouns. Articles answer the question *Which one?*

The article *the* is called the *definite article.*

KEY CONCEPT The **definite article** *the* refers to a specific person, place, or thing. ■

The word *the* notes one particular person, place, or thing.

EXAMPLES: the canoe

the trumpeter swan

A and *an*, the other two articles, are called *indefinite articles*. These two articles are not as specific as *the*.

KEY CONCEPT *A* and *an*, the other two articles, are called **indefinite articles.** They point out a type of person, place, or thing, but they do not refer to a specific one. ■

EXAMPLES: a pond (perhaps one of several)

an old sweater (any one of many)

You should also know when to use *a* and when to use *an*. *A* is used before consonant sounds. *An* is used before vowel sounds. Notice that you choose between *a* and *an* based on sound. The letter *h*, a consonant, may sound like either a consonant or a vowel. The letters *o* and *u* are also problems. They are vowels, but they sometimes sound like consonants.

| USING *A* AND *AN* ||
A With Consonant Sounds	*An* With Vowel Sounds
a yellow hat	an endangered water bird
a happy time (*h* sound)	an honest person
a onetime nesting area	(no *h* sound)
(*w* sound)	an old map (*o* sound)
a unicorn (*y* sound)	an uncle (*u* sound)

More Practice

Language Lab
CD-ROM
• Using Modifiers lesson
On-line
Exercise Bank
• Section 16.1
Grammar Exercise Workbook
• pp. 23–24

🖊 Spelling Tip

Before a word beginning with a consonant, *the* is pronounced "thə" *(the swan)*. Before a vowel, *the* is pronounced "thē" *(the only swan)*. However it is pronounced, it is always spelled the same way.

Connecting to Literature
Have students locate and read the complete story "The Third Wish" in the Bronze Level of *Prentice Hall Literature: Timeless Voices, Timeless Themes.* Have them analyze Aiken's use of adjectives in any story passage of ten or more lines.

Exercise 2 Distinguishing Between Definite and Indefinite Articles On your paper, write the articles that will complete each of the following sentences correctly. The word in parentheses tells you which kind of article to use.

EXAMPLE: (Definite) ambulance raced up (indefinite) one-way street.
ANSWER: The, a

1. (Indefinite) lake is (indefinite) ideal place for swans to live.
2. (Definite) water must not be too deep.
3. Swans must be able to reach (definite) bottom to find food.
4. (Indefinite) lake with gently sloping sides is (definite) best.
5. This allows (definite) birds to get in and out of (definite) water easily.
6. (Definite) plants growing in and around (indefinite) lake are very important to swans.
7. They provide (indefinite) essential supply of nest material and (indefinite) marvelous place to nest.
8. Some types of swans may spend (indefinite) entire year on (definite) same lake.
9. Other swans, especially those living in (indefinite) cold climate, have to leave before (definite) winter sets in.
10. (Definite) following spring, they return to (definite) same lake.

GRAMMAR IN LITERATURE

from **The Third Wish**
Joan Aiken

In this excerpt from "The Third Wish," you can see examples of articles (in red) and other adjectives (in blue).

The primroses were just beginning but the trees were still bare, and it was cold; the birds had stopped singing an hour ago.

As Mr. Peters entered a straight, empty stretch of road he seemed to hear a faint crying, and a struggling and thrashing, as if somebody was in trouble far away in the trees.

▲ Critical Viewing What are some *definite* traits of a swan that make it stand out from other birds? [**Compare and Contrast**]

Adjectives • 339

Answer Key

> **Exercise 2**

1. A, an
2. The
3. the
4. A, the
5. the, the
6. The, a
7. an, a
8. an, the
9. a, the
10. The, the

Critical Viewing

Compare and Contrast Possible response: The swan is larger than most other birds.

> **Step-by-Step Teaching Guide**

Grammar in Literature

1. Discuss how the definite articles identify specific things and the indefinite do not. (*The* before primroses, trees, and birds implies those which are in the place where the story occurs, and no others. *An* is used for hour because no definite time is given. *A* stretch, *a* crying, and *a* struggling are vague: a part of a longer road and unidentified sounds.)

2. Ask students to describe the information the other adjectives contribute. (The other adjectives give descriptions that help create the scene. They add details and give us sensory information, such as how it felt, what it looked like, what Mr. Peters heard.)

3. Discuss how removing the articles and other adjectives would affect this passage. (Readers would know very little about what was happening.)

More About the Writer

Joan Aiken has written numerous children's books, including the award-winning *The Wolves of Willoughby Chase*. This novel is the first of a series of stories set in an imaginary seventeenth-century England with a fictitious Stuart, King James III. The stories tell of the adventures of Dido, an impish Cockney child, and her friend Simon, a penniless art student later discovered to be a long-lost Duke.

Using Nouns as Adjectives

1. Occasionally, nouns will function as adjectives. A noun used as an adjective will modify another noun and answer the question *What kind?* or *Which one?*

2. On the chalkboard, write a few phrases with nouns used as adjectives, such as *baseball cap, infield fly, home plate,* and *curve ball.* In each of these phrases, the noun is being used to describe another noun. A baseball cap is a specific style of cap, an infield fly is a particular kind of fly ball, and so on.

3. Point out the words *salesperson* and *waterfowl* in the chart on this page. Explain that, because these are compound nouns, they offer another example of nouns used as adjectives. The first part of each of these compound words functions as an adjective. It describes the noun that follows it. *Sales* modifies *person,* and *water* modifies *fowl.* Ask students to suggest other compound words that fit this pattern. (Possible responses: classroom, grasshopper, basketball)

Answer Key

1. waterfowl (family)
2. winter (season)
3. wedge (formation)
4. flight (pattern)
5. flock (member), air (resistance)
6. leader (goose), point (position)
7. formation (leaders), flight (speed)
8. summer (home)
9. Wildlife (experts), waterfowl (protection)
10. goose (population), migration (periods)

Critical Viewing

Identify Possible responses: goose eggs, goose quill, goose feathers, bird house, bird nest, duck blind, duck-billed platypus

---

16.1

Using Nouns as Adjectives

Nouns can sometimes be used as adjectives. A noun used as an adjective usually comes directly before another noun and answers the question *What kind?* or *Which one?*

NOUNS	USED AS ADJECTIVES
shoe	a *shoe* salesperson (*What kind* of salesperson?)
waterfowl	the *waterfowl* refuge (*Which* refuge?)

▶ **Exercise 3** Identifying Nouns Used as Adjectives On your paper, write the noun(s) used as an adjective in the following sentences. Next to each adjective, write the noun it modifies.

EXAMPLE: A duck feather floated through the air.
ANSWER: duck (feather)

1. As with other members of the waterfowl family, geese gather in large flocks each autumn.
2. They travel long distances to spend the winter season in warm climates.
3. While migrating, geese often fly in a wedge formation.
4. This V flight pattern helps the birds fly for a greater distance than they could if they traveled alone.
5. It also provides an uplift that helps each flock member more easily overcome any air resistance.
6. When the leader goose tires, it rotates back into the formation and another goose flies to the point position.
7. When the geese honk while flying, they are encouraging the formation leaders to keep up their flight speed.
8. Flocks will return year after year to the same summer home.
9. Wildlife experts have set up refuges in these areas for waterfowl protection.
10. On some refuges, the goose population may increase to half a million birds for short times during migration periods.

▼ Critical Viewing Try to think of at least five phrases in which the word *duck, goose,* or *bird* is used as an adjective—for example, *bird song.* **[Identify]**

Using Proper Adjectives

A *proper adjective* begins with a capital letter. There are two types of proper adjectives:

KEY CONCEPT A **proper adjective** is (1) a proper noun used as an adjective or (2) an adjective formed from a proper noun. ■

A proper noun used as an adjective does *not* change its form. It is merely placed in front of another noun.

PROPER NOUNS	USED AS PROPER ADJECTIVES
Truman	the *Truman* library (*Which* library?)
Florida	*Florida* wetlands (*What kind* of wetlands?)
December	*December* weather (*What kind* of weather?)

When an adjective is formed from a proper noun, the proper noun does change its form.

PROPER NOUNS	PROPER ADJECTIVES FORMED FROM PROPER NOUNS
America	*American* history (*Which kind* of history?)
Victoria	*Victorian* ideas (*What kind* of ideas?)

Exercise 4 Recognizing Proper Adjectives On your paper, write the proper adjective(s) in each of the following sentences. Then, write the noun each proper adjective modifies.

EXAMPLE: An Austrian tourist watched the geese in flight.
ANSWER: Austrian (tourist)

1. Snow geese live in the Arctic region surrounding the North Pole.
2. Some spend winters along the Atlantic coast.
3. The Canada goose is another popular North American bird.
4. It usually lays its eggs during warm March or April days.
5. Some geese gather in winter at California refuges.

More Practice

Language Lab
CD-ROM
• Using Modifiers lesson
On-line
Exercise Bank
• Section 16.1
Grammar Exercise Workbook
• pp. 23–26

Adjectives • 341

Using Proper Adjectives

1. Briefly review proper nouns with students. Personal names of people and places are always capitalized. So are months of the year (January), days of the week (Tuesday), brand names (Frisbee), and certain periods in history (Renaissance). Explain that these nouns are also capitalized when they are used as adjectives.

2. Tell students that they can often recognize adjectives formed from proper nouns by the ending *-ish, -an,* or *-ian.* Point to the examples on the page such as *Victorian* and *American* and challenge students to suggest others. (Possible examples: Egyptian, Elizabethan, Italian, Mexican, Spanish) Warn students that there are many proper adjectives that do not take these endings (e.g., Israeli, French, Dutch, etc.).

Customize for
More Advanced Students

Give students a list of 15 or 20 proper nouns that they are likely to see in history, art history, geography, music, or literature classes. Possible nouns include *Mozart, Renaissance, Wagner, Turkey, Poland, Caesar, Shakespeare,* and *Shaw.* Make sure that several of your choices will take unusual endings (such as *Shavian* for *Shaw*). Challenge pairs of students to find the adjectival form of all the words.

Answer Key

Exercise 4

1. Arctic (region)
2. Atlantic (coast)
3. Canada (goose), North American (bird)
4. March, April (days)
5. California (refuges)

STANDARDIZED TEST PREPARATION WORKSHOP

Grammar and Usage Some standardized test questions measure students' ability to use adjectives and adverbs appropriately. Share the following example with students:

I like cats because they are ___ animals.

A friendly
B friend
C nicely
D quietly

The correct choice is item **A.** B is a noun, and C and D are both adverbs, which cannot modify the noun *animals.*

Using Compound Adjectives

1. Review compound words with students and have them give a few examples. (Possible responses: *trashcan, paperweight, milkshake*) Explain that compound adjectives, like other compound words, are composed of more than one word.

2. Point out that many compound adjectives are hyphenated. Direct students' attention to some of the examples on the page, such as *well-known*. Explain that the hyphen helps a reader visually connect both parts of the compound adjective. The hyphen shows that the two adjectives are linked and that together, they modify the following noun. Other compound adjectives are written as one word (coldblooded, lifelong). Encourage students to use a dictionary to check the spelling when they are in doubt.

Answer Key

> **Exercise 5**

1. web-footed (birds)
2. fan-shaped (tail)
3. black-necked (swan), snow-white (body)
4. backward-facing (teeth)
5. Pintail (ducks), surface-feeding (birds)
6. wedge-shaped (head), trumpet-like (call)
7. high-pitched (call)
8. canvasback (duck), high-powered (wings)
9. saltwater (marshes), coastline (refuges)
10. freshwater (lakes), seacoast (homes)

16.1

Using Compound Adjectives

Adjectives, like nouns, can be compound.

> **KEY CONCEPT** A **compound adjective** is made up of more than one word. ■

Most *compound adjectives* are written as hyphenated words. Some are written as combined words, as in "a *runaway* horse." If you are unsure about how to write a compound adjective, look up the word in a dictionary.

HYPHENATED	COMBINED
a *well-known* actress	a *featherweight* boxer
a *full-time* job	a *freshwater* lake

> **Exercise 5** Recognizing Compound Adjectives In the following sentences, find the compound adjectives and write them on your paper. Next to each adjective, write the noun it modifies.

EXAMPLE: After the accident, the oil-covered highway slowed traffic for hours.

ANSWER: oil-covered (highway)

1. Ducks, geese, and swans are web-footed birds that come in all sizes, shapes, and colors.
2. The ruddy duck has a broad, fan-shaped tail and a small body.
3. The black-necked swan of South America has a snow-white body.
4. To help in catching fish, merganser ducks have sharp, backward-facing teeth.
5. Pintail ducks are surface-feeding birds, named for their pointed tails and wingtips.
6. The trumpeter swan has a wedge-shaped head and a unique trumpet-like call.
7. The whistling swan has a very high-pitched call.
8. The canvasback duck has high-powered wings, making it among the fastest ducks in North America.
9. During the fall, they migrate from northern lakes and ponds to saltwater marshes and other coastline refuges.
10. Some swans also migrate from freshwater lakes and rivers to seacoast homes.

> **More Practice**

Language Lab
CD-ROM
• Using Modifiers lesson
On-line
Exercise Bank
• Section 16.1
Grammar Exercise
Workbook
• pp. 25–28

☑ ONGOING ASSESSMENT: Prerequisite Skills

If students have difficulty with compound adjectives, you may find it necessary to review the following to assure coverage of prerequisite knowledge.

In the Textbook	Print Resources	Technology
Compound Nouns, pp. 297–298	Grammar Exercise Workbook, pp. 3–4	Language Lab CD-ROM, Using Nouns; On-Line Exercise Bank, Section 14.1

Using Nouns and Pronouns as Adjectives

▲ Critical Viewing
How do you think pintail ducks got their name? **[Relate]**

▷ **KEY CONCEPT** A noun or pronoun is used as an adjective if it modifies a noun. ■

EXAMPLES: The <u>duck</u> pond sometimes freezes in winter.
We see the ducklings on <u>this</u> side of the pond.
<u>Which</u> ducks are the males?

In the first example, the noun *duck* functions as an adjective modifying *pond*. In the second example, the demonstrative pronoun *this* modifies *side*, and in the third example, the interrogative pronoun *Which* modifies *ducks*.

Using Possessive Nouns and Pronouns as Adjectives

These personal pronouns are often called *possessive adjectives*: *my, your, his, her, its, our,* and *their*. They are adjectives because they are used before nouns and answer the question *Which one?* They are pronouns because they have antecedents.

EXAMPLE: The ducks flapped their wings.

Their is an adjective because it modifies *wings*. At the same time, it is a pronoun because it stands for the antecedent *ducks*.

Note About *Possessive Nouns:* Possessive nouns function as adjectives when they modify a noun.

The pond is on Mr. <u>Smith's</u> property.
The <u>duck's</u> feathers are colorful.

Adjectives • 343

Using Nouns and Pronouns as Adjectives

1. Review pronouns with students. Ask them what types of pronouns they remember (personal, demonstrative, interrogative, indefinite).

2. Point out that most of these pronouns can be used as adjectives, but not all. With personal pronouns, only the possessive form acts as an adjective. With interrogative pronouns, *what, which,* and *whose* act as adjectives, but *who* and *whom* do not. For indefinite pronouns, you may wish to go through the list (p. 307) with students and have them determine which ones can be used as adjectives (e.g., *both* or *neither*). Point out that some indefinites can become adjectives if they are made possessive (e.g., *everyone's, nobody's*).

3. Point out that, since possessive forms are used only if there is something that is possessed, possessive forms are always adjectives—they always modify the thing possessed. This applies to both pronouns and nouns: *Mr. Smith's dog, his dog, nobody's dog.*

4. (Demonstrative and interrogative pronouns used as adjectives are covered in greater depth on pp. 345–346, so focus students' attention on the possessive forms now.)

Critical Viewing

Relate The name describes the shape of the duck's tail.

☑ **ONGOING ASSESSMENT: Monitor and Reinforce**

If students miss more than two items in Exercises 3–5, refer them to the following for additional practice:

In the Textbook	Print Resources	Technology
Section Review, Ex. 11–12, p. 347	Grammar Exercise Workbook, pp. 23–26	Language Lab CD-ROM, Using Modifiers; On-Line Exercise Bank, Section 16.1

⏲ **TIME SAVERS!**

📄 **Answers on Transparency**
Use the Grammar Exercises Answers on Transparencies for Chapter 16 to have students correct their own or one another's exercises.

🖥 **On-Line Exercise Bank**
Have students complete the exercises on computer. The Auto Check feature will grade their work for you!

Customize for
ESL Students

Some students may confuse English possessives with plurals. Remind students to look for and use apostrophes. An apostrophe before or after the final *s* in a noun always indicates a possessive in English. Point out that the apostrophe indicates the possessive form only for nouns, however, not for possessive pronouns.

Customize for
ESL Students

Some students may confuse English possessives with plurals. Remind students to look for and use apostrophes. An apostrophe before or after the final *s* in a noun always indicates a possessive in English. Point out that the apostrophe indicates the possessive form only for nouns, however, not for possessive pronouns.

Answer Key

▶ **Exercise 6**

	Possessive Adjective	Noun Modified	Antecedent
1.	their	explorations	Europeans
2.	his	diary	Columbus
3.	its	size	humming-bird
4.	his	patron	Columbus
5.	her	garden	queen
6.	our	school	my brother and I
7.	its	skin	humming-bird
8.	her	neighbors	woman
9.	their	lives	humming-birds
10.	his	book	Audubon

Critical Viewing

Assess Possible answers: They can hover in space like insects or helicopters. They can flap their wings extremely rapidly. They are brilliantly colored.

Integrating Spelling Skills

It's or Its Write *its* and *it's* on the chalkboard and ask students which is the contraction meaning "it is" or "it has" and which is the possessive form of *it.* Explain that unlike possessive nouns, *its* has no apostrophe. Point out that no other possessive pronoun has an apostrophe either. Students can use this pattern to help themselves remember never to use *it's* as a possessive.

▶ **Exercise 6** **Identifying Possessive Adjectives** In each of the following sentences, a possessive adjective is underlined. On your paper, make three columns, as shown in the example. Write the underlined word in the first column. Then, write the noun it modifies in the second column and its antecedent in the third.

EXAMPLE: The puppy was chasing <u>its</u> tail.

ANSWER:

Possessive Adjective	Noun Modified	Antecedent
its	tail	puppy

1. Europeans first spotted hummingbirds during <u>their</u> explorations of the New World.
2. In <u>his</u> diary, Christopher Columbus wrote accounts of hummingbirds.
3. At first, he thought the hummingbird was an insect because of <u>its</u> size.
4. He brought several hummingbirds back to Spain as presents for <u>his</u> patron, Queen Isabella.
5. The queen let them fly free in <u>her</u> garden.
6. My brother and I found an article about hummingbirds in the library in <u>our</u> school.
7. We learned that the hummingbird was hunted because of <u>its</u> colorful skin.
8. Every fashionable European woman wanted to impress <u>her</u> neighbors with objects made of hummingbird skin.
9. To meet the demand, hundreds of thousands of hummingbirds lost <u>their</u> lives.
10. Audubon included several paintings of hummingbirds in <u>his</u> book of art prints.

▼ Critical Viewing
What are some special qualities that hummingbirds possess? **[Assess]**

344 • Adjectives and Adverbs

☑ **ONGOING ASSESSMENT: Prerequisite Skills**

If students have difficulty with adjectives derived from nouns and pronouns, you may find it necessary to review the following to assure coverage of prerequisite knowledge.

In the Textbook	Print Resources	Technology
Nouns and Pronouns, pp. 294–311	Grammar Exercise Workbook, pp. 1–12	Language Lab CD-ROM, Using Nouns, Using Pronouns; On-Line Exercise Bank, Section 16.1

Using Demonstrative Adjectives

This, *that*, *these*, and *those*—the four demonstrative pronouns—are often used as demonstrative adjectives.

PRONOUN: We saw *that*.

ADJECTIVE: *That* lake is home to many geese.

PRONOUN: What are *these*?

ADJECTIVE: *These* gulls are searching for food.

▶ **Exercise 7** **Recognizing Demonstrative Adjectives** Write the demonstrative pronoun in each of the following sentences. If it is used as a pronoun, write *pronoun*. If it is used as an adjective, write the noun it modifies.

EXAMPLE: I learned that last year.
ANSWER: that (pronoun)

EXAMPLE: I did well on that test.
ANSWER: that (test)

1. Those are yellow-legged gulls gathered on the beach, searching for food.
2. These gulls have dark-yellow legs and a distinctive red spot on their lower jaw.
3. That one is a herring gull.
4. These two types of sea gulls are very similar and are often mistaken for each other.
5. This is how you can tell the difference between the two kinds of gulls.
6. Notice the pinkish-colored legs on these herring gulls and the smaller red spots on their jaws.
7. There are other differences between the two birds besides those.
8. The feathers of this bird are slightly darker than those of the other.
9. These darker feathers belong to the herring gull.
10. Do you think you can remember all of this?

▶ **More Practice**

Language Lab CD-ROM
• Using Modifiers lesson
On-line Exercise Bank
• Section 16.1
Grammar Exercise Workbook
• pp. 29–30

Adjectives • **345**

Step-by-Step Teaching Guide

Using Demonstrative Adjectives

1. Review demonstrative pronouns with students. Copy the two example adjective sentences on the chalkboard. Then rewrite them with the pronoun *the* instead of *that* or *these*. Ask students to explain the difference in meaning. (*That lake* and *these gulls* are more emphatic phrases than *the lake* and *the gulls*. Also, they are pointing something out, or *demonstrating*.)

2. Demonstrate to students how a dialogue could be created by switching adjectives. *"I want the paint." "Which paint?" "That paint."*

3. Work through the first few sentences in Exercise 7 with students. Point out that the key to recognizing whether or not a demonstrative pronoun is being used as an adjective is the presence or absence of a modified word.

Answer Key

▶ **Exercise 7**

1. Those—pronoun
2. These—gulls
3. That—one
4. These—types
5. This—pronoun
6. these—gulls
7. those—pronoun
8. this—bird, those—pronoun
9. These—feathers
10. this—pronoun

☑ **ONGOING ASSESSMENT: Assess Mastery**

Use the following resources to assess students' mastery of adjectives.

In the Textbook	Print Resources	Technology
Chapter Review, Ex. 29–32, p. 356 Standardized Test Preparation Workshop, pp. 358–359	Grammar Exercise Workbook, pp. 21–30	Language Lab CD-ROM, Using Modifiers; On-Line Exercise Bank, Section 16.1

⏱ **TIME SAVERS!**

🗎 **Answers on Transparency**
Use the Grammar Exercises Answers on Transparencies for Chapter 16 to have students correct their own or one another's exercises.

🖥 **On-Line Exercise Bank**
Have students complete the exercises on computer. The Auto Check feature will grade their work for you!

Using Interrogative Adjectives

1. Write the word *interrogative* on the chalkboard and ask students to define it. If necessary, remind them that to interrogate means to question. Therefore, interrogative adjectives ask questions.

2. Point out that, as with demonstrative pronouns used as adjectives, the key is to determine whether or not *which, what,* and *whose* are modifying a word or standing alone.

Integrating Vocabulary Skills

Students may be confused about when to use the words *which* and *what.* Explain that they should use *which* when selecting one item from a set. *Which* always implies the words *of those.* Have students try adding this phrase to some "which" sentences.

Which is your favorite dress?

*Which **of those** dresses is your favorite dress?*

If the new sentence makes sense, then *which* is correct. In all other cases, students should use *what.* Remembering this rule will help students use these two words correctly in their own writing.

Customize for
Bodily/Kinesthetic Learners

Challenge students to locate and rehearse the classic Abbott and Costello routine "Who's on First?" for a class performance. Everyone will enjoy the characters' confusion over the names of the men who play the nine positions: Who, What, I Don't Know, and so on. Ask performers and audience to explain the source of the confusion (the use of interrogative pronouns and statements in place of names).

Using Interrogative Adjectives

Which, what, and *whose*—three of the interrogative pronouns—can be used as *interrogative adjectives.*

PRONOUN: *Which* do you think he will choose?

ADJECTIVE: *Which* parrot do you think he will buy?

PRONOUN: *Whose* can that be?

ADJECTIVE: *Whose* macaw can that be?

> **Exercise 8** **Recognizing Interrogative Adjectives** Write the interrogative pronoun in each of the following sentences. If it is used as a pronoun, write *pronoun.* If it is used as an adjective, write the word it modifies.

EXAMPLE: What do you want?
ANSWER: What (pronoun)

EXAMPLE: What words can she speak?
ANSWER: What (words)

1. Which is the most interesting pet to own?
2. What tips should you learn before purchasing a macaw?
3. Which pet shop carries the healthiest macaws?
4. Whose idea was it to come to this pet store?
5. What are we supposed to do to prepare our home for the new parrot?
6. Whose voice does the parrot seem to be imitating?
7. Which are the most unusual sounds that your bird makes?
8. Which brand of food is the most popular?
9. Whose is the best Web site for locating information about macaws?
10. What items did you put inside the parrot's cage?

346 • Adjectives and Adverbs

◯ Learn More

For more practice with pronouns, refer to Chapter 14.

▼ Critical Viewing
Which colors can you spot in this macaw's feathers? **[Distinguish]**

Answer Key

> **Exercise 8**

1. Which—pronoun
2. What—tips
3. Which—pet shop
4. Whose—idea
5. What—pronoun
6. Whose—voice
7. Which—pronoun
8. Which—brand
9. Whose—pronoun
10. What—items

Critical Viewing
Distinguish Colors identified may include red, orange, yellow, green, blue, white, and black.

Section 16.1 Section Review

GRAMMAR EXERCISES 9–15

Exercise 9 Recognizing Adjectives and the Words They Modify Copy each sentence. Draw an arrow from each underlined adjective to the word it modifies.

1. The swan is a <u>graceful</u> <u>water</u> bird.
2. Like geese, swans have a <u>flattened</u> bill.
3. They also have <u>long</u> necks, <u>short</u> tails, and <u>webbed</u> feet.
4. <u>Most</u> swans are <u>larger</u> than ducks.
5. Swans live in <u>mild</u> or <u>cold</u> climates.

Exercise 10 Distinguishing Between Definite and Indefinite Articles Rewrite each sentence, filling in the kind of article indicated in parentheses.

1. Swans nest along (definite) shores of ponds and marshes during summer.
2. Some move to (indefinite) large lake or bay for (definite) winter season.
3. Swans feed mostly on plants that they find under (definite) water.
4. Because of its webbed feet, (indefinite) swan is (indefinite) excellent swimmer.
5. The swan's long neck helps it locate (indefinite) underwater meal.

Exercise 11 Identifying Nouns and Pronouns Used as Adjectives Write the nouns and pronouns used as adjectives and the noun each one modifies.

1. The wings of a duck are small for its body weight.
2. Its rapid wing beat helps a duck to stay airborne.
3. The record speed for a duck is more than 70 miles per hour.
4. What factors affect flight altitude?
5. Weather conditions can affect this altitude.

Exercise 12 Recognizing Proper and Compound Adjectives Write the proper and compound adjectives below and the noun each one modifies.

1. In 1903, the first American wildlife refuge was established.
2. The flamingo once lived in the wild in Florida coastline areas.
3. The flamingos of the Caribbean area have coral-red feathers.
4. South American flamingos have pinkish-white feathers.
5. One group that lives on the African continent has many wingtips.

Exercise 13 Find It in Your Reading Read this sentence from "The Third Wish" by Joan Aiken. List all of the adjectives you find in the sentence.

. . . Then he took her to his house in a remote and lovely valley and showed her all his treasures—the bees in their white hives, the Jersey cows, the hyacinths, the silver candlesticks, the blue cups and the luster bowl for putting primroses in.

Exercise 14 Find It in Your Writing Select a writing sample from your portfolio that contains several different kinds of adjectives. Circle the adjectives, and tell what word each modifies.

Exercise 15 Writing Application Imagine that you live in a house near a shoreline. Write a description of different birds you see when you look out your window. Use several kinds of adjectives in your description. Circle each adjective.

ASSESS

Section Review

Each of these exercises correlates to a concept in the section on adjectives, pages 336–346. These exercises may be used for more practice, for reteaching, or for review of the Key Concepts presented.

Answer Key

Exercise 9

1. arrow from *graceful* to *bird*; arrow from *water* to *bird*
2. arrow from *flattened* to *bill*
3. arrow from *long* to *necks*; arrow from *short* to *tails*; arrow from *webbed* to *feet*
4. arrow from *Most* to *swans*; arrow from *larger* to *swans*
5. arrow from *mild* to *climates*; arrow from *cold* to *climates*

Exercise 10

1. Swans nest along **the** shores of ponds and marshes during summer.
2. Some move to **a** large lake or bay for **the** winter season.
3. Swans feed mostly on plants that they find under **the** water.
4. Because of its webbed feet, **a** swan is **an** excellent swimmer.
5. The swan's long neck helps it locate **an** underwater meal.

Exercise 11

1. its—weight, body—weight
2. its—beat, wing—beat
3. record—speed
4. flight—altitude
5. Weather—conditions, this—altitude

continued

Answer Key continued

Exercise 12

1. American—refuge, wildlife—refuge
2. Florida—coastline, coastline—areas
3. Caribbean—area, coral-red feathers
4. South American—flamingos, pinkish-white—feathers
5. African—continent

Exercise 13

Find It in Your Reading

his, remote, lovely, all, his, their, white, Jersey, silver, blue, luster

Exercise 14

Find It in Your Writing

Challenge students to make their use of adjectives more precise, colorful, and descriptive.

Exercise 15

Writing Application

Have students draw a box around any proper and compound adjectives in their descriptions. Ask volunteers to share their descriptions. Discuss how their use of adjectives contributes to the description.

⏱ **TIME SAVERS!**

🔲 **Answers on Transparency** Use the Grammar Exercises Answers on Transparencies for Chapter 16 to have students correct their own or one another's exercises.

💻 **On-Line Exercise Bank** Have students complete the exercises on computer. The Auto Check feature will grade their work for you!

PREPARE and ENGAGE

Adverbs

Interest GRABBER Write on the board *He runs ____.* Ask students to suggest words that could be used to complete the sentence (*very swiftly, slowly, away, often*). Have students suggest another phrase, and repeat the exercise. Point out that the words they are suggesting are, like adjectives, modifying another word and making it more precise.

Activate Prior Knowledge

Write on the board: *She sings beautifully. They quietly whispered. Those shoes are really dirty.* Ask students to identify the word that each underlined word modifies (*sings, whispered, dirty*). Ask students to name the parts of speech of these modified words (verb, verb, adjective). Tell students that, in this section, they will learn more about these modifying words, called *adverbs*.

TEACH

Step-by-Step Teaching Guide

Using Adverbs That Modify Verbs

1. After students have read the Key Concept on this page, ask them why they think it is important to use words that modify verbs (possible answers: to give more information about what is happening, to be more descriptive).

2. Review the four questions that adverbs answer. Point out that "In what way?" could, if it helps students, be stated as "How?"

3. Have students suggest some other words (new adverbs for the verbs listed or new adverb/verb combinations) that illustrate answers to the four questions.

Answer Key

Exercise 16

1. In what way?
2. When?
3. In what way?
4. Where?, Where?
5. In what way?, In what way?

Adverbs can modify three different parts of speech:

▶ **KEY CONCEPT** An **adverb** modifies a verb, an adjective, or another adverb. ■

Although adverbs may modify adjectives and other adverbs, they generally modify verbs.

Using Adverbs That Modify Verbs

An adverb that modifies a verb will answer one of these four questions: *Where? When? In what way? To what extent?*

ADVERBS THAT MODIFY VERBS

Where?	
push *upward*	travels *everywhere*
fell *there*	go *outside*

When?	
arrived *yesterday*	swims *often*
comes *daily*	exhibits *yearly*

In What Way?	
works *carefully*	chews *noisily*
speaks *well*	acted *willingly*

To What Extent?	
hardly ate	*almost* cried
really surprised	*partly* finished

▶ **Exercise 16** Identifying How Adverbs Modify Verbs
Decide which question each underlined adverb answers and write it on your paper: *Where? When? In what way?* or *To what extent?*

1. One of California's main attractions is the coastline, which stretches <u>continuously</u> along the western border of the state.
2. Some people enjoy watching the gray whales as these whales migrate <u>yearly</u> to the California coast.
3. Others <u>intently</u> view the tide pools for hours at a time.
4. The ocean life seems to disappear as the water rushes <u>in</u> and <u>out</u>.
5. The seals <u>calmly</u> sunbathe on some of the rocky cliffs and swim <u>lazily</u> in the ocean waters.

348 • Adjectives and Adverbs

▶ **More Practice**
Language Lab CD-ROM
• Using Modifiers lesson
On-line Exercise Bank
• Section 16.2
Grammar Exercise Workbook
• pp. 31–34

⏱ TIME AND RESOURCE MANAGER

Resources
Print: Grammar Exercise Workbook, pp. 31–36; Hands-on Grammar Activity Book, Chapter 16
Technology: Language Lab CD-ROM, Using Modifiers; On-Line Exercise Bank, Section 16.2

In-Depth Coverage	Accelerated Pace
• Work through all key concepts, pp. 348–354. • Assign and review Exercises 16–22. • Read and discuss Grammar in Literature, p. 352. • Do the Hands-on Grammar Activity, p. 354.	• Assign pp. 348–354 for independent student review. • Assign Section Review Exercises 23–25, p. 355.

Using Adverbs That Modify Adjectives

An adverb modifying an adjective answers only one question: *To what extent?*

ADVERBS THAT MODIFY ADJECTIVES	
To What Extent?	
very upset	*extremely* tall
definitely wrong	*not* hungry

▶ **Exercise 17** Recognizing Adverbs That Modify Adjectives
On your paper, write the adverb in each of the following sentences. After each adverb, write the adjective it modifies.

EXAMPLE: California is the most productive state for certain crops.

ANSWER: most (productive)

1. California's central valley has soil abundantly rich in nutrients.
2. The state's warm weather allows for an unusually long growing season.
3. Farmers are able to grow many different kinds of fruits and vegetables.
4. The broccoli and spinach that are grown in California are dark green and nutritious.
5. California avocados are tasty, but they have a very high fat content.
6. Grapes and peaches are extremely sweet fruits that many people enjoy.
7. Cantaloupes and honeydew melons are packed in very large containers for shipping to market.
8. Plums and apricots are small fruits, but they have unusually large seeds.
9. The constantly humid weather of southern California is good for growing oranges.
10. California's delicious fruits and vegetables are widely known throughout the world.

▲ **Critical Viewing**
Use adverbs modifying adjectives to describe how magnificent this coastline is. [Describe]

✸ Grammar and Style Tip

Adding a descriptive adverb can improve your writing by creating a more vivid picture in the reader's mind.

Adverbs • 349

Using Adverbs That Modify Other Adverbs

1. Point out that adverbs modifying adverbs are similar to adverbs modifying adjectives—in both cases, the question being answered is "To what extent?"

2. Suggest that students look over the previous two pages to see examples of adverbs that answer the question of extent for both verbs and adjectives.

3. To give students more practice, after they have finished Exercise 18, you may wish to have them suggest other adverbs that could have been used in the exercise items, either retaining the meaning or changing it.

Answer Key

▶ **Exercise 18**

1. quite (successfully)
2. almost (entirely)
3. too (greatly)
4. very (often)
5. only (slightly)
6. quite (easily)
7. extremely (high)
8. quite (frequently)
9. rather (silently)
10. most (definitely)

Critical Viewing

Analyze Students may suggest that the bald eagle is proud, stately, fierce. Encourage them to use adverbs to modify their adjectives.

16.2

Using Adverbs That Modify Other Adverbs

Sometimes, adverbs sharpen the meaning of other adverbs. An adverb modifying another adverb answers one question: *To what extent?* In the following chart, each example contains two adverbs. The first adverb in each modifies the second.

ADVERBS MODIFYING ADVERBS
To What Extent?
moved *very quickly*   *not completely* wrong
climbed *almost over*   *only just* recognizable

▶ **Exercise 18** Recognizing Adverbs That Modify Other Adverbs In each sentence, find the adverb that modifies another adverb by answering the question, *To what extent?* On your paper, write this adverb and the adverb it modifies.

EXAMPLE: The French visitors to California spoke too rapidly for me to understand them.

ANSWER: too (rapidly)

1. Many animals have adapted quite successfully to life in the California desert.
2. The grizzly bear almost entirely disappeared from the state in the 1920's.
3. Cougars and bobcats too greatly populate the foothills and woodlands.
4. They very often prey on herds of deer and other small animals.
5. The mountain lion population has only slightly increased over the past twenty years.
6. Smaller animals—such as marmots, raccoons, and chipmunks—are quite easily spotted in the forest.
7. The golden eagle and bald eagle can be seen soaring extremely high above the trees.
8. Smaller birds can quite frequently be heard chirping their own songs.
9. Reptiles slither rather silently through the underbrush.
10. California most definitely has the largest variety of animals in the United States.

▼ Critical Viewing What qualities of the bald eagle earned it the status of national symbol of the United States of America? **[Analyze]**

✎ STANDARDIZED TEST PREPARATION WORKSHOP

Grammar and Usage Many standardized test questions ask students to choose the best change to a sentence in order to make it correct. Often these choices involve understanding the correct usage of adverbs. Give the following example to students:

We quickly ran out of the house in order to catch the school bus, but the bus was late.

Which is the BEST change, if any, to make to this sentence?

A Move *quickly* after *out*

B Change *late* to *lately*

C Change *quickly* to *quick*

D Make no change

The correct answer is item **D**. The sentence is correct and requires no changes. Items B and C create incorrect parts of speech, and item A results in awkward construction.

Finding Adverbs in Sentences

The chart below shows examples of possible locations of adverbs. Arrows point to the words that the adverbs modify.

LOCATION OF ADVERBS IN SENTENCES	
Location	**Example**
At the Beginning of a Sentence	*Silently*, she approached the ocean.
At the End of a Sentence	She approached the ocean *silently*.
Before a Verb	She *silently* approached the ocean.
After a Verb	She tiptoed *silently* into the ocean.
Between Parts of a Verb Phrase	She had *silently* entered the ocean.
Before an Adjective	Her father was *always* quiet.
Before Another Adverb	Her father spoke *rather* quietly.

Exercise 19 **Locating Adverbs in Sentences** Each of the following sentences contains an adverb. Copy the sentences onto your paper, and underline each adverb. Then, draw arrows pointing from the adverbs to the words they modify.

EXAMPLE: She has <u>never</u> forgotten the tree's

<u>consistently</u> blossoming flowers.

1. Trees have been effectively used for many things.
2. Loggers carefully cut down the necessary trees.
3. Often, the trees are taken to a sawmill.
4. The trees are made into lumber there.
5. This lumber is sometimes used to build homes.

Spelling Tip

The adverb *almost* sounds like the two words *all* and *most*. However, when writing it, bring the two words together and drop one of the *l*'s to make the word *almost*.

More Practice

Language Lab CD-ROM
• Using Modifiers lesson
On-line Exercise Bank
• Section 16.2
Grammar Exercise Workbook
• pp. 35–36

Finding Adverbs in Sentences

1. Be sure students understand that there are many correct positions for adverbs. Arrows can help them identify the word or words the adverbs modify.

2. Have students identify the subject and verb in the sentences in Exercise 19. Next, they should look at the other words in the sentence and think about which questions they answer and which parts of speech they modify. In sentence 1, for example, *effectively* answers the question *In what way?* about the verb phrase *have been used*.

Answer Key

Exercise 19

1. Trees have been <u>effectively</u> used for many things. (arrow from *effectively* to *have been*; arrow from *effectively* to *used*)
2. Loggers <u>carefully</u> cut <u>down</u> the necessary trees. (arrow from *carefully* to *cut*; arrow from *down* to *cut*)
3. <u>Often</u>, the trees are taken to a sawmill. (arrow from *Often* to *are taken*)
4. The trees are made into lumber <u>there</u>. (arrow from *there* to *are made*)
5. This lumber is <u>sometimes</u> used to build homes. (arrow from *sometimes* to *is used*)

☑ **ONGOING ASSESSMENT: Monitor and Reinforce**

If students miss more than two items in Exercises 17 or 18, or more than one item in Exercises 16 or 19, refer them to the following for additional practice:

In the Textbook	Print Resources	Technology
Section Review, Ex. 23–24, p. 355	Grammar Exercise Workbook, pp. 31–34	Language Lab CD-ROM, Using Modifiers; On-Line Exercise Bank, Section 16.2

⏱ **TIME SAVERS!**

📃 **Answers on Transparency** Use the Grammar Exercises Answers on Transparencies for Chapter 16 to facilitate correction by students.

💻 **On-Line Exercise Bank** Have students complete the exercises on computer. The Auto Check feature will grade their work for you!

Grammar in Literature

1. Read aloud the excerpt from "The Californian's Tale" to students.

2. Ask students which question each of the adverbs answers (*plainly* and *caressingly* both answer *In what way?*)

More About the Writer

Missouri native Samuel Clemens got his pen name, Mark Twain, from his days as a steamboat pilot on the Mississippi River. "Mark twain" was a depth measurement pilots used. Twain wrote literature in nearly every category: children's stories, travel narratives, historical fiction, tall tales, and even a detective novel, *Pudd'n'head Wilson.* Twain's Wilson was the first literary detective to use fingerprints to solve a case.

Connecting to Literature

Have students locate and read the complete story "The Californian's Tale" in the Bronze Level of *Prentice Hall's Timeless Voices, Timeless Themes.* Have them identify other adverbs in the story and the words they modify.

Adverb or Adjective?

1. Have a volunteer read the text about *-ly* endings aloud. Tell students that another *-ly* word that may confuse them is *early.* *Early* can be either an adjective or an adverb.

    He telephoned her very <u>early</u> that morning.

    She was awakened by the <u>early</u> call.

    In the first sentence, *early* is an adverb answering the question *When?* about the verb *telephoned.* In the second sentence, it is an adjective describing *What kind?* of call.

2. Warn students that they cannot automatically create an adverb by adding the suffix *-ly* to a verb or an adjective. If an adjective already ends in *-ly,* students will have to create a prepositional phrase to say what they want to say.

GRAMMAR IN LITERATURE

from **The Californian's Tale**
Mark Twain

In the following passage, two adverbs have been highlighted. Although these adverbs end in -ly, it is important to remember that not all adverbs do.

. . . The delight that was in my heart showed in my face, and the man saw it and was pleased; saw it so *plainly* that he answered it as if it had been spoken.
"All her work," he said *caressingly*; "she did it all herself—every bit," and he took the room in with a glance which was full of affectionate worship.

Adverb or Adjective?

Some words can function as adverbs or as adjectives, depending on their use in a sentence. An adjective will modify a noun or pronoun and will answer one of the questions *What kind? Which one? How many?* or *How much?* An adverb will modify a verb, an adjective, or another adverb and will answer one of the questions *Where? When? In what way?* or *To what extent?*

ADVERB MODIFYING VERB:	Lumberjacks work *hard.*

ADJECTIVE MODIFYING NOUN:	Lumberjacks enjoy *hard* work.

You should know also that while most words ending in *-ly* are adverbs, some are not. Several adjectives also end in *-ly.* These adjectives are formed by adding *-ly* to nouns.

ADJECTIVES WITH -ly ENDINGS:	A *kingly* feast. A *friendly* person.

More Practice

Language Lab CD-ROM
• Using Modifiers lesson
On-line Exercise Bank
• Section 16.2
Grammar Exercise Workbook
• pp. 31–34

352 • Adjectives and Adverbs

Incorrect	She smiled friendlyly.
Correct	She smiled in a friendly way.

The whole phrase *in a friendly way* answers the question *In what manner?* about the verb *smiled. Friendly* cannot be made into a one-word adverb because it already ends in *-ly.*

▶ **Exercise 20** Distinguishing Between Adverbs and Adjectives On your paper, write whether the underlined word in each sentence is an adverb or an adjective.
1. Some fruit trees bloom <u>earlier</u> than others.
2. Usually, the blossoms don't last <u>long</u>.
3. Sharing the fruit from one's trees is a <u>neighborly</u> gesture.
4. In autumn, it seems that the leaves of our oak tree fall <u>last</u>.
5. Squirrels act <u>fast</u> to collect and store the acorns.
6. The Japanese maple is <u>slow</u> to shed its leaves.
7. Its branches spread <u>wide</u>, shading a large area.
8. Another tree with <u>wide</u> branches is the elm.
9. The long branches of the willow tree dip <u>close</u> to the water.
10. The seeds of many trees are carried <u>far</u> away by winds.

▶ **Exercise 21** Writing Sentences With Adjectives and Adverbs Use each of the following words in two sentences, first as an adjective and then as an adverb.
1. daily
2. hard
3. fast
4. early
5. wide

▶ **Exercise 22** Revising Sentences by Adding Adverbs and Adjectives Revise each sentence about the photograph by adding adjectives and adverbs.
1. The trees reach into the sky.
2. The angle of the photograph reinforces the size of the trees.
3. The trunks are like poles.
4. Not much light reaches the ground.
5. The sunlight filters through the branches.

▼ Critical Viewing
Use adjectives and adverbs to describe the feeling you get from these trees. **[Relate]**

Adverbs • 353

Critical Viewing

Relate Have students identify each adjective and adverb in their descriptions.

Answer Key

▶ **Exercise 20**

1. adverb	6. adjective
2. adverb	7. adverb
3. adjective	8. adjective
4. adverb	9. adverb
5. adverb	10. adverb

▶ **Exercise 21**

Possible answers:
1. We get a <u>daily</u> newspaper. It arrives at 7 A.M. <u>daily</u>.
2. My dad likes what he calls "<u>hard</u> news." I try <u>hard</u> to read it, but prefer the travel section.
3. A <u>fast</u> truck brings newspapers from the plant. The newspaper deliverer distributes them <u>fast</u>.
4. <u>Early</u> delivery is expected. People who wake up <u>early</u> want their papers.
5. A <u>wide</u> variety of papers is delivered. Sometimes they are thrown <u>wide</u> of the door.

▶ **Exercise 22**

Possible answers:
1. The <u>towering</u> trees reach <u>high</u> into the sky.
2. The angle of the photograph <u>greatly</u> reinforces the <u>enormous</u> size of the trees.
3. The <u>long, narrow</u> trunks are <u>very much</u> like poles.
4. Not much light reaches <u>down</u> to the <u>dark</u> ground <u>below</u>.
5. The sunlight filters <u>softly</u> through the <u>large, leafy</u> branches.

Customize for

Less Advanced Students

Ask students to go back over Exercise 20, identifying the word or words each underlined adverb or adjective modifies. (bloom, do last, gesture, fall, act, maple, spread, branches, dip, away)

☑ **ONGOING ASSESSMENT: Assess Mastery**

Use the following resources to assess students' mastery of adverbs.

In the Textbook	Print Resources	Technology
Chapter Review, Ex. 33–35, p. 357 Standardized Test Preparation Workshop, pp. 358–359	Grammar Exercise Workbook, pp. 31–36	Language Lab CD-ROM, Using Modifiers; On-Line Exercise Bank, Section 16.1

Adjective or Adverb?

Teaching Resources: Hands-on Grammar Activity Book, Chapter 16

1. Remind students that most adverbs are spelled differently from related adjectives: for example, *easy, easily; slow, slowly.* Encourage students to be careful in selecting words that really do act as both adjectives and adverbs.

2. As a further activity, you may want to have students add words to their middle strips that are either adjectives or adverbs but *not* both, including some "tricky" adjectives like *friendly.*

3. Discuss how using a frame like this might help students identify the function of a word of which they are unsure.

4. Explain that if a word doesn't seem to make sense with the verb or noun displayed, they should change the verbs and nouns until something does work. For example, *a fast tree* doesn't make sense, but *a fast ball* does.

Find It in Your Reading

Have students share the adverbs and adjectives they have found, and create a master list on the board. This will also give you the opportunity to correct cases where students have incorrectly used an adjective form as an adverb (e.g., *slow* vs. *slowly*).

Find It in Your Writing

Ask students to read a few improved sentences, pointing out adjectives and adverbs they've added. If students feel that their writing does not need additional adjectives and adverbs, you may either ask them to share the modifiers they have used or encourage them to find more precise modifiers (e.g., *towering 100 feet above us* vs. *very high; shimmering in the sunlight* vs. *pretty*).

Hands-on Grammar

Adjective or Adverb?

Create a window frame for sliding word strips, as shown in the model below. Then, create three word strips that are narrow enough to fit through the slots in the frame. One strip of paper should list nouns, such as *avocado, highway, gold,* and *surfer.* The second strip of paper should list verbs, such as *drive, run, eat, speak.* The third strip of paper should list words that you want to test for function. These should be adjectives, adverbs, and modifiers that can function as both adjectives and adverbs, such as *hard, wide, fast, daily.*

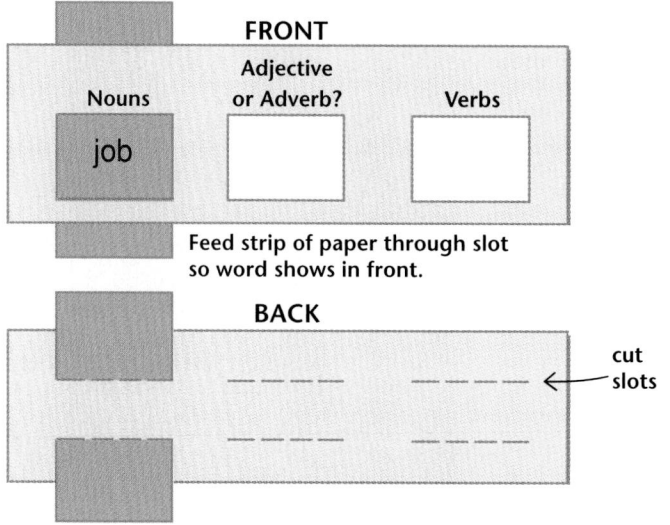

Feed the strips into the slots, as shown in the illustration. Slide each strip to reveal different words. For each combination, decide whether the word in the center window can modify the noun in the left window, the verb in the right window, or both. Tell whether the word functions as an adjective, an adverb, or both. Note that not all word combinations will make sense.

Find It in Your Reading In your reading, find examples of words that can function both as adverbs and as adjectives. Create strips to challenge a partner to identify how these words function when they modify different parts of speech.

Find It in Your Writing Review a piece of writing from your portfolio and identify sentences that could be made more descriptive by adding adjectives and adverbs. Challenge yourself to use colorful, precise words, rather than vague words such as *big* or *very.*

354 • Adjectives and Adverbs

⏱ TIME SAVERS!

Hands-on Grammar Book Use the Hands-on Grammar activity sheet for Chapter 16 to facilitate this activity.

354

Section 16.2 *Section Review*

GRAMMAR EXERCISES 23–28

Exercise 23 Identifying Adverbs
On your paper, write the adverb in each sentence.

1. Lakes and rivers in California frequently attract many tourists.
2. The Sacramento River flows south from Mount Shasta.
3. The San Joaquin and Sacramento rivers have tributaries that mainly drain into the central valley.
4. Dams have been used successfully to create small lakes.
5. These lakes continuously provide recreation such as fishing and boating.

Exercise 24 Recognizing Adverbs and the Words They Modify
For each of the following sentences, write the adverbs and the part of speech modified.

1. California has extremely varied climates and geographical features.
2. The very active San Andreas Fault runs through northern California.
3. Often, people travel north to see the redwoods.
4. In the northwestern part of the state is the remarkably rugged Sierra Nevada mountain range.
5. To appreciate the best view of the Sierra Nevada, you must get up early.
6. Do you think you will ever visit central California?
7. There, you can sample delicious fruits.
8. Oranges, however, are very widely grown.
9. In southern California, there is too little rainfall to support many crops.
10. We had good weather almost every day.

Exercise 25 Distinguishing Between Adverbs and Adjectives
On your paper, write whether the underlined word is an adjective or an adverb.

1. We took a <u>long</u> hike through the pine forest.
2. We walked <u>straight</u> down the path.
3. The <u>early</u> morning is the best time to take photographs here.
4. The rangers patrol the area <u>daily</u>.
5. They prepare <u>daily</u> reports on what they find.

Exercise 26 Find It in Your Reading
Identify at least five adverbs in this excerpt from "The Californian's Tale" by Mark Twain.

Thirty-five years ago I was out prospecting on the Stanislaus, tramping all day long with pick and pan and horn, and washing a hatful of dirt here and there, always expecting to make a rich strike, and never doing it.

Exercise 27 Find It in Your Writing
Review several pieces of work from your portfolio. Identify the adverbs you have used. Challenge yourself to increase the detail in one piece by adding adverbs.

Exercise 28 Writing Application
Write a postcard message to someone who lives in another state. Share details about the interests and attractions a tourist in your state might visit. Use adverbs to add details about *when, where, in what way,* and *to what extent.*

Answer Key

Exercise 23

1. frequently
2. south
3. mainly
4. successfully
5. continuously

Exercise 24

1. extremely—adjective
2. very—adjective
3. often—verb, north—verb
4. remarkably—adjective
5. early—verb
6. ever—verb
7. There—verb
8. very—adverb, widely—verb
9. too—adjective
10. almost—adjective

Exercise 25

1. adjective
2. adverb
3. adjective
4. adverb
5. adjective

Exercise 26

Find It in Your Reading
out, long, here, there, always, never

Exercise 27

Find It in Your Writing
Students can trade papers with partners, and discuss passages that might need more detail.

continued

Answer Key continued

Exercise 28

Writing Application
Students can compose their postcards on the computer and E-mail them to the recipients.

CHAPTER REVIEW

Each of these exercises correlates to a concept in the chapter on adjectives and adverbs, pages 336–354. These exercises may be used for more practice, for reteaching, or for review of the Key Concepts presented.

Answer Key

Exercise 29

1. live (performance), real-life (audience)—compound
2. written (text)
3. Broadway (play)—proper, difficult (job)
4. first (task), each (part)
5. Some (roles)
6. makeup (technique)—compound, complete (costume)
7. many (roles)
8. character (makeup), different (actor)
9. United States (high schools)—proper, dramatic arts (program)—compound
10. huge hometown (crowd)—compound, heartfelt (performance)—compound

Exercise 30

1. a
2. The
3. the
4. The, the, an
5. the

Exercise 31

Sentences will vary. Samples are given.

1. I grew up in a Mississippi river town.
2. We are going to see a Broadway play.
3. I hear that it is a heartbreaking story.
4. My mother wants me to wear a bluish-green dress.
5. There's nothing like a hometown picnic!
6. Many of the people here are European visitors.
7. We are going to visit Aunt Cecilia, who is an absent-minded relative.
8. Be careful driving on those snow-covered roads!
9. I think an April rain is relaxing.
10. Would you like to see a Shakespearean comedy?

Exercise 32

1. this—ADJ, semester
2. my—ADJ, studies
3. its—ADJ, history
4. those—PN
5. What—ADJ, kind

356

GRAMMAR EXERCISES 29–37

Exercise 29 Recognizing Adjectives and the Words They Modify
On your paper, write the adjective(s) (excluding articles) in each sentence. Then, write the word each one modifies. If the adjective is a proper or compound adjective, label it that way on your paper.

1. A play is a live performance before a real-life audience.
2. The script is the written text that the actors memorize.
3. The director of a Broadway play has a difficult job.
4. The first task of the director is to select the actors for each part.
5. Some roles require an actor to sing and dance.
6. Makeup technique is important in establishing the complete costume of an actor.
7. For many roles, the appearance of the performer is not changed dramatically.
8. In character makeup, however, an actor looks very different.
9. Many United States high schools have some kind of dramatic arts program.
10. A huge hometown crowd turns out for the heartfelt performance.

Exercise 30 Distinguishing Between Definite and Indefinite Articles Write the article(s) that will correctly complete each of the following sentences. The word in parentheses tells you which kind of article to use.

1. Have you purchased (indefinite) ticket for the play yet?
2. (Definite) box office opens again tomorrow at 10:00 A.M.

3. Let's try to sit close to (definite) stage.
4. (Definite) critic gave (definite) play (indefinite) excellent review.
5. She said (definite) acting was superb.

Exercise 31 Writing Sentences With Proper and Compound Adjectives Write a sentence about each topic below.

1. a Mississippi river town
2. a Broadway play
3. a heartbreaking story
4. a bluish-green dress
5. a hometown picnic
6. European visitors
7. an absent-minded relative
8. snow-covered roads
9. an April rain
10. a Shakespearean comedy

Exercise 32 Identifying Pronouns Used as Adjectives On your paper, write the underlined word in each sentence. If the word functions as a pronoun, label it *PN*. If the word functions as an adjective, label it *ADJ*, and write the word it modifies.

1. My favorite class this semester was drama.
2. It helped me decide to focus my studies on the dramatic arts.
3. Colleges and universities offer many courses in dramatic literature and its history.
4. There are many career options available to those who are interested.
5. What kind of career in the theater sounds most interesting to you?

Exercise 33 **Identifying Adverbs and the Words They Modify** On your paper, write the adverb in each of the following sentences. After each adverb, write the word it modifies.

1. Local theaters often depend on their own members to do set construction.
2. Sets are frequently constructed from large frames covered with painted canvas.
3. Lighting also helps to create an illusion.
4. Usually, the director, the set designer, and the lighting designer will meet.
5. It is vitally important that the designers and the director understand one another.
6. If many people help, a set can be built very quickly.
7. Painting and sanding are not difficult jobs.
8. Carpentry and electrical wiring of the set are more complicated tasks.
9. Some jobs require highly specialized knowledge.
10. The process of set building is definitely rewarding.

Exercise 34 **Distinguishing Between Adjectives and Adverbs** On your paper, write whether the underlined word in each sentence functions as an adjective or an adverb.

1. Set building is <u>hard</u> work.
2. We arrive <u>early</u> to begin construction.
3. Everyone is <u>friendly</u>.
4. Everyone works <u>hard</u>, but nobody complains.
5. We do not take a <u>long</u> lunch break.
6. Mary arrived too <u>late</u> for lunch.
7. The <u>early</u> shift is working now.
8. She was sorry to arrive <u>last</u>.
9. She hoped the others had not been waiting <u>long</u>.
10. Usually, Mary is not <u>late</u>.

Exercise 35 **Revising Sentences With Adjectives and Adverbs** Revise each sentence by adding at least one adjective and one adverb.

1. We were sad about the end of summer.
2. Many people think snails are delicious.
3. The rowboat drifted.
4. I will finish the dishes.
5. The leaves fell.
6. The play had an ending.
7. The trip will be dangerous.
8. My friend has moved.
9. He climbed trees.
10. They brought a list to the market.

Exercise 36 **Writing Application** Write about a performance you've seen. Use adverbs and adjectives to add details to your writing. Identify the question that each modifier answers. Challenge yourself to add modifiers that answer any remaining questions.

Exercise 37 **CUMULATIVE REVIEW** **Parts of Speech** On your paper, write each underlined word. Label each word *noun, pronoun, linking verb,* or *action verb.*

(1) A <u>set designer</u> (2) <u>studies</u> the (3) <u>play</u> before deciding on a set design. (4) <u>Music</u>, doorbells, whistles, and telephones (5) <u>are</u> just a few of the effects for which the sound designer is responsible. The director (6) <u>meets</u> with (7) <u>his</u> or <u>her</u> production team. Then, team members (8) <u>present</u> their ideas to the <u>group</u>. (9) <u>This</u> is an important part of the process, because it allows (10) <u>everyone</u> to share his or her thoughts.

Exercise 33

1. often, depend
2. frequently, constructed
3. also, helps
4. Usually, will meet
5. vitally, important
6. very; quickly, built
7. not, difficult
8. more, complicated
9. highly, specialized
10. definitely, rewarding

Exercise 34

1. adjective
2. adverb
3. adjective
4. adverb
5. adjective
6. adverb
7. adjective
8. adverb
9. adverb
10. adjective

Exercise 35

Sentences will vary. Possible answers:

1. very sad, a hot summer
2. cooked snails, especially delicious
3. blue rowboat, drifted aimlessly
4. quickly finish, dirty dishes
5. colorful leaves, fell quietly
6. very boring play, unusually sad
7. climbing trip, very dangerous
8. best friend, moved far away
9. effortlessly climbed, enormous trees
10. usually brought, long list, outdoor market

continued

Answer Key continued

Exercise 36

Writing Application
If any students "review" the same performance, have them compare their opinions and modifiers.

Exercise 37

Cumulative Review

1. set designer—noun
2. studies—action verb
3. play—noun
4. Music—noun
5. are—linking verb
6. meets—action verb
7. his, her—pronouns
8. present—action verb, group—noun
9. This—pronoun
10. everyone—pronoun

Lesson Objectives

1. To employ standard English usage, including parts of speech
2. To use adjectives and adverbs appropriately
3. To answer different types and levels of questions such as multiple choice

Step-by-Step Teaching Guide

Standard English Usage

Teaching Resources: Standardized Test Preparation Workbook, pp. 31–32

1. Remind students to read each sentence carefully.
2. When confronted with a fill-in-the-blank sentence, tell students they will have to rely on context clues to help them choose the right answer.
3. Tell students to make sure they reread the sentence with their choice in place to check their work.

Standardized Test Preparation Workshop

Standard English Usage: Adjectives and Adverbs

Knowing when to use an adverb or adjective is one of the skills measured on standardized tests. When answering a question that tests these skills, read the entire passage first. Then, ask yourself what type of description is needed for a word in the sentence—an adjective will tell *what kind, how much,* and *how many,* and an adverb will tell *when, where,* or *how.* Then, choose the modifier that will add that information.

The following test item will give you practice with questions that test your ability to choose the correct modifier.

Sample Test Item

Directions Read the passage, and choose the letter of the word or group of words that belongs in each space.

When examining the details of some paintings, there is no doubt that the artist's hand moved _____ and deliberately over the canvas, taking time and great care to create a masterpiece.

1 A slow
   B slowly
   C quick
   D quickly

Answers and Explanations

The correct answer is *B* because the modifier needs to tell how the hand moved. It had to be a modifier that described an action—the adverb *slowly.* Since the movement is described as deliberate, it could not have been done quickly.

TEST-TAKING TIP

Direct students' attention to the sample test item on the page. Explain to them that the word *deliberately* provides two important clues as to the correct choice. First, it is an adverb preceded by the word *and.* Students should realize that the correct choice is also an adverb, which eliminates A and C. Second, as stated in the explanation, *deliberate* does not imply a quick speed, so the correct choice is B.

Practice 1 **Directions:** Read the passage, and choose the letter of the word or group of words that belongs in each space.

Artist Mary Cassatt painted __(1)__ renderings of mother and child. Her impressionistic techniques create a __(2)__ soft image that is natural and captures the relationship between mother and child. She studied and worked in France when it was __(3)__ for her to achieve status as a woman artist in America. Her work *The Banjo Lesson* shows a woman playing the banjo with a __(4)__ girl watching __(5)__ over her shoulder.

1   **A**   beautiful
      B   beautifully
      C   artistically
      D   beauteously

2   **F**   real
      G   really
      H   perfect
      J   reality

3   **A**   hardly
      B   perfect
      C   difficult
      D   serious

4   **F**   young
      G   beautifully
      H   youthfully
      J   some

5   **A**   daily
      B   interested
      C   intense
      D   intently

Practice 2 **Directions:** Read the passage, and choose the letter of the word or group of words that belongs in each space.

Diana Ong is a pioneer in the __(1)__ field of using computer graphics programs as a medium for fine art. Because painting on a computer __(2)__ translates hand movements on a pressure-sensitive pad into images that seem to appear __(3)__ on screen, Ong says she feels like her ideas travel __(4)__ from her brain to her hand to her computer. She is one of the first __(5)__ artists in this field.

1   **A**   artistically
      B   back
      C   technical
      D   technically

2   **F**   usually
      G   never
      H   usual
      J   hardly

3   **A**   magic
      B   magical
      C   never
      D   magically

4   **F**   direction
      G   directly
      H   really
      J   very

5   **A**   really
      B   major
      C   minor
      D   male

Answer Key

Practice 1
1. A
2. G
3. C
4. F
5. D

Practice 2
1. C
2. F
3. D
4. G
5. B

In-Depth Lesson Plan

LESSON FOCUS	PRINT AND MEDIA RESOURCES
DAY 1 — **Recognizing Prepositions** Students learn to recognize and use prepositional phrases and understand their functions in sentences (360–365).	**Teaching Resources** *Grammar Exercise Workbook, pp.37–38; Grammar Exercises Answers on Transparencies,* Ch. 17 **Language Lab** CD-ROM, Prepositional Phrases; *On-Line Exercise Bank,* Section 17.1
DAY 2 — **Prepositions Used in Sentences** Students learn to distinguish prepositions from adverbs and do the Hands-On Grammar activity (pp. 366–369).	**Teaching Resources** *Grammar Exercise Workbook, pp.39–40; Grammar Exercises Answers on Transparencies,* Ch. 17; *Hands-On Grammar Activity Book,* Ch. 17 **Language Lab** CD-ROM, Prepositional Phrases; *On-Line Exercise Bank,* Section 17.2
DAY 3 — **Review and Assess** Students review chapter and demonstrate mastery of use of prepositions and prepositional phrases (pp. 370–373).	**Teaching Resources** *Formal Assessment,* Ch. 17; *Grammar Exercises Answers on Transparencies,* Ch. 17

Accelerated Lesson Plan

LESSON FOCUS	PRINT AND MEDIA RESOURCES
DAY 1 — **Prepositions** Students cover concepts and usage of prepositions as determined by Diagnostic Test (pp. 360–369).	**Teaching Resources** *Grammar Exercise Workbook, pp.37–40; Grammar Exercises Answers on Transparencies,* Ch. 17; *Hands-On Grammar Activity Book,* Ch. 17 **Language Lab** CD-ROM, Prepositional Phrases; *On-Line Exercise Bank,* Section 17.1–2
DAY 2 — **Review and Assess** Students review chapter and demonstrate mastery of use of prepositions and prepositional phrases (pp. 370–373).	**Teaching Resources** *Formal Assessment,* Ch. 17; *Grammar Exercises Answers on Transparencies,* Ch. 17

Options for Adapting Lesson Plans

HOMEWORK
Have students complete any section of the chapter for homework.

FEATURES
Extend coverage with the Grammar in Literature feature (p. 363), and the Standardized Test Preparation Workshop (p. 372).

TECHNOLOGY
Students can use the On-Line Exercise Bank to complete the exercises on computer. The Auto Check feature will grade their work.

INTEGRATED SKILLS COVERAGE

Grammar in Literature
SE p. 363

Reading
Find It In Your Reading, SE pp. 365, 368, 369

Writing
Find It In Your Writing, SE pp. 365, 368, 369
Writing Application SE pp. 365, 369

Viewing and Representing
Critical Viewing SE pp. 360, 363, 364, 366, 367

ASSESSMENT SUPPORT

Standardized Test Preparation SE p. 372; ATE pp. 364, 370
Standardized Test Preparation Workbook, pp. 33–34
Formal Assessment, Ch. 17

MEETING INDIVIDUAL NEEDS

Verbal/Linguistic Learners, ATE p. 364

Less Advanced Students ATE p. 367. See also Ongoing Assessment, p. 363

ESL Students ATE p. 373

BLOCK SCHEDULING

Pacing Suggestions
For 90-minute Blocks
• Administer the Diagnostic Test to students to determine instructional coverage.
• Have students complete the necessary exercises in class. Use the Hands-on Grammar activity to provide a change of pace.

Resources for Varying Instruction
• *Language Lab* **CD-ROM** If your students have access to hardware, a 90-minute block provides an ideal opportunity for students to work on computer.

Professional Development Support
• *How to Manage Instruction in the Block* This Teaching Resource provides management and activity suggestions.

MEDIA AND TECHNOLOGY

For the Student
• *Language Lab* **CD-ROM**, Prepositions, Prepositional Phrases
• *On-Line Exercise Bank,* Ch. 17

For the Teacher
• *Resource Pro* **CD-ROM**

WRITING AND GRAMMAR WEB SITE

The Interactive Writing and Grammar Web site provides a wide array of support for students, teachers, and parents. Grammar support includes:

• *On-Line Exercise Bank* with Auto Check scoring
• Diagnostic and assessment support

www.phschool.com

LITERATURE CONNECTIONS

Grammar in Literature selection from *Prentice Hall Literature: Timeless Voices, Timeless Themes,* Bronze
"All Summer in a Day," by Ray Bradbury, SE p. 363

▶ *Lesson Objectives*

1. To recognize prepositions and prepositional phrases and understand their functions in sentences
2. To distinguish between prepositions and adverbs
3. To employ standard English usage in writing for audiences, including parts of speech
4. To use prepositional phrases to elaborate written ideas

Critical Viewing

Describe Students may use prepositions such as *below, next to,* or *behind.*

Chapter 17 Prepositions

When you look at the night sky, the moon is *above* your head, *in* the sky. If there is no moonlight, darkness may be all *around* you.

Words like *above, in,* and *around* are called prepositions. Prepositions show relationships between words in a sentence. This chapter will introduce prepositions and show how they are used to relate words to each other.

▲ **Critical Viewing**
Describe the position of the moon in relationship to Earth in this picture. What preposition did you use? **[Describe]**

☑ ONGOING ASSESSMENT: Diagnose

If students miss more than one item in each category, direct them to the relevant pages of the text and assign exercises for practice and review.

Prepositions	Diagnostic Test Items	Teach	Practice	Section Reviews	Chapter Review
Skill Check A					
Identify Prepositions	A 1–5	p. 362	Ex. 1	Ex. 3, 5	Ex. 16, 19
Skill Check B					
Compound Prepositions	B 6–10	p. 362–364	Ex. 2	Ex. 4–5	Ex. 16, 19
Skill Check C					
Prepositional Phrases	C 11–20	p. 366	Ex. 9	Ex. 11	Ex. 17

Diagnostic Test

Directions: Write all answers on a separate sheet of paper.

Skill Check A. Identify the preposition(s) in each sentence.

1. The moon and Earth are held together by gravitational pull.
2. The moon moves in an orbit around Earth.
3. From Earth, we see different phases of the moon.
4. These phases occur as the moon moves into Earth's shadow.
5. When the moon moves around Earth, the sun lights the part we see, while Earth shades the part we don't see.

Skill Check B. Identify a compound preposition in each sentence.

6. Out of all the celestial bodies in our solar system, Earth is the only one that has water in three forms: solid, liquid, and gas.
7. Water covers 70 percent of the land on top of Earth's crust.
8. Plants and animals living on Earth recycle water by means of respiration.
9. In addition to the water vapor exhaled through respiration, all the water in living things returns to Earth when the living things die.
10. Rain occurs because of water evaporation and condensation.

Skill Check C. Identify the prepositional phrase(s) in each sentence.

11. The moon has a strong influence on Earth.
12. Tides occur as a result of the moon's effect on Earth.
13. The gravity of the moon pulls Earth's water toward it.
14. The rising of water underneath the moon is called high tide.
15. During high tide, the water level on beaches rises.
16. When Earth rotates on its axis, the waters affected by the moon also change.
17. Any water directly under the moon will be at high tide.
18. However, the moon also creates a high tide on the opposite side of Earth.
19. Water withdraws from spots between the two tidal bulges, creating low tides.
20. There are two high tides and two low tides along the shore every day.

Skill Check D. Write *prep* if the underlined word in each sentence is used as a preposition. Write *adv* if it is being used as an adverb.

21. Have you ever gazed at the moon as you walked <u>about</u> at night?
22. Scientists have different theories <u>about</u> the moon.
23. Some scientists think that the moon once orbited the sun, and Earth attracted the moon when it came <u>near</u>.
24. Others say that the moon and Earth were formed at the same time <u>by</u> the same dust.
25. One thing we do know is that the moon above is the same age as the Earth <u>beneath</u> our feet.

Answer Key

Diagnostic Test

Each item in the diagnostic test corresponds to a specific section in the chapter. This will enable you to tailor instruction to the particular needs of your students. See "Ongoing Assessment: Diagnose" below for further details.

Skill Check A

1. by
2. in, around
3. From, of
4. into
5. around

Skill Check B

6. Out of
7. on top of
8. by means of
9. In addition to
10. because of

Skill Check C

11. on Earth
12. of the moon's effect, on Earth
13. of the moon, toward it
14. of water, underneath the moon
15. During high tide, on beaches
16. on its axis, by the moon
17. under the moon, at high tide
18. on the opposite side, of Earth
19. from spots, between the two tidal bulges
20. along the shore

Skill Check D

21. adv
22. prep
23. adv
24. prep
25. prep

☑ **ONGOING ASSESSMENT: Diagnosis** *continued*

Prepositions	Diagnostic Test Items	Teach	Practice	Section Reviews	Chapter Review
Skill Check D					
Prepositions as Adverbs	D 21–25	p. 367	Ex. 10	Ex. 12–13	Ex. 19
Cumulative Reviews and Applications				Ex. 6–8 13–15	Ex. 21

⏱ **TIME SAVERS!**

📄 **Answers on Transparency**
Use the Grammar Exercises Answers on Transparencies for Chapter 17 to facilitate correction by students.

💻 **On-Line Exercise Bank**
Have students complete the Diagnostic Test on computer. The Auto Check feature will grade their work for you!

Show students a pencil and a mug (or other container). Challenge them to list every possible position the pencil can take relative to the container: it can be *in* the container, *beside* the container, *near* the container, *behind* the container, and so on. List students' answers on the chalkboard. Explain that the words they suggested are prepositions.

Activate Prior Knowledge

Ask students whether they have ever left a book or their homework at home and then made a phone call to describe its location to someone who would bring it to them. Have students write down the words they used to describe where the item could be found. Have volunteers read their descriptions aloud and see how many prepositions they used.

TEACH

Step-by-Step Teaching Guide

Recognizing Prepositions

1. Emphasize that prepositions show a relationship between two things. Prepositions often show a physical relationship; words such as *behind, inside,* and *opposite* show where two things are in relation to each other.

2. Compound prepositions function the same way other prepositions do; they show a relationship between two things. Compound prepositions contain more than one word. Point out that many of the words in compound prepositions are prepositions: *in* addition *to, on* account *of.*

3. Students can test whether a phrase is a compound preposition by substituting a one-word preposition for it. If the substitution works, the phrase is probably a compound preposition.

   The pencil was in back of *the container.*

   The pencil was behind *the container.*

Section 17.1 # Recognizing Prepositions

Prepositions function as connectors, relating one word to another within a sentence. They allow a speaker or writer to express the link between separate items, such as their relative location or direction.

▶ **KEY CONCEPT** A **preposition** relates the noun or pronoun following it to another word in the sentence. ■

Theme: Space
....
In this section, you will learn about prepositions. All the examples and exercises are about space.
....
Cross-Curricular Connection: Science

FIFTY COMMON PREPOSITIONS				
about	behind	during	off	to
above	below	except	on	toward
across	beneath	for	onto	under
after	beside	from	opposite	underneath
against	besides	in	out	until
along	between	inside	outside	up
among	beyond	into	over	upon
around	but	like	past	with
at	by	near	since	within
before	down	of	through	without

Prepositions consisting of more than one word are called *compound prepositions*.

COMPOUND PREPOSITIONS		
according to	by means of	instead of
ahead of	in addition to	next to
aside from	in back of	on account of
as of	in front of	on top of
because of	in place of	out of

Because prepositions have different meanings, using a particular preposition will affect the way other words in a sentence relate to one another. In the following sentence, for example, notice how each preposition changes the relationship between *passed* and *City Hall.*

EXAMPLE: The parade *passed*
$\left\{ \begin{array}{l} \text{near} \\ \text{by} \\ \text{in front of} \\ \text{behind} \\ \text{opposite} \end{array} \right\}$
 City Hall.

⏱ TIME AND RESOURCE MANAGER

Resources
Print: Grammar Exercise Workbook, pp. 37–38
Technology: Language Lab CD-ROM, Prepositional Phrases; On-Line Exercise Bank, Section 17.1

In-Depth Coverage	Accelerated Pace
• Work through all key concepts, pp. 362–364.	• Assign p. 362–364 for independent student review.
• Assign and review Exercises 1–2.	
• Read and discuss Grammar in Literature, p. 363.	• Assign Section Review Exercise 3–5, p. 365.

Critical Viewing

Connect Students may use prepositions such as *above, around, over,* or *on top of.*

Answer Key

> **Exercise 1**

Sample sentences are given.

1. beyond; NASA sent its first satellite into space.
2. in, around; It moved into orbit, rocketing through space.
3. of; Scientists gathered information about its orbit.
4. From; Because of these measurements, scientists found that Earth is not perfectly round.
5. for; This satellite transmitted messages during its six-year voyage.
6. During; Through all that time, it used solar power.
7. to; In addition to satellite launches, lunar missions were soon planned.
8. on; One year later, a Russian probe made a trip to the moon.
9. of; *Luna 3* was launched soon afterward, and it took many pictures from outer space.
10. into; Someday, astronauts may drill through the moon's crust, so they can test the inner rocks.

> **Exercise 1** Identifying Prepositions in Sentences
Identify the preposition(s) in each of the following sentences. Then, rewrite each sentence using a different preposition.

EXAMPLE: The scientist walked around the globe.

ANSWER: around; The scientist walked <u>behind</u> the globe.

1. NASA sent its first satellite beyond Earth's atmosphere.
2. It moved in an orbit around Earth.
3. Scientists gathered measurements of the satellite's orbit.
4. From these measurements, they found that Earth is slightly pear-shaped.
5. The satellite transmitted messages for six years.
6. During that time, it used solar power.
7. Missions to the moon were soon planned.
8. One year later, a Russian probe landed on the moon.
9. *Luna 3* was launched soon afterward, and it took many pictures of the moon.
10. Someday, astronauts may drill into the moon's interior to test its composition.

▲ Critical Viewing
Which prepositions could be used to talk about the relationship of the clouds to Earth? **[Connect]**

More Practice

Language Lab CD-ROM
• Prepositional Phrases lesson

On-line Exercise Bank
• Section 17.1

Grammar Practice Workbook
• pp. 37–38

GRAMMAR IN
LITERATURE

from **All Summer in a Day**
Ray Bradbury

Notice how the highlighted prepositions show the relationships between words in the sentences. Prepositions often show relationships of time or space.

It had been raining *for* seven years; thousands upon thousands *of* days compounded and filled *from* one end *to* the other *with* rain, *with* the drum and gush *of* water, *with* the sweet crystal fall *of* showers and the concussion *of* storms so heavy they were tidal waves come *over* the islands. A thousand forests had been crushed *under* the rain and grown up a thousand times to be crushed again. And this was the way life was forever *on* the planet Venus. . . .

Recognizing Prepositions • 363

Step-by-Step Teaching Guide

Grammar in Literature

1. Read or have a volunteer read aloud the passage.
2. Have students meet in small groups. Ask them to identify which words are connected by the prepositions. Then, have them discuss the specific time or space relationship shown by each preposition.

More About the Writer

Ray Bradbury began to write almost by accident. When he was a boy, he couldn't afford to buy the sequel to a novel he had read, so he wrote his own. This was the beginning of his award-winning career as a science fiction writer.

☑ **ONGOING ASSESSMENT: Monitor and Reinforce**

If students miss more than two items in Exercise 1 or 2, refer them to the following for additional practice.

In the Textbook	Print Resources	Technology
Section Review, Ex. 3–4, p. 365	Grammar Exercise Workbook, pp. 37–38	Language Lab CD-ROM, Prepositional Phrases; On-Line Exercise Bank, Section 17.1

Customizing for
Verbal/Linguistic Learners

Point out the way in which Bradbury uses prepositions in the excerpt on the previous page to help readers visualize the fictional setting of Venus. Challenge students to write brief descriptions of settings they are familiar with, using prepositions to make the descriptions vivid and clear. Have students share their descriptions with partners.

Critical Viewing

Relate Students may say that, in addition to its bright orange color, many clouds cover the surface of Venus.

Answer Key

▶ **Exercise 2**

1. next to; Venus is one planet near Earth in our solar system.
2. According to; In the past, people thought that Venus was much like Earth.
3. by means of; However, because of new technology, we now know that Venus is very different from Earth.
4. instead of; Because of the way Venus spins, its sun rises in the west.
5. in order to; Because of the atmosphere, humans would need scuba gear to breathe.
6. next to; The air pressure near the surface is 21 times greater than that on Earth.
7. In addition to; Besides the surface atmosphere, Venus has three layers of clouds.
8. instead of; Due to the sulfuric acid clouds, a space probe could quickly be destroyed.
9. at the top of; The clouds above the atmosphere are thin and hazy, and the wind always blows from east to west.
10. Because of; Due to so many clouds, the surface can't be seen clearly.

▶ **Exercise 2** Identifying and Using Compound Prepositions

Identify the compound preposition in each sentence below. Then, rewrite the sentence using a different compound preposition or a one-word preposition.

EXAMPLE: A cloud passed in front of the moon.
ANSWER: in front of; A cloud passed <u>before</u> the moon.

1. In our solar system, one planet next to Earth is Venus.
2. According to old theories, Venus was much like Earth.
3. However, by means of new technology, we now know that Venus is very different from Earth.
4. For example, on Venus the sun rises in the west instead of in the east.
5. The air is so thick at the surface that humans would need scuba gear in order to breathe.
6. The air pressure next to the surface is twenty-one times greater than that on Earth.
7. In addition to the conditions at the surface, Venus also has three layers of clouds in its atmosphere.
8. These clouds are composed of sulfuric acid instead of water vapor and could quickly destroy a space probe.
9. The clouds at the top of the atmosphere are thin and hazy, and the wind always blows from east to west.
10. Because of the clouds surrounding Venus, its surface can't be seen clearly from space.

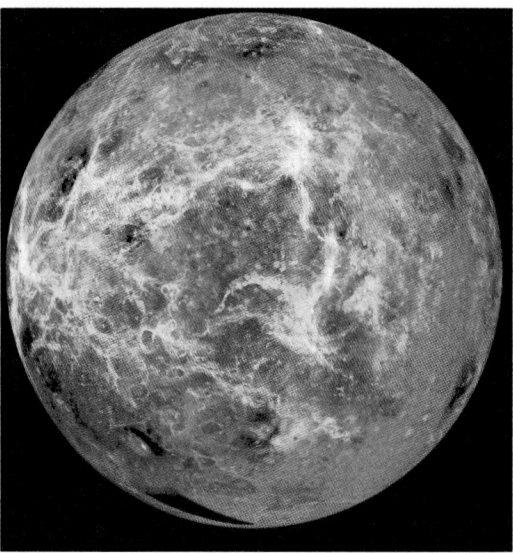

Venus

▶ **More Practice**

Language Lab CD-ROM
• Prepositional Phrases lesson

On-line Exercise Bank
• Section 17.1

Grammar Practice Workbook
• pp. 37–38

◀ **Critical Viewing** Create a sentence about Venus beginning with "In addition to its bright orange color, . . ." **[Relate]**

✏ STANDARDIZED TEST PREPARATION WORKSHOP

Grammar and Usage Standardized tests often ask students to identify certain grammatical elements in a sentence. Use the following example to help students practice identifying different types of prepositions:

She jumped on the diving board, launching her body into space and splashing into the pool.

What kind of prepositions does this sentence contain?

A simple   B compound
C both   D none

Students should recognize that the correct choice is item **A.** Compound prepositions are made of more than one word, and all three prepositions in this sentence are one word. Item **D** is incorrect because the sentence contains three prepositions (on, into, into).

Section 17.1 Section Review

GRAMMAR EXERCISES 3–8

Exercise 3 Identifying Prepositions
Identify the preposition(s) in each sentence below.

1. Neil Armstrong, Michael Collins, and Edwin Aldrin, Jr., rocketed outside Earth's atmosphere on July 16, 1969.
2. They landed on the moon that same week.
3. On July 20, Neil Armstrong stepped out the door of *Apollo 11*.
4. He was the first person in history to walk on the moon.
5. The astronauts collected rocks from the moon.
6. On July 24, they returned to Earth.
7. Since that time, five other ships have carried people to the moon.
8. These flights ended in 1972 with *Apollo 17*.
9. With the information we have collected from the moon, we have answered many questions.
10. We now know that the moon has no life forms of any kind.

Exercise 4 Identifying Compound Prepositions Identify only the compound prepositions in the following sentences.

1. Aside from Jupiter, Saturn is the largest planet.
2. On a solar system chart, it appears in back of Jupiter.
3. It is in front of Uranus.
4. Saturn is easily recognized through a telescope because of its wide rings.
5. In addition to its rings, Saturn also has many moons that orbit it.

Exercise 5 Classifying Prepositions
Copy the following paragraph. Underline the prepositions. Double-underline the compound prepositions.

From Earth, Saturn's rings look like smooth ice. However, according to information gathered by *Pioneer 11*, Saturn's rings include pieces of frozen rock. Instead of solid stationary objects, Saturn's rings are actually millions of tiny orbiting objects. When *Pioneer 11* was above the rings, the radiation readings were high. When it passed through the rings, the radiation readings under the rings were lower than those during takeoff from Earth.

Exercise 6 Find It in Your Reading
Write the prepositions you find in the following excerpt from "All Summer in a Day."

A few cold drops fell on their noses and their cheeks and their mouths. The sun faded behind a stir of mist. A wind blew cool around them. They turned and started to walk back toward the underground house, their hands at their sides, their smiles vanishing away.

Exercise 7 Find It in Your Writing
Look through a sample of your own writing. Identify the prepositions you have used.

Exercise 8 Writing Application
Write a brief description of the scene outside your classroom window. Use prepositions to tell where things are in relation to one another.

PREPARE and ENGAGE

Interest GRABBER Have students look at the descriptions they wrote for the Activate Prior Knowledge on page 362. Have them underline all the prepositions they used. Next, have students circle what each preposition refers to. Use this exercise to help students understand that the object of the preposition always answers a question: *Inside what? From where? For how long? Near what?*

Activate Prior Knowledge

Have students review the Grammar in Literature paragraph on page 363. Ask them what noun or pronoun follows each highlighted preposition. The answers to this question will be the objects of each preposition. From this, they can determine each prepositional phrase.

TEACH

Step-by-Step Teaching Guide

Prepositions Used in Sentences; Preposition or Adverb?

1. Have a student read aloud the Key Concept at the top of the page. Ask volunteers to identify the prepositional phrases in the Key Concept sentence (*in a sentence*). Explain that *sentence* is the object of the preposition *in.*

2. Help students recognize a preposition used as an adverb. Remind them that an adverb answers the questions *Where?, When?, In what way?,* and *To what extent?* If a word that seems like it might be a preposition has no object and answers one of these questions, it is being used as an adverb.

Critical Viewing

Speculate During a solar flare, gases shoot high above the sun's surface.

Section 17.2

Prepositions Used in Sentences

A preposition is never used by itself in a sentence. Instead, it appears as part of a phrase containing one or more other words.

▶ **KEY CONCEPT** A **preposition** in a sentence always introduces a prepositional phrase. ■

Prepositional Phrases

A *prepositional phrase* is a group of words that begins with a preposition and ends with a noun or pronoun. The noun or pronoun following the preposition is the *object of the preposition.*

Some prepositional phrases contain just two words—the preposition and its object. Others are longer because they contain modifiers.

EXAMPLES: from the solar system
             in place of the old, broken antenna

▶ **Exercise 9** **Identifying Prepositional Phrases** Write the prepositional phrase(s) appearing in each of the following sentences. Underline the preposition. Circle the object of the preposition.

EXAMPLE: The telescope is on the roof.
ANSWER: on the (roof)

1. Mars is the fourth planet from the sun.
2. For 687 Earth days Mars revolves around this giant star.
3. Two moons revolve around the planet.
4. Deimos orbits Mars once in thirty hours, while Phobos orbits in only eight hours.
5. The surface of Mars is red and rusty.
6. Huge dust storms blow across the rocky ground.
7. The dust mixed with the wind makes the air pink.
8. Sometimes the storms can last for several months!
9. The atmosphere on Mars is thin, so asteroids can easily crash into its surface.
10. Because of these crashes, Mars is scarred by craters.

366 • Prepositions

Theme: Space
In this section, you will learn about prepositional phrases. All the examples and exercises tell more about space.

Cross-Curricular Connection: Science

▼ **Critical Viewing** Which preposition would you use to introduce a phrase about the action of this solar flare? **[Speculate]**

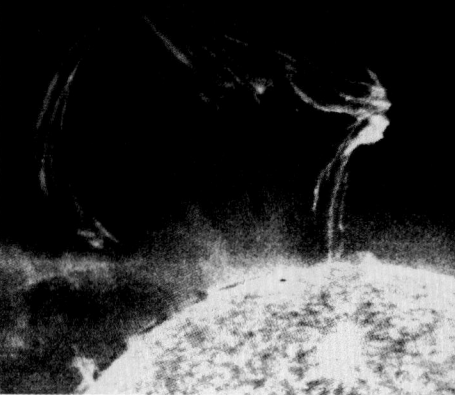
A Solar Flare

⏱ **TIME AND RESOURCE MANAGER**

Resources
Print: Grammar Exercise Workbook, pp. 39–40; Hands-on Grammar Activity Book, Chapter 17
Technology: Language Lab CD-ROM, Prepositional Phrases; On-Line Exercise Bank, Section 17.2

In-Depth Coverage	Accelerated Pace
• Work through all key concepts, pp. 366–367. • Assign and review Exercises 9–10. • Read and discuss the Hands-on Grammar Activity, p. 368.	• Assign pp. 366–367 for independent student review. • Assign Section Review Exercises 11–12, p. 369.

Preposition or Adverb?

Some words can be used either as prepositions or as adverbs. When a word is used as a preposition, it begins a prepositional phrase and is followed by the object of the preposition. If the word has no object, it is probably being used as an adverb.

PREPOSITION: The broken panel was *outside* the spacecraft.
ADVERB: The astronauts slowly stepped *outside*.
PREPOSITION: An asteroid belt appears *before* Jupiter.
ADVERB: I had not realized that *before*.

Exercise 10 Distinguishing Between Prepositions and Adverbs In each of the following pairs of sentences, one sentence contains a word used as a preposition and the other contains the same word used as an adverb. Find the word that appears in both sentences. If the word acts as a preposition, write the prepositional phrase on your paper and underline the preposition. If the word acts as an adverb, write it down and label it *adverb*.

EXAMPLE: The planetarium is down the road.
ANSWER: down the road
EXAMPLE: She examined the rock and then put it down.
ANSWER: down (adverb)

1. Pieces of asteroids that pass through Earth's atmosphere are called meteors.
   They are called meteors only while they are passing through.
2. Once they land on the ground they are called meteorites.
   Eager to examine the meteorite, the scientist switched the electron microscope on.
3. Meteors rain down every day somewhere on Earth.
   Sometimes, people climb down the craters that were created by meteorites.
4. However, most meteorites are so small that a person might walk right by without noticing one.
   Micrometeorites are space-dust particles that have been captured by Earth's magnetic field.
5. Meteor showers are tiny particles a comet leaves behind.
   We watched a recent shower from the field behind our home.

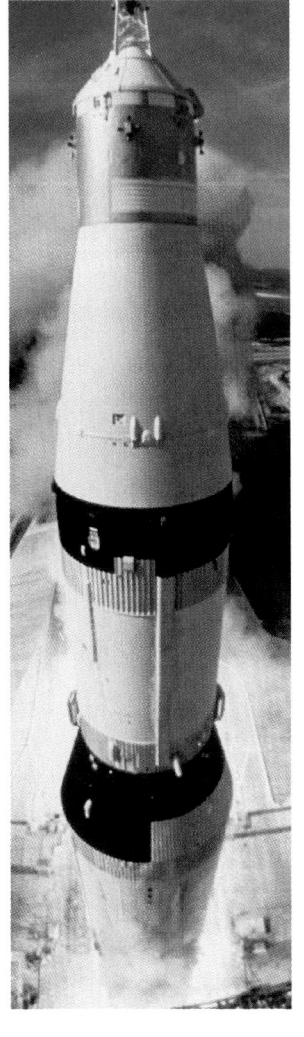

▲ **Critical Viewing** Create two sentences about this picture. In the first, use *up* as an adverb. In the second, use *up* as a preposition. How are the sentences different? **[Contrast]**

Prepositions Used in Sentences • 367

ONGOING ASSESSMENT: Prerequisite Skills

If students have difficulty with adverbs, you may find it necessary to review the following to assure coverage of prerequisite knowledge.

In the Textbook	Print Resources	Technology
Adverbs, pp. 348–353	Grammar Exercise Workbook, pp. 31–36	Language Lab CD-ROM, Prepositional Phrases; On-Line Exercise Bank, Section 16.2

Customize for
Less Advanced Students

If students are having trouble distinguishing between the use of a word as a preposition and its use as an adverb, you may want to give them additional practice. Scan the list of common prepositions to find obvious examples, such as *in, outside, over, since, before, after.* Then you may either create sentence pairs using these words and have students determine which is used as a preposition and which as an adverb, or you can list the words on the board and have students create sentences and then analyze them as a class to determine use.

Answer Key

Exercise 9 (page 366)

1. from the (sun)
2. For 687 Earth (days); around this giant (star)
3. around the (planet)
4. in thirty (hours); in only eight (hours)
5. of (Mars)
6. across the rocky (ground)
7. with the (wind)
8. for several (months)
9. on (Mars); into its (surface)
10. Because of these (crashes); by (craters)

Exercise 10

1. prep: through Earth's atmosphere; adverb: through
2. prep: on the ground; adverb: on
3. adverb: down; prep: down the craters
4. adverb: by; prep: by Earth's magnetic field
5. adverb: behind; prep: behind our home

Critical Viewing

Contrast Everyone was excited when the rocket went *up. Up* the road from her house, the rocket was launched. In the first sentence, *up* acts as an adverb because it modifies the verb "went." In the second sentence, *up* is a preposition in the prepositional phrase, *up* the road.

Preposition Pop-up

Teaching Resourses: Hands-on Grammar Activity Book, Chapter 17

1. If you wish to have students do the activity in class, be prepared with paper, scissors, paper fasteners, and string.

2. Have students refer to their Hands-on Grammar Activity Book or give them copies of the relevant pages for this activity. Have students carefully follow the directions to make the pop-ups.

3. As an extension, you may want to have students trade their lists with another student. Then they must demonstrate the prepositions on their partner's lists using the paper shape.

Find It in Your Reading

Have students bring in the excerpts. Students can work in pairs to check that they can correctly illustrate the prepositions.

Find It in Your Writing

Challenge students to incorporate more prepositional phrases in their writing even if all the prepositions on their lists have been used.

Hands-on Grammar

Preposition Pop-up

Fold a piece of stiff, colored cardboard or paper in half lengthwise. Cut into the fold, about halfway across the folded paper. Unfold the paper, and pop up the cut-out by reversing the fold. This pop-up should create a "shelf" of paper when you leave the paper partly folded. Use a paper fastener to attach a piece of string to the corner of the paper. To the end of the string, attach a paper shape, such as a star. Then, move the star to show the meaning of various prepositions. For example, put the star through the opening, under the shelf, or on the shelf. Record on the paper all the prepositions you can demonstrate with your pop-up.

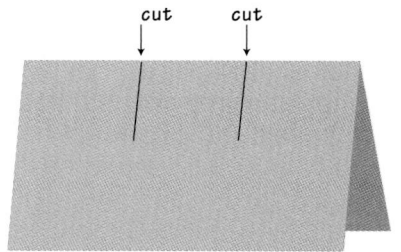

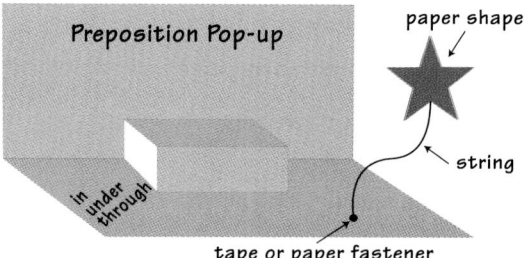

Find It in Your Reading Find examples of prepositions in a short story, novel, or textbook. Challenge yourself to find a way to use pop-ups to illustrate these prepositions.

Find It in Your Writing Look through your portfolio to find at least one use of each of the prepositions you have recorded on your pop-up. For any that you cannot find in your own writing, challenge yourself to add a sentence to your writing, using the preposition. Discuss with a partner what detail was added when you added the prepositional phrase.

368 • Prepositions

🕐 **TIME SAVERS!**

Hands-on Grammar Book
Use the Hands-on Grammar activity sheet for Chapter 17 to facilitate this activity.

☑ **ONGOING ASSESSMENT: Assess Mastery**

Use the following resources to assess mastery of prepositions.

In the Textbook	Technology
Chapter Review, Ex. 16–20, pp. 370–371 Standardized Test Preparation Workshop, pp. 372–373	On-Line Exercise Bank, Chapter 17

Section 17.2 Section Review

GRAMMAR EXERCISES 11–15

Exercise 11 Identifying
Prepositional Phrases Identify the
prepositional phrase(s) in each sentence.

1. Quasars are the brightest objects in
   the universe.
2. They occur when two galaxies collide
   with each other.
3. The collision, however, does not send
   pieces flying through the universe.
4. Because of the huge amount of empty
   space in the universe, galaxies can
   pass through each other.
5. Millions of stars form a galaxy, and
   between any two stars there are light
   years of space.
6. When galaxies move near each other,
   gravity pulls them out of shape.
7. The great arms of the galaxies become
   twisted.
8. Sometimes, they don't separate from
   each other.
9. In the center of some large galaxies
   exists a massive black hole.
10. When one galaxy's gas and dust pass
    on top of another galaxy's black hole,
    the matter is sucked into a whirlpool.

Exercise 12 Distinguishing
Between Prepositions and Adverbs
Label the underlined item a *preposition* or
an *adverb*. If it is a preposition, write its
object.

1. Black holes are created <u>from</u> giant
   exploding stars.
2. The matter <u>inside</u> the core is so heavy
   that it collapses in on itself.
3. Matter that comes close to the hole
   gets swallowed <u>up</u>.
4. Once it is sucked <u>in</u>, it cannot leave.
5. The black hole closest to us is more
   than 4,800 light years <u>beyond</u> Earth.

Exercise 13 Find It in Your
Reading Identify the prepositions in
the following excerpt from "All Summer in
a Day." Which word, used as an adverb,
could function as a preposition? Which
words used as prepositions could also
function as adverbs? Explain and give
examples.

> They walked slowly down the hall in
> the sound of cold rain. They turned
> through the doorway to the room in the
> sound of the storm and thunder. . . .
> They walked over to the closet door
> slowly and stood by it.
>   Behind the closet door was only
> silence.
>   They unlocked the door, even more
> slowly, and let Margot out.

Exercise 14 Find It in Your
Writing Review a piece of writing from
your portfolio. Underline each prepositional phrase you have used. Circle the preposition. Look for at least two places you can
use a prepositional phrase to add detail to
your writing.

Exercise 15 Writing Application
Write a brief description of the night
sky. Underline the prepositional phrases
you use in your sentences. Circle the
prepositions. Use at least five of the following prepositions in your description.

above	along
beyond	beside
near	opposite
next to	over
between	with

ASSESS and CLOSE

Section Review

Each of these exercises correlates
to a concept in the section on
prepositions used in sentences, pages
366–368. The exercises may be used
for more practice, for reteaching, or
for review of the Key Concepts
presented.

Answer Key

Exercise 11

1. in the universe
2. with each other
3. through the universe
4. Because of the huge amount; of
   empty space; in the universe;
   through each other
5. of stars; between any two stars;
   of space
6. near each other; out of shape
7. of the galaxies
8. from each other
9. In the center; of some large
   galaxies
10. on top of another galaxy's black
    hole; into a whirlpool

Exercise 12

1. preposition, stars
2. preposition, core
3. adverb
4. adverb
5. preposition; Earth

Exercise 13

Find It in Your Reading
down, in, of, through, to, in, of, to,
by, Behind; *over* can be used as a
preposition; *down* and *in* can be
used as adverbs: I fell *down*. The
doctor is *in*.

continued

Answer Key continued

Exercise 14

Find It in Your Writing
You may want to have students exchange their
pieces so that they can check each other's work.

Exercise 15

Writing Application
Invite volunteers to read their descriptions aloud
to the class. Encourage students to raise their
hands when they hear prepositions.

⏱ TIME SAVERS!

Answers on Transparency
Use the Grammar Exercises
Answers on Transparencies for
Chapter 17 to facilitate
correction by students.

On-Line Exercise Bank
Have students complete the
exercises on computer. The Auto
Check feature will grade their
work for you!

CHAPTER REVIEW

Each of these exercises correlates with a section in the chapter on prepositions, pages 362–369. The exercises may be used for more practice, for reteaching, or for review of the Key Concepts presented.

Answer Key

> **Exercise 16**

1. for, of
2. in
3. at, to
4. with
5. for
6. According to, before, in
7. on, by means of
8. in, next to
9. Because of, by
10. In addition to, of, of

> **Exercise 17**

1. of (ice) and (minerals)
2. near the (sun), of the (comet)
3. behind (it)
4. To (us), like a (tail)
5. Because of this (activity), around (Earth)
6. to the (core)
7. in a different (orbit), around (Earth)
8. With scientific (calculations), to (us)
9. In the (past), of (doom)
10. of a (hero), on its (way), to (heaven)

> **Exercise 18**

1. preposition
2. preposition
3. preposition
4. adverb
5. adverb
6. preposition
7. preposition
8. preposition
9. preposition
10. preposition

> Chapter **17**

Chapter Review

GRAMMAR EXERCISES 16–22

> **Exercise 16** Identifying

Prepositions Find the preposition(s), including compound prepositions, in each sentence.

1. A star can burn for billions of years.
2. Small stars are cooler in the middle, so they burn very slowly.
3. Average-size stars are hotter at the core due to their greater gravity.
4. Some massive stars are so hot they emit light with a bluish color.
5. Their fusion is so intense that giant stars live for only a few million years.
6. According to historians, before 1781, scientists believed there were six planets in our solar system.
7. Then, on March 13, 1781, by means of his telescope, William Herschel saw an unusual star.
8. It moved in a circular orbit next to Saturn.
9. Because of strong evidence gathered by scientists, Uranus was declared a planet.
10. In addition to several moons, the atmosphere of Uranus includes a group of thin black rings.

> **Exercise 17** Identifying

Prepositional Phrases Write the prepositional phrase(s) in each sentence. Underline the preposition and circle the object(s).

1. A comet is a ball of ice and minerals that orbits the sun.
2. When it gets near the sun, some of the comet melts away.
3. When it melts, it leaves gases and dust particles behind it.
4. To us, the particles look like a tail.
5. Because of this activity, comets get smaller each time they go around Earth.

6. Eventually, they melt to the core.
7. Each comet is in a different orbit around Earth.
8. With scientific calculations, we can predict when a comet will come closest to us.
9. In the past, comets were sometimes considered warnings of doom.
10. Some people thought a comet was the soul of a hero on its way to heaven.

> **Exercise 18** Distinguishing

Between Prepositions and Adverbs Label the underlined word a *preposition* or an *adverb*.

1. Except for the sun, Jupiter is the largest celestial body <u>in</u> our solar system.
2. It was named <u>by</u> ancient people after the king of the Roman gods.
3. Jupiter has a faint ring that circles the planet <u>around</u> its equator.
4. Its clouds are so thick they can't be seen <u>through</u>.
5. Storms that do not blow <u>over</u> quickly rage on the planet.
6. One storm, the Great Red Spot, has been blowing <u>on</u> Jupiter for 300 years!
7. <u>Within</u> the thick layer of clouds, temperatures are low, but they are significantly greater near Jupiter's core.
8. Io, a moon of Jupiter, orbits <u>within</u> a magnetic field that surrounds the planet.
9. Io moves <u>through</u> the magnetic current and creates an electrical field that a spaceship could not penetrate.
10. The electrical current is 5 million amperes, while the current <u>inside</u> a 100-watt light bulb is one ampere.

✎ STANDARDIZED TEST PREPARATION WORKSHOP

Grammar and Usage Standardized tests often measure a student's ability to rewrite sentences by combining ideas. Occasionally, prepositions are used to combine these ideas. Share the following example with students:

> *My mother told me something. She told me that we are going on vacation next month.*

Choose the letter of the best way to rewrite the sentences.

A We are going on vacation next month with my mother.

B According to my mother, we are going on vacation next month.

C Due to my mother telling me something, we are going on vacation next month.

D We are going on vacation next month, on account of my mother.

The best choice is item **B**. Item A, while correct, does not retain the meaning of the two original sentences. Item C and D also do not retain the original meaning.

Exercise 19 Classifying

Prepositions and Adverbs Label each underlined item a *preposition, compound preposition, prepositional phrase,* or *adverb.*

1. <u>According to</u> scientific measurements, Ganymede is Jupiter's biggest moon.
2. Its craters make it look much <u>like</u> our moon.
3. However, it also has great plates of ice above and a core of molten iron <u>below the surface.</u>
4. The second biggest moon, Callisto, has rings that were raised <u>by shock waves.</u>
5. A large asteroid smashed <u>into</u> the moon and formed a crater.
6. <u>Because of</u> the force of the crash, clouds of steam and water erupted.
7. Europa is almost as large as Earth's moon, and <u>as a result of</u> its moving plates, it has few crater marks.
8. Scientists think that <u>underneath the icy surface</u> there is an ocean of liquid water.
9. They believe there is an active core <u>of rock-metal.</u>
10. The moon Io is approximately the size <u>of our moon.</u>
11. However, <u>instead of</u> a quiet, peaceful surface like our moon, Io has at least ten active volcanoes.
12. Volcanoes blast <u>out</u> enough matter to cover the entire moon every million years.
13. The surface is eroded by radiation from Jupiter, and it is always being struck <u>by lightning arcs.</u>
14. Until a probe passed <u>by,</u> it was believed that Jupiter had only twelve moons.
15. Every year, scientists learn more <u>about the moons</u> of Jupiter.

Exercise 20 Supplying

Prepositional Phrases Supply a prepositional phrase to complete each sentence.

1. The moon travels ___?___.
2. Gravity holds the moon ___?___.
3. Life ___?___ would be impossible without the warmth of the sun.
4. Scientists are searching for new galaxies ___?___.
5. Advancements ___?___ have given scientists the ability to search farther than ever before.

Exercise 21 Writing Application

Write ten original sentences that include the following items. Underline the required items in each sentence.

1. prepositional phrase starting with the word *over*
2. the word *near* used as an adverb
3. two prepositional phrases, one starting with *in* and the other starting with *out*
4. any compound preposition
5. the compound preposition *because of*
6. two prepositional phrases—one starting with a compound preposition and the other starting with *outside*
7. the word *around* used both as an adverb and as a preposition
8. two prepositional phrases—one starting with *on* and the other with *under*
9. the word *near* used as a preposition and *Saturn* used as the object of the preposition
10. two compound prepositions

Exercise 22 CUMULATIVE REVIEW

Nouns, Verbs, Adjectives, and Adverbs
Write a sentence using each word as the part of speech indicated in parentheses.

1. test (noun)
2. space (noun)
3. space (adjective)
4. hard (adverb)
5. test (verb)

Answer Key continued

Exercise 22

Cumulative Review
Possible reponses are given.

1. How did you do on the test?
2. I would love to travel in outer space.
3. We got that data by sending out a space probe.
4. He hit the ball hard.
5. She will test us on prepositions.

Exercise 19

1. compound preposition
2. preposition
3. prepositional phrase
4. prepositional phrase
5. preposition
6. compound preposition
7. compound preposition
8. prepositional phrase
9. prepositional phrase
10. prepositional phrase
11. compound preposition
12. adverb
13. prepositional phrase
14. adverb
15. prepositional phrase

Exercise 20

Possible responses are given.

1. around Earth
2. in its orbit
3. on Earth
4. beyond our own
5. in technology

Exercise 21

Writing Application
Possible responses are given.

1. Can you see the plane flying <u>over that building</u>?
2. The asteroid came <u>near.</u>
3. <u>In a few more years,</u> my dog will be too old to run <u>out the door.</u>
4. <u>In addition to plastic cups,</u> we need forks and knives for the picnic.
5. <u>Because of</u> the rain, the party is being postponed.
6. <u>According to the principal,</u> everyone should meet <u>outside the school</u> at 2 o'clock.
7. I have to run some laps <u>around the track,</u> but will you be <u>around</u> later?
8. My cat chased the mouse <u>on the driveway</u> and then <u>under the porch.</u>
9. The space probe is almost <u>near</u> the planet <u>Saturn.</u>
10. I am standing <u>in back of</u> Felipe and <u>in front of</u> Billy.

continued

Step-by-Step Teaching Guide

Using Prepositions

Teaching Resources: Standardized Test Preparation Workbook, pp. 33–34

1. Remind students to read the directions carefully so that they know what they are being asked to do.

2. Have students read every choice carefully. Encourage them to think about which one makes the most sense without changing the meaning of the original sentences.

Standardized Test Preparation Workshop

Using Prepositions

Standardized test questions measure your ability to choose the best way to combine ideas or rewrite sentences. Often, your knowledge of prepositions will help you respond successfully to these items. Before you answer this type of question, first read the entire passage. Then, choose the answer choice that best uses prepositional phrases to connect similar ideas and eliminate unnecessary words.

The following test item will give you practice with questions that measure your ability to use prepositional phrases.

Test Tips

- Identify repeated ideas in the passages chosen.
- Combining those ideas with a prepositional phrase will provide the best rewrite.

Sample Test Item	Answer and Explanation
Directions Read the passage, and choose the letter of the best way to write the underlined sentences. (1) A typewriter has keys. The keys were originally arranged in alphabetical order. Christopher Sholes found that in this arrangement the letters used most kept jamming; he devised a system, still used today, where the letters were arranged according to how often they were used. 1 A A typewriter has keys of the alphabet that were originally arranged in alphabetical order. 　B The keys of a typewriter were originally arranged in alphabetical order. 　C The typewriter has keys that are arranged in alphabetical order. 　D A typewriter has keys, and the keys of the typewriter were originally arranged in alphabetical order.	The best answer is *B*. Since both sentences are about typewriter keys, it is logical to combine the repeated information with the prepositional phrase *of a typewriter*.

372 • Prepositions

✏ TEST-TAKING TIP

Remind students that prepositions show relationships between words in the sentence. So, in using prepositions to combine repeated information, it is important to consider the relation that is being established. Does one thing cause another (*because of, due to, by means of, on account of*)? Is something being added or subtracted (*with, without, in addition to*)? Is the relationship one of space (*in, through, beside, out, on, in back of*) or time (*during, before, after*)?

Here is an example. *My mother gave us some advice. She said that we need to get enough sleep before a big test.*

The relationship is that of source: the advice came from the mother. The sentences could be combined by using the compound preposition "according to". *According to my mother, we need to get enough sleep before a big test.*

Practice 1 **Directions:** Read the passage, and choose the letter of the best way to write the underlined sentences.

(1) The 1890s marked the invention of the zipper. Whitcomb Judson thought he had found a winner when he invented the zipper, but he waited nearly thirty years for it to catch on. (2) In 1917, a contract for 10,000 zippers for uniforms helped them gain popularity. The U. S. Navy held the contract.

1 **A** In the 1890's, the zipper was invented. Whitcomb Judson thought he had found a winner when he invented the zipper, but he waited nearly thirty years for it to catch on.
 B In the 1890's, Whitcomb Judson thought he had found a winner when he invented the zipper, but he waited nearly thirty years for it to catch on.
 C Whitcomb Judson thought he had found a winner when he invented the zipper, but he waited nearly thirty years in the 1890's for it to catch on.
 D Whitcomb Judson thought he had found a winner when he invented the zipper, but he waited nearly thirty years for it to catch on in the 1890's.

2 **F** In 1917, a contract for 10,000 zippers for uniforms helped them gain popularity with the U. S. Navy.
 G With the U.S. Navy, in 1917, a contract for 10,000 zippers for uniforms helped them gain popularity.
 H In 1917, a contract for 10,000 zippers for uniforms helped zippers gain popularity. The U. S. Navy held the contract for the 10,000 zippers.
 J In 1917, a contract with the U.S. Navy for 10,000 zippers for uniforms helped zippers gain popularity.

Practice 2 **Directions:** Read the passage, and choose the letter of the best way to write the underlined sentences.

The southeast is Brazil's economic heartland. It is home to forty percent of the population. (1) The region has a mostly humid subtropical climate and fertile soil. Farmers can easily grow great quantities of cash crops. The most important crop is coffee. (2) Thousands of people migrated to the southeast region of Brazil. They migrated during the 1800's.

1 **A** Farmers can easily grow great quantities of cash crops in the region with a humid subtropical climate and fertile soil.
 B Because of the region's mostly humid subtropical climate and fertile soil, farmers can easily grow great quantities of cash crops.
 C The region has a mostly a humid subtropical climate and fertile soil; according to farmers, they easily grow great quantities of cash crops.
 D In the region is mostly a humid subtropical climate and fertile soil. Farmers can easily grow great quantities of cash crops.

2 **F** By thousands of people migrating to the southeast region of Brazil, they migrated during the 1800's.
 G In thousands, people migrated to the southeast region of Brazil. They migrated during the 1800's.
 H During the 1800's, thousands of people migrated to the southeast region of Brazil.
 J Thousands of people migrated to the southeast region of Brazil, and they did so during the 1800's.

Answer Key

Practice 1
1. B
2. J

Practice 2
1. B
2. H

Customize for ESL Students

Students who are less proficient in English may have difficulty with these exercises if words are unfamiliar. You might need to discuss the original sentences to make certain that students know not only what all the words mean, but also which ones are most important to the meaning of the sentence. If necessary, work through both practice items as a class, discussing why the various rewrites do or do not work.

In-Depth Lesson Plan

	LESSON FOCUS	PRINT AND MEDIA RESOURCES
DAY 1	**Conjunctions** Students learn to recognize and use conjunctions and understand their functions in sentences (pp. 374–380).	**Teaching Resources** *Grammar Exercise Workbook,* pp.41–42; *Grammar Exercises Answers on Transparencies,* Ch. 18 **On-Line Exercise Bank,** Section 18.1
DAY 2	**Interjections** Students learn to recognize and use interjections and understand their functions in sentences and do the Hands-on Grammar activity (pp. 381–384).	**Teaching Resources** *Grammar Exercise Workbook,* pp.43–44; *Grammar Exercises Answers on Transparencies,* Ch. 18 *Hands-on Grammar Activity Book,* Ch. 18 **On-Line Exercise Bank,** Section 18.2
DAY 3	**Review and Assess** Students review chapter and demonstrate mastery of use of conjunctions and interjections (pp. 385–387).	**Teaching Resources** *Formal Assessment,* Ch. 18; *Grammar Exercise Answers on Transparencies,* Ch. 18

Accelerated Lesson Plan

	LESSON FOCUS	PRINT AND MEDIA RESOURCES
DAY 1	**Conjunctions and Interjections** Students cover concepts and usage of conjunctions and interjections as determined by Diagnostic Test (pp. 374–384).	**Teaching Resources** *Grammar Exercise Workbook,* pp. 41–44; *Grammar Exercises Answers on Transparencies,* Ch. 18 *Hands-on Grammar Activity Book,* Ch. 18 **On-Line Exercise Bank,** Section 18.1, 18.2
DAY 2	**Review and Assess** Students review chapter and demonstrate mastery of use of conjunctions and interjections (pp. 385–387).	**Teaching Resources** *Formal Assessment,* Ch. 18; *Grammar Exercise Answers on Transparencies,* Ch. 18

Options for Adapting Lesson Plans

HOMEWORK

Have students complete any section of the chapter for homework.

FEATURES

Extend coverage with the Grammar in Literature feature (p. 378), and the Standardized Test Preparation Workshop (p. 387).

TECHNOLOGY

Students can use the On-Line Exercise Bank to complete the exercises on computer. The Auto Check feature will grade their work.

INTEGRATED SKILLS COVERAGE

Grammar in Literature
SE pp. 378, 382

Reading
Find It In Your Reading, SE pp. 380, 383, 384

Writing
Find It In Your Writing, SE pp. 380, 383, 384
Writing Application SE pp. 380, 384

Spelling
SE p. 378

Workplace Skills
Integrating Workplace Skills ATE p. 379

Viewing and Representing
Critical Viewing SE pp. 374, 377, 379, 381

ASSESSMENT SUPPORT

Standardized Test Preparation SE p. 387; ATE pp. 377, 383

Standardized Test Preparation Workbook, pp. 35–36

Formal Assessment, Ch. 18

MEETING INDIVIDUAL NEEDS

ESL Students ATE p. 381

Less Advanced Students ATE p. 377. See also Ongoing Assessment, p. 378.

Bodily/Kinesthetic Learners, ATE p. 381

Visual/Spatial Learners, ATE p. 377

BLOCK SCHEDULING

Pacing Suggestions
For 90-minute Blocks
- Administer the Diagnostic Test to students to determine instructional coverage.
- Have students complete the necessary exercises in class. Use the Hands-on Grammar activity to provide a change of pace.

Professional Development Support
- *How to Manage Instruction in the Block* This Teaching Resource provides management and activity suggestions.

MEDIA AND TECHNOLOGY

For the Student
- *On-Line Exercise Bank,* Ch. 18

For the Teacher
- *Resource Pro* CD-ROM

WRITING AND GRAMMAR WEB SITE

The Interactive Writing and Grammar Web site provides a wide array of support for students, teachers, and parents. Grammar support includes:

- *On-Line Exercise Bank* with Auto Check scoring
- Diagnostic and assessment support

www.phschool.com

LITERATURE CONNECTIONS

Grammar in Literature selection from *Prentice Hall Literature: Timeless Voices, Timeless Themes,* Bronze:
"The Dying Detective," from a story by Sir Arthur Conan Doyle, Michael and Mollie Hardwick, SE pp. 378, 382

Chapter 18 Conjunctions and Interjections

A small piece of evidence can aid detectives in making connections that will help them solve a crime. In grammar, small words called **conjunctions** can aid you in connecting ideas. Conjunctions can connect individual words and groups of words, as well as combine sentences.

Interjections are another small part of speech that can add a special meaning to a sentence. An **interjection** is a part of speech that expresses feeling or emotion.

▲ **Critical Viewing**
What words might the detective use to express surprise, interest, or shock? **[Analyze]**

374 • Conjunctions and Interjections

Diagnostic Test

Directions: Write all answers on a separate sheet of paper.

Skill Check A. Identify the coordinating conjunction in each sentence. Then, tell which words or groups of words each conjunction joins.

1. Police and scientific researchers cooperate to solve mysteries.
2. Fingerprints are gathered at the scene of the crime, and then they must be matched to a suspect.
3. When a suspect is arrested, his or her fingerprints are taken.
4. People have long been aware of the ridges in fingerprints, but fingerprints were not used to solve crimes until the 1880's.
5. Fingerprints are invisible to the naked eye, so detectives dust a surface with a fine powder to make the prints visible.
6. Fingerprints are kept on file, for they might be needed later.
7. There are three basic fingerprint patterns, but these are further broken down into smaller categories.
8. Fingerprinting is fun, yet it can be very messy.
9. You will need a piece of paper and an ink pad to ink your finger.
10. Ink each finger, and press it firmly on the paper.

Skill Check B. Identify the correlative conjunction in each sentence. Then, tell which words or groups of words are connected.

11. Detectives both gather and study fingerprints as clues.
12. Fingerprints are not only different from person to person, but also from finger to finger on the same person.
13. Fingerprints can be removed from either rough surfaces, such as paper, or hard surfaces, such as metal.
14. Both skin oils and dirt on the fingertips make fingerprints.
15. Whether in court or at the crime scene, experts will collect needed evidence.
16. Both the police and the lab scientist must have positive proof before the case goes to court.
17. The test results will either prove or disprove their hypothesis.
18. Neither the prosecution nor the defense will know the decision of the jury until the jury returns to the courtroom.
19. The jury will either acquit or convict the accused, depending on the evidence.
20. The lawyer will try to build a strong case, whether with testimony or with physical evidence.

Skill Check C. Identify the interjections below. Then, tell what emotion is expressed.

21. Huh! There are only three basic fingerprint patterns!
22. Wow! Fingerprinting is exciting.
23. Oops! We didn't think my fingerprints would be seen.
24. Well, when they use a special powder, they can see them.
25. Ugh! How do I get all this fingerprinting ink off my fingers?

Conjunctions and Interjections • 375

Skill Check A

1. *and* connects *Police, scientific researchers*
2. *and* connects *Fingerprints are gathered at the scene of the crime, then they must be matched to a suspect*
3. *or* connects *his, her*
4. *but* connects *People have long been aware of the ridges in fingerprints, fingerprints were not used to solve crimes until the 1880's*
5. *so* connects *Fingerprints are invisible to the naked eye, detectives dust a surface with a fine powder to make the prints visible*
6. *for* connects *Fingerprints are kept on file, they might be needed later*
7. *but* connects *There are three basic fingerprint patterns, these are further broken down into smaller categories*
8. *yet* connects *Fingerprinting is fun, it can be very messy*
9. *and* connects *piece of paper, an ink pad*
10. *and* connects *Ink each finger, press it firmly on the paper*

Skill Check B

11. *Both . . . and* connects *gather, study*
12. *Not only . . . but also* connects *different from person to person, from finger to finger on the same person*
13. *either . . . or* connects *rough surfaces such as paper, hard surfaces such as metal*
14. *Both . . . and* connects *skin oils, dirt*
15. *Whether . . . or* connects *in court, at the crime scene*
16. *Both . . . and* connects *the police, the lab scientist*
17. *Either . . . or* connects *prove, disprove*
18. *Neither . . . nor* connects *the prosecution, the defense*
19. *Either . . . or* connects *acquit, convict*
20. *Whether . . . or* connects *with testimony, with physical evidence*

Skill Check C

21. Huh (surprise)
22. Wow (excitement)
23. Oops (regret)
24. Well (impatience)
25. Ugh (disgust)

ONGOING ASSESSMENT: Diagnose *continued*					
Conjunctions and Interjections	**Diagnostic Test Items**	**Teach**	**Practice**	**Section Review**	**Chapter Review**
Skill Check C					
Interjections	C 21–25	p. 381–382	Ex. 11–12	Ex. 13–15	Ex. 23–24
Cumulative Reviews and Applications				Ex. 8–10 16–18	Ex. 26

Ask students what they think the word *conjunction* means. (joining together, combining) Tell students that they will be learning about a part of speech, called *the conjunction,* that joins together words in a sentence.

Activate Prior Knowledge

Ask students to write four words that begin a sentence, such as *That house is green.* Then have them trade papers with a partner and complete each sentence, using *and* or *but.*

TEACH

Step-by-Step Teaching Guide

Coordinating Conjunctions

1. Point out to students that conjunctions make it possible to have more than one noun, verb, or other part of speech in a sentence. WIthout conjunctions, they might write: *I stopped at the store. I bought books. I bought paper.* With conjunctions, they can write: *I stopped at the store and bought books and paper.*

2. Explain that when conjunctions are described as connecting words, it doesn't mean that they are always adding words together. *And* adds things. However, *but* and *yet* contrast things, while *or* indicates a choice between one thing and another.

3. Review the seven coordinating conjunctions shown and ask students to suggest sentences using each.

Answer Key

Exercise 1

1. *and* connects *analyze clues, solve crimes*
2. *but* connects *they gather evidence, they take it back*
3. *yet* connects *fascinating, difficult*
4. *for* connects *analysis must be precise, if it's not*
5. *so* connects *The detective must gather evidence carefully, every clue remains intact*

Conjunctions

Conjunctions are like links in a chain; they help you join words and ideas. The conjunction you use often indicates the relationship between the words or groups of words connected.

▶ **KEY CONCEPT** A **conjunction** connects words or groups of words. ∎

Coordinating Conjunctions

A **coordinating conjunction** connects similar words or groups of words. ∎

COORDINATING CONJUNCTIONS						
but	and	nor	for	so	or	yet

The coordinating conjunctions are circled in these examples:

CONNECTING WORDS: The *pen* and *paper* contained fingerprints.
We will *win* or *lose* the case.

CONNECTING PREPOSITIONAL PHRASES: The forensic specialist sprinkled powder *on the doorknob* and *along the windowsill.*

CONNECTING TWO CLAUSES: *The expert examined the evidence,* but *she could not confirm the identity of the burglar.*

▶ **Exercise 1** Recognizing Coordinating Conjunctions
Identify the coordinating conjunction in each sentence below. Then, tell which words or groups of words are joined by it.

EXAMPLE: He wants a career in medicine or forensic science.

ANSWER: *or* connects *medicine* and *forensic science.*

1. Detectives analyze clues and solve crimes.
2. They gather evidence at the crime scene, but they take it back to the police laboratory for examination.
3. It is a fascinating yet difficult procedure.
4. The analysis must be precise, for if it's not, wrong conclusions could be drawn.
5. The detective must gather evidence carefully, so every clue remains intact.

In this section, you will learn about conjunctions. All the examples, sentences, and questions are about forensics—the use of science to gather and evaluate evidence in a criminal investigation.

Cross-Curricular Connection: Science

▶ **More Practice**
Language Lab CD-ROM
• Combining Sentences
On-line Exercise Bank
• Section 18.1
Grammar Practice Workbook
• pp. 41-42

🕐 **TIME AND RESOURCE MANAGER**

Resources
Print: Grammar Exercise Workbook, pp. 41–42
Technology: On-Line Exercise Bank, Section 18.1

In-Depth Coverage	Accelerated Pace
• Work through key concepts, pp. 376–379. • Assign and review Exercises 1–4. • Read and discuss Grammar in Literature, p. 378.	• Assign pp. 376–379 for independent student review. • Assign Section Review Exercises 5–7, p. 380.

Correlative Conjunctions

Correlative conjunctions are *pairs* of words that connect similar kinds of words or groups of words.

CORRELATIVE CONJUNCTIONS		
both . . . and	neither . . . nor	whether . . . or
either . . . or	not only . . . but also	

The correlative conjunctions are circled in these examples:

CONNECTING NOUNS: (Either) the small *van* (or) the *bus* will pick us up.

CONNECTING PRONOUNS: (Neither) *he* (nor) *she* is to be blamed.

CONNECTING VERBS: Every morning she (both) *runs* (and) *swims.*

CONNECTING PREPOSITIONAL PHRASES: She'll come—(whether) *by train* (or) *by plane*, I can't say.

CONNECTING TWO CLAUSES: (Not only) *can they sing,* (but) *they can* (also) *tap-dance.*

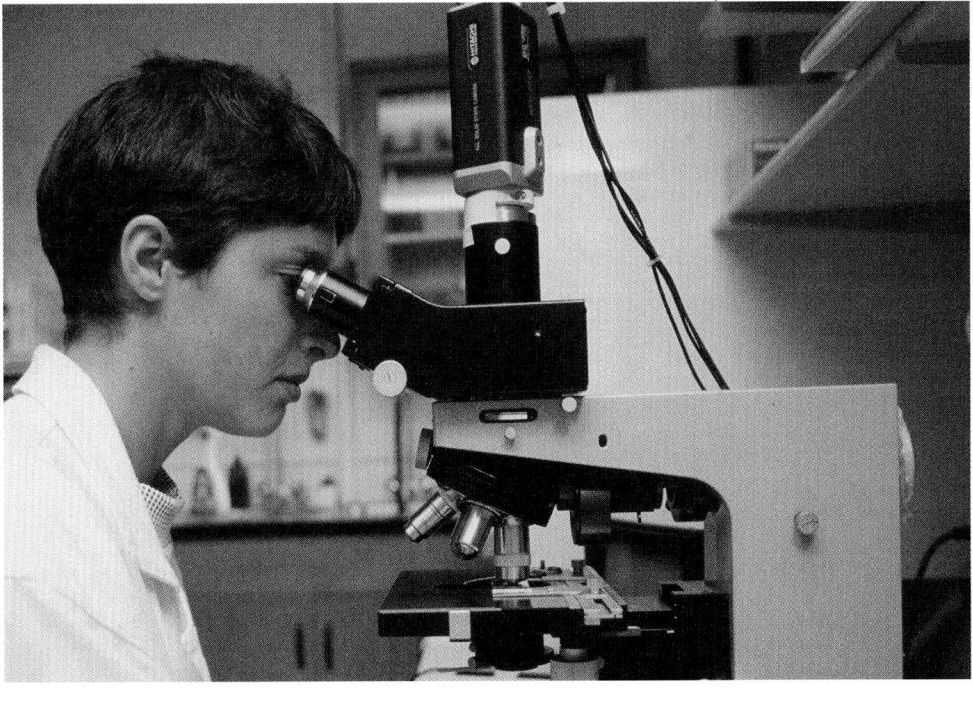

▼ **Critical Viewing**
How important are small details that can be seen with this microscope? How important are small words in sentences? **[Connect]**

Conjunctions • **377**

Correlative Conjunctions

1. Stress to students that correlative conjunctions always occur in pairs. Give these examples: I will have *either* a hamburger (noun) *or* a hot dog (noun) for lunch. I will *neither* yell (verb) *nor* run (verb) in the halls.

2. Be sure that students understand that correlative conjunctions connect *similar* kinds or groups of words; that is, a pair of nouns, a pair of verbs, a pair of pronouns, a pair of prepositional phrases, and so on.

Customize for
Visual/Spatial Learners

Write the five example sentences from this page on strips of paper. Then highlight the conjunctions and cut the strips apart before the second part of the conjunction. Mix up the strips. Have students work individually to match the strips (without looking at their textbooks).

Critical Viewing

Connect Students may suggest that small things, such as microbes, can play a major role in the health of a person. In the same way, the small words *but* and *and* can affect the overall meaning of a sentence.

Customize for
Less Advanced Students

Point out to students that correlative conjunctions always come in pairs. For example:

Both Mary *and* I are going to the circus.
We will eat *either* at home *or* in a restaurant.

Point out to students that, just as one correlative conjunction in the pair balances the other, the two items they link must also balance. Draw a pair of balance scales on the board, labeling one *both* and the other *and*. Underneath, list the pairs of words and phrases, such as *Mary, I, in the rain, in the sun, drives*. Have students match pair words and phrases from the list. For each pair, write one word or phrase on one side of the balance and the other on the other side. Have students call out if two are not parallel—whether they will "tip" the scales.

✒ STANDARDIZED TEST PREPARATION WORKSHOP

Grammar and Usage Many standardized tests require students to choose the correct version of a sentence. Write the following sentence on the board and ask students to choose the correct version.

I can either finish my homework or my brother wants me to play with him.

A I can either finish my homework and my brother wants me to play with him.

B I can either finish my homework nor play with my brother.

C I can either finish my homework then play with my brother.

D I can either finish my homework or play with my brother.

E No change

Students should recognize that item **D** is correct. Correlative conjunctions connect similar kinds of words or groups of words. In item D, two verb phrases (*finish my homework, play with my brother*) are connected by the correlative conjunction *either . . . or*. Item B is incorrect because *either . . . nor* is not a correlative conjunction.

377

Grammar in Literature

1. Have a volunteer read aloud the passage by Sir Arthur Conan Doyle.

2. Have students identify the conjunctions by type: *and* (coordinating), *Whether . . . or* (correlative).

3. Point out that, in this passage, the parallel elements used with correlative conjunctions are understood, rather than stated: *Whether he likes it or he does not like it.* Tell students to remember that this can happen both when they are identifying conjunctions and when they are using them.

More About the Author

Sir Arthur Conan Doyle was an English physician who began writing stories in the 1880's in order to supplement his income. His famous and beloved fictional detective, Sherlock Holmes, is a master of deductive reasoning who solves crimes by seeing clues that others miss.

Answer Key

Exercise 2

1. *not only . . . but also* connects *today's crimes, past crimes*
2. *either . . . or* connects *disease, poison*
3. *whether . . . or* connects *analyzing an ancient skeleton, studying a more recent one*
4. *both . . . and* connects *a comparison microscope, a polarized-light microscope*
5. *not only . . . but also* connects *magnifies an object, gives a side-by-side view*

Exercise 3

1. and
2. neither
3. Either
4. either
5. but also

18.1

GRAMMAR IN
LITERATURE

from **The Dying Detective**
from a story by Sir Arthur Conan Doyle
Michael and Mollie Hardwick

Notice how the author uses one coordinating and one pair of correlative conjunctions in the passage. The conjunctions are shown in blue italics.

WATSON. . . . You go along, Mrs. Hudson, *and* leave this to me. *Whether* he likes it *or* not, I shall ensure that everything possible is done.

▶ **Exercise 2** Identifying Correlative Conjunctions Identify the correlative conjunctions in each sentence below. Then, tell which words or groups of words are joined.

1. Forensic science solves not only today's crimes, but also past crimes.
2. Old bones can give clues to death by either disease or poison.
3. Whether analyzing an ancient skeleton or studying a more recent one, scientists use the same techniques.
4. Both a comparison microscope and a polarized-light microscope are used to compare evidence.
5. A comparison microscope not only magnifies an object but also gives a side-by-side view.

▶ **Exercise 3** Supplying Correlative Conjunctions Supply the second half of the correlative conjunction in each sentence.

1. The polarized light microscope can show both the shape ___?___ the thickness of a fiber.
2. Often, ___?___ a comparison microscope nor a polarized light microscope gives the whole story.
3. ___?___ in a crime lab or at an archaeological site, a forensic scientist should use the best tools.
4. Working ___?___ together or alone, scientists investigate the evidence.
5. Not only scientists ___?___ detectives work to uncover the facts.

378 • Conjunctions and Interjections

🖋 **Spelling Tip**

When confronted with difficult words, look for smaller words inside larger ones, such as *junction* inside of *conjunction*.

▶ **More Practice**

Language Lab CD-ROM
• Combining Sentences
On-line Exercise Bank
• Section 18.1
Grammar Practice Workbook
• pp. 41-42

☑ **ONGOING ASSESSMENT: Monitor and Reinforce**

If students miss more than two items in Exercises 2, 3, or 4, refer them to the following for additional practice.

In the Textbook	Print Resources	Technology
Section Review, Ex. 5 and 6, p. 380	Grammar Exercise Workbook, pp. 41–42	On-Line Exercise Bank, Section 18.1

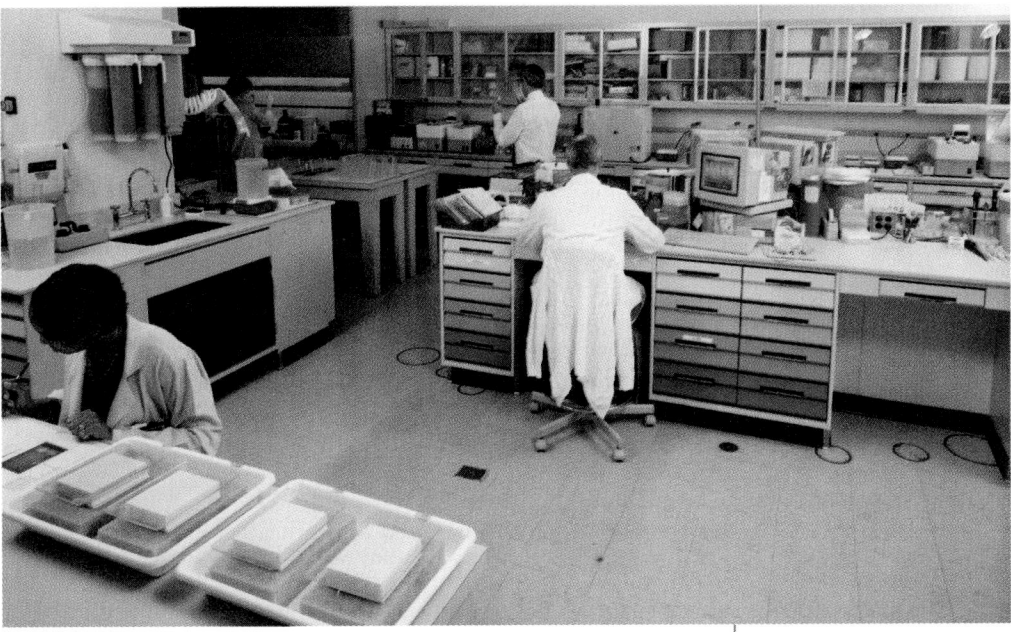

▲ Critical Viewing
Using a single sentence, describe what two people in this picture are doing. What conjunction did you use? **[Connect]**

▶ **Exercise 4** **Combining Sentences Using Conjunctions**

Combine each pair of sentences below using either a coordinating or a correlative conjunction.

EXAMPLE: Mary wanted to be a detective.
Mary wanted to be a doctor.

ANSWER: Mary wanted to be *either* a detective *or* a doctor.

1. Kim had not been to a police lab before. Lashonda had not been to a police lab before.
2. They saw the detectives at work. They saw evidence being examined.
3. They were interested in the work. They did not want to be detectives.
4. The class enjoyed the visit. They wrote a thank-you note.
5. Kim wrote a report about the visit. Lashonda wrote a report about the visit.
6. They didn't just write reports. They gave an oral presentation.
7. Kim wasn't sure that she would give the presentation. She wasn't sure that she would not give the presentation.
8. Kim got a good grade on the presentation. Lashonda got a good grade on the presentation.
9. Lashonda wants to be a veterinarian. She might be a teacher instead.
10. She likes animals. She enjoys working with children.

Conjunctions • **379**

Critical Viewing

Connect Possible response: Both people are working, but they are not working together; *but*

Answer Key

▶ **Exercise 4**

Sample responses are given.

1. Neither Kim nor Lashonda had been to a police lab before.
2. They saw the detectives at work and evidence being examined.
3. They were interested in the work, yet they did not want to be detectives.
4. The class enjoyed the visit, so they wrote a thank-you note.
5. Both Kim and Lashonda wrote reports about the visit.
6. Not only did they write reports, but they also gave an oral presentation.
7. Kim wasn't sure whether she would give the presentation or not.
8. Both Kim and Lashonda got good grades on the presentation.
9. Lashonda wants to be a veterinarian, but she might be a teacher instead.
10. She not only likes animals, but also enjoys working with children.

Integrating Workplace Skills

Sherlock Holmes is known for his exceptional problem-solving skills. Ask students to name other occupations that require problem-solving skills, and list them on the board. Then, have students explain how each occupation uses these skills. Doctor, football player, and teacher will be obvious. But even a clerk at the video store has problems to solve—ten customers want to rent a new movie, but there are only three copies in stock. What might he or she do?

Section Review

Each of these exercises correlates with a concept in the section on conjunctions, pages 376–379. These exercises may be used for more practice, for reteaching, or for the review of the Key Concepts presented. Answers for all chapter exercises are available in *Grammar Exercises Answers on Transparencies* in your teaching resources.

Answer Key

▶ Exercise 5

1. (Neither) the judge (nor) the jury had ever heard of fingerprints before.
2. The lawyer asked the jury (whether) they believed the finger smudges (or) the witnesses.
3. (Either) all the witnesses were lying (or) this new science of matching fingerprints was pure nonsense.
4. The prosecutor had fifteen people press their index fingers to drinking glasses, (and) then one of them also pressed a finger on the judge's desk.
5. The prosecutor matched a fingerprint from one of the glasses to the one on the desk, (so) people were convinced.

▶ Exercise 6

1. and—coordinating
2. or—coordinating
3. not only . . . but also—correlative
4. for—coordinating
5. NC
6. Whether . . . or—correlative
7. yet—coordinating
8. Neither . . . nor—correlative
9. Either . . . or—correlative
10. Whether . . . or—correlative

▶ Exercise 7

Answers will vary. Samples are given.

An expert was brought in for the job of matching the one print on the judge's desk to one of the fifteen on the glasses. Not only did the expert match the one fingerprint to the correct person, but he also did it in only four minutes. Both the judge and the jury were surprised at this new way of proving evidence.

GRAMMAR EXERCISES 5–10

▶ **Exercise 5** Recognizing Conjunctions Copy each sentence onto your paper. Circle the conjunction, and underline the words or groups of words that are joined by it.

1. Neither the judge nor the jury had ever heard of fingerprints before.
2. The lawyer asked the jury whether they believed the finger smudges or the witnesses.
3. Either all the witnesses were lying or this new science of matching fingerprints was pure nonsense.
4. The prosecutor had fifteen people press their index fingers to drinking glasses, and then one of them also pressed a finger on the judge's desk.
5. The prosecutor matched a fingerprint from one of the glasses to the one on the desk, so people were convinced.

▶ **Exercise 6** Identifying Types of Conjunctions In each of the following sentences, find the conjunction and label it *coordinating* or *correlative*. If a sentence does not contain a conjunction, write *NC* for "no conjunction."

1. After detectives have evidence and a suspect, the case goes to trial.
2. A trial is the process by which the accused is found guilty or not guilty.
3. The evidence is shown not only to the judge, but also to the jury.
4. The prosecution must prove the case, for the defendant is presumed innocent until proven guilty.
5. The accused's lawyer can question witnesses after the prosecutor presents the evidence to the jury.
6. Whether by argument or by evidence, the lawyer must build a strong case.
7. In one case, witnesses swore that a defendant was at the theater, yet fingerprints at the crime scene were his.
8. Neither his wife nor the other witnesses would change their stories.
9. Either the suspect was lying or the fingerprints were not his.
10. Whether or not he knew it, his fingerprints betrayed him.

▶ **Exercise 7** Revision Practice: Sentence Combining Where appropriate, use conjunctions to combine sentences in this paragraph.

An expert was brought in to match the single print on the judge's desk to one of the fifteen on the glasses. The expert matched the one fingerprint to the correct person. He did it in only four minutes. The judge was surprised at this new kind of evidence. The jury was surprised at this new kind of evidence.

▶ **Exercise 8** Find It in Your Reading
In a chapter in your social studies book, find examples of at least two of the different conjunctions that connect similar words or groups of words.

▶ **Exercise 9** Find It in Your Writing
Look through examples of your own writing to find conjunctions. Challenge yourself to use conjunctions to combine at least two sentences in one piece of writing.

▶ **Exercise 10** Writing Application
Write a description of a person you know well. Use conjunctions to combine ideas as you describe his or her personality and qualities. Circle the conjunctions you use.

▶ Exercise 8

Find It in Your Reading
When they finish, have students rewrite the sentences without the conjunctions. Ask them to decide which versions are easier to read, and to explain their reasoning.

▶ Exercise 9

Find It in Your Writing
In order to make sure students choose conjunctions that enhance the meaning of the text, rather than choosing them at random, ask them to share examples of their changes.

▶ Exercise 10

Writing Application
For a variation, have students exchange papers with a partner and then identify the conjunctions and connected words in each other's work.

Section 18.2 Interjections

The *interjection* is the part of speech that is used least often.

▶ **KEY CONCEPT** An **interjection** is an exclamation that expresses feeling or emotion. ■

In the examples below, the interjections are circled. Notice that interjections are set off by either one or two commas or an exclamation point. Generally, use commas to set off interjections expressing mild emotion, and exclamation points to set off those expressing strong emotion.

SURPRISE: (Oh,) we did not expect you today.
JOY: (Goodness!) How good it is to see you!
PAIN: (Ouch!) He stubbed his toe!
HESITATION: I can't explain, (uh,) exactly how it happened.
IMPATIENCE: (Tsk!) I think we've waited long enough.

The following chart lists some common interjections.

INTERJECTIONS			
Wow	Whew	Uh . . .	Well
Hey	Aaack	Er . . .	Huh
Oh	Ugh	Say	Hmmm

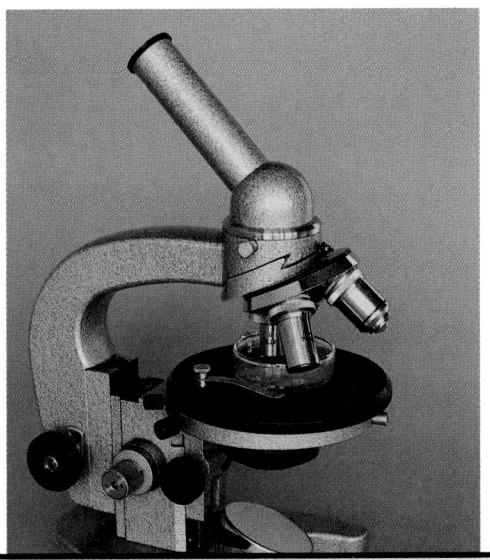

Grammar and Style Tip

Interjections are used to express both strong and mild feelings. Use them to help written dialogue sound like real speech.

◀ Critical Viewing
What interjections might someone use when he or she looks through a microscope? **[Speculate]**

Interjections • 381

PREPARE and ENGAGE

Interest GRABBER Use the Hands-on Grammar Activity on p. 383 to introduce interjections. Materials and procedures are specified in the Step-by-Step Teaching Guide.

Activate Prior Knowledge

Interjections are common in cartoons and comic strips. Have students bring to class a newspaper comics page and have them identify any interjections they find.

TEACH

Step-by-Step Teaching Guide

Interjections

1. Have students read the examples given and suggest other interjections they know. Then, ask them to match interjections to such emotions as happiness, boredom, contemplation, satisfaction, etc.

2. Tell students that only interjections that show strong emotion are punctuated with an exclamation mark. Others are set off by commas. Ask students to suggest interjections that require an exclamation mark and interjections that do not.

Critical Viewing

Speculate Students may suggest: *Wow! Oh! Ugh! Gee!*

Customize for
Bodily/Kinesthetic Learners

Interjections are about strong emotions. Have students take turns acting out an interjection using facial expressions and body gestures. Have the rest of the class guess which interjection the student is expressing.

Customize for
ESL Students

Students from other cultures may have difficulty understanding the emotions communicated by different inflections of voice, as well as the interjections themselves. After inviting volunteers to demonstrate examples of interjections in their home languages, have English-speaking volunteers demonstrate examples from the book.

🕐 TIME AND RESOURCE MANAGER

Resources
Print: Grammar Exercise Workbook, pp. 43–44; Hands-on Grammar Activity Book, Chapter 18
Technology: On-Line Exercise Bank, Section 18.2

In-Depth Coverage	Accelerated Pace
• Work through the key concept, p. 381. • Assign and review Exercises 11–12. • Read and discuss Grammar in Literature, p. 382. • Do the Hands-on Grammar Activity, p. 383.	• Assign pp. 381–382 for independent student review. • Assign Section Review Exercises 13–15.

381

Grammar in Literature

1. Have two volunteers read aloud the dialogue from the passage.

2. Guide them to use the correct inflection for the interjections. Discuss with students the types of inflections of voice used to communicate different emotions.

3. Make a list of interjections, and have students practice saying them aloud with different voice inflections. How might an interjection have different meanings depending on how it is said?

Answer Key

Exercise 11

Answers may vary. Samples are given.

1. Wow! I can't believe Lafarge committed the crime!
2. Uh, I know that sounds hard to believe.
3. Hey, how did they prove it?
4. Well, they used toxicology, the science that studies poisons.
5. Golly, Marie had no chance of not being convicted!
6. Say, do you know a lot about forensics?
7. Ugh, I think it's a very unpleasant topic.
8. Oh! I didn't know you felt that way.
9. Er . . . I'm afraid I'm a little squeamish.
10. Hey, don't be upset. It's nothing to worry about.

Exercise 12

Answers will vary. Sample response given.

> Jake: Hey! Are you going home after school?
>
> Me: Um . . . I think so. Why?
>
> Jake: Well, my dad is painting our kitchen and the whole house smells like paint.
>
> Me: Ugh! Do you want to stay for dinner?
>
> Jake: Wow! That would be great!

18.2

GRAMMAR IN LITERATURE

from **The Dying Detective**

from a story by Sir Arthur Conan Doyle
Michael and Mollie Hardwick

Sir Arthur Conan Doyle uses an interjection to make his characters' speech sound believable. The interjections are highlighted in blue italics.

WATSON. Holmes? It's I—Watson.

HOLMES. [Sighs] *Ahh*! *Well*, Watson? We . . . we seem to have fallen on evil days.

WATSON. *My dear fellow*!
[*He moves to reach for* HOLMES's *pulse.*]

HOLMES. [Urgently] *No, no*! Keep back!

WATSON. *Eh*?

Exercise 11 Recognizing Interjections Rewrite each of the following sentences using an appropriate interjection in place of the feeling shown in parentheses. Punctuate each interjection according to the feeling expressed.

EXAMPLE: (Disappointment) we lost again.

ANSWER: Aw, we lost again.

1. (Surprise) I can't believe Lafarge committed the crime!
2. (Hesitation) I know that sounds hard to believe.
3. (Impatience) how did they prove it?
4. (Hesitation) they used toxicology, the science that studies poisons.
5. (Amazement) Marie had no chance of not being convicted!
6. (Interest) do you know a lot about forensics?
7. (Disgust) I think it's a very unpleasant topic.
8. (Surprise) I didn't know you felt that way!
9. (Embarrassment) I'm afraid I'm a little squeamish.
10. (Reassurance) don't be upset. It's nothing to worry about.

Exercise 12 Writing Dialogue With Interjections Recall a memorable conversation you had in the last several days. Capture the conversation in a written dialogue like the one by Conan Doyle. Use at least four interjections.

More Practice

On-line
Exercise Bank
• Section 18.2
Grammar Practice Workbook
• pp. 43–44

☑ ONGOING ASSESSMENT: Assess Mastery

Use the following resources to assess student mastery of conjunctions and interjections

In the Textbook	Technology
Chapter Review, Ex. 19–24, pp. 385–386 Standardized Test Preparation Workshop, p. 387	On-Line Exercise Bank, Sections 18.1–2

Hands-on Grammar

Interjections Wheel

Cut two circles from stiff paper or cardboard, approximately four inches in diameter. On one of the circles, write emotions or feelings such as *surprise* or *joy*. Do not limit yourself to the examples shown on this wheel. On the other circle, write interjections that express the emotions you have written on the first circle.

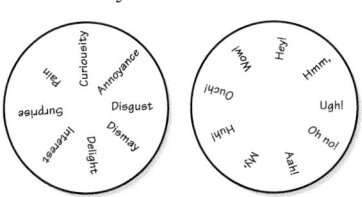

Next, cut two windows in a piece of 6 $\frac{1}{2}$-by-8 $\frac{1}{2}$ inch cardboard. The windows should be large enough so that the words you have written on the circles can fit into them. Label the paper as shown.

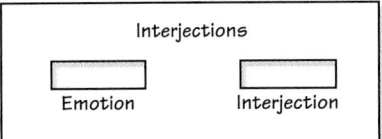

Front

Use paper fasteners to attach the circles to the back of the window sheet. Adjust so that the words show through the windows.

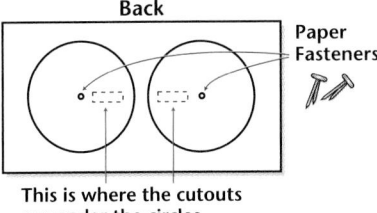

Back

This is where the cutouts are under the circles.

Spin the first wheel to choose an emotion. Spin the other wheel to find the corresponding interjection. Make up a sentence that appropriately uses the interjection to show the emotion. Write the sentence on loose-leaf paper or tell it to a partner. Continue spinning until you have tried all the combinations that make sense.

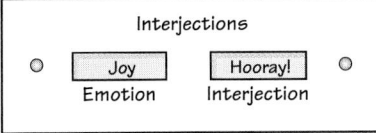

Front

Find It in Your Reading Find examples of interjections in a story or novel you have recently read.

Find It in Your Writing Find examples of interjections in a narrative you have written. If you cannot find any, challenge yourself to add one or two to the dialogue in the narrative.

Interjections • 383

Step-by-Step Teaching Guide

Interjections Wheel

Teaching Resources: Hands-on Grammar Activity Book, Chapter 18

1. Have students refer to their Hands-on Grammar Activity books or give them copies of the relevant pages for this activity.

2. You may wish to have students complete this activity in small groups.

3. Have students work together to create lists of emotions and interjections *before* they construct the wheels. This will prevent them from making errors on their wheels.

4. Remind students that not all combinations of emotions and interjections will make sense. If the group agrees, the interjection wheel can be spun again until an appropriate one appears.

Find It in Your Reading

Have students write down the interjections they find. Encourage volunteers to read to the class passages from their selected stories or novels that contain interjections.

Find It in Your Writing

Have students write the interjections they find in or add to their narratives. Then have them write down the emotions conveyed by each interjection.

STANDARDIZED TEST PREPARATION WORKSHOP

Grammar and Usage Some standardized tests measure students' ability to recognize the proper use of conjunctions. Share the following example with students:

My sister is deciding _____ or not to go on the school camping trip.

Which of the following choices best completes the sentence?

A if
B whether
C neither
D either

The correct answer is item **B**. Item A is not a conjunction, and both items C and D would require a different sentence construction in order to be correct.

⏱ TIME SAVER!

✋ **Hands-on Grammar Activity Book**
Use the Hands-on Grammar activity sheet for Chapter 18 to facilitate this activity.

Section Review

Each of these exercises correlates with the section on interjections on pages 381–383. These exercises may be used for more practice, for reteaching, or for review of the Key Concept presented.

Answer Key

Exercise 13

1. Wow!	6. Goodness!
2. Uh	7. uh
3. Well	8. Oh
4. Hey	9. Um
5. Gee!	10. Well

Exercise 14

Answers may vary. Samples are given.

1. Huh	6. Hurray!
2. Er	7. Phew!
3. Bravo!	8. Wow!
4. Um	9. Ugh!
5. So	10. Hey

Exercise 15

Answers may vary. Samples are given.

1. Hey!	4. Alas,
2. Well,	5. Oh well,
3. Golly,	

Exercise 16

Find It in Your Reading
Well, Dear me! goodness gracious, Oh

Exercise 17

Find It in Your Writing
Have students meet with partners and read aloud both versions of their dialogue. Which sounds more realistic? Why?

GRAMMAR EXERCISES 13–18

> **Exercise 13** Identifying Interjections Identify the interjection in each numbered item.

1. Wow! Did you know that there's a machine that can tell whether you are lying?
2. Uh, no, what is it called?
3. Well, it's called a polygraph.
4. Hey, do you want to see one?
5. Gee! I think that would be exciting!
6. Goodness! Do you think they will show us how it works?
7. I can't say. It depends, uh, on how busy they are.
8. Oh, I think it would be interesting to see someone being tested.
9. Um, they won't let you watch.
10. Well, we won't know for certain if we don't ask, so let's go.

> **Exercise 14** Supplying Interjections For each emotion, suggest an interjection that could be used to express that emotion.

1. shock	6. joy
2. anxiety	7. relief
3. pride	8. excitement
4. hesitation	9. disgust
5. curiosity	10. interest

> **Exercise 15** Writing With Interjections Add an interjection to each sentence in the following dialogue. Be sure to use the correct punctuation.

1. __?__ I just finished *The Dying Detective!*
2. __?__ did you enjoy it?
3. __?__ it was one of the best mysteries I've ever read.
4. __?__ I'm not a mystery fan!

5. __?__ then you probably wouldn't enjoy it.

> **Exercise 16** Find It in Your Reading Identify examples of interjections in the following dialogue from *The Dying Detective.*

MRS. HUDSON. Well, you know what he is for coming in at all hours. I was just taking my lamp to go to my bed on Wednesday night when I heard a faint knocking at the street door. I . . . I found Mr. Holmes there. He could hardly stand. Just muttered to me to help him up to his bed here, and he's barely spoken since.
WATSON. Dear me!
MRS. HUDSON. Won't take food or drink . . .
WATSON. But, goodness gracious, Mrs. Hudson, why did you not send for another doctor in my absence?
MRS. HUDSON. Oh, I told him straightaway I was going to do that, sir . . .

> **Exercise 17** Find It in Your Writing Revise a piece of dialogue from your own writing by adding interjections.

> **Exercise 18** Writing Application Write ten sentences using the following interjections. Make sure that you capitalize and punctuate correctly.

1. my	6. whew
2. well	7. goodness
3. oh	8. hurray
4. oops	9. tsk
5. wow	10. amazing

⏱ TIME SAVERS!

🗒 **Answers on Transparency**
Use the Grammar Exercises Answers on Transparencies for Chapter 18 to facilitate correction by students.

💻 **On-Line Exercise Bank**
Have students complete the exercises on computer. The Auto Check feature will grade their work for you!

> **Exercise 18**

Writing Application
Answers will vary. Samples are given.

1. My! You've gotten very tall!
2. Well, I guess we could wait until tomorrow.
3. Oh! Were you talking to me?
4. Oops! I didn't mean to put that there.
5. Wow! Have you ever seen anything so beautiful?
6. Whew! That was a close call!
7. Goodness! How did you manage to make such a mess?
8. Hurray! I knew you'd win the race!
9. Tsk! You really should have told me the truth.
10. Amazing! I can't believe I did so well on that test!

Chapter 18 Chapter Review

GRAMMAR EXERCISES 19–26

Exercise 19 Recognizing **Coordinating Conjunctions** Identify the coordinating conjunctions in the following sentences. Some sentences may contain more than one.

1. Francisco and Michael had to write a report on forensic science, so they decided to visit a police lab.
2. They asked the lab assistant to explain forensic science and the vocabulary that it uses.
3. He told them that a hypothesis is a theory based on observed facts and that it is used to explain evidence.
4. A hypothesis must be proved or disproved through laboratory testing.
5. Evidence is gathered at the crime scene, but it is examined in the lab.
6. Evidence is anything that can prove the guilt or innocence of a suspect.
7. A pathologist is a doctor who specializes in determining the cause of death or disease.
8. Toxicology is the science that studies poisons and their effects.
9. A polygraph is an instrument that measures changes in a person's blood pressure, breathing, heartbeat, and perspiration while being questioned.
10. Many defendants take a polygraph test, yet the results cannot be used as evidence in court.

Exercise 20 Using **Coordinating Conjunctions** Identify the coordinating conjunctions in each sentence. Then, tell which words or groups of words are joined by the conjunction.

1. The boys were eager to learn, so they asked many questions.
2. They learned about magnifying glasses but were more interested in microscopes.
3. They learned that a microscopic look

at cut fibers or other materials can reveal how the cuts were made.
4. Scientists had known about fingerprints for some time, but it wasn't until the late 1800's that police used them to solve crimes.
5. There are three basic fingerprint patterns: loop, arch, and whorl.
6. An eyewitness is a person who actually sees a crime happening and can give a report of it.
7. It was time for the lab assistant to leave, but the boys didn't want to leave.
8. They had learned many new and fascinating things during their visit.
9. The boys asked if they could come back, for they wanted to learn more.
10. Francisco wants to study forensic science, yet he knows it will require work.

Exercise 21 Recognizing **Correlative Conjunctions** Write down the correlative conjunctions and the words or groups of words they join in each sentence below. Then, circle the conjunctions.

1. Students in Mr. Smith's science class were not only assigned to collect samples, but they were also asked to make presentations of their experiences.
2. Class members wondered whether they would find samples or be disappointed.
3. Their presentations could be either oral or written.
4. Both Carlos and Ricardo decided to go camping by the lake to gather samples for their project.
5. The teacher told them to look not only for fossils, but also for arrowheads.
6. They could collect them either separately or as a team.
7. Neither Carlos nor Ricardo had done anything like this before.
8. The boys enjoyed not only the camping but also the challenge. *(continued)*

Chapter Review • **385**

CHAPTER REVIEW

Each of these exercises correlates with a concept in the chapter on conjunctions and interjections, pages 376–384. These exercises may be used for more practice, for reteaching, or for review of the Key Concepts presented.

Answer Key

Exercise 19

1. and, so	6. or
2. and	7. or
3. and	8. and
4. or	9. and
5. but	10. yet

Exercise 20

1. *so* connects *The boys were eager to learn, they asked many questions*
2. *but* connects *learned about magnifying glasses, more interested in microscopes*
3. *or* connects *cut fibers* and *other materials*
4. *but* connects *Scientists had known about fingerprints for some time, it wasn't until the late 1800's that police used them to solve crimes*
5. *and* connects *loop, arch, whorl*
6. *and* connects *sees a crime happening, can give a report of it*
7. *but* connects *It was time for the lab assistant to leave, the boys didn't want to leave*
8. *and* connects *new, fascinating*
9. *for* connects *The boys asked if they could come back, they wanted to learn more*
10. *yet* connects *Francisco wants to study forensic science, he knows it will require work*

Exercise 21

1. (not only) assigned to collect samples, (but also) asked to make presentations
2. (whether) they would find samples (or) be disappointed
3. (either) oral (or) written
4. (Both) Carlos (and) Ricardo
5. (not only) for fossils (but also) for arrowheads
6. (either) separately (or) as a team
7. (Neither) Carlos (nor) Ricardo
8. (not only) the camping (but also) the challenge

Note: items 9 and 10 are on p. 386.

9. (Both) Margaret (and) Juanita
10. (not only) to sketch footprints (but also) to collect fur samples

Exercise 22

1. and—coordinating
2. and—coordinating
3. not only . . . but also—correlative
4. whether . . . or—correlative
5. or—coordinating
6. or—coordinating
7. Both . . . and—correlative
8. and—coordinating
9. and—coordinating
10. Not only . . . but also—correlative

Exercise 23

Conjunctions: and, whether . . . or, and
Interjection: Oh!

Exercise 24

Answers may vary. Samples are given.

1. Gee
2. Wow
3. My
4. Ouch
5. Gosh

Exercise 25

1. whether
2. either
3. Gee!
4. Hey
5. Not only

Exercise 26

Writing Application
When they finish, have students tell whether each is a coordinating or a correlative conjunction.

TIME SAVERS!

Answers on Transparency
Use the Grammar Exercises Answers on Transparencies for Chapter 18 to facilitate correction by students.

On-Line Exercise Bank
Have students complete the exercises on computer. The Auto Check feature will grade their work for you!

Chapter Review Exercises cont'd.

9. Both Margaret and Juanita wanted to go to the mountains for their project.
10. They decided not only to sketch footprints, but also to collect fur samples.

Exercise 22 Classifying
Conjunctions Identify the conjunctions you find in the paragraph. Then, tell whether each conjunction is *coordinating* or *correlative*.

[1] We can learn about past civilizations from studying their burial sites and dwellings. [2] Archaeologists study the remains of ancient human life and collect various samples as well. [3] They specialize not only in finding clues but also in putting the clues together. [4] Using the clues available, archaeologists determine how people lived, whether by hunting or by farming. [5] A stone ax or an arrowhead can provide valuable information. [6] Artifacts—such as a basket full of seeds, a wooden post, or the bones of animals—help the scientists learn something about the physical environment. [7] Both archaeologists and historians work together to create a picture of the past. [8] Historians study writings, and archaeologists study physical remains. [9] Around 1770, Thomas Jefferson uncovered an Indian burial mound and carefully wrote down what was contained in the mound. [10] Not only did he list the items he took from the mound, but he also noted the order in which they were found.

Exercise 23 Identifying
Conjunctions and Interjections Identify the conjunctions and interjections in the following excerpt from *The Dying Detective*.

WATSON. . . . You're sick and as helpless as a child. Whether you like it or not, I'm going to examine you and treat you.
HOLMES. [*Sneering*] If I'm to be forced to

have a doctor, let him at least be someone I've some confidence in.
WATSON. Oh! You . . . After all these years, Holmes, you haven't . . . confidence in me?

Exercise 24 Supplying
Interjections Supply an interjection to complete each sentence.

1. ___?___, forensic science is interesting!
2. ___?___! Did you see that fiber under the microscope?
3. ___?___, it really looks strange.
4. ___?___, my eyes are getting tired from looking through the microscope.
5. ___?___! How do scientists do this hour after hour every day?

Exercise 25 Using Conjunctions
and Interjections Supply a conjunction or an interjection to complete each sentence.

1. Juanita wanted to know ___?___ she should make the plaster casts or collect the fur samples.
2. Their teacher told them to collect their samples ___?___ in the early morning or in the late evening.
3. ___?___ This is an interesting project.
4. ___?___ I think I hear a snake!
5. ___?___ did their class learn from this experience, but they also had fun.

Exercise 26 Writing Application
Write a comparison of two things. Circle the conjunctions you used to connect words and ideas.

Standardized Test Preparation Workshop

Standard English Usage: Conjunctions

Some standardized test questions are designed to measure your mastery of the conventions of English, including the proper use of conjunctions.

The following test item will give you practice in answering these types of questions.

Test Tip

Conjunctions connect related ideas. If an answer choice connects ideas that are unrelated, eliminate it.

Sample Test Item

Directions Read the passage, and choose the letter of the best word or words to complete the sentence.

Sculptor Henry Moore was inspired not only by unusual pebbles, _____ by unusual shells.
  A and also
  B but also
  C and
  D yet

Answer and Explanation

The best answer is *B*. The words *but also* complete the correlative conjunction begun with *not only*.

> **Practice**   **Directions** Read the passage, and choose the letter of the best word or words to complete the sentence.

1 Moore was a great sketch artist _____ he is best known for his sculptures.
  A so
  B and
  C yet
  D but also

2 His sculptures _____ drawings can be seen in museums.
  F yet
  G so
  H and
  J but also

3 He enjoyed nature,_____ he spent much of his time outside.
  A or
  B so
  C whether
  D but also

4 He is known not only for his sketches _____ for his sculpture.
  F yet
  G so
  H and
  J but also

► **Lesson Objectives**

• To use conjunctions to connect ideas meaningfully.

Step-by-Step Teaching Guide

Using Conjunctions

Teaching Resources: Standardized Test Preparation Workbook, pp. 35–36

1. Remind students to read the directions carefully. Sometimes, they may be misled by a question because they haven't carefully read the directions.

2. Have a volunteer identify the conjunction (or part of the conjunction) in the sample sentence. (not only)

3. Ask students what the rest of the correlative must be (but also).

Answer Key

> **Practice 1**

1. C
2. H
3. B
4. J

🖊 **TEST-TAKING TIP**

Tell students that it is important to read the whole sentence before picking a conjunction. Suggest that they look for clues, such as parallel structures or comparison and contrast. Another important clue can be part of a correlative conjunction, since these are consistent (that is, *either* always goes with *or*, etc.) If the answer doesn't jump out at them, suggest that students read the sentence with each suggestion in place, to see whether it makes sense.

CUMULATIVE REVIEW

Answer Key

Exercise A

1. Milky Way: singular, proper; galaxies: plural, common
2. sun: singular, common
3. Supergiants: compound, plural, common; stars: plural, common
4. committee: collective, singular common
5. Ptolemy: singular, proper

Exercise B

1. interrogative, singular
2. personal, plural; personal, singular; indefinite, plural
3. demonstrative, plural; personal, plural
4. demonstrative, plural; personal, plural
5. interrogative, singular

Exercise C

1. vary: action, transitive; expand: action, intransitive; contract: action, intransitive
2. become: linking; can: helping verb; fade: action, intransitive
3. last: action, intransitive; will: helping verb
4. be: linking; may: helping verb
5. say: action, transitive; has: action, transitive

Exercise D

1. adjective; tint
2. adverb; located
3. adjective; mythology
4. adjective; club
5. adverb; represent
6. adjective; stars
7. adjective; group
8. adverb; named
9. adverb; see
10. adjective; light-years

Exercise E

1. of, solar system
2. until, invention; of, telescope; in, seventeenth century
3. at, universities; in, Copenhagen, Leipzig
4. at, night; with, observations; of, stars
5. until, 1601; of, motion

Cumulative Review

PARTS OF SPEECH

Exercise A Classifying Nouns

Identify the underlined nouns in the following sentences as *collective, compound, common* or *proper*, and *singular or plural*.

1. The Milky Way is one of several hundred million galaxies.
2. The sun, the closest star to the Earth, is a typical star.
3. Supergiants are the largest known stars.
4. A committee of astronomers gave numbers to some stars.
5. In the second century A.D., Ptolemy compiled the first catalog of stars.

Exercise B Classifying Pronouns

Label the underlined pronouns in the following sentences *personal, demonstrative, interrogative, indefinite,* and *singular* or *plural.*

1. Who designated stars by Greek letters?
2. Johann Bayer listed them in a star atlas in 1603; it included many that Ptolemy had not cataloged.
3. John Flamsteed listed these stars according to their constellations.
4. Most of our modern catalogs are not like those used earlier; instead, they use copies of photographs.
5. Which of the charts includes the southern sky?

Exercise C Recognizing and Classifying Verbs Write the verbs in the following sentences. Label each *action* or *linking.* Include and identify all helping verbs. Classify action verbs as *transitive* or *intransitive.*

1. Many stars vary their brightness when

they expand and contract.
2. They can become very brilliant and then fade within days.
3. Some stars' cycles will last for years.
4. Most variations in brightness may be invisible to the human eye.
5. Scientists say that even the sun has a cycle of brightness.

Exercise D Recognizing Adjectives and Adverbs Label the underlined words in the following sentences *adjectives* or *adverbs.* Then, write the word each modifies.

1. The star called Rigel in the constellation Orion has a bluish-white tint.
2. Orion is located almost squarely on the celestial equator.
3. The stars form a picture of Orion, a hunter from Greek mythology.
4. He is standing with an uplifted club.
5. Three bright stars accurately represent his belt.
6. To the south, three fainter stars form his sword.
7. Another constellation, Pleiades, is a loose group of almost 3,000 stars.
8. The cluster was initially named by the Greeks after the mythological "Seven Sisters."
9. Observers can sometimes see up to twelve of the stars without a telescope.
10. Pleiades lies 375 light-years from our solar system.

Exercise E Recognizing Prepositions Write the prepositions in the following sentences, and then write the object of the preposition.

1. Tycho Brahe, a Danish astronomer, made measurements of the solar system.

2. This data was the most reliable until the invention of the telescope in the seventeenth century.
3. Brahe studied law and philosophy at universities in Copenhagen and Leipzig.
4. At night, he was busy with his observations of the stars.
5. Johannes Kepler, his assistant until 1601, used Brahe's data to formulate his three laws of planetary motion.

Exercise F Identifying Conjunctions Write the conjunctions in the following sentences and label them *coordinating* or *correlative*.

1. Both North Star and Pole Star are names for the star that roughly marks the direction of the North Pole.
2. Pole Star has been used by sailors, for they needed to find their direction when sailing at night.
3. It is used today for determining latitudes and other measurements.
4. Not only is Polaris the current North Star, but it also is part of the Little Dipper constellation.
5. Polaris is very accurate, but in the future, other stars will point more accurately to the North Pole.

Exercise G Recognizing Interjections Write an interjection that replaces the feeling shown in parentheses in the following sentences.

1. __(surprise)__! Did you see that meteor shower last night?
2. __(hesitation)__, I wasn't sure what that was.
3. __(disappointment)__, did that happen while I was sleeping?
4. __(amazement)__! I couldn't believe my eyes.
5. __(agreement)__, it is a natural event.

Exercise H Identifying All the Parts of Speech Write the part of speech of the underlined words in the following paragraph. Be as specific as possible.

These large comets <u>were</u> first <u>explained</u> by Tycho Brahe. Sir Isaac Newton and <u>Edmund Halley</u> made important observations about comets. The <u>American</u> astronomer Fred Whipple first described comets as a "dirty <u>snowball</u>," a combination of ice and dust. <u>Gee</u>, that doesn't sound very scientific, <u>but</u> it is true. <u>Many</u> of the different comets pass by the Earth. Some are <u>easily</u> visible to the human eye.

Exercise I Revising Sentences Revise each sentence according to the directions in parentheses.

1. Halley's Comet is a famous comet. (Add an adverb that modifies *famous*.)
2. Halley's Comet was discovered by Edmond Halley. (Replace *Halley's Comet* with a pronoun.)
3. Before he made his discovery, people believed that comets traveled at random, with no set path. (Replace *he* with a proper noun.)
4. Halley believed, however, that comets traveled regular patterns. (Add a preposition before *regular*.)
5. Halley's Comet takes a time—approximately seventy-seven years—to travel its orbit. (Add an adjective to modify *time* and another adjective to modify *orbit*.)

Exercise J Writing Application Write a short narrative about a trip into outer space. Underline at least one noun, pronoun, verb, adjective, adverb, preposition, conjunction, and interjection. Then, label the part of speech of each as specifically as possible.

Cumulative Review • 389

Exercise F
1. Both . . . and, correlative
2. for, coordinating
3. and, coordinating
4. Not only . . . but also, correlative
5. but, coordinating

Exercise G
Answers will vary. Samples are given.
1. Hey
2. Um
3. Aw
4. Wow
5. Right

Exercise H
were: helping verb; explained: action verb; Edmond Halley: proper noun; American: proper adjective; snowball: compound noun; Gee: interjection; but: coordinating conjunction; Many: indefinite plural pronoun; easily: adverb

Exercise I
Answers will vary. Samples are given.
1. Halley's Comet is a <u>very</u> famous comet.
2. <u>It</u> was discovered by Edmond Halley.
3. Before <u>Halley</u> made his discovery, people believed that comets traveled at random, with no set path.
4. Halley believed, however, that comets traveled <u>in</u> regular patterns.
5. Halley's Comet takes a <u>long</u> time—approximately seventy-seven years—to travel its <u>regular</u> orbit.

Exercise J
Writing Application
Have students exchange papers with a partner to check each other's work.

Time and Resource Manager

In-Depth Lesson Plan

	LESSON FOCUS	PRINT AND MEDIA RESOURCES
DAY 1	**Subjects and Verbs** Students learn to recognize and use complete subjects and predicates that express a complete thought and do the Hands-On Grammar activity (pp. 392–399).	**Teaching Resources** *Grammar Exercise Workbook*, pp.45–48; *Grammar Exercises Answers on Transparencies*, Ch. 19; *Hands-on Grammar Activity Book*, Ch. 19 *On-Line Exercise Bank*, Section 19.1–2
DAY 2	**Compound Subjects and Verbs** Students learn to identify and use compound subjects and compound verbs (pp. 400–404).	**Teaching Resources** *Grammar Exercise Workbook*, pp.49–50; *Grammar Exercises Answers on Transparency*, Ch. 19 *On-Line Exercise Bank*, Section 19.3
DAY 3	**Imperative and Inverted Subjects** Students learn to recognize imperative and inverted subjects (pp. 405–409).	**Teaching Resources** *Grammar Exercise Workbook*, pp.51–54; *Grammar Exercises Answers on Transparency*, Ch. 19 *On-Line Exercise Bank*, Section 19.4
DAY 4	**Complements** Students learn to identify and use complements in sentences (pp. 410–419).	**Teaching Resources** *Grammar Exercise Workbook*, pp. 55–64; *Grammar Exercises Answers on Transparency*, Ch. 19 *On-Line Exercise Bank*, Section 19.5
DAY 5	**Review and Assess** Students review chapter and demonstrate mastery of use of subjects, predicates and complements (pp. 420–423).	**Teaching Resources** *Formal Assessment*, Ch. 19; *Grammar Exercises Answers on Transparency*, Ch. 19 *On-Line Exercise Bank*, Sections 19.1–5

Accelerated Lesson Plan

	LESSON FOCUS	PRINT AND MEDIA RESOURCES
DAY 1	**Subjects and Predicates** Students cover concepts and usage of subjects, predicates, compound subjects and predicates and imperative subjects as determined by Diagnostic Test (pp. 390–419).	**Teaching Resources** *Grammar Exercise Workbook*, pp.45–54; *Hands-on Grammar Activity Book*, Ch. 19; *Grammar Exercises Answers on Transparencies*, Ch. 19; *On-Line Exercise Bank*, Section 19.1–4
DAY 2	**Complements** Students learn to identify and use complements in sentences as determined by Diagnostic Test (pp. 410–409).	**Teaching Resources** *Grammar Exercise Workbook*, pp. 55–64; *Grammar Exercises Answers on Transparency*, Ch. 19 *On-Line Exercise Bank*, Section 19.5
DAY 3	**Review and Assess** Students review chapter and demonstrate mastery of use of adjectives and adverbs (pp. 420–423).	**Teaching Resources** *Formal Assessment*, Ch. 19; *Grammar Exercises Answers on Transparency*, Ch. 19 *On-Line Exercise Bank* Sections 19.1–5

Options for Adapting Lesson Plans

HOMEWORK
Have students complete any section of the chapter for homework.

FEATURES
Extend coverage with the Grammar in Literature feature (p. 397, 401), and the Standardized Test Preparation Workshop (p. 422).

TECHNOLOGY
Students can use the On-Line Exercise Bank to complete the exercises on computer. The Auto Check feature will grade their work.

INTEGRATED SKILLS COVERAGE

Grammar in Literature
SE pp. 397, 401

Writing
Find It In Your Writing, SE pp. 395, 398, 399, 404, 409, 419
Writing Application SE pp. 395, 399, 404, 409, 419, 421

Reading
Find It In Your Reading, SE pp. 395, 398, 399, 404, 409, 419

Testing Skills
ATE p. 407

Language
Language Highlight, ATE p. 410

Spelling
SE p. 408

Viewing and Representing
Critical Viewing, SE pp. 390, 393, 397, 400, 403, 405, 407, 411, 412, 414

Speaking and Listening
SE p. 413

ASSESSMENT SUPPORT

Standardized Test Preparation SE p. 422; ATE pp. 398, 406
Standardized Test Preparation Workbook, pp. 37–38
Formal Assessment, Ch. 19

MEETING INDIVIDUAL NEEDS

Less Advanced Students ATE pp. 402, 417. See also Ongoing Assessment, pp. 394, 397, 402, 408, 415, 417.
ESL Students ATE p. 413
More Advanced Students ATE p. 415
Bodily/Kinesthetic Learners, ATE p. 406
Verbal/Linguistic Students ATE p. 403

BLOCK SCHEDULING

Pacing Suggestions
For 90-minute Blocks
• Administer the Diagnostic Test to students to determine instructional coverage.
• Have students complete the necessary exercises in class. Use the Hands-on Grammar activity to provide a change of pace.

Professional Development Support
• *How to Manage Instruction in the Block* This teaching Resource provides management and activity suggestions.

MEDIA AND TECHNOLOGY

For the Student
• *On-Line Exercise Bank,* Ch. 19

For the Teacher
• *Resource Pro* **CD-ROM**

WRITING AND GRAMMAR WEB SITE

The Interactive Writing and Grammar Web site provides a wide array of support for students, teachers, and parents. Grammar support includes:

• *On-Line Exercise Bank* with Auto Check scoring
• Diagnostic and assessment support

www.phschool.com

LITERATURE CONNECTIONS

Grammar in Literature selection from *Prentice Hall Literature: Timeless Voices, Timeless Themes,* Bronze:
"Cat on the Go," by James Herriot, SE pp. 397, 401

Critical Viewing

Analyze Students may say the cat's eyes are round. Its fur is soft.

Chapter 19 Basic Sentence Parts

The eight parts of speech are the building blocks of language. Whenever you speak and write, you use these basic units to express ideas. Patterns of words that communicate ideas are called *sentences*.

Not every pattern of words is a sentence. For example, the pattern "Fed Jana cat her" is not a sentence because it does not communicate an idea. The same words in a different pattern can form a sentence when you say, "Jana fed her cat."

This chapter will introduce you to the basic sentence parts and describe how nouns, pronouns, verbs, and adjectives play key roles in sentences.

▲ **Critical Viewing**
In two complete sentences, describe the shape of the cat's eyes and the feel of its fur. [Analyze]

☑ ONGOING ASSESSMENT: Diagnose

If students miss more than one item in each category, direct them to the relevant pages of the text and assign exercises for practice and review.

Basic Sentence Parts	Diagnostic Test Items	Teach	Practice	Section Review	Chapter Review
Skill Check A					
Subjects and Predicates	A 1–5	pp. 392–393 396–398	Ex. 1, 10	Ex. 4, 11–12	Ex. 50
Skill Check B					
Complete Sentences	B 6–10	pp. 392–394	Ex. 2–3	Ex. 5–6	Ex. 51
Skill Check C					
Compound Subjects and Verbs	C 11–15	pp. 400–403	Ex. 16–19	Ex. 20–21	Ex. 52

Diagnostic Test

Directions: Write all answers on a separate sheet of paper.

Skill Check A. Copy each of the following sentences onto your paper. Underline the subject once and the verb twice. Then, draw a vertical line between the complete subject and the complete predicate.

1. Cats make excellent pets.
2. Responsible owners train their cats methodically.
3. The manx is an interesting breed.
4. My sister and I enjoy going to cat shows.
5. The wide variety of cats intrigues and entertains us.

Skill Check B. On your paper, write *sentence* for each group of words below that is a sentence. Write *incomplete* for each group of words below that is not a sentence.

6. Running along the shelf.
7. Although my cat is playful.
8. Since we spend so much time with her and enjoy her company.
9. She plays.
10. Her many playful qualities are charming.

Skill Check C. Each of the following sentences contains a compound subject, a compound verb, or both. On your paper, write the compound subjects and the compound verbs. Label each one a *compound subject* or a *compound verb.*

11. Dogs and cats sometimes fight.
12. Playful cats chase any small moving object and trap it.
13. Adult cats and kittens play together and wrestle with old socks.
14. Hungry cats stand in the kitchen and meow.
15. The gray kitten and its striped mother licked their paws and cleaned their faces.

Skill Check D. Copy each of the following sentences onto your paper. Label the direct objects *DO*, the indirect objects *IO*, the adverbs *ADV*, the prepositions *PREP*, and the objects of prepositions *OP*.

16. Scientists study the leopards, lions, and cheetahs of Africa.
17. These powerful predators fascinate them.
18. Which cats will you study during the next six months?
19. Send me a pamphlet about cats soon.
20. I will also access information about them on the Internet.

Skill Check E. In the following sentences, label the predicate nouns *PN*, the predicate pronouns *PP*, and the predicate adjectives *PA*.

21. The cougar is dangerous.
22. Purring leopards may seem gentle to zoo visitors.
23. Mrs. Gunderson is one of the zoo's animal handlers.
24. It is she who teaches many of the classes.
25. The facility is highly respected and a model for other zoos and wildlife centers.

Skill Check A

1. <u>Cats</u>|<u>make</u> excellent pets.
2. Responsible <u>owners</u>|<u>train</u> their cats methodically.
3. The <u>manx</u>|<u>is</u> an interesting breed.
4. <u>My sister and I</u>|<u>enjoy</u> going to cat shows.
5. The wide <u>variety</u> of cats|<u>intrigues</u> and <u>entertains</u> us.

Skill Check B

6. incomplete
7. incomplete
8. incomplete
9. sentence
10. sentence

Skill Check C

11. dogs and cats—compound subject
12. chase and trap—compound verb
13. cats and kittens—compound subject; play and wrestle—compound verb
14. stand and meow—compound verb
15. kitten and mother—compound subject; licked and cleaned—compound verb

Skill Check D

16. leopards, lions, cheetahs—DO; of—PREP; Africa—OP
17. them—DO
18. cats—DO; during—PREP; months—OP
19. me—IO; pamphlet—DO; about—PREP; cats—OP; soon—ADV
20. also—ADV; information—DO; about—PREP; them—OP; on—PREP; Internet—OP

Skill Check E

21. dangerous—PA
22. gentle—PA
23. one—PP
24. she—PP
25. respected—PA; model—PN

ONGOING ASSESSMENT: Diagnose *continued*

Basic Sentence Parts	Diagnostic Test Items	Teach	Practice	Section Review	Chapter Review
Skill Check D					
Direct and Indirect Objects	D 16–20	pp. 410–415	Ex. 34–39	Ex. 44	Ex. 54–56
Skill Check E					
Predicates	E 21–25	pp. 416–418	Ex. 40–43	Ex. 45	Ex. 54–56
Cumulative Reviews and Applications				Ex. 7–9, 13–15, 22–24, 31–33, 47–49	Ex. 58

Challenge several volunteers to come to the chalkboard and write the shortest complete sentences they can think of. Have the class try to identify any that are not sentences because they do not express a complete thought (*Hello! Yes. Why?*). Underline the subjects and circle the verbs in the complete sentences. Explain that these are the two necessary parts of every complete sentence. If any student has written a one-word command such as *Sit!*, explain that this is a complete sentence because the subject *you* is understood. (Students will learn more about this in Section 19.4, page 406.)

Activate Prior Knowledge

Write the following sentences on the board and ask students to identify what is missing from each one. Then ask them to rewrite each one so that it is a complete sentence.

The dog in the yard.

(no verb; The dog *is* in the yard.)

Is playing happily with string

(no subject; My cat is playing happily with string.)

TEACH

The Two Basic Parts of a Sentence

1. Point out that all subjects are nouns, pronouns, or other words or groups of words that function as such. (Students will learn more about other words that can function as subjects, including verbals, later in the book.) Emphasize, however, that not all nouns or pronouns are subjects.

2. Remind students that linking verbs describe the condition of a subject, and action verbs tell what the subject does or what is done to the subject.

I swim at the lake every day. (action)

I am happy. (linking)

Section 19.1 *The Basic Sentence*

In order to be considered complete sentences, all sentences must have two things: a subject and a verb.

The Two Basic Parts of a Sentence

Every sentence, regardless of its length, must have a subject and a verb.

KEY CONCEPT A **sentence** contains a subject and a verb and expresses a complete thought. ■

The Subject A sentence must have a *subject*. Subjects are usually found at or near the beginning of a sentence. Most subjects are nouns or pronouns.

KEY CONCEPT The **subject** of a sentence is the word or group of words that names the person, place, or thing that performs the action or is described. ■

In the following examples, each subject is underlined.

EXAMPLES: The <u>cat</u> is hungry.
<u>Mrs. Meow</u> broke her dish.
<u>She</u> knows several tricks.

The noun *cat* is the subject in the first sentence. It tells *what* is hungry. In the next sentence, *Mrs. Meow* tells *who* broke her dish. The pronoun *she* in the third sentence also tells *who:* Who knows several tricks? *She* knows.

The Verb As one of the basic parts of a sentence, the verb tells something about a subject.

KEY CONCEPT The **verb** in a sentence tells what the subject does, what is done to the subject, or what the condition of the subject is. ■

In the following examples, the verbs are underlined twice.

EXAMPLES: My cat <u>won</u> a ribbon.
The award <u>was given</u> in a big ceremony.
He <u>seems</u> tired now.

Won tells what *my cat* did. *Was given* explains what was done with *award*. *Seems*, a linking verb, tells something about the condition of *he* by linking the subject to *tired*.

Theme: Cats

In this section, you will learn about subjects and verbs and how sentences form complete thoughts. The examples and exercises in this section are about domestic and wild cats.

Cross-Curricular Connection: Science

⏱ TIME AND RESOURCE MANAGER

Resources
Print: Grammar Exercise Workbook, pp. 45–46
Technology: On-Line Exercise Bank, Section 19.1

In-Depth Coverage	Accelerated Pace
• Work through all key concepts, pp. 392–394. • Assign and review Exercises 1–3.	• Assign pp. 392–394 for independent student review. • Assign Section Review Exercises 4–6.

> **Exercise 1** Identifying Subjects and Verbs Copy each of the following sentences onto your paper. Underline the subject once and the verb twice.

EXAMPLE: The tiny <u>kitten</u> <u>cries</u> for its mother.

1. Cat associations sponsor cat shows.
2. These events attract many cat lovers.
3. Many owners exhibit their cats.
4. Hundreds of cats compete for a small number of prizes.
5. Many expert judges are at the show.
6. Each judge works independently.
7. Each association has its own set of rules.
8. Awards are given to ten winners in each category.
9. The event lasts all day.
10. Winners receive large ribbons.

Using Subjects and Verbs to Express Complete Thoughts

Every basic sentence must express a complete thought.

> **KEY CONCEPT** A group of words with a subject and a verb expresses a complete thought if it can stand by itself and still make sense. ■

COMPLETE THOUGHT: The <u>kitten</u> <u>sleeps</u> in the basket.

This example is a complete sentence because it expresses a *complete thought.*

INCOMPLETE THOUGHT: In the basket in the hall.

This incomplete thought contains two prepositional phrases. In this case, the phrases can become a sentence only after *both* a subject and a verb are added to them.

COMPLETE THOUGHT: The ^S <u>kittens</u> ^V <u>are</u> in the basket in the hall.

With a subject and a verb, this group of words makes sense. It can stand by itself as a sentence.

In grammar, incomplete thoughts are often called *fragments.*

More Practice

On-line
Exercise Bank
• Section 19.1
Grammar Exercise
Workbook
• pp. 45–46

▼ Critical Viewing
What is the subject of this picture? What verb could you use with that subject to express a complete thought about the picture? **[Analyze]**

The Basic Sentence • 393

Step-by-Step Teaching Guide

Using Subjects and Verbs to Express Complete Thoughts

1. Ask a volunteer to read aloud the key concept statement. Review with students that the subject is what the sentence is about, and the verb expresses what the subject is or does.
2. Tell students not to be misled by the length of a sentence. *I ran* is a complete thought and is a sentence. *Has four feet, a long tail, and striped fur* is not a complete thought; it has no subject, and is thus a sentence fragment.
3. Point out that, though a sentence can be as short as two words, a subject and verb do not guarantee a sentence. For example, "If he runs" has a subject and verb, but does not express a complete thought.

Critical Viewing

Analyze Most students will suggest that *cats* or *three cats* should be the subject of the sentence. Expect more variation in the verbs they choose.

Answers will vary. Possible answers are shown.

1. We saw a pride of lions pictured in the magazine.
2. A family of kittens that are born together is called a litter.
3. The kittens were playfully pouncing on each other.
4. The old lion had a large, beautiful mane.
5. Tigers and cheetahs can run very fast.
6. Many zoo animals are no longer kept in cages.
7. These zoo animals enjoy natural habitats.
8. Visitors can ride monorails through some large animal parks.
9. They can see the lions basking in the sun.
10. Photographing the animals is fun.

Exercise 3

Answers will vary. Sample sentences are given.

1. sentence
2. The cat's long <u>whiskers</u> <u>help</u> it judge the width of a space.
3. sentence
4. Our <u>cat</u> constantly <u>grooms</u> its fur.
5. sentence
6. All <u>cats</u> <u>have</u> remarkable night vision.
7. <u>Cats</u> <u>are</u> popular household pets in cities.
8. <u>We</u> <u>found</u> a litter of kittens.
9. The <u>cat</u> <u>chases</u> a ball of yarn.
10. sentence

19.1

▶ **Exercise 2** Correcting Incomplete Thoughts None of the following groups of words expresses a complete thought. On your paper, correct each one by adding the punctuation and words needed to make a basic sentence. Each group of words may come at the beginning, middle, or end of the sentence.

EXAMPLE: the sailors on the ship
ANSWER: The sailors on the ship found a stowaway cat.

1. a pride of lions
2. called a litter
3. playfully pouncing on each other
4. a large, beautiful mane
5. run very fast
6. no longer kept in cages
7. enjoy natural habitats
8. monorails through some large animal parks
9. lions basking in the sun
10. photographing the animals

▶ **Exercise 3** Recognizing Sentences Some of the numbered items below are sentences; the others are incomplete thoughts. If a group of words is a sentence, write *sentence* on your paper. If a group of words expresses an incomplete thought, add the words needed to make a sentence. Underline the subject once and the verb twice in each new sentence.

EXAMPLE: The kittens in the woodpile.
ANSWER: The <u>kittens</u> <u>hid</u> in the woodpile.

1. Cats have soft paws and sharp claws.
2. The cat's long whiskers.
3. The body of a cat is more flexible than a dog's.
4. Grooms its fur.
5. Cats purr.
6. Remarkable night vision.
7. Popular household pets.
8. A litter of kittens.
9. Chases a ball.
10. Finding warm places, cats sleep.

On-line
Exercise Bank
• Section 19.1
Grammar Exercise
Workbook
• pp. 45–46

⏱ TIME SAVERS!

🖺 **Answers on Transparency**
Use the Grammar Exercises Answers on Transparencies for Chapter 19 to facilitate correction by students.

🖥 **On-Line Exercise Bank**
Have students complete the exercises on computer. The Auto Check feature will grade their work for you!

✓ ONGOING ASSESSMENT: Monitor and Reinforce

If students miss more than two items in Exercises 1–3, refer them to the following for additional practice.

In the Textbook	Print Resources	Technology
Section Review, Ex. 4–6, p. 395	Grammar Exercise Workbook, pp. 45–46	On-Line Exercise Bank, Section 19.1

Section 19.1 Section Review

GRAMMAR EXERCISES 4–9

Exercise 4 **Recognizing Subjects and Verbs** Copy each of the following sentences onto your paper. Underline the subject once and the verb twice.

1. The lion has a most distinctive face.
2. One can distinguish the male lion from the female lion by the male's mane.
3. The mane makes the male lion appear more threatening.
4. Only mature males develop manes.
5. The lion's frightening roar adds to its fierce presence.
6. Lions are highly social animals.
7. They live in groups known as prides.
8. Unlike most other cats, lions hunt their prey in groups.
9. Many other animals try to run from lions.
10. Lions are counted among the animal kingdom's mightiest hunters.

Exercise 5 **Correcting Incomplete Thoughts** Rewrite the numbered items below, adding any words needed to make each fragment a complete sentence.

1. bring companionship to their owners
2. all young cats that like to play
3. live for ten to twenty years
4. although indoor cats may be healthy
5. spend much time hunting for food

Exercise 6 **Proofreading for Complete Sentences** If a group of words in the following list is a sentence, write *sentence* on your paper. If a group of words expresses an incomplete thought, add the words needed to make a sentence. Underline the subject once and the verb twice.

1. Cats depend on their highly developed senses.

2. Excellent sense of smell.
3 They see well.
4. Can see better at night.
5. Their padded paws make it possible to surprise their quarry.
6. Rely on their acute hearing.
7. Detects high-pitched sounds.
8. Its funnellike outer ears.
9. Their ears aid cats' survival.
10. Hearing loss could put a cat at risk.

Exercise 7 **Find It in Your Reading** Tell whether each underlined section of this excerpt from "Cat on the Go" expresses a complete thought.

(1) The upturned face had an anxious look. (2) I went down the long flights of steps two at a time (3) and when I arrived slightly breathless on the ground floor (4) Tristan beckoned me through (5) to the consulting room at the back of the house.

Exercise 8 **Find It in Your Writing** Choose a piece from your writing portfolio. Underline each subject once and each verb twice in the sentences of the first paragraph. Note that some sentences may have more than one subject and verb.

Exercise 9 **Writing Application** Write a description of an animal. When you are finished, underline the subject once and the verb twice in each sentence. Proofread your paper to eliminate any fragments by adding words to the sentence or connecting the group of words to another sentence. Some of your sentences may have more than one subject and verb.

Section Review • 395

ASSESS

Section Review

Each of these exercises correlates to a concept covered in the section on basic sentences, pages 392–394. The exercises may be used for more practice, for reteaching, or for review of the Key Concepts presented. Answers for all chapter exercises are available in *Grammar Exercises Answers on Transparencies* in your teaching resources.

Answer Key

Exercise 4

1. The <u>lion</u> <u>has</u> a most distinctive face.
2. <u>One</u> <u>can distinguish</u> the male lion from the female lion by the male's mane.
3. The <u>mane</u> <u>makes</u> the male lion appear more threatening.
4. Only mature <u>males</u> <u>develop</u> manes.
5. The lion's frightening <u>roar</u> <u>adds</u> to its fierce presence.
6. <u>Lions</u> <u>are</u> highly social animals.
7. <u>They</u> <u>live</u> in groups known as prides.
8. Unlike most other cats, <u>lions</u> <u>hunt</u> their prey in groups.
9. Many other <u>animals</u> <u>try</u> to run from lions.
10. <u>Lions</u> <u>are counted</u> among the animal kingdom's mightiest hunters.

Exercise 5

Answers will vary. Sample sentences are shown.

1. Pets bring companionship to their owners.
2. All young cats that like to play are appealing.
3. Most cats live for ten to twenty years.
4. Although indoor cats may be healthy, all cats should get fresh air sometimes.
5. Well-fed pet cats don't spend much time hunting for food.

Exercise 6

Answers will vary. Sample sentences are given.

1. sentence
2. All <u>cats</u> <u>have</u> an excellent sense of smell.
3. sentence
4. <u>Cats</u> <u>can see</u> better at night.
5. sentence
6. Like many wild animals, <u>cats</u> <u>rely</u> on their acute hearing.

continued

Answer Key continued

7. The cat's <u>ear</u> <u>detects</u> high-pitched sounds.
8. <u>It</u> <u>uses</u> its funnellike outer ears to channel sound.
9. sentence
10. sentence

Exercise 7

Find It in Your Reading
1. complete
2. complete
3. incomplete
4. complete
5. incomplete

Exercise 8

Find It in Your Writing
You may want to have students work with partners to check each other's work. Students should identify the subjects and verbs in their writing.

Exercise 9

Writing Application
Students can proofread a partner's description to eliminate any sentence fragments and to check that all subjects and verbs are underlined. Students should write complete sentences and identify subjects and verbs.

395

Interest GRABBER Challenge students to compose a very long sentence. Start with a short sentence, such as *I play.* Go around the room, having students add to the sentence, and write their additions on the chalkboard. For example: I play in the park on sunny days, but if it rains I play indoors until the rain stops , and then I go outside. Tell students that they will learn to classify all words in this sentence into two sentence parts.

Activate Prior Knowledge

Write the following sentence on the board: *My grandmother's gray cat chases the birds outside.* Ask students to identify the subject and the verb. Underline and draw a vertical line between the two words. Then ask students whether they know what function the other words in this sentence serve. Guide them to see that all the words to the left of the line are related to the subject *cat,* and all the words to the right are related to the verb *chases.*

TEACH

Step-by-Step Teaching Guide

Complete Subjects and Predicates

1. Help students differentiate between the simple subject/predicate and the complete subject/predicate. A simple subject is usually just one word. A simple predicate is a verb or verb phrase. Complete subjects and predicates include all the words that modify the simple subjects and predicates.

2. Warn students that introductory phrases set off by commas often belong to the predicate rather than the subject. When in doubt, students should try to identify the word an introductory phrase modifies. If it modifies the verb, it is part of the predicate; if not, it is part of the subject.

    As he talked, my thoughts drifted back to the last time we had met.

3. *As he talked* modifies the simple predicate *drifted,* not the subject, *my thoughts,* so it is part of the complete predicate.

Complete Subjects and Predicates

Have you ever seen tiles laid on a floor? First, a line is drawn down the center of the room. One tile is placed to the left of the line, and another is placed to the right. Then, more tiles are added in the same way: one to the left, and one to the right.

Imagine that the first tile on the left is a subject and the first tile on the right is a verb. You would then have a subject and a verb separated by a vertical line, as shown in the example:

EXAMPLE: Fur | flew.

Now, in the same way that you would add a few more tiles if you were tiling a floor, add a few more words:

EXAMPLE: Ginger fur | flew through the air.

At this point, you could add still more words:

EXAMPLE: Oscar's ginger fur | flew through the air.

The center line is important in laying tiles. It is just as important in dividing a sentence into two parts. All the words to the left of the line in the preceding examples are part of the *complete subject.* (The main noun in the complete subject, *fur,* is often called the *simple subject.*)

▶ **KEY CONCEPT** The **complete subject** of a sentence consists of the subject and any words related to it. ∎

As the examples above show, the complete subject may be just one word—*fur*—or several words—*Oscar's ginger fur.*

All the words to the right of the line in the preceding examples are part of the *complete predicate.* (The verb *flew,* or a verb phrase such as *had flown,* on the other hand, is often called the *simple predicate.*)

▶ **KEY CONCEPT** The **complete predicate** of a sentence consists of the verb and any words related to it. ∎

As the examples show, a complete predicate may be just the verb itself or the verb and several other words.

Theme: Cats

In this section, you will learn about complete subjects and predicates. The examples and exercises in this section are about cats in different parts of the world.

Cross-Curricular Connection: Science

Learn More

To review verbs, see Chapter 15.

⏱ TIME AND RESOURCE MANAGER

Resources
Print: Grammar Exercise Workbook, pp. 47–48; Hands-on Grammar Activity Book, Chapter 19
Technology: On-Line Exercise Bank, Section 19.2

In-Depth Coverage	Accelerated Pace
• Work through all key concepts, pp. 396–398. • Assign and review Exercise 10. • Read and discuss Grammar in Literature, p. 397. • Read and discuss Hands-on Grammar Activity, p. 398.	• Assign pp. 396–398 for independent student review. • Assign Review Exercise 11–12.

GRAMMAR IN LITERATURE

from Cat on the Go
James Herriot

In the following excerpt from James Herriot's "Cat on the Go," the complete subjects are underlined once, the complete predicates twice. The simple subjects are shown in blue; the verbs are shown in red.

He walked over and opened the door and our Oscar strode in with all his old grace and majesty. He took one look at Helen and leaped onto her lap. With a cry of delight she put down her cup and stroked the beautiful fur.

▶ **More Practice**

On-line
Exercise Bank
• Section 19.2
Grammar Exercise
Workbook
• pp. 47–48

▶ **Exercise 10** Recognizing Complete Subjects and Complete Predicates Copy each of the following sentences onto your paper. Underline the simple subject once and the verb twice. Then, draw a vertical line between the complete subject and the complete predicate.

EXAMPLE: The cat with the blue eyes | is a Siamese.

1. Cats have become very popular house pets over the years.
2. Leonardo da Vinci included cats in his work.
3. Several popular comic strips feature feline characters.
4. The first domestic cats in North America arrived with the colonists.
5. At one time, some people in Thailand and China worshiped cats as deities.
6. *Alice's Adventures in Wonderland* introduced the Cheshire cat.
7. Cat lovers of all ages collect cats of all kinds.
8. Phoenician sailors traded cats for other treasures.
9. The Renaissance was the golden age of cats.
10. Images of cats appeared on many Greek coins in the fifth century.

▼ Critical Viewing
Kitten waits. Add details to this simple subject and verb to form a sentence about *why* or *for what* the kitten waits.
[Draw Conclusions]

Complete Subjects and Predicates • 397

☑ **ONGOING ASSESSMENT: Monitor and Reinforce**

If students miss more than two items in Exercise 10, refer them to the following for additional practice:

In the Textbook	Print Resources	Technology
Section Review, Ex. 11–12, p. 399	Grammar Exercise Workbook, pp. 47–48; Hands-on Grammar Activity Book, Chapter 19	On-Line Exercise Bank, Section 19.2

Grammar in Literature

1. Have a volunteer read the excerpt. Have students explain how they recognize simple and complete subjects and predicates.

2. Point out that each sentence has a compound verb. Have volunteers identify each one. Tell students they will learn more about compound verbs in Section 19.3.

Conecting With Literature

Students can read the complete "Cat on the Go" in *Prentice Hall Literature: Timeless Voices, Timeless Themes,* Bronze.

Answer Key

▶ **Exercise 10**

1. Cats|have become very popular house pets over the years.
2. Leonardo da Vinci|included cats in his work.
3. Several popular comic strips| feature feline characters.
4. The first domestic cats in North America|arrived with the colonists.
5. Some people in Thailand and China| worshiped cats as deities [At one time]. (You may wish to explain to students that "at one time" is an adverb phrase and actually modifies the predicate. This will be covered in greater depth later.)
6. *Alice's Adventures in Wonderland*| introduced the Cheshire cat.
7. Cat lovers of all ages|collect cats of all kinds.
8. Phoenician sailors|traded cats for other treasures.
9. The Renaissance|was the golden age of cats.
10. Images of cats|appeared on many Greek coins in the fifth century.

Critical Viewing

Draw Conclusions Students may use physical descriptions of the kitten and suggest that it is waiting for food, its owner, or perhaps a mouse.

Sentence Part Flip Book

Teaching Resources: Hands-on Grammar Activity Book, Chapter 19

1. Explain to students that even nonsensical sentences are sentences. For example: *The little striped cat sang and danced very well* has a subject and predicate, so it is a sentence.

2. Encourage students to change their subjects or predicates so that singular or plural subjects have the correct form of the verb in the predicate.

Find It in Your Reading

Suggest that students first concentrate on finding sentences in which the complete subject precedes the complete predicate. As they become more proficient, they can recognize sentences in which parts of the predicate precede the subject.

Find It in Your Writing

Most students will tend to write in subject-verb order. Encourage them to look for sentences with variety in their work.

19.2

Hands-on Grammar

Sentence Part Flip Book

To explore the way subjects and predicates function, create a sentence parts flip book. Alone or with a partner, create two sets of index cards. On the first set, write the part of a sentence that tells the person, place, or thing that does the action, including all the adjectives, adverbs, phrases, and clauses that rename or describe the noun.

EXAMPLE: The cat with the orange stripe on its head

On the second set of cards, write actions or conditions.

EXAMPLE: wants us to feed it.

After you have created six or seven cards for each set, label a long, narrow strip of posterboard as shown.

Use a hole punch to put a hole in the top center of each card. Use a paper fastener to attach each set to the appropriate end of the posterboard strip. Attach the cards loosely enough so that you can swivel each card away to reveal the card beneath. Experiment with different combinations of cards to create different sentences with different complete subjects and complete predicates. If you used a wide variety of nouns, verbs, and modifiers, some of your sentences should be very humorous. No matter how silly the sentence, the subject indicates the doer of the action. The complete subject can contain a verb, as long as the verb is not the main action being performed by the subject in the sentence.

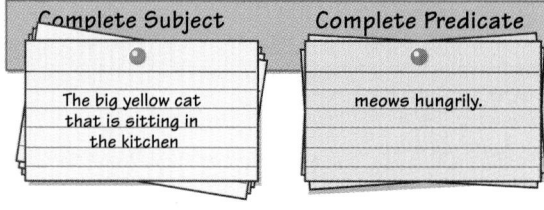

Find It in Your Reading Choose several sentences from a short story, and add them to your flip book. You may need to reorder some words to get all the words of the complete predicate on one card.

Find It in Your Writing Review your portfolio, and choose several sentences to add to the flip book. If necessary, reorder the words to get all the words of the complete predicate on one card.

398 • Basic Sentence Parts

✏️ STANDARDIZED TEST PREPARATION WORKSHOP

Grammar and Usage Some standardized test questions measure students' ability to recognize appropriate sentence construction. Share the following example with students:

My parents took me on a trip to France. And my brother, when I was ten years old.

Choose the letter of the best way to rewrite this.

A My parents took me and my brother on a trip to France. When I was ten years old.

B When I was ten years old, my parents took me and my brother on a trip to France.

C When I was ten years old. My parents took me and my brother on a trip to France.

D Correct as is

The correct choice is item **B**. It combines the clause *when I was ten years old* to form a complete sentence. The other choices merely change the order of the clause.

Section 19.2 *Section Review*

GRAMMAR EXERCISES 11–15

Exercise 11 Identifying Complete Subjects and Predicates Copy each of the following sentences onto your paper. Underline the subject once and the verb twice. Then, draw a vertical line between the complete subject and the complete predicate.

1. Leopards are members of the family of big cats.
2. The Latin name for the cat family is *Felidae.*
3. *Panthera pardus* is the Latin name for the leopard.
4. Leopards are good tree climbers.
5. They may be found in Africa and Asia.
6. The habitat of the Amur leopard is found in Korea.
7. The leopard's body is specifically designed to survive cold winters.
8. Its pale or yellowish-brown coat features widely spaced dark brown spots.
9. Its fur changes from a deep reddish yellow in the summer to a lighter shade in the winter.
10. An average adult female weighs from 62 to 132 pounds.

Exercise 12 Writing Sentences With Complete Subjects and Predicates Develop each item into a complete subject and predicate by adding details to the subject and verb. The first word of each of the following pairs is a noun that can be used as a subject. The second word is a verb.

	NOUN	VERB
1.	leopard	raced
2.	cougar	climbed
3.	cat	grooms
4.	antelope	escaped
5.	speed	helped

Exercise 13 Find It in Your Reading Rewrite each underlined section of this excerpt from James Herriot's "Cat on the Go." Then, draw a vertical line between the complete subject and the complete predicate. Finally, underline the simple subject once and the simple verb twice.

In this passage, the veterinarian Herriot and one of his partners struggle to save a cat's life.

Even now, when we are both around the sixty mark, <u>he often talks to me about the cat</u> he has had for many years. It is a typical relationship—<u>they tease each other unmercifully</u>—but it is based on real affection.

"It's no good, Triss," I said gently. "It's got to be done." I reached for the syringe but <u>something in me rebelled against plunging a needle into that mutilated body</u>. Instead I pulled a fold of the blanket over the cat's head.

Exercise 14 Find It in Your Writing Review a piece of writing from your portfolio. Choose several sentences, and identify the simple subject and the simple predicate in each. You may find that some sentences have more than one part, each containing a simple subject and a simple predicate.

Exercise 15 Writing Application Describe an animal that would make a good pet for your area. Identify the simple subject and simple predicate in each of your sentences. You may find that some sentences have more than one part, each containing a simple subject and a simple predicate.

Section Review • **399**

ASSESS

Section Review

Each of these exercises correlates to a concept covered in the section on basic subjects and predicates, pages 396–398. The exercises may be used for more practice, for reteaching, or for review of the Key Concepts presented. Answers for all chapter exercises are available in *Grammar Exercises Answers on Transparencies* in your teaching resources.

Answer Key

Exercise 11

1. <u>Leopards</u>|<u>are</u> members of the family of big cats.
2. The Latin <u>name</u> for the cat family| <u>is</u> *Felidae.*
3. <u>*Panthera pardus*</u>|<u>is</u> the Latin name for the leopard.
4. <u>Leopards</u>|<u>are</u> good tree climbers.
5. <u>They</u>|<u>may be found</u> in Africa and Asia.
6. The <u>habitat</u> of the Amur leopard| <u>is found</u> in Korea.
7. The leopard's <u>body</u>|<u>is</u> specifically <u>designed</u> to survive cold winters.
8. Its pale or yellowish-brown <u>coat</u>| <u>features</u> widely spaced dark brown spots.
9. Its <u>fur</u>|<u>changes</u> from a deep reddish yellow in the summer to a lighter shade in the winter.
10. An average adult <u>female</u>|<u>weighs</u> from 62 to 132 pounds.

Exercise 12

Answers will vary. Sample answers are given.

1. The leopard raced along the ground after the herd of zebras.
2. The cougar climbed to a wide low branch and stretched out for a nap.
3. The big cat grooms her cubs by licking their fur into place.
4. The terrified antelope escaped from the lion by leaping over some rocks.
5. The antelope's speed helped it get away.

Exercise 13

Find It in Your Reading

1. <u>he</u>| often <u>talks</u> to me about the cat
2. <u>they</u>|<u>tease</u> each other unmercifully
3. <u>something</u> in me|<u>rebelled</u> against plunging a needle into that mutilated body

continued

Answer Key continued

Exercise 14

Find It in Your Writing
You may want to have students work in pairs to complete this exercise. Pairs can work together to identify simple subjects and predicates in their own writing.

Exercise 15

Writing Application
When students have finished writing, have them trade their descriptions with a partner to check that they have correctly identified the simple subjects and predicates.

Compound Subjects and Compound Verbs

Some sentences have more than one subject. Some have more than one verb.

Recognizing Compound Subjects

A sentence containing more than one subject is said to have a *compound subject*.

▶ **KEY CONCEPT** A **compound subject** is two or more subjects that have the same verb and are joined by a conjunction such as *and* or *or*. ■

In the examples in the chart, the parts of the compound subject are underlined once. The verbs are underlined twice.

SENTENCES WITH COMPOUND SUBJECTS
Cats and kittens are popular as pets.
She and I will feed the cat.
Cats, dogs and other pets can learn to live together.

Theme: Cats

In this section, you will learn about compound subjects and verbs. The examples and exercises in this section tell more about cats.

Cross-Curricular Connection: Science

✿ Grammar and Style Tip

When using a compound subject, make sure the verb agrees in number with the subject. For instance, *My cat likes tuna* has a single subject: *cat.* Here's the same sentence with a plural subject: *My cat and my dog like tuna.*

◀ Critical Viewing Use a compound subject in a sentence describing the unusual features of this cat. [Describe]

⏱ TIME AND RESOURCE MANAGER

Resources
Print: Grammar Exercise Workbook, pp. 49–50
Technology: On-Line Exercise Bank, Section 19.3

In-Depth Coverage	Accelerated Pace
• Work through all key concepts, pp. 400–403. • Assign and review Exercises 16–18. • Read and discuss Grammar in Literature, p. 401.	• Assign pp. 400–403 for independent student review. • Assign Review Exercises 20–21.

> **Exercise 16** Recognizing Compound Subjects Each of
the following sentences contains a compound subject. Copy
the sentences onto your paper, and underline the simple subjects that make up each compound subject.

EXAMPLE: <u>Manx</u> and <u>Siamese</u> are two domestic cat breeds.

1. Indoor cats and outdoor cats require lots of attention.
2. A cat and her kittens should be fed a high-quality commercial cat food daily.
3. Food and water should always be put in the same place.
4. A litter box or pet door should be accessible to the cat.
5. People food and chemicals should be kept out of a cat's
   reach.
6. Fleas and mites can cause irritation to cats.
7. Dogs and small children can harm a cat.
8. Loose fur and dirt should be removed every week with a
   brush.
9. Toys, treats, and a scratching post help keep cats happy.
10. Cats and humans can be great friends.

> **More Practice**

On-line
Exercise Bank
• Section 19.3
Grammar Exercise
Workbook
• pp. 49–50

GRAMMAR IN
LITERATURE

from **Cat on the Go**
James Herriot

*Notice how the author has used compound subjects (in
blue) and compound verbs (in red) in this passage to name
people and show actions.*

"Well, I reckon I'd better leave 'im with you. You'll be going
to put him out of his misery. There's nothing anybody can
do about . . . about that?"

I *shrugged* and *shook* my head. The girl's eyes filled with
tears; she *stretched* out a hand and *touched* the emaciated
animal, then *turned* and *walked* quickly to the door.

"Thanks again, Marjorie," I called after the retreating
back. "And don't worry—we'll look after him."

In the silence that followed, *Tristan* and *I* looked down at
the shattered animal. . . .

Compound Subjects and Compound Verbs • 401

Answer Key

> **Exercise 16**

1. <u>Indoor cats</u> and <u>outdoor cats</u>
   require lots of attention.
2. A <u>cat</u> and her <u>kittens</u> should be
   fed a high-quality commercial
   cat food daily.
3. <u>Food</u> and <u>water</u> should always
   be put in the same place.
4. A <u>litter box</u> or <u>pet door</u> should
   be accessible to the cat.
5. <u>People food</u> and <u>chemicals</u>
   should be kept out of a cat's
   reach.
6. <u>Fleas</u> and <u>mites</u> can cause
   irritation to cats.
7. <u>Dogs</u> and small <u>children</u> can
   harm a cat.
8. Loose <u>fur</u> and <u>dirt</u> should be
   removed every week with a
   brush.
9. <u>Toys</u>, <u>treats</u>, and a <u>scratching
   post</u> help keep cats happy.
10. <u>Cats</u> and <u>humans</u> can be great
    friends.

Step-by-Step Teaching Guide

Grammar in Literature

1. Ask students to identify the
   compound subject in the
   literature model. (Tristan and I)
   Ask how students know this is a
   compound subject. (The two
   parts are joined by the word *and*;
   both parts share the verb *looked*.)

2. Point out the red text that
   identifies the compound verbs
   in the second paragraph. Ask
   students whether they can
   guess what a compound verb is.
   (multiple verbs showing actions
   performed by a subject)

More About the Writer

James Herriot was the pen name of
James Alfred Wight. Wight became a
veterinarian when he was only
twenty-four, after serving in the Royal
Air Force during World War II. During
the 1960s, he began writing a book
about his life as a veterinarian in a
Yorkshire village. The books he wrote
under the name James Herriot have
sold millions of copies, and a British
television series was based on them.

Recognizing Compound Verbs

1. Ask students to describe, in their own words, how compound verbs are similar to compound subjects (more than one item joined by a conjunction).

2. Point out in the chart that the verbs in a compound are not always right next to each other.

3. Ask students to define *verb phrases* and give an example (a verb that is made up of several words, a main verb plus helping verbs, such as *might have been handled* or *can be trained*).

4. Explain that, in addition to sharing subjects, compound verbs often share helping verbs. For example, in the sentence *The cat will jump and play*, the two verbs share the helping verb *will*– the cat will jump and the cat will play.

Answer Key

▶ **Exercise 17**

1. The cat <u>bites</u> and <u>shreds</u> with its teeth rather than chewing, as humans do.
2. The cat <u>uses</u> its senses and <u>depends</u> on them to survive and adapt in the environment.
3. The cat <u>tests</u> obstacles and <u>senses</u> changes in the environment through its whiskers.
4. The cat <u>tears</u> meat from bones, <u>laps</u> liquids, and <u>grooms</u> itself with its tongue.
5. The cat <u>can hear</u> a wide range of sounds and <u>focus</u> on them.

Customize for
Less Advanced Students

Students who have trouble understanding compound subjects and verbs can draw arrows from each part of a compound verb to its subject, and from each part of a compound subject to its verb. Students can use the sentences in Exercises 16 and 17 for practice. They will see that in each case, multiple arrows all arrive at the same point(s).

19.3

Recognizing Compound Verbs

Just as sentences can have compound subjects, they can have compound verbs. Compound verbs are also joined by conjunctions.

▶ **KEY CONCEPT** A **compound verb** is two or more verbs that have the same subject and are joined by a conjunction such as *and* or *or*. ■

In the following chart, the parts of the compound verbs are underlined twice. The subjects are underlined once.

SENTENCES WITH COMPOUND VERBS
<u>Kittens</u> <u>sleep</u>, <u>eat</u>, and <u>play</u>.
<u>I</u> have to <u>feed</u> the cat and <u>walk</u> the dog.
The <u>cat</u> <u>yawned</u>, <u>settled</u> into the blanket, and <u>fell</u> asleep.

Sometimes a sentence will have both a compound subject and a compound verb.

EXAMPLE: The <u>house</u> and the <u>garden</u> <u>face</u> the lake and <u>are protected</u> by hedges.

▶ **Exercise 17** Recognizing Compound Verbs Each of the following sentences contains a compound verb. Copy the sentences onto your paper, and draw two lines under the verbs that make up each compound verb.

EXAMPLE: The kitten <u>crawled</u> out of the box and <u>explored</u> the garage.

1. The cat bites and shreds with its teeth rather than chewing, as humans do.
2. The cat uses its senses and depends on them to survive in the environment.
3. The cat tests obstacles and senses changes in the environment through its whiskers.
4. The cat tears meat from bones, laps liquids, and grooms itself with its tongue.
5. The cat can hear a wide range of sounds and focus on them.

▶ **More Practice**

On-line
Exercise Bank
• Section 19.3
Grammar Exercise
Workbook
• pp. 49–50

☑ ONGOING ASSESSMENT: Monitor and Reinforce

If students miss more than two items in Exercises 16–18, refer them to the following for additional practice.

In the Textbook	Print Resources	Technology
Section Review, Ex. 20, p. 404	Grammar Exercise Workbook, pp. 49–50	On-Line Exercise Bank, Section 19.3

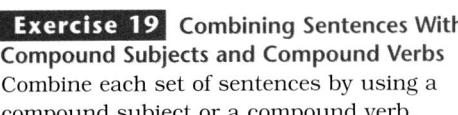

Exercise 18 Recognizing Compound Subjects and Compound Verbs Each of the following sentences contains a compound subject, a compound verb, or both. On your paper, write the compound subjects and the compound verbs. Then, label each one *compound subject* or *compound verb.*

1. For each domestic breed, a set of rules describes the ideal cat and mentions its faults.
2. The Manx, Russian blue, and Siamese began as naturally occurring varieties of domestic cats.
3. Curly-coated Rex breeds and the tailless Manx were developed and perfected by selective breeding.
4. Proper grooming and quality care are mandatory for all breeds of cats.
5. Bookstores and local humane societies sell or give away educational materials about proper cat care.
6. Fatal feline diseases and parasites are found frequently in the stray cat population.
7. Individuals and organizations work to reduce the stray cat population.
8. Declawed cats and kittens should not go outside unless confined to a covered enclosure.
9. Sometimes, outdoor cats have been struck by a car, poisoned by common pesticides, or injured by other animals.
10. However, outside cats hunt small animals, interact with other cats, and get plenty of exercise.

Exercise 19 Combining Sentences With Compound Subjects and Compound Verbs Combine each set of sentences by using a compound subject or a compound verb.

1. A cat's coat protects its skin. The coat also provides insulation.
2. The outercoat is one part of the cat's coat. The undercoat is the other part of the cat's coat.
3. The color of the coat varies among cats. The length of the coat also varies. The texture of the coat varies, too.
4. A cat's whiskers help it feel its way in the dark. A cat's whiskers can help it detect changes in wind direction.
5. The sense of smell is better in cats than in humans. The sense of hearing is better in cats than in humans.

▼ **Critical Viewing** What two things would you have to do in order to photograph a cat in such a stance? Explain in a sentence with a compound verb. **[Relate]**

Compound Subjects and Compound Verbs • **403**

Section Review

Each of these exercises correlates to a concept covered in the section on compound subjects and verbs, pages 400–403. The exercises may be used for more practice, for reteaching, or for review of the Key Concepts presented. Answers for all chapter exercises are available in *Grammar Exercises Answers on Transparencies* in your teaching resources.

Answer Key

▶ **Exercise 20**

1. <u>Cats</u>|<u>are</u> efficient hunters. *Neither*
2. Their <u>speed</u> and keen <u>eyesight</u>|<u>make</u> them a match for any other animal. *Compound subject*
3. Most <u>cats</u>|<u>hunt</u> at dusk or at night. *Neither*
4. <u>They</u>|<u>have</u> powerful legs and a muscular neck to help them catch prey. *Neither*
5. Most <u>cats</u>|<u>survive</u> on what they catch. *Neither*
6. An adult <u>lioness</u>|<u>needs</u> twelve pounds of meat per day. *Neither*
7. <u>Hunting</u> and <u>eating</u>|<u>take</u> a considerable amount of time. *Compound subject*
8. All <u>felines</u>, including domestic cats,|<u>attack</u> and <u>react</u> with lightning speed. *Compound verb*
9. <u>Lions</u>|<u>are</u> the only type of cat that hunts in groups. *Neither*
10. Most mother <u>cats</u> and their <u>young</u>|<u>hunt</u> and <u>eat</u> together. *Both*

▶ **Exercise 21**

Possible rewrite:

Scientists and zookeepers are researching the habits of leopards. Leopards see and hear very well. These solitary cats hunt and eat alone. They do not travel in groups as lions do. Leopards are similar to other big cats, however, because they sleep during the day and hunt at night. A leopard's diet includes wild boar and deer.

A leopard's physical abilities are amazing. Leopards can run at thirty-seven miles per hour and leap twenty feet horizontally. Great strength and nocturnal habits make the leopard a feared predator.

▶ **Exercise 22**

Find It in Your Reading
Compound subject: sentence two
Helen and I

GRAMMAR EXERCISES 20–24

▶ **Exercise 20** Identifying **Compound Subjects and Compound Verbs** Copy the following sentences onto your paper. Underline the subject(s) once and the verb(s) twice. Draw a vertical line between the complete subject and the complete predicate. Then, tell which sentences have compound subjects and/or compound verbs, and which have neither.

1. Cats are efficient hunters.
2. Their speed and keen eyesight make them a match for any other animal.
3. Most cats hunt at dusk or at night.
4. They have powerful legs and a muscular neck to help them catch prey.
5. Most cats survive on what they catch.
6. An adult lioness needs twelve pounds of meat per day.
7. Hunting and eating take a considerable amount of time.
8. All felines, including domestic cats, attack and react with lightning speed.
9. Lions are the only type of cat that hunts in a group.
10. Most mother cats and their young hunt and eat together.

▶ **Exercise 21** Revision Practice: **Combining Sentences With Compound Subjects and Compound Verbs** Revise the following passage by combining sentences as appropriate, using compound subjects or compound verbs.

Scientists are researching the habits of leopards. Zookeepers, too, research the habits of leopards. Leopards see very well. They also hear very well. These are solitary cats. They hunt alone. They eat alone. They do not travel in groups as lions do. Leopards are similar to other big cats, however, because they sleep during the

day. Leopards usually hunt at night. A leopard's diet includes wild boar. Leopards may also eat deer.

A leopard's physical abilities are amazing. A leopard can run at thirty-seven miles per hour. It can leap twenty feet horizontally. Great strength makes the leopard a feared predator. Its nocturnal habits also make it a feared predator.

▶ **Exercise 22** Find It in Your **Reading** Read the following passage from James Herriot's "Cat on the Go." Identify the sentence that has a compound subject, as well as the two parts of that compound subject.

Three nights later he was missing again. This time Helen and I didn't bother to search. We just waited. He was back earlier than usual. I heard the doorbell at nine o'clock. It was the elderly Mrs. Simpson peering through the glass. And she wasn't holding Oscar—he was prowling on the mat waiting to come in.

▶ **Exercise 23** Find It in Your **Writing** Review a piece of writing from your portfolio. Identify a sentence with a compound subject or a compound verb. If you can't find one, challenge yourself to add one to your writing.

▶ **Exercise 24** Writing Application Describe the habits of a species of wildlife. Use at least three sentences with a compound subject or verb.

▶ **Exercise 23**

Find It in Your Writing
Have partners exchange work and correctly identify compound subjects and verbs. Encourage students to revise by adding more compound subjects and verbs.

▶ **Exercise 24**

Writing Application
Ask volunteers to share their descriptions. Discuss the advantages of using compound verbs and/or subjects when writing.

Section 19.4 Special Problems With Subjects

In most sentences in English, the subject comes before the verb. This pattern is called *normal word order*. As long as the subject comes before the verb, the sentence is in normal word order, regardless of whether the subject and verb come near the beginning of the sentence, in the middle, or near the end.

NORMAL WORD ORDER: A <u>cheetah</u> <u>raced</u> across the plain.
On the nature program, <u>we</u> <u>saw</u> a cheetah.
As part of their daily routine, <u>cheetahs</u> <u>roam</u> their territory.

Not all sentences are in normal word order. In some, the verb comes before the subject. In others, such as questions, the subject can appear between parts of a verb phrase. In still others, the subject may seem to be missing altogether.

Finding subjects in sentences that are not in normal word order can be a problem. This section will give you practice in finding these difficult subjects.

Theme: Cats

In this section, you will learn about changes in word order in questions and in sentences beginning with *there* and *here*. The examples and exercises in this section are about wild cats.

Cross-Curricular Connection: Science

▼ Critical Viewing
Describe this cheetah in sentences beginning with "Wide is . . . ," "Spotted is . . . ," and "Sharp are. . . ." **[Analyze]**

Special Problems With Subjects • 405

PREPARE and ENGAGE

Interest GRABBER Write the following sentence on the board and ask students what is wrong with it:

Lasted three hours the trip.

Students should say that the subject belongs before the verb. Tell them that they will be learning about sentences in which the subject comes after the verb.

Activate Prior Knowledge

Have students turn back to Exercise 1 on page 393 of this chapter and list the subjects and verbs in those sentences. Ask students what pattern they can see in the placement of the subjects and verbs. (The subject always comes before the verb.) Challenge them to come up with sentences in which the verb comes first. Work with their examples, helping them to locate the subjects.

TEACH

Step-by-Step Teaching Guide

Normal Word Order

1. Point out to students that *normal* word order does not mean *correct* order. It is simply the order that is most common.

2. Ask students if they can think of examples where subjects come after verbs or are actually missing (questions, orders, etc.).

Critical Viewing

Analyze Students may say that wide is the cheetah's mouth, spotted is the cheetah's body, and sharp are the cheetah's teeth.

⏱ TIME AND RESOURCE MANAGER

Resources
Print: Grammar Exercise Workbook, pp. 51–54
Technology: On-Line Exercise Bank, Section 19.4

In-Depth Coverage	Accelerated Pace
• Work through all key concepts, pp. 405–408. • Assign and review Exercises 25–27.	• Assign pp. 405–408 for independent student review. • Assign Review Exercise 28–29.

Recognizing Subjects in Orders and Directions

1. Write a few short imperative sentences such as *Sit down! Be quiet! Run for your lives!* on the chalkboard. Challenge students to identify the subjects. If they are not sure, ask them who is supposed to perform the action in each sentence.

2. Students may have trouble understanding why *you* is the subject of an imperative sentence. Help them understand that *you,* the person being addressed in the sentence, is the person who will perform the action specified in the verb. Therefore, *you* is the subject.

Customize for
Bodily/Kinesthetic Learners

Have students choose partners. Give them a set of short imperative sentences like those at the top of this column. Each sentence should give a command or direction that can easily be performed in the classroom. Have one student give the first order or direction and have the partner follow the order. This physical activity will help them understand why the subject of the sentence is the person addressed: because he or she performs the action in the verb.

Answer Key

▶ **Exercise 25**

1. (you)
2. she
3. we
4. (you)
5. (you)
6. (you)
7. I
8. the lions
9. (you)
10. (you)

19.4

Recognizing Subjects in Orders and Directions

Stop! Finish your homework now. These sentences and others that give orders or directions seem not to have subjects. In fact, the subject in such cases is not stated, but understood.

▶ **KEY CONCEPT** In sentences that give orders or directions, the subject is understood to be *you.* ∎

The following chart lists examples of sentences that give orders or directions. The verbs are underlined twice. To the right, the same sentences are repeated with the understood subject in parentheses.

Orders or Directions	With Understood *You* Added
<u>Look</u> at the lion.	(You) <u>Look</u> at the lion.
After reading the background, <u>watch</u> the video.	After reading the background, (you) <u>watch</u> the video.
Leonard, <u>tell</u> us what lions eat.	Leonard, (you) <u>tell</u> us what lions eat.

▶ **Exercise 25** Recognizing Subjects That Give Orders or Directions On your paper, write the subject of each of the sentences that follow. Six of the ten sentences give orders or directions. The other four are ordinary sentences in normal word order.

EXAMPLE: Tom, help plan the field trip.
ANSWER: (you)

1. Jamie, watch the zookeeper feed the Siberian tigers.
2. She had better be careful!
3. We want to see the big cat exhibit.
4. Turn left just past the monkeys.
5. Call the Species Survival Plan to find out more about tiger facilities.
6. Find the cheetah area last.
7. I don't want to miss the ocelots.
8. Don't the lions get fed at 2:00?
9. Don't be late.
10. Anna, find the shortcut through the bird sanctuary.

▶ **More Practice**

On-line
Exercise Bank
• Section 19.4
Grammar Exercise Workbook
• pp. 51–52

⬥ STANDARDIZED TEST PREPARATION WORKSHOP

Grammar Standardized tests often ask students to identify a particular grammatical element in a sentence. Use this example to demonstrate finding the subject in a sentence.

Stop talking to me like that, Ross!

What is the subject of this sentence?

A Ross   B me
C that   D you

Item **D** is correct because the sentence is an order. The subject *you* is understood. *Me* is the object of a preposition. *That* is an adverb. *Ross* is a noun of direct address.

Finding Subjects in Questions

When the subject comes after the verb, a sentence is said to be in *inverted word order*. Inverted word order is found most often in questions.

KEY CONCEPT In questions, the subject often follows the verb. ■

Some questions in inverted word order begin with the words *what, which, whom, whose, when, where, why,* and *how.* Others begin with the verb itself or with a helping verb. In the sentences below, both the subject and the verb are underlined.

EXAMPLES: How <u>are</u> the <u>kittens</u> today?
<u>Did you feed</u> them in the morning?

If you ever have trouble finding the subject in a question, use this trick: Change the question into a statement. The subject will then appear in normal word order, before the verb.

Questions	Reworded as Statements
How <u>are</u> the <u>pups</u> today?	The <u>pups</u> <u>are</u> how today.
What <u>did</u> the <u>doctor</u> <u>say</u>?	The <u>doctor</u> <u>did</u> <u>say</u> what.
<u>Were</u> the <u>labels</u> ready?	The <u>labels</u> <u>were</u> ready.
<u>Did</u> <u>she</u> <u>bring</u> her camera with her?	<u>She</u> <u>did</u> <u>bring</u> her camera with her.

Not every question is in inverted word order. Some are in normal word order, with the subject before the verb.

EXAMPLES: <u>Who has</u> the camera?
<u>Whose story won</u> the writing contest?

Exercise 26 Finding the Subjects in Questions Copy the following sentences onto your paper. Underline the subject in each. Note that two of the sentences are in normal word order.

EXAMPLE: How did <u>you</u> get interested in leopards?

1. Where do leopards live?
2. A leopard can run at what speed?
3. What method do conservationists use to count leopard populations?
4. How are a cheetah's spots different from a leopard's?
5. Which scientists study the behavior of these big cats?

▼ Critical Viewing
Inverting normal sentence word order, ask a question about the differences between this leopard and other big cats. [Contrast]

Subjects in Sentences Beginning with *There* or *Here*

1. Have a volunteer read aloud the key concept. Work through the explanation and examples with students. Emphasize that *there* and *here* are words that show location and direction; this is why they usually function as adverbs.

2. Explain that *there* and *here* are not nouns and cannot function as nouns. This is why they can never be the subject of a sentence. When students see sentences beginning with *there* or *here,* they should look for nouns in the sentence and decide which is the subject. In the first sample sentence, *cage* cannot be the subject, because it is the object of the preposition *in.* Therefore, the subject must be *birds.*

Answer Key

▶ **Exercise 27**

1. Here are <u>answers</u> to your questions about the big cats.
2. There are <u>leopards</u>, <u>lions</u>, and <u>cheetahs</u> in this area.
3. There is a large <u>variety</u> of wildlife living on the savannah.
4. Here is a <u>picture</u> of a cheetah.
5. There was a <u>program</u> about the big cats on television last night.

19.4

Finding Subjects in Sentences Beginning With *There* or *Here*

A sentence beginning with *there* or *here* is usually in inverted word order.

▶ **KEY CONCEPT** *There* or *here* is never the subject of a sentence. ■

There has two uses in a sentence. First, it can be used simply as a sentence starter. *There* can also be used as an adverb at the beginning of a sentence. *Here* can be used in the same way. As adverbs, *there* and *here* point out *where.*

EXAMPLES:
                     V   S
        There <u>are</u> three <u>birds</u> in that cage.

                      V
        There <u>goes</u> the football <u>team.</u>

             V   S
        Here <u>is</u> the <u>recipe</u> for enchiladas.

If you have trouble finding the subject of a sentence beginning with *here* or *there,* reorder the sentence. The subject will then appear near the beginning.

Sentences Beginning With *There* and *Here*
There <u>are</u> two <u>lions</u> in that enclosure.
Here <u>is</u> the <u>exhibit.</u>

Reworded With Subjects Before Verbs
Two <u>lions</u> <u>are</u> in that enclosure.
The <u>exhibit</u> <u>is</u> here. ■

▶ **Exercise 27** Finding the Subjects in Sentences Beginning With *There* or *Here* Copy the following sentences onto your paper. Underline the subject in each.

1. Here are answers to your questions about the big cats.
2. There are leopards, lions, and cheetahs in this area.
3. There is a large variety of wildlife living on the savannah.
4. Here is a picture of a cheetah.
5. There was a program about the big cats on television last night.

🕯 Spelling Tip

Writers often confuse the spelling of *their* and *there.* Remember that *their* is a pronoun that shows possession (e.g., Children love *their* pet cats). *There* denotes place or the fact of something's existence (e.g., The cougar's cage is over *there,* or *There* is a rare species of cat in the zoo).

▶ **More Practice**

On-line
Exercise Bank
• Section 19.4
Grammar Exercise
Workbook
• pp. 53–54

☑ **ONGOING ASSESSMENT: Monitor and Reinforce**

If students miss more than two items in Exercises 25–27, refer them to the following for additional practice.

In the Textbook	Print Resources	Technology
Section Review, Ex. 28–30, p. 409	Grammar Exercise Workbook, pp. 51–54	On-Line Exercise Bank, Section 19.4

Section 19.4 *Section Review*

GRAMMAR EXERCISES 28–33

▶ **Exercise 28** Finding Subjects
in Orders, Questions, and Directions
On your paper, write the subject of each
sentence.

1. How heavy does a tiger get?
2. That tiger weighs up to 675 pounds.
3. Go to southeastern Asia or central
   India to see a Bengal tiger.
4. What do Bengal tigers eat?
5. Does the Bengal tiger inhabit grassy or
   swampy areas?
6. Where do Bengal tigers live?
7. Be cautious when observing tigers in
   their natural habitat.
8. Which tiger is not dangerous to man?
9. What is the Bengal tiger's classification?
10. Why are Bengal tigers protected?

▶ **Exercise 29** Finding Subjects in
Sentences Beginning With *There* or *Here*
Copy the following sentences. Underline
the subject in each.

1. There were several types of saber-
   toothed tigers.
2. There are fascinating exhibits about
   them.
3. Here, it is the most common mammal
   fossil found.
4. Here are saber-toothed tiger skeletons.
5. There are tar pits containing tiger
   skeletons at Rancho La Brea in
   California.

▶ **Exercise 30** Revising Sentences
Revise each of the following sentences
to begin with the subject. Make any other
minor changes that are necessary.

1. There is a large cat found on the
   grassy plains of Africa.
2. Although there are many fast cats,
   there are none as fast as the cheetah.

3. Seventy miles an hour a cheetah can
   run.
4. There are usually two to four cubs in a
   cheetah litter.
5. There are many predators—including
   hyenas, leopards, and lions—that pose
   a threat to young cheetahs.
6. There were once cheetahs throughout
   Africa, central Asia, and India.
7. Today, there are fewer cheetahs than
   in the past.
8. Declining are their numbers.
9. There are several reasons, such as
   predators and loss of habitat, that
   contribute to the problem.
10. Here is a picture of a cheetah.

▶ **Exercise 31** Find It in Your
Reading Read the following excerpt
from "Cat on the Go." Identify the subject
and the verb of each underlined part. If
necessary, reorder the sentence to find the
subject.

Tell me," I said. "This cat you lost.
What did he look like?

▶ **Exercise 32** Find It in Your
Writing Revise several sentences from
your own writing to begin with *There* or
Here. If you find a sentence already beginning with "There is . . ." or There are . . . ,"
try revising it to eliminate those words.

▶ **Exercise 33** Writing Application
Write a letter to a zoo or wildlife center,
asking for information on big cats. Include
three specific questions. Identify the subject
and verb in each of your questions.

Section Review • 409

Interest GRABBER Write the words *complement* and *complete* on the board. Tell students that both words come from the same Latin word and that their meanings are related. A complement makes something complete.

Activate Prior Knowledge

Ask students what a transitive verb is. If they don't remember, you may wish to direct them to page 316 in the text. (A transitive verb is an action verb that directs action from the performer of the action toward the receiver of the action.) Tell students that, in this lesson, they will learn to identify that "receiver of the action," as well as other complements.

TEACH

Step-by-Step Teaching Guide

Complements

1. Call students' attention to the examples of sentence fragments on this page. Point out that each one has a subject and a verb. Ask students to explain why these are not sentences. Review the term *complete thought*.

2. Write the following fragments on the board. Ask students how they would make each a complete sentence. Tell students that the words they are adding are the *complements*.

   Cat is. (fragment—My cat is big.)

   Mother told. (fragment—My mother told me to come home.)

Language Highlight

Even though *complement* (complete) and *compliment* (say something nice) don't mean the same thing, they both come from the Latin root *complere*, "to fill up or complete." However, while *complement* came into English directly from Latin, *compliment* came by way of French and Italian.

Section 19.5

Complements

In Section 19.1, a *complete thought* was defined as a group of words that contains a subject and a verb and that can stand by itself and still make sense. Sometimes, just a subject and a verb by themselves will express a complete thought. The following sentences, for example, do express complete thoughts.

EXAMPLES: Snakes slither.   Lizards scurry.
             ˢ   ᵛ   ˢ   ᵛ

Sometimes, however, a subject and verb alone will not express a complete thought.

EXAMPLES: Tracy fed.   That is.   It seems.
             ˢ   ᵛ   ˢ   ᵛ   ˢ   ᵛ

These sentences need other words to complete the thoughts begun by the subjects and verbs. The words needed are complements.

▶ **KEY CONCEPT** A **complement** is a word or group of words that completes the meaning of a subject and a verb. ■

Complements usually appear right after the verb or very close to it. Most complements are nouns, pronouns, or adjectives. In the examples below, the complements are labeled and boxed.

                              COMPLEMENT
EXAMPLES: Tracy <u>fed</u> the [lizard.]

                        COMPLEMENT
            That <u>is</u> a [problem.]

                      COMPLEMENT
            It <u>seems</u> [sick.]

▶ **Exercise 34**   Adding Complements   On your paper, write one word to complete each sentence.
1. The snake looks ___?___.
2. It feels ___?___.
3. The lizard seems ___?___.
4. Its skin is ___?___.
5. We like ___?___.

The next three parts of this section describe three types of complements: *direct objects*, *indirect objects*, and *subject complements*. The first part focuses on direct objects.

Theme: Reptiles

In this section, you will learn about direct and indirect objects and predicate nouns and adjectives. The examples and exercises in this section are about reptiles.

Cross-Curricular Connection: Science

▶ **More Practice**

On-line Exercise Bank
• Section 19.5
Grammar Exercise Workbook
• pp. 55–60, 65–66

⏱ **TIME AND RESOURCE MANAGER**

Resources
Print: Grammar Exercise Workbook, pp. 55–64
Technology: On-Line Exercise Bank, Section 19.5

In-Depth Coverage	Accelerated Pace
• Work through all key concepts, pp. 410–418. • Assign and review Exercises 34–43.	• Assign pp. 410–417 for independent student review. • Assign Review Exercise 44–45.

Recognizing Direct Objects

Direct objects follow action verbs.

KEY CONCEPT A **direct object** is a noun or pronoun that receives the action of a verb. ■

You can find a direct object by asking *What?* or *Whom?* after an action verb.

EXAMPLES:

                           DO

My older brother found a grass snake.

Found *what?* Answer: a grass snake.

          DO

I told Ricky not to take it home.

Told *whom?* Answer: Ricky

Grass snake and *Ricky* are the direct objects of the verbs in the examples. In the first sentence, *grass snake* answers the question *Found what? Ricky*, in the second sentence, answers the question *Told whom?*

Like subjects and verbs, direct objects can be compound. That is, one verb can have two or more direct objects.

EXAMPLES:

                 DO   DO

The lizard eats crickets and other bugs.

Eats *what?* Answer: crickets, bugs

                     DO   DO

The committee chose Mrs. Franks, Mr. Lynch,

         DO

and Ms. Rossi to organize the reptile show.

Chose *whom?* Answer: Mrs. Franks, Mr. Lynch, and Ms. Rossi.

◄ **Critical Viewing**
What do you notice, like, or dislike about this snake? Answer with a sentence containing a compound direct object. **[Evaluate]**

Complements • 411

Answer Key

▶ **Exercise 34** *(page 410)*

Answers will vary. Possible answers are shown.

1. slimy
2. smooth
3. tired
4. scaly
5. reptiles

Step-by-Step Teaching Guide

Recognizing Direct Object

1. Read aloud the key concept. Emphasize the phrase *receives the action of a verb.* Make sure students understand that only action verbs can take direct objects. Linking verbs cannot do this because they show no action for an object to receive.

   Ya Su opened the door.

   Ya Su was amazed.

   Opened is an action verb; *door* is its direct object.

   Was is a linking verb; it links the subject *Ya Su* to the adjective *amazed.*

2. Point out that all direct objects are nouns or pronouns. Adjectives, adverbs, or other parts of speech can follow action verbs, but they are not direct objects.

   Fury filled my heart, but I sat quietly.

   Heart is the direct object of *filled;* it is a noun. *Quietly* is not the direct object of *sat.* It is an adverb that modifies this verb.

Critical Viewing

Evaluate Possible sentence: I notice the snake's beady eyes and patterned skin.

▶ **Exercise 35**

1. Scales cover a snake's <u>body</u>.
2. Snakes do not have <u>legs</u> or <u>arms</u>.
3. Snakes lose their <u>fangs</u> periodically.
4. Some species also shed their <u>skin</u>.
5. Snakes eat <u>rats</u>, <u>mice</u>, and <u>frogs</u>.

▶ **Exercise 36**

1. The crocodile family includes crocodiles, alligators, and caimans.
2. Crocodiles inhabit Asia, Africa, and some areas of North America.
3. The hardy crocodile can survive droughts and cool weather.
4. Crocodiles eat birds and mammals.
5. For nesting sites, a crocodile might choose a sandy beach or a muddy bank.

Critical Viewing

Evaluate Most students will enjoy answering the question and suggesting that they might be the objects the hungry alligator wished to eat.

19.5

▶ **Exercise 35** Recognizing Direct Objects Each of the following sentences contains either a simple or a compound direct object. Copy the sentences onto your paper, and underline each direct object.

EXAMPLE: Snakes often scare <u>people</u>.

1. Scales cover a snake's body.
2. Snakes do not have legs or arms.
3. Snakes lose their fangs periodically.
4. Some species also shed their skin.
5. Snakes eat rats, mice, and frogs.

▶ **Exercise 36** Combining Sentences With Compound Direct Objects Combine each pair or group of sentences by using a compound direct object. You may make other minor changes as necessary.

EXAMPLE: We saw alligators at the zoo. We saw crocodiles, too.
ANSWER: We saw alligators and crocodiles at the zoo.

1. The crocodile family includes crocodiles. It also includes alligators. Caimans are also part of the crocodile family.
2. Crocodiles inhabit Asia. They are also found in Africa. Crocodiles also live in some areas of North America.
3. The hardy crocodile can survive droughts. It can also survive cool weather.
4. Crocodiles eat birds. They also eat mammals.
5. For nesting sites, a crocodile might choose a sandy beach. It might choose a muddy bank instead.

◀ Critical Viewing
If you were suddenly the direct object of a hungry alligator, what might its actions be? **[Evaluate]**

⏱ **TIME SAVERS!**

📄 **Answers on Transparency**
Use the Grammar Exercises Answers on Transparencies for Chapter 19 to facilitate correction by students.

💻 **On-Line Exercise Bank**
Have students complete the exercises on computer. The Auto Check feature will grade their work for you!

Finding Direct Objects in Questions

In normal word order, a direct object follows a verb. In questions, which are often in inverted word order, the position of a direct object often changes as well.

▶ **KEY CONCEPT** A direct object in a question will sometimes be found before the verb. ■

In the chart below, questions are paired with sentences reworded in normal word order. Compare the positions of the direct objects in each.

Questions	Sentences With Normal Word Order
DO What <u>does</u> a snake <u>eat</u>?	DO A <u>snake</u> <u>does eat</u> what.
DO Which T-shirt <u>do</u> <u>you</u> <u>like</u>?	DO <u>You</u> <u>do like</u> which T-shirt.
DO Whom <u>did</u> <u>you</u> <u>meet</u> in the cafeteria?	DO <u>You</u> <u>did meet</u> whom in the cafeteria.

In each of the three questions, the direct object appears before, rather than after, the verb. To locate the direct object in a question, put the sentence into normal word order. Then, the direct object will be found in its usual position after the verb.

▶ **Exercise 37** Finding Direct Objects in Questions Copy each of the sentences below, and underline the direct object.

EXAMPLE: <u>What</u> should we take with us to Reptile Park?

1. Whom did you invite to come with us?
2. What will you do with those interesting photographs?
3. Which reptile do you like?
4. Which species of reptile shall we visit first?
5. What should we see next?
6. Which reptiles can you touch?
7. Whom have they chosen to talk to us?
8. Whose questions will the guide answer?
9. What effect does the weather have on reptiles?
10. What reptile book shall I buy?

▶ **Speaking and Listening Tip**

With a partner, take turns reading the questions in Exercise 37 aloud. First, read each one as it is written, and then read it again as a statement with normal word order. Pay attention to the changing position of the direct objects.

▶ **More Practice**

On-line
Exercise Bank
• Section 19.5
Grammar Exercise
Workbook
• pp. 55–60

Finding Direct Objects in Questions

1. Explain that *which, what, who, whom,* and *whose* are all interrogative pronouns. One way to find the direct object of a question beginning with one of these words is to answer the question, find the direct object in the answer, then identify the pronoun that the noun replaces. That pronoun is the direct object in the question. Sentence 1 in Exercise 37 might be answered *I invited Carmen.* Since *Carmen* replaces *whom, whom* is the direct object in the question.

2. Warn students not to reorder every interrogative sentence. Certain questions are already in normal word order. Answering these questions will help students find the direct objects.

   Who called you last night?

   Answer: Rick called me last night.

   Me is the direct object in the answer. *Me* replaces the pronoun *you,* so *you* is the direct object of the question.

Customize for
ESL Learners

Make sure students know that the sample sentences in the right half of the chart are not correct English sentences. Challenge students to revise them so that they become correct sentences. Help students see that if they change the interrogative pronouns *what, which,* and *whom* to pronouns such as *it, this,* and *him,* the sentences are correct.

Answer Key

▶ **Exercise 37**

1. <u>Whom</u> did you invite to come with us?
2. <u>What</u> will you do with those interesting photographs?
3. Which <u>reptile</u> do you like?
4. Which <u>species</u> of reptile shall we visit first?
5. <u>What</u> should we see next?
6. Which <u>reptiles</u> can you touch?
7. <u>Whom</u> have they chosen to talk to us?
8. Whose <u>questions</u> will the guide answer?
9. What <u>effect</u> does the weather have on reptiles?
10. What reptile <u>book</u> shall I buy?

Recognizing Indirect Objects

1. Emphasize the fact that there is never an indirect object unless there is a direct object.

2. Ask students to suggest sentences that include indirect objects.

3. Caution students not to confuse indirect objects with objects of a preposition (refer them to Ch. 17, p. 366, if they need to review). In the sentence "I gave Tina the letter," Tina is an indirect object. However, in :"I gave the letter to Tina," Tina is the object of the preposition *to*. The idea is the same in both sentences, but the part of speech is not.

4. Point out to students that while an indirect object and object of a preposition are not the same thing, one can help them discover the other. Students can find an indirect object by rewording a sentence to include the word *to* or *for*. The indirect object in the original sentence will appear as the object of *to* or *for* in the reworded sentence, as in the example "I gave Tina the letter," "I gave the letter *to* Tina."

Critical Viewing

Connect Students may suggest that the Gila monster is giving them a scary or confused look. The indirect object would be the student; the direct would be the look.

Recognizing Indirect Objects

Sentences with direct objects may also have another kind of complement, called an *indirect object.* An indirect object is found only in a sentence that has a direct object.

▶ **KEY CONCEPT** An **indirect object** is a noun or pronoun that comes after an action verb and before a direct object. It names the person or thing that something is given to or done for. ■

Always look for the direct object first in a sentence. Then, look for an indirect object before it. An indirect object answers the question *To or for whom?* or *To or for what?* after the action verb.

EXAMPLES:
          IO   DO
Lucy told [him] the [news.]
Told to *whom?*   Answer: him

          IO   DO
I gave each [paper] a [number.]
Gave to *what?*   Answer: paper

Most sentences with indirect objects will follow the same pattern: Subject + Action Verb + Indirect Object + Direct Object. An indirect object will almost always come between the verb and the direct object.

Like direct objects, indirect objects can be compound. The verb can be followed by two or more indirect objects.

EXAMPLE:
                    IO   IO   DO
He gave his lizard and turtle their food.
Gave to *what?* Answer: lizard, turtle

◀ Critical Viewing Use an indirect object and a direct object in a sentence describing the kind of look this Gila monster seems to be giving you. [Connect]

> **Exercise 38** Recognizing Indirect Objects Each of the following sentences contains a direct object and an indirect object. Some indirect objects are compound. Copy the sentences onto your paper, and underline each indirect object.

EXAMPLE: We gave <u>John</u> a surprise for his birthday.

1. Yesterday, I gave John a pet lizard.
2. He will give his pet special treats.
3. We gave his lizard the name Lizzy.
4. John told his brother and sister details about Lizzy.
5. We made Lizzy a new home.
6. I showed my teacher and classmates the new habitat.
7. It gives her some space to grow.
8. John feeds Lizzy bugs.
9. We gave Mary a picture.
10. John gave me a picture of Lizzy, too.
11. We built her an outdoor enclosure for the warm days.
12. Everyone asks John and his family questions about her.
13. They tell them facts about lizards.
14. With Lizzy, they give them demonstrations.
15. Sometimes, when Lizzy is with them, people give them frightened looks.

> **Exercise 39** Combining Sentences With Compound Indirect Objects Combine each pair or group of sentences by using compound indirect objects. You may make other minor changes as needed.

EXAMPLE: Have you shown your teacher the snake article?
Have you shown your classmates the article?

ANSWER: Have you shown your teacher and your classmates the snake article?

1. Mr. Benson assigned Steve a report on snakes. He assigned me a report on snakes as well.
2. We gave Mary a book with facts on crocodiles. We also gave a book to Keisha.
3. We asked Mr. Benson some questions. We asked Tom some questions, too.
4. Mr. Benson showed Lucy several Internet sources. He also showed me the sources.
5. I will read the class my report. I might read my family the report instead.

> **More Practice**

On-line
Exercise Bank
• Section 19.5
Grammar Exercise
Workbook
• pp. 61–62

Complements • 415

Customize for
More Advanced Students

Challenge students to rewrite the sentences in Exercises 38 and 39, substituting pronouns for all indirect objects that are nouns. For example, students would rewrite Exercise 38.1 as *Yesterday, I gave him a pet lizard.* Have students exchange papers with partners. Each student should make sure that the partner has used the correct pronouns.

Answer Key

> **Exercise 38**

1. Yesterday, I gave <u>John</u> a pet lizard.
2. He will give his <u>pet</u> special treats.
3. We gave his <u>lizard</u> the name Lizzy.
4. John told his <u>brother</u> and <u>sister</u> details about Lizzy.
5. We made <u>Lizzy</u> a new home.
6. I showed my <u>teacher</u> and <u>classmates</u> the new habitat.
7. It gives <u>her</u> some space to grow.
8. John feeds <u>Lizzy</u> bugs.
9. We gave <u>Mary</u> a picture.
10. John gave <u>me</u> a picture of Lizzy, too.
11. We built <u>her</u> an outdoor enclosure for the warm days.
12. Everyone asks <u>John</u> and his <u>family</u> questions about her.
13. They tell <u>them</u> facts about lizards.
14. With Lizzy, they give <u>them</u> demonstrations.
15. Sometimes, when Lizzy is with them, people give <u>them</u> frightened looks.

> **Exercise 39**

1. Mr. Benson assigned Steve and me a report on snakes.
2. We gave Mary and Keisha a book with facts on crocodiles.
3. We asked Mr. Benson and Tom some questions.
4. Mr. Benson showed Lucy and me several Internet sources.
5. I will read the class or my family the report.

☑ **ONGOING ASSESSMENT: Monitor and Reinforce**

If students miss more than two items in Exercises 34–39, refer them to the following for additional practice.

In the Textbook	Print Resources	Technology
Section Review, Ex. 44–45, p. 419	Grammar Exercise Workbook, pp. 55–64	On-Line Exercise Bank, Section 19.5

Predicate Nouns and Pronouns

1. Review linking verbs. Remind students that linking verbs show no action. They describe a state or condition of the subject.

2. Review objects of prepositions with students. A preposition and its object or objects function together as a phrase, as one part of speech. Prepositional phrases add descriptive detail to sentences, but they do not function as direct or indirect objects or as predicate nouns or pronouns.

Answer Key

▶ **Exercise 40**

1. The largest lizard is the Komodo <u>dragon</u>.
2. Komodo dragons are huge <u>monsters</u>.
3. The dragon's home is the Indonesian <u>island</u> of Komodo.
4. The Komodo dragon is really one <u>type</u> of lizard—the monitor.
5. The second-largest monitor lizard is Australia's giant <u>perentie</u>.

19.5

Recognizing Subject Complements

Action verbs can be followed by direct objects and indirect objects. Linking verbs can be followed by another kind of complement, called a *subject complement*.

▶ **KEY CONCEPT** A **subject complement** is a noun, a pronoun, or an adjective that follows a linking verb and tells something about the subject. ∎

Predicate Nouns and Pronouns

Nouns and pronouns used as subject complements follow linking verbs.

▶ **KEY CONCEPT** A **predicate noun** or **predicate pronoun** follows a linking verb and renames or identifies the subject. ∎

PREDICATE NOUNS AND PRONOUNS	
Sentences	Relationships
PN A lizard is a reptile.	lizard = reptile
PP The leader will be he.	leader = he

A predicate noun or predicate pronoun is never the object of a preposition. In the following sentence, *superstars* is not a predicate noun. It is the object of the preposition *of*.

EXAMPLE: Steve Young <u>was</u> one of football's superstars.
(PP / OBJ OF PREP)

▶ **Exercise 40** Recognizing Predicate Nouns and Pronouns
Copy the following sentences onto your paper, and underline each predicate noun or predicate pronoun.
1. The largest lizard is the Komodo dragon.
2. Komodo dragons are huge monsters.
3. The dragon's home is the Indonesian island of Komodo.
4. The Komodo dragon is really one type of lizard—the monitor.
5. The second largest monitor lizard is Australia's giant perentie.

416 • Basic Sentence Parts

Journal Tip

This section focuses on several types of reptiles. In your journal, note some facts about the reptiles that especially interest you, along with your impressions of these creatures. You can review your notes later to find a possible topic for a report.

▶ **More Practice**

On-line
Exercise Bank
• Section 19.5
Grammar Exercise
Workbook
• pp. 65–66

⏱ **TIME SAVERS!**

🖨 **Answers on Transparency**
Use the Grammar Exercises Answers on Transparencies for Chapter 19 to facilitate correction by students.

💻 **On-Line Exercise Bank**
Have students complete the exercises on computer. The Auto Check feature will grade their work for you!

⏱ **TIME AND RESOURCE MANAGER**

Resources
Print: Grammar Exercise Workbook, pp. 65–68
Technology: On-Line Exercise Bank, Section 19.5

In-Depth Coverage	Accelerated Pace
• Work through all key concepts, pp. 416–418. • Assign and review Exercises 40–43.	• Assign pp. 416–418 for independent student review. • Assign Review Exercise 45.

Predicate Adjectives

A linking verb may also be followed by a predicate adjective.

KEY CONCEPT A **predicate adjective** follows a linking verb and describes the subject of the sentence. ■

Because a predicate adjective comes after a linking verb, it is considered part of the complete predicate of a sentence. In spite of this, a predicate adjective does *not* modify the words in the predicate. Instead, the predicate adjective describes the subject of the sentence.

PREDICATE ADJECTIVES	
Sentences	Relationships
Her <u>story</u> <u>seems</u> [PA strange] to us.	strange story
Komodo dragons are [PA huge].	huge Komodo dragons

Exercise 41 Recognizing Predicate Adjectives Copy each sentence and underline the predicate adjectives.

1. The long, thin cobra is olive brown.
2. It is unbelievably scary.
3. This snake's bite can be lethal.
4. It is extremely poisonous.
5. Cobras are useful to a snake charmer.
6. The music of the snake charmer is enchanting.
7. However, snakes are deaf.
8. The motion of the snake charmer, though, is fascinating to the snake.
9. The charmer must remain calm as the cobra flares its hood menacingly.
10. Snake charmers may be brave, but I think they are extremely foolish.

◀ Critical Viewing
Use several vivid predicate adjectives to fill in the blank: This Komodo dragon is/seems/might become _____.
[Infer]

Complements • 417

ONGOING ASSESSMENT: Monitor and Reinforce

If students miss more than two items in Exercises 40–43, refer them to the following for additional practice.

In the Textbook	Print Resources	Technology
Section Review, Ex. 45, p. 419	Grammar Exercise Workbook, pp. 65–68	On-Line Exercise Bank, Section 19.5

Customize for

Less Advanced Students

Have students practice building sentences that use subject complements. Suggest a subject, and then ask students to suggest nouns, pronouns, or adjectives that could follow a linking verb and complete the sentence. Encourage them to include a prepositional phrase in their suggestions when possible (e.g. "one of a kind," etc.).

Step-by-Step Teaching Guide

Predicate Adjectives

1. Emphasize that like all other adjectives, predicate adjectives modify nouns. This means that they describe the subject of the sentence, not the verb. This rule will help students disregard the adjective's location.

2. Go over Exercise 41 with students. If students identify *unbelievably* in sentence 2 or *extremely* in sentence 10 as a predicate adjective, remind them that adjectives must modify nouns. *Unbelievably* and *extremely* modify adjectives and answer the question *In what manner?* Therefore, they are adverbs. (The suffix *-ly* also is a clue that these are adverbs.)

Answer Key

Exercise 41

1. The long, thin cobra is <u>olive brown</u>.
2. It is unbelievably <u>scary</u>.
3. This snake's bite can be <u>lethal</u>.
4. It is extremely <u>poisonous</u>.
5. Cobras are <u>useful</u> to a snake charmer.
6. The music of the snake charmer is <u>enchanting</u>.
7. However, snakes are <u>deaf</u>.
8. The motion of the snake charmer, though, is <u>fascinating</u> to the snake.
9. The charmer must remain <u>calm</u> as the cobra flares its hood menacingly.
10. Snake charmers may be <u>brave</u>, but I think they are extremely <u>foolish</u>.

Critical Viewing

Infer Students may say the Komodo dragon is frightening.

417

Compound Subject Complements

1. Review the meaning of *compound* with students. Remind them that *compound* always implies sharing. The parts of a compound subject share a verb or verbs; the parts of a compound verb share a subject or subjects; and the parts of a compound subject complement all refer back to the same subject or subjects.

2. Write the first example sentence on the chalkboard. Draw arrows from each predicate noun to the subject, *owners*. Have students try the same thing with the other two example sentences. This demonstration will help them see how both predicate nouns and predicate adjectives can share the same subject.

Answer Key

▶ Exercise 42

1. large—PA; dangerous—PA
2. long—PA; heavy—PA
3. beautiful—PA; frightening—PA
4. poisonous—PA; carnivorous—PA
5. rabbits—PN; mice—PN; gophers—PN
6. desert—PN; forest—PN
7. smooth—PA; scaly—PA
8. bone—PN; cartilage—PN
9. taste—PN; smell—PN
10. loud—PA; soft—PA

▶ Exercise 43

Answers will vary. Sample answers are given.

1. My turtle is green.
2. Her cat is her best friend.
3. I would be amazed and terrified.
4. My three favorite animals are deer, dogs, and elephants.
5. The hardest workers were he and I.

19.5

Compound Subject Complements

Like other sentence parts, subject complements can be compound. That is, a linking verb may be followed by two or more predicate nouns, pronouns, or adjectives.

EXAMPLES: The snake's <u>owners</u> <u>are</u> Nancy^{PN} and Melissa.^{PN}

The report <u>writers</u> <u>were</u> Maureen^{PN} and he.^{PP}

The <u>rattlesnake</u> <u>looks</u> mean^{PA} and dangerous.^{PA}

▶ **Exercise 42** Recognizing Compound Subject Complements Write the parts of each subject complement in the following sentences. The complements may be predicate nouns (PN) or predicate adjectives (PA). Label them correctly.

EXAMPLE: The assignment is a report or project.
ANSWER: report (PN), project (PN)

1. The diamondback rattlesnake is large and dangerous.
2. Rattlesnakes grow long and heavy.
3. They appear both beautiful and frightening.
4. Rattlesnakes are poisonous and carnivorous.
5. A rattlesnake's prey can be rabbits, mice, or gophers.
6. Their home is either the desert or the forest.
7. The snake's skin is smooth but scaly.
8. A rattlesnake's skeleton is bone and cartilage.
9. The rattlesnake's most important senses are taste and smell.
10. The sound of their rattles may be loud or soft.

▶ **Exercise 43** Writing Sentences With Subject Complements Write sentences with subject complements, following the directions below.
1. Use a predicate adjective in a sentence describing a turtle.
2. Use a predicate noun in a sentence about a pet.
3. Write a sentence with compound predicate adjectives, describing how you would feel if you came upon a Komodo dragon in the wild.
4. Use compound predicate nouns in a sentence about three favorite animals.
5. Use compound predicate pronouns in a sentence about yourself and a friend.

418 • Basic Sentence Parts

More Practice

On-line
Exercise Bank
• Section 19.5
Grammar Exercise
Workbook
• pp. 67–68

☑ ONGOING ASSESSMENT: Assess Mastery

Use the following resources to assess student mastery of hard-to-find subjects and subject complements.

In the Textbook	Technology
Chapter Review, Ex. 53–56, pp. 420–421 Standardized Test Preparation Workshop, pp. 422–423	On-Line Exercise Bank, Section 19.5

Section 19.5 Section Review

GRAMMAR EXERCISES 44–49

> **Exercise 44** Recognizing Direct Objects and Compound Direct Objects

On your paper, write only the nouns or pronouns that make up each direct object or compound direct object.

1. Rattlesnakes frighten people.
2. The sun warms their skin and their blood.
3. Whose opinion do you value on the care and feeding of snakes?
4. Their rattles warn people and other intruders of their presence.
5. They use rocks and trees to conceal themselves.
6. Their tongues sense temperature changes and people.
7. I will take you to find more information on snakes.
8. Before eating prey, poisonous snakes paralyze it.
9. If undisturbed, rattlesnakes won't attack us.
10. Large birds of prey eat snakes and other small reptiles.

> **Exercise 45** Recognizing Compound Subject Complements

Write the subject complements in the following sentences. Label predicate nouns *PN*, predicate pronouns *PP*, and predicate adjectives *PA*.

1. My friend is knowledgeable and concerned about hawksbill turtles.
2. It was he and I who wrote a report on them.
3. The hawksbill is passive and graceful.
4. Its natural habitat is warm seas.
5. This species is neither quick nor powerful.

> **Exercise 46** Revision Practice: Sentence Combining Combine sentences in the following paragraph by using compound complements.

The sea turtle is an excellent swimmer. It is also a good diver. It eats mollusks. It also eats shellfish. One type of sea turtle is the hawksbill. Another interesting type of sea turtle is the green turtle. Hawksbill turtles are beautiful. They are rare.

> **Exercise 47** Find It in Your Reading Read an article about reptiles in an encyclopedia, on a Web page, or in a science textbook. Identify at least three examples of subject complements that are used in the article.

> **Exercise 48** Find It in Your Writing Review some of the finished work in your writing portfolio. Identify any places where you have used subject complements. Challenge yourself to add two more sentences—one containing compound predicate adjectives and the other containing compound predicate nouns.

> **Exercise 49** Writing Application Write a short description of a reptile. Circle the complements in each sentence, and identify direct and indirect objects, as well as predicate nouns, pronouns, or adjectives.

Section Review • **419**

ASSESS and CLOSE

Section Review

Each of these exercises correlates to a concept covered in the section on complements, pages 410–418. The exercises may be used for more practice, for reteaching, or for review of the Key Concepts presented.

Answer Key

> **Exercise 44**

1. people
2. skin, blood
3. opinion
4. people, intruders
5. rocks, trees
6. changes, people
7. you
8. it
9. us
10. snakes, reptiles

> **Exercise 45**

1. knowledgeable—PA; concerned—PA
2. he—PP; I—PP
3. passive—PA; graceful—PA
4. seas—PN
5. quick—PA; powerful—PA

> **Exercise 46**

The sea turtle is an excellent swimmer and a good diver. It eats mollusks and shellfish. Two types of sea turtles are the hawksbill and the green turtle. Hawksbill turtles are beautiful and rare.

> **Exercise 47**

Find It in Your Reading
Have students identify both the subjects and their complements.

continued

Answer Key continued

> **Exercise 48**

Find It in Your Writing
Tell students to begin by writing simple sentences, and then elaborate by adding the compound predicate adjectives and compound predicate nouns.

> **Exercise 49**

Writing Application
Have students exchange their descriptions with a partner to check that they have correctly identified the sentence parts.

⏱ **TIME SAVERS!**

🖼 **Answers on Transparency**
Use the Grammar Exercises Answers on Transparencies for Chapter 19 to facilitate correction by students.

💻 **On-Line Exercise Bank**
Have students complete the exercises on computer. The Auto Check feature will grade their work for you!

CHAPTER REVIEW

These exercises correlate to the concepts taught on basic sentence parts, pages 392–418. The exercises may be used for more practice, for reteaching, or for review of the Key Concepts presented. Answers for all chapter exercises are available in *Grammar Exercises Answers on Transparencies* in your teaching resources.

Answer Key

Exercise 50

1. <u>Tennis</u>|<u>is</u> a great personal sport.
2. The only <u>equipment</u> needed |<u>is</u> a racquet and a ball.
3. The <u>players</u>|<u>must learn</u> how to score.
4. Two or four <u>people</u>|<u>can play</u> the game.
5. A special <u>court</u>|<u>is</u> necessary to play tennis.

Exercise 51

1. sentence
2. fragment
3. sentence
4. fragment
5. fragment

Exercise 52

Answers will vary. Sample answers are given.

1. skates
2. companies; sell
3. trails
4. pads
5. perform

Exercise 53

1. (you)
2. (you)
3. you
4. game
5. tickets

Exercise 54

1. Serious runners often run <u>marathons</u>.—DO
2. Marathon runners are <u>dedicated</u>.—PA
3. They are outstanding <u>athletes</u>.—PN
4. Spectators at a marathon give the <u>runners</u> <u>encouragement</u>.—IO, DO
5. Their cheers add <u>excitement</u> to the race.—DO
6. A runner usually feels <u>tired</u> but <u>proud</u> at the end of the marathon.—PA, PA

Chapter 19 Chapter Review

GRAMMAR EXERCISES 50–59

Exercise 50 Identifying Complete Subjects and Complete Predicates
Copy each of the sentences below onto your paper. Underline the subject once and the verb twice. Then, draw a vertical line between the complete subject and the complete predicate.

1. Tennis is a great personal sport.
2. The only equipment needed is a racquet and a ball.
3. The players must learn how to score.
4. Two or four people can play the game.
5. A special court is necessary to play tennis.

Exercise 51 Recognizing Complete Thoughts On your paper, copy each group of words below. Label complete thoughts *sentence*. Label incomplete thoughts *fragment*.

1. The Frisbee hit the market in 1957.
2. Sailed through the air.
3. Frisbees have been manufactured by many companies.
4. Taken anywhere, with a leash.
5. Many dogs, but mostly my dog.

Exercise 52 Completing Sentences With Compound Subjects and Compound Verbs Each of the following sentences contains a single subject and verb and one or two blanks. On your paper, rewrite the sentences, filling in each blank with another noun or verb that would create a logical compound.

1. Skateboards and ___?___ are very popular.

2. Many stores and ___?___ buy and ___?___ inline skates.
3. Beach boardwalks and ___?___ are common places to use inline skates.
4. Helmets and ___?___ are important safety equipment for this sport.
5. Serious inline skaters practice and ___?___ tricks on specially constructed ramps.

Exercise 53 Locating Hard-to-Find Subjects On your paper, write the subject of each sentence. If the subject is understood, write it in parentheses.

1. Stay off the grass!
2. Wear the proper equipment for all sports.
3. On which field will you be playing?
4. There was another game played this afternoon.
5. Here are the tickets for tonight's football game.

Exercise 54 Identifying All Kinds of Complements Each of the following sentences contains one or more complements. Copy the sentences onto your paper. Underline each complement, and tell whether it is a direct object, an indirect object, a predicate noun, or a predicate adjective.

1. Serious runners often run marathons.
2. Marathon runners are dedicated.
3. They are outstanding athletes.
4. Spectators at a marathon give the runners encouragement.
5. Their cheers add excitement to the race.
6. A runner usually feels tired but proud at the end of a marathon.

7. In a way, each participant is a <u>winner</u>.—PN
8. Big marathons make <u>news</u> throughout the world.—DO
9. Many marathons raise <u>money</u> for charities.—DO
10. The organizers of these marathons are busy <u>people</u>.—PN

7. In a way, each participant is a winner.
8. Big marathons make news throughout the world.
9. Many marathons raise money for charities.
10. The organizers of these marathons are busy people.

Exercise 55 Recognizing Parts of Sentences Write the following sentences, and label the direct objects *DO*, the predicate nouns *PN*, and the predicate adjectives *PA*.

1. Water-skiing is both fun and exciting.
2. The best water-skiers on the trip were Mindy and Tanya.
3. This morning, the lake was calm and smooth.
4. We like Lake Shasta and Lake Powell for water-skiing.
5. Water-skiers must be strong and steady to stay up on their skis.

Exercise 56 Completing Sentences With Complements
Complete each sentence by adding a complement. You may add other words as needed to make sense. Tell whether the complement you add is a direct object, a predicate noun, or a predicate adjective.

1. We watched ___?___.
2. It was ___?___.
3. Which runner was ___?___?
4. That runner seems ___?___.
5. She won ___?___.
6. They played ___?___.
7. Someone asked ___?___.
8. They made ___?___.
9. We are ___?___.
10. He felt ___?___.

Exercise 57 Revision Practice: Sentence Combining Combine some sentences in the following paragraph by using compound complements. You may make other minor changes as necessary.

Of all the backyard games, badminton is my favorite. The equipment is not expensive. It isn't hard to set up, either. You need a net. You also need some racquets. You need a "birdie," too. Two or four people play the game. Badminton resembles tennis. Badminton and tennis are played with a net. They are both played with racquets as well. However, tennis is played with a tennis ball that can bounce on the ground during play. Badminton is played with a "birdie" that must not touch the ground during play. Last week, my brother and I played badminton. The game was fast. It was also exciting.

Exercise 58 Writing Application
Write an explanation of an activity you enjoy. Identify the simple subject and simple predicate of each sentence.

Exercise 59 CUMULATIVE REVIEW
Parts of Speech Read the following paragraph. Then, on your paper, write the part of speech of each underlined word.

(1) Buzz, an irritable, ugly old tortoise, moved into a pond in our back yard. (2) The big pond was just the right size for him. (3) He built a nest and chased all the ducks and geese away. (4) Then, he befriended our dog, Spike. (5) He and Spike became inseparable. (6) Soon, Buzz seemed different. (7) He appeared happy. (8) Spike gave him affection. (9) It seemed that Buzz had wanted affection and a friend all along. (10) Who frightened the ducks and geese?

Exercise 55
1. fun—PA; exciting—PA
2. Mindy—PN; Tanya—PN
3. calm—PA; smooth—PA
4. Lake Shasta—DO; Lake Powell—DO
5. strong—PA; steady—PA

Exercise 56
Sample answers are given.
1. television—DO
2. exciting—PA
3. best—PA
4. happy—PA
5. a prize—DO
6. games—DO
7. questions—DO
8. baskets—DO
9. tired—PA
10. sad—PA

Exercise 57
Answers may vary. Possible rewrite:
Of all the backyard games, badminton is my favorite. The equipment is neither expensive nor hard to set up. You need a net, some racquets, and a "birdie." Two or four people play the game. Badminton resembles tennis. Both use a net and racquets. However, tennis is played with a tennis ball that can bounce on the ground during play, while badminton is played with a "birdie" that must not touch the ground during play. Last week, my brother and I played badminton. The game was fast and exciting.

Exercise 58
Writing Application
Ask a volunteer to read his or her explanation to the class. After the explanation has been read through once, have the volunteer reread a few sentences, one at a time. After each sentence is read, ask the class to identify the simple subject and predicate.

Exercise 59
1. adjective
2. preposition
3. adverb
4. possessive pronoun (used as an adjective)
5. coordinating conjunction
6. adjective
7. linking verb
8. pronoun
9. noun
10. interrogative pronoun

Recognizing Appropriate Sentence Construction

Teaching Resources: Standardized Test Preparation Workbook, pp. 37–38

1. As students read each test item, remind them to look for clues to inappropriate sentence construction.

2. Have students refer to the sample test item on this page.

3. Guide them to see that the first sentence, while containing a subject and a verb, begins with the word *If*. This means that this is a dependent clause, not a complete sentence.

Standardized Test Preparation Workshop

Recognizing Appropriate Sentence Construction

Knowing how to use the basic parts of a sentence correctly is the foundation for building good writing. Standardized tests measure your ability to identify a complete sentence. Every sentence must contain a subject (the *who* or *what* that performs the action) and a verb (the action the subject is performing) and express a complete thought. If one of these parts is missing, you have an incomplete sentence, or a fragment. When answering these test questions, check each group of words for a subject and a verb, and then determine whether it expresses a complete thought. Finally, choose the group of words that contains all of the elements of a complete sentence to replace any sentence fragments.

The following question will give you practice with the format used for testing your knowledge of basic sentence parts.

Test Tips

• Remember that a verb can either follow or come before its subject.
• Also, a form of *be* can be the main verb of a sentence, but it does not express action; instead, it links words together.

Sample Test Item	Answer and Explanation
Choose the letter of the best way to write each underlined section. If the underlined section needs no change, choose "Correct as is." If inventors weren't able to pursue their ideas. We would still have to get up and walk to the television to change the channel. **A** If inventors weren't able to pursue their ideas. We would still have to get up, and walk to the television to change the channel. **B** If inventors weren't able to pursue their ideas, we would still have to get up and walk to the television. To change the channel. **C** If inventors weren't able to pursue their ideas, we would still have to get up and walk to the television to change the channel. **D** Correct as is	The correct answer is *C*. The sentence fragment "If inventors weren't able to pursue their ideas" contains a subject—*inventors*—and a verb—*pursue*—but it does not express a complete idea. Answer *C* combines the fragment with the complete sentence that follows by making the fragment an introductory clause.

422 • Basic Sentence Parts

✏ TEST-TAKING TIP

Have students read each of the choices carefully. Tell them to immediately eliminate any choice that does not follow appropriate sentence construction. For example, in the sample test item, choices A and B both contain incomplete sentences. These choices can be eliminated, making the process of choosing the right answer much easier.

▶ **Practice 1** **Directions:** Choose the letter of the best way to write the underlined section. If the underlined section needs no change, choose "Correct as is."

King Camp Gillette was a traveling
    (1)
hardware salesman, from Fond du Lac

Wisconsin. Invented the first razor with

disposable blades. While shaving with the
                        (2)
long, single-edged razor used at the time. He

realized only a small part—the blade—of it

was really needed.

1 **A** King Camp Gillette was a traveling hardware salesman from Fond du Lac, Wisconsin, who invented the first razor with disposable blades.

B King Camp Gillette was a traveling hardware salesman. From Fond du Lac, Wisconsin, invented the first razor with disposable blades

C King Camp Gillette was a traveling hardware salesman and inventor from Fond du Lac, Wisconsin. The first razor with disposable blades.

D Correct as is

2 **F** While shaving with the long, single-edged razor used at the time, he realized only a small part of it—the blade—was really needed.

G While shaving with the long, single-edged razor. Used at the time, he realized only a small part of it—the blade—was really needed.

H While shaving with the long, single-edged razor used at the time, he realized, only a small part of it. The blade was really necessary.

J Correct as is

▶ **Practice 2** **Directions:** Choose the letter of the best way to write the underlined section. If the underlined section needs no change, choose "Correct as is."

By creating a razor with disposable blades.
        (1)
Gillette created a smaller, safer razor.

Safety razors were not an instant success. In
                                            (2)
1903, only 51 razors and 168 blades were

sold. However, two years later, sales of
                    (3)
90,000 razors and 12,400,000 blades.

1 **A** Gillette created a smaller, safer razor, and by creating a razor with disposable blades.

B Gillette created a smaller, safer razor. When creating a razor with disposable blades.

C By creating a razor with disposable blades, Gillette created a smaller, safer razor.

D Correct as is

2 **F** Safety razors were not an instant success, in 1903, only 51 razors and 168 blades were sold.

G In 1903, sold only 51 razors and 168 blades. Not an instant success.

H Safety razors, not an instant success in 1903. Only 51 razors and 168 blades were sold.

J Correct as is

3 **A** Two years later, sales of 90,000 razors and 12,400,000 blades.

B However, two years later, sales climbed to 90,000 razors and 12,400,000 blades.

C However, climbed to 90,000 razors and 12,400,000 blades.

D Correct as is

▶ **Practice 1**
1. A
2. F

▶ **Practice 2**
1. C
2. J
3. B

In-Depth Lesson Plan

	LESSON FOCUS	PRINT AND MEDIA RESOURCES
DAY 1	**Prepositional Phrases** Students learn to identify and use prepositional phrases and phrases that act as adverbs (pp. 426–429).	**Teaching Resources** *Grammar Exercise Workbook*, pp. 69–78; *Grammar Exercises Answers on Transparencies*, Ch. 20; **On-Line Exercise Bank**, Section 20.1
DAY 2	**Verbal and Participial Phrases** Students learn to identify and use verbal, participial, infinitive and appositive phrases (pp. 430–437).	**Teaching Resources** *Grammar Exercise Workbook*, pp. 69–78; *Grammar Exercises Answers on Transparencies*, Ch. 20; **On-Line Exercise Bank**, Section 20.1
DAY 3	**Clauses** Students learn to identify and use adjective and adverb clauses (pp. 438-442).	**Teaching Resources** *Grammar Exercise Workbook*, pp. 79–86; *Grammar Exercises Answers on Transparencies*, Ch. 20; **On-Line Exercise Bank**, Section 20.2
DAY 4	**Sentence Classification** Students learn to identify simple, compound and complex sentences and do the Hands-On Grammar Activity (pp. 443–449).	**Teaching Resources** *Grammar Exercise Workbook*, pp. 79–86; *Grammar Exercises Answers on Transparencies*, Ch. 20; *Hands-on Grammar Activity Book*, Chapter 20 **On-Line Exercise Bank**, Section 20.2
DAY 5	**Review and Assess** Students review chapter and demonstrate mastery of use of phrases and clauses (pp. 450–453).	**Teaching Resources** *Formal Assessment*, Ch. 20; *Grammar Exercises Answers on Transparencies*, Ch. 20; **On-Line Exercise Bank**, Section 20.1

Accelerated Lesson Plan

	LESSON FOCUS	PRINT AND MEDIA RESOURCES
DAY 1	**Phrases** Students cover concepts and usage of phrases as determined by Diagnostic Test (pp. 426–437).	**Teaching Resources** *Grammar Exercise Workbook*, pp. 69–78; *Grammar Exercises Answers on Transparencies*, Ch. 20; **On-Line Exercise Bank**, Section 20.1
DAY 2	**Clauses** Students cover concepts and usage of clauses as determined by Diagnostic Test (pp. 438–447).	**Teaching Resources** *Grammar Exercise Workbook*, pp. 79–86; *Grammar Exercises Answers on Transparencies*, Ch. 20; *Hands-on Grammar Activity Book*, Chapter 20 **On-Line Exercise Bank**, Section 20.2
DAY 3	**Review and Assess** Students review chapter and demonstrate mastery of use of phrases and clauses (pp. 450–453).	**Teaching Resources** *Formal Assessment*, Ch. 20; *Grammar Exercises Answers on Transparencies*, Ch. 20; **On-Line Exercise Bank**, Section 20.1

Options for Adapting Lesson Plans

HOMEWORK

Have students complete any section of the chapter for homework.

FEATURES

Extend coverage with the Grammar in Literature feature (p. 447), and the Standardized Test Preparation Workshop (p. 452).

TECHNOLOGY

Students can use the On-Line Exercise Bank to complete the exercises on computer. The Auto Check feature will grade their work.

INTEGRATED SKILLS COVERAGE

Grammar in Literature
SE p. 447

Reading
Find It In Your Reading, SE pp. 437, 448, 449

Writing
Find It In Your Writing, SE pp. 437, 448, 449
Writing Application SE pp. 437, 449, 451
Grammar and Style SE pp. 426, 434, 446

Speaking and Listening ATE p. 434

Spelling SE pp. 426, 441

Vocabulary
ATE pp. 427, 438, 446

Technology SE p. 445

Real-World Connection ATE p. 442

Viewing and Representing
Critical Viewing SE pp. 424, 427, 429, 432, 435, 439, 440, 444

ASSESSMENT SUPPORT

Standardized Test Preparation SE p. 452; ATE p. 431
Standardized Test Preparation Workbook, pp. 39–40
Formal Assessment, Ch. 20

MEETING INDIVIDUAL NEEDS

Less Advanced Students ATE pp. 428, 439. See also Ongoing Assessment pp. 429, 435, 442, 446.
ESL Students ATE p. 428
More Advanced Students ATE p. 442
Verbal/Linguistic Learners ATE p. 431
Musical/Rhythmic Learners ATE p. 439

BLOCK SCHEDULING

Pacing Suggestions
For 90-minute Blocks
• Administer the Diagnostic Test to students to determine instructional coverage
• Have students complete the necessary exercises in class. Use the Hands-on Grammar activity to provide a change of pace.

Professional Development Support
• *How to manage Instruction in the Block* This Teaching Resource provides management and activity suggestions.

MEDIA AND TECHNOLOGY

For the Student
• *On-Line Exercise Bank*, Ch. 20

For the Teacher
• *Resource Pro* CD-ROM

WRITING AND GRAMMAR WEB SITE

The Interactive Writing and Grammar Web site provides a wide array of support for students, teachers, and parents. Grammar support includes:

• *On-Line Exercise Bank* with Auto Check scoring
• Diagnostic and assessment support

www.phschool.com

LITERATURE CONNECTIONS

Grammar in Literature selections from *Prentice Hall Literature: Timeless Voices, Timeless Themes,* Bronze:
"The Treasure of Lemon Brown," Walter Dean Myers, SE p. 447
"The Chase," from *An American Childhood,* Annie Dillard, SE p. 437

► Lesson Objectives

1. To recognize phrases in sentences
2. To distinguish between adjective phrases and adverb phrases
3. To understand and recognize verbals, including participles and infinitives
4. To distinguish between independent and subordinate clauses
5. To distinguish between adjective and adverb clauses
6. To distinguish among simple, compound, and complex sentences

Critical Viewing

Describe Students may say *appears very threatening, at the horizon, touching the ground, approaching rapidly,* or *it looks like a tornado.*

Chapter 20 Phrases and Clauses

A **phrase** is a group of words that functions in a sentence as a single part of speech. Phrases do not contain a subject and a verb. For example, in the sentence "I just started reading an excellent book about tornadoes," *about tornadoes* acts as a prepositional phrase. In this chapter, you will learn about prepositional phrases, verbal phrases, and appositive phrases. Each type of phrase has a different use in a sentence.

Just as the development of a tornado depends on a variety of factors, such as temperature and wind, sentences depend on individual clauses to make complete thoughts. A **clause** is a group of words with its own subject and verb. Unlike a phrase, a clause is sometimes, but not always, a complete sentence. In this chapter, you will learn the difference between independent and dependent clauses, as well as how to recognize adjective and adverb clauses.

▲ Critical Viewing
What groups of words would you use to describe the storm in this photograph? **[Describe]**

☑ **ONGOING ASSESSMENT: Diagnose**

If students miss more than one item in each category, direct them to the relevant pages of the text and assign exercises for practice and review.

Phrases and Clauses	Diagnostic Test Items	Teach	Practice	Section Review	Chapter Review
Skill Check A					
Prepositional Phrases	A 1–5	pp. 426–429	Ex. 1–3	Ex. 9	Ex. 35, 38
Adverb and Adjective Phrases	A 1–5	pp. 426–429	Ex. 1–3	Ex. 9	Ex. 35, 38
Skill Check B					
Participial Phrases	B 6–10	pp. 430–433	Ex. 4–6	Ex. 10–13	Ex. 37–38
Skill Check C					
Appositive Phrases	C 11–15	pp. 434–435	Ex. 7–8	Ex. 14–15	Ex. 36, 38

Diagnostic Test

Directions: Write all answers on a separate piece of paper.

Skill Check A. Copy the prepositional phrase in each sentence below, labeling each one *adjective phrase* or *adverb phrase*.

1. The study of weather is called meteorology.
2. Meteorologists make predictions about the weather.
3. Their forecasts are broadcast on television and radio.
4. People listen with a mixture of trust and disbelief.
5. With the help of new technology, accuracy is improving.

Skill Check B. Identify the verbal phrases in the following sentences as *participial* or *infinitive*. Indicate how each phrase is used and the word(s) it modifies.

6. Feared wherever they occur, tornadoes are the most violent storms.
7. A tornado consists of winds swirling in the shape of a funnel.
8. Blowing at speeds up to 200 miles per hour, tornado winds can tear up just about anything in the path of the storm.
9. These devastating storms may travel at up to 60 miles per hour.
10. People build storm cellars in which to shelter during tornadoes.

Skill Check C. In each sentence, identify the appositive phrase.

11. Hurricanes, another kind of storm, may spread out over 200 miles.
12. Hurricanes are caused by areas of low pressure in the trade winds, strong ocean winds that blow towards the equator.
13. Winds in a hurricane swirl around the eye, its calm center.
14. Wall clouds, the clouds surrounding the eye, produce heavy rains.
15. Hurricane Gilbert, the most violent hurricane on record for the Western Hemisphere, struck the West Indies and Mexico in 1988.

Skill Check D. Copy the sentences below, underlining every adjective or adverb clause. Label each one *adjective* or *adverb*.

16. A harmonica, which produces a sound when you blow into it, is an example of a wind instrument.
17. Whenever air is forced through the harmonica, it vibrates the individual reeds.
18. Because the reeds are vibrating, the air around them vibrates.
19. Anyone who plays the harmonica will find that all the holes on the front are of different sizes.
20. Different sounds are created when air passes through the holes.

Skill Check E. Identify each sentence below as *simple, compound,* or *complex.*

21. The National Federation of Music Clubs is the largest charitable music group in the world.
22. It publishes *Music Clubs* magazine and supports music causes.
23. The federation offers scholarships to young musicians, who each receive $5,000 awards.
24. Sponsoring National Music Week is another of its activities.
25. The group was founded in 1898; it is located in Indianapolis.

✓ ONGOING ASSESSMENT: DIAGNOSE *continued*

Phrases and Clauses	Diagnostic Test Items	Teach	Practice	Section Review	Chapter Review
Skill Check D					
Adjective and Adverb Clauses	D 16–20	pp. 438–442	Ex. 19–22	Ex. 28–30	Ex. 39–40
Skill Check E					
Kinds of Sentences	E 21–25	pp. 443–448	Ex. 23–27	Ex. 31	Ex. 41–42
Cumulative Reviews and Applications				Ex. 16–18, 32–34	Ex. 44

Answer Key

Each item in the diagnostic test corresponds to a specific section in the chapter, enabling you to tailor instruction as needed. See "Ongoing Assessment: Diagnose" below for further details.

Skill Check A

1. of weather—adjective
2. about the weather—adjective
3. on television and radio—adverb
4. with a mixture of trust and disbelief—adverb
5. of new technology—adjective

Skill Check B

6. Feared wherever they occur—participial—adjective—tornadoes
7. swirling in the shape of a funnel—participial—adjective—winds
8. Blowing at speeds up to 200 miles per hour—participial—adjective—tornado winds
9. devastating—participial—adjective—storms
10. to shelter during tornadoes—infinitive—adjective—which

Skill Check C

11. another kind of storm
12. strong ocean winds that blow toward the equator
13. its calm center
14. the clouds surrounding the eye
15. the most violent hurricane on record for the Western Hemisphere

Skill Check D

16. which produces a sound (adjective) when you blow into it (adverb)
17. Whenever air is forced through the harmonica (adverb)
18. Because the reeds are vibrating (adverb)
19. who plays the harmonica (adjective)
20. when air passes through the holes (adverb)

Skill Check E

21. simple
22. simple
23. complex
24. simple
25. compound

Write three very short sentences and one phrase on the chalkboard, such as *He sent flowers. She threw them away. He apologized. For hurting her feelings.* Ask students to pick out the item that does not belong, and challenge them to explain why. Explain that a group of words that functions as a single part of speech and that does not contain a subject and verb is called a phrase.

Activate Prior Knowledge

Have students share some of the prepositions they learned in Chapter 17, and list them on the chalkboard. Ask volunteers to make up sentences that include these prepositions. Remind students that groups of words that begin with prepositions are called *prepositional phrases.*

TEACH

Step-by-Step Teaching Guide

Prepositional Phrases

1. Use the textbook page to demonstrate prepositional phrases and how they function. For example, have students identify the prepositions and their objects in the first Key Concept (of words, in a sentence, as a single part of speech of speech).

2. Remind students that the object of the preposition is always a noun or pronoun. Point out that adjectives or other words often come between the preposition and its object. Explain that, while these adjectives are part of the prepositional phrase, they are not the object of the preposition.

3. Help students see that a phrase functions as a single part of speech. Write some sentences with prepositional phrases on the chalkboard. Have students identify the phrases and explain how each one functions as a unit.

   Example: He sang German songs about love and death.

The prepositional phrase *about love and death* functions as one unit describing the songs. It serves the same purpose as the one-word adjective *German*, which also describes the songs.

Section 20.1

Phrases

There are many types of phrases, but they all have one thing in common: The words that make up a phrase work together as one.

> **KEY CONCEPT** A **phrase** is a group of words that functions in a sentence as a single part of speech. Phrases do *not* contain a subject and a verb. ■

Recognizing Prepositional Phrases

By itself, a *prepositional phrase* has at least two parts: a preposition and a noun or pronoun that is the object of the preposition.

EXAMPLE:
PREP OBJ
near airports

The object of the preposition may be modified by one or more adjectives.

EXAMPLE:
PREP ADJ ADJ OBJ
near busy urban airports

The object may also be compound.

EXAMPLE:
PREP OBJ OBJ
near busy urban highways and airports

No matter how long a prepositional phrase is or how many different parts of speech it contains, a prepositional phrase in a sentence always acts as if it were a one-word adjective or adverb.

Phrases That Act as Adjectives

A prepositional phrase that acts as an adjective in a sentence is called an *adjective phrase.*

> **KEY CONCEPT** An **adjective phrase** is a prepositional phrase that modifies a noun or pronoun by telling *what kind* or *which one.* ■

One-word adjectives modify nouns or pronouns. Adjective phrases also modify nouns and pronouns. However, instead of coming before the noun or pronoun, an adjective phrase usually comes after it.

Theme: Severe Weather

In this section, you will learn about different types of phrases. The examples and exercises in this section are about severe weather events such as hurricanes, tornadoes, and thunderstorms.

Cross-Curricular Connection: Science

💡 Spelling Tip

Although the preposition *through* is pronounced the same way as the verb *threw*, they are spelled differently.

⚙ Grammar and Style Tip

Because prepositional phrases act as adjectives and adverbs, you can use them in your sentences to add description and to clarify action.

⏱ TIME AND RESOURCE MANAGER

Resources
Print: Grammar Exercise Workbook, pp. 69–78
Technology: On-Line Exercise Bank, Section 20.1

In-Depth Coverage	Accelerated Pace
• Work through all key concepts, pp. 426–435. • Assign and review Exercises 1–8.	• Assign pp. 426–435 for independent student review. • Assign Review Exercises 9–15.

Adjectives	Adjective Phrases
The *asphalt* roadway began there.	The roadway *with two lanes* began there.
The *angry* rancher stopped us.	The rancher *with the angry face* stopped us.

Adjective phrases answer the same questions as one-word adjectives do. *What kind* of highway began there? *Which* rancher stopped us?

An adjective phrase can modify almost any noun or pronoun in a sentence.

MODIFYING SUBJECT:	The sound *of the wind* scared us.
MODIFYING A DIRECT OBJECT:	It rattled windows *in the room.*

When two adjective phrases appear in a row, the second phrase may modify the object of the preposition in the first phrase or both phrases may modify the same word.

MODIFYING THE OBJECT OF A PREPOSITION:	The weather vane *on the roof of the barn* spun wildly.
MODIFYING THE SAME WORD:	There was a smell *of rain in the air.*

Exercise 1 Identifying Adjective Phrases Copy the sentences below onto your paper. Then, underline each prepositional phrase used as an adjective, and draw an arrow from it to the word it modifies.
1. Changes in air pressure can cause wind movement.
2. An anemometer measures the speed of the wind.
3. Cups on the anemometer catch the wind.
4. Rushes of air spin the cups.
5. A speedometer on the axle of the anemometer indicates the wind speed.

▼ Critical Viewing
Write two sentences about this photograph. Include one phrase beginning with *below* and another beginning with *near.* [Analyze]

More Practice

Language Lab CD-ROM
• Prepositional Phrases lesson

On-line Exercise Bank
• Section 20.1

Grammar Exercise Workbook
• pp. 69–70

Phrases • 427

Phrases That Act as Adjectives

1. Review adjectives with students. Remind them that adjectives are descriptive words that answer the questions *What kind? Which one? How many?* or *How much?*

2. Have students look again at the Key Concept thay analyzed. Ask if "of words" is an adjective phrase and have them explain their answers. (Yes; it answers the question *What kind?* about the noun group.)

Integrating Vocabulary Skills

Latin Roots Have students find the derivation of the word *adjective* in the dictionary. They will note that it is made of the Latin prefix *ad-*, meaning "toward," and the Latin root *jacere*, meaning "to throw." The literal meaning of *adjective* is something that has been added to (thrown at) something else. Have students come up with other English words with the root *ject (project, object, conjecture, objective, inject, eject)*. Help them see how all these words vary in meaning based on their prefixes or suffixes.

Answer Key

Exercise 1

1. Changes <u>in air pressure</u> can cause wind movement. [arrow to *changes*]
2. An anemometer measures the speed <u>of the wind</u>. [arrow to *speed*]
3. Cups <u>on the anemometer</u> catch the wind. [arrow to *Cups*]
4. Rushes <u>of air</u> spin the cups. [arrow to *Rushes*]
5. A speedometer <u>on the axle</u> of <u>the anemometer</u> indicates the wind speed. [arrows from *on* to *speedometer;* from *of* to *axle*]

Critical Viewing

Analyze Students may say that the lightning is *below the clouds* and that one bolt of lightning is striking *near the other.*

☑ **ONGOING ASSESSMENT: Prerequisite Skills**

If students have difficulty with adverb and adjective phrases, you may find it necessary to review the following to assure coverage of prerequisite knowledge.

In the Textbook	Print Resources	Technology
Adjectives and Adverbs, pp. 334–359 Prepositions, pp. 360–373	Grammar Exercise Workbook, pp. 21–40	Language Lab CD-ROM, Using Modifiers; On-Line Exercise Bank, Sections 16–17.

Phrases That Act as Adverbs

1. Make sure that students understand the difference between adjectives and adverbs. Both are modifiers—words that describe other words. However, adjectives modify nouns and pronouns; adverbs modify other parts of speech.

2. Read aloud the sample sentences on the page to the class. Point out that in the chart, the phrase *to the barn* answers the question *Where?* and the phrase *at exactly eleven o'clock* answers the question *When?*

Customize for
Less Advanced Students

If students have trouble distinguishing between adverb phrases and adjective phrases, have them look at the word a phrase modifies. If it is a noun or a pronoun, the phrase is an adjective phrase. If it is an adverb, adjective, or verb, then the phrase is an adverb phrase.

Example: *The nearsighted rhinoceros squinted through the grass at the herd of zebras.*

The phrase *through the grass* modifies *squinted. Squinted* is a verb, so this is an adverb phrase. It answers the question *Where?*

The phrase *of zebras* modifies *herd. Herd* is a noun, so this is an adjective phrase. It answers the question *What kind?*

Customize for
ESL Students

Help students to remember the difference between adverbs and adjectives by reminding them that the word *adverb* contains the word *verb.* This will help students remember that adverbs modify verbs.

20.1

Phrases That Act as Adverbs

A prepositional phrase that acts as an adverb modifies the same parts of speech as a one-word adverb does.

▶ **KEY CONCEPT** An **adverb phrase** is a prepositional phrase that modifies a verb, an adjective, or an adverb. Adverb phrases point out *where, when, in what way,* or *to what extent.* ■

Adverb phrases are used in the same way as one-word adverbs, but they sometimes provide more precise details.

Adverbs	Adverb Phrases
Bring your saddle *here.*	Bring your saddle *to the barn.*
The parade began *early.*	The parade began *at exactly eleven o'clock.*

Adverb phrases can modify verbs, adjectives, and adverbs.

MODIFYING A VERB: Raindrops fell *in heavy torrents.* (Fell *in what way?*)

MODIFYING AN ADJECTIVE: The day was warm *for December.* (Warm *in what way?*)

MODIFYING AN ADVERB: The tornado struck suddenly, *within minutes of the warning.* (Suddenly *to what extent?*)

Adverb phrases, unlike adjective phrases, are not always located near the words they modify in a sentence.

EXAMPLE: *During the storm,* ranchers chased the herd.

Two or more adverb phrases can also be located in different parts of the sentence and still modify the same word.

EXAMPLE: *In an instant,* a tornado tore *through our house.*

▶ **Exercise 2** Identifying Adverb Phrases Each of the sentences below contains at least one prepositional phrase used as an adverb. Copy the sentences onto your paper. Then, underline each adverb phrase, and draw an arrow from it to the word it modifies.

EXAMPLE: Thunderstorms are heavy rainstorms

accompanied <u>by thunder and lightning</u>.

1. Thunderstorms form within large cumulonimbus clouds.
2. Cumulonimbus clouds form when warm air collides with a cold front.
3. Warm, humid air is forced upward into the sky.
4. At the higher altitude, the warm air cools.
5. In a short time, the cooling air creates dense thunderheads.
6. Heavy rain falls and is sometimes accompanied by hail.
7. Inside the clouds, thunderstorms produce strong upward and downward drafts.
8. When a downdraft strikes the ground, the air spreads in all directions.
9. In some instances, the spreading air produces wind bursts called "wind shear."
10. Wind shear has caused airplane accidents during takeoff and landing.

▶ **Exercise 3** Revising With Adverb Phrases Complete each of the sentences below with an adverb phrase that answers the question in parentheses.

EXAMPLE: The fog thickened (to what extent?).

ANSWER: The fog thickened <u>through the night</u>.

1. The weather balloon floated north (when?).
2. Take your umbrella (where?).
3. He ran (in what way?) to get out of the storm.
4. Flowing quickly down the mountain, the runoff from the rain spilled (to what extent?).
5. The clouds gathered and darkened (to what extent?).

More Practice

Language Lab CD-ROM
• Prepositional Phrases lesson
On-line Exercise Bank
• Section 20.1
Grammar Exercise Workbook
• pp. 71–72

▼ **Critical Viewing**
Describe what you imagine happened in the scene pictured below. Be sure to include the ideas *where, when, in what way,* and *to what extent.* **[Infer]**

Phrases • **429**

Answer Key

▶ **Exercise 2**

1. Thunderstorms form <u>within large cumulonimbus clouds</u>. [arrow to *form*]
2. Cumulonimbus clouds form when warm air collides <u>with a cold front</u>. [arrow to *collides*]
3. Warm, humid air is forced upward <u>into the sky</u>. [arrow to *upward*]
4. <u>At the higher altitude</u>, the warm air cools. [arrow to *cools*]
5. <u>In a short time</u>, the cooling air creates dense thunderheads. [arrow to *creates*]
6. Heavy rain falls and is sometimes accompanied <u>by hail</u>. [arrow to *accompanied*]
7. <u>Inside the clouds</u>, thunderstorms produce strong upward and downward drafts. [arrow to *produce*]
8. When a downward draft strikes the ground, the air spreads <u>in all directions</u>. [arrow to *spreads*]
9. <u>In some instances</u>, the spreading air produces wind bursts called wind shear. [arrow to *produces*]
10. Wind shear has caused airplane accidents <u>during takeoff and landing</u>. [arrow to *caused*]

▶ **Exercise 3**

Answers will vary.

Sample answers:

1. in the morning
2. from the closet
3. at a fast speed
4. over the whole valley
5. in large, thick masses

Critical Viewing

Infer Students may say that during the storm, the wind was so powerful that it caused a great deal of damage.

☑ **ONGOING ASSESSMENT: Monitor and Reinforce**

If students miss more than two items in Exercises 1–3, refer them to the following for additional practice.

In the Textbook	Print Resources	Technology
Section Review, Ex. 9, p. 436	Grammar Exercise Workbook, pp. 69–72	Language Lab CD-ROM, Prepositional Phrases; On-Line Exercise Bank, Section 20.1

Participles

1. Write a few present participles used as adjectives on the chalkboard: *flying trapeze, tumbling acrobats, laughing clowns.* Have each student contribute a phrase that follows this pattern. Ask students to identify the part of speech of each participle. Help them see that although the first words are verbs, they are being used as adjectives because they describe the nouns that follow.

2. Repeat step 1 using past participles such as *spoiled food, blown leaves, turned dirt.* Point out that past participles are often irregular.

3. Have student volunteers read the key concepts aloud and give their own examples for each one.

20.1

Recognizing Verbal Phrases

To understand the next two kinds of phrases, you must learn about *verbals.* A *verbal* is any verb that is used in a sentence not as a verb, but as another part of speech. The verbals discussed in the next two sections are *participles* and *infinitives.* Participles are used as adjectives. Infinitives are used as nouns, adjectives, or adverbs.

Although they are used as nouns, adjectives, or adverbs, verbals keep certain characteristics of verbs. They can be modified by an adverb or adverb phrase. They can also be followed by a complement, such as a direct object. A verbal used with a modifier or a complement is called a *verbal phrase.*

Participles

Participles are verb forms with two basic uses. When they are used with helping verbs, they are verbs. When they are used alone to modify nouns or pronouns, they become adjectives.

▶ **KEY CONCEPT** A **participle** is a form of a verb that is often used as an adjective. ■

There are two kinds of participles: *present participles* and *past participles.* Each kind can be recognized by its ending. All present participles end in *-ing.*

EXAMPLES: talking   doing   eating   wanting

Most past participles, however, end either in *-ed* or in *-d.*

EXAMPLES: opened   jumped   played   moved

Other past participles end in *-n, -t, -en,* or another irregular ending.

EXAMPLES: grown   felt   bought   eaten   held

In the following chart, both present and past participles are used in sentences as adjectives.

Present Participles	Past Participles
A *walking* tour was arranged.	The *cooked* food won't spoil.
Playing, she grabbed his hand.	He was by then, of course, a *grown* man.

Participles, like other adjectives, tell *what kind* or *which one.*

Participial Phrases

A participle can be expanded into a *participial phrase* by adding a complement or modifier.

KEY CONCEPT A **participial phrase** is a present or past participle and its modifiers. The participle can be modified by an adverb or adverb phrase or a complement. The entire phrase acts as an adjective in a sentence. ■

Participles can be expanded in many different ways.

PARTICIPIAL PHRASES
The instructor, *speaking slowly*, explained the use of skis.
The skier, *choosing her slope*, looked at its features carefully.
The esteemed poet, *honored by the award*, expressed his thanks.

The first participial phrase is formed by adding the adverb *slowly* to the participle *speaking*. The second is formed by adding the direct object *her slope* to the participle *choosing*. The third is formed by adding the adverb phrase *by the award* to the participle *honored*.

In the chart, each participial phrase is located after the noun it modifies. It could also go at the beginning of the sentence.

EXAMPLE: *Honored by the award*, the esteemed poet expressed his thanks.

Exercise 4 Recognizing Participial Phrases Copy the sentences below onto your paper. Then, underline each participial phrase and draw an arrow pointing from it to the word it modifies.

EXAMPLE: On the table, I saw several packages wrapped in gold paper.

1. Known for its cold weather, Minnesota has an abundance of snow.
2. My neighbor needed help shoveling his sidewalk.
3. Gripping the shovel, I went to work.
4. The driveway, covered in ice, seemed huge.
5. Finishing up, we went inside to warm our hands.

More Practice

On-line
Exercise Bank
• Section 20.1
Grammar Exercise Workbook
• pp. 75–78

Participial Phrases

1. Remind students that, though they are made up of several words, participial phrases, like other phrases, function as a single part of speech.

2. Explain that, though a prepositional phrase always begins with a preposition, not all participial phrases begin with participles. For example, in "The professor, often just called Doc, was a popular speaker," the phrase "often just called Doc" is a participial phrase modifying "The professor."

3. Point out that many of the participial phrases in the text contain prepositional phrases acting as adverbs.

Customize for
Verbal/Linguistic Learners

Challenge students to write three sentences about a circus, a baseball game, or some other event involving a lot of physical activity. Have them read their sentences aloud. Then challenge them to add at least two verbals (verbs that act as adjectives or adverbs) to each sentence. Read the sentences aloud again, and discuss how the verbals add a sense of motion and liveliness to their writing.

Answer Key

Exercise 4

1. <u>Known for its cold weather</u>, Minnesota has an abundance of snow. [arrow to *Minnesota*]
2. My neighbor needed help <u>shoveling his sidewalk</u>. [arrow to *help*]
3. <u>Gripping the shovel</u>, I went to work. [arrow to *I*]
4. The driveway, <u>covered in ice</u>, seemed huge. [arrow to *driveway*]
5. <u>Finishing up</u>, we went inside to warm our hands. [arrow to *we*]

STANDARDIZED TEST PREPARATION WORKSHOP

Grammar and Usage Standardized tests often require students to identify particular grammatical elements in sentences. Write the following sentence on the board and have students identify the participle:

The tenor and soprano <u>sang</u> <u>softly</u>
                                    A   B

together, <u>walking</u> slowly across the
                  C

stage as the curtain <u>fell</u>.
                              D

Students can eliminate item B, because it is not a verb. Items A and D are verbs that function as verbs, telling what the *singers* and the *curtain* did. Item **C** is the correct choice. *Walking* is the first word of a participial phrase that describes the singers.

Infinitives and Infinitive Phrases

1. Explain that an infinitive form of a verb always begins with the word *to: to walk, to swim, to ride, to laugh.* When students see a verb immediately after the word *to,* they know they have found an infinitive rather than a prepositional phrase.

   Example: *I wanted to call Pamela, but I was afraid she would refuse to speak to me.*

   To call and *to speak* are infinitives. *To me* is a prepositional phrase, because *me* is a pronoun, not a verb.

2. Have students give their own examples of infinitives and infinitive phrases in sentences. Have other students identify the part of speech each functions as.

Critical Viewing

Compare and Contrast Encourage students to suggest very different scenes, perhaps a beach or other warm scene. They may want to use infinitive phrases about their favorite sports or outdoor activities in their comparisons.

20.1

Infinitives and Infinitive Phrases

Infinitives are verb forms that are used as nouns, adjectives, and adverbs. Like participles, they can be combined with other words to form phrases.

▶ **KEY CONCEPT** An **infinitive** is a verb form that can be used as a noun, an adjective, or an adverb. The word *to* usually appears before the infinitive. ■

EXAMPLES: It is important *to listen.*
            He is the one *to ask.*

▶ **KEY CONCEPT** An **infinitive phrase** is an infinitive with modifiers or a complement, all acting together as a single part of speech. ■

EXAMPLES: It is important *to listen carefully.*
            It is not polite *to listen through the keyhole.*
            I want *to hear the news.*
            They want *to give you a present.*

▼ Critical Viewing
Write a short paragraph comparing this nature scene with your favorite natural scenery. Use infinitives and infinitive phrases in your comparison. **[Compare and Contrast]**

Using Infinitive Phrases

An infinitive phrase can be used in a sentence as a noun, an adjective, or an adverb. As a noun, an infinitive phrase can function as a subject, object, or appositive.

USED AS A SUBJECT: *To listen carefully* is important.

USED AS AN OBJECT: She wanted *to listen carefully.*

USED AS AN ADJECTIVE: You can rely on me *to listen carefully.*

USED AS AN ADVERB: They waited *to listen carefully* to her.

USED AS AN APPOSITIVE: His suggestion, *to listen carefully*, was appreciated.

> **Exercise 5** Identifying Infinitive Phrases and Their Functions Copy the infinitive phrase(s) in each of the following sentences onto your paper, and then write how each phrase functions in the sentence.

EXAMPLE: To reach the top was her goal.
ANSWER: To reach the top (subject)

1. We wanted to get home as soon as possible.
2. To drive up the hill was impossible.
3. Our decision, to stop and get a cup of coffee, proved to be the wrong one.
4. The snow seemed to pile up more quickly than before.
5. We had no choice except to drive on.
6. To understand the problem required us to listen.
7. The boys were about to jump when their mother arrived.
8. The soldier tried to follow orders.
9. My dream, to fly an airplane, was finally coming true.
10. No one seemed to know he was there.

> **Exercise 6** Writing Sentences With Infinitive Phrases
Write sentences using each of the following infinitive phrases according to the function indicated in parentheses.
1. to become a doctor (object)
2. to travel to Russia (subject)
3. to roast the chestnuts (direct object)
4. to study harder (appositive)
5. to wait until summer (object of preposition)
6. to bake a cake (appositive)
7. to see them again (predicate noun)
8. to go camping (object of preposition)
9. to learn about art (subject)
10. to visit grandmother's house (direct object)

> **More Practice**
On-line
Exercise Bank
• Section 20.1

Answer Key

> **Exercise 5**
1. to get home—noun, object
2. To drive up the hill—noun, subject
3. to stop and get a cup of coffee—noun, appositive; to be the wrong one—noun, object
4. to pile up—adjective, predicate adjective
5. to drive on—noun, object of preposition
6. to understand the problem—noun, subject; to listen—noun, object
7. to jump—noun, object of preposition
8. to follow orders—noun, object
9. to fly an airplane—noun, appositive
10. to know—adjective, predicate adjective

> **Exercise 6**
Answers will vary. Sample answers given.
1. She wanted to become a doctor.
2. To travel to Russia can be enjoyable.
3. Ann started to roast the chestnuts.
4. His resolution, to study harder, was quickly broken.
5. I was about to wait until summer before buying a computer, but my grandmother gave one to me for my birthday.
6. His job, to bake a cake, would be done in an hour.
7. His plan was to see them again.
8. We were about to go camping when it started to rain.
9. To learn about art was Peter's goal.
10. Maria went to visit grandmother's house.

Phrases • 433

☑ **ONGOING ASSESSMENT: Assess Mastery**

Use the following resources to assess students' mastery of phrases.

In the Textbook	Technology
Chapter Review, Ex. 36–38, p. 450 Standardized Test Preparation Workshop, pp. 452–453	On-Line Exercise Bank, Section 20.1

⏱ **TIME SAVERS!**

Answers on Transparency
Use the Grammar Exercises Answers on Transparencies for Chapter 20 to facilitate correction by students.

On-Line Exercise Bank
Have students complete the exercises on computer. The Auto Check feature will grade their work for you!

Appositives in Phrases

1. Explain that an appositive is a noun or pronoun that renames another noun or pronoun. For example, in the example sentence on page 434, the name *Pablo Picasso* is a proper noun that renames the noun *painter.*

2. Point out that appositives and appositive phrases are often set off by commas when the appositive phrase is not essential to understanding the sentences. These are also known as **nonrestrictive** appositives.

   Example: *Charlie Chaplin, a silent-movie star, wrote the stories for most of his films.*

3. The subject of this sentence is *Charlie Chaplin,* and the verb is *wrote.* The appositive phrase *a silent-movie star* is not essential to the sentence's meaning and is therefore set off with commas.

Integrating Speaking Skills

Remind students that a comma indicates a natural pause in a sentence. Have students read aloud the sentences in Exercise 7 on page 435, paying close attention to the meaning of the words. Students will see that their natural instinct is to pause at each comma. This exercise will help them remember to set off most appositives and appositive phrases with commas.

20.1

Recognizing Appositive Phrases

Appositives are nouns or pronouns placed directly after other nouns or pronouns to give additional information about these words. Appositives are often set off from the rest of the sentence by commas or dashes.

▶ **KEY CONCEPT** An **appositive** is a noun or pronoun placed after another noun or pronoun to identify, rename, or explain the preceding word. ■

Note the way appositives are used in the chart below:

APPOSITIVES
The painter *Pablo Picasso* lived in Spain.
I want to visit Spain's famous museum, *The Prado*.
His painting *Guernica* impressed my father.

▶ **KEY CONCEPT** An **appositive phrase** is a noun or pronoun with modifiers. It stands next to a noun or pronoun and adds information or details.

The modifiers in the phrase are usually adjectives or adjective phrases.

APPOSITIVE PHRASES
Willa Cather, *an American novelist*, wrote *My Ántonia*.
Lisbon, *a thriving port in Portugal*, has often been the scene of espionage.
The shopping center—*a network of cars, shops, and people*—provides many jobs.

Appositives and appositive phrases can be compound.

EXAMPLE: The two settings, *a city in England* and *a city in Russia*, are contrasted in the book.

Grammar and Style Tip

Using appositives can add important details to the nouns in your sentences, which can make your writing more clear and more interesting.

☑ **ONGOING ASSESSMENT: Prerequisite Skills**

If students have difficulty with appositives and appositive phrases, you may find it necessary to review the following to assure coverage of prerequisite knowledge.

In the Textbook	Print Resources	Technology
Nouns and Pronouns, pp. 294–313 Adjectives, pp. 334–347	Grammar Exercise Workbook, pp. 1–12, 21–30	Language Lab CD-ROM, Using Nouns, Using Pronouns, Using Modifiers; On-Line Exercise Bank, Sections 14 and 16.1

▶ **Exercise 7** Identifying Appositives and Appositive Phrases
Underline the appositive or appositive phrase in the sentences
below. Then, draw an arrow to the word each one modifies.

1. Kublai Khan, the Mongol emperor of China, sent a fleet of
   ships carrying a huge army to attack Japan.
2. A typhoon, a powerful Pacific Ocean hurricane, struck the
   fleet.
3. The ships were buffeted by hurricane-force winds, some
   measuring more than 119 kilometers per hour.
4. The typhoon actually saved the Japanese from their enemies, the Chinese.
5. The Japanese gave the storm a special name, *kamikaze,*
   which means "divine wind."

▶ **Exercise 8** Combining Sentences Using Appositives and
Appositive Phrases Combine each pair of sentences to form a
single sentence containing an appositive or appositive phrase.

EXAMPLE: Pilgrims were also known as Separatists. The
             Pilgrims decided to establish a colony in the New
             World.

ANSWER: The Pilgrims, a group also known as Separatists,
             decided to establish a colony in the New World.

1. In 1620, a group of English Pilgrims set sail for North
   America. They were colonists seeking religious freedom.
2. Their ship was thrown off course by rough seas and
   storms. Their ship was named the *Mayflower.*
3. Instead of landing near the Hudson River, the *Mayflower*
   was blown to the Cape Cod peninsula. The Cape Cod
   peninsula is a spot farther east.
4. John Winthrop was one of the leaders of the Pilgrims.
   Winthrop thought the landing spot was a good place for
   their colony.
5. The newest settlement could thank a storm for its beginnings. The settlement was named Plymouth Colony.

▶ **More Practice**

On-line
Exercise Bank
• Section 20.1
**Grammar Exercise
Workbook**
• pp. 73–74

◀ **Critical Viewing**
Imagine that you are
below the clouds, in
the midst of this
storm. Write two sen-
tences that include
appositive phrases to
describe the storm.
[Describe]

Phrases • 435

▶ **Exercise 7**

1. the Mongol emperor of China—
   modifies *Kublai Khan*
2. a powerful Pacific Ocean
   hurricane—modifies *typhoon*
3. some measuring more than
   119 kilometers per hour—
   modifies *winds*
4. the Chinese—modifies *enemies*
5. *kamikaze*—modifies *name*

▶ **Exercise 8**

1. In 1620, a group of English
   Pilgrims, colonists seeking
   religious freedom, set sail for
   North America.
2. Their ship, the *Mayflower,* was
   thrown off course by rough seas
   and storms.
3. Instead of landing near the
   Hudson River, the *Mayflower*
   was blown to the Cape Cod
   peninsula, a spot farther east.
4. John Winthrop, one of the
   leaders of the Pilgrims, thought
   the landing spot was a good
   place for their colony.
5. The newest settlement,
   Plymouth Colony, could thank a
   storm for its beginning.

Critical Viewing

Describe Students may write that
the huge storm, a hurricane, is
battering the land.

☑ **ONGOING ASSESSMENT: Monitor and Reinforce**

If students miss more than two items in Exercises 4–8, refer them to the following for additional
practice.

In the Textbook	Print Resources	Technology
Section Review, Ex. 10–15, pp. 436–437	Grammar Exercise Workbook, pp. 73–78	On-Line Exercise Bank, Section 20.1

⏱ **TIME SAVERS!**

📄 **Answers on Transparency**
Use the Grammar Exercises
Answers on Transparencies for
Chapter 20 to facilitate
correction by students.

💻 **On-Line Exercise Bank**
Have students complete the
exercises on computer. The Auto
Check feature will grade their
work for you!

Section Review

Each of these exercises correlates with a concept in the section on phrases, pages 426–435. The exercises may be used for more practice, for reteaching, or for review of the Key Concepts presented.

Answer Key

Exercise 9

Sample answers:

1. With little warning, the storm struck.
2. It came from out of nowhere.
3. Jan, in a raincoat and boots, ran outside.
4. The town was in the eye of the storm.
5. School opened in spite of the weather report.
6. Lightning was above the clouds.
7. A burst of mud and rain hit the umbrella.
8. It was torn by gusting winds.
9. Jan ran inside as fast as she could.
10. The storm was just a blip on the radar screen.

Exercise 10

1. frozen—participle
2. to visit—infinitive
3. amazing—participle
4. to believe—infinitive
5. snow-producing—participle

Exercise 11

1. interrupted by a blizzard
2. to fall less rapidly
3. Continuing for several hours
4. snow-clogged roads
5. to drive home, to turn back
6. newly frozen
7. Skidding on the ice
8. changing to sleet as it got warmer
9. To be safe
10. to last two days

Exercise 12

Sample answers:

1. Those plants, _growing without roots_, are very unusual. (arrow to _plants_)
2. Fertilizer is used _to improve the soil_. (arrow to _used_)
3. Delicate roses, _blooming only in the summer_, are my favorite. (arrow to _roses_)

Section 20.1 Section Review

GRAMMAR EXERCISES 9–18

> **Exercise 9** Writing Sentences Using Adjective and Adverb Phrases
Write ten sentences, each using a prepositional phrase according to the instructions in parentheses.

1. with little warning (as an adverb phrase)
2. from out of nowhere (as an adverb phrase)
3. in a raincoat and boots (as an adjective phrase)
4. in the eye of the storm (as an adjective phrase)
5. in spite of the weather report (as an adverb phrase)
6. above the clouds (as an adjective phrase)
7. of mud and rain (as an adjective phrase)
8. by gusting winds (as an adverb phrase)
9. as fast as she could (as an adverb phrase)
10. on the radar screen (as an adjective phrase)

> **Exercise 10** Identifying Participles and Infinitives On your paper, identify the participle or infinitive in the following sentences.

1. Snow is frozen precipitation.
2. Ski resorts are fun to visit when there is a lot of snow.
3. Between 1971 and 1972, Mt. Rainier had an amazing 1,122 inches of snow.
4. It might be hard to believe, but Syracuse, New York, is the snowiest large city.
5. Nearly every area in the United States receives snow-producing storms.

> **Exercise 11** Identifying Verbal Phrases On your paper, write the participial phrase or the infinitive phrase in the following sentences.

1. The day, interrupted by a blizzard, seemed very long.
2. That afternoon, the snow began to fall less rapidly.
3. Continuing for several hours, the blizzard covered the highway with snow.
4. The snow plows could not clear the snow-clogged roads.
5. He attempted to drive home, but was forced to turn back.
6. Newly frozen ice lay beneath the snow.
7. Skidding on the ice, two trucks nearly collided.
8. The snow, changing to sleet as it got warmer, made the roads dangerous.
9. To be safe, several roads were closed.
10. The storm was predicted to last two days.

> **Exercise 12** Writing Sentences With Verbal Phrases On your paper, write ten sentences using the verbal phrases below. Underline each phrase and draw an arrow pointing from it to the word it modifies.

1. growing without roots
2. to improve the soil
3. blooming only in the summer
4. dropping to -30°F in the winter
5. to avoid weeds
6. to prepare for planting
7. caught in the direct sun
8. to dig rapidly
9. to write about gardening
10. nourished by the sun and rain

436 • Phrases and Clauses

---

4. The temperature, _dropping to −30°F in the winter_, is a balmy 70°F in summer. (arrow to _temperature_)
5. Check your garden often _to avoid weeds_. (arrow to _Check_)
6. Turn the soil over _to prepare for planting_. (arrow to _turn_)

7. A small plant, _caught in the direct sun_, looked beautiful. (arrow to _plant_)
8. Try _to dig rapidly_. (arrow to _try_)
9. I asked my mother _to write about gardening_. (arrow to _asked_)
10. Her garden flourished, _nourished by the sun and rain_. (arrow to _garden_)

> **Exercise 13** Adding Verbal
Phrases to Sentences On your paper,
complete each sentence below by filling in
the blank according to the instructions in
parentheses.

1. Living near the Arctic Circle, the Inuit
have learned ___?___ . (infinitive
phrase)
2. The Inuit, ___?___ , are isolated. (participial phrase)
3. ___?___ , they catch fish and hunt
whales and seals. (infinitive phrase)
4. Clothing, ___?___ , varies from area to
area. (participial phrase)
5. Caribou skin, ___?___ , is lightweight
and warm. (participial phrase)

> **Exercise 14** Identifying
Appositive Phrases On your paper,
write the appositive phrase found in each
sentence in the following paragraph.

(1) Satellites and weather balloons, two
important weather-prediction tools, have
been greatly improved in recent years. (2)
Short-range forecasts, predictions for up
to five days, are now fairly reliable. (3)
Weather balloons carry instruments into
the troposphere, the lowest layer of
Earth's atmosphere. (4) The instruments
gauge three important measurements,
temperature, air pressure, and humidity.
(5) The first weather satellite was
launched in 1960, the year before my
father was born.

> **Exercise 15** Identifying
**Appositives and the Nouns They
Modify** On a separate sheet of paper,
write the appositives and appositive phrases in the following sentences, and indicate
the noun each one renames.

1. A barometer, an instrument that
measures changes in air pressure,
helps in forecasting weather.

2. There are two kinds of barometers—
mercury barometers and aneroid
barometers.
3. A mercury barometer consists of a
glass tube that is open at the bottom
and partially filled with mercury, a
metallic element.
4. The space in the tube above the mercury is almost a vacuum, an airless
area.
5. Increases in air pressure will cause
the column of mercury in the tube
to rise above its normal level,
76 centimeters.

> **Exercise 16** Find It in Your
Reading List the prepositional and participial phrases you find in these sentences from "The Chase" by Annie Dillard.

He chased us silently over picket
fences, through thorny hedges,
between houses, around garbage
cans, and across streets. Every time
I glanced back, choking for breath,
I expected he would have quit.

> **Exercise 17** Find It in Your
Writing Look through your writing
portfolio. Find examples of sentences that
contain prepositional phrases, participial
phrases, or infinitive phrases. Underline
any phrases you find, and tell how they
are used. If your writing does not contain
any of these types of phrases, then revise
your writing to include them.

> **Exercise 18** Writing Application
Write a brief description of a rainstorm
or snowstorm. Include sentences that contain prepositional phrases, participial
phrases, infinitive phrases, and appositive
phrases in your description.

Section Review • 437

> **Exercise 13**
Possible answers are given.
1. to live comfortably
2. living in the Far North
3. To eat
4. made from the skins of animals
5. preferred by many

> **Exercise 14**
1. two important weather-prediction tools
2. predictions for up to five days
3. the lowest layer of Earth's atmosphere
4. temperature, air pressure, and humidity
5. the year before my father was born

> **Exercise 15**
1. an instrument that measures changes in air pressure—renames *barometer*
2. mercury barometers and aneroid barometers—renames *kinds*
3. a metallic element—renames *mercury*
4. an airless area—renames *vacuum*
5. 76 centimeters—renames *level*

> **Exercise 16**
Find It in Your Reading
Prepositional phrases: over picket fences, through thorny hedges, between houses, around garbage cans, across streets
Participial phrase: choking for breath

> **Exercise 17**
Find It in Your Writing
Have students exchange papers with a partner and make sure all phrases have been correctly identified.
continued

Answer Key continued

> **Exercise 18**
Writing Application
If students are having trouble using participial phrases, have them brainstorm for a list of verbs that might be associated with a storm. They can then change the forms of these verbs so that they may be used as participles.

TIME SAVERS!

Answers on Transparency
Use the Grammar Exercises Answers on Transparencies for Chapter 20 to facilitate correction by students.

On-Line Exercise Bank
Have students complete the exercises on computer. The Auto Check feature will grade their work for you!

Write the following clauses on the board:

She went to the concert

Since she went to the concert

Ask students: Both of these examples contain a subject and verb. Only one is a complete sentence. Which one? Why?

Elicit that the second one is not a complete sentence because it needs more information to make it a complete thought.

Activate Prior Knowledge

Write the words *dependent* and *independent* on the board. Have students brainstorm qualities they associate with each term. Then, have them predict the meaning of the terms *independent clause* and *dependent clause.*

TEACH

Step-by-Step Teaching Guide

Clauses

1. Make sure students understand the difference between *independent* and *subordinate* clauses. The name independent is a helpful reminder that this type of clause can stand on its own as a sentence.

2. *Because, since, that, which, when,* and *as* are other words that frequently begin a subordinate clause. Point out that these words show relationships. One event can happen *after, because of,* or *since* another. These words at the beginning of a subordinate clause show its relationship to the independent clause.

Integrating Vocabulary Skills

Dictionary Use Have students use dictionaries to define *subordinate.* This definition (inferior, lower in rank) will help them learn that a subordinate clause is not as strong as an independent clause. Point out that subordinate clauses are called *dependent clauses.* They modify independent clauses; they cannot stand on their own.

Section 20.2

Clauses

There are two basic kinds of clauses: *independent clauses* and *subordinate clauses.*

KEY CONCEPT An **independent clause** has a subject and a verb and can stand by itself as a complete sentence. ■

INDEPENDENT CLAUSES:

The air vibrated.

In the morning, he began to play the cello.

KEY CONCEPT A **subordinate clause**, also known as a dependent clause, has a subject and a verb but cannot stand by itself as a complete sentence. It is only part of a sentence. ■

SUBORDINATE CLAUSES:

after she performed her solo

while the band practiced in the garage

Why is the thought in a subordinate clause *not* complete? Part of the answer is found in the first word of each clause. Such words as *after* and *while* will often make a clause *dependent* on another clause. To make a complete thought from a subordinate clause, it is necessary to add an independent clause.

In the following example, the subordinate clause is italicized; the independent clause is not.

EXAMPLE:

After she performed, Debbie felt relieved.

Exercise 19 Identifying and Classifying Clauses Copy the following sentences, underlining the independent clauses once and the subordinate clauses twice. Some sentences have no subordinate clause.

1. The singer was terrific.
2. Before she came out on stage, the band played several instrumental numbers.
3. The guitar player, who was especially good, played one solo with his teeth.
4. The music was extremely loud.
5. The audience cheered wildly when she began singing the first song.
6. The lights focused on her as she sang and danced.
7. In the middle of the concert, the band took a break.
8. My favorite song was called "In the Midnight Hour."
9. Everyone sang along as they performed the last song.
10. When the curtain closed and the lights came on, we knew the show was over.

Theme: Music

In this section, you will learn about different types of clauses and how to classify sentences by structure. The examples and exercises in this section are about music and musicians.

Cross-Curricular Connection: Music

More Practice

Language Lab CD-ROM
• Varying Sentence Structure lesson
• Combining Sentences lesson

On-line Exercise Bank
• Section 20.2

⏱ TIME AND RESOURCE MANAGER

Resources
Print: Grammar Exercise Workbook, pp. 79–86; Hands-on Grammar Activity Book, Chapter 20
Technology: On-Line Exercise Bank, Section 20.2

In-Depth Coverage	Accelerated Pace
• Work through all key concepts, pp. 438–447.	• Assign pp. 438–447 for independent student review.
• Assign and review Exercises 19–27.	• Assign Review Exercises 28–31.
• Read and discuss Grammar in Literature, p. 447.	
• Read and discuss the Hands-on Grammar Activity, p. 448.	

Adjective Clauses

A subordinate clause will sometimes act as an adjective in a sentence.

KEY CONCEPT An **adjective clause** is a subordinate clause that modifies a noun or a pronoun. ■

Like one-word adjectives and adjective phrases, an *adjective clause* answers w*hat kind* or *which one.*

Recognizing Adjective Clauses Most adjective clauses begin with the words *that, which, who, whom,* and *whose.* Sometimes, an adjective clause begins with an adverb, such as *since, where,* or *when.*

The adjective clauses in the following chart are italicized. The arrow in each sentence points from the adjective clause to the word in the independent clause that the adjective clause modifies. Notice that the adjective clauses come right after the words they modify.

ADJECTIVE CLAUSES
The student *whom I asked for help* turned pages of music for me. (*Which* student?)
By pushing the pedal *that is connected to the drum*, you will make sound. (*Which* pedal?)
The harp, *which was played in ancient Egypt*, was forbidden for women to play. (*Which* harp?)
In the centuries *since that time*, other instruments with strings have been invented. (*Which* centuries?)
The piano, *whose strings are hit by hammers to produce sound*, can be made louder or softer by foot pedals. (*What kind* of piano?)
At the moment *when the pedal is pushed*, the damper inside the piano changes the tone. (*Which* moment?)
People *who make stringed instruments* have to keep in mind the size, shape, material, and string tension of the instrument in order to create the perfect sound. (*What kind* of people?)

▲ **Critical Viewing**
In a short paragraph, use independent and subordinate clauses to compare this cello with other stringed instruments. How are they similar? How are they different? **[Distinguish]**

Clauses • **439**

Step-by-Step Teaching Guide

Adjective Clauses

1. Tell students that an adjective clause is a clause used as an *adjective.* Therefore, it describes a noun or pronoun in the sentence and will usually follow the noun or pronoun it is modifying.

2. Make sure students understand that some adjective clauses begin with an adverb. Tell them that even though the clause starts with an adverb, it still modifies a noun or pronoun, making it an adjective clause.

   This is the house where I used to live.

3. The adjective clause *where I used to live* modifies *house* by answering the question "Which house?" Notice that this clause begins with an adverb.

Customize for
Musical/Rhythmic Learners

Let partners choose a song whose words they know. They should write out the lyrics, then highlight the dependent and independent clauses in different colors. Point out that in song lyrics, sound and rhythm often supercede the rules of grammar. For this reason, students might see some dependent clauses that stand alone.

Customize for
Less Advanced Students

Provide practice by giving students the following subordinate clauses. Ask them to add an independent clause before or after each one to make a complete sentence.

   because it snowed

   when I am grown up

   while I was walking in the park

Critical Viewing

Distinguish Answers will vary. A sample is given.

The violin and cello are both stringed instruments that require a bow when played. However, because of its smaller size, the violin can be tucked beneath the chin of its player, whereas the larger cello must stand upright to be played.

> **Exercise 19** *(page 438)*

1. The singer was terrific.
2. Before she came out on stage, the band played several instrumental numbers.
3. The guitar player, who was especially good, played one solo with his teeth.
4. The music was extremely loud.
5. The audience cheered wildly when she began singing the first song.
6. The lights focused on her as she sang and danced.
7. In the middle of the concert, the band took a break.
8. My favorite song was called "In the Midnight Hour."
9. Everyone sang along as they performed the last song.
10. When the curtain closed and the lights came on, we knew the show was over.

Answer Key

20.2

▶ **Exercise 20** Identifying Adjective Clauses Copy the following sentences, and underline the adjective clause in each.

1. A person who is willing to devote much time and effort to it may find a career in music satisfying.
2. For a future in music, start taking lessons from a teacher who has excellent credentials.
3. After high school, you can enroll in a conservatory, which is a specialized music school.
4. Students who are inquisitive can find many ways to use their interest in music.
5. Many musicians who study in conservatories plan to become professional composers or performers.

▶ **Exercise 21** Writing Sentences With Adjective Clauses
Use each of the adjective clauses below to write a complete sentence.

EXAMPLE: that the band featured

ANSWER: The instrument *that the band featured* was an electronic keyboard.

1. whose talent is exceptional
2. where the newest bands play
3. which has a beautiful sound
4. who are in professional orchestras
5. that you can find in the music field
6. which is played the loudest
7. where I buy printed music
8. that plays the lowest notes
9. who enjoy classical music
10. whom I wanted to hear

▶ **More Practice**

On-line
Exercise Bank
• Section 20.2
Grammar Exercise
Workbook
• pp. 79–80

▶ Critical Viewing Use adjective clauses to describe the qualities that these brass instruments share. [Classify]

440 • Phrases and Clauses

Adverb Clauses

Subordinate clauses can also be used as adverbs.

KEY CONCEPT An **adverb clause** is a subordinate clause that modifies a verb, an adjective, or an adverb. ■

Adverb clauses can answer any of the following questions about the words they modify: *Where? When? In what way? To what extent? Under what conditions?* or *Why?* Adverb clauses begin with *subordinating conjunctions*. The following chart lists a number of common subordinating conjunctions:

COMMON SUBORDINATING CONJUNCTIONS	
after	so that
although	than
as	though
as if	unless
as long as	until
because	when
before	whenever
even though	where
if	wherever
in order that	while
since	

A subordinating conjunction always introduces the adverb clause. In a sentence, the conjunction will usually appear in one of two places—either at the beginning, when an adverb clause begins the sentence, or in the middle, connecting the independent clause to the subordinate clause.

EXAMPLES:

ADVERB CLAUSE   IND CLAUSE
Since you expect to be late, I will prepare dinner.

ADVERB CLAUSE   IND CLAUSE
Whenever you are late, I expect you to call.

IND CLAUSE   ADVERB CLAUSE
I will prepare dinner *since* you expect to be late.

IND CLAUSE   ADVERB CLAUSE
I expect you to call *whenever* you are late.

KEY CONCEPT A **subordinating conjunction** introduces an adverb clause. ■

🖋 Spelling Tip

Be careful when writing the word *although.* You may be tempted to write *all though,* but the subordinating conjunction *although* is one word with only one *l.*

Adverb Clauses

1. Remind students that a conjunction is a word used to connect other words or groups of words. Challenge them to recall the seven coordinating conjunctions they learned in Chapter 18.

2. Explain that subordinating conjunctions also link groups of words. They do this by making one group of words dependent upon the other.

3. Read the examples on this page. Point out that the word *since* links the clauses by creating a cause-and-effect relationship. The effect needs, or is dependent upon, the cause.

4. Have students turn to the chart on page 442 for additional examples of adverb clauses.

☑ ONGOING ASSESSMENT: Prerequisite Skills

If students have difficulty with adjective and adverb clauses, you may find it necessary to review the following to assure coverage of prerequisite knowledge.

In the Textbook	Print Resources	Technology
Pronouns, pp. 301–309 Conjunctions, pp. 376–380	Grammar Exercise Workbook, pp. 7–12, 41–42	Language Lab CD-ROM, Using Pronouns; On-Line Exercise Bank, Sections 14.2 and 18.1

Real-World Connection

Witnesses to crimes often appear in court. Sometimes they are asked a question such as, Will you please describe what you saw? Witnesses have to recount accurately the order in which things happened. Adverb clauses that begin with the words *before, after, while, when,* and *since* help the lawyers and jurors piece together the precise sequence of events.

Answer Key

▶ **Exercise 22**

Sample answers:

1. A musical composition begins <u>when a composer writes some music</u>.
2. The composer expands on the idea <u>until the music develops the proper sound and rhythm</u>.
3. <u>Unless someone plays the music</u>, it will never be heard.
4. Musicians practice <u>until the music is played perfectly</u>.
5. <u>When the two musicians get together</u>, the result can be very exciting.
6. <u>Whenever the music begins</u>, people are silent.
7. <u>If the music catches on with the public</u>, it may become a best seller.
8. Listeners call in <u>so that their songs are played on the radio</u>.
9. <u>Since music influences our emotions</u>, movies use music to add intensity to a scene.
10. Many beautiful poems become songs <u>after a composer sets poetry to music</u>.

Customize for
More Advanced Students

Challenge students to review the sentences they wrote for Exercise 22 and identify the word or words each adverb clause modifies. Suggest that, if all the adverb clauses modify verbs, they try writing two or three sentences in which the adverb clauses modify adjectives or adverbs.

20.2

In the chart below, the adverb clauses are italicized. The arrows point to the words the clauses modify. Notice that each clause answers *Where? When? In what way? To what extent? Under what conditions?* or *Why?* about the word it modifies.

ADVERB CLAUSES	
Modifying Verbs	Put the package *wherever you find room*. (Put *where?*)
	The concert will begin *when the conductor enters*. (Will begin *when?*)
	Leo spoke *as if he were frightened*. (Spoke *in what manner?*)
	I will have some lemonade *if you do too*. (Will have *under what conditions?*)
Modifying an Adjective	I am tired *because I have been chopping wood all day*. (Tired *why?*)
Modifying an Adverb	She knows more *than the other engineers do*. (More *to what extent?*)

▶ **Exercise 22** Writing Sentences With Adverb Clauses Use each of the adverb clauses below to write a complete sentence.

EXAMPLE: before we performed

ANSWER: *Before we performed*, we practiced daily.

1. when a composer writes some music
2. until the music develops the proper sound and rhythm
3. unless someone plays the music
4. until the music is played perfectly
5. when the two musicians get together
6. whenever the music begins
7. if the music catches on with the public
8. so that their songs are played on the radio
9. since music influences our emotions
10. after a composer sets poetry to music

▶ **More Practice**

On-line
Exercise Bank
• Section 20.2
Grammar Exercise Workbook
• pp. 81–82

442 • Phrases and Clauses

☑ **ONGOING ASSESSMENT: Monitor and Reinforce**

If students miss more than two items in Exercise 19 or 22, refer them to the following for additional practice.

In the Textbook	Print Resources	Technology
Section Review, Ex. 28–30, p. 449	Grammar Exercise Workbook, pp. 79–82	On-Line Exercise Bank, Section 20.2

Classifying Sentences by Structure

All sentences can be classified according to the number and kinds of clauses they contain.

The Simple Sentence The *simple sentence* is the most common type of sentence structure.

▶ **KEY CONCEPT** A **simple sentence** consists of a single independent clause. ■

Simple sentences vary in length. Some are quite short; others can be several lines long. All simple sentences, however, contain just one subject and one verb. They may also contain adjectives, adverbs, complements, and phrases in different combinations.

Simple sentences can also have various compound parts. They can have a compound subject, a compound verb, or both. Sometimes, they will also have other compound elements, such as a compound direct object or a compound phrase.

All of the following sentences are simple sentences. The subjects are underlined once, and the verbs are underlined twice.

ONE SUBJECT AND VERB:	The <u>monsoon</u> <u>came</u>.
COMPOUND SUBJECT:	<u>Landslides</u> and <u>avalanches</u> <u>are</u> common.
COMPOUND VERB:	The <u>door</u> <u>squeaked</u> and <u>rattled</u>.
COMPOUND SUBJECT AND VERB:	My <u>mother</u> and <u>father</u> <u>said</u> goodbye and <u>left</u> on vacation.
COMPOUND DIRECT OBJECT:	^{DO} ^{DO} He <u>opened</u> the letter and the box.
COMPOUND PREPOSITIONAL PHRASE:	^{PREP PHRASE} It <u>can rain</u> from the east or ^{PREP PHRASE} from the west.

What does a simple sentence *not* have? First, a simple sentence never has a subordinate clause. Second, it never has more than one independent clause.

Step-by-Step Teaching Guide

The Simple Sentence

1. Emphasize that a simple sentence never has more than one subject or verb. A compound subject, such as *mother and father,* is not considered two subjects. It is a compound subject linked by the conjunction *and.* In the same way, a compound verb such as *squeaked and rattled* functions as one verb.

2. Go over the sentences in Exercise 23 (page 444) with students. Remind them to ignore all the prepositional phrases and direct objects as they look for the subjects and verbs. Encourage them not to allow the descriptive elements in the sentence to distract them from accurately identifying the subject and verb.

✓ ONGOING ASSESSMENT: Prerequisite Skills

If students have difficulty with simple and compound sentences, you may find it necessary to review the following to assure coverage of prerequisite knowledge.

In the Textbook	Print Resources	Technology
Basic Sentence Parts, pp. 390–423 Conjunctions, pp. 376–380	Grammar Exercise Workbook, pp. 41–42, 45–68	On-Line Exercise Bank, Sections 18.1 and 19

Answer Key

Exercise 23

1. <u>style</u> <u>emerged</u>
2. <u>Miles Davis</u>, <u>musicians</u> <u>were</u> <u>influenced</u>, <u>adopted</u>
3. <u>approach</u> <u>blended</u>
4. <u>musicians</u> <u>used</u>
5. <u>players</u> <u>created</u>, <u>experimented</u>
6. <u>cellos</u>, <u>flutes</u>, <u>tubas</u> <u>were featured</u>
7. <u>groups</u> <u>became</u>
8. <u>critics</u> <u>objected</u>, <u>wrote</u>
9. <u>sound</u> <u>became</u>
10. <u>concerts</u> <u>became</u>

Critical Viewing

Support Students may say that their favorite instrument is the piano. They like the sound.

Step-by-Step Teaching Guide

The Compound Sentence

1. Emphasize the key points of a compound sentence. Just as a compound subject has two or more nouns joined by a conjunction, a compound sentence has two or more independent clauses, usually joined by a conjunction.

2. Have students apply this test to decide whether a sentence is compound: Can they break it into two complete sentences simply by eliminating the conjunction? If they can, it is a compound sentence.

   Example: Tad arrived very late, but Julio had waited for him.

   Tad arrived very late. Julio had waited for him.

   This becomes two complete sentences when the conjunction *but* is eliminated. Therefore, it is a compound sentence.

3. Point out that the independent clauses in a compound sentence are closely related, so that the joining makes sense because it adds more information to the original remark. If the two (or more) clauses are not related, they should be broken into separate sentences.

444

20.2

> **Exercise 23** Recognizing Simple Sentences Copy each simple sentence below onto your paper, and underline the subject once and the verb twice. Notice that some of the subjects and verbs are compound.

EXAMPLE: Miles Davis <u>played</u> the trumpet and <u>made</u> more than fifty jazz recordings.

1. In the late 1940's, a new style of jazz emerged, known as cool jazz.
2. Miles Davis and other young musicians were influened by and adopted this new style.
3. Their approach to cool jazz blended strong rhythms with flowing melodies.
4. The musicians used softer tones, syncopation, and a more even beat than other jazz players.
5. Cool-jazz players also created complex harmonies and experimented on new instruments.
6. For the first time, cellos, flutes, and tubas were featured in jazz performances.
7. Throughout the 1950's, many jazz groups became identified with this new sound.
8. Some music critics objected to the new style and wrote negative reviews.
9. The new sound became popular with college students and intellectuals.
10. Jazz concerts became more popular than ever before.

The Compound Sentence A *compound sentence* is made up of more than one simple sentence.

> **KEY CONCEPT** A **compound sentence** consists of two or more independent clauses. ∎

In most compound sentences, the independent clauses are joined by a comma and a coordinating conjunction (*and, but, for, nor, or, so,* or *yet*). They may also be connected with a semicolon (;) or a colon (:).

EXAMPLES: Jamal manned a two-day music festival, <u>and</u> eight bands agreed to play.

All the bands performed on the first day<u>;</u> two were missing the second day.

Notice in both of the preceding examples that there are two separate and complete independent clauses, each with its own subject and verb. Like simple sentences, compound sentences never contain subordinate clauses.

444 • Phrases and Clauses

> **More Practice**

Language Lab CD-ROM
• Varying Sentence Structure lesson

On-line Exercise Bank
• Section 20.2

Grammar Practice Workbook
• pp. 83–86

▼ Critical Viewing
Use simple sentences to identify your favorite musical instrument and explain why you prefer it. **[Support]**

▷ **Exercise 24** Recognizing Compound Sentences The sentences below are compound sentences. Copy each onto your paper. Then, underline the subject once and the verb twice in each independent clause.

EXAMPLES: Country <u>music</u> <u><u>has become</u></u> very popular today, and several <u>radio stations</u> <u><u>feature</u></u> country artists.

1. Country music is played all over the country, but its roots are in the Appalachian region.
2. Actually, the history of country music goes back to Europe; settlers brought folk ballads with them to their new homeland.
3. Appalachian musicians used different instruments to play the folk ballads, and they tried different singing styles.
4. Radio played an important role in spreading country music, for people in remote areas were able to hear it.
5. Singers in the Southwest added a western swing style, so they called their blend country western music.

The Complex Sentence *Complex sentences* contain subordinate clauses, which can be either adjective clauses or adverb clauses.

▷ **KEY CONCEPT** A **complex sentence** consists of one independent clause and one or more subordinate clauses. ∎

In a complex sentence, the independent clause is often called the *main clause.* The main clause has its own subject and verb, as does each subordinate clause.

EXAMPLES:

MAIN CLAUSE   SUBORD. CLAUSE
<u>January 26, 1947,</u> <u><u>is</u></u> the day that <u>India</u> <u><u>won</u></u> its independence.

SUBORD. CLAUSE   MAIN CLAUSE
Because the <u>day</u> <u><u>is</u></u> so important, many of the <u>festivities</u> <u><u>are</u></u> official.

In the next example, the complex sentence is more complicated because the main clause is split by an adjective clause.

```
                    ┌──── MAIN CLAUSE ────────────┐
                    │  ┌──SUBORD. CLAUSE──┐        │
EXAMPLE:    Schoolchildren, who have the day off, participate
            in an exciting parade.
```

The two parts of the independent clause form one main clause: *Schoolchildren participate in an exciting parade.*

⊛ **Technology Tip**

When typing on a computer, make sure to put only one space after every comma or period.

Step-by-Step Teaching Guide

The Complex Sentence

1. Emphasize that the identifying mark of a complex sentence is its subordinate clause or clauses. Have students turn back to page 438, if necessary, to review subordinate clauses. Point out that only complex sentences include subordinate clauses.

2. Discuss the sentences in Exercise 25 (page 446) with students. Help them identify the subordinate clauses that make these sentences complex.

Integrating Vocabulary Skills

Word Meanings Tell students that a *compound* contains two or more of something. A compound word is made up two smaller words. A compound in chemistry is made up of two or more elements, such as H_2O. A compound sentence contains two independent clauses. *Complex* means "complicated," "involved," or "intricate"—a combination of different things that work together. A complex sentence contains two different things, an independent clause and a subordinate clause(s).

Answer Key

Exercise 25

1. Rock-and-roll <u>melodies</u> <u>are</u> simple, (<u>which</u> <u>makes</u> them easy to play and sing).
2. (When <u>singers</u> <u>perform</u> on stage), <u>people</u> in the audience <u>sing</u> along with them.
3. The electric <u>guitars</u> (that some <u>musicians</u> <u>play</u>) <u>add</u> exciting sounds to the songs.
4. Teenage <u>girls</u> in the audience often <u>screamed</u> (while <u>Elvis Presley</u> <u>performed</u> on stage).
5. (Though <u>Presley</u> <u>was</u> very popular), several other <u>singers</u> <u>sold</u> just as many records.

Exercise 26

1. simple	6. complex
2. complex	7. compound
3. compound	8. simple
4. complex	9. simple
5. compound	10. complex

> **Exercise 25** Recognizing Complex Sentences The following are complex sentences. Copy each onto your paper. Underline the subject once and the verb twice in each clause. Then, put parentheses around each subordinate clause.

EXAMPLE: (Since many <u>teenagers</u> <u>love</u> to dance), <u>they</u> <u>enjoy</u> rock-and-roll music.

1. Rock-and-roll melodies are simple, which makes them easy to play and sing.
2. When singers perform on stage, people in the audience sing along with them.
3. The electric guitars that some musicians play add exciting sounds to the songs.
4. Teenage girls in the audience often screamed while Elvis Presley performed on stage.
5. Though Presley was very popular, several other singers sold just as many records.

> **Exercise 26** Identifying the Structure of Sentences On your paper, identify the structure of each of the following sentences as *simple, compound,* or *complex.*

EXAMPLE: When the Beatles arrived in New York in 1964, they began a "British invasion" of American music.

ANSWER: complex

1. The Beatles consisted of four musicians in their twenties.
2. Because they were quite poor, they struggled at first.
3. They could not afford music lessons, so they taught themselves to play and sing.
4. They had been playing together for several years before they had their first hit record.
5. They listened to many American recordings, and then they added new ideas to their music.
6. Because the group's voices blended so well, many of their songs feature strong harmonies.
7. The Beatles had long hair, but they wore suits on stage.
8. Others, such as the Rolling Stones, had a different image.
9. They wore casual clothes and sang more raucous songs.
10. Whereas the Beatles sang a lot of love songs, the Rolling Stones focused on blues.

> **More Practice**
>
> Language Lab CD-ROM
> • Varying Sentence Structure lesson
> • Combining Sentences lesson
> On-line Exercise Bank
> • Section 20.2
> Grammar Exercise Workbook
> • pp. 83–86

Grammar and Style Tip

A complex sentence is a good way to effectively combine two simple sentences.

TIME SAVERS!

Answers on Transparency Use the Grammar Exercises Answers on Transparencies for Chapter 20 to facilitate correction by students.

On-Line Exercise Bank Have students complete the exercises on computer. The Auto Check feature will grade their work for you!

✓ ONGOING ASSESSMENT: Monitor and Reinforce

If students miss more than two items in Exercises 23–26, refer them to the following for additional practice.

In the Textbook	Print Resources	Technology
Section Review, Ex. 31, p. 449	Grammar Exercise Workbook, pp. 83–86	On-Line Exercise Bank, Section 20.2

GRAMMAR IN LITERATURE

from **The Treasure of Lemon Brown**

Walter Dean Myers

In the following passage, the writer has used simple, compound, and complex sentences.

The person who called himself Lemon Brown peered forward, and Greg could see him clearly. He was an old man. His black, heavily wrinkled face was surrounded by a halo of crinkly white hair and whiskers that seemed to separate his head from the layers of dirty coats piled on his smallish frame. His pants were bagged to the knee, where they were met with rags that went down to the old shoes. The rags were held on with strings, and there was a rope around his middle. Greg relaxed. He had seen the man before, picking through the trash on the corner and pulling clothes out of a Salvation Army box.

▶ **Exercise 27** **Revising the Structure of Sentences** On your paper, rewrite the following sentences according to the directions in parentheses.

EXAMPLE: Bob Dylan influenced many musicians during the 1960's. He is credited with inventing folk rock. (combine to make one compound sentence)

ANSWER: Bob Dylan influenced many musicians during the 1960's, and he is credited with inventing folk rock.

1. Dylan made an important contribution to rock, but he was originally a folk singer. (Break into two simple sentences.)
2. He began his career in New York City. He recorded in Nashville. (Combine into a complex sentence.)
3. His early songs contained a strong social message, but later Dylan's music became more personal. (Change from a compound to a complex sentence.)
4. Later, Dylan played his songs on electric instruments. He used a strong rock beat. This style became known as folk rock. (Combine to make one complex sentence.)
5. Many of Dylan's original fans did not like his electrified music. They even booed at many of his performances. (Combine to make one compound sentence.)

Clauses • 447

Grammar in Literature

1. Have students break up this passage into individual sentences and identify each as simple, compound, or complex. (compound *and* complex, simple, complex, complex, compound, simple, simple) Call on individuals to explain their answers, so that the whole class can get the benefit of everyone's reasoning.
2. Point out the variety of sentence length and structure in Myers's writing. Ask students how the passage would sound if all the sentences were short, like "He was an old man."
3. Discuss some of the benefits of using a variety of sentence types within a passage.

More About the Writer

Walter Dean Myers was born in 1937 in West Virginia but grew up in the lively, bustling community of Harlem in New York City. Because Myers left West Virginia so early, he always thought of Harlem as home. Many of his novels are about young African Americans growing up in urban communities like his own.

Connecting with Literature

Students can find the complete text of Walter Dean Myers's "The Treasure of Lemon Brown" in *Prentice Hall Literature: Timeless Voices, Timeless Themes*, BRONZE.

Answer Key

▶ **Exercise 27**

Possible answers:

1. Dylan made an important contribution to rock. He was originally a folk singer.
2. Although he began his career in New York City, he recorded in Nashville.
3. While his early songs contained a strong social message, Dylan's later music became more personal.

continued

Answer Key continued

4. Later, Dylan played his songs on electric instruments using a strong rock beat, a style that became known as folk rock.
5. Many of Dylan's original fans did not like his electrified music, and they even booed at many of his performances.

Silly Sentence Structures

Teaching Resources: Hands-on Grammar Activity Book, Chapter 20

1. Have students refer to their Hands-on Grammar activity books, or give them copies of the relevant pages for this activity.

2. Be sure students understand that each clause they write must have a subject and a verb.

3. To limit results a little, you may want to specify that subjects should be of a particular type, say animals.

4. If students enjoy this activity, have them swap clauses to see how the sentence changes.

Find It in Your Reading

Ask students to share one example each of complex and compound sentences they found.

Find It in Your Writing

Work with a partner. Change two of your partner's sentences into another structure. For example, if a sentence is compound, change it to two simple sentences.

20.2

Hands-on Grammar

Silly Sentence Structures

Explore compound and complex sentences by building silly sentence structures. First, create a set of coordinating conjunctions. On individual cards, write *and, but, for, so,* and *yet.* Write a comma in front of each word.

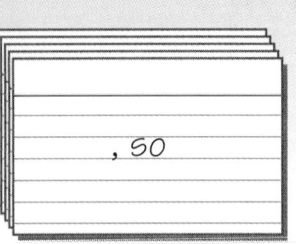

Next, create a set of subordinating conjunctions—connecting words used in complex sentences. Use the following words: *after, although, because, before, since, unless,* and *where.* Do not use commas in front of these words. Mix the two sets of cards together and place them face down so that the words cannot be seen.

Work with a partner to create two clauses. Decide who will write the clause that begins the sentence and who will write the clause that ends the sentence. Capitalize and use end punctuation accordingly. Write your clauses on separate strips of paper. Lay the two strips with the finished clauses next to each other. Draw one of the face-down connecting cards and place it between the two strips. Read the resulting sentence, and decide whether it is a compound or a complex sentence.

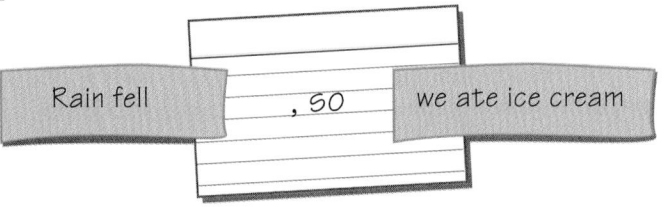

Continue joining clauses until you have used each of the cards at least once. Remember, you are creating these silly sentences to explore sentence structure. In your own writing, you should join only related ideas.

Find It in Your Reading In a short story or a textbook, find examples of compound and complex sentences using the coordinating and subordinating conjunctions on your cards. Write each sentence you find on the back of the appropriate card.

Find It in Your Writing Look through a piece of your writing to find examples of compound and complex sentences. If you cannot find at least three examples of each, challenge yourself to combine sentences, if possible.

☑ **ONGOING ASSESSMENT: Assess Mastery**

Use the following resources to assess students' mastery of kinds of sentences.

In the Textbook	Technology
Chapter Review, Ex. 41–42, p. 451 Standardized Test Preparation Workshop, pp. 452–453	On-Line Exercise Bank, Section 20.2

Section 20.2 Section Review

GRAMMAR EXERCISES 28–34

Exercise 28 Writing Sentences Using Dependent and Independent Clauses Identify each of the following clauses as independent or dependent.

1. Tuareg, which is a tribe in Africa
2. music is the heart of a Tuareg party
3. the singer plays an instrument with only one string
4. when the men pass around a bowl
5. musicians sing in a high voice

Exercise 29 Writing Sentences Using Adjective Clauses Write sentences using each of the following adjective clauses correctly.

1. that a composer wants to convey
2. when we are sad
3. who inspires us to dance
4. who find music relaxing
5. which is enjoyed by all
6. who leads the group
7. that it became a fan favorite
8. which the dancers ignored
9. whose name we shall never forget
10. where the fans gathered to celebrate

Exercise 30 Writing Sentences Using Adverb Clauses Write sentences using each of the following adverb clauses correctly.

1. when you write music
2. if a song is difficult to sing
3. because it sounds strange
4. as the group performed
5. although they played well
6. before we arrived at the concert
7. even though they danced for hours
8. unless the guitar was too loud
9. while we were watching
10. until the recording was complete

Exercise 31 Identifying Sentence Structure Identify each sentence in the following paragraph as *simple, compound,* or *complex.*

(1) Asian musicians use different instruments from those used by Western musicians, so their music sounds different. (2) While most Western music has harmony, traditional Chinese music has no harmony. (3) Two Chinese stringed instruments, the quin and the pipa, are very popular. (4) Bamboo grows extensively in Japan, and many Japanese instruments are made from bamboo. (5) One bamboo flute, which is called the *shakuhachi,* can be found in every Japanese orchestra.

Exercise 32 Find It in Your Reading Look back at the passage from "The Treasure of Lemon Brown" on page 447. Write down three adjective clauses you identify in the selection. Write three original sentences using the adjective clauses you have identified.

Exercise 33 Find It in Your Writing Look through your writing portfolio and choose a piece of writing in which you have used simple, compound, and complex sentences. Identify at least one example of each.

Exercise 34 Writing Application Imagine that you have attended a concert of your favorite musical group. Write a brief review of the performance using a variety of sentence structures.

ASSESS AND CLOSE

Section Review

Each of these exercises correlates to a concept in the section on clauses, pages 426–448. The exercises may be used for more practice, for reteaching, or for review of the Key Concepts presented.

Answer Key

Exercise 28

1. dependent
2. independent
3. independent
4. dependent
5. independent

Exercise 29

Sample answers:
1. Music is an expression of feelings that a composer wants to convey.
2. It consoles us when we are sad.
3. A good composer is one who inspires us to dance.
4. Those who find music relaxing listen frequently.
5. The best song is that which is enjoyed by all.
6. Carlos, who leads the group, is a great singer.
7. The fact that it became a fan favorite was ignored.
8. The directions, which the dancers ignored, were very complex.
9. The choreographer, whose name we shall never forget, was applauded.
10. The stadium where the fans gathered to celebrate was packed.

Exercise 30

Sample answers:
1. When you write music, you should start simply.
2. If a song is difficult to sing, practice longer.
3. Don't stop because it sounds strange.
4. The audience was quiet as the group performed.
5. Although they played well, other performances were better.
6. Our friends took their seats before we arrived at the concert.
7. They were not tired even though they danced for hours.
8. They loved the music unless the guitar was too loud.
9. While we were watching, the conductor arrived.
10. We did not leave until the recording was complete.

Answer Key continued

Exercise 31

1. compound
2. complex
3. simple
4. compound
5. complex

Exercise 32

Find It in Your Reading
The adjective clauses are the following: who called himself Lemon Brown, that seemed to separate his head from the layers of dirty coats piled on his smallish frame, where they were met with rags, that went down to the old shoes.

Exercise 33

Find It in Your Writing
If they find a passage that lacks a variety in sentence structure, challenge students to separate or combine sentences to add variety where appropriate.

Exercise 34

Writing Application
You might want to show students a music review from a recent newspaper or magazine so they can get a sense of what to include in their work.

CHAPTER REVIEW

These exercises correlate to the concepts taught in the chapter on phrases and clauses, pages 426–449. The exercises may be used for more practice, for reteaching, or for review of the Key Concepts presented. Answers for all chapter exercises are available in *Grammar Exercises Answers on Transparencies* in your teaching resources.

Answer Key

Exercise 35

1. of power, adjective
2. in a tornado, adjective
3. on Earth, adverb
4. from a dark cloud, adverb
5. over the ground, adverb; in a narrow path, adverb
6. during violent thunderstorms, adverb
7. for tornadoes, adjective
8. of dollars, adjective; in damage, adjective
9. into the air, adverb
10. for tornadoes, adverb

Exercise 36

Possible answers:
1. In 1989, a year of devastating weather, Hurricane Hugo struck.
2. Hugo killed 18 people in Charleston, a city in South Carolina.
3. Guadeloupe, a French-owned island, was also hit by Hugo.
4. Hugo, a hurricane of only medium strength, was one of the most costly storms in history.
5. The Caribbean and the southern United States, the worst hit areas, were declared disaster areas.

Exercise 37

Possible answers:
1. Acid rain containing sulfuric and nitric acid falls to Earth.
2. Water mixed with air containing sulfur dioxide and nitrogen oxides creates acid rain.
3. These chemicals are caused by automobiles, factories, and other sources burning fossil fuels.
4. Acid rain has polluted thousands of lakes and streams, killing fish and other aquatic life.
5. The Clean Air Act, amended in 1990, tightened emissions standards.

Exercise 38

1. appositive
2. prepositional
3. appositive
4. prepositional
5. participial
6. prepositional
7. participial
8. appositive
9. prepositional
10. appositive

Chapter 20 Chapter Review

GRAMMAR EXERCISES 35–44

Exercise 35 Identifying Prepositional Phrases On your paper, write the prepositional phrase(s) in the sentences below, and identify whether each acts as an *adjective* or an *adverb*.

1. A tornado is a display of power.
2. The winds in a tornado are incredibly turbulent.
3. Tornado winds are the most violent winds that occur on Earth.
4. A funnel descends from a dark cloud.
5. It whirls over the ground in a narrow path.
6. Tornadoes occur during violent thunderstorms.
7. Spring and summer are the typical seasons for tornadoes.
8. Tornadoes can cause millions of dollars in damage.
9. Strong tornadoes can lift cars, homes, and animals into the air.
10. The National Weather Service continually looks for tornadoes.

Exercise 36 Revising Sentences Using Appositives and Appositive Phrases Combine each of the following sentence pairs by using appositives or appositive phrases.

1. In 1989, Hurricane Hugo struck. That was a year of devastating weather.
2. Charleston is a city in South Carolina. Hugo killed eighteen people in Charleston.
3. Guadeloupe is a French-owned island. Guadeloupe was also hit by Hugo.
4. Hugo was a hurricane of only medium strength. Hurricane Hugo was one of the most costly storms in history.
5. The worst-hit areas were the Caribbean and the southern United States. These areas were declared disaster areas.

450 • Phrases and Clauses

Exercise 37 Revising Sentences Using Participial Phrases Use participial phrases to combine each of the following sentence pairs.

1. Acid rain contains sulfuric and nitric acids. The polluted rain falls to Earth.
2. Water mixes with air containing sulfur dioxide and nitrogen oxides. The combination creates acid rain.
3. These chemicals are caused by automobiles, factories, and other sources. The sources burn fossil fuels.
4. Acid rain has polluted thousands of lakes and streams. This pollution kills fish and other aquatic life.
5. The Clean Air Act was amended in 1990. The act tightened emissions standards.

Exercise 38 Classifying Different Kinds of Phrases Label each of the underlined phrases below a *prepositional phrase*, a *participial phrase*, or an *appositive phrase*.

(1) Meteorologists study hurricanes, a type of tropical storm. (2) Any tropical storm with winds over 39 miles per hour receives a name. (3) The eye-wall, the area around the eye of the storm, can produce 2 inches of rain hourly. (4) Flooding is a threat in low-lying areas. (5) Meteorologists using satellite data are able to track hurricanes. (6) The Saffir-Simpson scale designates five levels of hurricanes. (7) Beginning over warm waters, a hurricane picks up moisture. (8) Hurricanes, the most destructive of natural disasters, cause devastation. (9) The center of a hurricane is calm. (10) Typhoons, a type of hurricane, occur in the western Pacific.

Exercise 39 Classifying and Writing Sentences With Phrases and Clauses Classify each numbered item below as a *phrase*, an *independent clause*, or a *dependent clause*. Then, write a sentence using each.

1. who play in the orchestra
2. a gentle, flowing melody
3. most musicians played off-key
4. when the conductor raised the baton
5. drums beat out a steady rhythm

Exercise 40 Identifying Adjective and Adverb Clauses Copy the following sentences. Underline and identify the adjective and adverb clauses. Draw an arrow to the word each clause modifies.

1. The arts, which differ greatly in each Indian state, have been highly developed in India for thousands of years.
2. Indian music is based on a different scale from the one Western culture uses.
3. Its harmonies, which have different sounds as a base, are distinctive.
4. Even though the music is different, the instruments are similar to those of the Western world.
5. In India, some stringed instruments look like long guitars, although they have many more strings.

Exercise 41 Identifying Sentence Structures Identify the sentences below as *simple, compound,* or *complex.*

(1) Johann Sebastian Bach came from a musical family, and several of his sons also became composers. (2) He lived in Germany and served as a violinist, organist, and choir director. (3) Bach wrote hundreds of compositions, but he did not gain fame during his lifetime. (4) Most of Bach's compositions were ignored until long after he died. (5) When they are played today, Bach's compositions please audiences.

Exercise 42 Revising to Vary Sentence Structure On a separate sheet of paper, revise the following paragraph. Combine some of the simple sentences into compound and complex sentences.

In India, you can see ancient architecture in monasteries and shrines. These structures were built by Buddhist monks. On the walls, you can see beautiful frescoes. The frescoes are paintings on fresh plaster. Hindu temples offer another kind of architecture. Hindu temples feature tall towers. They have curving sides and taper at the top. In southern India, there are rectangular pyramids. The steps are carved to tell stories.

Exercise 43 CUMULATIVE REVIEW Sentence Parts On your paper, label the underlined word(s) in each sentence *subject, verb, direct object, indirect object, predicate noun,* or *predicate adjective.*

(1) Wolfgang Amadeus Mozart was a child prodigy. (2) He first composed and performed music at the age of five. (3) There have been few people as talented as Mozart. (4) His father gave him piano lessons. (5) Soon, Mozart surpassed his father in musical ability. (6) Mozart's father was willing to give up his own career to manage his son's. (7) Mozart's music is still popular today. (8) It is featured in concerts around the world. (9) Have you ever listened to a composition by Mozart? (10) I have several CDs in my collection.

Exercise 44 Writing Application Write a paragraph about a song or musician that you enjoy. Use adjective and adverb phrases in your paragraph, and include simple, compound, and complex sentences.

Chapter Review • 451

Exercise 39

1. dependent clause
2. phrase
3. independent clause
4. dependent clause
5. independent clause

Exercise 40

1. which differ greatly in each Indian state—adjective [arrow to *arts*]
2. from the one Western culture uses—adjective [arrow to *different*]
3. which have different sounds as a base,—adjective [arrow to *harmonies*]
4. Even though the music is different,—adverb [arrow to *are*]
5. although they have many more strings—adverb [arrow to *look*]

Exercise 41

1. compound
2. simple
3. compound
4. complex
5. complex

Exercise 42

Possible answer:

In India, you can see ancient architecture in monasteries and shrines which were built by Buddhist monks. On the walls, you can see beautiful frescoes, which are paintings on fresh plaster. Hindu temples offer another kind of architecture, featuring tall towers with curving sides that taper at the top. In southern India, there are rectangular pyramids whose steps are carved to tell stories.

Exercise 43

Cumulative Review

1. predicate noun
2. verb, verb (or compound verb)
3. subject
4. indirect object
5. direct object
6. predicate adjective
7. predicate adjective
8. verb
9. subject
10. direct object

Exercise 44

Writing Application
When they finish, have students exchange papers with a partner. Then have them underline and label all adjective and adverb phrases. Finally, have them write down the type of each sentence and make sure that a variety of types was used.

Step-by-Step Teaching Guide

Revising and Editing

Teaching Resources: Standardized Test Preparation Workbook, pp. 39–40

1. Remind students that sentences with repeated information can often be combined into complex sentences using phrases and clauses.

2. Have students cover the Answers and Explanations column in their textbooks. Ask them to identify the repeated information in the sample test item. (folk tales) Explain to them that the sentences then can be combined without changing the meaning of either sentence.

Standardized Test Preparation Workshop

Revising and Editing

Knowledge of grammar is tested on standardized tests. Questions that measure your ability to use phrases and clauses reveal your understanding of basic sentence construction and style. Remember that a phrase is a group of words without a subject and a verb that acts as a single part of speech, and a clause is a group of words that contains a subject and a verb. Use the following strategies when answering questions that test your knowledge of phrases and clauses:

- First, read the entire passage to get an idea of the author's purpose.
- Focus on the underlined words, and note any similarities between underlined sentences. Can they be combined by using a phrase or clause without changing meaning?
- Choose the answer that best uses a phrase or clause to combine similar ideas without changing the meaning.

The following will give you practice with the format of questions that test rules of standard grammar.

Test Tip

Although an answer choice may make sense, it may not be the best way to rewrite the original. Read every choice carefully before deciding on your answer.

Sample Test Item	Answer and Explanation
Choose the letter of the best way to write the underlined section. If the underlined section needs no change, choose "Correct as is." Many cultures have folk tales. These folk (1) tales communicate important values and ideas. A Many cultures have folk tales that communicate important values and ideas. B Many cultures have folk tales, and these folk tales communicate important values and ideas. C Folk tales, which communicate important values and ideas, belong to few cultures. D Correct as is.	The correct answer is *A*. This is the best rewrite of the two sentences because it combines related ideas without changing the meaning. Changing the second sentence into a clause eliminates the repetition of the words *folk tales*.

452 • Phrases and Clauses

✎ TEST-TAKING TIP

Remind students that questions like the ones here involve improving given sentences through revision and editing. Therefore, students always should compare each of the choices to the original version to make sure that none of the information is missing or has changed. Point out that in item 3 of Practice 1, choice C incorrectly omits the information about how many versions of the folk tale exist. Once students have excluded choices that change the meaning of the original sentences, they can focus on identifying the best revision remaining.

Practice 1 **Directions:** Choose the letter of the best way to write each underlined section. If the underlined section needs no change, choose "Correct as is."

One popular folk tale is the story of Cin-
(1)
derella. The story is known and loved

around the world. It is the story of a poor,
(2)
hard-working girl. She suffers under an

evil stepmother. There are more than 900
(3)
versions of Cinderella. The oldest is

more than a thousand years old. Most
(4)
Americans are familiar with the story writ-

ten in the 1600's. It is the only one with a

fairy godmother and a midnight time limit.

There are many differences between the
(5)
stories. The poor girl always escapes her

stepmother, marries the prince, and lives

happily ever after.

1 A One popular folk tale is the story of Cinderella, and the story is known and loved around the world.

B One popular folk tale, known and loved around the world, is the story of Cinderella.

C Known and loved around the world is one popular folk tale. This is the story of Cinderella.

D Correct as is.

2 F It is the story of a poor, hard-working girl; she suffers under an evil stepmother.

G Suffering under an evil stepmother is the poor, hard-working girl.

H It is the story of a poor, hard-working girl who suffers under an evil stepmother.

J Correct as is.

3 A There are more than 900 versions of this Cinderella, the oldest is more than a thousand years old.

B There are more than 900 versions; the oldest is more than a thousand years old.

C The oldest of the versions is more than a thousand years old.

D Correct as is.

4 F Most Americans are familiar with the story written in the 1600's. Although it is the only one with a fairy godmother and a midnight time limit.

G Most Americans are familiar with the story written in the 1600's, the only one with a fairy godmother and a midnight time limit.

H Written in the 1600's, most Americans are familiar with the story, the only one with a fairy godmother and a midnight time limit.

J Correct as is.

5 A The poor girl always escapes her stepmother, marries the prince, and lives happily ever after.

B There are many differences between the stories, and the poor girl always escapes her stepmother, marries the prince, and lives happily ever after.

C Although there are many differences between the stories, the poor girl always escapes her stepmother, marries the prince, and lives happily ever after.

D Correct as is.

Practice 1
1. B
2. H
3. B
4. J
5. C

Time and Resource Manager

In-Depth Lesson Plan

	LESSON FOCUS	PRINT AND MEDIA RESOURCES
DAY 1	**The Four Functions of a Sentence** Students learn to identify and write declarative, interrogative, imperative, and exclamatory sentences (pp. 456–459).	**Teaching Resources** *Grammar Exercise Workbook,* pp. 87–88; *Grammar Exercises Answers on Transparencies,* Ch. 21 ***On-Line Exercise Bank,*** Section 21.1
DAY 2	**Combining Sentence Parts** Students learn how to use compound subjects and verbs and join clauses (pp. 460–464).	**Teaching Resources** *Grammar Exercise Workbook,* pp. 89–92; ***Language Lab*** **CD-ROM,** Sentence Style; ***On-Line Exercise Bank,*** Section 21.2
DAY 3	**Vary Sentence Beginnings** Students learn to vary sentence beginnings (pp. 465–468).	**Teaching Resources** *Grammar Exercise Workbook,* pp. 91–93; ***On-Line Exercise Bank,*** Section 21.3
DAY 4	**Sentence Fragments** Students learn to identify and correct sentence and other kinds of fragments (pp. 469–473).	**Teaching Resources** *Grammar Exercise Workbook,* pp. 95–110; ***Language Lab*** **CD-ROM,** Problems With Sentences; ***On-Line Exercise Bank,*** Section 21.4
DAY 5	**Run-on Sentences** Students learn to identify and correct run-on sentences and other common errors. They can also do the Hands-on Grammar activity (pp. 473–483).	**Teaching Resources** *Grammar Exercise Workbook,* pp. 95–110; *Hands-on Grammar Activity Book,* Chapter 21 ***Language Lab*** **CD-ROM,** Problems With Sentences; ***On-Line Exercise Bank,*** Section 21.4
DAY 6	**Review and Assess** Students review chapter and demonstrate mastery of use of effective sentences (pp. 484–486).	**Teaching Resources** *Formal Assessment,* Ch. 21 ***On-Line Exercise Bank,*** Section 21.1

Accelerated Lesson Plan

	LESSON FOCUS	PRINT AND MEDIA RESOURCES
DAY 1	**Effective Sentences** Students cover concepts and usage of the following: declarative, imperative, interrogative, and exclamatory sentences; sentence parts; and combining sentences as determined by the Diagnostic Test (pp. 456–464).	**Teaching Resources** *Grammar Exercise Workbook,* pp. 87–90; *Grammar Exercises Answers on Transparencies,* Ch. 21 ***Language Lab*** **CD-ROM,** Sentence Style; ***On-Line Exercise Bank,*** Sections 21.1–2
DAY 2	**Vary Sentence Beginnings and Sentence Fragments** Students cover concepts and usage of varied sentence beginnings and sentence fragments as determined by the Diagnostic Test (pp. 465–473).	**Teaching Resources** *Grammar Exercise Workbook,* pp. 91–110; *Hands-on Grammar Activity Book,* Chapter 21 ***Language Lab*** **CD-ROM,** Problems With Sentences; ***On-Line Exercise Bank,*** Sections 21.3–4
DAY 3	**Run-On Sentences and Other Usage Problems** Students cover concepts and usage of run-on sentences and other usage problems as determined by the Diagnostic Test (pp. 473–483).	**Teaching Resources** *Grammar Exercise Workbook,* pp. 95–110; *Hands-on Grammar Activity Book,* Chapter 21 ***Language Lab*** **CD-ROM,** Problems With Sentences; ***On-Line Exercise Bank,*** Section 21.4
DAY 4	**Review and Assess** Students review chapter and demonstrate mastery of concepts (pp. 484–487).	**Teaching Resources** *Formal Assessment,* Ch. 21; ***On-Line Exercise Bank,*** Section 21.1

Options for Adapting Lesson Plans

HOMEWORK

Have students complete any section of the chapter for homework.

FEATURES

Extend coverage with the Grammar in Literature feature (pp. 457, 465), and the Standardized Test Preparation Workshop (p. 486).

TECHNOLOGY

Students can use the On-Line Exercise Bank to complete the exercises on computer. The Auto Check feature will grade their work.

INTEGRATED SKILLS COVERAGE

Grammar in Literature
SE pp. 457, 465

Reading
Find It In Your Reading, SE pp. 459, 464, 468

Writing
Find It In Your Writing, SE pp. 459, 464, 468, 483
Writing Application, SE pp. 459, 464, 468, 483, 485

Spelling
SE p. 478

Language Highlight
ATE p. 467

Workplace Skills
ATE p. 475

Speaking Skills
ATE p. 479

Viewing and Representing
Critical Viewing SE pp. 454, 457, 461, 462, 467, 469, 472, 474, 477, 480

ASSESSMENT SUPPORT

Standardized Test Preparation SE p. 486; ATE pp. 466, 474

Standardized Test Preparation Workbook, pp. 41–42

Formal Assessment, Ch. 21

MEETING INDIVIDUAL NEEDS

Less Advanced Students ATE pp. 476, 481, 487. See also Ongoing Assessment pp. 458, 461, 462, 467, 471, 472, 475, 477, 480
ESL Students ATE pp. 479, 481
Verbal/Linguistic Students ATE p. 461
Logical/Mathematical Learners ATE p. 479

BLOCK SCHEDULING

Pacing Suggestions
For 90-minute Blocks
• Administer the Diagnostic Test to students to determine instructional coverage
• Have students complete the necessary exercises in class. Use the Hands-on Grammar activity to provide a change of pace.

Resources for Varying Instruction
• *Language Lab* **CD-ROM** If your students have access to hardware, a 90-minute block provides an ideal opportunity for students to work on computer.

Professional Development Support
• *How to manage Instruction in the Block* This Teaching Resource provides management and activity suggestions.

MEDIA AND TECHNOLOGY

For the Student
• *Language Lab* **CD-ROM** Sentence Style, Problems With Sentences
• *On-Line Exercise Bank,* Ch. 21

For the Teacher
• *Resource Pro* **CD-ROM**

WRITING AND GRAMMAR WEB SITE

The Interactive Writing and Grammar Web site provides a wide array of support for students, teachers, and parents. Grammar support includes:

• *On-Line Exercise Bank* with Auto Check scoring
• Diagnostic and assessment support

www.phschool.com

LITERATURE CONNECTIONS

Related selections from *Prentice Hall Literature: Timeless Voices, Timeless Themes,* Bronze:
from *Tiger: A Biography of Tiger Woods,* by John Strege, SE p. 457
"Rikki-tikki-tavi," by Rudyard Kipling, SE p. 465

► **Lesson Objectives**

1. To distinguish among the four types of sentences.
2. To change and correct sentences and clauses in various ways.
3. To write in complete sentences, varying the types, and use appropriately punctuated independent and dependent clauses.

Critical Viewing

Evaluate Students may suggest lack of subject-verb agreement, mistakes in spelling, incorrect use of vocabulary, mistakes in verb tense, or mistakes in pronoun case.

Chapter 21 Effective Sentences

▲ **Critical Viewing**
What are some problems that can block sentences from achieving their goal? **[Evaluate]**

The sentence is a basic unit of communication. You use sentences every day—to ask questions, give directions, make statements, express emotion, or share information. Some of your sentences may be short and direct, and others may be long and complicated. In either case, you will need to follow certain rules and suggestions to make sure your sentences are correct, interesting, and meaningful. Putting words together in effective sentences is the first step in making sure that you are communicating clearly.

In this chapter, you will learn about the different functions of sentences. You will also learn how to combine ideas in sentences and how to vary the style of your sentences. Finally, you will learn how to avoid some of the problems that writers often confront when they are writing sentences.

454 • Effective Sentences

If students miss more than one item in each category, direct them to the relevant pages of the text and assign exercises for practice and review.

Effective Sentences	Diagnostic Test Items	Teach	Practice	Section Review	Chapter Review
Skill Check A					
The Four Types of Sentences	A 1–5	pp. 456–458	Ex. 1	Ex. 2–4	Ex. 45
Skill Check B					
Sentence Combining	B 6–10	pp. 460–463	Ex. 8–11	Ex. 12–14	Ex. 46
Skill Check C					
Varying Sentence Beginnings	C 11–15	pp. 465–467	Ex. 18–20	Ex. 21–23	Ex. 46

Diagnostic Test

Directions: Write all answers on a separate sheet of paper.

Skill Check A. Identify each sentence as *declarative, interrogative, imperative,* or *exclamatory,* and indicate which end mark to use.
1. Look at this article about Jim Thorpe
2. Didn't he win two Olympic gold medals in track and field events
3. He was also one of the first professional football stars
4. What an amazing athlete he was
5. Isn't there a town in Pennsylvania named after Jim Thorpe

Skill Check B. Combine each pair of sentences into one compound or complex sentence.
6. Soccer is the most popular sport in most of the world. Soccer has not always been a popular sport in the United States.
7. Today, many American children play soccer at school. They play soccer in organized leagues on weekends.
8. Sports are good for children. Sports teach children cooperation.
9. The net seems large. Scoring a goal is difficult.
10. A goal is scored. Everyone cheers.

Skill Check C. Rearrange each sentence to begin with the part of speech indicated in parentheses.
11. Pele joined Brazil's top soccer league at age sixteen. (preposition)
12. He became a star player quickly. (adverb)
13. Brazil relied on his skills to win three World Cup titles. (infinitive)
14. One trick was kicking a ball backwards over his head. (participle)
15. Pele remarkably scored 1,282 goals in 1,363 matches. (adverb)

Skill Check D. On your paper, write *F* if the numbered item below is a fragment, *RO* if it is a run-on, *MM* if it contains a misplaced modifier, and *DN* if it contains a double negative.
16. Two sports were invented in Massachusetts in the 1890's, one was basketball and the other was volleyball.
17. The net suspended between seven and eight feet above the ground.
18. Standing at the back, the ball is sent over the net by a server.
19. The other team can't hit the ball no more than three times.
20. They must return the ball, if not, the other team gets a point.

Skill Check E. Choose the word that best completes the sentence.
21. I am a good player (accept, except) for my strength.
22. Once, I hit the ball hard, with an unexpected (affect, effect).
23. The ball sailed over the other team and landed in (their, there, they're) bleachers.
24. The reason I hit the ball so hard was (because, that) I was thinking of the upcoming math test.
25. I will try not to hit the ball (to, too, two) hard in the future.

Effective Sentences • 455

ONGOING ASSESSMENT: Diagnose *continued*

Effective Sentences	Diagnostic Test Items	Teach	Practice	Section Review	Chapter Review
Skill Check D					
Avoiding Sentence Problems	D 16–25	pp. 469–482	Ex. 27–38	Ex. 39–42	Ex. 47–48
Cumulative Reviews and Applications				Ex. 5–7, 15–17, 24–26, 43–44	Ex. 52

Answer Key

Diagnostic Test

• Each item in the Diagnostic Test corresponds to a specific section in the chapter on effective sentences. This will enable you to tailor instruction to the particular needs of your students. See "Ongoing Assessment: Diagnose" below for further details.

• Answers for the Diagnostic Test and all chapter exercises are available in *Grammar Exercises Answers on Transparencies* in your Teaching Resources.

Skill Check A
1. imperative, period
2. interrogative, question mark
3. declarative, period
4. exclamatory, exclamation mark
5. interrogative, question mark

Skill Check B
Answers will vary. Samples are given.
6. Soccer is the most popular sport in most of the world, but it has not always been a popular sport in the United States.
7. Today, many American children play soccer in school and in organized leagues on weekends.
8. Sports are good for children because they teach them cooperation.
9. The net seems large, but scoring a goal is difficult.
10. Everyone cheers when a goal is scored.

Skill Check C
Answers will vary. Samples are given.
11. At age sixteen, Pele joined Brazil's top soccer league.
12. Quickly, he became a star player.
13. To win three World Cup titles, Brazil relied on his skills.
14. Kicking a ball backwards over his head was one trick.
15. Remarkably, Pele scored 1,282 goals in 1,363 matches.

Skill Check D
16. RO
17. F
18. MM
19. DN
20. RO

Skill Check E
21. except
22. effect
23. their
24. that
25. too

Activate Prior Knowledge

Play a matching game with students. Write these definitions on the chalkboard: *gives orders or directions, expresses strong emotion, presents facts or information,* and *asks questions.* To the right, list the four types of sentences, but not in the same order as their definitions. Challenge students to use their prior knowledge of the terms *declarative, imperative, interrogative,* and *exclamatory* (or words that sound like these) to match each type of sentence with its definition.

TEACH

Step-by-Step Teaching Guide

Declarative and Interrogative Sentences

1. Have a student read aloud the first key concept statement. Explain that the word *declare* means "to make something clear"—to state a fact.

2. Point out that a declarative sentence ends with a period. A sentence that gives facts or information and ends with an exclamation mark is called an exclamatory sentence. Its meaning is not changed by the punctuation mark, but its tone is. A declarative sentence is spoken more quietly.

3. Point out that an interrogative sentence, since it asks a question, ends with a question mark. Students can also recognize interrogative sentences by the words with which they begin. Generally, a question begins with *how, what, when, where, who,* or *why.*

Section 21.1

Classifying the Four Functions of a Sentence

Sentences can be classified according to what they do. Some sentences present facts or information in a direct way; others pose questions to the reader or listener; still others present orders or directions. A fourth type of sentence expresses strong emotion. These four types of sentences are called *declarative, interrogative, imperative,* and *exclamatory.* Each type of sentence has a different purpose and is constructed in a different way.

The type of sentence you are writing determines the punctuation mark you use to end the sentence. The three end marks are the period (.), the question mark (?), and the exclamation mark (!).

Declarative sentences are the most common type. They are used to state or "declare" facts.

▶ **KEY CONCEPT** A **declarative sentence** states, or declares, an idea and ends with a period. ■

DECLARATIVE: Soccer is a team sport.
Golf is a sport that can be played throughout a lifetime.
Although most schools fund team sports, many students choose to participate in individual sports.

Interrogative means "asking." An *interrogative sentence* is a question. What end mark do you think you would use after an interrogative sentence?

▶ **KEY CONCEPT** An **interrogative sentence** asks a question and ends with a question mark. ■

INTERROGATIVE: What is your best time in the one-mile run?
Where is the county track meet being held this year?
Who is the fastest runner on the school track team?

The word *imperative* is related to the word *emperor,* a person who gives commands. *Imperative sentences* are like emperors: They give commands.

Theme: Sports and Games

In this section, you will learn about the four functions sentences can perform. The examples and exercises in this section are about sports and games.

Cross-Curricular Connection: Physical Education

⏱ TIME AND RESOURCE MANAGER

Resources
Print: Grammar Exercise Workbook, pp. 87–88; Grammer Exercises Answers on Transparencies, Ch. 21
Technology: On-Line Exercise Bank, Section 21.1

In-Depth Coverage	Accelerated Pace
• Work through all key concepts, pp. 456–458. • Assign and review Exercise 1. • Read and discuss Grammar in Literature, p. 457.	• Assign pp. 456–458 for independent student review. • Assign Section Review Exercises 2–4.

GRAMMAR IN LITERATURE

from Tiger: A Biography of Tiger Woods

John Strege

In the following passage, the last sentence is an imperative sentence. The other sentences Earl [Tiger Woods's father] speaks are declarative. Since many imperative sentences leave the you understood, the final sentence might also have been spoken as "Do what you want to do."

"Tiger," Earl said, "you're not out there playing for me. You're out there playing for yourself. On the golf course you're the boss. You do what you want to do."

▶ **KEY CONCEPT** An **imperative sentence** gives an order or a direction and ends with either a period or an exclamation mark. ■

Most imperative sentences start with a verb. In this type of imperative sentence, the subject is understood to be *you.*

IMPERATIVE: Follow my instructions carefully.
Run as hard as you can!

Notice the punctuation at the end of these examples. In the first sentence, the period suggests that a mild command is being given in an ordinary tone of voice. The exclamation mark at the end of the last sentence suggests a strong command, one given in a loud voice.

▶ Critical Viewing Describe the question you might ask about the result of this shot, as well as the end mark you would use. **[Question]**

Tiger Woods tees off during a golf tournament.

The Four Functions of a Sentence • 457

Grammar in Literature

1. Ask a volunteer to read aloud the literature excerpt. Have students explain why each sentence is either declarative or imperative.

2. Challenge students to rewrite some of the sentences in the literature model as exclamatory sentences. Ask them how this alters their impression of Earl Woods's statements to Tiger. (Students may say the exclamatory mood makes him seem angry or excited.)

Responding to Literature

Have students locate and read more of the selection in the Bronze Level of *Prentice Hall Literature: Timeless Voices, Timeless Themes.* Have students choose paragraphs and identify the categories of the sentences.

Critical Viewing

Question Answers will vary, but students may ask what teeing off in golf means and what the result of teeing off should be. (To hit the ball as close as possible to a distant hole.) Students should say that the end mark they would use is a question mark.

1. declarative (.)
2. interrogative (?)
3. imperative (! or .)
4. interrogative (?)
5. exclamatory (!)
6. imperative (.)
7. interrogative (?)
8. declarative (.)
9. interrogative (?)
10. exclamatory (!)
11. interrogative (?)
12. exclamatory (!)
13. declarative (.)
14. declarative (.)
15. exclamatory (!)

21.1

► **KEY CONCEPT** An **exclamatory sentence** conveys strong emotion and ends with an exclamation mark. ■

EXCLAMATORY: She's going to crash into that hurdle!
                What an outstanding runner she is!

To *exclaim* means to "shout out." *Exclamatory sentences* are used to "shout out" emotions such as happiness, fear, delight, or anger.

► **Exercise 1** Identifying the Four Types of Sentences Read each of the following sentences carefully, and identify it as *declarative, interrogative, imperative,* or *exclamatory*. After each answer, write the appropriate punctuation mark to end that sentence.

EXAMPLE: Do you plan to run in the relay
ANSWER: interrogative (?)

1. The World Cup is the most famous international soccer competition
2. Isn't it held every year
3. Grab the soccer ball, and throw it to me
4. Do you know which country's team won the first World Cup trophy
5. I want to know right now
6. Look up Uruguay in the encyclopedia
7. Does it say that Uruguay's team won the first World Cup in 1930
8. Pele was a Brazilian soccer star
9. Did I read that he played in the United States for several seasons
10. That was the most exciting game I have ever seen
11. Can you dribble the ball with your feet
12. What an amazing header she took
13. She scored the winning goal in the last minute of the over-time period
14. When France won the World Cup, fans in Paris cheered all night long
15. No night was as exciting as that one

► **More Practice**

On-line
Exercise Bank
• Section 21.1
Grammar Exercise
Workbook
• pp. 87–88

☑ **ONGOING ASSESSMENT: Monitor and Reinforce**

If students miss more than two items in Exercise 1, refer them to the following for additional practice.

In the Textbook	Print Resources	Technology
Section Review, Ex. 2–4, p. 459	Grammar Exercise Workbook, pp. 87–88	On-Line Exercise Bank, Section 21.1

Section 21.1 Section Review

GRAMMAR EXERCISES 2–7

Exercise 2 Identifying the Four Types of Sentences Read each sentence carefully, and identify it as *declarative, interrogative, imperative,* or *exclamatory.*

1. Horseshoes is an easy game to play.
2. The iron stakes are set 40 feet apart.
3. Pound the stakes into the ground carefully.
4. The stakes should stick out of the ground 15 inches.
5. How do you score the game?
6. A ringer is a throw in which the shoe hooks the stake.
7. Show me how to throw.
8. I love to play horseshoes!
9. How many people can play at one time?
10. I won the game!

Exercise 3 Supplying the Correct Punctuation Mark Copy each sentence below onto your paper. Add the appropriate end mark, and identify the sentence type.

1. There are many fun and simple yard games
2. Get the neighborhood together, and have some fun
3. My favorite games are games of tag
4. Do you know any new forms of tag
5. You're it
6. Try to reach home base before I touch you
7. How will the game end
8. Count slowly by fives to one hundred
9. I am going to duck behind the big azalea bush
10. Stay out of the street
11. You never touched me
12. When do you have to go home
13. I am wearing my new sneakers
14. No, you cannot borrow them
15. Can you come over tomorrow, so we can play again

Exercise 4 Revising to Write the Four Types of Sentences Rewrite each sentence below to fit the function indicated in parentheses. Add the appropriate end mark.

1. Are the world's greatest badminton players from Indonesia (declarative)
2. A badminton smash can go over 200 miles per hour (exclamatory)
3. More than one million Americans play badminton regularly (interrogative)
4. You can get more information by writing to the U.S. Badminton Association (imperative)
5. They have a team (interrogative)

Exercise 5 Find It in Your Reading Read this declarative sentence from *Tiger: A Biography of Tiger Woods.* Write an *imperative* sentence, an *interrogative* sentence, and an *exclamatory* sentence that might have been part of Earl Woods's lecture to his son.

Earl's lecture, delivered at decibels with which Tiger was unfamiliar, centered on the theme that golf owes no one anything, least of all success, and that quitting is a flagrant foul, intolerable.

Exercise 6 Find It in Your Writing Look through your portfolio for examples of all four types of sentences. If you can't find examples of each, challenge yourself to revise a piece of writing to vary your sentence types.

Exercise 7 Writing Application Write a short explanation of how to play your favorite sport. Include each of the four types of sentences.

Section Review • 459

ASSESS

Section Review

Each of these exercises correlates to one of the concepts taught in the section on four functions of a sentence, pages 456–458. The exercises may be used for more practice, for reteaching, or for review of the Key Concepts presented. Answers for all chapter exercises are available in *Grammar Exercises Answers on Transparencies* in your teaching resources.

Answer Key

Exercise 2

1. declarative	6. declarative
2. declarative	7. imperative
3. imperative	8. exclamatory
4. declarative	9. interrogative
5. interrogative	10. exclamatory

Exercise 3

1. There are many fun and simple yard games. declarative
2. Get the neighborhood together, and have some fun! imperative
3. My favorite games are games of tag. declarative
4. Do you know any new forms of tag? interrogative
5. You're it! exclamatory
6. Try to reach home base before I touch you. imperative
7. How will the game end? interrogative
8. Count slowly by fives to one hundred. imperative
9. I am going to duck behind the big azalea bush. declarative
10. Stay out of the street! imperative, exclamatory
11. You never touched me. declarative
12. When do you have to go home? interrogative
13. I am wearing my new sneakers. declarative
14. No, you cannot borrow them. declarative
15. Can you come over tomorrow, so we can play again? interrogative

---

Answer Key continued

4. Write to the U.S. Badminton Association for more information.
5. Do they have a team?

Exercise 5

Find It in Your Reading
Answers will vary. Samples are given.

Imperative:	Never quit!
Interrogative:	Don't you know how intolerable quitting is?
Exclamatory:	Golf owes no one anything!

Exercise 6

Find It in Your Writing
Students can trade papers with partners to check for correct end punctuation.

Exercise 7

Writing Application
Students can compile their explanations into a class sports book.

Exercise 4

Answers will vary. Samples are given.

1. The world's greatest badminton players are from Indonesia.
2. A badminton smash can go over 200 miles per hour!
3. Do more than one million Americans play badminton regularly?

continued

some of it aloud to students. Make sure its text is written in short sentences. Ask students whether they think this book is easy to read. Ask why. (Students should cite the easy vocabulary and the short sentences.) Compare this children's book to a selection from students' literature anthology. Point out the difference in sentence length.

Activate Prior Knowledge

Review conjunctions as words that connect ideas. Ask what purpose a conjunction serves in a compound sentence. Use the sample sentences on this page to show how conjunctions can make short sentences into a longer one.

TEACH

Step-by-Step Teaching Guide

Combining Sentence Parts

1. Write this brief story with very short subject-verb sentences on the chalkboard:

   Tino got up from the bench. Tino chose a bat. Tino left the dugout. Tino went to home plate. The pitcher threw the ball. Tino hit a home run.

2. Ask a student to read it aloud. Have students comment on the style of the story and suggest ways they might alter the sentences to make the story more interesting. Introduce the idea of combining sentences.

3. Review compound subjects and verbs. Remind students that each part of a compound subject takes the same verb, and that all parts of a compound verb share the same subject. The subject of each short sentence in the second example at the right is Lisa; the two predicates can be made into one compound predicate that describes both of the things Lisa did.

Sentence Combining

Books written for very young readers present information in short, direct sentences. While these short sentences make the book easy to read, they don't make the book enjoyable or interesting to older readers. Writing for mature readers should include sentences of varying lengths and complexity to create a flow of ideas. One way to achieve sentence variety is to combine sentences—to express two or more related ideas or pieces of information in a single sentence. Look at the first two examples below. Then, look at how the two ideas are combined in different ways in the last three sentences.

EXAMPLES: We went to the zoo.
            We saw monkeys.

COMBINED: We went to the zoo and saw monkeys.
            We saw monkeys at the zoo.
            We saw monkeys when we went to the zoo.

Combining Sentence Parts

In the examples and exercises below, you will learn several different ways to combine sentences in order to write in a more mature and interesting way.

► **KEY CONCEPT** Sentences can be combined by using a compound subject, a compound verb, or a compound object. ■

EXAMPLE: Moira enjoyed watching the monkeys.
                   Tom enjoyed watching the monkeys.

COMPOUND
SUBJECT: Moira and Tom enjoyed watching the
                   monkeys.

EXAMPLE: Lisa played the game.
                   Lisa won a stuffed animal.

COMPOUND
VERB: Lisa played the game and won a stuffed
                   animal.

EXAMPLE: Scott rode the roller coaster.
                   Scott rode the Ferris wheel.

COMPOUND
OBJECT: Scott rode the roller coaster and the
                   Ferris wheel.

Theme: Fun Places

In this section, you will learn different ways to combine sentences to make your writing more interesting. The examples and exercises in this section are about fun places to visit.

Cross-Curricular Connection: Social Studies

⏱ **TIME AND RESOURCE MANAGER**

Resources
Print: Grammar Exercise Workbook, pp. 89–92
Technology: Language Lab CD-ROM, Sentence Style; On-Line Exercise Bank, Section 21.2

In-Depth Coverage	Accelerated Pace
• Work through all key concepts, pp. 460–463. • Assign and review Exercises 8–11.	• Assign pp. 460–463 for independent student review. • Assign Section Review Exercises 12–14.

▷ **Exercise 8** Combining Sentences Combine each pair of sentences in the way that makes the most sense. Identify what parts of the two sentences you made compound as you combined them.

1. My class went to the amusement park. We also went to the zoo.
2. At the amusement park, the carousel played music. It also rang bells.
3. Jen rode the carousel. Todd rode the carousel, too.
4. The carousel was too mild for Glenn. The Ferris wheel was too mild for Glenn.
5. He preferred the log flume. He rode it three times in a row.
6. At lunch, we ate sandwiches. We ate apples for lunch. We also ate raisins.
7. I enjoyed the roller coaster. I enjoyed the carousel. I enjoyed the Ferris wheel.
8. No one wanted to end our day at the amusement park. No one wanted to go home.
9. The class trip to the amusement park was fun. It was exciting.
10. Everyone thanked our chaperones. Everyone asked them to come back next year.

▷ **More Practice**

Language Lab CD-ROM
• Varying Sentence Structure lesson
On-line Exercise Bank
• Section 21.2
Grammar Exercise Workbook
• pp. 89–92

◀ **Critical Viewing** Use a compound verb to describe the ways in which this carousel pony might combine fun and fear for a young rider. [**Draw Conclusions**]

Sentence Combining • **461**

☑ **ONGOING ASSESSMENT: Prerequisite Skills**

Prerequisite Skills If students have difficulty with compound subjects and verbs, you may find it necessary to review the following to assure coverage of prerequisite knowledge.

In the Textbook	Print Resources	Technology
Compound Subjects and Compound Verbs, pp. 400–403	Grammar Exercise Workbook, pp. 49–50	Language Lab CD-ROM, Sentence Style; On-Line Exercise Bank, Section 21.2

Step-by-Step Teaching Guide

Joining Clauses

1. Review independent clauses. Remind students that an independent clause is a sentence; it can stand alone because it has both a subject and a verb and expresses a complete thought.

2. Point out that only sentences on the same topic should be combined into longer sentences. In the examples, the second sentence in each pair discusses the same topic as the first. If two short independent clauses are unrelated by topic, they should not be combined. Remind students that a sentence should express a complete thought. It should not discuss two unrelated thoughts.

3. Review use of the semicolon: It indicates a halt in a sentence, not just a pause for breath. A semicolon marks the end of a complete thought and a shift, but not a total change, in subject or mood. It functions as a coordinating conjunction and comma do.

4. Subordinate clauses cannot stand on their own because they do not express complete thoughts. A subordinate clause always has to be joined to an independent clause. Remind students that a subordinate clause is used to clarify ideas presented in the independent clause.

Critical Viewing

Infer Answers will vary. Possible responses: The riders were excited, and they screamed for another ride. The riders were scared, but they tried hard not to show it.

Joining Clauses

Use a compound sentence when combining related ideas of equal weight. To create a compound sentence, join the two independent clauses with a comma and a coordinating conjunction. Common conjunctions include *and, but, nor, for, so, or,* and *yet.* You can also link the two sentences with a semicolon (;) if they are closely related.

▶ **KEY CONCEPT** Sentences can be combined by joining two independent clauses to create a compound sentence. ■

EXAMPLE:	The wind whipped against our faces. The screams of other riders excited us.
COMPOUND SENTENCE:	The wind whipped against our faces, and the screams of other riders excited us.
EXAMPLE:	The ride lasted just a few minutes. My stomach continued to rumble for several hours.
COMPOUND SENTENCE:	The ride lasted just a few minutes, but my stomach continued to rumble for several hours.
EXAMPLE:	The roller coaster is such fun. It's very popular.
COMPOUND SENTENCE:	The roller coaster is such fun; it's very popular.

▶ **Exercise 9** Combining Sentences
Combine each pair of sentences by joining the clauses, following the instructions in parentheses.
1. The roller coaster had six loops. It was the wildest one Mark had ever ridden. (comma and conjunction)
2. He wanted to ride it several times. The lines were too long. (comma and conjunction)
3. Lynette was determined to ride it again. She waited in line. (comma and conjunction)
4. The amusement park had a wide variety of rides. All of us found something we liked. (semicolon)
5. This is my favorite amusement park. The rides are all really exciting. (semicolon)

▼ **Critical Viewing** After coming out of the big twist, how do you think these riders feel? What sounds are they making? Answer with a compound sentence. [Infer]

☑ **ONGOING ASSESSMENT: Monitor and Reinforce**

If students miss more than one item in Exercises 8–11, refer them to the following for additional practice.

In the Textbook	Print Resources	Technology
Section Review, Ex. 12–14, p. 464	Grammar Exercise Workbook, pp. 89–92	Language Lab CD-ROM, Sentence Style; On-Line Exercise Bank, Section 21.2

> **KEY CONCEPT** Sentences can be combined by changing one of them into a subordinate clause. ■

Combine sentences into a complex sentence to emphasize the relationship between two ideas, one of which depends on the other. A subordinating conjunction will help readers understand the relationship. Common subordinating conjunctions are *after, although, because, before, since,* and *unless.*

EXAMPLE:	We were frightened. The ride went so fast.
COMBINED WITH A SUBORDINATE CLAUSE:	We were frightened because the ride went so fast.

> **Exercise 10** Combining Sentences With Subordinating Conjunctions Combine each pair of sentences with a subordinating conjunction.
> 1. We rode the carousel. We rode the Ferris wheel.
> 2. Jamie rode the log flume to cool off. The day was so hot.
> 3. Brendan tried the roller coaster. He doesn't like loops.
> 4. Arthur promised to ride the monster coaster. It was closed.
> 5. We went home. The sun went down.

> **KEY CONCEPT** Sentences can be combined by changing one of them into a phrase. ■

When combining sentences in which one of the sentences simply adds details, change one of the sentences into a phrase.

EXAMPLE:	My team plays tomorrow. We play the Cougars.
COMBINED:	My team plays against the Cougars tomorrow.
EXAMPLE:	My team will play against the Cougars. It is the only undefeated team in the league.
COMBINED:	My team will play against the Cougars, the only undefeated team in the league.

> **Exercise 11** Using Phrases to Combine Sentences
> Combine the following pairs of sentences by rewriting information from one sentence as a phrase and adding it to the other.
> 1. Our class went to the amusement park. We went there for the entire day.
> 2. The whole class went. We traveled by bus.
> 3. The roller coaster thrilled us. The roller coaster has six loops.
> 4. This roller coaster is not for everyone. This roller coaster is the fastest in the area.
> 5. The trip to the amusement park was fun. It was on Tuesday.

> ⊙ **Learn More**
>
> For a more complete list of subordinating conjunctions, turn to Chapter 20.

> ▶ **More Practice**
>
> **Language Lab CD-ROM**
> • Varying Sentence Structure lesson
> **On-line Exercise Bank**
> • Section 21.2
> **Grammar Exercise Workbook**
> • pp. 89–92

Sentence Combining • 463

Answer Key

> ▶ **Exercise 9** (page 462)
> 1. The roller coaster had six loops, and it was the wildest one Mark had ever ridden.
> 2. He wanted to ride it several times, but the lines were too long.
> 3. Lynette was determined to ride it again, so she waited in line.
> 4. The amusement park had a wide variety of rides; all of us found something we liked.
> 5. This is my favorite amusement park; the rides are all really exciting.

> ▶ **Exercise 10**
>
> Answers will vary. Samples are given.
> 1. We rode the carousel after we rode the Ferris wheel.
> 2. Jamie rode the log flume to cool off because the day was so hot.
> 3. Brendan tried the roller coaster, although he doesn't like loops.
> 4. Arthur promised to ride the monster coaster before it was closed.
> 5. We went home after the sun went down.

> ▶ **Exercise 11**
>
> Answers will vary. Samples are given.
> 1. Our class went to the amusement park for the entire day.
> 2. The whole class went on the bus.
> 3. The roller coaster with its six loops thrilled us.
> 4. This roller coaster, the fastest in the area, is not for everyone.
> 5. The trip to the amusement park on Tuesday was fun.

☑ ONGOING ASSESSMENT: Assess Mastery

Use the following resources to assess student mastery of combining sentences.

In the Textbook	Technology
Chapter Review, Ex. 46, p. 484	Language Lab CD-ROM, Sentence Style; On-Line Exercise Bank, Section 21.2

> ⊙ **TIME SAVERS!**
>
> 🖶 **Answers on Transparency**
> Use the Grammar Exercises Answers on Transparencies for Chapter 21 to facilitate correction by students.
>
> 🖥 **On-Line Exercise Bank**
> Have students complete the exercises on computer. The Auto Check feature will grade their work for you!

Section Review

Each of these exercises correlates to the instruction on sentence combining, pages 460–463. The exercises may be used for more practice, for reteaching, or for review of the Key Concepts presented. Answers for all chapter exercises are available in *Grammar Exercises Answers on Transparencies* in your Teaching Resources.

Answer Key

▶ Exercise 12

1. Roller coasters and Ferris wheels can be found in almost every amusement park.
2. Most amusement parks have games and food stands.
3. You can enjoy the rides and spend time with your friends at an amusement park.
4. Some amusement parks offer special discounts or two-for-one tickets.
5. When we go to the amusement park, we arrive early and stay late.

▶ Exercise 13

Answers will vary. Samples are given.

1. Amusement parks have permanent rides, but traveling carnivals have rides that can be disassembled and moved.
2. We went to the state fair last year because we wanted to see the 4-H judging.
3. Although we left before dawn, the parking area was already crowded when we arrived.
4. We left right after lunch because it rained.
5. Next month, we might go to a theme park; we haven't decided which one.
6. I want to go to one with lots of rides; my parents want to go to one nearby.
7. The drive might be long, but I think it's worth the time.
8. There are many reasons to go to a theme park, but the main one is to have fun.
9. People in costumes greet guests, and the greeting makes everyone feel festive.
10. There is so much to see that you probably can't see it all in one day.

▶ Exercise 14

Answers will vary. Samples are given.

GRAMMAR EXERCISES 12–17

▶ **Exercise 12** Combining Sentence Parts Combine each pair of sentences by creating a compound subject, verb, or object.

1. Ferris wheels can be found in almost every amusement park. Roller coasters can be found in almost every amusement park.
2. Most amusement parks have games. Most also have food stands.
3. You can enjoy the rides at an amusement park. You can spend time with your friends at an amusement park.
4. Some amusement parks offer special discounts. Some amusement parks offer two-for-one tickets.
5. When we go to the amusement park, we arrive early. We also stay late.

▶ **Exercise 13** Combining Clauses Combine each pair of sentences into a single compound or complex sentence.

1. Amusement parks have permanent rides. Traveling carnivals have rides that can be disassembled and moved.
2. We went to the state fair last year. We wanted to see the 4-H judging.
3. We left before dawn. The parking area was already crowded when we arrived.
4. We left right after lunch. It rained.
5. Next month, we might go to a theme park. We haven't decided which one.
6. I want to go to one with lots of rides. My parents want to go to one nearby.
7. The drive might be long. I think it's worth the time.
8. There are many reasons to go to a theme park. The main one is to have fun.
9. People in costumes greet guests. The greeting makes everyone feel festive.
10. There is so much to see. You probably can't see it all in one day.

464 • Effective Sentences

▶ **Exercise 14** Using Phrases to Combine Sentences Combine each pair of sentences by changing one of them into a phrase.

1. We planned a family outing. It was a trip to the zoo.
2. We saw monkeys there. The monkeys were in a large habitat.
3. We rode the monorail. It went around the park.
4. The monorail is comfortable and convenient. It is the best way to see the whole park quickly.
5. We saw hundreds of animals. The animals were below the monorail.

▶ **Exercise 15** Find It in Your Reading Read the following sentences from "Zoo" by Edward D. Hoch. Identify the ideas that have been combined, and state each idea as a separate sentence.

All day long it went like that, until ten thousand people had filed by the barred cages [that were] set into the side of the spaceship. Then, as the six-hour limit ran out, Professor Hugo once more took the microphone in hand.

▶ **Exercise 16** Find It in Your Writing Look through your portfolio for a paragraph that contains several short sentences. Combine two of the short sentences to form one longer sentence.

▶ **Exercise 17** Writing Application Write a paragraph about a fun place you have visited with your family or friends. Combine ideas, using one of the ways suggested in this section.

---

1. For our family outing, we planned a trip to the zoo.
2. We saw monkeys in a large habitat.
3. We rode the monorail around the park.
4. The monorail, comfortable and convenient, is the best way to see the whole park quickly.
5. We saw hundreds of animals below the monorail.

▶ Exercise 15

Find It in Your Reading
Answers will vary. A sample is given.

All day long, people filed by the barred crates. The crates were set into the side of the spaceship. Ten thousand people filed by. Six hours went by. Professor Hugo took the microphone in his hand.

▶ Exercise 16

Find It in Your Writing
Students should check subject-verb agreement in their new sentences.

▶ Exercise 17

Writing Application
Have some students read their combined sentences aloud. Have others identify phrases, coordinating conjunctions, subordinating conjunctions, and compound subjects, verbs, and objects.

Section 21.3 *Varying Sentences*

Varying the length and form of the sentences you write can help create a rhythm, achieve an effect, or emphasize the connections between ideas. There are several ways you can introduce variety in the sentences you write.

Varying Sentence Length

Reading too many long sentences in a row is as uninteresting as reading too many short sentences. When you want to emphasize a point or surprise a reader, insert a short, direct sentence to interrupt the flow of several long sentences.

Some longer sentences contain only one main idea and should not be broken into separate sentences. Other sentences contain two or more ideas and might be shortened by breaking up the ideas.

LONGER SENTENCE:	You may have learned that many animals in many parts of the world fear snakes, but the mongoose does not.
TWO SENTENCES:	You may have learned that many animals in many parts of the world fear snakes. The mongoose does not.

> **Theme: Real and Fictional Animals**
>
> In this section, you will learn how to make your writing more interesting by varying your sentences. The examples and exercises in this section are about real and fictional animals.
>
> **Cross-Curricular Connection: Science**

GRAMMAR IN LITERATURE

from **Rikki-tikki-tavi**
Rudyard Kipling

In the following passage, the last sentence is emphasized because it is shorter and simpler than the preceding sentences.

. . . When a snake misses its stroke, it never says anything or gives any sign of what it means to do next. Rikki-tikki did not care to follow them, for he did not feel sure that he could manage two snakes at once. So he trotted off to the gravel path near the house, and sat down to think. It was a serious matter for him.

Varying Sentences • 465

⏱ **TIME AND RESOURCE MANAGER**

Resources
Print: Grammar Exercise Workbook, pp. 91–94; Grammer Exercises Answers on Transparencies, Ch. 21
Technology: On-Line Exercise Bank, Section 21.3

In-Depth Coverage	Accelerated Pace
• Work through all key concepts, pp. 465–467. • Assign and review Exercises 18–20. • Read and discuss Grammar in Literature, p. 465.	• Assign pp. 465–467 for independent student review. • Assign Review Exercises 21–23.

PREPARE and ENGAGE

Interest GRABBER Read aloud Abraham Lincoln's Gettysburg Address. Point out the great variety in length among its ten sentences: two short, simple sentences with linking verbs, and eight long sentences with multiple clauses of all different types. The sentences vary in length from 10 to 82 words. Have students discuss the way this variety affects them.

Activate Prior Knowledge

Use the Gettysburg Address to demonstrate the variety of ways to begin sentences. The first sentence begins with an adverb phrase, the second with the adverb *now*, the next two with the pronoun subject *we*.

TEACH

Step-by-Step Teaching Guide

Varying Sentence Length

1. Explain to students that varying sentence length is one easy way to create an interesting rhythm in their writing.

2. Encourage students to review their writing for long sentences.

Step-by-Step Teaching Guide

Grammar in Literature

1. Have a volunteer read aloud the literature excerpt. Ask students to discuss the effect of the short final sentence. (Students may suggest that the word *serious* stands out.)

2. Have students try to split up the first three long sentences in this excerpt into shorter ones. Then have them compare and contrast their versions with the original. (Students may say that the prose sounds choppy when they break up the long sentences.)

More About the Author

British writer Rudyard Kipling spent many years in India, his birth country. His famous works *Just So Stories, Kim, Rikki-Tikki-Tavi* and *Barrack-Room Ballads* are set there. Kipling worked as a journalist and war correspondent and wrote short stories, fairy tales, poetry, and adventure stories.

Exercise 18

Sample answers:

1. The mongoose views the snake as a dangerous enemy. The snake reacts to the mongoose in the same way.
2. The mongoose can be found in India and Jamaica.
3. The mongoose in Rudyard Kipling's story seems quite friendly with people. His behavior does not truly reflect the behavior of a wild mongoose.
4. The devious, clever snake in the story is constantly trying to catch Rikki-tikki-tavi.
5. In the end, the family is very grateful to the little mongoose. It has good reason to be thankful.

Step-by-Step Teaching Guide

Varying Sentence Beginnings

1. Write the following sentence on the chalkboard: *Omar, oddly enough, was the first to arrive that morning.* Challenge students to change the word order of this sentence so that it says the same thing in a new way. (Sample answers: Oddly enough, Omar was the first to arrive that morning. The first to arrive that morning, oddly enough, was Omar. That morning, oddly enough, Omar was the first to arrive.)

2. Explain that varying sentence beginnings is not always necessary or desirable. Repetition and parallel structure are very effective devices in writing. Read aloud the beginning of Charles Dickens's *A Tale of Two Cities.* (It is actually one long sentence, but students will not realize this, and it is an excellent example of repetition that works.)

> *It was the best of times, it was the worst of times, it was the age of wisdom, it was the age of foolishness, it was the epoch of belief, it was the epoch of incredulity, it was the season of Light, it was the season of Darkness, it was the spring of hope, it was the winter of despair . . .*

continued

466

21.3

▶ **Exercise 18** **Forming Short Sentences** On a separate sheet of paper, rewrite the following sentences by breaking each into two sentences or forming a simpler, more direct sentence.

EXAMPLE: The mongoose is an animal that can fight with snakes because it is quick and agile. (Rewrite as a more direct sentence.)

ANSWER: The quick and agile mongoose is able to fight snakes.

1. The mongoose views the snake as a dangerous enemy, and the snake reacts to the mongoose in the same way. (Break into two sentences.)
2. The mongoose can be found in India, and it can be found in Jamaica. (Rewrite as a more direct sentence.)
3. The mongoose in Rudyard Kipling's story seems quite friendly with people, but his behavior does not truly reflect the behavior of a wild mongoose. (Break into two sentences.)
4. The snake in the story is devious and clever, and he is constantly trying to catch Rikki-tikki-tavi. (Rewrite as a more direct sentence.)
5. In the end, the family is very grateful to the little mongoose, and it has good reason to be thankful. (Break into two sentences.)

Varying Sentence Beginnings

Another way to vary your sentences is to start your sentences in different ways. For instance, you can start sentences with different parts of speech.

Start with a noun (or an article and a noun).	Birdhouses, surprisingly, are not difficult to make.
Start with an adverb.	Surprisingly, birdhouses are not difficult to make.
Start with an infinitive.	To make birdhouses is, surprisingly, not difficult.
Start with a gerund.	Making birdhouses is, surprisingly, not difficult.

💡 Spelling Tip

Remember that in words such as *grateful* and *thankful,* the suffix *-ful* is spelled with only one *l.*

 **STANDARDIZED TEST PREPARATION WORKSHOP**

Effective Sentences Many standardized tests require students to choose among a set of possible revisions to a given sentence. Share with students the following example:

We were running late we missed the party.

Which of the following is the best revision?

A We were running late, we missed the party.

B Because we were running late, we missed the party.

C We were running late, but we missed the party.

D Correct as is

Item **B** is the best revision because it creates a dependent clause, making a complex sentence that logically relates the two ideas expressed in the original run-on.

Step-by-Step Teaching Guide *continued*

> **Exercise 19** **Varying Sentence Beginnings** Rearrange each sentence to begin with the part of speech indicated in parentheses.
> 1. The snake silently slithered through the grass. (adverb)
> 2. The mongoose was hiding in the tall weeds. (participle)
> 3. The snake would have to be quick to catch the mongoose. (infinitive)
> 4. Cautiously, the mongoose peeked around the corner. (article and noun)
> 5. The mongoose cleverly waited until the snake had gone away. (adverb)

You can also vary sentence beginnings by reversing the traditional subject-verb order.

Subject-Verb Order	Verb-Subject Order
The snake is waiting.	Waiting is the snake.
The boy watched cautiously.	Cautiously watched the boy.

> **Exercise 20** **Inverting Subject-Verb Order** Rewrite each of the following sentences by inverting the subject-verb order to verb-subject order. Rearrange the rest of the words in the sentence as needed.
> 1. The land is full of wildlife.
> 2. In the air the humming of insects vibrates.
> 3. Some type of living thing exists under every rock.
> 4. Numerous animal species appear at the water's edge.
> 5. The sun dawns on a new day.

More Practice

Language Lab CD-ROM
• Varying Sentence Structure lesson

On-line Exercise Bank
• Section 21.3

Grammar Exercise Workbook
• pp. 91–92

◀ **Critical Viewing** In two or three sentences, tell what this pair of mongooses might be watching. Use a different beginning for each sentence. **[Speculate]**

Varying Sentences • 467

3. Go over the sample verb-subject sentences on page 467 and work through Exercise 20 with the class. Ask students to give their reactions to these sentences. (Students may think they sound poetic, affected, or old-fashioned.) Ask when they think they might want to use sentences with a verb-subject pattern. (Possible answers: in writing poetry; as dialogue for a character who is not fluent in English)

Answer Key

> **Exercise 19**

1. Silently, the snake slithered through the grass.
2. Hiding in the tall weeds was the mongoose.
3. To catch the mongoose, the snake would have to be quick.
4. The mongoose peeked cautiously around the corner.
5. Cleverly, the mongoose waited until the snake had gone away.

> **Exercise 20**

1. Full of wildlife is the land.
2. In the air vibrates the humming of insects.
3. Under every rock exists some type of living thing.
4. At the water's edge appear numerous animal species.
5. On a new day dawns the sun.

Critical Viewing

Speculate Possible answers: The mongooses watched the snake alertly. Being distracted for even one instant was not an option.

Language Highlight

Irregular Plural Ask students to give the word for more than one mongoose. They will probably say *mongeese.* Explain that although the plural of *goose* is *geese,* the plural of *mongoose* is *mongooses. Mongoose* is from an Indian word for this small mammal.

☑ **ONGOING ASSESSMENT: Monitor and Reinforce**

If students miss more than two items in Exercises 18–20, refer them to the following for additional practice.

In the Textbook	Print Resources	Technology
Section Review, Ex. 21–23, p. 468	Grammar Exercise Workbook, pp. 91–94	On-Line Exercise Bank, Section 21.3

Section Review

Each of these exercises correlates to the instruction on varying sentences, pages 465–467. The exercises may be used for more practice, for reteaching, or for review of the Key Concepts presented. Answers for all chapter exercises are available in *Grammar Exercises Answers on Transparencies* in your Teaching Resources.

Answer Key

Exercise 21

Answers will vary. Samples are given.

1. Artists and writers have created many paintings, statues, stories, and movies portraying lions as symbols of courage.
2. The lion is a universal symbol in literature and art. It is featured in works from China, Greece, and Rome.
3. Aesop's popular fable about a lion teaches a good lesson.
4. The Sphinx, a character from Greek and Egyptian mythology, has the head of a human and the body of a lion.
5. Even today, the lion is a popular subject. It has been featured in movies such as *The Lion King*.

Exercise 22

Answers will vary. Samples are given.

1. To teach a lesson, Aesop used the fable "The Fox and the Crow."
2. Sitting in a tree with a piece of cheese in her beak is a crow.
3. Nearby, a fox spies on the crow.
4. The plan of the fox is to trick the crow.
5. Getting her cheese is his goal.
6. To distract the crow's attention, the fox flatters her.
7. Slyly, he asks her to sing just one song.
8. Opening her mouth to sing, the crow drops the cheese.
9. In a flash, the fox snaps up the cheese.
10. To end the fable, Aesop adds a moral.

GRAMMAR EXERCISES 21–26

> **Exercise 21** Revising Long Sentences Rewrite the following sentences by breaking each into two sentences or forming a simpler, more direct sentence.

1. Artists and writers have often used lions as symbols of courage, and lions have been portrayed in many paintings, statues, stories, and movies. (Rewrite as a more direct sentence.)
2. The lion is a universal symbol in literature and art, and it is featured in works from China, Greece, and Rome. (Break into two sentences.)
3. A popular fable by Aesop is about a lion, and the fable teaches a good lesson. (Rewrite as a more direct sentence.)
4. The Sphinx is a character from Greek and Egyptian mythology, and it has the head of a human, and it also has the body of a lion. (Rewrite as a more direct sentence.)
5. Even today, the lion is a popular subject, and it has been featured in movies such as *The Lion King*. (Break into two sentences.)

> **Exercise 22** Varying Sentence Beginnings Rearrange each sentence below to begin with the part of speech indicated in parentheses.

1. Aesop used the fable "The Fox and the Crow" to teach a lesson. (infinitive)
2. A crow is sitting in a tree with a piece of cheese in her beak. (participle)
3. A fox nearby spies on the crow. (adverb)
4. To trick the crow is the fox's plan. (article and noun)
5. His goal is to get her cheese. (gerund)
6. The fox flatters her to distract the crow's attention. (infinitive)

468 • Effective Sentences

7. He asks her slyly to sing just one song. (adverb)
8. The crow drops the cheese on opening her mouth to sing. (participle)
9. The fox snaps up the cheese in a flash. (preposition)
10. Aesop adds a moral to end the fable. (infinitive)

> **Exercise 23** Inverting Subject-Verb Order Invert the subject-verb order in the following sentences.

1. A leopard is hunting in the dark.
2. Its senses are alert to any movement.
3. Its prey is caught by surprise.
4. Two lions are gaining on the giraffe.
5. The chase ends not long after.

> **Exercise 24** Find It in Your Reading Notice the use of long and short sentences in this passage from "The Fox and the Crow." Which parts of the long sentence are independent clauses?

> The Crow lifted up her head and began to caw her best, but the moment she opened her mouth the piece of cheese fell to the ground, only to be snapped up by Master Fox. "That will do," said he. "That was all I wanted."

> **Exercise 25** Find It in Your Writing Find examples of long sentences in compositions in your portfolio. Rewrite them, forming shorter, more direct sentences.

> **Exercise 26** Writing Application Write a paragraph about your favorite fictional animal. Use both short and long sentences in your paragraph.

Exercise 23

1. Hunting in the dark is a leopard.
2. Alert to any movement are its senses.
3. Caught by surprise is its prey.
4. Gaining on the giraffe are two lions.
5. Not long after ends the chase.

Exercise 24

Find It in Your Reading
Independent clauses are "The Crow lifted up her head and began to caw her best" and "the piece of cheese fell to the ground." As extra practice, ask students to rewrite the first long sentence into several shorter ones.

Exercise 25

Find It in Your Writing
Have students explain which types of sentences they prefer and why.

Exercise 26

Writing Application
Have students read some of their paragraphs aloud. Have the class discuss the variety of sentences in each paragraph.

Section 21.4 *Avoiding Sentence Problems*

Correcting Sentence Fragments

Some groups of words, even though they have a capital at the beginning and a period at the end, are not complete sentences. They are *fragments*.

> ▶ **KEY CONCEPT** A **fragment** is a group of words that does not express a complete thought. ■

A sentence expresses a complete thought; a fragment does not. A fragment can be a group of words with no subject; a group of words that includes a possible subject but no verb; a group of words with a possible subject and only part of a possible verb; or even a subordinate clause standing alone.

FRAGMENTS	COMPLETED SENTENCES
In the early evening.	The flight arrived *in the early evening.*
Felt happy and relaxed.	I *felt happy and relaxed.*
The sign in the corridor.	*The sign in the corridor* is surprising.
The train coming around the bend.	*The train* was *coming around the bend.*
When she first smiled.	*When she first smiled,* the whole world seemed to light up.

> ▶ **Exercise 27** Recognizing Sentence Fragments Each of the following is either a sentence or a fragment. Write *F* if it is a fragment and *S* if it is a complete sentence.

EXAMPLE: Tourists climbing pyramids.
ANSWER: F

1. The parched sands of the desert.
2. The streets of Cairo are narrow and winding.
3. We shopped.
4. Bought a souvenir in the open bazaar.
5. Since there is very little rain in the area.

Theme: Ancient and Modern Egypt

In this section, you will learn how to avoid problems that make your sentences incorrect or hard to understand. The examples and exercises in this section are about ancient and modern Egypt.

Cross-Curricular Connection: Social Studies

▼ Critical Viewing
Use complete sentences to describe the environmental conditions that may cause fragments to fall from this ancient statue. [Speculate]

The Sphinx rises majestically in the Egyptian desert.

PREPARE and ENGAGE

Interest GRABBER Write the following sentences and fragments on the chalkboard:

Ate the whole cake.

It was Tamika's birthday.

All her friends were invited.

Jumped on the table.

Big pet dog.

Ask students to identify any items that are not sentences and explain why they are not. Explain that these groups of words are fragments.

Activate Prior Knowledge

Review the definition of a sentence. Remind students that a sentence must have a subject and a verb, and it must express a complete thought. Any group of words that does not fit this definition is a fragment. Students should not confuse very short sentences with fragments. *I won!* is a sentence: It has a subject and a verb.

TEACH

Step-by-Step Teaching Guide

Correcting Sentence Fragments

1. Have a volunteer read each fragment and completed sentence on this page.
2. Encourage students to complete the fragments in other ways.

Answer Key

▶ **Exercise 27**

1. F
2. S
3. S
4. F
5. F

Critical Viewing

Speculate Some students may have heard of the effects of acid rain on the Sphinx. Others may describe rain, wind, and desert sands as forces that work to wear away the stone. Explain that scientists began work to preserve the stone in the 1970's.

🕐 TIME AND RESOURCE MANAGER

Resources
Print: Grammar Exercise Workbook, pp. 95–110; Hands-on Grammar Activity Book, Chapter 21; Grammer Exercises Answers on Transparencies, Chapter 21
Technology: Language Lab CD-ROM, Problems With Sentences; On-Line Exercise Bank, Section 21.4

In-Depth Coverage	Accelerated Pace
• Work through all key concepts, pp. 469–481. • Assign and review Exercises 27–38. • Read and discuss Hands-on Grammar, p. 482.	• Assign pp. 469–481 for independent student review. • Assign Review Exercises 39–42.

Correcting Phrase and Clause Fragments

1. Review phrases: A phrase does not have a subject and a verb. It adds descriptive details to a sentence. Most phrases function as adverbs or adjectives, describing how, where, or when something was done, or what something or someone looks like.

2. Many phrases begin with prepositions. Remind students that if a verb follows the preposition *to,* it is an infinitive and not a prepositional phrase. In the sentence *Damon decided to walk to the park, to walk* is an infinitive, and *to the park* is a prepositional phrase.

3. Emphasize the difference between phrases and clauses. Phrases do not have subjects and verbs; clauses do. Review the list of subordinating conjunctions on page 441. Emphasize that if one of these words appears before a subject and verb in a sentence, a second, independent clause must appear.

21.4

Correcting Phrase Fragments

A phrase by itself is a fragment. It cannot stand alone because it does not have a subject and a verb.

KEY CONCEPT A phrase should not be capitalized and punctuated as if it were a sentence. ■

A *phrase fragment* can be corrected by adding it to a nearby sentence. The example below shows a prepositional phrase following a complete sentence.

FRAGMENT:	The travelers rode camels. *On the morning of March 4.*
ADDED TO NEARBY SENTENCE:	The travelers rode camels *on the morning of March 4.*

You can also correct a phrase fragment by adding to the phrase whatever is needed to make it a complete sentence. This method often requires adding a subject and a verb.

CHANGING PHRASE FRAGMENTS INTO SENTENCES

Phrase Fragment	Complete Sentence
In the ancient tomb	The treasure was found *in the ancient tomb.*
Touching his hand	*Touching his hand,* she asked for her father's advice.
To observe Ramadan	Sam learned *to observe Ramadan.*

▶ **Exercise 28** Changing Phrase Fragments Into Sentences
Use each of the following phrase fragments in a sentence. You may use the phrase at the beginning, at the end, or in any other position in the sentence. Check to see that each of your sentences contains a subject and a verb.

EXAMPLE: In the morning after breakfast.
EXPANDED: Sheri visited the mosque in the morning after breakfast.

1. To grow crops.
2. Waiting for rain.
3. In the Nile River.
4. Lost in the desert.
5. In Egypt.

▶ **More Practice**
Language Lab
CD-ROM
• Sentence Fragments lesson
On-line
Exercise Bank
• Section 21.4
Grammar Exercise
Workbook
• pp. 95–98

Correcting Clause Fragments

All clauses have subjects and verbs, but some cannot stand alone as sentences.

▶ **KEY CONCEPT** A subordinate clause should not be capitalized and punctuated as if it were a sentence. ■

Subordinate clauses do not express complete thoughts. Although a subordinate adjective or adverb clause has a subject and a verb, it cannot stand by itself as a sentence. (See Chapter 20 for more information about subordinate clauses and the words that begin them.)

Like phrase fragments, *clause fragments* can usually be corrected in either of two ways: (1) by attaching the fragment to a nearby sentence, or (2) by adding whatever words are needed to turn the fragment into a sentence.

Notice how the following clause fragments are corrected using the first method.

FRAGMENT:	The class enjoyed the poem. *That I recited to them as part of my oral report on Egypt.*
ADDED TO NEARBY SENTENCE:	The class enjoyed the poem *that I recited to them as part of my oral report on Egypt.*
FRAGMENT:	I'll give my report today. *As long as you give yours, too.*
ADDED TO NEARBY SENTENCE:	I'll give my report today *as long as you give yours, too.*

To change a clause fragment into a sentence by the second method, you must add an independent clause to the fragment.

CHANGING CLAUSE FRAGMENTS INTO SENTENCES

Clause Fragment	Complete Sentence
That you described.	I found the necklace *that you described.*
	The necklace *that you described* has been found.
When he knocked.	I opened the door *when he knocked.*
	When he knocked, I opened the door.

⊘ Learn More

For more information about sentences and fragments, turn to Chapter 19.

Answer Key

21.4

▶ **Exercise 29** Changing Clause Fragments Into Sentences
Use each of the clause fragments below in a sentence. Make sure that each sentence contains an independent clause.

EXAMPLE: That she wanted to use.

EXPANDED: I lent her the camera *that she wanted to use.*

1. If you send me a postcard from Cairo.
2. Which has an average temperature between 55 degrees and 70 degrees in the cool season.
3. That she taught us about the Nile River.
4. Who we thought were friendly and polite.
5. When the Nile River flooded the valley.

▶ **Exercise 30** Changing Fragments Into Sentences
Decide what is missing in each fragment, and then rewrite it as a complete sentence.

EXAMPLE: In the fall of each year.

EXPANDED: *In the fall of each year,* the Nile River floods.

1. Countries in Africa.
2. Where there are deserts, mountains, and rivers.
3. The third pyramid that we visited.
4. Saving money for a trip to Egypt.
5. In the morning.
6. Frightened by the mummy.
7. To listen to the music in the marketplace.
8. Whom you met in Sinai.
9. Four blankets in Egypt.
10. While they crossed the Suez Canal.

▶ **More Practice**

Language Lab CD-ROM
• Sentence Fragments lesson
On-line Exercise Bank
• Section 21.4
Grammar Exercise Workbook
• pp. 95–98

▼ Critical Viewing Explain the impression these pyramids make on you, and tell why. **[Connect]**

472 • Effective Sentences

▶ **Exercise 31** Revising to Correct Fragments in a **Paragraph** There are five fragments in the following paragraph. Rewrite the entire paragraph, correcting each fragment. You may correct a fragment by attaching it to a nearby sentence or by adding words to it to form a new sentence.

EXAMPLE: Needed a translator.
EXPANDED: Because we could not speak Arabic, *we needed a translator.*

(1) Before written records existed. (2) Egypt was established. (3) In the northeastern part of Africa. (4) Today, Egypt's capital is Cairo. (5) The most populated city in Africa. (6) Cairo is the center of government, industry, and business. (7) Important for commerce, transportation, and education. (8) The Nile River is a major resource for Cairo. (9) It is a waterway for transportation. (10) Water for irrigation.

Correcting Run-ons

A fragment is an incomplete sentence. A *run-on,* on the other hand, crowds together complete ideas without using the punctuation needed to see their relationship.

▶ **KEY CONCEPT** A **run-on** is two or more complete sentences that are not properly joined or separated. ∎

Run-ons are usually the result of haste. Learn to check your sentences carefully to see where one sentence ends and the next one begins.

Two Kinds of Run-ons There are two kinds of run-ons. The first one is made up of two sentences that are run together without any punctuation between them. The second type of run-on consists of two or more sentences separated only by a comma.

WITH NO PUNCTUATION: I use our library often the reference section is my favorite part.

WITH ONLY A COMMA: The library contains a wealth of information about Egypt, it is located on the second floor.

A good way to distinguish between a run-on and a sentence is to read the words aloud. Your ear will tell you whether you have one or two complete thoughts and whether you need to make a complete break between the thoughts.

📝 **Journal Tip**

In your journal, take notes on some of the facts about Egypt that interest you. Then, review them later to find a topic for a report.

Sample rewrite: Egypt was established in the northeastern part of Africa before written records existed. Today, Egypt's capital is Cairo, the most populated city in Africa. Cairo, the center of government, industry, and business, is important for commerce, transportation, and education. The Nile River is a major resource for Cairo. It is a waterway for transportation and provides water for irrigation. Rich soil deposited by the river is good for farming.

Step-by-Step Teaching Guide

Correcting Run-ons

1. Make sure students understand that run-on sentences and long sentences are not the same thing. You can create a long sentence that is grammatically correct:

   For our vacation, my mother, father, two sisters, brother, aunt, uncle, and I spent two weeks at the seashore, where we swam, lay in the sun, built sand castles, and had picnics.

2. A correct sentence must include a subject and verb for each clause, and must connect the clauses properly with conjunctions, punctuation marks, or both.

1. S
2. RO
3. RO
4. S
5. RO

Critical Viewing

Analyze Students may suggest size, type of decoration or symbols, and elaborate carving. Details of the image may suggest other indications of status.

Step-by-Step Teaching Guide

Three Ways to Correct Run-ons

1. Have volunteers read aloud the key concept statements on these two pages.

2. Have students try different methods of correcting each sample sentence and then discuss the results.

3. Explain that which method a writer uses to correct a run-on sentence is largely a matter of style. Most run-on sentences can be corrected by any of the three methods shown.

21.4

Exercise 32 Recognizing Run-ons On your paper, write *S* if the item is a sentence and *RO* if the item is a run-on.

EXAMPLE: At nine, Tutankhamen became king of Egypt, at eighteen he died.

ANSWER: RO

1. After Narmer unified the northern and southern kingdoms of Egypt, he became Egypt's first king.
2. The kings of ancient Egypt were known as pharaohs, they were believed to have been chosen and favored by the gods.
3. Egyptians worshiped the pharaohs as though they were gods, some people even said that the pharaohs were the sons of the gods.
4. Cheops is one of the better-known pharaohs of Egypt, and his tomb is visited by millions of people every year.
5. The Egyptians constructed one pyramid in a twenty-year time period it is not surprising that it took so long to cut, move, and assemble the two million stone blocks, which weigh more than two tons each.

Three Ways to Correct Run-ons

There are three easy ways to correct a run-on sentence.

Using End Marks **End marks** are periods, question marks, and exclamation marks.

KEY CONCEPT Use an end mark to separate a run-on into two sentences. ■

Properly used, an end mark splits a run-on into two shorter but complete sentences.

RUN-ON: The ancient Egyptians left remarkable monuments to their civilization, their huge temples and pyramid tombs still stand along the Nile today.

CORRECTED SENTENCES: The ancient Egyptians left remarkable monuments to their civilization. Their huge temples and pyramid tombs still stand along the Nile today.

▲ **Critical Viewing** What elements of this image reflect the status of the individual? Answer in complete sentences. **[Analyze]**

 **Learn More**

For help in identifying conjunctions, see Chapter 18.

STANDARDIZED TEST PREPARATION WORKSHOP

Grammar and Usage Standardized tests often ask students to choose an incorrect item from a group. Ask students which of the sentences in the following passage is incorrect and should be rewritten.

A Ben waited for his turn to cross the stage and get his diploma.

B He watched his friend Sylvia shake hands with the principal as her turn came.

C Sylvia looked out over the audience, she saw Ben and smiled at him.

D As Ben accepted the principal's congratulations, he was blinded momentarily by the flash from his mother's camera.

Item **C** is a run-on sentence. The other sentences in the passage are long but correct.

Using Commas and Coordinating Conjunctions

Sometimes the two parts of a run-on are related and should be combined into a compound sentence.

KEY CONCEPT Use a comma and a coordinating conjunction to combine two independent clauses into a compound sentence. ■

The most common coordinating conjunctions are *and, but, or, for,* and *nor.* To separate the clauses properly, use both a comma and a conjunction.

| RUN-ON: | I want to go on a Nile cruise, I need more money. |
| CORRECTED SENTENCE: | I want to go on a Nile cruise, but I need more money. |

Using Semicolons You can sometimes use a semicolon to connect the two parts of a run-on.

KEY CONCEPT Use a semicolon to connect two closely related ideas. ■

Do not overuse the semicolon. Use a semicolon only when the ideas in both parts of the sentence are closely related.

| RUN-ON: | The first train to Luxor leaves at 6:05, the express doesn't leave until an hour later. |
| CORRECTED SENTENCE: | The first train to Luxor leaves at 6:05; the express doesn't leave until an hour later. |

Exercise 33 **Revising to Correct Run-ons** Correct the following run-ons, using one of the methods you have learned.
1. There are three pyramids at Giza, a sphinx is also there.
2. A sphinx is a monster it has a human head and a lion's body.
3. The Great Sphinx is in Giza, it is called the Father of Terror because of its size and location.
4. Imagine standing next to the Great Sphinx, it is 66 feet tall.
5. If you could put the statue on a football field, it would cover almost the entire field, it is 242 feet long.
6. The Great Sphinx faces the Nile River, which is toward the east, its back faces the three great pyramids.
7. The age of the creature is unknown, evidence shows that it may be older than the pyramids.
8. There are many chambers in the Great Sphinx, an ancient passageway leads to one in the center of the statue.
9. Engraved in the body are several drawings, they are known as hieroglyphics.
10. Hieroglyphics are pictures that are symbols for sounds and words they were used as a writing system.

⚙ Grammar and Style Tip

Words such as *however, therefore, thus,* and *consequently* are effective words to start a sentence that may have originally been part of a run-on. These words connect the ideas in the sentences and clarify their meaning.

More Practice

Language Lab CD-ROM
• Run-on Sentences lesson
On-line Exercise Bank
• Section 21.4
Grammar Exercise Workbook
• pp. 99–102

Avoiding Sentence Problems • 475

Answer Key

Exercise 33

Answers will vary. Samples are given.
1. There are three pyramids at Giza; a sphinx is also there.
2. A sphinx is a monster; it has a human head and a lion's body.
3. The Great Sphinx is in Giza. It is called the Father of Terror because of its size and location.
4. Imagine standing next to the Great Sphinx! It is 66 feet tall.
5. If you could put the statue on a football field, it would cover almost the entire field. It is 242 feet long.
6. The Great Sphinx faces the Nile River, which is towards the East. Its back faces the three great pyramids.
7. The age of the creature is unknown; evidence shows that it may be older than the pyramids.
8. There are many chambers in the Great Sphinx, and an ancient passageway leads to one in the center of the statue.
9. Engraved in the body are several drawings. They are known as hieroglyphics.
10. Hieroglyphics are pictures that are symbols for sounds and words. They were used as a writing system.

Integrating Workplace Skills

Ask students to suggest examples of when workers need to use complete sentences and when they are unnecessary. Start with these examples:

Bus driver: "The next stop on this route is Main Street." Too much

"Next stop Main Street." Enough

Construction worker: "Bricks!"

"Watch out for the bricks!" or *"Don't drop the bricks!"* Better, more specific

☑ ONGOING ASSESSMENT: Monitor and Reinforce

If students have difficulty with Exercise 32 or 33, refer them to the following for additional practice.

In the Textbook	Print Resources	Technology
Section Review, Ex. 40, p. 483	Grammar Exercise Workbook, pp. 99–102	Language Lab CD-ROM, Problems With Sentences; On-Line Exercise Bank, Section 21.4

⏱ TIME SAVERS!

Answers on Transparency Use the Grammar Exercises Answers on Transparencies for Chapter 21 to facilitate correction by students.

On-Line Exercise Bank Have students complete the exercises on computer. The Auto Check feature will grade their work for you!

Correcting Misplaced Modifiers

1. Go over the first example sentence on the page and ask what is funny about it. (The lake didn't have an outboard motor.) Explain that readers usually assume that a modifier refers to the last noun before it in the sentence. Therefore, a modifier should usually be placed just after the noun it describes.

2. Go over the second example and again ask for the humor. (The sand wasn't walking.) Point out that the introductory clause is a modifier, and that it ends in a comma. In this type of sentence, the modifier always refers to the first noun or pronoun after the comma. Therefore, students must be careful to word their sentences to put the correct noun right after the comma that ends the modifier. Demonstrate this with the second corrected sentence on the page. The sentence has been rewritten so that the pronoun *we,* not the noun *sand,* immediately follows the comma.

Answer Key

Exercise 34

1. MM
2. C
3. C
4. MM
5. MM

Customize for
Less Advanced Students

Give students extra practice by having them rewrite sentences 1, 4, and 5 in Exercise 34 to make them correct. Have partners go over the new sentences together and make sure they are correct. Partners can work together to resolve any disagreements.

Correcting Misplaced Modifiers

If a phrase or clause acting as an adjective or adverb is not placed near the word it modifies, the meaning of the sentence may be unclear.

▶ **KEY CONCEPT** A *modifier* should be placed as close as possible to the word it modifies. ■

A modifier placed too far away from the word it modifies is called a *misplaced modifier.*

MISPLACED MODIFIER: We rented a boat at the lake with an outboard motor.

The misplaced phrase *with an outboard motor* makes it seem as though the lake has an outboard motor.

CORRECTED SENTENCE: At the lake, we rented a boat with an outboard motor.

Below is a somewhat different type of misplaced modifier.

MISPLACED MODIFIER: *Walking to the pyramid,* the sand felt hot under our feet.

In this sentence, *walking to the pyramid* should modify a person. Instead, it incorrectly modifies sand.

CORRECTED SENTENCE: *Walking to the pyramid,* we felt the hot sand under our feet.

▶ **Exercise 34** Recognizing Misplaced Modifiers Check the placement of the modifier in each sentence. If it is correct, write *C* on your paper. If it is misplaced, write *MM.*

EXAMPLE: My brother Richard bought a loaf of bread at the open bazaar that was warm and crusty.

ANSWER: MM

1. Originally, tools and weapons were used by the people that were made of stone and organic materials.
2. Later, people made tools of copper and other metals.
3. People who were richer or more influential were buried in graves that were larger and more ornate.
4. Early civilizations built ships for trade along the Nile River that were large and efficient.
5. Two domains emerged in Egypt that became known as the northern and the southern kingdoms.

476 • Effective Sentences

💚 Spelling Tip

Remember that the sound *us* at the end of an adjective is often spelled *-ious;* for example, *cautious, ambitious.*

▶ **More Practice**

Language Lab CD-ROM
• Misplaced Modifiers lesson
On-line Exercise Bank
• Section 21.4
Grammar Exercise Workbook
• pp. 103–106

▶ **Exercise 35** Revising to Correct Misplaced Modifiers On your paper, rewrite the following sentences to correct problems caused by misplaced modifiers. In each rewritten sentence, underline the modifier that was misplaced in the original. Then, draw an arrow from the modifier to the word it modifies.

EXAMPLE: My brother Richard bought a loaf of bread at the open bazaar that was warm and crusty.

ANSWER: At the open bazaar, my brother Richard bought

a loaf of bread that was warm and crusty.

1. In the dynastic period, King Narmer of ancient Egypt who was later called "the founder" unified the northern and southern kingdoms.
2. Built of stone, kings were buried in pyramids during the early dynastic period of Egypt.
3. Pyramids were the burial chambers of kings that increased in complexity and size as time passed.
4. Egyptians built temples, buildings, and statues to honor the kings next to the pyramids.
5. During the fifth dynasty, temples were built that were dedicated to the sun god.
6. The king demanded labor to build the pyramids and temples by many people.
7. Mastabas covered the graves of the royal family and government officials, which are large stone structures with many rooms.
8. In this time period, Egyptian paintings were done mostly on mastabas of food, drink, and objects to benefit the dead.
9. Using military power, other countries felt the expanding influence of Egypt.
10. The pharaohs eventually reduced the power of officials in provinces of Egypt who threatened the control of the king.

▼ **Critical Viewing** How does this sculpture convey that the subject is a queen? In your answer, use a sentence with an adjective or adverb clause. **[Evaluate]**

This bust of Queen Nefertiti is thousands of years old.

Avoiding Sentence Problems • **477**

Answer Key

▶ **Exercise 35**

Sample rewrites are given. Note that sometimes rewrites change modifiers into other parts of speech.

1. In the dynastic period of ancient Egypt, King Narmer, <u>who was later called "the founder,"</u> unified the northern and southern kingdoms. (arrow to *King Narmer*)
2. Kings were buried in pyramids <u>built of stone</u> during the early dynastic period of Egypt. (arrow to *pyramids*)
3. Pyramids, the burial chambers of kings, <u>increased in complexity and size as time passed</u>. (arrow to *Pyramids*)
4. Egyptians built temples, buildings, and statues <u>next to the pyramids</u> to honor the kings. (arrow to *built*)
5. Temples <u>dedicated to the sun god</u> were built during the fifth dynasty. (arrow to *Temples*)
6. The king demanded labor <u>by many people</u> to build the pyramids and temples. (arrow to *labor*)
7. Mastabas, <u>which are large stone structures with many rooms,</u> covered the graves of the royal family and government officials. (arrow to *Mastabas*)
8. In this time period, Egyptian paintings <u>of food, drink, and objects to benefit the dead</u> were done mostly on mastabas. (arrow to *paintings*)
9. Egypt, <u>using military power,</u> made other countries feel its expanding influence. (arrow to *Egypt*)
10. The pharaohs eventually reduced the power of <u>provincial</u> officials who threatened the control of the king. (arrow to *officials*)

Critical Viewing

Evaluate Sample sentence: The headdress that she wears is like a crown.

☑ ONGOING ASSESSMENT: Monitor and Reinforce

If students have difficulty with Exercise 34 or 35, refer them to the following for additional practice.

In the Textbook	Print Resources	Technology
Section Review, Ex. 41, p. 483	Grammar Exercise Workbook, pp. 103–106	Language Lab CD-ROM, Problems with Sentences; On-Line Exercise Bank, Section 21.4

 **TIME SAVERS!**

Answers on Transparency Use the Grammar Exercises Answers on Transparencies for Chapter 21 to facilitate correction by students.

On-Line Exercise Bank Have students complete the exercises on computer. The Auto Check feature will grade their work for you!

Avoiding Double Negatives

1. Use a few sample sentences with double negatives to demonstrate that two negatives equal one positive. Have students try this with a few more sentences until they understand the reason that double negatives and positives are the same thing:

   I will not go to no operas.

   Not go to no means the same thing as *will go.*

2. On occasion, a double negative can be used to make a positive statement especially emphatic.

   "I can't meet Yuri!" Esther cried, appalled.

   "You can't not meet him!" Joshua said solemnly.

   Joshua uses a double negative to emphasize his positive statement—that Esther must meet Yuri. Because he uses two negatives, his statement is positive. Students will occasionally see and hear this usage, usually in fiction and drama.

Answer Key

1. The tour guide wouldn't let anybody explore alone. The tour guide would let nobody explore alone.
2. She said she didn't want anyone to get lost. She said she wanted no one to get lost.
3. Because of the bright sun outside, we couldn't see anything when we first entered the underground tomb. Because of the bright sun outside, we could see nothing when we first entered the underground tomb.
4. We hadn't read any descriptions of the Temple of Luxor before we visited it. We had read no descriptions of the Temple of Luxor before we visited it.
5. The Temple of Luxor is not like any other Egyptian temple. The Temple of Luxor is like no other Egyptian temple.
6. There were no words that could adequately express our feelings about the temple. There weren't any words that could adequately express our feelings about the temple.

21.4

Avoiding Double Negatives

Negative words, such as *nothing* and *not*, are used to deny or to say *no*. Some people mistakenly use *double negatives*—two negative words—when only one is needed.

▶ **KEY CONCEPT** Avoid writing sentences that contain double negatives. ■

The sentences on the left in the following chart contain double negatives. Notice on the right how each can be corrected in either of two ways.

Double Negatives	Corrected Sentences
The lightning didn't damage nothing.	The lightning did*n't* damage anything. The lightning damaged *nothing*.
I haven't no time now.	I have*n't* any time now. I have *no* time now.
She never told us nothing about the thunderstorm.	She *never* told us anything about the thunderstorm. She told us *nothing* about the thunderstorm.

▶ **Exercise 36** Revising to Correct Double Negatives The following sentences contain double negatives, which are underlined. Correct each sentence in two ways.

EXAMPLE: We did<u>n't</u> want to miss <u>no</u> sites along the Nile.
ANSWER: We didn't want to miss any sites along the Nile.
We wanted to miss no sites along the Nile.

1. The tour guide would<u>n't</u> let <u>nobody</u> explore alone.
2. She said she did<u>n't</u> want <u>no one</u> to get lost.
3. Because of the bright sun outside, we could<u>n't</u> see <u>nothing</u> when we first entered the underground tomb.
4. We had<u>n't</u> read <u>no</u> descriptions of the Temple of Luxor before we visited it.
5. The Temple of Luxor is <u>not</u> like <u>no</u> other Egyptian temple.
6. There were<u>n't</u> <u>no</u> words that could adequately express our feelings about the temple.
7. We could<u>n't</u> <u>hardly</u> believe our eyes at the treasures inside.
8. For thousands of years, the temple was buried under sand, and <u>no one</u> knew <u>nothing</u> about it.
9. Was<u>n't</u> there <u>nothing</u> written about the temple by biographers of Alexander the Great?
10. After visiting Egypt, we would<u>n't</u> want to go <u>nowhere</u> else.

Spelling Tip

As you can see in the chart on this page, *thunderstorm* is a compound word and should not be written as *thunder storm* unless interrupted by the word *lightning*—for example, "They traveled through many thunder and lightning storms."

▶ **More Practice**

Language Lab CD-ROM
• Avoiding Double Negatives lesson
On-line Exercise Bank
• Section 21.4
Grammar Exercise Workbook
• pp. 107–108

7. We could hardly believe our eyes at the treasures inside. We couldn't believe our eyes at the treasures inside.
8. For thousands of years, the temple was buried under sand, and no one knew anything about it. For thousands of years, the temple was buried under sand, and people knew nothing about it.

9. Was there nothing written about the temple by biographers of Alexander the Great? Wasn't there anything written about the temple by biographers of Alexander the Great?
10. After visiting Egypt, we would want to go nowhere else. After visiting Egypt, we wouldn't want to go anywhere else.

Avoiding Common Usage Problems

This section contains fifteen common usage problems in alphabetical order. Some of the problems are expressions that you should avoid in both your speaking and your writing. Others are words that are often confused because of similar spellings or meanings.

(1) accept, except Do not confuse the spelling of these words. *Accept*, a verb, means "to take what is offered" or "to agree to." *Except*, a preposition, means "leaving out" or "other than."

VERB:	She *accepted* responsibility for the others.
PREPOSITION:	Everyone *except* him wanted to ride a camel.

(2) advice, advise Do not confuse the spelling of these related words. *Advice*, a noun, means "an opinion." *Advise*, a verb, means "to give an opinion."

NOUN:	My friend gave me *advice* about hotels in Cairo.
VERB:	My friend *advised* me to find a good guide.

(3) affect, effect *Affect*, a verb, means "to influence" or "to cause a change in." *Effect*, usually a noun, means "result."

VERB:	The sandstorm *affected* the caravan.
NOUN:	What is the *effect* of getting sand in your ears?

(4) at Do not use *at* after *where*.

INCORRECT:	Do you know *where* we're *at*?
CORRECT:	Do you know *where* we are?

(5) because Do not use *because* after *the reason*. Eliminate one or the other.

INCORRECT:	*The reason* I am sad is *because* our trip was canceled.
CORRECT:	I am sad *because* our trip was canceled.
	The reason I'm sad is *that* our trip was canceled.

> **Exercise 37** Avoiding Common Usage Problems Choose the correct word in parentheses, and write it on your paper.
> 1. Everyone (accept, except) James took pictures in the tomb.
> 2. The reason James didn't take pictures was (because, that) the batteries for his flash had run down.
> 3. We all gave him (advice, advise) about buying new batteries.
> 4. The hotel where we (were, were at) had a gift shop.
> 5. Our suggestions had no (affect, effect) on James's actions.

> **More Practice**
> On-line
> Exercise Bank
> • Section 21.4
> Grammar Exercise Workbook
> • pp. 109–110

Avoiding Common Usage Problems

1. Go through the usage problems here and on the next two pages with the whole class. Read, or have volunteers read, each of the fifteen explanations.

2. Students have probably heard the expression *Where are we at?* many times. This is a common expression in a certain American dialect. A writer whose characters were uneducated or from a certain geographical area might use this expression in dialogue. However, it is not considered acceptable.

3. Explain that the expression *reason is because* is redundant. The word *because* already includes the word *cause,* so it already signals the reader that a reason for something will be given. This is why the word *reason* is not needed.

continued

Integrating Speaking Skills

Pronunciation Have students try speaking aloud the easily confused words in Usage Problems 1–3. Help them with pronunciation as needed. Emphasize that the two words in each pair are pronounced somewhat differently. For example, the *s* in *advise* sounds like a *z*, while the *c* in *advice* is pronounced *s*. Encourage students to speak clearly so that their listeners will always know which of the easily confused words they are using.

Answer Key

> **Exercise 37**

1. except	4. were
2. that	5. effect
3. advice	

Customize for
ESL Students

Students who speak Spanish may have particular difficulty with the concept of the double negative, because in Spanish double negatives are used as single negatives are used in English. Use sample sentences such as *He didn't sing none of the songs well* to help them understand that in English, the literal meaning of a double negative is the same as a single positive.

Customize for
Logical/Mathematical Learners

Explain to students that a double negative in English works the same way as a double negative in math: $-(-2)$ is the same as $+2$. Challenge students to write some simple mathematical equations with positive and negative numbers. Students can play math tutors, explaining to the class why double negative signs in math equal single positive signs.

⏱ TIME SAVERS!

📄 **Answers on Transparency** Use the Grammar Exercises Answers on Transparencies for Chapter 21 to facilitate corrections by students.

💻 **On-Line Exercise Bank** Have students complete the exercises on computer. The Auto Check feature will grade their work for you!

479

4. Students are probably familiar with the expression *I'm not into that.* This is a slang expression; students should not use it as a model for when to use the preposition *into.*

5. Explain that *kind of* and *sort of* mean *type of.* Although they are commonly used in colloquial speech to mean *rather* or *somewhat,* this usage is not acceptable in standard English.

Colloquial | *I kind of like that music.*

Standard | *What kind of music is it?*

Challenge students to rephrase *I kind of like that music* in standard English. (Possible answers: I rather like that music; I occasionally enjoy music like that.)

Critical Viewing

Contrast Answers will vary. Possible response: The painted image is different from the image on page 474 in size, dress, and grandeur.

21.4

(6) beside, besides These two prepositions have different meanings and cannot be interchanged. *Beside* means "at the side of" or "close to." *Besides* means "in addition to."

EXAMPLES: We picnicked *beside* the Nile.
No one *besides* us had blankets on which to sit.

(7) different from, different than *Different from* is preferred over *different than.*

EXAMPLE: The pyramids were *different from* what I expected.

(8) farther, further *Farther* is used to refer to distance. *Further* means "additional" or "to a greater degree or extent."

EXAMPLES: We walked much *farther* than he. After he raised his voice, I listened no *further.*

(9) in, into *In* refers to position. *Into* suggests motion.

POSITION: The tourists are *in* the tomb.
MOTION: They walked *into* a hall before a pharaoh's shrine.

(10) kind of, sort of Do not use *kind of* or *sort of* to mean "rather" or "somewhat."

INCORRECT: This CD of Egyptian music is *sort of* new.
CORRECT: This CD of Egyptian music is *rather* new.

(11) like *Like,* a preposition, means "similar to" or "in the same way as." It should be followed by an object. Do not use *like* before a subject and a verb. Use *as* or *that* instead.

PREPOSITION: The pyramids looked *like* giant triangles.
INCORRECT: This stew doesn't taste *like* it should.
CORRECT: This stew doesn't taste *as* it should.

(12) that, which, who *That* and *which* refer to things. *Who* refers only to people.

THINGS: The photograph *that* I took won first prize.
PEOPLE: The dancer *who* performed is my cousin.

▲ **Critical Viewing**
Contrast the image of the man in this painting with the one on page 474. Use the word *different* in your response. **[Contrast]**

Technology Tip

Most word processors have a grammar-check feature. Practice some of these special problems on the computer. Observe to see whether the word processor catches usage errors or double negatives.

480 • Effective Sentences

| ☑ **ONGOING ASSESSMENT: Monitor and Reinforce** |

If students have difficulty with Exercise 37 or 38, refer them to the following for additional practice.

In the Textbook	Print Resources	Technology
Section Review, Ex. 42, p. 483	Grammar Exercise Workbook, pp. 107–110	On-line Exercise Bank, Section 21.4

(13) their, there, they're Do not confuse the spelling of these three words. *Their*, a possessive adjective, always modifies a noun. *There* is usually used either as a sentence starter or as an adverb. *They're* is a contraction of *they are*.

POSSESSIVE ADJECTIVE:	The tourists boarded *their* bus.
SENTENCE STARTER:	*There* are many tours available.
ADVERB:	The tour guide is standing over *there*.
CONTRACTION:	*They're* trying to board the bus now.

(14) to, too, two Do not confuse the spelling of these words. *To* plus a noun is a prepositional phrase. *To* plus a verb is an infinitive. *Too*, with two *o*'s, is an adverb and modifies adjectives and other adverbs. *Two* is a number.

PREPOSITION:	*to* the house	*to* Egypt
INFINITIVE:	*to* meet	*to* hide
ADVERB:	*too* sad	*too* quickly
NUMBER:	*two* clouds	*two* camels

(15) when, where, why Do not use *when*, *where*, or *why* directly after a linking verb such as *is*. Reword the sentence.

INCORRECT:	To see the Sphinx is *why* we came to Egypt.
CORRECT:	We came to Egypt to see the Sphinx.

▶ **Exercise 38** **Avoiding Common Usage Problems** On your paper, write the correct form from the choices in parentheses.

1. (Beside, Besides) seeing the Temple of Luxor, we visited the pyramids at Giza.
2. Luxor is (the place where, where) the pharaohs lived around 2000 B.C.
3. I climbed (farther, further) up the steps of the Great Pyramid than did either of my brothers.
4. The true story of how the Great Pyramid was built is (different from, different than) what I had heard before.
5. The myth that he made slaves build the pyramid earned Pharaoh Khufu a (kind of, somewhat) negative reputation.
6. Instead, Khufu employed farmers (which, who) were out of work because (there, their) land was flooded by the Nile.
7. Each huge limestone block used in the Great Pyramid seems almost (to, too) heavy to have been lifted into place.
8. Only the high priests were permitted to walk (in, into) the burial chamber of some of the pyramids.
9. We entered the ancient burial chamber (as, like) the high priests might have done thousands of years ago.
10. The camels (who, that) carried us across the desert are standing (beside, besides) the palm tree over (their, there).

▶ **More Practice**

On-line Exercise Bank
• Section 21.4
Grammar Exercise Workbook
• pp. 109–110

Avoiding Sentence Problems • **481**

Answer Key

▶ **Exercise 38**

1. Besides
2. the place where
3. farther
4. different from
5. somewhat
6. who, their
7. too
8. into
9. as
10. that, beside, there

Customize for
Less Advanced Students

Make, or have students make, a set of flashcards with the easily confused or misused boldface words from these three pages on one side and the definition and usage rules on the other side. The cards can be kept in class for reference. Partners can drill each other on the definitions and usage rules of each word. Encourage students who have trouble with Exercise 37 or 38 to practice with the flashcards.

Customize for
ESL Students

For some students learning English as a second language, homophones can be problematic. If necessary, explain in greater detail the differences among *their/there/they're* and *to/too/two*. Point out that the difference is made clear by the context or by how the word is used in the sentence.

☑ **ONGOING ASSESSMENT: Monitor and Reinforce**

Use the following resources to assess student mastery of effective sentences.

In the Textbook	Print Resources	Technology
Chapter Review, Ex. 47–51, pp. 484–485 Standardized Test Preparation Workshop, pp. 486–487	Formal Assessment, Chapter 21	On-Line Exercise Bank, Chapter 21

⏱ **TIME SAVERS!**

📑 **Answers on Transparency** Use the Grammar Exercises Answers on Transparencies for Chapter 21 to facilitate correction by students.

💻 **On-Line Exercise Bank** Have students complete the exercises on computer. The Auto Check feature will grade their work for you!

481

Sentence Breakup and Makeup

Teaching Resources: Hands-on Grammar Activity Book, Chapter 21

1. Have students refer to their Hands-on Grammar Activity books or give them copies of the activity sheet.

2. Have one student explain what a fragment is. Have another student explain what a run-on is. Have students make a chart that points out how the two are alike and how they differ. (Neither is a correct complete sentence. Fragments are missing parts while run-ons have too many parts.)

3. Ask students whether they think it is easier to correct a fragment or a run-on. Have them explain their reasoning and give examples.

Find It in Your Reading

You may want to let students check television or radio programs for fragments and run-ons. Remind students that these elements occur much more frequently in dialogue.

Find It in Your Writing

Encourage students with e-mail access to check their e-mails for fragments and run-ons. Ask them to correct five of their most confusing examples.

21.4

Hands-on Grammar

Sentence Breakup and Makeup

Practice correcting run-ons and fragments by doing this *Sentence Breakup and Makeup* activity.

First, form an even number of groups of four or five students each. Designate half the groups *Run-ons*, and half *Fragments*. Each group should cut eight to ten strips of colored paper—one color for run-ons and another for fragments. Next, each group of *Run-ons* students should brainstorm for **fragments**, and write one on each strip of paper; *Fragments* students should do the same, but with **run-on sentences**. You should end up with two fragments or run-on sentences for each member of the group. When finished, fold each strip two or three times, and place all of them in an envelope labeled either "Run-ons" or "Fragments." See the example below.

Then, each *Run-ons* group should pair up with a *Fragments* group, and exchange envelopes. Each group member draws two strips from the envelope. It is then the job of *Run-ons* group members to "break up" the run-on sentences, writing the corrections on the back of the strip of paper. It is the job of each *Fragments* group member to "make up"—or complete—the sentences by adding whatever is necessary to the fragments. After finishing, the two groups should exchange strips and check the corrections.

Find It in Your Reading Run-on sentences and fragments don't usually occur in formal writing. However, fragments often do appear in the dialogue of a story. Look through a story you have read, and identify one or two fragments in the dialogue. Challenge yourself to turn them into sentences.

Find It in Your Writing Review an essay in your portfolio, and note any run-on sentences or fragments. Then, correct them, using the methods presented in this section.

482 • Effective Sentences

Section Review

ASSESS and CLOSE

Section Review

Each of these exercises correlates to the instruction on avoiding sentence problems, pages 469–482. The exercises may be used for more practice, for reteaching, or for review of the Key Concepts presented. Answers for all chapter exercises are available in *Grammar Exercises Answers on Transparencies* in your Teaching Resources.

GRAMMAR EXERCISES 39–44

▶ **Exercise 39** **Revising to Correct Fragments** Correct the fragments in the following paragraph by adding them to a nearby sentence or by adding words to them to form new sentences.

Some records of early people have survived. Especially pictures on stone. From southern Africa to the Sahara, archaeologists have studied paintings on rock cliffs and cave walls. The paintings, which show the tools, weapons, and food-gathering methods of early people. The rock art of the Sahara lets us look at the lives of people. Who once lived there. Figures moving in graceful patterns. The paintings also reveal that herds of animals once roamed the Sahara.

▶ **Exercise 40** **Revising to Correct Run-ons** Rewrite each of these run-ons correctly.

1. Egyptians had many gods, they represented nature and ideas.
2. There were gods of the sun and moon, there were gods of the sky and earth.
3. The Nile flooded its valley every year, there was even a god of the Nile flood.
4. The Egyptians had many gods, there were gods of truth, learning, and craftsmanship.
5. When a relative died, Egyptians would turn to the god Osiris this god gave them hope for life after death.

▶ **Exercise 41** **Revising to Correct Misplaced Modifiers** Rewrite these sentences to correct any misplaced modifiers.

1. To serve as burial places, pharaohs built large and elaborate tombs.
2. Archaeologists found treasures in the tomb of King Tutankhamen made of wood, gold, and precious stones.

3. Imagine a crown on the mummy of pure gold and precious stone.
4. Looking through the treasures, six chariots made of wood, rope, and leather were discovered by archaeologists.
5. A beautiful collar was found on the mummified body of King Tut in the shape of a vulture and a cobra.

▶ **Exercise 42** **Revising to Correct Double Negatives and Usage Errors** Rewrite these sentences, correcting any double negatives or usage errors.

1. Accept for a small strip of fertile land along the Nile, most of Egypt is desert.
2. Farmers can't grow no crops in the desert area because it is to dry.
3. The reason the Nile valley is kind of overcrowded is because most of Egypt's population lives their.
4. Dams built along the Nile have had both a positive and a negative affect.
5. No one wants to see none of the ancient sites washed away by redirected river water.

▶ **Exercise 43** **Find It in Your Writing** Look through your portfolio to see whether you have used fragments, run-ons, or misplaced modifiers in any of your compositions. Rewrite the incorrect sentences, and explain how you have corrected the errors.

▶ **Exercise 44** **Writing Application** Write a description of an interesting place you have visited. Use a variety of short and long sentences, but make sure you have not included any fragments or run-ons. Check for other errors that might make your sentences less effective.

Section Review • 483

Answer Key

▶ **Exercise 39**

Sample rewrite: Some records of early people have survived, especially pictures on stone. From southern Africa to the Sahara, archaeologists have studied paintings on rock cliffs and cave walls. The paintings show the tools, weapons, and food-gathering methods of early people. The rock art of the Sahara lets us look at the lives of people who once lived there. Figures move in graceful patterns. The paintings also reveal that herds of animals once roamed the Sahara.

▶ **Exercise 40**

Answers will vary. Samples are given.

1. Egyptians had many gods. They represented nature and ideas.
2. There were gods of the sun and moon; there were gods of the sky and earth.
3. The Nile flooded its valley every year, and there was even a god of the Nile flood.
4. The Egyptians had many gods. There were the gods of truth, learning, and craftsmanship.
5. When a relative died, Egyptians would turn to the god Osiris. This god gave them hope for life after death.

▶ **Exercise 41**

1. Pharaohs built large and elaborate tombs to serve as burial places.
2. Archaeologists found treasures made of wood, gold, and precious stones in the tomb of King Tutankhamen.
3. Imagine a crown of pure gold and precious stone on the mummy.
4. Looking through the treasures, archaeologists discovered six chariots made of wood, rope, and leather.

continued

Answer Key continued

5. A beautiful collar in the shape of a vulture and a cobra was found on the mummified body of King Tut.

▶ **Exercise 42**

1. Except for a small strip of fertile land along the Nile, most of Egypt is desert.
2. Farmers can grow no crops in the desert area because it is too dry.
3. The reason the Nile valley is somewhat overcrowded is that most of Egypt's population lives there.
4. Dams built along the Nile have had both a positive and a negative effect.

5. No one wants to see any of the ancient sites washed away by redirected river water.

▶ **Exercise 43**

Find It in Your Writing
Students may want to display their funniest sentences with misplaced modifiers.

▶ **Exercise 44**

Writing Application
Suggest that students share their descriptions with someone who has visited the same place or with a friend they made there.

CHAPTER REVIEW

Each of these exercises correlates to a section of the chapter on effective sentences, pages 456–483. The exercises may be used for more practice, for reteaching, or for review of the Key Concepts presented.

Answer Key

Exercise 45

Answers will vary. Samples are given.

1. What an unusual tax system ancient Egyptians had!
2. You could pay taxes by doing work for the government.
3. Could people pay their taxes by joining the army?
4. Look at this picture of the pyramids.
5. Many people worked on the pyramids to pay their taxes.

Exercise 46

Sample rewrite: The ancient Egyptian writing system consisted of several hundred picture signs. These signs were called hieroglyphics. Some of the signs represented sounds; others represented ideas. Most words were formed with both sound and idea signs, but words could be made of just one of the two kinds. Egyptians used hieroglyphics for both communication and decoration.

Exercise 47

1. run-on
2. misplaced modifier
3. fragment
4. fragment
5. run-on

Sample rewrite: Alexander the Great's ambition was to conquer the world and spread Greek culture. To establish a capital for his kingdom in Egypt, he founded Alexandria in 332 B.C. Alexandria was located on the northern Mediterranean coast of Egypt, which was an ideal site because of its natural resources. There was sufficient water from Lake Maryut, and the Nile River provided a transportation waterway and irrigation. The island of Pharos made a good site for anchoring ships that were delivering goods.

Exercise 45 **Writing the Four Types of Sentences** Rewrite each sentence to fit the function indicated in parentheses. Add the appropriate end mark.

1. The tax system in ancient Egypt was how unusual? (exclamatory)
2. Could you pay taxes by doing work for the government? (declarative)
3. Some people joined the army as a way to pay their taxes. (interrogative)
4. You can look at this picture of the pyramids. (imperative)
5. Did many people work on the pyramids to pay their taxes? (declarative)

Exercise 46 **Combining Sentences and Varying Sentence Length** Rewrite this paragraph, combining some short sentences and leaving others short for emphasis.

(1) Ancient Egyptians had a writing system. (2) It consisted of several hundred picture signs. (3) These signs were called hieroglyphics. (4) Some of the signs represented sounds. (5) Other signs represented ideas. (6) A word could be written using only sound signs. (7) A word could be written using only idea signs. (8) Most words were a combination. (9) Egyptians used hieroglyphics for writing down ideas. (10) They used hieroglyphics for decoration.

Exercise 47 **Revising to Correct Fragments, Run-ons, and Misplaced Modifiers** Identify each numbered item in the following paragraph as a *fragment, run-on,* or *misplaced modifier.* Then, rewrite the paragraph, correcting the errors.

(1) The ambition of Alexander the Great was to conquer the world, he also wanted

484 • Effective Sentences

to spread Greek culture. (2) To establish a capital for his kingdom in Egypt, Alexandria was founded in 332 B.C. by Alexander the Great. (3) Located on the northern Mediterranean coast of Egypt. (4) Ideal site because of its natural resources. (5) There was sufficient water from Lake Maryut, the Nile River provided a transportation waterway and irrigation, the island of Pharos made a good site for anchoring ships to deliver their goods.

Exercise 48 **Revising to Correct Fragments, Run-ons, and Misplaced Modifiers** Rewrite this paragraph, correcting all sentence errors. Some sentences may be correct.

(1) Originally, Egyptians buried their dead kings, queens, and nobles in the dry deserts that bordered the Nile River, the dry soil preserved the bodies in their graves. (2) However, these graves could be dug up easily by animals or robbers. (3) Decided to build tombs. (4) There was not sufficient heat from the sun inside the tomb to dry a body. (5) In order to preserve the bodies. (6) Egyptians used a process known as mummification. (7) First, they removed the brain and all other large organs from the body. (8) Packing it in salt, they dried the body. (9) Linen rags were then put into the body cavity soaked with scented resins. (10) The bodies were finally wrapped in bandages, they were placed in elaborate wooden coffins. (11) Took seventy days to complete the process. (12) Jewels and magic charms were placed between layers of bandage. (13) To protect the mummy's spirit. (14) Intricately engraved, some pharaohs' mummies were covered with gold masks. (15) Over the centuries, these valuable mummies attracted robbers they pillaged many of the tombs.

Exercise 48

Sample rewrite: Originally, Egyptians buried their dead kings, queens, and nobles in the dry deserts that bordered the Nile River. The dry soil preserved the bodies in their graves. However, these graves could easily be dug up by animals or robbers, so the Egyptians decided to build tombs. Inside the tomb, there was not sufficient heat from the sun to dry a body. In order to preserve the bodies, Egyptians used a process known as mummification. First, they removed the brain and all other large organs from the body. They packed the body in salt to dry it. Linen rags soaked with scented resins were then put into the body cavity. The bodies were finally wrapped in bandages and placed in elaborate wooden coffins. It took seventy days to complete the process. Jewels and magic charms were placed between layers of bandages to protect the mummy's spirit. Some pharaohs' mummies were covered with intricately engraved gold masks. Over the centuries, these valuable mummies attracted robbers, who pillaged many of the tombs.

21 EFFECTIVE SENTENCES
Chapter Review

Exercise 49 Revising to Correct Double Negatives On your paper, write *C* for each sentence that is correct, and *DN* for each sentence that contains a double negative. Then, correct the double negatives.

1. Most people don't know nothing about camels.
2. You won't find no animals as well suited for desert life as a camel.
3. Because a camel has short hair, its body doesn't hold no heat for very long.
4. Because a camel sweats very little, it doesn't lose water it needs to survive.
5. Sand doesn't never get into a camel's eyes because of its long lashes.
6. A camel's large feet help it to walk on sand without sinking into it.
7. Camels can shut their nostrils so no sand doesn't get into them.
8. Did you know that camels don't store no water in their humps?
9. The hump contains stored fat that nourishes the camel so it won't starve, even during a long journey.
10. In cool weather, a camel can go six months without drinking no water.

Exercise 50 Identifying and Correcting Usage Problems The following sentences contain underlined words or phrases. On your paper, write *yes* if the underlined word or phrase contains a usage problem and *no* if it does not. Correct each problem.

1. Anwar Sadat was <u>different from</u> many modern Egyptian leaders.
2. Sadat was a man <u>which</u> was very concerned about peace in the Middle East.
3. When he was a young man, Sadat was only <u>sort of</u> interested in peace.
4. At the time, he was very angry that his country was forced to <u>except</u> being ruled by Great Britain.
5. Then, Sadat received valuable <u>advice</u> from Indian leader Mohandas Gandhi.

6. Gandhi's teachings about nonviolent revolt had a big <u>affect</u> on Sadat.
7. When he became Egypt's president, Sadat fought <u>to</u> wars against Israel.
8. The reason he decided to try a peaceful settlement was <u>because</u> the wars were draining Egypt's economy.
9. In 1979, Sadat stood <u>besides</u> Israeli leader Menachem Begin as they signed a historic peace treaty.
10. Sadat went <u>farther</u> toward establishing peaceful relations with Israel than some Egyptians wanted him to go, and he was later assassinated.

Exercise 51 Revision Practice
Rewrite the following paragraph, combining or revising sentences and correcting errors in sentence structure or usage.

(1) Cairo is a modern city. (2) Cairo is an ancient city, to. (3) The capital of Egypt and largest city in Africa. (4) Bustling with traffic and pedestrians. (5) You can find many bargains there. (6) You are willing to haggle with vendors in different shops and bazaars. (7) Most of Cairo's sixteen million residents are religious the city contains hundreds of mosques and several churches, and their is even one synagogue that dates back to the fourth century A.D. (8) You don't have to drive no further than a few miles west of downtown Cairo to reach the pyramids. (9) The only one of the Seven Wonders of the World that is still standing. (10) A sound and light show is held their most nights the combination of the ancient structures and modern technology has an affect on anyone which attends the show.

Exercise 52 Writing Application
Explain what you find most intriguing or interesting about Egypt. Vary the length and form of the sentences you use. Proofread your writing to correct any errors, especially those discussed in this chapter.

Chapter Review • **485**

1. DN Most people don't know anything about camels.
2. DN You will find no animals (or: You won't find any animals) as well suited for desert life as a camel.
3. DN Because a camel has short hair, its body doesn't hold heat for very long.
4. C
5. DN Sand doesn't get into a camel's eyes because of its long lashes.
6. C
7. DN Camels can shut their nostrils so no sand gets into them (or: so sand doesn't get into them).
8. DN Did you know that camels don't store any water in their humps (or: store no water in their humps)?
9. C
10. DN In cool weather, a camel can go six months without drinking any water.

Exercise 50

1. no
2. yes, who
3. yes, somewhat
4. yes, accept
5. no
6. yes, effect
7. yes, two
8. yes, that
9. yes, beside
10. yes, further

Exercise 51

Sample rewrite: The ancient city of Cairo is a modern city, too. It is the capital of Egypt and the largest city in Africa. Cairo is bustling with traffic and pedestrians. You can find many bargains in shops and bazaars if you are willing to haggle with vendors.
continued

Answer Key continued

Most of Cairo's sixteen million residents are religious. The city contains hundreds of mosques and several churches. There is even one synagogue that dates back to the fourth century A.D. You don't have to drive any farther than a few miles west of downtown Cairo to reach the pyramids, the only one of the Seven Wonders of the World that is still standing. A sound and light show is held there most nights. The combination of the ancient structures and modern technology has an effect on anyone who attends the show.

Exercise 52

Writing Application
Students who are especially intrigued with Egypt can get together to do research and present their report to the class.

⏱ TIME SAVERS!

🖼 **Answers on Transparency**
Use the Grammar Exercises Answers on Transparencies for Chapter 21 to facilitate correction by students.

🖥 **On-Line Exercise Bank**
Have students complete the exercises on computer. The Auto Check feature will grade their work for you!

Step-by-Step Teaching Guide

Effective Sentences

Teaching Resources: Standardized Test Preparation Workbook, pp. 41–42

1. Remind students that the best choice among different revisions to a given sentence may not necessarily be the same one they might write on their own.

2. If students cannot decide between two possible choices, encourage them to choose the revision that varies from the other sentences in the given passage. While splitting a run-on sentence into two choppy sentences may not be grammatically incorrect, it may not represent the best choice.

Standardized Test Preparation Workshop

Effective Sentences

Whether you are writing an e-mail or an essay for a test, using sentences correctly and effectively is critical to achieving logical, clear communication. Because this skill is so important, standardized tests often evaluate your ability to write effectively. When choosing the most effective sentence, use the following strategies:

- Avoid choosing **run-on** sentences in which two or more complete sentences are written as if they were a single sentence.

- Identify **sentence fragments** in your choices. **Fragments** are missing either a subject or a verb or in some other way do not complete a thought.

- Do not choose sentences with **misplaced modifiers** that confuse the reader and change the meaning of the passage.

- Choose a sentence that will add variety by using a different type of sentence beginning.

- Avoid choosing a sentence that will repeat the same format as the others and create a sequence of choppy sentences.

Sample Test Item	Answer and Explanation

Directions: Read the passage, and answer the questions that follow.
 	
The artist painted with black, gray, and dark green on hulking canvasses. (1) At the chic gallery downtown.
 	
1 Which of the following revisions best corrects part 1?
 	
  A She displayed her works at the chic downtown gallery.
  B The artist in the chic gallery downtown.
  C Displayed at the chic gallery downtown.
  D Correct as is.
	The correct answer is *A*. The original item and the other answer choices are sentence fragments. Choice *A* is a complete sentence.

✎ TEST-TAKING TIP

Tell students that they can quickly look at the choices in a test question to see which ones can be eliminated immediately. Any choice that is a run-on or fragment can be eliminated. This will make choosing the best revision easier by decreasing the number of possible choices.

> **Practice 1** **Directions:** Carefully read the following passage. Choose the letter of the best revision for each sentence.

(1) It was only two days into the grueling Iditarod race. (2) A cold wind raged across Alaskan snow, it blew into great drifts. (3) Like sand dunes in an Arabian desert. (4) The lone musher's whip sang out over the heads of the exhausted dogs. (5) His eyes ached from the cold. (6) He looked across the barren expanse. (7) He saw no sign of the next checkpoint he should have been there long ago. (8) Even his breath was beginning to freeze on the fleecy scarf his daughter had given him, leaving for the dangerous journey into the Alaskan wilderness.

1 Which of the following is the best revision for part 2?

  A A cold wind raged, blowing Alaskan snow into great drifts.

  B Wind blew the snow into great drifts.

  C A cold wind raged and, it blew into great drifts.

  D Correct as is

2 Which of the following is the best revision for part 3?

  F The drifts were like sand dunes in an Arabian desert.

  G Like sand dunes in an Arabian desert blew the snow.

  H Like sand dunes were the drifts in an Arabian desert.

  J Correct as is

3 Which of the following is the best revision for part 4?

  A The lone musher's whip. Sang out over the heads of the exhausted dogs.

  B The lone musher's whip sang out over the exhausted heads of the dogs.

  C The lone musher's whip; sang out over the exhausted heads of the dogs.

  D Correct as is

4 Which of the following is the best way to rewrite parts 5, 6, and 7?

  F His eyes ached from the cold; he looked across the barren expanse, he saw no sign of the next checkpoint, he should have been there long ago.

  G Eyes aching from the cold, he looked across the barren expanse. He saw no sign of the next checkpoint, where he should have been long ago.

  H His eyes ached from the cold, and he looked across the barren expanse. He saw no sign of the next checkpoint. He should have been there long ago.

  J Correct as is

5 Which of the following is the best way to rewrite part 8?

  A His breath was beginning to freeze on the fleecy scarf his daughter had given him before he made the dangerous journey into the Alaskan wilderness.

  B His daughter had given him before leaving on the dangerous journey into the Alaskan wilderness the fleecy scarf on which his breath was beginning to freeze.

  C His breath was beginning to freeze on the fleecy scarf. His daughter had given him before leaving for the dangerous journey into the Alaskan wilderness.

  D Correct as is

> **Practice 1**

1. A
2. F
3. D
4. G
5. A

Customize for
Less Advanced Students

Some students may be tempted to think that each sentence needs revision, and they may thus always avoid choosing "Correct as is." Remind them that if none of the choices make a better sentence(s), then they should not hesitate to leave the original version as is.

Exercise A

1. <u>Look</u> at this globe. (*you* is the implied subject; imperative)
   Here <u>is</u> <u>Australia</u> down in the Southern Hemisphere. (declarative)
2. Wow! What a surprise <u>that</u> <u>is</u>! (exclamatory)
3. <u>Aborigines</u> first <u>migrated</u> there and <u>remained</u> undisturbed until the seventeenth century. (declarative)
4. Didn't the first European <u>settlers</u> <u>arrive</u> at Botany Bay in 1788? (interrogative)
5. <u>Were</u> <u>they</u> British convicts? (interrogative)
   Please <u>answer</u> the question. (<u>you</u> is the implied subject; imperative)

Exercise B

1. high, predicate adjective
2. landmass, predicate noun
3. interior, indirect object; name, direct object
4. area, predicate noun
5. strange, predicate adjective

Exercise C

1. prepositional
2. appositive
3. participial
4. prepositional
5. prepositional, prepositional
6. participial
7. participial
8. appositive
9. participial
10. prepositional

Exercise D

1. subordinate, adjective
2. subordinate, adverb
3. independent
4. subordinate, adjective
5. subordinate, adverb

Cumulative Review

PHRASES, CLAUSES, AND SENTENCES

Exercise A Recognizing Subjects, Predicates, and Sentence Types

Copy these sentences, underlining each simple subject once, and each simple predicate twice. Then, identify each sentence as *declarative, interrogative, imperative,* or *exclamatory.*

1. Look at this globe. Here is Australia down in the Southern Hemisphere.
2. Wow! What a surprise that is!
3. Aborigines first migrated there and remained undisturbed until the seventeenth century.
4. Didn't the first European settlers arrive at Botany Bay in 1788?
5. Were they British convicts? Please answer the question.

Exercise B Identifying Complements

Write the complements in the following sentences, and label each *direct object, indirect object, predicate noun,* or *predicate adjective.*

1. Australia's mountains are not high.
2. In fact, Australia is almost the world's flattest landmass.
3. Australians gave the interior the name *Outback.*
4. The Central-Eastern Lowlands is an area extending from the Great Dividing Range to the Great Western Plain.
5. The Nullarbor Plain seems strange with its caverns and tunnels.

Exercise C Recognizing Phrases

Identify the underlined phrases as *prepositional, appositive,* or *participial.*

1. The climate of Australia varies <u>from region</u> to region.

2. The southern states—<u>warm, temperate regions</u>—have four seasons.
3. <u>Located in the Southern Hemisphere,</u> Australia has seasons opposite those in the Northern Hemisphere.
4. Queensland, <u>on the north coast</u>, experiences a great deal of rain.
5. However, <u>in the drier grasslands,</u> unpredictable rainfall must be supplemented <u>by irrigation.</u>
6. The deserts, <u>making up most of central and western Australia,</u> receive even less rainfall.
7. <u>Applying many modern irrigation techniques,</u> Australia has increased its agricultural production.
8. The Australian Alps, <u>a mountain range in New South Wales,</u> receives heavy snowfall.
9. <u>Lying in the temperate zone,</u> Tasmania has heavy rainfall and frequent winter storms.
10. Hot and dry winds are common <u>in the southern states.</u>

Exercise D Recognizing Clauses

Identify the underlined clauses as *independent* or *subordinate.* Identify the subordinate clauses as *adjective* or *adverb.*

1. The platypus is an aquatic mammal of the Monotreme order <u>that has a bill like a duck.</u>
2. The spiny anteater is also categorized as a Monotreme <u>because it is an egg-laying mammal.</u>
3. <u>While the kangaroo is a marsupial,</u> it is still a type of mammal.
4. Possums and koalas are marsupials <u>that live in trees.</u>
5. Marsupials are animals that give birth to live young <u>even though the young are then nourished in an external pouch.</u>

Exercise E Recognizing Sentence Structure
Label each sentence *simple*, *compound*, or *complex*.

1. Kangaroos' powerful hind legs are used for hopping, and their thick, long tails are used for balancing.
2. The large red or gray kangaroo may stand as tall as seven feet.
3. Wallabies and kangaroo rats are smaller animals that are also members of the kangaroo family.
4. Although it does not bark, the dingo is a dog-like animal.
5. Rabbits, foxes, and cats were introduced into Australia by Europeans.

Exercise F Varying Sentences
Rewrite the following sentences according to the instructions in parentheses.

1. Australia has two species of crocodiles. (Start with "Actually.")
2. The larger crocodile lives in the northern coastal swamps and can grow to be twenty feet long. (Revise the sentence so that it begins with "Living in the northern coastal swamp.")
3. Smaller species of crocodiles can be found living contentedly in inland fresh water. (Revise sentence to begin with "In inland fresh waters.")
4. More than 370 species of lizards are living in Australia. (Invert the subject-verb order.)
5. About 100 species of venomous snakes live in Australia. (Start with "Australia" as the subject, and change the verb as necessary.)

Exercise G Combining Sentences
Rewrite the following sentences according to the instructions in parentheses.

1. Australian waters contain hundreds of sharks. Some are a danger to humans. (Combine into a compound sentence.)
2. Edible shellfish are abundant. Oysters, abalone, and crayfish have been exploited. (Combine by turning one sentence into a subordinate clause.)
3. Seals live around the southern coast. They also inhabit the surrounding islands. (Combine by making a compound verb.)
4. The waters around Australia support many fish. There are also many aquatic mammals. (Combine sentences by creating a compound direct object.)
5. The Queensland lungfish breathes with a single lung. It does this instead of using gills. (Combine by changing one sentence into a phrase.)

Exercise H Identifying and Revising Sentence Problems
Label the error in each sentence *fragment, run-on, double negative, misplaced modifier,* or *common usage problem*. Then, correct the errors.

1. Believe the Aborigines were always in Australia.
2. By taking advantage of low sea levels that allowed land travel, researchers think the Aborigines migrated to Australia.
3. Tasmania was once part of Australia, a rise in sea level made Tasmania an island.
4. The Aborigines didn't have no domesticated animals other than the dingo.
5. There most recent history features the use of tools.

Exercise I Writing Application
Write a short description of a place you have visited. Vary the length and structure of your sentences. Circle at least three phrases and three clauses. Try to avoid fragments, run-ons, double negatives, misplaced modifiers, and the common usage problems you have studied.

Exercise E
1. compound
2. simple
3. complex
4. complex
5. simple

Exercise F
Answers may vary. Sample responses are given.

1. Actually, Australia has two species of crocodiles.
2. Living in the northern coastal swamp, the larger crocodile can grow to be twenty feet long.
3. In inland fresh waters, smaller species of crocodiles can be found living contentedly.
4. Living in Australia are more than 370 species of lizards.
5. Australia is home to about 100 species of venomous snakes.

Exercise G
Answers may vary. Sample responses are given.

1. Australian waters contain hundreds of sharks, and some are a danger to humans.
2. Since edible shellfish are abundant, oysters, abalone, and crayfish have been exploited.
3. Seals live around the southern coast and also inhabit the surrounding islands.
4. The waters around Australia support many fish and aquatic mammals.
5. The Queensland lungfish breathes with a single lung instead of using gills.

Exercise H
1. fragment; I believe the Aborigines were always in Australia.
2. misplaced modifier; Researchers think the Aborigines migrated to Australia by taking advantage of low sea levels that allowed land travel.
3. run-on; Tasmania was once part of Australia, but a rise in sea level made Tasmania an island.
4. double negative; The Aborigines didn't have any domesticated animals other than the dingo.
5. common usage problem; Their most recent history features the use of tools.

Exercise I
Writing Application
Have students exchange papers with a partner. Partners should proofread the description, noting any errors and identifying what the errors are.

In-Depth Lesson Plan

LESSON FOCUS	PRINT AND MEDIA RESOURCES
DAY 1 — **Four Principal Parts and Irregular Verbs** Students learn and apply concepts of four principal parts of regular and irregular verbs (pp. 492–499).	*Language Lab* CD-ROM, Using Verbs; *On-Line Exercise Bank*, Section 22.1 **Teaching Resources** *Grammar Exercise Workbook*, pp. 111–114
DAY 2 — **Basic Forms of the Six Tenses** Students learn and apply the forms of the six tenses of verbs (pp. 500–503).	*Language Lab* CD-ROM, Using Verbs; *On-Line Exercise Bank*, Section 22.2 **Teaching Resources** *Grammar Exercise Workbook*, pp. 115–116
DAY 3 — **Progressive Forms of Verbs** Students learn and apply progressive verb forms (pp. 504–507).	*Language Lab* CD-ROM, Using Verbs; *On-Line Exercise Bank*, Section 22.2 **Teaching Resources** *Grammar Exercise Workbook*, pp. 117–118 *Hands-on Grammar Activity Book*, Chapter 22
DAY 4 — **Troublesome Verbs** Students learn to use the correct form of troublesome verbs and do the Hands-on Grammar Activity (pp. 508–513).	*Language Lab* CD-ROM, Using Verbs; *On-Line Exercise Bank*, Section 22.3 **Teaching Resources** *Grammar Exercise Workbook*, pp. 119–120; *Hands-on Grammar Activity Book*, Chapter 22
DAY 5 — **Review and Assess** Students review chapter and demonstrate mastery of verb tense concepts (pp. 514–517).	*On-Line Exercise Bank*, Sections 22.1–3 **Teaching Resources** *Formal Assessment*, Ch. 22

Accelerated Lesson Plan

LESSON FOCUS	PRINT AND MEDIA RESOURCES
DAY 1 — **Four Principal Parts and Irregular Verbs** Students cover concepts and usage of principal parts of verbs as determined by Diagnostic Test (pp. 492–499).	*Language Lab* CD-ROM, Using Verbs; *On-Line Exercise Bank*, Section 22.1 **Teaching Resources** *Grammar Exercise Workbook*, pp. 111–114
DAY 2 — **Basic and Progressive Forms of the Six Tenses** Students cover the basic forms of the six tenses and six progressive forms of verbs as determined by the Diagnostic Test (pp. 500–507).	*Language Lab* CD-ROM, Using Verbs; *On-Line Exercise Bank*, Section 22.2 **Teaching Resources** *Grammar Exercise Workbook*, pp. 115–118 *Hands-on Grammar Activity Book*, Chapter 22
DAY 3 — **Troublesome Verbs** Students cover troublesome verb pairs as determined by the Diagnostic Test (pp. 508–513).	*Language Lab* CD-ROM, Using Verbs; *On-Line Exercise Bank*, Section 22.3 **Teaching Resources** *Grammar Exercise Workbook*, pp. 119–120
DAY 4 — **Review and Assess** Students review chapter and demonstrate mastery of verb tense concepts (pp. 514–517).	*On-Line Exercise Bank*, Sections 22.1–3 **Teaching Resources** *Formal Assessment*, Ch. 22

Options for Adapting Lesson Plans

HOMEWORK

Have students complete any section of the chapter for homework

FEATURES

Extend coverage with the Grammar in Literature feature (p. 505), and the Standardized Test Preparation Workshop (p. 516).

TECHNOLOGY

Students can use the On-Line Exercise Bank to complete the exercises on computer. The Auto Check feature will grade their work.

INTEGRATED SKILLS COVERAGE

Grammar in Literature
SE p. 505

Reading
Find It In Your Reading, SE pp. 499, 506, 507, 513

Writing
Find It In Your Writing, SE pp. 499, 506, 507, 513
Writing Application SE pp. 499, 507, 513, 515

Language Highlight
ATE p. 509

Speaking and Listening
ATE p. 511

Vocabulary
ATE p. 511

Real-World Connection
ATE p. 496

Viewing and Representing
Critical Viewing SE pp. 490, 494, 497, 501, 503, 510

ASSESSMENT SUPPORT

Standardized Test Preparation SE p. 516; ATE pp. 494, 502

Standardized Test Preparation Workbook, pp. 43–44

Formal Assessment, Ch. 22

MEETING INDIVIDUAL NEEDS

Less Advanced Students ATE p. 496. See also Ongoing
Assessment ATE pp. 493, 497, 501, 505.

ESL Students ATE pp. 495, 505

More Advanced Students ATE p. 494, 502

Bodily/KinestheticLearners ATE p. 510

Visual/Spatial Learners ATE pp. 504, 511

BLOCK SCHEDULING

Pacing Suggestions
For 90-minute Blocks
• Administer the Diagnostic Test to students to determine instructional coverage
• Have students complete the necessary exercises in class. Use the Hands-on Grammar activity to provide a change of pace.

Resources for Varying Instruction
• *Language Lab* CD-ROM If your students have access to hardware, a 90-minute block provides an ideal opportunity for students to work on computer.

Professional Development Support
• *How to Manage Instruction in the Block* This Teaching Resource provides management and activity suggestions.

MEDIA AND TECHNOLOGY

For the Student
• *Language Lab* CD-ROM, Using Verbs
• *On-Line Exercise Bank,* Ch. 22

For the Teacher
• *Resource Pro* CD-ROM

WRITING AND GRAMMAR WEB SITE

The Interactive Writing and Grammar Web site provides a wide array of support for students, teachers, and parents. Grammar support includes:

• *On-Line Exercise Bank* with Auto Check scoring
• Diagnostic and assessment support

www.phschool.com

LITERATURE CONNECTIONS

Related selection from *Prentice Hall Literature: Timeless Voices, Timeless Themes,* Bronze:
"Rip Van Winkle," by Washington Irving, SE p. 505

▶ *Lesson Objectives*

1. To recognize the four principal parts of regular and irregular verbs.

2. To recognize and understand the use of the past and past participles of regular and irregular verbs.

3. To use verb tenses appropriately and consistently in writing.

4. To use the correct forms of troublesome verbs.

Critical Viewing

Analyze Students may suggest such verbs as *watch/watched, eat/ate, drive/drove, sing/sang.*

Chapter 22 *Using Verbs*

Usage refers to the way a word or expression is used in a sentence. Verb usage is an area that can cause many problems. Since verbs have many forms and uses, you may find yourself occasionally using them incorrectly in your writing.

If you were writing a report on exotic birds, for instance, you would want to choose the correct forms of verbs, you would want to write in the correct verb tenses, and you would want to avoid certain mistakes that people often make in using verbs.

This chapter will help you learn to use verbs correctly in your speaking and in your writing.

▲ **Critical Viewing**
Think of three verbs that describe what these flamingos are doing. **[Analyze]**

✓ ONGOING ASSESSMENT: Diagnose					
If students miss more than one item in each category, direct them to the relevant pages of the text and assign exercises for practice and review.					
Using Verbs	**Diagnostic Test Items**	**Teach**	**Practice**	**Section Review**	**Chapter Review**
Skill Check A					
Principal Parts of Regular and Irregular Verbs	A 1–10	pp. 492–498	Ex. 1–6	Ex. 7–10	Ex. 37–39
Skill Check B					
Tenses and Forms of Verbs	B 11–20	pp. 500–506	Ex. 14–20	Ex. 21–24	Ex. 40–41, 43

Diagnostic Test

Directions: Write all answers on a separate sheet of paper.

Skill Check A. Identify the principal part used to form each underlined verb (*present, present participle, past,* or *past participle*). Label the verb *regular* or *irregular.*

1. Storks <u>possess</u> long legs, webbed toes, and strong, straight bills.
2. Artists <u>have</u> often <u>drawn</u> pictures of them.
3. One species, the white stork, <u>migrated</u> from its native Asia.
4. We saw that the head, neck, and body of the stork <u>were shimmering in the sunlight.</u>
5. Spreading its wings, it <u>displayed</u> partly black tips.
6. Its long legs <u>extended</u> from a white body.
7. Its neck <u>arched</u> gracefully.
8. Storks <u>have fed</u> on eels and other fish, amphibians, reptiles, young birds, and small mammals.
9. We noticed that one <u>was flying</u> over a marsh, looking for food.
10. A guide told us that the white stork <u>makes</u> a nest of sticks and reeds.

Skill Check B. Copy each of the following verbs onto your paper, supplying the tense indicated in parentheses.

11. The stork (surprise—future) you as you learn more about it.
12. It never (make—present perfect) a sound as far as we know.
13. That is to say, the stork (have—present) no voice.
14. The visitors (see—past) one fly powerfully through the air.
15. They learned that it (reach—future perfect) a very high altitude soon after liftoff.
16. Another type of stork, the black stork, (live—present perfect progressive) in Europe and Asia.
17. This stork (inhabit—future perfect progressive) Africa, as well.
18. People (confuse—present perfect) the white stork with a similar stork, the maguari.
19. The maguari (frequent—past perfect progressive) marshes and savannas in search of food.
20. However, the maguari stork (make—present perfect progressive) its home in South America rather than Europe and Asia.

Skill Check C. Choose the correct word from the pair in parentheses, and write it on your paper.

21. We could (of, have) seen the albatross if we had looked closely.
22. Some bird-watchers (saw, seen) them wandering great distances over the ocean.
23. They (lie, lay) on the ocean surface when they sleep, rocking with the waves.
24. The ocean (isn't, ain't) just temporary lodgings for the albatross; it's home.
25. The only time it (sets, sits) its webbed foot on land is at breeding time.

Using Verbs • 491

Answer Key

Diagnostic Test

Each item in the diagnostic test corresponds with a specific concept in the sections in the Using Verbs chapter. This will enable you to tailor instruction to the particular needs of your students. See "Ongoing Assessment: Diagnose" below for further details.

Skill Check A

1. present, regular
2. past participle, irregular
3. past, regular
4. present participle, regular
5. past, regular
6. past, regular
7. past, regular
8. past participle, irregular
9. present participle, irregular
10. present, irregular

Skill Check B

11. will surprise
12. has made
13. has
14. saw
15. will have reached
16. has been living
17. will have been inhabiting
18. have confused
19. had been frequenting
20. has been making

Skill Check C

21. have
22. saw
23. lie
24. isn't
25. sets

✓ ONGOING ASSESSMENT: Diagnose *continued*

Using Verbs	Diagnostic Test Items	Teach	Practice	Section Review	Chapter Review
Skill Check C					
Troublesome Verbs	C 21–25	pp. 508–512	Ex. 28–30	Ex. 31–33	Ex. 42
Cumulative Reviews and Applications				Ex. 11–13, 25–27, 34–36	Ex. 45–46

⏲ TIME SAVERS!

Answers on Transparency Use the Grammar Exercises Answers on Transparencies for Chapter 22 to facilitate correction by students.

On-Line Exercise Bank Have students complete the Diagnostic Test on computer. The Auto Check feature will grade their work for you!

Verbs have different forms to express time. The form of the verb *walk* in the sentence "They *walk* very fast" expresses action in the present. In "They *walked* too far from home," the form of the verb shows that the action happened in the past. In "They *will walk* home from school," the verb expresses action in the future. These forms of verbs are known as *tenses.* To use the tenses of a verb correctly, you must know the *principal parts* of the verb.

KEY CONCEPT A verb has four **principal parts:** the *present*, the *present participle*, the *past*, and the *past participle.* ■

Here, for example, are the four principal parts of the verb *walk.*

THE FOUR PRINCIPAL PARTS OF *WALK*			
Present	Present Participle	Past	Past Participle
walk	(am) walking	walked	(have) walked

The first principal part, called the present, is the form of the verb that is listed in a dictionary. Notice also the helping verbs in parentheses before the second and fourth principal parts. These two principal parts must be combined with helping verbs before they can be used as verbs in sentences. The result will always be a verb phrase.

Here are four sentences, each using one of the principal parts of the verb *walk.*

EXAMPLES: He *walks* toward us in a hurry.
June *was walking* behind us a minute ago.
They *walked* to the park.
We *have walked* three miles in search of our friends.

The way the past and past participle of a verb are formed shows whether the verb is *regular* or *irregular.*

Using Regular Verbs

Most verbs are *regular*, which means that their past and past participle forms follow a standard, predictable pattern.

KEY CONCEPT The past and past participle of a **regular verb** are formed by adding *-ed* or *-d* to the present form. ■

To form the past and past participle of a regular verb such as *chirp* or *hover*, you simply add *-ed* to the present. With regular verbs that already end in *e*—verbs such as *move* and *charge*—you simply add *-d* to the present.

PRINCIPAL PARTS OF REGULAR VERBS			
Present	**Present Participle**	**Past**	**Past Participle**
chirp	(am) chirping	chirped	(have) chirped
hover	(am) hovering	hovered	(have) hovered
move	(am) moving	moved	(have) moved
charge	(am) charging	charged	(have) charged

Exercise 1 Recognizing the Principal Parts of Regular Verbs The verb or verb phrase in each of the following sentences is underlined. Identify the principal part used to form each verb.

EXAMPLE: Ginny is watching a hummingbird in flight.

ANSWER: present participle

1. Hummingbirds have consumed tiny insects and nectar from our flowers for years.
2. They hover in front of these flowers to get the food.
3. They gather nectar from each blossom.
4. When they have finished, they move on.
5. A hummingbird's heart beats up to 1,200 times a minute.
6. Have you ever noticed a hummingbird flying backward?
7. This skill enables hummingbirds to move away from a flower easily.
8. Some are living in mountain areas over 15,000 feet high.
9. Their small wings are beating constantly.
10. We learned that a hummingbird breathes over 250 times a minute.

> **More Practice**
>
> Language Lab CD-ROM
> • Using Verbs: Principal Parts of Verbs lesson
> On-line Exercise Bank
> • Section 22.1
> Grammar Exercise Workbook
> • pp. 111–112

The Four Principal Parts of Verbs • **493**

Step-by-Step Teaching Guide

Regular Verbs

1. Tell students that *most* verbs in English are regular, with the past and past participle formed by adding *-d* or *-ed*.

2. Explain that when a verb ends in *–y* after a consonant, the *–y* changes to *i* before adding *–ed* (*try + ed = tried*, not *tryed*). When the verb ends in a single consonant after a single short vowel, the final consonant is doubled before adding *–ed* (*stop + ed = stopped*, not *stoped*). Doubling the consonant applies to creating the present participle, as well (*stop, stopping*).

3. Tell students that these spelling changes do not make the words irregular, because the past and past participle are still formed by adding *–d* or *–ed*.

4. Have students think of five regular verbs and write down the past and past participle of each. Have students share some of the verbs they selected.

Answer Key

> **Exercise 1**

1. past participle
2. present
3. present
4. past participle
5. present
6. past participle
7. present
8. present participle
9. present participle
10. past

Topic Bank

The thematic emphasis on exotic birds provides students with a number of research and writing possibilities. Students may wish to explore the following:

• comparing and contrasting the nesting habits of several birds

• describing various types of flightless birds

• identifying and explaining unique characteristics of birds

☑ ONGOING ASSESSMENT: Monitor and Reinforce

If students miss more than two items in Exercises 1 or 2, refer them to the following for additional practice.

In the Textbook	Print Resources	Technology
Section Review, Ex. 7–8, p. 499	Grammar Exercise Workbook, pp. 111–112	Language Lab CD-ROM, Using Verbs; On-Line Exercise Bank, Section 22.1

Exercise 2

1. create
2. used
3. design
4. viewed
5. structure
6. fastened
7. stayed
8. incubate
9. looking
10. wondering

Critical Viewing

Analyze Students may say that the hummingbird is hovering and fluttering beside the flower.

Customize for
More Advanced Students

Point out that the present form of a verb is sometimes used to describe action that is past. For example, a book reviewer might say, "She writes with a fluid style." Also, someone relating historic events might write, "At this point, General Lee contemplates his options." Explain that these are known as the critical and historic present. Discuss with students why the present tense works in these cases.

22.1

▲ **Critical Viewing** Use the present participles of *hover* and *flutter* to explain the actions of this hummingbird. **[Analyze]**

Exercise 2 **Using the Principal Parts of Regular Verbs**

Copy each of the following sentences onto your paper, writing the principal part of the verb indicated in parentheses.

EXAMPLE: They have (look—past participle) everywhere for a hummingbird nest.

ANSWER: They have *looked* everywhere for a hummingbird nest.

1. Every season, hummingbirds (create—present) small cup-shaped nests for their young.
2. Some have (use—past participle) spider webs and pieces of bark in their nests.
3. The hermit hummingbirds (design—present) their nests differently, however.
4. They have been (view—past participle) as unique among hummingbirds.
5. They (structure—present) their nests long and hanging.
6. They have (fasten—past participle) these long nests to large leaves.
7. The female hummingbirds (stay—past) in the nest once eggs were laid.
8. The females (incubate—present) the two white eggs alone.
9. Those visitors are (look—present participle) at a hummingbird's nest.
10. I am (wonder—present participle) if the birds will migrate.

More Practice

Language Lab CD-ROM
• Using Verbs: Principal Parts of Verbs lesson
On-line Exercise Bank
• Section 22.1
Grammar Exercise Workbook
• pp. 111–112

494 • Using Verbs

✎ **STANDARDIZED TEST PREPARATION WORKSHOP**

Grammar and Usage Standardized tests often require students to identify the usage of a word in the context of a sentence. Share the following example with students.

I watched the birds at the zoo last week.

What is the principal part of the underlined verb?

A present   **B** present participle
C past   **D** past participle
E None of the above

Students should recognize that *watched* is the past form of *watch* since *-ed* is added to the verb. Therefore, item **C** is correct.

Using Irregular Verbs

While most verbs are regular, many very common verbs are *irregular*—their past and past participle forms do not follow a predictable pattern. These are the verbs that cause the most problems.

▶ **KEY CONCEPT** The past and past participle of an **irregular verb** are not formed by adding *-ed* or *-d* to the present form. ■

IRREGULAR VERBS WITH THE SAME PAST AND PAST PARTICIPLE			
Present	**Present Participle**	**Past**	**Past Participle**
bring	(am) bringing	brought	(have) brought
build	(am) building	built	(have) built
buy	(am) buying	bought	(have) bought
catch	(am) catching	caught	(have) caught
fight	(am) fighting	fought	(have) fought
find	(am) finding	found	(have) found
get	(am) getting	got	(have) got *or* (have) gotten
hold	(am) holding	held	(have) held
lay	(am) laying	laid	(have) laid
lead	(am) leading	led	(have) led
lose	(am) losing	lost	(have) lost
pay	(am) paying	paid	(have) paid
say	(am) saying	said	(have) said
sit	(am) sitting	sat	(have) sat
spin	(am) spinning	spun	(have) spun
stick	(am) sticking	stuck	(have) stuck
swing	(am) swinging	swung	(have) swung
teach	(am) teaching	taught	(have) taught

Check a dictionary whenever you are in doubt about the correct form of an irregular verb.

IRREGULAR VERBS WITH THE SAME PRESENT, PAST, AND PAST PARTICIPLE			
Present	**Present Participle**	**Past**	**Past Participle**
bid	(am) bidding	bid	(have) bid
burst	(am) bursting	burst	(have) burst
cost	(am) costing	cost	(have) cost
hurt	(am) hurting	hurt	(have) hurt
put	(am) putting	put	(have) put
set	(am) setting	set	(have) set

Using Irregular Verbs

1. Explain to students that, unlike regular verbs, irregular verbs do not form the past or past participle by adding *-ed.*

2. As you review the verb charts with students, note that irregular verbs form the present participle in the "regular" way by adding *-ing.*

3. Suggest to students that the best way to learn the past and past participle forms of irregular verbs is to memorize them.

4. To demonstrate how students can use a dictionary to check whether a verb is regular or irregular, have them look up the words *chirp* and *run.* Point out that the entry for *chirp,* a regular verb, includes no verb forms, so the past and past participle must be *chirped.* In contrast, *fly,* an irregular verb, does list another verb form for the past and past participle, *flew.*

Customize for
ESL Students

Pronunciation of some irregular verbs may be an issue for ESL students. Point out, for example, that the present tense of *lead* rhymes with *need.* The past tense, *led,* rhymes with *red.*

Real-World Connection

Read to students each of these warnings from a TV weather forecast and ask which would cause them to take precautions:

A big storm approaches.

A big storm is approaching.

A big storm approached.

A big storm has approached.

Why do students think it is important for weather forecasts to use the correct forms of verbs?

Customize for
Less Advanced Students

Ask students to identify verbs on this chart that have given them difficulty in speaking or writing. As a class, read the parts aloud, then have students copy them in their notebooks.

IRREGULAR VERBS THAT CHANGE IN OTHER WAYS			
Present	Present Participle	Past	Past Participle
arise	(am) arising	arose	(have) arisen
be	(am) being	was	(have) been
begin	(am) beginning	began	(have) begun
blow	(am) blowing	blew	(have) blown
break	(am) breaking	broke	(have) broken
choose	(am) choosing	chose	(have) chosen
come	(am) coming	came	(have) come
do	(am) doing	did	(have) done
draw	(am) drawing	drew	(have) drawn
drink	(am) drinking	drank	(have) drunk
drive	(am) driving	drove	(have) driven
eat	(am) eating	ate	(have) eaten
fall	(am) falling	fell	(have) fallen
fly	(am) flying	flew	(have) flown
freeze	(am) freezing	froze	(have) frozen
give	(am) giving	gave	(have) given
go	(am) going	went	(have) gone
grow	(am) growing	grew	(have) grown
know	(am) knowing	knew	(have) known
lie	(am) lying	lay	(have) lain
ride	(am) riding	rode	(have) ridden
ring	(am) ringing	rang	(have) rung
rise	(am) rising	rose	(have) risen
run	(am) running	ran	(have) run
see	(am) seeing	saw	(have) seen
shake	(am) shaking	shook	(have) shaken
sing	(am) singing	sang	(have) sung
sink	(am) sinking	sank	(have) sunk
speak	(am) speaking	spoke	(have) spoken
spring	(am) springing	sprang	(have) sprung
swear	(am) swearing	swore	(have) sworn
swim	(am) swimming	swam	(have) swum
take	(am) taking	took	(have) taken
tear	(am) tearing	tore	(have) torn
throw	(am) throwing	threw	(have) thrown
wear	(am) wearing	wore	(have) worn
write	(am) writing	wrote	(have) written

Exercise 3 Completing the Principal Parts of Irregular Verbs On your paper, make four columns with the principal parts of verbs as the heads. Then, write the missing parts of the following irregular verbs. See how many you can fill in without looking back at the charts.

EXAMPLE:	Present	Present Participle	Past	Past Participle
	_____	_____	began	_____
ANSWER:	begin	beginning	began	begun

	Present	Present Participle	Past	Past Participle
1.	put	_____	_____	put
2.	_____	swinging	swung	_____
3.	choose	_____	chose	chosen
4.	rise	rising	_____	_____
5.	drink	_____	drank	_____
6.	hurt	hurting	_____	hurt
7.	_____	going	went	_____
8.	_____	_____	came	_____
9.	set	setting	_____	_____
10.	eat	_____	ate	_____

Exercise 4 Using the Principal Parts of Irregular Verbs For each of the following sentences, identify the irregular verb(s) and the principal part(s) used.

EXAMPLE: I found a Web site devoted to ostriches.

ANSWER: found (past)

1. The ostrich never flies.
2. Those ostriches are running.
3. As that one has matured, its legs have grown very powerful.
4. We have drawn pictures of ostriches.
5. We begin our study of a new animal this week.

More Practice

Language Lab
CD-ROM
• Using Verbs: Principal Parts of Verbs lesson
On-line
Exercise Bank
• Section 22.1
Grammar Exercise Workbook
• pp. 113–114

▼ Critical Viewing
What qualities of an ostrich make it seem "irregular" compared to most other birds? Use two or three irregular verbs in your answer. **[Compare and Contrast]**

The Four Principal Parts of Verbs • **497**

Answer Key

▶ **Exercise 3**

1. putting, put
2. swing, swung
3. choosing
4. rose, risen
5. drinking, drunk
6. hurt
7. go, gone
8. come, coming, come
9. set, set
10. eating, eaten

▶ **Exercise 4**

1. flies—present
2. are running—present participle
3. have grown—past participle
4. have drawn—past participle
5. begin—present

Critical Viewing

Compare and Contrast Students may say that an ostrich cannot fly but instead can run very fast.

☑ **ONGOING ASSESSMENT: Monitor and Reinforce**

If students miss more than two items in Exercises 3–6, refer them to the following for additional practice.

In the Textbook	Print Resources	Technology
Section Review, Ex. 9–10, p. 499	Grammar Exercise Workbook, pp. 113–114	Language Lab CD-ROM, Using Verbs; On-Line Exercise Bank, Section 22.1

⏱ **TIME SAVERS!**

 **Answers on Transparency** Use the Grammar Exercises Answers on Transparencies for Chapter 22 to facilitate correction by students.

🖳 **On-Line Exercise Bank** Have students complete the exercises on computer. The Auto Check feature will grade their work for you!

22.1

Exercise 5 Using the Past Participle of Irregular Verbs

For each of the following sentences, write the past participle of the verb in parentheses.

EXAMPLE: Charlayne has (choose) the parakeet.

ANSWER: chosen

1. Have you ever (see) a great spotted kiwi?
2. They have been (find) only in New Zealand and on nearby islands.
3. Like the large ostrich, kiwis have never (fly) through the air.
4. We had not (know) that kiwis hide themselves beneath their thick plumage.
5. Often, we see that kiwis have (come) to forage for food such as worms, seeds, and berries.

Exercise 6 Supplying the Correct Principal Part of Irregular Verbs For each of the following sentences, write the principal part of the verb given in parentheses.

EXAMPLE: You should have (bring—past participle) binoculars with you.

ANSWER: You should have *brought* binoculars with you.

1. Researchers have (study—past participle) the Chilean flamingo.
2. It has been (find—past participle) in the Andes Mountains.
3. The flamingo (feed—present) by dipping its head under water.
4. I am (watch—present participle) one trap food in its bill.
5. The same one (catch—past) a lot of food earlier today.
6. The flamingo's upper jaw (fit—present) over its lower jaw like the lid of a box.
7. We are (learn—present participle) that the food source (affect—present) the color of the flamingo's feathers.
8. Yesterday, we (see—past) the greater flamingo, which is larger than other flamingos.
9. It had (build—past participle) a nest on a cone-shaped mound in the water.
10. Then, it (take—past) good care of its young for seventy-five days.

More Practice

Language Lab
CD-ROM
• Using Verbs: Principal
  Parts of Verbs lesson
On-line
Exercise Bank
• Section 22.1
Grammar Exercise
Workbook
• pp. 113–114

☑ **ONGOING ASSESSMENT: Assess Mastery**

Use the following resources to assess student mastery of the four principal parts of verbs.

In the Textbook	Technology
Chapter Review, Ex. 37–39, p. 514	On-Line Exercise Bank, Section 22.1

Section 22.1 *Section Review*

GRAMMAR EXERCISES 7–13

Exercise 7 Identifying Regular and Irregular Verbs Label the following verbs *regular* or *irregular.*

1. fly
2. hover
3. run
4. eat
5. hurt
6. sing
7. chirp
8. move
9. begin
10. catch

Exercise 8 Identifying Principal Parts of Regular Verbs Identify the principal part used to form each underlined regular verb in the sentences below.

1. The cattle egret, a species of heron, once <u>inhabited</u> only Africa.
2. By the 1870's, it <u>had crossed</u> the Atlantic to South America.
3. It <u>reached</u> Florida in 1942.
4. It now <u>frequents</u> areas across both North and South America.
5. It <u>is living</u> in almost all of the United States.

Exercise 9 Recognizing Principal Parts and Regular or Irregular Verbs Identify the principal part used to form each underlined verb in the following sentences. Then, specify whether the verb is *regular* or *irregular.*

1. Scientists <u>have given</u> the common name of *ibis* to about thirty different species, including the sacred ibis.
2. These long-necked, long-legged birds <u>are living</u> throughout the world.
3. They <u>inhabit</u> areas of Africa, Turkey, and North and South America.
4. Historians studying ancient Egyptians <u>have written</u> about the sacred ibis.
5. It <u>became</u> a religious symbol in Egypt.

Exercise 10 Supplying the Correct Principal Part Copy the following sentences onto your paper. Supply the correct principal part. If there is no helping verb in the sentence, do not add one.

1. Some bird-watchers have (mistake) the ibis for the heron.
2. My biology teacher (speak) about a major difference between these birds.
3. The heron has always (fly) with its head back and its neck bent into an S-curve.
4. Flying ibises can be (see) with their necks straight and heads held forward.
5. We have (learn) that cranes, like ibises, fly with their necks straight.

Exercise 11 Find It in Your Reading Identify the principal part used to form each underlined word in these sentences from "The Hummingbird That Lived Through Winter" by William Saroyan.

The new life of the little bird <u>was</u> magnificent. It <u>spun</u> about in the little kitchen, <u>going</u> to the window, coming back to the heat, <u>suspending</u>, circling as if it were summertime and it <u>had</u> never <u>felt</u> better in its whole life.

Exercise 12 Find It in Your Writing Look through your writing portfolio. Find several examples of regular and irregular verbs. Identify the principal part of each verb you find.

Exercise 13 Writing Application Describe the habits of a bird or other animal in your area. Identify the four principal parts of the verbs you use.

Section Review • 499

Exercise 7

1. irregular
2. regular
3. irregular
4. irregular
5. irregular
6. irregular
7. regular
8. regular
9. irregular
10. irregular

Exercise 8

1. past
2. past participle
3. past
4. present
5. present participle

Exercise 9

1. past participle—irregular
2. present participle—regular
3. present—regular
4. past participle—irregular
5. past—irregular

Exercise 10

1. mistaken
2. spoke
3. flown
4. seen
5. learned

Exercise 11

Find It in Your Reading
was—past
spun—past
going—present participle
suspending—present participle
had felt—past participle

Exercise 12

Find It in Your Writing
Students should identify the principal parts of the verbs in their sentences. Suggest that students rewrite their sentences using a different verb form in each.

continued

Answer Key continued

Exercise 13

Writing Application
Students should identify the principal part of each verb they use, and then list the three remaining principal parts of each verb.

Invite students to complete the sentences below with the specified form of the verb *own*.

Right now, I ___ a pet flamingo. (present)

When I was five, I ___ a parakeet. (past)

When I am fifteen, I ___ ___ a pet ostrich. (future)

I ___ ___ hummingbirds, too. (present perfect)

By the time I was eight, I ___ ___ five birds. (past perfect)

By the time I am twenty, I ___ ___ ___ birds for fifteen years. (future perfect)

Activate Prior Knowledge

Point out to students that we can anticipate what will have happened in the future. Therefore, we use the future perfect tense. Encourage students to think ahead to things they will have done or seen by the time they are eighty years old. Ask them to respond in this form:

I will have ___.

Tell students that they will learn more about the future perfect tenses and other verb tenses in this section.

TEACH

The Basic Forms of the Six Tenses

1. Explain to students that a verb has six tenses to show when something happens or exists, has happened or existed, or will happen or exist.

2. Remind them that they already know three of the tenses: present, past, and future.

3. Indicate the other three tenses on the chart: present perfect, past perfect, and future perfect, and point out that these tenses are formed with helping verbs and the past participle of the main verb.

4. Take time to point out that each tense carries a specific meaning, giving verbs the power to "tell time" with great precision in only a few words.

The Tenses and Forms of Verbs

In English, verbs have six *tenses*. Each of the six tenses has a *basic* form and a *progressive* form. This section will explain first the basic forms and then the progressive forms.

> **KEY CONCEPT** A **tense** is a form of a verb that shows when something happens or when something exists. ∎

The Basic Forms of the Six Tenses

The chart below shows the *basic* forms of the six tenses, using *begin* as an example. The first column gives the name of each tense. The third column gives the principal part needed to form each tense. Only three of the four principal parts are used in the basic forms: the present, the past, and the past participle.

BASIC FORMS OF THE SIX TENSES OF *BEGIN*		
Tense	**Basic Form**	**Principal Part Used**
Present	I begin	Present
Past	I began	Past
Future	I will begin	Present
Present Perfect	I have begun	Past Participle
Past Perfect	I had begun	Past Participle
Future Perfect	I will have begun	Past Participle

Study the chart carefully. First, learn the names of the tenses. Then, learn the principal parts needed to form them. Notice also that only the last four tenses need helping verbs.

> **Exercise 14** Supplying Verb Tenses Complete each sentence below with the verb and tense indicated in parentheses.

EXAMPLE: Rip Van Winkle ___?___ (fall—past) asleep in the Catskill Mountains.

ANSWER: fell

1. Hiking in the Catskills, we ___?___ (lose—past) our compass.
2. Before we ___?___ (go—past perfect) far, we found an arrowhead.
3. We ___?___ (find—present perfect) several during our hikes.
4. By the end of the day, we ___?___ (hike—future perfect) about ten miles.
5. Next time, we ___?___ (keep—future) an eye on our compass.

Grammar and Style Tip

Whenever it makes sense in your writing, use different tenses to make your ideas more precise. For instance, when you write in the present tense, you might also use the present perfect to clarify some ideas.

⏱ TIME AND RESOURCE MANAGER

Resources
Print: Grammar Exercise Workbook, pp. 115–118; Hands-on Grammar Activity Book, Chapter 22
Technology: Language Lab CD-ROM, Using Verbs; On-Line Exercise Bank, Section 22.2

In-Depth Coverage	Accelerated Pace
• Work through all key concepts, pp. 500–506. • Assign and review Exercises 14–20. • Read and discuss Grammar in Literature, p. 505. • Do the Hands-on Grammar Activity, p. 506.	• Assign pp. 500–506, for independent student review. • Assign Section Review Exercises 21–24.

> **Exercise 15** Identifying the Basic Forms of Verbs Identify the tense of each underlined verb in the following sentences.

EXAMPLE: We <u>have completed</u> our study of the early settlement of New York.

ANSWER: present perfect

1. I often <u>had wondered</u> about the history of New York.
2. "If I ask my mom," I thought, "she <u>will tell</u> me it is rich in history."
3. She <u>will say</u>, "It extends back to the settlement of the area by Native Americans."
4. They first <u>occupied</u> New York's shores and river valleys.
5. Archaeological sites <u>exist</u> all the way from downstate Staten Island to upstate Lake Champlain.
6. Archaeologists <u>have found</u> evidence of ancient sites.
7. Some of these sites <u>had been</u> home to Cayuga and Seneca Native Americans.
8. For food, members of the ancient culture <u>had relied</u> on hunting and gathering.
9. A later culture <u>substituted</u> agriculture for hunting and gathering.
10. After more research, I <u>will have learned</u> other interesting facts about New York history.

> **More Practice**

Language Lab CD-ROM
• Using Verbs: Verb Tense lesson
On-line Exercise Bank
• Section 22.2
Grammar Exercise Workbook
• pp. 115–116

▼ Critical Viewing
Use future and future perfect verb tenses to tell what you think will become of this forest. [Assess]

The Tenses and Forms of Verbs • 501

Answer Key

> **Exercise 14** *(page 500)*

1. lost
2. had gone
3. have found
4. will have hiked
5. will keep

> **Exercise 15**

1. had wondered—past perfect
2. will tell—future
3. will say—future
4. occupied—past
5. exist—present
6. have found—present perfect
7. had been—past perfect
8. had relied—past perfect
9. substituted—past
10. will have learned—future perfect

Critical Viewing

Assess Possible response: People will use the natural resources found in this forest. By the time I am old, we will have cut down many trees.

☑ **ONGOING ASSESSMENT: Monitor and Reinforce**

If students miss more than two items in Exercises 14 or 15, refer them to the following for additional practice.

In the Textbook	Print Resources	Technology
Section Review, Ex. 21, p. 507	Grammar Exercise Workbook, pp. 115–116	Language Lab CD-ROM, Using Verbs; On-Line Exercise Bank, Section 22.2

⏱ **TIME SAVERS!**

 **Answers on Transparency** Use the Grammar Exercises Answers on Transparencies for Chapter 22 to facilitate correction by students.

🖥 **On-Line Exercise Bank** Have students complete the exercises on computer. The Auto Check feature will grade their work for you!

1. Explain that conjugating a verb is naming a verb's six forms that go with each of the singular and plural pronouns. Conjugating is a way to determine which verb and which pronoun to use together.

2. Invite students to use the chart on page 502, substituting other verb forms. This chart will help students do the exercises in this section.

3. To demonstrate the precise distinctions, ask volunteer students to explain the difference between the past and past perfect and the future and future perfect.

Customizing for
More Advanced Students

Ask students to construct a chart similar to the one on this page and conjugate a verb of their choice. Have them find the two instances in which the verb form differs from the other forms in the same tense, breaking the pattern. (third-person singular present and third-person singular present perfect)

22.2

Conjugating the Basic Forms of Verbs

Conjugating verbs can help you become familiar with the many forms of verbs.

▶ **KEY CONCEPT** A **conjugation** is a list of the singular and plural forms of a verb in a particular tense. ■

Each tense in a conjugation has six forms that fit with first-, second-, and third-person forms of the personal pronouns.

To conjugate any verb, begin by listing its principal parts. For example, the principal parts of the verb *hide* are *hide*, *hiding*, *hid*, and *hidden*. The following conjugation of *hide* shows all of the basic forms of this verb in the six tenses.

CONJUGATION OF THE BASIC FORMS OF *HIDE*		
	Singular	**Plural**
Present	I hide you hide he, she, it hides	we hide you hide they hide
Past	I hid you hid he, she, it hid	we hid you hid they hid
Future	I will hide you will hide he, she, it will hide	we will hide you will hide they will hide
Present Perfect	I have hidden you have hidden he, she, it has hidden	we have hidden you have hidden they have hidden
Past Perfect	I had hidden you had hidden he, she, it had hidden	we had hidden you had hidden they had hidden
Future Perfect	I will have hidden you will have hidden he, she, it will have hidden	we will have hidden you will have hidden they will have hidden

---

✎ STANDARDIZED TEST PREPARATION WORKSHOP

Using Verbs Many standardized tests measure students' knowledge of verb usage. Share the following sample question with students:

Read the sentence and choose the letter of the word or group of words that belongs in the space.

My father and I ___ to see my uncle before he left for Europe.

A hope   **C** were hoping

B will hope   **D** have been hoping

Only item **C** makes sense in terms of the time frame of the sentence, indicated by the phrase *he left*.

Relate Students may say that the artist idealized his subject.

Answer Key

> **Exercise 16**

1. It existed. It will exist. It has existed. It had existed. It will have existed.
2. You moved. You will move. You have moved. You had moved. You will have moved.
3. We brought. We will bring. We have brought. We had brought. We will have brought.
4. They began. They will begin. They have begun. They had begun. They will have begun.
5. I went. I will go. I have gone. I had gone. I will have gone.

> **Exercise 17**

1. Two major Native American language groups <u>emerged</u> in northeastern North America after A.D. 1000.
2. Archaeologists <u>have identified</u> these groups as the Algonquian and the Iroquoian.
3. The group that <u>had spoken</u> Algonquian soon spread the language.
4. These Algonquian tribes <u>include</u> the Mahican, the Delaware, and the Wappinger.
5. This knowledge <u>will bring</u> new understanding of the area's history.

Exercise 16 Conjugating the Basic Forms of Verbs The following sentences are written in the present tense. Rewrite each sentence in each of the other five tenses.

1. It exists.
2. You move.
3. We bring.
4. They begin.
5. I go.

▲ Critical Viewing In this painting, do you think the artist's vision was idealized or realistic? Use past tense forms in your answer. **[Relate]**

Exercise 17 Supplying the Correct Tense Copy each of the following sentences onto your paper, supplying the basic form of the verb indicated in parentheses.

EXAMPLE: Diane (buy—past) a book on New York history.
ANSWER: Diane *bought* a book on New York history.

1. Two major Native American language groups (emerge—past) in northeastern North America after A.D. 1000.
2. Archaeologists (identify—present perfect) these groups as the Algonquian and the Iroquoian.
3. The group that (speak—past perfect) Algonquian soon spread the language.
4. These Algonquian tribes (include—present) the Mahican, the Delaware, and the Wappinger.
5. This knowledge (bring—future) new understanding of the area's history.

> **More Practice**

Language Lab CD-ROM
• Using Verbs: Verb Tense lesson
On-line Exercise Bank
• Section 22.2
Grammar Exercise Workbook
• pp. 115–116

The Tenses and Forms of Verbs • **503**

🕑 **TIME SAVERS!**

Answers on Transparency Use the Grammar Exercises Answers on Transparencies for Chapter 22 to facilitate correction by students.

On-Line Exercise Bank Have students complete the exercises on computer. The Auto Check feature will grade their work for you!

1. Tell students that the progressive forms of verbs show action that is continuing or is in progress.

2. Explain that there is a progressive form for each of the six verb tenses. Each progressive verb form contains a form of the verb *be* plus the present participle.

3. Encourage students to use the chart on page 504 as they work with progressive forms of verbs.

Customize for
Visual/Spatial Learners

Cut three tagboard strips about 12 inches long. On one, print this sentence horizontally: *The runner ___ racing.* On another, print these names of progressive verb forms: present progressive, past progressive, future progressive, present perfect progressive, past perfect progressive, and future perfect progressive. On the final strip, print these helping verbs vertically: *are, were, will be, has been, had been, will be.* Ask students to use the strips to complete the sentence in each of the six ways, with the corresponding label next to each.

Answer Key

Exercise 18

1. present perfect progressive
2. present progressive
3. future progressive
4. past perfect progressive
5. past progressive
6. present perfect progressive
7. past perfect progressive
8. past perfect progressive
9. future perfect progressive
10. present perfect progressive

Exercise 19

1. was
2. had been
3. is
4. will be
5. will have been

22.2

The Six Progressive Forms of Verbs

Each of the six tenses introduced in this section also has a progressive form, which indicates continuing action. The present participle and a form of the verb *be* are used to make all six progressive forms.

The following chart, using *sing* as an example, shows the progressive forms of the six tenses.

PROGRESSIVE FORMS OF THE SIX TENSES OF *SING*		
Tense	**Progressive Form**	**Principal Part**
Present	I am singing	
Past	I was singing	
Future	I will be singing	
Present Perfect	I have been singing	Present Participle
Past Perfect	I had been singing	
Future Perfect	I will have been singing	

Exercise 18 Identifying the Progressive Forms of Verbs
Study the preceding chart. Then, identify the tense of each of the following verbs.

EXAMPLE: will have been waiting
ANSWER: future perfect progressive

1. has been going
2. is progressing
3. will be eating
4. had been exploring
5. was explaining
6. have been staying
7. had been building
8. had been thinking
9. will have been having
10. have been giving

Exercise 19 Supplying Helping Verbs for Progressive
Forms For each sentence below, supply the helping verbs necessary to form the progressive tense indicated in parentheses.

EXAMPLE: We (present perfect) hoping to visit the *Half Moon* exhibit.
ANSWER: We *have been* hoping to visit the *Half Moon* exhibit.

1. In 1609, aboard his ship *Half Moon*, Henry Hudson (past) searching for a Northwest passage to Asia.
2. He (past perfect) sailing for six months when he discovered the wide river that would bear his name.
3. Now, the New Netherland Museum in New York (present) exhibiting a replica of the *Half Moon.*
4. It (future) sailing around as an example of living history.
5. By 2005, the *Half Moon* replica (future perfect) giving visitors a taste of the era of exploration for almost fifteen years.

Spelling Tip

When forming the progressive form of verbs, be careful with verbs that end in *c*, such as *picnic*. To avoid having the *c* join with the *i* to make an *s* sound, add a *k* after the *c* to form *picnicking.*

GRAMMAR IN LITERATURE

from **Rip Van Winkle**
Washington Irving

The legend of "Rip Van Winkle" is set in the Dutch colony of New Netherland. In this passage from the story, notice the use of past tense and past progressive forms of both regular and irregular verbs.

On waking, he *found* himself on the green knoll whence he had first seen the old man of the glen. He *rubbed* his eyes—it *was* a bright sunny morning. The birds *were hopping* and *twittering* among the bushes, and the eagle *was wheeling* aloft, and *breasting* the pure mountain breeze. "Surely," *thought* Rip, "I have not slept here all night."

▶ **Exercise 20** Supplying the Correct Form of Progressive Verbs On your paper, rewrite each sentence, supplying the indicated progressive form of the verb in parentheses.

EXAMPLE: The threat of fire (worry—past progressive) leaders of Albany.

ANSWER: The threat of fire *was worrying* leaders of Albany.

1. A new law passed in 1670 (prohibit—future progressive) thatched roofs.
2. Other laws (require—present perfect progressive) that streets be kept clear of flammable materials.
3. The mayor (appoint—past perfect progressive) wardens to report fire hazards.
4. The wardens (fine—present progressive) violators of fire laws.
5. By 1732, the city (purchase—past progressive) its first fire engine.

▶ **More Practice**

Language Lab
CD-ROM
• Using Verbs: Verb Tense lesson
On-line
Exercise Bank
• Section 22.2
Grammar Exercise Workbook
• pp. 117–118

The Tenses and Forms of Verbs • 505

✓ **ONGOING ASSESSMENT: Monitor and Reinforce**

If students miss more than two items in Exercises 18, 19, or 20, refer them to the following for additional practice.

In the Textbook	Print Resources	Technology
Section Review, Ex. 21–22, 24, p. 507	Grammar Exercise Workbook, pp. 117–118	Language Lab CD-ROM, Using Verbs; On-Line Exercise Bank, Section 22.2

Verb Fortune Teller

Teaching Resources: Hands-on Grammar Activity Book, Chapter 22

1. Have students refer to their *Hands-on Grammar Activity Book* or give them copies of relevant pages for this activity.

2. Make sure students select both regular and irregular verbs. You may want to assign verbs to students.

Find It in Your Reading

Have students underline the verbs they find. Then, on a separate sheet of paper, have them list each verb and its tense or form.

Find It in Your Writing

You may want to have students complete this activity in pairs so that they can check each other's work.

22.2

Hands-on Grammar

Verb Fortune Teller

Practice verb tenses and forms with a "fortune teller." Take a 6 1/2-inch-square sheet of paper, and fold in the corners so they meet in the middle. Turn the paper over, and again fold in the corners. Then, crease the paper by folding it in half, and in half again. You will have a small square. Unfold only the small square, and lay the paper flat so that four square sections are facing upward. Write a different verb on each of the four squares. (See example A.)

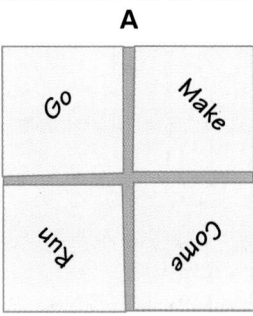

A

Next, turn the paper over, and on each of the eight triangular sections, write a different verb tense or form—for example, *present perfect, future progressive, past perfect, future, past, past perfect progressive.* (See example B.) Then, lift up each triangle, and write underneath it the corresponding forms of the verb on the back of the square. Each verb will have two forms.

Finally, refold the square so that the verbs are on the outside. Place your thumbs and index fingers in each of the four slots formed by the small squares, and pinch them together. You should be able to open and close the square in two directions, exposing different verb tenses each time. (See example C.)

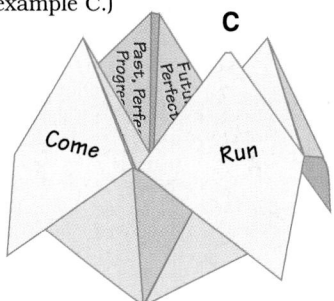

B

C

With a partner, take turns choosing a verb from the other's "fortune teller." After opening and closing the square in different directions four or five times, each person must give the form of the verb indicated on the triangle. Check your answers by lifting up the triangle.

Find It in Your Reading Read two or three paragraphs of a story or article, and see how many different verb tenses and forms you recognize.

Find It in Your Writing Review the verbs in a piece of your writing, and make sure you used and formed the tenses correctly.

⏱ **TIME SAVERS!**

✋ **Hands-on Grammar**
Use the Hands-on Grammar Activity Sheet for Chapter 22 to facilitate this activity.

☑ **ONGOING ASSESSMENT: Assess Mastery**

Use the following resources to assess student mastery of the tenses and forms of verbs.

In the Textbook	Technology
Chapter Review, Ex. 40–41, 43, pp. 514–515	On-Line Exercise Bank, Section 22.2

Section **22.2** *Section Review*

GRAMMAR EXERCISES 21–27

Exercise 21 Identifying Basic and Progressive Tenses Identify the tense of the underlined verb in the following sentences.

1. The Iroquois <u>are</u> fascinating to study.
2. For years, historians <u>have been disagreeing</u> on where the Iroquois first lived.
3. The debate <u>will</u> probably <u>continue</u> until more evidence is found.
4. Perhaps you <u>will be learning</u> about the famous Iroquois Confederacy.
5. Five Iroquois tribes <u>had united</u> in 1570.
6. They <u>formed</u> the Iroquois Confederacy.
7. This group <u>has</u> sometimes <u>been called</u> the Five Nations.
8. It <u>includes</u> the Mohawk, Onandaga, Cayuga, Oneida, and Seneca tribes.
9. In the 1600's, the Iroquois <u>had been extending</u> the area where they lived.
10. The confederacy <u>added</u> a sixth tribe, the Tuscarora, in the early 1700's.

Exercise 22 Forming Progressive Tenses of Verbs Write the tense indicated for each verb below.

1. present perfect progressive of *resist*
2. future progressive of *rename*
3. past perfect progressive of *grow*
4. present progressive of *become*
5. past progressive of *help*

Exercise 23 Revising Verb Forms Revise the following sentences by writing the correct form of the underlined verb. If the verb is used correctly, write *correct*.

(1) New York State has <u>have</u> a full and rich history. (2) The state <u>receive</u> its name from the Duke of York in the 1660's. (3) Before that, its name <u>be</u> New Netherland, since it had <u>begin</u> as a Dutch settlement. (4) Dutch leaders <u>run</u> the colony for years. (5) In fact, many places still <u>bear</u> Dutch names.

Exercise 24 Supplying the Correct Progressive Form Copy each of the following sentences onto your paper, supplying the progressive form of the verb indicated in parentheses.

(1) In 1665, Governor Nicolls called a meeting of settlers who (live—past perfect progressive) around Long Island. (2) He told them he (refuse—past progressive) their request for an assembly. (3) "However," he said, "I (give—present progressive) you a small degree of self-government." (4) "From this time on, you (elect—future progressive) your own town boards and constables." (5) By the Tricentennial of the United States, citizens (enjoy—future perfect progressive) freedom for more than 400 years.

Exercise 25 Find It in Your Reading Look back through the passage from "Rip Van Winkle" on page 505. Locate one verb in present perfect tense and one in past perfect tense.

Exercise 26 Find It in Your Writing Look through your writing portfolio. Find examples of sentences with verbs in different basic and progressive tenses. Identify the tense of each verb.

Exercise 27 Writing Application Write several sentences about the history of a place that you have visited or read about. Try to use different tenses in your sentences. Make sure you can identify the tense you use in each sentence.

Section Review • 507

Answer Key continued

Exercise 26

Find It in Your Writing
Students should identify the tenses of verbs in their writing. Have students rewrite each sentence using another verb form.

Exercise 27

Writing Application
Students should use different forms of verb tenses and list the verb tenses they used in their sentences.

ASSESS

Section Review
Each of these exercises correlates to a concept covered in the section on tenses and forms of verbs, pages 500–506. These exercises may be used for more practice, for reteaching, or for review of the Key Concepts presented. Answers for all chapter exercises are available in *Grammar Exercises Answers on Transparencies* in your teaching resources.

Answer Key

Exercise 21

1. present
2. present perfect progressive
3. future
4. future progressive
5. past perfect
6. past
7. present perfect
8. present
9. past perfect progressive
10. past

Exercise 22

1. has/have been resisting
2. will be renaming
3. had been growing
4. am/is/are becoming
5. was/were helping

Exercise 23

1. had
2. received
3. was, begun
4. ran *or* had run *or* had been running
5. correct

Exercise 24

1. In 1665, Governor Nicolls called a meeting of settlers who <u>had been living</u> around Long Island.
2. He told them he <u>was refusing</u> their request for an assembly.
3. "However," he said, "I <u>am giving</u> you a small degree of self-government."
4. "From this time on, you <u>will be electing</u> your own town boards and constables."
5. By the Tricentennial of the United States, citizens <u>will have been enjoying</u> freedom for more than 400 years.

Exercise 25

Find It in Your Reading
present perfect—have (not) slept
past perfect—had (first) seen

continued

Write the following sentences on the board and ask students to correct the errors.

My mother told me not to lay around all summer, so I got a job. (lie)

Cleaning the elephant cages at the circus ain't fun. (isn't)

I should of known that before I applied for the position. (have)

Tomorrow I will ask my boss to rise my salary. (raise)

Activate Prior Knowledge

Invite students to cite instances of incorrect grammar they have encountered in advertisements, magazines, newspapers, or Web sites. Ask students to jot down those they remember, and compare them with errors covered in this section.

TEACH

Step-by-Step Teaching Guide

Troublesome Verbs

1. Point out to students that English can be a difficult and inconsistent language, with many verbs and other words that can be confused.

2. Encourage students to keep lists of verbs that they find troublesome.

3. Tell students that listening carefully will help them remember and choose the correct verbs. Correct verb usage will become habitual over time.

Section 22.3 *Troublesome Verbs*

Many people have problems with the verbs listed in this section. Some of the problems arise when the wrong principal part is used. Other problems are caused when the meanings of certain pairs of verbs are confused. As you read through the list, concentrate on those verbs that have caused you difficulty in the past. Then, use the exercises to test your understanding. When you are writing and revising your compositions, refer to this section for help in checking your work.

ain't **Ain't** is not correct English. Avoid using it in speaking and in writing.

INCORRECT:	This *ain't* the Statue of Liberty.
CORRECT:	This *isn't* the Statue of Liberty.

did, done **Done** is a past participle and can be used as a verb only with a helping verb such as *have* or *has*. If you find you are using *done* without a helping verb, try using *did* instead. Otherwise, add the helping verb before *done*.

INCORRECT:	I *done* all my studying of New York.
CORRECT:	I *did* all my studying of New York.
	I *have done* all my studying of New York.

gone, went **Gone** is the past participle of *go* and can be used as a verb only with a helping verb such as *have* or *has*. **Went** is the past of *go* and is never used with a helping verb.

INCORRECT:	The Martins *gone* on vacation to New York.
	Niva *has went* along with them.
CORRECT:	The Martins *have gone* on vacation to New York.
	The Martins *went* on vacation to New York.
	Niva *has gone* along with them.
	Niva *went* along with them.

have, of In conversation, the words *have* and *of* sound very much alike. Be careful not to write *of* when you really mean the helping verb *have* or its contraction *'ve*.

INCORRECT:	He *should of* apologized.
CORRECT:	He *should have* apologized.
	He *should've* apologized.

Theme: Historic New York

In this section, you will learn about several different verbs that often give writers and speakers trouble. The examples and exercises in this section will tell you more about the history of New York State.

Cross-Curricular Connection: Social Studies

⏱ **TIME AND RESOURCE MANAGER**

Resources
Print: Grammar Exercise Workbook, pp. 119–120
Technology: Language Lab CD-ROM, Using Verbs; On-Line Exercise Bank, Section 22.3

In-Depth Coverage	Accelerated Pace
• Work through pp. 508–512. • Assign and review Exercises 28–30.	• Assign pp. 508–512 for independent student review. • Assign Section Review Exercises 31–33.

> **Exercise 28**   Avoiding Problems With Troublesome Verbs

For each of the following sentences, choose the correct verb from the pair in parentheses, and write it on your paper.

EXAMPLE: (Ain't, Aren't) you ready to leave yet?

ANSWER: Aren't

1. In 1682, Thomas Dongan (did, done) become governor of the New York colony.
2. Students of American politics should (of, have) heard of him.
3. However, he (isn't, ain't) as well known as he should be.
4. The Charter of Liberties he proposed for New York (did, done) a lot to promote democracy there.
5. His actions have (gone, went) down in history as early examples of American democratic principles at work.

lay, lie These verbs cause many problems because some of their forms are alike and have similar meanings. The first step in learning to distinguish between *lay* and *lie* is to memorize their principal parts.

PRINCIPAL PARTS: lay   laying   laid   laid
                       lie   lying   lay   lain

Next, compare the meaning and use of the two verbs.

Lay usually means "to put (something) down" or "to place (something)." This verb is almost always followed by a direct object. In the examples below, the direct objects are labeled.

                           DO
EXAMPLES: The captain *lays* his map on the galley table.

                           DO
            The colonists *have laid* cobblestones to pave the new road.

Lie usually means "to rest in a reclining position." It can also mean "to be situated." *Lie* is never followed by a direct object.

EXAMPLES: My father usually *lies* down after dinner.
            The food *had lain* in the sun all afternoon.

When using *lay* and *lie*, pay special attention to one particular area of confusion: *Lay* is the present tense of *lay*. *Lay* is also the past tense of *lie*.

PRESENT TENSE OF *LAY*:   The settlers always *lay* their clothes out in the sun to dry.

PAST TENSE OF *LIE*:   Because she was tired, my mother *lay* down for a nap after dinner.

More Practice

Language Lab CD-ROM
• Using Verbs: Troublesome Verb Pairs lesson
On-line Exercise Bank
• Section 22.3
Grammar Exercise Workbook
• pp. 119–120

Answer Key

> **Exercise 28**

1. did
2. have
3. isn't
4. did
5. gone

☑ **ONGOING ASSESSMENT: Monitor and Reinforce**

If students miss more than two items in Exercise 28–30, refer them to the following for additional practice.

In the Textbook	Print Resources	Technology
Section Review, Ex. 31–33, p. 513	Grammar Exercise Workbook, pp. 119–120	On-Line Exercise Bank, Section 22.3

TIME SAVERS!

Answers on Transparency Use the Grammar Exercises Answers on Transparencies for Chapter 22 to facilitate correction by students.

On-Line Exercise Bank Have students complete the exercises on computer. The Auto Check feature will grade their work for you!

Critical Viewing

Speculate Students may say that the man is raising his hand as he rises in the boat in order to raise the attention of someone onshore.

Customize for
Bodily/Kinesthetic Learners

Students may find it easier to distinguish between *raise* and *rise*, *lie* and *lay*, *sit* and *set* if they act out the different meanings in class. Note that students will need props for some words.

raise, rise *Raise* has several common meanings: "to lift (something) upward," "to build (something)," "to grow (something)," or "to increase (something)." Its principal parts are *raise, raising, raised,* and *raised. Raise* is usually followed by a direct object.

EXAMPLES:
DO
Raise the colonial flag higher.

DO
Colonists in New Netherland *raised* their children to speak Dutch.

Rise, on the other hand, is usually not followed by a direct object. *Rise* means "to get up," "to go up," or "to be increased." Its principal parts are *rise, rising, rose,* and *risen. Rise* is usually followed by an adverb or a prepositional phrase.

EXAMPLES:
The moon will *rise* at 8:00 P.M.
The sailors *have been rising* before 5:00 A.M. each day.
The waves *have risen* steadily, and the colonists' boat has been unable to land.

▼ **Critical Viewing** Use the verbs *raise* and *rise* correctly to describe the man at the rear of the canoe-like boat and suggest the purpose of his gesture. **[Speculate]**

saw, seen *Seen* is a past participle and can be used as a verb only with a helping verb such as *have* or *has.* If you find you are using *seen* without a helping verb, try using *saw* instead. Otherwise, make sure to add a helping verb before *seen.*

INCORRECT: We *seen* important changes in colonial rule.
               The governor *seen* how the colonists responded.

CORRECT: We *saw* important changes in colonial rule.
             We *have seen* important changes in colonial rule.
             The governor *saw* how the colonists responded.
             The governor *had seen* how the colonists responded.

set, sit These verbs are often confused. The first step in learning to distinguish between *set* and *sit* is to learn their principal parts.

PRINCIPAL PARTS: set   setting   set   set
                         sit   sitting   sat   sat

Set commonly means "to put (something) in a certain place." It is usually followed by a direct object.

                       DO
EXAMPLES: *Set* the candle on top of the mantle.
                           DO
             He *is setting* maps of New York in the rack.
                      DO
             Felix *set* the clock back an hour.
                          DO
             The king *has set* a new governor over the colony.

Sit usually means "to be seated" or "to rest." In its usual meanings, *sit* is never followed by a direct object. In the following examples, the words following the verbs are adverbs and prepositional phrases.

EXAMPLES: The duke's castle *sits* high up on that mountain.

             The governor's council *has been sitting* in a private session for several hours.

             Queen Mary *sat* for a portrait.

             A book on New York history *has sat* on that library shelf for two weeks.

📓 Journal Tip

This chapter contains information on the history of New York State. In your journal, take notes on some of the facts and topics that interest you. Then, you can review them later to find a subject for a report.

Integrating Speaking and Listening Skills

Tell students to choose one half-hour TV show and watch and listen very carefully. They should note every time someone uses words or grammar incorrectly. Tomorrow they can bring in their lists of errors and tell how to correct them. Students may wish to do this with a partner.

Integrating Vocabulary Skills

Dialect Explain that people from different parts of the United States use some words differently. For example, in some regions, people often use *set* to mean "sit," as in "Come over and set for a while." Dialect is usually a very old form of a language and is not considered incorrect. Students should always be aware of standard usage, however.

Customize for
Visual/Spatial Learners

Ask students to create simple drawings to show the differences between verbs that are often confused. Challenge them to try to show differences between past and present in their drawings.

1. lay
2. sit
3. rise
4. saw
5. lie

▶ **Exercise 30**

1. correct
2. The charters he passed could've (or could have) done a lot for New York before the Revolutionary War.
3. The newly crowned King James II, former Duke of York, saw a different course for New York, however.
4. correct
5. Now, both New York and New England lay within the new colony's boundaries.
6. A royal governor was to sit and watch closely over the colony.
7. King James should have seen how unhappy New Yorkers were about being linked with New England.
8. Their anger rose even more when the king dismissed Governor Dongan.
9. correct
10. After that, several New Yorkers had gone to meet with Governor Andros in his Boston offices.

22.3

▶ **Exercise 29** Avoiding Problems With Troublesome Verbs

For each of the sentences below, choose the correct verb from the pair in parentheses, and write it on your paper.

EXAMPLE: The governor (sat, set) the idea before the Colonial Assembly.

ANSWER: set

1. The idea for the Charter of Liberties came to Governor Dongan one night as he (lay, laid) in his bed.
2. According to the charter, a group of colonial legislators would (sit, set) together to discuss and pass new laws.
3. They would also decide how high the tax rate must (rise, raise) to meet the colony's needs.
4. The charter also (saw, seen) to it that citizens would be guaranteed trial by jury and freedom of worship.
5. According to the charter, many important decisions would (lie, lay) with the people themselves instead of with the governor.

▶ **Exercise 30** Revising to Correct Misused Verbs Rewrite each sentence below on your paper, correcting any misused verbs. If a verb is used correctly, write *correct.*

1. Sadly, the groundwork for liberty laid by Governor Dongan was torn up before it could be put into effect.
2. The charters he passed could of done a lot for New York before the Revolutionary War.
3. The newly crowned King James II, former Duke of York, seen a different course for New York, however.
4. He set New York within the boundaries of New England.
5. Now, both New York and New England laid within the new colony's boundaries.
6. A royal governor was to set and watch closely over the colony.
7. King James should have saw how unhappy New Yorkers were about being linked with New England.
8. Their anger raised even more when the king dismissed Governor Dongan.
9. They raised protests when they were placed under Sir Edmund Andros, the New England governor.
10. After that, several New Yorkers had went to meet with Governor Andros in his Boston offices.

▶ **More Practice**

Language Lab CD-ROM
• Using Verbs: Troublesome Verb Pairs lesson
On-line Exercise Bank
• Section 22.3
Grammar Exercise Workbook
• pp. 119–120

☑ **ONGOING ASSESSMENT: Assess Mastery**

Use the following resources to assess student mastery of troublesome verbs.

In the Textbook	Technology
Chapter Review, Ex. 42, p. 515	On-Line Exercise Bank, Section 22.3

Section 22.3 Section Review

GRAMMAR EXERCISES 31–36

Exercise 31 Recognizing Verbs That Use Direct Objects Write each verb on your paper. Write *yes* next to each verb that usually takes a direct object and *no* next to each one that does not.

1. raised
2. laid
3. lie
4. rise
5. sat
6. set
7. lay (past tense)
8. rose
9. sit
10. lay (present tense)

Exercise 32 Revising to Correct Misused Verbs On your paper, rewrite each incorrect sentence, and correct the misused verb. Write *correct* if the verb is used correctly.

1. She laid down for a nap.
2. The council will raise the issue.
3. They should've acted more quickly.
4. The king should of left the colony alone.
5. The matters have went before the king.
6. James done a terrible job of ruling.
7. The level of unhappiness has raised.
8. We seen to it that our views were noted.
9. The governor sat the plans for the city before the colonists.
10. They saw the plans and protested.

Exercise 33 Revising to Correct Usage of Troublesome Verbs Rewrite the following sentences, correcting the misused verbs. If the verb is used correctly, write *correct*.

1. Tensions raised between the English and the French in the 1680's.
2. It ain't hard to see why: They both wanted American colonies.
3. New York lay between the opposing forces.

4. Each nation would of liked to control New York's lakes.
5. They both seen the importance of controlling the Mohawk and Hudson rivers, along with the lakes.
6. The Iroquois, who held a strategic position near the waterways, did remain neutral at first.
7. However, in the French and Indian War, they had went into battle.
8. Some Iroquois were persuaded to raise up in arms to help the British.
9. Other Iroquois sat an alliance with the French.
10. In 1763, the British, with Iroquois help, won the war and seen to it that the French left New York for good.

Exercise 34 Find It in Your Reading Look through magazines and newspapers to find sentences in which troublesome verbs are used correctly.

Exercise 35 Find It in Your Writing Look through your writing portfolio. Find examples of sentences in which you have used some of the troublesome verbs discussed in this section. Make certain that you have used them correctly.

Exercise 36 Writing Application Imagine that you are upset at the dismissal of Governor Dongan by King James II (see Exercise 30). Write a brief letter to the king, raising some issues about what you think he should have done. Try to use some of the troublesome verbs discussed in this section.

Answer Key continued

Exercise 35

Find It in Your Writing
Students should correct any verbs they have used incorrectly in their writing. Ask students to try rewriting the sentences to avoid using troublesome verbs.

Exercise 36

Writing Application
You might allow students to do further library research on this period of New York history.

ASSESS and CLOSE

Section Review

Each of these exercises correlates to a concept covered in the section on troublesome verbs, pages 508–512. The exercises many be used for more practice, for reteaching, or for review of the Key Concepts presented. Answers for all chapter exercises are available in *Grammar Exercises Answers on Transparencies* in your teaching resources.

Answer Key

Exercise 31

1. raised—yes
2. laid—yes
3. lie—no
4. rise—no
5. sat—no
6. set—yes
7. lay—no
8. rose—no
9. sit—no
10. lay—yes

Exercise 32

1. She <u>lay</u> down for a nap.
2. correct
3. correct
4. The king should <u>have</u> left the colony alone.
5. The matters have <u>gone</u> before the king.
6. James <u>did</u> a terrible job of ruling.
7. The level of unhappiness has <u>risen</u>.
8. We <u>have seen</u> (or <u>saw</u>) to it that our views were noted.
9. The governor <u>set</u> the plans for the city before the colonists.
10. correct

Exercise 33

1. rose
2. isn't
3. correct
4. have
5. saw
6. correct
7. gone
8. rise
9. set
10. saw

Exercise 34

Find It in Your Reading
Students should find examples of correct verb usage of troublesome verbs. Have students look for examples of such verbs not listed in these pages.

continued

CHAPTER REVIEW

Each of these exercises correlates with concepts covered in the chapter on using verbs, pages 490–512. These exercises may be used for more practice, for reteaching, or for review of the Key Concepts presented. Answers for all exercises are available in *Grammar Exercises Answers on Transparencies* in your teaching resources.

Answer Key

> **Exercise 37**

1. present participle, regular
2. past, regular
3. past participle, irregular
4. present, regular
5. past participle, regular
6. past participle, irregular
7. past, irregular
8. past, irregular
9. present participle, regular
10. past participle, irregular

> **Exercise 38**

Answers will vary; samples follow.

1. We have found a great deal of information at the library. (irregular)
2. She wished she could have been there. (regular)
3. They left the theater after the movie. (irregular)
4. My parents have stayed at a hotel. (regular)
5. I have tied her shoelaces so that she won't trip. (regular)
6. He gave her a big kiss. (irregular)
7. How many clubs did you belong to last year? (regular)
8. James presented the award last night. (regular)
9. The kittens have done very well. (irregular)
10. I have seen that movie too! (irregular)

> **Exercise 39**

1. past
2. past
3. present
4. past participle
5. past
6. present participle
7. past participle
8. present
9. present participle
10. past participle

Chapter 22 Chapter Review

GRAMMAR EXERCISES 37–46

> **Exercise 37** Identifying Principal Parts and Regular and Irregular Verbs

Identify the principal part used to form each of the following verbs. Then, label the verb *regular* or *irregular*.

1. fetching
2. practiced
3. have found
4. type
5. have listed
6. has put
7. fell
8. laid
9. raising
10. have lain

> **Exercise 38** Using and Identifying Regular and Irregular Verbs

Write a sentence for each verb below—five should be in the past tense, and five in the present perfect tense. Then, label each verb *regular* or *irregular*.

1. find
2. wish
3. leave
4. stay
5. tie
6. give
7. belong
8. present
9. do
10. see

> **Exercise 39** Recognizing Principal Parts Used to Form Tenses

Identify the principal part used to form each underlined verb.

1. In July 1776, the New York Congress <u>ratified</u> the Declaration of Independence.
2. Then, it <u>changed</u> its own name to the Convention of Representatives of the State of New York.
3. New York <u>drafts</u> its first state constitution the next year.
4. They <u>had decided</u> to set up a legislature.
5. Consequently, the first legislature <u>met</u> in Kingston later that same year.
6. The citizens of New York <u>were holding</u> their first election as a state in 1777.

7. Soon, they <u>had chosen</u> George Clinton as their first governor.
8. He also <u>serves</u> as a delegate to the Second Continental Congress.
9. New constitutions and elections <u>were appearing</u> all over New England.
10. The revolutionary spirit <u>had caught</u> fire there.

> **Exercise 40** Identifying and Using Verb Tenses

Identify the tense of each of the following verbs, indicating whether it is in basic or progressive form. Then, write a sentence using each one.

1. have been washing
2. have extended
3. will name
4. am knowing
5. had been noticing
6. will have been entering
7. had patterned
8. have worked
9. was writing
10. will have fainted

> **Exercise 41** Identifying the Tenses of Verbs

Write the tense of the underlined verb in each sentence below.

1. The American Revolution <u>had lasted</u> eight years when it ended in 1783.
2. Almost one third of the battles <u>had been fought</u> in New York State.
3. Americans <u>were capturing</u> key forts on Lake Champlain during early fighting.
4. By September 1776, the British <u>are occupying</u> New York City.
5. They <u>hold</u> it until the end of the war.
6. The Americans <u>will be experiencing</u> a victory at Saratoga in October 1777.

> **Exercise 40**

Sentences will vary.

1. present perfect progressive
2. present perfect
3. future
4. present progressive
5. past perfect progressive
6. future perfect progressive
7. past perfect
8. present perfect
9. past progressive
10. future perfect

> **Exercise 41**

1. past perfect
2. past perfect
3. past progressive
4. present progressive
5. present
6. future progressive
7. future
8. past
9. past progressive
10. future perfect

7. This victory <u>will become</u> a turning point of the war.
8. The British <u>planned</u> to occupy Albany.
9. From Albany, they <u>were going</u> to control the Hudson River.
10. By controlling the Hudson, they think they <u>will have cut</u> New England off from the other colonies.

> **Exercise 42** Revising Usage of Troublesome Verbs Rewrite the following sentences, correcting the verbs. If a verb is used correctly, write *correct.*

1. When the Iroquois seen the Revolution break out, they didn't know which side to support.
2. They couldn't decide if they should have went with the Americans or not.
3. They thought perhaps they should just set quietly and wait.
4. They also couldn't agree if they should lie low and remain neutral.
5. Some individual Iroquois tribes laid plans to join with the British.
6. That is just what the Mohawks done.
7. In the summer of 1779, an American army was risen to fight the Mohawks.
8. The ending to this story ain't pleasant.
9. The American army went on to a decisive victory.
10. The Mohawks realized that they should of sided with the Americans.

> **Exercise 43** Using Verb Tenses On your paper, write logical sentences, using the verbs and tenses given below.

1. Use the present tense of *like* in a sentence about a friend.
2. Use the past tense of *want* in a sentence about your lunch.
3. Use the future tense of *go* in a sentence about next weekend.
4. Use the present perfect tense of *finish* in a sentence about your homework.
5. Ask a question using the present progressive tense of *think.*

> **Exercise 44** Supplying the Correct Tense On your paper, supply the form of the verb indicated in parentheses.

(1) After the Revolution ended, many New Yorkers (oppose—past perfect) a strong national government. (2) They (prefer—past progressive) to retain a weaker structure that (place—past) more power with the states. (3) When delegates (draw—past) up the U.S. Constitution in 1787, Alexander Hamilton was the only New Yorker to sign the final draft. (4) He (hope—past perfect progressive) that more New Yorkers would join him. (5) New York finally (ratify—past) the Constitution.

> **Exercise 45** Revision Practice Rewrite the paragraph below, correcting all errors in verb usage.

(1) In the 1750's, Samuel Stringer become one of Albany's leading citizens. (2) He had came to Albany in the 1750's while he holded a position as a surgeon with the British army. (3) Soon, Stringer had took in his new city. (4) He builded up a successful medical practice in Albany, and his income steadily raised. (5) Many people thunk that Stringer would of supported the British during the Revolution. (6) However, he done just the opposite. (7) He seen that his loyalty was with the revolutionary movement. (8) In 1775, he was chose for the post of chief physician of all the hospitals in the North. (9) He begun work on a new hospital to train American army doctors. (10) Following the war, Stringer starts the first medical library in Albany.

> **Exercise 46** Writing Application Write a paragraph about an important person in your city or town. Use at least three different verb tenses in your paragraph. Try to use both progressive and basic forms.

Chapter Review • 515

---

1. When the Iroquois <u>saw</u> the Revolution break out, they didn't know which side to support.
2. They couldn't decide if they should have <u>gone</u> with the Americans or not.
3. They thought perhaps they should just <u>sit</u> quietly and wait.
4. correct
5. correct
6. That is just what the Mohawks <u>did</u>.
7. In the summer of 1779, an American army was <u>raised</u> to fight the Mohawks.
8. The ending to this story <u>isn't</u> pleasant.
9. correct
10. The Mohawks realized that they should <u>have</u> sided with the Americans.

> **Exercise 43**

Sample sentences are given.

1. I like spending time with my friend Carla.
2. I wanted peanut butter and jelly for lunch.
3. We will go to the beach next weekend.
4. I have finished my homework.
5. Can you tell me what I am thinking?

> **Exercise 44**

1. had opposed
2. were preferring; placed
3. drew
4. had been hoping
5. ratified

> **Exercise 45**

1. In the 1750's, Samuel Stringer <u>became</u> one of Albany's leading citizens.
2. He had <u>come</u> to Albany in the 1750's while he <u>held</u> a position as a surgeon with the British army.
3. Soon, Stringer had <u>taken</u> in his new city.
4. He <u>built</u> up a successful medical practice in Albany, and his income steadily <u>rose</u>.
5. Many people <u>thought</u> that Stringer would <u>have</u> supported the British during the Revolution.
6. However, he <u>did</u> just the opposite.
7. He <u>saw</u> that his loyalty was with the revolutionary movement.
8. In 1775, he was <u>chosen</u> for the post of chief physician of all the hospitals in the North.
9. He <u>began</u> work on a new hospital to train American army doctors.

continued

Answer Key continued

10. Following the war, Stringer <u>started</u> the first medical library in Albany.

> **Exercise 46**

Writing Application
Students' paragraphs should contain at least three different verb tenses. Have students count the uses of each verb tense, and write more sentences using the tense they used least.

Using Verbs

Teaching Resources: Test Preparation Workbook, pp. 43–44

1. Explain to students that they should look for other verbs in the passage, as well as other context clues, to get an idea of the time frame. This will help them choose the correct verb tense or form.

2. In the sample passage, the word *yesterday* and the verb *rode* indicate that the action occurred in the past, which rules out A and B. The word *when* suggests that one past action was continuing when another occurred. A past progressive tense is indicated, which rules out A and B.

3. Have a volunteer explain his or her thinking for question 2.

Standardized Test Preparation Workshop

Using Verbs

Your knowledge of verb usage is frequently measured on standardized tests. Your ability to determine the correct tense of a verb—present, present perfect, past, past perfect, future, and future perfect and their progressive forms—is tested when you must choose a verb or verb phrase to complete a sentence. When choosing a verb, first read the sentence aloud and determine when the action is taking place. Then, choose a verb that indicates the same point in time or tense as the sentence.

The following test items will give you practice with the format of questions that test verb usage.

Test Tip

• Read the sentence quietly to yourself several times. Each time, substitute one of the answer choices in place of the blank. Eliminate those choices that sound awkward or change the meaning of the sentence.

Sample Test Items	Answers and Explanations

Read the passage, and choose the letter of the word or group of words that belongs in each space.
 	
Yesterday, I ____(1)____ my bike when I ____(2)____ my mother call me. Then I rode home.
 	
1 **A** riding
  B will have been riding
  C had ridden
  D was riding
	The correct answer is *D.* The passage hints at a continuing action that took place at the time of another past event. Therefore, the past progressive form *was riding* is the correct choice for completing the sentence.

2 **F** heard
  G had heard
  H had been hearing
  J was hearing
	The correct answer is *F.* The passage indicates an action that occurred in the past. The *had* in G and H implies that the action happened before the bike riding, while *was hearing* implies a continuing action, which doesn't make sense. Therefore, the past tense verb *heard* is the correct choice for completing the sentence.

TEST-TAKING TIP

When dealing with questions that test students' knowledge of verb tenses, it might help students to write the tense names in "chronological" order, from past to present to future. This way, when they determine the time frame of a sentence or passage, they can look at the order of tenses to check which tense would work correctly in the context of the passage's time frame.

> **Practice 1** **Directions:** Read the passage, and choose the letter of the word or group of words that belongs in each space.

Often, a bicycle __(1)__ by those who __(2)__ the age of sixteen or do not have access to mass transit. However, whatever your size or shape, you __(3)__ the benefits of bike riding. Just hop on, and you __(4)__ on your way. No doubt you __(5)__ that, although bikes __(6)__ easy to use, they __(7)__ a danger if not used properly. Soon, in most areas, wearing a helmet __(8)__ the law. Also, use of hand signals __(9)__ required. By following the rules, you __(10)__ a safer environment for yourself and others on the road.

1 A rode
  B has been riding
  C is riding
  D is ridden

2 F don't reach
  G have not reached
  H are not reaching
  J have not been reaching

3 A enjoy
  B will have enjoyed
  C enjoyed
  D had enjoyed

4 F have been
  G will be
  H will have been
  J were

5 A have learned
  B were learning
  C learn
  D had learned

6 F are being
  G were being
  H are
  J have been

7 A present
  B did present
  C were presenting
  D have presented

8 F become
  G have become
  H became
  J will have become

9 A was
  B will have been
  C will be
  D have been

10 F create
  G have been creating
  H will have created
  J had created

> **Practice 1**
1. D
2. G
3. B
4. G
5. A
6. H
7. A
8. J
9. C
10. F

In-Depth Lesson Plan

	LESSON FOCUS	PRINT AND MEDIA RESOURCES
DAY 1	**Nominative and Objective Pronouns** Students learn and apply concepts of the nominative and objective case of pronouns (pp. 520–524).	*Language Lab* **CD-ROM,** Using Pronouns; *On-Line Exercise Bank,* Section 23 **Teaching Resources** *Grammar Exercise Workbook,* pp. 121–124; *Grammar Exercises Answers on Transparency,* Ch. 23
DAY 2	**Possessive Pronouns** Students learn and apply concepts of the possessive case of pronouns and do the Hands-on Grammar activity (pp. 525–527).	*Language Lab* **CD-ROM,** Using Pronouns; *On-Line Exercise Bank,* Section 23 **Teaching Resources** *Grammar Exercise Workbook,* pp. 125–126; *Grammar Exercises Answers on Transparency,* Ch. 23; *Hands-on Grammar Book,* Ch. 23
DAY 3	**Review and Assess** Students review chapter and demonstrate mastery of pronoun cases (pp. 528–531).	*On-Line Exercise Bank,* Section 23 **Teaching Resources** *Grammar Exercises Answers on Transparency,* Ch. 23; *Formal Assessment,* Ch. 23

Accelerated Lesson Plan

	LESSON FOCUS	PRINT AND MEDIA RESOURCES
DAY 1	**Pronoun Case** Students cover concepts and usage of pronoun case as determined by the Diagnostic Test (pp. 518–527).	*Language Lab* **CD-ROM,** Using Pronouns; *On-Line Exercise Bank,* Section 23 **Teaching Resources** *Grammar Exercise Workbook,* pp. 121–126; *Grammar Exercises Answers on Transparency,* Ch. 23; *Hands-on Grammar Book,* Ch. 23
DAY 2	**Review and Assess** Students review chapter and demonstrate mastery of use of pronoun case (pp. 528–531).	*On-Line Exercise Bank,* Section 23 **Teaching Resources** *Grammar Exercises Answers on Transparency,* Ch. 23; *Formal Assessment,* Ch. 23

Options for Adapting Lesson Plans

HOMEWORK
Have students complete any section of the chapter for homework.

FEATURES
Extend coverage with the Grammar in Literature feature (p. 525), and the Standardized Test Preparation Workshop (p. 530).

TECHNOLOGY
Students can use the On-Line Exercise Bank to complete the exercises on computer. The Auto Check feature will grade their work.

INTEGRATED SKILLS COVERAGE

Grammar in Literature
SE p. 525

Reading
Find It In Your Reading, SE p. 527

Writing
Find It In Your Writing, SE p. 527
Writing Application SE pp. 529

Speaking and Listening
SE p. 521

Spelling
SE p. 525

Real-World Connection
ATE p. 524

Viewing and Representing
Critical Viewing, SE pp. 518, 522, 524, 526

ASSESSMENT SUPPORT

Standardized Test Preparation SE p. 530; ATE pp. 523, 526
Standardized Test Preparation Workbook, pp. 45–46
Formal Assessment, Ch. 23

MEETING INDIVIDUAL NEEDS

Less Advanced Students ATE pp. 521, 523, See also Ongoing Assessment, pp. 521, 522
ESL Students ATE p. 524
More Advanced Students ATE pp. 521, 522

BLOCK SCHEDULING

Pacing Suggestions
For 90-minute Blocks
• Administer the Diagnostic Test to students to determine instructional coverage
• Have students complete the necessary exercises in class. Use the Hands-on Grammar activity to provide a change of pace.

Resources for Varying Instruction
• *Language Lab* CD-ROM If your students have access to hardware, a 90-minute block provides an ideal opportunity for students to work on computer.

Professional Development Support
• *How to Manage Instruction in the Block* This Teaching Resource provides management and activity suggestions.

MEDIA AND TECHNOLOGY

For the Student
• *Language Lab* CD-ROM, Using Pronouns
• *On-Line Exercise Bank,* Ch. 23

For the Teacher
• *Resource Pro* CD-ROM

WRITING AND GRAMMAR WEB SITE

The Interactive Writing and Grammar Website provides a wide array of support for students, teachers, and parents. Grammar support includes:

• *On-Line Exercise Bank* with Auto Check scoring
• Diagnostic and assessment support

www.phschool.com

LITERATURE CONNECTIONS

Related selections from *Prentice Hall Literature: Timeless Voices, Timeless Themes,* Bronze:
"Was Tarzan a Three-Bandage Man?," by Bill Cosby, SE p. 525

Chapter
23 Using Pronouns

Lesson Objectives

1. To understand and recognize the nominative, objective, and possessive cases.
2. To write with increasing accuracy when using the pronoun case.

Critical Viewing

Infer Students may say that the batter is about to swing *his* bat. *He* is getting ready.

23 Using Pronouns

There are three different kinds, or cases, of personal pronouns: nominative, objective, and possessive. Pronouns are used to give writing variety. For example, when reading or writing about the history of baseball, it would be monotonous to repeat the noun *Brooklyn Dodgers* every time a reference to this team is made. Using a pronoun such as *they* allows the writing to flow more smoothly.

▲ **Critical Viewing**
What is about to happen in this photograph? Use the personal pronouns *he* and *his* in your answer. **[Infer]**

✔ **ONGOING ASSESSMENT: Diagnose**

If students miss more than one item in each category, direct them to the relevant pages of the text and assign exercises for practice and review.

Using Pronouns	Diagnostic Test Items	Teach	Practice	Chapter Review
Skill Check A				
Pronoun Case	A 1–5	pp. 520–521	Ex. 1	Ex. 10
Skill Check B				
Nominative Case	B 6–10	pp. 521–522	Ex. 2–3	Ex. 11
Skill Check C				
Objective Case	C 11–15	pp. 523–524	Ex. 4–6	Ex. 12

Diagnostic Test

Directions: Write all answers on a separate sheet of paper.

Skill Check A. List the personal pronouns in the sentences below. Label each pronoun *nominative, objective,* or *possessive.*

1. Our team is the wild-card team, and it will be included in the playoffs.
2. It was the Cougars who won in their division, and they will now be in the playoffs as well.
3. They are an excellent team, and we will probably see them in the county championship series.
4. The league also has All-Star Games, but it holds those in the summer.
5. The All-Star Game matches the best players in each league, so you should try to see one someday!

Skill Check B. Write each underlined pronoun in the nominative case. Then, label the pronoun subject *(S)* or predicate pronoun *(PP)*.

6. Jenny and I started our careers in T-ball with my father's help.
7. It was he who coached our first team.
8. Jenny knows that no one hits as well as she can.
9. It was she who led our team to victory this season.
10. Next year, we are going to play without the T-ball stand.

Skill Check C. Identify how each underlined pronoun in the objective case is used.

11. Baseball uses equipment such as balls, bats, gloves, cleats, helmets, and pads; all players use one or more of them.
12. The gloves and cleats were used by her.
13. The coach showed us the cork center of the baseball.
14. Knowing the equipment well helps us in the game.
15. He is the catcher, so the larger, more padded glove belongs to him.

Skill Check D. Write the correct possessive pronoun from the pair in parentheses.

16. The manager is responsible for giving the team (its, it's) strategy.
17. It is (his', his) choice who plays first base.
18. Umpires have complete authority over the game; therefore, the responsibility of enforcing rules is (their's, theirs).
19. That manager is (ours, our's).
20. (My, Mine) dad is an umpire, and he removed the pitcher from the game.

Answer Key

Diagnostic Test

Each item in the Diagnostic Test corresponds to a specific section in the Using Pronouns chapter. This will enable you to tailor instruction to the particular needs of your students. See "Ongoing Assessment: Diagnose" on the bottom of page 518 for further details.

Skill Check A

1. Our—possessive; it—nominative
2. It—nominative; their—possessive; they—nominative
3. They—nominative; we—nominative; them—objective
4. it—nominative
5. you—nominative

Skill Check B

6. I—S
7. It—S; he—PP
8. she—S
9. It—S; she—PP
10. we—S

Skill Check C

11. object of a preposition
12. object of a preposition
13. indirect object
14. direct object
15. object of a preposition

Skill Check D

16. its
17. his
18. theirs
19. ours
20. My

✓ ONGOING ASSESSMENT: Diagnose *continued*

Using Pronouns	Diagnostic Test Items	Teach	Practice	Chapter Review
Skill Check D				
Possessive Case	D 16–20	pp. 525–526	Ex. 7–8	Ex. 13
Cumulative Reviews and Applications				Ex. 15–16

⏱ TIME SAVERS!

Answers on Transparency Use the Grammar Exercises Answers on Transparencies for Chapter 23 to facilitate correction by students.

On-Line Exercise Bank Have students complete the Diagnostic Test on computer. The Auto Check feature will grade their work for you!

PREPARE and ENGAGE

Interest GRABBER Use the Hands-on Grammar activity on page 527 to introduce the topics to students. Materials and procedures are specified in the Step-by-Step Guide on that page of this Teacher's Edition.

Activate Prior Knowledge

Have students work in pairs. Ask them to write a brief five- or six-sentence story in which each of them is a character in the story. However, they may use each person's name only once in the story. Ask students what they substituted for their names (probably nicknames, names referring to relationships, and pronouns).

TEACH

The Three Cases of Personal Pronouns

1. Direct students' attention to the chart, noting that each case has a specific function or functions within a sentence.

2. Review subject, predicate pronoun, direct object, indirect object, and object of a preposition using the following examples:

   I am happy. (subject)

   The drummer is he. (predicate pronoun)

   Dad drove me *to school.* (direct object)

   Al gave you *the ball.* (indirect object)

   Bill brought the bicycle to me. (object of preposition)

3. Point out to students that objective and possessive cases might be easier to remember if they notice that all uses of the objective case contain the word *object*, and realize that another word for *ownership* is *possession*.

Answer Key

▶ **Exercise 1** *(p. 521)*

1. possessive
2. nominative
3. objective
4. nominative
5. objective

520

Many pronouns change form according to usage. *Case* is the relationship between a pronoun's form and its use. This chapter will explain the three cases and show you how to use the various forms of pronouns correctly.

The personal pronouns listed in Section 14.2 are presented in three groups: those that refer to the person speaking; those that refer to the person spoken to; and those that refer to the person, place, or thing spoken about. Pronouns can also be grouped according to three cases.

▶ **KEY CONCEPT** Pronouns have three cases: *nominative*, *objective*, and *possessive*. ■

Identifying the Three Cases of Personal Pronouns

The personal pronouns are grouped in the following chart according to the three cases.

THE USES OF PERSONAL PRONOUNS BY CASE	
Nominative Case	**Use in Sentence**
I, we you he, she, it, they	Subject of a Verb Predicate Pronoun
Objective Case	**Use in Sentence**
me, us you him, her, it, them	Direct Object Indirect Object Object of a Preposition
Possessive Case	**Use in Sentence**
my, mine, our, ours your, yours his, her, hers, its, their, theirs	To Show Ownership

SUBJECT OF A VERB:	<u>We</u> badly wanted to see the game.
PREDICATE NOMINATIVE:	It was <u>they</u> who got the tickets.
DIRECT OBJECT:	Please give me <u>them</u>.
INDIRECT OBJECT:	Please give <u>me</u> the tickets.
OBJECT OF A PREPOSITION:	Please give the tickets to <u>me</u>.
TO SHOW OWNERSHIP:	They are <u>our</u> tickets, not theirs.

520 • Using Pronouns

Theme: Baseball

In this chapter, you will learn about using pronouns. The examples and exercises are about baseball.

Cross-Curricular Connection: Physical Education

🔵 Learn More

Pronouns are used to replace nouns. For more information on nouns, refer to Chapter 14.

⏱ TIME AND RESOURCE MANAGER

Resources
Print: Grammar Exercise Workbook, pp. 121–126; Hands-on Grammar Activity Book, Chapter 23
Technology: Language Lab CD-ROM, Usisng Pronouns; On-Line Exercise Bank, Section 23

In-Depth Coverage	Accelerated Pace
• Work through all key concepts, pp. 520–526. • Assign and review Exercises 1–8. • Read and discuss Grammar in Literature, p. 525. • Do the Hands-on Grammar Activity, p. 527.	• Assign pp. 520–526 for independent student review. • Review Ex. 8 (Checking the Case of Personal Pronouns), p. 526.

> ◄ **Exercise 1** Identifying Case Identify the case of the personal pronouns that are underlined in the following sentences.

EXAMPLE: Didn't Richard give <u>her</u> the directions?

ANSWER: objective

1. Baseball got <u>its</u> start from other stickball games.
2. <u>It</u> is similar to a game called rounders.
3. During the Civil War, the game was introduced to <u>us</u> by traveling soldiers.
4. <u>They</u> played and provided free entertainment, while owners of the ball fields made profits.
5. The players became professional in 1869, when owners of the ball fields first began to pay <u>them</u>.

Using the Nominative Case

Personal pronouns in the nominative case have two uses in sentences:

> ◄ **KEY CONCEPT** Use the nominative case for the subject of a verb. ■

SUBJECTS: *I* collect baseballs.
              She wrote a letter to the President.

> ◄ **KEY CONCEPT** Use the nominative case when a pronoun is used as a predicate nominative. ■

A predicate nominative renames the subject. Pronouns used as predicate nominatives always follow a form of the verb *be* or a verb phrase ending in *be* or *been*.

PREDICATE   It is *she*.
NOMINATIVE: It might have been *they*.

To make sure you are using the correct case of a personal pronoun in a compound subject, use just the pronoun with the verb in the sentence. In the following examples, "Me collect" clearly sounds wrong. The nominative case *I* is correct and should be used.

INCORRECT: Gina and *me* collect stamps.
             Me and Gina collect stamps.

CORRECT: Gina and *I* collect stamps.

More Practice

Language Lab
CD-ROM
• Using Pronouns lesson
On-line
Exercise Bank
• Section 23
Grammar Exercise
Workbook
• pp. 121–122

Speaking and Listening Tip

Accustom yourself to using nominative pronouns correctly. With one or two classmates, take turns reading aloud the correct examples on this page and Exercises 2 and 3 on the next page.

Using the Nominative Case

1. Ask students to define subject and linking verb, and give an example of each in a sentence.

2. Point out that identifying a subject—especially a compound subject—and linking verbs in a sentence can help students determine when the nominative case should be used.

3. Have students read the examples, and then have volunteers write sentences on the board to demonstrate understanding of correct usage.

Customize for
Less Advanced Students

Review linking verbs, which students learned about in Chapter 15. Review conjugations of the verb *to be* with students, pointing out how it is used in the nominative case. For example: It *was they* who rescued the dog.

Customize for
More Advanced Students

Have students work with partners to write a three-sentence paragraph about baseball in which each sentence contains a pronoun in a different case. Example: *I* like the New York Yankees. (nominative) *My* team has won more World Series than any other. (possessive) I have followed *them* for years. (objective)

Using Pronouns • 521

☑ **ONGOING ASSESSMENT: Prerequisite Skills**

If students have difficulty with the three cases of personal pronouns, you may find it necessary to review the following to assure coverage for prerequisite knowledge.

In the Textbook	Print Resources	Technology
Pronouns, pp. 301–309 Linking Verbs, pp. 320–325	Grammar Exercise Workbook, pp. 7–12, 15–18	On-Line Exercise Bank, Sections 14.2 and 15.2

23

Exercise 2 Identifying the Use of Personal Pronouns in the Nominative Case Write each nominative pronoun in the following sentences, and indicate how each one is used.

EXAMPLE: She memorized the rules of the game.
ANSWER: She (subject)

1. Josh Gibson hit approximately 800 home runs in the 17 years he played baseball.
2. Many of his statistics are undocumented, but they are known to be outstanding.
3. It is known that Gibson had a lifetime batting average of .347.
4. Some people were opposed to integrating professional baseball; it was they who opposed the signing of African American players.
5. Josh Gibson died the year that Jackie Robinson signed with the Dodgers. Soon, we saw the integration of professional major league baseball.

Exercise 3 Using Personal Pronouns in the Nominative Case Complete each of the following sentences by writing an appropriate nominative pronoun. Then, indicate how each pronoun is used in the sentence.

EXAMPLE: ___?___ think that this photograph is best.
ANSWER: We (subject)

1. ___?___ were excited when he won Rookie of the Year in 1947.
2. ___?___ was an exciting and controversial time in baseball.
3. The person who made the Dodgers the first multiracial team was ___?___ .
4. The biggest fans of Jackie Robinson were Jenny, Sarah, and ___?___ .
5. ___?___ read every baseball biography.

▲ Critical Viewing Use the nominative pronouns it and he in a sentence describing one of Jackie Robinson's achievements in baseball. **[Relate]**

522 • Using Pronouns

Using the Objective Case

Personal pronouns in the objective case have three uses:

KEY CONCEPT Use the objective case (1) for a direct object, (2) for an indirect object, and (3) for the object of a preposition. ■

DIRECT OBJECTS:	Kate invited *me* to the game.
	The dog chased *us* across the lawn.
INDIRECT OBJECTS:	Diego wrote *her* a letter.
	I told *them* the story.
OBJECTS	Were they talking to *me?*
OF PREPOSITIONS:	Give this message to *them.*

Mistakes with pronouns in the objective case usually occur only when the object is compound.

INCORRECT:	Kate invited Ron and *I* to the game.
	Diego wrote his mother and *she* a letter.
	Were they talking about Lois and *I?*

Again, to check whether the case of the personal pronoun is correct, use the pronoun by itself after the verb or preposition. In the preceding examples, "Kate invited I," "Diego wrote she," and "Were they talking about I?" all sound wrong. Objective pronouns are needed.

CORRECT:	Kate invited Ron and *me* to the game.
	Diego wrote his mother and *her* a letter.
	Were they talking about Lois and *me?*

Exercise 4 Identifying the Use of Personal Pronouns in the Objective Case Write the objective pronouns in the sentences below, and indicate how each one is used.

EXAMPLE:	Baseball has given us many exciting moments.
ANSWER:	us (indirect object)

1. Baseball teams have undergone many changes over the years; World War II caused them to lose many players.
2. When a player had to go to war, there was no one to play for him.
3. Latin American players played for us at that time.
4. If a woman was interested in baseball, the All-American Girl's Baseball League gave her a chance to play.
5. From 1943 to 1954, the league helped promote women athletes and made them into celebrities.

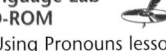

More Practice

Language Lab CD-ROM
• Using Pronouns lesson
On-line Exercise Bank
• Section 23
Grammar Exercise Workbook
• pp. 123–124

Step-by-Step Teaching Guide

Using the Objective Case

1. Remind students that pronouns, like nouns, can be receivers of action. The objective case is used when nouns and pronouns receive action (when they are *objects*).

2. Explain that picking a pronoun based on what sounds right is not as reliable as identifying how the pronoun is used in a sentence or phrase. Review the examples to make sure that students can correctly identify direct and indirect objects and objects of prepositions.

3. Point out to students that *it* and *you* function both as nominative and objective pronouns. This may make determining a pronoun's case in an existing sentence a bit more difficult, which is why it is important to understand how sentence structure determines case.

Customizing for
Less Advanced Students

To help students better understand direct and indirect objects, review how action verbs relate to direct and indirect objects. You could also briefly review prepositions to help students identify prepositional phrases and their objects.

Answer Key

Exercise 4

1. them—direct object
2. him—object of a preposition
3. us—object of a preposition
4. her—indirect object
5. them—direct object

STANDARDIZED TEST PREPARATION WORKSHOP

Grammar and Usage Standardized tests often ask students to identify the grammatically correct version of a sentence. Share the following example with students:

Which of the following sentences is correct?

A. She told Yin and I to meet her at 6 o'clock.

B. Her told Yin and me to meet her at 6 o'clock.

C. She told Yin and me to meet she at 6 o'clock.

D. She told Yin and me to meet her at 6 o'clock.

Students should identify item **D** as the correct version. The other versions all contain errors in pronoun cases.

TIME SAVERS!

Answers on Transparency
Use the Grammar Exercises Answers on Transparencies for Chapter 23 to facilitate correction by students.

On-Line Exercise Bank
Have students complete the exercises on computer. The Auto Check feature will grade their work for you!

23

▶ **Exercise 5** Using Personal Pronouns in the Objective Case

Complete each of the following sentences by writing an appropriate objective pronoun. Then, indicate how each pronoun is used in the sentence.

EXAMPLE: Why didn't Edwin invite ___?___ to the game?
ANSWER: me (direct object)

1. If we hadn't recruited women and players from other countries, there would have been no one to play for ___?___ .
2. When a player returned after the war, the coach would give ___?___ his position back.
3. Foreign players continued to play for ___?___ even after the return of the veterans.
4. The girl's league lasted only a few years because people didn't follow ___?___ after the regular players returned.
5. Baseball still gives ___?___ many issues to consider.

◀ Critical Viewing Why do you think these women are so happy? Answer using the objective-case pronouns *her* and *them*. **[Draw Conclusions]**

▶ **Exercise 6** Writing Sentences With Objective Pronouns

Write five sentences about an event or activity that has caught your interest. Use objective pronouns as indicated. Of course, you may use other pronouns in your sentences as necessary.

1. *me* or *us* as an indirect object
2. *it* or *them* as a direct object
3. *me*, *us*, or *them* as the object of a preposition
4. *him* or *her* as a direct object
5. *them* or *it* as the object of a preposition

Using the Possessive Case

Personal pronouns in the possessive case show ownership.

▶ **KEY CONCEPT** Use the possessive case of personal pronouns to show possession before nouns. Also, use certain personal pronouns by themselves to show possession. ■

BEFORE NOUNS: The bat found *its* target.
                  Have you seen *their* gloves?
BY THEMSELVES: Is this hat *yours* or *his*?

Notice that personal pronouns ending in -s are never written with an apostrophe.

INCORRECT: *Our's* is the last seat in the row.
               That lemonade is *his'*, not *her's*.
CORRECT: *Ours* is the last seat in the row.
               That lemonade is *his*, not *hers*.

The possessive form of *it* is *its*. *It's* is a contraction for *it is*.

CONTRACTION: *It's* time to start the game.
POSSESSIVE
PRONOUN: A team is only as good as *its* players.

GRAMMAR IN
LITERATURE

from **Was Tarzan a Three-Bandage Man?**
Bill Cosby

In this passage, the nominative pronouns are blue, the objective pronouns are red, and the possessive pronouns are green. What noun does each pronoun replace?

"Why *you* walkin' like that?" said *my* mother one day.
"This is Jackie *Robinson's* walk," *I* proudly replied.
"There's somethin' wrong with *his* shoes?"
"*He's* the fastest man in baseball."
"*He'd* be faster if *he* didn't walk like that. *His* mother should make *him* walk right."

Step-by-Step Teaching Guide

Using the Possessive Case

1. Point out that pronouns differ from nouns in that, rather than adding 's to form the possessive, you use a different word—a possessive pronoun.

2. Review the key concept with students, going over the examples to make sure they understand the two ways possessive pronouns can be used.

3. Practice using possessive pronouns by asking questions, such as the following, and having students answer with a possessive pronoun:

   Whose classroom is this? (ours)

   Whose desk is that? (mine, his, hers)

   Whose desk is this [teacher's desk]? (yours)

4. Have students rewrite their one-word answers into statements that use the noun with the possessive pronoun:

   This is our *classroom.*

   This is my/his/her *desk.*

   That is your *desk.*

Step-by-Step Teaching Guide

Grammar in Literature

1. Have a volunteer read aloud the passage by Bill Cosby.

2. Ask students to identify who is speaking each of the last three lines of dialogue. (line 3—mother, line 4—narrator, line 5—mother)

3. Discuss with students how the use of different pronoun cases helps readers understand what is being said. For instance, if *his* was changed to *the*, how would the reader know if the shoes being discussed were the narrator's, the mother's, or Jackie Robinson's?

More About the Writer

Bill Cosby is an American comedian, actor, and writer. Cosby became the first African American to star in a prime time TV show when he took on a leading role in the adventure series *I Spy* in the 1960's. His *The Cosby Show* was the most popular show on TV in the 1980's. Cosby has been recognized for his work as a humanitarian and educator throughout his career.

525

Spelling Tip

The possessive pronoun *their* does not follow the "i before e except after c" rule.

Answer Key

> **Exercise 7**

1. its
2. his
3. theirs
4. ours
5. his
6. yours
7. It's
8. his
9. yours
10. his

> **Exercise 8**

1. me—I
2. His'—His
3. correct
4. I—me
5. correct; your's—yours
6. I—me
7. correct
8. him—he; correct
9. his'—his
10. me—I

Critical Viewing

Relate Students may say that the ball is worn along *its* seams or the player claimed *his* home run ball.

23

> **Exercise 7** Using Personal Pronouns in the Possessive
Case For each of the following sentences, write the correct personal pronoun from the choices in parentheses.

EXAMPLE: Now that Kim has gone away to school, this room is all (your's, yours).

ANSWER: yours

1. The team plays (it's, its) best at home.
2. The first baseman took (his', his) place near the base.
3. The field is (their's, theirs) to play on until they get three outs.
4. That designated hitter is (our's, ours), but he doesn't play on the field.
5. Center field is (his', his) responsibility.
6. The shortstop position is (your's, yours), so stand between second and third base.
7. (It's, Its) the infielders who throw players out at bases.
8. I play catcher, and the pitching position is (his', his).
9. I always forget which position is (your's, yours).
10. The fastball is (his', his) best pitch.

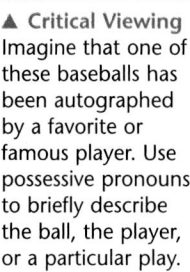

> **Exercise 8** Checking the Case of Personal Pronouns
Write the underlined pronouns in the following sentences that are incorrect. Then, write the form of the pronoun that should be used in formal writing. For sentences with no errors, write *correct*.

EXAMPLE: Is this uniform your's?

ANSWER: your's—yours

1. The three players to strike out were Alex, Willy, and <u>me</u>.
2. <u>His'</u> hit was a high fly ball.
3. When <u>our</u> favorite team came to town, we went to the game.
4. When deciding who should hit first, the coach couldn't decide between her and <u>I</u>.
5. <u>You</u> will be happy to hear that the right-field position is now <u>your's</u>.
6. The coach showed Jose and <u>I</u> the batting order.
7. <u>It's</u> the second out of the inning.
8. It was <u>him</u> who took <u>my</u> glove.
9. The pitcher could not believe that <u>his'</u> was the winning team.
10. Kevin, Larry, and <u>me</u> are playing on the same team.

▲ Critical Viewing
Imagine that one of these baseballs has been autographed by a favorite or famous player. Use possessive pronouns to briefly describe the ball, the player, or a particular play. [Relate]

> **More Practice**

Language Lab CD-ROM
• Using Pronouns lesson
On-line Exercise Bank
• Section 23
Grammar Exercise Workbook
• pp. 125–126

526 • Using Pronouns

⊘ **TIME SAVERS!**

📋 **Answers on Transparency**
Use the Grammar Exercises Answers on Transparencies for Chapter 23 to facilitate correction by students.

🖥 **On-Line Exercise Bank**
Have students complete the exercises on computer. The Auto Check feature will grade their work for you!

✏ **STANDARDIZED TEST PREPARATION WORKSHOP**

Grammar and Usage Standardized tests measure students' abilities to recognize correct pronoun usage. Share the following example with students:

Read the sentence and choose the letter of the word that belongs in the space.

Kaitlin and I are taking ___ to the baseball game.

A she   **C** her
B they   **D** we

The correct choice is item **C**. The sentence structure demands a direct object after the verb, and *her* is the only objective pronoun.

Hands-on Grammar

Pronoun Case Checker

Errors in pronoun case often occur when the first-person singular pronoun is used as part of a compound. Many people have the tendency to use the nominative case *I* in all situations. In many cases, however, the objective case is correct. Use a pronoun case checker to illustrate that the correct case of a pronoun can often be determined by eliminating the rest of the compound.

On a strip of paper, write the following sentence, in which the object of the preposition is compound.

Fold the paper so that the first-person singular pronouns fold over the other words in the compound. By eliminating the other words, you can more easily recognize that the objective case is correct in this situation.

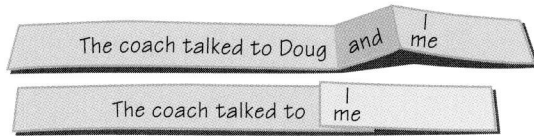

Complete strips for each of the following sentences. Fold each one so that only the first-person pronoun shows. Determine which case is correct.

Find It in Your Reading Look through a short story you are reading, and find sentences with compound objects that contain a first-person pronoun. Complete a sentence strip to check that the case is correct.

Find It in Your Writing Use a pronoun case checker to check the case of any compound pronouns in your own writing.

Step-by-Step Teaching Guide

Pronoun Case Checker

Teaching Resources: Hands-on Grammar Activity Book, Chapter 23

1. Have students refer to the Hands-on Grammar Activity books or give them copies of the relevant pages for this activity.
2. You may want to have students complete the activity in pairs.
3. Students should say that the objective case is correct for all three sentences.
4. Point out to students that the same technique could be used to check subjects. For example, in the sentence "Kendra and (I/me) talked to the coach," students might use *me*, but covering *Kendra and* will show that *I* would be the correct choice.

Find It in Your Reading

When students are finished, have them present their paper strips to the class.

Find It in Your Writing

If students cannot find any appropriate sentences, have them write three sentences with compound pronouns to check.

☑ ONGOING ASSESSMENT: Assess Mastery

Use the following resources to assess mastery of using pronouns in the proper case.

In the Textbook	Technology
Chapter Review, Exercises 10–14, pp. 528–529 Standardized Test Preparation Workshop, pp. 530–531	On-Line Exercise Bank, Section 23

⏱ TIME SAVERS!

✋ **Hands-on Grammar**
Use the Hands-on Grammar activity sheet for Chapter 23 to facilitate this activity.

ASSESS and CLOSE

Chapter Review

Each of these exercises correlates to a section of the chapter on using pronouns, pages 518–527. These exercises may be used for more practice, for reteaching, or for review of the Key Concepts presented.

Answer Key

Exercise 9

1. their
2. They
3. them
4. their
5. you
6. her
7. their
8. he
9. His
10. It, he, him
11. she
12. her
13. his
14. us
15. He

Exercise 10

1. us—objective
2. them—objective
3. We—nominative; my— possessive
4. us—objective
5. He—nominative
6. His—possessive
7. her—possessive
8. They—nominative
9. him—objective
10. his—possessive
11. ours—possessive
12. us—objective
13. him—objective
14. She—nominative; they— nominative
15. They—nominative

Exercise 11

1. subject
2. subject
3. predicate pronoun
4. subject
5. predicate pronoun
6. subject
7. predicate pronoun
8. subject
9. subject
10. predicate pronoun

GRAMMAR EXERCISES 9–16

Exercise 9 Identifying Personal Pronouns List the personal pronouns used in the sentences below.

1. Baseball players field the ball with their gloves.
2. They wear uniforms to differentiate between teams.
3. Spectators watch them play from the stands.
4. Professional players are not allowed to wear their hats backwards.
5. Baseball camps can teach you basic skills.
6. A high earned run average made her very valuable.
7. After the winning run, the players threw their hats in the air.
8. Over the left-field wall is where he hit the ball.
9. His batting average is the highest on the team.
10. It was he who struck him out.
11. Throwing curve balls is what she does best.
12. The coach asked her to pinch-hit.
13. Caring for the balls and bats is his responsibility.
14. The mascot entertains us between innings.
15. He hit the ball that the pitcher threw.

Exercise 10 Distinguishing Case List the pronouns from the sentences below. Label each pronoun *nominative*, *objective*, or *possessive*.

1. Ballplayers entertain us with winning runs and fast throws.
2. The team bus will take them to the games.
3. We played against my brother's team.
4. The outfielder threw us a ball.
5. He hit a grand slam.

6. His uniform number is six.
7. José was her biggest fan.
8. They played in the rain.
9. The foul ball was hit by him.
10. The catcher's glove was his.
11. The balls and bats are ours.
12. The pitcher struck us both out.
13. The umpire gave him the mask.
14. She hoped they would make the playoffs.
15. They sometimes missed games because of the weather.

Exercise 11 Identifying the Use of Personal Pronouns in the Nominative Case Identify whether the underlined pronoun in the nominative case is used as the subject of a verb or as a predicate nominative.

1. She hit the ball over third base.
2. Eventually, he caught the fly ball.
3. The player with the best record is he.
4. We have tickets to the series.
5. The best hitters are Tom, Joe, and he.
6. I caught the foul ball.
7. It was he who walked.
8. He struck out all three hitters.
9. I had great seats at the last game.
10. It was we who enjoyed the mascot's antics.

Exercise 12 Determining the Use of Personal Pronouns in the Objective Case Identify how each underlined pronoun in the objective case is used.

1. Who will pitch for them in the next game?
2. The coach showed him the playbook.
3. This season has prepared her for the championship game.
4. When you find the uniform, bring it to the game.

528 • Using Pronouns

5. The manager made a mistake and told <u>them</u> the team's strategy.
6. The umpire called Judy and <u>her</u> out.
7. The play was a secret between Jane and <u>me</u>.
8. As the season progressed, the coach had greater expectations of <u>us</u>.
9. The manager presented <u>him</u> with the MVP award.
10. The pitcher caught the ball and then threw <u>it</u> home.

Exercise 13 Supplying Personal Pronouns in the Possessive Case Write an appropriate possessive pronoun to complete each sentence below.

1. The coach told the team about ___?___ new plays for the championship game.
2. The bats are ___?___ , but we can use them.
3. How many of the fans are ___?___ , and how many are ___?___ ?
4. He told me it's now ___?___ turn at bat.
5. I think this equipment is ___?___ .

Exercise 14 Revising to Eliminate Problems in the Case of Personal Pronouns For each sentence, replace any incorrect underlined pronoun with a correct one. If the pronoun is not wrong, write *correct.*

1. The players at bat will be Patti, Maxine, and <u>me</u>.
2. <u>Her</u> and <u>I</u> have practiced hard, and <u>our</u> playing ability has improved.
3. When the players arrived, the manager let <u>them</u> onto the field.
4. The coach couldn't decide between her and <u>I</u>.
5. You will be happy to know that the position is now <u>your's</u>.
6. The team needs to change <u>its</u> habits.
7. The trainer asked Tom and <u>he</u> to stretch.
8. The victory is <u>theirs</u>.

9. Steve, Jerry, and <u>me</u> will celebrate after the game.
10. The team had <u>it's</u> best season ever.

Exercise 15 Writing Application
Write an article about a sports event. Use three nominative pronouns, three objective pronouns, and four possessive pronouns.

Exercise 16 CUMULATIVE REVIEW Problems With Sentences, Usage, Shifts in Verb Tense, and Pronouns Revise the following paragraph, correcting sentence errors, usage problems, unnecessary shifts in verb tense, and misused pronouns.

(1) The team members told I that they were not frozen in terror on opening night. (2) They will know that they rose above being nervous. (3) First, too team members busted (4) there legs in a skiing accident. (5) Then, the manager caught a cold. (6) Two days before the first game, the uniform rental agency admitted that the uniforms were still on a field in a neighboring state! (7) Nevertheless, it became clear that the affect of all these difficulties (8) was to draw the team together. (9) The manager gave his' best wishes to the team, (10) and they will perform with confidence. (11) The players hoped to play a good game they were nervous but knew they were ready. (12) Any game you see on that field is good. (13) Their always ready to perform (14) in spite of any obstacles that you face. They always play a good game. (15) Even when its difficult.

1. object of a preposition
2. indirect object
3. direct object
4. direct object
5. indirect object
6. direct object
7. object of a preposition
8. object of a preposition
9. indirect object
10. direct object

Exercise 13
Answers may vary. Samples are given.

1. our
2. theirs
3. ours, theirs
4. your
5. yours

Exercise 14

1. I
2. she; correct; correct
3. correct
4. me
5. yours
6. correct
7. him
8. correct
9. I
10. its

Exercise 15

Writing Application
Have volunteers read their articles to the class. You may want to suggest that students jot down the pronouns they hear. Then ask the class to name pronouns from the article for each of the cases.

continued

Answer Key continued

Exercise 16

Cumulative Review
Answers will vary. Sample revision is given.

(1) The team members told me that they were not frozen in terror on opening night. (2) They knew that they had risen above being nervous. (3) First, two team members broke (4) their legs in a skiing accident. (5) Then, the manager caught a cold. (6) Two days before the first game, the uniform rental agency admitted that the uniforms were still on a field in a neighboring state! (7) Nevertheless, it became clear that the effect of all these difficulties (8) was to draw the team together. (9) The manager gave his best wishes to the team, (10) and they performed with confidence. (11) The players hoped to play a good game. They were nervous but knew they were ready. (12) Any game you see on that field is good. (13) The players are always ready to perform (14) in spite of the obstacles that they face. They always play a good game, (15) even when it's difficult.

⏱ TIME SAVERS!

📄 Answers on Transparency Use the Grammar Exercises Answers on Transparencies for Chapter 23 to facilitate correction by students.

💻 On-Line Exercise Bank Have students complete the exercises on computer. The Auto Check feature will grade their work for you!

Lesson Objectives

- To write with increasing accuracy when using the pronoun case.

Using Pronouns

Teaching Resources: Standardized Test Preparation Workbook, pp. 45–46

1. Lead students through the first sample question.

2. As mentioned in the explanation, since the sentence needs the rest of the compound subject, the nominative case is needed. This eliminates A and D since they are objective. Item B is a better choice than C to complete the sentence.

3. Have a volunteer follow this process of elimination for the second sample question.

Standardized Test Preparation Workshop

Using Pronouns

Standardized tests measure your knowledge of the rules of standard grammar, such as correct pronoun usage. Questions test your ability to use the three cases of personal pronouns correctly. When answering these questions, determine what type of pronoun is needed in the sentence—nominative case pronouns are used as subjects or predicate pronouns; objective case pronouns are used as direct objects, indirect objects, or objects of prepositions; and possessive case pronouns are used to show ownership.

The following test item will give you practice with the format of questions that test your knowledge of pronoun usage.

Test Tip

When an object or subject is compound, check to see if the case is correct by using only the pronoun in the compound construction—for example, *She invited Kate and I/me.* Correct: *She invited me.* Incorrect: *She invited I.*

Sample Test Items	Answers and Explanations

Read the passage, and choose the letter of the word or group of words that belongs in each space.
 	
Last night, Brooke and ___(1)___ watched a program on President Kennedy. Although ___(2)___ presidency was brief, he is one of the presidents most remembered.
 	
1 A me
   B I
   C them
   D us
	The correct answer is *B.* Since the sentence calls for a subject, a pronoun in the nominative case is the only choice. Therefore, the nominative pronoun *I* best completes the sentence.

2 F he
   G him
   H his
   J my
	The correct answer is *H.* Since the sentence calls for a word that shows ownership, a pronoun in the possessive case is the only choice. *My* is possessive, but doesn't make sense in context. Therefore, the possessive pronoun *his* best completes the sentence.

✎ TEST-TAKING TIP

Explain to students that one of the best ways to answer questions such as these is to first eliminate choices by determining the case required to complete the sentence. After eliminating these choices, students can substitute the remaining ones to see which best completes the sentence.

Practice 1 **Directions:** Read the passage, and choose the letter of the word or group of words that belongs in each space.

____(1)____ group was assigned a presentation on President John F. Kennedy. Finding information on ____(2)____, especially ____(3)____ years as president, has not been too difficult for ____(4)____. Each member has a specific job to fulfill. I am in charge of assigning and collecting research, but Brooke is the group leader. It is ____(5)____ who makes the final decisions. ____(6)____ help her keep group members on task, but ____(7)____ don't always appreciate when Brooke or ____(8)____ remind ____(9)____ of ____(10)____ jobs.

1   **A**   He
      B   Him
      C   Our
      D   Its

2   **F**   it
      G   he
      H   him
      J   her

3   **A**   his
      B   him
      C   our
      D   her

4   **F**   we
      G   us
      H   him
      J   its

5   **A**   her
      B   she
      C   him
      D   his

6   **F**   Me
      G   I
      H   Him
      J   Her

7   **A**   them
      B   they
      C   him
      D   her

8   **F**   me
      G   I
      H   him
      J   her

9   **A**   them
      B   they
      C   him
      D   her

10   **F**   her
      G   their
      H   our
      J   us

Answer Key

Practice 1

1. C
2. H
3. A
4. G
5. B
6. G
7. B
8. F
9. A
10. G

In-Depth Lesson Plan

	LESSON FOCUS	PRINT AND MEDIA RESOURCES
DAY 1	**Subject-Verb Agreement** Students learn the concept of number of noun, pronoun, and verb and agreement with singular and plural subjects (pp. 534–537).	*Language Lab* CD-ROM, Subject-Verb Agreement; *On-Line Exercise Bank*, Section 24.1 **Teaching Resources** *Grammar Exercise Workbook*, pp. 127–130; *Grammar Exercises Answers on Transparencies*, Ch. 24
DAY 2	**Subject-Verb Agreement continued** Students learn and apply the concepts of compound subject agreement and agreement in inverted word order sentences, and indefinite pronoun agreement (pp. 538–547).	*Language Lab* CD-ROM, Subject-Verb Agreement; *On-Line Exercise Bank*, Section 24.1 **Teaching Resources** *Grammar Exercise Workbook*, pp. 131–134; *Grammar Exercises Answers on Transparencies*, Ch. 24; *Hands-on Grammar Activity Book*, Ch. 24
DAY 3	**Pronoun-Antecedent Agreement** Students learn and apply the concepts of personal and indefinite pronoun-antecedent agreement (pp. 548–553).	*Language Lab* CD-ROM, Using Pronouns; *On-Line Exercise Bank*, Section 24.2 **Teaching Resources** *Grammar Exercise Workbook*, pp. 135–136; *Grammar Exercises Answers on Transparencies*, Ch. 24
DAY 4	**Review and Assess** Students review chapter and demonstrate mastery of use of agreement between subjects and verbs and pronouns and antecedents (pp. 554–557).	*On-Line Exercise Bank*, Sections 24.1–2 **Teaching Resources** *Grammar Exercises Answers on Transparencies*, Ch. 24; *Formal Assessment*, Ch. 24

Accelerated Lesson Plan

	LESSON FOCUS	PRINT AND MEDIA RESOURCES
DAY 1	**Subject-Verb Agreement** Students cover concepts and usage of subject-verb agreement as determined by Diagnostic Test (pp. 534–547).	*Language Lab* CD-ROM, Subject-Verb Agreement; *On-Line Exercise Bank*, Section 24.1 **Teaching Resources** *Grammar Exercise Workbook*, pp. 127–134; *Grammar Exercises Answers on Transparencies*, Ch. 24; *Hands-on Grammar Activity Book*, Ch. 24
DAY 2	**Pronoun-Antecedent Agreement** Students learn and apply the concepts of personal and indefinite pronoun-antecedent agreement (pp. 548–553).	*Language Lab* CD-ROM, Using Pronouns; *On-Line Exercise Bank*, Section 24.2 **Teaching Resources** *Grammar Exercise Workbook*, pp. 135–136; *Grammar Exercises Answers on Transparencies*, Ch. 24
DAY 3	**Review and Assess** Students review chapter and demonstrate mastery of use of agreement between subjects and verbs and pronouns and antecedents (pp. 554–557).	*On-Line Exercise Bank*, Sections 24.1–2 **Teaching Resources** *Grammar Exercises Answers on Transparencies*, Ch. 24; *Formal Assessment*, Ch. 24

Options for Adapting Lesson Plans

HOMEWORK

Have students complete any section of the chapter for homework.

FEATURES

Extend coverage with the Grammar in Literature feature (p. 545), and the Standardized Test Preparation Workshop (p. 556).

TECHNOLOGY

Students can use the On-Line Exercise Bank to complete the exercises on computer. The Auto Check feature will grade their work.

INTEGRATED SKILLS COVERAGE

Grammar in Literature
SE p. 545

Reading
Find It In Your Reading, SE pp. 546, 547, 553

Writing
Find It In Your Writing, SE pp. 546, 547, 553
Writing Application SE pp. 547, 553, 555

Spelling
SE pp. 535, 551

Speaking and Listening
SE p. 540

Language Highlight
ATE p. 541

Workplace Skills
ATE p. 551

Viewing and Representing
Critical Viewing, SE pp. 532, 535, 537, 539, 541, 543, 544, 548, 552

ASSESSMENT SUPPORT

Standardized Test Preparation SE p. 556; ATE pp. 538, 543

Standardized Test Preparation Workbook, pp. 47–48

Formal Assessment, Ch. 24

MEETING INDIVIDUAL NEEDS

Less Advanced Students ATE pp. 538, 543. See also Ongoing Assessment, pp. 535, 537, 539, 545, 549, 550.

ESL Students ATE pp. 534, 549

Gifted/Talented Students ATE p. 549

BLOCK SCHEDULING

Pacing Suggestions
For 90-minute Blocks
- Administer the Diagnostic Test to students to determine instructional coverage.
- Have students complete the necessary exercises in class. Use the Hands-on Grammar activity to provide a change of pace.

Resources for Varying Instruction
- *Language Lab* **CD-ROM** If your students have access to hardware, a 90-minute block provides an ideal opportunity for students to work on computer.

Professional Development Support
- *How to Manage Instruction in the Block* This Teaching Resource provides management and activity suggestions.

MEDIA AND TECHNOLOGY

For the Student
- *Language Lab* **CD-ROM** Subject-Verb Agreement, Using Pronouns
- *On-Line Exercise Bank,* Ch. 24

For the Teacher
- *Resource Pro* **CD-ROM**

WRITING AND GRAMMAR WEB SITE

The Interactive Writing and Grammar Website provides a wide array of support for students, teachers, and parents. Grammar support includes:

- *On-Line Exercise Bank* with Auto Check scoring
- Diagnostic and assessment support

www.phschool.com

LITERATURE CONNECTIONS

Related selection from *Prentice Hall Literature: Timeless Voices, Timeless Themes,* Bronze:
A Christmas Carol: Scrooge and Marley, dramatized by Israel Horovitz, SE p. 545

Chapter 24 Making Words Agree

Have you ever seen people dressed in green on St. Patrick's Day? Have you watched fireworks on the Fourth of July?

Just as special events can "fit" with certain celebrations, subjects and verbs must fit together in sentences. For example, you would never say, "*I are* the winner!" or "*Is they* your best friends?" You would hear that something is wrong with these sentences. The problem is that the subjects and verbs do not *agree*.

In most of the sentences you speak and write, the subjects and verbs agree almost automatically. You would probably say, "*I am* the winner!" or "*Are they* your best friends?" In some sentences, however, you might be tempted to make a verb agree with a word that is not the subject. In such a case, check to find the real subject and make sure that it agrees with its verb. Pronouns and the words they stand for must also agree. This chapter will explain the rules of agreement and how to make parts of sentences work together correctly.

▲ Critical Viewing
Describe what is happening in this photograph in a sentence that begins "Bursts of color . . . ." Be sure your verb agrees with this subject. **[Analyze]**

532 • Making Words Agree

☑ **ONGOING ASSESSMENT: Diagnose**

If students miss more than one item in each category, direct them to the relevant pages of the text and assign exercises for practice and review.

Making Words Agree	Diagnostic Test Items	Teach	Practice	Section Review	Chapter Review
Skill Check A, B, and C					
Singular and Plural Subjects	A 1, 4, 6, 8 B 15,17,18	pp. 534–537	Ex. 1–3, 6–7, 10	Ex. 11, 13	Ex. 27–28, 30–31
Compound Subjects	A 3, 7 B 13,19	pp. 538–541	Ex. 4–7, 10	Ex. 12–13	Ex. 27–28, 30–31
Confusing Subjects	A 2, 5, 9–10 B 11–12, 14, 16, 20 C 21–22, 25	pp. 542–546	Ex. 8–10	Ex. 12–13	Ex. 27–28, 30–31

Diagnostic Test

Directions: Write all answers on a separate sheet of paper.

Skill Check A. For the following sentences, choose the correct word from each pair in parentheses.

1. Celebrations (is, are) ways in which we remember important events.
2. Some celebrations (comes, come) in the form of holidays, others as feasts or festivals.
3. Customs and traditions (plays, play) important roles in the way we celebrate.
4. For many people, traditions (has, have) been passed from generation to generation.
5. Each person (celebrates, celebrate) an event in his or her own way.
6. Mary (cheers, cheer) when she gets an *A* on an exam.
7. I hope either Joey or Nate (has, have) a large party after (his, their) graduation.
8. The students at school (holds, hold) a victory dance after winning a big game.
9. Almost everyone (enjoys, enjoy) a celebration.
10. What events (does, do) you like to celebrate?

Skill Check B. In some of the sentences below, subjects and verbs do not agree in number. If a sentence is correct, write *correct* on your paper. If it is incorrect, rewrite the sentence correctly.

11. Several holidays throughout the year has big celebrations.
12. Many children dresses up in costumes for parties.
13. Leslie and her family stays up until midnight on New Year's Eve.
14. Both Ed and Neil spend Thanksgiving at their grandmother's house.
15. Michael likes St. Patrick's Day parades because people usually wear green.
16. Neither Kit nor Stewart want to miss the fireworks on July fourth.
17. Danny said that Christmas are his favorite holiday.
18. His family have many long-standing Christmas traditions.
19. Jason and Tom prefers birthday celebrations.
20. There are always a big party with all of his friends.

Skill Check C. All of the following sentences are in the present tense. On your paper, write a verb or pronoun to complete each sentence, making sure to maintain agreement.

21. She follows holiday customs from _____?_____ native land.
22. The holidays of some countries differ from _____?_____.
23. In Mexico, Carlos and _____?_____ family celebrate Cinco de Mayo.
24. After a successful harvest, people in some cultures have a feast to celebrate _____?_____ good fortune.
25. Anybody who celebrates that holiday must be following the ways of _____?_____ ancestors.

Making Words Agree • **533**

Diagnostic Test

Each item in the Diagnostic Test corresponds to a specific section in the agreement chapter. This will enable you to tailor instruction to your students' particular needs. See "Ongoing Assessment: Diagnose" on the bottom of pages 532–533 for further details.

Skill Check A

1. are	6. cheers
2. come	7. has, his
3. play	8. hold
4. have	9. enjoys
5. celebrates	10. do

Skill Check B

11. Several holidays throughout the year <u>have</u> big celebrations.
12. Many children <u>dress</u> up in costumes for parties.
13. Leslie and her family <u>stay</u> up until midnight on New Year's Eve.
14. correct
15. correct
16. Neither Kit nor Stewart <u>wants</u> to miss the fireworks on July fourth.
17. Danny said that Christmas <u>is</u> his favorite holiday.
18. His family <u>has</u> many long-standing Christmas traditions.
19. Jason and Tom <u>prefer</u> birthday celebrations.
20. There <u>is</u> always a big party with all of his friends.

Skill Check C

Answers may vary. Samples are given.

21. her
22. ours
23. his
24. their
25. his or her

☑ ONGOING ASSESSMENT: Diagnose *continued*					
Making Words Agree	**Diagnostic Test Items**	**Teach**	**Practice**	**Section Review**	**Chapter Review**
Pronoun-Antecedent Agreement	C 23–24	pp. 548–552	Ex. 17–20	Ex. 21–23	Ex. 29–31
Cumulative Review and Applications				Ex. 14–16, 24–26	Ex. 34–35

⏱ **TIME SAVERS!**

📖 **Answers on Transparency** Use the Grammar Exercises Answers on Transparencies for Chapter 24 to facilitate corrections by students.

💻 **On-Line Exercise Bank** Have students complete the Diagnostic Test on computer. The Auto Check feature will grade their work for you!

Interest GRABBER Have students look around the room or out of the window and write two singular and two plural nouns that name what they see. Have them exchange lists with a partner and write sentences using each noun.

Activate Prior Knowledge

Write the following sentences on the chalkboard, and ask students to identify the incorrect sentence. Discuss how the sentences illustrate the rule for forming singular and plural verbs.

We walk to school every day. (correct)

Sheila eat her lunch with us. (incorrect—verb should be *eats*)

Toby and Cheryl live on the same street. (correct)

TEACH

Step-by-Step Teaching Guide

Recognizing the Number of Nouns and Pronouns

1. Review singular and plural nouns with students. Be sure that students understand that collective nouns such as *team, group, class,* and *crew* generally act as singular nouns requiring singular verbs.

2. Review singular and plural verbs in the third person.

3. Have students make a list of irregular plural noun forms, such as *calves, teeth, feet, children, men, women* and those that do not change, such as *fish, sheep, deer.*

Customize for
ESL Students

Students may be surprised to learn that only nouns, pronouns, and verbs show number. In many languages, articles and adjectives must also agree. Explain to students that they can focus on subject-verb agreement without worrying about modifiers.

Section 24.1

Agreement Between Subjects and Verbs

Subject-verb agreement has one main rule:

▶ **KEY CONCEPT** A verb must agree with its subject in number. ■

The number of a word can be either singular or plural. Singular words indicate *one.* Plural words indicate *more than one.* Only nouns, pronouns, and verbs have number.

Recognizing the Number of Nouns and Pronouns

Most of the time, it is easy to tell whether a noun or pronoun is singular or plural. Compare, for example, the singular and plural forms of the nouns in the following chart:

NOUNS	
Singular	**Plural**
custom	customs
box	boxes
knife	knives
mouse	mice

Most nouns are made plural by adding *-s* or *-es* to the singular form (friend**s** and box**es**). Some nouns become plural in other ways (kni**ves** and m**ice**). Pronouns have different forms to indicate singular and plural. For example, *I, he, she, it,* and *this* are singular. *We, they,* and *these* are plural. *You, who,* and *some* are either singular or plural.

▶ **Exercise 1** Recognizing the Number of Nouns and Pronouns On your paper, indicate whether each of the following words is *singular* or *plural.*

EXAMPLE: children—plural

1. turkey
2. geese
3. Thanksgiving
4. they
5. it
6. I
7. veteran
8. festivals
9. shamrocks
10. we
11. fireworks
12. women
13. street fair
14. flag
15. feasts

Theme: Holidays and Celebrations

In this section, you will learn about the singular and plural forms of nouns and verbs. The examples and exercises are about holidays and celebrations.

**Cross-Curricular Connection:
Social Studies**

▶ **More Practice**

Language Lab CD-ROM
• Subject-Verb Agreement lesson
On-line Exercise Bank
• Section 24.1
Grammar Exercise Workbook
• pp. 127–128

⏱ **TIME AND RESOURCE MANAGER**

Resources
Print: Grammar Exercise Workbook, pp. 127–134
Technology: Language Lab CD-ROM, Subject-Verb Agreement; On-Line Exercise Bank, Section 24.1

In-Depth Coverage	Accelerated Pace
• Work through all key concepts, pp. 534–545. • Assign and review Exercises 1–10. • Read and discuss Grammar in Literature, p. 545. • Do the Hands-on Grammar Activity, p. 546.	• Assign pp. 534–545 for independent student review. • Review Checking Agreement in Sentences with Unusual Word Order and Checking Agreement With Indefinite Pronouns, pp. 542–543, and assign Exercises 8–9.

Recognizing the Number of Verbs

Like nouns, verbs have singular and plural forms. Problems involving the number of verbs normally involve the third-person forms in the present tense (*she wants, they want*) and certain forms of the verb *be* (*I am; he is* or *was; we are* or *were*).

SINGULAR AND PLURAL VERBS IN THE PRESENT TENSE	
Singular	**Plural**
The girl *runs*.	The girls *run*.
The boy *plays*.	The boys *play*.
I *am* happy.	We *are* happy.
This *was* great!	Those *were* great!

Exercise 2 Recognizing the Number of Verbs On your paper, write the verb from the choices in parentheses that agrees in number with the pronoun. After each answer, write whether the verb is *singular* or *plural*.

EXAMPLE: they (meets, meet)
ANSWER: meet (plural)

1. this (is, are)
2. he (votes, vote)
3. I (is, am)
4. she (gives, give)
5. we (is, are)
6. it (bark, barks)
7. they (was, were)
8. we (has, have)
9. those (has been, have been)
10. they (counts, count)

▶ Critical Viewing
Write a sentence describing this dog. Then, identify the number of the verb(s) you have used. [**Apply**]

Agreement Between Subjects and Verbs • 535

Step-by-Step Teaching Guide

Recognizing the Number of Verbs

1. Review with students singular and plural verbs, especially the third-person forms. These verbs will most likely confuse students when dealing with subject-verb agreement.

2. Write the following verbs on the chalkboard. Ask students whether each verb is in the singular or plural form.

   walks (singular)

   was (singular)

   are (plural)

Answer Key

Exercise 1 *(page 534)*

1. singular	9. plural
2. plural	10. plural
3. singular	11. plural
4. plural	12. plural
5. singular	13. singular
6. singular	14. singular
7. singular	15. plural
8. plural	

Exercise 2

1. is—singular
2. votes—singular
3. am—singular
4. gives—singular
5. are—plural
6. barks—singular
7. were—plural
8. have—plural
9. have been—plural
10. count—plural

Critical Viewing

Apply Students' answers will vary, but they should correctly identify the number of each verb they have used.

💡 **Spelling Tip**

If a noun ends in *fe* (such as *knife*), its plural is usually formed by changing *fe* to *ve* and adding *s* (*knives*).

☑ **ONGOING ASSESSMENT: Prerequisite Skill**

If students have difficulty with subject-verb agreement, you may wish to review the following to assure coverage for prerequisite knowledge.

In the Textbook	Print Resources	Technology
Nouns and Pronouns, pp. 296–309 Basic Sentence Parts, pp. 392–419	Grammar Exercise Workbook, pp. 1–12, 45–54	Language Lab CD-ROM, Nouns and Pronouns; On-Line Exercise Bank, Sections 14.1–14.2, 19.1–19.4

Making Verbs Agree With Singular and Plural Subjects

1. Be sure that students understand the basic rule of subject-verb agreement. A singular subject must have a singular verb. A plural subject gets a plural verb.

2. Review with students that the subject of a sentence is who or what the sentence is about, and that it is always a noun, noun phrase, or pronoun.

3. With the exception of the verb *be*, only the present and present perfect tenses change verb form. Illustrate this with the following examples on the chalkboard:

   Singular: *Louie's Diner makes great fries.*

   Plural: *Kay's and The Fry Guy also make great fries.*

   Singular: *Kim has made a salad.*

   Plural: *The girls have made a salad.*

4. A phrase placed between a subject and verb can be a source of confusion. Students may be tempted to make the verb agree with the nonsubject noun because it is closer to the verb. The basic rule always holds true: A verb must agree with its subject.

   Independence Day, along with the fireworks, is exciting to Kate. (The verb is agrees with the subject, Independence Day.)

24.1

Making Verbs Agree With Singular and Plural Subjects

To check for agreement between a subject and a verb, begin by determining the number of the subject. Then, make sure the verb has the same number.

▶ **KEY CONCEPT** A singular subject must have a singular verb. A plural subject must have a plural verb. ■

In the following examples, the subjects are underlined once and the verbs are underlined twice.

SINGULAR SUBJECT AND VERB:	<u>Jeff</u> always <u>has</u> a good time at the beach. <u>She</u> <u>was</u> here earlier today. A <u>picnic</u> <u>is being planned</u> for Independence Day.
PLURAL SUBJECT AND VERB:	The <u>surfers</u> always <u>have</u> a good time at the beach. <u>They</u> <u>were</u> here earlier today. <u>Picnics</u> <u>are being planned</u> for Independence Day.

All the subjects in the preceding examples stand next to or near their verbs. Often, however, a subject is separated from its verb by a prepositional phrase. In these cases, it is important to remember that the object of a preposition is never the subject of a sentence.

▶ **KEY CONCEPT** A prepositional phrase that comes between a subject and its verb does *not* affect subject-verb agreement. ■

In the first example below, the subject is *arrival*, not *firemen*, which is the object of the preposition *of*. Because *arrival* is singular, the plural verb *have caused* cannot agree with it. In the second example, the subject is the plural *cheers*, not *crowd*; therefore, it takes the plural verb *were heard*.

INCORRECT:	The <u>arrival</u> of the firemen <u>have caused</u> much excitement at the picnic.
CORRECT:	The <u>arrival</u> of the firemen <u>has caused</u> much excitement at the picnic.
INCORRECT:	The <u>cheers</u> of the crowd <u>was heard</u> several blocks away.
CORRECT:	The <u>cheers</u> of the crowd <u>were heard</u> several blocks away.

Exercise 3 Making Verbs Agree With Singular and Plural
Subjects For each of the following sentences, choose the
correct verb from the pair in parentheses, and write it on your
paper.

EXAMPLE: People often (gathers, gather) on holidays.

ANSWER: gather

1. Independence Day (commemorates, commemorate) the
   beginning of our freedom from English rule.
2. The Declaration of Independence (was, were) signed by
   many leading statesmen.
3. More than two hundred years (has, have) passed since this
   great event.
4. This holiday (occurs, occur) every Fourth of July.
5. Many cities around the nation (has, have) parades and
   other special celebrations.
6. Marching bands in a parade often (wears, wear) red, white,
   and blue uniforms.
7. Some people in the parade (likes, like) to dress up as
   American colonists.
8. The decorations seen around town (uses, use) the colors of
   the flag.
9. A picnic with hot dogs and apple pie (seems, seem) like a
   good summertime meal.
10. A bright display of fireworks (is, are) often the grand finale
    of this day of fun and pride.

More Practice

**Language Lab
CD-ROM**
• Subject-Verb
  Agreement lesson
**On-line
Exercise Bank**
• Section 24.1
**Grammar Exercise
Workbook**
• pp. 129–130

◄ **Critical Viewing**
What sounds do
fireworks make?
Answer this question
in a sentence using
two colorful plural
verbs. [**Analyze**]

Agreement Between Subjects and Verbs • 537

Answer Key

► **Exercise 3**

1. commemorates
2. was
3. have
4. occurs
5. have
6. wear
7. like
8. use
9. seems
10. is

Critical Viewing

Analyze Students may say that
when fireworks are lit, they hiss,
crackle, and loudly pop.

✓ **ONGOING ASSESSMENT: Monitor and Reinforce**

If students miss more than two items in Exercise 1, 2, or 3, refer them to the following for additional
practice.

In the Textbook	Print Resources	Technology

Section Review Ex. 11, p. 547
Chapter Review Ex. 27, p. 554
	Grammar Exercise Workbook,
	  pp. 127–130
		Language Lab CD-ROM,
		  Subject-Verb Agreement;
		  On-Line Exercise Bank,
		  Section 24.1

⏱ **TIME SAVERS!**

 **Answers on Transparency**
Use the Grammar Exercises
Answers on Transparencies for
Chapter 24 to facilitate
correction by students.

💻 **On-Line Exercise Bank**
Have students complete the
exercises on computer. The Auto
Check feature will grade their
work for you!

Making Verbs Agree With Compound Subjects

1. Compound subjects can be confusing. Write the following sentences on the board:

   Inez and Tomoko <u>are</u> *here.*

   Inez <u>or</u> Tomoko <u>is</u> here.

   The <u>Garcias and the Tanakas</u> <u>are</u> here.

   The <u>Garcias or Tomoko</u> <u>is</u> here.

   Inez <u>or the Tanakas</u> <u>are</u> here.

2. Review the sentences. Point to the underlined words and review the rules for compound subject–verb agreement.

Subject	Verb
singular and singular	= *plural*
singular or singular	= *singular*
plural and plural	= *plural*
plural or singular	= *singular*
singular or plural	= *plural*

3. Be sure students understand that *each* and *every* are modifiers that denote singularity and require a singular verb.

Customize for
Less Advanced Students

Review with students that the conjunctions *or, neither . . . nor,* and *either . . . or* join subjects that are different. Compound subjects linked by these conjunctions are frequently singular, but not always. Example: *Neither the Garcias nor the Tanakas have come.*

Answer Key

> **Exercise 4**

1. are
2. is
3. makes
4. buys
5. is
6. tastes
7. is
8. are
9. works
10. is

24.1

Making Verbs Agree With Compound Subjects

A compound subject is made up of two or more subjects joined by a conjunction such as *or, nor,* or *and.*

> **KEY CONCEPT** Two or more singular subjects joined by *or* or *nor* must have a singular verb. Two or more plural subjects joined by *or* or *nor* must have a plural verb. ■

INCORRECT:	Either the <u>turkey</u> or the <u>stuffing</u> <u>are</u> cooking.
CORRECT:	Either the <u>turkey</u> or the <u>stuffing</u> <u>is</u> cooking.
CORRECT:	Neither the <u>potatoes</u> nor the <u>peas</u> <u>are</u> done.

> **KEY CONCEPT** When singular and plural subjects are joined by *or* or *nor*, the verb must agree with the closer subject. ■

SINGULAR SUBJECT CLOSER:	Neither the <u>lights</u> nor the <u>wreath</u> <u>is</u> in the box.
PLURAL SUBJECT CLOSER:	Neither the <u>wreath</u> nor the <u>lights</u> <u>are</u> in the box.

> **Exercise 4** **Making Verbs Agree With Compound Subjects Joined by *or* or *nor*** For each of the sentences listed below, choose the correct verb from the pair in parentheses, and write it on your paper.

EXAMPLE:	Neither the twins nor their dog (has, have) remained long at the parade.
ANSWER:	has

1. Either historical occasions or distinguished persons (is, are) commemorated on secular holidays.
2. Neither Father's Day nor Mother's Day (is, are) celebrated in many foreign countries.
3. Usually, Bob or Liz (makes, make) a gift for Mother.
4. Either Anne or her sister (buys, buy) her mother a card.
5. Concert tickets or a fancy dinner (is, are) a great gift.
6. Often, either Chinese or Italian food (tastes, taste) good.
7. Sunday or Monday (is, are) the day for holidays.
8. Either flowers or balloons (is, are) delivered to the house.
9. Neither Mom nor Dad (works, work) on a holiday.
10. Neither Groundhog Day nor Valentine's Day (is, are) a national holiday.

> **More Practice**
> Language Lab CD-ROM
> • Subject-Verb Agreement lesson
> On-line Exercise Bank
> • Section 24.1
> Grammar Exercise Workbook
> • pp. 131–132

✎ STANDARDIZED TEST PREPARATION WORKSHOP

Grammar and Usage Standardized tests often measure students' ability to recognize errors in sentence construction. Provide students with the following sample test item:

Identify the underlined word or phrase in the following sentence which contains an error:

<u>Both</u> <u>Isabelle and Marcus</u> <u>visits</u>
A   B   C

their <u>parents</u> for Thanksgiving. <u>No error</u>
D   E

The correct answer is item **C**. The compound subject *Isabelle and Marcus* requires a plural verb, not a singular one.

Critical Viewing

Connect Students may say that, unlike the six marchers in the middle, neither the marcher at the right end nor the marcher at the left end is carrying a flag.

▶ **KEY CONCEPT** A compound subject joined by *and* is usually plural and must have a plural verb. ■

And usually acts as a plus sign. Whether the parts of the compound subject are all singular, all plural, or mixed in number, they usually add up to a subject that takes a plural verb.

EXAMPLES: The boy and girl are waiting for the parade.
The boys and girls are waiting for the parade.
The boys and the girl are waiting for the parade.

This rule has two exceptions. First, if the parts of the compound subject taken together are thought of as a single unit, then the compound subject is considered singular and must have a singular verb.

SINGULAR COMPOUND
SUBJECT: Bacon and eggs is a very popular breakfast. (Bacon + eggs = one breakfast)

The second exception involves the words *every* and *each*. Either of these words before a compound subject indicates the need for a singular verb.

SINGULAR COMPOUND
SUBJECT: Every town and village celebrates.

▲ **Critical Viewing**
In a sentence using *neither . . . nor,* explain how the marchers at each end of the row differ from those in the middle. **[Connect]**

Agreement Between Subjects and Verbs • **539**

☑ **ONGOING ASSESSMENT: Monitor and Reinforce**

If students miss more than two items in Exercises 4–7, refer them to the following for additional practice.

In the Textbook	Print Resources	Technology
Section Review Exercise 12, p. 547	Grammar Exercise Workbook, pp. 131–134	Language Lab CD-ROM, Subject-Verb Agreement; On-Line Exercise Bank, Section 24.1

⏱ **TIME SAVERS!**

Answers on Transparency Use the Grammar Exercises Answers on Transparencies for Chapter 24 to facilitate correction by students.

 **On-Line Exercise Bank** Have students complete the exercises on computer. The Auto Check feature will grade their work for you!

Answer Key

▶ **Exercise 5**

1. are
2. have been
3. learns
4. pays
5. mark
6. is
7. visit
8. honor
9. commemorate
10. are

▶ **Exercise 6**

1. are
2. observe
3. remembers
4. call
5. honors
6. delivers
7. have
8. celebrate
9. honor
10. celebrates

▶ **Exercise 5** Making Verbs Agree With Compound Subjects Joined by *and* Choose the correct verb from the pair in parentheses, and write it on your paper.

1. Memorial Day and Veterans Day (is, are) national holidays.
2. Soldiers and sailors (has been, have been) remembered on these days for many years.
3. Each boy and girl in school (learns, learn) that General John Alexander Logan originated Memorial Day.
4. Nearly every city and town (pays, pay) tribute to those killed in battle.
5. Parades and speeches (marks, mark) this day's importance.
6. In some towns, the tombstone or grave marker of every deceased service person (is, are) decorated with an American flag.
7. My family and I (visits, visit) Arlington National Cemetery every year on this important holiday.
8. Both Veterans Day and Memorial Day (honors, honor) those who served in America's armed forces.
9. While both Memorial Day and Veterans Day (commemorates, commemorate) all those who served, Veterans Day is dedicated to those who survived the fighting.
10. World War II and the Vietnam War (is, are) two wars that people think of on Memorial Day.

▶ **Exercise 6** Avoiding Errors in Subject-Verb Agreement

On your paper, write the correct verb from the pair in parentheses.

1. Veterans Day and Armistice Day (is, are) different names for the same holiday.
2. The Allied countries that fought in World War I (observes, observe) this holiday.
3. Each country (remembers, remember) those who served in this war.
4. Americans (calls, call) the holiday Veterans Day.
5. This day (honors, honor) veterans of all wars.
6. The President always (delivers, deliver) a speech on Veterans Day to pay tribute to those who served.
7. Great Britain and Canada (has, have) different names for this holiday.
8. Both countries (celebrates, celebrate) the day on November 11.
9. France and Italy also (honors, honor) the soldiers who fought in World War I on this day.
10. Neither Bolivia nor Kenya (celebrates, celebrate) this holiday.

▶ **Speaking and Listening Tip**

After choosing the correct verb, read each sentence aloud to a partner. As you read, stress the conjunction that connects the two parts of the compound subject.

▶ **More Practice**

Language Lab
CD-ROM
• Subject-Verb Agreement lesson
On-line
Exercise Bank
• Section 24.1
Grammar Exercise Workbook
• pp. 131–132

⊘ **TIME SAVERS!**

🔲 **Answers on Transparency**
Use the Grammar Exercises Answers on Transparencies for Chapter 24 to facilitate correction by students.

🖥 **On-Line Exercise Bank**
Have students complete the exercises on computer. The Auto Check feature will grade their work for you!

▶ **Exercise 7** Correcting Errors in Subject-Verb Agreement
In some of the sentences below, subjects and verbs do not
agree in number. If a sentence is correct, write *correct*. If it
is incorrect, rewrite the sentence correctly.

EXAMPLE: Neither the moon nor the stars is visible tonight.

ANSWER: Neither the moon nor the stars are visible
             tonight.

1. Neither Valentine's Day nor Memorial Day are celebrated
   in September.
2. However, a law in the United States declare that the first
   Monday in September is Labor Day.
3. Most people in the business world are given a holiday from
   work on Labor Day.
4. Many in my class, including Joe, is looking forward to
   Valentine's Day this year.
5. Kara or Sue plan to send him a card.

◀ Critical Viewing
Tell about gift-giving
on Valentine's Day in
a sentence that
begins "Roses or
chocolate . . . ."
[Evaluate]

Agreement Between Subjects and Verbs • **541**

Answer Key

▶ **Exercise 7**

1. Neither Valentine's Day nor
   Memorial Day <u>is</u> celebrated in
   September.
2. However, a law in the United
   States <u>declares</u> that the first
   Monday in September is Labor
   Day.
3. correct
4. Many in my class, including Joe,
   <u>are</u> looking forward to
   Valentine's Day this year.
5. Kara or Sue <u>plans</u> to send him a
   card.

Language Highlight

Although people in America and
England both speak the same
language, they spell many words
differently. For example, in England
labor is spelled *labour*, *tire* is spelled
tyre, *curb* is spelled *kerb*, and *jail* is
spelled *gaol*.

Critical Viewing

Evaluate Students may say that
roses or chocolate is given on
Valentine's Day as a token of the
admirer's love for the admired.

Checking Agreement in Sentences With Unusual Word Order

1. Provide additional examples of sentences with inverted word order.

   There is a parking space.

   Here is the theater.

   There are our seats.

   Here are some programs.

2. Show students how to find the subject in inverted sentences by reading it in the more familiar, subject-first order:

   A parking space is there.

   The theater is here.

   Our seats are there.

   Some programs are here.

3. Review the inverted word order of questions. Tell students that to find the subject in questions, they can read the question in subject-first order, as they did the sentences above.

   Where is the lobby?

   The lobby is where?

   When is intermission?

   The intermission is when?

Answer Key

> **Exercise 8**

1. customs—are
2. gifts—are
3. you—do know
4. box—is
5. holidays—are
6. they—have chosen
7. bells—were rung
8. children—have been
9. string—was
10. he—is waiting

⏲ TIME SAVERS!

Answers on Transparency
Use the Grammar Exercises Answers on Transparencies for Chapter 24 to facilitate correction by students.

On-Line Exercise Bank
Have students complete the exercises on computer. The Auto Check feature will grade their work for you!

542

24.1

Checking Agreement in Sentences With Unusual Word Order

In most sentences, the subject comes before the verb. In some sentences, however, this normal word order is turned around, or inverted. In other sentences, the helping verb comes before the subject even though the main verb follows the subject.

▶ **KEY CONCEPT** When a subject comes after the verb, the subject and verb still must agree with each other in number. ■

Sentences beginning with *there* or *here* are almost always in inverted word order. In the following sentences, the subjects are underlined once and the verbs are underlined twice.

EXAMPLES:　There <u>were</u> several <u>books</u> about holidays.
　　　　　　Here <u>is</u> a <u>book</u> about the holiday.

The contractions *there's* and *here's* both contain the singular verb *is*: *there is* and *here is*. Do not use these contractions with plural subjects.

INCORRECT:　Here's the <u>keys</u> to the house.
CORRECT:　　Here <u>are</u> the <u>keys</u> to the house.

Many questions are also in inverted word order.

EXAMPLE:　Where <u>are</u> the <u>keys</u> to the house?

▶ **Exercise 8** Checking Agreement in Sentences With Inverted Word Order On your paper, write the subject in each of the following sentences. Choose the correct verb from the pair in parentheses, and write it next to the subject.

EXAMPLE:　There (is, are) a few new rules in this pamphlet.
ANSWER:　　rules—are

1. There (is, are) many different customs associated with holidays in December.
2. Where (is, are) the gifts?
3. Which customs (does, do) you know?
4. Here (is, are) a big box of decorations.
5. There (is, are) some holidays very close together.
6. Which day (has, have) they chosen?
7. When (was, were) the bells rung?
8. Where (has, have) the children been?
9. There (was, were) a string of lights decorating the house.
10. Why (is, are) he waiting?

✹ Grammar and Style Tip

You can make your writing more interesting by varying the style of your sentences. Inverting the subject-verb order of some sentences helps to create variety.

▶ **More Practice**

Language Lab CD-ROM
• Subject-Verb Agreement lesson

On-line Exercise Bank
• Section 24.1

Grammar Exercise Workbook
• pp. 133–134

Checking Agreement With Indefinite Pronouns

Indefinite pronouns used as subjects can also cause agreement problems.

Some pronouns are always singular: *anyone, everyone, someone, anybody, everybody, somebody, each,* and *either.*

ALWAYS SINGULAR:	<u>Each</u> of the banners <u>is</u> blue.
	<u>Everyone</u> in the first five rows <u>was</u> delighted by the play.
	<u>Either</u> of those hats <u>is</u> warm.

Some pronouns are always plural: *both, few, many, others,* and *several.*

ALWAYS PLURAL:	<u>Few</u> <u>have chosen</u> a gift yet.
	<u>Many</u> <u>are waiting</u> until they finish reading the book.
	<u>Several</u> <u>have</u> not <u>started</u> reading the book.

▶ **KEY CONCEPT** Many indefinite pronouns can take either a singular or a plural verb. The choice depends upon the meaning given to the pronoun. ■

The following indefinite pronouns can be singular or plural: *all, any, more, most, none,* and *some.*

SINGULAR:	<u>Some</u> of the milk <u>is</u> frozen.
PLURAL:	<u>Some</u> of the cookies <u>are</u> frozen, too.

With an indefinite pronoun that can be either singular or plural, the antecedent of the pronoun determines its number. In the example above, *some* is singular when it refers to *milk,* plural when it refers to *cookies.*

▶ Critical Viewing Describe what these two students are doing, first in a sentence that begins *Each of . . . ,* and then in a sentence that begins with *Both of . . . .* [Compare]

Agreement Between Subjects and Verbs • 543

Checking Agreement With Indefinite Pronouns

1. Review indefinite pronouns. Encourage students to examine each pronoun for clues as to whether it is singular or plural.

2. Singular indefinite pronouns show their singularity. For example, the word *one* attached to *every, any,* or *some* always denotes singularity. *Each* and *either* discriminate between single things.

3. Similarly, *few, many,* and *several* all mean more than one.

4. Review the use of *some* with the following examples:

    Some of the parade was fun.

    Some of the stores were having sales.

   Point out that the verb takes its cue from the antecedent of the pronoun *some.* In the first sentence, *parade* is singular, so the verb is singular. In the second sentence, *stores* is a plural antecedent, so the verb is plural.

Customize for
Less Advanced Students

A prepositional phrase after the indefinite pronouns *each, either,* and *neither* can be confusing. To help students remember that these indefinite pronouns are always singular, tell students to imagine adding the suffix *-one* to the pronoun so that *Neither of you was responsible* becomes *Neither* [one] *of you was responsible.*

Critical Viewing

Compare Students may say that *each of* the students is reading, and *both of* the students are concentrating.

🖉 STANDARDIZED TEST PREPARATION WORKSHOP

Grammar and Usage Standardized tests often require students to select the item that best completes a sentence. Write the following question on the board and ask students to choose the best answer.

Most of the birds in this area ___ flown south for the winter.

A has   **B** is
C have   **D** none of the above

The indefinite pronoun *most* can be singular or plural. Since *birds* is plural, the verb must be plural in order to agree. Item **C** is the only plural verb form. Item **C** is the only choice that makes sense for the sentence.

Answer Key

> **Exercise 9**

1. were
2. have been
3. Does
4. have
5. have
6. were
7. was
8. tells
9. want
10. enjoys

Critical Viewing

Draw Conclusions Students may suggest that anyone who sees such a large wooden soldier would be taken aback by its size.

24.1

> **Exercise 9** Checking Agreement With Indefinite Pronouns

For each of the following sentences, choose the correct verb from the pair in parentheses, and write it on your paper.

EXAMPLE: Most of the story (was, were) written from a child's point of view.

ANSWER: was

1. Many of the children in school (was, were) performing in the program.
2. Several (has been, have been) helping with the props.
3. (Does, Do) anyone know if there is a large audience?
4. All of the children (has, have) costumes.
5. Some of the people (has, have) not arrived yet.
6. All of the children (was, were) given scripts.
7. Each of the songs (was, were) practiced.
8. Every boy and girl in the program (tells, tell) about a holiday.
9. Both Jeff and Patty (wants, want) to do well.
10. Everyone (enjoys, enjoy) hearing the children laugh with delight.

◄ Critical Viewing These girls are expressing very different attitudes. How do you think others might react to this large wooden soldier? Begin your answer with *Anyone who . . . .* [**Draw Conclusions**]

544 • Making Words Agree

GRAMMAR IN LITERATURE

from A Christmas Carol: Scrooge and Marley

dramatized by Israel Horovitz

In the following lines, the subjects are highlighted in red, the verbs in blue. In both examples, plural subjects take plural verbs. All is an indefinite pronoun that is plural in this case.

SCROOGE sits near the tiny low-flamed fire, sipping his gruel. There *are* various *pictures* on the walls: *all* of them now *show* likenesses of MARLEY. SCROOGE blinks his eyes.

Exercise 10 Supplying Verbs Rewrite the following sentences, supplying a verb that completes each one logically. Make sure the verbs you use agree with their subjects.

EXAMPLE: Most of the children ___?___ parts in the holiday pageant.

ANSWER: Most of the children have parts in the holiday pageant.

1. There ___?___ many reasons to celebrate.
2. Each of the children ___?___ about a holiday tradition.
3. Here ___?___ the children now.
4. Most ___?___ their parts.
5. Everyone ___?___ to do well.
6. Where ___?___ the sign for the beginning of the show?
7. ___?___ they made popcorn for the guests?
8. There ___?___ several other programs like this one.
9. All ___?___ wonderful.
10. Each ___?___ special.
11. Anyone who ___?___ the show will come away smiling.
12. Amy and Matt ___?___ looking forward to attending.
13. Neither of them ___?___ ever ___?___ the holiday pageant.
14. Before this year, there ___?___ no live music.
15. However, this year there ___?___ a pianist and a cellist.

More Practice

Language Lab CD-ROM
• Subject-Verb Agreement lesson
On-line Exercise Bank
• Section 24.1
Grammar Exercise Workbook
• pp. 133–134

Agreement Between Subjects and Verbs • **545**

Grammar in Literature

1. Have a volunteer read aloud the excerpt.
2. Tell students that *A Christmas Carol* is a famous novel by Charles Dickens in which the wealthy miser Ebenezer Scrooge learns the importance of generosity and love.
3. Work with students to rewrite the second sentence as follows:

   Various pictures are on the walls. They all now show likenesses of Marley.

More About the Author

Israel Horovitz is an American playwright, novelist, and essayist. He and two friends founded the Gloucester Stage Company theater in Gloucester, Massachusetts, in 1979 to act as a "safe harbor" for playwrights and new plays.

Answer Key

Exercise 10

Some answers may vary. Samples are given.

1. are
2. tells
3. are
4. know
5. wants
6. is
7. Have
8. have been
9. were
10. was
11. sees
12. are
13. has; seen
14. was
15. are

✓ ONGOING ASSESSMENT: Monitor and Reinforce

If students miss more than two items in Exercises 8, 9 or 10, refer them to the following for additional practice.

In the Textbook	Print Resources	Technology
Section Review Exercises 12–13, p. 547 Chapter Review Exercises 27–28, p. 554	Grammar Exercise Workbook, pp. 133–134	Language Lab CD-ROM, Subject-Verb Agreement; On-Line Exercise Bank, Section 24.1

Agreement Flip Book

Teaching Resources: Hands-on Grammar Activity Book, Chapter 24

1. Have students refer to their Hands-on Grammar Activity Books or give them copies of the relevant pages for this activity.

2. You may want to have students work in pairs so that they can check the accuracy of each others' sentences.

3. As an extension, have students create cards without the colored lines. They will have to check the accuracy of agreement on their own.

Find It in Your Reading

You may want to assign the same story for all students to use.

Find It in Your Writing

Have students keep a list of the errors in agreement they find. This way they will know the areas in which they need extra practice.

24.1

Hands-on Grammar

Agreement Flip Book

Make an Agreement Flip Book to see how subjects and verbs must "match up" in order to agree. On lined index cards, write the following nouns and verbs, and underline them in green: *boy, girl, man, woman, child, dog, cat, plays, eats, thinks, waits, goes, runs, walks.* Write the following nouns and verbs, and underline them in orange: *boys, girls, men, women, children, dogs, cats, play, eat, think, wait, go, run, walk.* Use the lines on the index cards as guides to ensure that each word and its underlining are the same distance from the bottom of each card.

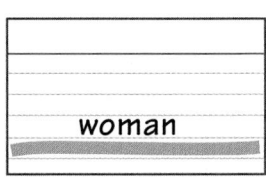

Punch a hole in the top center of each index card. Use a paper fastener to fasten the cards to a cardboard strip. Make sure all the nouns are on the left and all the verbs are on the right, but do not worry about keeping each side in a particular order.

paper fasteners

Create different combinations of nouns and verbs by rotating the top cards up. When the colors of the underlining match, the verb form agrees with the noun. Use the word pair in a sentence. Create another flip book, using nouns and verbs related to a topic of interest to you, such as sports, music, or computers.

Find It in Your Reading Create a flip book with five nouns and verbs from a short story in your literature book. Use the singular and plural forms of each word you choose.

Find It in Your Writing Choose a piece of writing from your portfolio. Underline singular subjects and verbs in red. Underline plural subjects and verbs in blue. If the colors in a sentence do not match, check the subject-verb agreement. (Ask your teacher for help in evaluating sentences that have more than one verb.)

546 • Making Words Agree

Hands-on Grammar
Use the Hands-on Grammar activity sheet for Chapter 24 to facilitate this activity.

✓ **ONGOING ASSESSMENT: Assess Mastery**

Use the following resources to assess mastery of subject-verb agreement.

In the Textbook	Technology
Chapter Review, Exercises 27–28 pp. 554–555 Standardized Test Preparation Workshop, pp. 556–557	Language Lab CD-ROM, Subject-Verb Agreement; On-Line Exercise Bank, Section 24.1

Section 24.1 Section Review

GRAMMAR EXERCISES 11–16

Exercise 11 Recognizing the Number of Nouns, Pronouns, and Verbs On your paper, write whether the noun-verb or pronoun-verb pair in each sentence is singular or plural.

1. You are welcome.
2. The children on stage sing beautifully.
3. The light gleams in the window.
4. People cheer at the celebration.
5. Music plays during the ceremony.
6. The teachers clap for the students.
7. Banners decorate the stage.
8. Balloons add a festive air.
9. The final song is sung.
10. Everyone leaves the auditorium.

Exercise 12 Making Verbs Agree With Their Subjects In some of the sentences below, subjects and verbs do not agree in number. If a sentence is correct, write *correct* on your paper. If it is incorrect, rewrite the sentence correctly.

1. Either Joe or his twin brothers graduate from high school this year.
2. English and math is required for graduation.
3. Cap and gown have become standard attire at graduations.
4. Neither Mike nor Amy want to speak at the ceremony.
5. Dances and parties are common celebrations of graduation.
6. Each graduating boy and girl receive a diploma.
7. Here is a group of teachers and the principal.
8. There are the students.
9. Do either Mikael or Tomas have a speech prepared?
10. Most students are happy when the ceremonies begin.

Exercise 13 Revising for Subject-Verb Agreement Copy the following paragraph into your notebook. Correct any errors in subject-verb agreement.

(1) There's many different ways to celebrate holidays. (2) Some families has special traditions and customs. (3) A few of these has been passed from generation to generation. (4) Often a custom or holiday come from other countries. (5) How does people in another country celebrate?

Exercise 14 Find It in Your Reading Read the following excerpt from *A Christmas Carol*. Identify which of the underlined subjects and verbs are singular, and which are plural. Explain why the verb agrees with any compound subjects you find.

SCROOGE. They owe me money and I will collect. I will have them jailed, if I have to. . . . [MARLEY *moves* towards SCROOGE; *two steps. The* spotlight stays *with him.*] MARLEY. [*Disgusted*] He and I were partners for I don't know how many years.

Exercise 15 Find It in Your Writing Choose an early draft of a piece of writing from your portfolio. Check the subject-verb agreement in all sentences. Explain any corrections you make.

Exercise 16 Writing Application Write an explanation of how you celebrate a special occasion. In each sentence, underline the subject once and the verb twice. Indicate whether the subject is plural or singular.

Section Review • 547

ASSESS

Section Review

Each of these exercises correlates with a concept in the section on subject-verb agreement, pages 534–546. These exercises may be used for more practice, for reteaching, or for review of the Key Concepts presented. Answers for all chapter exercises are available in *Grammar Exercise Answers on Transparencies* in your teaching resources.

Answer Key

Exercise 11

1. singular or plural
2. plural
3. singular
4. plural
5. singular
6. plural
7. plural
8. plural
9. singular
10. singular

Exercise 12

1. correct
2. English and math <u>are</u> required for graduation.
3. Cap and gown <u>has</u> become standard attire at graduations.
4. Neither Mike nor Amy <u>wants</u> to speak at the ceremony.
5. correct
6. Each graduating boy and girl <u>receives</u> a diploma.
7. Here <u>are</u> a group of teachers and the principal.
8. correct
9. <u>Does</u> either Mikael or Tomas <u>have</u> a speech prepared?
10. correct

Exercise 13

1. There <u>are</u> many different ways to celebrate holidays.
2. Some families <u>have</u> special traditions and customs.
3. A few of these <u>have</u> been passed from generation to generation.
4. Often a custom or holiday <u>comes</u> from other countries.
5. How <u>do</u> people in another country celebrate?

Exercise 14

Find It in Your Reading
1. They owe—plural
2. I will collect—singular
3. Marley moves—singular
4. spotlight stays—singular
5. He and I were—plural; compound subject joined by *and* takes a plural verb

continued

Answer Key continued

Exercise 15

Find It in Your Writing
Students should correct errors in subject-verb agreement.

Exercise 16

Writing Application
Ask volunteers to share their accounts with the class. Discuss how identifying subjects and verbs makes it easier to ensure agreement.

Interest GRABBER Have each student make a list of ten nouns, then exchange papers with a partner. Ask students to write a pronoun that could replace each of the nouns on the list.

Activate Prior Knowledge

Write the following sentence on the chalkboard:

Either Marta or Jennie will bring (her/their) dog to the parade.

Ask students to decide which pronoun correctly completes the sentence and to explain their choices.

TEACH

Step-by Step Teaching Guide

Making Personal Pronouns and Antecedents Agree

1. Be sure that students understand that personal pronouns must agree with their antecedents in number and gender. Ask them to list pronouns that can replace a singular, masculine noun *(John)(he,him,his)*. Continue, providing singular feminine nouns, singular neutral nouns, etc.

2. Ask students to list given names of people, places, or things. Then have them write sentences in which they use both the noun and pronoun replacement in the same sentence.

3. Review the common error of shifts in person. Explain that there is no "trick" to this. It simply involves keeping track of what they ar writing about. In the example, the sentences are about Stephanie, not an undefined "you."

4. Remind students that *and* joins like items, making the antecedents they link plural.

   Franco and Tomasso are lending me their hockey sticks.

Critical Viewing

Analyze Students may say the people, the buildings in the background, or the many pieces of materials used to make the tower.

Agreement Between Pronouns and Antecedents

An **antecedent** is the word or words for which a pronoun stands. A pronoun's antecedent may be a noun, a group of words acting as a noun, or even another pronoun. This section will explain the ways in which pronouns must agree with their antecedents. If you are not sure that you can quickly recognize pronouns and antecedents, review Section 14.2 before continuing with this section.

Making Personal Pronouns and Antecedents Agree

Personal pronouns should agree with their antecedents in three important ways:

▶ **KEY CONCEPT** A personal pronoun must agree with its antecedent in person, number, and gender. ■

Person tells whether a pronoun refers to the person speaking (first person), the person spoken to (second person), or the person, place, or thing spoken about (third person). *Number* tells whether the pronoun is singular (referring to one) or plural (referring to more than one). *Gender* tells whether a third-person-singular antecedent is masculine or feminine.

EXAMPLE: I told *David* to bring a bathing suit with *him*.

In the example above, the pronoun *him* is third person and singular. It agrees with its masculine antecedent, *David*, which is also third person (the person spoken about) and singular.

Avoiding Shifts in Person Shifts in person usually involve the careless use of *you* (the second-person pronoun) to refer to a noun in the third person.

INCORRECT: *Stephanie* has learned French. This is the language *you* need to know when *you* go to Paris.

CORRECT: *Stephanie* has learned French. This is the language *she* needs to know when *she* goes to Paris.

Whenever you use the word *you*, make sure it refers to the person to whom you are speaking or writing and not to any other person.

▲ Critical Viewing
What parts of this picture could you refer to using a plural pronoun? [Analyze]

⏱ TIME AND RESOURCE MANAGER

Resources
Print: Grammar Exercise Workbook, pp. 135–136
Technology: Language Lab CD-ROM, Using Pronouns; On-Line Exercise Bank, Section 24.2

In-Depth Coverage	Accelerated Pace
• Work through all key concepts, pp. 548–552. • Assign and review Exercises 17–20.	• Assign pp. 548–552 for independent student review. • Assign Section Review Exercises 21–23, p. 553.

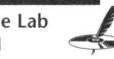

Avoiding Problems With Number and Gender

Making pronouns and antecedents agree in number and gender may sometimes be a little more difficult. Problems may arise, for example, when the antecedent is a compound joined by *or* or *nor*, or when the gender of the antecedent is not known.

KEY CONCEPT Use a singular personal pronoun to refer to two or more singular antecedents joined by *or* or *nor*. ■

Two or more singular subjects joined by *or* or *nor* must have a singular verb. In the same way, two or more singular antecedents joined by *or* or *nor* must have a singular pronoun.

INCORRECT: Either *Becca* or *Megan* will take *their* backpack.

CORRECT: Either *Becca* or *Megan* will take *her* backpack.

If a compound antecedent is joined by *and*, however, the pronoun should be plural.

EXAMPLE: *Becca* and *Megan* will take *their* backpacks.

KEY CONCEPT When the gender of a third-person-singular antecedent is not known, you may make the pronoun agree in one of these three ways: (1) Use *he or she*, *him or her*, *his or hers*. (2) Rewrite the sentence so that the antecedent and pronoun are plural. (3) Rewrite the sentence to eliminate the pronoun. ■

Exercise 17 Making Pronouns and Antecedents Agree
Rewrite each of the following sentences, filling in the blank with an appropriate pronoun.

EXAMPLE: My parents had left ___?___ travel brochures all over the living room.

ANSWER: My parents had left their travel brochures all over the living room.

1. Jack was excited about ___?___ visit to New York City.
2. He and his family planned ___?___ trip well.
3. They learned that a tourist must watch ___?___ luggage carefully.
4. Each boy selected the places ___?___ wanted to visit.
5. The family members will have ___?___ picture taken at the Statue of Liberty.

More Practice

Language Lab
CD-ROM
• Pronoun-Antecedent Agreement lesson
On-line
Exercise Bank
• Section 24.2
Grammar Exercise
Workbook
• pp. 135–136

Agreement Between Pronouns and Antecedents • 549

ONGOING ASSESSMENT: Prerequisite Skill

If students have difficulty with pronoun-antecedent agreement, you may wish to review the following to assure coverage for prerequisite knowledge.

In the Textbook	Print Resources	Technology
Nouns and Pronouns, pp. 296–309 Basic Sentence Parts, pp. 392–419	Grammar Exercise Workbook, Exercises 1–12, 47–50	Language Lab CD-ROM, Nouns and Pronouns; On-Line Exercise Bank, Section 24.2

Exercise 18

1. <u>Mary</u> knows that <u>she</u> could get lost in a big city.
2. Either <u>Curtis</u> or <u>Tim</u> will bring <u>his</u> city map today.
3. It is the <u>statue</u> or that tall <u>tree</u> that is casting <u>its</u> shadow over the sidewalk.
4. The <u>drivers</u> should know that <u>they</u> can only turn left on that one-way street.
5. The <u>taxicab</u> and the delivery <u>truck</u> made <u>their</u> way through the busy traffic.
6. <u>Tourists</u> know that <u>they</u> have many cultural activities from which to choose in a big city.
7. <u>Elsa</u> is planning to go shopping in the city, where <u>she</u> has a large selection of stores from which to choose.
8. Either <u>Sandra</u> or <u>Audrey</u> will spend <u>her</u> vacation visiting relatives in a big city.
9. <u>Al</u> likes to visit Manhattan, where <u>he</u> can do a lot of sightseeing without a car.
10. <u>Joe</u> and <u>Marc</u> know that <u>they</u> could spend a whole day in Central Park.

Critical Viewing

Describe Answers will vary. Sample answer: George and I enjoy going to the park every day, where we race our toy boats across the lake.

24.2

Exercise 18 Revising Sentences to Eliminate Pronoun
Shift Each sentence below contains one error in pronoun-antecedent agreement. Rewrite each sentence correctly, underlining the pronoun that you have changed and its antecedent.

EXAMPLE: A member of the girls' tour spends much of their time sightseeing.

ANSWER: A <u>member</u> of the girls' tour spends much of <u>her</u> time sightseeing.

1. Mary knows that you could get lost in a big city.
2. Either Curtis or Tim will bring their city map today.
3. It is the statue or that tall tree that is casting their shadow over the sidewalk.
4. The drivers should know that you can only turn left on that one-way street.
5. The taxicab and the delivery truck made its way through the busy traffic.
6. Tourists know that you have many cultural activities from which to choose in a big city.
7. Elsa is planning to go shopping in the big city, where you have a large selection of stores from which to choose.
8. Either Sandra or Audrey will spend their vacation visiting relatives in a big city.
9. Al likes to visit Manhattan, where you can do a lot of sightseeing without a car.
10. Joe and Marc know that you could spend a whole day in Central Park.

More Practice

Language Lab
CD-ROM
• Pronoun-Antecedent Agreement lesson
On-line
Exercise Bank
• Section 24.2
Grammar Exercise Workbook
• pp. 135–136

▼ Critical Viewing
Using at least two pronouns, write a sentence describing a scene that could take place in a park like this one. Make sure your pronouns agree in number. [Describe]

550 • Making Words Agree

☑ **ONGOING ASSESSMENT: Monitor and Reinforce**

If students miss more than two items in Exercises 17–20, refer them to the following for additional practice.

In the Textbook	Print Resources	Technology
Section Review, Exercises 21–24, p. 553 Chapter Review, Exercise 29, p. 554	Grammar Exercise Workbook, pp. 135–136	Language Lab CD-ROM, Subject-Verb Agreement; On-Line Exercise Bank, Section 24.2

Making Personal Pronouns and Indefinite Pronouns Agree

Indefinite pronouns (listed in Chapter 14, p. 307) are words such as *each, everybody, either,* and *one.* Pay special attention to the number of a personal pronoun when the antecedent is a singular indefinite pronoun.

KEY CONCEPT Use a singular personal pronoun when its antecedent is a singular indefinite pronoun. ■

Do not be misled by a prepositional phrase that follows an indefinite pronoun. The personal pronoun agrees with the indefinite pronoun, not with the object of the preposition.

Incorrect	Correct
One of the cats has lost *their* collar.	*One* of the cats has lost *its* collar.
Everyone in the two groups expressed *their* opinion.	*Everyone* in the two groups expressed *his or her* opinion.

Exercise 19 Making Personal Pronouns and Indefinite Pronouns Agree For each of the following sentences, choose the correct personal pronoun from the choices given in parentheses, and write it on your paper.

EXAMPLE: One of these houses has a weather vane on (its, their) roof.
ANSWER: its

1. Every one of the towns has a city hall at (its, their) center.
2. Some of the homes have fences around (its, their) yards.
3. Each street has trees shading (its, their) sidewalk.
4. Neither of the towns has (its, their) own television station.
5. Every child rides the bus to (his or her, their) school.
6. Both of those towns are famous for (its, their) history.
7. Each of the towns has (its, their) own mayor.
8. Many in this town grow (its, their) own vegetables.
9. Everyone in that town keeps (its, his or her) lawn neat.
10. Each town's news is published in (its, their) local paper.

✔ Spelling Tip

Make sure that you are using *their, there,* and *they're* correctly in your writing. If you're unsure which is appropriate, check the definitions of these three words in a dictionary.

Making Personal Pronouns and Indefinite Pronouns Agree

1. Introduce the key concept and the boxed sentences. Stress that the common error here is to confuse the object of the preposition (*cats*) with the indefinite pronoun (*one*).

2. Give students the following sentences for practice.

   Each of the dogs is on (its/their) leash.

   All of the dogs did (its/their) best in the show.

   Some of the dogs wear (its/their) ribbons on their collars.

Answer Key

Exercise 19
1. its
2. their
3. its
4. its
5. his or her
6. their
7. its
8. their
9. his or her
10. its

Integrating Workplace Skills

Many jobs involve writing. Employees may write letters to customers or clients. They may write instructions for how to use products. They may even write advertisements for their goods or services. Errors in agreement are one of the most common mistakes in grammar. Careful attention to agreement can help a writer avoid creating confusion for the reader.

☑ ONGOING ASSESSMENT: Assess Mastery

Use the following resources to assess mastery of pronoun-antecedent agreement.

In the Textbook	Technology
Chapter Review, Ex. 29–31 pp. 554–555	Language Lab CD-ROM, Subject-Verb Agreement; On-Line Exercise Bank, Section 24.2

⏲ TIME SAVERS!

Answers on Transparency Use the Grammar Exercises Answers on Transparencies for Chapter 24 to facilitate correction by students.

On-Line Exercise Bank Have students complete the exercises on computer. The Auto Check feature will grade their work for you!

24.2

> **Exercise 20** Revising Sentences to Eliminate Errors in **Pronoun-Antecedent Agreement** Most of the following sentences contain errors in pronoun-antecedent agreement. Find the sentences with errors, and rewrite them on your paper. Write *correct* for those sentences without errors.

EXAMPLE: Each of the brochures has a map printed on their cover.

ANSWER: Each of the brochures has a map printed on its cover.

1. Most large cities offer its residents a choice of sports teams to follow.
2. Jess believes that you can attend many sporting events in a large city.
3. Neither Judy nor Carol has their tickets to the basketball game.
4. Not one of the available seats was as close as it looked in the diagram.
5. Several of the fans were attending his first professional sporting event.
6. Each of the players has their own fan club.
7. All of the teams wear its colors proudly.
8. Some of the teams play their games out of town.
9. Each of the fans must provide his or her own transportation to the game.
10. Patsy forgot her bus schedule, which you really needed to get around in a big city.

More Practice

Language Lab
CD-ROM
• Pronoun-Antecedent Agreement lesson
On-line
Exercise Bank
• Section 24.2
Grammar Exercise Workbook
• pp. 135–136

◀ Critical Viewing
What features do the buildings in this photograph have in common? Use the words *its* and *their* in your answer, and make sure they agree with their antecedents.
[Analyze]

Section 24.2 *Section Review*

GRAMMAR EXERCISES 21–26

> **Exercise 21** Making Personal
Pronouns Agree For each of the following sentences, choose the correct personal pronoun from the pair in parentheses, and write it on your paper.

1. A city is a community where thousands, or even millions, of people make (its, their) homes.
2. According to the United Nations, any place that has more than 20,000 people living within (its, their) boundaries is considered a city.
3. Over forty percent of the people in the world make (its, their) homes in cities.
4. Some people don't like living far from (his, their) neighbors.
5. Neither Jim nor Larry moved (his, their) family from a farm town to the city.

> **Exercise 22** Making Pronouns
and Antecedents Agree Supply a personal pronoun to complete each sentence.

1. John lives with ___?___ parents in a small town.
2. Neither John nor Wally has ___?___ own car.
3. Both of them ride the bus to ___?___ school.
4. Wally says ___?___ can walk to school in about thirty minutes.
5. Each student has ___?___ own locker.

> **Exercise 23** Revising Sentences
to Eliminate Errors in Pronoun-Antecedent Agreement The following sentences contain errors in pronoun-antecedent agreement. Rewrite them on your paper, correcting the errors.

1. Every day, Bob and Jane walk together to a city college in her neighborhood.
2. Monica said that you have many classes from which to choose.
3. Everyone at the college selects their own class schedule.
4. Mr. Roberts hosts his or her drama class on Friday evenings at a local theater.
5. Each student in the class purchases their own ticket to the theater.

> **Exercise 24** Find It in Your
Reading Read the following excerpt from "The Monsters Are Due on Maple Street." Identify the number of each pronoun, as well as its antecedent.

MRS. GOODMAN *comes through her porch door, glass of milk in hand. The entry hall, with table and lit candle, can be seen behind her.*

Outside, the camera slowly pans down the sidewalk, taking in little knots of people who stand around talking in low voices. At the end of each conversation they look toward LES GOODMAN'S *house. . . .*

> **Exercise 25** Find It in Your
Writing Review a piece of writing from your portfolio. Check pronoun-antecedent agreement—especially agreement between personal pronouns and indefinite pronouns.

> **Exercise 26** Writing Application
Write a description of your town, village, or city. Underline all the pronouns you use. Make sure that each agrees with its antecedent.

553

Each of these exercises correlates with a concept covered in the chapter on agreement, pages 532–553. These exercises may be used for more practice, for reteaching, or for review of the Key Concepts presented. Answers for all exercises are available in *Grammar Exercises Answers on Transparencies* in your Teaching Resources.

Answer Key

▶ Exercise 27

1. pace—is
2. amount—makes
3. towns—have
4. everyone—knows
5. Most—are
6. stores—are
7. Each—has
8. barber—cuts
9. Several—attend
10. people—live

▶ Exercise 28

Answers will vary. Samples are given.

1. goes; goes
2. likes
3. are
4. is
5. are
6. like
7. like
8. holds
9. are
10. is

▶ Exercise 29

1. its
2. his
3. he
4. he or she
5. they
6. his or her
7. their
8. he
9. his or her
10. he

continued

Chapter 24 *Chapter Review*

GRAMMAR EXERCISES 27–34

▶ **Exercise 27** Identifying Subjects and Checking for Agreement On your paper, write the subject of each of the following sentences. Choose the correct verb from the pair in parentheses, and write it next to the subject.

1. The slower pace of life (is, are) one reason many people choose to live in a small town.
2. The amount of traffic (makes, make) it is easy to get around.
3. Some towns (has, have) only one stoplight.
4. Quite often, everyone in a small town (knows, know) everyone else.
5. Most of the townspeople (is, are) very friendly.
6. The grocery and the department stores (is, are) located down the street.
7. Each of the stores (has, have) an awning over the front door.
8. The barber next door still (cuts, cut) hair for one dollar.
9. Several of the children (attends, attend) school in another town.
10. How many people (lives, live) in your town?

▶ **Exercise 28** Supplying Appropriate Verbs Rewrite each of the following sentences, supplying an appropriate verb in the present tense.

1. When Stan __?__ home, Vinnie __?__ with him for a visit.
2. Vinnie __?__ to ride the horses at Stan's house.
3. All of the horses __?__ very gentle.
4. Each of the boys __?__ an excellent rider.
5. Many hours __?__ spent riding over the foothills nearby.

6. Both Stan and Vinnie __?__ to ride their horses fast.
7. The boys __?__ to swim and fish in a pond near the house.
8. Stan __?__ the record for the largest fish caught in the pond.
9. There __?__ many outdoor activities to enjoy in the country.
10. When the week is over, Vinnie __?__ sad to go back to the city.

▶ **Exercise 29** Checking for Agreement Between Pronouns and Antecedents For each of the following sentences, choose the correct word from the pair given in parentheses, and write it on your paper. Note that the antecedent for a pronoun may appear in a previous sentence.

1. Every city offers (its, their) residents opportunities for work and play.
2. Jack studied large cities in (his, their) social studies class.
3. A typical city, (he, they) told me, covers many square miles.
4. Everyone living in a city has choices as to how (he or she, they) will travel to work.
5. Many people work in the city, but it's the suburbs where (he or she, they) live.
6. Everyone living in the suburbs can choose (his or her, their) means of travel to work.
7. Some choose buses or trains, while others use (his, their) cars.
8. Jack would like to visit a large city because (you, he) will see interesting, different neighborhoods.
9. Almost any city dweller can be found living in close proximity to (his or her, their) neighbors.
10. Neither Jim nor his brother could decide which city (he, they) would like most to visit.

1. have 4. minds
2. is 5. have; their
3. have

► **Exercise 30** **Using All the Rules**
of Agreement For each of the following
sentences, choose the correct word from
the pair given in parentheses.

1. Lil and her family (has, have) an
apartment in a big city.
2. There (is, are) an amusement park in
the big city.
3. Most of the rides at the park (has,
have) very long lines.
4. Neither Mary nor Lil (minds, mind)
waiting for the rides.
5. Both of the girls (has, have) decided
that Italian food is (her, their) favorite.

► **Exercise 31** **Revising Sentences**
to Eliminate Problems in Agreement
Rewrite the sentences below, eliminating
any errors in agreement and making any
other minor changes needed.

1. There's many reasons people like to
live in either a small town or a big city.
2. Each type of city has their own attractions and problems.
3. Neither a small town nor a large city
are apt to satisfy everyone.
4 My brother thinks that small towns is
too boring.
5. He likes big cities because you can do
so much.

► **Exercise 32** **Revising a Paragraph**
to Eliminate Problems in Agreement
Rewrite the paragraph below, correcting all
errors in agreement.

(1) Holidays is celebrated in both small
towns and big cities. (2) However, each of
the holidays are celebrated differently. (3)
There's more big parades in a big city. (4)
Each small-town storekeeper is likely to
close their store for a holiday. (5) Both big
cities and small towns usually celebrate its
founders' days. (6) Almost everyone say
they like a fireworks display. (7) Either a

picnic or a dance are also great ways to
celebrate. (8) Civic leaders likes to give
speeches at these events. (9) Cultural
traditions of the community is featured at
many celebrations. (10) Almost everybody
have a good time.

► **Exercise 33** **Writing Sentences**
With Correct Agreement Write five
sentences, using combinations of the words
listed below. Be sure subjects and verbs,
and pronouns and antecedents, agree.

she	travel	fly	packs	they
suitcase	taxi	them	friend	Ellen
tourist	her	hers	theirs	map

► **Exercise 34** **Writing Application**
Write five sentences about how a
favorite holiday is celebrated in your city
or town. In each sentence, underline the
subject once and the verb twice. Write
in the present tense, and make sure the
subject and verb agree in every sentence.

► **Exercise 35** **CUMULATIVE**
REVIEW Problems With Verbs,
Pronouns, and Agreement Revise the following paragraph, correcting errors in verb
and pronoun usage and agreement.

(1) John and his family has a special way
of celebrating New Year's Eve. (2) To prepare, they have spent the evening making
food. (3) Each of them have their own specialty. (4) John's specialty will be apple pie.
(5) After they have finished in the kitchen,
the family will watch their favorite movie
again. (6) They had seen it so many times,
everyone know the dialogue by heart. (7)
While the family watches, one member
serves they. (8) This year, John says, it is
him who must serve. (9) Neither John nor
his brothers has to go to bed early on that
night. (10) All of them, even his youngest
brother, stays up until midnight.

Chapter Review • 555

► **Exercise 31**

1. There are many reasons people
like to live in either a small town
or a big city.
2. Each type of city has its own
attractions and problems.
3. Neither a small town nor a large
city is apt to satisfy everyone.
4. My brother thinks that small
towns are too boring.
5. He likes big cities because he can
do so much.

► **Exercise 32**

1. Holidays are celebrated in both
small towns and big cities.
2. However, each of the holidays is
celebrated differently.
3. There are more big parades in a
big city.
4. Each small-town storekeeper is
likely to close his or her store for
a holiday.
5. Both big cities and small towns
usually celebrate their founders'
days.
6. Almost everyone says he or she
likes a fireworks display.
7. Either a picnic or a dance is also
a great way to celebrate.
8. Civic leaders like to give
speeches at these events.
9. Cultural traditions of the
community are featured at many
celebrations.
10. Almost everybody has a good
time.

► **Exercise 33**

Answers will vary. Sample responses
are given.

1. Ellen asked for a tourist map.
2. She and her mother fly to
Europe.
3. To prepare, each of them packs a
suitcase.
4. A taxi takes them to the airport.
5. They travel with a friend of
theirs.

continued

Answer Key continued

► **Exercise 34**

Writing Application
Subjects and verbs should agree in students'
sentences.

► **Exercise 35**

Cumulative Review
(1) John and his family have a special way of
celebrating New Year's Eve. (2) To prepare, they
spend the evening making food. (3) Each of
them has his or her own specialty. (4) John's

specialty is apple pie. (5) After they have
finished in the kitchen, the family watches their
favorite movie again. (6) They have seen it so
many times, everyone knows the dialogue by
heart. (7) While the family watches, one
member serves them. (8) This year, John says, it
is he who must serve. (9) Neither John nor his
brothers have to go to bed early on that night.
(10) All of them, even his youngest brother,
stays up until midnight.

Standardized Test Preparation Workshop

Recognizing Appropriate Sentence Construction

Standardized tests frequently test your knowledge of the rules of subject-verb agreement. When checking a sentence for errors, first identify the subject. Next, identify the type of subject: singular, plural, or compound. Then, apply the rules of agreement to make sure that the verb in the sentence agrees with the subject.

The following questions will give you practice with different formats used for items that test knowledge of subject-verb agreement.

Sample Test Items	Answers and Explanations

Directions: Identify the underlined word or phrase that contains an error in the following sentence.
 	
Neither Carolyn nor her visitors hears the
   (A)   (B)   (C)
 	
car approaching. No error.
   (D)   (E)
	The correct answer is *C*. The compound subject of the sentence is *Neither Carolyn nor her visitors*. When a singular and a plural subject are joined by *or* or *nor*, the verb must agree with the subject closest to it. In this case, the subject *visitors* is plural, so the plural verb *hear* should be used in the sentence.

Directions: Choose the revised version of the following sentence that eliminates all errors in grammar, usage, and mechanics. Neither Carolyn nor her visitors hears the car approaching. A Either Carolyn or her visitors hear the car approaching. B Neither Carolyn nor her visitors hear the car approaching. C Carolyn, and her visitors, hears the car approaching. D The car approaching are not heard by Carolyn or her visitors.	The correct answer is *B*. The compound subject of the sentence is *Neither Carolyn nor her visitors*. When a singular and a plural subject are joined by *or* or *nor*, the verb must agree with the subject closest to it. In this case, the subject *visitors* is plural, so the plural verb *hear* should be used in the sentence. Answers *A* and *C* change the meaning of the sentence. Answer *D* contains an error in agreement.

556 • Making Words Agree

Practice 1 **Directions:** Identify the underlined word or phrase that contains an error in each of the following sentences.

1 The president and vice president
           (A)
wave as they move through the crowd.
  (B)   (C)   (D)
No error.
(E)

2 Each one wears pins made for them
    (A)   (B)
by the children of Cedar Grove.
  (C)   (D)
No error.
(E)

3 My sister and I is attending their
    (A)   (B)
address to the community. No error.
  (C)   (D)   (E)

4 Here is the doors to get
 (A) (B)   (C)
into the community center. No error.
     (D)   (E)

5 Either my sister or I hope to ask them
    (A)   (B)
questions about environmental concerns.
  (C)   (D)
No error.
(E)

Practice 2 **Directions:** Choose the revised version of each numbered sentence that eliminates all errors in grammar, usage, and mechanics.

1 The study of American presidents often reveal that they was once simply average citizens.

  A The study of American presidents often reveal that they were once simply average citizens.

  B The study of American presidents often reveals that they was once simply average citizens.

  C The study of American presidents often reveals that they were once simply average citizens.

  D The study of American presidents which reveal that they was once simply average citizens.

2 Perhaps our greatest president, Abraham Lincoln came from very humble beginnings, but neither poverty nor lack of formal education hold a man of Lincoln's brilliance and integrity back.

  F Perhaps our greatest president, Abraham Lincoln came from very humble beginnings, but neither poverty nor lack of formal education holds a man of Lincoln's brilliance and integrity back.

  G Perhaps our greatest president, Abraham Lincoln come from very humble beginnings. However, neither poverty nor lack of formal education holds a man of Lincoln's brilliance and integrity back.

  H Perhaps our greatest president, Abraham Lincoln comes from very humble beginnings, but neither poverty nor lack of formal education hold a man of Lincoln's brilliance and integrity back.

  J Perhaps our greatest president, Abraham Lincoln come from very humble beginnings, but neither poverty nor lack of formal education holds a man of Lincoln's brilliance and integrity back.

Standardized Test Preparation Workshop • 557

Answer Key

Practice 1

1. E
2. B
3. B
4. A
5. E

Practice 2

1. C
2. F

Chapter 25 Time and Resource Manager

In-Depth Lesson Plan

LESSON FOCUS	PRINT AND MEDIA RESOURCES
DAY 1 — **Using Modifiers** Students learn and apply the concepts of forming the comparative and superlative degree of modifiers and do the Hands-on Grammar activity (pp. 560–566).	*Language Lab* **CD-ROM**, Using Modifiers; *On-Line Exercise Bank*, Section 25.1 **Teaching Resources** *Grammar Exercise Workbook*, pp. 137–142; *Grammar Exercises Answers on Transparencies*, Ch. 25; *Hands-on Grammar Book*, Chapter 25
DAY 2 — **Troublesome Modifiers** Students learn and apply the correct comparative and superlative degree of irregular and troublesome modifiers (pp. 567–571).	*Language Lab* **CD-ROM**, Using Modifiers; *On-Line Exercise Bank*, Section 25.2 **Teaching Resources** *Grammar Exercise Workbook*, pp.143–144; *Grammar Exercises Answers on Transparencies*, Ch. 25
DAY 3 — **Review and Assess** Students review chapter and demonstrate mastery of use of comparative and superlative degrees of modifiers (pp. 572–573).	*On-Line Exercise Bank*, Sections 25.1–2 **Teaching Resources** *Formal Assessment*, Ch. 25; *Grammar Exercises Answers on Transparencies*, Ch. 25

Accelerated Lesson Plan

LESSON FOCUS	PRINT AND MEDIA RESOURCES
DAY 1 — **Using Modifiers Through Troublesome Modifiers** Students cover concepts and usage of modifiers as determined by Diagnostic Test (pp. 558–573).	*Language Lab* **CD-ROM**, Using Modifiers; *On-Line Exercise Bank*, Sections 25.1–2 **Teaching Resources** *Grammar Exercise Workbook*, pp. 137–144; *Grammar Exercises Answers on Transparencies*, Ch. 25; *Hands-on Grammar Book*, Chapter 25
DAY 2 — **Review and Assess** Students review chapter and demonstrate mastery of use of comparative and superlative degrees of modifiers (pp. 572–573).	*On-Line Exercise Bank*, Sections 25.1–2 **Teaching Resources** *Formal Assessment*, Ch. 25; *Grammar Exercises Answers on Transparencies*, Ch. 25

Options for Adapting Lesson Plans

HOMEWORK
Have students complete any section of the chapter for homework.

FEATURES
Extend coverage with the Grammar in Literature feature (p. 564), and the Standardized Test Preparation Workshop (p. 574).

TECHNOLOGY
Students can use the On-Line Exercise Bank to complete the exercises on computer. The Auto Check feature will grade their work.

INTEGRATED SKILLS COVERAGE

Grammar in Literature
SE p. 564

Reading
Find It In Your Reading, SE p. 566, 570, 571

Writing
Find It In Your Writing, SE p. 566, 570, 571
Writing Application SE pp. 566, 571, 573
ATE p. 562

Spelling
SE p. 561

Technology
SE p. 564

Speaking and Listening
ATE p. 563

Viewing and Representing
Critical Viewing, SE pp. 558, 562, 565, 567, 568

ASSESSMENT SUPPORT

Standardized Test Preparation SE p. 574; ATE pp. 564, 568
Standardized Test Preparation Workbook, pp. 49–50
Formal Assessment, Ch. 25

MEETING INDIVIDUAL NEEDS

Less Advanced Students ATE p. 560, see also Ongoing Assessment, pp. 561, 563, 569
More Advanced Students ATE pp. 561, 568

BLOCK SCHEDULING

Pacing Suggestions
For 90-minute Blocks
• Administer the Diagnostic Test to students to determine instructional coverage.
• Have students complete the necessary exercises in class. Use the Hands-on Grammar activity to provide a change of pace.

Resources for Varying Instruction
• *Language Lab* **CD-ROM** If your students have access to hardware, a 90-minute block provides an ideal opportunity for students to work on computer.

Professional Development Support
• *How to Manage Instruction in the Block* This Teaching Resource provides management and activity suggestions.

MEDIA AND TECHNOLOGY

For the Student
• *Language Lab* **CD-ROM** Using Modifiers
• *On-Line Exercise Bank,* Ch. 25

For the Teacher
• *Resource Pro* **CD-ROM**

WRITING AND GRAMMAR WEBSITE

The Interactive Writing and Grammar Website provides a wide array of support for students, teachers, and parents. Grammar support includes:

• *On-Line Exercise Bank* with Auto Check scoring
• Diagnostic and assessment support

www.phschool.com

LITERATURE CONNECTIONS

Related selection from *Prentice Hall Literature: Timeless Voices, Timeless Themes,* Bronze:
from "Lochinvar" by Sir Walter Scott, SE p. 564

Lesson Objectives

1. To recognize how to form and use the comparative and superlative degrees of modifiers.

2. To demonstrate how to use *more* and *most* to form the comparative and superlative degrees of three-syllable modifiers.

3. To understand how to correctly use troublesome adjectives and adverbs.

4. To clarify and support spoken ideas with evidence and examples.

Critical Viewing

Analyze Students may say the player on the left is wearing a brighter color, but the player on the right appears to be more interested in playing.

Chapter 25 Using Modifiers

Adjectives and adverbs can be used in comparing people, places, or things. The form of an adjective or adverb depends on the kind of comparison that is being made.

The following example shows how adjectives change form: "Ben Attow is a *high* mountain in Scotland (1,032 meters). It is *higher* than Ben Hope (927 meters). Ben Nevis is the *highest* mountain in Scotland (1,343 meters)." Adverbs also change form, as shown in these sentences: "Ian plays the bagpipes *well*. Mary plays the bagpipes *better* than Ian does, but Angus plays the bagpipes *best* of all." These different forms of adjectives and adverbs are known as *degrees of comparison*.

▲ **Critical Viewing**
Use adjectives and adverbs to compare these two bagpipe players. Which one is wearing a *brighter* color? Which one appears to be *more interested* in playing music? **[Analyze]**

558 • Using Modifiers

✓ ONGOING ASSESSMENT: Diagnose

If students miss more than one item in each category, direct them to the relevant pages of the text and assign exercises for practice and review.

Using Modifiers	Diagnostic Test Items	Teach	Practice	Section Review	Chapter Review
Skill Check A					
Degrees, Two Syllables or Less	A 1–5	pp. 560–561	Ex. 1–2	Ex. 8, 10	Ex. 22
Skill Check B					
Degrees, Three or More Syllables	B 6–10	p. 562	Ex. 3	Ex. 8, 10	Ex. 22
Skill Check C					
Irregular Modifiers	C 11–15	p. 563	Ex. 4–6	Ex. 9, 11	Ex. 23–24

Diagnostic Test

Directions: Write all answers on a separate sheet of paper.

Skill Check A. Write the comparative and superlative degrees of the following modifiers. Whenever possible, use the *-er* and *-est* forms.

1. nervous
2. quick
3. painful
4. short
5. quiet

Skill Check B. Write the comparative and superlative degrees of the following modifiers.

6. generous
7. attractive
8. suddenly
9. capable
10. powerfully

Skill Check C. Indicate the degree of the underlined word in each of the following sentences.

11. Judy and Mark enjoyed the Highland games in Scotland <u>more</u> than the rest of the trip.
12. Judy thought the <u>best</u> part of the Highland games was the Scottish dancing.
13. Mark thought the shot-put event was <u>better</u> than the dancing.
14. The tallest athlete threw the shot the <u>farthest</u>.
15. Judy also thought the musicians played <u>well</u>.

Skill Check D. Revise the following sentences, correcting all errors in degree. If the sentence contains no errors, write *correct*.

16. Mark realized more sooner than Judy that the Scottish castles were just ahead.
17. They wondered which of the two castles had the highest tower.
18. Judy grew more fonder of the castles as she explored them.
19. Balmoral Castle is the most famous of the two castles.
20. Mark liked the other castle better.

Skill Check E. Revise the sentences below that contain errors in degree or usage. If a sentence contains no errors, write *correct*.

21. The kilt looked badly after the dance.
22. There were fewer dancers in the Highland fling than in the sword dance.
23. Mark just reached his seat one minute before the dance began.
24. Judy thought the dancer performed good.
25. There only were seven dancers (not eight) for the Scottish reel.

☑ ONGOING ASSESSMENT: Diagnose *continued*

Using Modifiers	Diagnostic Test Items	Teach	Practice	Section Review	Chapter Review
Skill Check D					
Using Comparative and Superlative Degrees of Modifiers	D 16–20	p. 565	Ex. 7	Ex. 12	Ex. 25–26
Skill Check E					
Troublesome Adjectives and Adverbs	E 21–25	pp. 567–570	Ex. 15–16	Ex. 17–18	Ex. 27–29
Cumulative Review and Applications				Ex. 12–14 Ex. 19–21	Ex. 30

Answer Key

- Each item in the Diagnostic Test corresponds with a concept covered in the Using Modifiers chapter. This will enable you to tailor instruction to your students' particular needs. See "Ongoing Assessment: Diagnose" on the bottom of pages 558–559 for further details.

- Answers for the Diagnostic Test and all chapter exercises are available in *Grammar Exercises Answers on Transparencies* in your teaching resources.

Skill Check A

1. more nervous, most nervous
2. quicker, quickest
3. more painful, most painful
4. shorter, shortest
5. quieter, quietest

Skill Check B

6. more generous, most generous
7. more attractive, most attractive
8. more suddenly, most suddenly
9. more capable, most capable
10. more powerfully, most powerfully

Skill Check C

11. comparative
12. superlative
13. comparative
14. superlative
15. positive

Skill Check D

16. Mark realized sooner than Judy that the Scottish castles were just ahead.
17. They wondered which of the two castles had the higher tower.
18. Judy grew fonder of the castles as she explored them.
19. Balmoral Castle is the more famous of the two castles.
20. correct

Skill Check E

21. The kilt looked bad after the dance.
22. correct
23. Mark reached his seat just one minute before the dance began.
24. Judy thought the dancer performed well.
25. There were only seven dancers (not eight) for the Scottish reel.

Activate Prior Knowledge

Have students work in pairs. Ask each to write a few sentences in which he or she describes what the partner is wearing and doing. Have them exchange papers and identify the adjectives and adverbs in the sentences.

TEACH

Step-by-Step Teaching Guide

Regular Modifiers With One or Two Syllables

1. Tell students that the -er and -est suffixes are used for the regular formation of the comparative and superlative degrees of modifiers unless they sound awkward.

2. Point out the spelling change that occurs when -er or -est is added to words ending in y.

3. Review the use of more and most with students. For one- or two-syllable adjectives, there is no general rule. Students need to rely on sound. More just rather than juster is correct.

4. Tell students that adjectives of more than two syllables and adverbs ending in -ly form their comparative and superlative degrees using more and most.

   more wonderful, most wonderful
   more quickly, most quickly

5. Remind students that not all words ending in -ly are adverbs. For example: the adjectives lovely, lovelier, loveliest.

Customize for
Less Advanced Students

Review with students that adjectives modify nouns, and adverbs modify verbs, adjectives, and other adverbs. Practice making comparisons to reinforce the concept that comparative has to do with a comparison of two things while superlative involves the comparison of three or more things.

Section 25.1

Comparison of Adjectives and Adverbs

You may recall from Chapter 16 that adjectives and adverbs are modifiers. Adjectives can modify nouns or pronouns. Adverbs can modify verbs, adjectives, or other adverbs. These two parts of speech can be either *regular* or *irregular*. Luckily, most adjectives and adverbs in English are regular—that is, their comparative and superlative degrees are formed in predictable ways. How these degrees are formed depends on the number of syllables in the positive form.

> **KEY CONCEPT** Most adjectives and adverbs have three degrees of comparison: the *positive*, the *comparative*, and the *superlative*. ■

The *positive* degree is used when no comparison is being made. This is the form listed in a dictionary. The *comparative* degree is used when two things are being compared. The *superlative* degree is used when three or more things are being compared.

Regular Modifiers With One or Two Syllables

The comparative and superlative degrees of most adjectives and adverbs of one or two syllables can be formed in either of two ways:

> **KEY CONCEPT** Use -er or *more* to form the comparative degree and -est or *most* to form the superlative degree of most one- and two-syllable modifiers. ■

Adding -er for the comparative degree and -est for the superlative degree are the most common ways to form these degrees.

COMPARATIVE AND SUPERLATIVE DEGREES FORMED WITH *-ER* AND *-EST*		
Positive	**Comparative**	**Superlative**
fast	faster	fastest
tall	taller	tallest
narrow	narrower	narrowest
sunny	sunnier	sunniest

Theme: Scotland

In this section, you will learn about degrees of comparison. The examples and exercises are about Scotland.

Cross-Curricular Connection: Social Studies

Learn More

To learn more about adjectives and adverbs, refer to Chapter 16.

⏱ TIME AND RESOURCE MANAGER

Resources
Print: Grammar Exercise Workbook, pp. 137–142
Technology: Language Lab CD-ROM, Using Modifiers; On-Line Exercise Bank, Section 25.1

In-Depth Coverage	Accelerated Pace
• Work through all key concepts, pp. 560–565. • Assign and review Exercises 1–7. • Read and discuss Grammar in Literature, p. 564.	• Assign pp. 560–565 for independent student review. • Review Irregular Adjectives and Adverbs, pp. 563–564, and assign Exercises 4–6.

More and *most* can also be used to form the comparative and superlative degrees of most one- and two-syllable modifiers. These words should not be used when the result sounds awkward, as in "A greyhound is *more fast* than a beagle."

Notice in the following chart that two of the examples from the preceding chart—*narrow* and *sunny*—can be used with *more* and *most*. *More* and *most* are also used to form the comparative and superlative degrees of most adverbs ending in *-ly* and of one- and two-syllable modifiers that would sound awkward with *-er* and *-est*.

COMPARATIVE AND SUPERLATIVE DEGREES FORMED WITH *MORE* AND *MOST*

Positive	Comparative	Superlative
narrow	more narrow	most narrow
sunny	more sunny	most sunny
quickly	more quickly	most quickly
just	more just	most just

Use *-er* and *-est* with the last two examples above. Notice how awkward they sound. If you are not sure which form to use, say the words aloud and it will become clear.

► **Exercise 1** Forming the Comparative and Superlative Degrees of One- and Two-Syllable Modifiers Write the comparative and superlative degrees of the following modifiers. If the degrees can be formed in either way, write the *-er* and *-est* forms.

1. high
2. smart
3. mean
4. pretty
5. clear
6. brightly
7. tall
8. late
9. young
10. slowly

► **Exercise 2** Supplying Modifiers Copy the following sentences, supplying the form of the modifier indicated in parentheses.
1. Scotland is (small—comparative) than the United States.
2. The Highlands is the (rugged—superlative) area.
3. The River Clyde is Scotland's (important—superlative) river.
4. The Tay, the (long—superlative) river, is 120 miles long.
5. Before engineers widened the Clyde River in the 1700's, it was (narrow—comparative) and (shallow—comparative) than it is now.

💡 **Spelling Tip**

When adjectives and adverbs end with a consonant plus *-y*, drop the *-y* and add *-ier* or *-iest*. Words ending with the suffix *-ly* are an exception to this rule.

► **More Practice**

Language Lab CD-ROM
• Using Modifiers lesson
On-line Exercise Bank
• Section 25.1
Grammar Exercise Workbook
• pp. 137–138

Customize for
More Advanced Students

Have students use a dictionary to determine the comparative and superlative degrees of the following modifiers:

easy (easier, easiest)

eager (more eager, most eager)

nervous (more nervous, most nervous)

hopeful (more hopeful, most hopeful)

careless (more careless, most careless)

Answer Key

► **Exercise 1**

1. higher, highest
2. smarter, smartest
3. meaner, meanest
4. prettier, prettiest
5. clearer, clearest
6. more brightly, most brightly
7. taller, tallest
8. later, latest
9. younger, youngest
10. more slowly, most slowly

► **Exercise 2**

1. Scotland is smaller than the United States.
2. The Highlands is the most rugged area.
3. The River Clyde is Scotland's most important river.
4. The Tay, the longest river, is 120 miles long.
5. Before engineers widened the Clyde River in the 1700's, it was narrower and shallower than it is now.

☑ **ONGOING ASSESSMENT: Prerequisite Skills**

If students have difficulty with comparatives and superlatives, you may wish to review the following to assure coverage for prerequisite knowledge.

In the Textbook	Print Resources	Technology
Adjectives and Adverbs, pp. 336–357	Grammar Exercise Workbook, pp. 21–36	Language Lab CD-ROM, Using Modifiers; On-Line Exercise Bank, Section 16

⏱ **TIME SAVERS!**

📄 **Answers on Transparency** Use the Grammar Exercises Answers on Transparencies for Chapter 25 to facilitate correction by students.

🖥 **On-Line Exercise Bank** Have students complete the exercises on computer. The Auto Check feature will grade their work for you!

Regular Modifiers With Three or More Syllables

1. Tell students the three-or-more-syllables rule is clear because there are no exceptions. Remind them that some one- and two-syllable adjectives also form the comparative and superlative degrees using *more* and *most*.

2. Give students the following words for additional practice:

   capable (more, most)

   correct (more, most)

   necessary (more, most)

   brave (both ways)

Answer Key

> **Exercise 3**

1. more envious, most envious
2. more talented, most talented
3. more secretly, most secretly
4. more comfortable, most comfortable
5. more delicate, most delicate
6. more friendly, most friendly; friendlier, friendliest
7. more original, most original
8. more recently, most recently
9. more natural, most natural
10. more emotionally, most emotionally

Critical Viewing

Compare Answers will vary depending on where students live. Many will say that the area in the photo appears quieter, more mountainous, more majestic, or more old-fashioned than their hometown.

Integrating Writing Skills

Remind students that, although modifiers add detail to description, they lose impact if they are used incorrectly. Ask students to review a selection from their recent writings to check whether they have used the correct form of the comparative and superlative degree for modifiers.

25.1

Regular Modifiers With Three or More Syllables

When an adjective or adverb has three or more syllables, its comparative and superlative degrees are easy to form.

> **KEY CONCEPT** Use *more* and *most* to form the comparative and superlative degrees of all modifiers of three or more syllables. ■

Never use *-er* or *-est* with modifiers of more than two syllables.

DEGREES OF MODIFIERS WITH THREE OR MORE SYLLABLES		
Positive	**Comparative**	**Superlative**
popular	more popular	most popular
affectionate	more affectionate	most affectionate
intelligently	more intelligently	most intelligently

> **Exercise 3** Forming the Comparative and Superlative Degrees of Modifiers With More Than Two Syllables On your paper, write the comparative and superlative degrees of the following modifiers.

EXAMPLE: beautiful

ANSWER: more beautiful, most beautiful

1. envious
2. talented
3. secretly
4. comfortable
5. delicate
6. friendly
7. original
8. recently
9. natural
10. emotionally

▼ **Critical Viewing** What modifiers would you use to compare this scene to the area where you live? **[Compare]**

Irregular Adjectives and Adverbs

A few adjectives and adverbs are *irregular*. Their comparative and superlative degrees must be memorized.

KEY CONCEPT Memorize the irregular comparative and superlative forms of certain adjectives and adverbs. ■

The following chart lists the most common irregular modifiers.

DEGREES OF IRREGULAR ADJECTIVES AND ADVERBS

Positive	Comparative	Superlative
bad	worse	worst
badly	worse	worst
far (distance)	farther	farthest
far (extent)	further	furthest
good	better	best
well	better	best
many	more	most
much	more	most

Exercise 4 **Recognizing the Degree of Irregular Modifiers**
On your paper, indicate the degree of the underlined word in each of the following sentences.

EXAMPLE: We could see <u>farther</u> as the fog lifted.
ANSWER: comparative

1. The head of a clan was called the chief, and the clan members served him <u>well</u>.
2. <u>Most</u> clan members were both the chief's tenants and his relatives.
3. Out of the three clans, the Clan Stewart had the <u>most</u> members.
4. The Clan Campbell had <u>more</u> members than the Clan MacDonald.
5. The Clan Fergusson can be traced the <u>furthest</u> back in history.
6. The clans in the Highlands of Scotland fought <u>many</u> battles long ago.
7. The Scottish Clan MacDonald fought even <u>more</u> battles against the Clan Campbell.
8. The warriors looked <u>bad</u> after a long battle.
9. The clans became <u>more</u> tired as they fought.
10. The <u>most</u> impressive characteristic of a Scottish clan is the loyalty of its members.

Grammar and Style Tip

When you write, try not to overuse the various forms of *good* and *bad*. Be as precise as possible when writing descriptions.

More Practice

Language Lab
CD-ROM
• Using Modifiers lesson
On-line
Exercise Bank
• Section 25.1
Grammar Exercise
Workbook
• pp. 139–140

Comparison of Adjectives and Adverbs • 563

Irregular Adjectives and Adverbs

1. Although they are included here, you may wish to refer students to the usage of *bad/badly* and *good/well,* taught on page 567 in Section 25.2, Troublesome Adjectives and Adverbs.

2. Review the two uses of *far.* Help students to understand the distinction between distance (Our houses are *far* apart) and extent (That comment went too *far*).

3. Let students know that *far* is an example of a word that has two distinct but related meanings. Help them see that the confusion arises because both meanings involve quantity, but one quantity is of distance, while the other is of extent or degree.

Answer Key

Exercise 4

1. positive
2. superlative
3. superlative
4. comparative
5. superlative
6. positive
7. comparative
8. positive
9. comparative
10. superlative

Integrating Speaking and Listening Skills

Students do not learn bad usage from what they read. Most usage errors occur in what they hear around them, on television, and in movies. Have students work in pairs, each student telling in a few brief sentences how someone did something well or badly. The partner should write the sentences as they are being said. Then students can review their sentences for correct use of *well* and *good, bad* and *badly.*

✓ ONGOING ASSESSMENT: Monitor and Reinforce

If students miss more than two items in Exercise 1, 2, or 3, refer them to the following for additional practice.

In the Textbook	Print Resources	Technology
Section Review, Ex. 8, 10, p. 566 Chapter Review, Ex. 22, p. 572	Grammar Exercise Workbook, pp. 137–140	Language Lab CD-ROM, Using Modifiers; On-Line Exercise Bank, Section 25.1

More Practice

Language Lab
CD-ROM
• Using Modifiers lesson
On-line
Exercise Bank
• Section 25.1
Grammar Exercise
Workbook
• pp. 141–142

Exercise 5

1. more
2. best
3. worst
4. better
5. farthest

Exercise 6

Some of the <u>most violent</u> struggles in Scottish history occurred during the late 900's. Each king from 900 to 1005 gained control by killing his predecessor. Each one was <u>worse</u> than the one before. One of my teacher's favorite plays, *Macbeth*, is based on this period in history. Even though the play itself is violent, the actual events were probably <u>bloodier</u> than the play.

Step-by-Step Teaching Guide

Grammar in Literature

1. Read or have a volunteer read aloud the Scott passage.

2. Ask students to replace the italicized adjectives with other positive, comparative, or superlative adjectives. Do they like their revision better? Why or why not?

More About the Author

Sir Walter Scott (1771–1832) was a Scottish novelist and poet of the Romantic Era. Scott's most famous works include the romantic poem *The Lady of the Lake* and the novels *Ivanhoe* and *Quentin Durward*. Fittingly for one who wrote about knights and heroes, Scott was knighted in 1820.

▶ **Exercise 5** Using the Comparative and Superlative Degrees of Irregular Modifiers Copy the following sentences, supplying the form of the modifier indicated in parentheses.

EXAMPLE: The fog seems (bad—comparative) this morning.

ANSWER: The fog seems worse this morning.

1. Judy and Mark hiked (much—comparative) in the Highlands than in the Border Country.
2. The (good—superlative) part of the hike was the beautiful scenery.
3. The weather was the (bad—superlative) on the first day of the trip.
4. The weather turned (good—comparative) after that.
5. That was the (far—superlative) trip they had ever taken.

▶ **Exercise 6** Revising a Passage to Eliminate Errors With Modifiers In your notebook, revise the following passage. Correct any errors in the way modifiers are used.

Some of the violentest struggles in Scottish history occurred during the late 900's. Each king from 900 to 1005 gained control by killing his predecessor. Each one was badder than the one before. One of my teacher's most favorite plays, *Macbeth*, is based on this period in history. Even though the play itself is violent, the actual events were probably more bloodier than the play.

GRAMMAR IN
LITERATURE

from **Lochinvar**
Sir Walter Scott

In the following excerpt, the positive and superlative forms of the irregular adjective good *are italicized in* blue.

O, young Lochinvar is come out of the West,
Through all the wide Border his steed was the *best,*
And save his *good* broadsword he weapons had none;
He rode all unarmed, and he rode all alone.

🖥️ **Internet Tip**

Adjectives generally do not help to narrow your searches on the Internet. Avoid including adjectives as key words because they will link to topics unrelated to your search.

🖊️ STANDARDIZED TEST PREPARATION WORKSHOP

Grammar and Usage Standardized tests often ask students to recognize correct usage within a given sentence. Give students the following example:

I had the <u>better</u> time of my life on our vacation to Scotland.

Is the underlined word used correctly? If not, choose the appropriate correction.

A most better
B best
C good
D no change

Students should see that this sentence requires the superlative form of *good,* because more than three things are being compared *(time of my life).* The correct choice is item **B**.

Comparative and Superlative Degrees

Remember the following rules when you use the comparative and superlative degrees:

KEY CONCEPT Use the **comparative** degree to compare *two* people, places, things, or occurrences. Use the **superlative** degree to compare *three or more* people, places, things, or occurrences. ■

COMPARE TWO:	These bagpipes sound *better* than those. The bagpipes sound *better* now. (present compared to past)
COMPARE MORE THAN TWO:	Cameron is the *best* bagpipe player in town. (Cameron compared to all others.)

Do not combine the use of *-er* and *more* to form the comparative degree or *-est* and *most* to form the superlative degree.

INCORRECT:	This assignment is *more easier* than I thought. Edinburgh is the *most beautifulest* city in Scotland.
CORRECT:	This assignment is *easier* than I thought. Edinburgh is the *most beautiful* city in Scotland.

▲ Critical Viewing
Use at least one comparative and one superlative modifier to describe the place pictured here. **[Apply]**

Exercise 7 Correcting Errors in Degree On your paper, revise the sentences that contain errors in degree. Write *correct* if the sentence contains no errors.

EXAMPLE:	This mountain is the *highest* of the two.
ANSWER:	This mountain is the *higher* of the two.

1. The sword dance is more harder than the Scottish reel.
2. Bagpipe music is played most softly for dances than for parades.
3. The bagpipes are played most loud during a parade.
4. Bagpipe bands have been formed in more areas of the world where large numbers of Scots have settled.
5. Bagpipe music is a more bigger part of the Highland games than tossing the caber is.

Learn More

To practice using modifiers in a standardized test format, see the Standardized Test Preparation Workshop on pages 574–575.

Comparison of Adjectives and Adverbs • 565

Step-by-Step Teaching Guide

Comparative and Superlative Degrees

1. Review the key concept, reinforcing the 1-2-3 rule of degree.

   To describe 1 thing, use the positive degree.

   To compare 2 things, use the comparative degree.

   To compare 3 or more things, use the superlative degree.

2. Use the following examples to give students practice identifying degrees:

   Maria is a fast runner. (positive)

   Maria is faster than Roy. (comparative)

   Maria is the fastest runner in the class. (superlative)

3. The use of *more* with the comparative degree of an adjective is the equivalent of using a double negative. Emphasize to students that only one is required.

Answer Key

Exercise 7

1. The sword dance is harder than the Scottish reel.
2. Bagpipe music is played more softly for dances than for parades.
3. The bagpipes are played loudest during a parade.
4. Bagpipe bands have been formed in most areas of the world where large numbers of Scots have settled.
5. Bagpipe music is a bigger part of the Highland games than tossing the caber is.

Critical Viewing

Apply Students may suggest that the mountains of Scotland are its *most beautiful* natural element. Students may also note that the mountain on the left side of the picture rises *higher* than the mountain on the right.

☑ ONGOING ASSESSMENT: Assess Mastery

Use the following resources to assess student mastery of using modifiers.

In the Textbook	Technology
Chapter Review, Ex. 22–26, p. 572	Language Lab CD-ROM, Using Modifiers; On-Line Exercise Bank, Section 25.1

GRAMMAR EXERCISES 8–14

> **Exercise 8** Identifying the Comparative and Superlative Degrees
On your paper, label the following modifiers *comparative* or *superlative*.

1. more compact
2. coolest
3. greasier
4. rounder
5. moldiest

> **Exercise 9** Recognizing the Degree of Irregular Modifiers On your paper, indicate the degree of the underlined word in each of the following sentences.

1. Mark and Judy had a <u>bad</u> scare on their way to the Border Country.
2. They had an even <u>worse</u> time getting to the Lowlands.
3. Judy thought the kilt the mannequin was wearing looked <u>good</u>.
4. Mark looked <u>better</u> in the kilt than the mannequin did.
5. The store owner looked <u>best</u> in the kilt.

> **Exercise 10** Forming the Comparative and Superlative Degrees
On your paper, write the comparative and superlative degrees of the modifiers below.

1. fresh
2. clammy
3. carefully
4. correctly
5. confident

> **Exercise 11** Using the Comparative and Superlative Degrees of Irregular Modifiers Copy each of the following sentences onto your paper, supplying the form of the modifier requested in parentheses.

1. Scotland has (many—comparative) mountains in the Highlands than in the Lowlands.

2. The Border Country is the (good—superlative) place to see castles.
3. The Tay River flows (far—comparative) than the Tweed River.
4. Loch Ness is the (much—superlative) famous lake in Scotland.
5. The (bad—superlative) part of visiting Scotland was leaving.

> **Exercise 12** Find It in Your Reading Identify the comparative and superlative degrees of the underlined modifiers in the following excerpt from "Lochinvar."

So <u>faithful</u> in love, and so dauntless in war,/There never was knight like the <u>young</u> Lochinvar. . . ./But, ere he alighted at Netherby gate,/The bride had consented, the gallant came <u>late</u>. . . ./"There are maidens in Scotland more <u>lovely</u> by far/That would <u>gladly</u> be bride to the young Lochinvar."

> **Exercise 13** Find It in Your Writing In a draft from your portfolio, find examples of modifiers in the comparative or superlative degree. Challenge yourself to add two modifiers that will add detail to your writing.

> **Exercise 14** Writing Application
Write a letter to a travel agent requesting information about Scotland. Use modifiers of different degrees to indicate the level of interest you have in different features of the country.

Section 25.2 *Troublesome Adjectives and Adverbs*

The common adjectives and adverbs listed below often cause problems in both speaking and writing.

(1) bad, badly *Bad* is an adjective. Use it after linking verbs, such as *are, appear, feel, look,* and *sound. Badly* is an adverb. Use it after action verbs, such as *act, behave, do,* and *perform.*

                   LV
INCORRECT: Jan looked *badly* after the trip.

                  LV
CORRECT: Jan looked *bad* after the trip.

                AV
INCORRECT: I did *bad* on the test.

               AV
CORRECT: I did *badly* on the test.

(2) fewer, less Use the adjective *fewer* to answer the question "How many?" Use the adjective *less* to answer the question "How much?"

HOW MANY: *fewer* calories   *fewer* chores
HOW MUCH: *less* food   *less* work

(3) good, well *Good* is an adjective. *Well* can be either an adjective or an adverb, depending on its meaning. A common mistake is the use of *good* after an action verb. Use the adverb *well* instead.

                    AV
INCORRECT: The children have behaved *good* all day.

                    AV
CORRECT: The children have behaved *well* all day.

As adjectives, *good* and *well* have slightly different meanings, which are often confused. *Well* usually refers simply to a person's or an animal's health.

EXAMPLES: Janet felt *good* after the hike.
              The fresh bread smells *good.*
              That puppy is not *well.*

(4) just When used as an adverb, *just* often means "no more than." When *just* has this meaning, place it right before the word it logically modifies.

Theme: Scotland

In this section, you will learn about degrees of comparison. The examples and exercises tell more about Scotland.
• • • • • • • • • • • • • • • • • • • •
Cross-Curricular Connection: Social Studies

▼ Critical Viewing
How can using language carefully help to improve communication, both at home and abroad? **[Evaluate]**

Troublesome Adjectives and Adverbs • **567**

PREPARE and ENGAGE

Interest GRABBER Select a description of a recent event in a local newspaper or magazine. Read the description and omit all the adjectives and adverbs. Ask students whether the description was interesting. What would they suggest to make it more interesting and exciting?

Activate Prior Knowledge

Write these sentences on the board. Ask students to identify the usage errors. Which part of speech is used incorrectly?

The new banana swordfish ice cream tastes very badly.

However, chocolate-chip anchovy tastes well.

TEACH

Step-by-Step Teaching Guide

Troublesome Adjectives and Adverbs

1. Review common errors in the use of *bad.* Mistakes often occur in confusing adjective and adverb forms.

2. To give students an alternative way of keeping *fewer* and *less* straight, have them remember that *fewer* refers to a group of countable things.

   I had <u>less</u> time than I expected, so I answered <u>fewer</u> of the homework questions.

3. Review common errors in the use of *well* and *good.* The most frequent error is using *good* as an adverb to modify an action verb. Use the following to demonstrate. *He played well. He is a good player.* Some confusion arises from some students' failure to recognize linking verbs such as *tastes* or *seems.*

continued

Critical Viewing

Evaluate Students may point out that choosing one's words carefully can prevent misunderstandings and confusion, which is especially important in communicating with people from different cultures.

4. Tell students that *just* can be used as either an adverb or an adjective. As an adverb, it has meanings in addition to the one given here. It can mean "simply" or "truly" (The weather is just glorious). It can also mean "precisely" or "exactly" (This color is just right).

5. As an adjective, *just* means "honorable" or "fair" (He is a just man).

6. When using *only*, think about which word is being modified. Note in the examples that *only* should be close to the word or phrase that is being singled out: *only* she, *only* answered, *only* that question, *only* from me.

Critical Viewing

Make a Judgment Students might say that their lives were more luxurious and free from cares and worries than the lives of common folk.

Customize for
More Advanced Students

Have students use a dictionary to clarify meanings for *just,* then write a brief paragraph in which they use the word *just* as an adverb with two different meanings, and also as an adjective.

25.2

▲ **Critical Viewing** Based on the picture, what can you guess about the lives of the people who lived in this castle? [**Make a Judgment**]

| INCORRECT: | Do you *just* want one baked potato with your steak? |
| CORRECT: | Do you want *just* one baked potato with your steak? |

(5) only The position of *only* in a sentence sometimes affects the sentence's entire meaning. Consider the meaning of these sentences:

EXAMPLES: *Only* she answered that question. (Nobody else answered that question.)
She *only* answered that question. (She did nothing else with the question.)
She answered *only* that question. (She answered that question and no other question.)

Mistakes involving *only* usually occur when its placement in a sentence makes the meaning unclear.

| UNCLEAR: | *Only* take advice from me. |
| BETTER: | Take advice *only* from me. |

Whenever you use *only* in a sentence, make sure it indicates your exact meaning.

568 • Using Modifiers

✎ STANDARDIZED TEST PREPARATION WORKSHOP

Grammar and Usage Standardized tests measure students' ability to use modifiers correctly. Share the following sample test question with students:

Choose the letter of the modifier that best completes the sentence.

Ana and William said that the movie was even ___ than they thought it would be.

| A bad | C worse |
| B badder | D worst |

Students should recognize that the comparative form of *bad* is required to compare two viewpoints. Items **A** and **D** offer a positive and a superlative form. Item **B** can be eliminated because it is not a grammatical word. The correct choice is item **C**.

Exercise 15 Correcting Errors Caused by Troublesome
Modifiers In the sentences that follow, each underlined modifier is used incorrectly. On your paper, revise each sentence, correcting the misused modifier.

EXAMPLE: The team played <u>bad</u> yesterday.
ANSWER: The team played badly yesterday.

1. Scotland <u>only</u> is attached to England; it is not part of England.
2. The people from Scotland are called Scots or Scottish, but they will react <u>bad</u> to being called English.
3. The Scots and the English have lived in peace for <u>less</u> centuries than they have lived at war with each other.
4. It is <u>fewer</u> time than you might imagine since the Scots' last battle with the English.
5. The clans in the Highlands of Scotland fought <u>good</u> in their battles with the English.

Exercise 16 Identifying and Correcting Errors Caused by
Troublesome Adjectives and Adverbs Rewrite the sentences below that contain errors in the use of modifiers. If a sentence contains no errors, write *correct*.

EXAMPLE: There are less flowers in the garden now.
ANSWER: There are fewer flowers in the garden now.

1. When they weren't fighting against England, few clans got along good.
2. Before the English tried to break up the clans, the people of Scotland spoke Gaelic, but only about 2 percent of Scots speak it today.
3. After England tried to break up the clans, many Scots were recruited into Highland regiments and fought for the royalty that had treated them so bad.
4. The Clan MacDonald marched to war very good.
5. The Highland troops looked badly after the war.
6. The Highland warriors didn't feel good after the battle.
7. The internal rivalry for chieftainship in the fifteenth century left some in the Clan Campbell feeling badly.
8. The English fought good, but the Scots won the battle.
9. The Scots fought especially good in the last battle at Culloden.
10. Castles were not built only by kings: Many noble families also had strongholds from which they could defend themselves against their enemies.

More Practice

Language Lab
CD-ROM
• Using Modifiers lesson
On-line
Exercise Bank
• Section 18
Grammar Exercise
Workbook
• pp. 143–144

Troublesome Adjectives and Adverbs • 569

Answer Key

▶ **Exercise 15**

1. Scotland is only attached to England; it is not part of England.
2. The people from Scotland are called Scots or Scottish, but they will react badly to being called English.
3. The Scots and the English have lived in peace for fewer centuries than they have lived at war with each other.
4. It is less time than you might imagine since the Scots' last battle with the English.
5. The clans in the Highlands of Scotland fought well in their battles with the English.

▶ **Exercise 16**

1. When they weren't fighting against England, few clans got along well.
2. correct
3. After England tried to break up the clans, many Scots were recruited into Highland regiments and fought for the royalty that had treated them so badly.
4. The Clan MacDonald marched to war very well.
5. The Highland troops looked bad after the war.
6. The Highland warriors didn't feel well after the battle. (or *correct*)
7. The internal rivalry for chieftainship in the fifteenth century left some in the Clan Campbell feeling bad.
8. The English fought well, but the Scots won the battle.
9. The Scots fought especially well in the last battle at Culloden.
10. correct

☑ ONGOING ASSESSMENT: Monitor and Reinforce

If students miss more than two items in Exercise 15 or 16, refer them to the following for additional practice.

In the Textbook	Print Resources	Technology
Section Review, Ex. 17–18, p. 571	Grammar Exercise Workbook, pp. 143–144	Language Lab CD-ROM, Using Modifiers; On-Line Exercise Bank, Section 25.2

⏱ TIME SAVERS!

🖺 **Answers on Transparency**
Use the Grammar Exercises Answers on Transparencies for Chapter 25 to facilitate correction by students.

🖥 **On-Line Exercise Bank**
Have students complete the exercises on computer. The Auto Check feature will grade their work for you!

Troublesome Modifiers Fold-Up

Teaching Resources: Hands-on Grammar Activity Book, Chapter 25

1. Have students refer to their Hands-on Grammar Activity books or give them copies of the relevant pages for this activity.

2. Before students begin making their fold-ups, you may want to work together as a class to make a list of other troublesome modifiers. Students can then make fold-ups for these modifiers.

Find It in Your Reading

You may want to have students complete this activity with a partner.

Find It in Your Writing

As an extension, have students select a piece of their own writing. Tell them to check their work using their fold-ups.

25.2

Hands-on Grammar

Troublesome Modifiers Fold-Up

Create a fold-up booklet to keep in your folder as a handy reference for using troublesome modifiers such as *bad, badly* and *good, well.* Cut a strip of colored paper approximately three inches wide. Fan-fold the strip into sections approximately 1 inch deep. (The number of folds you make will depend on the length of the strip you've created.)

On one side of the strip, write ADJ for *adjective.* In each section, write a linking verb followed by the adjective. The example below shows several linking verbs followed by *bad*, the adjective.

On the reverse side of the same strip, write ADV for *adverb* in the top section. Then, in each section, write an action verb followed by the adverb. In the example, the adverb *badly* is used.

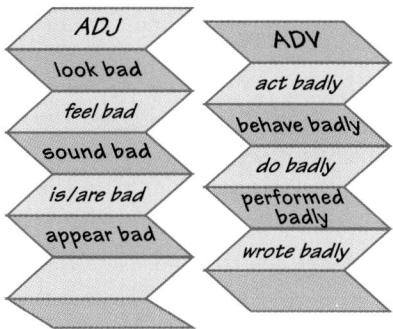

Keep your fold-up in your notebook or folder. Tape additional fan-folded strips to the end as you find more examples of words with which you would use the adjective and the adverb. Create a separate strip for *good* and *well.*

Find It in Your Reading Look through a short story or novel to find uses of these adjectives and adverbs that do not already appear on your fold-up. Add to the list.

Find It in Your Writing Use your fold-ups when you proofread your writing.

⏱ **TIME SAVERS!**

✋ **Hands-on Grammar Book**
Use the Hands-on Grammar activity sheet for Chapter 25 to facilitate this activity.

☑ **ONGOING ASSESSMENT: Assess Mastery**

Use the following resources to assess mastery of troublesome adjectives and adverbs.

In the Textbook	Technology
Chapter Review, Ex. 28–29, p. 573	Language Lab CD-ROM, Using Modifiers; On-Line Exercise Bank, Section 25.2

Section Review

GRAMMAR EXERCISES 17–21

Exercise 17 Correcting Errors in
Adjective and Adverb Usage Rewrite
the following paragraph, correcting all
errors in adjective and adverb usage.

Judy and Mark are excited to visit
Scotland. (1) However, only they can travel
for a few days. (2) They are planning on
using their time good. Judy wants to be
sure they go on a hike in the Highlands
and see some castles. (3) She has also
heard that the dancers and bagpipe music
at the Highland games are really well. (4)
She wants to see the dancers bad. (5)
Mark wants just to be sure to visit the
Highland games. (6) He's heard the tossing-the-caber event is especially well. (7)
They are planning on spending fewer time
in the Border Country and more time
focusing on the tourist attractions. (8) The
trip is going to be for less days than they
would like. (9) However, they are going to
make the best of it and not feel badly. (10)
Whatever happens, the trip is going to be a
well one.

Exercise 18 Correcting Errors
**Caused by Troublesome Adjectives and
Adverbs** Rewrite the sentences below that
contain errors in the use of modifiers. If a
sentence contains no errors, write *correct*.

1. Mark, Judy, Natalie, and Sam can only
   visit Scotland for three days.
2. They were just given eight bus tickets
   to last the whole vacation.
3. They will have to only ride the bus
   when they are traveling long distances.
4. Mark and Sam want to see the
   Highland games badly.
5. Luckily, the friends just reached their
   seats one minute before the bus left
   for the games.
6. Natalie only had made four reservations for the Highland games.

7. When they arrived, they were very surprised to see fewer than one hundred
   spectators in attendance.
8. They would sit only in the front seats;
   otherwise, it would be hard to see the
   Highland athletes.
9. Only after the last event were they
   ready to leave.
10. They all felt well and decided to go on
    a hike in the Highlands.

Exercise 19 Find It in Your
Reading In the following passage from
"Lochinvar," identify one word that could
be replaced by *only* or *just*. Replace the
word, and then explain why the replacement is possible.

> "And now I am come, with this lost love
> of mine,
>
> To lead but one measure, drink one cup
> of wine. . . ."

Exercise 20 Find It in Your
Writing Review a piece of writing in your
portfolio to check your usage of troublesome
adjectives and adverbs.

Exercise 21 Writing Application
Write a brief description of a place you
have visited or would like to visit. Use the
comparative and superlative forms of modifiers to compare this place to another.
Review your work to make sure you have
avoided any problems with modifiers.

ASSESS and CLOSE

Section Review

Each of these exercises correlates
with a concept covered in the
Glossary of Troublesome Adjectives
and Adverbs, pages 567–570. These
exercises may be used for more
practice, for reteaching, or for review
of the Key Concepts presented.
Answers for all chapter exercises are
available in *Grammar Exercises
Answers on Transparencies* in your
teaching resources.

Exercise 17

Judy and Mark are excited to visit
Scotland.

(1) However, they can travel for
only a few days. (2) They are planning
on using their time well. Judy wants
to be sure they go on a hike in the
Highlands and see some castles.
(3) She has also heard that the
dancers and bagpipe music at the
Highland games are really good.
(4) She wants to see the dancers
badly. (5) Mark just wants to be sure
to visit the Highland games. (6) He's
heard the tossing-the-caber event is
especially good. (7) They are
planning on spending less time in
the Border Country and more time
focusing on the tourist attractions.
(8) The trip is going to be for fewer
days than they would like.
(9) However, they are going to make
the best of it and not feel bad.
(10) Whatever happens, the trip is
going to be a good one.

Exercise 18

1. Mark, Judy, Natalie, and Sam can
   visit Scotland for only three days.
2. They were given just eight bus
   tickets to last the whole vacation.
3. They will have to ride the bus
   only when they are traveling
   long distances.
4. correct
5. Luckily, the friends reached their
   seats just one minute before the
   bus left for the games.
6. Natalie had made only four
   reservations for the Highland
   games.
7. correct
8. They would sit in the front seats
   only; otherwise, it would be hard
   to see the Highland athletes.
9. correct
10. They all felt good and decided to
    go on a hike in the Highlands.
    continued

Exercise 19

Find It in Your Reading
The word *but* can be replaced by *only* or *just*
because it means "no more than."

Exercise 20

Find It in Your Writing
When they finish, have students make a "Guide
to Troublesome Modifiers" page to keep in their
portfolios for future reference.

Exercise 21

Writing Application
Ask volunteers to share their descriptions with
the class. Discuss how modifiers enable a writer
to share details and feelings about a place.

CHAPTER REVIEW

Each of these exercises correlates with a section of the chapter on using modifiers, pages 560–571. These exercises may be used for more practice, for reteaching, or for review of the Key Concepts presented. Answers for all chapter exercises are available in *Grammar Exercises Answers on Transparencies* in your Teaching Resources.

Answer Key

Exercise 22

1. brighter, brightest
2. more intelligent, most intelligent
3. cuter, cutest
4. more natural, most natural
5. lazier, laziest
6. more difficult, most difficult
7. more ordinary, most ordinary
8. cleaner, cleanest
9. skinnier, skinniest
10. more gorgeous, most gorgeous
11. muddier, muddiest
12. more dangerous, most dangerous
13. more, most
14. more elaborate, most elaborate
15. worse, worst

Exercise 23

1. comparative
2. comparative
3. superlative
4. superlative
5. positive

Exercise 24

1. better
2. more
3. best
4. worse
5. Most

Exercise 25

Answers may vary. Samples are given.

1. best—superlative; good, better
2. creative—positive; more creative, most creative
3. good—positive; better, best
4. more—comparative; much, most
5. most interesting—superlative; interesting, more interesting

Exercise 26

1. On the Island of Lewis, there is a great circle of standing stones, together with a group of cairns, which is one of the most important relics of the Bronze Age in the whole of Britain.

GRAMMAR EXERCISES 22–30

Exercise 22 Forming the **Comparative and Superlative Degrees of Modifiers** On your paper, write the comparative and superlative degrees of the following modifiers.

1. bright	9. skinny
2. intelligent	10. gorgeous
3. cute	11. muddy
4. natural	12. dangerous
5. lazy	13. much
6. difficult	14. elaborate
7. ordinary	15. bad
8. clean	

Exercise 23 Recognizing the **Degree of Irregular Modifiers** On your paper, indicate the degree of each underlined word in the following sentences.

1. The Isles are <u>more</u> north than the Highlands.
2. The Border Country is <u>farther</u> south than the Highlands.
3. Out of all the regions of Scotland, the Isles are the <u>farthest</u> north.
4. <u>Most</u> of the people in the Isles earn their living by fishing.
5. The weather there is not always <u>good</u>.

Exercise 24 Using the **Comparative and Superlative Degrees of Irregular Modifiers** Copy each of the following sentences onto your paper, supplying the form of the modifier requested in parentheses.

1. The Scottish reel dancer felt (good—comparative) after drinking a tall glass of water.
2. The bagpipe player knows the music to (many—comparative) Scottish dances than the dancer does.

3. Which dance did you like the (good—superlative)?
4. The Highland dancer was not nervous before the performance, but she felt (bad—comparative) after she tripped on stage.
5. (Many—superlative) Highland dancers wear kilts when they perform.

Exercise 25 Supplying Modifiers Copy the following sentences, supplying a modifier for each blank space. Identify the form you have used. Then, write the other two forms.

1. "Lochinvar" is the ___?___ poem we've read this semester.
2. The author must have been ___?___.
3. The poem we read last week was not as ___?___.
4. Usually, I enjoy reading fiction ___?___ than I like reading poems.
5. The ___?___ part of this poem was the ending.

Exercise 26 Correcting Errors in **Degree** Revise the sentences below that contain errors in degree. If the sentence contains no errors, write *correct*.

1. On the Island of Lewis, there is a great circle of standing stones, together with a group of cairns, which is one of the more important relics of the Bronze Age in the whole of Britain.
2. Writings about Scotland by the Roman historian Tacitus date farther back in history.
3. Most modern Scots are descended from the Celtic tribes that inhabited the region before the Romans came to Britain.
4. Before the nineteenth century, the

---

2. Writings about Scotland by the Roman historian Tacitus date further back in history.
3. correct
4. Before the nineteenth century, the Scots were a more warlike people than they are today.
5. The worst battle with the English was the battle of Culloden Moor.

Scots were a most warlikest people than they are today.

5. The worse battle with the English was the battle of Culloden Moor.

Exercise 27 Revising to Eliminate Errors in Adjective and Adverb Usage

Revise the following paragraph, correcting all errors in adjective and adverb usage.

(1) Scotland is the more northern part of Great Britain. (2) It just extends 274 miles north from its border with England. Topographically, Scotland can be divided into three main regions: (3) The Highlands make up the northern two thirds, where Scotland's higher mountain, Ben Nevis, is found. (4) Central Scotland is called the Lowlands and has much isolated hills. (5) It is the more densely populated area. The third region is called the Border Country, as it is located on the English border. (6) Scotland has had a better national system of education for several centuries. (7) Now, fewer than 1 percent of the population is unable to read. (8) Of Scotland's twelve universities, the older is Saint Andrews, established in 1411. (9) Although Scotland has a large percentage of literate people, there are less jobs available for them. (10) More Scots leave Scotland to seek employment elsewhere.

Exercise 28 Choosing the Correct Modifier

Choose the correct word to complete each sentence.

1. I felt (bad, badly) that I missed the slide show on Scotland.
2. They didn't feel (bad, badly) about killing another king.
3. There were (fewer, less) people willing to support a weak king.
4. If a king ruled (good, well), people would continue to support him.
5. If a battle went (good, well), a king could keep his throne.

6. Thank goodness there is (fewer, less) violence now than there was in ancient times.
7. Do you think you did (good, well) on the test about Scottish history?
8. I hope I didn't do too (bad, badly).
9. I wish there had been (fewer, less) questions about Duncan and Macbeth.
10. Although I think I told the story (good, well), I couldn't remember all the dates.

Exercise 29 Revising to Eliminate Errors Caused by Troublesome Adjectives and Adverbs

Revise the sentences below that contain errors in the use of modifiers. If a sentence contains no errors, write *correct.*

1. Although kilts are the traditional men's clothing of Scotland, less Scots wear them today than in days of old.
2. Originally, the kilt just was a large piece of cloth Scots wrapped around their waists and put over their shoulders.
3. Wearing a kilt as clothing was not its only use; a kilt also doubled as a blanket.
4. A traditional kilt was made of thick material and would endure good.
5. Most Scots just had one kilt and wore it every day.

Exercise 30 Writing Application

Make a travel brochure for a country that interests you. Use modifiers in sentences that highlight the unique features of the country. For example, "Scotland has more lakes than you could visit in a year." Then, meet with a partner to check for any errors in your usage of modifers and to discuss whether the modifiers you chose are the most effective for your purpose.

Chapter Review • 573

Answer Key

Exercise 27

1. Scotland is the most northern part of Great Britain.
2. It extends just 274 miles north from its border with England. Topographically, Scotland can be divided into three main regions:
3. The Highlands make up the northern two thirds, where Scotland's highest mountain, Ben Nevis, is found.
4. Central Scotland is called the Lowlands and has many isolated hills.
5. It is the most densely populated area. The third region is called the Border Country, as it is located on the English border.
6. Scotland has had a good national system of education for several centuries.
7. Now, less than 1 percent of the population is unable to read.
8. Of Scotland's twelve universities, the oldest is Saint Andrews, established in 1411.
9. Although Scotland has a large percentage of literate people, there are few jobs available for them.
10. Many Scots leave Scotland to seek employment elsewhere.

Exercise 28

1. bad	6. less
2. bad	7. well
3. fewer	8. badly
4. well	9. fewer
5. well	10. well

Exercise 29

1. Although kilts are the traditional men's clothing of Scotland, fewer Scots wear them today than in days of old.
2. Originally, the kilt was just a large piece of cloth Scots wrapped around their waists and put over their shoulders.
3. correct
4. A traditional kilt was made of thick material and would endure well.
5. Most Scots had just one kilt and wore it every day.

Exercise 30

Writing Application
Ask students which countries they selected for this exercise. Have them share some of the modifiers they used and features they highlighted in their writing.

Lesson Objectives

• To use the comparative and superlative forms of adjectives and adverbs appropriately.

Forms of Comparison

Teaching Resources: Standardized Test Preparation Workbook, pp. 49–50

1. Encourage students to create a graphic organizer to display the information on this page. Putting this information in graphic form may help them remember the strategies for using the comparative and superlative forms of adjectives and adverbs.

2. Point out to students that in item 2, the positive form is required. *More important* is incorrect because the fight for independence is not compared to another belief or ideal. Remind students that the comparative form of an adjective usually will appear with the word *than*, which signals a comparison between two things:

   Your apple is sweeter **than** *mine.*

   Your dog is more affectionate **than** *mine.*

Standardized Test Preparation Workshop

Standard English Usage: Forms of Comparison

Standardized test questions often measure your ability to use modifiers correctly. One way this is done is by testing your ability to choose the correct form of comparison to complete a sentence. Use the following strategies to help you determine which form to use in a sentence:

• If no comparison is being made, use the positive form of the modifier.

• If one thing or action is compared to another thing or action, use the comparative degree of the modifier—the form ending in *-er* or preceded by *more*.

• If one thing or action is being compared to more than one other thing or action, use the superlative degree of the modifier—the form ending in *-est* or preceded by *most*.

• Be aware that some modifiers have special forms, such as *good, bad, much,* and *many*.

The following sample items will give you practice in answering these types of standardized test questions.

Test Tip

Be careful not to choose a double comparison, such as *more easier*, to complete a sentence. The correct form is *easier*.

Sample Test Items	Answers and Explanations

Choose the letter of the modifier that best completes each sentence.
 	
There were ___(1)___ soldiers in the Texas army than in the Mexican army. Although the odds were not in their favor, the people of Texas believed that fighting for their independence was ___(2)___ .
 	
1   A   little
     B   least
     C   fewer
     D   most little
	The correct answer for item 1 is *C, fewer*. The comparison is being made between the two armies, so the comparative form should be used.

2   F   important
     G   importantest
     H   more important
     J   most important
	The correct answer for item 2 is *F, important*. The fight for independence is not being compared to anything else, so the positive form is used.

574 • Using Modifiers

✎ TEST-TAKING TIP

Remind students to reread the sentence with their choice in place. They should make sure their choice sounds correct in the context of the sentence. Most incorrect choices can be identified by placing them in the sentence in question.

▶ **Practice** **Directions:** Choose the letter of the modifier that best completes each sentence.

One of the ___(1)___ battles in American history happened at the Alamo. Many historians even believe that the Battle of the Alamo was the ___(2)___ massacre ever to take place on American soil. At an ___(3)___ time, the Alamo had been a chapel attached to the Spanish mission, San Antonio de Valero. At the time of the battle, the Alamo had become a fort, protecting a small band of Texans against ___(4)___ than 2,000 Mexican troops. Davy Crockett, one of the ___(5)___ Americans at the time, fought the Mexicans under the command of Colonel William Barret Travis. When the smoke finally cleared at the Alamo, ___(6)___ was left of the band of Texans who had resisted. ___(7)___ than twenty women and children survived the battle and all the men defending the Alamo were killed. The battle of the Alamo gave Sam Houston ___(8)___ time to gather troops to save the independence movement. He retreated ___(9)___ east while being pursued by Santa Anna. Houston then turned on the army and a day ___(10)___ captured Santa Anna and made him sign a peace treaty.

1 A bloody
  B bloodier
  C bloodiest
  D more bloody

2 F bad
  G worse
  H most bad
  J worst

3 A early
  B earlier
  C earliest
  D more early

4 F many more
  G most
  H more
  J many

5 A most famous
  B more famous
  C famouser
  D famousest

6 F less
  G little
  H least
  J littler

7 A Most few
  B Fewer
  C Fewest
  D Few

8 F more
  G most
  H much
  J many

9 A most farther
  B farthest
  C far
  D farther

10 F latest
  G more later
  H later
  J late

▶ **Practice**

1. C
2. J
3. B
4. H
5. A
6. G
7. B
8. F
9. D
10. H

▶ **Exercise A**

1. present participle
2. past participle
3. past
4. past
5. present participle

▶ **Exercise B**

1. present perfect progressive; making present participle
2. present perfect; taken past participle
3. present progressive; looking present participle
4. past perfect progressive; hoping present participle
5. future; go present
6. past perfect; been past participle
7. present; are present
8. future perfect; shopped past participle
9. future; find present
10. present perfect; found past participle

▶ **Exercise C**

1. us (objective), our (possessive)
2. I (nominative), my (possessive), me (objective), she (nominative)
3. Her (possessive), ours (possessive)
4. their (possessive)
5. his/her (possessive)
6. they (nominative)
7. their (possessive)
8. we (nominative), our (possessive)
9. You (nominative), its (possessive)
10. it (nominative)

continued

Cumulative Review

USAGE

▶ **Exercise A** Recognizing the **Principal Parts of Verbs** Identify the principal part used to form the underlined verbs in the following sentences as *present, present participle, past,* or *past participle.*

1. Steve <u>is buying</u> my birthday presents at the local shopping center.
2. He <u>has found</u> some of the lowest prices at one of the stores.
3. Last year, I think I <u>paid</u> too much for his gift.
4. First, I put it in layaway, and I <u>went</u> back to get it a week later.
5. This year, I hope to enter the stores only once because I <u>am going</u> to make a list.

▶ **Exercise B** Recognizing Verb Tense Identify the tense of each underlined verb or verb phrase in the following sentences. Then, write the principal part used to form the tense.

1. For our vacation, I <u>have been making</u> a list of things that I think I will need.
2. It seems as though summer <u>has taken</u> a long time to arrive.
3. I <u>am looking</u> forward to a shopping trip with my mom and my best friend.
4. I <u>had been hoping</u> we would go this weekend, and we are!
5. We <u>will go</u> to the outlet center that has opened several miles away.
6. Before the outlets opened, the location <u>had been</u> mainly farmland.
7. We were sorry to see the farms go, but we <u>are</u> happy now to buy some of our favorite brands at discounted prices.
8. By the time we finish, we <u>will have shopped</u> for hours.
9. Nowadays, you <u>will find</u> outlet centers just off interstate highways all across the country.

10. Discount stores <u>have found</u> success in Canada and Western Europe, as well.

▶ **Exercise C** Identifying Pronoun **Case** Identify the case of each personal pronoun in the following sentences as *nominative, objective,* or *possessive.*

1. Most of us shop at our local supermarkets.
2. I remember my great-grandmother telling me that she grew up in a town without a supermarket.
3. Her times were very different from ours.
4. Before the Great Depression of the 1930's, most people bought their food and household items in many different shops.
5. For example, a person would buy his or her meat at a butcher shop, bread at a bakery, and milk and cheese at a dairy.
6. When supermarkets arrived on the scene, combining self-service with lower prices, they experienced immediate growth.
7. In addition, the spread of the automobile meant that shoppers could drive to a store and fill their cars with packaged groceries.
8. Now, in one place, we can buy all our food, cleaning products, greeting cards, batteries, and much, much more.
9. You can see how the supermarket got its name!
10. The theory of supermarkets has spread to other types of stores; it is called "low-cost mass distribution."

Exercise D Revising to Eliminate Errors in Agreement Revise the following sentences, eliminating errors in agreement. If a sentence has no errors, write *correct*.

1 A common sight in stores is the "sale" sign.
2. There is chains in many types of businesses.
3. Each town and city has their own branches of certain fast-food restaurants, banks, movie theaters, gas stations, and supermarkets.
4. The products or services of each branch of a particular chain is almost always the same.
5. The chicken burrito that a person buys for their lunch at one fast-food restaurant will be just like the chicken burrito sold at another branch of the same chain.
6. Each of us probably has our own favorites.
7. Developers of the first chain stores were not sure that they would be successful.
8. However, the lower prices and convenience has made chains very popular.
9. Usually in charge of a chain store is managers rather than an individual owner.
10 Managers make the day-to-day decisions concerning their particular stores.

Exercise E Writing Sentences With Modifiers Write sentences according to the instructions. Be careful to use the correct forms of modifiers, and make sure your comparisons are complete and logical.

1. Using the comparative form of *expensive*, write a sentence about a shoe store.
2. Using the superlative form of *comfortable*, write a sentence about a new pair of shoes.
3. Using the superlative form of *friendly*, write a sentence about the salesperson.
4. Using the comparative form of *few*, write a sentence about job opportunities at this shoe store.
5. Using the comparative form of *far*, write a sentence about the distance of the store from your home.
6. Using the positive form of *good*, write a sentence about transportation into town.
7. Using the comparative form of *bad*, write about the service in another shoe store.
8. Using the superlative form of *much* as an adverb, describe the variety of styles in the shoe store.
9. Using the comparative form of *quickly*, write about a decision about a pair of shoes.
10. Using the superlative form of *good*, describe a purchase.

Exercise F Revising to Eliminate Various Usage Errors Rewrite the following paragraph, correcting errors in agreement and in the usage of verbs, pronouns, and modifiers.

As usual, my parents, brothers, sister, and me had different ideas about where we should go this summer. Each of my two brothers has their own favorite place for fishing, while my sister was insisting on the beach. My parents and me have different ideas. My father thinks that us should see someplace new; he wanted to camp and fish at the shore. His idea is not the most popularest since the rest of us want to be closer to stores, movies, and other conveniences. My mother wants to visit a city because you can do so much there. I think we should of drawn straws instead of arguing for so long.

Exercise G Writing Application Describe a store in which you like to shop. Use a consistent verb tense, and check carefully for problems in agreement or in the usage of verbs, pronouns, and modifiers.

Answer Key continued

Exercise F

As usual, my parents, brothers, sister, and <u>I</u> <u>have</u> different ideas about where we should go this summer. Each of my two brothers has <u>his</u> own favorite place for fishing, while my sister <u>insists</u> on the beach. My parents and <u>I</u> have different ideas. My father thinks that <u>we</u> should see someplace new; he <u>wants</u> to camp and fish at the shore. His idea is not the <u>most popular</u> since the rest of us want to be closer to stores, movies, and other conveniences. My mother wants to visit a city because <u>she</u> can do so much there. I think we should <u>have</u> drawn straws instead of arguing for so long.

Exercise G

Writing Application
Have students exchange their completed descriptions to correct each other's work.

Exercise D *(page 577)*

1. correct
2. There <u>are</u> chains in many types of businesses.
3. Each town and city has <u>its</u> own branches of certain fast-food restaurants, banks, movie theaters, gas stations, and supermarkets.
4. The products or services of each branch of a particular chain <u>are</u> almost always the same.
5. The chicken burrito that a person buys for <u>his or her</u> lunch at one fast-food restaurant will be just like the chicken burrito sold at another branch of the same chain.
6. Each of us probably has <u>his or her</u> own favorites.
7. correct
8. However, the lower prices and convenience <u>have</u> made chains very popular.
9. Usually in charge of a chain store <u>are</u> managers rather than an individual owner.
10. correct

Exercise E

Answers will vary. Sample responses are given.

1. The shoes in this store are more expensive than the ones in the store I like.
2. These new shoes are the most comfortable I have ever owned.
3. That is the friendliest salesperson in the world!
4. Tim said there are fewer jobs available at this store than there were last week.
5. The store is farther from my home than from yours.
6. I wish we had a good transportation system in this town.
7. I've heard that the service in Sam's Shoes is worse than the service here.
8. I was most happy with the selection of shoes.
9. She told me to make my decision more quickly than I could.
10. This purchase was my best buy yet!

continued

In-Depth Lesson Plan

	LESSON FOCUS	PRINT AND MEDIA RESOURCES
DAY 1	**End Marks and Commas** Students learn correct usage of periods, question marks, exclamation marks, and commas in sentences, and do Hands-on Grammar Activity (pp. 580–599).	*Language Lab* CD-ROM, Punctuation; *On-Line Exercise Bank,* Sections 26.1–2 **Teaching Resources** *Grammar Exercise Workbook,* pp. 145–158; *Grammar Exercises Answers on Transparencies,* Ch. 26; *Hands-on Grammar Activity Book,* Ch. 26
DAY 2	**Semicolons and Colons** Students learn correct usage of semicolons and colons (pp. 600–605).	*On-Line Exercise Bank,* Section 26.3 **Teaching Resources** *Grammar Exercise Workbook,* pp. 159–162
DAY 3	**Quotation Marks** Students learn correct usage of quotation marks (pp. 606–617).	*On-Line Exercise Bank,* Section 26.4 **Teaching Resources** *Grammar Exercise Workbook,* pp. 163–168
DAY 4	**Hyphens and Apostrophes** Students learn correct usage of hyphens and apostrophes (pp. 618–629).	*On-Line Exercise Bank,* Section 26.5 **Teaching Resources** *Grammar Exercise Workbook,* pp. 169–174
DAY 5	**Review and Assess** Students review chapter and demonstrate mastery of use of punctuation (pp. 630–633).	**Teaching Resources** *Formal Assessment,* Ch. 26

Accelerated Lesson Plan

	LESSON FOCUS	PRINT AND MEDIA RESOURCES
DAY 1	**End Marks and Commas** Students cover concepts and usage of end marks and commas as determined by Diagnostic Test (pp. 580–599).	*Language Lab* CD-ROM, Punctuation; *On-Line Exercise Bank,* Sections 26.1–2 **Teaching Resources** *Grammar Exercise Workbook,* pp. 145–158; *Grammar Exercises Answers on Transparencies,* Ch. 26; *Hands-on Grammar Activity Book,* Ch. 26
DAY 2	**Other Punctuation** Students cover concepts and usage of semicolons, colons, quotation marks, hyphens, and apostrophes as determined by Diagnostic Test (pp. 600–629).	*On-Line Exercise Bank,* Sections 26.3–5 **Teaching Resources** *Grammar Exercise Workbook,* pp. 159–174; *Grammar Exercises Answers on Transparencies,* Ch. 26
DAY 3	**Review and Assess** Students review chapter and demonstrate mastery of use of punctuation (pp. 630–633).	*On-Line Exercise Bank,* Sections 26.1–5 **Teaching Resources** *Formal Assessment,* Ch. 26

Options for Adapting Lesson Plans

HOMEWORK

Have students complete any stage of the lesson for homework.

FEATURES

Extend coverage with the Grammar in Literature features (p. 591, 612, 627), and the Standardized Test Preparation Workshop (p. 632).

TECHNOLOGY

Students can use the On-Line Exercise Bank to complete the exercises on computer. The Auto Check feature will grade their work.

INTEGRATED SKILLS COVERAGE

Grammar in Literature
SE pp. 591, 612, 627

Reading
Find It In Your Reading, SE pp. 584, 598, 599, 605, 617, 629

Writing
Find It In Your Writing, SE pp. 584, 598, 599, 605, 617, 629
Writing Application SE pp. 584, 599, 605, 617, 629, 631

Speaking and Listening
ATE p. 583

Workplace Skills
ATE p. 604

Technology
SE p. 603; ATE pp. 614, 622

Real-World Connection
ATE p. 613

Spelling
SE p. 610

Viewing and Representing
Critical Viewing   SE pp. 578, 581, 582, 586, 589, 595, 597, 601, 603, 606, 609, 610, 619, 620, 622, 624

ASSESSMENT SUPPORT

Standardized Test Preparation Workshop SE p. 632; ATE p. 588

Standardized Test Preparation Workbook, pp. 51–52

Formal Assessment, Ch. 26

MEETING INDIVIDUAL NEEDS

Less Advanced Students See Ongoing Assessment, pp. 590, 602, 613, 622, 627

ESL Students ATE pp. 590, 623

Verbal/Linguistic Learners ATE p. 609

Gifted and Talented Students ATE p. 597

BLOCK SCHEDULING

Pacing Suggestions
For 90-minute Blocks
• Administer the Diagnostic Test to students to determine instructional coverage.
• Have students complete the necessary exercises in class. Use the Hands-on Grammar activity to provide a change of pace.

Resources for Varying Instruction
• *Language Lab* **CD-ROM** If your students have access to hardware, a 90-minute block provides an ideal opportunity for students to work on computer.

Professional Development Support
• *How to Manage Instruction in the Block* This Teaching Resource provides management and activity suggestions.

MEDIA AND TECHNOLOGY

For the Student
• *Language Lab* **CD-ROM** Punctuation
• *On-Line Exercise Bank,* Ch. 26

For the Teacher
• *Resource Pro* **CD-ROM**

WRITING AND GRAMMAR WEB SITE

The Interactive Writing and Grammar Web site provides a wide array of support for students, teachers, and parents. Grammar support includes:

• On-Line Exercise Bank with Auto Check scoring
• Diagnostic and assessment support

www.phschool.com

LITERATURE CONNECTIONS

Related selections from *Prentice Hall Literature: Timeless Voices, Timeless Themes,* Bronze:
"Yeh-Shen: A Cinderella Story From China," by Ai-Ling Louie, SE p. 591
"The Lion and the Statue," by Aesop, SE p. 612
from *Golden Girls: The 1998 U.S. Women's Hockey Team,* Johnette Howard, SE p. 627

Lesson Objectives

1. To use periods, question marks, and exclamation marks correctly with declarative, imperative, interrogative, and exclamatory sentences and interjections.

2. To use commas correctly in a variety of situations.

3. To use semicolons correctly to join independent clauses and in sentences where additional commas would cause confusion.

4. To use colons correctly as introductory devices and in some special writing situations.

5. To use quotation marks correctly.

6. To use other punctuation marks correctly with quotation marks, and appropriately in paragraphs when writing dialogue.

7. To use underlining correctly with titles and certain names.

8. To use hyphens correctly with numbers, with word parts and compound words, and to divide words correctly at the end of lines.

9. To use apostrophes correctly.

Critical Viewing

Speculate Students may say that the girls might stop if they saw a friend, to admire the scenery, to discuss how close they are to their destination, to rest before continuing their journey.

Chapter 26 Punctuation

▲ Critical Viewing
What are some reasons these girls might pause or stop during their walk? **[Speculate]**

All languages have symbols that help people make sense of the words they speak and write. For example, periods let a reader know where a thought ends and a new thought begins. In the English language, symbols such as these are called punctuation marks.

Punctuation marks tell readers to pause, to stop, or to read in a questioning, commanding, or surprised tone. Punctuation marks also connect certain ideas with other ideas or set ideas apart.

In this chapter, you will learn the correct use of punctuation marks.

578 • Punctuation

☑ ONGOING ASSESSMENT: Diagnose

If students miss more than one item in each category, direct them to the relevant pages of the text and assign exercises for practice and review.

Punctuation	Diagnostic Test Items	Teach	Practice	Section Review	Chapter Review
Skill Check A					
End Marks	A 1–5	pp. 580–583	Ex. 1–4	Ex. 5–8	Ex. 73
Skill Check B					
Commas	B 6–10	pp. 585–598	Ex. 12–24	Ex. 25–27	Ex. 74–76
Skill Check C					
Semicolons and Colons	C 11–15	pp. 600–604	Ex. 31–36	Ex. 37–39	Ex. 77–78

Diagnostic Test

Directions: Write all answers on a separate sheet of paper.

Skill Check A. Rewrite the following sentences, adding end marks.

1. There are two types of pandas: giant pandas and red pandas
2. What is the difference between the two
3. Giant pandas weigh twenty-five times more than red pandas do
4. The United States received two giant pandas in 1972 from the Chinese government
5. A baby panda weighs only five ounces How amazing

Skill Check B. Rewrite these sentences, adding needed commas.

6. China the most populated country in the world is located in the eastern portion of Asia.
7. To the north it borders Russia Mongolia and North Korea.
8. China covers about 3695000 square miles and it includes hundreds of islands off its coastline.
9. China and its people I think would be fascinating to study.
10. On September 23 1999 my aunt and uncle flew from San Francisco California to Beijing China to visit.

Skill Check C. Rewrite the following sentences, adding semicolons and colons where necessary.

11. So much of China's early art was encouraged by its emperors in fact, artists were employed by their government.
12. Some of these dynasties produced important art the Shang dynasty, the Zhou dynasty, and the Han dynasty.
13. The Shang dynasty produced artifacts of several types ceramics, bronze containers, and jade.
14. The Zhou dynasty followed the Shang it produced rich treasures.
15. Our letter to the Chinese embassy began, "Dear Sir or Madam Please send me travel brochures about your beautiful country."

Skill Check D. Add quotation marks and underlining where needed in the following sentences.

16. What have you learned this year about China? my grandmother asked me.
17. Oh, a great deal! I replied. My favorite topic is Chinese art.
18. Did you read the article about China in the Los Angeles Times? she asked.
19. The Good Earth by Pearl S. Buck is about a girl's life in China.
20. Why did you say, I read that book already?

Skill Check E. Add hyphens and apostrophes where needed below.

21. During the 1800's, China and England fought over trade.
22. The all powerful British army fought against the Chinese.
23. Chinese commanders couldnt defend themselves completely.
24. The Chinese emperor agreed to pay twenty one million dollars.
25. Finally, Chinas major cities were opened for trade.

Punctuation • 579

ONGOING ASSESSMENT: Diagnose *continued*

Punctuation	Diagnostic Test Items	Teach	Practice	Section Review	Chapter Review
Skill Check D					
Quotation Marks and Underlining	D 16–20	pp. 606–616	Ex. 43–51	Ex. 52–54	Ex. 80
Skill Check E					
Hyphens and Apostrophes	E 21–25	pp. 618–628	Ex. 58–65	Ex. 66–69	Ex. 81

Answer Key

Diagnostic Test

- Each item in the Diagnostic Test corresponds with a concept covered in the chapter on punctuation marks. This will enable you to tailor instruction to your students' particular needs. See "Ongoing Assessment: Diagnose" below for further details.
- Answers for the Diagnostic Test and all chapter exercises are available in *Grammar Exercises Answers on Transparencies* in your Teaching Resources.

Skill Check A

1. period
2. question mark
3. exclamation mark (or period)
4. period
5. period, exclamation mark

Skill Check B

6. China, the most populated country in the world,
7. Russia, Mongolia, and
8. 3,695,000 square miles, and
9. people, I think,
10. On September 23, 1999, San Francisco, California, to Beijing, China,

Skill Check C

11. emperors; in fact
12. art: the Shang
13. types: ceramics
14. Shang; it
15. Madam: Please

Skill Check D

16. "What have you learned this year about China?" my grandmother asked me.
17. "Oh, a great deal!" I replied. "My favorite topic is Chinese art."
18. "Did you read the article about China in the <u>Los Angeles Times</u>?" she asked.
19. <u>The Good Earth</u> by Pearl S. Buck is about a girl's life in China.
20. Why did you say, "I read that book already"?

Skill Check E

21. 1800's
22. all-powerful
23. couldn't
24. twenty-one
25. China's

Activate Prior Knowledge

Model for students being in a hurry. Act out for the class speaking so quickly you can hardly be understood. Now repeat the same information more slowly. Discuss how by slowing down, the natural pauses between phrases and sentences become apparent, allowing hearers to understand you.

TEACH

Step-by-Step Teaching Guide

Using the Period

1. Explain that punctuation is the framework of the sentence, telling the reader, speaker, or listener when and how to connect ideas, pause, stop, or indicate a question or exclamation. Without punctuation, words and sentences would run together.

2. Explain that the period is the most commonly used punctuation mark. It serves several functions.

3. Write the following sentences on the board, circling the periods and asking students how each period is used.

   Family names come before given names in China.

   Think about what that would mean.

   A United States citizen called Mr. Sam Smith would be called Mr. Smith Sam in China.

4. Explain that periods are used to end a statement of fact or opinion, as in sentences 1 and 3 on the board. The second sentence gives a direction and it also ends with a period. Periods are also used after abbreviations, such as Mr., Dr., etc., or St.

End Marks

Punctuation is an accepted set of symbols used to give specific directions to the reader. These are the most common punctuation marks:

COMMON PUNCTUATION MARKS					
period	.	comma	,	quotation marks	" "
question mark	?	semicolon	;	hyphen	-
exclamation mark	!	colon	:	apostrophe	'

Sentences, words, and phrases may all be concluded with one of the three *end marks* in the first column of the chart.

KEY CONCEPT There are three end marks: the *period (.)*, the *question mark (?)*, and the *exclamation mark (!)*. They usually indicate the end of a sentence. ■

Using the Period

The end mark used most often is the period.

KEY CONCEPT Use a period to end a declarative sentence—that is, to end a statement of fact or opinion. ■

DECLARATIVE SENTENCE:	China is a country in Asia.

KEY CONCEPT Use a period to end an imperative sentence—that is, to end a direction or command. ■

IMPERATIVE SENTENCES:	Use a calligraphy pen to draw the characters. Listen carefully to the tour guide.

KEY CONCEPT Use a period after initials and most abbreviations. ■

INITIALS:	R. F. Nordstrom
TITLES:	Mr. Mrs. Dr. Sgt. Jr.

Note that when an abbreviation is located at the very end of a sentence, only one period is required.

EXAMPLE:	Be sure to include Jack Jenkins, Jr.

580 • Punctuation

Theme: China

In this section, you will learn how end marks are used to conclude sentences, end abbreviations, and indicate strong emotion. The examples and exercises in this section are about China's history and culture.

Cross-Curricular Connection: Social Studies

More Practice

Language Lab CD-ROM
• Punctuation lesson
On-line Exercise Bank
• Section 26.1
Grammar Exercise Workbook
• pp. 145–148

⏱ TIME AND RESOURCE MANAGER

Resources
Print: Grammar Exercise Workbook, pp. 145–148
Technology: Language Lab CD-ROM, Punctuation; On-Line Exercise Bank, Section 26.1

In-Depth Coverage	Accelerated Pace
• Work through all key concepts, pp. 580–583. • Assign and review Exercises 1–4.	• Assign pp. 580–583 for independent student review. • Assign Review Exercises 5–8.

> **Exercise 1** Using the Period Copy each of the sentences below onto your paper, adding the missing periods.

EXAMPLE: Mrs M L Richards organized the China tour

ANSWER: Mrs. M. L. Richards organized the China tour.

1. Mr Marco Polo traveled to China in the 1200's
2. He described his travels upon returning to Italy in AD 1295
3. Tell us about your adventures in China, Marco
4. The Chinese had developed a pony express system that traveled as far as Ping Avenue
5. In the 1700's, American ships sailed to China from Salem, Massachusetts
6. One ship was under the command of Capt Cyrus Lincoln from Richmond, Virginia
7. Take us to see the Great Wall of China
8. Sgt E Snow reported on Mao Zedong's regime for US newspapers
9. In 1972, Mao invited President Richard M Nixon to tour China
10. The President was accompanied by Mrs Nixon and an advisor, Dr Elliot Sanderson, Jr

Using the Question Mark

The *question mark* is most commonly used to end an interrogative sentence, one that asks a question requiring an answer.

> **KEY CONCEPT** Use a question mark to end an interrogative sentence—that is, to end a direct question. ■

The following are direct questions requiring answers:

INTERROGATIVE SENTENCES: Who turned in a paper with no name on it?

    How much money will the trip cost?

Sometimes, a single word or a phrase is used to ask a question. In this situation, the word or phrase is punctuated with a question mark just as a complete sentence would be.

> **KEY CONCEPT** Use a question mark to end an incomplete question in which the rest of the question is understood. ■

EXAMPLES: You said that the airplane landed. Where?

    She wants to join our tour group. But how?

▼ **Critical Viewing** How do you know this picture was taken during a modern period of history? **[Infer; Support]**

> **Exercise 1**

1. Mr. Marco Polo traveled to China in the 1200's.
2. He described his travels upon returning to Italy in A.D. 1295.
3. Tell us about your adventures in China, Marco.
4. The Chinese had developed a pony express system that traveled as far as Ping Avenue.
5. In the 1700's, American ships sailed to China from Salem, Massachusetts.
6. One ship was under the command of Capt. Cyrus Lincoln from Richmond, Virginia.
7. Take us to see the Great Wall of China.
8. Sgt. E. Snow reported on Mao Zedong's regime for U.S. newspapers.
9. In 1972, Mao invited President Richard M. Nixon to tour China.
10. The President was accompanied by Mrs. Nixon and an advisor, Dr. Elliot Sanderson, Jr.

Step-by-Step Teaching Guide

Using the Question Mark

1. Let students know that the question mark ends not only interrogative sentences, but incomplete questions relating to prior sentences. Question marks also are used to end a statement intended as a question.

2. Write the following sentences on the board.

   Direct Question: Have you ever been to China? When did you go?

   Incomplete Question: You mentioned that you went on a trip to China. When?

3. Erase the question marks and replace them with periods. Ask students if the sentences still make sense.

Critical Viewing

Infer; Support Students may say that the picture shows cars, skyscrapers, paved roads, modern dress, and lighted signs.

1. Where did the Taiping Rebellion take place?
2. Who started the rebellion? Why?
3. How many people fought during the rebellion?
4. Did the natural disasters have anything to do with the start of the rebellion?
5. Hong Xiuguah, leader of the rebels, crowned himself king. But how?

Step-by-Step Teaching Guide

Using the Exclamation Mark

1. Exclamation marks can end sentences, punctuate commands, or follow descriptive words of emotional outbursts called *interjections*.

2. Write the following sentences on the board. Point out that *Watch out!* is a command, and *Wow!* is an interjection.

   I can't believe you have been to China!

   Watch out!

   Wow! It is amazing how much Chinese you have learned.

3. Ask students to identify the different emotions expressed in the sentences on the board. Write a few of their responses beneath the examples. Their responses might include such emotions as surprise, fear, envy, amazement, disbelief, annoyance, shock.

Critical Viewing

Respond Possible responses: fear, anxiety, amazement, surprise, dislike.

26.1

▶ **Exercise 2** **Using the Question Mark** Copy each item below, adding the missing question marks.

EXAMPLE: Which desk is yours

ANSWER: Which desk is yours?

1. Where did the Taiping Rebellion take place
2. Who started the rebellion   Why
3. How many people fought during the rebellion
4. Did the natural disasters have anything to do with the start of the rebellion
5. Hong Xiuguah, leader of the rebels, crowned himself king. But how

Using the Exclamation Mark

Exclamation marks are used to punctuate sentences that show strong feelings.

▶ **KEY CONCEPT** Use an exclamation mark to end an exclamatory sentence—that is, to end a statement showing strong emotion. ∎

EXAMPLE: You surprised me!

▶ **KEY CONCEPT** Use an exclamation mark after an imperative sentence if the command is urgent and forceful. ∎

EXAMPLE: Move away from the fire!

▶ **KEY CONCEPT** Use an exclamation mark after an interjection expressing strong emotion. ∎

EXAMPLE: Goodness! I forgot to bring my homework.

Too many exclamation marks can make your writing too emotional, however. Be sure to use them sparingly.

▶ Critical Viewing What strong emotions does this Chinese lion sculpture make you feel? **[Respond]**

TIME SAVERS!

Answers on Transparency
Use the Grammar Exercises Answers on Transparencies for Chapter 26 to facilitate correction by students.

On-Line Exercise Bank
Have students complete the exercises on computer. The Auto Check feature will grade their work for you!

☑ **ONGOING ASSESSMENT: Monitor and Reinforce**

If students have difficulty with Exercise 1, 2, 3, or 4, refer them to the following for additional practice.

In the Textbook	Print Resources	Technology
Section Review, Ex. 5–8, p. 584	Grammar Exercise Workbook pp. 145–148	Language Lab CD-ROM, Punctuation; On-Line Exercise Bank, Section 26.1

> **Exercise 3** Using the Exclamation Mark Copy each item below, adding the missing exclamation marks and periods.

EXAMPLE: Stop Don't forget your money

ANSWER: Stop! Don't forget your money.

1. Hooray The Taiping Rebellion has ended
2. Thirty million people were affected
3. The Taiping rebels fought to abolish torture and to increase personal freedom How brave
4. The Qing regime needs our support
5. Thank goodness The British and French came to the assistance of the Qing regime.
6. It was the largest rebellion of modern China Amazing
7. You can't overestimate the impact of the Taiping Rebellion
8. Imagine The leader was just a country teacher
9. What an amazing act of courage to fight the oppressors
10. They truly risked their lives

> **Exercise 4** Revising to Correct the Use of End Marks

Revise the following sentences, correcting the use of punctuation marks as necessary. If a sentence is punctuated correctly, write *correct.*

EXAMPLE: China's cities are on the move. How!

ANSWER: China's cities are on the move. How?

1. Daily life in China's major cities has really changed in recent years? In what ways?
2. In 1980, Dr Jay Arena and his family visited several cities in China!
3. What do you think they found on their travels?
4. They saw many small, cramped one-story houses and people riding bicycles everywhere.
5. There must have been 2 million bikes racing by them at once. Amazing.
6. If Dr Arena went to China now, would he see big differences!
7. Today, he would stare up at high-rise apartment and office buildings on Chonwenmen Wai St in Beijing.
8. Would he be surprised to see thousands of cars and buses racing by him! Absolutely!
9. These changes are not all good, however. Why?
10. Today, air pollution has become a major problem in cities both in China and in the United States!

More Practice

Language Lab
CD-ROM
• Punctuation lesson
On-line
Exercise Bank
• Section 26.1
Grammar Exercise
Workbook
• pp. 145–148

End Marks • 583

1. Hooray! The Taiping Rebellion has ended.
2. Thirty million people were affected! (or .)
3. The Taiping rebels fought to abolish torture and to increase personal freedom. How brave!
4. The Qing regime needs our support!
5. Thank goodness! The British and French came to the assistance of the Qing regime.
6. It was the largest rebellion of modern China. Amazing!
7. You can't overestimate the impact of the Taiping Rebellion! (or .)
8. Imagine! The leader was just a country teacher.
9. What an amazing act of courage to fight the oppressors!
10. They truly risked their lives!

1. Daily life in China's major cities has really changed in recent years. In what ways?
2. In 1980, Dr. Jay Arena and his family visited several cities in China.
3. correct
4. correct
5. There must have been 2,000,000 bikes racing by them at once. Amazing!
6. If Dr. Arena went to China now, would he see big differences?
7. Today, he would stare up at high-rise apartment and office buildings on Chonwenmen Wai St. in Beijing.
8. Would he be surprised to see thousands of cars and buses racing by him? Absolutely!
9. correct
10. Today, air pollution has become a major problem in cities both in China and the United States.

ONGOING ASSESSMENT: Assess Mastery

Use the following resources to assess student mastery of end marks.

In the Textbook	Technology
Chapter Review, Ex. 74, p. 630	On-Line Exercise Bank, Section 26.1

Integrating Speaking and Listening Skills

Select a short excerpt from *Prentice Hall Literature, Timeless Voices, Timeless Themes,* Bronze level that contains many questions and exclamations. Have students read the excerpt aloud using the appropriate inflections to indicate questions and exclamations. Have the rest of the class listen and identify question marks or exclamation points.

Section Review

Each of these exercises correlates with the instruction on end marks, pages 580–583. These exercises may be used for more practice, for reteaching, or for review of the Key Concepts presented. Answers for all chapter exercises are available in *Grammar Exercises Answers on Transparencies* in your Teaching Resources.

Answer Key

Exercise 5

1. Mon.	4. Sgt.
2. Dr.	5. Jr.
3. P. T.	

Exercise 6

1. Rice is the main food in China.
2. In fact, the Chinese word *fan* means both rice and meal.
3. Believe it or not, there are 7,000 ways to make rice!
4. Sometimes Chinese people say they "can't eat rice."
5. What does that expression mean?
6. "Cannot eat rice" means that one is ill.
7. What do you think the expression "broken the rice bowl" indicates?
8. It means that someone has lost a job.
9. My, how interesting these expressions are!
10. Do other foods have symbolic meanings?

Exercise 7

1. Good manners in China are different from American manners. declarative
2. Oh, all right, you can slurp soup. declarative
3. Don't point chopsticks at people. imperative
4. Wait! It is rude to eat before everyone is at the table. exclamatory, declarative
5. Why are you moving the food around? interrogative

Exercise 8

1. How impolite. (or !)
2. Rapping on the table three times shows gratitude for a full cup of tea.
3. What is usually eaten first in China?
4. Plain rice is the first food tasted.

Section Review

GRAMMAR EXERCISES 5–11

Exercise 5 Using a Period with Abbreviations On your paper, add a period to each abbreviation.

1. Mon	4. Sgt Cally
2. Dr Smith	5. John Jones, Jr
3. PT Barnum	

Exercise 6 Using End Marks Add a period, exclamation point, or question mark to each sentence below. (In some cases, you may need two end marks.)

1. Rice is the main food in China
2. In fact, the Chinese word *fan* means both rice and meal
3. Believe it or not, there are 7,000 ways to make rice
4. Sometimes Chinese people say they "can't eat rice"
5. What does that expression mean
6. "Cannot eat rice" means that one is ill
7. What do you think the expression "broken the rice bowl" indicates
8. It means that someone has lost a job
9. My how interesting these expressions are
10. Do other foods have symbolic meanings

Exercise 7 Identifying Declarative, Imperative, Interrogative, or Exclamatory Statements Identify each sentence as *declarative, imperative, interrogative,* or *exclamatory,* and then add the appropriate punctuation mark.

1. Good manners in China are different from American manners
2. Oh, all right you can slurp soup
3. Don't point chopsticks at people
4. Wait It is rude to eat before everyone is at the table
5. Why are you moving the food around

Exercise 8 Revising to Correct End Marks Revise these sentences, correcting the use of end marks as necessary.

1. How impolite?
2. Rapping on the table three times shows gratitude for a full cup of tea?
3. What is usually eaten first in China!
4. Plain rice is the first food tasted!
5. Wow. Some Chinese foods are unusual!
6. Imagine eating bear paws, frog legs, iguanas, snakes, or camel hooves!
7. Those exotic meals are eaten in China!
8. Are you willing to taste them.
9. How do the Chinese remedy bad breath.
10. Just chew tea leaves!

Exercise 9 Find It in Your Reading Read this paragraph from "Yeh-Shen: A Cinderella Story From China." Why has the writer used three different end marks?

That day Yeh-Shen turned many a head as she appeared at the feast. All around her people whispered, "Look at that beautiful girl! Who can she be?"

Exercise 10 Find It in Your Writing Look through your portfolio to find examples of sentences with each type of end mark. Explain why you used each mark. Then, rewrite each sentence so that it calls for a different end mark.

Exercise 11 Writing Application Imagine that you are dining at a Chinese restaurant. Write a dialogue between the waiter and yourself. Include declarative sentences, questions, and exclamations in your dialogue.

---

5. Wow! Some Chinese foods are unusual.
6. Imagine eating bear paws, frog legs, iguanas, snakes, or camel hooves!
7. Those exotic meals are eaten in China.
8. Are you willing to taste them?
9. How do the Chinese remedy bad breath?
10. Just chew tea leaves.

Exercise 9

Find It in Your Reading
The period ends a declarative sentence. The exclamation point ends an exclamatory sentence. The question mark ends an interrogative sentence. By varying the end marks, the author is able to indicate the people's wonderment and curiosity.

Exercise 10

Find It in Your Writing
Students might choose to revise a paragraph, rewriting each sentence to conclude with a different end mark.

Exercise 11

Writing Application
Students can practice speaking/listening skills by reading aloud their dialogues to the class.

Commas

Using Commas to Separate Basic Elements

While an end mark signals a full stop, a comma signals a brief pause. It may be used to separate basic elements in a sentence or to set off elements added to a sentence.

Many people use more commas than are necessary, while others use fewer than they should. To avoid the overuse or underuse of commas, include a comma in your writing only when you know that a specific rule applies.

This section presents the rules that you need to know to use commas correctly.

Commas With Compound Sentences A compound sentence consists of two or more independent clauses joined by one of the coordinating conjunctions *(and, but, for, nor, or, so,* and *yet).*

▶ **KEY CONCEPT** Use a comma before the conjunction to separate two independent clauses in a compound sentence. ■

Notice that each of the following sentences is compound because it is made up of more than one complete thought. In the first sentence, a comma and the conjunction *and* separate the independent clauses. In the second, a comma and the conjunction *but* separate the independent clauses.

| COMPOUND SENTENCES: | Marco Polo was fascinated with China, *and* he took home many souvenirs. |
| | He told Italian friends about China, *but* they did not believe his stories. |

Remember to use a comma before a conjunction only when there are complete thoughts on both sides of the conjunction. Do not use a comma when there is just a word, phrase, or subordinate clause on either side of the conjunction.

WORDS:	Polo visited *cities* and *farming areas.*
PHRASES:	The Chinese established systems *for delivering mail* and *for carrying goods.*
SUBORDINATE CLAUSES:	Kublai Khan was a man *who ruled strictly* but *who could also be kind.*

In some compound sentences, the independent clauses are very brief, and the meaning is clear. When this occurs, the comma before the conjunction may be omitted.

| EXAMPLE: | Jonathan listened carefully but he heard nothing. |

Theme: China

In this section, you will learn how commas are used to separate or set off elements in sentences. The examples and exercises in this section will tell you more about China's history and culture.

**Cross-Curricular Connection:
Social Studies**

Commas • 585

⏱ TIME AND RESOURCE MANAGER

Resources
Print: Grammar Exercise Workbook, pp. 149–158; Hands-on Grammar Activity Book, Chapter 26; Grammar Exercises Answers on Transparancies, Chapter 26
Technology: Language Lab CD-ROM, Punctuation; On-Line Exercise Bank, Section 26.2

In-Depth Coverage	Accelerated Pace
• Work through all key concepts, pp. 585–597. • Assign and review Exercises 12–24. • Read and discuss Grammar in Literature, p. 591. • Do the Hands-on Grammar Activity, p. 598.	• Assign pp. 585–597 for independent student review. • Assign Section Review Exercises 25–27, p. 599.

PREPARE and ENGAGE

Interest GRABBER Ask students to write one sentence in which they discuss at least three different ways they like to eat ice cream. Have them read their sentence aloud to the class at a normal speed but without pausing. Next, have them read their sentences aloud, pausing more times than makes sense. Discuss how the comma, used correctly, creates neither too many nor too few pauses.

Activate Prior Knowledge

Ask students to remember the last time they went shopping at the supermarket. What are five items that their family always buys? On a piece of paper have them complete the sentence:

At the supermarket, my family always buys . . .

Ask them how they separated each item from the next in their list. Point out how without commas, for example, *milk eggs bread* would all seem like one thing.

TEACH

Step-by-Step Teaching Guide

Commas With Compound Sentences

1. Let students know that the purpose of the comma is to separate ideas. Commas in a sentence make ideas easier to recognize and read.

2. Have students review compound sentences in Chapter 20.

3. Write the following sentences on the board, circling the comma and the word *and* in the first sentence, and the word *and* in the second sentence.

   China is very far away from the United States, and it takes a long time to travel to China from here.

   China is very large and very diverse in its regional cultures.

Point out that the first sentence can be made into two sentences. In the second sentence, the phrase after the conjunction *and* could not stand on its own as a complete sentence, so no comma is necessary.

► **Exercise 12**

1. B.C., and
2. equipment, so
3. states, but
4. cloth, and
5. system, yet

► **Exercise 13**

1. society, but; time the
2. large, for; servants and
3. power, for; matters and
4. watched and; descendants, so
5. die, yet; still considered

Critical Viewing

Identify; Support Students may mention land and water, nature and architecture, or people and nature.

26.2

► **Exercise 12** Using Commas With Compound Sentences

Read each sentence below, and decide where a comma is needed. On your paper, write the word before the comma, the comma, and the conjunction following the comma.

1. The Shang dynasty has been dated from 1700 to 1027 B.C. and Shang rulers helped to shape Chinese civilization.
2. Shang bronze workers used their skills to improve farming equipment so farmers were able to produce more food.
3. Shang rulers divided their kingdom into separate states but they also set up a single capital city.
4. The rulers wore silk cloth and they learned to read from books made of bamboo and wood.
5. Under Shang rule, the Chinese developed a writing system yet most of the written records have disappeared.

► **Exercise 13** Revising Sentences to Correct Comma Usage

Revise each sentence, correcting any misuses of commas.

1. The kingdom was a well-developed society but over time, the government became weaker.
2. The tombs of Shang kings could be very large for the kings were buried with their servants, and belongings.
3. The king held tremendous power for he headed state matters, and was also the leader of the religion.
4. The Shang believed that dead ancestors watched, and guided their descendants so the Shang revered their dead ancestors.
5. Ancestors might die yet they were still, considered part of the living family.

► **More Practice**

Language Lab CD-ROM
• Punctuation lesson
On-line Exercise Bank
• Section 26.2
Grammar Exercise Workbook
• pp. 149–152

▼ Critical Viewing
What different elements are joined together in this photo? **[Identify; Support]**

586 • Punctuation

☑ **ONGOING ASSESSMENT: Prerequisite Skills**

If students have difficulty with the use of commas in compound sentences, you may find it necessary to review the following to assure coverage of prerequisite knowledge.

In the Textbook	Print Resources	Technology
Sentence Structure, pp. 445–447	Grammar Exercise Workbook, pp. 83–86	Language Lab CD-ROM, Combining Sentences; On-Line Exercise Bank, Section 20.2

Commas Between Items in a Series When three or more similar items appear in a series, commas are needed to separate them.

▶ **KEY CONCEPT** Use commas to separate three or more words, phrases, or clauses in a series. ■

Notice in the following examples that the number of items in the series is one more than the number of commas needed. For example, in the first sentence, there are three items in the series that are separated by two commas.

SERIES OF WORDS:	The beverages included *fruit juice, ginger ale,* and *jasmine tea.*
SERIES OF PHRASES:	Ceramic vases were placed *on the table, on the mantel,* and *on the windowsill.*
SERIES OF CLAUSES:	We needed to know *where we would catch the plane, when it would leave,* and *how much baggage we were allowed.*

One exception to the rule for using commas in a series occurs when each item is separated from the others by a conjunction.

EXAMPLE: My sister collects stamps and coins and pottery.

▶ **Exercise 14** Using Commas Between Items in a Series
Copy these sentences, adding commas where they are needed.
1. Many historical sites are found in Beijing, such as the Old Palace Museum the Wall of Nine Dragons and the Museum of Chinese Art.
2. Beijing is a city that connects the past present and future.
3. The emperors of ancient Beijing could be found governing China from the Forbidden City enjoying recreation at the Summer Palace or praying at the Temple of Heaven.
4. The four Buddhist temples housed in Beijing are the Yunju Temple the Dazhong Temple the Fahai Temple and the Yonghegong Temple.
5. Beijing has beautiful scenery as the Great Wall surrounds it the Yan Shan Mountains overlook it and the Grand Canal runs by it.

▶ **Exercise 15** Writing Sentences With Commas Write five sentences in which you convey what you know about China. Three of the sentences should be compound sentences containing commas, and two should use commas to separate items in a series.

⚙ **Grammar and Style Tip**

Some writers view the comma preceding the conjunction as optional; most professional writers, however, add the last comma to avoid confusion.

Commas • 587

☑ **ONGOING ASSESSMENT: Monitor and Reinforce**

If students miss more than one item in Exercise 12, 13, 14, or 15, refer them to the following for additional practice.

In the Textbook	Print Resources	Technology
Section Review, Ex. 25, p. 599	Grammar Exercise Workbook, pp. 149–150	Language Lab CD-ROM, Punctuation; On-Line Exercise Bank, Section 26.2

Step-by-Step Teaching Guide

Commas Between Items in a Series

1. Explain to students that separating each item in a series by commas makes the sequence of items clear to the reader.

2. Write the following sentences on the board, circling the commas and the words, phrases, or clauses that follow them.

   The Chinese practice many art forms, such as carving, painting, and calligraphy.

   The ancient martial art of tai chi is often practiced privately indoors, in school studios, or in large groups outside.

   Building the Great Wall challenged workers, required much manpower, and took many years.

   Point out that these sentences show three different types of lists, or series. The first is a series of words, the second is a series of phrases, and the third is a series of clauses.

3. Explain that the exception to using commas in a series is when each item is separated by a conjunction. Use the sentence below to illustrate.

   Dorothy, the Tin Man, the Scarecrow, and the Cowardly Lion were afraid of meeting lions and tigers and bears.

Answer Key

▶ **Exercise 14**

1. the Old Palace Museum, the Wall of Nine Dragons, and the Museum of Chinese Art.
2. past, present, and future.
3. governing China from the Forbidden City, enjoying recreation at the Summer Palace, or praying at the Temple of Heaven.
4. the Yunju Temple, the Dazhong Temple, the Fahai Temple, and the Yonghegong Temple.
5. scenery, as the Great Wall surrounds it, the Yan Shan Mountains overlook it, and the Grand Canal

▶ **Exercise 15**

Have students check partners' writing for three compound sentences and two sentences with items in a series. Be sure commas are used correctly.

587

Commas Between Adjectives

1. Tell students that commas are also used to separate adjectives when more than one modifies a noun. In this way, the adjectives are like items in a series. However, commas are used to separate only adjectives that are of equal importance.

2. Let students know that they can test whether the adjectives are equally important and therefore need a comma separating them. Can the word *and* be placed in between the adjectives without changing the meaning of the sentence?

3. Write the following sentences on the board. Explain that the first needs commas because it passed the *and* test. The second sentence does not need commas because the *and* test will not work.

   Flavorful, spicy *soups are common in Chinese cuisine.*

   Several different *spices are used to make a Chinese soup.*

4. The second way students can determine whether the adjectives are of equal rank is by changing their order. If the order can be changed without changing the meaning of the sentence, then commas should be used. If not, students should not use a comma.

5. Write the following sentences on the board. Explain that the first needs commas because it stands up to the order-change test. The second does not need commas because the test does not work.

   I asked to taste a mild, sweet *soup so I wouldn't burn my mouth.*

   I was offered several special *choices to try.*

26.2

Commas Between Adjectives Sometimes adjectives need to be separated by commas.

▶ **KEY CONCEPT** Use commas to separate adjectives of equal rank. ■

Two methods can be used to help decide whether two or more adjectives are of equal rank. First, if the word *and* can be placed between the adjectives without changing the meaning of the sentence, then the adjectives are of equal rank. Second, if the order of the adjectives can be changed, then they are equal.

Study the following examples. Then, try both methods for deciding whether the adjectives are of equal rank.

EXAMPLES: You have made a *simple, polite* request.
Flavorful, spicy, nutritious soups are common in Chinese cuisine.

If you tried both methods on these examples, you learned that the adjectives are of equal rank. Therefore, commas are needed to separate them. In other sentences, however, placing an *and* between the adjectives or changing their order would alter the meaning of the sentence.

▶ **KEY CONCEPT** Do not use commas to separate adjectives that must stay in a specific order. ■

Apply the two methods for determining whether the adjectives are of equal rank to the following examples.

EXAMPLES: I read descriptions of *several ancient* temples in my guidebook.
Some colorful birds perched on the temple roof.

As you can see, the italicized adjectives in the examples cannot be separated by *and*, and their order cannot be changed without destroying the meaning of the sentences. Therefore, no commas should be added.

Note About *Commas With Adjectives:* A comma should never be used to separate the last adjective in a series from the noun it modifies.

INCORRECT: An efficient, helpful, interesting, guide led our party.

CORRECT: An efficient, helpful, interesting guide led our party.

588 • Punctuation

✎ STANDARDIZED TEST PREPARATION WORKSHOP

Grammar and Usage Many standardized tests require students to identify correctly punctuated sentences. Have students read the sentence below, then choose the correct revision.

The Chinese invented the printing press, gunpowder and advanced methods of glazing pottery.

A The Chinese invented the printing press, gunpowder, and advanced methods of glazing pottery.

B The Chinese invented the printing press gunpowder and advanced methods of glazing pottery.

C The Chinese, invented the printing press, gunpowder, and advanced methods of glazing pottery.

D Correct as is

The correct answer is **A** because commas separate the items in a series.

▶ Critical Viewing
In what ways does
the poster show that
men and women
have equal rank?
[Infer; Support]

▶ **Exercise 16** Using Commas Between Adjectives Copy the
underlined adjectives onto your paper, adding commas only in
those places where they are needed.
1. Traditionally, Chinese families wished for <u>strong</u> <u>sturdy</u>
   sons.
2. Sons often carried on <u>their</u> <u>family's</u> traditions.
3. The birth of a daughter was not always accompanied by a
   <u>warm</u> <u>joyous</u> celebration.
4. Marriages were arranged in <u>traditional</u> <u>Chinese</u> families.
5. Sons were expected to remain in their <u>old</u> <u>family</u> home
   even after they married.

▶ **Exercise 17** Revising Sentences to Correct the Use of
Commas Between Adjectives Revise the following sentences,
adding or removing commas as appropriate.
1. When a woman married, she had to leave her home to join
   a new unfamiliar family.
2. Every, young bride was expected to obey her husband's
   mother.
3. Some mothers-in-law treated the new, family member in a
   harsh cruel manner.
4. It wasn't until the early, twentieth century that efforts
   were made to change women's social, status in China.
5. An early custom of foot binding, which produced sore
   mangled deformed feet, has been mostly discontinued.

🔗 **Learn More**

To review adjectives,
refer to Section 16.1:
Adjectives.

Commas • 589

☑ **ONGOING ASSESSMENT: Monitor and Reinforce**

If students miss more than one item in Exercise 16, or 17, refer them to the following for additional
practice.

In the Textbook	Print Resources	Technology
Section Review, Ex. 25, p. 599	Grammar Exercise Workbook, pp.151–152	Language Lab CD-ROM, Punctuation; On-line Exercise Bank, Section 26.2

Commas After Introductory Material

1. Point out that a sentence's introductory word, phrase, or clause is often set apart, but it always tells something about the main idea of the sentence.

2. Ask students whether they know how a writer shows that introductory words are set apart from the rest of a sentence.

3. Write the following sentences on the board, underlining the introductory material and the comma that follows it.

   Look, there's the Great Wall!

   Outside the hotel, we saw the men and women practicing tai chi in the park.

   When I come back from China, I am going to publish my travel journal.

Customize for
ESL Students

Nonnative speakers may pause often when they speak English because they are uncertain of vocabulary or grammar. As a result, it may be difficult for them to hear the natural pauses that are often a guide to proper comma usage. Assign students a passage from a book in which commas are used. Ask them to read the passage aloud to a partner, paying close attention to the pauses in the flow of the sentences wherever there are commas. The more fluent partner may reread from the passage, using careful inflection to illustrate comma pauses.

26.2

Using Commas to Set Off Added Elements

Commas are used not only to separate similar kinds of words and groups of words but also to set off—that is, set apart—certain parts of a sentence from the rest.

As you read the rules for commas used to set off added elements, remember that commas should be used in your writing only when a specific rule applies.

Commas After Introductory Material Sometimes, a sentence begins with introductory material. Generally, the extra word or words are set off from the rest of the sentence by a comma.

▶ **KEY CONCEPT** Use a comma after an introductory word, phrase, or clause. ■

The following examples illustrate three types of introductory material:

KINDS OF INTRODUCTORY MATERIAL	
Introductory Words	*Well*, I need a minute to decide. *Tom*, where are you? *Please*, put some clams in the chowder.
Introductory Phrases	*In the vibrant city of Hong Kong*, trade is booming. *Located on the coast of China*, Hong Kong is an important port. *To visit Hong Kong*, you need a passport.
Introductory Clauses	*If the British had not relented*, they might still rule Hong Kong. *Where there is bustling trade*, there you will find a colorful night life as well.

When a prepositional phrase of only two words begins a sentence, a comma is not absolutely necessary.

EXAMPLES: *At night* we heard the crickets.
For hours we nervously remained awake.

☑ ONGOING ASSESSMENT: Monitor and Reinforce

If students miss more than one item in Exercise 18 or 19, refer them to the following for additional practice.

In the Textbook	Print Resources	Technology
Section Review, Ex. 26, p. 599	Grammar Exercise Workbook, pp. 153–154	Language Lab CD-ROM, Punctuation; On-Line Exercise Bank, Section 26.2

GRAMMAR IN LITERATURE

from Yeh-Shen: A Cinderella Story From China

Retold by Ai-Ling Louie

Notice how the writer has used commas to separate items in a series and to set off added elements. Do the commas make it easier to read the story?

. . . This time the big fish saw Yeh-Shen's familiar jacket and heaved itself onto the bank, expecting to be fed. But the stepmother, having hidden a dagger in her sleeve, stabbed the fish, wrapped it in her garments, and took it home to cook for dinner.

Exercise 18 Using Commas With Introductory Material
For each of the following sentences, write the introductory material, the missing comma, and the word following the comma.
1. Oh I'm so excited to fly to Hong Kong!
2. Located on China's southern coast Hong Kong consists of the Kowloon Peninsula and several islands.
3. Though Hong Kong covers only 400 square miles over six million people live there.
4. As you can tell when you visit Hong Kong it is one of the most crowded places in the world.
5. Please will you tell me more about Hong Kong?

Exercise 19 Revising the Use of Commas With Introductory Material Revise the paragraph below, adding or deleting commas where necessary.
(1) During the twentieth century Hong Kong became an economic power in Asia. (2) An important manufacturing center it contains factories specializing in textiles, clothing, and electronic equipment. (3) While Hong Kong workers produce many, goods nearly all of their products are exported to other countries. (4) Up until recent, times the colony belonged to the British. (5) Determined the Chinese government demanded, that Hong Kong be returned to Chinese control.

> **More Practice**
> **Language Lab CD-ROM**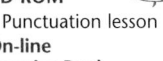
> • Punctuation lesson
> **On-line Exercise Bank**
> • Section 26.2
> **Grammar Exercise Workbook**
> • pp. 153–154

Commas • 591

Step-by-Step Teaching Guide

Grammar in Literature

1. Have a volunteer read aloud the passage from "Yeh-Shen" on page 591.
2. Ask students to explain how the commas make it possible to link several actions undertaken by the stepmother.
3. Revise the excerpt, replacing the commas with periods (". . . onto the bank. It expected . . ."). Read it to students and ask how this change affected the flow of the story.

Responding to Literature

The full text of "Yeh-Shen: A Cinderella Story from China," can be found in the Bronze level of *Prentice Hall Literature: Timeless Voices, Timeless Themes,* matched with a Native American Cinderella story. Tell students that versions of the Cinderella story—a poor but virtuous girl suffers at the hands of her evil stepmother and stepsisters—can be found all over the world. More than nine hundred versions exist, including one that has been traced back more than a thousand years to China.

Answer Key

> **Exercise 18**

1. Oh, I'm
2. coast, Hong Kong
3. miles, over
4. Hong Kong, it
5. Please, will

> **Exercise 19**

1. century, Hong Kong
2. center, it
3. many goods, nearly
4. recent times, the
5. Determined, the; demanded that

> **TIME SAVERS!**

Answers on Transparency
Use the Grammar Exercises Answers on Transparencies for Chapter 26 facilitate correction by students.

On-Line Exercise Bank
Have students complete the exercises on computer. The Auto Check feature will grade their work for you!

591

Commas With Parenthetical Expressions

1. Explain that a parenthetical phrase is not essential to the main idea of the sentence. The sentence would stand on its own and make sense if the parenthetical expression was removed.

2. Write the following examples on the chalkboard:

   Hold on a minute, Sue, I want to get a picture of this statue.

   It is not going to be possible, unfortunately, to see the full collection of Ming Dynasty vases.

   China is a huge landmass and, most important, has the largest population of any country on Earth.

3. Have students isolate and circle the parenthetical phrase in each sentence.

Answer Key

Exercise 20

1. The Chinese, I think, do not get enough credit for their many technological advances.
2. Nevertheless, some Chinese inventions deserve recognition.
3. Did you know, for example, that Chinese naval captains were the first to use magnetic compasses?
4. Sailors all over the world, therefore, can thank the Chinese for helping them find their way.
5. Helene, can you think of any other tools that were invented in China?

Commas With Parenthetical Expressions

A *parenthetical expression* is a word or phrase that is not essential to the rest of the sentence. These words or phrases generally add extra information to the basic sentence.

KEY CONCEPT Use commas to set off parenthetical expressions. ■

Parenthetical expressions are sometimes written at the beginning of a sentence as introductory material. They may also be written in the middle or at the end of a sentence. A parenthetical expression in the middle of a sentence needs a comma before it and a comma after it to set it off. If it is written at the end of the sentence, only one comma is needed.

Examples of parenthetical expressions are shown below:

KINDS OF PARENTHETICAL EXPRESSIONS	
Names of People Being Addressed	Watch, *Frank*, while I show you another early Chinese invention. Stop whispering, *Pamela and Dan*.
Certain Adverbs	You are, *therefore*, the person I would choose. Your answer is incorrect, *however*.
Common Expressions	One Chinese invention, *on the other hand*, helped sailors all over the world. They are not given enough credit, *I believe*.

Exercise 20 Using Commas With Parenthetical Expressions

Copy each of the following sentences, adding commas to set off the parenthetical expressions.

EXAMPLE: Their garden however survived the storm.

ANSWER: Their garden, however, survived the storm.

1. The Chinese I think do not get enough credit for their many technological advances.
2. Nevertheless some Chinese inventions deserve recognition.
3. Did you know for example that Chinese naval captains were the first to use magnetic compasses?
4. Sailors all over the world therefore can thank the Chinese for helping them find their way.
5. Helene can you think of any other tools that were invented in China?

More Practice

Language Lab CD-ROM
• Punctuation lesson
On-line Exercise Bank
• Section 26.2
Grammar Exercise Workbook
• pp. 155–156

☑ ONGOING ASSESSMENT: Monitor and Reinforce

If students miss more than one item in Exercise 20 or 21, refer them to the following for additional practice.

In the Textbook	Print Resources	Technology
Section Review, Ex. 26, p. 599	Grammar Exercise Workbook, pp. 155–156	Language Lab CD-ROM, Punctuation; On-Line Exercise Bank, Section 26.2

Commas With Nonessential Expressions Sometimes, it is difficult to decide when to set off material with commas. Knowing whether a word, phrase, or clause is essential or nonessential to the meaning of a sentence helps.

▶ **KEY CONCEPT** Use commas to set off nonessential expressions. Do not set off essential material with commas. ■

Notice that each nonessential expression in the chart below can be left out without changing the meaning of the sentence.

APPOSITIVES AND APPOSITIVE PHRASES	
Essential	The Chinese thinker *Confucius* taught the importance of tradition.
Nonessential	Confucius, *a Chinese thinker*, taught the importance of tradition.
	The importance of tradition was taught by Confucius, *a Chinese thinker.*

PARTICIPIAL PHRASES	
Essential	The man *leading a European expedition to China* was Marco Polo.
Nonessential	Marco Polo, *leading a European expedition to China*, arrived there in 1275.
	Marco Polo arrived in 1275, *leading a European expedition.*

ADJECTIVE CLAUSES	
Essential	The invaders *who swept into China in the 1200's* ruled with an iron hand.
Nonessential	The Mongols, *who swept into China in the 1200's*, ruled with an iron hand.
	The country was ruled by the Mongols, *who swept into China in the 1200's.*

▶ **Exercise 21** Using Commas With Nonessential Expressions If the underlined material in a sentence below is nonessential, add a comma or commas as needed. Otherwise, write *E.*

EXAMPLE: The patient had typhoid a contagious disease.
ANSWER: The patient had typhoid, a contagious disease.

1. <u>As early as A.D. 100</u> the Chinese had set up medical schools.
2. The doctors <u>who were trained in these schools</u> learned many advanced techniques.
3. They timed a person's pulse <u>or heart rate</u> to diagnose illness.
4. Anesthetics <u>which render patients unconscious during operations</u> were first used in China.
5. Acupuncture <u>another Chinese invention</u> was used to ease pain.

Commas With Nonessential Expressions

1. Explain that one way to avoid using too many commas is to understand when a word, phrase, or clause requires a comma to set it off.

2. Point out that some words, phrases, and clauses are essential to the sentence. A sentence loses its meaning if an essential word or phrase is taken away. Commas are not used here.

3. Write the following sentences on the board, underlining the essential phrase or clause. Have students explain why each underlined example is an essential part of the sentence.

   The famous Chinese philosopher <u>Confucius</u> had fascinating ideas about society. (who)

   The student <u>studying hard</u> is a senior. (which one)

4. Explain that some words, phrases, and clauses are nonessential to the sentence. The sentence could stand on its own if a nonessential word or phrase were taken away. Commas, therefore, should be used to set them apart.

5. Write the following sentences on the board, underlining the nonessential phrase or clause. Have students explain why each example is a nonessential part of the sentence. Have them compare the nonessential to the essential phrases still written on the board.

   Confucius, <u>the famous Chinese philosopher</u>, had fascinating ideas about society. (detail/modifier)

   The student, <u>by studying hard</u>, is trying to win a scholarship. (detail/modifier)

Answer Key

▶ **Exercise 21**

1. As early as A.D. 100, the Chinese had set up medical schools.
2. E
3. They timed a person's pulse, or heart rate, to diagnose illness.
4. Anesthetics, which render patients unconscious during operations, were first used in China.
5. Acupuncture, another Chinese invention, was used to ease pain.

Using Commas in Special Situations

1. As in other circumstances, the use of commas to separate dates, geographical names, and other special material from the rest of the sentence prevents information from running together and confusing the reader.

2. Write the following sentences on the board.

   Tuesday, July 4, was a day of celebration for everyone.

   On December 31, 1999, everyone celebrated the turn of the century.

3. Explain the optional rule of using a comma to separate a month from a year. Stress the importance of consistency in any optional grammatical rule. When one style of usage has been chosen, students should continue to use it throughout any piece of written work.

Answer Key

> **Exercise 22**

1. On January 1, 2000, lion and dragon dances were performed in Hangzhou to greet the new year.
2. February 10 was the date of the Spring Flower Fair in Guangzhou, China.
3. A carnival in Beijing, China, on June 17, 2000, featured an opera and an acrobatic performance.
4. Our flight left from Seoul, South Korea, on Thursday, June 10, and landed in Seattle, Washington, seven hours later.
5. We planned a showing of our China slides in Tacoma, Washington, on Tuesday, July 6, 2000.

⏱ TIME SAVERS!

Answers on Transparency
Use the Grammar Exercises Answers on Transparencies for Chapter 26 to facilitate correction by students.

On-Line Exercise Bank
Have students complete the exercises on computer. The Auto Check feature will grade their work for you!

26.2

Using Commas in Special Situations

Commas are also used to set off dates, geographical names, and other special material.

Commas With Dates and Geographical Names

Commas are used to separate the different parts of some dates and geographical names. The following rule applies to dates consisting of several parts:

▶ **KEY CONCEPT** When a date is made up of two or more parts, use a comma after each item except in the case of a month followed by a day. ■

Notice in the following examples that commas are not used to set off a month followed by a numeral standing for a day. Commas are used, however, when the month and date are used as an appositive to rename a day of the week.

EXAMPLES: On July 12, 1979, Aunt Mai arrived in this country with just a few possessions.

Tuesday, March 18, was carefully circled on his calendar.

When a date contains only a month and a year, commas are unnecessary.

EXAMPLE: I will graduate in June 2004.

▶ **KEY CONCEPT** When a geographical name is made up of two or more parts, use a comma after each item. ■

EXAMPLES: They lived in Marietta, Georgia, for several years and then moved to Sarasota, Florida.

My friend Pedro was born in El Salto, Durango, Mexico.

> **Exercise 22** Using Commas With Dates and Geographical Names Add commas where necessary.
> 1. On January 1 2000 lion and dragon dances were performed in Hangzhou to greet the new year.
> 2. February 10 was the date of the Spring Flower Fair in Guangzhou China.
> 3. A carnival in Beijing China on June 17 2000 featured an opera and an acrobatic performance.
> 4. Our flight left from Seoul South Korea on Thursday June 10 and landed in Seattle Washington seven hours later.
> 5. We planned a showing of our China slides in Tacoma Washington on Tuesday July 6 2000.

▶ **More Practice**

Language Lab CD-ROM
• Punctuation lesson
On-line Exercise Bank
• Section 26.2
Grammar Exercise Workbook
• pp. 157–158

▶ Critical Viewing
How did the Great Wall set apart China from its enemies? [Speculate]

▶ **Exercise 23** Writing a Letter Using Commas to Separate Dates and Geographical Names Imagine that you have had the opportunity to travel to China. Write a letter or a postcard to a friend describing your experiences. Use the photographs and the information in this section for material. In your letter or postcard, include at least four place names and two dates separated by commas. For a challenge, include a sentence using a comma for each of the other purposes you have learned in this chapter.

Commas in Addresses, Letters, Numbers, and Quotations

Commas are also used in other situations; these include addresses, letter salutations and closings, numbers, and quotations. The following rule governs the use of commas in addresses:

▶ **KEY CONCEPT** Use a comma after each item in an address that is made up of two or more parts. ■

In the following example, commas are needed after the name, street, and city. Notice, however, that no comma separates the state from the ZIP Code.

EXAMPLE: She is corresponding with her friend Arlene Blackwell, 32 Birdsong Avenue, Falmouth, Massachusetts 02540.

Notice, however, that when the same address is written in three lines—name, street, town, and state—on an envelope, most of the commas are not necessary.

EXAMPLE: Arlene Blackwell
32 Birdsong Avenue
Falmouth, MA 02540

Commas • 595

3. Ask a student to volunteer a pen-pal's first name, and write Dear ___ on the board, followed by a comma. Then write a closing sentiment on the board different from the examples given in the book, such as *Yours truly* or *Best wishes.*

4. Point out that commas are also used to set apart quotations; the number of commas needed depends on the placement of the quote in the sentence. Write the following sentences on the board, circling the commas for emphasis.

Sue said under her breath, "I hope I get to rest before I finish my tour of the museum."

"I would like to rest," Sue said, "before seeing the rest of the museum!"

"This museum is wonderful but very large," Sue murmured tiredly.

26.2

The next rule covers the use of commas in salutations and closings in letters.

▶ **KEY CONCEPT** Use a comma after the salutation in a personal letter and after the closing in all letters. ■

SALUTATIONS: Dear Kaori,   My dear Ann,
CLOSINGS: With affection,   Sincerely,

Using commas according to the following rule makes it easier to read large numbers:

▶ **KEY CONCEPT** With numbers of more than three digits, add a comma before every third digit, counting from the right. ■

EXAMPLES: 2,532 bricks
            a population of 1,860,421
            82,471,908 grains of sand

Note About *Commas With Numbers:* No commas should be used with ZIP Codes, telephone numbers, page numbers, or serial numbers.

ZIP CODE: 14878
TELEPHONE NUMBER: (607) 555-1328
PAGE NUMBER: on page 1817
SERIAL NUMBER: 402 36 4113

A final use of the comma is to show where a direct quotation begins and ends.

▶ **KEY CONCEPT** Use commas to set off a direct quotation from the rest of a sentence. ■

The placement of the commas depends upon the "he said/she said" part of the sentence. As you study the following examples, notice the correct placement of the commas. (See Section 26.4 for more information about punctuating quotations.)

EXAMPLES: Gordon murmured with a yawn, "This is a dull movie."

           "I thought," Lydia said, "that you liked martial arts movies."

           "It's the third time I've seen this one," Gordon replied.

▶ **More Practice**
Language Lab CD-ROM
• Punctuation lesson
On-line Exercise Bank
• Section 26.2
Grammar Exercise Workbook
• pp. 157–158

▶ **Exercise 24** Using Commas in Other Situations Copy each item below onto your paper, adding commas where they are needed.

EXAMPLE: "My sister is studying Chinese literature" he said.

ANSWER: "My sister is studying Chinese literature," he said.

1. The Chinese philosopher Confucius once said "He who learns but does not think is lost; he who thinks but does not learn is in danger."
2. "By nature" said Confucius "people are pretty much alike; it is learning and practice that set them apart."
3. Dear Amy   Sincerely   Jenny Ling
4. On page 1341 of the atlas, I read that the population of Shanghai is approximately 14329600.
5. The atlas was published by Jayson Books 1437 Langston Blvd. Savannah Georgia 31406.
6. Jayson Books
   1437 Langston Blvd.
   Savannah GA 31406
7. Go to the Temple of the Jade Buddha 170 Anyuan Lu Putuo Shanghai China to see two of China's most famous jade Buddhas.
8. Our tour leader said "Each Buddha is carved from a single piece of white jade."
9. The Yuyuan Garden in Shanghai was planted before the year 1600 and contains more than 1100 different flowers and trees.
10. Standing majestically above Shanghai's harbor is a 1535-foot-high television tower.

▶ Critical Viewing How does a ballerina signal the end of her performance? [Relate]

Commas • 597

Exercise 24

1. The Chinese philosopher Confucius once said, "He who learns but does not think is lost; he who thinks but does not learn is in danger."
2. "By nature," said Confucius, "people are pretty much alike; it is learning and practice that set them apart."
3. Dear Amy,
   Sincerely,
   Jenny Ling
4. On page 1341 of the atlas, I read that the population of Shanghai is approximately 14,329,600.
5. The atlas was published by Jayson Books, 1437 Langston Blvd., Savannah, Georgia 31406.
6. Jayson Books
   1437 Langston Blvd.
   Savannah, GA 31406
7. Go to the Temple of the Jade Buddha, 170 Anyuan Lu, Putuo, Shanghai, China, to see two of China's most famous jade Buddhas.
8. Our tour leader said, "Each Buddha is carved from a single piece of white jade."
9. The Yuyuan Garden in Shanghai was planted before the year 1600 and contains more than 1,100 different flowers and trees.
10. Standing majestically above Shanghai's harbor is a 1,535-foot-high television tower.

Critical Viewing

Relate Possible responses: she bows, stops dancing, she leaves the stage.

Customize for
Gifted and Talented Students

Have students research Chinese ballet and traditional dance forms. Have them select the story from one ballet or dance and write a summary of its plot, making sure to use commas correctly.

☑ **ONGOING ASSESSMENT: Monitor and Reinforce**

If students have difficulty with Exercise 22, 23, or 24, refer them to the following for additional practice.

In the Textbook	Print Resources	Technology
Section Review, Ex. 27, p. 599	Grammar Exercise Workbook, pp. 157–158	Language Lab CD-ROM, Punctuation; On-line Exercise Bank, Section 26.2

Punctuation Circles

Teaching Resources: Hands-on Grammar Activity Book, Chapter 26

1. Have students refer to their Hands-on Grammar Activity books or give them copies of relevant pages for this activity.

2. Be sure students understand that sometimes two or more ways to punctuate are correct. It is often difficult, for example, to decide whether a sentence is a statement or an exclamation.

3. If sticky dots are not easily available, students can use different colored pencils or pens to draw colored circles.

4. To challenge students, also input the sentences without capitalization and have them supply this, too.

Find It in Your Writing

Have students swap writing samples with a partner and see if they each punctuate the same way.

Find It in Your Reading

Have students work with a partner. Each takes the same article, and they compare how they punctuated it.

26.2

Hands-on Grammar

Punctuation Circles

1. Choose a passage from a short story in your literature book. Ideally, it should be a passage that includes dialogue.

2. Input the passage using a word-processing program. Use a large font size—14 or 16 points. Omit all of the punctuation as you input. Print out your completed passage.

3. Obtain packets of differently colored sticky dots at an office supply store.

4. Read the selection aloud. Following the chart below, place the appropriate colored sticky dots in places where you feel punctuation is needed, based on the sound of your reading.

5. Compare the pattern of circles in your version of the passage with the original passage. What did you punctuate differently? Why? What did you punctuate the same? Why?

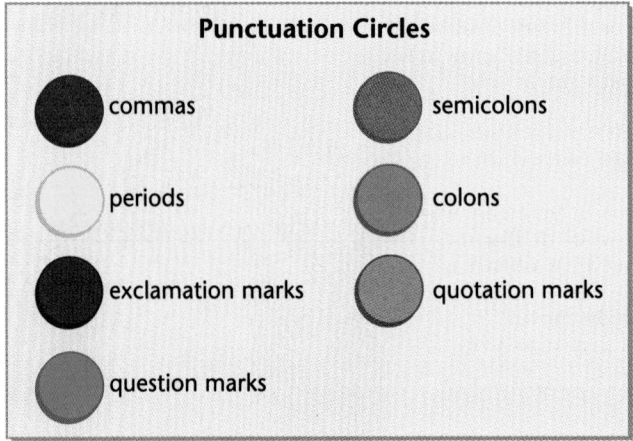

Punctuation Circles

- commas
- periods
- exclamation marks
- question marks
- semicolons
- colons
- quotation marks

Find It in Your Writing Try the above activity with a piece of your own writing. Choose a piece of writing from your portfolio. Eliminate the punctuation, and complete the steps above. How does your color-coded version compare with your original?

Find It in Your Reading Select an article from a newsmagazine. Choose a passage that especially interests you. Then, follow the steps outlined above.

⏱ TIME SAVERS!

✋ **Hands-on Grammar Book**
Use the Hands-on Grammar activity sheet for Chapter 26 to facilitate this activity.

☑ ONGOING ASSESSMENT: Assess Mastery

Use the following resources to assess student mastery of commas.

In the Textbook	Technology
Chapter Review, Ex. 75–77, p. 630	On-Line Exercise Bank, Section 26.2

Section 26.2 Section Review

GRAMMAR EXERCISES 25–30

Exercise 25 Revising the Use of Commas in Compound Sentences, Between Adjectives, and Between Items in a Series Revise the following sentences, adding or deleting commas as needed.

1. For Chinese children, school begins at the age of seven but many children participate in day care earlier, in life.
2. A fast-paced active time opens their days at school.
3. Children have the opportunity to play sports such as Ping-Pong swimming, or basketball.
4. They participate in many exciting challenging festivals such as the Lantern Festival the Qing Ming Festival and Liberation Day.
5. Children enjoy listening to a talented animated, storyteller and, they are encouraged to make up stories of their own.

Exercise 26 Revising the Use of Commas to Set Off Added Elements Rewrite the following sentences, adding commas to set off introductory, parenthetical, or nonessential material.

1. Much of China's ancient art contains jade a very valuable gem.
2. Because jade is very durable it can be used for detailed carving without breaking.
3. Nephrite which is one of the minerals that jade comes from is difficult to find.
4. Jade's rarity of course increases its value.
5. Did you know Stephen that if a jade piece is made from dark green stone it is more prized by collectors of Chinese art?

Exercise 27 Using Commas in Other Situations Copy each sentence, adding commas where they are needed.

1. I wrote to the Chinese National Tourist Office 333 West Broadway Suite 201 Glendale California 91204.
2. On Thursday October 14 2000 I received a response to my letter.
3. Enclosed was a videotape about Tianjin China's third-largest city which has a population of 12000000.
4. An announcer said "Tianjin's history dates back over 4000 years."
5. "Even though it is a very large city" the announcer added "Tianjin has a small-town feel about it."

Exercise 28 Find It in Your Reading Read this passage from "Yeh-Shen: A Cinderella Story From China," and explain the purpose of each comma.

. . . She hurried down to the pond, but she was unable to see the fish, for Yeh-Shen's pet wisely hid itself. The step-mother, however, was a crafty woman, and she soon thought of a plan. She walked home and called out, "Yeh-Shen, go and collect some firewood."

Exercise 29 Find It in Your Writing Look through your portfolio to find a paragraph with four or more commas. Explain the purpose of each comma.

Exercise 30 Writing Application Write a brief description of an interesting place you have visited. Include at least two commas in each sentence of your description.

Section Review • 599

ASSESS

Section Review

Each of these exercises correlates with the instruction on commas, pages 585–598. These exercises may be used for more practice, for reteaching, or for review of the Key Concepts presented. Answers for all chapter exercises are available in *Grammar Exercises Answers on Transparencies* in your Teaching Resources.

Answer Key

Exercise 25

1. For Chinese children, school begins at the age of seven, but many children participate in day care earlier in life.
2. A fast-paced, active time opens their days at school.
3. Children have the opportunity to play sports such as Ping Pong, swimming, or basketball.
4. They participate in many exciting, challenging festivals, such as the Lantern Festival, Qing Ming Festival, and Liberation Day.
5. Children enjoy listening to a talented, animated storyteller, and they are encouraged to make up stories of their own.

Exercise 26

1. Much of China's ancient art contains jade, a very valuable gem.
2. Because jade is very durable, it can be used for detailed carving without breaking.
3. Nephrite, which is one of the minerals that jade comes from, is difficult to find.
4. Jade's rarity, of course, increases its value.
5. Did you know, Stephen, that if a jade piece is made from dark green stone, it is more prized by collectors of Chinese art?

Exercise 27

1. I wrote to the Chinese National Tourist Office, 333 West Broadway, Suite 201, Glendale, California 91204.
2. On Thursday, October 14, 2000, I received a response to my letter.
3. Enclosed was a videotape about Tianjin, China's third-largest city, which has a population of 12,000,000.

continued

Answer Key continued

4. An announcer said, "Tianjin's history dates back over 4,000 years."
5. "Even though it is a very large city," the announcer added, "Tianjin has a small-town feel about it."

Exercise 28

Find It in Your Reading
The first comma separates the two parts of a compound sentence. The second comma separates another independent clause. The third and fourth commas surround a parenthetical expression. The fifth comma separates parts of a compound sentence. The sixth comma separates a direct quotation from the rest of the sentence. The seventh separates a direct address.

Exercise 29

Find It in Your Writing
Have students explain their use of commas and revise to improve comma usage.

Exercise 30

Writing Application
Students can trade their descriptions with a partner to check for frequency and accuracy of comma use.

Ask students why some intersections have yield signs, while others have stop signs. (Yield signs encourage drivers to slow down and watch for other cars without stopping.) Sometimes sentences come to a long pause without stopping. Let students know that the colon and semicolon may be compared to a yield sign.

Activate Prior Knowledge

Ask students to answer the following question: If you mixed together the rules for a comma and the rules for a period, what kind of punctuation would you get? (chaotic. Sentences would stop and start choppily.) As they try to answer the question, elicit the general rules governing commas and periods (commas are a pause, while periods are a full stop).

Step-by-Step Teaching Guide

Semicolons and Colons

1. Write a semicolon on the board and ask students to describe what it looks like. (a period over a comma). Explain that semicolons are used to join complete ideas in sentences. They help avoid confusion when there are already many commas in a sentence. One way to imagine them is almost like an auxiliary period, halfway between a period and a comma.

2. Write a colon on the board and ask students to describe what it looks like. (two periods one on top of the other). Students who use the Internet will be familiar with the e-mail convention of sending a smile (set colon, set close parentheses), or wink (set semicolon, set close parentheses). Suggest to students that they think of a colon as a pair of eyes that signal, "Stop and look." A colon indicates a stop in a sentence that draws the reader's special attention to what follows.

Section 26.3

Semicolons and Colons

The *semicolon* looks like a period over a comma (;). The semicolon signals a less final pause than a period but a stronger separation than a comma.

Semicolons are used to join complete ideas within sentences and to avoid confusion in sentences already containing several commas.

The *colon* looks like two periods, one above the other (:). Colons can be used to introduce lists of items and in certain other special situations.

Using Semicolons to Join Independent Clauses

The following rule governs the use of semicolons with independent clauses:

▶ **KEY CONCEPT** Use a semicolon to join independent clauses that are not already joined by the conjunctions *and, but, for, not, or, so,* or *yet.* ■

The following examples show independent clauses joined by a comma and a conjunction.

CLAUSES WITH COMMA:	The Wright brothers read books about flying, and they dreamed of building a flying machine. Their first flight lasted just 12 seconds, for the plane traveled only 120 feet.

Notice, however, that when the comma and conjunction are omitted from the sentence, a semicolon must replace them.

CLAUSES WITH SEMICOLON:	The Wright brothers read books about flying; they dreamed of building a flying machine. Their first flight lasted just 12 seconds; the plane traveled only 120 feet.

A semicolon should be used only when there is a close relationship between the two independent clauses. If the clauses are not very closely related, they should be written as separate sentences with a period or other end mark to separate them.

INCORRECT:	The Wright brothers' first flight lasted just 12 seconds; the plane had a 40-foot wing span.
CORRECT:	The Wright brothers' first flight lasted just 12 seconds. The plane had a 40-foot wing span.

600 • Punctuation

Theme: The History of Flight

In this section, you will learn how semicolons and colons are used in sentences. The examples and exercises in this section are about flying machines and the history of flight.

Cross-Curricular Connection: Social Studies

▶ **More Practice**

On-line Exercise Bank
• Section 26.3
Grammar Exercise Workbook
• pp. 159–160

⏱ TIME AND RESOURCE MANAGER

Resources
Print: Grammar Exercise Workbook, pp. 159–162; Grammar Exercises Answers on Transparencies, Chapter 26
Technology: Language Lab CD-ROM, Punctuation; On-Line Exercise Bank, Section 26.3

In-Depth Coverage	Accelerated Pace
• Work through all key concepts, pp. 600–604. • Assign and review Exercises 31–36.	• Assign pp. 600–604 for independent student review. • Assign Section Review Exercises 37–39.

Semicolons Used to Join Independent Clauses

1. Remind students that independent clauses could stand by themselves. They are often joined by a comma and a conjunction, as shown in the comma section, but a semicolon alone may also be used.

2. Write the following sentences on the board. Ask the students whether there is anything different in the meaning of the two sentences. (Since there is no difference in meaning, both forms are correct.)

   The astronauts on board Apollo 13 *faced a challenging mission, and they knew it would put their abilities to the test.*

   The astronauts on board Apollo 13 *faced a challenging mission; they knew it would put their abilities to the test.*

3. Write the following sentence on the board and ask students why it should not have a semicolon. Change the sentence into two sentences on the board.

   The astronauts on board Apollo 13 *faced a challenging mission; the space shuttle was designed to withstand tremendous atmospheric pressure.*

▲ **Critical Viewing**
How might you describe these astronauts in a single sentence containing two independent clauses joined by a semicolon? **[Describe]**

▶ **Exercise 31** Using Semicolons to Join Independent Clauses
Read each sentence below, and decide where a semicolon is required. On your paper, write the word before each semicolon, the semicolon, and the word that follows it.

EXAMPLE: The first astronauts faced many uncertainties however, the flights were completed successfully.

ANSWER: uncertainties; however

1. American plans to send a man into space required careful planning therefore, the process took several years.
2. Precautions were taken in case of a failure for example, an ejection seat was designed.
3. Parachutes were included to cushion the Mercury capsule's fall into the ocean the water was also expected to help break the impact.
4. Ham, a chimpanzee, went on a trial run into space his flight lasted 18 minutes.
5. Alan Shepard was the first man from the United States launched into space however, his mission did not reach the speed and altitude required to orbit Earth.

Answer Key

▶ **Exercise 31**

1. planning; therefore
2. failure; for
3. ocean; the
4. space; his
5. space; however

Critical Viewing

Describe Possible responses: They might feel as though they are flying or swimming; they might be disoriented. They are having fun floating around; however, it must be hard to get used to the sensation.

Semicolons and Colons • **601**

☑ **ONGOING ASSESSMENT: Prerequisite Skills**

If students have difficulty with the use of semicolons to join independent clauses, you may find it necessary to review the following to assure coverage of prerequisite knowledge.

In the Textbook	Print Resources	Technology
Clauses, pp. 438–449	Grammar Exercise Workbook, pp. 79–82	On-Line Exercise Bank, Section 20.2

Using Semicolons to Avoid Confusion

1. Write the following sentence on the chalkboard. Circle the commas and semicolons to clarify the difference between how the semicolons and the commas are used within the whole.

   The spectators, standing alertly; the relatives, waving signs; and the ground crew, wishing them luck, all made the launch unforgettable for the astronauts.

2. Point out that the last complete item in the series does not need a semicolon.

Answer Key

> **Exercise 32**

1. NASA has many facilities, including the John F. Kennedy Space Center, Merritt Island, Florida; the Lyndon B. Johnson Space Flight Center, Houston, Texas; and the George C. Marshall Space Flight Center, Huntsville, Alabama.

2. The types of orbits are the circular, in which the spacecraft maintains a constant distance from Earth; the elliptical, in which the spacecraft travels faster closer to Earth; the inclined, which forms an angle with the equator; and the polar, which carries the spacecraft over both poles.

3. The conveniences of space shuttles have been improved with collections of books, tapes, and computer games; nutritious, appetizing foods; and permanent shower stalls.

4. The first crew to land on the moon consisted of Neil Armstrong, the first person to walk on the moon; Edwin Aldrin, who accompanied Armstrong to the moon; and Michael Collins, who piloted the *Columbia.*

5. Microgravity, or weightlessness, affects the fuel, which must be pumped with high-pressure gas; air currents, which must be circulated by fans; and the astronauts' vestibular system, the inner ear organs, which control balance and directional signals.

> **Exercise 33**

Have students work with partners to check their work.

602

26.3

Using Semicolons to Avoid Confusion

Sometimes, to avoid confusion, semicolons are used to separate items in a series.

> **KEY CONCEPT** Consider the use of semicolons to avoid confusion when items in a series already contain commas. ■

When the items in a series already contain several commas, semicolons can be used to make a sentence easier to read. Semicolons are placed at the end of all but the last complete item in the series.

EXAMPLE: The fans, cheering loudly; the band, playing a rousing march; and the cheerleaders, turning cartwheels, helped inspire the team to play well.

> **Exercise 32** Using Semicolons to Avoid Confusion Copy each sentence below, adding semicolons where they are needed.
> 1. NASA has many facilities, including the John F. Kennedy Space Center, Merritt Island, Florida the Lyndon B. Johnson Space Flight Center, Houston, Texas and the George C. Marshall Space Flight Center, Huntsville, Alabama.
> 2. The types of orbits are the circular, in which the spacecraft maintains a constant distance from Earth the elliptical, in which the spacecraft travels faster closer to Earth the inclined, which forms an angle with the equator and the polar, which carries the spacecraft over both poles.
> 3. The conveniences of space shuttles have been improved with collections of books, tapes, and computer games nutritious, appetizing foods and permanent shower stalls.
> 4. The first crew to land on the moon consisted of Neil Armstrong, the first person to walk on the moon Edwin Aldrin, who accompanied Armstrong to the moon and Michael Collins, who piloted the *Columbia.*
> 5. Microgravity, or weightlessness, affects the fuel, which must be pumped with high-pressure gas air currents, which must be circulated by fans and the astronauts' vestibular system, the inner-ear organs, which control balance and directional signals.

> **Exercise 33** Writing Sentences Using Semicolons Write five sentences of your own about airplane travel. Each sentence should include a semicolon.

> **More Practice**
> Language Lab
> CD-ROM
> • Punctuation lesson
> On-line
> Exercise Bank
> • Section 26.3
> Grammar Exercise
> Workbook
> • pp. 159–160

☑ ONGOING ASSESSMENT: Monitor and Reinforce

If students have difficulty with Exercise 32, 33, or 34, refer them to the following for additional practice.

In the Textbook	Print Resources	Technology
Section Review, Ex. 38, p. 605	Grammar Exercise Workbook, pp. 159–160	Language Lab CD-ROM, Punctuation; On-Line Exercise Bank, Section 26.3

Using Colons as Introductory Devices

KEY CONCEPT Use a colon before a list of items following an independent clause. ■

In the following example, the colon directs the reader's attention to the list directly following it. The words before the colon make up an independent clause that expresses a complete idea.

EXAMPLE: Sandor's model airplane collection included many different items: a Piper Cub, a P-51 Mustang, a Heinkel Salamander, and a Spitfire.

Notice that a colon should never be used directly after a verb or a preposition.

INCORRECT: The magazine included: an article on model planes, a column about radio controls, and a ballooning poster.
             Features in the magazine were on: model planes, radio controls, and ballooning.
CORRECT: Some features in the magazine were the following: an article on model planes, a column about radio controls, and a poster on ballooning.

Exercise 34 Using Colons to Introduce Lists of Items
Read each sentence below, and decide where a colon is needed. On your paper, write the word before the colon, the colon, and the word following the colon.

EXAMPLE: Balloon festivals were held in three cities Chicago, Denver, and San Francisco.
ANSWER: cities: Chicago

1. Hot-air balloons were used for many things racing, exploration, weather forecasting, and recreation.
2. The first passengers of a hot-air balloon were the following animals a duck, a rooster, and a sheep.
3. People tried many methods to control the direction of hot-air balloons rudders, feathered oars, and steam engines.
4. Many types of fuel were used to keep the balloon elevated smoke, hydrogen, helium, and propane.
5. The nylon or Dacron balloon fabric comes in a variety of patterns climbing swirls, herringbone slashes, checkerboards, and stripes.

 **Internet Tip**

Colons are used in Internet addresses but should be omitted from Internet searches.

▼ **Critical Viewing**
What list of items might you come up with to describe this photograph? **[Connect]**

Using Colons as Introductory Devices

1. Let the students know that the words before the colon express the main idea of the sentence, and the colon clues the reader that the list that follows relates directly to that main idea.

2. Remind students of their grocery store shopping list exercise from page 585. Write the following sentence on the board.

   At the grocery store, my family always buys the following items: bread, milk, eggs, juice, and fruit.

3. Point out the rule that a colon should never follow a verb or preposition. Write the following sentences on the board to illustrate this idea. Circle the verb to emphasize that the example is incorrect.

   At the grocery store, my family always buys: bread, milk, eggs, juice, and fruit.

Critical Viewing

Connect Ask students to write their responses in a sentence using a colon. Possible response: The hot-air balloon is a feast for the eyes: colorful fabric panels, a graceful shape, an inspiring upward sweep, and a thrillingly tiny figure in the basket.

Answer Key

Exercise 34

1. things: racing
2. animals: a
3. balloons: rudders
4. elevated: smoke
5. patterns: climbing

Using Colons in Special Situations

Ask students to tell you what time it is. Write the time on the board, highlighting the colon. Next, ask students to imagine that they are writing a letter to the President of the United States. Write on the board the greeting *Dear Mr. President:*, again showing the correct use of the colon. Lastly, have students remember a warning label that they have seen recently on a product such as a cleaning solution. Write the following on the board: *Warning: Contents dangerous if swallowed.* Circle the colon for emphasis.

Answer Key

▶ **Exercise 35**

1. The plane will arrive at 6:30 P.M.
2. Caution: Rocket Launch Area
3. Dear Dr. Von Braun:
4. To Whom It May Concern:
5. Warning: Earplugs Required in Hangars
6. The 9:30 P.M. plane isn't expected to land until 12:15 A.M.
7. Dear Sir or Madam:
8. Note: All passengers must report for the flight before 7:15 A.M.
9. Dear Mr. Wright:
10. Since the plane is scheduled at 9:50 A.M., we should arrive at the airport by 8:30.

▶ **Exercise 36**

Have students work with a partner. The partner should check for the correct number and use of colons and semicolons in the e-mail.

Integrating Workplace Skills

Many workers see notices containing colons on the job. A sign at a construction site might read WARNING: HARD-HAT AREA. Bus and truck drivers see signs saying DANGER: DEER CROSSING. Even teachers are confronted with colons, such as "Please submit your budget requests by 3:00 P.M. today."

604

26.3

Using Colons in Special Situations

Use a colon in a number of special writing situations to show time with numerals, to end salutations in business letters, and to signal important ideas.

The chart shows the uses of the colon in these special situations:

SPECIAL USES OF THE COLON	
Numbers Giving the Time	12:25 P.M. 3:00 A.M.
Salutations in Business Letters	Gentlemen: Dear Ms. Brown:
Labels Used to Signal Important Ideas	**Caution:** High voltage **Warning:** Trespassers will be prosecuted.

▶ **Exercise 35** Using Colons in Special Situations Copy the sentences, adding the colon missing from each.
1. The plane will arrive at 630 P.M.
2. Caution Rocket Launch Area
3. Dear Dr. Von Braun
4. To Whom It May Concern
5. Warning Earplugs Required in Hangars
6. The 930 P.M. plane isn't expected to land until 1215 A.M.
7. Dear Sir or Madam
8. Note All passengers must report for the flight before 715 A.M.
9. Dear Mr. Wright
10. Since the plane is scheduled at 950 A.M., we should arrive at the airport by 830.

▶ **Exercise 36** Writing an E-mail With Colons and Semicolons Imagine that you have just visited NASA as part of a school trip. Write an e-mail to a classmate who did not take part in the trip. In your e-mail, use at least four semicolons and three colons. Use semicolons and colons for each of the functions that you have learned in this section.

604 • Punctuation

▶ **More Practice**

Language Lab
CD-ROM
• Punctuation lesson
On-line
Exercise Bank
• Section 26.3
Grammar Exercise
Workbook
• pp. 161–162

☑ **ONGOING ASSESSMENT: Assess Mastery**

Use the following resources to assess student mastery of colon and semicolon usage.

In the Textbook	Technology
Chapter Review, Ex. 78–79, pp. 630–631	On-Line Exercise Bank, Section 26.3

Section 26.3 Section Review

GRAMMAR EXERCISES 37–42

Exercise 37 Revising the Use of Semicolons in Independent Clauses
Rewrite each sentence below, adding or deleting semicolons where necessary.

1. Paul MacCready wasn't satisfied with airplane models in a box as a result, he designed his own.
2. Some of them had wings three feet long however, they weighed only 1/15 of an ounce.
3. Paul's models crashed often however, they were easily repaired.
4. At age fifteen, Paul was an expert model builder he won the National Junior Model Airplane Championship.
5. When he was older, Paul built gliders one of his inventions set a world record; for human-powered flight.

Exercise 38 Revising the Use of Semicolons to Avoid Confusion Rewrite this passage, replacing commas with semicolons where necessary to avoid confusion.

Prior to *Apollo 11* came *Apollo 8*, launched in December 1968, *Apollo 9*, launched in March 1969, and *Apollo 10*, launched in May 1969. A series of satellites had also been sent up to take pictures of the moon. The satellites included the Ranger probes, which took pictures and then crashed, the Surveyor probes, and the Luna probes, which were sent up by the Soviets.

The three parts of *Apollo 11* were the command module, which Collins piloted, the lunar module, which Armstrong and Aldrin landed on the moon, and the Saturn V rocket booster, which powered the craft out of orbit.

Exercise 39 Using Colons Correctly Colons are needed below. On your paper, write the word before the colon, the colon, and the word that follows it.

1. Do you know who set each of these flight records flying across the Atlantic, flying around the world, and flying around the world without refueling?
2. The *Voyager* had three designers Dick Rutan, Burt Rutan, and Jeana Yeager.
3. Jeana Yeager brought two key assets to the project team her knowledge of rocketry and her organizational skills.
4. During tests, the team found three major problems leakage, engine malfunctions, and stalls in rainstorms.
5. There were several emergency personnel at Mission Control a doctor, a weather expert, and a radio operator.

Exercise 40 Find It in Your Reading Explain why the author used a colon in this passage from "Icarus and Daedalus" by Josephine Preston Peabody.

. . . He forgot Crete and the other islands that he had passed over: he saw but vaguely that wingèd thing in the distance before him that was his father Daedalus.

Exercise 41 Find It in Your Writing Look through your portfolio for passages containing compound sentences or lists of items. Rewrite five passages, using semicolons or colons correctly.

Exercise 42 Writing Application Write a paragraph describing an unusual flight or car trip you have taken. Include several sentences in which you use semicolons or colons correctly.

Answer Key continued

Exercise 40

Find It in Your Reading
The colon introduces the sentence that explains and illustrates the preceding sentence. Ask students to explain whether they would leave the sentence as is, or rewrite it as two sentences.

Exercise 41

Find It in Your Writing
Challenge students to rewrite a partner's sentences, using commas and conjunctions instead of semicolons and colons.

Exercise 42

Writing Application
Have students trade descriptions with a partner to check for correct punctuation. Challenge students to revise their paragraphs to contain one more semicolon and one more colon.

Activate Prior Knowledge

Ask students to imagine that they are journalists. How could they ensure that their readers know and understand exactly what was said by the people who were interviewed? Have students themselves ever been quoted in a newspaper or magazine?

Step-by-Step Teaching Guide

Direct and Indirect Quotations

1. Explain to students that in fiction, quotation marks are used for invented dialogue between fictional characters; in other forms of written communication, such as journalism, quotations are used a number of ways.

2. Write the following sentences on the board and point out how quotation marks signal the difference between the exact quotes and the rest of the sentence.

   "The last time I was camping in the woods, I saw a bear," said Bob.

   Jennifer replied calmly, "Yes, but it turned out to be only a raccoon."

3. Write the following sentences on the chalkboard and point out that it would be unnecessary to use quotation marks since no direct quote is made.

   Bob mentioned that he saw a bear the last time he went hiking.

   Jennifer was thinking that it was time for a little practical joke.

Critical Viewing

Speculate Possible responses: "Go away!" "Here, kitty, kitty." "Help!"

Quotation Marks and Underlining

Using Quotation Marks With Direct Quotations

When you write research papers or essays, you may sometimes wish to use the exact words from a book to support your own ideas. When you write fiction, you may sometimes want your characters to speak in their own words to make the story more vivid and interesting. *Quotation marks* identify the exact spoken or written words of others that you are including in your writing. These punctuation marks are used in all kinds of writing situations.

Study this section carefully. It should help you use quotation marks with greater confidence in your own writing.

Direct and Indirect Quotations Before you can use quotation marks correctly, you must first be able to tell the difference between *direct* and *indirect quotations.*

▶ **KEY CONCEPT** A **direct quotation** represents a person's exact speech or thoughts and is enclosed in quotation marks (" "). ■

EXAMPLES: Janine said, "Tomorrow we are going hiking."
"I hope we don't see any wild animals," thought Martin.

Indirect quotations do not repeat the exact words a person said or thought. Instead, an indirect quotation paraphrases, or explains, what someone said or thought.

▶ **KEY CONCEPT** An **indirect quotation** reports only the general meaning of what a person said or thought and does not require quotation marks. ■

EXAMPLES: Janine said that we would go hiking tomorrow.
Martin hoped they wouldn't see any wild animals.

606 • Punctuation

Theme: Carnivorous Mammals

In this section, you will learn how quotation marks are used with direct quotations and how quotation marks and underlining are used with titles. The examples and exercises in this section are about meat-eating mammals.

Cross-Curricular Connection: Science

▼ Critical Viewing
What would you say if you encountered this African lion directly? **[Speculate]**

⏱ TIME AND RESOURCE MANAGER

Resources
Print: Grammar Exercise Workbook, pp. 163–168; Grammar Exercises Answers on Transparencies, Chapter 26
Technology: Language Lab CD-ROM, Punctuation; On-Line Exercise Bank, Section 26.4

In-Depth Coverage	Accelerated Pace
• Work through all key concepts, pp. 606–616. • Assign and review Exercises 43–51. • Read and discuss Grammar in Literature, p. 612.	• Assign pp. 606–616 for independent student review. • Assign Section Review Exercises 52–54.

Exercise 43 Distinguishing Between Direct and Indirect Quotations Identify each of the following as a *direct quotation* or an *indirect quotation*. Then, add proper punctuation to the direct quotations.

1. Carnivorous mammals help to regulate the balance of nature, explained the ranger.
2. Carla wondered what kind of animals were carnivores.
3. Cats, dogs, weasels, bears, and foxes are all carnivores, said Jamal.
4. The ranger added, Carnivores have well-developed canine teeth.
5. Kent realized that his puppy was an example of a carnivorous mammal.
6. Did you know that carnivores live in all parts of the world except Antarctica? asked Kari.
7. My teacher told me that most live on land, but some spend time in water.
8. Spencer wondered when the tour would begin.
9. I can't wait to see the bear cub, declared Theresa.
10. Here comes the wildlife tour bus, yelled the ranger.

Exercise 44 Revising Indirect Quotations as Direct Quotations Rewrite each of the indirect quotations from the previous exercise to make them direct quotations, adding the appropriate punctuation.

Direct Quotations With Introductory, Concluding, and Interrupting Expressions Quotations are generally accompanied by expressions such as *he said* or *she replied*. Expressions of this kind can introduce, conclude, or interrupt the quoted material. The following rules describe how to punctuate quotations with expressions that come before the direct quotation, after the direct quotation, or in the middle of the direct quotation.

KEY CONCEPT When an introductory expression precedes a direct quotation, place a comma after the introductory expression, and write the quotation as a full sentence. ■

EXAMPLES: Timothy told his friend, "I had a great time at camp."
    Ginnie added, "We went on trips to the zoo and to a wildlife park."

More Practice

Language Lab
CD-ROM
• Punctuation lesson
On-line
Exercise Bank
• Section 26.4
Grammar Exercise
Workbook
• pp. 163–164

Answer Key

> **Exercise 43**

1. D; "Carnivorous mammals help to regulate the balance of nature," explained the ranger.
2. I
3. D; "Cats, dogs, weasels, bears, and foxes are all carnivores," said Jamal.
4. D; The ranger added, "Carnivores have well-developed canine teeth."
5. I
6. D; "Did you know that carnivores live in all parts of the world except Antarctica?" asked Kari.
7. I
8. I
9. D; "I can't wait to see the bear cub," declared Theresa.
10. D; "Here comes the wildlife tour bus!" yelled the ranger.

> **Exercise 44**

2. Carla asked, "What kind of animals are carnivores?"
5. Kent said, "My puppy is an example of a carnivorous mammal."
7. My teacher told me, "Most live on land, but some spend time in water."
8. "When will the tour begin?" wondered Spencer.

> *Step-by-Step Teaching Guide*

Direct Quotations With Introductory, Concluding, and Interrupting Expressions

1. Write the following sentence on the board, underlining the introductory expression and pointing out the use of the capital *W* and the end punctuation.

   Dylan worried out loud, "What if I forget the safety precautions I learned about how to avoid mountain lions?"

continued

ONGOING ASSESSMENT: Monitor and Reinforce

If students have difficulty with Exercise 43 or 44, refer them to the following for additional practice.

In the Textbook	Print Resources	Technology
Section Review, Ex. 52, p. 617	Grammar Exercise Workbook, pp. 163–164	Language Lab CD-ROM, Punctuation; On-Line Exercise Bank, Section 26.4

2. Explain that when a *concluding* expression follows a direct quotation, the quotation is written as a full sentence but ends with a comma or any end punctuation *other than a period.* This is because the quote is included inside the sentence but does not finish it. Rewrite the example used in suggestion 1 as follows, underlining the concluding punctuation:

> *"What if I forget the safety precautions I learned about how to avoid mountain lions?" Dylan worried out loud.*

3. Let students know that when a one-sentence direct quotation is divided in two by an *interrupting* expression, the two halves of the quote must each be surrounded by their own quotation marks, and the first half must end with a comma to show that the quotation has been interrupted but is not finished. Furthermore, the interrupting expression must not be capitalized as if it were the beginning of a new sentence, because it is not. The interrupting expression is followed by a comma to show that the rest of the quote is now picking up where the interruption left off. Write the following example on the board.

> *"If I forget the safety precautions I learned about how to avoid mountain lions," worried Dylan, "then I don't plan to leave my tent!"*

4. Explain that there is one more example of an *interrupting* expression, and that is when it is used between a two-sentence direct quotation. In this case, the first quote is ended with a comma, question mark, or exclamation point but not a period. The period comes after the interrupting expression, as it is this which ends the first sentence. The second direct quote is written as its own complete sentence. Write the following sentences on the board.

> *"I might forget the safety precautions I learned about how to avoid mountain lions," worried Dylan out loud. "If so, I don't plan to leave my tent!"*

26.4

▶ **KEY CONCEPT** When a concluding expression follows a direct quotation, write the quotation as a full sentence ending with a comma, question mark, or exclamation mark inside the closing quotation mark. Then, write the concluding expression. ▪

Notice the kinds of punctuation placed before the final quotation marks in the examples below. In the first example, a comma signals a pause rather than a full stop. The final end mark is not used until the end of the concluding expression. In the last two examples, however, end marks are necessary before the final quotation mark.

EXAMPLES: "I think you would have fun at our camp," Timothy said.
"What activities does the camp offer?" inquired Kamilla.
"It's everything anyone could want!" exclaimed Ginnie enthusiastically.

Because concluding expressions are not complete sentences, they do not begin with capital letters. Notice also that the closing quotation marks are always placed outside the punctuation at the end of the direct quotations.

Interrupting expressions are governed by their own punctuation rule.

▶ **KEY CONCEPT** When a one-sentence direct quotation is separated by an interrupting expression, end the first part of the direct quotation with a comma and a quotation mark. Place a comma after the interrupting expression. Then, use a new set of quotation marks to enclose the rest of the quotation. ▪

Notice the following details in the examples below: (1) the comma inside the quotation mark at the end of the first part of the quotation; (2) the small letter at the beginning of the interrupting expression; (3) the comma inserted after the interrupting expression; (4) the small letter at the beginning of the second part of the quotation; and (5) the end mark inside the last quotation mark.

EXAMPLES: "Since the camp is located on a lake," explained Ginnie, "we can go swimming and boating and water-skiing."
"Do you think," interrupted Kamilla, "that I could learn to water-ski?"

Sometimes, a quotation is made up of two sentences, with a complete sentence on each side of the interrupting expression. A final rule is needed for this situation.

5. Have students practice the key concepts in this section by rewriting the sample sentences on pages 607–608 with introductory, concluding, and interrupting expressions. Students may also compose their own sentences using all three expression forms.

▲ **Critical Viewing**
What conversation might you have with your friends if you saw this grizzly bear in its natural habitat? How would you capture the conversation in writing? **[Speculate]**

▶ **KEY CONCEPT** When two complete sentences in a direct quotation are separated by an interrupting expression, end the first quoted sentence with a comma, question mark, or exclamation mark and a quotation mark. Next, place a period after the interrupter. Then, write the second quoted sentence as a full quotation. ■

Read the examples below carefully and notice the following details: (1) the different kinds of punctuation at the end of the first quoted sentence; (2) the small letter at the beginning of the interrupting expression; (3) the period following the interrupting expression; (4) the capital at the beginning of the second quoted sentence; and (5) the end mark inside the last quotation mark.

EXAMPLES: "We practically came face to face with a grizzly bear on one of our hikes in Alaska," said Juan. "It was exciting and scary at the same time."
"That's amazing!" exclaimed Jenna. "How close did you get?"
"I'd say we were about fifty feet away," responded Juan. "We were so close we could see its teeth."

Exercise 45

1. "Wolf pups learn to hunt by playing with each other," explained Virginia.
2. "Did you know that wolves hunt caribou and elk?" asked Kunal. "They must be quick and clever."
3. "When wolves gather to hunt," said Saba, "they howl to warn other wolves to stay out of their territory."
4. "Wolves," added Joseph, "are careful that they are downwind from their prey."
5. "Wait!" exclaimed Anna. "Don't wolves hunt in packs?"
6. Mica smiled and answered, "They hunt in a single line until the chase starts."
7. "Often the prey gets away," said Stephen. "Wolves chase many more animals than they catch."
8. "The objective," stated Lorelei, "is to chase the animal until it becomes weak."
9. Viora commented, "The hunt can take many hours."
10. "Sometimes the wolves give up because the prey is too fast," concluded Doug.

Exercise 46

Have students swap dialogues with partners to check for the correct use of quotations.

Critical Viewing

Hypothesize Possible responses: "I live in the woods." "I howl at the moon." Write some of their suggestions on the board following the introductory phrase, "The coyote says . . ."

26.4

> **Exercise 45** **Writing Direct Quotations With Introductory, Concluding, and Interrupting Expressions** Copy each of the sentences below onto your paper, correcting punctuation and capitalization as needed.

EXAMPLE: Do wolves live in these woods he asked.
ANSWER: "Do wolves live in these woods?" he asked.

1. Wolf pups learn to hunt by playing with each other explained Virginia.
2. Did you know that wolves hunt caribou and elk asked Kunal they must be quick and clever.
3. When wolves gather to hunt said Saba they howl to warn other wolves to stay out of their territory.
4. Wolves added Joseph are careful that they are downwind from their prey.
5. Wait exclaimed Anna don't wolves hunt in packs?
6. Mica smiled and answered They hunt in a single line until the chase starts.
7. Often the prey gets away said Stephen Wolves chase many more animals than they catch.
8. The objective stated Lorelei is to chase the animal until it becomes weak.
9. Viora commented The hunt can take many hours.
10. Sometimes the wolves give up because the prey is too fast concluded Doug.

> **Exercise 46** **Writing an Original Dialogue** Imagine that you are on a wilderness trip and that you have just seen the coyote in this picture. Write a dialogue in which you describe what you have seen to your friends. Check to see that you have used correct punctuation.

▶ Critical Viewing What could a coyote say to you about living in the wild and hunting food? Write your answer in dialogue form. [Hypothesize]

💡 Spelling Tip

To make the plural of many words that end in *f*, change the *f* to *v* and add *-es*. For example, the plural of *wolf* is *wolves*.

⏱ TIME SAVERS!

📃 **Answers on Transparency** Use the Grammar Exercises Answers on Transparencies for Chapter 26 to facilitate correction by students.

💻 **On-Line Exercise Bank** Have students complete the exercises on computer. The Auto Check feature will grade their work for you!

☑ ONGOING ASSESSMENT: Monitor and Reinforce

If students have difficulty with Exercise 45 or 46, refer them to the following for additional practice.

In the Textbook	Print Resources	Technology
Section Review, Ex. 52, p. 617	Grammar Exercise Workbook, pp. 163–164	Language Lab CD-ROM, Punctuation; On-line Exercise Bank, Section 26.4

Quotation Marks With Other Punctuation Marks

You may sometimes find it hard to decide whether another punctuation mark should go inside or outside the quotation marks. If you study the three rules and the examples that follow, you should be able to make these decisions correctly.

KEY CONCEPT Always place a comma or a period *inside* the final quotation mark. ■

EXAMPLES: "We saw a puma today," Uncle Joe said.
            He added, "It was standing on a high rock."

KEY CONCEPT Place a question mark or an exclamation mark *inside* the final quotation mark if the end mark is part of the quotation. ■

In the following examples, notice that the sentences themselves are declarative. In the first example, however, the quoted material asks a question. In the second, the quoted material shows strong emotion. In these cases, the end marks are placed with the quotations, inside the quotation marks.

EXAMPLES: Jane asked, "Have you seen the fox anywhere?"
            Her sister exclaimed, "No, and I don't want to!"

Remember that it is not necessary to use two end marks. In the following examples, the quoted material requires a question mark and the entire sentence appears to need a period. Because two final punctuation marks are never used, the period is dropped.

INCORRECT: George thought, "Where are we going?".
CORRECT: George thought, "Where are we going?"

In some situations, the entire sentence requires a question mark or an exclamation mark. In these cases, the placement of the final punctuation changes.

KEY CONCEPT Place a question mark or an exclamation mark *outside* the final quotation mark if the end mark is part of the entire sentence and not part of the quotation. ■

Both quotations in the following examples are declarative. The first sentence is a question; the second sentence is an exclamation.

EXAMPLES: Why did you say, "I prefer cats to dogs"?
            Don't ever say "I can't"!

More Practice

Language Lab
CD-ROM
• Punctuation lesson
On-line
Exercise Bank
• Section 26.4
Grammar Exercise
Workbook
• pp. 165–166

Quotation Marks With Other Punctuation Marks

1. Students are often confused when they have to use quotation marks in conjunction with other punctuation marks. Help them narrow the rules to remember by pointing out that no punctuation mark ever goes inside the first quotation mark.

2. Then, point out that periods and commas always go inside the second punctuation mark.

3. Question marks and exclamation points usually go inside the second quotation mark as well. Write the following sentences on the board to reinforce the exceptions to this rule.

   The man asked, "Why don't I like dogs?"

   Why did the man say, "I don't like dogs"?

   In the first sentence, the man being quoted is asking a question, so the question mark belongs inside of the quotation mark with his question. In the second example, the entire sentence is a question with the man's statement being the direct object of the sentence. Putting the question mark outside the quotes in this case shows that the entire sentence is a question.

4. Ask students to create two new sentences to illustrate this rule.

Grammar in Literature

1. Have a volunteer read aloud the excerpt from "The Lion and the Statue."

2. After noting how the writer used quotation marks, ask another student to reread the passage. Tell the class to listen for how the reader's voice changes when reading the parts inside the quotation marks.

3. Reinforce the idea that all punctuation marks give us information about what we are reading. They can affect our tone of voice, how long we pause before or after a phrase or sentence, and how we understand what we've read.

Answer Key

▶ **Exercise 47**

1. Dana commented, "There are seven species of bears."
2. Shay asked the zookeeper, "What do bears eat?"
3. Didn't you hear him say, "They eat rodents, fish, berries, and grubs"?
4. Chad yelled across the room, "Bears like honey, too!"
5. Nathaniel questioned, "Don't the bees sting the bears?"
6. Eric answered, "The bear's thick fur protects it from the bee stings."
7. Did the park attendant say, "Bears sometimes raid garbage cans for a snack"?
8. Sarah said, "One bear's hunting ground ranges from ten to twelve square miles."
9. Did I hear the ranger say, "Bears are peaceful animals"?
10. The ranger exclaimed, "Bears attack only when they or their cubs are threatened!"

⏱ TIME SAVERS!

Answers on Transparency
Use the Grammar Exercises Answers on Transparencies for Chapter 26 to facilitate correction by students.

On-Line Exercise Bank
Have students complete the exercises on computer. The Auto Check feature will grade their work for you!

26.4

GRAMMAR IN
LITERATURE

from **The Lion and the Statue**
Aesop

Notice how the writer has used quotation marks with other punctuation marks in the direct quotes in this passage.

. . . The Man contended that he and his fellows were stronger than lions by reason of their greater intelligence. "Come now with me," he cried, "and I will soon prove that I am right." So he took him into the public gardens and showed him a statue of Hercules overcoming the Lion and tearing his mouth in two.

"That is all very well," said the Lion, "but proves nothing, for it was a man who made the statue."

▶ **Exercise 47** Using End Marks With Direct Quotations

Read each sentence below, and decide whether the missing end marks go inside or outside the quotation marks. Copy each sentence onto your paper, adding the missing punctuation.

EXAMPLE: He asked the lifeguard, "When can we swim"

ANSWER: He asked the lifeguard, "When can we swim?"

1. Dana commented, "There are seven species of bears"
2. Shay asked the zookeeper, "What do bears eat"
3. Didn't you hear him say, "They eat rodents, fish, berries, and grubs"
4. Chad yelled across the room, "Bears like honey, too"
5. Nathaniel questioned, "Don't the bees sting the bears"
6. Eric answered, "The bear's thick fur protects it from the bee stings"
7. Did the park attendant say, "Bears sometimes raid garbage cans for a snack"
8. Sarah said, "One bear's hunting ground ranges from ten to twelve square miles"
9. Did I hear the ranger say, "Bears are peaceful animals"
10. The ranger exclaimed, "Bears attack only when they or their cubs are threatened"

Quotation Marks for Dialogue

Quotation Marks for Dialogue A conversation between two or more people is called a *dialogue*.

KEY CONCEPT When writing dialogue, begin a new paragraph with each change of speaker. ■

In the following example of dialogue, capitalization and punctuation are used as they would be for any quotations. Remember, however, to indent whenever a new speaker talks.

EXAMPLE: "Why don't we go to San Diego for a vacation?" Grandfather asked.

Surprised, Danielle replied, "Why do you want to go to San Diego? Let's go somewhere else. I'd like to visit an interesting zoo or wildlife park."

"You can't be serious!" exclaimed Grandfather. "San Diego has one of the most famous zoos in the world, or we could visit Sea World and see Shamu, the trained killer whale."

"In that case," said Danielle, "maybe I should reconsider."

Exercise 48 Revising to Punctuate Dialogue Correctly
The example of dialogue below is missing some punctuation marks and indentations. Read the selection carefully, and decide where punctuation marks and indentations are required. Then, copy the paragraphs onto your paper, making the necessary changes. You should have seven paragraphs when you finish.

(1) What exclaimed Darlene, pointing at a strange-looking animal in the cage, is that? (2) Don't you know? asked Mitch. (3) That's a short-tailed weasel. (4) I've never seen a weasel before. (5) What do they do? wondered Darlene. (6) They chase squirrels, mice, and other rodents replied Mitch. (7) The weasel eats earthworms, snakes, lizards, frogs, and small birds. (8) How does it catch its prey? Darlene asked (9) It sneaks its thin body into burrows and narrow crevices to capture its food noted Mitch. (10) I wouldn't want one to sneak up on me! Darlene exclaimed.

More Practice
Language Lab CD-ROM
• Punctuation lesson
On-line Exercise Bank
• Section 26.4
Grammar Exercise Workbook
• pp. 165–166

Quotation Marks for Dialogue

1. Review with students that paragraphs are used to show transitions between, or to separate, ideas in a text. Point out that a new speaker talking is by definition a new idea, so every time they use quotation marks to indicate a new speaker, they must indent for a new paragraph.

2. Ask for a volunteer to share a brief conversational exchange he or she had today. Write a small part of the exchange on the board, using quotation marks and proper indentation.

3. Use the example on the board to illustrate how each part of the conversation indicates a new idea or perspective.

Real-World Connection

Ask students whether they can think of a time when they were misquoted or when someone was misquoted in the news. Discuss the importance of quotation marks when they set apart the actual words spoken by an individual.

Answer Key

Exercise 48

P indicates new paragraph.
1. P "What," exclaimed Darlene, pointing at a strange-looking animal in the cage, "is that?"
2. P "Don't you know?" asked Mitch.
3. "That's a short-tailed weasel."
4. P "I've never seen a weasel before.
5. What do they do?" wondered Darlene.
6. P "They chase squirrels, mice, and other rodents," replied Mitch.
7. "The weasel eats earthworms, snakes, lizards, frogs, and small birds."
8. P "How does it catch its prey?" Darlene asked.
9. P "It sneaks its thin body into burrows and narrow crevices to capture its food," noted Mitch.
10. P "I wouldn't want one to sneak up on me!" Darlene exclaimed.

✓ **ONGOING ASSESSMENT: Monitor and Reinforce**

If students have difficulty with Exercise 47 or 48, refer them to the following for additional practice.

In the Textbook	Print Resources	Technology
Section Review, Ex. 52–53, p. 617	Grammar Exercise Workbook, pp. 165–166	Language Lab CD-ROM, Punctuation; On-Line Exercise Bank, Section 26.4

Underlining and Other Uses of Quotation Marks

1. Review the basic rules of underlining with students.

2. Create several columns with these headings, leaving room beneath each so that you can record students' responses: Long Written Works; Major Artistic Works; Movies; Individual Air, Sea, Space, and Land Craft.

3. Ask students to name entries for each category and write them underneath the appropriate heading, underlining as you go. If students suggest entries that should not be underlined, you may wish to list these in a separate column and place quotation marks around them to illustrate titles that are treated differently, such as titles of poems.

Technology Tip

When students work on a computer, they should use the italics function, not the underline, for these names and titles.

26.4

Underlining and Other Uses of Quotation Marks

Certain titles and names should be underlined in your writing. Other titles should be enclosed in quotation marks. Quotation marks are used in all types of writing and printing. Underlining, however, is used only for handwritten or typed materials. Printed materials use italics instead of underlining.

UNDERLINING: <u>The Hobbit</u>

ITALICS: *The Hobbit*

Underlining Long written works that are made up of several parts should be underlined whenever they are written or typed. For example, the title of a book should be underlined.

> **KEY CONCEPT** Underline titles of long written works and titles of publications that are published as a single work. ■

The following chart shows some of the titles that are covered by this rule:

WRITTEN WORK TITLES THAT ARE UNDERLINED	
Title of a Book	<u>Black Beauty</u>
Title of a Play	<u>What Price Glory?</u>
Title of a Long Poem	<u>The Wasteland</u>
Title of a Magazine	<u>Popular Mechanics</u>
Title of a Newspaper	the <u>Miami Herald</u>
	the <u>Chicago Tribune</u>

The titles of other kinds of major works should also be underlined.

> **KEY CONCEPT** Underline the titles of movies, television and radio series, and works of art and music. ■

ARTISTIC WORK TITLES THAT ARE UNDERLINED	
Title of a Movie	<u>Revenge of the Pink Panther</u>
Title of a Television Series	<u>Little House on the Prairie</u>
Title of a Long Musical Work	<u>The Magic Flute</u>
Title of a Record Album	<u>Long Distance Voyager</u>
Title of a Painting	<u>The Passage of the Delaware</u>
Title of a Sculpture	<u>Bird in Space</u>

⚙ Grammar and Style Tip

Be sure to underline titles of performance artists' cassettes, videos, compact discs, and other performances.

KEY CONCEPT Underline the names of individual air, sea, space, and land craft. ∎

AIR: the <u>Hindenburg</u> (zeppelin)

SEA: the <u>Leonardo da Vinci</u> (ship)

SPACE: <u>Voyager 2</u> (spaceship)

LAND: the <u>Southwest Limited</u> (train)

Exercise 49 **Underlining Titles and Names** On your paper, write the items in the following sentences that require underlining, and then underline them.

EXAMPLE: Enid Bagnold's novel National Velvet has been a classic for years.

ANSWER: <u>National Velvet</u>

1. Cherie Mason, a naturalist, wrote about nursing an injured fox back to health in her book Wild Fox.
2. The book was reviewed in both Zoo Times magazine and the Los Angeles Times.
3. In Once a Wolf, author Stephen Swinburne explores why people fear wolves and sometimes mistreat them.
4. Our science teacher showed the film Tigers in the Snow to her third-period class.
5. The television series Call of the Wild is based on the famous book by Jack London.
6. If you want to learn why wolves howl, read Mary Ling's book Amazing Wolves, Dogs, and Foxes.
7. Eyewitness: Bear will be shown on the Public Broadcasting System station later this week.
8. Peter and the Wolf is one of my favorite musical pieces.
9. Two articles in the Detroit Free Press focused on Zoo Story, a new sculpture on display at the Fine Arts Museum.
10. Laika, the first dog in space, flew aboard the Soviet craft Sputnik 2 but did not survive the trip.

Exercise 50 **Writing Dialogue With Titles and Names** Write an imaginary dialogue with friends in which you discuss books and magazines you have read and movies you have seen. Check your use of quotation marks and underlining.

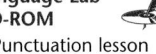

More Practice

Language Lab CD-ROM
• Punctuation lesson

On-Line Exercise Bank
• Section 26.4

Grammar Exercise Workbook
• pp. 167–168

Answer Key

▶ **Exercise 49**

1. <u>Wild Fox</u>
2. <u>Zoo Times</u>, <u>Los Angeles Times</u>
3. <u>Once a Wolf</u>
4. <u>Tigers in the Snow</u>
5. <u>Call of the Wild</u>
6. <u>Amazing Wolves, Dogs, and Foxes</u>
7. <u>Eyewitness: Bear</u>
8. <u>Peter and the Wolf</u>
9. <u>Detroit Free Press</u>, <u>Zoo Story</u>
10. <u>Sputnik 2</u>

▶ **Exercise 50**

Have students swap dialogues with a partner and check for the correct use of quotation marks and underlining.

☑ ONGOING ASSESSMENT: Monitor and Reinforce

If students have difficulty with Exercise 49, 50 or 51, refer them to the following for additional practice.

In the Textbook	Print Resources	Technology
Section Review, Ex. 54, p. 617	Grammar Exercise Workbook, pp. 167–168	Language Lab CD-ROM, Punctuation; On-Line Exercise Bank, Section 26.4

⏱ TIME SAVERS!

🔲 **Answers on Transparency**
Use the Grammar Exercises Answers on Transparencies for Chapter 26 to facilitate correction by students.

🖥 **On-Line Exercise Bank**
Have students complete the exercises on computer. The Auto Check feature will grade their work for you!

Quotation Marks

1. Refer to the lists of long written works and major artistic works on page 614.

2. Point out that that these works are often made up of smaller parts. Go down the list and have students name the smaller parts that comprise longer works (articles in magazines, episodes of TV shows, songs on record albums or CDs, and so on).

3. Ask students to name several examples and put them on the board in quotation marks.

Answer Key

▶ **Exercise 51**

1. "The Tiger Who Would Be King"
2. "Zoo"; Super SciFi Tales
3. "The Grizzly Bear"; Our World of Animals
4. "The Lion and the Bulls"; Aesop's Fables
5. National Geographic; "The Wonders of Wolves"

26.4

Quotation Marks The titles of short written works and works that are part of longer works are generally enclosed in quotation marks.

▶ **KEY CONCEPT** Use quotation marks around the titles of short written works. ■

WRITTEN WORK TITLES THAT TAKE QUOTATION MARKS	
Title of a Short Story Chapter From a Book	"The Richer, the Poorer" "Hazel's Decision" from Watership Down
Title of a Short Poem Title of an Article	"The Concord Hymn" "Windmills: Alternative Energy Sources"

▶ **KEY CONCEPT** Use quotation marks around the titles of episodes in a series, songs, and parts of a long musical composition. ■

ARTISTIC WORK TITLES THAT TAKE QUOTATION MARKS	
Title of an Episode Title of a Song Title of a Part of a Long Musical Work	"The Nile" from Cousteau Odyssey "The Best Things in Life Are Free" "The Storm" from the William Tell Overture

▶ **Exercise 51** Using Quotation Marks With Titles Copy the titles in the sentences below onto your paper, adding quotation marks or underlining as needed.

EXAMPLE: How Much Is That Doggy in the Window? was a hit record in the 1950's.

ANSWER: "How Much Is That Doggy in the Window?"

1. Thurber's The Tiger Who Would Be King is a modern fable.
2. Zoo by Edward Hoch is included in Super SciFi Tales.
3. The Grizzly Bear is the first episode in the new PBS series, Our World of Animals.
4. You should read The Lion and the Bulls in Aesop's Fables.
5. This month's National Geographic contains a great article, The Wonders of Wolves.

616 • Punctuation

▶ **More Practice**

Language Lab CD-ROM
• Punctuation lesson
On-line Exercise Bank
• Section 26.4
Grammar Exercise Workbook
• pp. 167–168

⏱ **TIME SAVERS!**

Answers on Transparency Use the Grammar Exercises Answers on Transparencies for Chapter 26 to facilitate correction by students.

On-Line Exercise Bank Have students complete the exercises on computer. The Auto Check feature will grade their work for you!

☑ **ONGOING ASSESSMENT: Assess Mastery**

Use the following resources to assess student mastery of quotation marks and underlining.

In the Textbook	Technology
Chapter Review, Ex. 81, p. 631	On-Line Exercise Bank, Section 26.4

Section Review

GRAMMAR EXERCISES 52–57

Exercise 52 Revising Direct Quotations With Introductory, Concluding, and Interrupting Expressions
Rewrite each quotation below, adding needed quotation marks and other punctuation marks.

1. I thought I heard something howling during the night, I said.
2. It was probably just coyotes singing to each other my mom said Howling is their trademark.
3. The farmer down the road commented Those coyotes are my enemies because they snatch my chickens and my ducks.
4. They are also my friends he added because they prey on mice and rabbits that eat my crops
5. Unlike humans the farmer said coyote babies are ready to be on their own when they're less than a year old That's pretty amazing

Exercise 53 Revising the Use of End Marks in Direct Quotations Revise the following items, correcting capitalization and the use of punctuation where necessary.

1. Abby stated, "The tiger is the largest member of the cat family".
2. Katie asked, "Just how big does a grown tiger get"?
3. Didn't you hear the zookeeper say, "a male tiger can grow to weigh 420 pounds and can be 9 feet long, including his tail."
4. Ariel exclaimed, "No wonder deer, antelope, and wild pigs avoid tigers"!
5. Were you surprised when the zookeeper said, "Tigers especially enjoy dining on porcupines?"

Exercise 54 Punctuating Titles
Copy the titles in the sentences below onto your paper, either enclosing them in quotation marks or underlining them.

1. My favorite episode of Wild Kingdom was entitled Cats on the Run.
2. Its host, Marlin Perkins, was featured in an article in the New York Daily News entitled TV's Cat Man.
3. Camille Saint-Saens takes listeners to a pretend zoo with his composition The Carnival of the Animals.
4. The sculpture Three Cougars is on the cover of this month's Zoology Today.
5. Ogden Nash's poem The Hippopotamus is very clever.

Exercise 55 Find It in Your Reading Look back at the passage from "The Lion and the Statue" on page 612. Explain why the passage needs to be divided into two paragraphs.

Exercise 56 Find It in Your Writing Review a story or a report from your portfolio, and either add three direct quotations or rewrite three indirect quotations to make them direct quotations. Use correct punctuation.

Exercise 57 Writing Application
Use a reference book or the Internet to find information about a carnivorous mammal that interests you. Write a dialogue in which you explain facts about the animal to one of your classmates. Be sure to start a new paragraph for each new speaker.

Section Review • 617

Ask students to think about things that are joined together. They might suggest things such as a truck and a trailer, the links of a chain, a television and a VCR, peanut butter and jelly. Point out that joining things together often increases what they are able to do. Tell them that words operate in the same way: By linking some words together you can give them additional meaning.

Activate Prior Knowledge

Write several hyphenated words on the board, including *twenty-one, never-ending, mid-July.* Ask students to think of others. Write these on the board too. Point out that the examples on the board all follow slightly different rules.

Step-by-Step Teaching Guide

Using Hyphens for Numbers

1. Briefly review the rules for using hyphens with numbers. Emphasize the twenty-one through ninety-nine rule.

2. Write this list on the board:

   21 = twenty-one   50 = fifty
   74 =   90 =   93 =
   99 = ninety-nine

3. Ask students to fill in the missing numbers. Point out that hyphens are used when two numbers such as a 7 and a 4 are linked together to make 74. Reiterate that hyphens are used only between twenty-one and ninety-nine.

4. Explain that a hyphen is also used when two numbers are written together to make a fraction that acts as an adjective. Point out that the linked numbers of the fraction have been joined by the hyphen to make a new kind of word: an adjective. Provide the following examples on the board:

   Four fifths of the students voted.

   He won by a four-fifths majority.

5. Ask students to create two more related sentences that illustrate how a fraction becomes an adjective.

1. thirty-four   4. one-fourth
2. ninety-six   5. twenty-six
3. correct

618

Section 26.5
Hyphens and Apostrophes

The *hyphen* (-) is used to combine some numbers and some word parts and to show a connection between the syllables of words that are broken at the ends of lines.

The *apostrophe* (') is used mainly in two situations: (1) to show possession in nouns and pronouns or (2) to indicate missing letters in contractions.

Using Hyphens for Numbers

Some compound numbers and fractions require the use of the hyphen.

▶ **KEY CONCEPT** Use a hyphen when writing out compound numbers from *twenty-one* through *ninety-nine*. ■

EXAMPLES: Before she fell asleep, Tracy counted to *fifty-three*.
We bought *seventy-seven* tickets for the game.

▶ **KEY CONCEPT** Use a hyphen when writing fractions that are used as adjectives. ■

EXAMPLE: A *two-thirds* vote of approval was necessary.

When a fraction is used as a noun, do not use a hyphen.

EXAMPLE: *Two thirds* of the players come from California.

▶ **Exercise 58** Using Hyphens With Numbers Read the following sentences carefully to decide where hyphens are needed. If words in a sentence need a hyphen, rewrite the words correctly on your paper. If a sentence does not have any missing hyphens, write *correct*.

EXAMPLE: Three fourths of the students attended the game.
ANSWER: correct

1. Cynthia Cooper was named the WNBA's first Most Valuable Player when she was thirty four years old.
2. The eight original WNBA teams had ninety six players.
3. Over one tenth of the players were of international origin.
4. The Charlotte Sting was made up of one fourth North Carolina State alumni.
5. Zheng Haixia of the Los Angeles Sparks averaged twenty six points for China during the 1994 World Championship.

In this section, you will learn how hyphens are used to combine or connect words and how apostrophes are used to show possession or replace missing letters. The examples and exercises in this section are about women athletes.

Cross-Curricular Connection: Physical Education

⏱ TIME AND RESOURCE MANAGER

Resources
Print: Grammar Exercise Workbook, pp. 169–174; Grammar Exercises Answers on Transparencies Chapter 26
Technology: On-Line Exercise Bank, Section 26.5

In-Depth Coverage	Accelerated Pace
• Work through all key concepts, pp. 618–628. • Assign and review Exercises 58–65.	• Assign pp. 618–628 for independent student review. • Assign Section Review Exercises 66–70.

Using Hyphens for Word Parts and Compound Words

Hyphens are also used to separate certain prefixes (which begin words) and suffixes (which end words). The next two rules govern the use of hyphens with prefixes and suffixes.

KEY CONCEPT Use a hyphen after a prefix that is followed by a proper noun or adjective. ■

EXAMPLES: The softball tournament takes place in mid-July.
The pro-Atlanta fans sat together in the stands.

Three other prefixes and one suffix always require the use of hyphens.

KEY CONCEPT Use a hyphen in words with the prefixes *all-*, *ex-*, and *self-*, and in words with the suffix *-elect*. ■

EXAMPLES: all-powerful   self-employed
ex-football player   president-elect

In many instances, compound words also require the use of hyphens.

KEY CONCEPT In many cases, a hyphen is used to connect two or more nouns that are used as one compound word. ■

Compound nouns are written in several ways. Some are written as one word. Others are written as separate words. Still others require hyphens. Unless you are sure how a compound word is spelled, consult a dictionary.

ONE WORD: ballplayer
                 shortstop
                 footstep
                 earthquake

SEPARATE WORDS: seat belt
                 sweet potato
                 waiting room
                 time limit

WITH HYPHENS: son-in-law
                 secretary-treasurer
                 great-grandmother
                 six-year-olds

► **More Practice**

On-line
Exercise Bank
• Section 26.5
Grammar Exercise Workbook
• pp. 169–170

▼ Critical Viewing
What compound words would you use to describe the girl in this picture? **[Describe]**

Using Hyphens for Word Parts and Compound Nouns

1. Write the following sentence on the board.

   From mid-June to mid-September, the off-season time of the year for the NBA, fans of professional women's basketball become all-powerful at the box office.

   Ask students to identify each of the hyphen rules used in the sample sentence, then challenge them to create their own sentences using as many of the rules as possible.

2. Write students' suggestions on the board, working with the class to see whether the sentences fit the rules outlined for prefixes with proper nouns and adjectives, as well as the rules for *all-, ex-, self-,* and *-elect*.

3. Read over the list of compound nouns with students and have them suggest words that they think might be compound nouns, while several volunteers check the words in a dictionary. This will reinforce the idea that students can always check the dictionary for the spelling of compound nouns when they are uncertain about hyphen usage.

Critical Viewing

Describe Possible answers might include *self-assured, pro-team,* or age related words such as *eleven-year-old.*

619

Using Hyphens for Compound Words

1. Tell students that adjectives can be joined by hyphens just as numbers and nouns can be. Explain that compound modifiers—one adjective modifying a second adjective before a noun—create new hyphenated words with new meanings.

2. List the following phrases on the board.

   mass-produced sneakers

   well-fed athletes

   never-ending glory

   happy-go-lucky player

3. Ask students to analyze each phrase, telling which word is the noun and which is the adjective modifying the other adjective. Students should pay special attention to the rules for compound modifiers that come after the nouns they modify (they sometimes don't use hyphens). Remind them to look up words about which they're uncertain, and reiterate that if words are hyphenated in the dictionary, they are always hyphenated.

Critical Viewing

Describe Encourage students to build from on-page words such as *never-ending sound, full-court press* and then create original words.

26.5

Compound modifiers follow a different rule.

▶ **KEY CONCEPT** Use a hyphen to connect a compound modifier that comes before a noun. ■

In a compound modifier, the hyphen shows that the first modifier describes the second modifier, not the noun.

EXAMPLES: The team used a *full-court* press to slow down the opposing players.
The seven *well-fed* puppies curled up together for a nap.

Sometimes, a compound modifier comes after a noun. Generally, no hyphen is needed in this situation.

BEFORE: The *never-ending* sound of cheering thrilled the players.

AFTER: The sound of cheering was *never ending*.

It is wise, however, to consult a dictionary when you use compound modifiers after nouns.

EXAMPLES: The *happy-go-lucky* goalie rarely worries.
The goalie is *happy-go-lucky*.

You should also remember a final rule when you write compound modifiers:

▶ **KEY CONCEPT** Do not use a hyphen with a compound modifier that includes a word ending in *-ly*, or in a compound proper adjective or a compound proper noun acting as an adjective. ■

INCORRECT: poorly-written letter   South-American tourist
CORRECT: poorly written letter   South American tourist

▲ Critical Viewing
What compound modifiers might you use to describe the action pictured here? [Describe]

▶ **Exercise 59** Using Hyphens With Word Parts and Compound Words Decide whether hyphens are needed in the phrases below. If a phrase is correct as it is, write *correct*. If a phrase needs hyphenation, rewrite it correctly.

EXAMPLE: an old fashioned story

ANSWER: an old-fashioned story

1. a first round draft pick
2. during the mid season playoffs
3. a mass-produced product
4. a two time champion
5. the all star team
6. a sports oriented family
7. the ten week season of games
8. an All American choice
9. the off-season games
10. WNBA licensed merchandise

Rules for Dividing Words at the End of a Line

Hyphens serve a useful purpose when they are used to divide words at the ends of lines. They should not, however, be used more often than is necessary. Following are several rules that determine how to divide a word at the end of a line.

The first rule for dividing words at the end of a line is the most important rule for you to remember and use whenever you divide words:

▶ **KEY CONCEPT** If a word must be divided, always divide it between syllables. ■

EXAMPLE: The coach's pep talks, usually quite inspir-
             ing, are often characterized by wild hand ges-
             tures and frequent shouts.

In addition to the preceding rule, other details also affect word division. As the following example indicates, a hyphen used to divide a word should never be placed at the beginning of the second line. It must be placed at the end of the first line.

INCORRECT: To make one large room, knock down this par
             -tition.

CORRECT: To make one large room, knock down this par-
             tition.

▶ **More Practice**

On-line
Exercise Bank
• Section 26.5
Grammar Exercise
Workbook
• pp. 169–170

Hyphens and Apostrophes • 621

Integrating Technology Skills

Point out that computer word-processing programs have made end-of-line hyphen use infrequent. Have students experiment with the text-wrap feature in a word-processing program by typing several sentences. Point out that on typewriters, words don't automatically shift down to the next line, so a typist must know hyphenation rules. Show students how to work with left, center, right, and justified alignment. Point out that they will still use the rules for dividing words at the end of a line in handwritten papers.

Critical Viewing

Analyze Possible responses: The defender is moving the ball to the side. She is stepping to the side to divert attention away from the ball.

26.5

▶ **KEY CONCEPT** One-syllable words should never be divided, even if they seem long or look like two-syllable words. ■

INCORRECT: fif-th   brow-se   stra-ight
CORRECT: fifth   browse   straight

When a one-syllable word does not fit at the end of a line, just leave the space and write the word, without a hyphen, on the next line.

If you are uncertain about the division of syllables in a specific word, consult a dictionary.

▶ **KEY CONCEPT** Avoid dividing a word so that a single letter stands alone. ■

The following words are correctly broken into syllables. They should usually not, however, be divided at the end of a line.

SYLLABLES: i-dle   a-lone   ink-y

▶ **KEY CONCEPT** Avoid dividing proper nouns or proper adjectives. ■

POOR: Eliza-beth   Ger-man
BETTER: Elizabeth   German

▶ **KEY CONCEPT** Divide a hyphenated word only immediately following the existing hyphen. ■

INCORRECT: It was a post-sea-
              son soccer game.
CORRECT: It was a post-
              season soccer game.

▶ **Critical Viewing** How is the defender trying to divide the striker's attention? **[Analyze]**

622 • Punctuation

▶ **Exercise 60** **Using Hyphens to Divide Words** If a word in the list below can be divided, write the part of the word that would appear at the end of a line. If a word should not be divided, write the complete word.

EXAMPLE: exhaust

ANSWER: ex-

1. backboard
2. net
3. mass-produced
4. scrimmage
5. game
6. defense
7. uniform
8. winning
9. teammate
10. Comets

Using Apostrophes to Form Possessives of Nouns

Use apostrophes with nouns to show ownership.

▶ **KEY CONCEPT** Add an apostrophe and *s* to show the possessive case of most singular nouns. ■

EXAMPLES: The bat *of the player* becomes the *player*'s bat.
The idea *of Coach Long* becomes *Coach Long*'s idea.

Even when a singular noun already ends in *s*, an apostrophe and *s* should usually be added to show possession.

EXAMPLES: The shape *of the lens* becomes the *lens*'s shape.
The fastball *of Jen Wells* becomes *Jen Wells*'s fastball.
The impact *of loss* becomes the *loss*'s impact.

▶ **KEY CONCEPT** Add just an apostrophe to show the possessive case of plural nouns ending in *s* or *es*. ■

EXAMPLES: The flavor *of the strawberries* becomes the *strawberries*' flavor.
The buzzing *of the bees* becomes the *bees*' buzzing.

▶ **More Practice**

On-Line
Exercise Bank
• Section 26.5
Grammar Practice Workbook
• pp. 169-170

Hyphens and Apostrophes • **623**

Customize for
ESL Students

Nonnative English speakers are often uncomfortable using the apostrophe and -*s* to form possessives. They may opt instead for the safer and more obvious *the book of the woman* instead of *the woman's book,* or *the class of the teacher* instead of *the teacher's class.* Give students extra practice by having them tell you, in speaking or writing, about things that belong to them or to their friends and family. Encourage them to experiment with using the apostrophe and -*s* to show possession.

Answer Key

▶ **Exercise 60**

1. back-
2. net
3. mass-
4. scrim-
5. game
6. de-
7. uni-
8. win-
9. team-
10. Comets

Step-by-Step Teaching Guide

Using Apostrophes to Form Possessives of Nouns

1. Begin by reviewing with students that *possessive* indicates "ownership." Write the sentence below on the board and have a student read it aloud.

   The soccer ball of the girl and the Frisbee of the boy were left out in the backyard of their neighbor.

2. Point out that this way of showing possession or ownership is awkward and repetitive. With the class, rewrite the sentence using the first rule: Add an apostrophe and *s* to show the possessive case of most singular nouns.

   The girl's soccer ball and the boy's Frisbee were left in their neighbor's backyard.

3. Review the variations in the formation of the possessive and write the following sentences on the board.

   The orders of the coaches were drowned out by the shouting of the women as they called out to the goalie, the target of their shots.

   The coaches' orders were drowned out by the women's shouting as they called out to the goalie, their shots' target.

4. Read both sentences with students to illustrate the efficiency with which the apostrophe shows possession. Ask for volunteers to explain the use of the apostrophe in each part of the second sentence.

5. Plural possessives are likely to cause the most confusion. Ask each student to suggest one plural noun. Write them on the board. Then have students come to the board and add an apostrophe or apostrophe -*s* to each word.

623

Singular:

1. trainer's
2. team's
3. racket's
4. swimmer's
5. muscle's
6. toss's
7. track's
8. champion's
9. game's
10. skate's

Plural:

11. gymnasts'
12. softballs'
13. athletes'
14. feet's
15. goals'
16. trophies'
17. coaches'
18. skis'
19. teeth's
20. races'

Critical Viewing

Describe Possible answers include

the school's

the girls'

the ninth-grade's

Encourage the use of both singular and plural possessives.

26.5

Forming the possessive of plural nouns that do not already end in *s* requires a different rule.

► **KEY CONCEPT** Add an apostrophe and *s* to show the possessive case of plural nouns that do not end in *s* or *es*. ■

EXAMPLES: The tournament *of women* becomes the *women's* tournament.
The game *of the children* becomes the *children's* game.

The following two steps can help you decide where to place the apostrophe and whether an *s* is needed when you form possessives. First, determine the owner of the quality or object involved. Ask yourself, "To whom does it belong?" Second, if the answer to this question is a singular noun, follow the rule for forming singular possessives. If the answer is a plural noun, follow the rules for forming plural possessives.

If you wish to use the phrase *the mountains beauty*, ask yourself, "To what does the beauty belong?" If the answer is "the mountain," then the possessive is singular: *the mountain's beauty*. If the answer is "the mountains," then the possessive is plural: *the mountains' beauty*.

► **Exercise 61**   Using Apostrophes to Form Possessives of Nouns   The first ten of the following nouns are singular. The last ten are plural. Make two columns on your paper, labeled as in the example. Then, write the correct possessive form for each word in the appropriate column.

EXAMPLE: volleyball player
ANSWER: <u>Singular</u>   <u>Plural</u>
volleyball player's

1. trainer   11. gymnasts
2. team   12. softballs
3. racket   13. athletes
4. swimmer   14. feet
5. muscle   15. goals
6. toss   16. trophies
7. track   17. coaches
8. champion   18. skis
9. game   19. teeth
10. skate   20. races

▼ Critical Viewing
What possessive nouns might you use to describe a volleyball team? **[Describe]**

⏱ **TIME SAVERS!**

🗂 **Answers on Transparency**
Use the Grammar Exercises Answers on Transparencies for Chapter 26 to facilitate correction by students.

🖥 **On-Line Exercise Bank**
Have students complete the exercises on computer. The Auto Check feature will grade their work for you!

Using Apostrophes With Pronouns

Both indefinite pronouns and personal pronouns can indicate possession. Here are two rules to follow to show possession:

> **KEY CONCEPT** Use an apostrophe and *s* with indefinite pronouns to show possession. ■

EXAMPLES: everyone's plan   each one's decision
somebody's book   one another's ideas

> **KEY CONCEPT** Do *not* use an apostrophe with possessive personal pronouns. ■

The following personal pronouns show possession: *my, mine, your, yours, his, her, hers, its, our, ours, their,* and *theirs.* Some of these pronouns are generally used as adjectives.

EXAMPLES: *Your* batting stance is unusual.
Carrie broke *her* glasses.

Others can be used as subjects, direct objects, and subject complements.

EXAMPLES: *Yours* is a good idea.
Give me *mine.*
This jacket is *his.*

Whatever the use, a possessive personal pronoun should never include an apostrophe.

> **Exercise 62** Using Apostrophes With Pronouns Rewrite each of the following sentences, replacing the blank(s) with the possessive forms of appropriate indefinite pronouns or personal pronouns.

EXAMPLE: They borrowed __?__ jackets.
ANSWER: They borrowed each other's jackets.

1. When she was eight, Olympic champion Dorothy Hamill received the first pair of ice skates that were really __?__ .
2. __?__ father saw how much __?__ little girl enjoyed skating, so he decided she could take lessons.
3. Soon Dorothy and __?__ mom were adjusting __?__ schedules to include daily practice at the ice rink.
4. Dorothy learned quickly, and soon __?__ skating skills were as good as __?__ .
5. In __?__ estimation, she was bound for success.

▶ **More Practice**

Language Lab
CD-ROM
• Punctuation lesson
On-line
Exercise Bank
• Section 26.5
Grammar Exercise
Workbook
• pp. 171–172

Using Apostrophes With Pronouns

1. Help students make the distinction between personal and indefinite pronouns in the following sentences.

   The volleyball belonged to my friend. It was hers.

   The volleyball belonged to the school. It was everyone's.

2. Point out that in the first sentence, the pronouns *my* and *hers* refer to a specific person, and that in both cases it is incorrect to use an apostrophe and *-s* to show possession. In the second sentence, however, the pronoun *everyone's* refers to a general group of people that it would be impossible to name specifically. Thus it is an indefinite pronoun and uses an apostrophe and *-s* to show possession.

Answer Key

▶ **Exercise 62**

1. When she was eight, Olympic champion Dorothy Hamill received the first pair of ice skates that were really hers.
2. Her father saw how much his little girl enjoyed skating, so he decided she could take lessons.
3. Soon Dorothy and her mom were adjusting their schedules to include daily practice at the ice rink.
4. Dorothy learned quickly, and soon her skating skills were as good as anyone's.
5. In everyone's estimation, she was bound for success.

☑ ONGOING ASSESSMENT: Monitor and Reinforce

If students have difficulty with Exercise 61 or 62, refer them to the following for additional practice.

In the Textbook	Print Resources	Technology
Section Review, Ex. 69, p. 629	Grammar Exercise Workbook, pp. 171–172	Language Lab CD-ROM, Punctuation; On-Line Exercise Bank, Section 26.5

Using Apostrophes With Contractions

1. Put the following sentences on the board to illustrate the usefulness and efficiency of contractions. Tell students that this will help them to notice which letters are replaced by an apostrophe as they review the list of common contractions.

   I am certain that you would not be pleased if we could not go with you to the movies.

   I'm certain that you wouldn't be pleased if we couldn't go with you to the movies.

2. Have a student read both sentences out loud. Discuss the awkward formality of the first sentence and the quicker flow of the second. Tell students that contractions help writing to sound more like ordinary speech.

3. Use this opportunity to make the point that contractions should never be used in formal writing. Write the following opening from a letter on the board to reinforce that rule.

   Dear Mr. President,

   I do not agree that higher taxes cannot be avoided.

   Dear Mr. President,

   I don't agree that higher taxes can't be avoided.

4. Ask students which version seems more formal and correct.

26.5

Using Apostrophes With Contractions

Contractions are shortened forms of words or phrases.

▶ **KEY CONCEPT** Use an apostrophe in a contraction to indicate the position of a missing letter or letters. ■

Contractions are often used in informal speaking and writing. For example, instead of saying, "I am ready," most people would probably say, "I'm ready."

The following chart shows some of the many contractions formed with verbs:

COMMON CONTRACTIONS WITH VERBS		
Verb + *not*	are not (aren't) is not (isn't) was not (wasn't) were not (weren't) cannot (can't)	could not (couldn't) did not (didn't) do not (don't) should not (shouldn't) would not (wouldn't)
Pronoun + the Verb *will*	I will (I'll) you will (you'll) he will (he'll) she will (she'll)	we will (we'll) they will (they'll) who will (who'll)
Pronoun or Noun + the Verb *be*	I am (I'm) you are (you're) he is (he's) she is (she's) it is (it's)	we are (we're) they are (they're) who is (who's) where is (where's) Andy is (Andy's)
Pronoun or Noun + the Verb *would*	I would (I'd) you would (you'd) he would (he'd) she would (she'd)	we would (we'd) they would (they'd) who would (who'd) Penny would (Penny'd)

In a contraction, the exact position of the missing letter or letters is indicated by the apostrophe.

INCORRECT: did'nt th'eyd
CORRECT: didn't they'd

Remember that you should avoid using contractions in formal speaking or writing.

INFORMAL WRITING: *What's* the solution?
FORMAL WRITING: *What is* the solution?

GRAMMAR IN LITERATURE

from **Golden Girls: The 1998 U.S. Women's Hockey Team**

Johnette Howard

Notice the contractions the writer has used in this passage. What word group does each contraction represent?

Sportswriters walked into the final grousing about having to cover it and walked out gushing that it was the best thing *they'd* ever seen. A felicitous line by *Washington Post* columnist Michael Wilbon, who called Mleczko "the first leftwinger *I've* ever had a crush on," was typical.

> **Exercise 63** Using Apostrophes With Contractions On your paper, write each of the underlined word groups as a contraction.

EXAMPLE: They are leaving at five.

ANSWER: They're

1. Who would have imagined that after only four years on skates, Dorothy Hamill would win the Novice Division at the National Championships?
2. I was not aware that Dorothy trained in Toronto, Canada, for one summer.
3. I cannot believe that the following January, Dorothy won the Eastern Championship in the Junior Division.
4. At Nationals the next month, Dorothy could not believe it when they announced she had won the school figures.
5. She knew she would do well on her freestyle program because she loved doing it the most.
6. She did not place first overall but took second place at the age of thirteen.
7. Dorothy would not be competing as a Junior again since she had passed the test qualifying her as a Senior Lady.
8. People were not too surprised when Dorothy took fifth place at the 1971 Nationals as a Senior Lady.
9. Dorothy, who is remembered most for her 1976 gold medal performance in Innsbruck, won many more competitions.
10. She will always be remembered for her classy skating, her bright smile, and her famous hairdo.

> **More Practice**
>
> Language Lab
> CD-ROM
> • Punctuation lesson
> On-line
> Exercise Bank
> • Section 26.5
> Grammar Exercise
> Workbook
> • pp. 173–174

☑ **ONGOING ASSESSMENT: Monitor and Reinforce**

If students have difficulty with Exercise 63, 64, or 65, refer them to the following for additional practice.

In the Textbook	Print Resources	Technology
Section Review, Ex. 69–70, p. 629	Grammar Exercise Workbook, pp. 171–174	Language Lab CD-ROM, Punctuation; On-Line Exercise Bank, Section 26.4

Exercise 64

Sentences will vary. Correct possessives follow.

1. goalie's
2. golf club's
3. tennis star's
4. winner's
5. team's
6. stadium's
7. track's
8. champions'
9. contest's
10. skates'
11. swimmers'
12. softballs'
13. athletes'
14. athlete's
15. competition's
16. skiers'
17. coaches'
18. racket's
19. bobsledders'
20. races'

Exercise 65

1. Romania's Nadia Comaneci.
2. everyone's curriculum
3. Nadia's parents knew she'd like
4. everyone else's in her class.
5. classmates' complaints.
6. They would say, "It's not fair.
7. Nadia was the tournament's
8. she wasn't happy
9. she'd improved
10. Nadia wouldn't lose in
11. Nadia's trophy case
12. By early 1976, she'd become
13. Nadia's name was on every fan's lips.
14. her coach's advice.
15. the judges' cards.

Exercise 64 Writing Sentences Using Apostrophes
Correctly Write a sentence in which you use the possessive form of each of the following nouns. Check to see that you have used apostrophes correctly in each sentence.

1. goalie
2. golf club
3. tennis star
4. winner
5. team
6. stadium
7. track
8. champions
9. contest
10. skates
11. swimmers
12. softballs
13. athletes
14. professional athlete
15. competition
16. skiers
17. coaches
18. racket
19. bobsledders
20. races

Exercise 65 Revising to Use Apostrophes Correctly
Rewrite the paragraph below, adding apostrophes where they are needed.

(1) Gymnastics became the most important thing in the life of Romanias Nadia Comaneci. (2) Gymnastics was part of everyones curriculum at her school. (3) Nadias parents knew shed like gymnastics because she was always running and jumping. (4) Soon her skills were better than everyone elses in her class. (5) Her teachers often heard classmates complaints. (6) They would say, "Its not fair. Nadia always beats us." (7) When she entered the National Championship of Romania at the age of eight, Nadia was the tournaments youngest competitor. (8) Nadia placed thirteenth that year, but she wasnt happy with her performance. (9) By the next year, shed improved greatly and the championship medal was hers. (10) Nadia wouldnt lose in a Romanian competition again. (11) Nadias trophy case began to fill with medals from international competitions. (12) By early 1976, shed become the best gymnast in the world. (13) At the 1976 Olympics in Montreal, Canada, Nadias name was on every fans lips. (14) The tiny fourteen-year-old carefully followed her coachs advice. (15) She did so well that she was first on all of the judges cards.

More Practice

On-line
Exercise Bank
• Section 26.5
Grammar Exercise
Workbook
• pp. 173–174

☑ **ONGOING ASSESSMENT: Assess Mastery**

Use the following resources to assess student mastery of punctuation.

In the Textbook	Technology
Chapter Review, Ex. 74–82, pp. 630–631 Standardized Test Preparation Workshop, pp. 632–633	On-Line Exercise Bank, Chapter 26

Section 26.5 Section Review

GRAMMAR EXERCISES 66–73

Exercise 66 Using Hyphens in Numbers Write out each number, adding hyphens where needed.

1. 21   2. 17   3. 64   4. 300   5. 33

Exercise 67 Using Hyphens With Word Parts and Compound Words If a phrase below needs hyphenation, rewrite it correctly. If a phrase is correct as it is, write *correct* on your paper.

1. third leading scorer
2. story that was basketball related
3. up to the minute scores
4. poorly thrown pass
5. world class players

Exercise 68 Using Hyphens to Divide Words If a word below can be divided, write the part that would appear at the end of a line. If the word cannot be divided, write the complete word.

1. playing
2. spectators
3. award-winning
4. mini-rounds
5. professional
6. award
7. Monarchs
8. scoring
9. coach
10. rebound

Exercise 69 Using Apostrophes to Form Possessives of Nouns Write the possessive form of each noun below.

1. crowd
2. judges
3. women
4. gymnasts
5. apparatus
6. competitors
7. fan
8. goalie
9. winners
10. James

Exercise 70 Revising to Add Apostrophes and Hyphens Rewrite the paragraph below, adding apostrophes and hyphens where they are needed.

(1) Tara Lipinskis figure skating career started at age three. (2) It didnt begin on blades, however. (3) She was a roller skating champ before shed ever thought about ice skating. (4) At age six, Tara tried skating on ice and wasnt successful at first. (5) She ignored her friends laughter as she flopped on the ice. (6) Within 45 minutes, Taras natural ability took over. (7) Soon, to everyones amazement, she was skating forward and backward. (8) She quickly got her parents permission to take lessons. (9) Tara proved there wasnt any jump she couldn't do. (10) In 1998, she won the Womens Figure Skating gold medal.

Exercise 71 Find It in Your Reading Explain why hyphens and apostrophes are used in this passage from Johnette Howard's "Golden Girls."

In winning the six-team inaugural women's Olympic tournament with a 6–0 record, the U.S. team eclipsed Picabo Street as America's feel-good story of the Winter Games.

Exercise 72 Find It in Your Writing Review your work to find five examples of possessive nouns. Check to see that you've punctuated them correctly, and make any necessary corrections.

Exercise 73 Writing Application Find out about a famous female athlete. Write a biography that includes possessive nouns and contractions.

Section Review • 629

ASSESS and CLOSE

Section Review

Each of these exercises correlates with the instruction on hyphens and apostrophes, pages 618–628. These exercises may be used for more practice, for reteaching, or for review of the Key Concepts presented. Answers to all chapter exercises are available in *Grammar Exercises Answers on Transparencies* in your Teaching Resources.

Answer Key

Exercise 66

1. twenty-one
2. seventeen
3. sixty-four
4. three hundred
5. thirty-three

Exercise 67

1. third-leading
2. correct
3. up-to-the-minute
4. correct
5. world-class

Exercise 68

1. play-
2. spec- (or specta-)
3. award-
4. mini-
5. pro- (or profes-, or profession-)
6. award
7. Monarchs
8. scor-
9. coach
10. re-

Exercise 69

1. crowd's
2. judges'
3. women's
4. gymnasts'
5. apparatus's
6. competitors'
7. fan's
8. goalie's
9. winners'
10. James's

Exercise 70

1. Tara Lipinski's skating career started at age three.
2. It didn't begin on blades, however.
3. She was a roller-skating champ before she'd ever thought about ice skating.
4. At age six, Tara tried skating on ice and wasn't successful at first.
5. She ignored her friends' laughter as she flopped on the ice.

continued

629

Answer Key continued

6. Within 45 minutes, Tara's natural ability took over.
7. Soon, to everyone's amazement, she was skating forward and backward.
8. She quickly got her parents' permission to take lessons.
9. Tara proved there wasn't any jump she couldn't do.
10. In 1998, she won the Women's Figure Skating gold medal.

Exercise 71

Find It in Your Reading
Six-team is a compound modifier. Women's is a plural possessive. *America's* is a singular possessive. *Feel-good* is a compound modifier.

Exercise 72

Find It in Your Writing
Have students write sentences to use the plural possessives they find.

Exercise 73

Writing Application
Students can post their minibiographies on a female-sports-heroes bulletin board.

CHAPTER REVIEW

Each of these exercises correlates with a section of the chapter on punctuation, pages 578–629.

Answer Key

Exercise 74

1. Why did Philip Wrigley establish strict rules for players in the All-American Girls Professional Baseball League?
2. He wanted to show the public that women could be athletic and charming!
3. Wow! The players had so many rules.
4. They received a beauty kit as well as a handbook to reinforce good grace.
5. That's unbelievable!

Exercise 75

1. Originally, softball was an indoor sport, but in 1895 outdoor games began.
2. Pitcher, shortstop, and center fielder are all positions in softball.
3. The inside of a softball is made with a rubbery, stretchy material.
4. The Amateur Softball Association sets rules, so umpires join the association.
5. Some guidelines for slow-pitch softball include ten players, a 12-inch ball, and no base stealing.

Exercise 76

1. In gymnastics, four main events are judged, I believe.
2. Sue, did you know that on the uneven bars, gymnasts must stay in motion?
3. If gymnasts use the whole length of the balance beam, their scores go up.
4. Rhythmic gymnastics, which involves holding an object and dancing, isn't as popular as traditional gymnastics.
5. The balance beam, the best-known apparatus, is only four inches wide.

Exercise 77

1. On December 8, 1941, the United States entered World War II, and many male baseball players went to war.
2. Philip Wrigley turned to women and formed the All-American Girls Baseball League on February 17, 1943.
3. Tryouts were held at Wrigley Field, Chicago, Illinois.

GRAMMAR EXERCISES 74–83

Exercise 74 Revising the Use of **End Marks** Revise these sentences, correcting end marks where necessary.

1. Why did Philip Wrigley establish strict rules for players in the All-American Girls Professional Baseball League.
2. He wanted to show the public that women could be athletic and charming!
3. Wow. The players had so many rules!
4. They received a beauty kit as well as a handbook to reinforce good grace?
5. That's unbelievable?

Exercise 75 Revising the Use of **Commas** Revise the following, adding or deleting commas where necessary.

1. Originally softball was an indoor sport but in 1895, outdoor games began.
2. Pitcher shortstop, and center fielder are all, positions in softball.
3. The inside of a softball is made with a rubbery stretchy material.
4. The Amateur, Softball Association sets rules so umpires join the association.
5. Some guidelines for slow-pitch softball, include ten players a 12-inch ball and no base stealing.

Exercise 76 Revising the Use of **Commas** Revise the following, adding or deleting commas where necessary.

1. In gymnastics four, main events are judged I believe.
2. Sue did you know that on the uneven, bars gymnasts must stay in motion?
3. If gymnasts use the whole length of the balance beam their scores go up.
4. Rhythmic gymnastics which involves

630 • Punctuation

holding an object and dancing isn't as popular as traditional gymnastics.
5. The balance beam the best-known apparatus is only four inches wide.

Exercise 77 Using Commas in **Dates and Places** Write the dates and places in each sentence, adding needed commas.

1. On December 8 1941 the United States entered World War II, and many male baseball players went to war.
2. Philip Wrigley turned to women and formed the All-American Girls Baseball League on February 17 1943.
3. Tryouts were held at Wrigley Field Chicago Illinois.
4. Players came from places such as Red Hill Pennsylvania and Popular Point Manitoba Canada.
5. The Racine Belles from Racine Wisconsin won the 1946 championship on Monday September 16 by just one run.

Exercise 78 Using Semicolons Replace the comma and conjunction with a semicolon in the sentences below.

1. Bela Karolyi was excited, for he wanted to coach Svetlana Boginskaya.
2. Svetlana was only twenty-three, but she was one of the oldest competitors.
3. When she was little, Svetlana hated following rules, and her parents wanted her to learn a disciplined sport.
4. As Svetlana grew, the skills became more difficult, and practicing also seemed monotonous and routine.
5. Svetlana stuck with gymnastics longer than many other young women, and she became a world champion.

4. Players came from places such as Red Hill, Pennsylvania, and Popular Point, Manitoba, Canada.
5. The Racine Belles from Racine, Wisconsin, won the 1946 championship on Monday, September 16, by just one run.

Exercise 78

1. Bela Karolyi was excited; he wanted to coach Svetlana Boginskaya.
2. Svetlana was only twenty-three; she was one of the oldest competitors.
3. When she was little, Svetlana hated following rules; her parents wanted her to learn a disciplined sport.
4. As Svetlana grew, the skills became more difficult; practicing also seemed monotonous and routine.
5. Svetlana stuck with gymnastics longer than many other young women; she became a world champion.

Exercise 79 Using Colons Add colons where appropriate.

1. There are four events in women's gymnastics balance beam, floor exercise, vault, and uneven bars.
2. **Warning** Beware of Slippery Bars
3. Dominique Moceanu's success involves many things her discipline, her genes, her tenacity, and her positive attitude.
4. Dominique trained in many states Illinois, Florida, California, and Texas.
5. Dear Ms. Moceanu

Exercise 80 Revising to Apply All Punctuation Rules Revise the following passage, adding, deleting, and correcting punctuation marks where necessary. Also, begin new paragraphs wherever necessary.

(1) During the documentary the commentator said of Olga Korbut; Besides the difficult stunts she had an expression of joy, as she performed! (2) He added before Olga you couldn't sell a thousand tickets to a gymnastics event? (3) Nadia Comaneci scored even, higher than Olga he continued but she did not have as much impact on the sport. (4) Generations of gymnasts were inspired by Olga pointed out one of those interviewed during the one hour special; (5) Those gymnasts included Mary Lou Retton the gold medal champion in the womens all-around in 1984. (6) Mary Lou Retton had the same coach as Nadia Comaneci, Bela Karolyi the announcer informed the audience (7) Can you imagine having two such, accomplished students! (8) After the announcer made this remark the program traced Retton's career and her connection to Karolyi. (9) The program concluded with a tribute to the womens team of 1996? (10) I found the program so interesting; that I taped it and watched it, again.

Exercise 81 Adding Quotation Marks and Underlining Write the titles below on your paper, adding quotation marks or underlining them.

1. A book called The Development and Decline of the All-American Girls Professional Baseball League, 1943–1954 is a great source of statistics and rules.
2. In the chapter Life in the League, readers get a glimpse into how the players lived their lives on and off the field.
3. Magazines such as Life and Esquire wrote articles about the AAGPBL.
4. Phil Stack mocked the hard-working female baseball players through his short poem All-American Babe.
5. A TV documentary entitled When Diamonds Were a Girl's Best Friend aired in 1987.

Exercise 82 Using Hyphens and Apostrophes Rewrite these sentences, adding needed hyphens or apostrophes.

1. One fourth of the AAGPBL championships were won by Fort Waynes Daisies.
2. Jean Faut, one of the leagues best players, was twenty one years old when she began playing.
3. While they were poorly paid professional athletes, AAGPBL players salaries were increased if they made the all star team.
4. Angie Pottholf of the Lynx basketball team is involved in D.A.R.E., an anti drug educational program for children.
5. Her coach believes shes a terrific role model because she isnt selfish.

Exercise 83 Writing Application

Write a dialogue that you might have if you could interview a famous woman athlete. Proofread your work carefully for correct punctuation of dialogue.

Answer Key continued

5. A TV documentary entitled <u>When Diamonds Were a Girl's Best Friend</u> aired in 1987.

Exercise 82

1. One fourth of the AAGPBL championships were won by Fort Wayne's Daisies.
2. Jean Faut, one of the league's best players, was twenty-one years old when she began playing.
3. While they were poorly paid professional athletes, AAGPBL players' salaries were increased if they made the all-star team.
4. Angie Pottholf of the Lynx basketball team is involved in D.A.R.E., an anti-drug educational program for children.
5. Her coach believes she's a terrific role model because she isn't selfish.

Exercise 83

Writing Application
Have students work with a partner and check the punctuation of each other's dialogue.

Exercise 79

1. There are four events in women's gymnastics: balance beam, floor exercise, vault, and uneven bars.
2. **Warning:** Beware of Slippery Bars
3. Dominique Moceanu's success involves many things: her discipline, her genes, her tenacity, and her positive attitude.
4. Dominique trained in many states: Illinois, Florida, California, and Texas.
5. Dear Mrs. Moceanu:

Exercise 80

(1) During the documentary, the commentator said of Olga Korbut: "Besides the difficult stunts, she had an expression of joy as she performed." (2) He added, "Before Olga, you couldn't sell a thousand tickets to a gymnastics event." (3) "Nadia Comaneci scored even higher than Olga," he continued, "but she did not have as much impact on the sport." (4) "Generations of gymnasts were inspired by Olga," pointed out one of those interviewed during the one-hour special. (5) Those gymnasts included Mary Lou Retton, the gold medal champion in the women's all-around in 1984. (6) "Mary Lou Retton had the same coach as Nadia Comaneci, Bela Karolyi," the announcer informed the audience. (7) "Can you imagine having two such accomplished students!" (8) After the announcer made this remark, the program traced Retton's career and her connection to Karolyi. (9) The program concluded with a tribute to the women's team of 1996. (10) I found the program so interesting that I taped it and watched it again.

Exercise 81

1. A book called <u>The Development and Decline of the All-American Girls Professional Baseball League, 1943–1954</u> is a great source of statistics and rules.
2. In the chapter "Life in the League," readers get a glimpse into how the players lived their lives on and off the field.
3. Magazines such as <u>Life</u> and <u>Esquire</u> wrote articles about the AAGPBL.
4. Phil Stack mocked the hard-working female baseball players through his short poem "All-American Babe."

continued

Lesson Objectives

- To capitalize and punctuate correctly to clarify and enhance meaning.

Step-by-Step Teaching Guide

Punctuation

Teaching Resources: Standardized Test Preparation Workbook, pp. 51–52

1. Explain to students that they will encounter different types of questions that will each require different strategies. Remind them to read each set of directions carefully to determine what they are being asked to do.

2. Have students cover the "Answers and Explanations" column in their textbooks.

3. Tell them that in the first sample test item, they need to read the entire sentence to determine if there are any punctuation errors. Encourage students to read the sentence a second time.

4. In the second test item, they should focus on the underlined portion only.

Standardized Test Preparation Workshop

Punctuation

Some standardized tests include items that test your knowledge of punctuation rules. Most often, this testing involves identifying errors in punctuation. Remember these basic rules to help you identify such errors:

- End marks denote the end of a sentence and will identify the type of sentence. Use a period to end a declarative or imperative sentence, a question mark to end an interrogative sentence, and an exclamation mark to end an exclamatory sentence.

- Use commas to separate items in a series; after introductory words, phrases, or clauses at the beginning of a sentence; and to set off nonessential elements from the rest of the sentence.

- Quotation marks enclose direct quotations—a person's exact speech or thoughts.

- Abbreviations and titles of people end with a period.

Test Tip

Remember this exception: Postal abbreviations for states always have two capital letters and use no punctuation.

Sample Test Items	Answers and Explanations

Directions: Identify which, if any, part of each sentence contains a punctuation error.
1 A The rain, the cold,
  B and the fog,
  C made this winter bitter and dreary.
  D (No mistake)
	The correct answer for item 1 is *B*. There should be no comma between the last item in the series and the verb.

Directions: Read this passage, and decide which type of error, if any, appears in the underlined section.
 	
The <u>rush hour traffic in New York City prevented him</u> from making it to his meeting in Boston.
 	
2 A Spelling error
  B Capitalization error
  C Punctuation error
  D No error
	The correct answer for item 2 is *C*. There should be a hyphen between *rush* and *hour* because the two words are being used together as a compound adjective.

✎ TEST-TAKING TIP

As students read each test item, they should look for words and other clues to help them determine if a sentence is punctuated correctly. Share with students the following example:

Tonight we are having chicken, stuffing and green beans for dinner.

Students should see that a comma is missing after *stuffing*. These are items in a series and the word *and* should be a clue to students that a comma is needed.

> **Practice 1** Directions: Read this passage, and decide which type of error, if any, appears in the underlined section.

My father <u>Dr, Esteban,</u> was ecstatic to
(1)
<u>read that Tiger Woods had once again been</u>

<u>named Athlete of the Year.</u> <u>I knew he was</u>
(2)
<u>great!</u> <u>dad exclaimed</u> as he rushed into our
(3)
<u>house with the newspaper.</u>
(4)

He <u>excitedly, told us</u> that Woods would
(5)
now be in a prestigious group of <u>two time-</u>

<u>winners, including</u> Michael Jordan, Sandy
(6)
Koufax, and Carl Lewis. <u>He then sped back</u>

<u>across our street, Mitchell Rd., to alert the</u>

<u>neighborhood!</u>
(7)

1 A Spelling error
   B Capitalization error
   C Punctuation error
   D No error

2 F Spelling error
   G Capitalization error
   H Punctuation error
   J No error

3 A Spelling error
   B Capitalization error
   C Punctuation error
   D No error

4 F Spelling error
   G Capitalization error
   H Punctuation error
   J No error

5 A Spelling error
   B Capitalization error
   C Punctuation error
   D No error

6 F Spelling error
   G Capitalization error
   H Punctuation error
   J No error

7 A Spelling error
   B Capitalization error
   C Punctuation error
   D No error

> **Practice 2** Directions: Identify which, if any, part of each sentence contains a punctuation error.

1 A That was one of the most
   B gripping, nail biting
   C games I have ever attended.
   D (No mistake)

2 F When I left the game
   G it was tied;
   H I discovered who won when I got home.
   J (No mistake)

3 A The game lasted for four hours,
   B and by the time it ended,
   C it was past midnight.
   D (No mistake)

4 What punctuation rule explains the use of commas in this sentence: He then sped back across our street, Mitchell Rd., to alert the neighborhood!
   F use commas to separate items in a series
   G use commas to set apart parts of an address
   H use commas to set apart nonessential elements in a clause
   J None–they are incorrectly used in this sentence.

Practice 1

1. C
2. J
3. C
4. G
5. C
6. H
7. D

Practice 2

1. B
2. J
3. D
4. H

In-Depth Lesson Plan

	LESSON FOCUS	PRINT AND MEDIA RESOURCES
DAY 1	**Capitalization** To learn and apply concepts of capitalization (pp. 636–642).	*Language Lab* **CD-ROM**, Capitalization; *On-Line Exercise Bank*, Section 27 **Teaching Resources** *Grammar Exercise Workbook*, pp. 175–180; *Grammar Exercises Answers on Transparencies*, Ch. 27
DAY 2	**Capitalization (continued)** To learn and apply concepts of capitalization and do the Hands-on Grammar activity (pp. 643–649).	*Language Lab* **CD-ROM**, Capitalization; *On-Line Exercise Bank*, Section 27 **Teaching Resources** *Grammar Exercise Workbook*, pp. 181–186; *Grammar Exercises Answers on Transparencies*, Ch. 27; *Hands-on Grammar Book*, Ch. 27
DAY 3	**Review and Assess** Students review chapter and demonstrate mastery of use of capitalization (pp. 650–655).	*On-Line Exercise Bank*, Section 27 **Teaching Resources** *Formal Assessment*, Ch. 27; *Grammar Exercises Answers on Transparencies*, Ch. 27

Accelerated Lesson Plan

	LESSON FOCUS	PRINT AND MEDIA RESOURCES
DAY 1	**Capitalization** Students cover concepts and usage of capitalization determined by Diagnostic Test (pp. 636–649).	*Language Lab* **CD-ROM**, Capitalization; *On-Line Exercise Bank*, Section 27 **Teaching Resources** *Grammar Exercise Workbook*, pp. 175–186; *Grammar Exercises Answers on Transparencies*, Ch. 27
DAY 2	**Review and Assess** Students review chapter and demonstrate mastery of use of capitalization (pp. 650–655).	*On-Line Exercise Bank*, Section 27 **Teaching Resources** *Formal Assessment*, Ch. 27; *Grammar Exercises Answers on Transparencies*, Ch. 27

Options for Adapting Lesson Plans

HOMEWORK

Have students complete any section of the chapter for homework.

FEATURES

Extend coverage with the Grammar in Literature feature (p. 644), and the Standardized Test Preparation Workshop (p. 652).

TECHNOLOGY

Students can use the On-Line Exercise Bank to complete the exercises on computer. The Auto Check feature will grade their work.

INTEGRATED SKILLS COVERAGE

Grammar in Literature
SE p. 644

Reading
Responding to Literature SE p. 644
Find It in Your Reading SE p. 649

Writing
Find It in Your Writing SE p. 649
Writing Application SE p. 650; ATE p. 638

Technology
SE p. 638

Language
SE p. 642

Workplace Skills ATE pp. 641, 644

Real-World Connection ATE p. 645

Viewing and Representing
Critical Viewing SE pp. 634, 637, 642, 645, 646, 648
ATE p. 639

ASSESSMENT SUPPORT

Standardized Test Preparation SE p. 652; ATE p. 646
Standardized Test Preparation Workbook, pp. 53–54
Formal Assessment, Ch. 27

MEETING INDIVIDUAL NEEDS

Less Advanced Students ATE p. 635. See also Ongoing Assessments ATE pp. 643, 648.
ESL Students ATE pp. 640, 643
Visual/Spatial Learners ATE p. 638
Interpersonal Learners ATE p. 648

BLOCK SCHEDULING

Pacing Suggestions
For 90-minute Blocks
• Administer the Diagnostic Test to students to determine instructional coverage.
• Have students complete the necessary exercises in class. Use the Hands-on Grammar activity to provide a change of pace.

Resources for Varying Instruction
• *Language Lab* **CD-ROM** If your students have access to hardware, a 90-minute block provides an ideal opportunity for students to work on computer.

Professional Development Support
• *How to Manage Instruction in the Block* This teaching resource provides management and activity suggestions.

MEDIA AND TECHNOLOGY

For the Student
• *Language Lab* **CD-ROM,** Capitalization
• *On-Line Exercise Bank,* Ch. 27

For the Teacher
• *Resource Pro* **CD-ROM**

WRITING AND GRAMMAR WEB SITE

The Interactive Writing and Grammar Web site provides a wide array of support for students, teachers, and parents. Grammar support includes:
• *On-Line Exercise Bank* with Auto Check scoring
• Diagnostic and assessment support

www.phschool.com

LITERATURE CONNECTIONS

Related selection from *Prentice Hall Literature: Timeless Voices, Timeless Themes,* Bronze:
from "King Arthur: The Marvel of the Sword", by Mary MacLeod, SE p. 644

► *Lesson Objectives*

1. To understand and follow capitalization rules for sentences, proper nouns, proper adjectives, and titles.

2. To capitalize and punctuate correctly to clarify and enhance meaning by capitalizing titles, using hyphens, semicolons, colons, possessives, and sentence punctuation.

Critical Viewing

Connect Most students will answer Queen Elizabeth or Queen Elizabeth II.

Chapter 27 *Capitalization*

Capital letters are used to indicate important words. A beginning of a sentence or quotation, the word *I*, proper nouns and adjectives, a person's name, and titles are examples of words that are capitalized.

EXAMPLE: In my history class, I am learning about Queen Victoria of England.

In fact, a sentence without capitals can be somewhat confusing.

EXAMPLE: The slaterville art festival will show paintings by picasso from ann wilke's private collection.

When capitals are added, the sentence is easier to understand.

EXAMPLE: The Slaterville Art Festival will show paintings by Picasso from Ann Wilke's private collection.

▲ **Critical Viewing**
Elizabeth II was born Elizabeth Alexandra Mary Windsor. By what title is she best known? How would you capitalize it? **[Connect]**

634 • Capitalization

If students miss more than one item in each category, direct them to the relevant pages of the text and assign exercises for practice and review.

Capitalization	Diagnostic Test Items	Teach	Practice	Chapter Review
Skill Check A and C				
Capitals for Sentences, the Word *I*, Proper Nouns, Proper Adjectives, and Titles of People	A 1–10 C 16–25	pp. 636–646	Ex. 1–9	Ex. 12–15 16–17
Skill Checks B				
Capitals for Titles of Things	B 11–15	pp. 647–648	Ex. 10–11	Ex. 15–17
Cumulative Reviews and Applications				Ex. 18–19

Diagnostic Test

Directions: Write all answers on a separate sheet of paper.

Skill Check A. Each of the following sentences contains one or more words that should be capitalized. On your paper, rewrite the words, adding the missing capitals.

1. Studying british royalty can be confusing, i think.
2. in history I, a few of the rulers we studied were henry VIII, william the conqueror, elizabeth I, and queen victoria.
3. michael and i decided to study william I, while my brother chose to study george III.
4. i learned that william I was crowned on christmas day, 1066.
5. land was given to the normans, the french, and the flemish allies in exchange for their military duties.
6. william used bishop lanfranc, archbishop of canterbury, to administer his government when he was in france.
7. the treaty of abernethy in 1072 marked a truce between scotland's king malcolm iii and william.
8. the church of england was reorganized by lanfranc.
9. churches such as canterbury and durham cathedrals were built during this time.
10. landowners pledged their allegiance to william in the oath of salisbury.

Skill Check B. Rewrite each of the following titles, adding the missing capitals.

11. the story of britain	book
12. "down by the salley gardens"	short poem
13. the market cart	painting
14. the daily mirror	newspaper
15. paradise lost	long poem

Skill Check C. Rewrite the following sentences, correcting all errors in capitalization. If the sentence contains no capitalization errors, write *correct*.

16. aunt Dolly and uncle Pete went to england last month.
17. mom and dad decided to go with them.
18. During their visit, they saw the duke of Edinburgh.
19. He was riding in a parade with the queen mother.
20. My aunt and uncle, along with my mom and dad, spent the day at Trafalgar Square.
21. At three o'clock the next day, they met professor Nevis, who took them on a tour of the houses of parliament.
22. Lord and Lady Seymour sponsored a coronation ball.
23. The first dance was led by a prince.
24. A princess and judge Williams soon joined in.
25. Their postcard began, "dear gary, We wish you were here."

Customize for Less Advanced Students

You may need to explain to students that the Houses of Parliament may be likened to the Capitol Building in the United States. This information may help them in recognizing what needs to be capitalized.

PREPARE and ENGAGE

PREPARE and ENGAGE

Interest GRABBER Write the following sentence on the chalkboard:

once Upon A time, there was a LITTLE OLD woman named betsy who lived in a Shoe.

Ask students about their reaction to the sentence. Most students will probably say that the sentence looks funny because some of the words are capitalized incorrectly. Confirm that the sentence does not follow the proper rules of capitalization. Explain that in this chapter they will learn the rules and guidelines that govern the use of capitals.

Activate Prior Knowledge

Remind students that when they learned the alphabet, they learned two different ways to write every letter: lowercase and uppercase, or capital. Explain that this system gives readers information about the words in texts. Ask them to tell you some of the ways they think capital letters are used. (They might say that capitals are used in names, in titles, and so on.)

TEACH

Step-by-Step Teaching Guide

Using Capitals for Sentences and the Word *I*

1. Ask students to write a sentence about a historical event, such as "The Civil War began in 1861."

2. Have several students write their sentences on the board. Assuming that most students applied the first word capitalization rule correctly, ask students why. (The first word in a sentence is always capitalized to signal the start of a new idea.)

continued

Answer Key

▶ Exercise 1

1. Do	6. He
2. No	7. He
3. After	8. Collecting
4. Alfred	9. The
5. Athelstan	10. Edgar's

Using Capitals for Sentences and the Word *I*

Every sentence must begin with a capital letter. The word *I* must also be capitalized every time you use it.

Sentences The first word in a sentence must begin with a capital.

▶ KEY CONCEPT Capitalize the first word in declarative, interrogative, imperative, and exclamatory sentences. ■

DECLARATIVE:	Several members of the royal family were impatiently waiting for the ceremony to begin.
INTERROGATIVE:	Isn't anyone going to start?
IMPERATIVE:	Bow deeply when introduced to the Queen.
EXCLAMATORY:	What an unusual day this is!

There are also situations, especially in informal writing, in which only a part of a sentence is written out. A capital letter is still required for the first word in each partial sentence.

EXAMPLES:	Where?	For how much?	Never!

▶ Exercise 1 **Using Capitals to Begin Sentences** Copy the following items onto your paper, adding the missing capitals.

EXAMPLE:	what do you know about the kings of England?
ANSWER:	What do you know about the kings of England?

1. do you know who the first king of England was?
2. no, who was it?
3. after defeating the Mercians at the Battle of Ellandun, Egbert of Wessex became king in A.D. 825.
4. alfred the Great ruled all of England that wasn't occupied by the Danes in A.D. 886.
5. athelstan, the grandson of Alfred, was the first monarch to have his likeness officially reproduced on coins.
6. he was very much entitled to his reputation as a great warrior.
7. he defeated a combined force of Scots, Welsh, and Vikings in one battle.
8. collecting jewelry, art, and relics was how Athelstan liked to spend his social time.
9. the period from A.D. 959 to A.D. 975 was referred to as the reign of Edgar the Peaceable.
10. edgar's great-grandfather was Alfred the Great.

Theme: Great Britain

In this chapter, you will learn the rules of capitalization. The examples and exercises are about the history of Great Britain.

Cross-Curricular Connection: Social Studies

◉ Learn More

For additional information about capitalizing sentences, see Chapter 19: Basic Sentence Parts.

⏱ TIME AND RESOURCE MANAGER

Resources
Print: Grammar Exercise Workbook, pp. 175–186
Technology: Language Lab CD-ROM, Capitalization; On-Line Exercise Bank, Section 27

In-Depth Coverage	Accelerated Pace
• Work through all key concepts, pp. 636–648. • Assign and review Exercises 1–11.	• Assign pp. 636–648 for independent student review. • Assign Chapter Review Exercises 17.

The Word *I* The word *I* must be capitalized wherever it appears.

> **KEY CONCEPT** Always capitalize the word *I*. ∎

EXAMPLE: *I* watched the clock while *I* waited for you.

> **Exercise 2** Capitalizing the Word *I* Copy the following sentences, adding the missing capitals.

EXAMPLE: she and i have always been friends.
ANSWER: She and I have always been friends.

1. kelly and i are doing a report on Queen Victoria.
2. i didn't know she ruled for more than sixty-three years.
3. The Queen was rather stern, i think.
4. i learned that she was only eighteen years old when she became queen.
5. kelly asked if i could find more information on her nine children.

Using Capitals for Proper Nouns

An important use of capitals is to show that a word is a proper noun. It names a specific person, place, or thing.

> **KEY CONCEPT** Capitalize all proper nouns. ∎

Names of People The name of a specific person is perhaps the most common kind of proper noun.

> **KEY CONCEPT** Capitalize each part of a person's full name, including initials. ∎

EXAMPLES: Margaret Rose Windsor
             L. T. Cornwall

▶ **Critical Viewing** As a young woman, before being crowned Queen of England, what was most likely Victoria's title? How would you capitalize it? **[Speculate]**

Capitalization • **637**

> **More Practice**

Language Lab
CD-ROM
• Capitalization in Sentences lesson
On-line
Exercise Bank
• Chapter 27
Grammar Exercise Workbook
• pp. 175–176

Step-by-Step Teaching Guide continued

3. Write the following sentence on the board:

   I want to know more about the Boston Tea Party because i am interested in the Revolutionary War.

4. Ask students what is wrong with the sentence. (The word *i* needs to be capitalized.) Remind students that the word *I* is always capitalized regardless of its position in a sentence.

Answer Key

> **Exercise 2**

1. Kelly and I are doing a report on Queen Victoria.
2. I didn't know she ruled for more than sixty-three years.
3. The Queen was rather stern, I think.
4. I learned that she was only eighteen years old when she became queen.
5. Kelly asked if I could find more information on her nine children.

Step-by-Step Teaching Guide

Using Capitals for Proper Nouns

1. Write the following list on the chalkboard:

   person, city, holiday, ocean

2. Ask students to write the name of the first famous person, city, holiday, and ocean that they can think of. Ask several students to share their answers with the class, and write one for each category on the board.

3. Ask students to name the part of speech of the words on the board (nouns).

4. Explain that a proper noun names a specific person, place, or thing. Ask students to identify the pattern they see in how the words on the board are capitalized. (All of the proper nouns are capitalized while the common nouns are not.)

Critical Viewing

Speculate Students may suggest Princess Victoria. Explain that this is a title that is capitalized with a name.

Capitals for the Names of Geographical Places

1. Ask students to name the place in the world they would most like to study next in history.

2. Write several responses on the board and ask students what kind of nouns these are. (proper nouns)

3. Explain that the names of geographical places—that is, any places that can be found on a map—are proper nouns, so they are capitalized.

4. Ask students what kinds of geographical places can be found on a map. List them on the board and have students write an example of each.

   streets

   towns and cities

   countries

   continents

   mountains

   islands

   scenic spots

   bodies of water (lakes, bays, rivers)

5. Point out that the word for a general geographical feature is not capitalized (e.g., lake, river, mountain range). It is the names of individual features that are capitalized (e.g., Lake Michigan, Mississsippi River, Rocky Mountains).

Customize for
Visual/Spatial Learners

Provide students with outline maps of your state, with dots for major cities, lines for rivers, and so on. Ask students to label all of the geographical places shown on the map, using the correct rules for capitalization.

Integrating Writing Skills

Remind students to follow the rules of capitalization in all of their classes; not just English class. When writing about specific places and events in social studies, for example, they can refer to this textbook for answers to questions about capitalization.

27

Geographical Places The names of geographical places are also proper nouns.

▶ **KEY CONCEPT** Capitalize geographical names. ■

According to this rule, any place that can be found on a map should be capitalized. The following chart includes examples of different kinds of geographical names that need to be capitalized.

GEOGRAPHICAL NAMES	
Streets	Avenue of the Americas, Wildflower Drive
Towns and Cities Counties	Freeville, Youngstown, Cairo Dade County, Cook County
States and Provinces Nations Continents	Nebraska, Alberta India, Spain, United States of America North America, Antarctica, Asia
Valleys and Deserts Mountains	Death Valley, Kalahari Desert Cascade Range, Pike's Peak, Mount Everest
Sections of a Country Islands Scenic Spots	Gulf Coastal Plain, Northeast, South Corsica, Balearic Islands Grand Canyon, Riviera
Rivers and Falls Lakes and Bays Seas and Oceans	Danube, Colorado River, Victoria Falls Lake Champlain, Bay of Biscay Red Sea, Arctic Ocean

A compass point, such as south or northeast, is capitalized only when it names a specific geographical location. When a compass point refers to a direction, it is not capitalized.

EXAMPLES: The South is experiencing a serious drought.
Drive south for three miles, and you will arrive at the castle.

Technology Tip

Many towns and cities have Web sites that give information about the location's history, cultural events, and tourist attractions. Use the name of a place in a keyword search to get information about the place.

Other Proper Nouns Names of specific events and time periods also need to be capitalized.

▶ **KEY CONCEPT** Capitalize the names of specific events and periods of time. ■

The following chart contains examples of events and periods of time that require capitalization.

SPECIFIC EVENTS AND TIMES	
Historical Periods	Age of Enlightenment, Mesozoic Era, Middle Ages
Historical Events	World War II, Boston Tea Party
Documents	Declaration of Independence, Treaty of Paris
Days	Wednesday, Saturday
Months	December, October
Holidays	Washington's Birthday, Thanksgiving Day, Labor Day
Religious Days	Christmas, Passover, Ramadan
Special Events	Fiddlers' Convention, Boston Marathon

The names of seasons are an exception to the rule. Seasons of the year, despite the fact that they name a specific time of year, are not capitalized unless they are part of a title such as an event.

EXAMPLES: The most popular color this fall is rust.
This book is about a girl who travels in the summer.
Winter Carnival, Fall Fun Fair

Other proper nouns that need capitals are those that name specific groups.

▶ **KEY CONCEPT** Capitalize the names of various organizations, government bodies, political parties, and nationalities, as well as the languages spoken by different groups. ■

EXAMPLES: The ambassador attended the first session of the Austrian Parliament.
She delivered a brief address in German and received warm applause.

🔵 **Learn More**

For additional information about proper nouns, see Chapter 14.

Capitalization • **639**

Step-by-Step Teaching Guide

Capitals for the Names of Specific Events and Periods of Time

1. Write the following sentence on the chalkboard:

   In November next fall, my family will celebrate Veterans Day with my grandfather, who fought in World War II.

2. Ask students to identify all of the words that are capitalized in the sentence, *and* ask them why these words are capitalized. (They are all proper nouns.)

3. Explain that the names of specific events and periods of time are capitalized.

4. Direct students' attention to the word *fall* in the sentence on the board and explain that the names of seasons are not capitalized.

Step-by-Step Teaching Guide

Capitals for the Names of Various Organizations, Government Bodies, Political Parties, Races, and Nationalities

1. Explain to students that the names of organizations, government bodies, political parties, races, nationalities, and languages are capitalized.

2. Write the following sentence on the chalkboard:

   The members of the republican party met the leaders of the german government to discuss plans for the north atlantic treaty organization.

3. Ask students to identify the nouns in the sentence that need to be capitalized. (Republican Party, German, North Atlantic Treaty Organization)

Integrating Viewing and Representing Skills

Point out that on many maps, country names are written in all capitals, while city names follow the traditional style of capitalizing only the first letter. Ask students why mapmakers might choose to follow this style. (Students might say that this helps viewers distinguish between cities and countries.)

639

Capitals for References to Religions, Deities, and Religious Scriptures

1. Ask students to name all the religions they can think of. Write them on the board, capitalizing each.

2. Circle one religion about which students might have significant background knowledge.

3. Ask students to brainstorm a list of people, places, and things significant to this religion. Form a cluster or web on the board with the name of the religion in the center and students' responses on spokes.

4. When you have listed several words that need to be capitalized as well as several that don't need to be capitalized, stop and circle the capitalized nouns.

5. Ask students how these nouns differ from the other nouns listed. (These are proper nouns, so they are capitalized.)

6. Explain that names of religions, deities, and religious scriptures are capitalized.

Customize for
ESL Students

The rules of capitalization are not the same in languages other than English. For example, in French, Spanish, and Italian, the names of the languages would not be capitalized. Students not fluent in English may need both more examples and more practice covering what are considered proper nouns in English. You may wish to divide students into groups and have each group brainstorm for as many examples of each category of proper noun as possible. Have them share their answers with the class. This will make it easier for them to recognize those proper nouns when they read and write.

27

SPECIFIC GROUPS	
Clubs Organizations Institutions Businesses	Kiwanis Club National Governor's Association Massachusetts Institute of Technology Chemstrand Corporation
Government Bodies Political Parties	Congress, Supreme Court Democrats, Republican Party
Nationalities	Chinese, German, Nigerian, Iranian
Languages Spoken by Different Groups	English, Spanish, Italian, Swahili, Dutch

The proper nouns shown in the preceding chart are groups with which many people are familiar. All specific groups, however, must be capitalized, even if they are not well known.

In order to show respect, you should also use capitals for the names of the religions of the world and other related words.

▶ **KEY CONCEPT** Capitalize references to religions, deities, and religious scriptures. ■

The following chart presents a list of five of the world's major religions. Next to each religion are examples of some of the related religious words that you must be sure to capitalize in your writing.

RELIGIOUS REFERENCES	
Christianity	God, Lord, Father, Son, Holy Spirit, Bible, books of the Bible (Genesis, Deuteronomy, Psalms, and so on)
Judaism	God, Lord, Father, Prophets, Torah, Talmud, Midrash
Islam	Allah, Prophet, Mohammed, Koran
Hinduism	Brahma, Bhagavad Gita, Vedas
Buddhism	Buddha, Mahayana, Hinayana

Note in the following examples, however, that the words *god* and *goddess* in references to ancient mythology are not capitalized.

EXAMPLES: the god Jupiter
the goddess Juno

▶ **KEY CONCEPT** Capitalize the names of specific places and items. ■

This final rule applies to proper nouns such as monuments, memorials, buildings, celestial bodies, awards, the names of specific vehicles, and trademarks.

The following chart gives examples of some of these special places and items that you should capitalize in your writing.

OTHER SPECIAL PLACES AND ITEMS	
Monuments	Statue of Liberty
Memorials	Winston Churchill Memorial
Buildings	Houston Museum of Fine Arts, Empire State Building
Celestial Bodies *(except the moon and sun)*	Earth, Milky Way, Jupiter, Aries
Awards	Newbery Award, Nobel Peace Prize
Air, Sea, Space, and Land Craft	*Spirit of St. Louis, Monitor, Voyager 2*
Trademarks	Krazy Korn, Zenox

▶ **Exercise 3** **Capitalizing Proper Nouns** Each of the following sentences contains one or more names that need to be capitalized. On your paper, rewrite the names, adding the missing capitals.

EXAMPLE: chris, have you studied the life of King richard I?
ANSWER: Chris, Richard

1. Our class is studying richard the Lion-Hearted.
2. thomas told the class that richard I spent only seven months of his ten-year reign in england.
3. The class invited william r. taras to come and give a lecture on the king of england.
4. k. c. miller and marie lopez wondered where richard spent his years as king.
5. taras told us that besides spending a year on the Crusades, richard had been taken prisoner by the duke of Austria.

▶ **More Practice**

Language Lab CD-ROM
• Capitalization in Sentences lesson
• Proper Nouns lesson
On-line Exercise Bank
• Chapter 27
Grammar Exercise Workbook
• pp. 177–180

Step-by-Step Teaching Guide

Capitals for Names of Awards

1. Ask students why they think the names of awards are capitalized (they name specific things).

2. Have students name other awards with which they are familiar.

Answer Key

Exercise 4

1. Tower of London
2. Buckingham Palace, September, World War II
3. House of Commons, House of Lords
4. Whigs, Tories
5. Labor, Conservative

Exercise 5

1. Jerusalem
2. Acre, Palestine
3. Arsouf, Jaffa
4. Europe
5. France, Scotland

Critical Viewing

Relate Most students will suggest England and King Richard. Encourage more creative choices, too.

Language Highlight

Tell students that some brand-name products, such as Kleenex and Coke, have become so prevalent that we often think of them as common nouns. Remind students that these words are proper nouns and they must be capitalized. Challenge them to think of other examples.

KEY CONCEPT Capitalize the names of awards. ■

Notice in the following examples that *the* is not capitalized.

EXAMPLES: the Academy Awards, the Fulbright Scholarship, the Pulitzer Prize, Eagle Scout

Exercise 4 **Capitalizing Other Proper Names** Each of the following sentences contains one or more proper nouns that need to be capitalized. On your paper, rewrite the proper nouns, adding the missing capitals.

EXAMPLE: Jane Addams won the nobel peace prize in 1931.
ANSWER: Nobel Peace Prize

1. During our trip to England, we learned a great deal about the country's history, and we even visited the tower of london.
2. We also visited buckingham palace and learned that it had been bombed on september 12, 1940, during world war II.
3. We also visited the house of commons and the house of lords, where Britain's political officers meet.
4. The two major political parties in the early nineteenth century were called whigs and tories.
5. By the second half of the century, the party names were changed to labor and conservative.

Exercise 5 **Using Capitals for Geographical Names** Rewrite each geographical name, adding the missing capitals.

EXAMPLE: The capital of england is london.
ANSWER: England, London

1. Richard I set off to recapture the holy city jerusalem from the Muslim leader Saladin.
2. He demolished Saladin's forces at acre, in palestine.
3. He also defeated Saladin at arsouf, near jaffa.
4. On his way home through europe, the duke of Austria captured Richard.
5. John, who became king after Richard was killed, was constantly at war with france, scotland, and his own people.

▼ Critical Viewing What word or words would you capitalize in a sentence about the country King Richard ruled? **[Relate]**

TIME SAVERS!

Answers on Transparency Use the Grammar Exercises Answers on Transparencies for Chapter 27 to facilitate correction by students.

On-Line Exercise Bank Have students complete the exercises on computer. The Auto Check feature will grade their work for you!

Using Capitals
for Proper Adjectives

When a proper noun or a form of a proper noun is used to describe another noun, it is a proper adjective. As a proper adjective, it will generally need a capital.

KEY CONCEPT Capitalize most proper adjectives. ■

EXAMPLES: Arabian stallion   Spanish rice
               Senatorial candidate   British monarch

Many proper adjectives are formed from the brand names of products.

KEY CONCEPT Capitalize brand names used as adjectives. ■

EXAMPLES: Clearbright paint   Quickgrow grass seed

Exercise 6 Supplying Proper Adjectives On your paper, write a meaningful proper adjective to complete each of the following phrases. Be sure to capitalize the phrases correctly.

EXAMPLE: fashions
ANSWER: French fashions

1. __?__ shampoo   6. __?__ margarine
2. __?__ meatballs 7. __?__ music
3. __?__ imports   8. __?__ television
4. __?__ designer   9. __?__ potatoes
5. __?__ bread   10. __?__ cameras

Exercise 7 Capitalizing Proper Adjectives Capitalize the proper adjectives in the following sentences.
1. English artists were influenced by the italian artists of the fourteenth century.
2. Many works of art are on display at the tate Gallery in London.
3. We met french-, german-, and spanish-speaking visitors at the museum.
4. The elizabethan age brought about many changes in architecture.
5. The influences of european artists and architects can be seen in american art, as well.

More Practice
Language Lab
CD-ROM
• Proper Nouns and
  Proper Adjectives
  lesson
On-line
Exercise Bank
• Chapter 27
Grammar Exercise
Workbook
• pp. 181–182

Using Capitals for Proper Adjectives

1. Ask students what type of food they like best. Write their responses on the board in columns based on whether students describe food by ethnicity or taste. (If students don't identify food in one of the categories, list some for them.)

   Mexican food   *healthy food*
   Italian food   *spicy food*

2. Ask students what the difference is between the kinds of food listed in the right column and those listed in the left.

3. Explain that proper nouns that are used to describe other nouns, like the ones used to describe the food in the left column, are called proper adjectives. Point out that these kinds of adjectives usually are capitalized.

Answer Key

Exercise 6

Answers will vary. Samples are given.

1. Shine-ee shampoo
2. Swedish meatballs
3. German imports
4. Italian designer
5. French bread
6. Econospread margarine
7. Spanish music
8. American television
9. Idaho potatoes
10. Japanese cameras

Exercise 7

1. Italian
2. Tate
3. French-, German-, Spanish-
4. Elizabethan Age
5. European, American

Customize for
ESL Students

In English, adjectives usually precede nouns: French bread, lively puppy, ugly warthog. In some languages, however, adjectives follow nouns. Point out this difference and provide extra practice by giving students adjective-noun phrases and having them point to and name the part of speech of each word.

ONGOING ASSESSMENT: Monitor and Reinforce

If students have difficulty with Exercises 1–7, refer them to the following for additional practice.

In the Textbook	Print Resources	Technology
Section Review, Ex. 12–14, p. 650	Grammar Exercise Workbook, pp. 175–182	Language Lab CD-ROM, Capitalization, On-Line Exercise Bank, Ch. 27

Using Capitals for Titles of People

1. Write the following sentences on the board.

   When <u>Professor</u> Smith arrived for class on the day of the exam, one student asked, "Professor, will you tell us what's on the test?"

   The <u>professor</u> smiled and said no.

2. Explain why *professor* is capitalized twice in the first sentence but not in the second sentence: Titles are capitalized only when they are followed by the person's name, when they are used in a direct address, or when they are used as appositives.

3. Tell students that sometimes, to show respect for certain positions, a title will be capitalized for that position even when it is not followed by a name, such as the President of the United States, the Queen of England, etc.

Integrating Workplace Skills

In business, it is sometimes correct to break the rule about not capitalizing a person's title if the title stands alone. When writing business letters or memos, it is common to put a person's title after his or her name and to capitalize it:

   John Woo, Director

   Juanita Mendoza, Manager

Tell students that this is polite and shows respect for the person.

Grammar in Literature

1. Have a volunteer read aloud the excerpt from "King Arthur: The Marvel of the Sword."

2. Have students make a two-column chart in their notebooks. On the left, have them list all the common nouns in the passage. On the right, have them list all the proper nouns.

3. For each proper noun, have them point out the rule that explains why it is capitalized.

Using Capitals for Titles of People

Two major rules govern capitals in people's titles.

Social and Processional Titles One rule covers titles used before names and in direct address.

▶ **KEY CONCEPT** Capitalize the title of a person when the title is followed by the person's name, when it is used in place of a person's name, or when it is used as an appositive. ■

The following chart shows several common titles.

TITLES OF PEOPLE	
Social	Mister, Madam or Madame, Miss, Sir
Business	Doctor, Professor, Superintendent
Religious	Reverend, Father, Rabbi, Bishop, Sister
Military	Private, Ensign, Captain, General, Admiral
Government	President, Secretary of State, Ambassador, Senator, Representative, Governor, Mayor

The following examples show four titles in use.

BEFORE A NAME:	Detective O'Toole, Major Faulks, and Doctor Perkins have arrived.
IN DIRECT ADDRESS:	Look, Sergeant, the fingerprints match!
AS AN APPOSITIVE:	Charles, Prince of Wales, has arrived.

GRAMMAR IN LITERATURE

from King Arthur: The Marvel of the Sword
Mary MacLeod

Notice how capital letters are used with proper nouns that name people, places, and things in this passage.

When several years had passed, Merlin went to the Archbishop of Canterbury and counseled him to send for all the lords of the realm, and all the gentlemen of arms, that they should come to London at Christmas, and for this cause—that a miracle would show who should be rightly king of the realm.

644 • Capitalization

When writing names with numerals, such as King George I or John Smith III, always use Roman numerals, not Arabic numerals.

Connections With Literature

Students can read Mary MacLeod's "King Arthur: The Marvel of the Sword" in *Prentice Hall Literature: Timeless Voices, Timeless Themes,* Bronze level.

▶ **Exercise 8** Using Capitals for Social and Professional

Titles Each of the following sentences contains a title before a name, in direct address, or as an appositive. Rewrite each title, adding the missing capital.

EXAMPLE: A monarch I recently studied was queen Elizabeth.
ANSWER: Queen

1. One day I said to my teacher, "Tell me, professor Holmes, who in the royal family interests you most?"
2. She told me about prince Charles.
3. Even when king George VI ruled, prime minister Winston Churchill was a government leader.
4. It was sir Winston Churchill who was prime minister during World War II.
5. One of the famous military leaders of England during World War II was general Montgomery.
6. During talks at Yalta, president Roosevelt, prime minister Churchill, and premier Joseph Stalin of Russia discussed ways to end the war.
7. Today, queen Elizabeth dedicates many hours to charitable organizations.
8. In 1996, her daughter, princess Anne, had no fewer than 609 public engagements for charitable events.
9. Queen Elizabeth's son Charles, prince of wales, also champions a number of national and world causes.
10. Charles's older son, prince William, was christened by the archbishop of Canterbury.

Titles for Family Relationships Another rule applies to titles for family relationships.

▶ **KEY CONCEPT** Capitalize titles showing family relationships when the title is used with the person's name or as the person's name. The title may also be capitalized in other situations when it refers to a specific person, except when the title comes after a possessive noun or pronoun. ■

BEFORE A NAME:	We respect Uncle Frank's opinion.
IN PLACE OF A NAME:	We haven't seen Grandmother in almost a year.
AFTER POSSESSIVES:	Alan's father is the team's captain. No one knew my sister better.

Notice that the titles used in the last two examples are not capitalized because they are used after the possessive words *Alan's* and *my.*

▶ **More Practice**

Language Lab
CD-ROM
• Capitalization lesson
On-line
Exercise Bank
• Chapter 27
Grammar Exercise
Workbook
• pp. 183–184

▲ Critical Viewing
By what title might average English people address this woman? How would she be addressed by Princess Anne or by Prince William? **[Compare]**

Answer Key

▶ **Exercise 8**

1. Professor
2. Prince
3. King, Prime Minister
4. Sir
5. General
6. President, Prime Minister, Premier
7. Queen
8. Princess
9. Prince of Wales
10. Prince, Archbishop

Real-World Connection

Show students newspaper or magazine articles that capitalize stand-alone titles of people. Explain that different publications have a "house style," that is, their own preferred way of capitalizing. This is acceptable, as long as they follow their rules consistently.

Critical Viewing

Compare Most students will recognize Queen Elizabeth. She would be addressed as "Your Royal Majesty." Princess Anne is her daughter and would refer to her as Mother; Prince William is her grandson and would refer to her as Grandmother.

▶ *Step-by-Step Teaching Guide*

Titles for Family Relationships

1. Ask volunteers to write on the board a sentence describing something about one of their favorite relatives.
2. Have students point out all of the instances in which a title is used to show a family relationship. Underline these words as students point them out. For example:

   My <u>brother</u> is an excellent guitar player.

   <u>Uncle Bob</u> always makes the best chicken.
3. Explain that titles showing family relationships are capitalized when the title is used with the person's name, when it is used to refer to a specific person, and when it is used in a direct address. Titles referring to a specific person that follow a possessive noun or pronoun are not capitalized.

Answer Key

Critical Viewing

Speculate Expect students to recognize the military dress, medals, and ribbons and suggest military titles for the men in the foreground. Some may realize that this kind of reception would be given to members of the royal family. Family titles might include Mother, Father, Uncle, Aunt, etc.

Exercise 9 **Using Capitals for Family Titles** If a title in a sentence lacks a capital or if a title has been incorrectly capitalized, rewrite the title on your paper, correcting the error. If the sentence contains no error, write *correct*.

EXAMPLE: My sister and I are interested in British royalty.

ANSWER: correct

1. Do you like studying British royalty, mom?
2. No, but aunt Margaret enjoys it.
3. Her grandfather came from England.
4. Naturally, she and uncle Harold studied British history.
5. Their Mother met Lady Seymour.
6. Mother Stewart met her at a charity dinner.
7. Was your cousin Charles also at that dinner?
8. Did your Brother ever meet any royalty?
9. No, but his Sister-in-Law saw Prince William at a soccer tournament.
10. Sarah, my Grandmother, has this all written down in her personal journal.

▼ **Critical Viewing** What family and professional titles might some of the people in this picture have? How would you capitalize the titles? **[Speculate]**

✏ **STANDARDIZED TEST PREPARATION WORKSHOP**

Grammar and Usage Standardized tests often require students to identify correctly capitalized sentences. Ask students to choose the correctly capitalized version of the following sentence.

I called, "Hi, doctor" when I saw doctor jones, who was headed for a doctors' convention.

A I called, "Hi, Doctor" when I saw Doctor Jones, who was headed for a doctors' convention.

B I called, "Hi, Doctor" when I saw Doctor Jones, who was headed for a Doctors' convention.

C I called, "Hi, doctor" when I saw doctor Jones, who was headed for a doctors' convention.

The correct answer is item **A** because the title "doctor" is used with a person's name or in place of a person's name in the first two occurrences, but not in the third.

Using Capitals for Titles of Things

Titles of certain things require capitals also.

Written Works and Works of Art The titles of different kinds of written works and works of art must always be capitalized.

> **KEY CONCEPT** Capitalize the first word and all other important words in the titles of books, periodicals, poems, stories, plays, paintings, and other works of art. ■

Each word in a title of this kind should begin with a capital except for the articles (*a, an, the*). Articles and short prepositions or conjunctions should be capitalized only when they are used as the first or last word in a title.

EXAMPLES: A Separate Peace
Press and Sun-Bulletin
Young Woman With a Water Jug
"The Man That Corrupted Hadleyburg"

> **Exercise 10** **Using Capitals for Written Works and Works of Art** Rewrite each of the following titles, adding the missing capitals.

EXAMPLE: "of missing persons"
ANSWER: "Of Missing Persons"

1. first knight	(movie)
2. "the wanderer"	(poem)
3. you come too	(book)
4. oliver twist	(book/movie)
5. effect of the sun on the water	(painting)
6. kidnapped	(book)
7. "pomp and circumstance"	(musical work)
8. the shrimp girl	(painting)
9. "the cat who thought she was a dog and the dog who thought he was a cat"	(short story)
10. the adventures of ulysses	(book)

School Courses The titles of certain courses must also be capitalized.

> **KEY CONCEPT** Capitalize the title of a course when the course is a language or when the course is followed by a number. ■

EXAMPLES: French   History 3A   Math 203

Learn More

To practice responding to capitalization items in a standardized test format, use the Standardized Test Preparation Workshop on pages 652–653.

Step-by-Step Teaching Guide

Capitals for Written Works and Works of Art

1. Write the following list on the chalkboard:

   book, painting, magazine, song

2. Ask students to write an example of each of these. For example:

   book *The Call of the Wild*

   painting *Mona Lisa*

   magazine *Newsweek*

   song "The Star-Spangled Banner"

3. Ask students to name the difference between the nouns on the right and the nouns on the left. (The nouns on the right are specific examples of the nouns on the left; they are proper nouns.)

4. Explain that the titles of different written works and works of art are capitalized. However, articles, prepositions, and conjunctions of fewer than four letters are not capitalized in titles unless they are the first word.

Step-by-Step Teaching Guide

Capitals for School Courses

1. Write the names of the following courses on the board in two columns.

French	*French 102*
history	*History 150*
biology	*Biology 150*
German	*German 100*
math	*Math 400*

2. Tell students that the courses on the right all have numbers after them, indicating that they are specific courses. This makes them proper nouns, so they must be capitalized.

3. Direct students' attention to the courses on the left. These courses do not have numbers; however, some of them are capitalized because they are proper adjectives.

Answer Key

> **Exercise 10**

1. First Knight
2. "The Wanderer"
3. You Come Too
4. Oliver Twist
5. Effect of the Sun on the Water
6. Kidnapped
7. "Pomp and Circumstance"
8. The Shrimp Girl
9. "The Cat Who Thought She Was a Dog and the Dog Who Thought He Was a Cat"
10. The Adventures of Ulysses

Answer Key

1. History I
2. French
3. calculus
4. Drama I
5. Latin

Critical Viewing

Apply Students may say that they are performing an electrical experiment in Science II.

Customize for
Interpersonal Learners

Small groups of students can play "round-robin titles." Each student labels a piece of paper with a different category, such as book title, movie, song, story, art, and writes a title. Students pass their papers clockwise. The recipient checks the previous title for correct capitalization and adds a new title. If the capitalization is wrong, that student is out. Play continues until there is only one student left.

▲ **Critical Viewing** What subject is being studied by the students in this picture? Give an example of a sentence in which the name of the subject would be capitalized. **[Apply]**

▶ **Exercise 11** **Using Capitals for Courses** In each of the following sentences, choose the correctly written course title from the choices in parentheses and write it on your paper.

EXAMPLE: Lisa is a student in my (algebra, Algebra) class.
ANSWER: algebra

1. While studying (history I, History I), I became interested in English royalty.
2. Most royal children were required to learn (french, French), as well as other foreign languages.
3. Prince Charles studied (calculus, Calculus) at the Naval Academy.
4. Shakespeare's plays are studied today in (drama I, Drama I) classes.
5. The study of (Latin, latin) is beneficial for students studying biology and other sciences.

▶ **More Practice**

Language Lab
CD-ROM
• Capitalization lesson
On-line
Exercise Bank
• Chapter 27
Grammar Exercise
Workbook
• pp. 185–186

648 • Capitalization

✓ ONGOING ASSESSMENT: Monitor and Reinforce

If students have difficulty with Exercises 8–11, refer them to the following for additional practice.

In the Textbook	Print Resources	Technology
Chapter Review, Ex. 15–17	Grammar Exercise Workbook, pp. 183–186	Language Lab CD-ROM, Capitalization; On-Line Exercise Bank, Ch. 27

Hands-on Grammar

Capitals Card Catalog

Help yourself remember the categories of words that are capitalized by creating a Capitals Card Catalog based on the word *capitals*.

For each letter in C A P I T A L S, cut out several large squares. Use paper of a different color for each letter, or use markers to draw a different colored border for each letter. Next, print one letter of CAPITALS in the middle of each of eight squares. Then, on a square matching the color for each letter, write the categories shown on the examples below. Finally, write several examples of capitalized words beneath each category.

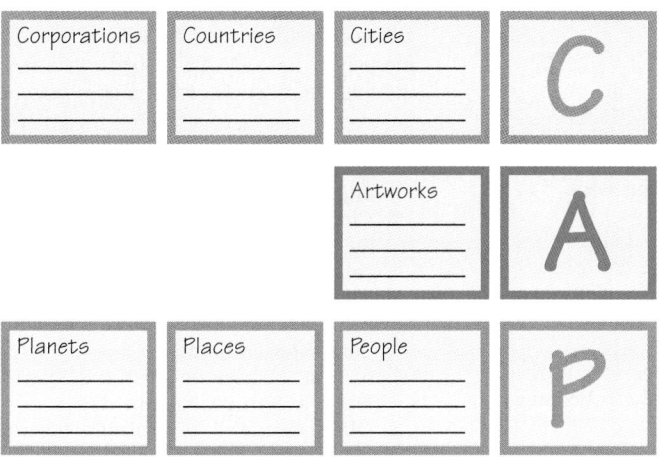

Continue making cards for the remaining letters, using these categories: **I**—The pronoun *I*, Institutions; **T**—Titles, Trademarks, Times of the year (months, days, holidays); **A**—Abbreviations, Adjectives (proper); **L**—Languages; **S**—States, Specific groups, Sentence beginnings. If you think of other categories for a letter, make additional cards.

Find It in Your Reading Look through a story or piece of nonfiction in your literature book, and see how many capitalized words you can find that fit into the categories in your Capitals Card Catalog. Add several of the words to your cards.

Find It in Your Writing Review an essay in your portfolio, and note where you used capital letters. Are they used correctly? Into which categories do they fit? Add several of the words to your Capitals Card Catalog.

Capitalization • **649**

Capitals Card Catalog

Teaching Resources: Hands-on Grammar Activity Book, Chapter 27

1. Have students refer to their Hands-on Grammar Activity books or give them copies of the relevant pages for this activity.

2. Remind students that not all words that fall into a category are capitalized. They must be proper nouns, not common nouns.

3. Some students may suggest categories that do not begin with one of the letters in *capitals*. Tell them these are valid choices but not for this activity.

4. Be sure that students have at least one category for each letter.

Find It in Your Reading

You may want to divide students into teams and assign each team one or two categories.

Find It in Your Writing

Allow students to use letters not in the word *capitals* if they wish for this exercise.

☑ ONGOING ASSESSMENT: Assess Mastery

Use the following resources to assess student mastery of capitalization.

In the Text	Technology
Chapter Review, Ex. 12–17, pp. 650–651 Standardized Test Preparation Workshop, pp. 652–653	On-Line Exercise Bank, Section 27

⊘ TIME SAVERS!

Hands-on Grammar
Use the Hands-on Grammar activity sheet for Chapter 27 to facilitate this activity.

CHAPTER REVIEW

Each exercise correlates with a concept in the chapter on capitalization, pages 636–649. The exercises may be used for more practice, for reteaching, or for review of the Key Concepts presented.

Answer Key

▶ **Exercise 12**

1. The
2. The Honorable
3. Lady
4. World
5. Her
6. Elizabeth
7. In
8. She
9. In
10. After

▶ **Exercise 13**

1. France, North Sea, Great Britain
2. Thames River, London
3. London, Stratford-on-Avon
4. Canterbury, Gloucester
5. Pennines, England

▶ **Exercise 14**

1. England
2. Parliament, Church of England
3. Parliament's, Parliament
4. Charles, Parliament
5. Cromwell, Huntingdon, Parliament's, Marston Moor, Naseby

▶ **Exercise 15**

1. Princess
2. *The Toronto Star*
3. Duke
4. Rail Canada
5. correct
6. Mayor
7. correct
8. royal visit, "O Canada," "Hail, Britannia"
9. correct
10. correct

GRAMMAR EXERCISES 12–19

▶ **Exercise 12** **Using Capitals to Begin Sentences** Copy any items onto your paper that require capital letters. Add the missing capitals.

1. the Queen Mother was born August 4, 1900.
2. the honorable Elizabeth Angela Marguerite Bowes-Lyon spent her childhood in Hertfordshire.
3. lady Elizabeth could speak fluent French by the age of ten.
4. world War I broke out on her fourteenth birthday.
5. her family's home was used as a hospital.
6. elizabeth and her older sisters were childhood friends of George V's children.
7. in January of 1923, she became engaged to Albert, Duke of York, second son of the king and queen.
8. she was married in Westminster Abbey on April 26, 1923.
9. in 1936, Albert ascended to the throne as George VI, and Elizabeth became queen.
10. after George VI died in 1952, his daughter Elizabeth became queen.

▶ **Exercise 13** **Capitalizing Geographical Names** Each of the following sentences contains one or more geographical names that need to be capitalized. On your paper, rewrite the names, adding the missing capitals.

1. Last summer, after we visited france, we decided to cross the north sea and visit great britain.
2. As we traveled up the thames river, we saw our first glimpse of the city of london.
3. We would be in london for only two

days before we traveled north to stratford-on-avon.
4. Also on the list of places to visit were canterbury, gloucester, and other cathedral towns.
5. The pennines, a mountain range in northern and central england, is the industrial center of the country.

▶ **Exercise 14** **Capitalizing Other Proper Nouns and Adjectives** Correct the proper nouns and proper adjectives in the following sentences. If a sentence has no errors, write *correct*.

1. A civil war was fought to decide who should rule england.
2. Charles I and parliament could not agree about how money should be raised for the church of england.
3. Charles failed to get parliament's consent, and so many townspeople supported parliament.
4. At first, charles had better soldiers and leaders than parliament did.
5. Oliver cromwell, a huntingdon gentleman, reorganized the parliament's forces and defeated the King at marston moor and naseby.

▶ **Exercise 15** **Using Capitals for Titles of People, Works, and Things** Capitalize and lowercase titles as needed in the following sentences.

1. On October 10, 1951, princess Elizabeth visited Canada.
2. Her visit was reported in all the major newspapers, including *the toronto star*.
3. Her husband, the duke of Edinburgh, made the trip with her.
4. Although the public train service, run by rail canada, is extensive, the duke

and princess traveled by private car.

5. The princess and duke made their television debut while there.

6. Windsor's mayor Cabot appeared with them.

7. Among the welcoming party was the mayor of Detroit.

8. Two songs that were often played during the Royal Visit were "o canada" and "hail, britannia."

9. Canada is home to many fine writers, including author Margaret Atwood.

10. Atwood's novel *The Robber Bride* is set in Toronto.

Exercise 16 Proofreading Sentences to Eliminate Errors in Capitalization Rewrite the sentences, adding or changing capitals as needed. If the sentence has no errors, write *correct*.

1. Last month, i read a book about Prince Charles.

2. I learned that he was born November 14, 1948.

3. he became heir apparent and the duke of Cornwall when his mother became Queen.

4. My sister, Kiera, asked if i knew where he went to school.

5. I told her he went to Cheam and Gordonstoun.

6. she wondered if he also went to school in australia.

7. in my reading, i learned that he had gone to school in melbourne.

8. this was the first time a Royal Family member had attended an overseas school.

9. cambridge university was where charles studied Archaeology.

10. He graduated from Cambridge in 1970.

Exercise 17 Proofreading a Paragraph to Eliminate Capitalization Errors Find the capitalization errors in the following paragraph, and write them on your paper, capitalizing correctly.

(1) in History class, i learned that princess Anne was the second child of queen Elizabeth. (2) she was born august 15, 1950, at clarence house in london. (3) at the age of twelve, she went to france to live for one year. (4) the Professor told my friend and me about her engagement to captain mark phillips. (5) he was a member of the dragoon guards. (6) on november 14, 1973, they were married. (7) i told the professor i had some pictures of their wedding. (8) princess Anne and captain Phillips had two children. (9) while doing this research, i found information about her charity work. (10) she spends long hours raising money for many charities.

Exercise 18 Writing Application
Write a short narrative story about your favorite vacation. Be sure to capitalize all the place names correctly.

Exercise 19 Writing Application
Write an ad for a grocery store, advertising five different products that are on sale. Be sure to use brand names and to capitalize brand names correctly.

Exercise 16

1. Last month I read a book about Prince Charles.
2. correct
3. He became heir apparent and the duke of Cornwall when his mother became queen.
4. My sister, Kiera, asked if I knew where he went to school.
5. correct
6. She wondered if he also went to school in Australia.
7. In my reading, I learned that he had gone to school in Melbourne.
8. This was the first time a royal family member had attended an overseas school.
9. Cambridge University was where Charles studied archaeology.
10. correct

Exercise 17

1. In, history, I, Princess, Queen
2. She, August, Clarence House, London
3. At, France
4. The, professor, Captain Mark Phillips
5. He, Dragoon Guards
6. On, November
7. I, I
8. Princess, Captain
9. While, I
10. She

Exercise 18

Writing Application
Students can rewrite their narratives without capital letters and challenge a partner to correct the usage errors.

Exercise 19

Writing Application
Have students check each other's ads for correct capitalization.

651

Proofreading for Spelling, Capitalization, and Punctuation Errors

Many standardized tests measure your ability to recognize errors within the context of a written passage. Often, a written passage is provided for you to proofread. Then, you will be asked to identify the type of error, if any. The following sample items will give you practice in responding to these types of test items

Sample Test Items	Answers and Explanations
Directions Read the passage, and decide which type of error, if any, appears in each underlined section. Sharon <u>glanced at her Aunt. Together,</u> (1) they had planned this surprise birthday party, and now it was time! As they waited for Uncle Bob to open the door, <u>they heard only</u> <u>the shufling feet of a few guests.</u> (2) 1 A Spelling error B Capitalization error C Punctuation error D No error	The correct answer is *B. Aunt* should not be capitalized because it is preceded by a possessive. Words designating family members are capitalized only when they are used in direct address (Are you ready, *Aunt*?), with the person's name (Is *Uncle Louis* ready?), or when used alone (Is *Mother* ready?).
2 F Spelling error G Capitalization error H Punctuation error J No error	The correct answer is *F.* There should be two *f*s in *shuffling*.

TEST-TAKING TIP

Because these types of standardized test questions require students to utilize three separate elements—spelling, capitalization, and punctuation—they may feel overwhelmed. Explain to students that it will help to first read the passage for sense. Then students can carefully go through the passage checking that all the words are spelled correctly. Next, they can check for proper capitalization of words. Finally, students can check the punctuation in the passage to see if there are any errors.

Practice 1 **Directions:** Read the passage and decide which type of error, if any, appears in each underlined section.

When *The Saturday Evening Post* a
_____
(1)
popular magazine was purchased by Cyrus
_____

Curtis in 1897, it contained only sixteen

unnillustrated pages and had a circula-
_____
(2)
tion of just 2,000. Over the years, the

Magazine shifted its focus from business
_____
(3)
to articles of general interest. Lively cover

illustrations were created by noteworthy
_____

artists; including Norman Rockwell.
_____
(4)

1 **A** Spelling error
   B Capitalization error
   C Punctuation error
   D No error

2 **F** Spelling error
   G Capitalization error
   H Punctuation error
   J No error

3 **A** Spelling error
   B Capitalization error
   C Punctuation error
   D No error

4 **F** Spelling error
   G Capitalization error
   H Punctuation error
   J No error

Practice 2 **Directions:** Read the passage and decide which type of error, if any, appears in each underlined section.

The city of Tenochtitlán began on an
_____
(1)
island in the middle of a swampy lake.
_____

There, the aztecs built their first temple.
_____
(2)
The city began to grow impressively after
_____
(3)
1385, when Acamapichtli was the King.

The European Bernal Díaz wrote "These
_____
towns and buildings rising from the water
_____
(4)
seemed like an enchanted vision."

1 **A** Spelling error
   B Capitalization error
   C Punctuation error
   D No error

2 **F** Spelling error
   G Capitalization error
   H Punctuation error
   J No error

3 **A** Spelling error
   B Capitalization error
   C Punctuation error
   D No error

4 **F** Spelling error
   G Capitalization error
   H Punctuation error
   J No error

Practice 1
1. C
2. F
3. B
4. H

Practice 2
1. D
2. G
3. B
4. H

Answer Key

> **Exercise 1**

1. There is an old palace located in the heart of Venice, Italy.
2. Called the Doges' Palace, it was the residence of the elected rulers.
3. The waterfront portion was built in 1340; the great balcony was added in 1404.
4. Whose paintings cover the inner waiting room, the Hall of the Cabinet, and the Hall of the Senate?
5. Many rooms and ceilings were decorated by these Italian painters: Tintoretto, Bellini, and Tiepolo.
6. The palace contained offices, meeting rooms, and law courts.
7. It also served as a prison, and it even held the famous Casanova.
8. Wow! You mean the notorious Italian adventurer?
9. The Doges' Palace is connected to the New Prisons by a small stone bridge, the Bridge of Sighs.
10. Do you know the origin of the bridge's name?

> **Exercise 2**

1. Did you hear the guide say, "Windsor Castle is the primary residence of British kings and queens"?
2. Begun in 1474, Saint George's Chapel was completed by King Henry VIII in 1528.
3. Tradition says that the Round Tower is built on the site where King Arthur's Knights of the Round Table met.
4. Valuable paintings, statues, and decorations are found in these state apartments: Saint George's Hall, the Waterloo Chamber, and the Throne Room.
5. Old Windsor was home to the Anglo-Saxon kings; in fact, William the Conqueror built a castle nearby.
6. Is that where Edward III met with the Knights of the Garter?
7. Leading from Home Park to Great Park, the tree-lined road is more than three miles long.
8. Did you know there was a very destructive fire there in 1992?
9. What! I can't believe it.

Cumulative Review

MECHANICS

> **Exercise 1** Proofreading Sentences to Correct Errors in End Marks, Commas, Semicolons, and Colons
Proofread the following sentences, inserting end marks, commas, semicolons, and colons where necessary. Eliminate unnecessary punctuation. Some items are questions.

1. There is an old palace located in the heart of Venice Italy
2. Called the Doges' Palace it was the residence of the elected rulers
3. The waterfront portion was built in 1340 the great balcony was added in 1404
4. Whose paintings cover the inner waiting room the Hall of the Cabinet, and the Hall of the Senate
5. Many rooms and ceilings were decorated by these Italian painters Tintoretto Bellini and Tiepolo
6. The palace contained offices meeting rooms and law courts
7. It also served as a prison: and it even held the famous Casanova
8. Wow You mean the notorious Italian adventurer
9. The Doges' Palace is connected to the New Prisons by a small stone bridge the Bridge of Sighs
10. Do you know the origin of the bridge's name

> **Exercise 2** Proofreading Sentences for All the Rules of Punctuation
Proofread the following sentences. Correct all punctuation errors. In the first sentence, the guide's words are directly quoted. Some items are questions.

1. Did you hear the guide say Windsor Castle is the primary residence of British kings and queens
2. Begun in 1474 Saint Georges Chapel

was completed by King Henry VIII in 1528
3. Tradition says that the Round Tower is built on the site where King Arthurs Knights of the Round Table met
4. Valuable paintings statues and decorations are found in these state apartments Saint George's Hall the Waterloo Chamber and the Throne Room
5. Old Windsor was home to the Anglo Saxon kings in fact William the Conqueror built a castle nearby
6. Is that where Edward III met with the Knights of the Garter
7. Leading from Home Park to Great Park the tree lined road is more than three miles long
8. Did you know there was a very destructive fire there in 1992
9. What I cant believe it
10. An article in the International Herald Tribune said it destroyed Saint George's Hall and the Waterloo Chamber.

> **Exercise 3** Proofreading a Page to Correct Punctuation Errors Proofread these paragraphs, supplying missing punctuation and correcting errors in usage of end marks, commas, semicolons, quotation marks, hyphens, and apostrophes.

Neuschwanstein Castle in Germany is one of the worlds best known castles? With it's turrets and tall archways; it looks like a medieval castle As a friend of mine who visited it exclaimed This castle is a real fairy-tale fantasy come true

It sits high on a hilltop overlooking the Alps, and a deep gorge. The castle was built between—1869 and 1886—for King Ludwig II. The room's feature murals and detailed carvings. The woodcarving in Ludwigs bedroom took four-teen carpen-

---

10. An article in the *International Herald Tribune* said it destroyed Saint George's Hall and the Waterloo Chamber.

> **Exercise 3**

Neuschwanstein Castle in Germany is one of the world's best-known castles. With its turrets and tall archways, it looks like a medieval castle. As a friend of mine who visited it exclaimed, "This castle is a real fairy-tale fantasy come true!"

It sits high on a hilltop overlooking the Alps and a deep gorge. The castle was built between 1869 and 1886 for King Ludwig II. The rooms feature murals and detailed carvings. The woodcarving in Ludwig's bedroom took fourteen carpenters 4 1/2 years to complete. Do you think you can pronounce *Neuschwanstein*?

ters 4 1/2 years to complete Do you think you can pronounce *Neuschwanstein.*

Exercise 4 Proofreading to Correct Errors in Capitalization
Revise the following sentences, adding the missing capital letters.

1. castles in europe developed from the ancient roman idea of walled cities.
2. from spain to transylvania, castles were almost always built for defensive purposes.
3. the word *castle* also refers to large residences like william randolph hearst's castle in san simeon, california.
4. the area of nairnshire in northern scotland is well known for cawdor castle.
5. segovia, spain, located on the eresma river, is known for the alcazar, a famous castle.
6. in torun, poland, there are the ruins of a castle of ancient knights.
7. the wittelsbach family, a german dynasty, took their name from their castle in bavaria.
8. one wittelsbach was count otto vi, who served the emperor frederick I; he was made a duke in 1180.
9. in 1020 bishop werner built habsburg castle on the aare river.
10. later divided into the austrian and spanish branches, the habsburg family ruled in europe for hundreds of years.
11. a result of world war I was the banishment of emperor charles I.
12. in england, king george III bought buckingham palace but sometimes lived at saint james's palace.
13. another castle, balmoral castle, is the british royal residence in scotland.
14. in central japan, the city of osaka features a park built on the site of a sixteenth-century castle.
15. on an island near tokyo, iwatsuki is a castle town that was founded in 1458.

Exercise 5 Revision Practice:
Dialogue Write the following sentences as a dialogue, inserting the proper capitalization and punctuation, and beginning a new paragraph with each new speaker.

stan i just read a book about castles but im confused about the difference between a castle and a palace said rebecca
from what i remember from history class replied stan castles used to be the same as fortresses
kate added oh like the tower of london where they kept prisoners
right you must have read shakespeares *richard III* exclaimed stan
richard put prisoners in the tower added kate
thats true said stan however british royalty lived in the tower of london until the time of queen elizabeth I
wait a second kate said i saw the movie *elizabeth* but i dont remember the name of her castle
stan replied as time went on, *castle* came to mean the same thing as a large mansion
i think i see said kate some palaces were originally fortresses and were rebuilt as luxurious resorts
buckingham palace was built only as a residence but never to be a safe place during battle said stan

Exercise 6 Writing Application
Write a brief dialogue in which you and a friend discuss your dream castle or palace. Be sure to follow all the rules of capitalization and punctuation.

Exercise 4
1. Castles in Europe developed from the ancient Roman idea of walled cities.
2. From Spain to Transylvania, castles were almost always built for defensive purposes.
3. The word *castle* also refers to large residences like William Randolph Hearst's castle in San Simeon, California.
4. The area of Nairnshire in northern Scotland is well known for Cawdor Castle.
5. Segovia, Spain, located on the Eresma River, is known for the Alcazar, a famous castle.
6. In Torun, Poland, there are the ruins of a castle of ancient knights.
7. The Wittelsbach family, a German dynasty, took their name from their castle in Bavaria.
8. One Wittelsbach was Count Otto VI, who served the Emperor Frederick I; he was made a duke in 1180.
9. In 1020, Bishop Werner built Habsburg Castle on the Aare River.
10. Later divided into the Austrian and Spanish branches, the Habsburg family ruled in Europe for hundreds of years.
11. A result of World War I was the banishment of Emperor Charles I.
12. In England, King George III bought Buckingham Palace but sometimes lived at Saint James's Palace.
13. Another castle, Balmoral Castle, is the British royal residence in Scotland.
14. In central Japan, the city of Osaka features a park built on the site of a sixteenth-century castle.
15. On an island near Tokyo, Iwatsuki is a castle town that was founded in 1458.

Exercise 5

"Stan, I just read a book about castles, but I'm confused about the difference between a castle and a palace," said Rebecca.

"From what I remember from history class," replied Stan, "castles used to be the same as fortresses."

Kate added, "Oh, like the Tower of London, where they kept prisoners?"

"Right, you must have read Shakespeare's *Richard III*!" exclaimed Stan.

continued

Answer Key continued

"Richard put prisoners in the tower," added Kate.

"That's true," said Stan. "However, British royalty lived in the Tower of London until the time of Queen Elizabeth I."

"Wait a second," Kate said. " I saw the movie *Elizabeth,* but I don't remember the name of her castle."

Stan replied, "As time went on, *castle* came to mean the same thing as a large mansion."

"I think I see," said Kate. "Some palaces were originally fortresses and were rebuilt as luxurious resorts."

"Buckingham Palace was built only as a residence but never to be a safe place during battle," said Stan.

Exercise 6

Writing Application
Have students check partner's dialogues for capitalization and punctuation.

1.

Rhonda	phoned

2.

Smoke	was rising

3.

Mick Bradley	has arrived

4.

Everyone	has been chosen

5.

Skyscrapers	sway

Sentence Diagraming Workshop

Sentences can be diagramed to show how their basic parts are related. In a diagram, each word is positioned to show its use in the sentence. This section will show you how to diagram the basic parts of a sentence.

Subjects and Verbs

In a diagram, the subject and the verb are placed on a horizontal line, separated by a vertical line. The subject is placed to the left. The verb is placed to the right.

EXAMPLE: Snow fell.

Snow	fell

Names and compound nouns are diagramed in the same way as *snow* in the example above. Verb phrases are diagramed in the same way as *fell*.

EXAMPLE: Robert Stone has been selected.

Robert Stone	has been selected

> **Exercise 1** **Diagraming Subjects and Verbs** Each of the following sentences contains a subject and a verb. Diagram each sentence, using the preceding examples as models.
> 1. Rhonda phoned.
> 2. Smoke was rising.
> 3. Mick Bradley has arrived.
> 4. Everyone has been chosen.
> 5. Skyscrapers sway.

Adjectives, Adverbs, and Conjunctions

In addition to a subject and a verb, many sentences contain adjectives, adverbs, and conjunctions. These parts of speech are added to a diagram in the following ways.

Adding Adjectives An adjective is placed on a slanted line directly below the noun or pronoun it describes.

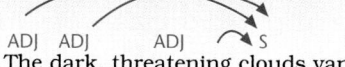

EXAMPLE: The dark, threatening clouds vanished.

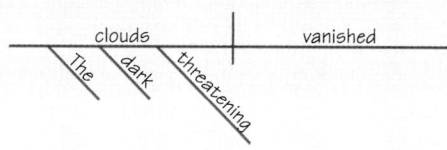

Adding Adverbs Adverbs, like adjectives, are placed on slanted lines. They are placed directly under the verbs, adjectives, or adverbs they modify.

EXAMPLE: My mother drove very slowly.

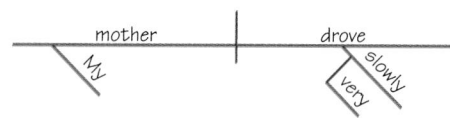

Adding Conjunctions Conjunctions are placed on dotted lines drawn between the words they connect.

EXAMPLE: The tired but friendly traveler smiled warmly
and gratefully.

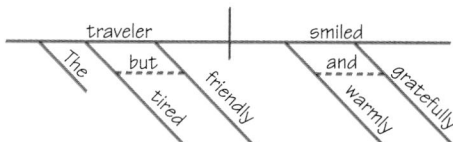

Sentence Diagraming Workshop • **657**

1.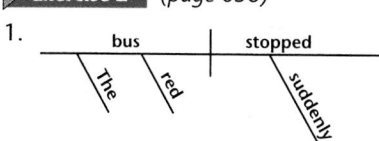

2.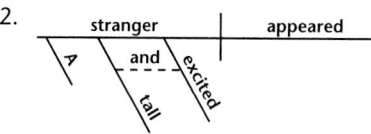

3.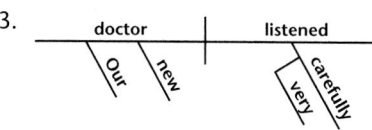

4.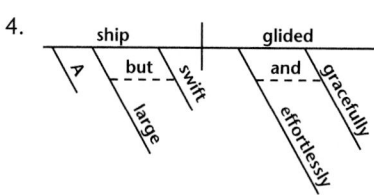

5.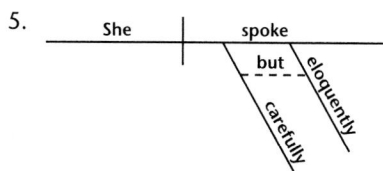

1.
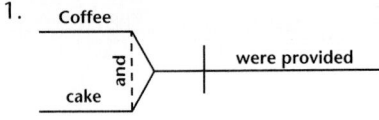

2.
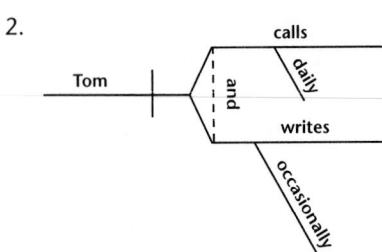

3.
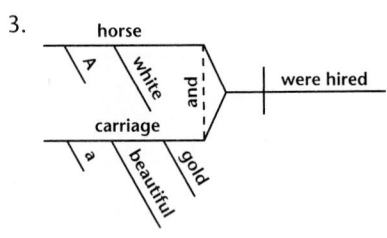

4.
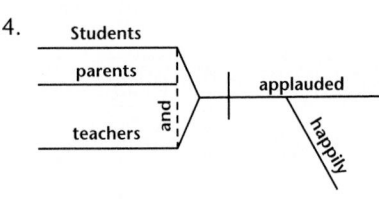

5.
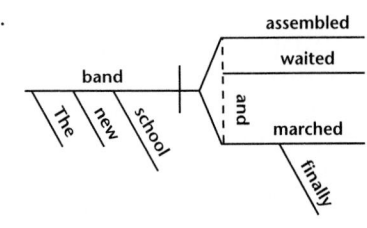

> **Exercise 2** Diagraming Sentences With Modifiers and Conjunctions Diagram each sentence below.
> 1. The red bus stopped suddenly.
> 2. A tall and excited stranger appeared.
> 3. Our new doctor listened very carefully.
> 4. A large but swift ship glided effortlessly and gracefully.
> 5. She spoke carefully but eloquently.

Compound Subjects and Verbs

To diagram a sentence with either a compound subject or a compound verb, you must split the main horizontal line.

Compound Subjects Each part of a compound subject is diagramed on a separate horizontal line. The conjunction that connects the subjects is placed on a dotted vertical line, as shown in the following example.

EXAMPLE: Red flags and blue banners appeared.

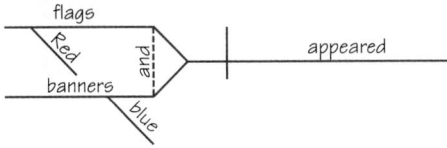

Compound Verbs The diagram for a compound verb is similar to the diagram for a compound subject.

EXAMPLE: Anne writes clearly and draws well.

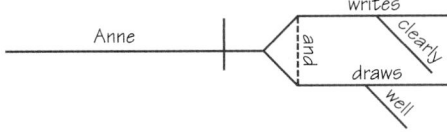

> **Exercise 3** Diagraming Compound Subjects and Compound Verbs Diagram the following sentences.
> 1. Coffee and cake were provided.
> 2. Tom calls daily and writes occasionally.
> 3. A white horse and a beautiful gold carriage were hired.
> 4. Students, parents, and teachers applauded happily.
> 5. The new school band assembled, waited, and finally marched.

Imperative Sentences

Diagrams for sentences that give orders or directions follow a pattern similar to those you already know. The understood subject *you* is in the regular subject position, but in parentheses.

EXAMPLE: Go today.

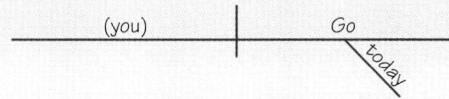

Exercise 4 **Diagraming Imperative Sentences** Diagram the following sentences, placing the understood subjects correctly.

1. Read slowly.
2. Look closely.
3. Choose very carefully.
4. Try harder!
5. Stand up now!

Complements

The three kinds of complements—direct objects, indirect objects, and subject complements—are all diagramed in different ways.

Direct Objects A direct object is placed on the same horizontal line as the subject and verb. The direct object follows the verb and is separated from it by a short vertical line.

EXAMPLE:
S   V   DO
Steven bought a notebook.

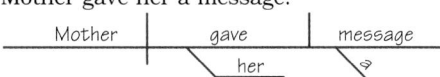

Indirect Objects An indirect object is the only complement that is not placed on the main horizontal line. Instead, it is placed on a short horizontal line extending from a slanted line directly below the verb.

EXAMPLE:
S   V   IO   DO
Mother gave her a message.

Sentence Diagraming Workshop • 659

Exercise 4

1.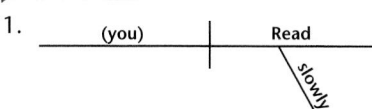

2.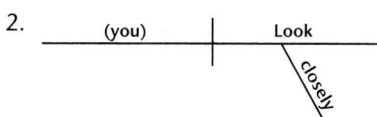

3.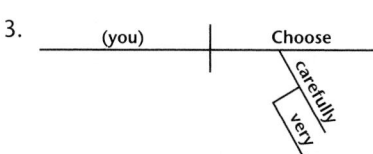

4.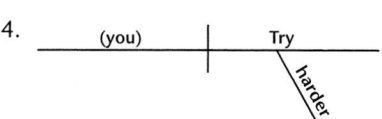

5.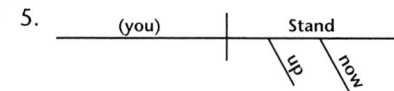

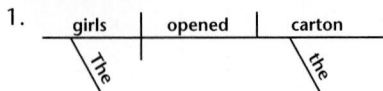

1.

2.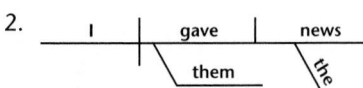

3.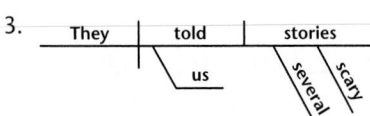

4.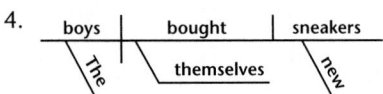

5.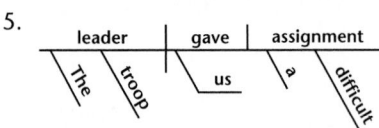

1.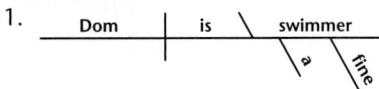

2.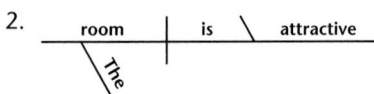

3.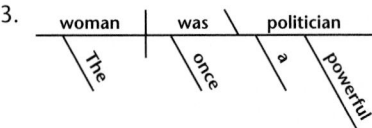

4.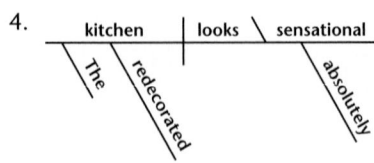

5.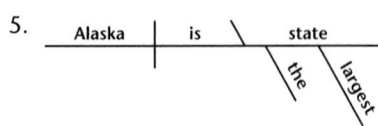

Subject Complements The subject complements—predicate nouns, predicate pronouns, and predicate adjectives—follow linking verbs. Like direct objects, they are placed on the same horizontal line as the subject and verb. They are positioned after the verb and separated from it by a slanted line that points back to the subject.

EXAMPLE:
```
        S    V              PN
      Fred was our last representative.
```

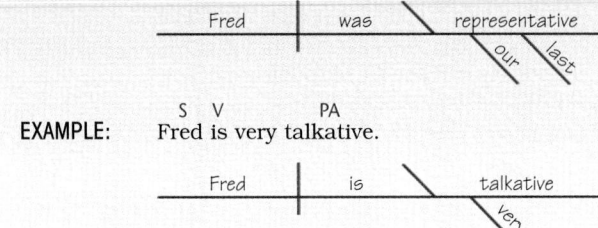

EXAMPLE:
```
        S   V       PA
      Fred is very talkative.
```

Exercise 5 Diagraming Direct Objects and Indirect Objects Diagram the following sentences.
1. The girls opened the carton.
2. I gave them the news.
3. They told us several scary stories.
4. The boys bought themselves new sneakers.
5. The troop leader gave us a difficult assignment.

Exercise 6 Diagraming Subject Complements Diagram the following sentences.
1. Dom is a fine swimmer.
2. The room is attractive.
3. The woman was once a powerful politician.
4. The redecorated kitchen looks absolutely sensational.
5. Alaska is the largest state.

660 • Sentence Diagraming Workshop

Exercise 7 *(page 661)*

Sample answers:
1. Tammy and Sue play soccer.

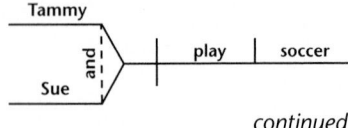

continued

Exercise 7 Writing and Diagraming Sentences Use the
following instructions to write five sentences of your own.
Then, correctly diagram each sentence.

EXAMPLE: Write a sentence that contains a compound verb.
ANSWER: The dog yawned lazily and stretched.

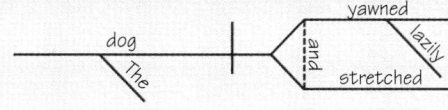

1. Write a sentence that contains a compound subject.
2. Write a sentence that contains two adjectives connected
   by *and.*
3. Write a sentence that gives an order.
4. Write a sentence that contains a subject complement.
5. Write a sentence that contains a direct object.

Prepositional Phrases

The diagram for a prepositional phrase is drawn under the
word it modifies. The diagram starts with a slanted line for the
preposition and continues with a horizontal line for the object
of the preposition. Adjectives that modify the object are placed
below it on slanted lines.

PREPOSITIONAL PHRASE:
PREP   OBJ OF PREP
on a cold morning

Adjective Phrases An adjective phrase is placed directly
under the noun or pronoun that the phrase modifies.

EXAMPLE:
S   V
A teacher from our school spoke briefly.

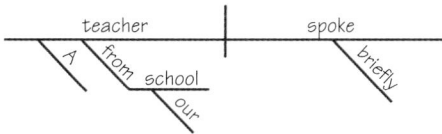

Sentence Diagraming Workshop • **661**

2. Our team won the long and
   exciting game.

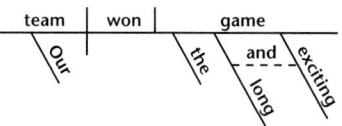

3. Watch this!

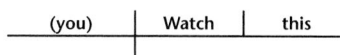

4. The goalie is my sister.

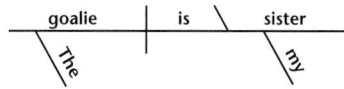

5. She blocked three kicks.

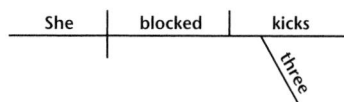

Exercise 8 (page 662)

1.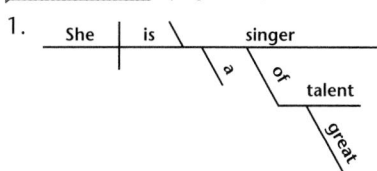

2.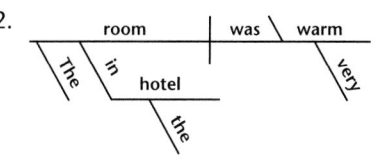

3.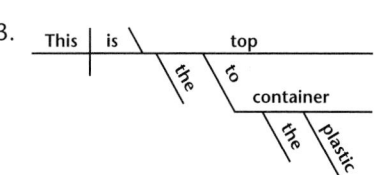

4.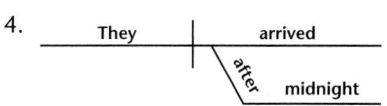

5.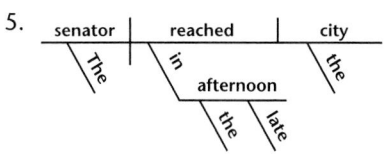

661

1.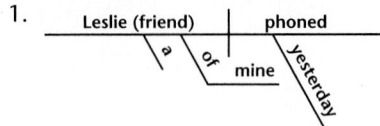

2.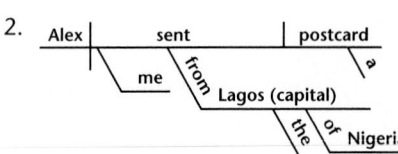

3.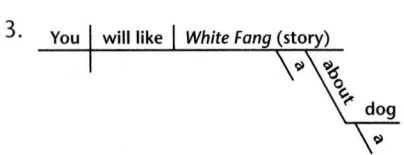

4.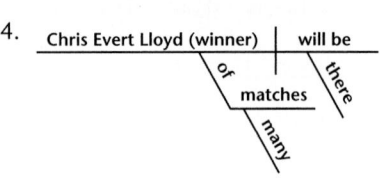

5.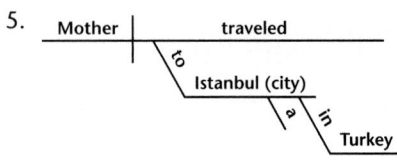

Adverb Phrases The diagram for an adverb phrase is also placed directly under the word it modifies.

EXAMPLE: His family fled to the country.

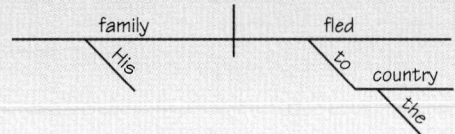

Exercise 8 **Diagraming Prepositional Phrases** Each of the following sentences contains one prepositional phrase. Diagram the sentences, using the preceding examples as models.
1. She is a singer of great talent.
2. The room in the hotel was very warm.
3. This is the top to the plastic container.
4. They arrived after midnight.
5. The senator reached the city in the late afternoon.

Appositives

To diagram an appositive, place it in parentheses next to the noun or pronoun it renames. Any adjectives or adjective phrases that modify the appositive are placed below it.

EXAMPLE: Bill spoke about Countee Cullen, an American poet.

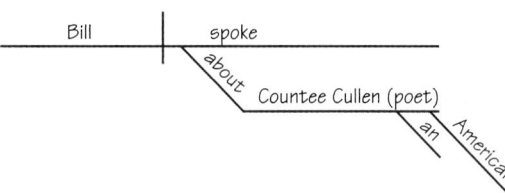

EXAMPLE: Albany, the capital of New York, is a river city.

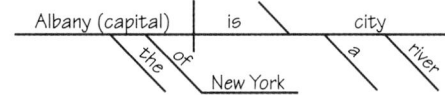

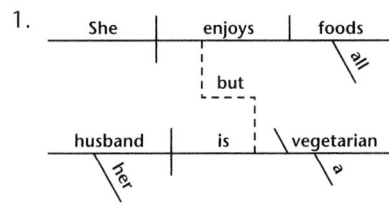

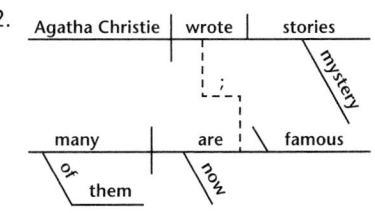

Exercise 9 Diagraming Appositive Phrases Diagram the following sentences, each of which contains an appositive phrase.

1. Leslie, a friend of mine, phoned yesterday.
2. Alex sent me a postcard from Lagos, the capital of Nigeria.
3. You will like *White Fang*, a story about a dog.
4. Chris Evert Lloyd, winner of many matches, will be there.
5. Mother traveled to Istanbul, a city in Turkey.

Compound Sentences

A compound sentence consists of two or more independent clauses. Each clause in a compound sentence is diagramed on a separate horizontal line, one above the other. The clauses are joined at the verbs with a dotted line in the shape of a step. Place the conjunction or semicolon on the horizontal part of the step.

EXAMPLE: Jeff fixed the toaster, and then he began his homework.

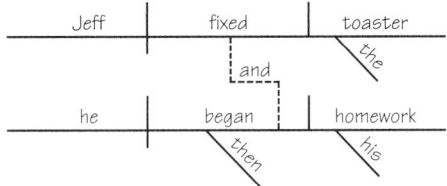

Exercise 10 Diagraming Compound Sentences Diagram each of the following compound sentences, using the preceding example as a model.

1. She enjoys all foods, but her husband is a vegetarian.
2. Agatha Christie wrote mystery stories; many of them are now famous.
3. He bought an expensive coin, but it was a forgery.
4. Hammurabi was a Babylonian king; he enacted a famous code of laws.
5. She has read many mysteries, but she dislikes spy stories.

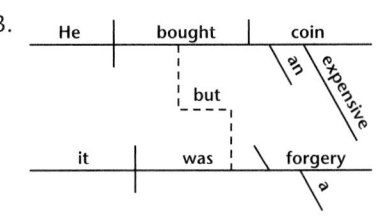

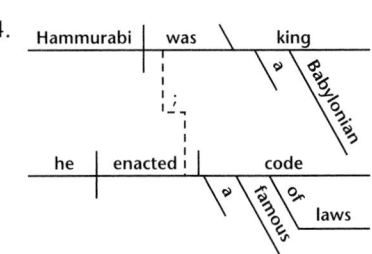

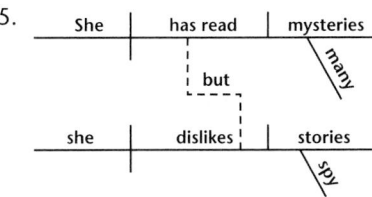

Sentence Diagraming Workshop • 663

1.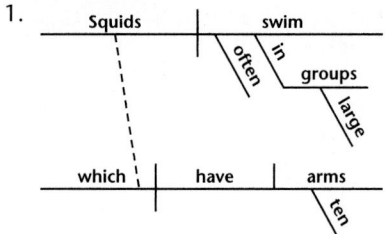

2.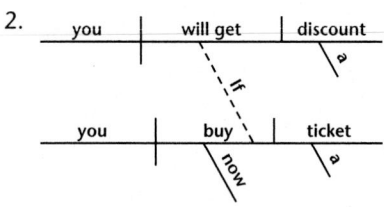

3.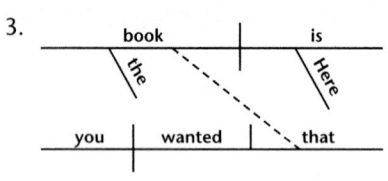

4.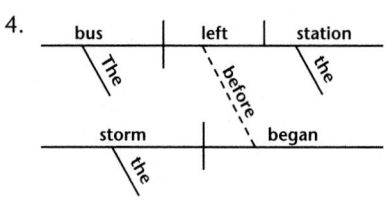

5.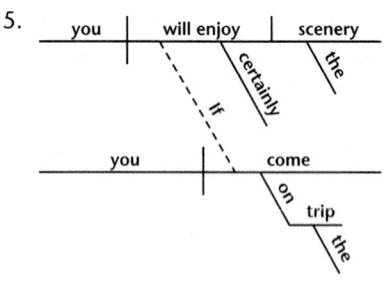

Complex Sentences

A complex sentence contains one independent clause and one or more subordinate clauses. In diagraming a complex sentence, each clause is placed on its own horizontal line.

Adjective Clauses An adjective clause is placed on a separate horizontal line underneath the independent clause, with a dotted line connecting the two clauses. This line connects the noun or pronoun modified in the independent clause with the pronoun that begins the adjective clause.

EXAMPLE: She is the pupil who won the speech contest.

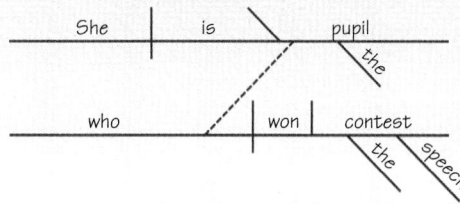

EXAMPLE: The antique car that you described is a Maxwell.

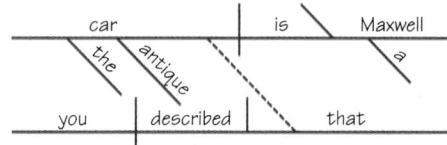

Adverb Clauses Like an adjective clause, an adverb clause is placed on a separate horizontal line underneath the independent clause. A dotted line connects the modified verb, adverb, or adjective in the independent clause with the verb in the adverb clause. The subordinating conjunction that begins the adverb clause is written on the dotted line.

EXAMPLE: I have known him since he was a boy.

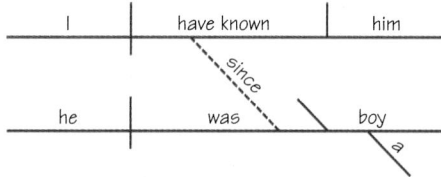

1. I saw that movie, but I didn't like it.

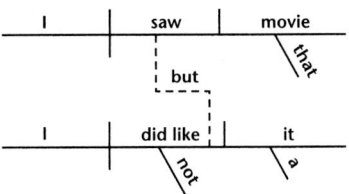

2. Math is easy; it's my favorite subject.

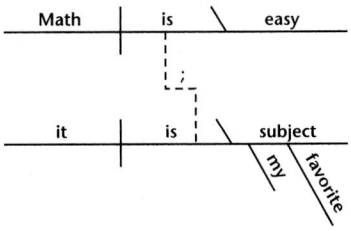

3. I bought the book that everyone is reading.

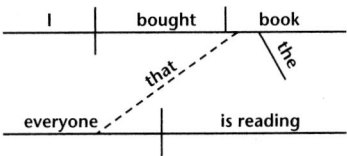

4. After I finish this book, I'll send it to you.

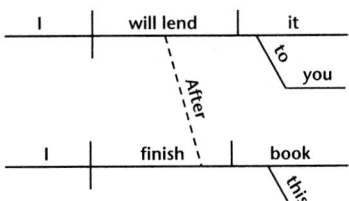

Exercise 11 Diagraming Subordinate Clauses Each of the following complex sentences contains either an adjective clause or an adverb clause. Diagram each sentence.

1. Squids, which have ten arms, often swim in large groups.
2. If you buy a ticket now, you will get a discount.
3. Here is the book that you wanted.
4. The bus left the station before the storm began.
5. If you come on the trip, you certainly will enjoy the scenery.

Exercise 12 Writing and Diagraming Compound and Complex Sentences Use the following instructions to write five sentences of your own. Then, correctly diagram each sentence. (If you use contractions, spell them out before diagraming the sentence.)

EXAMPLE: Write a complex sentence in which an adjective clause modifies the subject of the main clause.

ANSWER: The house that we rented overlooks the beach.

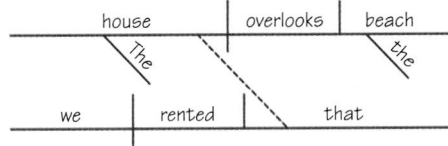

1. Write a compound sentence connected by the conjunction *but*.
2. Write a compound sentence connected with a semicolon.
3. Write a complex sentence in which an adjective clause modifies a direct object in the main clause.
4. Write a complex sentence beginning with an adverb clause.
5. Write a complex sentence in which an adverb clause follows the main clause.

5. I will wait until I hear from you.

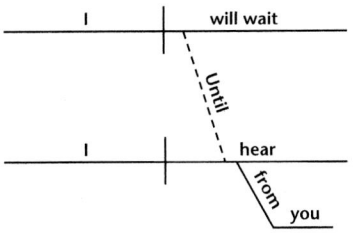

Lesson Objectives

1. To develop critical listening and effective speaking skills and apply them to various types of presentations

2. To understand and evaluate visual images and messages in a variety of media

3. To produce visual images, messages, and meanings that communicate with others

4. To expand vocabulary through reading and listening and by developing skills in using context, word structure, word origins, and reference tools to determine word meanings

5. To develop and apply reading strategies for a variety of purposes and texts

6. To develop study and research skills and become familiar with reference tools and the resources of libraries and the Internet

7. To develop skills in taking tests in various formats

8. To learn and apply specific communication and procedural skills of the workplace, including problem-solving and managing time and money

Academic and Workplace Skills

Responding to Fine Art

Strap Hangers by **William Low**

Use this painting to start a discussion about the definition of academic and workplace skills.

1. Have students examine the painting on pages 666–667. You might use the following questions to prompt discussion:

    If you didn't know the title of this painting, what details could you use to help you determine the subject matter? What kinds of books might the passengers be reading?

2. Students who aren't familiar with living in a city may not know what the people in the painting are doing or what the term *strap hangers* means. Explain to them that these people most likely are on their way to work.

3. Ask students to name professions in which writing is important. Ask students to identify other skills that are essential for people to master if they are to be successful in their careers. Students should see that writing and other communicative skills are important to almost every type of work.

In-Depth Lesson Plan

	LESSON FOCUS	PRINT AND MEDIA RESOURCES
DAY 1	**Speaking** Students learn the skills for clear and effective personal and public speaking (pp. 668–672).	**Teaching Resources** *Academic and Workplace Skills Activity Book,* pp. 1–4
DAY 2	**Listening** Students learn and practice the skills for effective listening (pp. 673–674).	**Teaching Resources** *Academic and Workplace Skills Activity Book,* p. 5
DAY 3	**Viewing and Representing** Students learn how to interpret a variety of graphics and coordinate visual images with language (pp. 675–687).	**Teaching Resources** *Academic and Workplace Skills Activity Book,* pp. 6–15

Accelerated Lesson Plan

	LESSON FOCUS	PRINT AND MEDIA RESOURCES
DAY 1	**Speaking and Listening** Students learn the basic skills for effective speaking and listening, in their personal lives and in the classroom.	**Teaching Resources** *Academic and Workplace Skills Activity Book,* pp.1–5
DAY 2	**Viewing and Representing** Students learn to interpret a variety of graphics and coordinate visual images with language.	**Teaching Resources** *Academic and Workplace Skills Activity Book,* pp. 6–15

Options for Adapting Lesson Plans

HOMEWORK

Have students complete any stage of the lesson for homework.

FEATURES

Extend coverage with the Standardized Test Preparation Workshop (p. 688).

TECHNOLOGY

Students can complete any stage of the lesson on computer. Have them print out their completed work.

INTEGRATED SKILLS COVERAGE

Viewing and Representing
Critical Viewing, SE pp. 668, 672, 677, 680, 685, 686, 687

Real-World Connection
ATE p. 670

Technology Skills
ATE p. 678

ASSESSMENT SUPPORT

Standardized Test Preparation, SE p. 688

Standardized Test Preparation Workbook, pp. 55–56

Formal Assessment, Ch. 28

MEETING INDIVIDUAL NEEDS

ESL Students ATE pp. 669, 673, 679

Less Advanced Students ATE pp. 672. See also Ongoing Assessment ATE pp. 670, 672, 674, 679, 680, 687

Bodily/Kinesthetic Learners ATE p. 687

BLOCK SCHEDULING

Pacing Suggestions
For 90-minute Blocks
• Have students complete the Speaking and Listening stages in a single period.
• Focus one class period on Viewing and Representing.

Professional Development Support
• *How to Manage Instruction in the Block* This Teaching Resource provides management and activity suggestions.

MEDIA AND TECHNOLOGY

For the Teacher
• *Resource Pro* CD-ROM

WRITING AND GRAMMAR WEB SITE

The Interactive Writing and Grammar Web site provides a wide array of support for students, teachers, and parents. Writing support includes

• Interactive revision checkers
• Scoring rubrics with complete models

www.phschool.com

Lesson Objectives

1. To determine the purposes for listening.
2. To monitor understanding of the spoken message and seek clarification as needed.
3. To listen to proficient, fluent models of oral reading.
4. To adapt spoken language such as word choice, diction, and usage to the audience, purpose, and occasion.
5. To use media to compare ideas and points of view.
6. To evaluate the purposes and effects of various media.

Critical Viewing

Analyze Students may suggest that they would use maps, graphs, charts, or video.

Chapter 28 Speaking, Listening, Viewing, and Representing

Listening and speaking are both part of one process: communicating. If you speak well, you can express your ideas clearly. If you listen well, you can remember more of what you hear. Speaking and listening are active processes that require you to think about how you want to express yourself and what you want to hear.

▲ Critical Viewing
This student is preparing to give a multimedia presentation. What different kinds of media would you use to make a presentation better? [Analyze]

668 • Speaking, Listening, Viewing, and Representing

🕐 TIME AND RESOURCE MANAGER	
Resources	
Print: Academic and Workplace Skills Activity Book, pp. 1–5	
In-Depth Coverage	**Accelerated Pace**
• Work through all key concepts, pp. 669–674. • Assign and review all the activities on pp. 669–674.	• Assign pp. 669–674 for independent student review.

Section 28.1 Speaking and Listening Skills

By developing good speaking and listening skills, you will be able to get more out of conversations, class discussions, and class presentations. Developing good speaking skills will enable you to contribute more effectively to class discussions, give formal presentations with greater confidence, and communicate your feelings and ideas to other people more easily. By developing good speaking and listening skills, you will be able to get more out of conversations, class discussions, and class presentations. The more fully you participate in class, the more profitable—and enjoyable—your classroom time will be.

Using Informal Speaking Skills

Informal speaking skills include talking with friends or family, speaking in class, giving directions, and making introductions.

KEY CONCEPT Develop informal speaking skills to build confidence about participating in class discussions, giving clear and accurate directions, and introducing people properly. ■

How to Participate in Class You can improve your speaking skills by taking part in class discussions. If you plan what you want to say before you say it and participate in class often, you will become more fluent, comfortable, and confident in your speaking. The following chart offers some suggestions for improving your participation in class discussions.

TAKING PART IN CLASS DISCUSSIONS

1. Set a goal for yourself about taking part in class.
2. Do whatever homework and reading assignments are required so that you are well prepared.
3. Decide on the points you would like to make before class begins.
4. Do not wait for the teacher to call on you. Raise your hand, and volunteer to contribute your thoughts.
5. Listen to the discussion carefully, and make sure that your points are relevant to the discussion.
6. Observe other students who make meaningful contributions to the class, and learn from their example.
7. Ask questions about what you do not understand or what you want to know more about.

PREPARE and ENGAGE

 Interest GRABBER Ask students to think of being moved or excited by a movie character. What did the actor say, and how did he or she say it, to make it memorable?

Activate Prior Knowledge

Ask students to remember the last time they said to someone, "You don't understand." Were they being unclear, or was the person not paying attention? In either case, what could they have done differently to make the other person get it?

TEACH

Step-by-Step Teaching Guide

Informal Speaking Skills; How to Participate in Class

1. Ask students to consider how much they participate in class now. For example, ask students how often they contribute ideas in whole-class discussions.

2. Based on this information, have students set a goal for themselves that will help them increase their participation. Elicit from students some strategies and actions they can take that will help them to meet these goals.

3. Direct students' attention to the chart of suggestions on how to take part in class discussions.

4. Ask students to select at least two strategies from the chart that will help them to meet their goals.

Customize for
ESL Students

Students who need the most practice speaking are those least likely to do so. Explain that part of their grade is based on class participation. They do not lose points if their comments have some grammatical mistakes or they can't think of the exact English word they want. And every time they try, they will get better.

Step-by-Step Teaching Guide

How to Give Directions

1. Choose two extroverted students. Have one follow the suggestions for giving directions and explain how to get from the classroom to the school library.

2. Have the other student explain how to get from your classroom to the school cafeteria. This student should mumble a sentence, suggest one wrong turn, and interrupt with a non sequitur ("Hey, Bill, I like your shirt").

3. Discuss the differences between the two explanations.

Step-by-Step Teaching Guide

How to Make Introductions

1. Read the two sample introductions in the book and ask students what information is included in the second that is not in the first. (The second introduction includes the first and last names of the person being introduced and more explicit information of interest about one of the participants.)

2. Ask students to get together in groups of three to practice introducing one another.

Real-World Connection

Students should not underestimate the importance of introductions, in both social and workplace situations. You may wish to have students write a brief introduction for a hypothetical speaker at a conference. Have students reinforce their speaking skills by delivering their introductions to the class.

Answer Key

Exercise 1

Answers will vary.

Exercise 2

Answers will vary. Directions should include short, clear sentences and specific, relevant details.

How to Give Directions You may be asked to give directions for how to get somewhere or how to do something. If you can give clear and accurate directions, people will be able to follow them easily.

The following chart offers some suggestions for giving clear and accurate directions.

SUGGESTIONS FOR GIVING DIRECTIONS

1. Think through the directions carefully before you speak.
2. Speak slowly so that your listeners can follow your directions without difficulty.
3. Choose your words carefully, being as specific as you can.
4. Use short sentences, so your listener can remember each one. Give only one step of the directions in each sentence.
5. Remember to give the most important details, but do not confuse your listener with unnecessary information.

How to Make Introductions How do you make a good introduction? The most important thing to remember is to pronounce the person's *full* name correctly. You should also include some interesting details about the person you are introducing.

Note the difference between these two introductions:

INTRODUCTIONS: Mom, this is David. I know him from school.

Mom, I'd like to introduce my friend, David Lawrence. He lives right down the street. We're in the same English class. David, this is my mother, Mrs. Joyce.

Exercise 1 Improving Class Participation Skills For each of your classes, keep a record of your contributions to class discussions for two weeks. Try to increase the number and the quality of your comments.

Exercise 2 Writing Directions and an Introduction Write clear and accurate directions to your house from school. Write an introduction presenting a famous person to your class. Then, give the directions and your introduction to a classmate, and have him or her evaluate them.

> **More Practice**
> Academic and Workplace Skills Activity Book
> • pp. 1–2

✓ ONGOING ASSESSMENT: Monitor and Reinforce

If students are having trouble including interesting or relevant details in their class comments or introductions, refer to the following option.

Have the student list ten details about himself or herself. Ask the student to consider which five are the most important, and then instruct the student to write an introduction of himself or herself, using the five details that he or she chose.

Using Formal Speaking Skills

Formal speaking generally refers to speaking in front of an audience, such as giving a class presentation or a speech.

Recognize Different Kinds of Speeches There are three main kinds of speeches: explanatory speeches, persuasive speeches, and entertaining speeches.

KEY CONCEPT Choose the kind of speech you will give by considering the purpose of the speech and your audience:

- An **explanatory** speech explains an idea or an event.
- A **persuasive** speech is used to get your audience to agree with your point of view or to take some action.
- An **entertaining** speech is given to amuse the audience. ■

Plan Your Speech Preparation is the most important part of a speech. When you are asked to give a speech, begin by thinking carefully about the purpose of your speech and your audience. This will help you determine the kind of speech to give, the topic of the speech, and the way to present the material.

KEY CONCEPT Choose a subject that you know or like, in order to interest your audience. ■

Choose your topic and gather information about it. Then, organize it in outline form. Next, write the main ideas and major details for your speech topic on note cards. You can refer to your note cards quickly and easily as you deliver your speech.

The following chart offers suggestions for preparing note cards for a speech.

PREPARING NOTE CARDS FOR A SPEECH

1. Print all information neatly on 3" x 5" index cards.
2. Write out quotations or facts that you want to remember.
3. Write out beginning and ending statements.
4. Rely mainly on key words and phrases or clear abbreviations to jog your memory.
5. Use a clear outline form, and indent all the details under the ideas they support.
6. Use underlining and capital letters to make important information stand out.
7. Number your cards to help keep them in order.

Formal Speaking Skills

1. Write the following speech topics on the chalkboard:

   Building the Golden Gate Bridge

   Stopping Pollution

   My Crazy Summer at Camp

2. Ask students what they think is the speaker's purpose in giving each of these speeches. They should remember the purposes for writing they have learned.

3. Ask students what kinds of audiences might be appropriate for each of the speeches listed above.

4. Have students work in small groups to brainstorm a list of possible topics they might present to the class in a speech.

5. Have students choose the three topics they think are most appropriate for a given purpose and audience.

Plan Your Speech

1. Ask students to look at the three topics they chose from their brainstormed list, then choose a topic for their speech.

2. Explain that the purpose of an outline of the speech is to organize its main points in the order in which they will be covered.

3. Once students have outlined their speeches, they can create note cards that include the main ideas and main supporting details. Explain to students that using note cards to deliver a speech allows the presenter to organize information and read it quickly.

4. Have partners practice applying the suggestions by making a sample note card for one of the points listed above in the sample outline.

Deliver Your Speech

1. When students have the content of their speeches decided, they can think about how to deliver their speeches.

2. Ask students what makes a good speaker. (A good speaker is clear, expressive, natural, relaxed, uses nonverbal cues, and speaks for an appropriate amount of time.)

3. Have students work in groups of four to practice their speeches. Instruct the listeners to choose a different aspect of the speaker's performance to critique. Encourage students to provide positive feedback first and to be constructive and respectful when offering suggestions for improvement.

Customize for
Less Advanced Students

A speech does not have to be long. A good two-minute speech is preferable to a five-minute speech that is full of irrelevant details. Encourage students to practice by themselves until they are comfortable—perhaps in the shower where no one can hear them.

Critical Viewing

Describe Students may note that Barbara Jordan's beaming smile and outraised arms are indicative of the audience's positive response to some aspect of her speech.

Answer Key

▶ **Exercise 3**

Topics will vary. Students should use note cards, and their speech presentations should demonstrate their understanding of the "Five Things to Remember When Delivering a Speech," such as pronouncing words clearly, using body language suited to their purposes, and being able to answer questions from the audience.

▶ **Exercise 4**

Make sure students respond constructively to each other's speeches.

28.1

Deliver Your Speech Practice giving your speech just as you plan to give it in class. Using the note cards you have prepared, deliver your speech several times alone, in front of a mirror, and then to your parents or a friend. The more practice you get, the more confidence you will have when you deliver your speech in class.

▶ **KEY CONCEPT** Practice your speech to gain confidence. ■

Use the suggestions in the following chart while practicing and delivering your speech.

FIVE THINGS TO REMEMBER WHEN DELIVERING A SPEECH
1. Do not read to your audience. Refer to your note cards, and speak in a natural, relaxed way.
2. Pronounce your words clearly, and do not speak too hurriedly or too slowly.
3. Use nonverbal language—such as movements, posture, facial expressions, and gestures—effectively while you practice and deliver your speech.
4. Stay within the time limit you were given for your speech.
5. Be prepared to answer questions from your audience.

▶ **Exercise 3** Planning and Delivering a Speech Prepare a short speech on a topic you enjoy or would be interested in researching. Gather information on this topic, and organize it in outline form. Next, write the information on note cards, following the suggestions in the chart on page 671. Then, practice giving the speech several times, following the suggestions in the chart above. As a final step, deliver your speech in class.

▶ **Exercise 4** Giving and Getting Feedback After delivering a speech or after listening to a speech, sit down with a group of your classmates and critique the speech. Discuss all aspects of the speech—content, presentation, body language, organization— and tell how the speech could be better.

▶ Critical Viewing Barbara Jordan, member of the House of Representatives from 1973 to 1979, delivers a speech at the Democratic National Convention in 1992. Describe her nonverbal language. [Describe]

▶ **More Practice**

Academic and Workplace Skills Activity Book
• pp. 3–5

672 • Speaking, Listening, Viewing, and Representing

☑ **ONGOING ASSESSMENT: Monitor and Reinforce**

If students have trouble planning or delivering their speeches, consider the following options.

Option 1 Provide students with the text of a famous speech, such as Abraham Lincoln's Gettysburg Address or John F. Kennedy's Inauguration Day speech. Meet with each student separately or in a group and discuss the organization of the speech.

Option 2 Show students videos of famous speeches such as Martin Luther King's "I have a dream . . ." speech or John F. Kennedy's Inauguration Day speech and have them assess the qualities of the speaker's delivery.

Listening Effectively

A good deal of your time in school is spent listening. To listen well, you must give the speaker your complete attention, and you must learn to identify and remember the speaker's main ideas and major details.

KEY CONCEPT Focus your attention on the speaker, and pay attention to the speaker's main points and details. ■

The ability to concentrate and pay attention is a skill that has to be learned. The chart below provides seven rules that will help you build your listening skills.

SEVEN RULES FOR LISTENING EFFECTIVELY

1. Pay attention and concentrate on what is being said. Avoid daydreaming by actively trying to listen, understand, and remember.
2. Do not look around at your friends in class, out the window, at books on your desk, or at anything else that would distract you from the speaker. Focus your eyes and ears on the speaker.
3. Concentrate on what the speaker is saying, and try not to be distracted by his or her looks or manner of speaking.
4. Block out any distractions, such as noises inside or outside the classroom, or any concerns or thoughts you had earlier in the day. Put all your energy into listening and taking in what is being said.
5. Put away anything that may detract from your paying attention to the speaker, such as books, magazines, and homework schedules.
6. Keep a pencil and paper handy so you can take notes, but avoid writing things unrelated to the discussion.
7. Try to find out in advance what main topic will be discussed. That way, you will have some idea of what to focus on while you are listening.

As you listen, identify the speaker's main idea and major details. These will help you decide what information you want to remember after the speaker has finished. Use the questions in the chart on the next page to help you identify this information.

Step-by-Step Teaching Guide

Listening Effectively

1. Good listening requires concentration and focus. These are skills that can be practiced and learned.
2. Ask students which of the following speeches they think they would find easier to understand and why:

   The Humor in Prime-Time TV Sitcoms

   Ethical Issues in Nuclear Physics

   Since, as they know, it is easier to understand things they are familiar with, finding out about the topic and material that will be discussed in a speech can help them to focus on what they hear and understand it better.

3. To elicit the rules for listening given in the book as well as other helpful strategies, ask students to get into groups and brainstorm a list of techniques they use when listening to help them to understand and remember the information they hear.

4. Create a list of good strategies on the board as the groups report their responses. Remind students that, since everyone learns in his or her own way, some of the strategies listed will work better for them than others.

Customize for
ESL Students

Students know that when they read, they can skim over some words they don't know and still understand the text. This is harder when listening to a speech, because it is the speaker who sets the pace. Encourage students to focus on the big idea of the speech and not be distracted by words they don't know. They can jot down these words (with phonetic spelling, if necessary) and ask what they mean later.

More Practice

Academic and
Workplace Skills
Activity Book
• pp. 6–7

Exercise 5

Encourage students to keep track of their progress. For example, they could keep a chart of listening skills and date each column, then compare the number of check marks on subsequent days.

Exercise 6

Main idea is underlined; major details are in italics.

1. There will be a <u>special performance</u> of *You're a Good Man, Charlie Brown* on *Friday night, October 21,* in the *Hayes Auditorium. Student tickets,* priced at $4.00, will be available *tomorrow only* from *8:30 to 1:30 in Room 242.* There will be no student tickets available at the time of the performance.
2. The <u>Explorer's Club</u> will have its <u>first meeting</u> *on Wednesday, April 6, at 3:30 P.M.* The *registration fee is $3.00,* and you must have a *permission slip signed by a parent.* Come to the *school gym,* and bring any suggestions or ideas for outings.

IDENTIFYING MAIN IDEA AND MAJOR DETAILS

1. What is the opening sentence about? This is often the topic sentence that tells you the general topic.
2. What is the last sentence about? This is often a restatement of the main topic.
3. What important points are being made about the topic?
4. What needs to be remembered about each point?
5. What clues is the speaker giving about something's importance? For example, does he or she begin by saying "Remember . . . ," "Most of all . . . ," or "To sum up . . . "?
6. Does the speaker repeat an idea or phrase a number of times, or emphasize its importance by his or her tone of voice or gestures?
7. What is written on the blackboard? What do the visual aids or supporting materials (if any) say about the main idea and major details?

Exercise 5 Developing Your Listening Skills Read through the rules for listening, and try to practice them in one particular class. At the end of the class, grade yourself on how well you listened by placing check marks in your notebook next to all the rules you followed. Continue to practice the rules in the same class until you have placed check marks next to all of them. Repeat the strategy for the rest of your classes.

Exercise 6 Practicing Listening Skills Work with another student on this exercise. One of you should read aloud the first announcement below, while the other listens for the main idea and major details, writing them down after the reading is completed. Then, switch roles and repeat the process with the second passage.

1. There will be a special performance of *You're a Good Man, Charlie Brown* on Friday night, October 21, in the Hayes Auditorium. Student tickets, priced at $4.00, will be available tomorrow only from 8:30 to 1:30 in Room 242. There will be no student tickets available at the time of the performance.
2. The Explorers' Club will have its first meeting on Wednesday, April 6, at 3:30 P.M. The registration fee is $3.00, and you must have a permission slip signed by a parent. Come to the school gym, and bring any suggestions or ideas for outings.

✓ ONGOING ASSESSMENT: Monitor and Reinforce

If students have trouble with Exercise 6, consider the following option.

Read aloud a list of wedding announcements or special interest announcements from your local newspaper to students. Instruct students to listen for and write down the main idea and major details of the announcements.

Viewing and Representing Skills

Section 28.2

Visual representation is an important way to communicate. Television programs, textbooks, and works of art are common types of media that use images to expand your view of the world. Graphic organizers, multimedia presentations, and performances are ways in which you can express yourself to the world. In this section, you will learn how to receive—and provide—information through visual representations.

Interpreting Maps, Graphs, and Photographs

Any map, graph, or photograph can provide a wealth of information. The key to the information these representations hold is your ability to interpret them.

▶ **KEY CONCEPT** Use your knowledge of the features of maps, graphs, and photographs to get information visually. ∎

Follow these general guidelines when reading a visual aid:

- **Determine Your Purpose** Knowing your purpose helps you focus on the information you need.
- **Read the Title, Caption, and Labels** The title or caption tells you what kind of information to expect.
- **Decode Symbols** Symbols are sometimes used to give information. Find out what they represent.
- **Look for Notable Features** Areas that stand out usually contain important information.
- **Link Information to Text** Determining the relationship between the visual elements and the text allows you to use the text to understand the visual elements better and vice versa.

Maps A map can do more than simply indicate the location of a state capital. For example, maps can identify population clusters, clarify wartime battle activities, and report weather forecasts.

Use these steps when interpreting maps:
1. Familiarize yourself with the map.
2. Find out which way is north on the map.
3. Look at the distance scale (usually found at the bottom of the map).

Graphs There will be times when you have to get information from graphs. Graphs provide a quick and easy way to compare several pieces of related information.

Viewing and Representing Skills • 675

⏱ TIME AND RESOURCE MANAGER

Resources
Print: Academic and Workplace Skills Activity Book, pp. 6–16

In-Depth Coverage	Accelerated Pace
• Work through all key concepts, pp. 675–687. • Assign and review all the activities on pp. 675–687.	• Assign pp. 675–687 for independent student review.

PREPARE and ENGAGE

🎖 **Interest GRABBER** Show students a map that displays roadways and ask them how they would figure out the best possible route between two points.

Activate Prior Knowledge

Ask students to name situations in which they have had to use a graph. Have them discuss why they think graphs are useful tools.

TEACH

Step-by-Step Teaching Guide

Interpreting Maps, Graphs, and Photographs

1. Visual aids such as these can add very helpful information about the subject. In order to use this information, students need to be able to interpret visuals.

2. Reading the title and caption of a visual aid can help students to focus on and understand the information provided by letting them know what kind of information to expect, while labels and symbols provide specific information or show the relationships between pieces of information.

3. Direct students' attention to the map of the Ancient Middle East. Ask what ancient cities are represented. (Baghdad, Babylon, Jerusalem, Bethlehem, Mecca, Ur, and Medina)

4. Ask students how they knew that these were ancient cities. (They interpreted the symbol for ancient city by using the key on the map.)

Step-by-Step Teaching Guide

Maps

Direct students' attention to the map in the book and ask them to answer the following questions and explain how they know.

- *Which ancient city on the map is located farthest north?*
- *What is the distance between Mecca and Babylon?*
- *In which modern nation is the site of Babylon located?*

Step-by-Step Teaching Guide

Line Graphs

A line graph shows a change in something over time. Refer to the first graph and ask the following questions:

- *What was measured to create this graph?* (rainfall)
- *Where was it measured?* (Iraq)
- *When was it measured?* (October 1998–March 1999)
- *What do the axes show?* (vertical: amount of rain; horizontal: months)
- *How much rain fell in February in Iraq?* (about 4.75 cm)

Step-by-Step Teaching Guide

Bar Graphs

1. Ask students how a bar graph differs from a line graph. (A bar graph compares amounts of several similar things.)

2. This bar graph provides an easy way to compare empires—the tallest bar is the longest empire. Discuss reasons why the graph can communicate more simply and effectively than, say, a paragraph explaining the same information in words.

Different kinds of graphs are used to show different kinds of information. The following discussion of the three main types of graphs you are likely to find in your reading provides steps to help you interpret each type.

A **line graph** shows changes that occurred over time. It features a line that connects points. The points, which may appear as actual dots, represent numbers or amounts of something.

Use these steps to interpret a line graph:

1. Read the labels. The labels tell you what the data represent and the time interval over which the data are being reported.
2. Read each axis of the graph. The axes are the main vertical line and the main horizontal line that make up the graph.
3. Compare and contrast the data.

A **bar graph** compares and contrasts amounts. In a bar graph, you read the "heights" or "lengths" of bars to see what numbers they represent.

Use these steps to interpret a bar graph:

1. Look at the heights or lengths of the bars.
2. Match the subject that goes with the bar to the number the bar reaches.
3. Compare and contrast the heights or lengths of the bars.

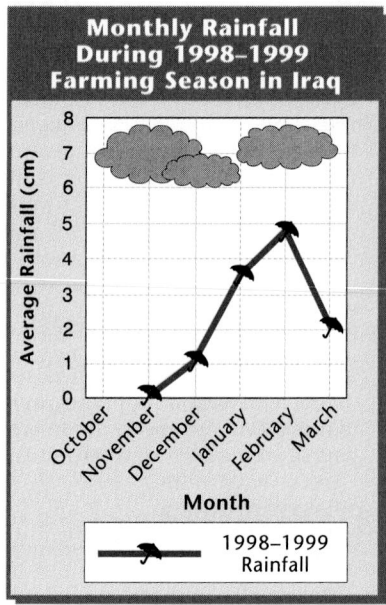

Monthly Rainfall During 1998–1999 Farming Season in Iraq

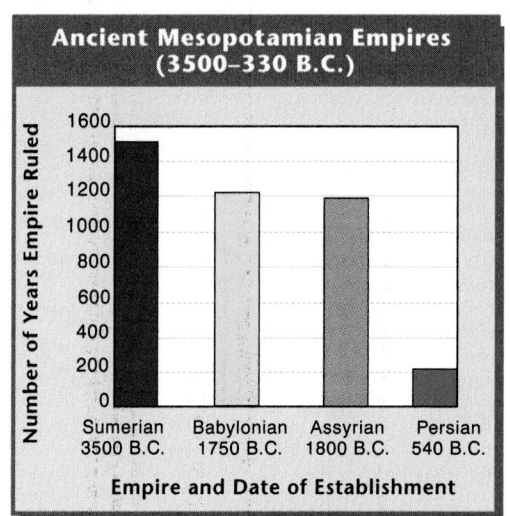

Ancient Mesopotamian Empires (3500–330 B.C.)

A **pie graph** shows the relationship of parts to a whole. It is in the shape of a circle that is divided into parts. The circle stands for 100 percent of something. Each part stands for a certain portion, or percentage, of the whole.

Use these steps to interpret a pie graph:

1. Look at the numbers that go with the individual parts.
2. Match the parts to the key.
3. Use the numbers and parts to make comparisons.

Photographs A photograph conveys meaning in a single, vivid burst. Whether it shows last year's solar eclipse or the facial expression of yesterday's home-run hero, a photograph allows you to be a witness to the event represented. Still, there is more to interpreting a photograph than just responding to its power. Use the caption and the main image of the photograph to identify what it is about—its main subject. Ask yourself these questions when you interpret a photograph:

- Which details are of particular interest?

- What do these details tell me about the main subject?

- What do other details tell me about the main subject?

Types of Land in Modern Iraq

13%
3%
9%
75%

Cultivated land
Forest & Woodland
Meadows & Pastures
Other

> **Exercise 7** Reading Information Visually Find an example of each type of visual aid (maps, graphs, and photographs). Using the general guidelines and steps for interpretation, describe each visual aid, and indicate the kinds of information you can learn from it.

▶ Critical Viewing Look at this stair detail of a Sumerian ziggurat (a temple tower) at ancient Ur, now in Iraq. What details are of particular interest to you? [Analyze]

Viewing and Representing Skills • **677**

Step-by-Step Teaching Guide

Pie Graphs

1. A pie graph shows parts of a whole. Stress that the entire pie represents 100%, or a whole. It does not equal 100 items. For example, a car dealer could use a pie graph to show what percent of annual sales of 683 cars were vans, sedans, and sports cars. 683 = 100% of sales. So 337 vans = 49% of the pie.

2. Ask students to look at the graph in the book. The full circle represents 100% of the land in Iraq; each piece of the pie represents a different type of land in that country.

3. Students should first look at the numbers that go with the parts of a pie graph and then match these parts with the key.

Step-by-Step Teaching Guide

Photographs

1. Have students look in their textbooks for pictures related to texts they have already read.

2. Ask students to follow the steps outlined in their books for interpreting photographs to determine what the photograph is showing and what it tells them about the main subject.

Answer Key

> **Exercise 7**

Answers will vary.

Critical Viewing

Analyze Students might say the long staircase, the bricks from which the temple is built, or the top of the tower.

Viewing Information Media Critically

1. Ask students how they get information about world and local events and people. (Most students get information from television.)

2. Ask students what kinds of TV programs and films provide information. Create a list on the board of students' answers.

3. Choose several different kinds of programs listed and ask students what kinds of information are provided by each.

4. Ask students which kind of program they think provides the most trustworthy information and why.

5. Stress that it is important to view all information media critically before accepting the ideas presented. The first step is to know what form of information media they are encountering and what kind of information that program provides.

6. Direct students' attention to the chart in their books listing nonprint information media. After students read the chart, discuss which media offer the most comprehensive information, which have ulterior motives, etc.

Integrating Technology Skills

Anyone can create a Web site on the Internet. Have students compare three Web sites with a similar topic: for example, the National Institute of Health's information on diet, a site advertising a commercial weight-loss product, and a site from a pharmaceutical company describing weight-loss medication. Ask students what efforts were made to give the site for the commercial weight-loss product an authoritative, objective, and scientific look.

28.2

Viewing Information Media Critically

When you view information media critically, you think carefully about what you see and hear. Because the media distribute large amounts of information, it is important to learn how to differentiate among various media, as well as to evaluate the information presented.

Kinds of Information Media Television, documentary films, and other media provide news and other information. The quality and importance of the information you get depend on the kind of program or film you are watching.

The chart that follows describes several forms of nonprint information media.

NEWS MEDIA CHART			
Form of News Media	Topic(s)	Coverage and Content	Point of View
Television News Program	Focuses on current events or critical news	Summaries of events illustrated by video clips, graphics, and interviews	Recounts information objectively
Documentary	Focuses on one topic of current or historical interest	In-depth stories presented through narration, interviews, and illustrations	Sometimes expresses opinions and viewpoints
Television Newsmagazine	Covers a variety of current topics	In-depth stories or short features illustrated by video clips and interviews	Presents some information objectively and other information with an opinion
Interview	Addresses current topics of social, political, or cultural interest	Questions to find out more about the subject	Presents the opinions of the person being interviewed
Editorial	Addresses current controversial topics	Commentary by a single person sometimes supported by statistics or facts	Presents the opinions of a single individual
Commercial	Advertises products—things, people, places, or ideas	Message of engaging images and catchy slogan used to present a product in a memorable way	Designed to make people want to purchase something

Evaluating Information From the Media After having determined the kind of program you are watching, it is helpful to go a step further and evaluate both the images represented and the language spoken in the program.

▶ **KEY CONCEPT** Learn to evaluate the images and language in the media to enhance your critical viewing skills. ■

Learning the following concepts will help prepare you to evaluate information from the media:

- **Facts and opinions** are important to separate when watching the media. A *fact* is a statement that can be proven to be true. An *opinion* is a viewpoint that cannot be proven to be true.
- **Loaded language and images** are emotional words and visuals used to persuade you to think a certain way.
- **Bias** is a tendency to think in a certain way. As you watch, consider whether the information is being presented in a one-sided way, or whether it takes all viewpoints into account.

Use the following strategies to increase your grasp of information from the media.

EVALUATING INFORMATION FROM THE MEDIA

1. Be aware of the kind of program you are watching, its purpose, and its limitations.
2. Listen and watch carefully.
3. Sort out facts from opinions.
4. Be aware of any loaded language or sensationalist images that might cause you to react in a certain way.
5. Listen for bias, and note any points of view not discussed.
6. Check surprising or questionable information in other sources.
7. View the complete program before reaching a conclusion.
8. Develop your own views about the issues, people, and information presented.

▶ **Exercise 8** Analyzing Information Media Watch a program that provides news or other information, including the commercials during the program. In an essay, identify the kind of program and describe the topics covered. Also, identify what each commercial is selling. Then, evaluate the information on each topic in the program and in the commercials, using the strategies listed above.

▶ **More Practice**

Academic and Workplace Skills Activity Book
• p. 8

☑ ONGOING ASSESSMENT: Monitor and Reinforce

If students are having trouble evaluating images and language in the media, consider the following option.

Ask the student to watch the local news on one channel and then the national news on another channel. Instruct the student to identify and describe a news event covered by both	programs. Then, have the students list any differences in both language and image between the two newscasts.

Step-by-Step Teaching Guide

Evaluating Information From the Media

1. Write the following statements on the board.
   - *There was very little rainfall in Iraq in November 1998.*
   - *It's wonderful that there was very little rainfall in Iraq in November 1998.*

2. Ask students what the difference is between these two statements. (The first statement is a fact because it can be proved. The second one is an opinion because it is a personal judgment.) Ask whether some people in Iraq might disagree with each statement, to get students to see that most people could not disagree with the first statement, but many could disagree with the second.

3. When evaluating information media, it is important to distinguish between ideas that can be proved and those that convey someone's personal feelings or biases.

4. Have several students describe commercials they have seen recently and describe the loaded nature of the information included.

5. Ask students whether commercials offer different viewpoints or opinions about the products being sold. (No. Commercials are biased—they show only one side.)

6. Direct students' attention to the strategies for evaluating information from the media and ask them to apply these strategies to evaluate any recent information media they have encountered.

Customize for
ESL Students

Loaded language can be hard to recognize because it often uses idioms, jargon, and clichés. On television it is usually easy to see loaded images. People drinking a certain soft drink are all beautiful and fun.

Answer Key

▶ **Exercise 8**

Answers will vary. Students should recognize kinds of programs and be able to differentiate between fact and opinion and to recognize examples of bias and loaded language and imagery.

Viewing Fine Art Critically

1. Students may be intimidated by fine art. Experts say that *Mona Lisa* is a great painting, but they don't like it. So they think they must be stupid.

2. It is all right to like some pieces of art but not others. There are many reasons why a viewer might respond to a painting: the colors are pretty; the shapes are interesting; it reminds him or her of a past experience. Assure students that there is no one right response.

3. Students can practice appreciating art by making up a story to go with Chagall's painting. Then, have them choose an abstract work from their book and make up a story about it too.

Answer Key

Exercise 9

Answers will vary. Sample responses are given.

1. The work is a painting.
2. The work depicts a scene: a farmyard with a building, a horse, a broken-down cart, another building, and hills in the distance.
3. Answers will vary. Students may note that the scene depicted is calm, but that the style of the painting is energetic.
4. The objects seem ordinary-sized.
5. The space seems crowded, almost as if the large building is ramming into the left side of the painting, crowding out the other objects.
6. The colors in the painting are white, brown, yellow, and blue—neutral and cool.
7. Most of the lines are straight and thick, except for the curvy lines on the roof of the house. The brushstrokes are wide and somewhat jumbled.
8. Dark areas include the background (sky and hills). Light areas include the foreground, primarily the house. The contrast makes the farmyard seem peaceful and the hills and sky threatening.

9. The lines of the farmhouse sweep in towards the left side of the painting, where they meet with the tight lines of the smaller building on the left, which point inward and straight across.
10. Answers will vary. Students may note that the energetic brushstrokes, the cramped look of the object on the left, and the sweep of lines in towards a spot on the left create a sense of unrest even in a calm scene.

28.2

Viewing Fine Art Critically

When you look at a painting, you may not find much information about the world. Instead, you will find a mood, a movement of color, or the drama of an event. Paintings, drawings, and photographs are all examples of visual fine art. Visual art uses line, shape, color, and motion to take your imagination on a journey. By interpreting these elements, you can travel farther on the journey that a work of art inspires.

▶ **KEY CONCEPT** Interpret the elements of art to understand the devices used to enrich your enjoyment of it. ■

To help you interpret a work of art, answer the following questions on the formal elements of art:

1. Is the work a painting? Is it a photograph? Is it a drawing?
2. Does the work depict a scene or tell a story? Is it abstract—using lines, colors, textures, and patterns to create a mood or to release energy, but without representing people or objects?
3. What is your response to the work? Do you find it joyful or sad, calm or energetic?
4. Do objects represented seem ordinary-sized, gigantic, or tiny?
5. How is space defined? Is there a lot of space between objects, only a little, or are both large and small distances represented?
6. Are the colors neutral (black, white, grays, and browns), cool (blues and greens), or warm (reds, oranges, and yellows)?
7. What kinds of lines are used? Are they thick or thin, straight or curvy? Are they bold or faint? In a painting, what kind of brushstrokes does the painter use?
8. Which areas are darkest and which are lightest? What mood does the contrast create?
9. The outlines or arrangements of objects can create "lines" that guide your eye through a work. In what directions do the lines in the work invite your eye to travel?
10. What elements of the work contribute to your reaction to it?

▶ **Exercise 9** Interpreting Fine Art Interpret the formal elements of the painting *The Farmyard*, by Russian-born artist Marc Chagall, by asking and answering the questions given above. Write your answers in your notebook.

▲ **Critical Viewing** What personal experiences or memories does this painting bring to mind? [Connect]

Critical Viewing

Answers will vary. Students should refer to details of the painting in explaining their answers.

Creating Graphic Organizers for Comprehension

When you need to comprehend a great deal of information or read an article with long descriptions, it is helpful to organize what you read.

KEY CONCEPT When you have a lot of information or technical data to present, consider putting that information into a visual form that is easy to view and comprehend. ■

Use the following strategies to construct graphic organizers:

- **Use Text Descriptions** Some types of writing give lots of descriptive information, often organized with headings and subheadings to indicate various sections. To help you understand all the information, create a graphic organizer, such as a concept map, that displays the information visually. For text with detailed descriptions, you may want to create a drawing to clarify the details. For example, a graphic image would help to visualize an architectural concept.

- **Look at Text Structure** The organization of a text can help you create graphic organizers. First, identify the text structure. Is it presented in comparison-and-contrast, cause-and-effect, main-idea-and-details, or chronological order? For comparison and contrast, a Venn diagram or a comparison chart can show similarities and differences. A flowchart can help you understand cause-and-effect relationships. An outline is one way to organize a main idea with many supporting details. One way to visualize chronological order is by creating a timeline.

- **Identify Your Purpose** Consider which parts of the text you want to present. Then, decide which type of graphic organizer will help you to present this information effectively. For instance, you might want to show what two story characters have in common, or chart three possible outcomes of a character's actions. Or you might want to compare and contrast the percentages of people who own mountain bikes and racing bikes.

> **More Practice**
>
> Academic and Workplace Skills Activity Book
> • p. 9–11

Step-by-Step Teaching Guide

Creating Graphic Organizers for Comprehension

1. Using a visual form to represent ideas can be a good way to understand and organize a large amount of information.

2. Text descriptions, text structure, and definition of purpose can help students to create graphic organizers efficiently and accurately.

3. Give students a sample plot map of a story they have read, such as "All Summer in a Day" or "Rikki-tikki-tavi," as a model of how to organize information visually.

4. Have students practice making graphic organizers of their own with a recently read text. Then, share graphic organizers to discuss how each person chose to organize the information.

5. Stress that graphic organizers should be designed so that the creator understands the ideas he or she is representing and the relationship between them.

ONGOING ASSESSMENT: Monitor and Reinforce

If students have trouble with Exercise 9, consider the following option.

Instruct the students to pick a piece of art that they are both familiar with and fond of, and	then have them write about two formal aspects of the artwork.

Graphic Organizers and Aids

1. The examples and descriptions of graphic organizers and aids on pages 682–683 provide students with an opportunity to review their uses and applications.

2. Remind students that charts, graphs, and tables come in many forms and provide information in useful formats for readers.

3. Diagrams and illustrations are often used to explain complicated processes or unfamiliar information. Maps can convey different kinds of information ranging from how to get from one place to another to what kind of geographical features exist in a particular region.

28.2

Charts, Graphs, and Tables To present columns of numbers, survey statistics, or other complex information, create a chart, graph, or table. A chart can be any shape or color and contain any type of information, such as the seating arrangement in your classroom. A graph, such as a bar or line graph, is a good way to show changes that take place over time. Tables enable you to present scientific and statistical information clearly and logically.

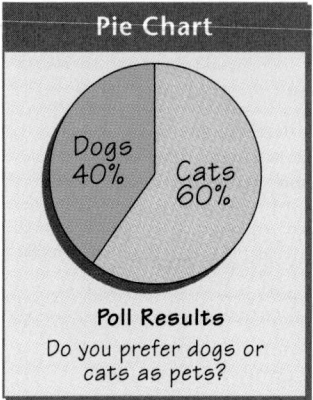

Pie Chart

Dogs 40%

Cats 60%

Poll Results
Do you prefer dogs or cats as pets?

Diagrams and Illustrations Diagrams and illustrations are line drawings that indicate the features of something. If you were describing an airplane, for example, you might create a diagram and label the plane's parts—the rudder, the landing gear, the wing—on the diagram.

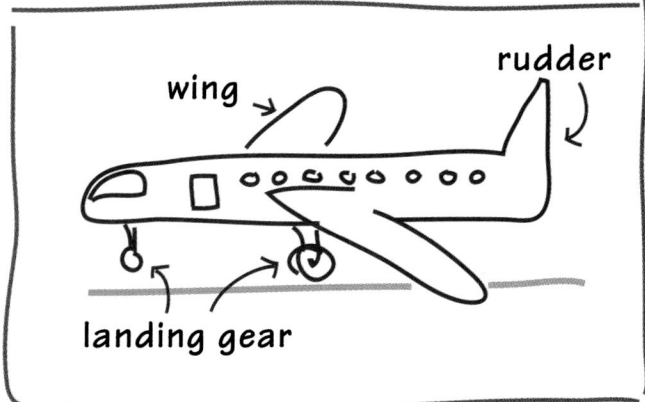

wing

rudder

landing gear

Maps If you are writing directions to someone's house or explaining the geography of several regions, it's probably best to present that information in map form. In fact, maps can show almost any type of information—for example, highway routes, geological formations, air currents, or hotel locations.

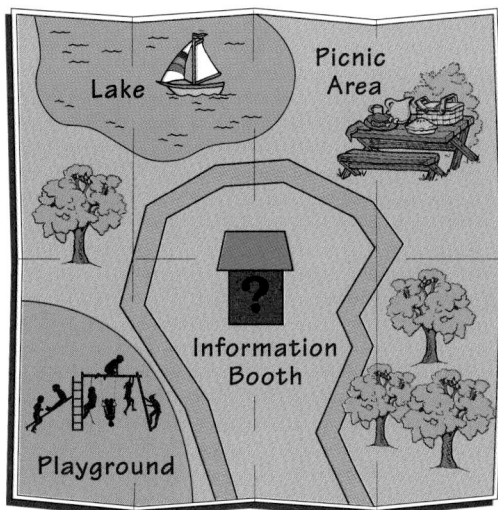

> **Exercise 10** Using Graphic Organizers and Aids Answer the following questions on a sheet of paper.
>
> 1. If you wanted to give a history of your town's population figures over the past century, what form of graphic organizer or aid would you choose to create? Why?
> 2. What forms of writing most typically contain graphic organizers or aids?

> **Exercise 11** Creating Graphic Organizers and Aids
> Complete each of the following assignments, using a sheet of paper of the appropriate size and kind. Use pens, pencils, or markers of different colors when necessary.
>
> 1. Draw a map of the route from your house to a friend's house. Show important landmarks and turns, but do not overload your map with unnecessary details.
> 2. Outline a section of your social studies or science textbook with a graphic organizer.
> 3. Take a poll of your class. Get their opinion on an issue or a question. Use a type of graph to present your data.

Answer Key

> **Exercise 10**

1. Point out that the activity instructions include the phrase "a history of your town's population figures." A bar or line graph is a good way to show changes that take place over time or compare populations at different times.
2. Answers may include textbooks, instruction manuals, historical articles, atlases, and so on.

> **Exercise 11**

Graphic organizers and aids will vary. Assess students' work for organization, clarity, and completeness.

Formatting to Create Effect

1. Have students study the image of the Skills Activity. Make a class list on the board of all the different formatting elements used in this example. Responses should include the following:

   Capitals—the words SKILLS ACTIVITY at the top of the page

   *Boldface—the **T** that begins the text on the page and the lesson title and headings*

   Numbered (or Lettered) Lists—the instructions under the heading TRY IT OUT

   Bulleted List—the list under the heading GET READY

2. Ask students to match the explanations given for the different elements of formatting with the ways they are used in the example.

Answer Key

> **Exercise 12**

Students can create professional-looking flyers on the computer. They may want to display them around the classroom or in school hallways.

28.2

Formatting to Create Effect

Any written work can be enhanced by using basic word-processing formatting features such as boldface, italics, capitals, and numbered and bulleted lists. Following are some tips for making the most of these features:

1. Capitals in heads call out important ideas and topics.
2. Boldface can direct the reader's attention to key concepts or ideas within a written work.
3. Italics give special emphasis to a written line or word.
4. Numbered lists can be used when you have steps to be followed in sequence.
5. Bulleted lists can be used for items that do not follow a particular order.

> **Exercise 12** Using Formatting to Create a Flyer Using the tips on formatting listed above, create a flyer advertising a special event at your school. Then, give reasons for your formatting choices.

> **More Practice**
>
> Academic and Workplace Skills Activity Book
> • p. 12

⏱ TIME AND RESOURCE MANAGER

Resources
Print: Academic and Workplace Skills Activity Book, pp. 12–15

In-Depth Coverage	Accelerated Pace
• Work through all key concepts, pp. 684–687 • Assign and review selected activities on pp. 684–687	• Assign pp. 684–687 for independent student review

Developing a Multimedia Presentation

In most multimedia presentations, the presenter gives an oral report, illustrating the main points with media selections. This type of presentation can be effective and memorable if it is well planned and executed.

KEY CONCEPT Multimedia presentations supply information through a variety of media, including text, slides, videos, music, maps, charts, and art. ∎

Tips for Preparing a Multimedia Presentation

- Create an outline of your report first, and then decide which parts to illustrate through the use of media.

- Choose a medium that is suited to your topic. For example, if you were discussing the art of Leonardo da Vinci, reproductions of his artwork and music selections from his time would enhance your presentation.

- Evenly space the media within your presentation. Don't bunch them up at the beginning or end of your presentation.

- Check to ensure that the media you've selected will be able to be seen or heard by everyone. A postage stamp, for example, is too small to be held up in front of a large audience. It would be better to photocopy it and enlarge the image.

- Before the presentation, check your equipment—slide projectors, overhead projectors, microphones, cassette players—to be sure that they are in working condition.

- Always have a backup plan in case anything goes wrong with the equipment.

- Plan to rehearse with the equipment the day before the presentation. Be sure you know the location of all controls—for focus or for volume, for example—and understand their use.

Exercise 13 Preparing a Multimedia Presentation Read through the saved writings in your portfolio. Select one that could be made into a multimedia presentation. Then, using an outline, select the media you'd like to include, and decide on the sequence of your presentation.

▲ **Critical Viewing**
What media is this student using to enhance her oral report? **[Interpret]**

More Practice

Academic and Workplace Skills Activity Book
• p. 13

Developing a Multimedia Presentation

1. Using a variety of media in a presentation to supply information can help make the facts and ideas expressed clear, meaningful, and interesting to the audience.

2. Ask students to brainstorm a list of the kinds of media available for their use in a multimedia presentation, and create a list on the board.

3. Ask students to consider the topics they selected earlier for their speeches and whether these topics could be made into a multimedia presentation.

4. Ask one student to volunteer his or her topic and the information gathered. Using the tips for preparing a multimedia presentation listed in the book, ask students to decide what forms of media could be used and when in the presentation.

Answer Key

Exercise 13

Students may want to work in small groups that contain at least one visual learner.

Critical Viewing

Interpret Students may suggest that the student in the photograph is using both a video and maps to make her presentation.

Creating a Video

1. Ask students what they think makes a good video.

2. Explain that video can be a powerful medium of expression and that video makers have many different purposes for creating pieces.

3. Ask students to recall the most recent video they have seen and to try to determine what the artist's purpose was in creating it.

4. Have students consider a topic or message that they may want to communicate to an audience and then share it with a partner.

5. Have partners read through the basic steps for creating a video before offering each other feedback about the feasibility of creating a video on the topic described.

Answer Key

> **Exercise 14**

If students do not have access to video equipment, they can create the video as an extended storyboard. If students do create videos, they may want to arrange a formal showing in the school auditorium.

Critical Viewing

Speculate Students may say they are shooting in a well-lit, quiet location, but they might improve the video by not shooting with light behind the girl.

28.2

Creating a Video

Video allows viewers to see the world as you see it. A video can communicate a message, entertain, or do both.

> **KEY CONCEPT** Create a video to inform or entertain your audience. ■

Although a video can last from seconds to hours, and subjects can range from the serious to the ridiculous, certain rules of thumb apply to all videography:

Basic Steps

1. Write out the story or message in the form of a shooting script. A shooting script contains lines to be spoken, or the dialogue among characters. It also contains directions about camera angles and descriptions of settings, costumes or wardrobe, and props.
2. Create a storyboard to show a clear sequence of events. A storyboard looks like a cartoon strip, with each important shot planned out.
3. Select locations for shooting, and get permission to use them.
4. Cast the roles or parts, and rehearse.
5. Write out a shooting schedule (the order in which scenes will be shot and who will be involved in each), and distribute it to all the characters.
6. Tape the scenes.
7. Edit the video. Store the video in a safe place.

Tips for Taping

- Hold the camera steady.
- Select a quiet location for shooting. Keep in mind that outdoor locations can be unpredictably noisy.
- When in doubt, shoot more. It's easier to cut scenes than to have to reassemble the cast and crew to refilm.
- Keep scenes simple and short.

> **Exercise 14** Create a Video Create a three-minute documentary. Write out the information you want to include in your documentary in the form of a shooting script. Next, create a storyboard. Select the location and actors for your documentary. Then, film and edit your work. Use the Tips for Taping to help you in your presentation.

▲ Critical Viewing
What tips for shooting a video are these students paying attention to? How could they improve their video shooting? **[Speculate]**

Performing or Interpreting

Communication through performance is an art that has existed since the dawn of history, if not before.

▶ **KEY CONCEPT** Performers use a variety of techniques to convey the meaning of a text or song. ■

Prepare to Perform

1. Write the text in a notebook, and highlight its most important words and ideas.
2. Read the text aloud several times, experimenting with the tone and pitch of your voice.
3. Practice using body language, including hand gestures and posture, to convey meaning.
4. Consider background music to enhance the mood.
5. Establish a mood through your choice of setting, costumes, and music.
6. Rehearse.

Keep in Mind

- Always speak more slowly than you think is necessary.
- Don't fidget.
- Periodically make eye contact with your audience, unless you are representing a character in a scene.

▶ **Exercise 15** **Preparing to Perform** Select a poem you would like to interpret. Copy it, highlighting its key ideas and words. Then, jot down performance notes, planning the effect you'd like your reading to have and the mood you'd like to set.

▲ **Critical Viewing**
Actor Albert Finney here plays Shakespeare's Hamlet. What mood does his body language convey? **[Infer]**

▶ **More Practice**

Academic and Workplace Skills Activity Book
- pp. 14–16

Reflecting on Your Speaking, Listening, Viewing, and Representing Skills

Review all the different kinds of speaking, listening, viewing, and representing purposes discussed in this section. Write a journal entry discussing these experiences. Begin your inquiry by asking yourself these questions:

- What experiences did I find the most enjoyable?
- What experiences were the most difficult?
- What experiences gave me the most information?
- What experiences presented the most information?
- What skills would I most like to improve? Why?

Viewing and Representing Skills • 687

Performing or Interpreting

1. Performance artists use more than just words to communicate their meaning.
2. Show students a performance on video, or ask students to recall a recent performance they saw in a movie or on TV.
3. Ask students to make a list of the techniques the performer used to convey his or her meaning.
4. Ask students to select a short reading or part of a favorite story.
5. Have students use the steps for preparing to perform before getting into small groups to perform their texts.
6. Ask audience group members to give the performer feedback on speed, body language, and eye contact after the performance.
7. Have the groups choose one person each to perform for the class.

Customize for
Bodily/Kinesthetic Learners

Some students may be able to express the meaning conveyed in a text more accurately or comfortably through physical interpretation. Give the option of interpreting a text through nonverbal means. Encourage them to follow the same steps to prepare their presentations.

Critical Viewing

Infer Students may conclude that Finney is sad or grieving because of the actor's bowed head and furrowed brow, as well as the fact that he is reaching towards his head with his hand.

Answer Key

▶ **Exercise 15**

Encourage students to read their selected poems to the class.

☑ **ONGOING ASSESSMENT: Monitor and Reinforce**

If students have difficulty with Exercise 15, try one of the following options.

Option 1 Have the student practice the poem in front of a mirror or in front of family members.	**Option 2** Suggest that the student learn a short poem. This way he or she can memorize the words and pay more attention to delivery.

Lesson Objectives

• To interpret ideas and information from maps, charts, and graphics

Step-by-Step Teaching Guide

Interpreting Graphic Aids

Teaching Resources: Standardized Test Preparation Workbook, pp. 55–56

1. Have students cover the "Answers and Explanations" column in their textbooks.

2. Have a volunteer read aloud the first question to the class.

3. Help students to see that the largest proportional increase from one bar to the next occurred between 1950 and 1952.

4. Direct students' attention to the second question. Ask students to answer the following questions for each possible choice listed:

   • Is this statement true?

   • Does it have any relation to the information provided in the text or in the graph?

5. Students should see that the only choice that is both true and related to the information is item G.

Standardized Test Preparation Workshop

Interpreting Graphic Aids

Some standardized tests contain questions testing your ability to gather details, draw conclusions, and interpret from the information provided in maps, charts, graphs, and other graphic aids. The sample item that follows will help you become familiar with these types of questions.

Test Tip

As you look at each graphic aid, examine legends, keys, and titles before drawing conclusions from the information.

Sample Test Items

Read the passage, study the graphic aid, and answer the questions that follow.

Before 1950, television was a novelty. As technology advanced and prices fell, television sets became more accessible. By the end of the decade, they were a common feature in American homes.

1 For each two-year period, consider how many times greater the number of homes with television sets was at the end of the period than at the beginning. During which period did the largest proportional growth occur?

   A 1950–1952
   B 1954–1956
   C 1956–1958
   D 1958–1960

Homes With Television Sets

(bar graph: Millions of Homes vs. Year 1948–1960)

Answers and Explanations

The correct answer is *A, 1950–1952*. During those years, the number of homes with television sets tripled.

2 What logical conclusion could you draw about the increase in television purchases?

   F Televisions were not as large as before.
   G Televisions became more affordable for the average family during the decade.
   H There was more advertising of televisions toward the end of the decade.
   J Television created new celebrities.

The correct answer is *G. Televisions became more affordable for the average family during the decade.* This is the most logical conclusion to draw, based on the information provided in the passage and the chart.

688 • Speaking, Listening, Viewing, and Representing

TEST-TAKING TIP

Maps usually contain a great deal of information. Some students may be overwhelmed when faced with the task of reading a map. Encourage students to familiarize themselves with the details and information contained in different kinds of maps. If you have an atlas in the classroom, have students work in groups to list the kinds of information they can learn from a particular map. This practice will help them when they are confronted with standardized test questions that require them to interpret maps.

▶ **Practice 1** **Directions:** Read the passage, study the map, and answer the questions that follow.

Egypt was first united in 3200 B.C. It was ruled by pharaohs during three great kingdoms: Old, Middle, and New. It developed along riverbanks, where great cities were built and civilizations developed.

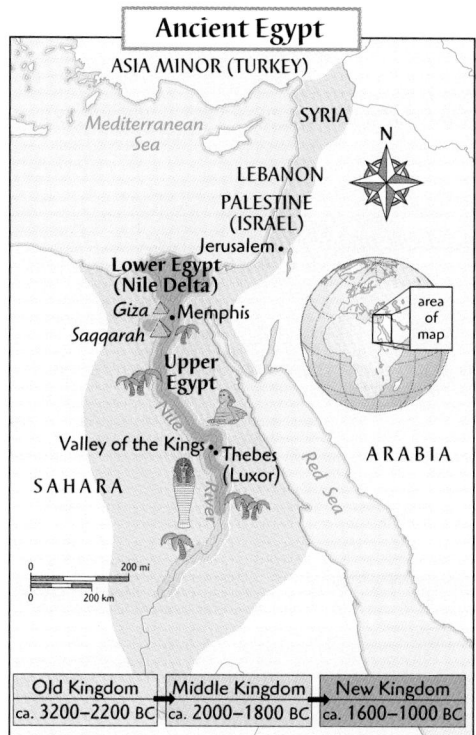

Ancient Egypt

Old Kingdom	Middle Kingdom	New Kingdom
ca. 3200–2200 BC	ca. 2000–1800 BC	ca. 1600–1000 BC

1 Which statement best describes how Egypt changed between 3200 and 1000 B.C.?

A The area of land Egypt ruled grew.
B The area of land Egypt ruled shrank.
C The Egyptian navy grew more powerful.
D The area of desert in Egypt grew.

2 Throughout the three kingdoms, where did the rule of the pharaohs remain strong?

F along the northern part of the Nile
G in the Sahara
H along the Mediterranean
J from Syria to Upper Egypt

3 Which of the following geographical features encouraged the rise of early civilizations?

A a good ocean harbor in a region with a cool climate
B a large river in a region with a warm climate
C a large desert surrounded by numerous mountains
D a good ocean harbor near a large jungle

4 Along which bodies of water did ancient civilizations in Egypt develop?

F Red Sea and Nile River
G Nile River, Atlantic Ocean, and Red Sea
H Mediterranean Sea
J Nile River

5 What direction would one take to travel from Thebes to Giza?

A north
B south
C west
D east

6 Approximately how many miles lie between Memphis and Thebes?

F 600 miles
G 30 miles
H 300 miles
J 10 miles

In-Depth Lesson Plan

	LESSON FOCUS	PRINT AND MEDIA RESOURCES
DAY 1	**Vocabulary** Students learn to develop vocabulary skills (pp. 691–694).	**Teaching Resources** *Academic and Workplace Skills Activity Book,* pp. 17–18
DAY 2	**Studying Words** Students learn how to systematically study words to build vocabulary (pp. 695–697).	**Teaching Resources** *Academic and Workplace Skills Activity Book,* pp. 19–21
DAY 3	**Word Parts and Origins** Students learn to study word parts and etymologies (pp. 698–701).	**Teaching Resources** *Academic and Workplace Skills Activity Book,* pp. 22–25
DAY 4	**Spelling** Students learn spelling skills (pp. 702–711).	**Teaching Resources** *Academic and Workplace Skills Activity Book,* pp. 26–33

Accelerated Lesson Plan

	LESSON FOCUS	PRINT AND MEDIA RESOURCES
DAY 1	**Vocabulary** Students learn skills for building their vocabulary (pp. 691–701).	**Teaching Resources** *Academic and Workplace Skills Activity Book,* pp. 17–25
DAY 2	**Spelling** Students learn spelling skills (pp. 702–711).	**Teaching Resources** *Academic and Workplace Skills Activity Book,* pp. 26–33

Options for Adapting Lesson Plans

HOMEWORK
Have students complete any section of the chapter for homework.

TECHNOLOGY
Students can use the On-Line Exercise Bank to complete the exercises on computer. The Auto Check feature will grade their work.

INTEGRATED SKILLS COVERAGE

Technology
SE p. 710

Viewing and Representing
Critical Viewing, SE pp. 690, 691, 693, 694, 700, 707, 709

ASSESSMENT SUPPORT

Standardized Test Preparation, SE p. 712
Standardized Test Preparation Workbook, pp. 57–58
Formal Assessment, Ch. 29

MEETING INDIVIDUAL NEEDS

ESL Students ATE pp. 692, 693, 703
Less Advanced Students ATE p. 693. See also Ongoing
Assessments, pp. 693, 695, 701, 710.

BLOCK SCHEDULING

Pacing Suggestions
For 90-minute Blocks
• Administer the Diagnostic Test to students to determine
instructional coverage.
• Have students complete the necessary exercises in class. Use
the Hands-on Grammar activity to provide a change of pace.

Professional Development Support
• *How to manage instruction in the block* This Teaching
Resource provides management and activity suggestions.

MEDIA AND TECHNOLOGY

For the Teacher
• *Resource Pro* **CD-ROM**

WRITING AND GRAMMAR WEB SITE

The Interactive Writing and Grammar Web site provides a wide
array of support for students, teachers, and parents. Grammar
support includes:

• On-Line Exercise Bank with Auto Check scoring
• Diagnostic and assessment support

www.phschool.com

Lesson Objectives

1. Apply knowledge of letter-word correspondences, language structure, and context to recognize words.

2. Use structural analysis to identify words, including knowledge of Greek and Latin roots and prefixes/suffixes.

3. Locate the meanings, pronunciations, and derivations of unfamiliar words using dictionaries, glossaries, and other sources.

Critical Viewing

Analyze Students should say that she is using a dictionary. Learning words helps to increase your vocabulary.

Chapter 29 Vocabulary and Spelling

An unfamiliar word can be like a roadblock. When you hear or read the word, your understanding of what's going on may grind to a halt. At the same time, hearing or reading an unfamiliar word can be like coming to a bridge. It is your chance to learn the word and cross over into new understanding. By learning a new word, you increase your ability to grasp the ideas of others and to communicate your own thoughts effectively. This chapter includes a number of methods for learning and remembering the new words you encounter. Choose the methods that you find most useful.

▲ **Critical Viewing**
What language tool is this student using? How can it help increase her vocabulary? **[Analyze]**

690 • Vocabulary and Spelling

⏱ TIME AND RESOURCE MANAGER

Resources
Print: Academic and Workplace Skills Activity Book, pp. 17–18

In-Depth Coverage	Accelerated Pace
• Work through all key concepts, pp. 691–694. • Assign and review Exercises 1–3.	• Assign pp. 691–694 for independent student review.

Section 29.1 Developing Your Vocabulary

What would we do without words? We could draw complicated pictures. We could grunt and point. But we are lucky enough to have inherited a well-developed written and spoken language complete with a wide variety of words. Human beings use language to communicate with each other. By building your vocabulary, you can communicate with others more effectively.

▶ **KEY CONCEPT** The most common ways to increase your vocabulary are listening, reading, and taking part in conversation. ■

Conversation You've been building your vocabulary since the day you were born! The words you learned as a toddler were ones you heard in conversation. By first listening to and then taking part in conversations, you learned the meanings and pronunciations of new words. Use the same strategy in your life today. Listen for unfamiliar words whenever you talk to teachers, people from different places, and people with interests that are different from your own. Find out what the words mean by asking or by looking the words up in a dictionary.

Works Read Aloud Another way to build your vocabulary is to listen to works of literature read aloud. Many works are available on audiocassette or CD. By listening, you will hear how unfamiliar words are pronounced and how they are used in context. You may even choose to read along while the work is being read so that you can see and hear new words.

Wide Reading The more you read, the more new words you will encounter. Soon, new words will become familiar words as you encounter them again and again. Read from a wide variety of sources to encounter the widest variety of words and to learn how the same word may be used in a variety of contexts.

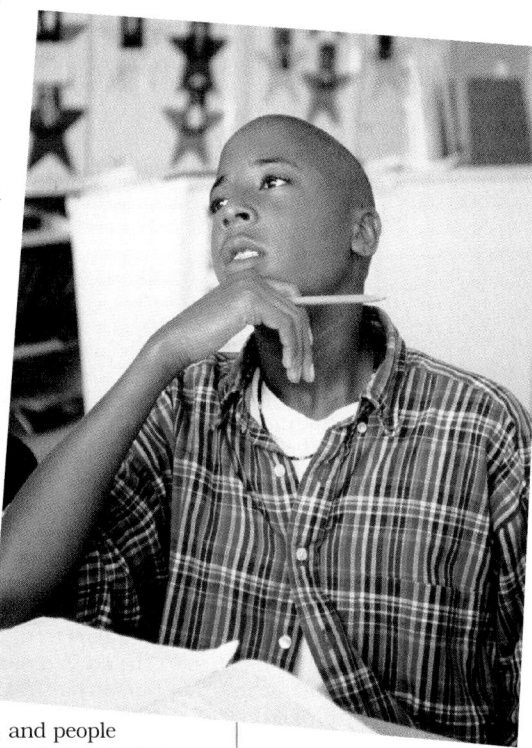

▲ Critical Viewing
Do you think this student is listening to someone speak or thinking about something he just read? Explain. **[Analyze]**

PREPARE and ENGAGE

Interest GRABBER Write the following zany *z* words on the chalkboard:

zabaglione

zarf

zebu

ziggurat

zonk

zoot suit

zori

zounds

Have eight groups each choose one word, find its definition, use it in a sentence, and report back to the class.

Activate Prior Knowledge

Ask students about the last time (before the Interest Grabber!) they learned a new word. You may want to help them by reiterating some of the places they may have picked up new vocabulary, such as science class, reading a book, watching TV, listening to someone speak. Ask students to talk about what makes them start using a new word in conversation. Students might share that they like the word, it's impressive, it describes something important to them, it's cool, or they have to use it in school assignments.

Critical Viewing

Analyze Students may suggest he is listening to someone because his eyes are focused on something in front of him and he appears to be listening. Others may think he is deep in thought.

Developing Your Vocabulary • 691

Recognizing Context Clues

1. Write the following sentences on the chalkboard:

   Monica was <u>ravenous</u> because she hadn't eaten anything since breakfast.

   Stanley <u>importuned</u> his mother, begging her to let him go to the ball game.

2. Ask students how they can figure out the meaning of the underlined words. Context clues should not be new to students. If necessary, point out that "she hadn't eaten . . ." is a clue that *ravenous* means "hungry." In the second sentence, *beg* is a synonym for *importune*.

3. Using context clues this way to understand a word can help students get the overall meaning of a text without stopping to look up the word. Looking up every unfamiliar word while reading can actually get in the way of overall comprehension.

Customize for
ESL Students

Tell students who are learning English that it is often impossible to figure out the meaning of an unknown idiom. *The history quiz was a piece of cake.* A quiz has nothing to do with cake. Students can ask someone what the idiom means. If they are shy, they can use the dictionary. The idiom is often listed as part of the entry for the main word, in this case *cake*.

Answer Key

Exercise 1

1. Students should cite *encouraged and supported artists* as a context clue.
2. Students should cite *rare opportunity* as a context clue.
3. Students should cite *filled the woods with color* as a context clue.
4. Students should cite *outraged child* as a context clue.
5. Students should cite *natural fabrics* as a context clue.

29.1

Recognizing Context Clues

If you carefully analyze the sentence or paragraph containing an unfamiliar word, you can sometimes determine the word's meaning.

▶ **KEY CONCEPT** The **context** of a word is the other words and the ideas that it is connected with. For instance, the rest of the sentence in which a word appears is part of its context. ■

USING CONTEXT CLUES

1. Read the sentence, concentrating on the unknown word.
2. Look for clues in the surrounding words.
3. Guess the possible meaning of the new word.
4. Substitute your meaning for the word. If the sentence does not make sense, try another guess.
5. Check the word's meaning in the dictionary.
6. Add it to your notebook.

Figurative Language *Figurative language*, which is language that is not meant to be taken literally, often uses familiar words in unfamiliar ways. For example, you might encounter the sentence, "The leaves pirouette in the wind." You might know the literal meaning of *pirouette*: "a dance movement in which the dancer spins on one toe." The context of the sentence shows, however, that leaves, not human dancers, are being referred to. Using your knowledge of the context, you can see that *pirouette* here means "spinning about like a dancer."

Idioms An *idiom* is an expression used with a special meaning, one different from what the words literally mean. For instance, "easy as pie" is an idiom meaning "extremely easy." Often, idioms used by people from an area or time other than your own will be unfamiliar. Use context clues to figure out the meaning. Compare unfamiliar idioms to expressions that you use for similar meanings.

▶ **Exercise 1** **Using Context Clues** Explain how context clues help you determine the meaning of each underlined word or group of words.
1. The arts <u>flourished</u> because patrons encouraged and supported artists.
2. Knowing this was a rare opportunity, the coach decided to <u>seize the moment</u>.
3. The <u>kaleidoscope</u> of autumn leaves filled the woods with color.
4. The baby sitter tried to <u>placate</u> the outraged child.
5. I prefer natural fabrics to <u>synthetic</u> ones.

⚙ **Grammar and Style Tip**

Use figurative language to add interest to stories and poems. Use idioms to make dialogue sound realistic.

▶ **More Practice**

Academic and Workplace Skills Activity Book
• pp. 17–18

Studying Meanings in the Content Areas

Use a Notebook and a Glossary

Learning words from context helps you incorporate them into your working vocabulary. This method takes time, though. To master a subject such as social studies or science, you need to have the meanings of special words right at your fingertips. Keep a special section of your notebook in each subject area to write the meanings and pronunciations of new words you encounter. Use the glossary at the back of your textbook to find the subject-specific meaning of unfamiliar words.

Social Studies In social studies, you are likely to encounter words that deal with types of government, political activity, and physical features of an area. Use categories such as these to group words based on what they name or describe. Make notes concerning similar or opposing ideas. For instance, you might note that democracy and dictatorship name opposite forms of government.

Science Unfamiliar words in science often have Latin origins. Categorize science words by their prefixes, suffixes, or roots. For example, you could group *photosynthesis* with *phototropism* because they both begin with *photo-*. Once you have learned that *photo-* means "of or produced by light," you will more easily remember the meanings of both words.

Current Events By listening to the news or reading a newspaper, you increase the likelihood that you will encounter the words you learned in science and social studies. The more times you hear or see a word used, the better you will understand its meaning. Use current event topics as a source of vocabulary reinforcement.

▶ **Exercise 2** Studying Words in the Content Areas Work with a partner to come up with a list of unfamiliar words in a chapter from your social studies or science book. Write the words on index cards, look up their definitions, and group the words in various ways. When you are satisfied that the words are logically grouped, record them in your notebook.

▼ Critical Viewing
This student may be writing unfamiliar words in his notebook. How will that help him to increase his vocabulary? **[Infer]**

Developing Your Vocabulary • 693

Use a Notebook and a Glossary

1. Using a variety of techniques to learn and remember new words will help students build their vocabulary.

2. Point out that they are learning new words every day in their other classes, but some of these words are probably forgotten because students don't use them very often.

3. They can help themselves remember these words by creating a special vocabulary glossary in their notebooks. They can do this with a divider or by folding a page in half to create a division that is easy to find.

4. Choose a recent word that students encountered in class and have them enter it into their vocabulary glossary. Next, ask students to enter the definition.

5. Encourage students to enter unfamiliar words they encounter in all of their classes in the same manner.

Customize for
Less Advanced and ESL Students

Students can make flashcards with a word on one side and the definition (including a drawing, if they wish) on the other side. Students can also include the word in their home language. Encourage partners to use the flashcards to quiz each other.

Critical Viewing

Infer Students may suggest that writing the words and their definitions reinforces understanding.

Answer Key

▶ **Exercise 2**

Responses will vary. Students should not just list unfamiliar words in a subject; they should also arrange them according to logical groupings.

☑ **ONGOING ASSESSMENT: Monitor and Reinforce**

If students have difficulty recording the proper pronunciation of words, try the following option.

Photocopy the pronunciation guide of a dictionary and hand the copies out to students.	Review the pronunciation symbols with students.

Using "Possible Sentences"

1. One of the best ways to remember the meanings of new words is to use them in sentences. Words are tools that help people communicate ideas and feelings, and the more students practice using these tools the better they'll become at expressing themselves.

2. Ask students to list five words from their vocabulary notebook or from something that they are currently reading. These should be words with which they're unfamiliar.

3. Tell them to write five new sentences using these words. Make sure that students don't simply write definitions from the dictionary. These should be sentences that come from their own imagination and their new understanding of the words.

Answer Key

▶ **Exercise 3**

Responses will vary.

Critical Viewing

Analyze Students may say that it makes communicating easier.

29.1

Using "Possible Sentences"

You can experiment with unfamiliar words by using the Possible Sentences strategy. This method increases your vocabulary and your understanding of words in context.

STEPS FOR USING POSSIBLE SENTENCES

1. Find an unfamiliar word in your reading, and use context clues to figure out its meaning.
2. Write a sentence for the unfamiliar word in your vocabulary notebook.
3. Check the actual meaning of the word in a dictionary.
4. Evaluate your sentence to see whether you have used the word correctly.
5. Revise your sentence to make it correct.

▶ **Exercise 3** Using Possible Sentences Using the steps mentioned above, apply the Possible Sentences strategy to increase your understanding of five vocabulary words from a novel, short story, or textbook you are reading.

◀ Critical Viewing Each of these people has a different set of vocabulary words. Why is it important for people to learn as many words as they can? **[Analyze]**

Section 29.2 Studying Words Systematically

Keeping a Vocabulary Notebook

KEY CONCEPT A vocabulary notebook will help you to learn new words. You can use the notebook, flashcards, and a tape recorder to help you review. Study and review new words a few times each week. ∎

Create a Vocabulary Notebook Keep a notebook available to list new words, along with a dictionary. On the top of each page in your notebook, write the chapter or book title. Divide your page into three sections, listing the word, its definition, and some examples of how to use it.

> Chapter 5: The Early Nation
>
> | Words | Definitions | Examples |
> |---|---|---|
> | anticipate (an tis' ə pāt) | look forward to; expect | Did the British anticipate an early end to the war? |
> | repeal (ri pēl') | withdraw officially or formally; revoke | Congress decided to repeal the law. |
> | embargo (im bär' gō) | a government order prohibiting the entry or departure of commercial ships to its ports | What is the purpose of imposing an embargo? |

Exercise 4 Setting Up a Vocabulary Notebook Select one of the subjects you are studying this year or one of the books you are reading for pleasure. As you read, jot down any unfamiliar words. When you have finished a chapter, look up unfamiliar words in a dictionary, and record the meaning in your notebook.

▶ **More Practice**
Academic and Workplace Skills Activity Book
• p. 19

Studying Words Systematically • **695**

PREPARE and ENGAGE

Interest GRABBER Ask students what they normally do when they come upon an unfamiliar word as they are reading. Tell them that they will be learning some useful strategies for understanding unfamiliar words.

Acitivate Prior Knowledge

Ask students to explain how they would find the correct spelling and meaning in the dictionary of a particular word.

TEACH

Step-by-Step Teaching Guide

Keeping a Vocabulary Notebook

1. This is not the same as the subject-area glossaries students created on page 693.
2. A vocabulary notebook (or a vocabulary section of a notebook) is for general words. *Photosynthesis* belongs in the science glossary. *Exasperate* belongs in a general vocabulary list because it isn't restricted to any discipline.
3. There is no point creating vocabulary lists if students never look at them again. They can review them any time—waiting at the bus stop, before a movie starts, and so on.

Answer Key

▶ **Exercise 4**

Responses will vary. Encourage students to share with class any new words they have learned.

⏱ TIME AND RESOURCE MANAGER

Resources
Print: Academic and Workplace Skills Activity Book, pp. 19–21

In-Depth Coverage	Accelerated Pace
• Work through all key concepts, pp. 695–697. • Assign and review Exercises 4–6.	• Assign pp. 695–697, for independent student review.

Studying New Words

1. Show students an example of a flashcard with the vocabulary word they entered into their notebook. The card should have the word written on one side and the definition and the subject it relates to on the other side.

2. Students can use flashcards alone or with a partner to quiz themselves on new words.

3. The same basic approach can be taken by recording the word on a tape recorder. Instead of hiding the definition on the back of the card, students should wait a moment to record the definition. This pause in the recording will allow them to guess the meaning of the word before hearing it.

Answer Key

▶ **Exercise 5**

Responses will vary. Definitions for the five sample words include:
1. an extraordinary event or person, especially a highly talented child
2. planned and acted together in secret
3. weird; eerie
4. fascinate
5. distinguished; highly repected

29.2

Studying New Words

Set a regular time to review new vocabulary words. Use one or more of the following methods to review:

Use Your Notebook Study the words you have recorded in your notebook. As you review, cover the definition of each word, and try to remember the meaning by looking at the word and the example sentence. Then, uncover the definition and read it. Create a new sentence using the word.

Write Sentences With Vocabulary Words Create sentences using the words in your notebook. Use the definition of the word, along with the word itself, in each sentence.

EXAMPLE: He *anticipates* a good party because he is *looking forward* to getting expensive gifts.

Use Flashcards On the front of an index card, write a word you want to remember. On the back, write the definition, the pronunciation, and a sentence that uses the word. Use these flashcards to test yourself or ask others to test you.

Front	Back
aptitude	natural ability or talent ap′tə tōod′ I'm afraid I have no <u>aptitude</u> for creative writing.

Use a Tape Recorder Record a vocabulary word. Pronounce the word carefully. Then, after a pause, record its definition. To review, play the tape. During the pause, recall the word's definition. Listen to the recorded definition to check yourself.

▶ **Exercise 5** Making Flashcards or Tapes Make a set of flashcards or tapes to study these words. Add words from your own reading or from assigned vocabulary lists.
1. prodigy   3. uncanny   5. eminent
2. conspired   4. intrigue

Using a Dictionary

A variety of resources can help you clarify the meaning, pronunciation, and correct usage of an unfamiliar word.

To find the exact meaning of a word, look it up in a dictionary. Record in a notebook the words you look up. Words in a dictionary are listed alphabetically. The dictionary entry will tell you the pronunciation of the word, the parts of speech it functions as, and its various meanings. In addition, most dictionaries provide the origins of the word—the words from which it grew. Reading the origins of a word can help you make associations with other words that share the origin.

Using Other Reference Aids

Thesaurus A thesaurus lists a word's synonyms (words with similar meanings) and sometimes antonyms (words with opposite meanings). Words in some thesauruses are listed alphabetically. In others, words are arranged by categories. The categories are listed in an alphabetical index. Remember to always check the meaning of an unfamiliar word in a dictionary before using it.

Synonym Finder Many word-processing programs have synonym finders in their menus. If you are drafting on-line, highlight a word for which you want to find a synonym and use the finder to check alternative words. Again, remember to always check the meaning of an unfamiliar word in a dictionary before using it.

Glossary A glossary is a list of terms and definitions specific to a field of study. Each of your textbooks probably has a glossary that lists the words you need to know and learn in that subject area.

Software Like most references, dictionaries and thesauruses are available in electronic form. Some can be purchased and loaded onto your hard drive; others are available on the Internet.

> **Exercise 6** Using Vocabulary Reference Aids Look up each of the following words in the references indicated. Compare and contrast the information found in each source.
> 1. respiration (science textbook glossary, dictionary)
> 2. pioneer (dictionary, thesaurus)
> 3. preeminent (dictionary, synonym finder)
> 4. rotation (science textbook glossary, on-line dictionary)
> 5. resource (social studies textbook glossary, thesaurus)

ⓠ Learn More

To see an annotated dictionary entry, go to Chapter 31, Study, Reference, and Test-Taking Skills.

💿 Technology Tip

Almost any reference available in print is also available on-line. Ask a reference librarian to show you how to find and use on-line dictionaries and thesauruses. Find out what other vocabulary-building tools are available on-line.

> **More Practice**
>
> Academic and Workplace Skills Activity Book
> • pp. 20–21

Using a Dictionary and Other Reference Aids

1. Display a dictionary page on an overhead projector. Choose one word and go through the parts of the entry: pronunciation, part(s) of speech, origin, definition(s), other forms of the word, and idioms or expressions containing the word.

2. A thesaurus lists words and their synonyms. It is especially useful when students notice that they are using the same word over and over in their writing and wish to find a replacement.

3. Have students practice finding synonyms for these overused and boring words: *said, good, pretty, really*.

Answer Key

> **Exercise 6**

Responses will vary. Students should see that a dictionary will give a word's pronunciation, meaning(s), and history; a thesaurus and synonym finder will list synonyms; textbook glossaries will give specialized definitions.

☑ ONGOING ASSESSMENT: Monitor and Reinforce

If students have difficulty using a dictionary or other reference aid, try one of the following options.

Option 1 Pair less abled students with more advanced students. Have each pair find a list of words in different reference aids.	**Option 2** Have students make a chart that lists different reference aids and the kinds of information they would find in each.

PREPARE and ENGAGE

 **Interest GRABBER** Write the following on the chalkboard:

cavate   clude   change   plode

Ask them what two letters they could add to the above to make them complete words.(*e* and *x*)

Activate Prior Knowledge

Write the following words on the chalkboard:

inhale   exhale

Ask students what each word means and how they are able to tell the two words apart.

TEACH

Step-by-Step Teaching Guide

Using Roots

1. Explain the difference between a base word and a root. A base word is an English word to which can be added prefixes and suffixes: *appear, disappear, appearance, disappeared.*

2. A root is usually a Latin or Greek word or word part. As in the example, the root *-gress* is not an English word.

3. Students can't always tell a root from a base word. *Happiness* is the base word *happy* + the suffix *-ness*. *Horrible* is <u>not</u> the base word *horror* + the suffix *-ible*. A quick look in the dictionary, at the word's origin, makes this clear.

Answer Key

Exercise 7

1. b; *-flect-* —to bend
2. g; *-mot-* —to move
3. d; *-met-* —measure, size
4. c; *-ped-* —foot
5. f; *-hap-* —chance or luck
6. e; *-mod-* —measure
7. a; *-manus-* —hand
8. j; *-pict-* —to paint
9. h; *-stan-* —to stand
10. i; *-sent-* —to feel

Exercise 8

1. e; *mot*—move
2. a; *ped*—foot
3. b; *manus*—hand
4. c; *mod*—measure
5. d; *hap*—chance or luck

Section 29.3 Studying Word Parts and Origins

Using Roots

Learning roots, the most basic parts of words, will help you learn the meanings of groups of words. For example, if you know that the root *-gress* means "to step or move forward," you have a key to the meaning of the following words: *regress, progress, retrogress, transgress, egress,* and *digress.*

> **KEY CONCEPT** A **root** is a word part that determines an important part of the meaning of a word. ■

FIVE COMMON ROOTS

Root	Meaning	Example
-mit- (-mis-)	to send	dis*miss* (to *send* away)
-mov- (-mot-)	to move	*motion, movement*
-ven- (-vent-)	to come	con*vene* (to *come* together)
-vert- (-vers-)	to turn	re*versal* (*turning* around)
-vid- (-vis-)	to see	*vision* (ability to *see*)

> **Exercise 7** **Learning Word Roots** Match the words in the first column with the words in the second column that appear to have the same root. Look up each pair of words in a dictionary. Identify the root they share, and write its meaning.

1. reflect   a. manuscript
2. motivate   b. deflect
3. dimension   c. centipede
4. pedal   d. immense
5. hapless   e. modify
6. model   f. happiness
7. manufacture   g. motion
8. picture   h. circumstance
9. distance   i. assent
10. sentence   j. depict

> **Exercise 8** **Using Roots to Determine the Meaning of Words** Match each word in the first column with its definition in the second column. Explain how the roots you learned in the previous exercise helped you to determine each answer.

1. motility   a. person walking
2. pedestrian   b. by hand
3. manual   c. one of a set of units
4. module   d. unfortunate accident
5. mishap   e. ability to move on one's own

698 • Vocabulary and Spelling

More Practice

Academic and Workplace Skills Activity Book
• pp. 22–23

⏱ TIME AND RESOURCE MANAGER

Resources
Print: Academic and Workplace Skills Activity Book, pp. 22–25

In-Depth Coverage	Accelerated Pace
• Work through all key concepts, pp. 698–701. • Assign and review Exercises 7–14.	• Assign pp. 698–701 for independent student review.

Using Prefixes

KEY CONCEPT A **prefix** is one or more syllables placed at the beginning of a word to change its meaning or to create a new word. ∎

FIVE COMMON PREFIXES		
Prefix	Meaning	Example
ex-	from, out	*ex*change (to change *from* one thing to another)
mis-	wrong	*mis*place (to put in the *wrong* place)
re-	back, again	*re*call (to call *back*)
trans-	over, across	*trans*port (to carry *over a* distance)
un-	not	*un*seen (*not* seen)

Exercise 9 Analyzing Prefixes Write each numbered word. Circle the prefix, and underline the base word. Then, write the letter of the definition for each word.

1. prepay
2. disassemble
3. uncooperative
4. exhale
5. retort

a. breathe out
b. pay before
c. not helpful
d. answer back
e. take apart

Exercise 10 Finding the Meanings of Prefixes Use a dictionary to find words beginning with the following prefixes. Give an example of a word beginning with each prefix. Define the word in a way that incorporates the meaning of the prefix.

1. ante-
2. hyper-
3. sub-
4. in-
5. tele-

Exercise 11 Using Prefixes to Determine Word Meanings Use what you have learned about prefixes to match each word in the left column with its probable definition in the right column. Check your answers in a dictionary.

1. preamble
2. misappropriate
3. transpose
4. unassailable
5. revive

a. change the places of two things
b. not able to be attacked
c. take for the wrong reason
d. bring back to health
e. introduction

Using Suffixes

1. Point out to students that different parts of speech can be identified by different suffixes. Have them carefully review the last column of the chart in their textbooks.

2. Encourage students to take a base word and find as many forms with different suffixes as they can, such as *happiness* and *happily*.

Answer Key

> **Exercise 12**

1. grati(tude); b
2. verb(ose); c
3. hero(ism); d
4. sens(ory); e
5. categor(ize); a

> **Exercise 13**

1. art—noun; artistic—adjective
2. excite—verb; excitement—noun
3. fresh—adjective; freshen—verb
4. quick—adjective; quickly—adverb
5. assist—verb; assistant—noun

Critical Viewing

Connect Students may say that the artist uses paints, canvas, brushes, and colors to express herself in her work.

29.3

Using Suffixes

> **KEY CONCEPT** A **suffix** is a letter, syllable, or group of syllables added to the end of a word to change its meaning or function or to form a new word. ∎

FOUR COMMON SUFFIXES			
Suffix	Meaning	Example	Part of Speech
-able (-ible)	capable of being	vis*ible*	adjective
-ly	in a certain way	swift*ly*	adverb/adjective
-ment	the result of	content*ment*	noun
-tion (-ion, -sion)	being the act or state of being	predic*tion*	noun

> **Exercise 12** Analyzing Suffixes Write each numbered word. Circle the suffix, and examine the root or base word. Then, write the letter of the definition for each word.

1. gratitude
2. verbose
3. heroism
4. sensory
5. categorize

a. to make categories
b. quality of being grateful
c. especially verbal or talkative
d. quality of being a hero
e. of the senses

> **Exercise 13** Identifying How Suffixes Change Word Function
Write each numbered pair of words. Then, write the part of speech for each word in the pair.

1. art, artistic
2. excite, excitement
3. fresh, freshen
4. quick, quickly
5. assist, assistant

▶ Critical Viewing The artist is expressing herself in a nonverbal way. Using details from the picture, identify the tools and materials the artist uses to express herself. **[Connect]**

> **More Practice**

Academic and Workplace Skills Activity Book
• pp. 24–25

Examining Word Origins

English is part of the Indo-European family of languages. Within that family, the closest relatives to English are other Germanic languages, such as Dutch and German. English is the most widely spoken language in the world. It has also borrowed the most from other languages. More than 70 percent of the words we call English are borrowed from other languages.

Understanding Historical Influences If English had developed in isolation, it would have fewer borrowed words. No language develops in complete isolation, however. Battles, travels, new inventions and technologies—each of these events or circumstances contributes to the growth and change of a language.

HISTORICAL INFLUENCES ON ENGLISH

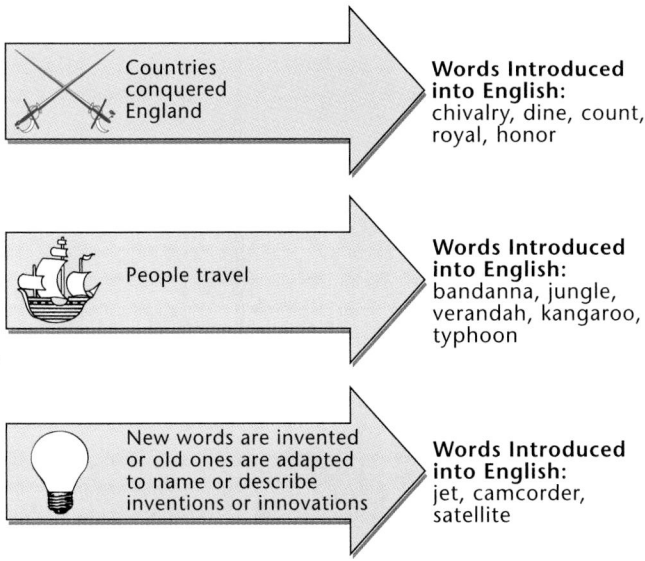

Countries conquered England → **Words Introduced into English:** chivalry, dine, count, royal, honor

People travel → **Words Introduced into English:** bandanna, jungle, verandah, kangaroo, typhoon

New words are invented or old ones are adapted to name or describe inventions or innovations → **Words Introduced into English:** jet, camcorder, satellite

Exercise 14 Analyzing Word Origins Look up each of the following words in a print or electronic dictionary. Then, write the language from which it comes.

1. camel
2. molasses
3. kosher
4. canoe
5. honor

Examining Word Origins

1. Display a page from a dictionary on an overhead projector. Review how to interpret the information on derivations.

2. Go through each word on the page and make tallies on the chalkboard of English words, Greek words, Latin words, and others.

Answer Key

▶ **Exercise 14**

1. camel—Old English from Latin from Greek from Hebrew or Phoenician
2. molasses—Portuguese from Latin
3. kosher—Yiddish from Hebrew
4. canoe—Spanish from Arawakan from Cariban
5. honor—Middle English from French from Latin

☑ **ONGOING ASSESSMENT: Prerequisite Skills**

If students have difficulty understanding how a dictionary provides information on word origins, try the following option.

Refer students to a reference aid that deals exclusively with word origins. These will usually be more in depth than a dictionary entry. Have	students find the origins of a few words of their choice.

Ask students whether they have ever heard of a mnemonic device. If no one has, explain that it is a memory aid that helps you remember something, such as the correct spelling of a word.

Activate Prior Knowledge

Ask students to name words they know that come from languages other than English. Ask them to spell the words for you.

TEACH

Step-by-Step Teaching Guide

Starting a Personal Spelling List

1. A spelling notebook is different from a vocabulary notebook. Students all know what *coolly* and *misspell* mean, but many of them spell the words *cooly* and *mispell*.

2. It is hard to recognize our own spelling mistakes, because the words look correct to us—otherwise we would not have misspelled them! Have friendly partners go through each other's recent writing to find misspelled words. Students can begin their personal spelling lists with these words.

Section 29.4

Improving Your Spelling

Starting a Personal Spelling List

▶ **KEY CONCEPT** Select the words the spelling of which you want to learn, enter them in your notebook, and study them regularly. ■

Record Frequently Misspelled Words Create a section just for words that you frequently misspell. Review corrected tests, essays, and homework to find your problem words. Add to the list any words that sound the same but have different spellings for different meanings, such as *they're*, *their*, and *there*. Each entry should include the word's spelling, pronunciation, and definition, and either a sentence or a memory aid.

Word	Pronunciation	Definition	Sentence
audience	ô′dē əns	a group assembled to see and hear a play or concert	Debbie saw her mother and father in the audience.
decision	di sizh ′ən	the act of deciding something	Jack had a difficult decision to make.
license	lī′səns	formal or legal permission to do something specified	Does your sister have a driver's license?

Include Derivatives A derivative is a word that is formed from another word. Once you know how to spell a base word—the word from which the others are formed—you can more easily learn to spell its derivatives.

BASE WORD: decide
DERIVATIVES: decision, decisive

BASE WORD: caution
DERIVATIVES: cautionary, cautious

Include derivatives in your spelling notebook. Underline the parts of the word that are always spelled with the same letters. Circle any parts that change.

EXAMPLE: regul**ar** regul**ate**, regul**ation**

⏱ TIME AND RESOURCE MANAGER	
Resources **Print:** Academic and Workplace Skills Activity Book, pp. 26–33	
In-Depth Coverage	**Accelerated Pace**
• Work through all key concepts, pp. 702–711. • Assign and review Exercises 15–27	• Assign pp. 702–711 for independent student review

Studying Your Spelling Words

Study your words regularly. Divide your list into groups of five or ten words, and study each group for a week. As you become more comfortable with this study method, you can test yourself on larger groups of words that include those you have learned and those you are in the process of mastering.

KEY CONCEPT Review your words several times a week. ■

A METHOD FOR STUDYING YOUR SPELLING WORDS

1. **Look** at each word. Notice any unusual features about the spelling of the word. For example, in the word *argument*, the *e* in *argue* is dropped before the ending is added. Concentrate on the part of the word that gives you the most trouble. Then, cover the word and try to picture it in your mind.

2. **Say** the word aloud. Then, sound the word out slowly, syllable by syllable.

3. **Spell** the word by writing it on a sheet of paper. Say each syllable aloud as you write it down.

4. **Compare** the word that you wrote on the paper with the word in your notebook. If you spelled the word correctly, put a small check in front of the word in your notebook. If you misspelled the word, circle the letter or letters on your paper that are incorrect. Then, start over again with the first step.

Exercise 15 Checking Spelling Skills Fill in the missing letter(s) in the words below. Add any words you misspelled to your personal spelling list.

1. accident___?___y
2. annivers___?___ry
3. cur___?___ous
4. di___?___appear
5. exer___?___
6. famil___?___r
7. n___?___ghbor
8. prob___?___bly
9. simil___?___
10. tomo___?___ow

Exercise 16 Identifying Commonly Misspelled Words
Look through your writing portfolio and through tests that have been returned to you. Find misspelled words and record them in your notebook. Study them. Have a partner test you on the words.

More Practice
Academic and Workplace Skills Activity Book
• pp. 26–27

Improving Your Spelling • 703

Using *ie* or *ei*

1. All of these words are good candidates for students' spelling notebooks.

2. Stress the key concept. It works 99 percent of the time for *ie/ei* words.

Answer Key

▶ **Exercise 17**

1. pierced
2. Reindeer
3. veil
4. siege
5. receipt

29.4

Applying Spelling Rules

In addition to studying words that give you particular trouble, study rules that apply to groups of words.

Using *ie* or *ei*

There are basic rules for *ie* and *ei* words. You will need to memorize certain exceptions to these rules.

▶ **KEY CONCEPT** Remember this rule: *i* before *e* except after *c* and when sounded as *ay*, as in *neighbor* and *weigh*. ■

When a word has a long *e* sound, use *ie*.
When a word has a long *a* sound, use *ei*.
When a word has a long *e* sound preceded by the letter *c*, use *ei*.

COMMON *ie* AND *ei* WORDS		
Long *e* Sound—Use *ie*	Long *a* Sound—Use *ei*	Long *e* Sound Preceded by *c*—Use *ei*
achieve	eight	ceiling
believe	freight	deceive
field	neighbor	perceive
grief	reign	receive
piece	vein	
thief	weigh	

Some of the exceptions to the preceding rules are listed in the next chart.

SOME EXCEPTIONS TO THE RULE		
either	neither	seize

▶ **Exercise 17** Spelling *ie* and *ei* Words Fill in the blanks below with either *ie* or *ei*. Check the spellings in a dictionary. Add difficult words to your personal spelling list.

1. Samantha went to the doctor to get her ears p__?__rced.
2. R__?__ndeer live in the colder regions of the world.
3. The bride wore a shoulder-length v__?__l.
4. The soldiers were ready for another s__?__ge.
5. The cashier stapled the rec__?__pt to the bag.

▶ **Technology Tip**

When you are working on a word processor, set the spelling checker to alert you immediately when a word is misspelled. The sooner you correct the word, the more likely you are to remember its correct spelling.

▶ **More Practice**

Academic and Workplace Skills Activity Book
• p. 28

Adding Suffixes

SPELLING CHANGES WHEN ADDING SUFFIXES

Word Ending	Rule	Examples
-y preceded by a consonant	Change y to i.	beauty, beautiful EXCEPTIONS: Most suffixes beginning with i: try, trying baby, babyish
-y preceded by a vowel	Make no change.	joy, joyous EXCEPTIONS: day, daily gay, gaily
-e	Drop the final e if suffix begins with a vowel.	love, lovable use, usable EXCEPTIONS: change, changeable peace, peaceable agree, agreeable
-e	Make no change if suffix begins with a consonant	hope, hopeful late, lately EXCEPTIONS: true, truly argue, argument
One-syllable word ending in a single consonant preceded by a single vowel	Double the final consonant if suffix begins with a vowel.	drop, dropped grin, grinned EXCEPTIONS: Words ending in x or w: mix, mixing blow, blowing
Word ending in a single consonant preceded by a single vowel and having the accent on the final syllable	Double the final consonant if suffix begins with a vowel.	permit, permitted EXCEPTIONS: Words in which the accent shifts when the suffix is added: refer´, ref´erence

Exercise 18 Working With Suffixes Make new words by combining words and suffixes. Check the spellings in a dictionary, and add difficult words to your list.

1. run + -er
2. value + -able
3. stop + -ed
4. hungry + -ly
5. dry + -ing
6. sleepy + -ly
7. mystery + -ous
8. commit + -ed
9. nerve + -ous
10. easy + -ly

Step-by-Step Teaching Guide

Adding Suffixes

1. Have volunteers read each entry in the chart.
2. For each entry, have students come up with additional examples.

Answer Key

▶ **Exercise 18**

1. runner
2. valuable
3. stopped
4. hungrily
5. drying
6. sleepily
7. mysterious
8. committed
9. nervous
10. easily

29.4

Adding Prefixes

▶ **KEY CONCEPT** When a prefix is added to a word, the spelling of the word stays the same. ■

EXAMPLES: un- + noticed = unnoticed
dis- + solve   = dissolve

▶ **Exercise 19** **Working With Prefixes** Make new words by combining the prefixes and words below.

1. dis- + appear
2. un- + necessary
3. mis- + behave
4. re- + entry
5. in- + experienced
6. dis- + satisfied
7. de- + press
8. im- + movable
9. co- + operate
10. re- + elect

Using Memory Aids

Because English contains words that come from many different languages, spelling rules do not always apply. Some words must be memorized. Help yourself remember the correct spelling of difficult words by making up a sentence that is a memory aid for spelling the word correctly.

▶ **KEY CONCEPT** Use memory aids to help remember difficult spelling words. ■

You can associate the troublesome part of a word with a word you know or find a short word within a longer word.

EXAMPLES: It is *wise* to *exercise*.
Will you *hand* me a *handkerchief*?

▶ **Exercise 20** **Making Memory Aids** Make up a memory aid for each of the following words.

1. believe
2. curious
3. familiar
4. calendar
5. cemetery
6. committee
7. knowledge
8. laboratory
9. misspell
10. secretary

▶ **Exercise 21** **Writing Your Own Memory Aids** Select five words from your personal spelling list that contain a shorter word. Write a memory aid in your notebook for each.

▶ **More Practice**

Academic and Workplace Skills Activity Book
• p. 30

Understanding the Influence of Other Languages and Cultures

Most languages have a set of rules for spelling and pronunciation that are very predictable and constant. More than 70 percent of English words, however, have been borrowed from other languages. A borrowed word may come with traces of its spelling and pronunciation in the original language. For this reason, English uses a wide variety of letters to spell the same sounds: One sound may have been spelled different ways in different languages. For related reasons, English words often contain "silent letters"—letters that are not pronounced. Read widely and study often to overcome the difficulties these inconsistencies present. When you are writing, use a print or electronic dictionary to confirm the spelling of any word about which you are unsure.

KEY CONCEPT Because other languages and cultures contribute to the spelling and pronunciation of words in English, different letters might be used in different words to spell the same sound. ■

EXAMPLES:
puff	cough	fuel	phone
giraffe	jump	page	
call	keep	pack	hike

Exercise 22 Choosing the Correct Spelling Select the correctly spelled word from each group. Check your answers in a dictionary. Enter misspelled words on your personal spelling list, and note the language from which each word originates.

1. spagetti   spaghetti   sphagetti
2. skunck   scunk   skunk
3. cayack   kyak   kayak
4. resteraunt   restaurant   restauraunt
5. scool   skool   school

▲ Critical Viewing Many of our words for foods come from other languages. Speculate what you think these people might be ordering. Use the names of foods from other countries. [Connect]

Step-by-Step Teaching Guide

Understanding the Influence of Other Languages and Cultures

This is another situation where there is no substitute for practice. The more often students use these words in speech and writing, the sooner they will automatically spell them correctly.

Answer Key

Exercise 22

1. spaghetti
2. skunk
3. kayak
4. restaurant
5. school

Critical Viewing

Connect Students should provide actual names of foods. Have them identify the country of origin for each food they name.

Forming Plurals

1. Memorizing spelling rules that apply to most words can help students know how to spell many other words without memorizing each one individually.

2. Ask students how to form the plural of the following words:

   chair

   bed

   shirt

   Explain that adding -*s* to a noun is the most common way to form plurals.

3. Write the following words on the chalkboard and ask students how to make them plural:

   batch

   toss

   wash

   mix

   In order to make these words plural, -*es* is added. The last letter(s) of the word determines this spelling rule. Words that end in *s, ss, x, z, zz, sh,* or *ch* get -*es* to form the plural.

4. Words that end in *o* also usually take -*es*. There are exceptions in addition to musical words: *avocados, zeros,* for example. As usual, when in doubt, look it up.

5. Words that end in *f* also follow a different plural rule. The *f* is most often changed to *v* and -*es* is added to form the plural: *wife/wives, life/lives.*

6. When a word ends in *ff*, -*s* is added to form the plural.

29.4

Forming Plurals

The plural form of a noun indicates that more than one person, place, or thing is being named. For instance, the plural form of *dog, dogs,* refers to more than one dog. Plural forms are either *regular* or *irregular.*

▶ **KEY CONCEPT** Regular nouns form their plurals by adding -*s* or -*es.* Most nouns have regular plural forms. ■

Some regular nouns change their spelling in the plural form. Check the chart below for examples that change slightly.

FORMING REGULAR PLURALS		
Word Ending	**Rule**	**Examples**
-s, -ss, -x, -z, -zz, -sh, -ch	Add -es.	bus, buses mass, masses fox, foxes buzz, buzzes crash, crashes punch, punches
-o preceded by a consonant	Add -es.	tomato, tomatoes EXCEPTIONS: solo, solos (and other musical terms)
-o preceded by a vowel	Add -s.	radio, radios
-y preceded by a consonant	Change y to i and add -es.	party, parties discovery, discoveries
-y preceded by a vowel	Add -s.	day, days monkey, monkeys
-ff	Add -s.	bluff, bluffs staff, staffs
-fe	Change f to v and add -es.	knife, knives
-f	Add -s. OR Change f to v and add -es.	chief, chiefs calf, calves leaf, leaves

> **KEY CONCEPT** Use a dictionary to look up the correct spelling of irregular plurals. Memorize them. ■

FORMING IRREGULAR PLURALS	
Rule	Examples
Add -en.	ox, oxen
Add -ren.	child, children
Change vowels.	goose, geese woman, women
Change vowels and one other letter.	mouse, mice
Use singular form as plural.	sheep, sheep deer, deer
Use plural form only.	clothes scissors

Most one-word compound nouns have regular plural forms. If one part of the compound noun is irregular, the plural form will also be irregular.

EXAMPLES: flashlight, flashlights (regular)
            snowman, snowmen (irregular)

Most compound nouns written with hyphens or as separate words form the plural by making the modified word—the word being described—plural.

EXAMPLES: son-in-law, sons-in-law
            suit of armor, suits of armor

> **Exercise 23** **Writing Plurals** Write the plural form for each of the following words. Use a dictionary if you need to. Add any difficult words to your personal spelling list.

1. class
2. valley
3. circus
4. sister-in-law
5. shelf
6. story
7. moose
8. potato
9. sheriff
10. diary

> ▶ Critical Viewing The best way to remember irregular plurals is to memorize them. Using this photograph for inspiration, think up a memory aid that you can use to remember that the plural of *moose* is *moose.* [**Connect**]

> **More Practice**
> Academic and Workplace Skills Activity Book
> • p. 31

Forming Irregular Plurals

1. This is one area where the "looks wrong" strategy works.

2. Students may not know the plural of *sheep* or *mouse,* but they will know that *sheeps* and *mouses* look wrong. And they certainly sound wrong. Ask students to try saying "I have three mouses as pets" without laughing.

3. Compound nouns that are hyphenated or more than one word can be tricky. Dictionary entries do not give the plural form of obvious or regular words (*dog, church*), but they do give irregular and compound plurals.

Answer Key

> **Exercise 23**

1. classes
2. valleys
3. circuses
4. sisters-in-law
5. shelves
6. stories
7. moose
8. potatoes
9. sheriffs
10. diaries

Critical Viewing

Connect Responses will vary. Have volunteers share the memory aids they have thought of. Discuss whether or not student strategies or memory aids can be applied to other words.

Improving Your Spelling • 709

Spelling Homophones

1. Illustrate homophones with these examples on the chalkboard.

   I can *see* the *sea* from my window.

   I *ate* *eight* bananas.

   If you pass *by* the store, please stop and *buy* milk.

2. Students make homophone errors not because they confuse *right* and *write*, but because they often work quickly (or while watching TV). Stress the necessity of proofreading their writing for these kinds of mistakes.

Integrating Technology Skills

The spell checker on a computer questions only things it does not recognize. *The dog wagged its tale* looks correct to a computer.

Answer Key

Exercise 24

1. Their
2. piece
3. tale
4. too
5. write

Exercise 25

Answers will vary. Samples are given.

1. The sum of 2 + 2 is 4. Some dogs are poodles.
2. I ate the whole bag of popcorn. There is a hole in my sock.
3. The park is a good site for a ballpark. A sunset is a beautiful sight.
4. You use a reel to catch fish. The dodo was a real bird.
5. Meet me at the skating rink at three o'clock. Hamburger is my favorite meat.

29.4

Spelling Homophones

> **KEY CONCEPT** Homophones are words that sound the same but have different meanings and may have different spellings. ∎

Be especially careful to use and spell the following homophones correctly.

EXAMPLES:

their:	a possessive pronoun that means "belonging to them"
they're:	a contraction for *they are*
there:	a place word or sentence starter, as in "There are five cookies."
tail:	a part of an animal
tale:	a story
piece:	a portion
peace:	the condition of not being at war
write:	to put words on paper
right:	correct
to:	begins a prepositional phrase or infinitive
too:	also
two:	a number

> **Exercise 24** Spelling Homophones Select the correct word from each pair in parentheses. Check your answers in a dictionary. Enter misspelled words on your personal spelling list, and review them.
> 1. (Their, They're) party is Saturday.
> 2. Would you like a (piece, peace) of pie?
> 3. I don't believe that (tail, tale) for a minute.
> 4. My sister wants to help, (to, too).
> 5. We were asked to (right, write) a letter.

> **Exercise 25** Writing Sentences With Homophones Write a sentence for each lettered word in each numbered pair. Check a dictionary to make sure you are spelling and using each word correctly.
> 1. (a) sum   (b) some
> 2. (a) whole   (b) hole
> 3. (a) site   (b) sight
> 4. (a) reel   (b) real
> 5. (a) meet   (b) meat

Technology Tip

Spelling checkers will not catch places where you have misused a homophone. Proofread all your work, even if you have used an electronic spelling checker.

> **More Practice**
> Academic and Workplace Skills Activity Book
> • p. 32

✓ **ONGOING ASSESSMENT: Monitor and Reinforce**

If students have difficulty differentiating between or among homophones, try the following option.

Have students create graphic organizers of their choice containing the homophones in their textbooks. Encourage them to find other examples to add and to create memory aids to help them distinguish between or among the homophones.

Proofreading and Using References

Proofread your written work thoroughly to make sure that you have eliminated all spelling errors. Keep a dictionary or glossary, with you as you proofread. Place a red checkmark on any words for which you want to check the spelling. Then, look up each word and correct the spelling if necessary.

> **KEY CONCEPT** Use dictionaries, electronic spelling checkers, and glossaries to check spellings. ■

> **Exercise 26** **Proofreading Sentences** Copy and proofread the following sentences. Correct any words that are written incorrectly. Use a dictionary, spelling checker, or glossary to confirm the spelling of any words about which you are unsure.
> 1. Sally goes to an excercise class three times a week.
> 2. I need a pair of scissers to open this package.
> 3. The soccer team worked hard to acheive its goal of a winning season.
> 4. Is it neccessary to make reservations ahead of time?
> 5. Jane didn't want to dissapoint her brother by missing his swim meet.

> **Exercise 27** **Proofreading a Paragraph** Copy and proofread the following paragraph. Write the corrected paragraph on a separate sheet of paper.
> The student awards diner was planed for Thusday night. Everyone was very exsited. Sum of the clases prepared posters and decorasions. Others were in charje of music. Althogh it had been on the calender for months, it still seemed as if the date arrivved to soon. The scool secretery made an announcemant in the morning. She gave the time that each comitte was expected to arrive. We couln't beleive that the big night was finaly hear.

Technology Tip

Most word-processing programs can alphabetize a list. Enter electronically your personal list of frequently misspelled words. Sort it alphabetically. Keep the alphabetized list in your folder as a "quick-check" list for proofreading.

Reflecting on Your Spelling and Vocabulary

Think about what you have learned by answering the following questions:
- Which technique do you find most effective for studying spelling words?
- Which do you find most helpful for studying vocabulary words?
- What do the techniques have in common? In what ways are they different?

Improving Your Spelling • 711

Proofreading and Using References

1. Write the following sentences on the chalkboard and ask students what is wrong with them:

   Pedro actualy enjoyed eating spinach. He hated vegetables?

2. The obvious errors are that *actually* is misspelled and the second sentence should end with a period. In addition, the two sentences do not make sense. If Pedro hates vegetables, then he wouldn't enjoy spinach.

3. The moral is that students need to proofread for spelling, punctuation, and sense.

4. Reading for mechanics (spelling, punctuation, subject-verb agreement, correctly placed modifiers, and so on) and for sense are different processes. Students may want to proofread for one at a time.

Answer Key

> **Exercise 26**

1. Sally goes to an <u>exercise</u> class three times a week.
2. I need a pair of <u>scissors</u> to open this package.
3. The soccer team worked hard to <u>achieve</u> its goal of a winning season.
4. Is it <u>neccessary</u> to make reservations ahead of time?
5. Jane didn't want to <u>disappoint</u> her brother by missing his swim meet.

> **Exercise 27**

The student awards dinner was planned for Thursday night. Everyone was very excited. Some of the classes prepared posters and decorations. Others were in charge of music. Although it had been on the calendar for months, it still seemed as if the date arrived too soon. The school secretary made an announcement in the morning. She gave the time that each committee was expected to arrive. We couldn't believe that the big night was finally here.

✓ ONGOING ASSESSMENT: Assess Mastery

Use one of the following options to assess students' mastery of vocabulary and spelling.

Self-Assessment Have students rate their mastery of each of the skills in the chapter and provide reasons for the ratings they give.	**Teacher Assessment** Use both students' responses to the exercises and your own observations to assess students' abilities.

Step-by-Step Teaching Guide

Using Context to Determine Word Meaning

Teaching Resources: Standardized Test Preparation Workbook, pp. 57–58

1. Review with students the ways in which they can use context clues to determine the meaning of a word.

2. Draw students' attention to the Test Tip. Explain to them that, even though they may know a meaning of a given word, they should still use context clues to determine the precise meaning of the word as it is used in the passage.

3. Review the two sample test items to reinforce the importance of using context clues.

Standardized Test Preparation Workshop

Using Context to Determine Word Meaning

The questions on standardized tests often require you to figure out the meaning of a word using the context of a passage. Using the group of words surrounding an underlined term or phrase will help you determine the meaning of idioms, expressions, words with multiple meanings, figurative language, and specialized and technical terms. Use the following strategies when answering these types of questions:

- Read the sentence carefully, focusing on the underlined word or words.

- Look for clues in the surrounding words.

- Use these clues to guess which answer choice best defines the meaning of the new word.

- Reread the passage, substituting your meaning for the new word to see whether it makes sense.

Test Tip

Just because you recognize an underlined word does not mean you know its definition. Some words have multiple meanings. Read the passage carefully and choose a word that best defines the underlined word in the context of the passage.

Sample Test Items	Answers and Explanations

Read the passage. Then, read each question that follows the passage. Decide which is the best answer to each question.
 	
In order to install your program on this <u>system</u>, you must first make sure your computer has enough <u>memory</u>.
 	
1 In this passage, the word *system* means—
 	
  A a method of organization
 	
  B a procedure
 	
  C a computer program
 	
  D the workings of a computer
	The correct answer is *D*. Although both *A* and *B* are correct definitions of the word, the only meaning that applies, using the context of the passage, is *the workings of a computer.*

2 The word *memory* in this passage means—
 	
  F the storing of things past learned
 	
  G the capacity for storing information
 	
  H remembering an event
 	
  J the power of recalling
	The correct answer is *G*. The word *memory* has a technical meaning. To fit the context of this passage, the word must refer to the capacity a computer has to store information for use at a later time.

712 • Vocabulary and Spelling

✐ TEST-TAKING TIP

If students come upon a completely unfamiliar word, tell them not to panic. Students can figure out unfamiliar words by carefully examining context clues. For example, in Practice 2, students may not know what chlorophyll is. However, if they carefully read the whole sentence, they will have all the clues they need to define the word. The passage states that "*green* leaves start to *fade* as they *stop producing chlorophyll.*" From these clues, students should see that chlorophyll is a green substance.

Practice 1 **Directions:** Read the passage. Then, read each question that follows the passage. Decide which is the best answer to each question.

The campaign <u>trail</u> to the presidency always proves to be exciting for all. Beginning with the first <u>primaries</u> held to decide upon candidates to the day in November when you choose the president, voters are constantly <u>bombarded</u> with political tactics aimed at getting their support. Voters must learn to <u>discern</u> between information and promises that have value and those that are last-ditch attempts at winning their votes.

1 In this passage, the word *trail* means—

A dragging behind

B aftermath

C a track through the wilderness

D a course to be followed

2 In this passage, the word *primaries* means—

F group of colors

G elections

H first occurrences

J celestial bodies

3 In this passage, the word *bombarded* means—

A bombed

B repeatedly giving

C subject to rapidly moving particles

D attacked

4 The word *discern* in this passage means—

F disapprove

G identify differences

H dislike

J collect

Practice 2 **Directions:** Read the passage. Then, read each question that follows the passage. Decide which is the best answer to each question.

During the <u>dog days of summer</u>, when the heat is most intense, a tree starts storing nutrients in its roots and trunk and cuts off the leaves. The green leaves start to fade as they stop producing <u>chlorophyll</u>. As the chlorophyll starts to break down, a <u>turning</u> leaf remains partly green with splotches of red and yellow. The colors were always present on the leaves, but the green pigment camouflaged them. Soon, the green fades away to reveal beautifully colored leaves <u>as vibrant as flames</u>.

1 In this passage, the expression *dog days of summer* means—

A days dogs don't have enough to drink

B time between July and September

C earliest days of summer

D final days of summer

2 The word *chlorophyll* means—

F green pigment

G chlorine

H a leaf's waxy coating

J oxygen

3 Here, the word *turning* means—

A thinking over

B rotating

C causing prejudice

D changing

4 In this passage, the expression *as vibrant as flames* means—

F as dangerous as fire

G as brightly colored as flames

H as toxic as fire

J as hot as flames

Answer Key

> **Practice 1**

1. D
2. G
3. D
4. G

> **Practice 2**

1. B
2. F
3. D
4. G

Time and Resource Manager

In-Depth Lesson Plan

	LESSON FOCUS	PRINT AND MEDIA RESOURCES
DAY 1	**Textbook Features** Students learn how to use sections and features of textbooks (pp. 714–716).	**Teaching Resources** *Academic and Workplace Skills Activity Book,* pp. 34–35
DAY 2	**Reading Strategies and Graphic Organizers** Students learn how to adapt reading strategies to different writing genres, practice the SQ4R method, interpret graphic organizers that accompany reading material, and create their own graphic content (pp. 717–720).	**Teaching Resources** *Academic and Workplace Skills Activity Book,* pp. 36–37
DAY 3	**Comprehending Nonfiction** Students learn a variety of ways to read and critically evaluate nonfiction (pp. 721–726).	**Teaching Resources** *Academic and Workplace Skills Activity Book,* pp. 38–43
DAY 4	**Reading Literature and Reading from Varied Sources** Students apply reading strategies to a variety of literary genres, and learn to read from a variety of sources (pp. 727–733).	**Teaching Resources** *Academic and Workplace Skills Activity Book,* pp. 44–51

Accelerated Lesson Plan

	LESSON FOCUS	PRINT AND MEDIA RESOURCES
DAY 1	**Textbook Features to Graphic Organizers** Students learn how to use the sections and features of textbooks, adapt reading strategies to different genres, and interpret and create graphic organizers (pp. 714–720).	**Teaching Resources** *Academic and Workplace Skills Activity Book,* pp. 34–37
DAY 2	**Nonfiction to Varied Sources** Students learn how to read nonfiction critically, apply reading strategies to fictional genres, and read from varied sources (pp. 721–733).	**Teaching Resources** *Academic and Workplace Skills Activity Book,* pp. 38–51

Options for Adapting Lesson Plans

HOMEWORK

Have students complete any stage of the lesson for homework.

FEATURES

Extend coverage with the Standardized Test Preparation Workshop (p. 734).

TECHNOLOGY

Students can complete any stage of the lesson on computer. Have them print out their completed work.

INTEGRATED SKILLS COVERAGE

Viewing and Representing
Critical Viewing, SE pp. 714, 723, 725, 728, 730, 733

Speaking and Listening
ATE p. 729

Real-World Connection
ATE p. 733

Technology Skills
SE p. 717

Workplace Skills
ATE p. 733

ASSESSMENT SUPPORT

Standardized Test Preparation Workshop, SE p. 734

Standardized Test Preparation Workbook, pp. 59–60

Formal Assessment, Ch. 30

MEETING INDIVIDUAL NEEDS

Less Advanced Students ATE pp. 720, 726. See also Ongoing Assessments ATE pp. 720, 726, 731

ESL Students ATE p. 731

BLOCK SCHEDULING

Pacing Suggestions
For 90-minute Blocks
- Have students complete the Textbook Features, Reading Strategies, and Graphic Organizers stages in a single period.
- Focus one class period on Nonfiction and Fiction.

Professional Development Support
- *How to Manage Instruction in the Block* This Teaching Resource provides management and activity suggestions.

MEDIA AND TECHNOLOGY

For the Teacher
- *Resource Pro* CD-ROM

WRITING AND GRAMMAR WEB SITE

The Interactive Writing and Grammar Web site provides a wide array of support for students, teachers, and parents. Writing support includes:

- Interactive revision checkers
- Scoring rubrics with complete models

www.phschool.com

30 Reading Skills

Critical Viewing

Analyze Students may note that the woman has just finished dining and is reading a newspaper. They may suggest that she takes a leisurely approach to reading.

Hobb Green Breakfast by Richard Schmid ©1999

Part of being a good reader involves adapting your reading style to fit the material you are reading and your purpose in reading it. For example, the right reading style for research may involve identifying and focusing on the most important information in the text. You must also know how to evaluate its reliability.

In this chapter, you will learn how to use a variety of reading skills to improve your comprehension of the materials that you read in school and on your own.

▲ **Critical Viewing**
What can you tell about the type of material this woman is reading and about her approach to reading? Explain.
[Analyze]

714 • Reading Skills

⏱ TIME AND RESOURCE MANAGER

Resources
Print: Academic and Workplace Skills Activity Book, pp. 34–37

In-Depth Coverage	Accelerated Pace
• Work through all key concepts, pp. 715–720. • Assign and review Exercises 1–5.	• Assign pp. 715–720 for independent student review.

Reading Methods and Tools

To understand more fully the contents of a book or article, you have to be able to identify and understand the main ideas it presents. Through the use of the special sections and features of your textbooks, reading techniques, and graphic organizers, you can improve your comprehension of the material.

Using Sections in Textbooks

Knowing how your textbook is organized will help you to apply your reading skills to it. Most textbooks have special sections to help you use them effectively. It is important to become familiar with these sections so that you know what they are and how to use them.

> **KEY CONCEPT** Use the special sections of your textbook to become familiar with the book's content. ∎

Table of Contents The table of contents is located at the front of a textbook. It lists the order in which sections and chapters appear and indicates the pages on which each section begins. It can be used to locate general information or a particular section.

Chapter Introduction and Summary A chapter introduction tells you the main ideas of a chapter. A chapter summary, often appearing at the end of a chapter, reviews the main points and other important information.

Glossary The glossary, located at the back of a book, is a list of terms with definitions. Generally, the glossary includes specialized terms that are used within the textbook. These terms are listed alphabetically.

Appendix Appendices are found at the back of a textbook. They contain useful additional, or supplementary, material.

Index The index is found at the back of a book. It lists alphabetically all the subjects covered in the book and indicates on which pages they are discussed. In an index, people are listed by their last names first. Titles or topics that begin with *a* or *the* are listed by the first main word.

> **More Practice**
>
> Academic and Workplace Skills Activity Book
> • p. 34

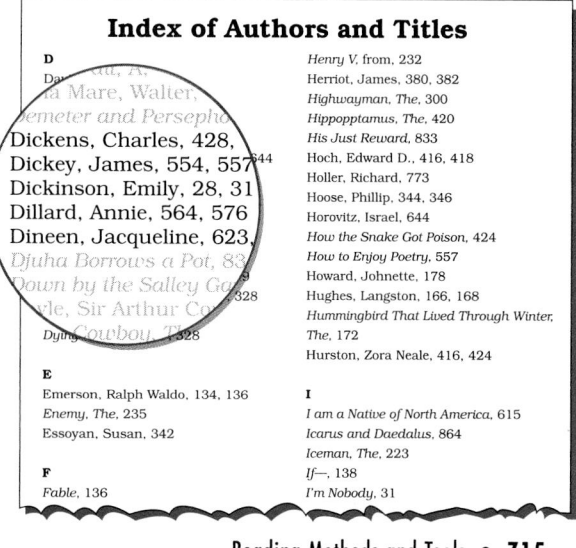

Index of Authors and Titles

Reading Methods and Tools • 715

Using Features of Textbooks

1. Ask students to read the title headings and subheadings of this section of their books and then tell what kind of information these headings provide about the section. (The title headings and subheadings indicate the main ideas and supporting ideas in the sections.)

2. Reading titles, headings, and subheadings before reading a textbook chapter can help students understand the organization of the text and therefore create expectations about what they will read. This important step in prereading will help them read more efficiently and with better comprehension.

3. Ask students what kinds of information they usually need to know in order to answer the questions at the end of each chapter in a textbook. (Students usually need to know the main ideas and the most important supporting points in a chapter.)

4. Reading the questions before they read the chapter can help students focus on the points that are most important. Answering these questions after they read can help them remember the information.

5. While reading, it is important to use the pictures and captions that accompany the text. A caption usually explains the picture and how it relates to the information in the text.

Answer Key

> **Exercise 1**

Responses will vary.

> **Exercise 2**

Responses will vary.

30.1

Using Features of Textbooks

In addition to using the special sections of your textbooks, you should use the textbook's special features to help you read and study the material.

> **KEY CONCEPT** Use the special features of your textbook to aid your reading and study of the material. ■

Titles, Headings, and Subheadings The material in textbooks is usually divided into manageable sections. The sections are labeled with titles, headings, and subheadings. The headings are usually larger than the rest of the text and appear in bold type. Often, they are printed in color. Main topics usually have larger headings; subtopics, smaller ones.

Questions and Exercises Questions and exercises are often provided at the ends of chapters or units. To help direct your reading, look over the questions before you begin. After you finish reading, use the questions to check your understanding.

Pictures and Captions The pictures that accompany the written text can often help you grasp meaning as you read. Look carefully at the photographs and the captions that accompany them, and think about how they relate to what you're reading.

> **Exercise 1** Examining the Sections in a Textbook
Examine two textbooks to become acquainted with their special sections. For each book, answer the following questions:
  1. According to the table of contents, how many units and chapters does the textbook have?
  2. Does the textbook have a glossary or an appendix? What are two pieces of information you can learn from each?
  3. Pick one subject covered in the textbook. Then, using the index, list all the information dealing with this topic.

> **Exercise 2** Examining the Features of a Textbook Answer the following questions about one of your other textbooks.
  1. How many headings and subheadings does the first chapter contain? Explain how the size of the headings helps you figure out the relationship between topics.
  2. Does the chapter have an introduction, a summary, or questions and exercises? What information can be learned from each?
  3. Find three pictures with captions in the textbook. How do the captions explain the picture? What information in the text does the picture help to explain?

Using Reading Strategies

There are a number of different strategies you can use to increase your understanding of the material you read. Three important ones are varying your reading style, learning Question-Answer Relationships, and using the SQ4R method.

▶ **KEY CONCEPT** Use a variety of reading strategies to gain a more complete understanding of the material you read. ■

Vary Your Reading Style The three types of reading styles are *skimming*, *scanning*, and *close reading*. Before you begin reading any material, consider your purpose, and then decide which reading style is the most suitable.

Skimming refers to looking over a text quickly to get a general idea of the information it contains. Look for highlighted or bold type, headings, and topic sentences.

Scanning involves searching through a text until you find a specific section or piece of information. Look for words related to the topic for which you are searching.

Close reading is the most deliberate, careful style of reading. The goal of a close reading is to thoroughly comprehend all of the information in the piece you are reading.

Use Question-Answer Relationships (QAR) One strategy for improving your reading ability is to ask and answer questions as you read. The first step in answering your questions is determining how and where the answer can be found. Following are four different methods for finding answers to different kinds of questions:

QUESTION-ANSWER RELATIONSHIPS
(How and Where to Find Answers)

RIGHT THERE
The answer is right there in the text, usually in one or two sentences. To answer this question, scan the text to locate information.

THINK AND SEARCH
The answer is in the text, but you need to think about the question's answer and then search for supporting evidence.

AUTHOR AND YOU
The answer is not only in the text. Answer this question by thinking about what the author says, what you know, and how these fit together.

ON YOUR OWN
The answer is, for the most part, not in the text. To answer this question, you need to draw from your own experiences. You can, however, use examples from the text.

🖳 Internet Tip

You can use each of these reading styles when you are using the Internet. *Skim* to get an overall sense of a site. *Scan* to find specific pieces of information on a site. Use *close reading* to read articles and other extended passages that interest you.

▶ **More Practice**
Academic and Workplace Skills Activity Book
• pp. 35–36

Step-by-Step Teaching Guide

Using Reading Strategies

1. Ask students to describe the difference between the way they read a fiction story and the way they read a textbook chapter. Elicit the idea that they have different purposes for reading each of these texts and that their purpose for reading helps them choose a reading style that fits their needs.

2. Have students give examples of works they would skim, scan, and read closely. (Possible answers: skim a dictionary to find a certain word; scan a long encyclopedia article to find a certain subtopic; closely read a science textbook)

Step-by-Step Teaching Guide

Using Question-Answer Relationships (QAR)

Have students copy the diagram into their notebooks. Remind them to refer to this chart as they read.

Using the SQ4R Method

1. The SQ4R method is helpful for any nonfiction textbook: science, history, math, and literature.

2. Have students practice the method with page 721.

   - *S: Survey the headings and note the exercise*

   - *Q: Ask, How can I read nonfiction critically? or What are ways to comprehend nonfiction?*

   - *R: Read the key concept and following text; take notes of main ideas; review the text and notes as necessary*

Answer Key

> **Exercise 3**

Responses will vary.

> **Exercise 4**

Responses will vary.

> **Exercise 3** Varying Reading Style and Using QAR Using the description of QAR on page 717, create and answer the four types of questions for your next reading assignment. Use the various reading styles to answer your questions: *Scan* the text to answer the Right There question, *skim* the text to answer the Think and Search question, and *closely read* the text to answer the Author and You question.

Use the SQ4R Method Another reading strategy that is especially appropriate for reading textbooks is called the SQ4R method, a systematic approach to reading that involves the six steps below. This method not only helps guide you as you read but also helps you retain information.

THE STAGES OF SQ4R

Survey — Preview the material you are going to read for these features: chapter title, headings, subheadings, introduction, summary, and questions or exercises.

Question — Turn each heading into a question about what will be covered under that heading. Ask the questions *who, what, when, where,* and *why* about it.

Read — Search for the answers to the questions that have been posed in the step above.

Recite — Orally or mentally recall questions and their related answers.

Record — Take notes to further reinforce the information. List the main ideas and the major details.

Review — Review the material on a regular basis, using some or all of the steps above.

> **Exercise 4** Using the SQ4R Method Use the SQ4R method to read a chapter in one of your textbooks. Write an explanation of how the method helped you learn and remember the information.

Using Graphic Organizers

A graphic organizer can be an effective tool for thinking and learning because it visually organizes information so you can review it more easily. A graphic organizer helps you arrange the material that you have read to show the relationships among various ideas and to prepare information for use in writing. The graphic organizer that you use depends on the nature of the material that you need to understand and learn.

▶ **KEY CONCEPT** Use graphic organizers to understand how ideas in a text are related. ■

Sunburst A sunburst organizer can help you break down a broad topic into key ideas and details. To create a sunburst organizer, draw a circle. Write the topic or idea that you want to describe inside the circle. Then, draw rays coming from that circle. At the end of each ray, draw a box. Write the ideas or details that explain, describe, or are associated with the larger idea or topic inside each box.

SUNBURST DIAGRAM

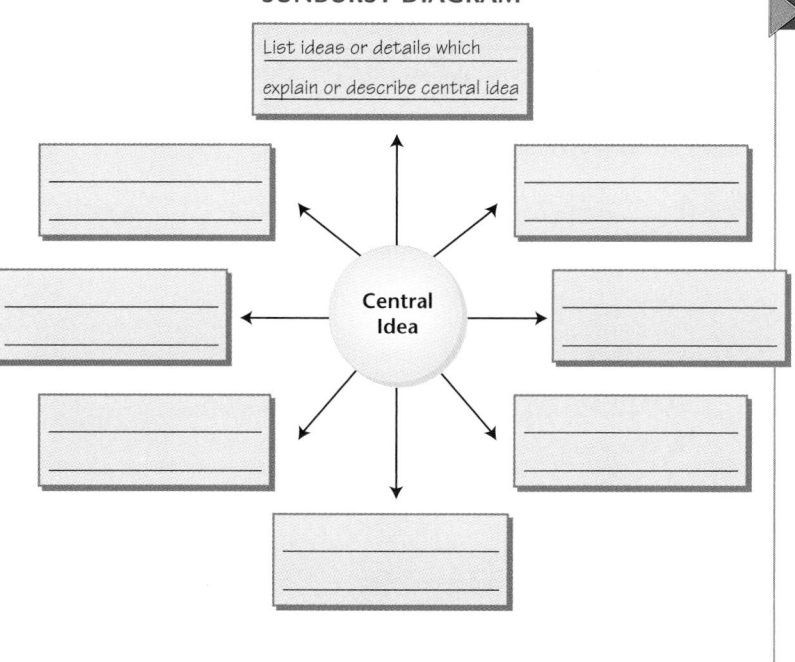

List ideas or details which
explain or describe central idea

Central Idea

🗐 Research Tip

Use graphic organizers to organize material from newspaper and magazine articles when you are preparing information from those sources for reports and presentations.

▶ **More Practice**

Academic and
Workplace Skills
Activity Book
• p. 37

Step-by-Step Teaching Guide

Using Graphic Organizers

1. Creating a visual representation of the information students read can help them create a record of the important points and the relationship among the points.

2. Point out that the sunburst is similar to word and character webs students have made when reading literature. This graphic also works for nonfiction to identify main idea and details.

continued

---

3. For practice, have partners draw a blank grid. They can choose a topic from their science textbook, then fill out the grid.

4. Point out that grids can be useful study tools before a test. Students can refer to grids they made earlier in the year and see what areas they should focus on in their review.

5. Venn diagrams are familiar to students from math and literature classes. They also can use a Venn diagram for history and science: for example, to compare and contrast the natural resources of two countries, or to compare and contrast mammals and birds.

Customize for
Less Advanced Students

Students may get overwhelmed by the task of finding characteristics and subtopics to enter into their graphic organizers. It may be difficult for them to see the words and phrases they need because they are struggling to decode basic meaning in whatever text they are reading. Having students underline or highlight important words and phrases before transferring them onto the graphic organizers may give them the intermediary step they need in order to complete the task successfully.

Answer Key

▶ **Exercise 5**

Responses will vary.

30.1

Grid A grid can help you sort information from nonfiction texts. Create a series of boxes, as in the example below. In the box in the upper left corner, write the topic of the section you are reading. In the three boxes to the right, note subtopics or main points into which the topic is divided in the text. In the boxes directly below the topic box, list characteristics or key details of each subtopic.

GRID ORGANIZER

Topic you are studying	Subtopic	Subtopic	Subtopic
Characteristic			
Characteristic			

Venn Diagram Use a Venn diagram to look at similarities and differences between two subjects. Draw two overlapping circles. In the area where the circles overlap, write the characteristics that the two subjects have in common. In the sections of the circles that do not overlap, list the differences.

VENN DIAGRAM

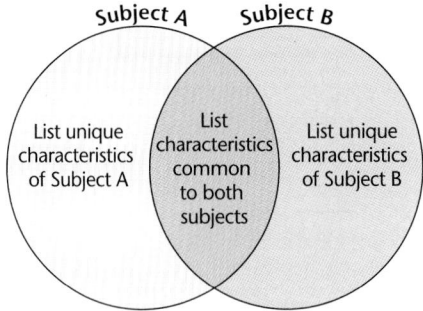

▶ **Exercise 5** Using Graphic Organizers Read a chapter from a textbook. Use one of the three graphic organizers described in this section to organize the information from that chapter. Explain why you chose the graphic organizer that you did.

720 • Reading Skills

☑ ONGOING ASSESSMENT: Monitor and Reinforce

If students are having trouble varying their reading strategies or effectively organizing information gleaned from their readings, try one of the following options.

Option 1 Have the students skim the front page of their local newspaper. Ask them to list the article headings on a sheet of paper. Then, have them scan one article from the front page and do a close reading of another. Remind your students of the QARs on p. 717.	**Option 2** Have students choose two topics that have obvious similarities and differences, such as softball and baseball. Then, have them draw a Venn diagram to organize their findings.

Reading Nonfiction Critically

Section 30.2

Nonfiction is writing that is based on fact. When you read nonfiction critically, you examine and question the ideas the author presents. You learn to distinguish between fact and opinion, to identify the author's purpose, and to recognize when language is being used to distort your understanding of the text. This section will guide you through a number of reading strategies that you can use to become a critical reader.

Comprehending Nonfiction

Before you begin to read a text critically, you need to have a general understanding of it. This process involves finding and interpreting important information, identifying the author's purpose, and understanding the relationship the material has to what you are studying.

▶ **KEY CONCEPT** Comprehending nonfiction involves understanding the author's purpose as well as the information presented in the writing. ■

Locate Main Ideas and Major Details The main ideas are the key points an author wishes to convey. The major details explain and support these main points.

Interpret What You Are Reading Paraphrase, or state in your own words, the information in the text, starting with the main ideas and major details. This technique will help you to remember ideas and their relationship to each other.

Identify the Author's Purpose for Writing After you have a general idea of the content, examine the writer's choice of words and details to determine the author's purpose. As you continue to read, look for additional information that supports this purpose.

Reflect on What You Have Read After you have finished reading, take a moment to think about what the author has written. Consider the following questions: How does the information relate to what you are studying? How does this information relate to your life?

▶ **Exercise 6** Comprehending Nonfiction Use the strategies mentioned above to read a chapter from one of your textbooks. Then, answer these questions: What main points and major details did you locate? What was the author's purpose? What details did you use to identify it? What is the importance of the information you read?

⊙ Learn More

These critical reading skills are also helpful when revising the ideas in your own writing. See Chapters 1, 2, and 3.

▶ **More Practice**

Academic and Workplace Skills Activity Book
• pp. 38–39

Step-by-Step Teaching Guide

Comprehending Nonfiction

1. Write the following paragraph on the chalkboard:

   Using clear and specific details in a descriptive essay is important because these details help get a reader interested. Sometimes these details are called showing details. *Showing details often involve the senses and create a word picture. They help the reader see and experience the action or state the writer describes.*

2. Ask students what the main idea of this paragraph is. (Details can enhance a descriptive essay.)

3. Finding the main idea in a text and putting it into their own words are two important strategies for understanding nonfiction.

4. Putting the information students read into their own words is called *paraphrasing.* It can help students determine if they have understood what they read. If they cannot paraphrase a paragraph, then they need to reread it carefully.

5. Once students understand the main point and main supporting points in a text and have paraphrased them, it is important to examine the language and details the author uses to identify his or her purpose for writing the text.

6. Finally, it is important for students to think about what they read and how it relates to what they already know and to their lives.

Answer Key

▶ **Exercise 6**

Responses will vary.

⊙ TIME AND RESOURCE MANAGER

Resources
Print: Academic and Workplace Skills Activity Book, pp. 38–43

In-Depth Coverage	Accelerated Pace
• Work through all key concepts, pp. 721–726. • Assign and review Exercises 6–11.	• Assign pp. 721–726 for independent student review.

Distinguishing Fact From Opinion

1. Write the following sentences on the chalkboard:

   Bill Clinton was elected president for two terms.

   It's wonderful that Bill Clinton was elected president for two terms.

   Ask students what is the difference between these two sentences. (One is a fact and one is an opinion.)

2. Review the difference between fact and opinion. A claim about a fact can be looked up and proved true or false. *Bill Clinton was elected for only one term* is false, but it is a claim about a fact; it is not an opinion.

3. Students can look for clues that identify opinions: *I believe; I think;* adjectives such as *good, bad, wonderful, terrible, best, worst,* and so on.

4. Students are often asked for their opinions, for example, in responses to literature. They can present any opinion, but they must support it. "'All Summer in a Day' is the best story I ever read" is not adequate. But if the student continues, "I empathized with Margot. I can imagine how awful it was for her to miss the only sun in seven years," the first statement is a supported opinion, which is fine.

Answer Key

Exercise 7

1. claim about a fact, true
2. opinion, unsupported
3. claim about a fact, true
4. claim about a fact, false
5. opinion, supported

30.2

Distinguishing Fact From Opinion

One of the keys to being a critical reader is being able to separate statements of fact from statements of opinion.

Facts A statement of fact can be *verified*, or proved to be true, using a written source (such as a dictionary, encyclopedia, or other reference book), an authority, a scientific experiment, or direct personal observation.

STATEMENT
OF FACT: The sun rises in the East and sets in the West.

The statement is a fact because it can be verified by a written source, such as an encyclopedia or a science textbook, or by direct personal observation.

Opinions A statement of opinion expresses a person's feelings, judgments, or predictions about a given situation. An opinion statement cannot be proved to be true or false. When you come across an opinion in a piece of writing, you should look to see whether the writer has supported the opinion with facts. Opinions that are backed up by facts are more worthy of acceptance than those that are not.

SUPPORTED   Solar energy is the most logical form of energy
OPINION: to develop because the sun will continue to release energy for another 5 billion years.

UNSUPPORTED: Solar energy is the best kind of energy, and in a few years, everyone will use solar energy instead of fossil fuels.

The first opinion statement is *worthy of serious consideration* because it is based on related facts. The second opinion statement, however, is *not* worthy of acceptance because it is not supported by facts.

▶ **Exercise 7** Distinguishing Between Fact and Opinion
Identify the first sentence in each numbered item as *fact* or *opinion*. If the statement is an opinion, tell whether it is *supported* or *unsupported*.

1. George Washington was a United States president.
2. George Washington was brave and honorable.
3. George Washington was a leader in the Revolutionary War.
4. He owned a great deal of land.
5. Mount Vernon, Washington's estate, is quite impressive. It covers about 500 acres of land and includes a mansion and fifteen smaller buildings.

🔲 **Research Tip**

Knowing the difference between fact and opinion will help you judge the accuracy of written material in such sources as editorials.

▶ **More Practice**

Academic and Workplace Skills Activity Book
• pp. 40–41

Identifying the Author's Purpose

Another part of being a critical reader is knowing how to determine the author's reason for writing. As you read, you should look for clues to help you identify the author's purpose. When you think you know what the author's purpose is, you should confirm this idea by linking it to details from the text.

> **KEY CONCEPT** Learn to identify the author's purpose by using clues found in the material. ■

Following are some common purposes:

- **To Inform** The writer presents a series of factual statements.

- **To Instruct** The writer provides a step-by-step explanation of an idea or process.

- **To Offer an Opinion** The writer presents his or her viewpoint on an issue and attempts to convince readers to accept that viewpoint.

- **To Sell** The writer uses persuasive techniques to convince readers to buy something.

- **To Entertain** The author tells an engaging, often amusing story, or looks at a subject in an amusing way.

> **Exercise 8** Determining the Author's Purpose Read the following sentences, and determine the author's purpose. Explain your answer.
> 1. This manual will guide you through the steps for cooking a dinner for seven people.
> 2. Due to its smaller mass, the moon's gravity is one sixth of the gravity on Earth.
> 3. I'm going to tell you about three unconventional ways to relieve stress.
> 4. It is easy to avoid failure—simply never try anything.
> 5. Our modems are the quickest and easiest to use in today's market.

▼ Critical Viewing
What clues can you identify in the picture that the girl is reading text meant to inform? [Analyze]

Identifying the Author's Purpose

1. Professional writers have the same purposes as student writers: to inform, instruct, offer an opinion, sell, and entertain.

2. Ask students for which purposes opinions would be appropriate. (instruct, offer opinion, sell, entertain)

Answer Key

> **Exercise 8**

1. instruct
2. inform
3. offer an opinion
4. entertain
5. sell

Critical Viewing

Analyze Students may say that the eggs in the girl's right hand and the girl's index finger on the book suggests that she is following a recipe in a cookbook.

Applying Forms of Reasoning

1. Write the following statement on the chalkboard:

   Jane exercises for two hours a day and eats only very healthy foods.

   Ask students what they can guess about Jane based on this information. (She is concerned about staying healthy.)

2. Students' guesses about Jane are called *inferences*. This form of reasoning is often necessary to interpret a text.

3. When information is not stated directly, it is necessary for readers to put together the details contained in a text and to infer the meaning.

4. When they are valid, generalizations are also a kind of inference based on a large number of facts and examples.

5. A valid generalization is one that is supported by a large number of facts or examples. A hasty generalization is invalid because it is not supported with enough information.

6. Write the following generalization on the chalkboard:

   Most people in this class have brown hair.

   Ask students how they might support this generalization. (They could count how many students have brown hair.)

7. It is necessary to decide whether generalizations are hasty or valid by asking questions about the support provided.

8. Have partners find a generalization in one of their textbooks, then decide if it is hasty or valid.

Answer Key

Exercise 9

1. Sports and exercise can increase a person's strength and fitness.
2. Schoolchildren are less active today than they were in the 1960's.

30.2

Applying Forms of Reasoning

As a critical reader, you should also use forms of reasoning —logical ways of thinking—to grasp underlying meaning and to make connections that extend beyond the text.

Make Inferences Sometimes, an author states his or her main ideas directly. In other cases, however, main ideas are implied, or conveyed indirectly. It is left up to you to piece together details to figure out what they mean or what message they convey. This is called **making inferences.**

INFORMATION: Stephen has been published in three different magazines.

INFERENCE: Stephen is a talented writer.

Make Generalizations You should also make generalizations, when appropriate, as you read. A **generalization** is a broad statement based on a large number of facts and examples.

INFORMATION: It rained on 25 out of 30 days this May.
GENERALIZATION: This May was a rainy month.

A *hasty generalization* is one based on too few examples, or one that fails to account for exceptions. Use these questions to make valid generalizations:

- What examples are presented, and how are they connected?
- Will the generalization hold true for all—or most—examples? Are there any exceptions to this statement?
- Are enough examples given to make a valid generalization?

▶ **Exercise 9** Making Inferences and Generalizations Read the following passage. Then, answer the questions that follow.

According to Health and Human Services tests, American youth have gotten heavier than they were in the 1960's. Young people spend an average of thirteen hours a week at sports or other exercise. They spend three to four times that watching television and playing video games. Schoolchildren's scores are now declining for strength, power, speed, agility, and cardiovascular fitness. The tests also report that less than half of the young population meets the required standards of physical conditioning. Just a few years ago, the number was much higher.

1. What can you infer about the effect of physical activity on a person's strength and fitness?
2. What generalization can you make about the habits of schoolchildren?

724 • Reading Skills

🔲 Research Tip

When you are conducting research on a topic, be careful to avoid making hasty generalizations based on a single source. Confirm your generalizations by consulting additional sources.

▶ **More Practice**

Academic and Workplace Skills Activity Book
• pp. 42–43

Analyzing the Text

Analyzing a text involves looking at the language a writer uses and examining how the writer organizes the information that is presented.

KEY CONCEPT Identify and understand the different uses of language, and recognize the various text structures. ■

Examine Authors' Language Authors sometimes use language in ways that can suggest how you should feel about a particular subject or issue. *Denotation, connotation,* and *jargon* are three ways that authors use language to affect your opinions and ideas about what you are reading.

Denotation and Connotation The exact meaning of a word is called its *denotation. Connotation,* on the other hand, refers to the feelings that a word stirs up. Often, writers carefully choose words with certain connotations. For example, if a writer is trying to convey a negative impression of a subject, he or she is likely to choose words with a negative connotation. Look at the different connotations of the words in the examples below:

EXAMPLES: Their furniture is *cheap.*
Their furniture is *inexpensive.*
The man was *dressed* in a *formal black suit.*
The gentleman was *outfitted* in an *elegant black tuxedo.*

Jargon *Jargon* is the use of specialized vocabulary intended for a specific audience—for example, sportswriters or doctors. Jargon is meant to have a very precise meaning, but it often hides, rather than reveals, meaning. The opposite of jargon is *direct language.*

Exercise 10 Analyzing Uses of Language
Look through magazines and newspapers. Find three examples of words with positive connotations, three examples with negative connotations, and three examples of jargon.

▶ Critical Viewing Describe this man's outfit in two ways—one using words with positive connotations, the other using words with negative connotations. [Describe]

Reading Nonfiction Critically • 725

Step-by-Step Teaching Guide

Analyzing the Text

1. Write the following sentences on the chalkboard:

   Jean finished the ski competition first.

   With an amazing and graceful performance, Jean finished the ski competition first.

2. Ask students what the difference is between these two sentences. (Although these sentences describe the same situation, the second sentence communicates a positive feeling, while the first sentence communicates information without attaching any judgments about the nature of Jean's performance.)

3. Ask students whether they feel differently about Jean's performance after reading each of the sentences. (The second sentence leaves a reader with a more positive feeling about the performance.)

4. Explain that both sentences denote the same event. However, the first sentence contains words with neutral connotations. The second sentence contains words with highly positive connotations. These words express the author's personal point of view and are designed to influence the way the reader feels about the subject described.

Critical Viewing

Describe Students may say that the man's tuxedo is *tailored* or *well-fitted,* which have positive connotations. Among words with negative connotations, students may suggest that the man's tuxedo is *stiff* or *stuffy-looking.*

Answer Key

Exercise 10

Responses will vary.

Identify Text Structure

1. Have students give examples of cause-and-effect relationships. Where do students think they might find nonfiction texts structured through cause and effect?

2. Most students will be readily familiar with texts structured in chronological order. Encourage students to look in *Prentice Hall Literature: Timeless Voices, Timeless Themes* for examples.

Customize for
Less Advanced Students

Students who are struggling with basic meaning will have difficulty identifying structures and the progression of ideas in texts. Having them summarize their understanding of the text's main points and/or encouraging them to discuss its meaning will help them build confidence. Once they understand the broadest points that are made in the text, they will be more able to tackle more sophisticated levels of meaning.

Answer Key

▶ **Exercise 11**

Responses will vary. You may want to narrow the range of topics that the students will research.

30.2

Identify Text Structure Writers structure their texts in different ways depending on their topic, form, and purpose for writing. Learn to recognize how an author structures a text so that you can understand the relationship among ideas and locate information easily. Following are some of the common types of organization:

Cause and Effect In a cause-and-effect structure, the writer presents a series of interrelated events or situations. One or more events or situations cause another event or situation to occur, which can then lead to other events or situations.

Chronological Order Chronological order is the arrangement of events in the order in which they occurred. Writers frequently use chronological order when telling a story or describing an event.

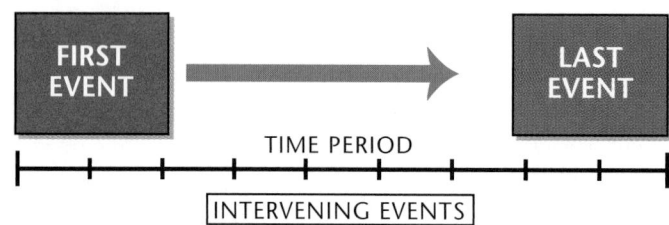

Order of Importance When writers create a persuasive argument, they often arrange their evidence in order of importance. One effective way to use order of importance is to begin with your second-best argument to capture audience interest. Then, build your other support in increasing order of importance, finishing with your most powerful point.

Spatial Order When writers are describing something, they often arrange details as they appear in space. For example, they might move from top to bottom.

▶ **Exercise 11** Analyzing Text Structures Conduct research, either in the library or on the Internet, to find four pieces of nonfiction, each following one of the organizations described above. Explain why each organizational pattern was used.

✓ ONGOING ASSESSMENT: Monitor and Reinforce

If students have difficulty with Exercises 9, 10, or 11, try one of the following options.

Option 1 Have students locate a piece of nonfiction on the Internet and identify words with positive connotations and negative connotations.	**Option 2** Have students work in small groups to identify text structure on nonfiction pieces that you provide.

Speaking and **Listening Tip**

Speakers also use these organizations when delivering public speeches. Think about the types of speeches for which each organization would be most appropriate.

Section 30.3
Reading Literary Writing

Literary writing refers to fiction, drama, and poetry. You can use some of the same strategies to read literary writing that you use to read nonfiction. However, there are some special strategies that will help you with these genres, or forms.

Reading Fiction

The following strategies will help you to increase your comprehension of short stories and novels.

Predict Read closely to find hints about what will happen next, and make predictions about these future events based on the clues that you find. As you read, check your predictions.

Identify With Characters When you imagine yourself as a character in a story or place yourself in the character's situation, you increase your understanding of the character's feelings and thoughts. As a result, the story comes alive.

Ask Questions Become involved in the story by asking questions about the characters, setting, and events. As you read, look for answers to your questions.

ACTIVE READING QUESTIONS

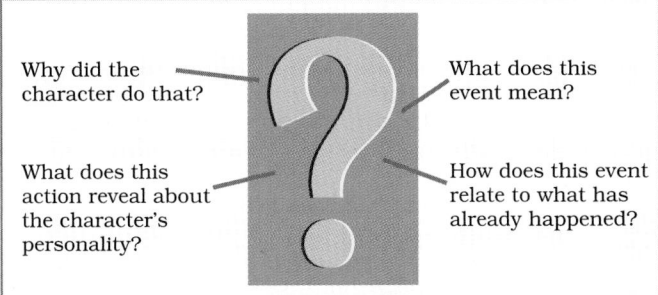

Why did the character do that?

What does this event mean?

What does this action reveal about the character's personality?

How does this event relate to what has already happened?

Make Inferences The theme, or central message, of a work of fiction is usually implied, or conveyed indirectly. To grasp this message, you need to make inferences, or draw conclusions, based on the characters' comments and actions, the outcome of events, and other details the writer provides.

> **Exercise 12** Reading Fiction Read a short story, and apply the strategies above. After you've finished, write an explanation of how the strategies affected your response to the story.

> **More Practice**
> Academic and Workplace Skills Activity Book
> • pp. 44–45

Reading Literary Writing • 727

⏱ TIME AND RESOURCE MANAGER

Resources
Print: Academic and Workplace Skills Activity Book, pp. 44–50

In-Depth Coverage	Accelerated Pace
• Work through all key concepts, pp. 727–731. • Assign and review Exercises 12–15.	• Assign pp. 727–731 for independent student review.

Reading Drama

1. Drama is different from stories in that it is only dialogue. There is no descriptive detail to accompany or explain the characters' words and actions.

2. Good fiction writers create pictures in the reader's mind. In drama, readers have to create their own pictures. Therefore, it is especially important to pay attention to the cast of characters and stage directions.

3. Have students look at "A Christmas Carol" in *Prentice Hall Literature: Timeless Voices, Timeless Themes*, Bronze and point out the elements listed.

Answer Key

Suggest a few plays for the students to look at and have them present their answers in class.

Critical Viewing

Deduce Students may mention information about the costumes, the sets, the lighting, and the ways the characters should speak and behave.

30.3

Reading Drama

Drama is a story designed to be performed on the stage. It is told mostly through what the actors say and do. Stage directions in the script contain instructions about how actors should move and how they should speak their lines. Sometimes, these stage directions contain information about the sets, costumes, lighting, and sound effects. Use the following strategies to increase your understanding of drama:

Read the Cast of Characters
Before the dialogue begins, there is usually a list of the characters who take part in the action. Reading this list can tell you the various relationships among the characters. It may also give a brief description of the characters to help you imagine who they are.

Use Stage Directions to Envision the Play
Use the information in the stage directions to create a mental picture of what is happening during the play, as well as a picture of what people look like and how they behave.

Review Events After Scenes or Acts
Dramas are often broken into acts or scenes. These breaks in the play give you a chance to review what has happened in the play. Pause at the end of each scene or act, summarize what has happened up to that point, and make predictions about what will happen in the next scene or act.

▲ **Critical Viewing**
What stage directions would you expect to find in a written version of this scene? **[Deduce]**

> **Exercise 13** Understanding Drama Read the first act or scene from a play. Then, answer the following questions.
> 1. What three pieces of information can you learn from reading the cast of characters?
> 2. Explain the significance of three stage directions. How do they contribute to your understanding of a mood, an action, or a character?
> 3. Summarize the events that occurred in the act or scene.
> 4. Predict what will happen in the next act or scene. Explain the basis for your predictions.
> 5. Read the next act or scene and check to see whether your predictions come true.

Reading Poetry

Poetry is a unique type of writing in which ideas are presented in verse. Poems are generally briefer than other forms of writing, and sound plays a more important role than in most other writing. Use the following strategies to help you understand and appreciate poetry:

Identify the Speaker The speaker is the imaginary voice that the poet uses to present the poem. Occasionally, the speaker is the poet. At other times, the speaker is a character invented by the poet. As you read, look for clues to help identify the speaker's personality, experiences, and perspective on life.

Experience Images Through Your Senses Poetry usually contains images, or word pictures, that appeal to one or more of your five senses. To experience these images more fully, use your senses to see, hear, smell, touch, and feel what the poet describes.

Read Lines According to Their Punctuation
Sometimes, readers make the mistake of pausing at the end of each line of a poem. Instead, you should read according to punctuation. When you see a comma, dash, or semicolon, pause before continuing with the poem. Stop longer at periods, question marks (remembering to read the material as you would a question), and exclamation points (remembering to stress the statements or exclamations).

Read the following excerpt from Walt Whitman's *Leaves of Grass*, pausing at the commas (shaded yellow), stopping longer at the periods, dashes, semicolons, and exclamation marks (shaded red), and continuing to read where it is shaded green.

Poets to come! orators, singers, musicians to come!
Not to-day is to justify me and answer what I am for,
But you, a new brood, native, athletic, continental,
    greater than before known,
Arouse! for you must justify me.

I myself but write one or two indicative words for
    the future,
I but advance a moment only to wheel and hurry
    back in the darkness.

I am a man who, sauntering along, without fully
    stopping, turns a casual look upon you and then
    averts his face,
Leaving it to you to prove and define it,
Expecting the main things from you.

> **Speaking** and **Listening Tip**
>
> One of the best ways to truly understand and appreciate a poem is to read it aloud. Listen to the sounds of the words and the rhythms of the lines. How does the poet use sound to enhance the poem's meaning?

> ▶ **More Practice**
>
> Academic and Workplace Skills Activity Book
> • pp. 46–49

Reading Poetry

1. Read aloud Whitman's poem as students follow along.

2. Ask students to choose an image in the poem that appeals to one of their five senses and to share the image with the class. Explain that creating images through their senses when reading a poem can help them discover the author's meaning.

3. Have students practice reading the poem aloud to partners, pausing when they see commas, colons, and periods.

Integrating Speaking and Listening Skills

Much poetry is meant to be read aloud. Select some short poems from *Prentice Hall Literature: Timeless Voices, Timeless Themes,* Bronze and have volunteers read these poems aloud to the class. Encourage the readers to discuss how reading a poem aloud differs from reading it to oneself. Then have the listeners discuss their experiences of hearing the poem read aloud.

Reading Myths, Legends, and Folk Tales

1. Myths attempt to explain actions of gods or natural occurrences. Ask students to give examples of myths they have read and the actions or occurrences they explained.

2. Legends are widely told stories about the past, and folk tales are stories about heroes and adventures.

3. Because these stories often tell something about the values and traditions of the cultures they come from, it is important to identify the cultural context in which a myth, legend, or folk tale takes place.

4. Have partners find a myth, legend, or folk tale in *Prentice Hall Literature: Timeless Voices, Timeless Themes* and fill in the chart with clues about the context.

5. Have pairs who chose the same story compare their charts.

Answer Key

> **Exercise 14**

Responses may vary.

1. The writer is the speaker.
2. It helps break up the images and ideas.
3. The image of a man "sauntering by" is quite vivid.
4. Responses will vary.

Critical Viewing

Evaluate Students may suggest that this is a good place because it appears quiet and peaceful.

Paraphrase the Lines Paraphrase, or restate in your own words, what you think each part of the poem is communicating. Putting the ideas into your own words will help you clarify and remember the meaning.

> **Exercise 14** Reading Poetry Reread the poem on page 729. After you have read the poem, answer the following questions.
> 1. Who is the speaker of the poem?
> 2. How did the punctuation (or lack of it) help you to understand the poem?
> 3. What sensory details did the poem have? Describe the images that these details created in your mind.
> 4. Paraphrase the poem.

Reading Myths, Legends, and Folk Tales

Myths are fictional tales that explain the actions of gods or heroes, or explain natural occurrences. **Legends** are widely told stories about the past that may or may not be based on fact. **Folk tales** are entertaining stories about heroes, adventurers, or mischief-makers. Like myths, folk tales often offer fictional explanations for natural occurrences. Although these stories are retold in writing, they come to us from the oral tradition—the passing along of stories by word of mouth. Each story reveals something about the values and traditions of the culture from which it comes.

◄ Critical Viewing
Does this look like a good setting for reading a piece of literary writing? Why or why not? [Evaluate]

Identify the Cultural Context Understanding the culture from which a myth, legend, or folk tale comes will help you to understand the ideas presented in it. Read any notes that accompany a story to find out more about the culture. While you read the story, look for details that tell you about the culture. Record these ideas in a chart like the one below.

Clues to Culture in "All Stories Are Anansi's"	
Clue	**What this clue says about the culture**
Anansi, spider Mmoboro, hornets Onini, python	shows a variety of animals and plant life in Ghana
Anansi wants to own stories	suggests storytelling is valued
conflict resolved by Nyame, the sky god	shows the religious beliefs of the culture

Predict Look for clues to help you make educated guesses about what will happen next. As you read ahead, revise your predictions as new details unfold, and check to see whether your predictions come true.

Recognize the Storyteller's Purpose Knowing why a legend, myth, or folk tale was told will help you understand why the characters in it behave in certain ways. It will also help you learn more about the culture itself. For example, knowing that a legend deals with how a terrible blizzard affected the land might lead you to conclude that its purpose is to find a way to explain changes in the weather.

> **Exercise 15** Reading Myths, Legends, and Folk Tales
Read a myth, legend, or folk tale from your literature textbook, and answer the following questions.
1. List details from the chart in this section, and explain what they suggest about the culture presented in the piece.
2. What predictions did you make about events in the piece? Were you correct? Why or why not?
3. What is the purpose of this piece? What does the purpose suggest about the culture's values or beliefs?

⊛ Technology Tip

Locate the Web site of a local cultural organization. What does it teach about this culture? How is this culture different from your own?

Customize for
ESL Students

Ask students from the same culture to work together to prepare a short oral, visual, or written presentation of a popular myth, legend, or folk tale from their home culture. They can present or distribute copies of their work and challenge the class to identify cultural details and recognize the purpose of the story.

Answer Key

> **Exercise 15**

Responses will vary.

☑ **ONGOING ASSESSMENT: Monitor and Reinforce**	
If students have difficulty with Exercises 12, 13, 14, or 15, try one of the following options.	
Option 1 Have students read a short story or play and write a summary.	**Option 2** Have students form small groups and discuss the themes, characters, images, etc. of a short story or poem.

Reading From Varied Sources

1. Remind students that the importance of reading extends far beyond the classroom. Ask students to suggest other ways they use reading skills during the course of a day and make a list on the chalkboard. Be sure students name *everything* they read: street signs, menus, names on gym lockers, the destination of a bus, the slogan on a friend's T-shirt, and so on. The point is that they read all day long, even though they aren't aware of it.

2. Ask students to tell when they have had to read each of the different kinds of documents listed in the textbook. Did they understand everything they read? If not, ask what strategies they used to help them—or what strategies they now know that they could have used.

Section 30.4

Reading From Varied Sources

You have a wide variety of sources from which you can choose reading material. You can read newspapers, magazines, advertisements, manuals, handbooks, textbooks, Web pages, or anthologies—collections of short works. What you read depends on why you are reading. Select material that is best suited to your purpose for reading.

Forms and Applications One of the most practical purposes for reading is to fill out forms and applications. Look over these texts carefully. Understanding what information is being requested and where you are expected to write it will help you fill out forms accurately. Look at the sample form below, and decide what information is being requested in each section. Follow any additional directions about how to fill out the form. Use the spaces and directions in italics to help you decide.

SAMPLE FORM

FORM A

Please print in blue or black ink.

Name (*last name first*)

Street

City   State

Date of Birth

MO   DAY   YR

Phone Number

Newspapers When you want to know what's going on in your community or the world, you can find out by reading a newspaper. Some newspapers are local—they cover events that affect a town, city, county, or region. Other newspapers are national—they cover events and issues that affect the entire country. If you are looking for news about a specific event, consider whether the event has local, national, or global impact. Choose the newspaper that will give the most thorough coverage to that particular type of event. Except for sections that are intended to offer a viewpoint, such as the editorial page, newspapers should report the news objectively, without including opinions.

732 • Reading Skills

Vocabulary Tip

When filling out a form or an application, use language as precisely as possible. Provide only the information asked for in the directions.

More Practice

Academic and Workplace Skills Activity Book
• p. 51

⏱ TIME AND RESOURCE MANAGER

Resources
Print: Academic and Workplace Skills Activity Book, p. 51

In-Depth Coverage	Accelerated Pace
• Work through pp. 732–733 with students.	• Assign pp. 732–733 for independent reading.

Magazines When you want to read about a specific area of interest, such as a hobby or sport, you can find information and ideas in a magazine. Some magazines deal with current events, but many magazines focus on attracting a specific audience with specific interests. You can find magazines on camping, computers, crafts, cooking, woodworking, and celebrities. Unlike newspapers, magazines usually offer an opinion or a point of view on the topic they present. Even magazines that cover current events or celebrities set a tone or take an attitude toward the subjects they cover.

Electronic Texts Electronic texts such as Web pages provide detailed, specific information on a wide variety of topics. Web pages may offer objective information, or they may present one person's opinion about a topic. Because Web pages come from such a wide variety of sources, it is vital that you evaluate the authority and background of the source before using or accepting any of the information presented. Some electronic texts are provided by retailers—companies that want to sell you something—and should be viewed as advertisements rather than as informational texts.

▲ Critical Viewing
What kinds of information would you expect these students to find?
[Deduce]

Anthologies If you discover that you enjoy a particular type of literature or a particular author, you might select an anthology or collection that focuses on your preference. There are anthologies that focus on a single author's work; on specific types of literature, such as poetry or drama; and on literature from certain periods, such as early American literature or modern short stories.

Reflecting on Your Understanding of Reading Strategies

Using the questions below as a guide, write a journal entry in which you reflect on what you have learned in this chapter.

- What strategies best helped me to study from my textbook? Why were they so helpful?
- How has my understanding of the uses of language changed?
- Which graphic organizers were most useful to me? Why?
- What are my most common purposes for reading?
- From what sources do I read most often?

Make Inferences and Predictions

Teaching Resources: Standardized Test Preparation Workbook, pp. 59–60

1. Remind students that to infer means to read between the lines. Students should not only pay attention to what a writer is saying, but how a writer says it.

2. Ask students how they can tell that the narrator is uncomfortable, even though the author never uses that word.

Standardized Test Preparation Workshop

Make Inferences and Predictions

The reading sections of standardized tests often measure your ability to make inferences. You can make inferences, or draw logical conclusions, about what you have read, about characters and stories, or about the author's purpose or point of view. Some questions require you to make a prediction or anticipate future actions or outcomes from the material you have read. Some tests will ask you to read a passage, think about it by responding to a question, and explain your response in writing.

The following sample test items will help you prepare for answering these types of questions on standardized tests.

Test Tip

Before answering difficult questions, first mark them. Then, answer all the easy questions. Finally, go back and use the majority of your time to work on those questions that you have marked.

Sample Test Items	Answers and Explanations
Read this passage from "The All-American Slurp" by Lensey Namioka. Then answer the questions that follow the passage. We had been invited to dinner by our neighbors, the Gleasons. After arriving at the house, we shook hands with our hosts and packed ourselves into a sofa. Our family of four sat stiffly in a row; my younger brother and I stole glances at our parents for a clue as to what to do next.	

1 The narrator feels—
 	
  A comfortable in this setting.
  B uncomfortable.
  C happy and excited.
  D sad.
	The answer is *B*. By using the information provided in the passage, you conclude that the narrator was uncomfortable with her surroundings.

Answer the following question. Base your answer on the passage from "The All-American Slurp." How does the narrator feel about her surroundings? Support your answer with details from the story.	Your answer should consist of a paragraph that includes a topic sentence and details from the passage that support it. One possible response: *The narrator is uncomfortable in her surroundings. She describes how her family withdrew to the safety of the couch but were not relaxed and sat stiffly. She and her brother don't know how to act and are looking to her parents for help.*

734 • Reading Skills

 TEST-TAKING TIP

Remind students that they should read each passage more than once. Also encourage them, whenever possible, to take notes about what they are reading.

Practice 1 **Directions:** Read the passage. Then, answer the questions that follow the passage.

The following excerpt from "Suzy and Leah" by Jane Yolen is a diary entry of a young girl who lived in a concentration camp and is now living in a refugee camp in the United States.

August 5, 1944

My dear *Mutti* (Mommy),

I have but a single piece of paper to write on. And a broken pencil. But I will write small so I can tell all. I address it to you, Mutti, though you are gone from me forever. I write in English, to learn better, because I want to make myself be understood.

Today another girl came. With more sweets. A girl with yellow hair and a false smile. Yonni and Zipporah and Ruth, my friends, all grabbed for the sweets. Like wild animals. Like . . . like prisoners. But we are no longer prisoners. Even though we are still penned in.

I stared at the yellow-haired girl until she was forced to look down. Then I walked away. When I turned to look back, she was gone. Disappeared. As if she had never been.

Leah

1 The author writes the story as diary entries—
- **A** to share the characters' personal thoughts and feelings.
- **B** to use a traditional story form.
- **C** to keep the reader guessing.
- **D** to create suspense.

2 Where is the girl's mother?
- **F** on a trip
- **G** living in another country
- **H** dead
- **J** in prison

3 The girl needs to learn English—
- **A** because it is required as her second language.
- **B** so she can work at her job.
- **C** so she can communicate in a new country.
- **D** because it is her hobby.

4 What is the best way to describe Leah's feelings toward the girl with the yellow hair?
- **F** dislikes her
- **G** admires her
- **H** believes she is kind
- **J** wants to be like her

5 If the girl with the yellow hair and Leah meet, they will—
- **A** instantly like each other.
- **B** become roommates.
- **C** probably not like each other at first.
- **D** not be able to communicate at all.

6 Leah stares at the girl because—
- **F** she is not in a regular home.
- **G** she thinks the girl is treating her like an animal.
- **H** she is jealous.
- **J** she doesn't like her hair.

Practice 2 **Directions:** Answer the following question. Base your answer on the passage from "Suzy and Leah."

READ, THINK, EXPLAIN What do Leah's reactions to the girl with the yellow hair (Suzy) tell you about Leah? Use details from the story to explain your answer.

Answer Key

Practice 1

1. A
2. H
3. C
4. F
5. C
6. G

Practice 2

Students' responses will vary.

In-Depth Lesson Plan

	LESSON FOCUS	PRINT AND MEDIA RESOURCES
DAY 1	**Basic Study Skills** Students form a study plan, find a place for study, and take notes (pp. 736–739).	**Teaching Resources** *Academic and Workplace Skills Activity Book,* pp. 52–53
DAY 2	**Library Books** Students select and use library books for their research (pp. 740–745).	**Teaching Resources** *Academic and Workplace Skills Activity Book,* pp. 54–55
DAY 3	**Dictionary** Students use a dictionary to find the spelling, meanings, and pronunciations of words, as well as other information (pp. 746–747).	**Teaching Resources** *Academic and Workplace Skills Activity Book,* p. 57
DAY 4	**Other Library Resources** Students locate and use reference works and nonbook library resources for their research (pp. 748–750).	**Teaching Resources** *Academic and Workplace Skills Activity Book,* p. 58
DAY 5	**Test-Taking Strategies** Students learn a variety of ways to take tests (pp. 751–755).	**Teaching Resources** *Academic and Workplace Skills Activity Book,* pp. 59–60

Accelerated Lesson Plan

	LESSON FOCUS	PRINT AND MEDIA RESOURCES
DAY 1	**Basic Study Skills to Dictionary** Students learn how to make a study plan, use library books to do research, and use a dictionary to find word meanings and pronunciations (pp. 736–747).	**Teaching Resources** *Academic and Workplace Skills Activity Book,* pp. 52–57
DAY 2	**Other Library Resources to Test-Taking Strategies** Students use electronic and print reference resources to do library research and learn a variety of test-taking strategies (pp. 748–755).	**Teaching Resources** *Academic and Workplace Skills Activity Book,* pp. 58–60

Options for Adapting Lesson Plans

HOMEWORK

Have students complete any stage of the lesson for homework.

FEATURES

Extend coverage with the Standardized Test Preparation Workshop (p. 756).

TECHNOLOGY

Students can complete any stage of the lesson on computer. Have them print out their completed work.

INTEGRATED SKILLS COVERAGE

Viewing and Representing
Critical Viewing, SE pp. 736, 737, 740, 743, 744, 749, 750, 755

Speaking and Listening
SE 739; ATE p. 753

Real-World Connection
ATE p. 739

Workplace
ATE p. 738

Language Highlight
ATE p. 745

Technology
SE pp. 738, 741, 745, 748, 752,

ASSESSMENT SUPPORT

Standardized Test Preparation Workshop, SE p. 756
Standardized Test Preparation Workbook, pp. 61–62
Formal Assessment, Ch. 31

MEETING INDIVIDUAL NEEDS

Less Advanced Students ATE p. 741. See also Ongoing Assessments ATE pp. 739, 749, 755.
More Advanced Students ATE p. 742
ESL Students ATE p. 743, 747
Verbal/Linguistic Learners ATE p. 747
Visual/Spatial Learners ATE p. 749

BLOCK SCHEDULING

For 90-minute Blocks
• Have students complete the Organization, Library Books, and Dictionary stages in a single period.
• Focus one class period on Other Print and Electronic References and Test-Taking Strategies.

Professional Development Support
• *How to Manage Instruction in the Block* This Teaching Resource provides management and activity suggestions.

MEDIA AND TECHNOLOGY

For the Teacher
• *Resource Pro* **CD-ROM**

WRITING AND GRAMMAR WEB SITE

The Interactive Writing and Grammar Web site provides a wide array of support for students, teachers, and parents. Writing support includes:

• Interactive revision checkers
• Scoring rubrics with complete models

www.phschool.com

1. To form a study plan, including setting up a study area and taking notes.
2. To locate meanings, pronunciations, and derivations of unfamiliar words using reference sources.
3. To select and use reference materials and resources for writing.
4. To develop strategies for taking tests.
5. To answer different types of test questions.

Critical Viewing

Speculate Students may say they are working on a research paper because they are using computers.

Chapter 31 Study, Reference, and Test-Taking Skills

▲ Critical Viewing
On what types of assignments might these students be working? On what do you base your answer? **[Speculate]**

Studying, researching, taking tests—all are vital skills to develop as you progress through your years at school. In this chapter, you will learn how to make the most of your study time. You will also learn more about retrieving information from print and electronic sources. Finally, you will receive valuable tips that can help improve your test scores.

🕐 TIME AND RESOURCE MANAGER	
Resources **Print:** Academic and Workplace Skills Activity Book, pp. 52–53	
In-Depth Coverage	**Accelerated Pace**
• Work through all key concepts, pp. 737–739. • Assign and review Exercises 1–4.	• Assign pp. 737–739 for independent student review.

Section 31.1 *Basic Study Skills*

Developing good study habits is an important first step toward success in school.

Forming a Study Plan

A study plan is a consistent, well-thought-out approach to studying that includes where and when you study.

▶ **KEY CONCEPT** Establish a study area that works well for you, and set aside regular periods for studying. ■

Choose a Study Setting Even though you can probably get some studying done at school, you should set up a study area at home. Make a habit of studying in the same place every day. Keep everything you need in your study area, so you will not have to interrupt your studies to hunt for pencils, paper, and so on. A good study area is

- free from distraction.
- equipped with a chair, desk, and reading lamp.
- well-organized and neat.

Create a Study Schedule You will have enough time to complete all of your homework and still have time for other activities if you plan your time carefully. At the beginning of each week, plan how you will use your study time each day. Vary the amount of time you spend on each subject, based on tests, projects, and long-term assignments that are scheduled.

▲ **Critical Viewing** Judging from this photograph, is this girl working in a good study area? Why? **[Analyze]**

▶ **More Practice**
Academic and Workplace Skills Activity Book
- p. 52

SAMPLE STUDY SCHEDULE		
	3:00–4:30	Sports Practice
Mon	5:00–6:00	Daily Assignments
	7:30–8:00	Review for Science Test (Weds)
	8:00–8:30	Work on Social Studies Paper
Tue	5:00–6:00	Daily Assignments
	7:30–8:30	Study for Science Test
Wed	5:00–6:00	Daily Assignments
	7:00–8:00	Work on Social Studies Paper
	8:00–8:30	Review for Math Test (Next Tues)

Basic Study Skills • **737**

Keeping an Assignment Book

1. Explain that most people use some sort of agenda in their professional life to keep themselves organized, meet their appointments, and get their work done.

2. An assignment book is like a student's agenda, used to keep track of the work that has been assigned as well as due dates.

Integrating Workplace Skills

Have students ask adult family members if they use some form of agenda or organizer and if so, why they find it helpful. Then, have students make a copy of a sample page of the agenda. Have them present this sample page to the class, describing how the day is structured by time slots and how it is organized into categories such as "To Do," "Appointments," and so on.

Answer Key

Exercise 1

Responses will vary. Make sure students select areas that will allow them to work without distraction.

Exercise 2

At the end of the week, have students discuss their experiences with keeping a schedule.

Exercise 3

At the end of the week, have students discuss the changes they made to their assignment books.

Keep an Assignment Book It is important to keep track of the papers, reading assignments, and tests due in each class. Do this by keeping an assignment book or a special assignment section in your notebook. Write down each assignment as you get it. This will help you plan what to work on in your scheduled time. Keeping an assignment book will help you to complete each assignment on time and to be prepared for any in-class discussions or tests.

KEY CONCEPT Use an assignment book to record homework assignments and due dates. ■

Use the following model to set up your assignment book:

Date	Subject	Assignment	Due	Completed
10/15	History	Read Ch. 6, pp. 55–75	10/18	✓
10/16	Math	Answer problems 1–20 on p. 42	10/17	
10/17	English	Answer questions on pp. 76 & 77	10/19	

Exercise 1 Describing Your Study Area If you already have a study area, write a brief description of it, and explain any ways it can be improved. If you do not, choose one. Then, write a short explanation of why you selected this place.

Exercise 2 Preparing a Study Schedule Create your own study schedule, using the sample schedule as a model. Follow the schedule for a week. Then, evaluate it and make any needed changes. Keep a copy in your notebook.

Exercise 3 Setting Up an Assignment Book In a special section of your notebook or in a separate notebook, set up an assignment book. Use it for a week. Then, if you find it necessary, revise it. You may want to make changes, such as leaving more room for writing assignments or using a red marker to indicate tests.

Technology Tip

Computer software is available to help you keep track of your assignments. Consult with your teacher or technology coordinator to consider databases or management programs you might use for this purpose.

Taking Notes

Taking good notes is an important and useful study skill. Taking notes in class helps you remember what you heard, and taking notes while reading helps you remember what you read. Later, you can use your notes to study for a test or just to review the information you have learned.

TIPS FOR TAKING NOTES

- Don't record every word; focus on capturing main ideas.
- Label your notes with the topic and date.
- Keep notes for different subjects in separate notebooks or in separate sections of a general notebook.

Modified Outlines One note-taking device that you can use to sort out main ideas and major details is a *modified outline*. List each main idea, and underline it. Place major details below the main idea, and number them. Jot down supporting details under each major detail.

SAMPLE MODIFIED OUTLINE

```
Solar System ───────────── Main idea
1. Sun ───────────────────── Major detail
    A star ─────────────┐
    Center of the solar system ┘─ Supporting details
2. Planets
    Nine planets
    Orbit the sun in west to east direction
    Most have moons or satellites
3. Asteroids, Meteoroids, and Comets
    Asteroids—fragments of rock
    Meteoroids—the result of asteroid collisions
    Comets—solid nucleus surrounded by
            frozen gases and dust particles
```

Summaries Writing a *summary* is another way of organizing information you've learned. After reading a chapter or attending a class, write one or more paragraphs stating the key points covered and explaining how the ideas are connected.

▶ **Exercise 4** Making a Modified Outline and a Summary
Create a modified outline and a summary of a chapter in your science or social studies textbook.

▶ **Speaking and Listening Tip**

Spoken summaries can also be an effective study tool. With a class-mate, take turns summarizing a lecture or a piece you have read. Check to see that you both have the same understanding.

▶ **More Practice**

Academic and Workplace Skills Activity Book
• p. 53

Basic Study Skills • **739**

Step-by-Step Teaching Guide

Taking Notes

1. Remind students of the story of Hansel and Gretel. Although breadcrumbs clearly weren't a good choice of material, leaving a trail behind you as you go through the forest to use again on the way back out, is exactly the idea behind note taking.

2. Taking notes is a tool for remembering what is studied. Notes show us what has been learned and help students retain the information so they can make use of it later. Good notes are just like a trail, which students can follow to revisit what they have learned, read, or heard.

3. Notes take two primary forms: outlines and summaries. An outline is a shorthand description made while studying or listening to a lecture. A summary, prepared afterward, is a condensed recap of the main ideas.

Real-World Connection

Explain to students that taking good notes is not just an important skill for school. People in a wide variety of jobs and situations are required to take notes. Ask students to brainstorm for a list of both jobs and daily situations in which they might have to take good notes.

Answer Key

▶ **Exercise 4**

You may want to have students present their outlines and summaries in order to check their work.

☑ **ONGOING ASSESSMENT: Monitor and Reinforce**

If students have difficulty with Exercise 3 or 4, try one of the following options.

Option 1 Have students use a daily planner as a model for their assignment books.	**Option 2** Have students work backward to create an outline from a piece of their own writing. This will help them see the structural connections between an outline and the finished product.

Activate Prior Knowledge

Encourage volunteers to share their experiences of using the school or local library.

TEACH

Step-by-Step Teaching Guide

Using the Library

1. Every library provides a listing of its materials. The library catalog is like a map of what can be found in a particular library, as well as a guide to finding the right resources when you have only a limited amount of information at the start.

2. Libraries have either a card catalog, a printed catalog, or an electronic catalog. In all of these, books are listed according to one of three pieces of information: title, author, or subject. It is not necessary to know all three, and this is one of the great advantages of using the library catalog.

continued

Critical Viewing

Analyze Students should say the author, the title, and the call number.

31.2 *Reference Skills*

The information explosion of recent years makes it possible to obtain more and more information on your own. Just about every major form of printed reference now has its electronic equivalent on CD-ROM, on-line, or both. Many of the works, in both printed and electronic form, are available at school or public libraries.

Using the Library

Whether you want to know the date of a president's birth or of the first space-shuttle flight, your best source of information will generally be the library. Both your school and public libraries hold a vast amount of knowledge.

Most school and public libraries contain some or all of these resources: fiction and nonfiction books, audiocassettes and videocassettes, periodicals (newspapers, magazines, and journals), information on microfilm, reference works in printed and electronic form, and computer access to the Internet.

Use the Library Catalog Whether you seek books for casual reading or for research, your search usually begins with the *library catalog*. The catalog will show you whether the library owns a particular book. It can also help you find

• books by an author when you don't know the titles.

• books on a subject when you don't know titles or authors.

> **KEY CONCEPT** Use the library catalog to identify and locate the books that a library contains. ■

The library catalog will be in one of these three forms:

Card Catalog A card catalog lists books on index cards. Each book has a separate *author card* and *title card*. If the book is nonfiction, it also has at least one *subject card*. Cards are filed alphabetically in small drawers, with author cards alphabetized by last names and title cards alphabetized by the first words of the titles, excluding *A*, *An*, and *The*.

▲ **Critical Viewing** What are the key pieces of information listed on the spines of these books? [Analyze]

> **More Practice**
> Academic and Workplace Skills Activity Book
> • pp. 54–55

🕐 TIME AND RESOURCE MANAGER

Resources
Print: Academic and Workplace Skills Activity Book, pp. 54–58

In-Depth Coverage	Accelerated Pace
• Work through all key concepts, pp. 740–750. • Assign and review Exercises 5–10.	• Assign pp. 740–750 for independent student review.

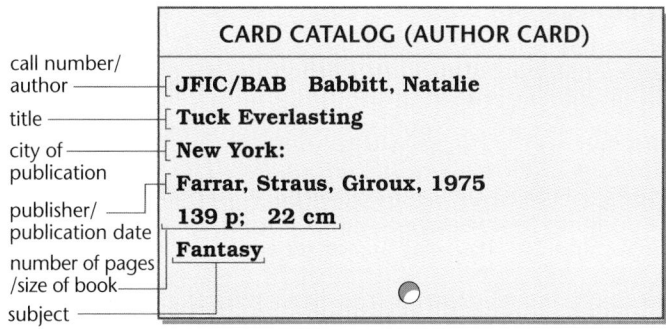

CARD CATALOG (AUTHOR CARD)

call number/author — JFIC/BAB Babbitt, Natalie

title — Tuck Everlasting

city of publication — New York:

publisher/publication date — Farrar, Straus, Giroux, 1975

number of pages/size of book — 139 p; 22 cm

subject — Fantasy

Printed Catalog A printed catalog lists information in printed booklets, with each book listed alphabetically by author, by title, and—if nonfiction—by subject. Often, there are separate booklets for author, title, and subject listings.

Electronic Catalog An electronic catalog lists entries in an on-line database that you can access from computer terminals in the library. Usually, you can find a book's catalog entry by typing in its title, key words in the title, its author's name, or an appropriate subject. Entries usually tell you

- whether the book is available or has been checked out.
- whether the book is available from other local libraries and may be obtained through an interlibrary loan system.

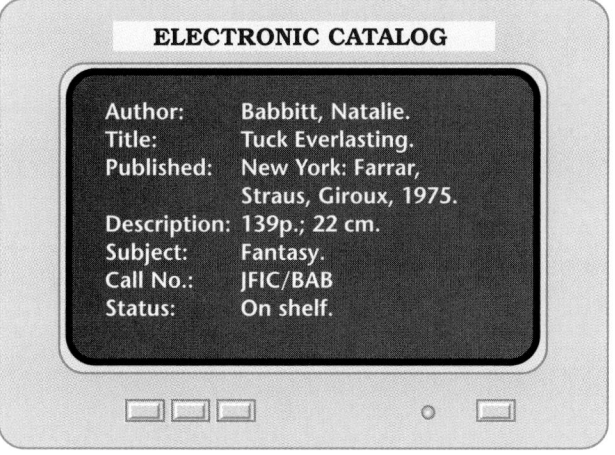

ELECTRONIC CATALOG

Author: Babbitt, Natalie.
Title: Tuck Everlasting.
Published: New York: Farrar,
             Straus, Giroux, 1975.
Description: 139p.; 22 cm.
Subject: Fantasy.
Call No.:   JFIC/BAB
Status: On shelf.

Technology Tip

Some electronic catalogs can be accessed remotely through a computer in your home or school. Ask your librarian if this feature is available and, if so, how to use it.

Step-by-Step Teaching Guide continued

3. Ask students to look at the example card on the page and answer the following questions.

- *What is the title of the book?* (Tuck Everlasting)
- *When was it published? (1975)*
- *How long is the book? (139 pages)*
- *What is the book's subject? (fantasy)*

Customizing for
Less Advanced Students

Some students may feel overwhelmed when faced with using a card catalog. Have students work in small groups to find information on a few books. You can provide the title and have groups identify the information shown on the card on this page.

Find Books on Library Shelves

1. You can take the class to the school library for this section, or you can bring to class several library books of fiction and nonfiction so that you can use their bindings as examples.

2. Explain that fiction books in the library are arranged in alphabetical order by author's last name. Libraries generally use a form of last name abbreviation to label the book's spine. (Point to the actual book as an example.) For nonfiction books, American librarian Melvil Dewey came up with the system of library organization called the Dewey Decimal System. The Dewey Decimal System separates nonfiction books into ten categories.

3. Explain the categories. General works include reference books. Social sciences are anthropology, political science, psychology, and sociology. Pure science is biology, chemistry, and physics. The arts include music, dance, and fine art.

Customizing for
More Advanced Students

Challenge students to devise alternate systems for organizing books. Have them compare their systems to the Dewey Decimal System.

Finding Books on Library Shelves

Libraries need a special method of organizing their books so that people can find them. The library distinguishes between two kinds of books—*fiction* and *nonfiction.*

Fiction Books In most libraries, fiction books are shelved in a special section, alphabetized by the authors' last names. In the library catalog and on the book's spine, a work of fiction may be labeled *F* or *FIC,* followed by one or more letters of an author's last name—for example, *FIC Paul* may appear on a novel by Gary Paulsen.

KEY CONCEPT Find fiction arranged alphabetically by the authors' last names. Find nonfiction on the shelves by using the call numbers. ■

Nonfiction Books Nonfiction books have call numbers. In most school and public libraries, the call numbers are based on the Dewey Decimal System. Books are arranged in number-letter order on the shelves—for example, 619.1, 619.2, 619.31A, 619.31D, 619.32A, 619.32P, 620.1. The system is named for an American librarian, Melvil Dewey, who suggested that books could be classified into ten main groups, as shown in following chart:

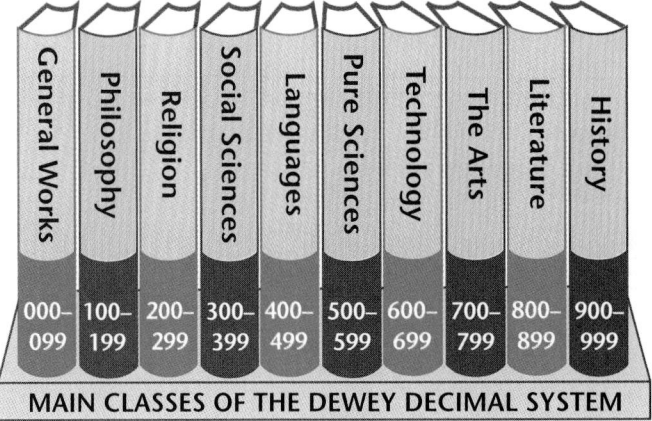

General Works	Philosophy	Religion	Social Sciences	Languages	Pure Sciences	Technology	The Arts	Literature	History
000–099	100–199	200–299	300–399	400–499	500–599	600–699	700–799	800–899	900–999

MAIN CLASSES OF THE DEWEY DECIMAL SYSTEM

Locating Biographies and Other Special Materials
Most libraries have separate sections for biographies and autobiographies, reference books, and young-adult books.

Biographies A *biography* is a factual account of a person's life. If that person wrote his or her own story, it is called an *autobiography*. In the library catalog and on the book's spine, a biography may be labeled *B* or *BIO*, or *921* (its Dewey Decimal number), followed by one or more letters of the subject's last name. For example, *BIO Lin* may appear on a biography of Abraham Lincoln.

Reference Materials Most libraries also have a special section for *reference books*. Frequently, the sources in the library's reference section are labeled *R* or *REF*.

Young Adult Books Books that are of interest to teenagers may be placed in a *young-adult section*. The letters *YA* or *J* (*Juvenile*) in front of the call number show that the book is in this section.

Nonprint Materials In addition to books, most libraries contain a variety of nonprint materials, including videos, audiotapes, audio CDs, CD-ROMs, and more. Libraries use a variety of symbols in catalog entries to indicate nonprint material, and these materials are usually kept in special sections of the building. Ask your librarian for help locating such materials.

▲ Critical Viewing
How would you tell which one of these drawers to look in for a particular book or subject area? [Analyze]

▶ **Exercise 5** **Using the Library Catalog and Finding Books on Shelves** When you visit your school or local library, use the catalog to answer the following questions.

1. What kind of catalog does the library use—card, printed, or electronic? Where is it located?
2. What are the titles, subjects, and call numbers of the books that your library carries by author Laurence Yep?
3. What are the titles, authors, and call numbers of three books about the solar system?
4. Arrange these fiction authors in the order in which you would find them on the library shelves: Louise Erdrich, Elizabeth Enright, Ralph Waldo Emerson.
5. Using the Dewey Decimal System, indicate the general subject matter you would expect to find in nonfiction books with these call numbers:

   a. 973.7G   **b.** 613.5A   **c.** 423F   **d.** 746R

**Using Periodicals
and Periodical Indexes**

1. Books are usually the place to find very detailed information on a given subject; periodicals, or magazines, journals, and newspapers that are published at regular periods, are the place to go for up-to-the-minute information. In many study endeavors, it is extremely important to learn about the latest discoveries, theories, or debates about a topic.

2. Ask students to suggest examples of topics for which it would be important to consult periodicals as well as books (scientific breakthroughs, evaluations of a recent movie, and so on).

3. A periodical index tells in a citation exactly when and where an article was published. This information is necessary to find the article in the library. An abstract is a brief summary of the article and can be helpful in determining whether that particular article will be useful to particular research.

4. Some electronic indexes actually provide the text of the article, but it is not always complete, in which case it is necessary to locate the article in the library. Library periodicals are usually kept in a special section and can be found in binders on shelves, behind a designated librarian's desk, or on microfilm or CD-ROM.

Critical Viewing

Analyze Students should say that she will use the information she is gathering to locate articles on her topic.

31.2

Using Periodicals and Periodical Indexes

Newspapers, magazines, and other printed materials that are published at regular intervals, or periods, are called **periodicals.** They may be issued daily, weekly, monthly, or at any other regular interval.

When to Use Periodicals Periodicals provide the most recent information about a wide variety of subjects. A book provides more detailed information, but will not include information, events, or developments that take place after its publication.

▶ **KEY CONCEPT** Use periodicals when you are researching a current event or development, or when you want to learn how an event was reported at the time it happened. ■

Using Periodical Indexes **Periodical indexes** contain *citations* that tell you precisely where and when an article was published. They may also contain *abstracts*, or brief summaries, of the articles. Indexes can be in print or electronic form. Many electronic indexes provide the full text for some or all of the articles cited.

▶ **KEY CONCEPT** Use a periodical index to find articles published in newspapers and magazines. ■

The most frequently used periodical index is the *Readers' Guide to Periodical Literature.* The *Readers' Guide* covers all types of periodicals. A sample entry from the *Readers' Guide* appears on the next page. Other periodical indexes focus on specific subjects, such as art and business.

Locating Periodicals If the periodical index does not provide the full text of an article, you need to find the article itself. Most libraries subscribe to many periodicals to which all library users have access. Current issues can usually be found on shelves in a special section of the library. Older issues may be available on CD-ROM or on microfilm.

▲ Critical Viewing
What is this student doing with the information she gathers from a periodical index? Why? [Analyze]

SAMPLE *READERS' GUIDE* ENTRY

Fruit ——————————————————————— Main subject
   See also   heading
   Cooking—Fruit   — Cross-references
   individual names of fruit
Fruit for all seasons. E. W. Stiles il *Nat Hist* ——— Author of article
93:42–53 Ag '84   ┌ Title of article
Fruit selection. N. Nevins. il *South Living* 19:144
Ag '84
Sweet summer sensations. il *Glamour*   — Magazine
82:188–99 Jl '84
Winter temptations. il *Glamour* 82:302–5+ N '84
     Diseases and pests —————— Subheading
   See also
   Codling moths
   Fruit flies
       Drying
Stretch summer flavor with dried produce. M.
Chason. il. *South Living* 19:188+ Je '84   — Volume: page
    Preservation   numbers and
Keeping fruit fresh [polyethylene film wrap] date
Consum Res Mag 67:2 F' 84   └ Illustrated
    Ripening
Ripe promises. E. W. Stiles. *Nat Hist* 93:51
Ag '84
    Varieties

Have you grown new fruit varieties? *Sunset*
172:256 Je '84

Exercise 6 **Using Periodicals** Visit your school or local library to answer the following questions.

1. What newspapers does the library carry?
2. Name two newsmagazines the library carries. How far back does each go, and in what format(s) are they given?
3. Use a periodical index to find citations for articles on a subject you are studying in science or social studies. Then, find at least one of the articles in your library.
4. Using a periodical index, locate a newspaper or magazine article about someone you admire in sports or another field. Read the article, and then write a summary.
5. Using a periodical index, find two recent articles on a current event.

Using Vertical Files Pamphlets containing current information on topics such as local government, educational programs, and local parks can also be a valuable research tool. Most often, pamphlets are stored in a vertical file—a file cabinet with large drawers. Ask your librarian whether the library's vertical files contain any pamphlets that might aid you in your research.

Internet Tip

Many leading newspapers and magazines now have free Internet Web sites where you can read current editions at no cost. The older articles are usually stored in a section called the *archives.*

More Practice

Academic and Workplace Skills Activity Book
• p. 56

Answer Key

Exercise 6

1–5. Responses will vary.

Language Highlight

A library may serve as an archive. The word *archive* is derived from the Greek word *archeion,* meaning "government house." An archive is a place where public or institutional records are stored or preserved.

Using Dictionaries

1. Write the word *mog* on the board. Ask students how they could learn what *mog* means, its part of speech, and its pronunciation. (All answers should lead to using the dictionary.)

2. Dictionaries now come in both print and electronic forms. The type and size of the dictionary being consulted should be determined by the nature of the search. If the word is a very obscure one (not in popular or common usage), an unabridged dictionary will be needed. Abridged dictionaries are fine to use when the word being looked up is not obscure, and, as they are smaller, they are often easier to use. A specialized dictionary is needed when the word is related to a specific field, particularly when it is a foreign word, or part of technical or occupational terminology. Usually, though, such words can be found in an unabridged dictionary.

3. Use a dictionary to demonstrate to the class the use of a thumb index and guide words.

4. Have students use an unabridged and abridged dictionary to find the word *mog*. Have them tell what it means, where the word comes from, its part of speech, and any other interesting facts. Then ask students to use *mog* in a sentence. (*Mog* is a verb meaning to move or plod from place to place. Its derivation is unknown. Forms are *mogged* and *mogging*. You may want to explain the abbreviation *Dial.,* which means dialect, a form of speech used by a particular group of people.)

Using Dictionaries

A dictionary is the first place you should look to find the spelling and meaning of words. Dictionaries also contain other information about words, such as their pronunciations.

Distinguishing Types of Dictionaries Like most references nowadays, dictionaries are available in both print and electronic forms. They also come in various types and sizes.

THREE TYPES OF DICTIONARIES	
Unabridged	Exhaustive study of the English language containing over 250,000 words
Abridged	Compact editions containing listings from 55,000 to 160,000 words
Specialized	Limited to words of a particular type or field, such as foreign languages or mathemathics

Finding Words in Dictionaries In *printed dictionaries*, all the items are listed in strict alphabetical order—that is, letter by letter, starting with *a* and finishing with *z*. To help speed a word search, use *guide words*, the large words at the top of each page that indicate the first and last words listed. In *electronic dictionaries*, you usually find a word simply by typing the word and having the computer search the dictionary database.

Understanding Dictionary Entries The information contained in a dictionary entry varies from dictionary to dictionary. Following are some of the elements you will find:

1. **Entry Word** A word and the information about it are called a *main entry*. The word itself is called an *entry word*. From it, you can confirm the word's spelling and learn how to break it into *syllables*. Dashes, dots, or spaces show the syllables.

2. **Pronunciation** Pronunciation is indicated by symbols that show how to say the word and which syllable to stress. To understand the symbols, consult the dictionary's *pronunciation key*. The syllable that gets the most emphasis usually has a heavy *primary stress*, which is shown by a heavy mark after it (´). Words of more than two syllables may also have a shorter, lighter, *secondary stress* mark (ˌ).

 **Spelling Tip**

Some words have more than one acceptable spelling. These will all be listed in a dictionary.

3. **Part-of-Speech Labels** These labels tell you how a word is used. This information is given in abbreviated form. When a word can be used as more than one part of speech, the meanings are grouped under each part-of-speech label.

4. **Plurals and Inflected Forms** The dictionary may also show the *plural forms of nouns* and *inflected forms of verbs*—past tense and participle forms—if there is anything irregular about their spelling.

5. **Etymology** The word's history, or etymology, usually appears in brackets near the start or end of the entry. Abbreviations used are explained in a key.

6. **Definitions** When a word has more than one definition, the dictionary will give the definitions a number and group them according to their part of speech.

7. **Idioms and Derived Words** The end of an entry may list and define *idioms*, or expressions, that contain the word. It may also list *derived words* formed by adding suffixes, such as *-ly* or *-ness*, to the entry word.

Usage labels indicate words that are rarely used in formal English. For example, (*Arch.*) indicates that a word is archaic and no longer used. *Field labels* indicate words used in certain fields, such as math.

SAMPLE DICTIONARY ENTRY

①──②───③────④────⑤
ear|ly (ur´lē) *adv., adj.* **-li|er, -li|est** [ME *erli* <OE *ærlic*, adv. (> *ærlic*, adj.) <*ær*, before (see ERE) + *-lice*, adv. suffix (see -LY², LIKE¹] ⑥**1** near the beginning of a given period of time or of a series, as of events; soon after the start **2** before the expected or customary time **3** in the far distant past; in ancient or remote times **4** in the near future; before much time has passed — ⑦**early on** at an early stage; near the beginning —**ear´li ness** *n.*

▶ **Exercise 7** **Working With a Dictionary** Use a dictionary to answer the following questions.
1. Which word is not spelled correctly?
   a. lollipop   b. gasoline   c. kindergarden   d. judgment
2. How many syllables are in the word *extravagance*?
3. What part of speech is the word *before*?
4. What is the origin of the word *silhouette*?
5. What are two definitions of the word *place*?

⊙ **Vocabulary Tip**

Etymologies can help you extend your vocabulary. Knowing a word's origin can help you remember its meaning. It will also help you figure out the meaning of related words.

▶ **More Practice**
Academic and Workplace Skills Activity Book
• p. 57

Customize for
ESL Students

Have students use an English dictionary and a dictionary for their first language to compare the English entry for *early* with the entry for its foreign-language equivalent. Have them find pronunciation, part of speech, and so on in both dictionaries.

Customize for
Verbal/Linguistic Learners

Have groups of students play "Dictionary." Students take turns looking up a word that is obscure or difficult and, without showing or telling the group what it means, they ask if anyone knows its meaning. When they have found a word that no one in the group knows, it is time for those who are guessing to write down what they imagine the word might mean, trying to make the definition as believable as possible. Students then read their made-up definitions out loud. Group members vote on the most believable and the most inventive definitions. If anyone's imaginary definition was right, they win the round. Points can also be given for most original answer or most believable.

Answer Key

▶ **Exercise 7**
1. c. the correct spelling is *kindergarten*
2. four
3. adv., prep., conj.
4. from Étienne de Silhouette, French minister of finance
5. Possible response: noun: space, room; verb: to put somewhere

Using Other Print and Electronic Reference

1. Whether students use a reference work in its printed or electronic form, consulting a reference work is an excellent way to obtain general information quickly and efficiently. Often, a reference work is helpful at the start of a research process, offering an overview of a subject before students proceed to study it in greater depth. A reference work is used in a similar way to a dictionary, when an explanation of a specific term, person, event, or place is needed.

2. Bring to class an example of each type of reference work—general encyclopedia, biographical reference, almanac, atlas, and thesaurus—if you do not conduct the lesson in the library.

3. A general encyclopedia provides the fundamental information needed to form a basic understanding of a given subject. A biographical reference provides information about important people from history or specific fields of endeavor; an almanac contains quick summaries of facts and statistics; an atlas is a geographical reference; and a thesaurus is a reference of language, providing synonyms and antonyms for the entry word.

4. Write the following questions on the board. Ask students which reference work would be most helpful in answering each one.

   - *What is the capital of South Africa? (atlas, almanac)*

   - *Which state in the United States gets the most rainfall? (atlas, almanac)*

   - *When did Abraham Lincoln begin his career in politics? (encyclopedia, almanac)*

   - *What is another word for reference? (thesaurus)*

   - *What is the history of the printing press, and how does it work? (encyclopedia)*

31.2

Using Other Print and Electronic References

A library's reference section includes other books and electronic resources that can help you in your studies. Listed below are a few of the resources you will find.

Print Encyclopedias When you are investigating an unfamiliar subject, one of the best places to start is a *general encyclopedia*. A general encyclopedia is a collection of articles that provide basic information on many subjects.

Most encyclopedias consist of several volumes. The spine of each book is marked with letters covering a part of the alphabet. Each volume contains articles on subjects that begin with those parts of the alphabet. At the top of each page, guide words show the subjects covered on that page.

CD-ROM Encyclopedias Encyclopedias on CD-ROM provide photographs, artwork, video, and audio to enhance the information on various topics. Generally, they have an alphabetical search feature that you can use to find topics.

WHEN TO USE AN ENCYCLOPEDIA

- Encyclopedias are a great source when you need information quickly for general interest or for a topic you're studying.

- Encyclopedias are a good starting point for research on a topic. However, they should *never* be your primary source of information for research papers.

Biographical References These books provide brief life histories of a variety of famous people. Some—such as *Current Biography*, *Merriam Webster's Biographical Dictionary*, and the *Biography Resource Center*—cover people from many walks of life; others, such as *Contemporary Authors* or *The International Who's Who of Women*, cover people in specific fields or areas.

Almanacs When you want to find specific facts quickly, you can check an *almanac*. These yearly publications are a source of facts and statistics in many areas. These include business, entertainment, government, population, sports, and current as well as historic events. They provide little background information. Most facts are represented in tables or charts.

Print Atlases Books of maps, called *atlases*, give information about geography. Maps show Earth's division into continents and countries, as well as the locations of cities, mountains, and oceans. Through the use of symbols and color, maps may also show climate, crops, and population. To find a specific map or location, use the index at the back of the atlas.

748 • Study, Reference, and Test-Taking Skills

Technology Tip

There are CD-ROM encyclopedias on a wide range of specialized topics, from baseball and football to visual arts and music.

More Practice

Academic and Workplace Skills Activity Book
• p. 58

CD-ROM Atlases Atlases are also available electronically on CD-ROM. The maps may be interactive, allowing you to see how to get from one place to another or to see changes over time. Generally, they include a search feature that makes it easy for you to find a specific location.

Thesauruses A thesaurus is a specialized dictionary that gives extensive lists of *synonyms*, or words with similar meanings, and may also list *antonyms*, or words with opposite meanings. Some thesauruses show words arranged by categories according to an alphabetical index. Others are arranged in strict alphabetical order, as a dictionary is.

Electronic Databases Electronic databases provide large collections of data on specific topics. Using one or more search features, you can easily access any piece of the data, piece together related information, or look at the information in different ways. Electronic databases are available both on CD-ROM and on the Internet.

▲ Critical Viewing
What types of references might this girl be using? On what do you base your answer? **[Speculate]**

▶ **Exercise 8** **Using Other Reference Works** Use printed or electronic reference works to find the following information. Indicate the type of reference you used.
1. the three largest cities in Texas and their population
2. three countries that border Switzerland
3. the first astronaut to walk on the moon and the date he landed there
4. the birthplace of English author Aldous Huxley and the names of two books that he wrote
5. five synonyms for the adjective *cold*

▶ **Exercise 9** **Using All Types of Reference Works** Explain at least two specific uses for each of the following types of references.
1. the encyclopedia
2. newspapers
3. almanacs
4. nonfiction books
5. pamphlets

Reference Skills • 749

Critical Viewing

Speculate Student responses will vary, but make sure that students support their answers with specific evidence from the photograph.

Customize for
Visual/Spatial Learners

Have students look in the reference works listed for the types of visual images used. For example, have them find a chart in an almanac, a photograph or illustration of a famous person in a biographical reference, a topographical map in an atlas, and an anatomical or scientific diagram in an encyclopedia. Have them make a collage of their findings in poster form for display in the classroom.

Answer Key

▶ Exercise 8

1. San Antonio, 1,114,130; Houston, 1,786,691; Dallas, 1,075,894 (almanac; some atlases may also contain this information.)
2. France, Germany, Austria, Italy (atlas)
3. Neil Armstrong, 1969 (encyclopedia)
4. Godalming, Surrey, England; *Brave New World, Crome Yellow* (encyclopedia)
5. Possible answers: *chilly, freezing, aloof, cool, unsympathetic* (thesaurus)

Answer Key

▶ Exercise 9

Answers will vary. Sample responses given.

1. The history of a particular country; a biography
2. current events; stock prices
3. population of a city; exports from a country
4. the story of a scientific discovery;
5. information about an organization; current events

☑ **ONGOING ASSESSMENT: Monitor and Reinforce**

If students have difficulty with Exercise 8 or 9, try one of the following options.

Option 1 Have students make a chart that lists different reference materials in the left column, and the information contained in each in the right column. Encourage students to refer to their charts when working with research materials.

Option 2 Have students work in small groups to find information in reference materials on subjects you provide.

Using the Internet

1. It is likely that students are quite familiar with the Internet. Lead a discussion of what the Internet is and how it works. Ask students if they know why connecting to the Internet is called going "on-line." Explain that the Internet is a worldwide network that connects computers together (as in a "web") through the use of phone and cable lines, which is where the term "going on-line" comes from. Ask students to share different ways they have already used the Internet.

2. A URL is another term for an Internet address, because it stands for Universal Resource Locator. Point out that *resource* truly is what the Internet is all about, but it is important for someone using the Web as a resource to realize that not all Web sites are of equal accuracy and value.

3. Ask students to explain ways that they have used search engines to find information on the Internet. Point out that library journals are also useful ways to learn about Internet sites that might have reliable information on a given topic.

Answer Key

> **Exercise 10**

Answers will vary.

Critical Viewing

Speculate Students may say that he does look interested because he is looking directly at the screen with an expression of concentration.

31.2

Using the Internet

The Internet provides access to an almost unlimited amount of information through a personal computer. Web sites consist of text, graphics, and sometimes audio or video displays, which you can download.

Locating Appropriate Web Sites Following are some strategies for finding information on the Internet:

- If you know a reliable Web site and its address (URL), simply type the address into your Web browser. Often, television programs, commercials, magazines, newspapers, and radio stations provide Web site addresses where you can find more information about a show, product, company, and so on.

- Consult library journals to learn addresses of Web sites that provide useful and reliable information.

- If you don't know particular Web sites, you can do a general search for a key term on a search engine. Try several search engines to discover which are best for each type of search. Some search engines are best for finding academic information. Others are best for hobbies and general interests.

- Remember to bookmark (or save to Favorite Places) the interesting and reliable sites you find while searching the Web.

Evaluating Web Sites Don't just assume that information is reliable because it is posted on the Web. Anyone with a computer can set up a Web site on any topic, regardless of that person's beliefs or how much that person knows about the topic. Critically evaluate a Web site by asking these questions:

1. Who or what is the source of the information on the site? Does that source have credentials, such as expertise in the field?
2. Does the source reflect a particular point of view on the topic? If so, you should consider this point of view before accepting any information that is presented.
3. Is the information up-to-date?
4. How does it compare to other information on the topic?

▼ **Critical Viewing** Does this student look interested in what he is finding on the Internet? On what do you base your answer? **[Speculate]**

> **Exercise 10** **Using the Internet to Write an Essay** On a library, school, or home computer, use the Internet to research the following topics. Record the names and addresses (URLs) of the Web sites you use as sources, and evaluate the effectiveness of each site.
> (1) Edgar Allan Poe (2) Russian czars (3) Yellowstone National Park (4) soccer (5) Egyptian pyramids

Section 31.3 *Test-Taking Skills*

Strategies for Taking Tests

Over the years, you will take a wide range of tests. These will include standardized tests, as well as the ones you take in school. Some will follow a multiple-choice format; others will require you to write an essay. Regardless of the type of test you take, there are strategies you can use to help you succeed. The most important strategy is to prepare thoroughly. Good time management and a familiarity with the types of questions you'll encounter will also contribute to your success.

KEY CONCEPT Budget your time between previewing the test, answering the questions, and proofreading. ■

PREVIEW THE TEST

1. Put your name on each sheet of paper you will hand in.
2. Look over the entire test to get an overview of the types of questions and how they are arranged.
3. Find out whether you lose points for incorrect answers. If you do, do not guess at answers.
4. Decide how much time you want to spend on each section of the test.
5. Plan to devote the most time to questions that are hardest or worth the most points.

ANSWER THE QUESTIONS

1. Answer the easy questions first. Put a check next to harder questions, and come back to them later.
2. If permitted, use scratch paper to jot down your ideas.
3. Read each question at least *twice* before answering.
4. Supply the single best answer, giving only one answer to a question unless the instructions say otherwise.
5. Answer all questions on the test unless you are told not to guess or there is a penalty for wrong guesses.
6. Do not change your first answer without a good reason.

PROOFREAD YOUR ANSWERS

1. Check that you have followed directions completely.
2. Reread test questions and answers. Make sure that you have answered all of the questions.

Test-Taking Skills • 751

⏱ TIME AND RESOURCE MANAGER

Resources
Print: Academic and Workplace Skills Activity Book, pp. 59–60

In-Depth Coverage	Accelerated Pace
• Work through all key concepts, pp. 751–755. • Assign and review Exercises 11–13.	• Assign pp. 751–755 for independent student review.

Answering Different Types of Questions

1. It is a good idea for students to familiarize themselves with the different kinds or types of objective questions which will likely be asked on an objective test. It is also important to understand the best strategies for answering them. These strategies are the same ones used by much older students taking such objective tests as the PSAT, ACT, SAT, and so on, so it is a good idea to learn about them now!

2. Using the examples given in the book of types of objective questions, have students take a piece of paper and cover the answer as well as the answering strategies box for each example in succession. Have them imagine that they are answering that question on a test. After they have chosen their answer, have them remove the piece of paper, check their answer, and then read the appropriate strategy suggestions. Lead a discussion after each example of how and why the strategies listed would be helpful.

31.3

Answering Different Types of Questions

If you are familiar with the different kinds of questions that are frequently asked on tests, you may improve your performance. It is also important to know various strategies for answering the different kinds of questions.

Answering Multiple-Choice Questions This kind of question asks you to choose from several possible responses.

EXAMPLE:
What is a URL?

a. an Internet service provider   c. a universal reference

b. an Internet Web site address   d. a periodical index

In the preceding example, the answer is *b*.

ANSWERING MULTIPLE-CHOICE QUESTIONS
1. Try answering the question before looking at the choices. If your answer is one of the choices, select that choice.
2. Eliminate the obviously incorrect answers, crossing them out if you are allowed to write on the test paper.
3. Change a question into a statement by inserting your answer to see whether the statement makes sense.

Answering Matching Questions Matching questions ask that you match items in one group with items in another.

EXAMPLE:

__ 1. negligible   a. causing fear or dread

__ 2. formidable   b. difficult to understand

__ 3. inscrutable   c. small or unimportant

In the preceding example, the answers are *c, a,* and *b*.

ANSWERING MATCHING QUESTIONS
1. Count each group to see whether items will be left over. Check the directions to see whether items can be used more than once.
2. Read all the items before you start matching.
3. Match the items you know first. If you can write on the paper, cross out the items when you use them.
4. Match remaining items about which you are less certain.

Internet Tip

You can find additional information, strategies, and practice on test-taking on the Internet.

More Practice

Academic and Workplace Skills Activity Book
• p. 59–60

Answering True/False Questions True/false questions require you to identify whether a statement is accurate or not.

EXAMPLE:

__ You should study only when you have a test.

__ You should proofread your answers on a test only when you think you made some mistakes.

__ If permitted, you should use scratch paper to write down ideas when taking a test.

In the preceding example, the answers are *F*, *F*, and *T*.

ANSWERING TRUE/FALSE QUESTIONS
1. If a statement seems true, be sure the entire statement is true.
2. Pay special attention to the word *not*, which often changes the meaning of a statement.
3. Pay special attention to the words *all*, *always*, *never*, *no*, *none*, and *only*. They often make a statement false.
4. Pay special attention to the words *generally*, *much*, *many*, *most*, *often*, *sometimes*, and *usually*. They often make a statement true.

Answering Fill-in Questions A fill-in question asks you to supply an answer in your own words. The answer may complete a statement or it may simply answer a question.

EXAMPLE: An __?__ in a periodical index summarizes the article.

OR: In a periodical index, what is a summary of an article called?

In the preceding example, the answer is *abstract*.

ANSWERING FILL-IN QUESTIONS
1. Read the question or incomplete statement carefully.
2. If you are completing a statement, look for context clues (such as *an*) that may signal the answer.
3. If you are answering a question, change it into a statement by inserting your answer to see whether that makes sense.

Answering Short-Answer Questions Short-answer questions require you to write briefly to demonstrate what you know about a specific topic. Make your answers as brief and direct as possible. However, be sure to include supporting facts and examples to back up your points.

Integrating Speaking and Listening Skills

Have students interview someone they know who has taken a standardized test, such as the SAT or ACT. Have them formulate in advance such questions as: Which types of questions did you find the easiest/most difficult? How did you prepare in advance? Which types of strategies did you use in making the test taking easier? How did you manage your time during the test? Have them present their interview findings to the class and lead a discussion of what the interviewee shared that struck them as important or useful.

Test-Taking Skills • 753

Answering Analogies

1. Review with students the definitions of *synonyms* and *antonyms*. Synonyms are words having the same or similar meanings. Antonyms are words with opposite meanings. Explain that pairs of synonyms or pairs of antonyms often appear as analogy itmes on tests. To answer such questions, students should look for a second pair of synonyms or antonyms among the answer choices.

2. The four other analogy relationships found on tests are more difficult. Have students answer the following analogies and tell what type each is.

   - *TAIL : DOG :: WHEEL :*
     a. wag b. car c. round
     (b; part to whole)
   - *CUT : SAW :: SEW :*
     a. needle b. slice c. sharp
     (a; function)
   - *MOUSE : RODENT :: SWITZERLAND :*
     a. rat b. country c. cheese
     (c; type)
   - *CLOUDS : RAIN :: SUN :*
     a. light b. storm c. plants
     (a; cause-effect)

Answer Key

▷ **Exercise 11**

Answers will vary.

31.3

Answering Analogies An analogy asks you to find pairs of words that express a similar relationship.

EXAMPLE: REDWOOD : TREE :: BEAR :
    a. cave   b. mammal   c. honey

In the preceding example, the answer is *b*. The relationship between the pairs of words is *type*. A redwood is a *type* of tree, and a bear is a *type* of mammal. The following chart lists common analogy relationships:

COMMON ANALOGY RELATIONSHIPS	
Relationship	**Example**
synonym	enormous : gigantic
antonym	love : hate
part-to-whole	receiver : telephone
type	boat : yacht
cause-effect	question : answer
function	telescope : magnify

Once you have learned the different analogy relationships, use these strategies to answer an analogy:

ANSWERING ANALOGIES
1. Create a sentence that describes the relationship between the given word pair.
2. If more than one choice seems to express the relationship, go back to the given word pair, and restate its relationship.
3. If you are unable to establish a relationship between the given word pair or to find a parallel relationship among the answers, look for a second meaning to a word.

Writing Essays for Tests On many tests, you will also be called on to write one or more essays. See Chapter 13, Writing for Assessment, for detailed, step-by-step instruction on writing in a test situation.

▶ **Exercise 11** Answering Different Types of Questions
Using a subject you are studying in a class, prepare a short objective test on the material. Write five multiple-choice questions, five matching questions, five true/false questions, and five fill-in questions. Exchange papers with another student, and take the other student's test, writing your answers on a separate sheet of paper. Then, exchange again, and grade the test.

⊙ Learn More

For more instruction and information on answering the various types of questions, consult the table of contents to see the topics covered in the *Standardized Test Preparation Workshops.*

Exercise 12 Answering Analogies For each analogy, identify the relationship between the given word pair. Then, use the strategies you have learned to determine each answer.

1. WRITER : AUTHOR :: HERO :
   a. villain   b. scribe   c. champion

2. PIANO : MUSIC :: CANDLE :
   a. light   b. sound   c. wax

3. DALMATIAN : DOG :: TULIP :
   a. spots   b. field   c. flower

4. GRACEFUL : AWKWARD :: WORDY :
   a. eloquent   b. clumsy   c. speechless

5. CHAPTER : NOVEL :: ACT :
   a. character   b. play   c. stage

Exercise 13 Analyzing a Test Essay Analyze an essay that you wrote for a recent test. Come up with at least two suggestions on how you could improve it.

▶ Critical Viewing What details in this photograph indicate that the student in the front is carefully studying the questions before getting started? [Analyze]

Reflecting on Your Study Skills

Think about the various methods you have learned for improving your study, reference, and test-taking skills. Decide which methods you will need to work on most. Use these questions to help you reflect:

- What changes do I need to make in my study area or study schedule?
- What changes do I need to make in my assignment book?
- Which area of the library is most unfamiliar to me? How could becoming more familiar with that part of the library improve my reference skills?
- Which type of test question do I prefer answering? Why?
- With which type of test question do I most frequently have problems?
- What can I do to improve my performance with these types of test questions?

Test-Taking Skills • 755

Answer Key

▶ **Exercise 12**

1. synonyms, c
2. cause-and-effect, a
3. type, c
4. antonyms, c
5. part-to-whole, b

Answer Key

▶ **Exercise 13**

Responses will vary.

Step-by-Step Teaching Guide

Reflecting on Your Study Skills

1. Remind students that studying, researching, and test-taking are all activities for which they can prepare themselves through practice and the acquisition of new skills.

2. Help them begin thinking about the journal questions listed in the textbook by having a brief discussion about which of these activities they find the easiest and which the most difficult.

3. Encourage them to write about the areas in which they feel they need to improve.

Critical Viewing

Analyze Students should say he is looking at the test carefully and he is not writing.

☑ **ONGOING ASSESSMENT: Monitor and Reinforce**

If students have difficulty with Exercise 12 or 13, try one of the following strategies.

Option 1 Provide students with more examples of analogies from test preparation materials. You might want to have students work with partners.	**Option 2** Have students refer to the different strategies covered in the writing section of their textbooks. Encourage them to use this information to evaluate their test essays.

1. To construct meaning from informational texts.

2. To establish a purpose for reading.

3. To determine a text's main ideas and how those ideas are supported with details.

4. To draw conclusions or generalizations and support them with text evidence.

Step-by-Step Teaching Guide

Constructing Meaning From Informational Texts

Teaching Resources: Standardized Test Preparation Workbook, pp. 61–62

1. Tell students that they should read the passage at least twice. The first time, they can read to get a general idea of what the passage is about. The second reading should be a closer one, in which they read the information carefully.

2. Suggest that students circle, underline, or highlight important information in the passage. For example, they can circle facts and underline opinions to help them distinguish between the two as they read.

Standardized Test Preparation Workshop

Constructing Meaning From Informational Texts

When you take a standardized test, you often must answer questions about a passage you have read. These questions test your ability to construct meaning from the information provided in the passage. When answering these types of questions, you will be required to do the following:

- Identify the main idea, stated or implied, of a section of the passage.
- Identify the best summary—a concise restating of the key points of the passage.
- Distinguish between facts and opinions.

The following sample item will give you practice answering these types of questions.

Test Tip

When answering a main-idea question, make sure your choice is entirely correct and includes as much relevant information as possible.

Sample Test Item	Answer and Explanation

Read the passage. Then, read each question that follows the passage. Decide which is the best answer to each question. Mercury is the smallest of planets and the one closest to the sun. It is not visible from a basic telescope. Because it is so close to the sun, Mercury experiences extremely hot temperatures. These hot temperatures have led scientists to believe that life does not exist on the planet.
 	
 1 What is the main idea of this passage?
 	
   A The planet is not visible from the novice astronomer's telescope.
 	
   B Mercury is the smallest and hottest planet.
 	
   C It is close to the sun.
 	
   D Mercury is a small planet.
	The correct answer is *B*. This is the only statement that includes all of the most relevant information from the passage.

✎ TEST-TAKING TIP

Students may be tempted to believe that the first sentence of a passage always contains the main idea. Remind students that main idea of a passage may, in fact, not be directly stated. To find the implied main idea of a passage, remind students to look for answers to the six questions *who, what, when, where, why,* and *how.* Answering this information will help them determine the main idea of a passage.

Answer Key

▶ **Practice**

1. A
2. J
3. B
4. H

▶ **Practice** **Directions:** Read each passage. Then, read each question that follows the passage. Decide which is the best answer to each question.

Venus is the closest planet to Earth and is a near twin in size. Venus provides scientists with a much more interesting subject for study than Earth. The average surface temperature on Venus is 887 degrees Fahrenheit, eight times hotter than any region on Earth. In addition, its atmosphere is dramatically different from that of Earth, consisting mostly of sulfuric acid and sulfur dioxide. Venus rotates only once every 243 days, in contrast to Earth, which rotates once every 24 hours.

1 What is the main idea of this passage?

A Although Venus is near to Earth and is also close in size, it differs in temperature, atmosphere, and rotation patterns.

B Venus rotates only once every 243 days, in contrast to Earth, which rotates once every 24 hours.

C Venus is hotter than Earth and also has a different atmospheric makeup.

D There are few similarities between Venus and Earth.

2 Which of the following is an OPINION expressed in the passage?

F Venus is the closest planet to Earth and is a near twin in size.

G The average surface temperature on Venus is 887 degrees Fahrenheit, eight times hotter than any region on Earth.

H Its atmosphere is dramatically different from that of Earth, consisting mostly of sulfuric acid and sulfur dioxide.

J Venus provides scientists with a much more interesting subject for study than Earth.

Early in its history, Mars was much more like Earth. Although both Earth and Mars used most of the carbon dioxide in their atmospheres to form carbonate rocks, Mars could not recycle it back into its atmosphere to sustain a significant greenhouse effect. Therefore, the surface of Mars is much colder than the surface of Earth would be at that distance from the sun. The thin atmosphere of Mars does produce a greenhouse effect, but it is only enough to raise the surface temperature by five degrees. It is unlikely that any life forms similar to humans could survive there.

3 What is the main idea of the passage?

A Mars was at one time more like Earth because both atmospheres had carbon dioxide.

B The surface of Mars is much colder than that of Earth.

C The atmosphere of Mars cannot produce as significant a greenhouse effect as the atmosphere of Earth can.

D Mars could not sustain life forms similar to humans.

4 Which of the following is the best summary of this passage?

F The greenhouse effect on both Earth and Mars is caused by the recycling of carbon dioxide into the atmosphere.

G Both Earth and Mars had carbon dioxide in their atmospheres that was used to form carbonate rocks.

H Because of its cold temperature, Mars could not sustain any life forms similar to humans.

J Because Mars cannot recycle the carbon dioxide from carbonate rocks, it cannot sustain a greenhouse effect as strong as Earth's.

Standardized Test Preparation Workshop • 757

Citing Sources and Preparing Manuscript

The presentation of your written work is important. Your work should be neat, clean, and easy to read. Follow your teacher's directions for placing your name and class, along with the title and date of your work, on the paper.

For handwritten work:

- Use cursive handwriting or manuscript printing, according to the style your teacher prefers. The penmanship reference below shows the accepted formation of letters in cursive writing.
- Write or print neatly.
- Write on one side of lined $8\frac{1}{2}$" x 11" paper with a clean edge. (Do not use pages torn from a spiral notebook.)
- Indent the first line of each paragraph.

- Leave a margin, as indicated by the guidelines on the lined paper. Write in a size appropriate for the lines provided. Do not write so large that the letters from one line bump into the ones above and below. Do not write so small that the writing is difficult to read.
- Write in blue or black ink.
- Number the pages in the upper right corner.
- You should not cross out words on your final draft. Recopy instead. If your paper is long, your teacher may allow you to make one or two small changes by neatly crossing out the text to be deleted and using a caret [^] to indicate replacement text. Alternatively, you might make one or two corrections neatly with correction fluid. If you find yourself making more than three corrections, consider recopying the work.

PENMANSHIP REFERENCE

Aa Bb Cc Dd Ee Ff
Gg Hh Ii Jj Kk Ll
Mm Nn Oo Pp Qq
Rr Ss Tt Uu Vv Ww
Xx Yy Zz 1 2 3 4 5 6 7 8 9 0

For word-processed or typed documents:

- Choose a standard, easy-to-read font.
- Type or print on one side of unlined $8\frac{1}{2}$" x 11" paper.
- Set the margins for the side, top, and bottom of your paper at approximately one inch. Most word-processing programs have a default setting that is appropriate.
- Double-space the document.
- Indent the first line of each paragraph.
- Number the pages in the upper right corner. Many word-processing programs have a header feature that will do this for you automatically.

- If you discover one or two errors after you have typed or printed, use correction fluid if your teacher allows such corrections. If you have more than three errors in an electronic file, consider making the corrections to the file and reprinting the document. If you have typed a long document, your teacher may allow you to make a few corrections by hand. If you have several errors, however, consider retyping the document.

For research papers:

Follow your teacher's directions for formatting formal research papers. Most papers will have the following features:

- Title page
- Table of Contents or Outline
- Works-Cited List

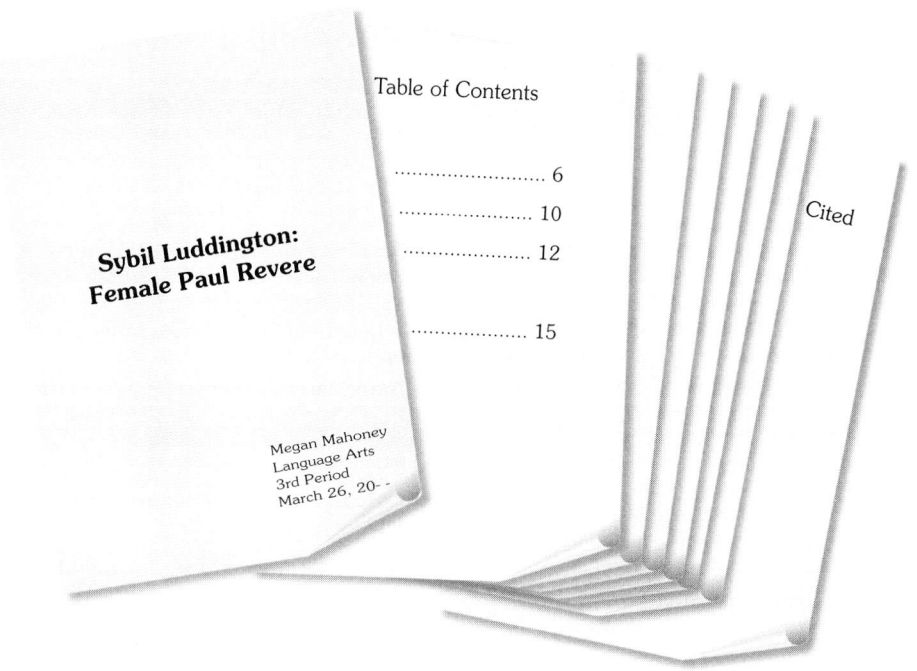

Table of Contents

.... 6

.... 10

.... 12

.... 15

Cited

Sybil Luddington:
Female Paul Revere

Megan Mahoney
Language Arts
3rd Period
March 26, 20- -

Incorporating Ideas From Research

Below are three common methods of incorporating the ideas of other writers into your work. Choose the most appropriate style by analyzing your needs in each case. In all cases, you must credit your source.

- **Direct Quotation:** Use quotation marks to indicate the exact words.
- **Paraphrase:** To share ideas without a direct quotation, state the ideas in your own words. While you haven't copied word-for-word, you still need to credit your source.
- **Summary:** To provide information about a large body of work—such as a speech, an editorial, or a chapter of a book—identify the writer's main idea.

Avoiding Plagiarism

Whether you are presenting a formal research paper or an opinion paper on a current event, you must be careful to give credit for any ideas or opinions that are not your own. Presenting someone else's ideas, research, or opinion as your own—even if you have rephrased it in different words—is *plagiarism*, the equivalent of academic stealing, or fraud.

You can avoid plagiarism by synthesizing what you learn: Read from several sources and let the ideas of experts help you draw your own conclusions and form your own opinions. Ultimately, however, note your own reactions to the ideas presented.

When you choose to use someone else's ideas or work to support your view, credit the source of the material. Give bibliographic information to cite your sources of the following information:

- Statistics
- Direct quotations
- Indirectly quoted statements of opinions
- Conclusions presented by an expert
- Facts available in only one or two sources

Crediting Sources

When you credit a source, you acknowledge where you found your information and you give your readers the details necessary for locating the source themselves. Within the body of the paper, you provide a short citation, a footnote number linked to a footnote, or an endnote number linked to an endnote reference. These brief references show the page numbers on which you found the information. To make your paper more formal, prepare a reference list at the end of the paper to provide full bibliographic information on your sources. These are two common types of reference lists:

- A **bibliography** provides a listing of all the resources you consulted during your research.
- A **works-cited list** indicates the works you have referenced in your paper.

Choosing a Format for Documentation

The type of information you provide and the format in which you provide it depend on what your teacher prefers. These are the most commonly used styles:

- **Modern Language Association (MLA) Style** This is the style used for most papers at the middle-school and high-school level and for most language arts papers.
- **American Psychological Association (APA) Style** This is used for most papers in the social sciences and for most college-level papers.
- *Chicago Manual of Style* **(CMS) Style** This is preferred by some teachers.

On the following pages, you'll find sample citation formats for the most commonly cited materials. Each format calls for standard bibliographic information. The difference is in the order of the material presented in each entry and the punctuation required.

MLA Style for Listing Sources

Book with one author	Pyles, Thomas. *The Origins and Development of the English Language.* 2nd ed. New York: Harcourt Brace Jovanovich, Inc., 1971.
Book with two or three authors	McCrum, Robert, William Cran, and Robert MacNeil. *The Story of English.* New York: Penguin Books, 1987.
Book with an editor	Truth, Sojourner. *Narrative of Sojourner Truth.* Ed. Margaret Washington. New York: Vintage Books, 1993.
Book with more than three authors or editors	Donald, Robert B., et al. *Writing Clear Essays.* Upper Saddle River, NJ: Prentice-Hall, Inc., 1996.
A single work from an anthology	Hawthorne, Nathaniel. "Young Goodman Brown." *Literature: An Introduction to Reading and Writing.* Ed. Edgar V. Roberts and Henry E. Jacobs. Upper Saddle River, NJ: Prentice-Hall, Inc., 1998. 376–385. [Indicate pages for the entire selection.]
Introduction in a published edition	Washington, Margaret. Introduction. *Narrative of Sojourner Truth.* By Sojourner Truth. New York: Vintage Books, 1993, pp. v–xi.
Signed article in a weekly magazine	Wallace, Charles. "A Vodacious Deal." *Time* 14 Feb. 2000: 63.
Signed article in a monthly magazine	Gustaitis, Joseph. "The Sticky History of Chewing Gum." *American History* Oct. 1998: 30–38.
Unsigned editorial or story	"Selective Silence." Editorial. *Wall Street Journal* 11 Feb. 2000: A14. [If the editorial or story is signed, begin with the author's name.]
Signed pamphlet	[Treat the pamphlet as though it were a book.]
Pamphlet with no author, publisher, or date	*Are You at Risk of Heart Attack?* n.p. n.d. [n.p. n.d. indicates that there is no known publisher or date]
Filmstrips, slide programs, and videotape	*The Diary of Anne Frank.* Dir. George Stevens. Perf. Millie Perkins, Shelley Winters, Joseph Schildkraut, Lou Jacobi, and Richard Beymer. Twentieth Century Fox, 1959.
Radio or television program transcript	"The First Immortal Generation." *Ockham's Razor.* Host Robyn Williams. Guest Damien Broderick. National Public Radio. 23 May 1999. Transcript.
Internet	*National Association of Chewing Gum Manufacturers.* 19 Dec. 1999 <http://www.nacgm.org/consumer/funfacts.html> [Indicate the date you accessed the information. Content and addresses at Web sites change frequently.]
Newspaper	Thurow, Roger. "South Africans Who Fought for Sanctions Now Scrap for Investors." *Wall Street Journal* 11 Feb. 2000: A1+ [For a multipage article, write only the first page number on which it appears, followed by a plus sign.]
Personal interview	Smith, Jane. Personal interview. 10 Feb. 2000.
CD (with multiple publishers)	Simms, James, ed. *Romeo and Juliet.* By William Shakespeare. CD-ROM. Oxford: Attica Cybernetics Ltd.; London: BBC Education; London: HarperCollins Publishers, 1995.
Article from an encyclopedia	Askeland, Donald R. (1991). "Welding." *World Book Encyclopedia.* 1991 ed.

APA Style for Listing Sources

The list of citations for APA is referred to as a Reference List and not a bibliography.

Book with one author	Pyles, T. (1971). *The Origins and Development of the English Language* (2nd ed.). New York: Harcourt Brace Jovanovich, Inc.
Book with two or three authors	McCrum, R., Cran, W., & MacNeil, R. (1987). *The Story of English.* New York: Penguin Books.
Book with an editor	Truth, S. (1993). *Narrative of Sojourner Truth* (M. Washington, Ed.). New York: Vintage Books.
Book with more than three authors or editors	Donald, R. B., Morrow, B. R., Wargetz, L. G., & Werner, K. (1996). *Writing Clear Essays.* Upper Saddle River, New Jersey: Prentice-Hall, Inc. [With six or more authors, abbreviate second and following authors as "et al."]
A single work from an anthology	Hawthorne, N. (1998) Young Goodman Brown. In E. V. Roberts, & H. E. Jacobs (Eds.), *Literature: An Introduction to Reading and Writing* (pp. 376–385). Upper Saddle River, New Jersey: Prentice-Hall, Inc.
Introduction to a work included in a published edition	[No style is offered under this heading.]
Signed article in a weekly magazine	Wallace, C. (2000, February 14). A vodacious deal. *Time, 155,* 63. [The volume number appears in italics before the page number.]
Signed article in a monthly magazine	Gustaitis, J. (1998, October). The sticky history of chewing gum. *American History, 33,* 30–38.
Unsigned editorial or story	Selective Silence. (2000, February 11). *Wall Street Journal,* p. A14.
Signed pamphlet	Pearson Education. (2000). *LifeCare* (2nd ed.) [Pamphlet]. Smith, John: Author.
Pamphlet with no author, publisher, or date	[No style is offered under this heading.]
Filmstrips, slide programs, and videotape	Stevens, G. (Producer & Director). (1959). *The Diary of Anne Frank.* [Videotape]. (Available from Twentieth Century Fox) [If the producer and the director are two different people, list the producer first and then the director, with an ampersand (&) between them.]
Radio or television program transcript	Broderick, D. (1999, May 23). The First Immortal Generation. (R. Williams, Radio Host). *Ockham's Razor.* New York: National Public Radio.
Internet	National Association of Chewing Gum Manufacturers. Available: http://www.nacgm.org/consumer/funfacts.html [References to Websites should begin with the author's last name, if available. Indicate the site name and the available path or URL address.]
Newspaper	Thurow, R. (2000, February 11). South Africans who fought for sanctions now scrap for investors. *Wall Street Journal,* pp. A1, A4.
Personal interview	[APA states that, since interviews (and other personal communications) do not provide "recoverable data," they should only be cited in text.]
CD (with multiple publishers)	[No style is offered under this heading.]
Article from an encyclopedia	Askeland, D. R. (1991). Welding. In *World Book Encyclopedia.* (Vol. 21 pp. 190–191). Chicago: World Book, Inc.

CMS Style for Listing Sources

The following chart shows the CMS author-date method of documentation.

Book with one author	Pyles, Thomas. *The Origins and Development of the English Language,* 2nd ed. New York: Harcourt Brace Jovanovich, Inc., 1971.
Book with two or three authors	McCrum, Robert, William Cran, and Robert MacNeil. *The Story of English.* New York: Penguin Books, 1987.
Book with an editor	Truth, Sojourner. *Narrative of Sojourner Truth.* Edited by Margaret Washington. New York: Vintage Books, 1993.
Book with more than three authors or editors	Donald, Robert B., et al. *Writing Clear Essays.* Upper Saddle River, New Jersey: Prentice-Hall, Inc., 1996.
A single work from an anthology	Hawthorne, Nathaniel. "Young Goodman Brown." In *Literature: An Introduction to Reading and Writing.* Ed. Edgar V. Roberts and Henry E. Jacobs. 376–385. Upper Saddle River, New Jersey: Prentice-Hall, Inc., 1998.
Introduction to a work included in a published edition	Washington, Margaret. Introduction to *Narrative of Sojourner Truth,* by Sojourner Truth. New York: Vintage Books, 1993. [According to CMS style, you should avoid this type of entry unless the introduction is of special importance to the work.]
Signed article in a weekly magazine	Wallace, Charles. "A Vodacious Deal." *Time,* 14 February 2000, 63.
Signed article in a monthly magazine	Gustaitis, Joseph. "The Sticky History of Chewing Gum." *American History,* October 1998, 30–38.
Unsigned editorial or story	*Wall Street Journal,* 11 February 2000. [CMS states that items from newspapers are seldom listed in a bibliography. Instead, the name of the paper and the relevant dates are listed.]
Signed pamphlet	[No style is offered under this heading.]
Pamphlet with no author, publisher, or date	[No style is offered under this heading.]
Filmstrips, slide programs, and videotape	Stevens, George. (director). *The Diary of Anne Frank.* 170 min. Beverly Hills, California: Twentieth Century Fox, 1994.
Radio or television program transcript	[No style is offered under this heading.]
Internet	[No style is offered under this heading.]
Newspaper	*Wall Street Journal,* 11 February 2000. [CMS states that items from newspapers are seldom listed in a bibliography. Instead, the name of the paper and the relevant dates are listed.]
Personal interview	[CMS states that, since personal conversations are not available to the public, there is no reason to place them in the bibliography. However, the following format should be followed if they are listed.] Jane Smith. Conversation with author. Wooster, Ohio, 10 February 2000.
CD (with multiple publishers)	Shakespeare, William. *Romeo and Juliet.* Oxford: Attica Cybernetics Ltd.; London: BBC Education; London: HarperCollins Publishers, 1995. CD-ROM.
Article from an encyclopedia	[According to CMS style, encyclopedias are not listed in bibliographies.]

Sample Works-Cited List (MLA)

Carwardine, Mark, Erich Hoyt, R. Ewan Fordyce, and Peter Gill. *The Nature Company Guides: Whales, Dolphins, and Porpoises.* New York: Time-Life Books, 1998.

Ellis, Richard. *Men and Whales.* New York: Knopf, 1991.

Whales in Danger. "Discovering Whales." 18 Oct. 1999. <http://whales.magna.com.au/DISCOVER>

Sample Internal Citations (MLA)

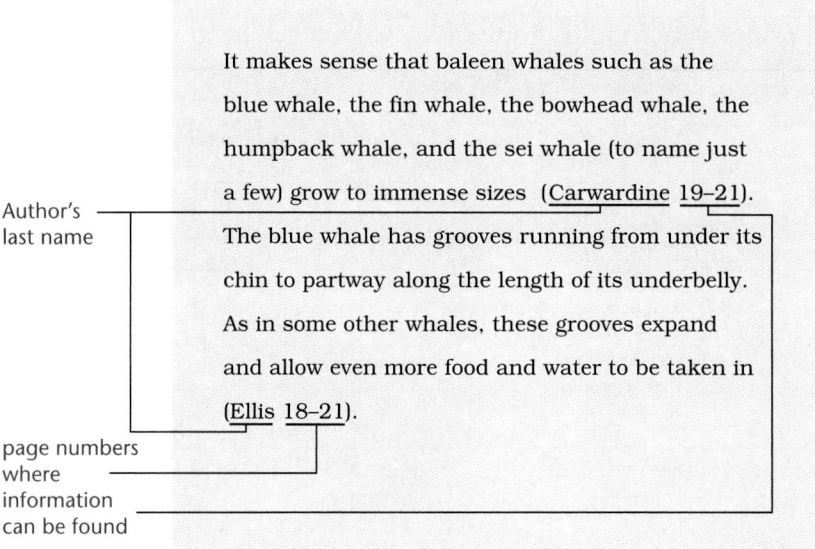

It makes sense that baleen whales such as the blue whale, the fin whale, the bowhead whale, the humpback whale, and the sei whale (to name just a few) grow to immense sizes (Carwardine 19–21). The blue whale has grooves running from under its chin to partway along the length of its underbelly. As in some other whales, these grooves expand and allow even more food and water to be taken in (Ellis 18–21).

Author's last name

page numbers where information can be found

Internet Research Handbook

Introduction to the Internet

The Internet is a series of networks that are interconnected all over the world. The Internet allows users to have almost unlimited access to information stored on the networks. Dr. Berners-Lee, a physicist, created the Internet in the 1980's by writing a small computer program that allowed pages to be linked together using key words. The Internet was mostly text-based until 1992, when a computer program called the NCSA Mosaic (National Center for Supercomputing Applications at the University of Illinois) was created. This program was the first Web browser. The development of Web browsers greatly eased the ability of the user to navigate through all the pages stored on the Web. Very soon, the appearance of the Web was altered as well. More appealing visuals were added, and sound was also implemented. This change made the Web more user-friendly and more appealing to the general public.

Using the Internet for Research

Key Word Search

Before you begin a search, you should identify your specific topic. To make searching easier, narrow your subject to a key word or a group of key words. These are your search terms, and they should be as specific as possible. For example, if you are looking for the latest concert dates for your favorite musical group, you might use the band's name as a key word. However, if you were to enter the name of the group in the query box of the search engine, you might be presented with thousands of links to information about the group that is unrelated to your needs. You might locate such information as band member biographies, the group's history, fan reviews of concerts, and hundreds of sites with related names containing information that is irrelevant to your search. Because you used such a broad key word, you might need to navigate through all that information before you find a link or subheading for concert dates. In contrast, if you were to type in "Duplex Arena and [band name]" you would have a better chance of locating pages that contain this information.

How to Narrow Your Search

If you have a large group of key words and still don't know which ones to use, write out a list of all the words you are considering. Once you have completed the list, scrutinize it. Then, delete the words that are least important to your search, and highlight those that are most important.

These **key search connectors** can help you fine-tune your search:

AND: narrows a search by retrieving documents that include both terms. For example: *baseball AND playoffs*

OR: broadens a search by retrieving documents including any of the terms. For example: *playoffs OR championships*

NOT: narrows a search by excluding documents containing certain words. For example: *baseball NOT history of*

Tips for an Effective Search

1. Keep in mind that search engines can be case-sensitive. If your first attempt at searching fails, check your search terms for misspellings and try again.

2. If you are entering a group of key words, present them in order, from the most important to the least important key word.

3. Avoid opening the link to every single page in your results list. Search engines present pages in descending order of relevancy. The most useful pages will be located at the top of the list. However, read the description of each link before you open the page.

4. When you use some search engines, you can find helpful tips for specializing your search. Take the opportunity to learn more about effective searching.

Other Ways to Search

Using On-line Reference Sites *How* you search should be tailored to *what* you are hoping to find. If you are looking for data and facts, use reference sites before you jump onto a simple search engine. For example, you can find reference sites to provide definitions of words, statistics about almost any subject, biographies, maps, and concise information on many topics. Some useful on-line reference sites:

    On-line libraries
    On-line periodicals
    Almanacs
    Encyclopedias

You can find these sources using subject searches.

Conducting Subject Searches As you prepare to go on-line, consider your subject and the best way to find information to suit your needs. If you are looking for general information on a topic and you want your search results to be extensive, consider the subject search indexes on most search engines. These indexes, in the form of category and subject lists, often appear on the first page of a search engine. When you click on a specific highlighted word, you will be presented with a new screen containing subcategories of the topic you chose. In the screen shots below, the category *Sports & Recreation* provided a second index for users to focus a search even further.

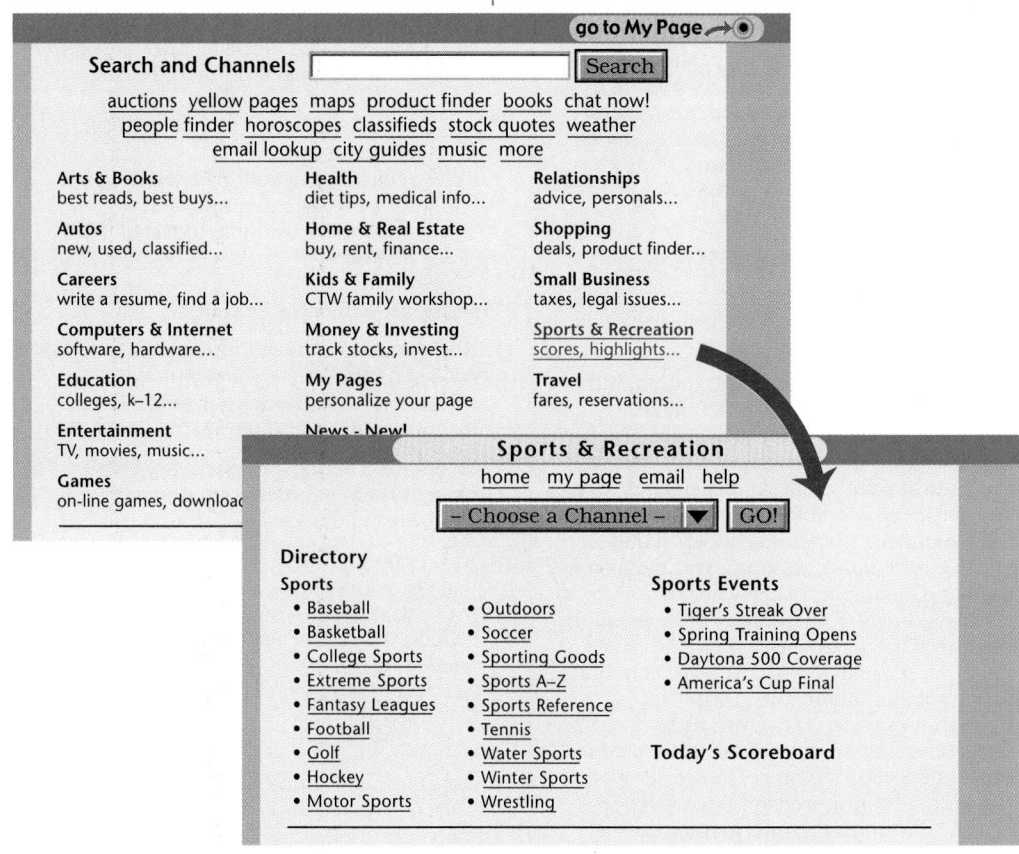

Evaluating the Reliability of Internet Resources

Just as you would evaluate the quality, bias, and validity of any other research material you locate, check the source of information you find on-line. Compare these two sites containing information on the poet and writer Langston Hughes:

Site A is a personal Web site constructed by a college student. It contains no bibliographic information or links to sites that he used. Included on the site are several poems by Langston Hughes and a student essay about the poet's use of symbolism. It has not been updated in more than six months.

Site B is a Web site constructed and maintained by the English Department of a major university. Information on Hughes is presented in a scholarly format, with a bibliography and credits for the writer. The site includes links to other sites and indicates new features that are added weekly.

For your own research, consider the information you find on Site B to be more reliable and accurate than that on Site A. Because it is maintained by experts in their field who are held accountable for their work, the university site will be a better research tool than the student-generated one.

Tips for Evaluating Internet Sources

1. Consider who constructed and who now maintains the Web page. Determine whether this author is a reputable source. Often, the URL endings indicate a source.

   - Sites ending in *.edu* are maintained by educational institutions.
   - Sites ending in *.gov* are maintained by government agencies (federal, state, or local).
   - Sites ending in *.org* are normally maintained by nonprofit organizations and agencies.
   - Sites with a *.com* ending are commercially or personally maintained.

2. Skim the official and trademarked Web pages first. It is safe to assume that the information you draw from Web pages of reputable institutions, on-line encyclopedias, on-line versions of major daily newspapers, or government-owned sites produce information as reliable as the material you would find in print. In contrast, unbranded sites or those generated by individuals tend to borrow information from other sources without providing documentation. As information travels from one source to another, the information has likely been muddled, misinterpreted, edited, or revised.

3. You can still find valuable information in the less "official" sites. Check for the writer's credentials and then consider these factors:

   - Don't let official-looking graphics or presentations fool you.
   - Make sure the information is updated enough to suit your needs. Many Web pages will indicate how recently they have been updated.
   - If the information is borrowed, see whether you can trace it back to its original source.

Respecting Copyrighted Material

Because the Internet is a relatively new and quickly growing medium, issues of copyright and ownership arise almost daily. As laws begin to govern the use and reuse of material posted on-line, they may change the way that people can access or reprint material.

Text, photographs, music, and fine art printed on-line may not be reproduced without acknowledged permission of the copyright owner.

Glossary of Internet Terms

attached file: a file containing information, such as a text document or GIF image, that is attached to an e-mail message; reports, pictures, spreadsheets, and so on transmitted to others by attaching these to messages as files

bandwidth: the amount of information, mainly compressed in bits per second (bps), that can be sent through a connection within a specific amount of time; depending on how fast your modem is, 15,000 bits (roughly one page of text) can be transferred per second

bit: a binary digit of computerized data, represented by a single digit that is either a 1 or a 0; a group of bits constitutes a byte

bookmark: a feature of your Web browser that allows you to place a "bookmark" on a Web page to which you wish to return at a later time

browser: software designed to present material accessed on the Web

bulletin-board system: a computer system that members access in order to join on-line discussion groups or to post announcements

case-sensitivity: the quality of a search engine that causes it to respond to upper- or lowercase letters in different ways

chat room: informal on-line gathering sites where people share conversations, experiences, or information on a specific topic; many chat rooms do not require users to provide their identity, so the reliability or safety of these sites is uncertain

cookie: a digitized piece of information that is sent to a Web browser by a Web server, intended to be saved on a computer; cookies gather information about the user, such as user preferences, or recent on-line purchases; a Web browser can be set to either accept or reject cookies

cyberspace: a term referring to the electronic environment connecting all computer network information with the people who use it

database: a large collection of data that have been formatted to fit a certain user-defined standard

digerati: a slang term to describe Internet experts; an offshoot of the term *literati*

download: to copy files from the Internet onto your computer

e-mail: electronic mail, or the exchange of messages via the Internet; because it is speedier than traditional mail and offers easier global access, e-mail has grown in popularity; e-mail messages can be sent to a single person or in bulk to a group of people

error message: a displayed communication or printout that reports a problem with a program or Web page

FTP site (file transfer protocol): a password-protected server on the Internet that allows the transfer of information from one computer to another

GIF (Graphic Interchange Format): a form of graphics used on the Web

graphics: information displayed as pictures or images instead of text

hits: items retrieved by a key word search; the number tracking the volume of visits to a Web site

home page: the main Web page for an individual or an organization, containing links to subpages within

HTML (HyperText Markup Language): the coding text that is the foundation for creating Web pages

interactivity: a quality of some Web pages that encourages the frequent exchange of information between user and computer

Internet: a worldwide computer network that supports services such as the World Wide Web, e-mail, and file transfer

JPEG (Joint Photo Experts Group, the developers)**:** a file format for graphics especially suited to photographs

K: a measurement of file size or memory; short for "Kilobyte," 1,000 bytes of information (see *bit*)

key word: search term entered into the query box of a search engine to direct the results of the search

link: an icon or word on a Web page that, when clicked, transfers the user to another Web page or to a different document within the same page

login: the procedure by which users gain access to a server or a secure Web site; usually the user must enter a specific user name and password

modem: a device that transfers data to a computer through a phone line. A computer's modem connects to a server, which then sends information in the form of digital signals. The modem converts these signals into waves, for the purpose of information reception. The speed of a modem affects how quickly a computer can receive and download information

newbie: jargon used to describe Internet novices

newsgroup: an on-line discussion group, where users can post and respond to messages; the most prevalent collection of newsgroups is found on USENET

query box: the blank box in a search engine where your search terms are input

relevance ranking: the act of displaying the results of a search in the order of their relevance to the search terms

search engines: tools that help you navigate databases to locate information; search engines respond to a key word search by providing the user with a directory of multiple Web pages about the key word or containing the key word

server: a principal computer that provides services, such as storing files and providing access to the Internet, to another computer

signature: a preprogrammed section of text that is automatically added to an e-mail message

surfing: the process of reading Web pages and of moving from one Web site to another

URL (Uniform Resource Locator): a Web page's address; a URL can look like this:

http://www.phwg.phschool.com or
*http://www.senate.gov/~appropriations/
labor/testimony*

usenet: a worldwide system of discussion groups, or newsgroups

vanity pages: Web sites placed on-line by people to tell about themselves or their interests; vanity pages do not have any commercial or informational value

virus: a set of instructions, hidden in a computer system or transferred via e-mail or electronic files, that can cause problems with a computer's ability to perform normally

Web page: a set of information, including graphics, text, sound, and video, presented in a browser window; a Web page can be found by its URL once it is posted on the World Wide Web

Web site: a collection of Web pages that are linked together for posting on the World Wide Web

W3: a group of Internet experts, including networking professionals, academics, scientists, and corporate interests, who maintain and develop technologies and standards for the Internet

WWW (World Wide Web): a term referring to the multitude of information systems found on the Internet; this includes FTP, Gopher, telnet, and http sites

zip: the minimizing of files through compression; this function makes for easier transmittal over networks; a receiver can then open the file by "unzipping" it

Internet Research Handbook • **769**

Commonly Overused Words

When you write, use the most precise word for your meaning, not the word that comes to mind first. Consult this thesaurus to find alternatives for some commonly overused words. Consult a full-length thesaurus to find alternatives to words that do not appear here. Keep in mind that the choices offered in a thesaurus do not all mean exactly the same thing. Review all the options, and choose the one that best expresses your meaning.

about approximately, nearly, almost, approaching, close to

absolutely unconditionally, perfectly, completely, ideally, purely

activity action, movement, operation, labor, exertion, enterprise, project, pursuit, endeavor, job, assignment, pastime, scheme, task

add attach, affix, join, unite, append, increase, amplify

affect adjust, influence, transform, moderate, incline, motivate, prompt

amazing overwhelming, astonishing, startling, unexpected, stunning, dazzling, remarkable

awesome impressive, stupendous, fabulous, astonishing, outstanding

bad defective, inadequate, poor, unsatisfactory, disagreeable, offensive, repulsive, corrupt, wicked, naughty, harmful, injurious, unfavorable

basic essential, necessary, indispensable, vital, fundamental, elementary

beautiful attractive, appealing, alluring, exquisite, gorgeous, handsome, stunning

begin commence, found, initiate, introduce, launch, originate

better preferable, superior, worthier

big enormous, extensive, huge, immense, massive

boring commonplace, monotonous, tedious, tiresome

bring accompany, cause, convey, create, conduct, deliver, produce

cause origin, stimulus, inspiration, motive

certain unquestionable, incontrovertible, unmistakable, indubitable, assured, confident

change alter, transform, vary, replace, diversify

choose select, elect, nominate, prefer, identify

decent respectable, adequate, fair, suitable

definitely unquestionably, clearly, precisely, positively, inescapably

easy effortless, natural, comfortable, undemanding, pleasant, relaxed

effective powerful, successful

emphasize underscore, feature, accentuate

end limit, boundary, finish, conclusion, finale, resolution

energy vitality, vigor, force, dynamism

enjoy savor, relish, revel, benefit

entire complete, inclusive, unbroken, integral

excellent superior, remarkable, splendid, unsurpassed, superb, magnificent

exciting thrilling, stirring, rousing, dramatic

far distant, remote

fast swift, quick, fleet, hasty, instant, accelerated

fill occupy, suffuse, pervade, saturate, inflate, stock

finish complete, conclude, cease, achieve, exhaust, deplete, consume

funny comical, ludicrous, amusing, droll, entertaining, bizarre, unusual, uncommon

get obtain, receive, acquire, procure, achieve

give bestow, donate, supply, deliver, distribute, impart

go proceed, progress, advance, move

good satisfactory, serviceable, functional, competent, virtuous, striking

great tremendous, superior, remarkable, eminent, proficient, expert

happy pleased, joyous, elated, jubilant, cheerful, delighted

hard arduous, formidable, complex, complicated, rigorous, harsh

help assist, aid, support, sustain, serve

hurt injure, harm, damage, wound, impair

important significant, substantial, weighty, meaningful, critical, vital, notable

interesting absorbing, appealing, entertaining, fascinating, thought-provoking

job task, work, business, undertaking, occupation, vocation, chore, duty, assignment

keep retain, control, possess

kind type, variety, sort, form

know comprehend, understand, realize, perceive, discern

like (adj) similar, equivalent, parallel

like (verb) enjoy, relish, appreciate

main primary, foremost, dominant

make build, construct, produce, assemble, fashion, manufacture

mean plan, intend, suggest, propose, indicate

more supplementary, additional, replenishment

new recent, modern, current, novel

next subsequently, thereafter, successively

nice pleasant, satisfying, gracious, charming

old aged, mature, experienced, used, worn, former, previous

open unobstructed, accessible

part section, portion, segment, detail, element, component

perfect flawless, faultless, ideal, consummate

plan scheme, design, system, plot

pleasant agreeable, gratifying, refreshing, welcome

prove demonstrate, confirm, validate, verify, corroborate

quick brisk, prompt, responsive, rapid, nimble, hasty

really truly, genuinely, extremely, undeniably

regular standard, routine, customary, habitual

see regard, behold, witness, gaze, realize, notice

small diminutive, miniature, minor, insignificant, slight, trivial

sometimes occasionally, intermittently, sporadically, periodically

take grasp, capture, choose, select, tolerate, endure

terrific extraordinary, magnificent, marvelous

think conceive, imagine, ponder, reflect, contemplate

try attempt, endeavor, venture, test

use employ, operate, utilize

very unusually, extremely, deeply, exceedingly, profoundly

want desire, crave, yearn, long

Commonly Misspelled Words

The list on these pages presents words that cause problems for many people. Some of these words are spelled according to set rules, but others follow no specific rules. As you review this list, check to see how many of the words give you trouble in your own writing. Then, read the instruction in the "Vocabulary and Spelling" chapter in the book for strategies and suggestions for improving your own spelling habits.

abbreviate	athletic	catastrophe	curious
absence	attendance	category	cylinder
absolutely	auxiliary	ceiling	deceive
abundance	awkward	cemetery	decision
accelerate	bandage	census	deductible
accidentally	banquet	certain	defendant
accumulate	bargain	changeable	deficient
accurate	barrel	characteristic	definitely
ache	battery	chauffeur	delinquent
achievement	beautiful	chief	dependent
acquaintance	beggar	clothes	descendant
adequate	beginning	coincidence	description
admittance	behavior	colonel	desert
advertisement	believe	column	desirable
aerial	benefit	commercial	dessert
affect	bicycle	commission	deteriorate
aggravate	biscuit	commitment	dining
aggressive	bookkeeper	committee	disappointed
agreeable	bought	competitor	disastrous
aisle	boulevard	concede	discipline
all right	brief	condemn	dissatisfied
allowance	brilliant	congratulate	distinguish
aluminum	bruise	connoisseur	effect
amateur	bulletin	conscience	eighth
analysis	buoyant	conscientious	eligible
analyze	bureau	conscious	embarrass
ancient	bury	contemporary	enthusiastic
anecdote	buses	continuous	entrepreneur
anniversary	business	controversy	envelope
anonymous	cafeteria	convenience	environment
answer	calendar	coolly	equipped
anticipate	campaign	cooperate	equivalent
anxiety	canceled	cordially	especially
apologize	candidate	correspondence	exaggerate
appall	capacity	counterfeit	exceed
appearance	capital	courageous	excellent
appreciate	capitol	courteous	exercise
appropriate	captain	courtesy	exhibition
architecture	career	criticism	existence
argument	carriage	criticize	experience
associate	cashier	curiosity	explanation

extension
extraordinary
familiar
fascinating
February
fiery
financial
fluorescent
foreign
forfeit
fourth
fragile
gauge
generally
genius
genuine
government
grammar
grievance
guarantee
guard
guidance
handkerchief
harass
height
humorous
hygiene
ignorant
illegible
immediately
immigrant
independence
independent
indispensable
individual
inflammable
intelligence
interfere
irrelevant
irritable
jewelry
judgment
knowledge
laboratory
lawyer
legible
legislature
leisure
liable

library
license
lieutenant
lightning
likable
liquefy
literature
loneliness
magnificent
maintenance
marriage
mathematics
maximum
meanness
mediocre
mileage
millionaire
minimum
minuscule
miscellaneous
mischievous
misspell
mortgage
naturally
necessary
negotiate
neighbor
neutral
nickel
niece
ninety
noticeable
nuclear
nuisance
obstacle
occasion
occasionally
occur
occurred
occurrence
omitted
opinion
opportunity
optimistic
outrageous
pamphlet
parallel
paralyze
parentheses

particularly
patience
permanent
permissible
perseverance
persistent
personally
perspiration
persuade
phenomenal
phenomenon
physician
pleasant
pneumonia
possess
possession
possibility
prairie
precede
preferable
prejudice
preparation
prerogative
previous
primitive
privilege
probably
procedure
proceed
prominent
pronunciation
psychology
publicly
pursue
questionnaire
realize
really
recede
receipt
receive
recognize
recommend
reference
referred
rehearse
relevant
reminiscence
renowned
repetition

restaurant
rhythm
ridiculous
sandwich
satellite
schedule
scissors
secretary
siege
solely
sponsor
subtle
subtlety
superintendent
supersede
surveillance
susceptible
tariff
temperamental
theater
threshold
truly
unmanageable
unwieldy
usage
usually
valuable
various
vegetable
voluntary
weight
weird
whale
wield
yield

Abbreviations Guide

Abbreviations, shortened versions of words or phrases, can be valuable tools in writing if you know when and how to use them. They can be very helpful in informal writing situations, such as taking notes or writing lists. However, only a few abbreviations can be used in formal writing. They are: *Mr., Mrs., Miss, Ms., Dr., A.M., P.M., A.D., B.C., M.A, B.A., Ph.D.,* and *M.D.*

The following pages provide the conventional abbreviations for a variety of words.

Abbreviations of Common Titles

Ambassador	Amb.	Lieutenant	Lt.
Attorney	Atty.	Major	Maj.
Brigadier-General	Brig. Gen.	President	Pres.
Brother	Br.	Professor	Prof.
Captain	Capt.	Representative	Rep.
Colonel	Col.	Reverend	Rev.
Commander	Cmdr.	Secretary	Sec.
Commissioner	Com.	Senator	Sen.
Corporal	Cpl.	Sergeant	Sgt.
Doctor	Dr.	Sister	Sr.
Father	Fr.	Superintendent	Supt.
Governor	Gov.	Treasurer	Treas.
Honorable	Hon.	Vice Admiral	Vice Adm.

Abbreviations of Academic Degrees

Bachelor of Arts	B.A. (or A.B.)	Esquire (lawyer)	Esq.
Bachelor of Science	B.S. (or S.B.)	Master of Arts	M.A. (or A.M.)
Doctor of Dental Surgery	D.D.S.	Master of Business Administration	M.B.A.
Doctor of Divinity	D.D.		
Doctor of Education	Ed.D.	Master of Fine Arts	M.F.A.
Doctor of Laws	LL.D.	Master of Science	M.S. (or S.M.)
Doctor of Medicine	M.D.	Registered Nurse	R.N.
Doctor of Philosophy	Ph.D.		

Abbreviations of States

State	Traditional	Postal Service	State	Traditional	Postal Service
Alabama	Ala.	AL	Montana	Mont.	MT
Alaska	Alaska	AK	Nebraska	Nebr.	NE
Arizona	Ariz.	AZ	Nevada	Nev.	NV
Arkansas	Ark.	AR	New Hampshire	N.H.	NH
California	Calif.	CA	New Jersey	N.J.	NJ
Colorado	Colo.	CO	New Mexico	N.M.	NM
Connecticut	Conn.	CT	New York	N.Y.	NY
Delaware	Del.	DE	North Carolina	N.C.	NC
Florida	Fla.	FL	North Dakota	N.Dak.	ND
Georgia	Ga.	GA	Ohio	O.	OH
Hawaii	Hawaii	HI	Oklahoma	Okla.	OK
Idaho	Ida.	ID	Oregon	Ore.	OR
Illinois	Ill.	IL	Pennsylvania	Pa.	PA
Indiana	Ind.	IN	Rhode Island	R.I.	RI
Iowa	Iowa	IA	South Carolina	S.C.	SC
Kansas	Kans.	KS	South Dakota	S.Dak.	SD
Kentucky	Ky.	KY	Tennessee	Tenn.	TN
Louisiana	La.	LA	Texas	Tex.	TX
Maine	Me.	ME	Utah	Utah	UT
Maryland	Md.	MD	Vermont	Vt.	VT
Massachusetts	Mass.	MA	Virginia	Va.	VA
Michigan	Mich.	MI	Washington	Wash.	WA
Minnesota	Minn.	MN	West Virginia	W. Va	WV
Mississippi	Miss.	MS	Wisconsin	Wis.	WI
Missouri	Mo.	MO	Wyoming	Wyo.	WY

Common Geographical Abbreviations

Apartment	Apt.	National	Natl.
Avenue	Ave.	Park, Peak	Pk.
Block	Blk.	Peninsula	Pen.
Boulevard	Blvd.	Point	Pt.
Building	Bldg.	Province	Prov.
County	Co.	Road	Rd.
District	Dist.	Route	Rte.
Drive	Dr.	Square	Sq.
Fort	Ft.	Street	St.
Island	Is.	Territory	Terr.
Mountain	Mt.		

Abbreviations of Traditional Measurements

inch(es)	in.	ounce(s)	oz.
foot, feet	ft.	pound(s)	lb.
yard(s)	yd.	pint(s)	pt.
mile(s)	mi.	quart(s)	qt.
teaspoon(s)	tsp.	gallon(s)	gal.
tablespoon(s)	tbsp.	Fahrenheit	F.

Abbreviations of Metric Measurements

millimeter(s)	mm	liter(s)	L
centimeter(s)	cm	kiloliter(s)	kL
meter(s)	m	milligram(s)	mg
kilometer(s)	km	centigram(s)	cg
milliliter(s)	mL	gram(s)	g
centiliter(s)	cL	Celsius	C

Other Commonly Used Abbreviations

about (used with dates)	c., ca., circ.	manager	mgr.
and others	et al.	manufacturing	mfg.
anonymous	anon.	market	mkt.
approximately	approx.	measure	meas.
associate, association	assoc., assn.	merchandise	mdse.
auxiliary	aux., auxil.	miles per hour	mph
bibliography	bibliog.	miscellaneous	misc.
boxes	bx(s).	money order	M.O.
bucket	bkt.	note well; take notice	N.B.
bulletin	bull.	number	no.
bushel	bu.	package	pkg.
capital letter	cap.	page	p., pg.
cash on delivery	C.O.D.	pages	pp.
department	dept.	pair(s)	pr(s).
discount	disc.	parenthesis	paren.
dozen(s)	doz.	Patent Office	pat. off.
each	ea.	piece(s)	pc(s).
edition, editor	ed.	poetical, poetry	poet.
equivalent	equiv.	private	pvt.
established	est.	proprietor	prop.
fiction	fict.	pseudonym	pseud.
for example	e.g.	published, publisher	pub.
free of charge	grat., gratis	received	recd.
General Post Office	G.P.O.	reference, referee	ref.
government	gov., govt.	revolutions per minute	rpm
graduate, graduated	grad.	rhetorical, rhetoric	rhet.
Greek, Grecian	Gr.	right	R.
headquarters	hdqrs.	scene	sc.
height	ht.	special, specific	spec.
hospital	hosp.	spelling, species	sp.
illustrated	ill., illus.	that is	i.e.
including, inclusive	incl.	treasury, treasurer	treas.
introduction, introductory	intro.	volume	vol.
italics	ital.	weekly	wkly
karat, carat	k., kt.	weight	wt.
left	L.		

Proofreading Symbols Reference

Proofreading symbols make it easier to show where changes are needed in a paper. When proofreading your own or a classmate's work, use these standard proofreading symbols.

insert	I proofr_aed.
delete	Ip proofread.
close up space	I proof read.
delete and close up space	I proofreade.
begin new paragraph	¶ I proofread.
spell out	I proofread (10) papers. (sp)
lowercase	I Proofread. (lc)
capitalize	i proofread. (cap)
transpose letters	I proofraed. (tr)
transpose words	I only proofread her paper. (tr)
period	I will proofread.
comma	I will proofread and she will help.
colon	We will proofread for the following errors.
semicolon	I will proofread she will help.
single quotation marks	She said, "I enjoyed the story The Invalid."
double quotation marks	She said, I enjoyed the story.
apostrophe	Did you borrow Sylvias book?
question mark	Did you borrow Sylvia's book ?/
exclamation point	You're kidding !/
hyphen	online /=/
parentheses	William Shakespeare 1564–1616

Student Publications

To share your writing with a wider audience, consider submitting it to a local, state, or national publication for student writing. Following are several magazines and Web sites that accept and publish student work.

Periodicals

Creative Kids P.O. Box 8813, Waco, TX 76714

Merlyn's Pen: The National Magazine of Student Writing P.O. Box 1058, East Greenwich, RI 02818

Skipping Stones P.O. Box 3939, Eugene, OR 97403

The McGuffey Writer McGuffey Foundation School, 5128 Westgate Drive, Oxford, OH 45056

Writing! General Learning Corporation, 900 Skokie Boulevard, Northbrook, IL 60062

On-line Publications

Stone Soup http://stonesoup.com/

MidLink Magazine http://longwood.cs.ucf.edu:80/~MidLink/

Wild Guess Magazine http://members.tripod.com/~WildGuess/

Contests

Annual Poetry Contest National Federation of State Poetry Societies, 3520 State Route 56, Mechanicsburg, OH 43044

National Written & Illustrated By . . . Awards Contest for Students Landmark Editions, Inc., 1402 Kansas Avenue, Kansas City, MO 64127

Paul A. Witty Outstanding Literature Award International Reading Association, Special Interest Group for Reading for Gifted and Creative Students, c/o Texas Christian University, P.O. Box 32925, Fort Worth, TX 76129

Seventeen Magazine Fiction Contest *Seventeen* Magazine, 850 Third Avenue, New York, NY 10022

The Young Playwrights Festival National Playwriting Competition 321 East 44th Street, Suite 906, New York, NY 10036

Glossary

A

accent: the emphasis on a syllable, usually in poetry

action verb: a word that tells what action someone or something is performing (*See* linking verb.)

active voice: the voice of a verb whose subject performs an action (*See* passive voice.)

adjective: a word that modifies a noun or pronoun by telling *what kind* or *which one*

adjective clause: a subordinate clause that modifies a noun or pronoun

adjective phrase: a prepositional phrase that modifies a noun or pronoun

adverb: a word that modifies a verb, an adjective, or another adverb

adverb clause: a subordinate clause that modifies a verb, an adjective, an adverb, or a verbal by telling *where, when, in what way, to what extent, under what condition*, or *why*

adverb phrase: a prepositional phrase that modifies a verb, an adjective, or an adverb

allegory: a literary work with two or more levels of meaning—a literal level and one or more symbolic levels

alliteration: the repetition of initial consonant sounds in accented syllables

allusion: an indirect reference to a well-known person, place, event, literary work, or work of art

annotated bibliography: a research writing product that provides a list of materials on a given topic, along with publication information, summaries, or evaluations

apostrophe: a punctuation mark used to form possessive nouns and contractions

appositive: a noun or pronoun placed after another noun or pronoun to identify, rename, or explain the preceding word

appositive phrase: a noun or pronoun with its modifiers, placed next to a noun or pronoun to identify, rename, or explain the preceding word

article: one of three commonly used adjectives: *a, an*, and *the*

assonance: the repetition of vowel sounds in stressed syllables containing dissimilar consonant sounds

audience: the reader(s) a writer intends to reach

autobiographical writing: narrative writing that tells a true story about an important period, experience, or relationship in the writer's life

B

ballad: a song that tells a story (often dealing with adventure or romance) or a poem imitating such a song

bias: the attitudes or beliefs that affect a writer's ability to present a subject objectively

bibliography: a list of the sources of a research paper, including full bibliographic references for each source the writer consulted while conducting research (*See* works-cited list.)

biography: narrative writing that tells the story of an important period, experience, or relationship in a person's life, as reported by another

blueprinting: a prewriting technique in which a writer sketches a map of a home, school, neighborhood, or other meaningful place in order to spark memories or associations for further development

body paragraph: a paragraph in an essay that develops, explains, or supports the key ideas of the writing

brainstorming: a prewriting technique in which a group jots down as many ideas as possible about a given topic

C

case: the form of a noun or pronoun that indicates how it functions in a sentence

cause-and-effect writing: expository writing that examines the relationship between events, explaining how one event or situation causes another

character: a person (though not necessarily a human being) who takes part in the action of a literary work

characterization: the act of creating and developing a character through narration, description, and dialogue

citation: in formal research papers, the acknowledgment of ideas found in outside sources

classical invention: a prewriting technique in which writers gather details about a topic by analyzing the category and subcategories to which the topic belongs

clause: a group of words that has a subject and a verb

climax: the high point of interest or suspense in a literary work

coherence: a quality of written work in which all the parts flow logically from one idea to the next

colon: a punctuation mark used before an extended quotation, explanation, example, or series and after the salutation in a formal letter

comma: a punctuation mark used to separate words or groups of words

comparison-and-contrast writing: expository writing that describes the similarities and differences between two or more subjects in order to achieve a specific purpose

complement: a word or group of words that completes the meaning of a verb

compound sentence: a sentence that contains two or more independent clauses with no subordinate clauses

conclusion: the final paragraph(s) of a work of writing in which the writer may restate a main idea, summarize the points of the writing, or provide a closing remark to end the work effectively (*See* introduction, body paragraph, topical paragraph, functional paragraph.)

conflict: a struggle between opposing forces

conjugation: a list of the singular and plural forms of a verb in a particular tense

conjunction: a word used to connect other words or groups of words

connotation: the emotional associations that a word calls to mind (*See* denotation.)

consonance: the repetition of final consonant sounds in stressed syllables containing dissimilar vowel sounds

contraction: a shortened form of a word or phrase that includes an apostrophe to indicate the position of the missing letter(s)

coordinating conjunctions: words such as *and, but, nor,* and *yet* that connect similar words or groups of words

correlative conjunctions: word pairs such as *neither . . . nor, both . . . and,* and *whether . . . or* used to connect similar words or groups of words

couplet: a pair of rhyming lines written in the same meter

cubing: a prewriting technique in which a writer analyzes a subject from six specified angles: description; association; application; analysis; comparison and contrast; and evaluation

D

declarative sentence: a statement punctuated with a period

demonstrative pronouns: words such as *this, that, these,* and *those* used to single out specific people, places, or things

denotation: the objective meaning of a word; its definition independent of other associations the word calls to mind (*See* connotation.)

depth-charging: a drafting technique in which a writer elaborates on a sentence by developing a key word or idea

description: language or writing that uses sensory details to capture a subject

dialect: the form of a language spoken by people in a particular region or group

dialogue: a direct conversation between characters or people

diary: a personal record of daily events, usually written in prose

diction: a writer's word choice

direct object: a noun or a pronoun that receives the action of a transitive verb

direct quotation: a drafting technique in which writers indicate the exact words of another by enclosing them in quotation marks

documentary: nonfiction film that analyzes news events or another focused subject by combining interviews, film footage, narration, and other audio/visual components

documented essay: research writing that includes a limited number of research sources, providing full documentation parenthetically within the text

drafting: a stage of the writing process that follows prewriting and precedes revising in which a writer gets ideas on paper in a rough format

drama: a story written to be performed by actors and actresses

E

elaboration: a drafting technique in which a writer extends his or her ideas through the use of facts, examples, descriptions, details, or quotations

epic: a long narrative poem about the adventures of a god or a hero

essay: a short nonfiction work about a particular subject

etymology: the history of a word, showing where it came from and how it has evolved into its present spelling and meaning

exclamation mark: a punctuation mark used to indicate strong emotion

exclamatory sentence: a statement that conveys strong emotion and ends with an exclamation mark

exposition: writing to inform, addressing analytic purposes such as problem and solution, comparison and contrast, how-to, and cause and effect

extensive writing: writing products generated for others and from others, meant to be shared with an audience and often done for school assignments (*See* reflexive writing.)

F

fact: a statement that can be proved true (*See* opinion.)

fiction: prose writing about imaginary characters and events

figurative language: writing or speech not meant to be interpreted literally

firsthand biography: narrative writing that tells the story of an important period, experience, or relationship in a person's life, reported by a writer who knows the subject personally

five *W*'s: a prewriting technique in which writers gather details about a topic by generating answers to the following questions: *Who? What? Where? When?* and *Why?*

fragment: an incomplete idea punctuated as a complete sentence

freewriting: a prewriting technique in which a writer quickly jots down as many ideas on a topic as possible

functional paragraph: a paragraph that performs a specific role in composition, such as to arouse or sustain interest, to indicate dialogue, to make a transition (*See* topical paragraph.)

G

generalization: a statement that presents a rule or idea based on particular facts

gerund: a noun formed from the present participle of a verb (ending in -*ing*)

gerund phrase: a group of words containing a gerund and its modifiers or complements that function as a noun

grammar: the study of the forms of words and the way they are arranged in phrases, clauses, and sentences

H

helping verb: a verb added to another verb to make a single verb phrase that indicates the time at which an action takes place or whether it actually happens, could happen, or should happen

hexagonal writing: a prewriting technique in

which a writer analyzes a subject from six angles: literal level, personal allusions, theme, literary devices, literary allusions, and evaluation

homophones: pairs of words that sound the same as each other yet have different meanings and different spellings, such as *hear/here*

how-to writing: expository writing that explains a process by providing step-by-step directions

humanities: forms of artistic expression including, but not limited to, fine art, photography, theater, film, music, and dance

hyperbole: a deliberate exaggeration or over-statement

hyphen: a punctuation mark used to combine numbers and word parts, to join certain compound words, and to show that a word has been broken between syllables at the end of a line

I

I-Search report: a research paper in which the writer addresses the research experience in addition to presenting the information gathered

image: a word or phrase that appeals to one or more of the senses—sight, hearing, touch, taste, or smell

imagery: the descriptive language used to re-create sensory experiences, set a tone, suggest emotions, and guide readers' reactions

imperative sentence: a statement that gives an order or a direction and ends with either a period or an exclamation mark

indefinite pronoun: a word such as *anyone*, *each*, or *many* that refers to a person, place, or thing, without specifying which one

independent clause: a group of words that contains both a subject and a verb and that can stand by itself as a complete sentence

indirect quotation: reporting only the general meaning of what a person said or thought; quotation marks are not needed

infinitive: the form of a verb that comes after the word *to* and acts as a noun, adjective, or adverb

infinitive phrase: a phrase introduced by an infinitive that may be used as a noun, an adjective, or an adverb

interjection: a word or phrase that expresses feeling or emotion and functions independently of a sentence

interrogative pronoun: a word such as *which* and *who* that introduces a question

interrogative sentence: a question that is punctuated with a question mark

interview: an information-gathering technique in which one or more people pose questions to one or more other people who provide opinions or facts on a topic

intransitive verb: an action verb that does not take a direct object (*See* transitive verb.)

introduction: the opening paragraphs of a work of writing in which the writer may capture the readers' attention and present a thesis statement to be developed in the writing (*See* body paragraph, topical paragraph, functional paragraph, conclusion.)

invisible writing: a prewriting technique in which a writer freewrites without looking at the product until the exercise is complete; this can be accomplished at a word processor with the monitor turned off or with carbon paper and an empty ballpoint pen

irony: the general name given to literary techniques that involve surprising, interesting, or amusing contradictions

itemizing: a prewriting technique in which a writer creates a second, more focused, set of ideas based on an original listing activity. (*See* listing.)

J

jargon: the specialized words and phrases unique to a specific field

journal: a notebook or other organized writing system in which daily events and personal impressions are recorded

K

key word: the word or phrase that directs an Internet or database search

L

layering: a drafting technique in which a writer elaborates on a statement by identifying and then expanding upon a central idea or word

lead: the opening sentences of a work of writing meant to grab the reader's interest, accomplished through a variety of methods, including providing an intriguing quotation, a surprising or provocative question or fact, an anecdote, or a description

learning log: a record-keeping system in which a student notes information about new ideas

legend: a widely told story about the past that may or may not be based in fact

legibility: the neatness and readability of words

linking verb: a word that expresses its subject's state of being or condition (*See* action verb.)

listing: a prewriting technique in which a writer prepares a list of ideas related to a specific topic. (*See* itemizing.)

looping: a prewriting activity in which a writer generates follow-up freewriting based on the identification of a key word or central idea in an original freewriting exercise

lyric poem: a poem expressing the observations and feelings of a single speaker

M

main clause: a group of words that has a subject and a verb and can stand alone as a complete sentence

memoir: autobiographical writing that provides an account of a writer's relationship with a person, event, or place

metaphor: a figure of speech in which one thing is spoken of as though it were something else

meter: the rhythmic pattern of a poem

monologue: a speech or performance given entirely by one person or by one character

mood: the feeling created in the reader by a literary work or passage

multimedia presentation: a technique for sharing information with an audience by enhancing narration and explanation with media, including video images, slides, audiotape recordings, music, and fine art

N

narration: writing that tells a story

narrative poem: a poem that tells a story in verse

nominative case: the form of a noun or pronoun used as the subject of a verb, as a predicate nominative, or as the pronoun in a nominative absolute (*See* objective case, possessive case.)

noun: a word that names a person, place, or thing

noun clause: a subordinate clause that acts as a noun

novel: an extended work of fiction that often has a complicated plot, many major and minor characters, a unifying theme, and several settings

O

objective case: the form of a noun or pronoun used as the object of any verb, verbal, or preposition, or as the subject of an infinitive (*See* nominative case, possessive case.)

observation: a prewriting technique involving close visual study of an object; a writing product that reports such a study

ode: a long formal lyric poem with a serious theme

onomatopoeia: words such as *buzz* and *plop* that suggest the sounds they name

open-book test: a form of assessment in which students are permitted to use books and class notes to respond to test questions

opinion: beliefs that can be supported but not proved to be true (*See* fact.)

oral tradition: the body of songs, stories, and poems preserved by being passed from generation to generation by word of mouth

outline: a prewriting or study technique that allows writers or readers to organize the presentation and order of information

oxymoron: a figure of speech that fuses two contradictory or opposing ideas, such as "freezing fire" or "happy grief"

P

parable: a short, simple story from which a moral or religious lesson can be drawn

paradox: a statement that seems to be contradictory but that actually presents a truth

paragraph: a group of sentences that share a common topic or purpose and that focus on a single main idea or thought

parallelism: the placement of equal ideas in words, phrases, or clauses of similar types

paraphrase: restating an author's idea in different words, often to share information by making the meaning clear to readers

parentheses: punctuation marks used to set off asides and explanations when the material is not essential

participial phrase: a group of words made up of a participle and its modifiers and complements that acts as an adjective

participle: a form of a verb that can act as an adjective

passive voice: the voice of a verb whose subject receives an action (*See* active voice.)

peer review: a revising technique in which writers meet with other writers to share focused feedback on a draft

pentad: a prewriting technique in which a writer analyzes a subject from five specified points: actors, acts, scenes, agencies, and purposes

period: a punctuation mark used to end a declarative sentence, an indirect question, and most abbreviations

personal pronoun: a word such as *I, me, you, we, us, he, him, she, her, they,* and *them* that refers to the person speaking; the person spoken to; or the person, place, or thing spoken about

personification a figure of speech in which a nonhuman subject is given human characteristics

persuasion: writing or speaking that attempts to convince others to accept a position on an issue of concern to the writer

phrase: a group of words without a subject and verb that functions as one part of speech

plot: the sequence of events in narrative writing

plural: the form of a word that indicates more than one item is being mentioned

poetry: a category of writing in which the final product may make deliberate use of rhythm, rhyme, and figurative language in order to express deeper feelings than those conveyed in ordinary speech (*See* prose, drama.)

point of view: the perspective, or vantage point, from which a story is told

portfolio: an organized collection of writing projects, including writing ideas, works in progress, final drafts, and the writer's reflections on the work

possessive case: the form of a noun or pronoun used to show ownership (*See* objective case, nominative case.)

prefix: one or more syllables added to the beginning of a word root (*See* root, suffix.)

preposition: a word that relates a noun or pronoun that appears with it to another word in the sentence to indicate relations of time, place, causality, responsibility, and motivation

prepositional phrase: a group of words that includes a preposition and a noun or pronoun

presenting: a stage of the writing process in which a writer shares a final draft with an audience through speaking, listening, or representing activities

prewriting: a stage of the writing process in which writers explore, choose, and narrow a topic and then gather necessary details for drafting

problem-and-solution writing: expository writing that examines a problem and provides a realistic solution

pronoun: a word that stands for a noun or for another word that takes the place of a noun

prose: a category of written language in which the end product is developed through sentences and paragraphs (*See* poetry, drama.)

publishing: a stage of the writing process in which a writer shares the written version of a final draft with an audience

punctuation: the set of symbols used to convey specific directions to the reader

purpose: the specific goal or reason a writer chooses for a writing task

Q

question mark: a punctuation mark used to end an interrogative sentence or an incomplete question

quicklist: a prewriting technique in which a writer creates an impromptu, unresearched list of ideas related to a specific topic

quotation mark: a punctuation mark used to indicate the beginning and end of a person's exact speech or thoughts

R

ratiocination: a systematic approach to the revision process that involves color-coding elements of writing for evaluation

reflective essay: autobiographical writing in which a writer shares a personal experience and then provides insight about the event

reflexive pronoun: a word that ends in -*self* or -*selves* and names the person or thing receiving an action when that person or thing is the same as the one performing the action

reflexive writing: writing generated for oneself and from oneself, not necessarily meant to be shared, in which the writer makes all decisions regarding form and purpose (*See* extensive writing.)

refrain: a regularly repeated line or group of lines in a poem or song

relative pronoun: a pronoun such as *that, which, who, whom,* or *whose* that begins a

subordinate clause and connects it to another idea in the sentence

reporter's formula: a prewriting technique in which writers gather details about a topic by generating answers to the following questions: *Who? What? Where? When?* and *Why?*

research: a prewriting technique in which writers gather information from outside sources such as library reference materials, interviews, and the Internet

research writing: expository writing that presents and interprets information gathered through an extensive study of a subject

response to literature writing: persuasive, expository, or narrative writing that presents a writer's analysis of or reactions to a published work

revising: a stage of the writing process in which a writer reworks a rough draft to improve both form and content

rhyme: the repetition of sounds at the ends of words

rhyme scheme: the regular pattern of rhyming words in a poem or stanza

rhythm: the form or pattern of words or music in which accents or beats come at certain fixed intervals

root: the base of a word (*See* prefix, suffix.)

rubric: an assessment tool, generally organized in a grid, to indicate the range of success or failure according to specific criteria

run-on sentence: two or more complete sentences punctuated incorrectly as one

S

salutation: the greeting in a formal letter

satire: writing that ridicules or holds up to contempt the faults of individuals or of groups

SEE method: an elaboration technique in which a writer presents a statement, an extension, and an elaboration to develop an idea

semicolon: a punctuation mark used to join independent clauses that are not already joined by a conjunction

sentence: a group of words with a subject and a predicate that expresses a complete thought

setting: the time and place of the action of a piece of narrative writing

short story: a brief fictional narrative told in prose

simile: a figure of speech in which *like* or *as* is used to make a comparison between two basically unrelated ideas

sonnet: a fourteen-line lyric poem with a single theme

speaker: the imaginary voice assumed by the writer of a poem

stanza: a group of lines in a poem, seen as a unit

statistics: facts presented in numerical form, such as ratios, percentages, or summaries

subject: the word or group of words in a sentence that tells whom or what the sentence is about

subordinate clause: a group of words containing both a subject and a verb that cannot stand by itself as a complete sentence

subordinating conjunction: a word used to join two complete ideas by making one of the ideas dependent on the other

suffix: one or more syllables added to the end of a word root (*See* prefix, root.)

summary: a brief statement of the main ideas and supporting details presented in a piece of writing

symbol: something that is itself and also stands for something else

T

theme: the central idea, concern, or purpose in a piece of narrative writing, poetry, or drama

thesis statement: a statement of an essay's main idea; all information in the essay supports or elaborates this idea

tone: a writer's attitude toward the readers and toward the subject

topic sentence: a sentence that states the main idea of a paragraph

topic web: a prewriting technique in which a writer generates a graphic organizer to identify categories and subcategories of a topic

topical paragraph: a paragraph that develops, explains, and supports the topic sentence related to an essay's thesis statement

transition: words, phrases, or sentences that smooth writing by indicating the relationship among ideas

transitive verb: an action verb that takes a direct object (*See* intransitive verb.)

U

unity: a quality of written work in which all the parts fit together in a complete, self-contained whole

V

verb: a word or group of words that expresses an action, a condition, or the fact that something exists while indicating the time of the action, condition, or fact

verbal: a word derived from the verb but used as a noun, adjective, or adverb (*See* gerund, infinitive, participle.)

vignette: a brief narrative characterized by precise detail

voice: the distinctive qualities of a writer's style, including diction, attitude, sentence style, and ideas

W

works-cited list: a list of the sources of a research paper, including full bibliographic references for each source named in the body of the paper (*See* bibliography.)

Index

Note: **Bold numbers** show pages on which basic definitions and rules appear.

A

Abbreviations, 580, 584, 632, 774–777
 academic degrees, 774
 commonly used, 777
 geographical, 776
 metric measurements, 776
 states, 775
 traditional measurements, 776
Abstracts, 195, **744**
Accent, **780**
accept, except, 479
Action shots, as image type, **69**
Action verbs, **87**, 314, **316**–319
 adverbs located after, 567
 direct objects follow, 411
 grammar exercises on, 319
 intransitive, **316**–317, 319
 mental, 318
 review exercises on, 319
 transitive, **316**–317, 319
Actions, 171, 254
 parts of speech and, 61, 314, 426, 504
 visible, 318
Active reading, 727
Active voice, **780**
Actors, as pentad category, 254
Addresses, 595, 750
Adjective clauses, **439**–440, 445, 593, **780**
 diagraming, 664
Adjective phrases, **426**–427, 434, 436, **780**
 diagraming, 661
Adjectives, **113**, **336**, **780**
 commas and, 114, 588–589
 compound, **342**, 620
 cumulative review exercises on, 371, 388
 demonstrative, 345
 diagraming, 657
 endings of, 352, 561
 forms of, 560–561
 help for troublesome, 567–570
 infinitives as, 430, 432–433
 interrogative, 346
 linking verbs and, 567
 modified by other parts of speech, 348–349, 428, 441–442
 as modifiers, 336–337, 352, 434
 nouns as, 340–341

participles as, 237, 430
possessive, **343**–344
predicate, 417–418, 451
pronouns as, 305
proper, **341**, 619, 622, 634, 643–644, 651
Adjectives and adverbs, 334–359, 558–575
 degrees of comparison, 558, **560**–566
 diagnostic tests on, 335, 559
 distinguishing between, **352**–353, 355
 grammar exercises on, 566, 571
 as modifiers, 334
 multiple functions of, 352
 review exercises on, 356–357, 572–573
 test preparation on, 358–359, 574–575
 usage of, 358, 567–571
 See also Adjectives; Adverbs
Adventure stories, 73
Adverb clauses, **441**–442, 445, **780**
 diagraming, 664
Adverb phrases, **428**–429, 436, **780**
 diagraming, 662
Adverbs, **211**, **348**, **780**
 cumulative review exercises on, 371, 388
 diagraming, 657
 distinguishing, from prepositions, 367, 369, 370
 endings of, 352, 561
 forms of, 560
 functions of, 348–350
 grammar exercises on, 355
 help for troublesome, 570
 infinitives as, 430, 432–433
 locations of, 351, 567
 modified by other adverbs, 348, 350
 modified by other parts of speech, 428, 441–442
 as modifiers, 348, 352
 as parenthetical expressions, 592
Advertisements, 45, **144**–145, 678
advice, advise, 479
Aerial view shots, as camera technique, 121
affect, effect, 479
Agencies, as pentad category, 254
Agreement errors, 576–577

Agreement rules. *See* Making words agree; Pronoun-antecedent agreement; Subject-verb agreement
ain't, 508
Aircraft, capitalization and, 615, 641
Allegory, **780**
Alliteration, **780**
Allusion, **780**
Almanacs, 748
Analogies, **312**–313, 754–755
Analysis, skills for, 94, **105**, 147
 analyze as key word, **156**
 media and technology, 95, 245
 nonfiction text and, 725–726
 peer review and, 113, 138
 for visual arts, 195, 675, 680–681
 writing purpose, 55, 157, 260
Annotated bibliography, **780**
Antecedents, **302**–303, 305–306, 343–344
 See also Pronoun-antecedent agreement
Anthologies, 733
Antonyms, **697**, 749
Apostrophes, 580, 618, 623–628, **780**
 contractions and, 525, 626–628
 grammar exercises on, 629
 showing ownership with, 623–624
Appendixes, 715
Applications
 filling out, 732
Appositive, **434**–435, 437, 593, **780**
 diagraming, 662
Appositive phrases, **434**–435, 437, 593, **780**
 diagraming, 663
apply, as key word, 105, 156
Archives, **745**
argue, as key word, **277**
Arguments
 end marks for, 139
 persuasion and, 125–127, 137
 pro or con, 105, 156
 refutation and, 143, 148–149
 rhythm and organization of, 132
 standardized tests and, 148–149
 types of, **127**, **131**–133
 See also Evidence
Art, fine. *See* Responding to Fine Art and Literature; Spotlight on the Humanities

Art, visual
  choosing subjects for, 195
  interpreting, 271, 675–677,
    680–683
  multimedia forms of, 271, 685
  See also type of, e.g., Movies
Articles, published, 4, 616
  in periodicals, 8, 115, 265, 745
Articles (parts of speech), **780**
  as adjectives, 338–339, 347, 356
  pronunciation of, 338
  in titles, 647, 715
Artistic works
  evaluating, 44, 146, 170, 288
  titles of, 614, 616, 647
Assessment, **274**
  See also Artistic works, evaluat-
    ing; Rubrics for Self-Assessment;
    Standardized Test Preparation
    Workshops; Tests; Writing for
    assessment
Assignments, class, 738
Associate, 105, 156
Assonance, **780**
at, 479
Atlases, maps in, 748–749
Attached file, **768**
Audiences, 8, **55**, **80**, 130, 171,
  671, **780**
  appropriate writing for, **18**,
    148–149, 204
  considering, 104, 204, 215,
    220, 255
  writing affected by, 55, 80,
    141, 181, 231
  See also Reader interest
Audio elements. *See* Sounds
Audiovisual equipment, 11, 685
Authors, 5, 9, 249, 257
  library catalogs and, 740–741
  main points of, 152–153
  purposes of, 126–127, 721, 723
  strategies of, 9, 23, 49, 73, 99,
    125, 151, 175, 199, 223, 249
  See also Spotlight on the
    Humanities
Autobiographical writing, 48–71,
  49, **780**
  drafting, 56–57
  editing and proofreading, 63
  photo essays as, 68
  prewriting, 52–55
  publishing and presenting, 64
  purpose of, 48–49
  revising, 58–62
  test preparation for, 70
  types of, **49**
Awards, capitalization and, 641

B

bad, badly, 567, 570
Balance in writing, 160, 209, 324
Ballad, **780**
Balloon help, computers and,
  219
Bandwidth, **768**
Bar graphs, 676, 682
Basic sentence parts, 390–423
  complements, **410**–419
  compound parts as, **400**–404
  diagnostic test on, 391
  function of, 392–395
  grammar exercises on, 395,
    399, 404, 409, 419
  review exercises on, 420–421
  subjects, **392**, 396–399,
    405–409
  test preparation on, 422–423
  verbs, **392**
Bays, names of, 638
be, 626
  forms of, 25, 320, 326, 422, 535
because, 479
beside, besides, 480
Bias, **147**, **679**, **780**
Bibliography, **760**–763, **780**
Biographies, **743**, 748, **780**
  firsthand, **67**
  sketches as, 223, 229, 232, 240
  See also Autobiographical
    writing
Bit, **768**
Block method, organization by,
  158, 160, 173, 279
Blueprinting, **52**, 178, **780**
Body, in compositions, **39**, 182,
  780
Boldface, function of, 684
Bookmarks, electronic, 750, **768**
Books, 45, 738
  finding, in libraries, 742–743
  reviews of, 249, 265
  titles of, 614, 616, 647
  See also Textbooks
Brainstorming, 7, 178, 179, 254,
  780
Brand names, capitalization and,
  643
Broadcast media, **45**
Browsing, 8, 252
Bulletin board system, electronic,
  768
Building elements of writing, 84,
  251, 260, 268
Building your portfolio, **27**
  autobiographical writing, 64
  cause-and-effect essay, 190

  comparison-and-contrast essay,
    166
  description, 115
  how-to essay, 215
  persuasive essay, 140
  research report, 240
  response to literature, 265
  short story, 89
  A Walk Through the Writing
    Process, 29
  writing for assessment, 284
  See also Portfolios, work to
    include in
Buildings, capitalization and, 641
Businesses, names of, 639–640
BUT Charts, 154

C

Call numbers, 742
Cameras
  techniques and, 69, 86, 104,
    121
  video, and uses, 157, 685–686
Candid photographs, **195**
Capitalization, 634–653
  diagnostic test on, 635
  in direct quotations, 608–609
  errors, proofreading for, 26,
    290–291, 652–653
  function of, 634, 684
  proper adjectives, **643**–646
  proper nouns, 63, 298,
    637–642, 647–648
  review exercises, 650–651
  sentence requirements for, 283,
    636
  state abbreviations and, 632
  on tests, 290–291
Captions, **195**, 229, 675
Careers, 9, 301–311, 374–387
Carets, revising with, 71, 149
Caricatures, **244**
Cartoons, storytelling devices in,
  95
Case, **780**
Case-sensitivity in search engines,
  768
Catalogs, library, 740–741
Causal connections, types of,
  183, **190**
Cause-and-effect essay, 174–197,
  175, **780**
  drafting, 182–183
  editing and proofreading, 189
  how-to essays and, 201
  order in, 38
  prewriting, 178–181

Index • **793**

Index • **795**

compound sentences and, 137, 444, 462
semicolons with, 600–601
simple sentences and, 443
Indexes, 131, 697, 715, 740–741, 744–745
Indirect objects, **414**–415, 451, 520, 523–524
Indirect quotations, **606**–607, **783**
Inferences, 100–101, **176**
making, 177, 724, 727
test preparation on, 734–735
Infinitive phrases, **432**–433, **783**
Infinitives, 430, **432**, 436, **783**
Informal English, **43**
Information media, 45, 678–679
analyzing, 679
and bias, 679
commercial , 678
comparing and contrasting newscasts, 45
comparing different media, 120, 170–171, 218, 288
documentary, 678
editorial, 678
evaluating varieties of, 679
facts and opinion in, 679
interview, 678
loaded language and images, 679
newsmagazine, 678
nonprint materials as, 675–677, 740–741, 743, 749
purposes of, 679
television news program, 678
See also Media and Technology Skills workshops
Informative writing. *See* Exposition
Insight, **56**
Inspirational arguments, 127
Institutions, names of, 639–640
Instructions
in how-to essays, 199, 201
imperative sentences as, 456–457
informative purpose of, 157, 723
recognizing subjects in, 406
revision strategy with, 184, 209
speaking skills for giving, 669–670
for test taking, 289
writing prompts as, **275**
Interactivity, electronic, **768**
Interjections, **381**–384, **783**
cumulative review exercises on, 389
function of, 374

grammar exercises on, 384
help on, 383
punctuation used with, 381–382, 582
Internet resources, 140, 239, 733, **765**, **768**
and copyright, 767
evaluating, 245, 750, 767
glossary of terms, **768**–769
key word search on, **765**
narrowing a search on, 765
nature of, 11, 45
on-line reference sites, 766
searching, 222, 231, 245, 564, 603, 750
subject searches, 766
Web sites, 8, 240, 731, 745, 750
Interpreting, **74**, 77, 721
Interrogatives
adjectives, 346
grammar exercises on, 584
pronouns, **306**, 346, **783**
sentences, **456**, 581, **783**
Interrupting expressions, 608–610
Interviews, 222–223, 228, 252, 678, 742, **783**
into, in, 480
Intransitive verbs, **316**–317, 319, **783**
Introductions, spoken, 670
Introductions, written, **783**
See also Openings
Inverted word order, **407**–409, 413, 467, 542
Investigations, 175, 193
Invisible-Ink technique, 202, **783**
Irony, **783**
Irregular parts of speech
adjectives, 564
modifiers, 563–564, 566
verbs, 492, 495–498, 505
Islands, names of, 638
Italics, 614, 684
Itemizing, 55, 81, 205, **783**

J

Jargon, **725**, **783**
Journals, 4, 10, 14, 416, **783**
JPEG format, **768**
Judgment, 249, 722
just, 567–568

K

Key elements, as topic sentences, 35, 41

Key words, **784**
as search tool, 765, **769**
in writing prompt, 277
kind of, sort of, 480

L

Labels, 604, 675, 747
Lakes, names of, 638
Land craft, names of, 615, 641
Landscapes, **195**
Language, 26, 94, 130, 138, 390
conventions of written, 43, 290–291, 725
figurative, 257, 272, **692**
loaded, 131, 133, 142, 147, **679**
variety used in, 213, 324
Language variety checker, 213
Languages, 578, 639–640, 647–648, 701
See also English language
lay, lie, 509
Layering process, 133, 159, **784**
Leads, 21, **39**, 208, **784**
expository, **161**
Learning logs, 4, **784**
Legal issues, as topics, 129
Legends, 730–731, **784**
Legibility, **784**
cursive *vs.* print, 758
manuscript preparation, 758–759
proofreading and, 26
less, fewer, 567
Letters
business, 43, 604
friendly, 43
sending, to build portfolios, 8, 140
writing, 249, 253, 596
Letters (alphabet), silent, 707
Library resources, 11, 265, 745
catalogs of, 740–741
librarians as, 131, 741–742
reference skills and, 222–223, 740–750
reference works as, 181, 697, 722, 744–749
using, to confirm details, 26, 261
lie, lay, 509
like, 480
Line graphs, 676, 682
Link, electronic, **769**
Linking verbs, **320**–325, **784**
action verbs distinguished from, 323–325

punctuation and, 590–591, 607, 610
purpose of, 73–74, 250
Opinions, **722**, **784**
  expert, 131, 222
  expressing, 263, 267, 723
  facts and, 147, 679, 722, 756–757
Oral tradition, 94, 730–731, **784**
  finding clues to culture, 730
Orders (arrangement)
  types of, **106**, **199**, **232**
  See also Word order
Orders (directions)
  diagraming, 659
  See also Instructions
Organization, 3, 145, 203
  analyzing, 134, 260, 725–726
  applying, 55, 106, 108, 122, 134, 217, 279
  chronological order, **38**, 71, 106, 182, 191–192, 199, 206, 209, 232, 279, 726
  clear, 249, 268
  comparison-and-contrast essays and, 151–152, 158, 160, 167, 172–173
  creating emphasis through, 132, 250
  logical order of, 32, 38–39, 122, 182, 184, 199, 201, 217, 220, 224, 285
  methods of, 71, 152, 158, 160, 167, 173, 232, 279
  spatial order, 38, 106, 726
  test preparation on, 46, 122, 272–273
  textbook, and reading skills, 715–716
  types of, **38**
  See also Classification; Structure in writing
Organization, revising. *See* Overall structure, revision strategies for
Organizations, names of, 639–640
Outlines, 257, **785**
  adding details to, 280
  making, 232, 279, 739
  matching, to written work, 234
Overall structure, revision strategies for, **15**, **23**
  analyze your organization, 108, 134, 160, 260
  build to a point, 84, 260
  check structure, 160, 184, 281
  circle details and points for strength, 109, 260

code details and points for support, 135, 160, 260
connect the steps, 58, 184
cut and paste for order, 108
evaluate pacing, 84
highlight main points, 134, 161
identify connections, 58, 185
match draft to outline, 234
tag high points, 134, 161
write a strong lead, 208
Oxymoron, **785**

coding connections, 59, 136, 185
finding the "tug," 185
illuminating for improvement, 85, 261
making applications, 24
marking patterns, 162
using steps, stacks, chains, and balances, 209
using transition words, 235
Parallelism, **785**
Paraphrasing, **721**, **760**, **785**
Parentheses, **785**
Parenthetical expressions, **592–593**
Participial phrases, **237**, **431**, 593, **785**
Participles, **237**, **430**–431, 436, **785**
Parts of speech, 390, 747
  actions in, 314
  connected with conjunctions, 376–377
  cumulative review exercises on, 421
  irregular, 492, 495–498, 505, 563–564, 566
  See also Diagnostic Tests
Parts of speech, cumulative review exercises on
  action verbs, 357
  adjectives, 371, 388
  adverbs, 371, 388
  agreement errors, 576–577
  conjunctions, 389
  interjections, 389
  linking verbs, 357
  modifiers, 577
  nouns, 331, 357, 371, 388
  prepositions, 388–389
  pronoun cases, 576
  pronouns, 331, 357, 388, 529
  verb tenses, 576
  verbs, 331, 357, 371, 388, 529, 576
  word usage errors, 577
Passive voice, **785**
Past participles
  as *-ed* or *-d* verbs, **237**
  end irregularly with *-en, -n,* or *-t,* 430
  helping verbs with, 511
  of irregular verbs, 495–497
  of regular verbs, 492–493
Past perfect tense, 500, 502, 504, 506, 516–517
Past tense, **492**
  basic form of, 500, 502

preparations for brief skit, 190
presentation diagrams, 190
reading events and occasions,
  64, 89
"Wall of Fame," 240
Web site of your design, 240
See also Building Your Portfolio
Portraits, **69, 195**
Positive degree, 560–564
  basis for comparative and
    superlative degrees, **560–562**
  using, of irregular modifiers,
    563–564
Possessive adjectives, 343–344
Possessive case, 520, 525–526,
  529–530, **785**
Possessive nouns, 343, 623–624
Possessive pronouns, 165, 625
"Possible Sentences" strategy, 694
Posters, 215, 265
Practice tests, across media, 289
Precise nouns, **61**
Precise words, 61, 138, 188, 263,
  267, 282, 500, 725
Predicate adjectives, 417–418
Predicate nouns, **416**, 418
Predicate pronouns, **416**, 418
Predicates
  cumulative review exercises on,
    451, 488
  grammar exercises on, 399
  nominative pronouns as,
    520–522
  as subject complements,
    416–417
Prediction, 722
  as reading strategy, 727, 731
  as reading-writing connection,
    50–51
  test preparation on, 734–735
Prefixes, **619, 699**, 706, **785**
Prepositional phrases, **366–367**,
  369, 372, 426, **785**
  compound, in simple sentences,
    443
  connected with conjunctions,
    376–377
  diagraming, 661
  subject-verb agreement not
    affected by, 537
Prepositions, **189**, 360–373, **362,
  785**
  capitalization of, in titles, 647
  classifying, 365, 371
  compound, **362**, 364–365
  cumulative review exercises on,
    388–389
  diagnostic test on, 361

distinguishing, from adverbs,
  367, 369, 370
functions of, 362, 366
grammar exercises, 365, 369
learning aids for, 368
objects of, **366**–367, 426, 520,
  523–524, 530
phrases with, 366–367, 369,
  372, 376–377, 426, 443, 537
preferred number of, 189
review exercises, 370–371
usage test on, 372–373
Present participles
  as *-ing* verbs, **237**
  end with *-ing,* 430
  of irregular verbs, 495–497
  of regular verbs, 492–493
Present perfect tense, 500, 502,
  504, 506, 516–517
Present tense, **492**
  basic form of, 500, 502–503
  progressive verb form and
    principal part in, 504, 506
  usage test on, 516–517
  as verb principal part, 492–493,
    495–497, 500, 502–503
Presentations,
  evaluating 45, 94, 121, 146–
    147, 170–171, 194, 218
  multimedia, 271, 685, **784**
  speech, 671–672
Presenting, **15, 785**
  See Publishing and Presenting
Prewriting, **15, 785**
  See Audiences; Choosing a
    topic; Gathering details;
    Narrowing your topic; Purposes
    for writing; Standardized Test
    Preparation Workshops
Print media, **45**, 253
  applying conventions of,
    290–291
  comparing and contrasting, with
    visual media, 155, 171, 288
  as electronic texts, 746, 748
  flip-through process and, 78,
    128, 178, 228
  library catalogs as, 740–741
Problem-and-solution essay, **217,
  785**
Problems, 23, 49
  avoiding, with sentences,
    469–485
  listening for, 164, 413, 473, 521
  subjects as special, 405–409
  word usage, 479–481,
    508–512, 529, 567–569

Product comparisons, writing,
  151, 166, 169
Professional titles, capitalization
  and, 644
Prompts for responding to
  media. *See* Critical Viewing
Prompts on tests, 12, **275–277,**
  279
  choice of, 276
  expository, 172, 196, 220
  key words as, 277
  responding to, 30, 70, 148
  test preparation on, 272–273
  See also Standardized Test
    Preparation Workshops
Pronouns, 165, **296, 301–309,
  786**
  antecedents of, **302**–303, 305–
    306, 343–344 (*see also*
    Pronoun-antecedent agree-
    ment)
  apostrophes and, 625
  appositives as, 434
  conjunctions and, 377
  contractions and, 626
  cumulative review exercises on,
    331, 359, 388, 529
  demonstrative, **305**, 345
  as direct objects, 411
  functions of, 164, 305
  grammar exercises on, 309
  indefinite, **306**–307, 543–545,
    551–553, 625
  as indirect objects, 414
  interrogative, **306**, 346
  modified by other parts of
    speech, 336–337, 426–427
  as objects of prepositional
    phrases, 426, 520, 523–524,
    530
  personal, 303–304, 343–344,
    518–531, 548–550, 551–553,
    625, 634, 637, 650
  plural, 502, 534–535
  possessive, 343–344, 520,
    525–526, 529, 625
  predicate, 416, 418, 520–522
  singular, 502, 534
  types of, **165, 303–307**
  See also Using pronouns
Pronoun-antecedent agreement,
  532, 548–553
  grammar exercises on, 553
  indefinite and personal, 551–552
  person and number, 165, 549
  personal pronouns and, 548–550
  See also Antecedents; Pronouns
Pronoun cases, 520–526, 528–530

storytelling devices of, 95
structure of, 73
timing in, 257
titles of, in quotation marks, 616
types of, **73**
Showing and telling, 83, 282
See also Publishing and presenting
Showing differences. *See* Contrast
Showing similarities. *See* Comparison
Signature, electronic, **769**
Simile, **118**, **787**
Simple sentences, 443–444, 446, 449
Simple subjects, 397
Single quotation marks, 264
Singular number, **165**, **534**–537
sit, set, 511
Sketches, written
  autobiographical, and their purpose, 49
  biographical, 223, 229, 232, 240
Skills assessments. *See* Rubrics for Self-Assessment; Standardized Test Preparation Workshops
Skimming, **717**
Social titles, capitalization and, 644–645
Songs, 270, 616
Sonnets, **787**
sort of, kind of, 480
Sounds
  article, before consonants or vowels, 338
  background, in multimedia projects, 271, 685
  homophones, 426, 525, 551, 707, 710
  long *a*, spelling, 704
  long *e*, spelling, 704
  poetry and, 729
  recording equipment for, 129, 696
  s, to avoid, 504
  spelling of, 426, 476, 525, 704
  See also Music
Spacecraft, 615, 641
Spatial order, **38**, 106, 726
Speaker, **787**
Speaking, listening, viewing, and representing, 668–689
  listening skills, 673–674
  representing skills, 681–687
  speaking skills, 338, 668–672, 726, 746

test preparation for, 688–689
  viewing skills, 675–680
Speaking skills 669–672
  class participation and, 669
  formal, 671
  giving directions, 670
  informal, 669
  making introductions, 670
  nonverbal language, 672
  planning a speech, 671
  preparation for, 669
  preparing note cards for, 671
  taking part in class discussions, 669
  varieties of speech, 671
Special events, names of, 639
Special places, capitalization and, 641
Special things, capitalization and, 641
Specific groups, capitalization and, 640
Speech, 726
  audience and, 271, 687
  delivering, 672
  evaluating speeches, 45, 147
  giving and getting feedback, 672
  nonverbal language, 672
  planning a speech, 671
  preparing note cards for, 671
  providing main idea and details, 671
  varieties of, 671
  volume, pitch, and tone, 271, 687
Spelling, 702–711
  -*c* endings of verbs and added *k*, 504
  -*tion,* for *shun* sound, 476
  adding prefixes, 706
  adding suffixes, 705
  apostrophes and, 623–624
  commonly misspelled words, 772–773
  dropping letters when, 351, 441, 466
  ei words, 704
  exceptions to, rules, 525, 561, 704–705, 708
  homophones, **710**
  hyphens and, 619
  ie words, 704
  influence of language and cultures on, 707
  personal notebook for, words, 378, 702, 706
  plural, 534–535, 610, 708–709

proofreading for, errors, 26, 290–291, 652–653, 711
  recording errors in, 702–703, 707
  Roman numerals in, 644
  rules, 704–706
  sounds and, 426, 476, 525, 704
  studying, 703, 706
  test preparation on, 220, 290–291
  word usage and, 328, 426, 479, 481, 551
  See also Dictionaries; Vocabulary and spelling
Spelling plurals
  add -*es* to singular nouns, 534
  add -*s* to singular nouns, 534
  add -*ves* to singular nouns ending in -*fe,* 534–535, 708
  change -*f* of singular nouns to -*v* and add -*es,* 610, 708
  learn special forms, 534–535, 709
Spotlight on the Humanities
  art, 270
  dance, 44
  drama, 194
  forms of self-expression, 10
  motion pictures, 120
  opera music, 146
  operettas, 170
  oral tradition, 94
  painting, 120, 270
  photography, 28, 68
  science fiction, 218
  theater, 244, 288
Spy camera, revision technique, 86
SQ4R Method, reading skills and, 718
Stacks, explanatory, 209
Standardized Test Preparation Workshops
  adjectives and adverbs, 358–359
  agreement, 556–557
  basic sentence parts, 422–423
  capitalization, 652–653
  cause-and-effect essay, 196–197
  comparison-and-contrast essay, 172–173
  conjunctions, 387
  constructing meaning, 756–757
  effective sentences, 486–487
  general strategies, 12–13
  how-to essay, 220–221
  inferences and predictions, 734–755

inverting word order for, 467, 542

sentence, as style element, **42,** 86, 225, 236, 460–468

in sentence beginnings, 24, 210, 466–467

using, of research sources, 231

using synonyms for, 213

Venn diagrams, 157, 173, 720

Verbs, 91, **314**–333, 542, **787**

action, **87,** 314, **316**–319, 411, 567

circling, as revision strategy, 25, 87, 186

common problems with, 508–512

in complete sentences, **392**–395, **422**

compound, **402**–404, 443, 460–461

conjugating, 502–503

conjunctions with, 377, 538–540

contractions with, 626

cumulative review exercises on, 331, 359, 371, 388, 451, 576

diagnostic tests on, 315, 491

diagraming, 656

forms of, in dictionaries, 747

grammar exercises on, 499, 507, 513

helping, **326**–329, 492, 511

linking, **320**–325, 416–418, 422, 567

main, 326–327

modified by other parts of speech, 348, 428, 441–442

participial forms of, 237, **430,** 492–498

plural, 163, 502, 538–539

principal parts of, 492–506

review exercises on, 330–331, 514–515

revision strategies for, 25, 87, 187–188

sentence requirements for, 283

in simple sentences, 443

singular, 163, 502, 538

with singular and plural subjects, 536–537

test preparations on, 332–333, 516–517

See also Subject-verb agreement; Subject-verb order; Using verbs; Verb phrases; Verb tenses

Verb phrases

grammar exercises on, 329

helping verbs and, **326**–329, 328–329, 492

usage test on, 516–517

Verb tenses, **187, 492**

consistent, with exceptions, 186

cumulative review exercises on, 529, 576

in dictionaries, 747

future, 492, 500–502

future perfect, 500–502, 504, 506

past, 492–493, 495, 496, 500, 502

past perfect, 500, 502, 504, 506

present, 492–493, 495, 497, 500, 502, 503

present perfect, 500, 502, 504, 506

Verbal phrases, **430, 787**

grammar exercises on, 436–437

Verbals, 430

infinitives, **432**

participles, **430**–431

Vertical files, 4, 745

Viewing skills

comparing and contrasting newscasts, 45

comparing different media, 120, 170–171, 218, 288

fine art, analyzing elements 680

graphs, 675

bar, 676

line, 676

pie, 677

link information to text, 675

maps, 675

notable features, 675

set a purpose, 675

symbols, 675

title caption and labels, 675

photographs, 675, 677

information media, 678

See also Critical Viewing, Information Media, Responding to Fine Art

Viewpoints, 49, 56, 122, 272

Vignettes, 99, 103, **787**

Virus, electronic, **769**

Visual media

comparing and contrasting, with print, 155, 171

formatting scripts for, 193, 686

graphic organizers as, 681–683

meaning and, 68–69, 95, 121

See also type of, e.g., Photographs

Vocabulary, 690–701, 711

development of, 691–694

listening and, 691, 693

notebooks for, words, 693–696

"Possible Sentences" strategy, 694

reading and, 691

studying word parts and origins, 698–701

studying words systematically, 695–697

in subject content areas, 693

using context, 692

Vocabulary and spelling, 690–713

reflecting on, 711

spelling improvement, 702–711

study tools for, 695–701

test preparation for, 712–713

vocabulary development, 690–694

See also Spelling; Vocabulary

Voice in writing, **3,** 729, **787**

See also Point of View

Vowels, 338, 705, 708

W

Waterfalls, names of, 638

Web page, **769**

See also Internet resources

Webs. *See* Topic webs

Web site, **769**

Weeding, as revision strategy, 59

well, good, 567

went, gone, 508

when, where, why, 481

which, who, that, 480

Word agreement. *See* Making words agree; Pronoun-antecedent agreement; Subject-verb agreement

Word choice, 153, 212

audiences and, 204

for cause-and-effect, 209

clichés, 336

double comparisons, 565, 574

double negatives, 478, 480

persuasion and, 130, 131, 133

precise, 3, 61, 138, 188, 263, 267, 282, 297, 563

repetition in, 86, 164, 212

revising (*see also* Revision strategies, word choice)

systematic study of, 695–697

test preparation on, 122, 149, 221

vivid, 3, 76, 83, 91, 161, 282, 336, 349

Word choice, revision strategies for, **15, 25,** 86, 209

The program authors would like to acknowledge the work of the following writers whose ideas have influenced the writing strategies presented in this series.

Brock, Paula. "Help Me, Quick." *R&E Journal* 2 (1998): 14-16.

Burke, Kenneth. *A Grammar of Motives.* Berkeley: University of California Press, 1969.

Cooper, Charles R., and Lee Odell. *Evaluating Writing: Describing, Measuring, Judging.* Urbana, IL: National Council of Teachers of English, 1977.

Corbett, Edward P. J., and Robert J. Connors. *Classical Rhetoric for the Modern Student.* New York: Oxford University Press, Inc., 1998.

Cowan, Gregory, and Elizabeth Swan. *Writing.* New York: John Wiley, 1980.

Elbow, Peter. *Writing Without Teachers.* New York: Oxford University Press, 1973.

Emig, Janet. *The Composing Process of Twelfth Graders.* Urbana, IL: National Council of Teachers of English, 1971.

Lane, Barry. *After the End: Teaching and Learning Creative Revision.* Portsmouth, NH: Heinemann Educational Books, Inc., 1993.

Rico, Gabriele Lusser. *Writing the Natural Way.* Los Angeles: J.P. Tarcher, 1983.

Rief, Linda. *Seeking Diversity.* Portsmouth, NH: Heinemann Educational Books, 1992.

Stillman, Peter R. *Families Writing.* Cincinnati, OH: Writer's Digest Books, 1989.

Acknowledgments

Staff Credits

The people who made up the *Prentice Hall Writing and Grammar: Communication in Action* team—representing design services, editorial, editorial services, electronic publishing technology, manufacturing and inventory planning, marketing, marketing services, market research, on-line services and multimedia development, product planning, production services, project office, and publishing processes—are listed below. Bold type denotes the core team members.

Ellen Backstrom, Betsy Bostwick, Evonne Burgess, **Louise B. Capuano, Sarah Carroll, Megan Chill,** Katherine Clarke, Rhett Conklin, Martha Conway, Harold Crudup, **Harold Delmonte,** Laura Dershewitz, Donna DiCuffa, Amy Fleming, Libby Forsyth, Ellen Goldblatt, Elaine Goldman, Jonathan Goldson, **Rebecca Graziano,** Rick Hickox, Kristan Hoskins, Jim Jeglikowski, Carol Lavis, **George Lychock,** Gregory Lynch, William McAllister, **Frances Medico,** Perrin Moriarty, Loretta Moser, Margaret Plotkin, Maureen Raymond, Shannon Rider, **Steve Sacco,** Gerry Schrenk, **Melissa Shustyk,** Annette Simmons, Robin Sullivan, **Elizabeth Torjussen, Doug Utigard**

Additional Credits

Ernie Albanese, Diane Alimena, Susan Andariese, Michele Angelucci, Penny Baker, Susan Barnes, Louise Casella, Lorena Cerisano, Cynthia Clampitt, Elizabeth Crawford, Ken Dougherty, Vince Esterly, Katty Gavilanes, Beth Geschwind, Michael Goodman, Diana Hahn, Jennifer Harper, Evan Holstrom, Alex Ivchenko, Leanne Korszoloski, Sue Langan, Rebecca Lauth, Dave Liston, Maria Keogh, Christine Mann, Vicki Menanteaux, Gail Meyer, Artur Mkrtchyan, LaShonda Morris, Karyl Murray, Omni-Photo Communications, Kim Ortell, Patty Rodriguez, Brenda Sanabria, Carolyn Sapontzis, Ken Silver, Slip Jig Image Research Services, Sunnyside, NY, Ron Spezial, Barbara Stufflebeem, Gene Vaughan, Karen Vignola, Linda Westerhoff

Grateful acknowledgment is made to the following for copyrighted material:

Addison-Wesley Educational Publishers
"Hans Christian Anderson" from *Children & Books* by Zena Southerland. Copyright © 1997 by Addison-Wesley Educational Publishers Inc. Used by permission.

Bantam Books
"The Eternal Frontier" from *Frontier* by Louis L'Amour, copyright © 1984 by Louis L'Amour Enterprises, Inc.

Curtis Brown, Ltd.
"Suzy and Leah" from *American Girl Magazine* by Jane Yolen. Copyright © 1993 by Jane Yolen.

The Curtis Publishing Company
Excerpt from *Luke Baldwin's Vow* by Morley Callaghan.

Reprinted from The Saturday Evening Post, copyright © 1947, The Curtis Publishing Company.

Frances Foster Books, Farrar, Straus and Giroux
Excerpt from *Holes* by Louis Sachar, copyright © 1998 by Louis Sachar.

Little Brown and Company
"How Many Flowers Fall in Wood" from T*he Complete Poems of Emily Dickinson* by Emily Dickinson, copyright © 1960 by Mary L. Hampson. Originally published by Little Brown and Company. Used by permission of The Harvard University Press.
"I'm Nobody! Who are You?" from *The Complete Poems of Emily Dickinson* by Emily Dickinson, copyright © 1960 by Mary L. Hampson. Originally published by Little Brown and Company. Used by permission of The Harvard University Press.

The Poynter Institute
"House of Memories" by Kaitlin Crockett (student model). The Poynter Institute, St. Petersburg, Florida.

Reader's Digest
"How Do Rainmakers Make it Rain?" from *How in the World?* Copyright © 1990 by The Reader's Digest Association Limited. First published as *How is it Done?* By The Reader's Digest Association Limited, London.

Scholastic Inc.
"Bat Attacks?" by Laura Allen from ScienceWorld Magazine. Copyright © 1998 by Scholastic, Inc.

St. Martin's Press
"Cat on the Go" from *All Things Wise and Wonderful* by James Herriot. Copyright © 1976, 1977 by James Herriot, St Martin's Press, Inc., New York, New York

University Press of New England
"The Bike" by Gary Soto from *A Summer Life.* Copyright © 1990 by University Press of New England. Used by permission.

Walker and Company
"Sarah Tops" from *The Key Word and Other Mysteries* by Isaac Asimov, copyright © 1977 by Isaac Asimov. Reprinted with permission from Walker and Company, 435 Hudson Street, New York, New York 10014 1-800-289-2553. All rights reserved.

Wayland (Publishers) Ltd.
Excerpt from *Wildlife at Risk: Pandas* by Gillian Standring. Copyright © 1991 Wayland (Publishers) Ltd. Reprinted by permission of the publisher.

Note: Every effort has been made to locate the copyright owner of material reprinted in this book. Omissions brought to our attention will be corrected in subsequent editions.

Photo Credits

Cover: (top) Stamp design ©United States Postal Service, All Rights Reserved; (bottom) ©Jerry Driendl/ FPG International Corp.; vi: (top) David Young-Wolff/ PhotoEdit; (bottom) Corel Professional Photos CD-ROM(™); vii: (top) Renate Hiller/ Monkmeyer; (bottom); Philip Gould/ CORBIS; ix: *March Wind,* © Robert Vickrey/Licensed by VAGA, New York, NY, Collection, Mrs. Nathan; x: *Early Carolina Morning,* 1978. From the Profile/Part 1: The Twenties series (Mecklenburg County), Collage on board. 29 x 41 in., Romare Bearden, © Romare Bearden Foundation/ Licensed by VAGA, New York, NY; xi: *Early Houses,* 1913, Lawren S. Harris, Gift of the Founders, Robert and Signe McMichael, McMichael Canadian Art Collection, 1976.25.5; xii: Michael Newman/PhotoEdit; xiii: *The King of Prospect Park Triptych,* 1994 (dark), Anders Knutsson, Courtesy of the artist; xiv: ©1997, VCG/FPG International Corp.; xv: The Kobal Collection; xvi: The Granger Collection, New York; xvii: *Dormer,* 1984–1987, Edward Rice, Morris Museum of Art, Augusta, Georgia; xviii: The Granger Collection, New York; xix: (top) Corel Professional Photos CD-ROM™; (bottom) Courtesy of the Library of Congress; xx: (top and middle) NASA; (bottom) Corel Professional Photos CD-ROM™; xxi: Corel Professional Photos CD-ROM™; xxii: (top) image ©Copyright 1998 PhotoDisc, Inc.; (bottom) Corel Professional Photos CD-ROM™; xxiii: Corel Professional Photos CD-ROM™; xxiv: (top) Siteman/Monkmeyer; (bottom) ©The Stock Market/Roy Morsch; xxv: (top) Tony Freeman/ PhotoEdit; (bottom) Rhoda Sidney/Monkmeyer 1: *The Students,* Eduard Von Gebhardt, SuperStock; 2: Myrleen Ferguson/ PhotoEdit; 5: Todd Powell/The Picture Cube; 6: Tony Stone Images; 7: Lynn Saville; 9: (top) Photo by Jean Hobbs. Courtesy of the author; (middle) Prentice Hall; (bottom) Prentice Hall; 10: SEF/Art Resource, NY; 14: ©1991, Arthur Tilleyr/FPG International Corp.; 27: Will Hart; 28: ©Elliot Erwitt, Magnum Photos, Inc.; 32: Corel Professional Photos CD-ROM™; 44: *Pavlova as Bacchante,* Sir John Lavery

(1856–1941), Glasgow Art Gallery and Museum, Scotland/ The Bridgeman Art Library; 48: Untitled, Pascal Milelli, Courtesy of the artist; 50: ©The Stock Market/Ted Horowitz; 53: *March Wind,* ©Robert Vickrey/Licensed by VAGA, New York, NY, Collection, Mrs. Nathan Allen; 57: CORBIS; 62: ©1998 VCG/FPG International Corp.; 65: ©The Stock Market/Ariel Skelley; 66: Bruce Coleman, Ltd./Natural Selection Stock Photography, Inc.; 68: Coco Chanel, ca. 1927, Berenice Abbott, vintage silver print, 3 x 2 1/4 in., The National Museum of Women in the Arts, Gift of Wallace and Wilhelmina Holladay; 72: *Early Carolina Morning,* 1978. From the Profile/Part 1: The Twenties series (Mecklenburg County), Collage on board. 29 x 41 in., Romare Bearden, © Romare Bearden Foundation/Licensed by VAGA, New York, NY; 74: American Museum of Natural History, Photo by R. Sheridan; 76: ©The Stock Market/Chris Rogers; 77: Catherine Ursillo/Photo Researchers, Inc.; 79: *Story Teller,* Velino Shije Herrera, National Museum of American Art, Washington DC/Art Resource, NY; 81: AP Photo/Steve Helber; 82: From SWAMP ANGEL by Anne Isaacs, illustrated by Paul O. Zelinsky, copyright ©1994 by Paul O. Zelinsky, illustrations. Used by permission of Dutton, a division of Penguin Putnam, Inc. ; 86: Photofest; 90: Fairfield Porter, *View of Bear Island Harbor,* c. 1950, acrylic on canvas, 23 3/4 x 29 3/4 inches, signed, lower right. Courtesy Martha Parrish & James Reinish, Inc., New York.; 92: ©CORBIS/Dewitt Jones; 93: CORBIS/ Stephanie Maze; 94: (top) Private Collection/ET Archive London/ SuperStock; (bottom) The Granger Collection, New York; 98: ©The Stock Market/Pete Saloutos; 100: ©James Blank/FPG International Corp.; 101: ©1994, Jim Cummins/FPG International Corp.; 103: *Fort George Hill,* 1915, Preston Dickinson, Munson-Williams-Proctor Institute Museum of Art, Utica, New York (Preston Dickinson, *Fort George Hill,* 1915, oil on canvas,14 x 17 in.); 104: Mary Kate Denny/PhotoEdit; 106: Courtesy of Megan Chill; 112: Nancy Sheehan/ PhotoEdit; 116: ©Peter Gridley/FPG

International Corp.; 117: Tommy Chandler, Elizabeth Whiting & Associates/CORBIS; 118: *Early Houses,* 1913, Lawren S. Harris, Gift of the Founders, Robert and Signe McMichael, McMichael Canadian Art Collection, 1976.25.5; 120: (top) *Spring,* ©1922, Georgia O'Keeffe, oil on canvas, 351/2 x 303/8", Frances Lehman Loeb Art Center, Vassar College, Poughkeepsie, New York, Bequest of Mrs. Arthur Schwab (edna Bryner, class of 1907) 1967.31.15, ©2000 The Georgia O'Keeffe Foundation/ Artists Rights Society (ARS), New York; (bottom) The Metropolitan Museum of Art, Gift of Georgia O'Keeffe through the generosity of The Georgia O'Keeffe Foundation and Jennifer and Joseph Duke, 1997 (1997.61.31), Photographic Services, The Metropolitan Museum of Art, New York, NY; 124: Corbis/Ted Streshinsky; 126: NASA; 129: *August Bargain Days,* John Ward Lockwood, Collection of The McNay Art Museum, Bequest of Marion Koogler McNay; 132: ©Ron Chapple/ FPG International Corp.; 141: Tony Freeman/PhotoEdit; 142: Michael Newman/PhotoEdit; 143: Wally McNamee/CORBIS; 144: ©2000 Office of Communications and Marketing, New York City Health and Hospitals Corporation; 146: (top) Giacomo Puccini (1858–1924), Italian composer, portrait photograph by Montabone of Milan, with Puccini's autograph, Private Collection/ The Bridgeman Art Library; (bottom) Scala/Art Resource, NY; 150: (top) *The King of Prospect Park Triptych,* 1994 (light), Anders Knutsson, Courtesy of the artist; (bottom) *The King of Prospect Park Triptych,* 1994 (dark), Anders Knutsson, Courtesy of the artist; 152: Philip Gould/CORBIS; 153: ©The Stock Market/Lew Long; 155: *Summer Days,* 1936, Georgia O'Keeffe, Photograph Copyright © 1999: Whitney Museum of American Art, New York, Gift of Calvin Klein, ©2001 The Georgia O'Keeffe Foundation/ Artists Rights Society (ARS), New York; 158: ©1995, Chip Simmons/FPG International Corp.; 160: ©1999, Anne-Marie Weber/FPG International Corp.; 164: M2Stock/Brian Calkins/

Photo Credits • 813

The Picture Cube; **167:** ©1990, Scott Markewitz/FPG International Corp.; **168:** CORBIS/Karl Weatherly; **169:** Dana White/PhotoEdit; **170:** (top) Jack Vartoogian; (bottom) *The Little White Girl,* James Abbott McNeill Whistler, Tate Gallery, London/Art Resource, NY; **174:** (left) ©1997, VCG/FPG International Corp.; (right) ©1998, Telegraph Colour Library/FPG International Corp.; **176:** Mary Fulton/Liaison Agency; **179:** © Paul Brach, *Ahola #6,* 1991, oil on canvas 51 1/2 x 61 1/2". Courtesy Bernice Steinbaum Gallery, Miami, FL; **182:** RUBE GOLDBERG™ and © Rube Goldberg Inc. Distributed by United Media; **187:** ©1998, VCG/FPG International Corp.; **188:** Tony Freeman/PhotoEdit; **191:** ©1999, Gene Ahrens/FPG International Corp.; **192:** Mark Richards/ PhotoEdit; **193:** Robert Brenner/PhotoEdit; **194:** (top) Illustration to "The Princess and the Pea" by Hans Christian Andersen, c. 1911, Edmund Dulac (1882–1953), Victoria & Albert Museum, London, UK/ The Bridgeman Art Library; (bottom) Photofest; **195:** Courtesy of the Library of Congress; **198:** Michael Newman/PhotoEdit; **200:** image ©Copyright 1998 PhotoDisc, Inc.; **203:** *Man Playing with Dog,* acrylic on board, 30" x 40", Serge Hollerbach, Courtesy of Sanders and Newman Gallery, PA; **204:** Tony Stone Images; **209:** Bill Aron/PhotoEdit; **213:** Mary Kate Denny/Tony Stone Images; **216:** ©StockFood America/Bischof; **218:** (top) The Kobal Collection; (bottom) Corel Professional Photos CD-ROM™; **222:** Le Roman, Rosa Ibarra/Omni-Photo Communications, Inc.; **224:** ©Zig Leszczynski/Animals Animals; **225:** ©Zig Leszczynski/Animals Animals; **229:** Dannielle Hayes/ Omni-Photo Communications, Inc.; **233:** ©The Stock Market/ Tom Brakefield; **235:** Corel Professional Photos CD-ROM™; **238:** Rudi Von Briel/ PhotoEdit; **243:** AP/Wide World Photos; **244:** (top) Photofest; (bottom) The Granger Collection, New York; **248:** Tonny Freeman/PhotoEdit; **250:** Archivo Iconografico, S.A./CORBIS; **251:** Tony Stone Images; **253:** Dormer, 1984–1987, Edward Rice, Morris Museum of Art, Augusta, Georgia; **255:** ©The Stock Market/Jose L. Palaez; **257:** John

Eastcott/Yva Momatiuk/The Image Works; **259:** ©Kolvoord/ The Image Works; **266:** Hulton Getty/Liaison Agency, Inc.; **267:** image ©Copyright 1998 PhotoDisc, Inc.; **268:** ©1994 Zefa Germany/The Stock Market; **269:** Christopher Bissell/Tony Stone Images; **270:** *Icarus,* plate 8 of the 'Jazz' series, 1943, Henri Matisse, Arts Council Collection, Hayward Gallery, London, UK/The Bridgeman Art Library, London/New York © 2001 Succession H. Matisse, Paris/Artists Rights Society (ARS), New York; **274:** Mark Richards/ PhotoEdit; **275:** Rene Magritte, Belgian (1898–1967), *Time Transfixed,* 1938, oil on canvas, 147 x 98.7 cm. Joseph Winterbotham Collection, 1970.426. Photograph ©1997, The Art Institute of Chicago, All Rights Reserved. © 2001 C. Herscovici, Brussels/Artists Rights Society (ARS), NY; **277:** ©The Stock Market/Michael Kevin Daly; **279:** ©1994, Stephen Simpson/ FPG International Corp.; **281:** David Young-Wolff/PhotoEdit; **285:** image©Copyright 1998 Photo-Disc, Inc.; **286:** David Young-Wolff/ PhotoEdit; **287:** Myrleen Ferguson/ PhotoEdit; **288:** (top) The Everett Collection; (bottom) The Granger Collection, New York; **292:** *Gardeners,* 1995, Judy Byford, The Grand Design, Leeds, England/SuperStock; **294:** David Young-Wolff/PhotoEdit; **298–314:** Corel Professional Photos CD-ROM™; **317–327:** Courtesy of the Library of Congress; **328:** National Archives at College Park; **334–353:** Corel Professional Photos CD-ROM™; **360–367:** NASA; **376:** Culver Pictures, Inc.; **379:** Corel Professional Photos CD-ROM™; **381:** Federal Bureau of Investigation; **383–423:** Corel Professional Photos CD-ROM™; **424:** AP/Wide World Photos; **425–427:** Corel Professionsl Photos CD-ROM **429:** NOAA; **432:** Corel Professional Photos CD-ROM™; **435:** NASA; **439 & 440:** Silver Burdett Ginn; **444 & 454:** Corel Professional Photos CD-ROM™; **457:** AP/Wide World Photos; **461:** Marc D. Longwood/Pearson Education/PH College; **462 & 465:** Corel Professional Photos CD-ROM™; **467:** Marc D. Longwood/Pearson Education/PH College; **469–501:** Corel Professional Photos CD-ROM™; **503 &**

510: Courtesy of the Library of Congress; **518:** Corel Professional Photos CD-ROM™; **522:** Courtesy of the Library of Congress; **524–532:** Corel Professional Photos CD-ROM™; **535:** Courtesy of Megan Chill; **537 & 539:** Corel Professional Photos CD-ROM™; **541:** image ©Copyright 1998 Photo-Disc, Inc.; **543:** Pearson Education; **544–550:** Corel Professional Photos CD-ROM™; **552–597:** Pearson Education/PH College; **601:** US Navy Office of Information, East; **603–634:** Corel Professional Photos CD-ROM™; **637 & 642:** Courtesy of the Library of Congress; **645–648:** Corel Professional Photos CD-ROM™; **666:** *Strap Hangers,* William Low, Courtesy of the artist; **668:** Stanley Rowin/The Picture Cube; **672:** UPI/CORBIS-BETTMANN; **677:** © Georg Gerster/Comstock, Inc.; **680:** La *Cour d'un Ferme,* Marc Chagall, Christie's Images, London, UK/Bridgeman Art Library, London/New York, ©2000 Artists Rights Society (ARS), New York/ADAGP, Paris; **685:** Siteman/Monkmeyer; **686:** Ken Karp Photography/PH Photo; **687:** Corel Professional Photos CD-ROM™; **690:** Renate Hiller/Monkmeyer; **691:** Mary Kate Denny/Tony Stone Images; **693:** ©The Stock Market/Roy Morsch; **694:** CORBIS; **700:** David Young-Wolff/ PhotoEdit; **707:** Paul A. Souders/COR-BIS; **709:** Corel Professional Photos CD-ROM™; **714:** *Hobb Green Breakfast,* by Richard Schmid ©1999; **723:** Michael Newman/PhotoEdit; **725:** image©Copyright 1998 Photo-Disc, Inc.; **728:** Bob Davis as Bob Cratchit, Kevin James Kelly as Charles Dickens and Richard Ooms as Ebneezer Scrooge in the Guthrie Theater's 1994 production of *A Christmas Carol* adapted by Barbara Field. Photo credit: Michal Daniel; **730:** Tony Freeman/PhotoEdit; **733:** Sidney/Monkmeyer; **736:** Tony Freeman/PhotoEdit; **737:** David Young-Wolff/PhotoEdit; **740:** Rhoda Sidney/Monkmeyer; **743:** Philip Gould/CORBIS; **744:** Michael Newman/PhotoEdit; **749:** Owen Franken/CORBIS; **750:** ©1999 Stephen Simpson/FPG International Corp.; **755:** Mimi Forsyth/Monkmeyer